AF213492

Juristic Concept of the Validity of Statutory Law

Andrzej Grabowski

Juristic Concept of the Validity of Statutory Law

A Critique of Contemporary Legal Nonpositivism

Translated by Małgorzata Kiełtyka

Springer

Andrzej Grabowski
Faculty of Law and Administration, Department of Legal Theory
Jagiellonian University
Kraków
Poland

Translation from the Polish language edition: PRAWNICZE POJĘCIE OBOWIĄZYWANIA PRAWA STANOWIONEGO. KRYTYKA NIEPOZYTYWISTYCZNEJ KONCEPCJI PRAWA, (c) Księgarnia Akademicka 2009. All rights reserved.

The book was written with financial support from Alexander von Humboldt-Stiftung and the Polish State Committee for Scientific Research (KBN).

The translation has been funded by the Foundation for Polish Science (FNP).

The publishing costs were partially covered by Alexander von Humboldt-Stiftung and the Jagiellonian University in Kraków.

ISBN 978-3-642-27687-3 ISBN 978-3-642-27688-0 (eBook)
DOI 10.1007/978-3-642-27688-0
Springer Heidelberg New York Dordrecht London

Library of Congress Control Number: 2013942383

© Springer-Verlag Berlin Heidelberg 2013
This work is subject to copyright. All rights are reserved by the Publisher, whether the whole or part of the material is concerned, specifically the rights of translation, reprinting, reuse of illustrations, recitation, broadcasting, reproduction on microfilms or in any other physical way, and transmission or information storage and retrieval, electronic adaptation, computer software, or by similar or dissimilar methodology now known or hereafter developed. Exempted from this legal reservation are brief excerpts in connection with reviews or scholarly analysis or material supplied specifically for the purpose of being entered and executed on a computer system, for exclusive use by the purchaser of the work. Duplication of this publication or parts thereof is permitted only under the provisions of the Copyright Law of the Publisher's location, in its current version, and permission for use must always be obtained from Springer. Permissions for use may be obtained through RightsLink at the Copyright Clearance Center. Violations are liable to prosecution under the respective Copyright Law.
The use of general descriptive names, registered names, trademarks, service marks, etc. in this publication does not imply, even in the absence of a specific statement, that such names are exempt from the relevant protective laws and regulations and therefore free for general use.
While the advice and information in this book are believed to be true and accurate at the date of publication, neither the authors nor the editors nor the publisher can accept any legal responsibility for any errors or omissions that may be made. The publisher makes no warranty, express or implied, with respect to the material contained herein.

Printed on acid-free paper

Springer is part of Springer Science+Business Media (www.springer.com)

Preface

This book was originally published in Polish (Księgarnia Akademicka, Kraków 2009) under the title *Prawnicze pojęcie obowiązywania prawa stanowionego. Krytyka niepozytywistycznej koncepcji prawa*. I decided to introduce minor changes and additions to the Polish text in order to make the content comprehensible for a non-Polish readership. Additionally, I removed those parts that were addressed exclusively to Polish readers.

I would like to thank Sławomira Wronkowska, Robert Alexy, Tomasz Gizbert-Studnicki, Ulfrid Neumann, Lech Morawski and Marek Zirk-Sadowski for their support and assistance in obtaining the finance for the translation of this book into English and for its subsequent publication by Springer-Verlag.

I express my gratitude to Alexander von Humboldt-Stiftung for a scholarship—which made it possible for me to analyse German nonpositivism—as well as for the financial support given for the publication of the English version of the book. I also thank the Polish State Committee for Scientific Research (*KBN*) for a research grant connected with developing the postpositivist concept of the validity of statutory law and the Foundation for Polish Science (*FNP*), which granted a subsidy to cover the costs of translating the book.

Last but not least, I greatly appreciate the help and accurate editorial guidance provided by Anke Seyfried, who supervised the publication of this book by Springer-Verlag.

Kraków, Poland
April 2012

Andrzej Grabowski

Preface

Abbreviations

AI	Ars Interpretandi. Jahrbuch für juristische Hermeneutik
AIC	Archivum Iuridicum Cracoviense
AI&L	Artificial Intelligence and Law
AJJ	The American Journal of Jurisprudence
APhD	Archives de Philosophie du Droit
APhF	Acta Philosophica Fennica
ARG	Argumentation
ARSP	Archiv für Rechts- und Sozialphilosophie
AS	Associations. Journal of Social and Legal Theory
AUL FI	Acta Universitatis Lodziensis – Folia Iuridica
AUMCS-G	Annales Universitatis Mariae Curie-Skłodowska. Sectio G
AUNC	Acta Universitatis Nicolai Copernici
AUS	Annales Universitatis Saraviensis
AUW	Acta Universitatis Wratislaviensis
BMS	Biblioteka Myśli Semiotycznej [Library of Semiotical Thought]
CC	Colloquia Communia
CLR	California Law Review
DZPh	Deutsche Zeitschrift für Philosophie
D&QP	Diritto & questioni pubbliche
ERK	Erkenntnis
GSiP	Gazeta Sądowa i Penitencjarna [Gazette of Judiciary and Penitentiary]
GSP	Gdańskie Studia Prawnicze [Gdańsk Legal Studies]
HLR	Harvard Law Review
IJSL	International Journal for the Semiotics of Law
IS	Isonomía
JL&S	Journal of Law and Society
JPh	Journal of Philosophy
JS	Juristische Schulung
JZ	Juristenzeitung
KAR	Krakauer-Augsburger Rechtsstudien
KiS	Kultura i Społeczeństwo [Culture and Society]

KSP	Krakowskie Studia Prawnicze [Kraków Legal Studies]
KVfGR	Kritische Vierteljahresschrift für Gesetzgebung und Rechtswissenschaft
LA	Logique et Analyse
LA NS	Logique et Analyse (Nouvelle série)
Lin&Ph	Linguistics and Philosophy
LT	Legal Theory
L&Ph	Law and Philosophy
MLR	Michigan Law Review
MSPhS	Minnesota Studies in the Philosophy of Science
M&W	Man and World
NHPh	Neue Hefte für Philosophie
NJW	Neue Juristische Wochenschrift
NP	Nowe Prawo [The New Law]
NYULR	New York University Law Review
OJLS	Oxford Journal of Legal Studies
OSNC	Orzecznictwo Sadu Najwyższego – Izba Cywilna [Records of the Supreme Court Rulings, the Civil Chamber]
OSNKW	Orzecznictwo Sadu Najwyższego – Izba Karna i Wojskowa [Records of the Supreme Court Rulings, the Penal and Military Chamber]
OTK ZU	Orzecznictwo Trybunału Konstytucyjnego. Zbiór Urzędowy [The Official Collection of the Jurisdiction of Constitutional Tribunal]
ÖZÖR (NF)	Österreichische Zeitschrift für öffentliches Recht (Neue Folge)
PAS	Proceedings of the Aristotelian Society
PhilRev	The Philosophical Review
PhQ	The Philosophical Quarterly
PhR	Philosophische Rundschau
PhS	Philosophical Studies
PiP	Państwo i Prawo [State and Law]
PL	Przegląd Legislacyjny [Review of Legislation]
PNUŚ	Prace Naukowe Uniwersytetu Śląskiego w Katowicach [Scientific Works of the Silesian University in Katowice]
PrS	Protosoziologie
PS	Przegląd Sejmowy [Parliamentary Review]
P&PA	Philosophy and Public Affairs
RF KUL	Roczniki Filozoficzne Katolickiego Uniwersytetu Lubelskiego [Philosophical Yearbook of the Catholic University in Lublin]
RIFD	Rivista internazionale di filosofia del diritto
RJ	Ratio Juris
RJBA	Revista Jurídica de Buenos Aires
RPEiS	Ruch Prawniczy, Ekonomiczny i Socjologiczny [Journal of Law, Economics and Sociology]
RPiE	Ruch Prawniczy i Ekonomiczny [Journal of Law and Economics]
RT	Rechtstheorie

SC	Studia Cywilistyczne [Studies on Civil Law]
SF	Studia filozoficzne [Philosophical Studies]
SFP	Studia z filozofii prawa [Studies in Legal Philosophy]
SIS	Sistema. Revista de ciencias sociales
SL	Studia Logica
SM	Studia Metodologiczne [Methodological Studies]
SP	Studia Prawnicze [Legal Studies]
SPE	Studia Prawno-Ekonomiczne [Studies on Law and Economics]
SPhL	Studies in the Philosophy of Law
SPP	Studia Prawa Prywatnego [Studies on Private Law]
SSL	Scandinavian Studies in Law
VVDS	Veröffentlichungen der Vereinigung der Deutschen Staatsrechtslehrer
YLJ	The Yale Law Journal
ZaW	Zeitschrift für allgemeine Wissenschaftstheorie
ZevK	Zeitschrift zum evangielischen Kirchenrecht
ZNUJ PNP	Zeszyty Naukowe Uniwersytetu Jagiellońskiego. Prace z nauk politycznych [Scientific Papers of Jagiellonian University. Studies on Political Sciences]
ZNUJ PP	Zeszyty Naukowe Uniwersytetu Jagiellońskiego. Prace prawnicze [Scientific Papers of Jagiellonian University. Legal Studies]
ZNUŁ NHS	Zeszyty Naukowe Uniwersytetu Łódzkiego. Nauki Humanistyczno-Społeczne [Scientific Papers of the University of Łódź. Humanistic and Social Sciences]
ZphF	Zeitschrift für philosophische Forschung
ZPh&phK	Zeitschrift für Philosophie und philosophische Kritik
ZSchwR	Zeitschrift für Schweizerisches Recht

For my Wife

Contents

Chapter 1
Introduction

What does it mean for a legal norm to be valid? Does the validity of legal norms depend solely on their due enactment and social efficacy, or conceivably on their moral rightness as well? Does legal validity imply membership in the legal system, or perhaps applicability or observance within that system? In what way do we recognise that legal norms are valid? What are the structure and the layout of juristic argumentation concerning legal validity? Are the courts occasionally bound by valid positive law to apply invalid legal norms or provisions? These are some of the theoretical and practical questions that I aim to answer in this book.

Undoubtedly, the characteristic feature of legal sciences is that many crucial jurisprudential issues have been notoriously debatable. One of them is the question of the validity of law (and legal norms in particular), which constitutes the subject of continuous controversy and reflection. This subject matter has been brought to the attention of the representatives of all legal professions: both to lawyers, who are practitioners (facing a number of specific problems concerning legal validity in the course of procedures involving making and applying law), as well as to legal scholars such as dogmaticians, historians, sociologists, theoreticians and philosophers of law (seeking to understand the essence of the validity of law and to develop its adequate theory). These are not easy tasks, given that the validity of law is often regarded, especially by theoreticians and philosophers of law, as "probably the most intricate problem of jurisprudence",[1] a problem which is "particularly puzzling and complicated".[2] It then merits tackling this problem that intrigues many lawyers, as it is not only of theoretical, but also of great practical importance.

---

[1] S. Wronkowska, 'O źródłach prawa i aktach normatywnych raz jeszcze' [Once More on Sources of Law and Normative Acts] in A. Nowicka *et al.* (eds.), *Prawo prywatne czasu przemian*, Poznań 2005, p. 119.

[2] J. Woleński, *Z zagadnień analitycznej filozofii prawa* [Some Problems in Analytical Legal Philosophy], Kraków 1980, p. 98.

A. Grabowski, *Juristic Concept of the Validity of Statutory Law*,
DOI 10.1007/978-3-642-27688-0_1, © Springer-Verlag Berlin Heidelberg 2013

The primary aim of this work is to examine the problem of the validity of law and to arrive at such a concept of it which would not only be accurate in terms of contemporary theory and philosophy of law, but that would also be helpful in solving at least some problems concerning legal validity that we encounter in legal practice. The direct inspiration for taking up the subject of legal validity was the belief that I came to whilst researching various approaches to settling problems concerning the validity of legal provisions and norms in the jurisdiction of the Polish Constitutional Tribunal.[3] They made me realise the need for developing a conception of the validity of law that would not only clarify the nature of this phenomenon, but that could also provide a theoretical basis for the settlement of such practical specific questions as, for example, the problems of the so-called prolonged validity of formally derogated legal provisions or the revival of the legal validity of provisions whose formal derogation was deemed unconstitutional by the Constitutional Tribunal. My belief was validated when I became familiar with the current state of research and the achievements of Polish theory and philosophy of law concerning this subject matter. Despite the fact that many outstanding representatives of our discipline were involved in issues of legal validity and that some competing conceptions of the validity of law were created, in my opinion, it is difficult to consider any of those specific conceptions as being singularly dominant. What also calls for a resumption of the subject concerning the validity of law is the fact that the last major work in the Polish theory of law devoted directly to legal validity was a monograph written by Wiesław Lang in 1962.[4] Considering that, paraphrasing the famous Gustav Radbruch's dictum concerning the science of law, one can assume that the characteristic feature of the theory and philosophy of law is that some research problems are still undertaken, and that each generation of scholars writes anew their own philosophy of law.[5] In our case, it will be the theory of law tentatively referred to as "postpositivist legal theory".

The concept of the validity of law is very complicated and may be considered from various research perspectives because it is related to a number of specific problems of analytical, normative, axiological and empirical (sociological or psychological) character. What therefore becomes essential is the task of defining the scope and methodology of the research here undertaken. I have assumed that the most appropriate way will be to examine the most basic and *prima facie* simplest topic; namely, the juristic concept of the validity of statutory law. This means that,

[3] *Cf.* A. Grabowski, B. Naleziński, 'Kłopoty z obowiązywaniem. Uwagi na tle orzecznictwa Trybunału Konstytucyjnego' [Problems with Validity. Comments on the Basis of the Constitutional Tribunal Jurisdiction], *SFP* 1 (2001), pp. 219–257.

[4] W. Lang, *Obowiązywanie prawa* [Validity of Law], Warszawa 1962. *Cf. idem*, 'Obowiązywanie normy prawnej w czasie w świetle logiki norm' [Validity of a Legal Norm in Time in the Light of Logic of Norms], *ZNUJ PP* 7 (1960), pp. 47–88. Lang presented an updated version of his theory in 'A Concept of the Validity of Law', *AIC* XXIX–XXX (1996–1997), pp. 87–101.

[5] G. Radbruch, *Rechtsphilosophie. Studienausgabe*, R. Dreier, St.L. Paulson (eds.), Heidelberg 1999, p. 117: "So ist es auch kein Wunder, daß jedes Zeitalter seine Rechtswissenschaft neu schreiben muß".

in principle, in the study I leave aside the problem of the non-juristic (for example, ethical, psychological or sociological) validity of law, as well as the issues related to the validity of non-statutory (e.g. customary) law. It should be noted that the analysis in question was carried out in the context of the continental system-type of statutory law (a system-type of *ius civile*); thus, my deliberations do not relate directly to the Polish or any other national legal system. Therefore, any potential application of the conception at issue in legal dogmatics or in the practice of law of a given state will be possible only after appropriate adjustment, taking into account the peculiarities of its legal culture (in particular, the normative conception of the sources of law appropriate to a given national system of law) as well as the regulation of the issue of legal validity by positive law.

The principal objectives of this study and its subject matter have a fundamental influence on the choice of the method applied in the course of analyses. The studies have been based on the methodological canon developed as a part of a general analytical philosophy and analytical theory and philosophy of law. The basic method applied is therefore a linguistic and conceptual analysis, combined with elements of logical analysis. I must admit that I use—in a methodologically unencumbered way—methods developed in the mainstream of the descriptionistic analytical philosophy of language and within reconstructionism.[6] I do believe that such a pattern is justified not only because of the complementary (rather than the antagonistic) nature of these two classical approaches.[7] A far more important reason is that limiting research to purely descriptive analyses would basically make it impossible to propose an appropriate definition of the juristic concept of the validity of statutory law, which constitutes a conclusion of the conception of legal validity that is elaborated in this study. It seems obvious to me that this definition cannot be of a purely descriptive (analytical) nature and that it must be regulative (analytical–synthetic) in form.[8] Otherwise, we would have to assume in advance that the study in question, instead of developing the discussion on the juristic concept of legal validity, merely describes its present state.

---

[6] For more on the mentioned trends of analytical philosophy *see* J. Kotarbińska, 'The Controversy over the Limits of Applicability of Logical Methods', *LA NS* 29 (1965), pp. 178–207; J. Woleński, *Z zagadnień analitycznej filozofii prawa*, *op. cit.*, pp. 33ff.; T. Gizbert-Studnicki, 'Teoria prawa, filozofia języka, lingwistyka' [Theory of Law, Philosophy of Language, Linguistics], *SF* 2–3 (1985), pp. 71ff.; Z. Ziembiński, 'Deskrypcjonistyczna i rekonstrukcjonistyczna analiza języka w prawoznawstwie' [Descriptionistic and Reconstructionistic Analysis of Language in Jurisprudence], *SP* 3–4 (1985), pp. 329–341.

[7] *See e.g.*, T. Gizbert-Studnicki, *ibidem*, p. 75; Z. Ziembiński, *ibidem*, p. 341; K. Opałek, J. Wróblewski, *Prawo. Metodologia, filozofia, teoria prawa* [Law. Methodology, Philosophy, Legal Theory], Warszawa 1991, pp. 106–107.

[8] I would like to stress at this point that I aim to develop a regulative definition that only clarifies the meaning of this concept, and not a definition of a purely stipulative (synthetic) character, since it would be, due to its arbitrary nature, probably useless in practice. *Cf.* A. Bator's comments on the definitions applied in legal studies, in 'O konserwatyźmie językowym nauki prawa' [On Linguistic Conservatism of the Science of Law] in H. Rot (ed.), *Prawo i prawoznawstwo wobec zmian społecznych*, Wrocław 1990, pp. 25ff.

The choice of the analytical method also entails certain consequences, among which two seem most important. Firstly, due to this method, a number of issues—usually considered as *par excellence* philosophical problems—come down to the level of linguistic and logical analysis. In this sense, the method in question is—if not aphilosophical—then at least anti-metaphysical. Philosophical minimalism of the undertaken analyses, being an inherent component of this method, nonetheless seems to me as the most appropriate form, if we consider that the subject of our debate is the juristic concept of the validity of statutory law, which may be constructed in a manner that is relatively independent of the adoption of certain ontological and epistemological standpoints.[9] Secondly, the analytical method allows for carrying out research in a generally assumptionless manner,[10] which should also be—in my view—regarded as its considerable advantage. I must admit, though, that when setting about the planned research, I made an assumption that I would try to formulate a conception of the validity of law so that the concepts of valid law and invalid law were dichotomous. I decided that—for theoretical, axiological and, above all, for practical reasons—the existence of any conceptual category of a "transitional" character, between valid and invalid law, would be highly undesirable, and a regulative definition of the juristic concept of the validity of statutory law would not properly fulfil its primary function, consisting of eliminating linguistic ambiguity and the vagueness of this concept.[11] Yet, I would

[9] It does not mean that in this study I do not make any assumptions of an ontological or epistemological nature. Indeed, they will be indicated in the relevant parts of the text. Yet, at this point I can only add that if I were to define the philosophical (theoretical) standpoint which provides the basis for my views presented below, I would refer to it as moderately realistic – for more on this *see* Chap. 6 at pp. 224–225 (the fourth objective of clarification).

[10] "Assumptionlessness" (which is a provisional translation of the German *Voraussetzungslosigkeit*) is naturally associated with E. Husserl's phenomenology. I do believe, though, that it may also be combined with *par excellence* analytical philosophy, as J. Szymura proves in his monograph *Język, mowa i prawda w perspektywie fenomenologii lingwistycznej J.L. Austina* [Language, Speech and Truth in the View of J.L. Austin's Linguistic Phenomenology], Wrocław/Warszawa/Kraków/Gdańsk/Łódź 1982, pp. 18ff., 129ff.

[11] By adopting this assumption, which refers to the conceptual level, obviously I have not eliminated the possibility of the existence of acts of law, norms or legal provisions contained in a specific "transitional" category between validity and invalidity. I decided, nonetheless, that even if the scope of such a category is not empty, after all, the cases falling within it will be eventually (i.e., after careful consideration by a specially authorised organ or by a competent interpreter) included in terms of the extension of the concepts of either valid or invalid law. *Tertium non datur*. Indeed, as A. Bator accurately stresses ('O konserwatyźmie językowym nauki prawa', *op. cit*., pp. 24–25), in respect to the language of legal studies oriented at practical problems, the finding that the norm N is "to some extent" valid is not acceptable due to its practical uselessness. Let us add that many theoreticians and dogmatists of law assume such a dichotomous standpoint, thus not allowing for any gradability of legal validity – *see e.g*., J. Raz, 'Legal Validity', *ARSP* 63 (1977), p. 339; R. Alexy, *Theorie der Grundrechte*, Baden-Baden 1985, p. 78 [English version: *A Theory of Constitutional Rights*, trans. J. Rivers, Oxford 2002, p. 49]; A. Marmor, 'Exclusive Legal Positivism' in J.L. Coleman, S.J. Shapiro (eds.), *The Oxford Handbook of Jurisprudence and Philosophy of Law*, Oxford 2002, p. 106. It is worth quoting a vivid comparison proposed by A. Peczenik and S. Urbina in 'Why Officials? On Legal Positivism Old and New', *RT* 27 (1995),

like to stress that it was the only significant conceptual assumption that was adopted in full awareness at the beginning of the research. Other assumptions will be identified and explained in the passages of this study that are devoted to the specific methodological issues associated with the analyses carried out in this book.[12]

The book consists of two parts, divided into chapters, in which various topics are examined in sections and subsections. The main conclusions of the undertaken analyses and the perspectives on further research are presented in the Epilogue, which also includes some comments on the methodology and on the postpositivist theory of law.

The aim of the first descriptive–critical part is to determine the conceptual consequences of a nonpositivist conception of law, elaborated by Ralf Dreier and Robert Alexy, in relation to the juristic concept of the validity of law. The essential question that I try to answer is whether the definition of the juristic concept of the validity of law should take into account the requirements of substantive (especially moral) correctness or rightness of law. What constitutes the basis of the deliberations at issue is a critical analysis of the German nonpositivist conception, with a particular emphasis on Alexy's and Dreier's argumentation in favour of the nonpositivist concept of law and the thesis on the necessary conceptual connection between law and morality (*Verbindungsthese*). What is primarily presented in this historical context are Dreier's and Alexy's nonpositivist definitions of law (Chap. 2); I further reconstruct the nonpositivist argumentation proposed by these authors (Chap. 3), and I undertake a multi-dimensional criticism of this argumentation at the analytical, normative and empirical level (Chap. 4). Then (in Chap. 5) I carry out the analysis of the theoretical correctness and practical relevance of nonpositivist definitions of law proposed by the German philosophers. I justify not only the theoretical but also the practical usefulness of distinguishing between the concepts of law and valid law, which is, roughly speaking, denied by the supporters of the nonpositivist understanding of law. I also discuss the arguments in favour of adopting an axiologically detached and impartial concept of the validity of law in the juristic discourse, resulting from the critical analysis of nonpositivism and modern legal positivism.

---

p. 142: "First of all, the concept 'valid law' according to its ordinary use, is like 'pregnancy': one is either pregnant or not, one cannot be pregnant to some extent". *Cf.* a different opinion, provided by R.S. Summers, 'Toward a Better General Theory of Legal Validity', *RT* 16 (1985), pp. 72ff. and 'Positivism, Natural Law and the Theory of Legal Validity' in *idem*, *Essays on the Nature of Law and Legal Reasoning*, Berlin 1992, pp. 52ff. In his papers, Summers presents arguments supporting the thesis that the positivist conceptual dichotomy of validity and invalidity is too strict and must be changed. L.J. Wintgens argues similarly in 'Legisprudence: Elements for a New Theory of Legislation', *AS* 3 (1999), p. 203 ff. where he does not hesitate in suggesting that the concept of being pregnant (treated as an analogue to the concept of formal validity) has a classifying character only due to technological development, while the formal validity of norms is construed by him as a classifying term purely by means of adopting the external perspective. *See* also A. Ross' standpoint, discussed in Chap. 7 at p. 316.

[12] *See* Chap. 6, pp. 217ff., Chap. 7, pp. 247ff., Chap. 8, pp. 360ff., and Chap. 9, pp. 455ff.

The main aim of the inquiries in the second—mostly purely analytical—part of the study is to undertake a clarification of the juristic concept of the validity of statutory law. This aim is accomplished in two stages: firstly, I try to eliminate the conceptual indeterminacy of this concept (Chaps. 6–8) and, later, its vagueness (Chap. 9).

In the first of the above-mentioned stages of research, I try to explain the concept of the validity of statutory law by means of a model analysis of the meaning of the phrase: "A norm of statutory law is valid". The purpose of the deliberation is to formulate such a noncriterial regulative definition, which would indicate an appropriate way of applying the juristic concept of the validity of statutory law and it would, thereby, eliminate its conceptual and semantic indeterminacy. The latter does not aim at developing proper criteria that would enable determining whether the norm of statutory law is valid (i.e. at the attempt to settle the problem of extension, associated with the vagueness of this concept, which has been undertaken in the penultimate chapter of my study). Instead, what is being attempted is a possibly exact specification of the meaning of this concept (i.e. determining the question of its intension). After an indispensable methodological introduction, which aims to characterise the manner in which the juristic concept of the validity of statutory law was undertaken (Chap. 6), the discussion shall focus on different possibilities of clarifying the intension of this concept (Chap. 7). To this end, I explore the conceptual relations that occur between the validity of norms and their membership in a legal system, their application and their applicability as well as their observance and efficacy. Since these analyses unexpectedly lead to the conclusion that the definition of the juristic concept of the validity of statutory law cannot be properly formulated on the basis of any of these five concepts (membership, application, applicability, observance, efficacy) or by means of some combination of these concepts, the need to find a proper way to elucidate the intension of the juristic concept of the validity of statutory law arises. Therefore, relying inter alia on the analysis of the types and modes of constructing juristic concepts, after presenting the linguistic and logical characteristics of pragmatically differentiated juristic utterances concerning the validity of law, I go on to formulate a regulative definition of the juristic concept of the validity of statutory law, based on the concept of legal situation and referring to the pragmatic conception of legal norm (Chap. 8).

The final stage of research, presented in Chap. 9, constitutes a discursive complement to the previous analyses, aiming, at least, to partially eliminate the vagueness of the juristic concept of the validity of statutory law. After a general presentation of the contemporary theories of legal argumentation and after a few critical comments regarding their suitability, further deliberations are focused on a conceptual distinction and the characterisation of the discourse on validity as a specific type of juristic discourse. In order to attempt the latter, I analyse the basic types and forms of the discourse on validity, their possible outcomes, as well as the mutual relations between the discourse of validity (*Geltungsdiskurs*), the discourse of justification (*Begründungsdiskurs*) and the discourse of application (*Anwedungsdiskurs*). Then I go on to present the argumentative characteristics of the juristic presumption of the validity of statutory law norms, based on the analysis of the structure and content of this presumption, discussing various methods of argumentation on legal validity and the initial identification of the rules governing the burden of such argumentation as well as discussing the issues pertaining to the classification of typical legal arguments, raised in a discourse of validity in a strict sense in order to rebut the above-mentioned presumption. In contrast to an earlier regulative definition of the juristic concept of the validity of statutory law (as formulated in Chap. 8), I present—though very generally—the ways of resolving specific problems of validity, in particular, in seeking answers to a fundamental practical question concerning the validity of the norms of statutory law. In the final sections of this chapter, I analyse the relations between the postpositivist juristic concept of the validity of statutory law and the principles *ignorantia iuris nocet* and *ignorantia legis neminem excusat* and I discuss the possibilities of applying the model of the validity discourse *sensu stricto* in legal science and legal practice.

In my work, I refer to a number of theories and specific concepts of contemporary analytical theory and philosophy of law and—above all—to the German nonpositivist conception of law (the output of which constitutes the subject matter of analysis in the first part of the study). Such a choice for the theoretical background for my analysis is not only justified by the unquestionably important role currently played by German theory and philosophy of law, but also by the very fact that this conception has so far been presented in a merely fragmentary way in the European and, particularly, in the Polish literature on the subject.[13] I believe that a detailed discussion of this conception and a multi-layered criticism, which is presented in this study,[14] could become the basis for rethinking and—perhaps—even modifying the conceptions of law which are typically positivistically-oriented

[13] For further detail *see* Chap. 4 at pp. 63ff.

[14] I would like to stress that my intention is not to give an overall presentation and critical analysis of this conception, but I aim primarily at making use of some ideas put forward in it. In other words, it would be an over-interpretation if the Reader treated the first part of this study as a monograph on German nonpositivism. On the other hand, it was particularly in the third and fourth chapters that I decided to devise a more detailed description of the analysed conception and to also identify in the footnotes – besides source texts – a number of recommendable studies that may be useful for those interested in developing their knowledge about the contemporary German nonpositivist concept of law and its critique. These decisions undoubtedly influenced the volume of the book and also made it necessary to discuss many topics that are only loosely related to the juristic concept of legal validity. What is even worse is that these decisions of mine expose this study to a certain kind of objection, aptly formulated by Z. Ziembiński: "If I write in a review that a certain theoretical book includes 999 footnotes out of 777 bibliographic entries, it will be treated as the highest praise in the eyes of a scholar having the soul of a documentary, and as a scathing critique in the eyes of those who feel disgust for erudite exhibitionism" (Z. Ziembiński, *Wstęp do aksjologii dla prawników* [Introduction to Axiology for Lawyers], Warszawa 1990, p. 51). *De gustibus non est disputandum.* In any case, my only intention is to facilitate further studies for all those who are interested in the topics analysed in this work, as well as criticism for those who consider the theses and argumentation presented in this work as unfounded. Furthermore, a number of footnotes have the character of cross references, thus avoiding useless repetitions in the main text.

and which dominate in the Polish theory and philosophy of law. I also hope that the postpositivist juristic concept of the validity of statutory law developed from the perspective of a nonpositivist conception of law, and based on the concept of legal situation and on the pragmatic concept of legal norm, will not be a conception that is devoid of practical application. Indeed, I do not intend to develop—as Lech Morawski neatly suggested—the "painstaking analytical theory of law".[15] I also try to analyse some theoretical conceptions—or even above all—having regard to the aspect of their suitability for the explanation and resolution of specific problems concerning legal validity that arise in the practice of lawmaking and law application. I consider such a practical approach as an important *differentia specifica* of the postpositivist theory of law.[16]

Summarising the preliminary comments, I assume that the primary purpose of this study is to develop a juristic concept of the validity of statutory law; whereas, its additional objective (subordinate to the principal one, which does not mean that it is without the utmost importance in itself) is a discussion and criticism of Ralf Dreier's and Robert Alexy's nonpositivist conception of law.[17]

---

[15] L. Morawski, *Co może dać nauce prawa postmodernism?* [What Postmodernism Can Offer to Legal Science?], Toruń 2001, pp. 12ff.

[16] For more on this *see* Chap. 6 at p. 223 and Epilogue at pp. 539ff.

[17] In this book, I, consequently, use the terms "nonpositivist conception of law" and "nonpositivism" as the English equivalents to the terms "nichtpositivistische Konzeption des Rechts" and "Nichtpositivismus"; i.e., the names used in German-language jurisprudential literature in reference to the conception of law elaborated by R. Dreier and R. Alexy. By doing so, I follow the logical pattern of term creation – *see e.g.*, Z. Ziembiński, *Practical Logic*, Warszawa/Dordrecht 1976, p. 33; *cf.* Chap. 4, pp. 70ff. The problem is that the terms usually used in the English jurisprudential literature: "non-positivist conception of law" and "non-positivism" are linguistically correct; however, they can easily give the wrong impression; namely, that Dreier's and Alexy's conception is the only non-positivist one. Arguably, the opposite is the case: the German nonpositivist conception of law is one of many non-positivist theories created in the legal theory of the second part of the twentieth century.

Part I
Critique of the Nonpositivist Conception of Law

Chapter 2
The Nonpositivist Concept of Law

2.1 Historical Background: The Role of "Radbruch's Formula"

The German nonpositivist conception of law has been developed since the mid-1980s of the twentieth century. This conception has not been created in a vacuum, since the criticism of legal positivism has been one of the main trends in the German post-war theory and philosophy of law. Initially, this criticism was associated with the "Second Renaissance" of the natural law theories that was observed in many countries—not just the post-totalitarian ones—during and immediately after World War II.[1] In the German region, this revival lasted about 20 years; nevertheless, the natural law theories—referring primarily to Christian moral philosophy—that were created in that period did not play a major role in the further development of the German philosophy of law.[2] The literature stresses the episodic nature of this renaissance,[3] and it even casts doubt on the general characteristics of this

[1] *See* H. Waśkiewicz, '"Drugie Odrodzenie" prawa naturalnego' ["Second Revival" of Natural Law], *RF KUL, Etyka* X/2 (1962), pp. 115–151.

[2] Broadly on the development and periodisation of post-war theory and philosophy of law in Germany *see* R. Dreier, 'Hauptströmungen gegenwärtiger Rechtsphilosophie in Deutschland', *ARSP* 81 (1995), pp. 155–163 and 'Deutsche Rechtsphilosophie in der zweiten Hälfte des 20. Jahrhunderts. Ein Rückblick' in R. Alexy (ed.), *Integratives Verstehen*, Tübingen 2005, pp. 215–223; U. Neumann, 'Rechtsphilosophie in Deutschland seit 1945' in D. Simon (ed.), *Rechtswissenschaft in der Bonner Republik*, Frankfurt am Main 1994, pp. 145–187; K. Opałek, 'Główne kierunki niemieckiej teorii i filozofii prawa po II wojnie światowej' [Main Currents in the German Theory and Philosophy of Law After the Second World War] in *idem*, *Studia z teorii i filozofii prawa*, Kraków 1997, pp. 11–44; M.E. Salas, '¿Qué pasa actualmente en la Teoría del Derecho alemana? Un breve bosquejo general', *DOXA* 24 (2001), pp. 204ff.; J. Zajadło, '"Trzecie odrodzenie" prawa natury? (Uwagi metodologiczne)' ["Third Revival" of Natural Law? (Methodological Remarks)], *CC* 6/41–1/42 (1988–1989), pp. 111–118.

[3] *See e.g.*, A. Kaufmann, 'Die Naturrechtsrenaissance der ersten Nachkriegsjahre – und was daraus geworden ist' in M. Stolleis (ed.), *Die Bedeutung der Wörter*, München 1991, pp. 105ff. and J. Zajadło, *Formuła Radbrucha* [Radbruch's Formula], Gdańsk 2001, pp. 85ff.

A. Grabowski, *Juristic Concept of the Validity of Statutory Law*,
DOI 10.1007/978-3-642-27688-0_2, © Springer-Verlag Berlin Heidelberg 2013

phenomenon as involving the "rebirth" of natural law.[4] Nonetheless, nobody denies that the most important conception, which arose during *Naturrechtsdiskussion* and which still plays a significant role both on the theoretical and practical level, is Gustav Radbruch's conception of "statutory injustice" (*gezetzliches Unrecht*)[5] and "suprastatutory law" (*übergesetzliches Recht*). Its essence boils down to two theses,[6] usually collectively known as "Radbruch's formula". According to the first one, labelled *Unerträglichkeitsthese* or *Unerträglichkeitsformel*, positive law is in force, even if it is to no purpose or is unjust in content, unless the extent to which this law contradicts justice reaches "such a level that cannot be borne" (*unerträgliches Maß*).[7] In such cases, the statute—as a "statutory injustice" (or, more precisely, "statutory unlawfulness" or "statutory un-law"[8])—should give way to justice; that is, to "suprastatutory law". It should be emphasised that this thesis is often equated with "Radbruch's formula"—such terminology is usually assumed by those who use the formula in the argument for the nonpositivist concept of law. They prefer to express it in lapidary forms: *extremes Unrecht ist kein Recht*[9] or *lex iniustissima non est lex.*[10] Radbruch's second thesis is called *Verleugnungsthese* or *Verleugnungsformel*. According to it, when positive law does not seek justice and, at the same time, deliberately denies (*verleugnen*) equality, which is the essence of

[4] U. Neumann, 'Rechtsphilosophie in Deutschland seit 1945', *op. cit.*, pp. 154ff.

[5] This book very often presents – both in quotes as well as in the text itself – the original wording of foreign terms or phrases translated into English, to help readers understand what I am writing about. I assume that familiarity with foreign language terminology often proves crucial in fully understanding the various jurisprudential concepts and the concept of legal validity, in particular. On the latter issue *see* Chap. 7 at pp. 267ff.

[6] *See e.g.*, St.L. Paulson, 'On the Background and Significance of Gustav Radbruch's Post-War Papers', *OJLS* 26/1 (2006), pp. 26ff. and J. Zajadło, *Dziedzictwo przeszłości* [Inheritance of the Past], Gdańsk 2007, pp. 206ff.

[7] G. Radbruch, 'Gesetzliches Unrecht und übergesetzliches Recht' in *idem*, *Rechtsphilosophie*, *op. cit.*, p. 216 [English version: 'Statutory Lawlessness and Supra-Statutory Law (1946)', trans. B. Litschewski Paulson, St.L. Paulson, *OJLS* 26/1 (2006), p. 7]. It should be added that these theses were presented by Radbruch for the first time in a slightly less complicated way in 'Fünf Minuten Rechtsphilosophie' in G. Radbruch, *ibidem*, pp. 209–210 [English version: 'Five Minutes of Legal Philosophy (1945)', trans. B. Litschewski Paulson, St.L. Paulson, *OJLS* 26/1 (2006), p. 14]. Radbruch's original theses are quoted in Chap. 4 at p. 74.

[8] The term "un-law" was coined (in a context of the corruption of law) by N. MacCormick, *Institutions of Law*, Oxford 2007, p. 278. I suppose that the most precise English translation of the German term *gezetzliches Unrecht* is "statutory un-law" and I frequently use this translation hereafter, instead of "statutory injustice" – a term more commonly used in jurisprudential works.

[9] R. Alexy, *Mauerschützen*, Hamburg/Göttingen 1993, p. 4, 'Bulygins Kritik des Richtigkeitsarguments' in E. Garzón Valdés *et al.* (eds.), *Normative Systems in Legal and Moral Theory*, Berlin 1997, note 8 at p. 237, and *O pojęciu i naturze prawa / On the Concept and the Nature of Law*, Warszawa 2006, pp. 32–33.

[10] A. Peczenik, 'Non-Positivist Conception of Law' in (teamwork ed.), *Teoria prawa*, Toruń 1998, p. 225; L. Morawski, *Główne problemy współczesnej filozofii prawa* [Main Problems of the Contemporary Philosophy of Law] Warszawa 1999, p. 265. In German literature, the term *lex iniustissima* in reference to Radbruch's *Unerträglichkeitsthese* is used by W. Ott, *Der Rechtspositivismus*, 2nd ed., Berlin 1992, p. 194.

justice, such a statute is not so much unjust law, but is simply devoid of the nature of law (*Rechtsnatur*). What merits mentioning at this point, is Radbruch's third argument, called *Wehrlosigkeitsthese*, which is, in fact, no longer a part of "Radbruch's formula",[11] but which certainly serves as its basic factual premise. It provides that it was legal positivism, with its belief *Gesetz ist Gesetz*, that made German lawyers vulnerable (*wehrlos*) in the face of statutes with arbitrary and criminal content. Finally, while two theses constituting "Radbruch's formula" are recognised in the jurisprudential literature as disputable, *Wehrlosigkeitsthese* (interpreted as a descriptive claim) is now regarded as a false argument.[12]

"Radbruch's formula", according to the interpretation popularised by Radbruch's most prominent follower—Arthur Kaufmann—gave rise to the search for another "third way" (*dritten Weg*) so as to go beyond both legal positivism and natural law theories.[13] Among the German jurisprudential conceptions that directly refer to Radbruch's philosophy of law and that attempt to overcome this classic dilemma, one can, for example, point to Kaufmann's legal hermeneutics.[14] Undoubtedly, a theory that consistently seeks to develop an alternative to the traditional positivist understanding of law, without being another version of the doctrine of natural law, is Ralf Dreier's and Robert Alexy's nonpositivist conception of law. In German theory and philosophy of law, it has a function similar to the role of Ronald Dworkin's anti-positivism within the Anglo-American philosophy of law.[15] Incidentally, a similar trend was assumed—albeit within the frames of

[11] Such a standpoint is commonly assumed in the German literature – *see e.g.*, U. Neumann, 'Ralf Dreiers Radbruch' in R. Alexy (ed.), *Integratives Verstehen*, *op. cit.*, pp. 141ff., in particular, note 5 at p. 141, and the references cited therein.

[12] *See e.g.*, H. Dreier, 'Die Radbruchsche Formel – Erkenntnis oder Bekenntnis?' in H. Mayer (ed.), *Staatsrecht in Theorie und Praxis*, Wien 1991, pp. 120–127, 134; W. Ott, F. Buob, 'Did Legal Positivism Render German Jurists Defenceless during the Third Reich?', *ARSP* Bh. 52 (1993), pp. 92–105; M. Walther, 'Hat der juristische Positivismus die deutschen Juristen im "Dritten Reich" wehrlos gemacht? Zur Analyse und Kritik der Radbruch-These' in R. Dreier, W. Sellert (eds.), *Recht und Justiz im "Dritten Reich"*, Frankfurt am Main 1989, pp. 334, 351–353; J. Zajadło, 'Formuła Radbrucha a paradygmat niepozytywistycznej teorii prawa' [Radbruch's Formula and the Paradigm of Nonpositivist Legal Theory], *GSP* VII (2000), pp. 690ff., *Formuła Radbrucha*, *op. cit.*, pp. 115ff., and *Dziedzictwo przeszłości*, *op. cit.*, pp. 212–213, 238ff.

[13] A. Kaufmann, 'Die Naturrechtsrenaissance der ersten Nachkriegsjahre – und was daraus geworden ist', *op. cit.*, pp. 105, 117ff. and 'Problemgeschichte der Rechtsphilosophie' in A. Kaufmann *et al.* (eds.), *Einführung in Rechtsphilosophie und Rechtstheorie der Gegenwart*, 7th ed., Heidelberg 2004, pp. 89ff. In Polish literature, a similar standpoint has been expressed by J. Zajadło, *Formuła Radbrucha*, *op. cit.*, pp. 101ff.

[14] For more detail (in Polish literature) *see* M. Piechowiak, *W poszukiwaniu ontologicznych podstaw prawa. Arthura Kaufmanna teoria sprawiedliwości* [In Search for Ontological Foundations of Law. Arthur Kaufmann's Theory of Justice] Warszawa/Poznań 1992; G. Skąpska, J. Stelmach, 'Stare i nowe interpretacje filozofii prawa Arthura Kaufmanna' [Old and New Interpretations of Arthur Kaufmann's Philosophy of Law], *CC* 6/41–1/42 (1988–1989), pp. 75–81.

[15] The standpoint – expressed here – concerning Dworkin's theory is based on the methodological characteristics of his theory carried out by H.L.A. Hart, who treats it as a "third alternative" or a "middle way" between natural law and legal positivism (which constitutes, incidentally, according

broadly construed legal positivism—by the creators of institutional legal positivism: Neil MacCormick and Ota Weinberger[16] and by many Anglo-American legal philosophers who opted for a soft positivism, contemporarily taking the form of divergent versions of inclusive legal positivism, which was referred to by some of its creators (e.g., by Jules Coleman) as incorporationism.[17] In the case of the latter approaches, however, the core problem is to find a positivist "third way" between hard positivism and Dworkin's anti-positivist integral theory of law.

2.2 The Nonpositivist Conception of Ralf Dreier and Robert Alexy

The period of *Naturrechtsdiskussion* in the German philosophy of law ended more or less in the mid-1960s of the last century, giving way to the so-called fundamental debate (*Grundlagendiskussion*), which focused mainly on the methodological and

to Hart, a confusion of these two jurisprudential positions) – *see* H.L.A. Hart, 'El nuevo desafío al positivismo jurídico', trans. L.L. Hierro, F. Laporta, J.R. de Páramo, *SIS* 36 (1980), pp. 5, 13, 15ff. and J.R. de Páramo, 'Entrevista a H.L.A. Hart', *DOXA* 5 (1988), p. 347. The term that refers to Dworkin's theory as "the third theory of law" (next to the concept of legal positivism and natural law theories) derives probably from J. Mackie, 'The Third Theory of Law', *P&PA* 7/1 (1983), pp. 3–16. In Polish literature, a similar interpretation of Dworkin's philosophy of law is expressed by L. Morawski, *Główne problemy współczesnej filozofii prawa*, *op. cit.*, p. 257, who treats Dworkin simply as one of the nonpositivists, and by M. Zirk-Sadowski, *Wprowadzenie do filozofii prawa* [Introduction to Legal Philosophy], Kraków 2000, p. 197, who attributes to Dworkin the creation of "the third way in jurisprudence". It should be noted, however, that many of Dworkin's critics regard his theory as simply being a natural law theory – *see e.g.*, O. Weinberger, 'Die Naturrechtskonzeption von Ronald Dworkin' in D. Mayer-Maly, P.M. Simons (eds.), *Das Naturrechtsdenken heute und morgen*, Berlin 1983, pp. 497–515.

[16] *See* N. MacCormick, 'Law, Morality and Positivism' in N. MacCormick, O. Weinberger, *An Institutional Theory of Law*, Dordrecht/Boston/Lancaster/Tokyo 1986, pp. 139ff. and O. Weinberger, 'Beyond Positivism and Natural Law' in *ibidem*, pp. 111–126.

[17] On the issue of not yet entirely determined terminology *see e.g.*, J.L. Coleman, 'Incorporationism, Conventionality, and the Practical Difference Thesis' in *idem* (ed.), *Hart's Postscript*, Oxford/New York 2001, pp. 99ff., in particular note 5 at p. 100; J. Waldron, 'Normative (or Ethical) Positivism' in *ibidem*, pp. 411–414; K.E. Himma, 'Inclusive Legal Positivism' in J.L. Coleman, S.J. Shapiro (eds.), *The Oxford Handbook of Jurisprudence and Philosophy of Law*, *op. cit.*, pp. 125ff.; M.H. Kramer, 'Throwing Light on the Role of Moral Principles in the Law: Further Reflections', *LT* 8 (2002), pp. 115–116 and *Where Law and Morality Meet*, Oxford 2004, pp. 2ff. In further considerations, the issue of soft positivism is left to one side and it is referred to only incidentally. This does not mean that the question of the relationship between law and morals cannot be analysed in the context of a dispute between the inclusive (soft) and exclusive (hard) legal positivism. It would, however, require a separate study. Let us add in this context that the choice of the German nonpositivist conception of law as the background to our analysis of legal validity is at least partly justified by the fact that this conception applies directly to the continental legal system of statutory law (rather than – as in the case of inclusive positivism – to a common law legal system) and, moreover, its basic theses constitute a far more radical attempt to refute hard legal positivism – for more on the latter issue *see* Chap. 4 at pp. 131ff.

theoretical issues of the social sciences, including jurisprudence. A characteristic feature for this stage of development in the German philosophy and theory of law was in creating several mutually competing trends of jurisprudential lines of thought, commencing the process of rehabilitating practical philosophy as well as overcoming previous isolation in relation to international studies.[18] Although the primary purpose of this debate was to develop an appropriate methodological canon of social science and jurisprudence, the criticism of legal positivism was also perceptible in the period at issue.[19] However, the emergence of a nonpositivist conception, based on new grounds (the most crucial of which is analytical philosophy of law and, in particular, the theory of legal discourse developed in the framework of the latter), took place after the debate, in the 1980s of the last century. This approach differs significantly from the earlier—natural law—attempts to break the positivist way of understanding the law. One of its characteristic features is indeed the fact that the creators and supporters of nonpositivism not only make use of the arguments of an axiological or normative nature, but also of purely analytic arguments. Besides, the concept of natural law in general does not occur in the conception at issue and its nonpositivist character can be most of all proven by the fact that it categorically rejects the thesis of the conceptual separation of law and morals (typically referred to in the German literature as *Trennungsthese* or—less often—as *Neutralitätsthese*[20]).

Ralf Dreier was a forerunner of the nonpositivist conception of law in the contemporary German theory and philosophy of law. The definition of law, as proposed by him, was first presented during a lecture delivered at Cornell Law School in September 1984,[21] and supplemented the positivist criteria of authoritative issuance and social effectiveness with the requirement of at least minimum

[18] *See* R. Dreier, 'Hauptströmungen gegenwärtiger Rechtsphilosophie in Deutschland', *op. cit.*, pp. 156ff.; J.E. Herget, *Contemporary German Legal Philosophy*, Philadelphia 1996, pp. 7ff.; U. Neumann, 'Rechtsphilosophie in Deutschland seit 1945', *op. cit.*, pp. 164ff.; K. Opałek, 'Główne kierunki niemieckiej teorii i filozofii prawa po II wojnie światowej', *op. cit.*, pp. 22ff.; M.E. Salas, '¿Qué pasa actualmente en la Teoría del Derecho alemana?', *op. cit.*, pp. 201ff.

[19] As noted by R. Dreier, based on the research carried out by his associates (*see idem*, 'Zur gegenwärtigen Diskussion des Verhältnisses von Recht und Moral in der Bundesrepublik Deutschland', *ARSP* Bh. 44 (1991), p. 55), 53 authors out of 99 German-language jurisprudential works, written between 1970–1989, rejected positivist argumentation supporting the thesis of the separation of law and morals.

[20] On a slightly opaque German terminology *see* Chap. 4 at p. 122ff.

[21] The text of the lecture was presented by Dreier in 'Der Begriff des Rechts', *NJW* 39 (1986), pp. 890–896 and in significantly revised English version: 'Some Remarks on the Concept of Law' in W. Krawietz *et al.* (eds.), *Prescriptive Formality and Normative Rationality in Modern Legal Systems*, Berlin 1994, pp. 109–124. It should be added that the postulate of formulating a "concept of law modified by practical reason" (*vernunftrechtlich modifizierter Rechtsbegriff*) can be found already in Dreier's early work 'Bemerkungen zur Rechtserkenntnistheorie', *RT* Bh. 1 (1979), p. 105, whereas the first proposal of nonpositivist concept of legal validity (but not yet the mere concept of law) was presented by Dreier in a study 'Recht und Moral' in *idem*, *Recht – Moral – Ideologie*, Frankfurt am Main 1981, p. 198.

ethical justification (minimum substantial correctness)—so characteristic for nonpositivism. According to the definition proposed by Dreier:

> Law consists of those norms which belong to the constitution of a system of norms organized in a state or on the international level, if this system is on the whole socially effective and, in a minimal sense, ethically justifiable, and of those norms which are laid down according to this constitution, if these, taken by themselves, are socially effective or have at least the chance to become socially effective and which are, in a minimal sense, ethically justifiable.[22]

This definition was later modified by Robert Alexy, the author who is rightly recognised as a leading representative of contemporary German nonpositivism and who also developed an extensive line of argument for the thesis of a necessary conceptual connection between law and morals. According to the approach proposed by Alexy, the law is a system of norms that:

1. Lays the claim to correctness (*Anspruch auf Richtigkeit*);
2a. Consists of the totality of norms that belong to a constitution by and large (*im großen und ganzen*) socially efficacious and that are not extremely unjust;
2b. As well as the totality of norms that are enacted in accordance with this constitution, norms that manifest a minimum social efficacy or the chance of becoming socially efficacious and that are not extremely unjust;
3. And, finally, comprises the principles and other normative arguments on which the procedure of law application is and/or must be grounded in order to satisfy the claim to correctness.[23]

The above-mentioned argument, claiming that Dreier's and Alexy's concept of law is not of a natural law character, though it is nonpositivist, can best be justified on the basis of a chart identifying the components of the definition of law, as proposed by Alexy.[24] Alexy assumes that the possible elements of the definition of law are due enactment (*ordnungsgemäße Gesetztheit*), social efficacy (*soziale*

---

[22] R. Dreier, 'Some Remarks on the Concept of Law', *op. cit.*, note 32 on pp. 123–124. *Cf. idem*, 'Der Begriff des Rechts', *op. cit.*, p. 896 and 'Göttliches und menschliches Recht', *ZevK* 32 (1987), p. 296.

[23] *See* R. Alexy, *Begriff und Geltung des Rechts*, Freiburg/München 1992, p. 201 [English version: *The Argument from Injustice. A Reply to Legal Positivism*, trans. B. Litschewski Paulson, St.L. Paulson, Oxford 2002, p. 127] and 'A Definition of Law' in W. Krawietz *et al.* (eds.), *Prescriptive Formality and Normative Rationality in Modern Legal Systems*, *op. cit.*, p. 102. The English translation and numbering of the elements of the definition (within its second part) have been modified.

[24] R. Alexy, 'A Definition of Law', *op. cit.*, pp. 101–102. Alexy presented the analysis of the definition of law (however without the diagram itself) firstly in *Begriff und Geltung des Rechts*, *op. cit.*, p. 29 [English version, p. 13]. *Cf.* R. Alexy, 'Law and Correctness', trans. K. Bock, in M.D. A. Freeman (ed.), *Legal Theory at the End of the Millennium*, Oxford 1998, p. 214 [German extended version: 'Recht und Richtigkeit' in W. Krawietz *et al.* (eds.), *The Reasonable as Rational?*, Berlin 2000, p. 16].

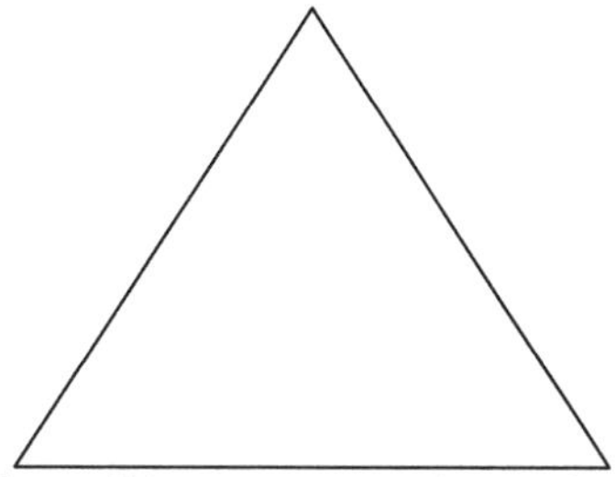

Fig. 2.1 The definitional triangle of law

Wirksamkeit) as well as substantial correctness (*inhaltliche Richtigkeit*). The area of the definition of law operating these elements is presented by the following scheme (see Fig. 2.1).

Alexy stresses that any positivist definitions of law are located on the line connecting point A with point C, whilst pure natural law concepts make use of the definitions of law within point B. Nonpositivist conceptions of law, on the other hand, are placed in the whole area of the triangle and, more precisely, these are the definitions contained between the line A–C, and the point B. Their characteristic feature is, therefore, that they call into question the positivist thesis of the separation of law and morals, modifying the positivist definition of law by supplementing it with—differently understood—requirements of substantial (e.g. moral) correctness or rightness.

Despite this clear justification for a nonpositivist—rather than natural law—character of Dreier's and Alexy's conception, it is worth pointing out the emerging voices in the literature that treat the conception at issue as an attempt at the renaissance of natural law thinking.[25] A notable example is the opinion expressed in relation to Dreier's nonpositivist conception by Werner Krawietz, who imputes that Dreier attempts to renew the tradition of natural law (or law of reason) by making morality the fundament of law (*Fundamentalisierung des Rechts durch Moral*).[26] A decisive role is taken in the assessment of this complaint through the analysis of the argumentation in favour of the nonpositivist conception of law, as

---

[25] *See e.g.*, E. Hilgendorf, 'Zur transzendentalpragmatischen Begründung von Diskursregeln', *RT* 27 (1995), p. 185; E. Bulygin, 'Is There a Conceptual Connection between Law and Morality?', *AS* 3 (1999), p. 45; M. La Torre, 'On Two Distinct and Opposed Versions of Natural Law: "Exclusive" versus "Inclusive"', *RJ* 19 (2006), pp. 207ff. In Polish literature, the opposite view, consisting of distinguishing nonpositivist conceptions from natural law ones is explicitly expressed by L. Morawski, 'Państwo prawa' [Law-Governed State] in M. Zirk-Sadowski (ed.), *Filozoficzno-teoretyczne problemy sądowego stosowania prawa*, Łódź 1997, p. 17. Anticipating the results of the analysis carried out in subsequent chapters, it can be clearly noted that referring to Dreier's and Alexy's conception as being of a natural law character is primarily persuasive in its purpose – however *cf.* Chap. 4, the text corresponding to note 158 at p. 100.

[26] W. Krawietz, 'Neues Naturrecht oder Rechtspositivismus? Eine kritische Auseinandersetzung mit dem Begriff des Rechts bei Ralf Dreier und Norbert Hoerster', *RT* 18 (1987), pp. 212ff.

stated by Dreier and Alexy, which I attempt to carry out in the following chapters. However, even at this stage, the possibility of a preliminary reply to the objection formulated by Krawietz arises. To carry this forward, the identification of both the positivist and nonpositivist elements used in the above-mentioned nonpositivist definitions of law is necessary. This operation will also be useful in the context of further analysis of nonpositivist argumentation, given that the structure and content of these definitions is undoubtedly a direct result of formulating and applying various nonpositivist arguments.

2.3 Some Remarks on the Construction of the Nonpositivist Definition of Law

The first observation that we will make when comparing the nonpositivist definitions of law proposed by Dreier and Alexy is finding significant differences in their construction and a diverse distribution of positivist and nonpositivist elements which are used in their formulations.

Let us first note that the definition of law proposed by Dreier is, on the one hand, much weaker—in terms of overcoming the positivist concept of law—than Alexy's definition. Two components of his definition are indeed positivist in nature, and only one is of a nonpositivist character. A preliminary prerequisite for recognising norms for components of the system of law is whether they are a part of the constitution of the state or interstate normative system or their establishment is in accordance with the lawmaking rules of such a system—it is the first purely positivist element. The constitution of this system is to be, in principle, socially effective, whereas norms that do not belong to it, though established in compliance with the latter, are to be characterised by at least a minimum level of social effectiveness or the possibility of such effectiveness—this is the second positivist element. Without a doubt, a positivist would easily reconcile these two conditions because they do not go beyond the paradigm of a positivist understanding of law. It is only the third element of Dreier's definition of law that determines its nonpositivist character; namely, the requirement of at least minimum ethical justification (or at least the possibility of such justification) of the norms that constitute the law. On the other hand, Dreier's definition, at least at first glance, is stronger than that of Alexy is, since the requirement of at least minimum ethical justification (namely at least minimum substantial correctness) of the norms is a positive prerequisite, allowing for the treatment of certain norms in terms of them belonging to the legal system. In Alexy's definition, by contrast, this condition is negatively formulated; namely, in the form of a lack of extreme injustice. In general, the application of Dreier's conception in determining whether a given norm constitutes an element of the legal system consists in firstly determining the scope of possible legal norms by means of two positivist criteria and only then is it subject to an additional nonpositivist test. What therefore seems legitimate is the view that Dreier only modifies the positivist concept of law, as it undoubtedly constitutes the starting point of the conception of law proposed by him.

The construction of Alexy's definition of law is far more complicated. The starting point for his definition of law is not a positivist conception of law—but—firstly, the three fundamental nonpositivist arguments: the argument from correctness (*Richtigkeitsargument*), the argument from injustice (*Unrechtsargument*)[27] and the argument from principles (*Prinzipienargument*), which respectively correspond to the three above-mentioned parts of his definition of law,[28] and secondly—what also underlies Alexy's nonpositivist conception—a discursive perception of the law as a system consisting not only of norms-rules, but also of norms-principles (which jointly constitute the "passive side" of legal system) and the procedures of the creation, application and discursive analysis of law (which form an "active side" of it).[29] Therefore, the extension of the nonpositivist concept of law is, on one hand, narrower than in the positivist conception—utterly unfair norms are eliminated from it—and, on the other hand, it is wider, because it also covers non-positivised principles and normative arguments, which serve the purpose of satisfying the claim to correctness. The basic nonpositivist condition, whose realisation allows us to refer to a given normative system as law, is the fact that this system adopts the claim to correctness (*Anspruch auf Richtigkeit*). This is, therefore, why Alexy's concept of law cannot be treated merely as a modification of the positivist one, since the nonpositivist concept of law is dominated—both in quantitative[30] and qualitative aspects—by the elements that legal positivists cannot agree to if they do not want to lose their positivistic identity.[31]

---

[27] I follow the typical translation of the German term *Unrechtsargument,* which is usually translated as "argument from (of) injustice" in the jurisprudential literature. However, it is worth noting that probably the better translation of this term is "argument from un-law", since *Unrecht* means "un-law". For more on this issue *see* Chap. 4 at pp. 70ff.

[28] R. Alexy, 'A Definition of Law', *op. cit.*, p. 103 and *Begriff und Geltung des Rechts, op. cit.*, pp. 201ff. [English version, pp. 127ff.]. It is worth adding that the argument from correctness is manifested not only in the first portion of Alexy's definition but it also influences the way in which its third portion has been formulated.

[29] *See* R. Alexy, 'Die Idee einer prozeduralen Theorie der juristischen Argumentation', *RT* Bh. 2 (1981), pp. 185ff., 'Rechtssystem und praktische Vernunft', *RT* 18 (1987), pp. 416ff., 'Idee und Struktur eines vernünftigen Rechtssystems', *ARSP* Bh. 44 (1991), pp. 36ff., and 'Ota Weinbergers Kritik der diskurstheoretischen Deutung juristischer Rationalität', *RT* Bh. 14 (1994), pp. 152ff. *Cf.* A. Aarnio, R. Alexy, A. Peczenik, 'The Foundation of Legal Reasoning', *RT* 12 (1981), pp. 272ff. and the monograph by J.-R. Sieckmann, *Regelmodelle und Prinzipienmodelle des Rechtssystems*, Baden-Baden 1990, in particular pp. 89ff.

[30] We should add here that the positivist requirements of due enactment and social efficacy occur only in the second part of Alexy's definition, while the remaining parts of his definition of law are purely nonpositivist.

[31] For more on "the problem of identity" of legal positivists *see* L. Morawski, 'Hard Positivism, Soft Positivism and Dead Positivism', trans. T.Z. Wolański, *Ius et Lex* I/1 (2005), pp. 156ff.

2.4 The Nonpositivist Conception of Law and the Concept of Legal Validity (Preliminary Remarks)

One cannot accurately assess the value and merits of Dreier's and Alexy's theory without a thorough analysis of the argumentation justifying the nonpositivist concept of law. However, before dealing with the latter, there are still a few preliminary observations to be made on the relationship between the concept of law proposed by them and the concept of legal validity. It should be noted that the main problem—which is to be clarified by the argumentation presented in this part of the work—is the question of the possibility of taking into consideration the requirements of substantial (e.g. moral) correctness and/or justice of law in the definition of the juristic concept of the validity of statutory law. In this context, one can observe that Dreier's and Alexy's conception does not make the discussion at issue easier, since the nonpositivist definitions of the concept of law—as outlined above—are constructed so that the concept of law embraces the concept of legal validity. In other words, both conceptual suggestions seek to construct a nonpositivist concept of law while meeting the function of the (nonpositivist?) concept of the validity of law.

Dreier presents the following justification for embracing the concept of validity to the concept of law. If the aim of our deliberations is to obtain juristic (rather than a sociological or ethical) definition of law—a jurisprudential definition, which also proves useful in legal dogmatics and in the application of law—then what should be deemed as paradigmatic in terms of a legal perspective is the point of view of a judge for whom the question of "What is the law?" boils down to the question: "What is the valid law?".[32] Thus—according to Dreier—the concepts of existing law, positive law and legally valid law (*rechtlich geltendes Recht*) are treated, from a juristic point of view, as synonymous.[33]

Alexy, on the other hand, justifies embracing the concept of validity in the concept of law primarily by means of the argument proclaiming that in this manner we avoid trivialising the problem of selecting the appropriate (positivist or nonpositivist) definition of law.[34] This trivialisation relies on the fact that when applying the concept of law, which does not include the element of validity, one can maintain (as, for example, Hans Kelsen put it in his classic formula) that the law can consist of the norms of any (moral) content.[35] In this trivial—yet failing to address

---

[32] R. Dreier, 'Some Remarks on the Concept of Law', *op. cit.*, pp. 114–115, 122.

[33] R. Dreier, 'Der Begriff des Rechts', *op. cit.*, p. 894 and 'Neues Naturrecht oder Rechtspositivismus? In Erwiderung auf Werner Krawietz', *RT* 18 (1987), p. 376.

[34] R. Alexy, 'On Necessary Relations between Law and Morality', *RJ* 2 (1989), p. 170 and *Begriff und Geltung des Rechts*, *op. cit.*, pp. 44–46 [English version, pp. 23–24].

[35] Original version: "Jeder beliebige Inhalt kann Recht sein, es gibt kein menschliches Verhalten, das als solches, kraft seines Gehalts, ausgeschlossen wäre, zum Inhalt einer Rechtsnorm zu werden" – *Reine Rechtslehre*, Leipzig/Wien 1934, p. 63. This was followed closely in the second revised edition of *Reine Rechtslehre*, Wien 1960, p. 201 [English version: *Pure Theory of Law*, trans. M. Knight, Berkeley/Los Angeles/London 1967, p. 198]. On the restrictions of this positivist principle accepted by Kelsen *cf.* Chap. 7, text to notes 256–263 at pp. 302–304.

the core issues—way, a positivist might seek to demonstrate that the necessary conceptual link between law and morality does not exist. However, such an argument does not apply when legal validity is incorporated into the concept of law. For the sake of our deliberations, it should be added at this point that—contrary to Alexy's argument—the proponents of legal positivism generally use the concept of law identified with the valid law, and they are far from claiming that the fact that law can have any content entails that the law should have any (moral) content, and the requirement of compliance with the law and of obedience to the law are conclusive.[36]

Leaving aside for the time being the question of whether the above-mentioned arguments should be regarded as sufficient for the adoption of the concept of law including its validity, one can point at serious doubts arising in connection with equating the law with the valid law.[37] At this point, we shall content ourselves with

---

[36] *See e.g.*, N. Hoerster, 'Zum begrifflichen Verhältnis von Recht und Moral', *NHPh* 17 (1979), p. 82; M. Kriele, 'Rechtspflicht und die positivistische Trennung von Recht und Moral' in *idem, Recht, Vernunft, Wirklichkeit*, Berlin 1990, pp. 454ff.; J. Woleński, 'O pozytywizmie prawniczym' [On Legal Positivism] in J. Pawlica (ed.), *Etyka a Prawo i Praworządność*, Kraków 1998, p. 15; differently: L. Morawski, 'Hard Positivism, Soft Positivism and Dead Positivism', *op. cit.*, pp. 175ff. It should be added that modern defenders of legal positivism often, in their deliberations, come to the conclusion that there is not even a *prima facie* obligation to obey the law – *see e.g.*, J. Raz, 'The Obligation to Obey the Law' in *idem, The Authority of Law*, Oxford 1979, pp. 233–249; M.B.E. Smith, 'Is There a Prima Facie Obligation to Obey the Law?', *YLJ* 82 (1973), pp. 950–976, or that the law (and the rule of recognition, in particular) does not impose any moral obligation at all – *see e.g.*, J.L. Coleman, 'On the Relationship between Law and Morality', *RJ* 2 (1989), pp. 66ff. According to H.L.A. Hart: "It seems clear that the mere existence of a legal system, irrespective of the character of its laws, is not sufficient in any intelligible theory of morality to establish that a person ought morally to do what its laws require him to do" ('Problems of the Philosophy of Law' in H.L.A. Hart, *Essays in Jurisprudence and Philosophy*, Oxford 1983, p. 118). Incidentally, this kind of evolution of the positivist standpoint was predicted almost fifty years ago by L.L. Fuller, 'Positivism and Fidelity to Law – A Reply to Professor Hart', *HLR* 71 (1958), p. 656, who claimed that: "I do not think it is unfair to the positivistic philosophy to say that it never gives any coherent meaning to the moral obligation of fidelity to law. [. . .]. The fundamental postulate of positivism – that law must be strictly severed from morality – seems to deny the possibility of any bridge between the obligation to obey the law and other moral obligations". When evaluating the controversy between positivism and nonpositivism, it can be noted that A. Peczenik argued, within his nonpositivist conception, in favour of the thesis concerning the existence of a *prima facie* moral obligation to obey the law regardless of its content – weakened, however, by excluding from the scope of validity of this obligation the "extremely immoral normative systems", which are by no means valid law – *see idem*, 'Non-Positivist Conception of Law', *op. cit.*, pp. 233–236 and 'Law, Morality, Coherence and Truth', *RJ* 7 (1994), p. 148. The views presented by Peczenik come as no surprise: the nonpositivist conception of law, which excludes from its scope extremely unjust legal systems or individual legal norms, can be consistently combined with the moral obligation to obey the law without any additional moral, theoretical or philosophical constraints.

[37] For more detail *see* T. Gizbert-Studnicki, A. Grabowski, 'Kilka uwag o niepozytywistycznej koncepcji prawa' [Some Remarks on the Nonpositivist Conception of Law] in I. Bogucka, Z. Tobor (eds.), *Prawo a wartości*, Kraków 2003, pp. 57ff. The argument quoted below comes from T. Gizbert-Studnicki.

paying attention to the most obvious yet most essential doubt. The consequence of Dreier's and Alexy's nonpositivist conception of law is, inter alia, the fact that the criteria normally understood as the criteria of the validity of law become, quite simply, the criteria of law. From a semantic point of view, the term "valid law" is therefore redundant. The attribute "valid" operates in this context as a confirming attribute; in this way, the extensions of the terms "law" and "valid law" are identical. Thus, the compound "invalid law" is either an empty term, because the attribute "invalid" is purely abolishing in its character, or one might consider that the attribute "invalid" is a modifying (abolishing-determining) attribute, which shifts the scope of the term "law" in the set of qualitatively different objects.[38] Therefore, if Dreier's and Alexy's suggestions were treated consistently, the application of the concept of the validity of law would become unnecessary. It seems, however, that such a depletion of the conceptual instrumentation of jurisprudence (resulting from equating both intension and extension of the concept of law with the concept of valid law, respectively) entails not only conceptual, but also practical difficulties in the description and in the analysis of many phenomena typical of modern systems of statutory law.[39]

[38] The terminology used here comes from K. Twardowski, 'Z logiki przymiotników' [From the Logic of Adjectives] in *idem*, *Wybrane pisma filozoficzne*, Warszawa 1965, pp. 373–375. For more on Twardowski's conception *see* Chap. 4 at pp. 77ff. The question as to whether the attribute "invalid" in reference to the law is of a purely abolishing character or rather of an abolishing-determining (modifying) one will be touched upon again in Chap. 5 at pp. 201ff.

[39] This point will be discussed in Chap. 5 at p. 207 and, indirectly, in Chap. 7 at pp. 351ff.

Chapter 3
Argumentation for the Nonpositivist Concept of Law

3.1 The Methodological Framework of Nonpositivist Argumentation

The creators of the German nonpositivist conception of law adopt a common methodological standpoint on the characteristics of the theory of law as a scientific discipline. In Alexy and Dreier's paper stating the main assumption of their programme—*The Concept of Jurisprudence* of 1990[1]—they opt in favour of a dualistic understanding of the theory of law as a discipline consisting of a general juristic theory of law (having the nature of an object-oriented theory) and of the juristic theory of legal science (having a metatheoretical character[2]). In their view, what distinguishes the theory of law from other legal disciplines (such as philosophy or the sociology of law) is neither the object of the study nor the methodology of the undertaken research, but is first and foremost a specific legal aspect (or perspective) of jurisprudential considerations, tantamount to the conclusion that the whole of the science of law aims at establishing "what persons in particular cases are legally obligated, prohibited, enabled or permitted to do"[3]; that is, at determining legal obligations imposed by the law on legal subjects. This implies a close link between legal theory and the theory of adjudication or even with the legal decision-making process.[4] In the context of such a program, the orientation of legal theory on the practice of its application (which indeed cannot be denied reason), it may not be surprising that those authors strongly reject an understanding of the concept of the

[1] The paper was published in *RJ* 3 (1990), pp. 1–13.

[2] *Ibidem*, p. 7.

[3] *Ibidem*, p. 3.

[4] *Ibidem*, pp. 3, 9, 13. What merits noting is a considerable similarity with an equally practical standpoint expressed by another distinguished critic of legal positivism, R. Dworkin, who treats jurisprudence as a "general part of adjudication, silent prologue to any decision at law" – quoted from *Law's Empire*, London 1986, p. 90. For more on this *see* Chap. 6, the fragment concerning the second goal of clarification at pp. 223–224.

A. Grabowski, *Juristic Concept of the Validity of Statutory Law*,
DOI 10.1007/978-3-642-27688-0_3, © Springer-Verlag Berlin Heidelberg 2013

theory of law based on the dichotomy between theory and practice, treating it as obsolete.[5]

With regard to the research methodology for the theory of law, Alexy and Dreier distinguish three dimensions: analytical, empirical and normative, which constitute the basis for jurisprudential considerations.[6] The analytical dimension serves mostly as the grounds for logical and conceptual analysis of basic legal and juristic concepts. The empirical dimension provides the basis for the consideration of such specific issues as the identification of valid positive law (being the subject of the general juristic theory of law) and the actual method for practising the respective legal sciences (being the subject of reflection of the general juristic theory of legal science), an examination of the ways in which jurists use factual premises in the normative argumentation and the analysis of the factual structures and functions of the law. In cases where there is a normative dimension in terms of jurisprudence, we encounter the problems of finding answers to two fundamental questions: "How the law should be?" and "How legal science should be performed?".[7] This dimension, therefore, constitutes the grounds for creating the theories of right or just law and a good legal science—which are mostly of an interdisciplinary character because they are, respectively, associated with the primary objective of the research of the philosophy of law (or more specifically, the ethics of law) and with normative theory and the ethics of science.

Before proceeding to a detailed discussion of a conceptual framework for nonpositivist argumentation, two additional remarks are required. The first concerns the nonpositivist argumentation developed by Dreier, which was created at least several years prior to the publication of the above-mentioned collective work on jurisprudential methodology. Hence, the metatheoretical position presented therein could not have been fully reflected in his nonpositivist argumentation.[8] The second remark concerns the argumentation developed by Alexy. At the time of launching this conception—which took place more or less simultaneously with the publication of *The Concept of Jurisprudence*—Alexy undoubtedly placed his nonpositivist conception within the theory of law. With time, nonetheless, and especially since taking up human rights issues (i.e., more or less since the mid-90s of the twentieth century), an important change in Alexy's research approach can be seen, involving the transition

[5] R. Alexy, R. Dreier, 'The Concept of Jurisprudence', *op. cit.*, p. 8.

[6] *Ibidem*, pp. 9–10.

[7] *Ibidem*, p. 10.

[8] It should be noted, however, that some theses expressed in 'The Concept of Jurisprudence' can already be traced to Dreier's early works. For instance, the thesis on perceiving the theory of law as the theory of positive law, which is primarily addressed to legal dogmatists, was formulated by Dreier in *Was ist und wozu Allgemeine Rechtstheorie?*, Tübingen 1975, pp. 23–24, 32. In addition, the conceptual distinction between the theory of law, the philosophy of law, and legal sociology on the basis of the differences in research aspects can be found in the paper published in 1979 – 'Bemerkungen zur Rechtserkenntnistheorie', *op. cit.*, p. 101. Both these theses are also included in the basic work that presents Dreier's nonpositivist argumentation – 'Der Begriff des Rechts', *op. cit.*, pp. 893–894.

from the theoretical (jurisprudential) level to the level of the philosophy of law. A significant manifestation of the new approach was the lecture delivered by Alexy during the XXI World Congress of the International Association for the Philosophy of Law and Social Philosophy (*IVR*) in Lund in 2003. Issues of moral appropriateness and the legitimisation of law, inclusion of morality into law and correctness, understood as one of the two essential features of law (the second—coercion), are treated therein as the basic problems of the philosophy of law (as opposed to the juristic theory of law).[9] This evolution of Alexy's metatheoretical position, though, appears to be of limited importance, given the correctness of his argumentation in favour of a nonpositivist conception of law.

When creating the nonpositivist conception of law, Dreier applies some indirectly correlated distinctions of a conceptual character.[10] He admits that the law is a very complex phenomenon that can be analysed from different research perspectives: for example, from a historical, sociological, ethical, logical, dogmatic, economic, linguistic or teleological perspective.[11] When it comes to the basic problem of developing the very concept of law, according to Dreier, three perspectives should be deemed most crucial; namely, juristic (characteristic of the theory of law), sociological (corresponding to the sociology of law) and ethical (typical of philosophical deliberations).[12] These three key perspectives correspond to three different concepts of law, whereas what differs between them is a distinct definition of the concept of valid law.[13] In his own nonpositivist conception of law, Dreier relies on two distinctions: firstly, on the differentiation—referring to a well-known distinction of H.L.A. Hart—between an internal perspective (the perspective of a participant) and an external perspective (the perspective of the observer)[14]; and secondly, he distinguishes between the concepts of law that contain or do not contain the concept of its validity.[15]

---

[9] R. Alexy, 'The Nature of Legal Philosophy', *AS* 7 (2003), pp. 67ff. *Cf. idem*, 'On Two Juxtapositions: Concept and Nature, Law and Philosophy. Some Comments on Joseph Raz's "Can There Be a Theory of Law?"', *RJ* 20 (2007), pp. 166ff. For more on the method of developing the philosophy of law, postulated by Alexy, *see* Chap. 4 at pp. 136–137.

[10] This situation underwent a change when Alexy developed – in a more ordered way – conceptual frames of nonpositivist argumentation, which were by and large accepted by Dreier (apart from a certain terminological specification, which is to be discussed later) – *see idem*, 'Zur gegenwärtigen Diskussion des Verhältnisses von Recht und Moral in der Bundesrepublik Deutschland', *op. cit.*, pp. 58–59.

[11] R. Dreier, 'Der Begriff des Rechts', *op. cit.*, p. 893.

[12] *Cf. ibidem*, pp. 893ff. and 'Some Remarks on the Concept of Law', *op. cit.*, p. 122.

[13] 'Der Begriff des Rechts', *op. cit.*, p. 894. Dreier had already presented the examples of these three definitions of the validity of the law (sociological, ethical and juristic – in a positivist and nonpositivist version) in his earlier work 'Recht und Moral', *op. cit.*, pp. 194 and 198, only to repeat them in 'Some Remarks on the Concept of Law', *op. cit.*, pp. 122ff.

[14] *See* 'Der Begriff des Rechts', *op. cit.*, pp. 890ff. and 'Some Remarks on the Concept of Law', *op. cit.*, p. 114. For more on this distinction *see infra*, note 23 at p. 27 and Chap. 6 at p. 226ff.

[15] 'Der Begriff des Rechts', *op. cit.*, p. 891 and 'Some Remarks on the Concept of Law', *op. cit.*, p. 115.

Distinctions adopted by Dreier can also be found in more systematically constructed conceptual frames of Alexy's nonpositivist argumentation.[16] They boil down to five distinctions: (1) a distinction between analytical and normative argumentation; (2) a distinction between the concept that does or does not contain the concept of its validity; (3) a distinction between the legal system understood as a system of norms and as a system of procedures; (4) a distinction between the perspective of a participant and observer; and (5) a distinction as to the two types of conceptual relations between law and morality; that is, classifying and qualifying relations.

The distinction between the analytical and normative argumentation in the debate on the concept of law identifies two basic forms of argumentation in favour of or against the thesis on the necessity of defining law in such a way that this definition contains moral elements (*Verbindungsthese*). Analytical arguments may justify the theses claiming that the inclusion of moral elements in the definition of law is conceptually necessary, possible or impossible. Normative arguments, on the other hand, may justify the theses claiming that the inclusion (or non-inclusion) of moral elements in the definition of this concept is necessary in order to achieve a particular purpose or to meet a certain standard. It should be noted that Alexy initially also allows for nonpositivist empirical arguments, yet he does not analyse them (and, in his later works, he does not even mention them), because he believes that they in fact constitute merely the components of analytical or normative argumentation and, furthermore, that they are rather on the peripheries of the main debate on the correctness of legal positivism.[17]

The issue of differentiating the concept of law by embracing or not embracing the concept of legal validity has already been touched upon.[18] So let us recall only that Alexy is strongly in favour of referring nonpositivist argumentation to the concept of law including the concept of its validity, recognising, nonetheless, the

[16] These frames are presented by Alexy in two papers introducing a complex analytical nonpositivist argumentation: 'On Necessary Relations between Law and Morality', *op. cit.*, pp. 170–173 and in an extended German-language version: 'Zur Kritik des Rechtspositivismus', *ARSP* Bh. 37 (1990), pp. 12–14. On distinguishing the issue of the participant's and the observer's perspective *cf. idem*, 'An Answer to Joseph Raz' in G. Pavlakos (ed.), *Law, Rights and Discourse*, Oxford/Portland 2007, pp. 37–55. It should be noted that Alexy also uses this framework in his normative argumentation, yet adding here a further distinction in the form of distinguishing the argument from injustice (*Unrechtsargument*), and the argument from principles (*Prinzipienargument*), which nonetheless – in my opinion – is of substantive character and which will be covered in subsequent points – *see* R. Alexy, 'Zur Verteidigung eines nichtpositivistischen Rechtsbegriffs' in W. Krawietz, G.H. von Wright (eds.), *Öffentliche oder private Moral?*, Berlin 1992, pp. 86–90. *Cf. idem, Begriff und Geltung des Rechts, op. cit.*, pp. 44–51 [English version, pp. 23–27] and 'A Definition of Law', *op. cit.*, pp. 103–104. *See* also *infra*, note 26 at p. 28.

[17] *See* R. Alexy, 'On Necessary Relations Between Law and Morality', *op. cit.*, p. 168, 'Zur Kritik des Rechtspositivismus', *op. cit.*, p. 10, 'Zur Verteidigung eines nichtpositivistischen Rechtsbegriffs', *op. cit.*, p. 86, *Begriff und Geltung des Rechts*, *op. cit.*, p. 40 [English version, p. 20], and 'A Definition of Law', *op. cit.*, p. 104. The issue of leaving aside empirical argumentation is discussed in Chap. 4 at pp. 181ff.

[18] *See* Chap. 2, pp. 20–22.

possibility of a dispute with legal positivism in relation to such a concept of law that does not embrace the concept of validity.[19] According to him, due to the introduction of the concept of validity to the concept of law, norms need no longer be conceived merely as "semantic entities",[20] yet our discussion is also being opened up on the institutional and social aspects of the law, associated with the processes of making, applying and enforcing the law.

The third distinction consists in distinguishing the legal system as a system of norms and as a system of procedures. Referring to methodological terminology introduced by Polish analytical philosopher Kazimierz Ajdukiewicz,[21] the first approach to the system of law relates to its apragmatic aspect (norms are treated as results of the procedures), whilst the second relates to its pragmatic aspect (the system of law is understood here as a set of procedures, perceived not as mere legal regulations but as activities—regulated by law—of making, justifying, interpreting, applying and enforcing the law).[22]

Distinguishing the perspective of the participant and the observer is another methodological distinction adopted by Alexy. Since these concepts are ambiguous, Alexy does not merely recall Hart's classic distinction of the internal and external point of view,[23] but he defines it anew. The participant's perspective (paradigm: judge's point of view) is assumed by someone who—within a given legal system—participates in a discussion concerning the issue of what a particular system requires, prohibits, permits and what kind of authority it grants, whilst the observer's perspective (e.g. a white American tourist travelling with his Afro-American wife to South Africa during the apartheid era[24]) is assumed by someone

[19] *See e.g.*, R. Alexy, 'On Necessary Relations between Law and Morality', *op. cit.*, note 1 at p. 168 and 'Zur Verteidigung eines nichtpositivistischen Rechtsbegriffs', *op. cit.*, note 13 at p. 88.

[20] R. Alexy, 'A Definition of Law', *op. cit.*, p. 103.

[21] K. Ajdukiewicz, *Logika pragmatyczna* [Pragmatic Logic], Warszawa 1975, pp. 173–177. This differentiation obviously refers to the famous distinction between acts and results developed by K. Twardowski – *see idem, O czynnościach i wytworach* [On Acts and Results], Kraków 1911, pp. 6ff.

[22] Alexy uses a different terminology here, which – taking into account the next distinction between the participant and observer – can easily cause misunderstanding. He writes (respectively) about the "external side" (*äußere Seite*) and the "internal side" (*innere Seite*) of the legal system – *see idem*, 'Zur Kritik des Rechtspositivismus', *op. cit.*, p. 12 and 'On Necessary Relations between Law and Morality', *op. cit.*, p. 171. Therefore, the terminology introduced by Ajdukiewicz seems to be more appropriate.

[23] *See* H.L.A. Hart, *The Concept of Law*, Oxford 1961, pp. 55ff., 86ff. On the indeterminacy of the concepts of participant and observer and on the issue of differentiating between an internal and external point of view *see e.g.*, N. MacCormick, *Legal Reasoning and Legal Theory*, Oxford 1978, pp. 275ff. For more on various points of view adopted in jurisprudential analyses *see* Chap. 6 at pp. 226–228.

[24] Alexy borrowed this example from N. Hoerster, 'Zur Verteidigung des Rechtspositivismus', *NJW* 39 (1986), p. 2481. I believe that Alexy's perspective of the observer corresponds with a well-known perspective of a Holmesian "bad man" who *ex definitione* is not interested in moral correctness of legal decisions: "A man who cares nothing for an ethical rule which is believed and practised by his neighbors is likely nevertheless to care a good deal to avoid being made to pay

who does not ask what is the proper (correct) decision in a given legal system, but asks what decisions are actually made under it.

What remains to be discussed is the distinction between the two types of conceptual relations between law and morality; namely, classifying and qualifying relations.[25] The characteristic feature of a classifying relation is that if a given norm or a system of norms does not meet certain moral criteria, they are not legal at all (they do not have the status of a legal norm or a legal system). A qualifying relation is the one where such a norm or a system of norms may in fact be regarded as legal, but they are defective legal norms or legal systems. What is very important, according to Alexy, is that such defectiveness is of a legal nature, and not only of a moral one.

Let us add that Alexy does not stop at elaborating the above-mentioned five distinctions (indeed, he does not exclude the further distinctions that may improve the reliability of the dispute that is in progress between positivists and nonpositivists), but he also examines the possibilities of their juxtaposition. It can be seen from a relatively simple calculation ($2^5 = 32$) that the conceptual frames of nonpositivist argumentation, adopted by him, help to identify 32 possible conceptual standpoints, which, taking into account the fact that these standpoints may be used not only by supporters of the thesis of the necessary conceptual connection between law and morality (nonpositivists), but also by supporters of the thesis on their separation (positivists), ultimately gives as many as 64 theoretical possibilities. It will soon be discussed, though, how Alexy, in his nonpositivist argumentation, explicitly adopts, in principle, only two[26] of the most basic methodological combinations (based on distinctions 2–5).

money, and will want to keep out of jail if he can" – O.W. Holmes, 'The Path of The Law', *HLR* 10 (1897), p. 459. However, *cf.* Chap. 6, note 43 at p. 226.

[25] Initially, Alexy referred to classifying relations as "defining relations" – *see idem*, 'On Necessary Relations between Law and Morality', *op. cit.*, pp. 171ff. and 'Zur Kritik des Rechtspositivismus', *op. cit.*, pp. 13ff. Nonetheless, in time, due to Dreier's criticism (*see idem*, 'Zur gegenwärtigen Diskussion des Verhältnisses von Recht und Moral in der Bundesrepublik Deutschland', *op. cit.*, pp. 58–59), who pointed out that such relations, referred to as "qualifying relations", are of a defining character as well, Alexy adopted the terminology provided by his mentor – *see* R. Alexy, 'Zur Verteidigung eines nichtpositivistischen Rechtsbegriffs', *op. cit.*, note 18 at p. 89.

[26] As we shall see later, in his nonpositivist argumentation Alexy uses one more distinction when considering the problem of the relation of law and morality in respect to particular norms and legal systems as a whole. In the majority of Alexy's works (the only exception here being 'Zur Verteidigung eines nichtpositivistischen Rechtsbegriffs', *op. cit.*, pp. 88–89) this distinction is not treated as a preliminary methodological distinction, but it already appears at the presentation stage of a substantive nonpositivist argumentation – *cf. idem*, 'On Necessary Relations between Law and Morality', *op. cit.*, pp. 173ff., 'Zur Kritik des Rechtspositivismus', *op. cit.*, pp. 14ff., *Begriff und Geltung des Rechts*, *op. cit.*, pp. 51ff. [English version, pp. 40ff.], and 'A Definition of Law', *op. cit.*, pp. 104ff.

3.2 Ralf Dreier's Nonpositivist Argumentation

The objective pursued by Dreier whilst developing his nonpositivist conception of law, is to reconstruct the juristic concept of law—the concept that is often vague and not fully realised by lawyers.[27] Therefore, it is not too surprising that, in his deliberations, Dreier assumes the perspective of a participant (and more specifically, a judge) and he creates the concept of law that includes the concept of its validity.[28] The nonpositivist juristic concept of law, although constructed partially empirically on the basis of the analysis of the German legal practice—in particular, the jurisdiction of the German federal courts and the Federal Constitutional Court (*Bundesverfassungsgericht*)—is, as Dreier repeatedly emphasised, of a normative rather than empirical or analytical nature.[29] According to the scholar of Göttingen, the juristic concept of law should define the "legitimate basis" (*legitime Bestimmungsgründe*) of judicial decisions.[30] In other words, it should be this concept that the judge should adopt in the course of adjudication.[31]

The strategy of Dreier's nonpositivist argumentation entails that he firstly accurately identifies the opponent of his nonpositivist conception, analysing the basic theses of legal positivism and the construction of the positivist definitions of law.[32] The foundation of the positivist concept of law is the Separation Thesis; that is, the thesis of the absence of any necessary relation between law and morality (*Trennungsthese*). It is usually expressed in the form of a theorem, which states that the law can have any content (even contrary to the fundamental principles of justice), or in the form of a postulate of a strict distinction between what law is, from what it should be. Consequently, positivist definitions of law are based—according to Dreier—on the combination of only two elements: the authoritativeness (*autoritative Gesetztheit*) and social effectiveness (*soziale Wirksamkeit*) of individual norms or systems of norms and granting advantage to any of these elements is usually caused by adopting a particular research perspective. Thus,

---

[27] R. Dreier, 'Der Begriff des Rechts', *op. cit.*, p. 890 and 'Neues Naturrecht oder Rechtspositivismus?', *op. cit.*, p. 368. Incidentally, Dreier believes that every lawyer also has his own philosophy of law; nonetheless, most lawyers are usually unaware of that, and this leads to disastrous consequences – *see idem*, *Was ist und wozu Allgemeine Rechtstheorie?*, *op. cit.*, p. 33.

[28] *Cf. supra*, p. 25 and Chap. 2 at p. 20.

[29] R. Dreier, 'Der Begriff des Rechts', *op. cit.*, pp. 894–895 and 'Some Remarks on the Concept of Law', *op. cit.*, p. 123. Dreier's standpoint is similarly characterised by Alexy, who claims that Dreier's nonpositivist argumentation refers to the normative necessity of the connection between law and morality – *see* R. Alexy, 'On Necessary Relations between Law and Morality', *op. cit.*, p. 173 and 'Zur Kritik des Rechtspositivismus', *op. cit.*, p. 12. Dreier fully accepts the interpretation provided by his disciple – *see idem*, 'Zur gegenwärtigen Diskussion des Verhältnisses von Recht und Moral in der Bundesrepublik Deutschland', *op. cit.*, p. 59.

[30] R. Dreier, 'Neues Naturrecht oder Rechtspositivismus?', *op. cit.*, p. 376.

[31] R. Dreier, 'Der Begriff des Rechts', *op. cit.*, pp. 894ff. For more on the strategy of developing the concept of law adopted by Dreier, *see* Chap. 5, note 32 together with the corresponding text at p. 200.

[32] *See* R. Dreier, *ibidem*, pp. 890–891, 894 and 'Some Remarks on the Concept of Law', *op. cit.*, pp. 113–115.

the definitions provided by the authors who highlight the element of the authoritative issuance of law usually take the participant's point of view (Dreier provides examples here of the definitions of law proposed by John Austin, Hans Kelsen and H.L.A. Hart), while the researchers who assume the observer's point of view pay more attention to the aspect of the social effectiveness of law (as, for example, in the definitions of law provided by Oliver Wendell Holmes, Max Weber, Theodor Geiger, Ernst Rudolf Bierling and Niklas Luhmann).[33] In further considerations, Dreier assumes that the positivist conception of law (which he refers his nonpositivist argumentation to) will be understood in terms of the conception developed within Kelsen and Hart's analytical theories of law, as a justification for which he provides not only their nature—a characteristic of modern positivism—but also the common research perspective of the participant—typical of both these theories and of his nonpositivist conception.[34]

Two classic arguments against the positivist perception of law play a fundamental role in Dreier's nonpositivist argumentation[35]: the argument from injustice

[33] Although the purpose of this chapter is description and reconstruction, rather than criticism of nonpositivist argumentation (which is carried out in the subsequent chapters), it seems crucial at this point to add that Dreier's analysis of the construction of positivist definitions of law encountered severe criticism by W. Krawietz, 'Neues Naturrecht oder Rechtspositivismus? Eine kritische Auseinandersetzung mit dem Begriff des Rechts bei Ralf Dreier und Norbert Hoerster', *op. cit.*, pp. 238ff. (the criticism concerned, inter alia, the understanding of M. Weber, T. Geiger and N. Luhmann's theories as "sociological positivism") as well as criticism of N. Hoerster, 'Zur Verteidigung des Rechtspositivismus', *op. cit*, p. 2481 (it referred to the fact that Dreier presented H. Kelsen and H.L.A. Hart's conceptions of law as descriptive, rather than as normative in nature). These criticisms were considered by Dreier as more or less justified – *see idem*, 'Neues Naturrecht oder Rechtspositivismus? In Erwiderung auf Werner Krawietz', *op. cit.*, p. 384 and 'Zur gegenwärtigen Diskussion des Verhältnisses von Recht und Moral in der Bundesrepublik Deutschland', *op. cit*, note 5 at p. 57.

[34] It comes as no surprise, though, that Dreier considers these two authors to be the representatives of twentieth-century legal positivism. What can be puzzling, nevertheless, is the fact that he lists them together. The main reason lies again in the sphere of the validity of law: despite obvious differences, both the conception of basic norms and rules of recognition contain the elements considered by Dreier as appropriate for positivism – next to authoritative issuance (which undoubtedly cannot be questioned) and social efficacy. In the case of Kelsen's *Grundnorm,* it is about the requirement contained in its formulation from *Reine Rechtslehre* that the constitution of a given system of law and norms established in accordance with the latter should be *im großen und ganzen* effective, whilst in the case of Hart's rule of recognition, this rule should be socially efficient (i.e., the results of its application should be accepted by the members of a given juristic community) – *see* R. Dreier, 'Der Begriff des Rechts', *op. cit*, p. 890, 'Some Remarks on the Concept of Law', *op. cit*, pp. 114–115, and 'Sein und Sollen. *Bemerkungen zur Reinen Rechtslehre Kelsens*' in *idem*, *Recht – Moral – Ideologie*, *op. cit*, pp. 222ff. Such standpoint presented by Dreier ought to be evaluated as a correct one. More on the similarities and differences between *Grundnorm* and the rule of recognition *see e.g.*, D. Beyleveld, R. Brownsword, 'Normative Positivism: The Mirage of the Middle-Way', OJLS 9/4 (1989), in particular pp. 497ff. and S. Delacroix, 'Hart's and Kelsen's Concepts of Normativity Contrasted', *RJ* 17 (2004), pp. 505ff. This issue is discussed in Chap. 7 at pp. 342ff.

[35] *See* 'Der Begriff des Rechts', *op. cit.*, pp. 891ff., 'Some Remarks on the Concept of Law', *op. cit.*, p. 115, and *Rechtsbegriff und Rechtsidee*, Frankfurt am Main 1986, pp. 26ff. In the

(*Unrechtsargument*), and the argument from principles (*Prinzipienargument*). The argument from injustice (known in German literature also as *Tyrannisargument*, *lex corrupta-Argument*, *Perversionsargument*, *Totalitarismusargument* or *Hitler-Argument*[36]) sets forth that there are norms or systems of norms that are unjust to such an extent that their legal validity and/or legal nature must be negated. The argument from principles, on the other hand, consists of determining that legal principles (understood in the sense given to that term by Ronald Dworkin) are an inherent part of all developed systems of law; therefore, due to their peculiar structure or nature of validity, they "blast" the positivist concept of law.

Dreier examines the argument from injustice (un-law) in two versions: first—referring to the different norms, and based on "Radbruch's formula" (more specifically, on *Unerträglichkeitsthese*, yet taking into account *Verleugnungsthese*), and the other—relating to the systems of law, and based on the formula developed by Martin Kriele.

In relation to the first version of *Unrechtsargument*, Dreier—justifying the validity of "Radbruch's formula"—refers first and foremost to empirical argument, noting that this formula, despite its vagueness, has proven very useful in the post-war German jurisdiction (in particular, in addition to a series of rulings assuming "Radbruch's formula", Dreier also cites the ruling of the German Federal Constitutional Court of 14 February 1968 in the case of the Eleventh Ordinance (*Verordnung*) of 25 November 1941 issued pursuant to the Statute on Reich Citizenship (*Reichsbürgergesetz*) of 15 September 1935, which, on the basis of racial grounds, deprived those German Jews who emigrated of their German nationality).[37] Dreier subsequently considers, also from a practical point of view, Hart's allegations against the formula and the way in which the latter advocated to resolve the issue of morally unacceptable consequences of wicked law, consisting of the legislator issuing retroactive laws.[38] Dreier reasonably asks what judges should do if the legislator does not meet this requirement. Should judges still continue to accept the positivist thesis of the separation of law and morality, basing their rulings on the positivist concept of law, even at the expense of harmed citizens? Dreier therefore concludes that "Radbruch's formula" is not only useful in practice, but it also constitutes an adequate modification of the juristic (judicial) concept of law.

---

following presentation we also take into consideration clarifications made by Dreier in 'Neues Naturrecht oder Rechtspositivismus?', *op. cit.* and 'Zur gegenwärtigen Diskussion des Verhältnisses von Recht und Moral in der Bundesrepublik Deutschland', *op. cit.*

[36] *See* K. Seidel, *Rechtsphilosophische Aspekte der "Mauerschützen"-Prozesse*, Berlin 1999, note 33 at p. 158, and the references cited therein; R. Dreier, 'Der Begriff des Rechts', *op. cit.*, p. 891; R. Alexy, *Begriff und Geltung des Rechts*, *op. cit.*, note 29 at p. 52 [English version, note 50 at p. 28].

[37] Due to its representative character, the theses of this ruling are quoted in full in Chap. 4 at p. 185.

[38] *See* H.L.A. Hart, 'Positivism and the Separation of Law and Morals', *HLR* 71 (1958), pp. 619ff. This and Hart's other objections are analysed in Chap. 4 at pp. 162ff.

The second version of the argument from injustice relates to the systems of law. It refers to Martin Kriele's thesis of a necessary connection between the legal and moral obligation of compliance to the law, yet it is formulated on the condition that law (a particular system of law), in principle, is ethically justified ("it takes into account the question of morality"[39]). Dreier does not examine the justification of this thesis, but he compares its impact with the consequences of applying "Radbruch's formula" as well as considering its usefulness in the practice of law. Kriele does not deny all regulations or institutions that belong to the totalitarian system of law their legal nature because some of them, namely, those not characteristic of only anti-democratic regimes, may have, as such, direct legitimacy.[40] Therefore, with regard to the consequences of "Radbruch's formula" and "Kriele's formula", Dreier notes that both these formulas fulfil the same function of eliminating iniquitous legal regulations. When analysing the usefulness of "Kriele's formula" in practice, he intimates as to the possibility of taking it into account in international law in relation to the problem of recognising emerging states (or governments) as lawful subject to this law, postulating in that respect an ethical modification of the existing doctrine pursuant to which international recognition is based solely on the criterion of the effectiveness of the new authority.

While the argument from injustice relates to periods of degeneration of systems of law, the argument from principles refers to the everyday practice of legal systems, so making it undoubtedly more important for a nonpositivist. The argument from principles (Dreier firstly refers to Dworkin's conception of principles[41] and, later, to the conception provided by Alexy[42]) takes two specific forms, as the distinction between principles from the ordinary legal rules can be viewed in terms of structural or validation differences (oriented to the issue of validity). Accordingly, *Prinzipienzargument* in its structural version constitutes a nonpositivist argument in the sense that principles—identifiable in any developed legal system—and, out of necessity, the procedures of weighing (*Abwägung*) them that accompany the latter, open up the legal system to morality, by requiring the judge (not only in the moral sense but also in the legal one)—as far as it is legally and actually possible—to fully implement moral ideas expressed in concrete principles. On the other hand, such an argument in its validating version questions the positivist concept of law, because at least some of the principles (namely, those that have not been positivised and thus formally incorporated into the system of law) constitute a part of valid law, though they do not meet the criteria of validity characteristic for standard legal rules (to use Dworkin's terminology—they do not meet the test of pedigree).

Dreier justifies the adequacy of the structural version of the argument from principles not only by referring to Dworkin and Alexy's theory of principles

---

[39] In the original version, this condition is as follows: "daß das Recht *'im großen und ganzen'* der Sittlichkeit Rechnung trägt" – M. Kriele, *Recht und praktische Vernunft*, Göttingen 1979, p. 117.

[40] *See ibidem*, pp. 120ff.

[41] *See* R. Dreier, 'Der Begriff des Rechts', *op. cit.*, pp. 892ff.

[42] *See* R. Dreier, 'Some Remarks on the Concept of Law', *op. cit.*, pp. 117ff.

(which has been left aside in the subsequent discussion, since these are well-known issues[43]), but also by formulating three particular theses of an explanatory nature that, at the same time, develop the content of *Prinzipienzargument*.[44] The first one is referred to as *Inkorporationsthese*, which states that every developed legal system incorporates the legal and ethical principles, that, nonetheless, do not undermine the positivist understanding of law when we interpret this thesis as merely pointing to the fact of positivising many principles by modern systems of law (as is presented by Dreier in the example of the positive constitutional law of Germany). The second thesis is, in turn, referred to as *Offenheitsthese*, and it states that such principles—already incorporated into the legal system—open the latter up to legal and ethical argumentation. It is not questioned by the positivist, but the fundamental difference appears in the following contentious issue: for a positivist, the consequence of such opening is the existence of a legally uncontrollable sphere of judicial discretion, while a nonpositivist understands here the argument from principles in such a way that also in this sphere the judge is legally bound by the principles that belong to a given legal system. Dreier strongly emphasises that the difference between positivism and nonpositivism is not of a purely verbal character (*Vokabelfrage*), but it is essential for the comprehension of law. In the sphere of judicial discretion, the judge does not have unlimited authority to make decisions consistent with his moral views (a classical positivist view), but also in this sphere he is bound to provide the legal justification for the decisions that have been made (a nonpositivist position). The question of how the judge is legally bound by the principles is explained by the last thesis—*Optimierungsthese*. As the name suggests, the fact that the judge is bound by principles imposes on her/him the obligation of maximal possible realisation of the principles that belong to the system, conceived—in reference to Alexy's analyses—as optimisation norms. Naturally, the implementation of this obligation is not simple, since the principles are not only (like any norm) subject to legal interpretation, but also to the specific pattern of their application, which is based on weighing and mutual balancing. It is another area where nonpositivism differs fundamentally from positivism because it recognises the legal (rather than ethical or moral) nature of these procedures. At this point, Dreier again relies on empirical arguments, paying attention to the category of the so-called *Wertordnungsrechtsprechungen*—occurring in the judicial practice of the German Federal Constitutional Court—in which the court have formulated a number of specific rules of weighing and collision. Given that, according to Dreier,

---

[43] *See* (in the Polish literature) T. Gizbert-Studnicki, 'Zasady i reguły prawne' [Legal Principles and Rules], *PiP* 3 (1988), pp. 16–26; L. Morawski, 'Zasady prawne – komentarz krytyczny' [Legal Principles – A Critical Commentary], *SFP* 1 (2001), pp. 71–81; M. Dybowski, 'Ronalda Dworkina koncepcja zasad prawa' [Ronald Dworkin's Conception of Legal Principles], *RPEiS* LXIII/3 (2001), pp. 99–115.

[44] *See* R. Dreier, *Rechtsbegriff und Rechtsidee*, *op. cit.*, pp. 28 ff. It should be added that in his later works, Dreier refers to the theses developed by Alexy – *see* R. Dreier, 'Some Remarks on the Concept of Law', *op. cit.*, p. 120 and 'Zur gegenwärtigen Diskussion des Verhältnisses von Recht und Moral in der Bundesrepublik Deutschland', *op. cit.*, p. 63.

Alexy showed in his *Theorie der Grundrechte* that *Werttheorie*—underlying the judgments of the German Constitutional Court—is equivalent to the theory of principles, because each value can be expressed in "the language of principles",[45] *Optimierungsthese* is not merely a normative postulate but it is gaining the status of an empirical thesis.

In conclusion, in Dreier's approach, the essence of the argument from principles in its structural form is to identify the phenomenon of open texture and vagueness of the regulations of positive law, which results in the existence of a sphere of judicial discretion, within which, nonetheless, the judge is bound by legal (and not just moral) principles and legal procedures of weighing principles that set out the pattern of making legal decisions.[46]

When analysing the argument from principles in its validity version, Dreier directly refers to Dworkin's conception,[47] focusing in particular on the criteria of the validity of these principles, which are no longer covered by the test of institutional support. In this regard, Dreier suggests two possible argumentative strategies.[48] The first one, contrary to Dworkin, lies in extending the sphere of application of the test of institutional support. The second one—preferred by Dreier—consists of two stages: in order to justify the legal validity of principles (and their affiliation to the legal system, despite its non-compliance with either the positivist test of pedigree or with the Dworkinian test of institutional support), it has to be proven first that every developed legal system contains a set of fundamental principles and subordinated principles that are related to the latter or that can be reasonably inferred from them. Then it must be proved that these principles have (in a given legal system) constitutional status—they are explicitly expressed or implicitly contained in the constitution of a given legal system. Yet, when assuming the latter strategy, as Dreier admits, the positivist concept of law remains intact in the aspect of legal validity.

The last argument used by Dreier is definitely of an indirect character, which—nevertheless—does not make it less important. In developing his nonpositivist conception, Dreier notes[49] that if we wanted to justify the universal (i.e., covering all actual and possible legal systems) nature of the concept of law proposed by him, we would have to rely on a more general theory that could justify such a claim. In this context, Dreier perceives the possibility of reasoning based on Karl-Otto Apel's transcendental pragmatics or on Jürgen Habermas' universal pragmatics. Dreier, nonetheless, chooses a different path, claiming that his nonpositivist conception

---

[45] *See* R. Alexy, *Theorie der Grundrechte*, *op. cit.*, pp. 125ff., in particular p. 133 [English version, pp. 86ff., in particular p. 92].

[46] R. Dreier, 'Some Remarks on the Concept of Law', *op. cit.*, p. 119.

[47] *See* R. Dworkin, *Taking Rights Seriously*, Cambridge (Mass.) 1977, pp. 68ff.

[48] *See* R. Dreier, 'Der Begriff des Rechts', *op. cit.*, p. 893 and 'Some Remarks on the Concept of Law', *op. cit.*, pp. 120–122.

[49] *See* R. Dreier, 'Der Begriff des Rechts', *op. cit.*, pp. 894–895, *Rechtsbegriff und Rechtsidee*, *op. cit.*, pp. 8–25, 36–37, and 'Some Remarks on the Concept of Law', *op. cit.*, pp. 109–113, 124.

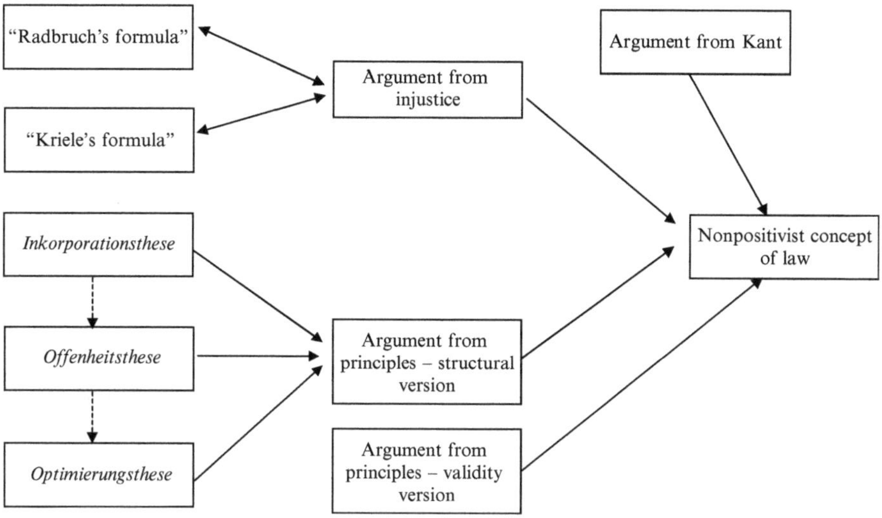

Fig. 3.1 Ralf Dreier's nonpositivist argumentation

falls within the tradition of the philosophy of Immanuel Kant. When analysing the Kantian concept of law, Dreier shows that one of the foundations of the concept of the philosopher from Königsberg is "orienting" law to reason. Therefore, what can be observed here is a connection with his nonpositivist conception, based on the identical premise.[50]

It should be added that after Alexy developed a more elaborate nonpositivist argumentation, despite a few minor critical remarks, it was accepted by Dreier.[51] Yet, it does not mean that Dreier gave up his own arguments, but rather that he treated both argumentations as complementary.

Let us conclude this synthetic presentation of Ralf Dreier's nonpositivist argumentation by presenting a diagram depicting its very clear and well-ordered structure (see Fig. 3.1 above).

3.3 Robert Alexy's Nonpositivist Argumentation

Ralf Dreier's nonpositivist argumentation can be treated as a point of departure for a far more complex and intricate argumentation in favour of the Connection Thesis (*Verbindungsthese*): the thesis on the necessary conceptual relation between law

[50] For more on this *see* R. Alexy, 'Ralf Dreier's Interpretation der Kantischen Rechtsdefinition' in *idem* (ed.), *Integratives Verstehen, op. cit.*, pp. 95–109.

[51] *See* R. Dreier, 'Zur gegenwärtigen Diskussion des Verhältnisses von Recht und Moral in der Bundesrepublik Deutschland', *op. cit.*, pp. 56ff.

and morality, elaborated by Dreier's disciple Robert Alexy. First, he developed his nonpositivist argumentation in favour of the analytical version of *Verbindungsthese* (namely, the thesis of the analytical necessity of providing a definition for the concept of law, containing moral elements)[52] and, subsequently, the one in favour of the normative version of *Verbindungsthese* (i.e., the thesis of the normative necessity of such a definition).[53] These two argumentations, with some small changes and numerous additions, were jointly presented in the book *Begriff und Geltung des Rechts* of 1992,[54] in which Alexy already treated them as a justification for a nonpositivist definition of law, which was proposed there for the first time.[55] Later, Alexy introduced certain, yet not very numerous, changes and additions in response to German and international criticism of his conception of law and nonpositivist argumentation. In order to provide a reliable description not only of Alexy's respective methods of argumentation, but also of the evolution of the arguments used by him, in the following sections we shall first deal with original versions of both his analytical and normative nonpositivist argumentations, and only then with the changes and additions introduced in *Begriff und Geltung des Rechts*. Further, yet not numerous, changes and additions to Alexy's arguments will be—not only due to editorial reasons—presented in the next chapter, because in this way their critical (polemical) origins can be best presented, and it will also allow for the assessment of the criticism of Alexy's nonpositivist argumentation.

Before we proceed with presenting the original versions of Alexy's analytical and normative argumentation, it should be noted that many components of this argument appeared long before he began to develop a nonpositivist conception of law. Already in Alexy's famous dissertation of 1976,[56] can we find many elements that were used later in his nonpositivist argumentation: the thesis which stipulates that legal discourse is a special case of general practical discourse (*Sonderfallthese*), the conception of a claim to correctness (*Anspruch auf Richtigkeit*) and the example of an erroneous judicial conviction used to justify the latter claim.[57] Moreover, it is already in this work that we may find the first, yet very general anticipation of his nonpositivist conception of law, since Alexy points out that his theory of legal argumentation and practical discourse implies rationality (*Vernünftigkeit*) of legislation, whilst the achievement of justice and rationality of the legal discourse require a just and rational social order.[58]

---

[52] *See* R. Alexy, 'On Necessary Relations between Law and Morality', *op. cit.* and 'Zur Kritik des Rechtspositivismus', *op. cit.*

[53] *See* R. Alexy, 'Zur Verteidigung eines nichtpositivistischen Rechtsbegriffs', *op. cit.*

[54] *See* R. Alexy, *Begriff und Geltung des Rechts*, *op. cit.*, pp. 51ff. [English version, pp. 27ff.].

[55] *Cf.* Chap. 2, p. 16.

[56] R. Alexy, *Theorie der juristischen Argumentation. Die Theorie des Rationalen Diskurses als Theorie der juristischen Begründung*, Frankfurt am Main 1978 [English version: *A Theory of Legal Argumentation. The Theory of Rational Discourse as Theory of Legal Justification*, trans. R. Adler, N. MacCormick, Oxford 1989].

[57] *Ibidem*, pp. 33–39, 263–272, 356–359 [English version, pp. 16–20, 212–220, 292–295].

[58] *Ibidem*, pp. 351, 359 [English version, pp. 289, 295]. *Cf.* Chap. 4 at pp. 138ff.

Alexy justifies the necessary relation between the claim to correctness and the law based on the example of two utterances, burdened—in his view—with an error of "performative contradiction" (*performativer Widerspruch*). The first example concerns the article in the new constitution, adopted by an honest minority ruling in a certain state, which states that "*X* is a sovereign, federal, and unjust republic". The second example, modified by Alexy under the influence of a critique of his original expression,[70] is presented in the form of the following convicting sentence: "The defendant is hereby sentenced to life imprisonment, albeit wrongly, because valid law was interpreted incorrectly".[71] According to Alexy, both these statements are defective because they are absurd in nature. The analysis of errors in the process of making them leads Alexy to the conclusion that they are not just technical, moral, conventional or legal errors,[72] but are primarily conceptual ones. Alexy argues that the authors of those utterances (that is, the creators of a new constitution and a judge) make a "performative contradiction", and thus, a conceptual error—since this is the only way that one can fully explain the absurdity of the statements quoted above.

In the first example, this contradiction takes place between the claim to justice, implicitly contained in the act of enacting the constitution (Alexy treats it as a special case of a more general claim to correctness[73]), and explicitly expressed in an assertion stating its injustice, presented in the article of the constitution. In the latter case, there is a contradiction between the claim to correctness implicitly contained in every act of jurisdiction (i.e., the claim to the proper application of law) and the assertion stating its inaccuracy, expressed explicitly in the quoted sentence. Thus—according to Alexy—the analysis at hand justifies the assertion that the claim to correctness is always adopted by the participants in legal discourse and, in this sense, it is immanent in law. As Alexy explained in his later works,[74] this is a deontological necessity, resulting from the structure of legal acts and from legal reasoning. Therefore, the claim to correctness is one of the essential characteristics

---

[70] The original example given in *Theorie der juristischen Argumentation*, *op. cit.*, p. 266: "Im Namen des Volkes, Herr N. wird, obwohl hierfür keine guten Gründe sprechen, zu zehn Jahren Freiheitsetzung verurteilt", has been criticised because of the ambiguity of the concept of good reason – *see* U. Neumann's review of Alexy's above-mentioned book, *PhR* 28 (1981), pp. 212ff.

[71] The wording of this sentence is taken from Alexy's latest works, in which he refers to the claim to correctness – *see idem*, 'On the Thesis of a Necessary Connection between Law and Morality: Bulygin's Critique', *RJ* 13 (2000), p. 140 and 'The Nature of Arguments about the Nature of Law' in L.H. Meyer *et al.* (eds.), *Rights, Culture, and the Law*, Oxford 2003, p. 11.

[72] Let us add that Alexy examines the possibility of a legal fault only in relation to the second example.

[73] *See* 'Zur Kritik des Rechtspositivismus', *op. cit.*, p. 20, 'On Necessary Relations between Law and Morality', *op. cit.*, p. 179, and 'The Nature of Legal Philosophy', *op. cit.*, p. 72. Alexy broadly analyses the relation between claim to correctness and claim to justice in 'Justicia como corrección', trans. A.I. Haquín, *DOXA* 26 (2003), pp. 163ff.

[74] *See* 'The Nature of Legal Philosophy', *op. cit.*, p. 72, 'Law, Discourse, and Time', *ARSP* Bh. 64 (1995), pp. 101ff.

of the law (or the system of law) as such—it is one of the so-called *universalium iuris*.

Another component of Alexy's analytical nonpositivist argumentation is a presentation of his theory of principles (*Prinzipientheorie*), by means of which he justifies the necessity (and not contingency) of incorporating moral principles into the legal system.[75] The starting point of the argument from principles is a distinction between legal principles and rules (modified by Alexy in relation to the original concept of Dworkin), according to which, principles are recognised as optimisation commands (*Optimierungsgebote*)—as norms requiring the implementation of a certain state of things to the highest possible extent, yet relativised to the existing actual and legal possibilities (of its realisation).[76] By means of the three theses: *Inkorporationsthese*, *Moralthese* and *Kohärenzthese*, Alexy justifies the necessity of the conceptual relation between law and morality. The Incorporation Thesis states that "every legal system that is at least minimally developed necessarily comprises principles".[77] Alexy understands this thesis in very general terms, explaining that it is merely contrary to the positivist thesis by stating that the fact as to whether or not principles are incorporated into the system of law at all depends entirely on the regulations of the positive law, and in this sense, such incorporation is not necessary (the so-called *These der kontingenten Inkorporation*). Yet, it is not inconsistent with another positivist thesis (the so-called *These der relativen Inkorporation*), which specifies that the issue of what principles should be incorporated into the system depends exclusively on the content of the positive law. In order to justify the correctness of *Inkorporationsthese*, Alexy considers the situation of a judge who must use the procedure of weighing (*Abwägung*) when adjudicating a hard case (*schweriger Fall*); that is, a case in which the adjudication does not stem directly from the norms of positive law. According to the author of the argumentation discussed, in any legal system that foresees the procedure of weighing and balancing, principles constitute its essential elements, because the judge's application of this procedure also constitutes the criterion for the occurrence of principles in a given system. Refuting a possible plea of a positivist who—despite even recognising the correctness of such argumentation—can also argue that these principles are of extra-systemic character and the requirement of

[75] *See* 'Zur Kritik des Rechtspositivismus', *op. cit.*, pp. 21–25.

[76] Alexy's theory of principles is presented in his works: 'Zum Begriff des Rechtsprinzips', *RT* Bh. 1 (1979), pp. 59–87, *Theorie der Grundrechte*, *op. cit.*, pp. 71ff. [English version, pp. 44ff.], 'Rechtsregeln und Rechtsprinzipien', *ARSP* Bh. 25 (1985), pp. 13–29, and 'Zur Struktur der Rechtsprinzipien' in B. Schilcher *et al.* (eds.), *Regeln, Prinzipien und Elemente im System des Rechts*, Wien 2000, pp. 31–52 [shortened English version: 'On the Structure of Legal Principles', *RJ* 13 (2000), pp. 294–304].

[77] R. Alexy, *Begriff und Geltung des Rechts*, *op. cit.*, p. 121. The translation is borrowed from *The Argument from Injustice*, *op. cit.*, p. 71. This thesis differs from Dreier's one – identically named – on two points: Alexy links it to "minimally developed systems of law" (rather than to "developed systems") and he writes about the incorporation of "principles" without their detailed specification (and not about "legal and ethical principles").

weighing them is a non-legal postulate of rationality, Alexy relies on two counterarguments. Firstly, he recalls the pragmatic approach to the legal system, adopted by him in this type of argumentation, under which the procedure of weighing (understood as the activity of law-applying authorities) belongs to the legal system. Secondly, to demonstrate that application of this procedure constitutes a judge's legal duty, he refers to the claim to correctness, arguing that in cases requiring judicial decisions, they are of a legal (and not just a moral) character. The judge is in fact—according to Alexy—legally obligated to make a proper (correct) weighing of the principles that are in collision, which can be best demonstrated when considering the legal correctness of a ruling in which the judge ultimately accepted that one of the principles was more important ("weightier") than the other, but based the decision on the other, less important principle.

Other theses that make up the argument from principles are already directed against the second positivist thesis—of the relativity of incorporation. The next thesis of the theory of principles, the Morality Thesis, states that the previously demonstrated necessity of the presence of principles in the legal system leads to the necessary connection of the law with any (not necessarily correct) morality. When justifying it, Alexy points out that in deciding hard cases we look for answers to practical questions: "*Was sein soll?*". Among the principles underlying the answers to such questions, there are undoubtedly those that belong to a certain morality. The third of the theses, the *Kohärenzthese*, is the first step to justifying the claim that the conceptual relation of law and any morality leads to a conceptual relation of law with correct morality (*richtige Moral*). It says that, "in the legal system there is a necessarily valid legal requirement to develop this system so that all principles, which can be considered in it, were included there and correctly weighed".[78] As can be readily seen, this thesis contains Dreier's *Optimierungsthese* and is based on the definition of principles as optimisation commands; that is, demanding their realisation to the greatest extent possible. To ensure such implementation and, at the same time, to satisfy the claim to correctness, the system of law should be based on a coherent moral system. The requirement of coherence, nevertheless, does not yet fully guarantee the necessity of a conceptual relation between law and correct morality, since one can easily imagine coherent, yet false morality.

At this point, we reach the third basis of *Richtigkeitsargument*; namely, the theory of practical discourse (expressed in the form of *Sonderfallthese*). The thesis that treats legal discourse as a special case of general practical discourse allows us to "shift" the theses of the procedural theory of discourse into the field of law.[79] If this thesis is true, then—according to Alexy—one can assess the necessity of a relation between law and universal morality, which is directly applicable with respect to modern legal systems and is also justifiable for premodern systems. This claim is based on the following reasoning. The claim to correctness,

---

[78] R. Alexy, 'Zur Kritik des Rechtspositivismus', *op. cit.*, p. 24.

[79] For more on this *see* A. Grabowski, 'Sonderfallthese – Its Critique and Interpretation', *RT* 34 (2003), pp. 371–392, and the references cited therein.

characteristic of practical discourse (and thus—according to the Special Case Thesis—also for legal discourse), implies a claim to justifiability (*Anspruch auf Begründbarkeit*), which, in turn, opens up a critical perspective on assessment and leads to qualifying the significance of justifiability. Justifiability of practical judgments assumes equal treatment of the participants involved in the discourse as well as universality of argumentation; that is, its correctness in respect to all possible participants of the discourse. This leads to a discursive ethics, built based on the idea of generalisability (*Verallgemeinerbarkeit*).[80] If a universal morality—manifested in the fundamental rights and principles of democracy—is a certain or universal morality, then the thesis of a necessary connection between law and correct morality appears to be justified. In conclusion, Alexy states that his nonpositivist analytical argumentation proves that there is a necessary conceptual connection between law and procedural and universalist morality.

The structure of the original version of Alexy's analytical nonpositivist argumentation can be synthetically presented in the form of a scheme (see Fig. 3.2 on the next page) that takes into account the methodological framework of argumentation adopted by him as well as its scope in terms of subject matter.[81]

3.3.2 *Alexy's Normative Argumentation*

Normative nonpositivist argumentation, developed by Alexy, does not merely consist of "adding normative arguments to analytical ones".[82] Although Alexy stresses the importance of conceptual arguments,[83] he admits that they have limited scope and power.[84] Moreover, he points out that a nonpositivist may even agree with a positivist thesis on the lack of any necessary conceptual relations between law and morality, thus defending his nonpositivist *Verbindungsthese* by means of non-analytical arguments (i.e., normative or, ultimately, empirical arguments).[85]

---

[80] Alexy refers here to Habermas' conception of universal pragmatics and to his own theory of legal discourse.

[81] In this scheme, I preserve Alexy's original terminology in terms of the scope and the content of the argument from correctness – *see supra*, note 68 at p. 40 and *infra*, pp. 54ff.

[82] R. Alexy, 'Zur Verteidigung eines nichtpositivistischen Rechtsbegriffs', *op. cit.*, p. 87.

[83] R. Alexy, 'On Necessary Relations between Law and Morality', *op. cit.*, p. 170 and 'Zur Kritik des Rechtspositivismus', *op. cit.*, p. 11.

[84] R. Alexy, 'Zur Verteidigung eines nichtpositivistischen Rechtsbegriffs', *op. cit.*, p. 87. What matters here is that – as it emerged in the analysis of nonpositivist analytical argumentation (*cf. supra*, p. 38) – "Radbruch's formula" cannot be justified by means of such arguments. According to Alexy, the latter can be done only by means of normative or practical arguments – *see idem*, 'A Definition of Law', *op. cit.*, p. 106.

[85] R. Alexy, 'On Necessary Relations between Law and Morality', *op. cit.*, pp. 168–170, 'Zur Kritik des Rechtspositivismus', *op. cit.*, pp. 10–11, and *Begriff und Geltung des Rechts*, *op. cit.*, pp. 40–41 [English version, pp. 20–21].

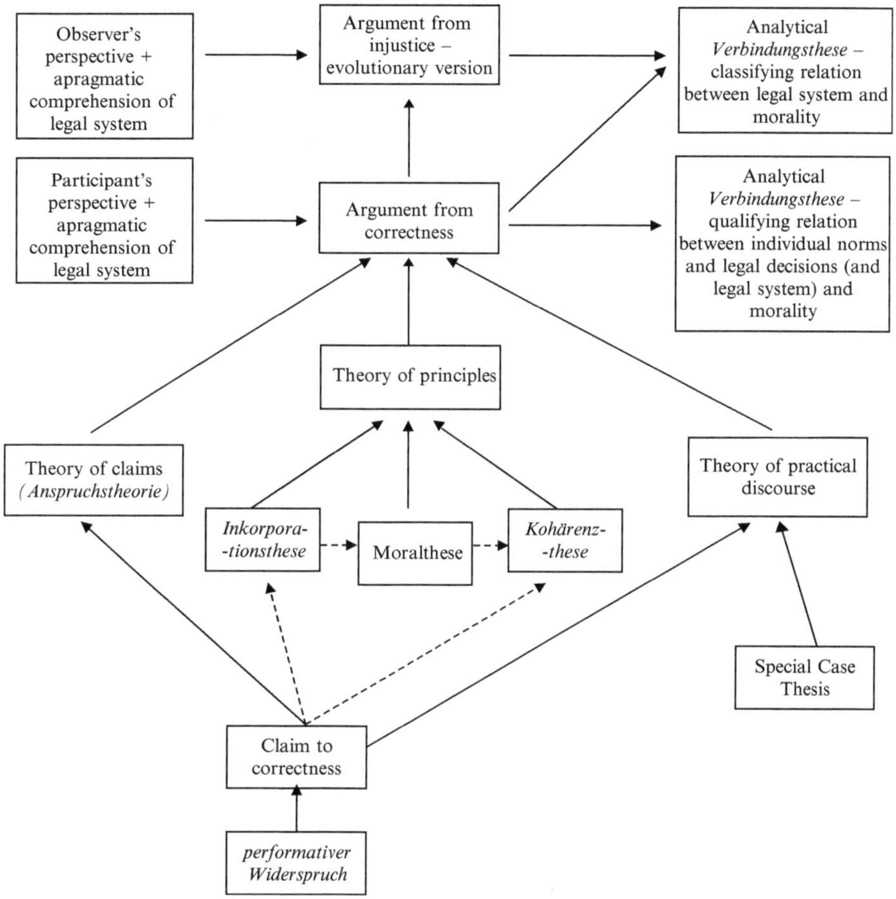

Fig. 3.2 Robert Alexy's original analytical nonpositivist argumentation

At the methodological level, for his normative argumentation Alexy assumes the point of view of the participant who seeks relations of a classifying character, taking place between legal norms and morality.[86] This argumentation is based on the argument from correctness and the argument from injustice (identified with "Radbruch's formula").[87]

---

[86] Although Alexy does not explain this directly, it seems that he understands law here in an apragmatic way (norms constitute the outcome of applied procedures of their issuance), yet when analysing the argument from language (*Sprachargument*), and the argument from efficiency (*Effektivitätsargument*), he takes into account (in the second case – indirectly) a pragmatic aspect of the legal system. It should also be added that, as in the case in analytical argumentation, Alexy applies here the concept of law that includes the concept of its validity.

[87] *See* R. Alexy, 'Zur Verteidigung eines nichtpositivistischen Rechtsbegriffs', *op. cit.*, pp. 88ff.

Before presenting this form of nonpositivist argumentation, the normative version of the Connection Thesis is specified by Alexy (in the context of the above-mentioned conceptual framework) in the form of an assertion, stating that stronger normative arguments argue for the fact that individual legal norms lose their legal character when they are extremely unjust. The starting point and the basis for justification of this thesis is again an argument from correctness (*Richtigkeitsargument*), understood, nonetheless, in a manner that is narrower than in analytical argumentation—it now corresponds with the theory of claims (*Anspruchstheorie*), presented in the frames of the latter argumentation. Alexy points out that with respect to singular norms, this argument leads merely to a relation of a qualifying character: if norms (similarly to respective legal decisions) do not satisfy or do not meet the claim to correctness, they do not lose their legal character or their binding force—they are only qualified as legally faulty. Accordingly, in order to move towards classifying relations between law and morality, it becomes necessary to examine the normative legitimacy of "Radbruch's formula" (understood by Alexy in reference to *Unerträglichkeitsthese*, but with the effect borrowed from *Verleugnungsthese*: individual norms lose their legal character after exceeding the threshold of extreme injustice). Alexy justifies the correctness of this formula by analysing and attempting to rebut the eight specific arguments raised against it in the jurisprudential debate.[88]

The first is the argument from language (*Sprachargument*), according to which the use of moral elements in the definition of the concept of law is linguistically pointless, because it deprives the nonpositivist of the possibility of conceptualising norms which, according to the nonpositivist conception, do not have a legal nature (for instance, the norms expressed in the example given by Dreier and Alexy of the Eleventh Ordinance to *Reichsbürgergesetz* of 1941). Alexy admits that this claim is correct, but only when adopting the external perspective of the observer; whereas, from the internal perspective of a participant (the judge), who pragmatically perceives the legal system (as a system of procedures–actions), the assessment is subject to a change. Indeed, if we assume that the judge should not apply the cited regulation, but—according to the claim to correctness—rule contrary to its wording, then without falling into a conflict, the judge cannot refer to this regulation as "the law", but at the most as "*prima facie* law", the legal nature of which is subsequently challenged in the course of adjudication and, in consequence, it is not the law ("[ist] im Ergebnis aber kein Recht").[89] Therefore, if there are any substantive legal reasons (which cannot be determined within a purely linguistic

[88] In his deliberations, Alexy mostly uses these arguments in the form presented by the leading German defender of legal positivism – N. Hoerster – *see idem*, 'Zur Verteidigung des Rechtspositivismus', *op. cit.*, p. 2482, 'Die rechtsphilosophische Lehre vom Rechtsbegriff', *JS* 27 (1987), pp. 184ff., and 'Zur Verteidigung der rechtspositivistischen Trennungsthese', *ARSP* Bh. 37 (1990), pp. 30–32; and by H.L.A. Hart – *see* 'Positivism and the Separation of Law and Morals', *op. cit.*, pp. 615ff.

[89] R. Alexy, *Begriff und Geltung des Rechts*, *op. cit.*, p. 74 [English version, p. 42].

analysis) in favour of the non-observance of such norms, then the argument from language—considered from the perspective of a participant—is erroneous.

The second normative counterargument is a formal argument from clarity (*Klarheitsargument*), according to which the positivist concept of law (which does not contain any moral elements) is clear and simple. What is more, its use does not blur the essence of the problem of unlawful statutes. According to a positivist, these are subject to moral criticism, which may lead to a refusal to obey such laws (which, in spite of this criticism remain as the law). Alexy's nonpositivist response to this objection consists of two elements. Firstly, he notes that a positivist approach to law may also result in conceptual confusion: firstly, it can be very unclear for a citizen if extremely unjust statutory regulations are treated as law. The source of confusion is different here than a mere nonpositivist understanding of law: the essence of the problem relates to a distinction between what is, from what is not extremely unjust. Secondly, legal nonpositivism by no means conceals the ethical nature of this problem, since it explicitly admits that this is a moral (ethical) problem which, nevertheless, (and that is the only difference) also becomes a legal problem in cases when extreme injustice (extreme iniquity) has been recognised.

The third counterargument is referred to as the argument from efficiency (*Effektivitätsargument*). In the context of Radbruch's *Wehrlosigkeitsthese*,[90] it calls into question the view that the inclusion of moral elements in the definition of law can provide effective protection against "statutory injustice". At this point, Alexy distinguishes two specific objections that undermine the effectiveness of the nonpositivist conception of law. The first one states that this conception does not prevent the development and application of an iniquitous law, since by means of a mere morally coloured definition of law one cannot change reality. The second argues that this conception can, uncritically, legitimise unjust laws. Accordingly, if we incorporate moral elements into the concept of law, then—according to the positivists—we risk the identification of the requirements of the law with morality (which implies the impossibility of any criticism of unjust laws). Since the second objection is most far-reaching, Alexy tries to rebut it in the first place, paying particular attention to the fact that the nonpositivist conception is based on a weak Connection Thesis (*schwache Verbindungsthese*), according to which, not every legal norm must be morally justified (such a view can be defined as *starke Verbindungsthese*; that is, the thesis of complete substantial conformity of law with morality[91]), yet extremely unjust norms cannot constitute law. Thus, it can be observed that nonpositivism does not deal with a positive equivalence of the two normative systems, but with the negative effects of morality on the law, thus leading to a rebuttal of the thesis of the possibility of law's uncritical legitimisation. The application of "Radbruch's formula" results only in rebutting the legitimisation of norms that exceed a threshold of extreme injustice, and not a—positive—

[90] *See* Chap. 2, p. 13.

[91] R. Alexy, *Begriff und Geltung des Rechts*, *op. cit.*, pp. 82ff. [English version, pp. 47ff.].

legitimisation of norms that fall below this threshold. On the other hand, in relation to the first objection—incidentally considered by Alexy as more justified—the defence of nonpositivism relies on taking into consideration two situations. Firstly, in a situation in which a nonpositivist conception of law is accepted in legal practice, therefore, judges not only have moral, but also legal grounds to oppose the laws that violate the elementary requirements of justice. In this sense, the acts of "statutory injustice" can be defeated, at least not less effectively than in cases involving practice that assumes a positivist standpoint. The second situation is the one in which we are already faced with a "state of un-law" (*Unrechtsstaat*). Alexy argues that, if earlier in such a state the nonpositivist concept of law was commonly accepted or approved to a considerable extent, then the judge who is to decide on the basis of unjust laws, has to take into account a threat—higher than in the case of a prior approval of a positivist position—of being made liable for using "statutory un-law" (*gesetzliches Unrecht*) after the collapse of that state. The "risk effect" (*Risikoeffekt*) of the nonpositivist conception of law may thus, even discreetly, affect the practice of law even in a lawless state. Thus, taking a nonpositivist position appears to be at least not less effective from the positivist one in combating moral injustice in evil states.

The fourth objection against nonpositivism takes the form of an argument from legal certainty (*Rechtssicherheitsargument*). According to this, a nonpositivist understanding of law poses a threat to legal certainty. Alexy admits that this argument is correct when it concerns a strong version of *Verbindungsthese*—because if every injustice allows for a refusal to abide by the law, we reach a state of anarchism. Yet, as mentioned above, the nonpositivist conception of law advocates only a weak version of the Connection Thesis. Hence, the objection at issue has very limited importance, since "Radbruch's formula" (and more precisely, *Unerträglichkeitsthese*), in principle, gives priority to the certainty of law over justice *sensu stricto* and purposiveness, and only in situations involving extreme blatant injustice does it prefer the opposite. Therefore, a weak version of the Connection Thesis—as assumed by nonpositivism—leads only to a marginal limitation of legal certainty. However, this view is only justified if we accept an assumption that it is usually possible to rationally identify and justify that a threshold of extreme injustice has been exceeded.

The argument from relativism (*Relativismusargument*) is strongly associated with the former one. It calls into question not only the possibility of making a distinction between the cases of extreme and non-extreme injustice, but also the possibility of objective cognition and rational justification of any assertions concerning justice. This argument stems from a relativistic metaethical position in which the inter-subjective justification of moral judgments is impossible. In response, Alexy admits that nonpositivism "presupposes an at least rudimentary [version] of non-relativistic ethics",[92] but the appropriateness of this assumption is

[92] *Ibidem*, p. 93 [English version, p. 53].

not considered in the work at issue.[93] Instead, he points to the fact (also cited by Radbruch) that there is strong conformity in terms of national and international practices with regard to fundamental human rights, and that this—in the context of legal practice—may bring us closer to a rebuttal of a relativistic ethical scepticism.

The sixth positivist objection can be referred to as the argument from democracy (*Demokratieargument*). According to this, the judge who relies on a nonpositivist conception of law and who refers to the demands of justice, can oppose the decisions of democratically legitimised legislators and thus violate the principle of the separation of powers, interfering into the realm of legislative authority. According to Alexy, this objection is inaccurate, since the result of a weak version of the Connection Thesis—as adopted by nonpositivism—is that judges interfere in the legislator's powers to a very limited extent (only in cases of extreme injustice): it is, in fact, a much less significant interference, for example, than in the judicial review of the constitutionality of laws. This comparison shows that if we accept the existence of the control of normative acts in terms of their constitutionality, this objection should be even more eagerly rejected.

The seventh objection assumes the form of the argument from superfluousness (*Unnötigkeitsargument*), and it states that we can use other legal measures to eliminate the consequences of "statutory injustice", which makes the reference to "Radbruch's formula" and its application unnecessary. The legislator may, in fact, repeal unjust laws (by means of retroactive laws) that were issued and applied during a previous unlawful state (*Unrechtsstaat*). When considering this argument, Alexy distinguishes between the cases in the area of penal law and the remaining ones. As for the former, Alexy argues—relying on dogmatic legal argument (consisting in recalling Article 103 Section 2 of the German Constitution, which grants constitutional status to the principle of *nulla poena sine lege poenali anteriori*[94])—that the prohibition of retroactivity in penal cases not only militates against the argument from superfluousness but it also shows that the real problem here is whether the application of "Radbruch's formula" in relation to unjust laws will not lead to circumventing the principle of *nulla poena sine lege*.[95] In relation to matters outside penal law, Alexy—like Dreier[96]—poses a question about how a

[93] These deliberations can be found in a number of other Alexy's works – in particular *see* 'A Discourse-Theoretical Conception of Practical Reason', trans. R. Adler, N. MacCormick, *RJ* 5 (1992), pp. 234ff. Alexy presents a range of different possibilities for justifying practical judgments (e.g. moral ones) in 'Menschenrechte ohne Metaphysik?', *DZPh* 52/1 (2004), pp. 17ff. The issues connected with this problem shall be analysed in Chap. 4 at pp. 86ff.

[94] The wording of this provision is as follows: "Eine Tat kann nur bestraft werden, wenn die Strafbarkeit gesetzlich bestimmt war, bevor die Tat begangen wurde".

[95] This problem is considered by Alexy as a part of the discussion concerning the argument from candour – *see* below.

[96] *Cf.* Dreier's argumentation in favour of "Radbruch's formula", discussed *supra* at pp. 30ff.

judge acts in a situation where the legislator remains passive after the collapse of a lawless state and he does not retroactively repeal unlawful laws. Arguing *ad absurdum*, Alexy apparently seriously wonders whether the judge should not, in this case, consistently apply unrepealed extremely unjust laws in order to persuade the legislator—at the cost of a citizen wronged in this way—to take appropriate legislative action. Naturally, if a judge followed such a pattern, she/he would not only undermine basic human rights, but would also be in conflict with the claim to correctness, associated with every judicial ruling. Thus, the application of "Radbruch's formula" and of the nonpositivist concept of law, here appears to be an effective remedy for the legislator's inactivity, making the argument from superfluousness in matters outside the penal law ineffective.

The last—eighth argument—against "Radbruch's formula" is the argument from candour (*Redlichkeitsargument*). This argument imputes a nonpositivist conception of law that, in criminal cases, leads to a circumvention of the *nulla poena sine lege* principle. According to Hart, who formulated this argument,[97] what is more fair than the application of "Radbruch's formula" is the enactment of criminal laws with retrospective force, without hiding the fact that in doing so we sacrifice the principle of *nulla poena sine lege*. Alexy admits that this is the strongest counterargument, yet it does not refute the nonpositivist conception of law. Firstly, a nonpositivist may assume that "Radbruch's formula" has very limited application in the field of penal law: the legal character of extremely unjust laws can be questioned by means of the formula, but in such a manner so as not to lead to a breach of the *nulla poena* principle. On the other hand, outside the domain of penal law, this formula would be fully applicable. According to another solution, preferred by Alexy, the application of "Radbruch's formula" does not result in creating new penal law provisions, which would justify the criminality of certain acts, but in the elimination of norms, which are undoubtedly extremely unjust and which justified a lack of criminality of certain human actions in unlawful states. In this way—as Alexy holds—we do not retroactively change the legal status, but we just eliminate those norms that obviously never had a legal nature.[98] In his opinion, one cannot speak of any unfairness in such an approach.

In conclusion, according to the philosopher from Kiel, stronger arguments militate in favour of adopting the weak version of *Verbindungsthese*, expressed by "Radbruch's formula", rather than for its rejection. The structure of his normative nonpositivist argumentation is presented in the following diagram (see Fig. 3.3).

[97] H.L.A. Hart, 'Positivism and the Separation of Law and Morals', *op. cit.*, pp. 619ff. and *The Concept of Law*, *op. cit.*, pp. 203–207.

[98] As Alexy writes, this is the joke (*Witz*) of "Radbruch's formula" – *see idem*, *Mauerschützen*, *op. cit.*, p. 33.

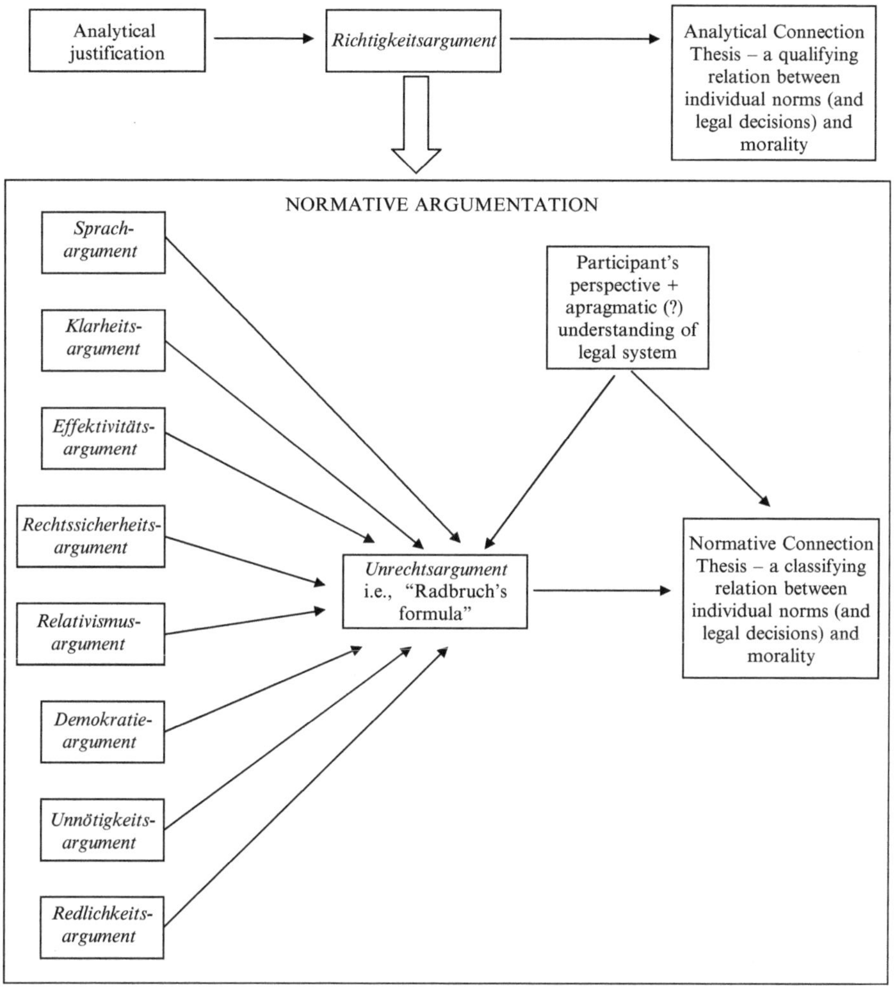

Fig. 3.3 Robert Alexy's original normative nonpositivist argumentation

3.3.3 Revisions and Supplements in *Begriff und Geltung des Rechts*

Alexy's nonpositivist argumentation was presented in a comprehensive manner in the book *Begriff und Geltung des Rechts* of 1992.[99] Although Alexy applied in this work an unchanged conceptual framework, previously established for analytical and normative argumentation, his presentation of nonpositivist argumentation has been significantly modified. In fact, Alexy treated the distinction between the perspective of

[99] R. Alexy, *Begriff und Geltung des Rechts*, *op. cit.*, pp. 39–136 [English version, pp. 20–81].

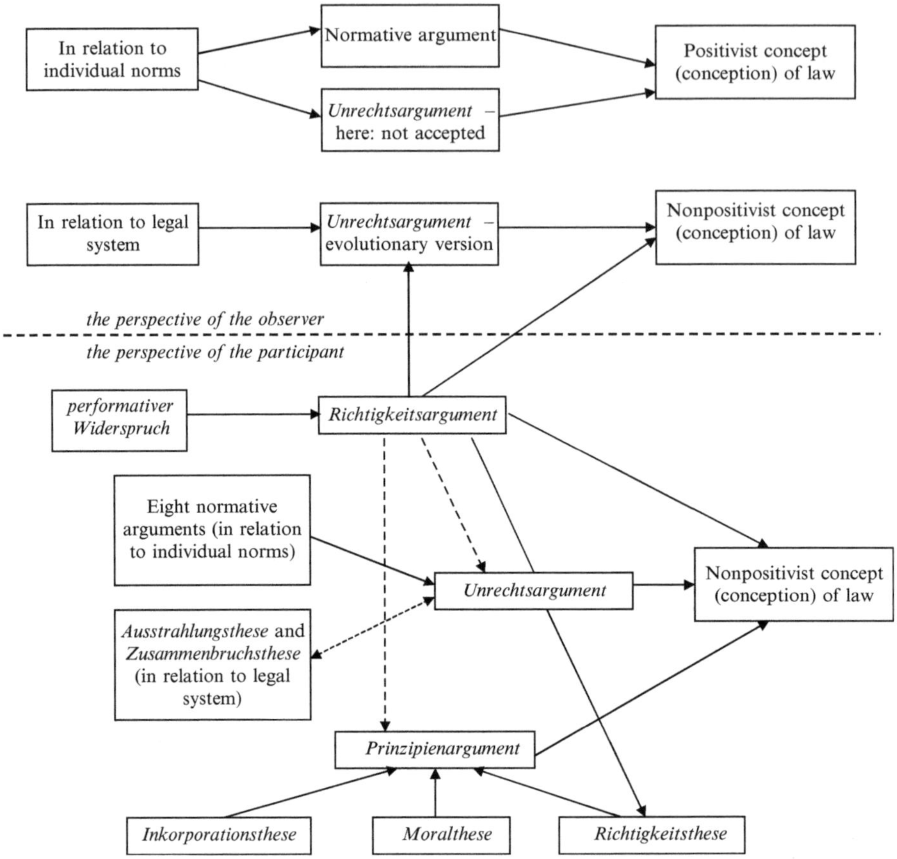

Fig. 3.4 Robert Alexy's nonpositivist argumentation (final version)

the observer and the one of the participant as a fundamental question. Let us begin the discussion of the revisions and supplements introduced by him with the scheme (see Fig. 3.4 above) showing the complex structure of this argumentation.

As explained by Alexy in the *Preface* to *Begriff und Geltung des Rechts*,[100] it constitutes only a part of a planned work co-written with Dreier and devoted to the theory of law.[101] It is no wonder then that Alexy uses several elements of Dreier's analysis, in particular, those concerning the positivist definitions of law, and he also refers to Dreier's normative nonpositivist argumentation. Similarly to him, Alexy crowns his deliberations with the formulation of the nonpositivist definition of law resulting therefrom.[102] The latter is associated with the first and fundamental

[100] *Ibidem*, p. 7 [English version, p. xv].

[101] Unfortunately, this planned work has not yet been published.

[102] *See* R. Alexy, *Begriff und Geltung des Rechts*, *op. cit.*, pp. 201ff. [English version, pp. 127ff.]. This definition has been presented in Chap. 2 at p. 16.

change in the manner of presenting Alexy's nonpositivist argumentation; as previously stated, the subject of the argumentation at issue no longer consists of two versions (analytical and normative) of nonpositivist *Verbindungsthese* but of the nonpositivist concept of law.

The comparison of the diagrams of the analytical and normative nonpositivist argumentation—provided in the previous sections—with the diagram reflecting the structure and substantive content of Alexy's argumentation in *Begriff und Geltung des Rechts* shows most of the revisions and supplements that have been introduced by him. In addition to the above-mentioned correction of the basic methodological distinction (i.e., distinguishing between the perspective of the observer and the participant), which Alexy used in order to re-organise the structure of his nonpositivist argumentation, the most important revisions and supplements include:

1. Incorporating a new normative argument within the argumentation carried out from the perspective of the observer, in regard to classifying relations between law and morality on the level of individual legal norms;
2. Changes in the understanding and justification of the argument from correctness and its role in the structure of nonpositivist argumentation;
3. Carrying out the analysis of the correctness of *Unrechtsargument* in relation to legal systems (from the perspective of a participant);
4. The change of name, content and partial change of the justification of the third thesis (now referred to as *Richtigkeitsthese*), together constituting the argument from principles.

Let us begin the discussion of the introduced modifications with a comment concerning the argumentation carried out from the perspective of an observer who examines the adequacy of the nonpositivist *Verbindungsthese* in relation to respective legal norms (*ad.* 1). In this regard, Alexy holds on to his standpoint—presented earlier within the analytical nonpositivist argumentation—assuming that in such a conceptual framework, the positivist conception of law is correct, whereas the nonpositivist one is unfeasible and unacceptable. The only novelty here is to consider the normative argument, formulated by Norbert Hoerster, that was previously discussed by Alexy only within the normative argumentation; namely, from the perspective of a participant rather than an observer.[103] Hoerster argues[104] that there is a need for an axiologically neutral term that would help to determine (call) the norms which—according to the nonpositivist definition of law—do not have a legal nature (for example, the norms contained in the often recalled example of the Eleventh Ordinance to *Reichsbürgergesetz* of 1941). He also points out that there is no suitable term that might constitute an alternative for the term "law". Alexy admits that the correctness of Hoerster's argument—though only from the perspective of the observer—weighs in favour of rejecting Radbruch's argument from

[103] *See* the discussion of linguistic argument *supra*, pp. 46–47.

[104] *See* N. Hoerster, 'Die rechtsphilosophische Lehre vom Rechtsbegriff', *op. cit.*, pp. 186–188 and 'Zur Verteidigung des Rechtspositivismus', *op. cit.*, p. 2481.

unlawfulness; namely, for the positivist *Trennungsthese* (with conceptual frames of the analysis adopted here).

The most far-reaching changes in Alexy's nonpositivist argumentation undoubtedly relate to the argument from correctness (*ad.* 2). Firstly, as already noted, the understanding of this argument is reduced here as compared to the one adopted in the original nonpositivist analytical argumentation.[105] In this new approach, this argument states that both singular norms or legal decisions and systems of law (treated as a whole) necessarily raise the claim to correctness (*Anspruch auf Richtigkeit*). Its content is therefore equivalent to what was previously referred to by Alexy as the theory of claims (*Anspruchstheorie*). Secondly, the argument from correctness (*Richtigkeitsargument*) is now justified exclusively by means of the analysis of the two above-mentioned examples of statements burdened with the error of "performative contradiction". Thus, the justification of *Richtigkeitsargument* already lacks the reference to the theory of claims (although the concept of *Anspruch auf Richtigkeit* obviously exists there), whereas neither the theory of principles (*Prinzipientheorie*) nor the theory of legal discourse, expressed in the form of *Sonderfallthese*, constitute the elements of the justification of this argument.[106] Thirdly—what should be regarded rather as a clarification of the relations taking place in the structure of the arguments developed earlier, than as its significant change—the argument from correctness—is treated by Alexy as the basis for other arguments (that is, the argument from injustice and the argument from principles), indispensable to justifying the nonpositivist conception of law; whereas this justification is made from the perspective of a participant in search of qualifying relations between law and morality.[107] In the case of *Unrechtsargument*, it should be understood in such a way that the eight normative arguments considered in the discussion on the correctness of this argument from the perspective of a participant are assessed in the context of the argument from correctness.[108] Yet, with regard to the argument from principles, the importance of the argument from correctness is primarily manifested in the fact that the third thesis of the theory of principles—now referred to as *Richtigkeitsthese*—constitutes, as Alexy argues,

[105] *Cf. supra*, note 68 at p. 40.

[106] Renouncing the application of *Sonderfallthese* can be explained by the fact that Alexy most probably noticed that its application in order to justify the argument from correctness could lead to a *circulus vitiosus*. Circularity of previous justificatory reasoning lies in the fact that in *Theorie der juristischen Argumentation*, *op. cit.*, pp. 263ff. [English version, pp. 213ff.], the claim to correctness (*Anspruch auf Richtigkeit*) – which is indeed the essence of the argument from correctness – constitutes one of the elements of justification of the Special Case Thesis that, in turn, has been used by Alexy to justify *Richtigkeitsargument* within the analytical nonpositivist argumentation – *see supra*, pp. 43–44. This remark implies that the change in the content and structure of the nonpositivist argumentation should undoubtedly be evaluated positively. *Cf.* however, *infra*, note 119 at p. 58.

[107] R. Alexy, *Begriff und Geltung des Rechts*, *op. cit.*, p. 64 [English version, pp. 35–36].

[108] *Ibidem*, pp. 70ff. [English version, pp. 40ff.].

"the result of applying the argument from correctness within the frames of the argument from principles".[109]

Another change in Alexy's nonpositivist argumentation is its supplementation (made in reference to Dreier's nonpositivist argumentation, based on the analysis of "Kriele's formula"[110]) with the analysis of the correctness of the argument from injustice in relation to legal systems, conducted from the perspective of the participant who seeks classifying relations between law and morality (*ad.* 3). For this purpose, Alexy considers what the consequences are in the situation when the legal system fails to comply with the claim to correctness. In his view, *Unrechtsargument* in such a conceptual framework can be reduced to the statement that, "[a] system of norms loses its legal character if it is – by and large – extremely unjust".[111] Given the ambiguity of the so-formulated thesis, Alexy presents and examines its two interpretations, assuming the form of the Extension Thesis (*Ausstrahlungsthese*) and the Collapse Thesis (*Zusammenbruchsthese*).

The first interpretation (*Ausstrahlungsthese*) states that a lack of legal character of the norms that constitute the substantive basis of the legal system implies a lack of legal character of all the norms typical for that system, and in this sense, it extends (radiates) to these norms.[112] In other words, respective legal norms lose their legal character, not because they are extremely unjust, but because they are a part of an extremely unlawful legal system. When analysing the acceptability of the argument from injustice, as interpreted in this way, however, one may draw the conclusion that it is untenable because it considerably affects the principle of legal certainty. Alexy points out that the analysis of "Radbruch's formula" from the perspective of a participant and in relation to individual norms has shown that legal certainty is a fundamental restriction of the scope in which this formula is applied in relation to the norms established in accordance with the lawmaking procedures of a given system, which are at the same time socially efficient. Certainty of law is also violated here due to the lack of clear criteria that allow for a strict distinction between the norms that are typical for a given system of law, from those that are not as well as for taking an appropriate decision as to the legal nature of norms that only marginally affect the extreme injustice of a particular legal system. Thus, when considering the legal nature, we should apply the criterion of extreme injustice only in relation to individual norms; otherwise we can indeed expect consequences that will substantially extend beyond the effects of applying the argument from injustice in relation to them. Alexy therefore concludes that although *Unrechtsargument* interpreted in the form of the Extension Thesis (*Ausstrahlungsthese*) can be credible and persuasive in other contexts (for example, in assessing the moral

[109] *Ibidem*, p. 130 [English version, p. 77]. The *Richtigkeitsthese* will be discussed in the final part of this section at pp. 57ff.

[110] *Cf. supra*, p. 32, and the references cited therein.

[111] R. Alexy, *Begriff und Geltung des Rechts*, *op. cit.*, p. 109 [English version, pp. 63–64].

[112] Alexy emphasises that his interpretation is consistent with Kriele's position – *see* R. Alexy, *ibidem*, p. 110 [English version, p. 64].

correctness or fairness of a legal system), it is not acceptable in the context of assessing the legal character of norms.

The second interpretation of the argument from injustice, presented in the form of the Collapse Thesis (*Zusammenbruchsthese*), is already based on the criterion of extreme injustice with respect to individual norms. This thesis states that the whole system of norms (understood as a system of law) breaks down and collapses when a great number of individual norms—that are especially important for this system—lose their legal nature due to their extreme injustice.[113] The legal system therefore collapses because, after applying the criterion of extreme injustice, not many of the legal norms remain within the system. Alexy admits that this thesis is correct, provided, however, that we take into account the change in the substantive identity of the system of law. The old system of law collapses, because after extremely iniquitous norms have been eliminated from it, it is substantively different, distinct from its predecessor—it becomes the new legal system. On the other hand, it is hard to speak about a "collapse" of an extremely unjust legal system if we take into account only its existence, because in such a situation—despite the loss of several norms—the legal system does not cease to exist after all. Alexy based such assessment on the assumption that in order for a legal system to exist, it is sufficient if a minimum set of norms preserves its legal character. In this context, Alexy considers the example of a system of law in which—in accordance with the constitution—only a dictator is entitled to issue norms. The dictator enacts 30 % of extremely unjust norms, 20 % of unjust norms, the same number of axiologically neutral norms and 30 % of norms that comply with justice. According to "Radbruch's formula", only 30 % of extremely unjust norms lose their legal character in this system. This may lead to the collapse of the entire system only when the situation of depriving the 30 % norms of their legal character entails that the norm which empowers the dictator to issue laws will be fully recognised as extremely unjust, and will lose its legal character and, thus, the other norms will also lose their legal character due to the loss of the legal basis for their validity. Yet, according to Alexy, it suffices that it was not a dictator, but a democratically elected parliament that was empowered to enact norms in the legal system at issue. In such a case, the possibility that the whole system collapses must be rejected because such a general norm of legislative competence cannot be considered as being extremely iniquitous. Therefore, Alexy concludes the analysis of the correctness of the argument from injustice in relation to the whole legal system, with the statement that the use of this argument does not lead to consequences exceeding the effects of its application in relation to individual norms.[114]

Further and final modifications in Alexy's nonpositivist argumentation concern the argument from principles (*ad.* 4). They consist of supplementing his critical introductory remarks to *Prinzipienargument* and a few minor improvements in the

[113] *Ibidem*, pp. 113–114 [English version, pp. 66–68].

[114] *Ibidem*, p. 117 [English version, p. 68].

justification of *Inkorporationsthese* and *Moralthese*.[115] The most important novelty is the change of the name, content and partial correction of the justification of the third thesis that makes up the argument from principles, now referred to as the Correctness Thesis (*Richtigkeitsthese*).[116] This thesis, which replaces an earlier *Kohärenzthese*, argues for the existence of a necessary connection of law to correct morality. Given that in the initial version of the analytical nonpositivist argumentation this thesis was justified not only within *Kohärenzthese*, but primarily by reference to the procedural theory of legal discourse, it is hardly surprising that the justification of *Richtigkeitsthese* contains elements that were previously used by Alexy.[117]

Alexy begins the justification of this thesis with an example of a legal system in which the fundamental constitutional principles (such as the principles of human dignity, freedom, equality, rule of law, democracy or the welfare state[118]) are consistent with the requirements of morality or, at least, acceptable by morality. In such a system, given the optimisation nature of the principles, the judge is legally obliged to seek optimal settlement in specific legal cases. According to Alexy, judicial argumentation related to the issue of weighing the principles (in cases, which, due to their complicated nature require such weighing) must be at least partly such an argumentation that has—in terms of its content—moral character. Thus, the claim to legal correctness (*Anspruch auf rechtliche Richtigkeit*), which, by means of *Richtigkietsargument*, is necessarily related to any judicial decision, includes a claim to moral correctness (*Anspruch auf moralische Richtigkeit*). Accordingly, there is a necessary relation between law and correct morality in the legal system in which positivised principles are consistent with morality or are acceptable from a moral point of view.

This statement might encounter an objection expressed by a positivist who contests the scope of its validity. Indeed, a doubt arises as to whether one can speak of the same necessary relation in cases of all systems of law, and thus also, in relation, for example, to the Nazi legal system, based on completely different principles. Alexy admits that in this context, the argument from principles encounters the argument from injustice; yet he tries to defend *Richtigkeitsthese*

---

[115] *Ibidem*, pp. 117ff. [English version, pp. 68ff.]. Briefly speaking, supplementing the analysis with the argument from principles consists of recalling – as was previously done by Dreier in his nonpositivist argumentation – the thesis, originating from Hart, about the open texture of law, which results in the existence of "an open sphere" (*Offenheitsbereich*) of positive law. According to the nonpositivist *Prinzipienargument*, in this sphere the judge is bound by positive law, which remains in a necessary connection with morality. This supplement also applies to the character of the relation between law and morality, justified by the argument from principles – Alexy points out that this is a conceptual relation, of a qualifying character for the participant of the legal system. Other changes – concerning the justification of *Inkorporationsthese* and *Moralthese* – are largely cosmetic in nature, and will therefore be ignored.

[116] *See ibidem*, pp. 129ff. [English version, pp. 76ff.].

[117] *See supra*, pp. 43–44.

[118] Alexy uses here the examples of legal principles that can be found in the German *Grundgesetz*.

without resorting to the latter. He assumes that the claim to correctness also preserves its validity in relation to the judge adjudicating on the basis of Nazi law. This claim entails, in fact, the claim to justifiability (*Anspruch auf Begründbarkeit*), which requires that it was possible to justify the judicial decision in relation to justifiable—and in that sense, correct morality. This position, nonetheless, allows for the possibility of further allegations being made by the opponents of the nonpositivist *Verbindungsthese*. They may claim that such a method of defending *Richtigkeitsthese* results in reducing this claim to such an extent that there is no longer any necessary connection between law and morality because, firstly, this defence deals only with the claim to correctness (rather than satisfying it) and, secondly, although this defence refers to "correct morality", it does not explain what this correctness should consist of. Alexy recognises both allegations, yet he does not think that they might rebut *Verbindungsthese*. He recalls that apart from the scope of application of the argument from injustice—and therefore in relation to the norms and decisions that do not exceed the threshold of extreme injustice—a necessary relation between law and correct morality can only assume the existence of the claim to correctness (and not fulfil this every time), because what can be examined here are only relations of qualifying rather than classifying character. The fact that violating the requirements of the correct morality does not result in the norm or legal decision losing their legal character, but it points at their necessary legal defectiveness (*rechtliche Fehlerhaftigkeit*).

Let us consider the last positivist objection. It can be seen that the nonpositivist argumentation at issue can also be criticised for merely referring to "correct morality", which is not sufficient. Importantly, this objection cannot be refuted by presenting a catalogue of moral rules which would unambiguously allow us to determine in every case whether a given norm or legal decision infringes on the requirements of correct morality. As far as the field of extreme injustice is concerned, there is a far-reaching agreement in this regard, whereas outside of this field, there is an equally far-reaching dispute. According to Alexy, it does not deny the possibility of a determination as to whether we deal with a just or an iniquitous legal norm or judicial decision. Such a resolution is possible due to the fact that the claim to correctness entails the claim to justifiability which, in turn, allows the requirements to be set, which must be met so that a certain morality need not be regarded as a false morality, and the requirements which must be met by it need to be met to the greatest extent possible in order for this morality to be considered as correct.[119]

Alexy concludes his reflections on *Richtigkeitsthese* by saying that they lead to the thesis of the necessary connection between law and the idea of correct

[119] Alexy does not discuss these requirements here, but he refers to *Theorie der juristischen Argumentation*, *op. cit.*, pp. 233ff. [English version, pp. 187ff.], where we find the rules and forms of general practical discourse, and then the outline of the theory of legal reasoning, undoubtedly also based on the Special Case Thesis. Thus, the circularity of Alexy's argument is preserved to a certain extent.

(i.e., justified) morality.[120] Although this idea lacks any substantive content, it may be filled by argumentation, because law does not only cover specific rules for the legal justification of decisions, but also the general rules for moral reasoning. Moreover, the idea of correct morality is perceived as a regulative idea (in a Kantian sense) and thus the claim to correctness directs us (in the frames of the argument from principles) towards the *ideale Dimension* of law that is necessarily related to law as such.[121]

[120] R. Alexy, *Begriff und Geltung des Rechts*, *op. cit.*, p. 136 [English version, p. 81].

[121] For more on this *see* Chap. 5, works cited in note 11 at p. 195, with the corresponding fragment of the text on the duality of the concept of law.

Chapter 4
Critique of Nonpositivist Argumentation

4.1 A Critique of the Nonpositivist Conception of Law

The nonpositivist conception of law stimulated yet another lively philosophical and jurisprudential debate in the on-going controversy between supporters and opponents of legal positivism. In Germany, this debate assumed the form of a multi-layered criticism directed both against the nonpositivist Connection Thesis (*Verbindungsthese*) as well as against the various components of Dreier's and Alexy's nonpositivist argumentation. The most challenged part of this argumentation—directly and indirectly—was Alexy's argument from correctness, based on the concept of the claim to correctness (*Anspruch auf Richtigkeit*). What can be distinguished in the German discussion are three basic controversies: between Dreier and Werner Krawietz[1]; between Dreier, Alexy and Norbert Hoerster[2]; and between the latter and Joachim Hruschka, the author who postulated the necessity of pre-positive law (*vorpositives Recht*)—having, in essence, the character of natural law and alluding to Radbruch's concept of suprastatutory law.[3] In addition, one can specify a number of works by authors who are the representatives of the middle and younger generations, and who directly or indirectly (within the critique

[1] *See* W. Krawietz, 'Neues Naturrecht oder Rechtspositivismus? Eine kritische Auseinandersetzung mit dem Begriff des Rechts bei Ralf Dreier und Norbert Hoerster', *op. cit.* and R. Dreier, 'Neues Naturrecht oder Rechtspositivismus? In Erwiderung auf Werner Krawietz', *op. cit.*

[2] *See* N. Hoerster, 'Zur Verteidigung des Rechtspositivismus', *op. cit.*, 'Die rechtsphilosophische Lehre vom Rechtsbegriff', *op. cit.*, and 'Zur Verteidigung der rechtspositivistischen Trennungsthese', *op. cit.*; R. Dreier, 'Zur gegenwärtigen Diskussion des Verhältnisses von Recht und Moral in der Bundesrepublik Deutschland', *op. cit.*; R. Alexy, 'On Necessary Relations between Law and Morality', *op. cit.*, 'Zur Kritik des Rechtspositivismus', *op. cit.*, and 'Zur Verteidigung eines nichtpositivistischen Rechtsbegriffs', *op. cit.*

[3] *See* J. Hruschka, 'Vorpositives Recht als Gegenstand und Aufgabe der Rechtswissenschaft', *JZ* 47 (1992), pp. 429–438 and 'Recht und Unrecht bei Norbert Hoerster', *ARSP* 79 (1993), pp. 421–424; N. Hoerster, 'Richtigstellung über den Rechtspositivismus', *ARSP* 79 (1993), pp. 416–420.

A. Grabowski, *Juristic Concept of the Validity of Statutory Law*,
DOI 10.1007/978-3-642-27688-0_4, © Springer-Verlag Berlin Heidelberg 2013

of Alexy's discursive theory of law and his theory of legal argumentation) raise objections to some components of nonpositivist argumentation—in particular, it is worth recalling here the works of Carl Braun,[4] Armin Engländer,[5] Peter Gril,[6] Klaus Günther,[7] Eric Hilgendorf,[8] Michel Paroussis[9] and Axel Tschentscher.[10] A separate debate, conducted primarily in the context of the trials over the "Berlin Wall shootings" (*Mauerschützenprozesse*),[11] concerns the issue of the correctness of "Radbruch's formula", which is of utmost importance for assessing the correctness of justifying the nonpositivist conception of law, given the reference to this

[4] *See* C. Braun, 'Diskurstheoretische Normenbegründung in der Rechtswissenschaft', *RT* 19 (1988), pp. 238–261.

[5] *See* A. Engländer, 'Zur begrifflichen Möglichkeit des Rechtspositivismus. Eine Kritik des Richtigkeitsarguments von Robert Alexy', *RT* 28 (1997), pp. 437–485, 'The Failure of Discourse Theory. Critical Remarks on Habermas' Moral and Legal Cognitivism', *AS* 4 (2000), pp. 223–251, *Diskurs als Rechtsquelle? Zur Kritik der Diskurstheorie des Rechts*, Tübingen 2002, and 'Moralische Richtigkeit als Bedingung der Rechtsgeltung? Eine erkenntnistheoretische Kritik', *ARSP* (2004), pp. 86–97.

[6] *See* P. Gril, 'Alexys Version einer transzendental-pragmatischen Begründung der Diskursregeln im Unterschied zu Habermas', *ARSP* 83 (1997), pp. 206–216 and *Die Möglichkeit praktischer Erkenntnis aus Sicht der Diskurstheorie. Eine Untersuchung zu Jürgen Habermas und Robert Alexy*, Berlin 1998, pp. 124ff.

[7] *See* K. Günther, *Der Sinn für Angemessenheit. Anwedungsdiskurse in Moral und Recht*, Frankfurt am Main 1988, pp. 257ff. [English version: *The Sense of Appropriateness. Application Discourses in Morality and Law*, trans. J. Farrell, Albany 1993, pp. 203ff.], 'Ein normativer Begriff der Kohärenz für eine Theorie der juristischen Argumentation', *RT* 20 (1989), pp. 184ff., and 'Critical Remarks on Robert Alexy's "Special-Case Thesis"', *RJ* 6 (1993), pp. 143–156. Günther's critique encountered Alexy's rejoinder – *see idem*, 'Normenbegründung und Normanwendung' in A. Aarnio *et al.* (eds.), *Rechtsnorm und Rechtswirklichkeit*, Berlin 1993, pp. 3–17 [English version: 'Justification and Application of Norms', *RJ* 6 (1993), pp. 157–170]. For more on this controversy *see* Chap. 9 at pp. 473ff.

[8] *See* E. Hilgendorf, *Argumentation in der Jurisprudenz. Zur Rezeption von analytischer Philosophie und kritischer Theorie in der Grundlagenforschung der Jurisprudenz*, Tübingen 1990, pp. 125ff., 223ff. and 'Zur transzendentalpragmatischen Begründung von Diskursregeln', *op. cit.*

[9] *See* M. Paroussis, *Theorie des juristischen Diskurses. Eine institutionelle Epistemologie des Rechts*, Berlin 1995, pp. 24ff.

[10] *See* A. Tschentscher, *Prozedurale Theorien der Gerechtigkeit. Rationales Entscheiden, Diskursethik und prozedurales Recht*, Baden-Baden 2000, pp. 217ff., 290ff. and 'Der Konsensbegriff in Vertrags- und Diskurstheorien', *RT* 33 (2002), pp. 43–59.

[11] Those who have so far taken part in this discussion – taking into account only the leading representatives of the German theory and philosophy of law – were, inter alia, R. Alexy, H. Dreier, R. Dreier, W. Hassemer, A. Kaufmann, U. Neumann and J.-R. Sieckmann (*see infra*, note 486 at p. 187). Among recent works on "Radbruch's formula", but that are no longer directly related to *Mauerschützenprozesse*, especially recommendable are those of W. Ott, 'Die Radbruch'sche Formel. Pro und Contra', *ZSchwR* 107 (1988), pp. 335–357; H. Dreier, 'Die Radbruchsche Formel – Erkenntnis oder Bekenntnis?', *op. cit.*; F. Saliger, *Radbruchsche Formel und Rechtsstaat*, Heidelberg 1995; A. Funke, 'Überlegungen zu Gustav Radbruchs "Verleugnungsformel". Ein Beitrag zur Lehre vom Rechtsbegriff', *ARSP* 89 (2003), pp. 1–16; B. Bix, 'Robert Alexy, Radbruch's Formula, and the Nature of Legal Theory', *RT* 37 (2006), pp. 139–149.

formula in Dreier's and Alexy's nonpositivist argumentation. When reporting on the state of the German debate, it is also worth mentioning the lack of monographs, or of studies that are more detailed on nonpositivism as well as the lack of direct references to nonpositivist definitions of law proposed by Dreier and Alexy. On the other hand, texts that take the nonpositivist concept of law as a conceptual basis for particular jurisprudential analyses can already be found in the German literature.[12]

The German nonpositivist conception of law has also encountered widespread criticism in the international forum. Although *tantum valet auctoritas quantum valet sua ratio*, however—not only because of the importance of the discussed problems, but also on account of the unquestioned authority of the scientists formulating objections to this conception—the critical works of Eugenio Bulygin and Ota Weinberger should be regarded as the most important. The critique of the Argentinean philosopher is primarily concerned with the justification of the argument from correctness and the modal character of conceptual relations between law and morality.[13] Weinberger, on the other hand, focused on the issue of practical reason and its role in the rational justification of practical judgments.[14] In the context of international debate, what is also worthy of mentioning is a monograph by Alfonso García Figueroa, in large part directly devoted to Alexy's nonpositivist

[12] *See e.g.*, D. Heckmann, *Geltungskraft und Geltungsverlust von Rechtsnormen. Elemente einer Theorie der autoritativen Normgeltungsbeendigung*, Tübingen 1997, pp. 15ff. and B. Hoffmann, *Das Verhältnis von Gesetz und Recht. Eine verfassungsrechtliche und verfassungstheoretische Untersuchung zu Art. 20 Abs. 3 GG*, Berlin 2003, pp. 158–160, 252ff.

[13] *See* E. Bulygin, 'Alexy und das Richtigkeitsargument' in A. Aarnio *et al.* (eds.), *Rechtsnorm und Rechtswirklichkeit*, *op. cit.*, pp. 19–24, 'Is There a Conceptual Connection between Law and Morality?', *op. cit.*, pp. 52ff., 'Alexy's Thesis of the Necessary Connection between Law and Morality', *RJ* 13 (2000), pp. 133–137ff., and the 'Alexy between Positivism and Non-Positivism', lecture presented at the 1st Conference on Philosophy and Law "Neutrality and Theory of Law", Girona 20–22 of May 2010 [http://www.te.gob.mx/ccje/Archivos/eugenio_bulygin.pdf]. Alexy's response to Bulygin's critique can be found in the works: 'Bulygins Kritik des Richtigkeitsarguments', *op. cit.*, 'On the Thesis of a Necessary Connection between Law and Morality: Bulygin's Critique', *op. cit.*, and the 'Between Positivism and Non-Positivism? A Third Reply to Eugenio Bulygin', lecture presented at the 1st Conference on Philosophy and Law "Neutrality and Theory of Law", Girona 20–22 of May 2010 [http://www.te.gob.mx/ccje/Archivos/r_aalexy.pdf].

[14] *See* O. Weinberger, 'Logische Analyse als Basis der juristischen Argumentation' in W. Krawietz, R. Alexy (eds.), *Metatheorie juristischer Argumentation*, Berlin 1983, pp. 185ff., 'Wartość, wartościowanie i doświadczanie wartości w argumentacji prawniczej' [Value, Evaluating and Experiencing Values in Legal Argumentation], trans. T. Gliwiński, *SP* 3–4 (1985), pp. 282ff., 'Typen der Rationalität in der juristischen Argumentation', *IJRG* 1992, pp. 369ff., 'Conflicting Views on Practical Reason. Against Pseudo-Arguments in Practical Philosophy', *RJ* 5 (1992), pp. 252–268, 'Grundlagenprobleme des Institutionalistischen Rechtspositivismus und der Gerechtigkeitstheorie', *RT* Bh. 14 (1994), pp. 253ff., and 'Basic Puzzles of Discourse Philosophy', *RJ* 9 (1996), pp. 172–181. Alexy refuted the most crucial objections raised by Weinberger in 'Nachwort (1991): Antwort auf einige Kritiker' in *idem*, *Theorie der juristischen Argumentation*, 2nd ed., Frankfurt am Main 1991, pp. 399ff. and 'Ota Weinbergers Kritik der diskurstheoretischen Deutung juristischer Rationalität', *op. cit.*

conception of law.[15] As a great number of philosophers and theorists of law took part in the discussion on the German nonpositivist conception of law,[16] one might have gained the impression that this discussion is now being undertaken as if it were closely aligned to the mainstream dispute concerning an adequate (and legitimate) form of legal positivism, which is already being conducted mainly among positivists. This controversy takes the form of a debate between the advocates of the soft—that is, inclusive legal positivism (in addition to H.L.A Hart, the representatives of this trend include Philip Soper, Jules Coleman, Wilfrid Waluchow, Matthew Kramer and José Juan Moreso)—and the supporters of the hard—that is, exclusive legal positivism (defended, inter alia, by Eugenio Bulygin, Joseph Raz, Scott Shapiro and Andrei Marmor).[17]

Finally, let me also present a few observations *pro domo sua*. In the Polish theory and philosophy of law, it has been very difficult up to now to be able to speak about any wider impact, reception or criticism of German nonpositivism. There are indeed numerous works in which the authors refer to Alexy's theory of juristic discourse,[18] to his theory of principles[19] or to a discursive justification of human

---

[15] A. García Figueroa, *Principios y positivismo jurídico. El no positivismo principialista en las teorías de Ronald Dworkin y Robert Alexy*, Madrid 1998, pp. 185ff. and 'La tesis del caso especial y el positivismo jurídico', *DOXA* 22 (1999), pp. 195–220.

[16] Due to the large number of works dealing with this subject, all of them cannot be listed here, yet many of them will be referred to in the course of this analysis.

[17] *See e.g.*, K.E. Himma, 'Inclusive Legal Positivism', *op. cit.*; J.L. Coleman, 'Inclusive Legal Positivism' in *idem*, *The Practice of Principle. In Defence of a Pragmatist Approach to Legal Theory*, Oxford/New York 2001, pp. 103–119; J.J. Moreso, 'In Defense of Inclusive Legal Positivism', *D&QP* 1 (2001), pp. 99–117; A. Marmor, 'Exclusive Legal Positivism', *op. cit.*; B. Leiter, 'Legal Realism, Hard Positivism, and the Limits of Conceptual Analysis' in J.L. Coleman (ed.), *Hart's Postscript*, *op. cit.*, pp. 355–370; M.H. Kramer, *Where Law and Morality Meet*, *op. cit.*

[18] *See e.g.*, J. Stelmach, *Kodeks argumentacyjny dla prawników* [An Argumentative Code for Lawyers], Kraków 2003; M. Smolak, *Uzasadnianie sądowe jako argumentacja z moralności politycznej* [Judicial Justification as the Argumentation from Political Morality], Kraków 2003, pp. 84ff.; B. Wojciechowski, 'Dyskursywny model sądowego stosowania prawa – wybrane aspekty' [Discursive Model of Judicial Application of Law – Selected Aspects] in J. Stelmach (ed.), *Filozofia prawa wobec globalizmu*, Kraków 2003, pp. 151–166 and *Dyskrecjonalność sędziowska. Studium teoretycznoprawne* [Judicial Discretion. A Jurisprudential Study], Toruń 2004, pp. 269ff.; B. Brożek, W. Cyrul, 'Zwischen Logik und Diskurs – Bemerkungen zur Geltung im globalen Rechtssystem', *KAR* 1 (2004), pp. 19–38.

[19] *See e.g.*, M. Smolak, *ibidem*, pp. 85ff.; P. Tuleja, *Stosowanie Konstytucji RP w świetle zasady jej nadrzędności (wybrane problemy)* [The Application of the Polish Constitution in the Light of the Principle of Its Superiority (Selected Problems)], Kraków 2003, pp. 155ff.; M. Dąbrowska-Kardas, 'Kara jako konflikt dóbr i kolizja norm w świetle koncepcji Roberta Alexy'ego konfliktu reguł i kolizji zasad. Rozważania na tle konstytucyjnych norm stanowienia i stosowania prawa' ['Punishment as a Conflict of Goods and Collision of Norms in the Light of Robert Alexy's Concept of the Conflict of Rules and Collision of Principles. Studies from the Perspective of Constitutional Norms of Enacting and Applying Law'], *PS* 4 (1996), pp. 20–33. Apart from its application, Alexy's conception of principles was also criticised from a jurisprudential point of view by L. Morawski, 'Zasady prawne – komentarz krytyczny', *op. cit.*, pp. 77ff.

rights,[20] but it is extremely difficult to find studies that relate directly to the nonpositivist conception of law. Nonetheless, it was in Polish legal theory that Lech Morawski developed the nonpositivist conception of the Law-Governed (i.e., Rule of Law) State (*Rechtsstaat*),[21] that is, to a considerable extent, original in relation to the German nonpositivist conception. What also merits noting is the paper published in Poland by Aleksander Peczenik, in which he presented his own version of a nonpositivist conception of law aimed mainly against positivist arguments involving the relativism of moral judgments.[22] In addition, thanks to a series of works by Jerzy Zajadło, devoted to "Radbruch's formula" (as well as to Radbruch's philosophy of law), this important component of nonpositivist argumentation has already been thoroughly described and researched in the Polish literature.[23]

Naturally, the question arises as to why Alexy's and Dreier's nonpositivism is not the subject of broader interest in Polish theory and philosophy of law. The answer may be—in my opinion—of a twofold (and to some extent Janus) nature. First, the nonpositivist conception of law has been *ab initio* rejected by our—to a considerable extent positivistically oriented—discipline. Such an assessment can be justified, inter alia, due to the harsh criticism that Morawski's nonpositivist conception has encountered.[24] Secondly, the silence of the representatives of our

---

[20] *See e.g.*, B. Wojciechowski, 'Uzasadnienie praw człowieka w koncepcji dyskursu prawniczego' [Justification of Human Rights in the Conception of Legal Discourse], *SPE* LXIII (2001), pp. 9–25.

[21] This concept was presented by Morawski in a number of studies: 'Spór o pojęcie państwa prawnego' [A Dispute over the Concept of the Law-Governed State], *PiP* 4 (1994), pp. 3–12, 'Zasada państwa prawnego – próba reinterpretacji' [The Principle of the Law-Governed State – An Attempt at Reinterpretation], *AUNC – Prawo* XXXV/304 (1996), pp. 3–22, 'Państwo prawa', *op. cit.*, and *Główne problemy współczesnej filozofii prawa*, *op. cit.*, pp. 257ff.

[22] *See* A. Peczenik, 'Non-Positivist Conception of Law', *op. cit. See* also his earlier study (co-written with S. Urbina), 'Why Officials? On Legal Positivism Old and New', *op. cit.*, in which on p. 159 they provide a nonpositivist definition of law (legal system), referring to Alexy's definition from *Begriff und Geltung des Rechts*, *op. cit.*

[23] *See* J. Zajadło, 'Gustaw Radbruch i antynomie współczesnej filozofii prawa' [Gustav Radbruch and the Antinomies of Modern Philosophy of Law], *CC* (1988–1989), pp. 63–74, 'Formuła Radbrucha – geneza, treść, zastosowanie' [Radbruch's Formula – Genesis, Content and Application], *PiP* 6 (2000), pp. 25–42, *Formuła Radbrucha*, *op. cit.*, and *Dziedzictwo przeszłości*, *op. cit.*, pp. 206ff.

[24] *See* H. Rot, 'W sprawie koncepcji prawa i praworządności' [On the Conception of Law and the Rule of Law], *PiP* 7–8 (1994), pp. 109–111 and K. Działocha, W. Gromski, 'Niepozytywistyczna koncepcja państwa prawnego a Trybunał Konstytucyjny' [Nonpositivist Conception of the Law-Governed State and the Constitutional Tribunal], *PiP* 3 (1995), pp. 4–16. Morawski replied to Rot's peculiar ideological criticism in his study 'Państwo prawne – odpowiedź na uwagi prof. H. Rota' [Law-Governed State – a Reply to Prof. H. Rot's Comments], *PiP* 12 (1994), pp. 84–87. Incidentally, the high temperature and persuasiveness of a debate between nonpositivists and positivists, or even using arguments *ad personam* can also be observed in international discussion – for example, O. Weinberger alleges in one place "that Alexy is anxious that he would lose his reputation if he were not able to offer practical knowledge" – *idem*, 'Conflicting Views on Practical Reason', *op. cit.*, note 15 at p. 264, whereas E. Bulygin admits that some of Alexy's claims "lie beyond his capacity of understanding" – *idem*, 'Alexy's Thesis of the Necessary Connection between Law and Morality', *op. cit.*, p. 135.

discipline can be explained by means of its specifically (and not necessarily pejoratively) understood isolationism, which at its core is an attempt not to yield to fashion, combined with a reluctance to follow the conceptions that are established abroad.[25] In my opinion, both answers contain a grain of truth. I do not think, however, that developing a position of Polish (or any other) theory of law against German nonpositivism, based on substantive analysis of Dreier's and Alexy's conception was pointless, not least because of the importance of both the philosophical and theoretical problems that this conception refers to and that it aims to resolve.

4.2 Controversial Points of Nonpositivist Argumentation

Up to now, several more or less complex objections against the various components of nonpositivist argumentation have been raised in the jurisprudential discussion on nonpositivism. The possibility of analysing all of the challenges at hand goes far beyond the scope of this work and its research objectives; therefore, in the criticism presented below, I refer only to some of these objections,[26] always trying to complement them with my own—hopefully thorough—analysis. I also introduce a few counterarguments against nonpositivist argumentation, which so far—to my knowledge—have not actually been raised by critics and commentators of Dreier's and Alexy's nonpositivist conception of law.

Before we proceed to the analysis, the objections and reservations against nonpositivism, which will be discussed in later parts of the work, will first be introduced. Accordingly, the criticism relating directly to the very nonpositivist

[25] *See* A. Peczenik, 'Stan obecny teorii i filozofii prawa w krajach zachodnich' [Current State of Theory and Philosophy of Law in Western Countries], *SFP* 2 (2003), pp. 13–14. In his opinion, in the crisis situation that the theory and philosophy of law in Western countries is currently facing, the Polish theory of law should maintain "respect for itself" and should refrain from "blind imitation of the West". Leaving aside the question as to whether Peczenik's thesis on the alleged crisis is adequate, or – rather – an exaggeration, it undoubtedly influenced many Polish scholars.

[26] What is especially important among the omitted issues is the critique of the argument from principles (*Prinzipienargument*), based, inter alia, on distinguishing legal principles and rules as introduced by Dworkin and as reformulated by Alexy. Taking into account the criticism of that fundamental element of nonpositivist argumentation and the very distinction of legal principles and rules, this argument also seems rather doubtful – *see e.g.*, H.-J. Koch, 'Zur Methodenlehre des Rechtspositivismus. Das Prinzipienargument – eine methodische Widerlegung des Rechtspositivismus?', *ARSP* Bh. 37 (1990), pp. 152–161; U. Neumann's review of R. Alexy's book: *Begriff und Geltung des Rechts*, *PrS* 6 (1994), pp. 245ff.; A. Engländer, *Diskurs als Rechtsquelle?*, *op. cit.*, pp. 136ff.; A. García Figueroa, *Principios y positivismo jurídico*, *op. cit.*, pp. 131ff., pp. 383ff.; L. Morawski, 'Zasady prawne – komentarz krytyczny', *op. cit.*; M. Kordela, 'Możliwość konstruowania ogólnej teorii zasad prawa. Uwagi do koncepcji Roberta Alexy'ego' [The Possibility of Constructing a General Theory of Legal Principles. Comments on Robert Alexy's Conception], *RPEiS* LXIX/2 (2007), pp. 11–28. *See* also comments concerning the dilemma of nonpositivism in the Epilogue at pp. 538–539.

definitions of law will be dealt with in Chap. 5. This is justified by substantive aspects because the issue of nonpositivist definitions of law is closely connected to the problem of including in the concept of law the concept of its validity, which shall become the object of critical reflection in the next chapter. Also due to substantive and editorial reasons, this chapter will not review some objections against Alexy's discursive theory of law and his theory of practical and legal discourse. The issues related to these objections will appear in Chap. 9, devoted—inter alia—to a discursive approach to the theory of law.[27] The reason for placing the above-mentioned critical analysis in the penultimate chapter of the work is that in this chapter, which covers the discourse on legal validity, I indirectly refer to the German theory of practical and legal discourse.

The order of the issues discussed below is based on the criterion of generality: I begin with the basic objections concerning the philosophical and jurisprudential foundations of the nonpositivist conception of law (Sects. 4.3–4.6), then I go on to the more specific ones relating to the nonpositivist argumentation of an analytical (Sect. 4.7), normative (Sect. 4.8) and empirical character (Sect. 4.9).

The first of the objections under consideration, although it has not yet been discussed in jurisprudential literature in the context of the German nonpositivist conception of law, constitutes a classic positivist challenge and it is undeniably of key importance. It concerns the self-contradiction of the nonpositivist thesis stating that "extremely unjust law is not law" as well as the conceptual consequences of recognising it as legitimate (Sect. 4.3). The second allegation discussed below is a typical metaethical objection. It questions the possibility of adopting a cognitivist standpoint in a traditional jurisprudential dispute over the so-called normative meaning and refers to the fact that norms and normative statements are usually grasped as linguistic entities that do not possess a logical value (Sect. 4.4). What is directly related to this objection is a more detailed third allegation that challenges the possibility of a discursive justification of the correctness of norms and normative statements (Sect. 4.5). In other words, the question concerns whether one can undertake the rehabilitation of practical reason by means of a discourse-theoretical conception of the latter (as expressed in the form of Alexy's procedural theory on practical discourse). The fourth allegation concerns the problem of the relation between the nonpositivist conception of law and legal positivism. After identifying on the version of legal positivism that is to be considered, in opposition to which the nonpositivist conception of law has been developed, this allegation, at first glance somewhat paradoxically disputes the nonpositivist nature of Dreier's and Alexy's conception (Sect. 4.6). The fifth objection relates to the justification of the argument from correctness, which is the basis of both analytical and normative nonpositivist argumentation presented by Alexy. According to its content, neither justification of *Richtigkeitsargument* by using a method based on the identification of

[27] Nevertheless, what will be discussed in this chapter is – due to its importance – the critique of O. Weinberger, concerning the role of practical discourse in justifying the correctness of norms, evaluations and other kinds of normative statements – *see infra*, pp. 84ff., 116ff.

"performative contradiction" of juridical speech acts, nor the justification by means of the argument from alternative, deserve to be accepted (Sect. 4.7). Next, I will analyse some—in my opinion, most crucial—objections that are related to nonpositivist normative argumentation (Sect. 4.8). Finally, the last part of the critical analyses in this chapter will be devoted to nonpositivist empirical argumentation (Sect. 4.9).

It should be noted that the following critical discussion will primarily refer to Alexy's nonpositivist conception and argumentation, which is undoubtedly more complex and far-reaching than Dreier's proposals. Furthermore, Alexy's argumentation was, largely, approved by Dreier.[28] The only exception to this focus will be during the analysis of nonpositivist empirical argumentation, which will devote more attention to the reasons formulated by Dreier.

4.3 *Lex iniustissima non est lex?*

The questions that we are going to discuss in this section refer to the thesis that is fundamental for the nonpositivist comprehension of the law. One may ask whether the thesis *extremes Unrecht ist kein Recht* (i.e., *lex iniustissima non est lex*) is self-contradictory. Can *gesetzliches Unrecht*—as stated by Radbruch in *Verleugnungsthese*—be regarded, without falling into *contradictio in adiecto*,[29] as entirely lacking the nature of law (*Rechtsnatur*) in the situation when the lawmaker consciously rejects equality, which is at the heart of justice? These questions reflect the content of the objection against argumentation justifying the nonpositivist conception, which—on account of its principal character and of the consequences resulting from it being valid—should be considered in the first place.

Let us begin with the observation that we are dealing with a renewed version of a well-known positivist objection against the natural law slogan of *lex iniusta non est lex* and of the conceptual consequences deriving from it.[30] The thesis claiming that an unjust law is not law can be found in the writings of Plato, Aristotle, Cicero, St. Augustine and St. Thomas Aquinas.[31] Yet, as John Finnis emphasises, this thesis cannot be considered as being fundamental for iusnaturalism, but only as a "subordinate theorem (slogan)" of natural law theories.[32] More importantly, the modern

[28] *See* Chap. 3, p. 35.

[29] Note that Radbruch was well aware of how paradoxical this thesis was for legal positivists, stressing that for the positivist's legal thinking, the concepts of *gesetzliches Unrecht* and *übergesetzliches Recht* are self-contradictory (they constitute "ein Widerspruch in sich") – *see idem*, 'Gesetzliches Unrecht und übergesetzliches Recht', *op. cit.*, p. 211 [English version, p. 1].

[30] *Cf. e.g.*, Hart's critique expressed in *The Concept of Law*, *op. cit.*, pp. 7–8, 203ff.

[31] Relevant quotes from the works of the authors recalled here are provided by N. Kretzmann, 'Lex iniusta non est lex. Laws on Trial in Aquinas' Court of Conscience', *AJJ* 33 (1988), pp. 100ff. and J. Finnis, *Natural Law and Natural Laws*, Oxford 1989, pp. 363ff.

[32] J. Finnis, *ibidem*, p. 351.

representatives of iusnaturalism are fully aware that this theorem should be used prudently so as to avoid the paradox arising from the assumption that an unjust law is not law.[33] What can be treated as an exemplification of such an approach is the analysis of Finnis, in which an attempt is made to explain why we cannot speak about an internal contradiction of the formulas under discussion.[34] The solution proposed by Finnis is based on the analysis of the standpoint expressed by St. Thomas and consists of differentiating the focal meaning of the term "law" (i.e., "law *simpliciter*") from its secondary meaning; that is, "law *secundum quid*". In taking this distinction into account, it can be stated (with some simplification) that the *lex iniusta* theorem does not contain any internal contradiction, as it provides only that unjust law *secundum quid* is not law *simpliciter*.[35] What seems far more important in the context of explaining the possible self-contradiction existing within "Radbruch's formula" is that Finnis—when analysing theories of natural law—stresses that its representatives have always claimed that "unjust LAWS are not law". Using the (capitalised) term "LAWS", Finnis emphasises that unjust laws (statutes) are formally valid law, and he even argues that there is not only a legal but a moral obligation to comply with them (dictated, for example, by the aim of respecting law as a whole).[36] For instance, in the natural law doctrine of St. Thomas Aquinas, unjust laws (i.e., laws that are inconsistent with *lex naturalis* yet not with *lex divina*) do not bind *in foro conscientae* their recipients and they should not be observed; however, if a failure to observe them is likely to lead to depravity (*scandalum*) or riots (*turbatio*), then we ought to obey them.[37]

---

[33] *See* J. Waldron, 'Normative (or Ethical) Positivism', *op. cit.*, pp. 416ff. For more on this issue *see* J.S. Russell, 'Trial by Slogan: Natural Law and Lex Iniusta Non Est Lex', *L&Ph* 19 (2000), pp. 433–449.

[34] *See* J. Finnis, *Natural Law and Natural Laws*, *op. cit.*, pp. 363ff.

[35] Note that in a similar manner, Alexy, analysing the merits of the positivist linguistic argument (*Sprachargument*) directed against "Radbruch's formula", states that the judge deciding the case on the basis of an extremely unjust law must avoid linguistic contradiction, recognising it as "*prima facie* law", which, however, is – all things considered – not law at all: "im Ergebnis [ist] kein Recht" (R. Alexy, 'Zur Verteidigung eines nichtpositivistischen Rechtsbegriffs', *op. cit.*, p. 93). Nonetheless, in his lecture *O pojęciu i naturze prawa / On the Concept and the Nature of Law*, *op. cit.*, p. 40, Alexy interprets the thesis of *lex iniusta non est lex* directly in the spirit of a qualifying rather than classifying relation, which is clearly inconsistent with the classifying nature of "hard" *Unrechtsargument* – *cf.* Chap. 3 at pp. 37ff. Therefore, in further discussion, this qualifying interpretation will be skipped, which does not change the fact that the solution proposed by Finnis is based on the qualifying and not classifying relation.

[36] J. Finnis, *Natural Law and Natural Laws*, *op. cit.*, pp. 364ff. The upper case emphasis comes from Finnis. In the literature in question, N. Kretzmann, 'Lex iniusta non est lex', *op. cit.*, pp. 104ff. and P. Łabieniec, *Prawo rozumu. O teorii prawa naturalnego Johna Finnisa* [Law of Reason. On John Finnis' Theory of Natural Law], Łódź 2004, pp. 48–49 draw attention to the fact that the slogan at hand deals with law that is understood as positive law (as laid down by man), which – in the technical sense – is valid law in spite of its wickedness.

[37] *See* N. Kretzmann, *ibidem*, pp. 116ff., who analyses the position of Aquinas against various forms of unjust law. In Polish jurisprudential literature, the moral obligation – dictated by some pressing reasons – to comply with an unjust law in the doctrine of St. Thomas, is emphasised by

4.3.1 Reconstruction of the Nonpositivist Standpoint

The analysis of the natural law position clearly shows that the nonpositivist argument from unlawfulness (*Unrechtsargument*) goes further than the theories of natural law. Generally speaking, the nonpositivists argue that—under "Radbruch's formula" (and more specifically under *Unerträglichkeitsthese*, which they refer to[38])—extremely unjust law is neither valid law (legally or morally) in any field or situation, nor it is law as such (as it is devoid of *Rechtsnatur*). It also turns out that the essence of the problem lies not so much in the outcome, whether this argument is vitiated by mistake of *contradictio in adiecto*, but—above all—in determining what is and how we can name something (i.e., norms enacted by a lawmaker and having social effectiveness) which, due to extreme injustice, is not law. Thus, the solution for the problem under discussion has to rely on the determination of relations between the concepts of law (*Recht*), un-law (*Unrecht*) and non-law (*Nicht-Recht*) in a satisfactory manner, if not even for a legal positivist, then at least for an analytical philosopher and legal practitioner.

First, let us try to characterise more neatly the semantic aspect of these relations. We shall refer here to the German debate, and specifically to the polemic between Norbert Hoerster and Joachim Hruschka, a substantial part of which concerns the issue under discussion.[39] These authors argue, inter alia, about the semantic role of the prefix *Un-* in the German language. Hoerster contends that the German prefix *Un-* usually expresses only a negative evaluation of something (so, in his opinion, it has—using the terminology of Kazimierz Twardowski[40]—merely a determining function). For example, *Untat* (crime) is from *Tat* (action), *Unwetter* (bad weather) is from *Wetter* (weather) and so forth. As the philosopher of Mainz claims, the concept of un-law (*Unrecht*) remains, therefore, in a relationship of inclusion (*Einschließungsverhältnis*) within the concept of law (*Recht*) because what is un-law due to moral reasons must, at the same time, be law.[41] Hruschka, on the other hand, claims that these concepts are mutually exclusive

---

Z. Ziembiński, '"Lex" a "ius" w okresie przemian' ["Lex" versus "Ius" in the Period of Transition], *PiP* 6 (1991), pp. 6–7.

[38] The fact that such reference to the classic statement of *Unerträglichkeitsthese* is not fully justified will be clarified soon.

[39] *See* the works listed in *supra*, note 3 at p. 61. This polemic has been analysed in J. Renzikowski, 'Naturrechtslehre versus Rechtspositivismus – ein Streit um Worte?', *ARSP* (1995), pp. 335–346; M.P. Förster, 'Auseinandersetzung zwischen Norbert Hoerster und Joachim Hruschka. Eine Stellungnahme zur antirechtspositivistischen Argumentation', *RT* 28 (1997), pp. 531–538; B. Hoffmann, *Das Verhältnis von Gesetz und Recht*, *op. cit.*, pp. 245ff.

[40] *See* K. Twardowski, 'Z logiki przymiotników', *op. cit.* For more on Twardowski's conception *see infra*, pp. 77ff. We will also use Twardowski's terminology in the subsequent deliberations.

[41] *See* N. Hoerster, 'Die rechtsphilosophische Lehre vom Rechtsbegriff', *op. cit.*, p. 185, 'Richtigstellung über den Rechtspositivismus', *op. cit.*, pp. 417–418 and 'Zum begrifflichen Verhältnis von Recht und Moral', *op. cit.*, pp. 80ff.

(*Ausschließungsverhältnis*),[42] since the prefix *Un-* normally has an abolitive function (in Twardowski's terminology). For example, *Ungnade* (disgrace) is not *Gnade* (grace), *Unsinn* (nonsense) is not *Sinn* (sense), *Unverstand* (stupidity) is not *Verstand* (reason) and so forth. These polemics show that the semantic analysis of ordinary languages does not allow for conclusively resolving the problem of relations between the concepts of *Recht* (law) and *Unrecht* (un-law).[43] Moreover, even if it were possible to find such an explicit solution, it would not entail a final resolution, because—as rightly pointed out by John L. Austin—a reference to ordinary language could and should be the "first word", but by no means the final step in applying the analytical method.[44]

In order to characterise the relations between the concepts of law (*Recht*), un-law (*Unrecht*) and non-law (*Nicht-Recht*), we therefore need to use a method of analysis that is different to a purely linguistic one. It seems that what may turn out useful is the application of one of the traditional methods of logical analysis, consisting of characterising these relations in terms of extensional relations. Accordingly, as far as the above is concerned, we dealt with the issues related to intension—now let us think primarily about the extension of the discussed terms.[45] The analysis of the views expressed by contemporary nonpositivists should be preceded by the analysis of Radbruch's position, since it will considerably facilitate our understanding of the essence of the contemporary controversy over the concept of extreme un-law (*extremes Unrecht*), which is derived from Radbruch's concept of statutory un-law (*gesetztliches Unrecht*), and arguably constitutes a modernised and slightly simplified equivalent of the latter.

Let us begin with the reconstruction of Radbruch's well-known classical position, presented in his paper *Gesetzliches Unrecht und übergesetzliches Recht* from January 1946.[46] As pointed out, in particular by commentators interpreting Radbruch's

[42] J. Hruschka, 'Recht und Unrecht bei Norbert Hoerster', *op. cit.*, p. 421.

[43] The rationale for this observation is not only the presented analysis concerning the German language, but also other languages – *see*, for example, comments on the English and Latin terminology presented by J. Renzikowski, 'Naturrechtslehre versus Rechtspositivismus – ein Streit um Worte?', *op. cit.*, p. 336. Similarly, the analysis of the Polish language gives equally inconclusive results: if, in fact, on the one hand, the un-law (unlawfulness) can be defined as "a state which is not regulated by laws" (thus "un-law" and "unlawfulness" would be synonymous with "non-law"), on the other hand, after all, one can also speak, for example, about "unlawfully undertaken eviction" or about "legislative unlawfulness" (and then un-law would "fall within" the frame of law understood pragmatically, yet applied or created in a manner inconsistent with that law).

[44] J.L. Austin, 'A Plea for Excuses' in *idem*, *Philosophical papers*, 3rd ed., J.O. Urmson, G.J. Warnock (eds.), Oxford/New York/Toronto/Melbourne 1979, p. 185.

[45] For more about the concepts of intension and extension that are used herein *see* Chap. 6 at pp. 218ff. As long as the analysis of intension usually entails consequences in relation to extension (except in the case of analysing the meaning of empty names), then the following analysis of extension will have to be based on the consideration of the intension (meaning) of the discussed terms.

[46] G. Radbruch, 'Gesetzliches Unrecht und übergesetzliches Recht' *op. cit.* ['Statutory Lawlessness and Supra-Statutory Law (1946)', *op. cit.*].

conception in the context of the theory of the Law-Governed State (*Rechtsstaat*) rather than in the context of the theory of the Unlawful State (*Unrechtsstaat*),[47] in this work, the philosopher from Heidelberg did not aim to define the conceptual borderline between law (*Recht*) and non-law (*Nicht-Recht*)[48] but to establish two other borderlines.[49] First, by means of using *Unerträglichkeitsthese*, essentially a vague boundary between an unjust law (*unrichtiges Recht*), which is, despite this injustice, a valid law, and unjust law which is already—in the terminology proposed by Knut Seidel[50]—"statutory un-law of the first category" (*gesetzliches Unrecht der ersten Kategorie*); that is, laws remaining in "unbearable" contradiction with justice and, therefore, invalid.[51] Secondly, by means of using *Verleugnungsthese*, Radbruch specified a sharp and obvious borderline—at least in his opinion—between unjust law and non-law, being already "statutory un-law of the second category" (*gesetzliches Unrecht der zweiten Kategorie*); that is, unlawfulness consisting of a "conscious denial" of equality (which is the essence of justice) by the statutes enacted by the Nazis. From the viewpoint of extensional relations, the classic form of Radbruch's conception of "statutory un-law"—expressed in the aforementioned work—can be presented by the following diagram (see Fig. 4.1 on the next page).

In terms of validity, *gesetzliches Unrecht* is a homogeneous class, because the interpretation of "Radbruch's formula" as a theory of the validity of law in an Unlawful State leads to the conclusion that both categories of "statutory un-law" are devoid of legal validity.[52] On the other hand, this diagram shows that in the context of extensional relations in which "statutory un-law" remains with the terms "law" and "non-law", it can be clearly seen that any homogeneity is out of question here,

[47] The distinction between these two modern interpretative contexts of "Radbruch's formula" was introduced by J. Zajadło, *Formuła Radbrucha*, *op. cit.*, pp. 69ff.

[48] What should be considered a more appropriate term here is *Nicht-Recht* (rather than *Nichtrecht*), as Radbruch – like the modern German nonpositivists (*e.g.*, M. Kriele, R. Dreier and R. Alexy) – is, in fact, not interested in the question of what is (in the positive sense) that which is not law. Thus, to emphasise that this is a class that is complementary to the universal set, we adopt a linguistic way of expressing this fact, proposed by Z. Ziembiński, *Practical Logic*, *op. cit.*, pp. 42ff. Moreover, the German literature also typically uses the term *Nicht-Recht* rather than *Nichtrecht – see e.g.*, N. Hoerster, 'Richtigstellung über den Rechtspositivismus', *op. cit.*, p. 418; M.P. Förster, 'Auseinandersetzung zwischen Norbert Hoerster und Joachim Hruschka', *op. cit.*; F. Saliger, *Radbruchsche Formel und Rechtsstaat*, *op. cit.*; K. Seidel, *Rechtsphilosophische Aspekte der "Mauerschützen"-Prozesse*, *op. cit.*; U. Neumann, 'Ralf Dreier's Radbruch', *op. cit.*, p. 142. On the other hand, the term *Nichtrecht* is used by H. Dreier, 'Gustav Radbruch und die Mauerschützen', *JZ* 52 (1997), pp. 421–434.

[49] *See e.g.*, F. Saliger, *ibidem*, pp. 17ff.

[50] K. Seidel, *Rechtsphilosophische Aspekte der "Mauerschützen"-Prozesse*, *op. cit.*, pp. 167ff.

[51] Although Radbruch does not explicitly claim that this law is not valid, the latter is obvious for his commentators, because without such a derogatory effect, differentiating such a category of "statutory un-law" would be meaningless – *see e.g.*, R. Dreier, St.L. Paulson, 'Einführung in die Rechtsphilosophie Radbruchs' in G. Radbruch, *Rechtsphilosophie*, *op. cit.*, p. 245.

[52] *See e.g.*, F. Saliger, *Radbruchsche Formel und Rechtsstaat*, *op. cit.*, p. 20 and K. Seidel, *Rechtsphilosophische Aspekte der "Mauerschützen"-Prozesse*, *op. cit.*, pp. 182ff., and the references cited therein.

Unjust (yet valid) law	Statutory un-law I° = *Unerträglichkeitsthese*	Statutory un-law II° = *Verleugnungsthese*
LAW (*RECHT*)		NON-LAW (*NICHT-RECHT*)

Fig. 4.1 Gustav Radbruch's conception of "statutory un-law" (classical version)

because the first category of statutory un-law is within the extension of law, while the second category is already non-law.[53] It seems that this heterogeneity can be explained by the different objectives and functions of Radbruch's specific theses, comprising the formula. *Unerträglichkeitsthese* seems to have, primarily a practical purpose, despite the vagueness of the borderline between the unjust (yet still valid) laws and unlawful (and thus invalid) ones indicated by it. It is worth noting that *Unerträglichkeitsthese* has already fulfilled its derogatory function in relation to unlawful laws in German and European jurisdiction,[54] whereas *Verleugnungsthese*—as emphasised by both the creators and supporters of the nonpositivist conception,[55] as well as by the authors referring to it with caution[56]—is devoid of such a practical function due to its subjective premise of "wilful denial" of equality, the satisfaction of which is hardly possible to prove. Therefore, it seems justified to claim that the primary objective of *Verleugnungsthese* may be considered to be the solution of the basic problem of the legal theory of cognition (*juristische Erkenntnistheorie*) concerning an epistemological issue of identifying law (i.e., answering the question—in its nature, essentially transcendental for a Neo-Kantian—of what can be recognised as

[53] *Cf.* a different view of K. Seidel, *ibidem*, p. 167, which has, nonetheless, resulted in him taking into consideration Radbruch's other writings on the problems of statutory unlawfulness. According to Seidel, the only difference between the two theses lies in the different means of recognition of these two categories of "statutory un-law". W. Ott draws attention, in this context, to the impreciseness of Radbruch's terminology – *see idem*, 'Die Radbruch'sche Formel', *op. cit.*, p. 335, whereas L.H. Meyer stresses the inconsistent manner of Radbruch's use of the term "statutory un-law" – *see idem*, '"Gesetzen ihrer Ungerechtigkeit wegen die Geltung absprechen". Gustav Radbruch und der Relativismus' in R. Alexy *et al.* (eds.), *Neukantianismus und Rechtsphilosophie*, Baden-Baden 2002, pp. 322–323, note 12. In Polish literature, a similar opinion on Radbruch's imprecise conceptual instrumentarium was expressed by J. Zajadło, *Formuła Radbrucha*, *op. cit.*, p. 105.

[54] *See infra*, pp. 184ff.

[55] *See* R. Dreier, 'Gesetzliches Unrecht im SED-Staat? Am Beispiel des DDR-Grenzgesetzes' in F. Haft *et al.* (eds.), *Strafgerechtigkeit*, Heidelberg 1993, pp. 57ff.; R. Dreier, St.L. Paulson, 'Einführung in die Rechtsphilosophie Radbruchs', *op. cit.*, p. 245; R. Alexy, *Mauerschützen*, *op. cit.*, p. 3, note 3 *in fine* (with reference to Dreier's work); J.-R. Sieckmann, 'Die "Radbruch'sche Formel" und die Mauerschützen', *ARSP* 87 (2001), p. 499.

[56] *See e.g.*, H. Dreier, 'Gustav Radbruch und die Mauerschützen', *op. cit.*, p. 423; A. Kaufmann, 'Die Radbruchsche Formel vom gesetzlichen Unrecht und vom übergesetzlichen Recht in der Diskussion um das im Namen der DDR begangene Unrecht', *NJW* 48 (1995), p. 82; K. Seidel, *Rechtsphilosophische Aspekte der "Mauerschützen"-Prozesse*, *op. cit.*, pp. 174–176; B. Bix, 'Robert Alexy, Radbruch's Formula, and the Nature of Legal Theory', *op. cit.*, pp. 140ff.

law).[57] Such justification does not alter the fact that the term "un-law" remains in a relationship at the crossing over (overlapping) of the extensions both of the term "law" and of the term "non-law", which exposes this conception to the charges of self-contradiction raised both by the positivists as well as by the supporters of iusnaturalism. The former may ask why the second category of statutory un-law (determined by means of *Verleugnungsthese*) is not law, but merely non-law. While the latter may call into question that the first category of statutory un-law (determined by means of *Unerträglichkeitsthese*) is still law.

Yet, should the plea of conceptual heterogeneity of statutory un-law be regarded as legitimate? Probably yes, but what weighs in favour of Radbruch is the fact that his original formulations of the two particular theses, contained in *Five Minutes of Legal Philosophy* from September 1945,[58] lead to other extensional relations between the terms under discussion. The original version of *Unerträglichkeitsthese*$_5$ (for the sake of distinguishing them, we add subscript 5 to the names of Radbruch's original theses) is as follows:

> It must be, however, borne deeply in the consciousness of the people and lawyers: there *can* be statutes to such extent unjust and socially harmful that validity, and indeed the character of law must be denied to them.

Whereas *Verleugnungsthese*$_5$ stated that:

> If statutes deliberately deny the pursuit of justice by, for example, arbitrarily granting and taking away from people the human rights – then such statutes lack validity; then the people owe them no obedience; then lawyers must find the courage to deny them the nature of law.[59]

As can be easily seen, in both theses Radbruch calls for denying the extremely unlawful laws their legal character. Thus, "statutory un-law" becomes a

---

[57] Such an interpretation of *Verleugnungsthese*, undertaken in the context of Neo-Kantian philosophy of law, the main representative of which was indeed Radbruch, was recently suggested by A. Funke, 'Überlegungen zu Gustav Radbruchs "Verleugnungsformel"', *op. cit.*, pp. 4ff. In my opinion, this interpretation constitutes a new important way of understanding the nature of *Verleugnungsthese*. So far, this thesis has been exclusively related to the ontological aspect of the concept of law (related to the question of the nature of law – for example, *see* B. Bix, *ibidem*, pp. 141ff.) rather than to any epistemological dimension (relating to the question of how we can recognise something as law).

[58] G. Radbruch, 'Fünf Minuten Rechtsphilosophie', *op. cit.* ['Five Minutes of Legal Philosophy (1945)', *op. cit.*].

[59] Let us quote the original formulations (*ibidem*, p. 210; *cf.* English version, p. 14). *Unerträglichkeitsthese*$_5$: "Das aber muß sich dem Bewußtsein des Volkes und der Juristen tief einprägen: es *kann* Gesetze mit einem solchen Maß von Ungerechtigkeit und Gemeinschädlichkeit geben, daß ihnen die Geltung, ja der Rechtscharakter abgesprochen werden muß". *Verleugnungsthese*$_5$: "Wenn Gesetze den Willen zur Gerechtigkeit bewußt verleugnen, z. B. Menschenrechte Menschen nach Willkür gewähren und versagen, dann fehlt diesen Gesetzen die Geltung, dann schuldet das Volk ihnen keinen Gehorsam, dann müssen auch die Juristenden den Mut finden, ihnen den Rechtscharakter abzusprechen".

Fig. 4.2 Gustav Radbruch's conception of "statutory un-law" (original version)

homogeneous class, remaining in the relation of an extensional inferiority (inclusion) vis-à-vis "non-law" (see Fig. 4.2 above).[60]

Turning now to the discussion and critique of a modern nonpositivist standpoint, let us note that it is precisely identical to Radbruch's original position. For Dreier, Alexy and other supporters of contemporary nonpositivism, the "extreme un-law" (*extremes Unrecht*) remains in the relation of inferiority (inclusion) vis-à-vis "non-law", since *extremes Unrecht ist kein Recht*. This is illustrated by the following diagram (see Fig. 4.3).

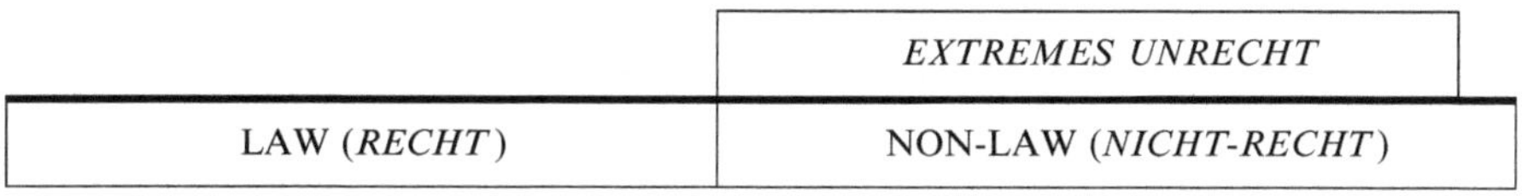

Fig. 4.3 The contemporary nonpositivist interpretation of "Radbruch's formula"

It can be concluded that the contemporary nonpositivist interpretation of "Radbruch's formula" corresponds to *Unerträglichkeitsthese*$_5$ rather than to the classic formulation of *Unerträglichkeitsthese* provided by Radbruch in *Gesetzliches Unrecht und übergesetzliches Recht*.[61] It follows that both Radbruch's original conception of "statutory un-law" and the position of modern nonpositivists can only encounter a positivist objection that can be briefly expressed in the form of the question: Why is "extreme un-law" (that is, "extremely unjust law") not law? Yet, is this objection accurate?

---

[60] For the sake of further consideration, the scheme disregards the irrelevant question of possible overlap (crossing) of the extensions of these two categories of un-law (unlawfulness).

[61] At most – as we pointed out earlier (*see* Chap. 3, p. 46) – it can be alternatively concluded that modern nonpositivists combine both Radbruch's theses from *Gesetzliches Unrecht und übergesetzliches Recht* in such way that they adopt the criterion of recognising "extreme un-law" from *Unerträglichkeitsthese*, but they attribute to it the effect specified in *Verleugnungsthese*. Yet, the relatively simplest explanation for such standpoint assumed by Dreier and Alexy is to remind that in their conception the concept of law embraces the concept of its validity. Thus, although Radbruch's *Unerträglichkeitsthese* causes only the loss of validity, for the creators of German nonpositivism the latter is synonymous with depriving such unlawful acts of their legal nature.

4.3.2 Discussion of the Positivist Objection

Before attempting to answer the latter question, we should now precisely define the subject and methodological context of the dispute between positivists and nonpositivists. Let us therefore recall that Alexy admitted that "Radbruch's formula" could not be justified analytically.[62] What is more, according to him, from the perspective of an observer who examines the various norms and legal decisions and, at the same time, apragmatically understands law and seeks relations of a classifying character, the positivist *Trennungsthese* is correct (extremely unjust law is law) and the nonpositivist *Verbindungsthese* must be rejected. Moreover, taking into account the analytical and evolutionary argument from un-law, the Nazi regime undoubtedly constituted law (the conclusion reached in the same methodological framework). Similarly, the analysis of applying *Unrechtsargument* in relation to legal systems (i.e., the application of "Kriele's formula"), undertaken already from the perspective of a participant who understands law pragmatically and seeks relations of classifying character, led him to conclude that it is groundless, as it goes beyond the scope of the argument from un-law in relation to individual norms and legal decisions. Thus, the controversy relates only to singular norms or legal decisions, analysed from the perspective of a participant who is in search of classifying relations between law that is understood pragmatically and just (justifiable) morality. Besides, the nonpositivist justification of the correctness of the claim that "extreme unlawfulness" is not law, is of a purely normative character (Alexy) or of an empirically-normative one (Dreier).

Our response to the positivist objection will consist of three remarks. The first point concerns the question as to whether the nonpositivist thesis *extremes Unrecht ist kein Recht* (*lex iniustissima non est lex*) is actually self-contradictory. Given the scope and methodological framework of such an objection—as specified above—such a positivist objection seems inaccurate, on account of the following counterargument. If the proponent of the positivist position maintains (as Hoerster does) that unlawful (extremely unjust) individual norms and legal decisions are law (from the perspective of a participant, because—let us emphasise it—this is the only perspective that the controversy at issue relates to), then his claim can be also challenged by the charge of *contradictio in adiecto*. A positivist, at the same time, claims that *extremes Unrecht ist Recht*, which is in evident contradiction with the positivist use of the term "un-law" from the perspective of a participant (e.g., a judge). For the sake of example, we can present here the view of the leading representative of legal positivism—Hans Kelsen—who applied the term "un-law" (*Unrecht*) to define "illegal behaviour" (*rechtswidrigen Verhaltens*).[63] This is a

[62] *See* Chap. 3, p. 38.

[63] *See e.g.*, H. Kelsen, 'Was ist juristischer Positivismus?', *JZ* 20 (1965), p. 465: "Als Recht wird *hier* eine *normative* Ordnung verstanden, die ein bestimmtes menschliches Verhalten dadurch herbeizuführen sucht, daß sie vorschreibt, daß im Falle eines gegenteiligen, des sogenannten

typical way, especially for the language of the dogmatics of law and jurisdiction, of using this concept (dogmatics and judges typically speak of an "unlawful act" or "unlawful behaviour"). Thus, we deal here with an apparent contradiction: while at the level of observance and application of law, "un-law" ("unlawfulness") remains in a relation of exclusion with "law", at the level of lawmaking, "un-law" should remain (according to positivists) in a relation of extensional inferiority (inclusion) vis-à-vis "law". The fact that this contradiction takes place between the concepts of un-law related to various pragmatic aspects of law (compliance with law and law application versus lawmaking), undoubtedly greatly weakens this counter-argument, but does not fully refute it,[64] as it can be illustrated by the following examples of statements consistent with the positivistic terminology: "although this norm is an extreme un-law, it is still law", and "this behaviour is against the law, therefore it is unlawful (un-law)".

The second remark concerns the problem of finding an axiologically neutral term (concept) for the acts (norms) that meet the nonpositivist test of "extreme unlawfulness". According to Hoerster's normative argument, we do not have any alternative, so we have to name such extremely unjust acts (norms) as "law".[65] Let us recall that such a normative positivist objection was accepted by Alexy in relation to the terminology used by the observer of a legal system; nonetheless, he did not agree with Hoerster's additional thesis—related to this objection—proclaiming that it is also valid for all possible research perspectives (methodological frameworks), especially for the terminology proper for the perspective of the participant, in relation to which, Alexy proposed using the concept of law *prima facie*.[66] This begs the observation that if the positivist does not want to use an axiologically involved term of "(extreme) un-law" and he is neither satisfied with the negative term "non-law", yet another—from a logical point of view—axiologically neutral and substantively positive term can be suggested to him.

In order to identify such a term, let us return briefly to the above-mentioned semantic dispute between Hoerster and Hruschka and analyse it using the conceptual apparatus of Twardowski's "logic of adjectives".[67] Let us recall that Hoerster argues that the use of the German prefix *Un-* typically stands for a negative evaluation of

rechtswidrigen Verhaltens, des 'Unrechts', ein Zwangsakt als Unrechtsfolge, als sogenannte Sanktion erfolgen soll".

[64] Yet, *see* a different view expressed by N. Hoerster, 'Zum begrifflichen Verhältnis von Recht und Moral', *op. cit.*, p. 80. He argues that the concepts expressed by adjectives or adverbs *recht* and *unrecht* (referring, for example, to behaviour) are mutually exclusive, but it has nothing to do with the relations that occur between these concepts expressed by means of the nouns *Recht* and *Unrecht*.

[65] *See* Chap. 3, pp. 46–47 (the discussion on the linguistic argument) and pp. 53ff.

[66] *See* R. Alexy, *Begriff und Geltung des Rechts*, *op. cit.*, p. 56, in particular, note 35 and pp. 72ff. [English version, pp. 30–31, in particular, note 56 and pp. 41ff.]. In this way, Alexy approaches the conceptual solution characteristic for natural law theories, as previously mentioned.

[67] The following analysis is undoubtedly of *per analogiam* character, because the prefixes are not adjectives; nevertheless, this analogy seems justified, since they may have similar semantic functions.

something, so—according to the "logic of adjectives"—it has a determining function. When using the examples given by Twardowski,[68] "un-law (unlawfulness)" would remain in a semantic relation to "law", analogous to the relation of the names "inexperienced man" and "man". The objection that can be raised against such a position is that "un-law" is not necessarily "law" that is complemented by a negative feature (evaluation): in fact, in some contexts, the state of un-law (unlawfulness) can be assessed positively.[69] Hruschka nonetheless maintains that the prefix *Un-* serves an abolitive function, which implies that "un-law" has nothing in common with the "law", just as "alleged shape" is not "shape". One can raise an objection against this view, consisting of the fact that the designates of the term "un-law" still have many features in common with the designates of the term "law"—for example, in the case of "statutory un-law" it was, like law, made by a lawmaker in the form of normative acts (mostly statutes), and then used by the Nazi or Communist courts and so forth. What is more, as emphasised earlier, from the viewpoint of an observer, even for nonpositivists, "un-law" is indeed "law". However, that is not all that can be achieved by using the method of analysis proposed by Twardowski. Using his division of adjectives based on the identification of the semantic functions that they fulfil, let us note that there are still two possibilities for the interpretation of the term "un-law" (*Unrecht*). First, the negative prefix *Un-* can—at least theoretically—serve a confirming function; namely, "un-law" would be semantically equivalent to "law", just as "true friend" is synonymous with "friend". Naturally, this interpretation seems *prima facie* absurd, and certainly unacceptable for the lawyer-participant, although in some contexts it is undoubtedly legitimate (for example, in the case of the views expressed by anarchists or modern alter-globalists for whom "un-law" is usually assessed as a synonym for the "law" of developed capitalist states). A final possibility is that this prefix has a complex abolitive-determining function (i.e., it modifies the meaning of the word that is prefixed). According to this interpretation, which we strongly advocate, the semantic relation between "un-law" and "law" would be similar to the relations between "artificial eye" and "eye" or between "counterfeit money" and "money". In this interpretation, the possibility of which has been omitted both by Hoerster and (admittedly, to a lesser extent) by Hruschka in their analyses, the term "un-law" would be in the relation of extensional contrariety (which is different from extensional contradiction)[70] vis-à-vis the term "law", because the linguistic content of these names would differ in their relevant (constitutive) features, yet have

[68] *See* K. Twardowski, 'Z logiki przymiotników', *op. cit.*

[69] As an example, let us quote an apropos aphorism from *Myśli nieuczesane* [Unkempt Thoughts] by S.J. Lec: "Where cruel laws govern, people miss un-law".

[70] *See e.g.*, Z. Ziembiński, *Practical Logic*, *op. cit.*, p. 45. Both extensional relations belong to the category of exclusive relations; however, in the case of contradiction, the extensions of two contradictory terms ('A' and 'non-A') together make up a universal class, whereas in the case of contrariety, the extensions of the terms involved (*e.g.* "dog" and "cat") are mutually exclusive as well, yet – taken together – they do not form a universal class. Let us remind you that – in our opinion – it is precisely the relation of contrariety that exists between "legal positivism" and "nonpositivism".

Fig. 4.4 The proposal of solution

some secondary (consecutive) common features—primarily of a formal nature. In light of this analysis, "un-law" is therefore not "law"—it is something that, using the terminology of constitutive rules, only erroneously may count as law, just as "counterfeit money" cannot be regarded as "money" (provided, of course, the fact of the forgery is noticed).

There remains, however, one unresolved question of how to denominate this statutory "extreme un-law" by means of a positive and axiologically neutral term. From a linguistic standpoint, taking into account the logical extensional relations between the names (terms),[71] for this purpose one can propose the use of the positive term "nonlaw" (*Nichtrecht*),[72] which seems to be neutral from the axiological point of view. The extension (denotation) of this concept would comprise all norms governing human behaviour, but not having the character of valid legal norms (in addition to the norms of "statutory un-law", it would also cover moral norms, as well as social or religious ones[73]). According to the proposed terminology, "law" and "nonlaw" are in the relation of extensional contrariety (which is different from the extensional contradiction that can be observed between the terms "law" and "non-law"), as illustrated by the following scheme (see Fig. 4.4 above).

The third remark concerns the question that already belongs to the practical (normative) sphere rather than to the theoretical (analytical) one. Even if we accept the earlier arguments in favour of the view that the nonpositivist thesis *extremes Unrecht ist kein Recht* is not self-contradictory (or at least that it is not "more"

[71] *See ibidem*, pp. 42–44. Following the logical convention adopted by Ziembiński and many other logicians, the term "nonlaw" would differ from the term "non-law", previously used in the analysis of extensional relations in the same way in which the term "nonconformist" (which refers to a person who does not accept the ways of thinking or behaving accepted by the majority of people) differs from the term "non-conformist" (meaning "whatever is not a conformist"; namely, a class complementary to the universal set, including "nonconformists", but also "dogs", "lamps", "airplanes" and so forth).

[72] The authors that use this term in the pattern suggested herein are M. Stolleis, *Recht im Unrecht. Studien zur Rechtsgeschichte des Nationalsozialismus*, Frankfurt am Main 1994, p. 7, note 1 and H. Dreier, 'Gustav Radbruch und die Mauerschützen', *op. cit.*, p. 423, wherein he states that "extremes Unrecht mutiert zu Nichtrecht". However, both German scholars presumably do not use the term *Nichtrecht* due to the logical reasons pointed out above.

[73] Naturally, identifying so many different types of norms, in addition, undoubtedly often contradictory (for example, taking into account the norms of the statutory un-law and moral norms), by means of one term, can raise reasonable substantive doubt; therefore, it should be emphasised again that we are referring here to the problem of a logical nature, only loosely connected with everyday legal terminology. Moreover, we are doing so only for the sake of positivistic conceptual needs.

self-contradictory than its positivist counterpart: *extremes Unrecht ist Recht*) and that "extreme un-law" can be included within the extension of an axiologically neutral term "nonlaw", a problem with a great practical significance still remains: should the norms and legal decisions exceeding the threshold of extreme injustice be called "un-law" or "nonlaw" and, therefore, be denied their nature of law? The practical importance of this question is obvious—if we assume, after nonpositivists, that "statutory un-law" was not law from the very beginning (*ex tunc*), then we deprive people involved in creating and applying this un-law of the basic exculpatory argument, proclaiming that they acted in accordance with valid law.

When analysing this problem, one should clearly distinguish its two temporal aspects (perspectives). First, the issue of naming extremely unjust acts and decisions by the lawyers of that time, looking at them from the perspective of a participant. Secondly, the issue of naming these legal acts from the perspective of a contemporary participant of a—post-totalitarian and democratic—system of law in which the basic human rights are respected. Before we proceed in discussing these two issues, let us add that in our deliberations we shall omit any purely moral arguments because they are irrelevant to the resolution of the issues that we are interested in. This argument certainly requires substantiation, if only because of its uncompromising and non-obvious character. The justification is fairly simple since, due to the nature of the dispute between positivists and nonpositivists, it is easy to see that any moral arguments will be dismissed outright by both parties as irrelevant or inadmissible. Simply put, we can say that the classic hard positivist shall reject moral argumentation because for him all the moral issues, though objectively certainly important, are outside the scope of the science of law. In other words, the fact that the law—as it is—must be distinguished from the law as it ought to be (since the time of John Austin), has been one of the fundamental theses of legal positivism and, therefore, the moral argument for the hard positivist remains legally irrelevant. Yet, a nonpositivist will also reject moral argumentation, albeit due to a completely different reason. For him, it is essential that the problems treated by the positivists as merely moral are considered as legal issues. Thus, even if a nonpositivist uses the moral argumentation, she/he will insist on considering that argument as a legal one and, accordingly, she/he will present typically legal reasons in favour of the accuracy of her/his position.[74]

[74] By way of example, let us note here the very consistent position expressed by Alexy, who, in his work 'Law, Discourse, and Time', *op. cit.*, pp. 105–107, tries to demonstrate, based on the analysis of the content and application of law concerning slavery during the Roman Empire, that even in this case, it must be accepted that the result of rational practical discourse has to be a thesis (important for the perspective of historical participants of the legal system of that time), proclaiming that at least some norms of contemporary Roman law (for example, allowing the killing of a slave without any reason or starving him to death) should be treated as extremely unjust, and so devoid of legal character (as Alexy writes, they are "no law"). With regard to the correctness of such arguments *see* U. Neumann, 'Ralf Dreier's Radbruch', *op. cit.*, pp. 155 ff., who rightly points out that adopting an internal point of view (i.e., the participant's perspective) is impossible in relation to the historical systems of law, because – what is self-evident – nobody can be a participant of a system that no longer exists (*ibidem*, p. 157).

Bearing in mind temporal relativisation, let us ask the first question: what should judges and other lawyers or officials of the Third Reich call (in legal and not moral terms) the legal norms and decisions which remain in "unbearable" contradiction with justice? In a broader context, this question naturally concerns lawyers-participants in all totalitarian regimes (Nazi, communist and others). Alexy and other nonpositivists argue that they should deny them their nature of law.[75] I think that the nonpositivist view is based on an idealism that is too far-reaching[76]—one can only agree that the participants of those systems could (in the legal sense) refer to such norms and decisions as "un-law" or "nonlaw". It should be noted that, according to Dreier's and Alexy's conception, the resolution of the legal problem of whether a legal norm or decision constitutes an "extreme unlawfulness" is based on a rational legal discourse, many initial assumptions of which certainly were not and are not met in totalitarian states. It is difficult, for example, to speak in any sense about the freedom (liberty) and equality of the panellists or about the unfettered nature of legal discourse in such states. Moreover, even if nonpositivists managed to justify—for example, by using formal-dogmatic argumentation—that they should deny these norms their legal nature, from a practical point of view such justification would be meaningless.[77] Indeed, if extremely unjust law was made and applied, the fact that the participants of a totalitarian system of law should have called it "un-law" will not change history and it will not of itself mean that the victims of the state apparatus of *Unrechtsstaat* cease to be injured—this fact could only constitute an initial argument in the subsequent lawsuits for rehabilitation and compensation. Finally, what must be held—in my opinion—as a decisive argument, is the fact that a nonpositivist can be faced with a danger that when she/he justifies her/his position by referring to extremely unjust laws and judicial decisions as "un-law", it will lead to the annihilation of the argument from un-law in the practical sense—an aspect that is the key to our deliberations. Namely, if she/he is able to show that the lawyers-participants of totalitarian legal systems ought (in the legal sense) to deny such norms their character of law without resorting to "Radbruch's

[75] *See* R. Alexy, *Begriff und Geltung des Rechts*, *op. cit.*, p. 75 [English version, p. 42] and 'Law, Discourse, and Time', *op. cit.*, pp. 104ff.

[76] I do not mean here, of course, "psychological idealism", consisting of the belief in the infinite psychological capability of human beings (especially judges) to bear the consequences of acting against the totalitarian state, but a "legal idealism", which consists of assuming that judges and other lawyers-participants of any (including the totalitarian) system of law, must always value the idea of law over its contents. In other words, they should always profess the precedence of *ius* over *lex*. Taking into consideration incidental psychological issues, we should add that, in a similar context, Alexy himself formulates the view that it is "certainly unfounded anthropological optimism" to count on the fact that every human is interested in striving for justice, or that her/his interest in justice justifiably prevails over any other reasons of action – *see* R. Alexy, 'Diskurstheorie und Menschenrechte' in *idem*, *Recht, Vernunft, Diskurs*, *op. cit.*, p. 142 [English version: 'Discourse Theory and Human Rights', *RJ* 9 (1996), p. 219].

[77] A similar argumentation – from the position of the institutional theory of law – is presented by U. Neumann, 'Problem obowiązywania prawa' [The Problem of Validity of Law], trans. A. Grabowski, *PiP* 7 (2007), pp. 45–46.

formula", she/he will, at the same time, justify that the latter is virtually useless in legal practice (jurisdiction).[78] Conversely, if she/he shows that, based on "Radbruch's formula" (namely, she/he assumes it as a premise of her/his reasoning), then she/he will not be allowed to use any practical arguments (normative, dogmatic and others) referring to the legal duty of judges and lawyers in the Unlawful States so as to justify the very formula and, hence, the argument from un-law. Without doubt, if a nonpositivist did this then her/his reasoning would be burdened with a logical fallacy of *curiculus vitiosus*.

Let us now discuss the second of the above issues. When looking from the perspective of a modern—post-totalitarian and democratic—system of law, should we (in the legal sense) refer *ex post* to legal norms and decisions exceeding the threshold of extreme injustice as "un-law" or "nonlaw" (i.e., deny them their legal character)? In answering such a practical question, we must ignore the fact that German and European jurisdiction has already provided a positive answer to this question,[79] because the fact that it happened, and still happens is undoubtedly of empirical character and, thus, it does not resolve the normative issue as to whether it should have happened or whether it should happen. When considering this multi-faceted issue, we shall focus only on one specific problem, which in our opinion is the most crucial. It is a problem concerning the practical consequences of giving a positive (namely nonpositivist) answer to such a question and, therefore, the consequences of assuming that currently we ought (in the legal sense[80]) to deny extremely unjust legal norms and decisions their character of law. A positivist will question such a solution, insisting that we use a nonpositivist, and therefore not neutral, but axiologically involved (entangled) concept of law.[81] On the other hand, the primary consequence of recognising as appropriate the nonpositivist response will deprive judges, prosecutors, officials and soldiers who shot people fleeing

[78] The fact that Radbruch acknowledged the need to formulate theses that make up a formula, shows that, for him, such a justification is impossible.

[79] *See infra*, pp. 184ff.

[80] The fact that, in a moral sense, we should do so, is not disputed even by positivists (*e.g.*, Hart or Hoerster – *see infra*, pp. 169ff). There is no doubt that at least part of the legislation and law enforcement practice of totalitarian states constituted "extreme injustice" from a moral point of view.

[81] *See e.g.*, N. Hoerster, 'Richtigstellung über den Rechtspositivismus', *op. cit.*, pp. 416ff. On the other hand, the positivist position based on *Neutralitätsthese* does not itself protect the positivist concept of law against the allegation of axiological involvement: *see e.g.*, J. Hruschka, 'Recht und Unrecht bei Norbert Hoerster', *op. cit.*, p. 423, who argues that such a seemingly neutral conceptual standpoint has yet serious practical consequences. In his opinion, if we assume, after the positivists that, for example, racist Nuremberg Laws constituted law, it has such a practical consequence that the judge who applies these laws cannot be accused of unlawful conduct. To put the matter in broad terms, the opponents of legal positivism can raise an objection against the latter that, because of its conceptual apparatus, it does not offer any (not just morally acceptable) way to solve the problem of the statutory un-law – *cf.* similar opinions from T. Mertens, 'Radbruch and Hart on the Grudge Informer: A Reconsideration', *RJ* 15 (2002), pp. 201ff. and F. Haldemann, 'Gustav Radbruch vs. Hans Kelsen: A Debate on Nazi Law', *RJ* 18 (2005), pp. 175ff.

through the Berlin Wall—namely, all the people who acted in the name and on behalf of a totalitarian state—of the possibility of using an exculpatory argument (or, at least, an argument greatly restricting their responsibility): "I have followed valid laws". Is such a positivist counterargument from consequences legally justified? Can one talk about depriving the above-mentioned categories of people of the possibility of exercising their rights by referring *ex post* to what they regarded as law, as "un-law" or "nonlaw" (moreover, with *ex tunc* effect)?

I think that the following legal argument, which has not yet been raised (to the best of my knowledge) in nonpositivist argumentation, fully justifies the rejection of the above positivist counterargument—even for the proponents of legal positivism. Let us formulate it as follows: if the addressees of legal norms are typically burdened with the liability of behaviour inconsistent with the law, not only in cases where they do not know the law, but also where they make a wrong interpretation (according to the rules *ignorantia iuris nocet* and *ignorantia legis neminem excusat*), then it should be even more the case that judges, prosecutors, officials and soldiers of *Unrechtsstaat* cannot be (in the legal sense) absolved from legal liability due to the fact that they considered as the law, something which, according to the assumption adopted in this linguistic analysis, has never been law.[82] Lawyers, bureaucrats and other people working in the apparatus of such a state may not now be treated as "better" or, using George Orwell's excellent description (from *Animal Farm*[83]), as "more equal" than other citizens, leaving aside the desire they may have in terms of preserving this privileged legal status.[84] This argument shows that the adopted nonpositivist solution need not be justified by nonpositivist arguments that a legal positivist would recognise as having the character of natural law or as purely moral, but it may be justified by means of positivist arguments, at least in so far as the principle of human equality before the law constitutes a principle of modern legal culture, usually even having a constitutional status. On the other hand, this argument does not yet resolve the issue of the liability of such persons. It is, in fact, a separate issue, as it can be argued that the principle of equality before the law—which constitutes the basis of this argument—interferes here with the principle *nullum crimen sine lege*

[82] For the purposes of this argument it is irrelevant whether and to what extent this principle allows for exceptions related to justifiable ignorance of the law; it is sufficient to assume that under this principle, a citizen (or more broadly: the addressee of a legal norm) generally will not be able to effectively rely on an erroneous interpretation of the law (or ignorance of the correct interpretation), as an exemption from her/his legal liability.

[83] G. Orwell, *Animal Farm* and *1984*, Orlando 2003, p. 80.

[84] At this point, a positivist may naturally claim that these categories of people in a totalitarian state usually held such a privileged status – even if not granted to them by law, then at least *de facto*. Nonetheless, this objection, in my opinion, does not refute the argument. What is decisive is that even in such a system there was the principle of *ignorantia iuris nocet (non excusat)* – at least in relation to "ordinary" citizens, which already suffices to refute such an objection.

penali anteriori (which can be treated, in the context of our deliberations, as a concretisation of the principle *lex retro non agit* within the domain of penal law).[85]

Thus, the considerations led us to the standpoint of proclaiming that, although from the perspective assumed by a historical participant of totalitarian legal systems, "extremely unjust" legal norms and decisions could be already referred to (in the legal sense) as "un-law" or "nonlaw", from the perspective of a modern participant of a democratic legal system, the above-mentioned positivist counterargument does not preclude a practical thesis that they should nowadays be considered (in the legal sense) as devoid of legal character.[86]

4.4 The Non-cognitivist Objection

The second basic objection against nonpositivist argumentation challenges the correctness of Alexy's cognitivist standpoint. This objection is raised by many critics of the nonpositivist conception of law and of the discourse-theoretical conception of practical reason, for example, Norbert Hoerster and Ota Weinberger. The former expresses it in the form of the Non-cognitivist Thesis (*Nonkognitivismusthese*)—epistemological in its nature—according to which there is no acceptable way to know absolutely valid norms of human conduct.[87] Accordingly, there are no norms that could be proved to be true. In this regard, this thesis challenges the existence of any natural law or law of reason.[88] Weinberger goes even further in his principled objections. He admits that he has "ever since" assumed a non-cognitivist standpoint,[89] treating the latter as a necessary precondition of practical philosophy. If practical sentences (norms, value judgments etc.) could be justified purely cognitively, there would be no room for acts of will or the valuation of acts, because they

[85] We shall return to the issue of the collision of these principles *infra*, pp. 169ff. In addition, these people will undoubtedly not be held liable for the ignorance of the law itself, but for their failure in complying with the law i.e., for their illegal behaviour.

[86] It does not obviously entail a complete justification of the practical correctness of "Radbruch's formula" from the perspective of a participant of the modern legal system, but only the rebuttal of one of the possible positivist counterarguments. Other normative counterarguments concerning the formula will be analysed *infra*, pp. 161ff. *See* also the analysis – closely associated with the above discussion – of an argument concerning the legal validity of norms, based on "Radbruch's formula", discussed in Chap. 9 at pp. 526ff.

[87] *See* N. Hoerster, 'Richtigstellung über den Rechtspositivismus', *op. cit.*, pp. 416, 418–419.

[88] However, it should be added that Hoerster certainly does not deny the possibility of a limited (non-absolute) rational justification of norms. He himself puts forward some proposals of inter-subjective justification of norms, based on the analysis of subjective interests and goals of individual actors in 'Rechtsethik ohne Metaphysik', *JZ* 37 (1982), pp. 267ff.

[89] *See* E. Bulygin, 'Entrevista con Ota Weinberger', *DOXA* 11 (1992), p. 314.

would merely constitute a logical consequence of purely descriptive cognition.[90] For Weinberger, a practical reason is no reservoir of practical sentences, or absolute values, nor any absolute and objective source of practical knowledge (because such knowledge does not exist at all), but only a logical (rational) ability to perform intellectual operations related to the practical human action.[91] Weinberger openly admitted that, despite the requirement for the non-emotional consideration of scientific issues, he failed to succeed in it in relation to the concept of discursive rationality.[92] What therefore comes as no surprise are his fierce objections (though easily understood on account of his practical experience, in particular, the need for exile after the fall of the Prague Spring[93]), which he raises against discursive theory, accusing the latter of fraudulent collectivisation of the practical reason, inspired by Neo-Marxist ideology which, incidentally, does not have anything in common with the ideals of democracy.[94] The act of basing the concept of correctness (or truth) of practical sentences on fulfilling, by practical discourse, the procedural rules of its rationality, or on reaching a consensus in the so-called ideal discourse (Weinberger refers to it as a "discourse of the Angels"[95]), which for him is absurd by definition,[96] is considered by him as tantamount to making the *ignoratio elenchi* mistake, because the beliefs of the participants of the discourse cannot, by any of these routes, be transformed into practical truth.[97] For Weinberger, the rationale of the practical judgments depends solely on the good reasons (*gute Gründe*) that justify the

[90] *See* O. Weinberger, 'Wertediskurs in Moral, Recht und Politik' in W. Krawietz *et al.* (eds.), *The Reasonable as Rational?*, *op. cit.*, p. 347.

[91] *See* O. Weinberger, 'Logische Analyse als Basis der juristischen Argumentation', *op. cit.*, p. 194 and 'Conflicting Views on Practical Reason', *op. cit.*, pp. 252–253, 266.

[92] *See* O. Weinberger, 'Grundlagenprobleme des Institutionalistischen Rechtspositivismus und der Gerechtigkeitstheorie', *op. cit.*, p. 266.

[93] *See* O. Weinberger, 'Aus intellektuellem Gewissen. Ein Rückblick auf mein wissenschaftliches Leben' in *idem, Aus intellektuellem Gewissen*, M. Fischer *et al.* (eds.), Berlin 2000, pp. 12ff. and E. Bulygin, 'Entrevista con Ota Weinberger', *op. cit.*, p. 313.

[94] *See* E. Bulygin, *ibidem*, pp. 317, 323 and O. Weinberger, 'Basic Puzzles of Discourse Philosophy', *op. cit.*, pp. 172ff.

[95] *See* O. Weinberger, 'Grundlagenprobleme des Institutionalistischen Rechtspositivismus und der Gerechtigkeitstheorie', *op. cit.*, p. 259.

[96] E. Bulygin, 'Entrevista con Ota Weinberger', *op. cit.*, p. 322.

[97] *See ibidem*, p. 321; *cf.* O. Weinberger, 'Grundlagenprobleme des Institutionalistischen Rechtspositivismus und der Gerechtigkeitstheorie', *op. cit.*, p. 258 and 'Wartość, wartościowanie i doświadczanie wartości w argumentacji prawniczej', *op. cit.*, p. 282. It has been most succinctly put by Weinberger in 'Basic Puzzles of Discourse Philosophy', *op. cit.*, p. 173: "*From an opinion there is no logically valid way to objective truth*. This concerns all real discourses in the same way as the so-called ideal discourse". *Ignorantio elenchi* (an ignorance of the subject matter of evidence) consists, therefore, of the fact that the authors of the discursive theory of practical reason do not actually prove the truth or correctness (rightness) of practical theses, but – at most – of the theoretical possibility of conducting rational practical discourses (including juristic ones).

latter—for example, on logical arguments or the ones based on experience.[98] A discourse conducted in accordance with the rules of rationality leads us only to the seemingly pseudo-legitimate cognitivism (*scheinbegründeten Kognitivismus*) rather than to practical cognition or objective rightness.[99] Thus, in Weinberger's assessment, Alexy's theory of practical discourse (and more broadly, discursive German philosophy), that is far too positively assessed by German philosophers, is essentially a dead end for legal hermeneutics, epistemology and the theory of science.[100]

4.4.1 Is Alexy a Cognitivist?

Allegations described above are certainly very important and they require a thorough discussion. Yet, before the analysis begins, we have to solve the preliminary problem of their adequacy. While studying the relevant jurisprudential literature, it can be easily observed that, apart from the commentators who claim that Alexy's metaethical standpoint is cognitivistic,[101] there are also views that regard it as intermediate between cognitivism and non-cognitivism.[102] It can, therefore, be seen that we should first discuss the issue of whether and to what extent Alexy's views are of a cognitivist character. This will allow us not only to better understand the essence of his conception of practical reason, but also to eliminate from further discussions such concerns and objections which prove to be inadequate and, therefore, irrelevant.

Going on to the reconstruction of Alexy's standpoint, let us recall that he repeatedly admits that nonpositivism "presupposes an at least rudimentary [version] of non-relativistic ethics".[103] Yet, he emphasises that by means of his discursive theory, he attempts to find a "middle way" (*Mittelweg*) between objectivistic

---

[98] *See* O. Weinberger, 'Logische Analyse als Basis der juristischen Argumentation', *op. cit.*, p. 203.

[99] *Ibidem*, p. 198.

[100] E. Bulygin, 'Entrevista con Ota Weinberger', *op. cit.*, p. 323, O. Weinberger, 'Wartość, wartościowanie i doświadczanie wartości w argumentacji prawniczej', *op. cit.*, p. 282. Incidentally, Weinberger's belief in such a positive evaluation of the contemporary German discursive philosophy seems to be exaggerated.

[101] Apart from Weinberger, a cognitivist character is attributed to Alexy's theory by E. Hilgendorf, *Argumentation in der Jurisprudenz*, *op. cit.*, p. 127 and 'Zur transzendentalpragmatischen Begründung von Diskursregeln', *op. cit.*, pp. 183ff.; F. Haft and E. Hilgendorf, 'Juristische Argumentation und Dialektik' in F. Haft *et al.* (eds.), *Strafgerechtigkeit*, *op. cit.*, pp. 107–108; A. Engländer, *Diskurs als Rechtsquelle?*, *op. cit.*, pp. 8, 89ff., 151 and 'Moralische Richtigkeit als Bedingung der Rechtsgeltung?', *op. cit.*, p. 86; J. Betegón, 'Sobre la pretendida corrección de la pretensión de corrección', *DOXA* 21/I (1998), p. 183.

[102] *See e.g.*, U. Neumann, *Juristische Argumentationslehre*, Darmstadt 1986, pp. 91ff.; M. Atienza, *Las Razones del Derecho. Teorías de la argumentatión jurídica*, Madrid 1993, p. 229 ; A. García Figueroa, *Principios y positivismo jurídico*, *op. cit.*, pp. 366ff.

[103] R. Alexy, 'Zur Verteidigung eines nichtpositivistischen Rechtsbegriffs', *op. cit.*, p. 102 and *Begriff und Geltung des Rechts*, *op. cit.*, p. 93 [English version, p. 53].

cognitivist theories and subjectivistic non-cognitivist theories.[104] Alexy's conception of practical correctness (*praktische Richtigkeit*) is expressed by the following definition: "Normative sentence (*normative Aussage*) N is correct (*richtig*) exactly when it can be the result of procedure P".[105] It is therefore not a consensus reached by the participants in the discourse (as in Habermas' discourse ethics[106]), but compliance with the procedural rules of rational discourse that constitutes the practical criterion of correctness or—as Alexy writes: "with the assumption of lenient theory of truth (*liberalen Wahrheitstheorie*)"[107]—of the practical truth of normative statements and norms. However, the result of rational discourse is neither merely objective nor just subjective. Its objectivity resulting from compliance with the rules of discourse does not eliminate the fact of subjectivity derived from participants in the discourse.[108] In addition, Alexy repeatedly emphasises that the concept of practical correctness used by him has a relative character: the correctness of the result of discourse indeed depends on the discourse rules, the degree of their compliance, the participants in the discourse and on its duration.[109] What is more, Alexy also introduces the concept of nonprocedural "absolute correctness" (*absolute Richtigkeit*), which, however, has only the role of a pure regulative idea in the Kantian sense; namely, something that by definition is

---

[104] *See* R. Alexy, 'Justicia como corrección', *op. cit.*, pp. 164–165 and 'Die juristische Argumentation als rationaler Diskurs' in R. Alexy, H.-J. Koch, L. Kuhlen, H. Rüßmann, *Elemente einer juristischen Begründungslehre*, Baden-Baden 2003, p. 117; M. Atienza, 'Entrevista a Robert Alexy', *DOXA* 24 (2001), p. 672.

[105] R. Alexy, 'Die Idee einer prozeduralen Theorie der juristischen Argumentation', *op. cit.*, p. 178 and A. Aarnio, R. Alexy, A. Peczenik, 'The Foundation of Legal Reasoning', *op. cit.*, p. 261.

[106] *See e.g.*, R. Alexy, 'Probleme der Diskurstheorie', *ZphF* 43 (1989), pp. 88–89. It should be noted that a lot of confusion about the critique of Alexy's theory seems to have its source in a failure to perceive significant differences between his conceptions and the conceptions of Habermas. Apart from the above problem of the role of consensus as the main criterion for practical correctness, the key differences between them relate to justification of discourse rules, the relation between morality and the theory of morality, the content of *Sonderfallthese*, human rights and their justification and, finally, the strict distinction of Is and Ought – *see* R. Alexy, *Theorie der juristischen Argumentation*, *op. cit.*, pp. 161ff. [English version, pp. 124ff.], 'Jürgen Habermas' Theorie des juristischen Diskurses' in *idem*, *Recht, Vernunft, Diskurs*, *op. cit.*, pp. 165–174, and 'The Special Case Thesis', *RJ* 12 (1999), pp. 376ff.; M. Atienza, *Las Razones del Derecho*, *op. cit.*, pp. 675–676. *Cf.* the review of some of these differences by P. Gril, 'Alexys Version einer transzendental-pragmatischen Begründung der Diskursregeln im Unterschied zu Habermas', *op. cit.* and *Die Möglichkeit praktischer Erkenntnis aus Sicht der Diskurstheorie*, *op. cit.*, pp. 129ff.; A. Engländer, *Diskurs als Rechtsquelle?*, *op. cit.*, pp. 15ff.

[107] R. Alexy, 'Die Idee einer prozeduralen Theorie der juristischen Argumentation', *op. cit.*, p. 178. Alexy also refers this rule to norms in 'Probleme der Diskurstheorie', *op. cit.*, p. 82. For more on the issue of the logical value of normative statements *see* his *Theorie der juristischen Argumentation*, *op. cit.*, note 5 at p. 222 [English version, note 5 at pp. 177–178], wherein Alexy indicates the arguments in favour of attributing truth-values to normative statements, yet calling into question whether it stands for the same "truth" as in the case of empirical statements.

[108] R. Alexy, 'Probleme der Diskurstheorie', *op. cit.*, pp. 88–89.

[109] *See ibidem*, pp. 92ff. *Cf.* R. Alexy, 'Nachwort (1991): Antwort auf einige Kritiker', *op. cit.*, p. 415 and 'Ota Weinbergers Kritik der diskurstheoretischen Deutung juristischer Rationalität', *op. cit.*, p. 151.

impossible to achieve, but which necessarily constitutes an objective of all discourses, not just "ideal discourses".[110] Obtaining absolute certainty (*absoluter Gewißheit*) in each issue by means of rational practical discourse is impossible, because the rules of this discourse, due to their perfect nature, can only be fulfilled approximately in real conditions.[111] Furthermore, even an "ideal discourse" that ends in success does not guarantee the final certainty (*endgültige Gewißheit*) of its outcome.[112] Therefore, Alexy's *Diskurstheorie*—as the author himself claims—is the theory that offers no definitive solutions or decisions (*nicht entscheidungs-definite Theorie*).[113] Thus, it seems that the characteristics of his conception of procedural practical correctness of normative statements and norms as a moderately cognitivist standpoint should be considered as reasonable.[114] Roughly speaking, one can say that Alexy's metaethical position does not categorically exclude the possibility of attributing truth-values to norms and other practical statements (which constitutes a definitional element of a pure, extreme cognitivist standpoint[115]), but, in its essence, it involves attributing to them the characteristics

[110] *See* R. Alexy, 'Probleme der Diskurstheorie', *op. cit.*, pp. 90ff., 'Ota Weinbergers Kritik der diskurstheoretischen Deutung juristischer Rationalität', *op. cit.*, pp. 148ff., 'Law, Discourse, and Time', *op. cit.*, p. 110, and 'Nachwort (1991): Antwort auf einige Kritiker', *op. cit.*, p. 414.

[111] *See e.g.*, R. Alexy, 'Rechtssystem und praktische Vernunft', *op. cit.*, p. 418 and 'Die juristische Argumentation als rationaler Diskurs', *op. cit.*, p. 119.

[112] R. Alexy, 'Probleme der Diskurstheorie', *op. cit.*, p. 87. It should, however, be added that Alexy refers this thesis to the consensuses obtained in "potentially endless ideal discourses", meaning such discourses, in which new arguments – so far ignored or overlooked – may still appear. Yet, by definition, the consensus achieved in actually completed ideal discourse in which all possible arguments have been presented and properly assessed, is of ultimately certain character – *see ibidem*, pp. 85–86. Well, it is hard to deny that the end of the world (or at least of the human race) will reconcile all participants in the discourse, but it would also probably not be questioned by Hoerster and Weinberger.

[113] R. Alexy, 'Die juristische Argumentation als rationaler Diskurs', *op. cit.*, p. 119 and 'Nachwort (1991): Antwort auf einige Kritiker', *op. cit.*, p. 411.

[114] *Cf.* A.C. Amato Mangiameli, 'Variazioni positivistiche e giusnaturalistiche sulla dialettica fra diritto e morale. Osservazioni in margine a "Begriff und Geltung des Rechts" di Robert Alexy', *RIFD* LXXI/1 (1994), pp. 8 and 30. She refers to Alexy's standpoint as "weak cognitivism" (*cognitivismo debole*). Alexy's standpoint is similarly characterised by A. García Figueroa, *Principios y positivismo jurídico*, *op. cit.*, once referring to it (p. 366) as "metaethical moderately cognitivist conception" (*la concepción metaética cognoscitivista moderada*) and then (p. 370) as "weak cognitivism" (*cognoscitivismo debil*). It can also be noted that this terminology is akin to a "revisionist" interpretation of Radbruch's post-war metaethical standpoint as "moderately relativistic" (*moderater metaethischer Relativismus*), proposed by L.H. Meyer, '"Gesetzen ihrer Ungerechtigkeit wegen die Geltung absprechen". Gustav Radbruch und der Relativismus', *op. cit.*, pp. 339ff.

[115] In Polish law theory, it is typical to distinguish three metaethical positions: cognitivistic, moderately non-cognitivist and extremely non-cognitivist – *see e.g.*, K. Opałek, 'Normen: Bedeutung und Performanz' in A. Aarnio *et al.* (eds.), *Rechtsnorm und Rechtswirklichkeit*, *op. cit.*, pp. 43ff., A. Peczenik, 'Coherence, Truth and Rightness in the Law' in P. Nerhot (ed.), *Law, Interpretation and Reality*, Dordrecht/Boston/London 1990, pp. 275ff. and *Scientia Juris*, Dordrecht 2005, pp. 167ff. The problems with an adequate characterisation of Alexy's

(values) of "practical and procedural correctness", not based on fully objective cognition (which brings this position closer to moderate non-cognitivism). Alexy's metaethical position results from the fundamental assumption of his theory of practical discourse (as well as his conception of practical reason), which consists of assuming that practical judgments (normative statements, evaluations and norms) are rationally justifiable (that is, they are subject to justification by means of rational practical argumentation).[116]

The explicitness of the above characteristics must be somewhat weakened since Alexy's metaethical position is subject to radicalisation when applying "Radbruch's formula", and hence, the nonpositivist conception of law in relation to the jurisdiction of German courts in cases relating to the "Berlin Wall shootings" (*Mauerschützenprozesse*). In the analysis of these trials, he accepts *par excellence* the cognitivist thesis of having a cognitive and objective character through certain types of practical judgment; namely, judgments about the extreme injustice of legal norms.[117] Nonetheless, in this context Alexy also grasps the cognitive and objective nature of practical judgments in a moderately cognitivist manner: they possess such qualities because they shall be subject to rational justification.[118] In this sense, we deal here with the radicalisation of having a verbal rather than a substantial character.

4.4.2 Preliminary Appraisal of the Non-cognitivist Objection

After explaining the essence of Alexy's moderately cognitivist position, we can now return to the main course of the analysis. The observation that is raised in relation to Hoerster's above-mentioned allegations is that the latter are not adequate

metaethical position in German literature presumably have their roots in the fact that one can usually differentiate in the latter only two extreme positions, namely cognitivism and non-cognitivism, without taking into consideration moderate intermediate positions – *see e.g.*, F. von Kutschera, *Grundlagen der Ethik*, Berlin/New York 1982, pp. 47ff.

[116] From the very beginning Alexy repeatedly emphasises this assumption. For example, in *Theorie der juristischen Argumentation*, *op. cit.*, note 6 at p. 264 [English version, note 6 at pp. 213–214] he states that: "Der Auffassung Kelsens liegt die Überzeugung zugrunde, daß Wert- und Verpflichtungsurteile nicht wahrheitsfähig oder rational begründbar sind und deshalb nicht Gegenstand einer wissenschaftlichen Behandlung sein können. Es ist die These dieser Untersuchung, daß letzteres nicht zutrifft". Similar views can be found in his papers: 'Die juristische Argumentation als rationaler Diskurs', *op. cit.*, p. 117 (in which he determines the possibility of a rational discussion about practical issues on the basis of the claim to correctness as *Grundidee der Diskurstheorie*), as well as in 'Law, Discourse, and Time', *op. cit.*, p. 109. *See* also Alexy's statements in M. Atienza, 'Entrevista a Robert Alexy', *op. cit.*, pp. 672, 685.

[117] R. Alexy, *Mauerschützen*, *op. cit.*, p. 23. Similarly in 'A Definition of Law', *op. cit.*, p. 106.

[118] R. Alexy, *Mauerschützen*, *op. cit.*, pp. 23ff., in particular, pp. 24–25, wherein Alexy emphasises that the existence of "extreme unlawfulness" is ultimately decided by the arguments that can withstand "the test of rational discourse" (*rationalen diskursiven Prüfung*), rather than our intuitions, or experiencing its obviousness.

with respect to Alexy's conception. Such judgment is justified, because, firstly, a scholar from Kiel treats the problem of attributing normative statements and norms with truth-value as a secondary one. Moreover, as Gril aptly notes,[119] the rightness of normative statements and norms depends, in Alexy's conception, entirely on their justifiability, rather than on assuming that they are attributed with logical value. Secondly, as already indicated above, in Alexy's conception, the result of rational discourse almost[120] never has an absolute or definitive character, but it is always relative and debatable.

The issue is no longer so straightforward in respect to Weinberger's objections regarding existence and the nature of practical reason as well as the possibility of practical knowledge by means of rational discourse. What should be primarily taken into consideration is that the non-cognitivist position, adopted by him, has contemporarily ceased to be self-evident or self-justified.[121] Moreover, not only the renaissance, but also even the advantage of cognitivist conceptions can be observed both in contemporary moral philosophy[122] and in the philosophy of law.[123]

---

[119] P. Gril, *Die Möglichkeit praktischer Erkenntnis aus Sicht der Diskurstheorie*, *op. cit.*, p. 157.

[120] The reason why this restriction needs to be added is explained *supra* in note 112 at p. 88. Let us note in this context, that also one of A. Kaufmann's objections against *Diskurstheorie* (*see idem*, *Rechtsphilosophie in der Nach-Neuzeit*, 2nd ed., Heidelberg, 1992, note 3 at p. 46), concerning the scientific unacceptability of an ultimately justified consensus reached in ideal conditions (assuming that something like this could occur), cannot be directly related to Alexy's theory of discourse. In fact, a universal (common) agreement, which is a cornerstone of the "ideal moral validity" of norms, constitutes only an ideal (not real) consequence of recognising the rules of discourse as valid – *see* the condition of "universal agreement" (*universeller Zustimmung*) formulated by Alexy in 'A Discourse-Theoretical Conception of Practical Reason', *op. cit.*, p. 236 [German version, pp. 15–16]. *Cf. idem*, 'Diskurstheorie und Menschenrechte', *op. cit.*, pp. 130–131 [English version, pp. 211–212].

[121] As J. Hruschka rightly observed in his criticism of Hoerster's non-cognitivist position, if *Nonkognitivismusthese* was treated as the statement on the impossibility (also in the future) of knowing absolutely valid norms, then this thesis would have the same logical value as the thesis put forward in the times of the Roman Empire: "There cannot be any non-Euclidean geometry" – *see idem*, 'Recht und Unrecht bei Norbert Hoerster', *op. cit.*, p. 423. It has to be added, however, that it is difficult to attribute such a timeless non-cognitivist thesis to Hoerster – *cf.* the argumentation of M.P. Förster, 'Auseinandersetzung zwischen Norbert Hoerster und Joachim Hruschka', *op. cit.*, p. 538.

[122] Let us indicate here, by way of example, the analysis presented by S. Darwall, A. Gibbard and P. Railton, who in a survey work 'Toward *Fin de siècle* Ethics: Some Trends', *PhilRev* CI (1992), pp. 121ff., distinguish the period of "The Great Expansion" of English cognitivist moral philosophy (ethics), which started more or less in the fifties of the last century.

[123] The authors that can be mentioned in this context, in addition to Alexy and Habermas, include, inter alia, M. Atienza, R. Dworkin, J. Finnis, L.L. Fuller, E. Garzón Valdés, O. Höffe, J. Kalinowski, D. Lyons, N. MacCormick, C.S. Nino, Ch. Perelman, J. Rawls, J. Ruiz Manero and many other authors of different versions of cognitivistically-oriented jurisprudential conceptions (i.e., approving the thesis of practical statements being attributed with the truth-value, or at least acknowledging the existence of practical reason, which allows, inter alia, at least sometimes, to overcome axiological scepticism or relativism). *See* also E. Bulygin, 'Entrevista con Ota Weinberger', *op. cit.*, p. 318, who expressly maintains that "ethical cognitivism seems to be a dominant trend in our time" and – on the issue of the revival of natural law theories within German

Therefore, the fundamental problem is not the admissibility of cognitivism within practical philosophy, but in finding an accurate answer to the question of whether Alexy's position is justified, and thus whether his discursive-theoretical concept of practical reason gives rise to being able to defend the basic thesis of the possibility of rational discursive justification of normative statements and norms.

4.5 Discursive Rehabilitation of Practical Reason?

Alexy presented his conception of practical reason (practical rationality[124]) at the XV World Congress of *IVR* in Göttingen in 1991. He defined practical reason (practical rationality) as the ability (*Vermögen*) to arrive at practical judgments based on a system of discourse rules.[125] The conditions of rational practical discourse (practical reasoning) were expressed in the form of a system of 28 rules of a general practical discourse[126]—developed by him 15 years earlier—which can be classified in different ways.[127] Since his conception of practical reason is rooted in the philosophy of Immanuel Kant, what constitutes the essential problem is the

philosophy of law – J. Zajadło, '"Trzecie odrodzenie" prawa natury?', *op. cit.*, pp. 111–118, and the references cited therein.

[124] Alexy uses the terms of "praktische Vernunft" (*practical reason*) and "praktische Rationalität" (*practical rationality*) as synonyms – *see idem*, 'Idee und Struktur eines vernünftigen Rechtssystems', *op. cit.*, note 1 at p. 30 and 'A Discourse-Theoretical Conception of Practical Reason', *op. cit.*, p. 232 [German version, p. 12]. Such a convention is followed by us when describing his conception of practical reason.

[125] *See* R. Alexy, 'A Discourse-Theoretical Conception of Practical Reason', *op. cit.*, p. 235 [German version, p. 15] and 'Die juristische Argumentation als rationaler Diskurs', *op. cit.*, p. 118.

[126] More precisely, it concerns 22 rules and 6 forms of arguments for general practical discourse – *see* R. Alexy, *Theorie der juristischen Argumentation*, *op. cit.*, pp. 234ff., 361ff. [English version, pp. 187ff., 297ff.] and 'Idee und Struktur eines vernünftigen Rechtssystems', *op. cit.*, pp. 30–33. I do not discuss the specific rules of discourse and neither do I carry out their critique, because they are not directly related to the nonpositivist conception (argumentation), and, even more so, with the problem of legal validity.

[127] Originally (in the works indicated in the previous note), Alexy distinguished six groups of rules and forms of general practical discourse: basic rules (*Grundregeln*), rationality rules (*Vernunftregeln*), rules for allocating the burden of proof (*Argumentationlastregeln*), argument forms (*Argumentformen*), justification rules (*Begründungsregeln*) and transition rules (*Übergangsregeln*). Note that in a later work, 'A Theory of Practical Discourse', trans. D. Frisby, in S. Benhabib, F. Dallmayr (eds.), *The Communicative Ethics Controversy*, Cambridge (Mass.)/ London 1990, p. 165, rationality rules are named as "rules of Reason". Nonetheless, when developing his conception of practical reason – *see idem*, 'A Discourse-Theoretical Conception of Practical Reason', *op. cit.*, p. 235 [German version, p. 15] – Alexy has identified only two groups of rules: those relating to the structure of arguments (*nota bene* also valid for monologues) and those governing the procedure of discourse; i.e., the so-called specific rules of discourse, to which the transcendental-pragmatic justification (presented below) is directly referred.

proper justification of the universality of these rules—because only in this way can the universal nature of practical rationality, defined by them, be proved.

The first specific problem consists of the justification of the universal character of discourse rules in substantive terms (i.e., as regards their contents). According to Alexy, it is justified in this aspect, since these rules require equal rights for all participants in the discourse.[128] At first glance, such reasoning seems to be indisputable,[129] yet it must be kept in mind that the general and broad character of the individual rules conferring equal rights on the discussants does not guarantee their full substantial universality in the above sense. First of all, these rules create a system in which normative conflicts may occur, requiring an interpretation that eliminates them. What is also evident in relation to any system of rules designed to function in social reality, in the formulations of discourse rules, ambiguous or vague expressions are frequently used.[130] It is thus clear that the justification of the universality of the rules in terms of their substantive aspect implicitly assumes the possibility of the existence of an unambiguous and, more importantly, a uniform interpretation of discourse rules, otherwise their substantively universal nature would be but an empty slogan. Without the existence of the practice of such an interpretation, it is hard to defend the thesis that discourse participants are granted equal rights.

The second, much more important problem is the justification of universal validity (*universelle Geltung*) of the rules of practical discourse. Alexy allows various forms of justification,[131] yet he himself uses two methods in his works. The first one consists of using the so-called principles of practical rationality. According to Alexy's analysis, these are the principle of consistency (*Konsistenz*),

---

[128] *See* R. Alexy, 'A Discourse-Theoretical Conception of Practical Reason', *op. cit.*, p. 239 [German version, p. 19].

[129] It should be noted though that the expression *jeder darf* (used by Alexy in the formulas of different rules of practical discourse), can be regarded as inaccurate due to its non-universal scope in terms of the validity of these rules – *cf. e.g.*, P. Gril, 'Alexy's Version einer transzendental-pragmatischen Begründung der Diskursregeln im Unterschied zu Habermas', *op. cit.*, p. 214 and *Die Möglichkeit praktischer Erkenntnis aus Sicht der Diskurstheorie*, *op. cit.*, p. 14; S. Wesche, 'Robert Alexys diskurstheoretische Menschenrechtsbegründung', *RT* 30 (1999), p. 86. For more on this issue *see infra*, pp. 100ff.

[130] Taking into account, for example, one of the rationality rules (2.1): "Everyone who can speak may take part in discourse", it can be easily noted that without a clear and uniform interpretation of the expression "everyone who can speak" – blurred in its nature – the substantive universality of discourse rules is out of the question. Such an interpretation naturally cannot be automatically guaranteed by the mere basic rule (1.4): "Different speakers may not use the same expression with different meanings".

[131] In particular, Alexy points to the possibility of technical, empirical, definitional and universal-pragmatic justification – *see idem*, *Theorie der juristischen Argumentation*, *op. cit.*, pp. 225ff. [English version, pp. 180ff.]. *Cf. idem*, 'A Theory of Practical Discourse', *op. cit.*, pp. 156–163.

principle of efficiency (*Zweckrationalität*), principle of testability (*Überprufbarkeit*), principle of coherence (*Kohärenz*), principle of generalisability (*Verallgemeinerbarkeit*) and the principle of sincerity (*Aufrichtigkeit*). These principles, which constitute an interpretation of the general idea of practical rationality, are reflected in the system of rules of rational practical discourse (which is, inter alia, the result of collisions occurring between these principles).[132] Nonetheless, in considerations on the conception of practical reason, Alexy resigns from this method of justification, probably due to the fact[133] that the dispute over practical reason does not concern the issue of the most general characteristics of rationality (which are reflected in the principles mentioned above), but it takes place at a slightly lower level of abstraction, being essentially a dispute between different conceptions of practical rationality (practical reason).[134] The second method, merely outlined in *Theorie der juristischen Argumentation* in the form of meta-discursive reasoning, based primarily on universal-pragmatic justification,[135] adopts within the conception of practical reason the form of ternary justification of the universal validity of the rules of practical discourse. The leading role in the justification proposed by Alexy is played by the weakened version of a transcendental-pragmatic argument (which has its source in the transcendental philosophy of Immanuel Kant), whereas its complementary elements are: an argument from maximisation of individual utility (referring to the philosophy of Thomas Hobbes) and an empirical anthropological thesis concerning human interest in correctness (referring to the Aristotelian tradition).[136]

---

[132] *See* A. Aarnio, R. Alexy, A. Peczenik, 'The Foundation of Legal Reasoning', *op. cit.*, pp. 266ff. It should be added that this way of justifying discourse rules has been suggested to Alexy by A. Peczenik – *see ibidem*, p. note 95 at 266. On the critique of this method, *see* M. Atienza, *Las Razones del Derecho*, *op. cit.*, pp. 217ff.

[133] Another reason why Alexy follows this pattern may be to avoid the circularity of reasoning. Provided that the principles of practical rationality express the idea of that rationality, and then they find expression in the rules of general practical discourse, which in turn define the practical rationality of decisions, such reasoning may be faced with an objection of indirect circularity – *see* T. Gizbert-Studnicki, 'Podstawy argumentacji prawniczej' [Foundations of Legal Argumentation], *AUW* 1772 (1995), p. 42.

[134] *See* R. Alexy, 'A Discourse-Theoretical Conception of Practical Reason', *op. cit.*, pp. 232–233 [German version, p. 12]. It is worth noting that, in this context, Alexy briefly discusses the contemporary conceptions of practical reason, referring to Aristotle's and Hobbes' historical models, treating them as an alternative to his own discursive conception, which constitutes the interpretation of Kant's universalistic ethics. What can be regarded as an additional reason for resigning from justifying discourse rules within the model of principles is that the latter fulfils mainly an explicative rather than justifying function – *see* A. Aarnio, R. Alexy, A. Peczenik, 'The Foundation of Legal Reasoning', *op. cit.*, pp. 266–267, 270.

[135] R. Alexy, *Theorie der juristischen Argumentation*, *op. cit.*, pp. 232–233 [English version, pp. 186–187]. *Cf.* A. Aarnio, R. Alexy, A. Peczenik, *ibidem*, pp. 270–272.

[136] The authors that the second and third component of the justification refer to, are identified by Alexy in 'Vorwort' to *Recht, Vernunft, Diskurs*, *op. cit.*, pp. 8–9 and in the paper 'Discourse Theory and Human Rights' in *Challenges to Law at the End of the 20th Century*, vol. II, Bologna 1995, p. 23. It should be noted that Alexy uses this method (*nota bene* slightly expanding his

Bearing in mind the requirements of clarity, the analysis of justifying the universal validity of practical discourse rules will be carried out in several steps. Firstly, we shall discuss the formal (logical) correctness of its first component; namely, a transcendental-pragmatic argument. Next, we shall focus on justifying the premises that occur in this argument and we will attempt to evaluate it. In the subsequent part of the analysis, we will examine the merits of the remaining elements of justification; namely, the argument from utility maximisation as well as the thesis concerning the human pursuit of correctness. Finally, in the last subsection we will try to formulate an overall assessment of discursive rehabilitation of practical reason, carried out by Alexy, in which we will reconsider Weinberger's non-cognitivist objections as previously indicated.

4.5.1 Logical Validity of the Transcendental-Pragmatic Argument

The transcendental-pragmatic argument is at the core of justifying the universality of practical discourse rules.[137] The hitherto assessment that recognises its logical accuracy is extremely laconic[138]; therefore, it is worth carefully examining its formal accuracy. Due to the fact that the transcendental-pragmatic argument is a version of a transcendental argument, we shall first focus on the general structure of the latter. In Alexy's approach, the transcendental argument consists of two premises and a conclusion. According to the first premise, certain things (representations, ideas, speech acts) are in some sense necessary (in his concrete transcendental-pragmatic version of that argument, Alexy uses the example of the speech act of assertion, as will be explained later in more detail). The second premise states the necessity for certain categories or rules, if the things referred to in the first premise are to be possible. The conclusion is the thesis that these categories or rules are "necessarily valid" (*notwendig gelten*). From a logical point of view, it seems at first glance that we are dealing here with a formally correct argument. If we leave outside the scope of our discussion a disputable issue

argumentation) also in relation to a discursive-theoretical justification of basic human rights – *see* in particular 'Diskurstheorie und Menschenrechte', *op. cit.*, pp. 132ff. [English version, pp. 23ff.]. In the subsequent discussion, the issue of the extended use of the method of discursive justification shall be omitted; in Polish literature this issue has been discussed by B. Wojciechowski, 'Uzasadnienie praw człowieka w koncepcji dyskursu prawniczego', *op. cit.*, pp. 14ff., while in German literature it is worth noting the work of S. Wesche, 'Robert Alexys diskurstheoretische Menschenrechtsbegründung', *op. cit.*

[137] *See* R. Alexy, 'A Discourse-Theoretical Conception of Practical Reason', *op. cit.*, pp. 239ff. [German version, pp. 19ff.] and 'Diskurstheorie und Menschenrechte', *op. cit.*, pp. 132ff. [English version, pp. 212ff.].

[138] The authors that advocate the logical correctness of Alexy's transcendental-pragmatic argument, based on the inference rule *modus ponendo ponens*, are S. Wesche, 'Robert Alexys diskurstheoretische Menschenrechtsbegründung', *op. cit.*, p. 83 and, indirectly, B. Wojciechowski, 'Uzasadnienie praw człowieka w koncepcji dyskursu prawniczego', *op. cit.*, p. 15.

of whether transcendental arguments can be analysed in a manner appropriate for deductive reasoning,[139] then the formal structure of the argument at hand seems to be as follows[140]:

1. $\Box x$ (first premise of transcendental argument)
2. $\Diamond x \rightarrow \Box y$ (second premise of transcendental argument[141])
3. $\Box y$ (conclusion of transcendental argument)

It is formally correct reasoning: if we add an enthymematic premise $\Box x \rightarrow \Diamond x$ (being one of the fundamental laws of modal logic), then under the law of transitivity and *modus ponendo ponens*,[142] or *modus ponendo ponens* used twice,[143] we

---

[139] What proves against this type of analysis is the fact that the nature of transcendental relations between premises and conclusion, as well as the relation expressed by the second premise of the transcendental argument is not identical to logical deductive inference. The second objection consists of a transcendental (and not purely modal) understanding of possibility and necessity. For more on various models of the analysis of transcendental arguments *see e.g.*, M.S. Gram, 'Do Transcendental Arguments Have a Future?', *NHPh* 14 (1978), pp. 23–56, particularly pp. 31ff., and the references cited therein; B. Brożek, *Rationality and Discourse. Towards a Normative Theory of Applying Law*, Warszawa 2007, pp. 163ff.

[140] In this scheme, the symbols $\Box$ and $\Diamond$ are modal operators of necessity and possibility, whereas the implication sign $\rightarrow$ stands for material implication. Undoubtedly, a problem emerges as to why, in order to write the second premise, we do not use the functor of strict implication $⥽$ (introduced by C.I. Lewis) and defined by the formula: $(p ⥽ q) \equiv {\sim}\Diamond(p \wedge {\sim}q)$. There are two reasons. First, given that the functor of strict implication is read: "if . . . , then necessarily . . ." and due to the formulation of the second premise, the consequent of which is $\Box y$, the application of strict implication would lead to redundant repetition, since this conditional premise would then have to be read as follows: "if x is possible, then necessarily y is necessary". Secondly, as will come to light in a moment, the modal logic alone is insufficient to express entirely the logical structure of the transcendental and transcendental-pragmatic argument, because in these arguments, deontic operators are also present. Therefore, we cannot use the language of modal logic, but we must use the language of the deontic system, based on modal logic, in the style of mixed systems of A.R. Anderson or Z. Ziemba. On the concepts and logical systems mentioned in this note *see e.g.*, Z. Ziemba, *Analityczna teoria obowiązku. Studium z logiki deontycznej* [Analytical Theory of Duty. Study of Deontic Logic], Warszawa 1983, pp. 29ff., 34ff. and 'Logika deontyczna' [Deontic Logic] in W. Marciszewski (ed.), *Logika formalna*, Warszawa 1987, pp. 320ff., and the references cited therein.

[141] Given the wording of this premise, doubts may arise as to whether the antecedent and the consequent of this implication should not be written in reverse order. Certainly not, because it is the possibility of certain things that entails the necessity of certain categories or rules, which we seek to justify. Note that in the notation of that conditional premise, the authors who undertake the logical formalisation of the transcendental argument assume that very order as obvious, without any additional commentary – *see e.g.*, St.L. Paulson, 'Lässt sich die Reine Rechtslehre transzendental begründen?', *RT* 21 (1990), p. 175 and 'On the Puzzle Surrounding Hans Kelsen's Basic Norm', *RJ* 13 (2000), p. 288; B. Brożek, *Rationality and Discourse*, *op. cit.*, pp. 163–164.

[142] 1. $\Box x$ [first premise], 2. $\Box x \rightarrow \Diamond x$ [enthymematic premise], 3. $\Diamond x \rightarrow \Box y$ [second premise], 4. $\Box x \rightarrow \Box y$ [2+3 under the law of transitivity of implication], 5. $\Box y$ [conclusion obtained from 1+4 by *modus ponendo ponens*].

[143] 1. $\Box x$ [first premise], 2. $\Box x \rightarrow \Diamond x$ [enthymematic premise], 3. $\Diamond x$ [1+2 by *modus ponendo ponens*], 4. $\Diamond x \rightarrow \Box y$ [second premise], 5. $\Box y$ [conclusion obtained from 3+4 by *modus ponendo ponens*].

obtain a logically correct inference. Yet, in my opinion, it is legitimately questionable that we are actually dealing with such a structure as the transcendental argument. Taking into account the above-cited conclusion of the transcendental argument, which points at the characteristic feature of "necessary validity", the structure of this inference can be more adequately presented as:

1. $\Box x$ (first premise of transcendental argument)
2. $\Diamond x \rightarrow \Box y$ (second premise of transcendental argument)
3. $\Box(\mathrm{O}y)$ (conclusion of transcendental argument[144])

Is this reasoning also logically correct? Let us note that this enthymeme lacks not only the $\Box x \rightarrow \Diamond x$ premise, but also an additional premise, which would allow us to establish the link between the second premise and the conclusion of the transcendental argument. Such an additional premise must have the form of $\Box y \rightarrow \Box(\mathrm{O}y)$ and the formal correctness of the argument is dependent on whether is it true. Thus, the question is whether the rules of practical discourse which are necessary in the transcendental sense are also necessarily (and—taking into account the purpose of Alexy's argument—also universally) valid in the transcendental sense or in any other sense.

Naturally, the author of such a great analytical skill as Alexy, probably predicted the above-mentioned doubts. The latter can be evidenced by the wording of the premises and conclusion of the transcendental-pragmatic argument. In this argument, Alexy tries to establish the necessary rules for making assertions (*Behauptung*).[145] The first premise of the transcendental-pragmatic argument states that assertions (understood in the way defined by Alexy in connection with the second premise) are necessary in a certain relative sense. Thus, we can write it as $\Box_{rs}a$. The second premise concerns that which is necessary as presupposed when performing an assertion. Its logical form is very difficult to interpret.[146] Alexy's

[144] Naturally, doubts arise as to how to adequately write this conclusion: other possible formalisations are $\Box\mathrm{O}y$ and $\mathrm{O}\Box y$. Moreover, a deontic operator O ("it is obligatory that...") can by replaced by a symbol of validity V. These doubts, given the brevity of Alexy's comments, must be left undecided. Besides, they are of little importance in the sense that – as we will see in a moment – the formulation of the conclusion in Alexy's transcendental-pragmatic argument no longer raises such doubts.

[145] *See* R. Alexy, 'A Discourse-Theoretical Conception of Practical Reason', *op. cit.*, pp. 239ff. [German version, pp. 19ff.] and 'Diskurstheorie und Menschenrechte', *op. cit.*, pp. 134ff. [English version, pp. 214ff.]. Let us add, for the sake of chronological accuracy, that this argument has been presented for the first time (in a simplified form) by Alexy in 'Nachwort (1991): Antwort auf einige Kritiker', *op. cit.*, pp. 417ff. and this *Nachwort* was first published as 'Postfacio: Respuesta a algunos críticos' in the Spanish edition of Alexy's dissertation, *Teoría de la argumentación jurídica. La teoría del discurso racional como teoría de la fundamentación jurídica*, trans. M. Atienza, I. Espejo, Madrid 1989, pp. 305ff.

[146] *See* how this premise was formulated in 'A Discourse-Theoretical Conception of Practical Reason', *op. cit.*, p. 239 [German version, pp. 19–20] and was slightly modified in 'Diskurstheorie und Menschenrechte', *op. cit.*, p. 134 [English version, p. 214]. My interpretation is based primarily on the Alexy's latter paper, the original fragments of which – taken from p. 134 – are quoted in the main text.

basic thesis is that in order for assertions to be possible, certain rules of making assertions have to be valid. Such rules must necessarily be assumed so that the assertions were possible. When interpreting literally the relevant passages of Alexy's texts, the second premise should be written as $\Diamond a \rightarrow (\Box y_a \equiv \mathrm{O}r_a \equiv \Box r_a)$, since the statements by which Alexy expresses this premise are presented by the formulas:

1. $\Diamond a \rightarrow \Box y_a$ ("Ich [...] beginne mit Thesen über das, was Behauptungen notwendig voraussetzen"),
2. $\Diamond a \rightarrow \mathrm{O}r_a$ ("[...] Behauptungen nur dann möglich sind, wenn irgendwelche Regeln des Behauptens gelten"),
3. $\Diamond a \rightarrow \Box r_a$ ("Das bedeutet, daß mit Behauptungen irgendwelche Regeln notwendig vorausgesetzt warden").

Moreover, as we can see, Alexy understands the latter statement as an explication of the meaning of the second one. Yet, it should be noted that within the first implication $\Diamond a \rightarrow \Box y_a$, whose antecedent is already adequate for the transcendental-pragmatic argument, the consequent still refers to the formula of a general transcendental argument, and is then modified by the third implication, which states that the sought y_a (a category or a rule necessary for making assertions) are rules for making speech acts of assertion r_a. Therefore, we can simplify—in my opinion—the logical formulation of the second premise of the transcendental-pragmatic argument to the following form: $\Diamond a \rightarrow (\Box r_a \equiv \mathrm{O}r_a)$. With regard to the logical form of expressing the conclusion, it should be noted that in Alexy's works it is subject to certain modifications. Initially, the conclusion of the transcendental-pragmatic argument speaks only of a hypothetical validity of discourse rules: "[t]hey are valid wherever and to the extent that there prevails an interest in correctness".[147] Yet, in the ultimate form, this conclusion takes a slightly different, two-element form, as Alexy also distinguishes the ideal and the real validity of discourse rules.[148] In his view, discourse rules are valid in a perfect sense when they are binding on all participants in the discourse, for whom the regulative ideas of truth or moral correctness have a positive value. This perfect validity is, in the context of ideas of correctness, of a categorical character. Nonetheless, in real terms (dependent on whether and to what extent human motivation and desire to comply with discourse rules actually exist), these rules are only hypothetically valid—it is "a factually limited validity".[149] Thus, this conclusion should be interpreted as the conjunction of

[147] R. Alexy, 'A Discourse-Theoretical Conception of Practical Reason', *op. cit.*, p. 242 [German version, p. 22].

[148] *See* R. Alexy, 'Diskurstheorie und Menschenrechte', *op. cit.*, pp. 141–142 [English version, pp. 218–219].

[149] *Ibidem*, p. 142 [English version, p. 219].

two arguments: the statement $\mathrm{O_{hip}}r_d$, which expresses, in a simplified form, the basic thesis included in the conclusion, namely a hypothetically (and actually limited) real validity of discourse rules as well as the statement $\Diamond\mathrm{O_{cat}}r_d$, which expresses, in a simplified form, an additional thesis of this conclusion; that is, the possibility[150] of a categorical and ideal validity of discourse rules in case of existence and in reference to those interested in moral correctness—namely, those for whom truth and moral correctness constitute the values to which they aspire.

The undertaken analysis leads to the following scheme, showing the logical structure of Alexy's transcendental-pragmatic argument:

1. $\Box_{\mathrm{rs}}a$ (first premise of transcendental-pragmatic argument)
2. $\Diamond a \rightarrow (\Box r_a \equiv \mathrm{O}r_a)$ (second premise of transcendental-pragmatic argument)
3. $\mathrm{O_{hip}}r_d$ ($\wedge$ $\Diamond\mathrm{O_{cat}}r_d$) (conclusion of transcendental-pragmatic argument)

In relation to such a reconstructed structure of the transcendental-pragmatic argument, it appears that Alexy's logical intuition does not fail, because the modifications of the content of premises and conclusion—as introduced by him—cause that, in contrast to the transcendental argument previously analysed, no objections can be raised with respect to the transcendental-pragmatic argument from the point of view of the logical correctness of the inferences that it expresses. Firstly, the enthymematic premise, which allows "linking" the explicit premises of this argument and assumes the form of $\Box_{\mathrm{rs}}a \rightarrow \Diamond a$, is correct. Accordingly, if speech acts of assertion are in a sense necessary, so, undoubtedly, are they possible. Secondly, due to this enthymematic premise, when applying *modus ponendo ponens*, we can, inter alia, infer $\mathrm{O}r_a$ from the explicit premises. Finally, from $\mathrm{O}r_a$ we can infer both $\mathrm{O_{hip}}r_d$ (because if the rules of discourse are valid, then it is even more the case that they are valid in a hypothetical way) as well as $\Diamond\mathrm{O_{cat}}r_d$ (because if the rules of discourse are valid, it is possible that they can be valid in a categorical, i.e., an unconditional, way). The last two statements certainly raise doubts, since Alexy formulates the second premise of the argument in relation to the rules concerning assertions, whereas his conclusions treat the different ways in which the rules of the whole practical discourse can be valid. This generalisation, nonetheless, seems legitimate[151]: for if we assume that the correctness of the

[150] Adding the modal characteristics of this additional thesis, not directly expressed in Alexy's wording on this element of the conclusion of the transcendental-pragmatic argument, is justified by the fact that during the discussion on the "argument from the individual utility (profit) maximisation", he states categorically that it was not possible to assert that all people treat the pursuit to a fair (i.e., just) resolution of the conflicts of interest as invariably primary to their other desires (R. Alexy, *ibidem*, p. 142 [English version, p. 219], *see* also *idem*, 'Nachwort (1991): Antwort auf einige Kritiker', *op. cit.*, p. 421). In this sense, his argumentation only proves that such people can exist. Thus, we can legitimately speak only of the possible ideal validity of discourse rules.

[151] *Cf.* a different opinion expressed by A. Engländer, *Diskurs als Rechtsquelle?*, *op. cit.*, pp. 55–59, 85–86, who questions the choice of the speech act of assertion that is significantly different from the normative speech acts (*normative Sprechakte*), and the fact that Alexy refers to it in the transcendental-pragmatic argument. In my view, this opinion is incorrect, mainly due to

transcendental-pragmatic argument can be justified in relation to assertions, then we can—accordingly—justify the validity of discourse rules concerning other speech acts, which will ultimately provide us with the justification of the validity of practical discourse rules relating to all speech acts that are performed within it (i.e., in the second premise we would be able to use $\mathrm{O}r_d$ instead of $\mathrm{O}r_a$).

Clearly, the formal logical correctness of the transcendental-pragmatic argument does not settle the question as to whether this argument deserves our approval. Apart from the correctness of the inference itself, what is needed in order to accept the argument is also the truth of the premises used. In other words, the fact that this argument is not burdened with *non sequitur* error, is of no significance in relation to the separate issue (which we examine in the next subsection) of whether the argument is not burdened with a material error.

4.5.2 *Justification of the Premises of the Transcendental-Pragmatic Argument*

The completed reconstruction of the logical structure of the transcendental-pragmatic argument allows for the precise identification of the statements, the veracity of which should be proved in order to consider it as correct also in the material sense. Firstly, it is indispensable to prove the truth of the first premise $\Box_{\mathrm{rs}}a$; namely, the thesis that the statements are necessary in some relative sense. Then we should prove the truth of the second premise $\Diamond a \rightarrow (\Box r_a \equiv \mathrm{O}r_a)$ which, due to its content, makes it necessary to prove two particular theses.[152] First, that it is these, and no other rules of making (formulating and expressing) assertions that are necessary to make assertions possible; that is, that r_a are identified and determined correctly in the context of the relation of $\Diamond a \rightarrow \Box r_a$. Second, that the necessity of these rules is equivalent to their validity; that is, that $\Box r_a \equiv \mathrm{O}r_a$.

Let us analyse the content of the transcendental-pragmatic argument in order to examine Alexy's argumentation by means of which he attempts to prove the

Alexy's very broad interpretation of the concept of assertion: according to him, what can also be expressed by means of an assertion are, inter alia, moral evaluative judgments or normative propositions – *see* R. Alexy, *Theorie der juristischen Argumentation*, *op. cit.*, pp. 89ff., 238 [English version, pp. 64ff., 191]. In this context, *see* also the critique of J.-R. Sieckmann, 'Human Rights and the Claim to Correctness in the Theory of Robert Alexy' in G. Pavlakos (ed.), *Law, Rights and Discourse*, *op. cit.*, pp. 194–195, 203ff.

[152] We leave aside the additional issue of determining the nature of the relation that occurs between the possibility and necessity in this premise: whether it is an analytic relation, an *a priori* synthetic one (concerning aprioric conditions of our abilities to make and understand assertions) or whether by means of it we only formulate a certain hypothesis explaining the possibility for making speech acts of assertion.

veracity of the indicated theses. As already pointed out above, in his version of the transcendental-pragmatic argument, Alexy uses the example of a speech act of assertion.[153] The first premise of this argument provides that the assertions (interpreted by Alexy as speech acts raising a claim to truth or correctness) are necessary in a certain relative sense (it is, inter alia, due to this fact, that Alexy calls his version of the transcendental-pragmatic argument "very weak"[154]). The main justification for this premise is the thesis that if someone has never made assertions or has never formulated arguments, then she/he does not participate in "the most general form of life (*Lebensform*) of human beings".[155] Thus, making an assertion is relatively necessary, if and until people finally and completely lose their basic ability to ask questions, to formulate assertions and their justification. Therefore, Alexy argues that all human "life forms" necessarily contain the "argumentative universals" expressed by discourse rules.

Going on to the analysis of the reasoning provided by Alexy, let us first explain two issues. Firstly, Alexy uses the term "form of life" in a different sense from that adopted by Ludwig Wittgenstein.[156] For the author of *Philosophischen Untersuchungen*, the *Lebensform* constitute a given framework for the development of various language games that, inter alia, allow for a non-ultimate justification of our actions (ultimate justification is, according to Wittgenstein, impossible—in this case, one has to say: "It is simply what I do"[157]). Meanwhile, Alexy sees "forms of life" in a natural law manner, explicitly admitting that at this point (but—as he emphasises—only herein) his discursive theory, attempting to explain human nature, refers to the tradition of the doctrines of natural law.[158] Secondly, one may wonder why Alexy assumes the need to make assertions as the first premise of the transcendental-pragmatic argument. The authors whose work Alexy refers to when developing his transcendental-pragmatic argument (such as Roderick

[153] The fact that the speech act is the entity whose necessity and conditions of possibility are under discussion provides the grounds for defining it as a transcendental-pragmatic argument.

[154] R. Alexy, 'A Discourse-Theoretical Conception of Practical Reason', *op. cit.*, p. 239 [German version, p. 19].

[155] *Ibidem*, p. 241 [German version, p. 21]. *See* also 'Diskurstheorie und Menschenrechte', *op. cit.*, p. 139, thesis 5 [English version, p. 217].

[156] *See* L. Wittgenstein, *Philosophische Untersuchungen/Philosophical Investigations*, trans. G.E.M. Anscombe, Oxford 1953, pp. 8 (I, § 19), 11–12 (I, § 23), 241 (I, § 241), 226 (II, § XI) and *Über Gewissheit/On Certainty*, trans. D. Paul, G.E.M. Anscombe, Oxford 1979, p. 46 (§ 358). The differences between Wittgenstein and Alexy in understanding *Lebensform* have been discussed by J. Betegón, 'Sobre la pretendida corrección de la pretensión de corrección', *op. cit.*, p. 182. *See* also R. Alexy, *Theorie der juristischen Argumentation*, *op. cit.*, pp. 71ff. [English version, pp. 49ff.] and A. Aarnio, R. Alexy, A. Peczenik, 'The Foundation of Legal Reasoning', *op. cit.*, pp. 278–279.

[157] L. Wittgenstein, *Philosophische Untersuchungen/Philosophical Investigations*, *op. cit.*, p. 85^{e} (I, § 217) and *Über Gewissheit/On Certainty*, *op. cit.*, p. 39 (§ 307).

[158] R. Alexy, 'Diskurstheorie und Menschenrechte', *op. cit.*, p. 141 [English version, p. 218]. As for the critique of applying the concept of "form of life" in Alexy's conception, *see* O. Weinberger, 'Logische Analyse als Basis der juristischen Argumentation', *op. cit.*, p. 213 and J. Betegón, 'Sobre la pretendida corrección de la pretensión de corrección', *op. cit.*, pp. 182ff.

Chisholm and Stanley Paulson[159]), assume a non-modal form of the first premise of the transcendental argument that merely states the existence (and not the necessity of it) of certain things or sensory data.[160] It can therefore be easy to see that it would be sufficient—in terms of logical correctness of the transcendental-pragmatic argument—to adopt the first condition in the form of a thesis about the existence of assertions, rather than the thesis about their necessity. The truth of such a condition would be, at least at first glance, easier to prove. The clarification of this issue seems to be the following. Alexy adopts a relative necessity of assertions as a starting point for his argument, since he is forced to do so by logical reasons. If he assumed that there are assertions (understood in the manner specified by him in connection with the second condition), then the transcendental argumentation in favour of the existence of practical reason would, accordingly, be insufficient, even if he managed to prove the veracity of such an existential condition. Let us recall that in the *Theory of Legal Argumentation* Alexy assumed that practical judgments may be reasonably justified; for example, by means of assertions formulated in the course of practical and juristic (legal) discourse.[161] Thus, if he now considered the existence of such assertions as one of the conditions to justify the existence of universal practical reason, then the circularity of such reasoning would be highly likely: the existence of practical assertions could yet be proved only on the basis of an assumption about the existence of practical reason and, on the other hand, the existence of practical assertions would justify the existence of such reason.[162]

Turning to the substantive assessment of the justification of the accuracy of the first premise of the transcendental-pragmatic argument—as presented by Alexy—the observation arises that it is so general that it can also be used to justify the need for other speech acts; in particular, those that the theory of rational practical discourse would seek to eliminate from the sphere of human reasoning. In this context, Peter Gril notes that it is the same way in which one can justify the necessity of lies, manipulation and deception in other people: this practice also exists in which every human being—at least to a minimum level—is involved.[163] The fact that in justifying this premise Alexy resorted to human abilities, brings us

[159] *See* R. Alexy, 'A Discourse-Theoretical Conception of Practical Reason', *op. cit.*, note 21 at p. 239 [German version, note 45 at p. 19] and 'Diskurstheorie und Menschenrechte', *op. cit.*, note 17 at p. 133 [English version, p. 213]. Alexy means here the papers of R. Chisholm, 'What is a Transcendental Argument?', *NHPh* 14 (1978), pp. 19–22 and of St.L. Paulson, 'Lässt sich die Reine Rechtslehre transzendental begründen?', *op. cit.*

[160] *See* R. Chisholm, *ibidem*, pp. 19ff., St.L. Paulson, *ibidem*, pp. 171ff. On the issue of reconstructing Kant's category of transcendental argument *see* St.L. Paulson, 'On the Puzzle Surrounding Hans Kelsen's Basic Norm', *op. cit.*, pp. 285ff. and M.S. Gram, 'Do Transcendental Arguments Have a Future?', *op. cit.*, pp. 24ff., and the references cited therein.

[161] *See supra*, p. 89, in particular note 116.

[162] *Nota bene*, such a justification would be of a purely empirical, rather than transcendental character.

[163] *See* P. Gril, 'Alexys Version einer transzendental-pragmatischen Begründung der Diskursregeln im Unterschied zu Habermas', *op. cit.*, p. 210 and *Die Möglichkeit praktischer Erkenntnis aus Sicht der Diskurstheorie*, *op. cit.*, pp. 142–143.

to the next—a much more serious—epistemological objection of naturalistic fallacy.[164] Even if we agree with Alexy that his theory of discourse does not consist in deducting norms from the facts (i.e., *Sollen* from *Sein*), but it is based on the reconstruction of a certain practice, undertaken from the perspective of its participant,[165] what must still raise doubts is the use of a number of empirical arguments (theses) to justify universal validity of practical discourse rules. This issue shall be further revisited, whereas now we will content ourselves with pointing out the above doubt. Nonetheless, in regard to the *meritum*, the following assessment can be made: assertions are actually relatively necessary; however, the degree of relativity as adopted by Alexy causes that this condition becomes trivial. What is even worse is that the universal validity of discourse rules seems to be, at this point, impossible to prove without assuming a corresponding relativisation (namely weakening) of that concept of universality.

The second transcendental-pragmatic premise provides that there are valid rules of discourse for making speech acts of assertion, which must be (if—let us repeat it again—transcendental-pragmatic reasoning is to succeed) necessary assumptions of the possibility of conducting these speech acts. What is more, Alexy rightly emphasises that the necessity has to be interpreted here in such a way that there can be no alternative discourse rules for making assertions.[166] Reconstruction of these rules is based on assuming the existence of the "core meaning" (*Kernbedeutung*) of the concept of assertion, which is confirmed by the differentiation of assertions from other speech acts. According to Alexy, assertions are only those speech acts that raise an implicit claim to truth or correctness (*Anspruch auf Wahrheit oder Richtigkeit*). This claim implies a claim to justifiability (*Anspruch auf Begründbarkeit*), which, in turn, entails a *prima facie* obligation to justify the assertion by the one who asserts in a situation where someone requests it.[167] Unfortunately, Alexy provides extremely laconic, not to say, rudimentary justification of such a clarification of the nature of assertions. In particular, he presents only

---

[164] The objection of naturalistic fallacy in relation to Alexy's justification is raised by J. Betegón, 'Sobre la pretendida corrección de la pretensión de corrección', *op. cit.*, p. 183 and – yet already in the context of the method of justification based on the identification of "performative contradiction" – by S. Wesche, 'Robert Alexys diskurstheoretische Menschenrechtsbegründung', *op. cit.*, pp. 84–85. A similar, but more substantively extensive complaint against the creators and supporters of German *Diskursethik* was raised by E. Hilgendorf, 'Moralphilosophie und juristisches Denken', *ARSP* 82 (1996), pp. 399–401.

[165] R. Alexy, 'Diskurstheorie und Menschenrechte', *op. cit.*, note 36 at p. 141 [English version, note 10 at p. 218].

[166] R. Alexy, 'A Discourse-Theoretical Conception of Practical Reason', *op. cit.*, p. 239 [German version, p. 20] and 'Diskurstheorie und Menschenrechte', *op. cit.*, p. 135 [English version, p. 214].

[167] *See* R. Alexy, 'A Discourse-Theoretical Conception of Practical Reason', *op. cit.*, pp. 240ff. [German version, pp. 20ff.], 'Diskurstheorie und Menschenrechte', *op. cit.*, pp. 135ff. [English version, pp. 214ff.], and 'Law and Correctness', *op. cit.*, p. 209ff. [German version, p. 6ff]. Let us recall that Alexy argues in a similar way within his analytical nonpositivist argumentation – *see* Chap. 3, p. 44.

two brief arguments for the correctness of defining assertions by means of the claim to truth or correctness. Alexy refers here to the determination of the intention of those who make assertions, as provided by Donald Davidson,[168] and he uses here the new example of a statement burdened with the error of "performative contradiction": "Ich behaupte, daß es regnet, und ich betone dabei, daß dies falsch ist", emphasising, however, that when showing a "performative contradiction", one cannot justify the rules of discourse, but at most one can show (*gezeigen*) that these rules are valid.[169] Moreover, given the results of the criticism of William Fusfield concerning the application of the method of justifying discourse rules based on recognition of the "performative contradiction" of statements by the creators of discursive ethics (especially Jürgen Habermas), Alexy admits that both his definition of the nature of assertions and the assumptions necessary for making assertions may be wrong.[170]

It could seem that such a weak justification is very easy to refute. Apparently, it simply suffices to provide other ways of defining the rules of making assertions (one can, for example, use pragmatic analysis of rules relating to speech acts of assertion as proposed by John Searle,[171] or—in Polish literature—by Tomasz Gizbert-Studnicki[172]) to demonstrate that the "non-alternativeness" (*Alternativlosigkeit*) of discourse rules established by Alexy and required for the validity of transcendental-pragmatic justification does not occur. One can also recall a thought experiment, proposed by the critic of discursive theories—Herbert Keuth, according to which the two philosophers—a realist and an idealist—disputing on the rules of making assertions, begin their discussion from the issue of adequacy of one of the rules, arriving in the course of the argumentation to the two sets of rules relevant to making assertions, in which there is no single common rule.[173] Such allegations,

---

[168] *See* R. Alexy, 'A Discourse-Theoretical Conception of Practical Reason', *op. cit.*, note 23 at p. 240 [German version, note 52 at p. 20,] and 'Diskurstheorie und Menschenrechte', *op. cit.*, note 26 at p. 135 [English version, note 5 at p. 214].

[169] R. Alexy, 'A Discourse-Theoretical Conception of Practical Reason', *op. cit.*, note 23 *in fine* at p. 240 [German version, note 52 *in fine* at p. 20] and 'Diskurstheorie und Menschenrechte', *op. cit.*, note 27 at pp. 135–136 [English version, note 6 at p. 216].

[170] *Ibidem. See* also R. Alexy, 'Law and Correctness', *op. cit.*, p. 213 [German version, pp. 10–11]. For more on Fusfield's criticism on how to justify the rules of practical discourse, based on the method of identifying *performativer Widerspruch* (in the context of justifying the necessity of assuming the claim to correctness in law) *see infra*, pp. 155ff.

[171] *See* J.R. Searle, *Speech Acts. An Essay in the Philosophy of Language*, London 1969, pp. 64ff. and J.R. Searle, D. Vanderveken, *Foundations of Illocutionary Logic*, Cambridge/London/New York/New Rochelle/Melbourne/Sydney 1985, pp. 37ff., 54ff., 183.

[172] *See* T. Gizbert-Studnicki, 'Stwierdzenie jako akt mowy' [A Statement as a Speech Act], *SF* 3 (1973), pp. 83–97, in particular, p. 94. In Polish jurisprudential literature *see* also the analysis of the concept of assertion and methods of their justification, presented by M. Zieliński and Z. Ziembiński, *Uzasadnianie twierdzeń, ocen i norm w prawoznawstwie* [Justifying Statements, Evaluations and Norms in Jurisprudence], Warszawa 1988, pp. 27ff., 93ff.

[173] *See* H. Keuth, 'Fallibilismus versus transzendentalpragmatische Letztbegründung', *ZaW* XIV/2 (1983), pp. 334ff.

moreover—most anticipated by Alexy are, in my opinion, inaccurate on the account of the relative necessity of making assertions—adopted in the first premise of the argument in question—are interpreted in a manner determined by Alexy. Such a premise does not indeed exclude a similar, relative necessity of making assertions understood differently. Yet, this analysis leads to the conclusion that the determination of the necessary conditions for making assertions is arbitrary to such an extent that possibilities exist for making assertions that are defined differently; that is, without doubt, a serious arbitrariness.[174] "Non-alternativeness" (*Alternativlosigkeit*) of the discourse rules as determined by Alexy is justified to an extent that depends on the degree of relative necessity of making assertions in accordance with the rules defined by him. Thus, we deal here only with "relative non-alternativeness"—which in itself sounds quite suspicious.[175] The analysis leads to an irresistible conclusion that the question of universal validity of discourse rules constitutes only a rhetorical-persuasive attempt because the universality of the necessity and validity of these rules is limited to such an extent that the application of this term seems to be entirely unauthorised, at least from the semantic point of view.

This brings us to a key point in the transcendental-pragmatic argument, in which there is a shift from modal necessity to deontic validity of the discourse rules defining the conditions under which the speech acts of assertions are made. As it is implicitly contained in the structure of the second premise of Alexy's argument, rather than expressed by him directly, it comes as no surprise that he does not provide any substantive reasons for such an inference. The author of the analysed argument is very brief here; he says only that "it is not disputed that the assertions are possible only if certain rules of asserting are valid".[176] One can agree with this statement only if the validity of these rules is understood in a purely instrumental-technical way (i.e., in the

[174] Many critics of transcendental-pragmatic justification of the universal validity of discourse rules claim that Alexy did not even prove the "non-alternativeness" (*Alternativlosigkeit*) of discourse rules proposed by him J. Betegón, 'Sobre la pretendida corrección de la pretensión de corrección', *op. cit.*, pp. 188–189; A. Engländer, *Diskurs als Rechtsquelle?*, *op. cit.*, *pp.* 58–59, 85; P. Gril, *Die Möglichkeit praktischer Erkenntnis aus Sicht der Diskurstheorie*, *op. cit.*, p. 150.

[175] It is worth noting that Alexy maintains that treating something (specifically, he means here the prohibition of retroactivity of the law as expressed in Article 103 Section 2 of the German *Grundgesetz*) as absolute and at the same time restricted is contradictory – *see* R. Alexy, *Der Beschluß des Bundesverfassungsgericht zu den Tötungen an der innerdeutschen Grenze vom 24. Oktober 1996*, Hamburg/Göttingen 1997, pp. 20–21. Therefore, the "relative non-alternativeness" would probably also be assessed by him – by analogy – as something intrinsically contradictory. In my opinion, it does not change the fact that at best we can speak of such non-absolute and non-universal "non-alternativeness" in relation to the discourse rules for assertions. The only competitive interpretation is the one indicated in the previous note; however, the total rejection of any "non-alternativeness" of discourse rules provided by Alexy is too strict for me.

[176] In the original: "Es besteht kein Streit darüber, daß Behauptungen nur dann möglich sind, wenn irgendwelche Regeln des Behauptens gelten" (quotation taken from 'Diskurstheorie und Menschenrechte', *op. cit.*, p. 134 [English version, p. 214]). Compare equally laconic assessments of this issue as formulated in 'A Discourse-Theoretical Conception of Practical Reason', *op. cit.*, p. 239 [German version, p. 20].

relation of means and ends).[177] In the language of the standard theory of speech acts, only meeting the necessary and sufficient conditions for a successful speech act allows us to make a fully felicitous ("happy") speech act (we cannot help but add that this statement is undoubtedly equally true, as trivial). Yet, it is difficult to talk about some other, for example, "moral" or "transcendental" (whatever that is supposed to mean) validity of these rules without providing any substantive justification for such a thesis.[178] Indeed, even if we accept that the discourse rules developed by Alexy are necessary to perform speech acts of assertion, there are no reasons why they should be automatically considered as valid in any non-instrumental sense of validity. It should also be noted that we are precluded here from using any arguments of an empirical nature, because if such a manner of justifying the validity of the discussed rules was followed by us, we would make a classic naturalistic fallacy. We cannot, therefore, justify their universal validity by the observance of these rules by the participants in a rational practical discourse or by their social acceptability or effectiveness.[179]

Before going on to further analysis, let us note that the formal logical correctness of the transcendental-pragmatic argument does not require proving the veracity of the equivalence $\Box r_a \equiv \mathrm{O}r_a$, but it is sufficient to justify the soundness of the implication $\Box r_a \rightarrow \mathrm{O}r_a$. Since the above reconstruction of the second premise of the transcendental-pragmatic argument, very succinctly expressed by Alexy, may be burdened with a mistake, for the purposes of further discussion let us therefore adopt its weaker interpretation as an implication. The problem, thus, is to justify the thesis according to which the necessity of rules of making assertions, as determined by Alexy, implies their non-instrumental validity. This problem cannot be resolved "transcendentally" without entering the

[177] What is certainly also possible is an epistemological interpretation of this relation: without knowledge of the rules of making assertions, we cannot clearly recognise and distinguish them from other speech acts. Yet, when applying such an interpretation, the problem of the validity of these rules does not arise at all – in order to identify the assertions it is sufficient to identify the rules according to which they are made.

[178] This justification can neither be based on the concept of "normative necessity", which is used by Alexy in a number of works and referred to in his later papers as "practical necessity", consisting of the necessity of achieving certain goals or meeting (complying with) certain norms or values and associated by Alexy with the concept of "being obligatory" – *see e.g.*, 'On Necessary Relations between Law and Morality', *op. cit.*, p. 169, 'Zur Kritik des Rechtspositivismus', *op. cit.*, p. 10, *Begriff und Geltung des Rechts*, *op. cit.*, pp. 41–42 [English version, pp. 21–22], 'The Nature of Arguments about the Nature of Law', *op. cit.*, p. 8, and 'The Nature of Legal Philosophy', *op. cit.*, pp. 71ff. Even if we leave aside the criticism of the very puzzling concept of normative (practical) necessity (*cf. e.g.*, E. Bulygin, 'Alexy's Thesis of the Necessary Connection between Law and Morality', *op. cit.*, p. 136, who evaluates it as "a rather obscure metaphor"), it is doubtful whether it can be used to justify the legitimacy of the discussed thesis – in doing so, we would have to accept that the necessity of discourse rules is of a normative (practical) rather than transcendental character. In addition, it would not be a substantive justification, but merely a terminological one and therefore arbitrary.

[179] It should also be added that even such a justification would be doomed to failure; since it is obvious that people hold discussions (often, effectively, that is conclusively), or they communicate with each other without complying with many rules of rational practical discourse.

domain of speculative metaphysics, which is definitely beyond the scope of this work and, more importantly, limited competence of its author. However, from the perspective of law and logic, which are often intertwined in our analyses, we can find three arguments, in light of which we can consider the correctness of the thesis expressed by the mentioned implication.

The first argument is based on the legal principle of *necessitum nulla est obligatio*,[180] in light of which the implication $\Box r_a \rightarrow Or_a$ at first glance appears to be incorrect (false). If we consider this principle as right (and there is no reason why we should deny it its practical rightness), then the necessity of discourse rules that belong to the world of *Sollen* exclude their validity in that world. Since this critical argument seems to be quite unintuitive, let us examine its legitimacy in the example. Alexy points out that by means of a transcendental-pragmatic argument one can directly justify only some of the most fundamental rules of practical discourse.[181] Let us therefore analyse the substantive correctness of the discussed implications with respect to the first of the basic rules (in Alexy's notation it is *Grundregel* 1.1): "Kein Sprecher darf sich widersprechen". If this is a necessary rule, without which a rational practical discourse (or at least performing acts of assertion) was impossible, then speaking about its (necessary) validity seems to have a similar sense to speaking about the validity of a rule requiring that every man should die. The principle of *necessitum nulla est obligatio* undoubtedly expresses the following relation of necessity and validity: "Since every man must die, then the rule that establishes an ought (obligation, duty) to die cannot be valid". Common sense tells us, however, that it is not necessary that each discussant did not express self-contradictory theses. *Grundregel* 1.1 can be a valid rule, because it is possible to break it. Daily life experience gives us confidence that this is indeed the case,

---

[180] When analysing this argument, we shall use the comments and examples of norms as provided by H. Kelsen, *Reine Rechtslehre*, 2nd ed., *op. cit.*, pp. 10–11, 98 [English version, pp. 11, 94–95] and *Allgemeine Theorie der Normen*, K. Ringhofer, R. Walter (eds.), Wien 1979, pp. 45, 113. Incidentally, in the legal discourse there are a number of topics related to necessity (e.g., *necessitas caret lege*, *necessitas legem frangit* or *necessitas non habet legem*), which, however, will not be considered here, since they express a different aspect of the relations between necessity (already relatively understood) and the law, consisting of the law being "neutralised" by necessity, which is incidentally largely approved and regulated by the modern positive law, for example, by means of penal institutions of the lawful self-defence and the state of necessity or civil law rules on limitation of liability due to *vis maior*. We come back to Kelsen's examples in Chap. 7 at p. 302.

[181] Alexy notes (*see idem*, 'Nachwort (1991): Antwort auf einige Kritiker', *op. cit.*, p. 418 and 'Diskurstheorie und Menschenrechte', *op. cit.*, pp. 130ff. [English version, pp. 211ff.]) that the justification by means of the transcendental-pragmatic argument focuses on non-monologue procedural rules of rationality (in particular, *Vernunftregeln* 2, 2.1–2.3). Nevertheless, I hope that by using the rule of non-contradiction in the analysis that follows, the analysis can hardly be considered as unfair manipulation; moreover, this attempt was prompted mainly by its illustrative character. Using the example of this rule seems to be perfectly legitimate, because Alexy determines the validity of the *Grundregeln* group (which is opened by the rule of non-contradiction) as "a precondition for the possibility (*Bedingung der Möglichkeit*) of every linguistic communication which give rise to any question of truth or correctness", that is also in a *par excellence* transcendental manner – R. Alexy, *Theorie der juristischen Argumentation*, *op. cit.*, p. 234 [English version, p. 188].

since many participants in the discussion (real discourses) do not observe this rule.[182] Thus, we come to the conclusion that the discussed argument does not refute the implication of $\Box r_t \rightarrow Or_t$ because Alexy certainly does not have in mind the necessity of a certain behaviour of the participants in the discourse, but the necessity of the rules that constitute this discourse as such. If a discussant violates the rule of non-contradiction of her/his own assertions, or some other rule of practical discourse, then she/he simply ceases to participate in rational practical discourse (in Alexy's understanding), because she/he violates one of its rules.

The second argument refers to the principle (topic): "What is inevitable, is permitted". Based on the logical analysis of this principle conducted by Jan Woleński,[183] one must point out—after the philosopher from Kraków—that it expresses a certain law of deontic logic (often assumed as an axiom of the standard system of this logic). Woleński shows that if we write this law as P(T), for example, in the form $P(p \vee {\sim}p)$,[184] then its negation ${\sim}P(p \vee {\sim}p)$ can be relatively easily converted into a formula $Op \wedge {\sim}Op$, which is an instance of deontic contradiction. What is more, Woleński stresses that even with such interpretations of the principle "What is inevitable, is permitted" which do not have a logical character—that is, such as where the necessity is understood, for example, as natural or axiological necessity—the negation of this principle also leads to a contradiction with the assumptions that are adopted in such extra-logical interpretations.[185] This principle thus expresses the following relation between necessity and validity of norms of specific content: "That which is necessary, must be allowed"; that is, $\Box p \rightarrow Pp$.[186]

Let us now consider the consequences of applying this principle to the evaluation of the correctness of the implication $\Box r_a \rightarrow Or_a$. First, there again arises an initial problem concerning the admissibility of such a method of analysis, because

[182] An analogous argumentation can be carried out in relation to other rules of practical discourse, because in a real discourse, arguably each of them may be infringed.

[183] *See* J. Woleński, 'Treść logiczna dwóch zasad prawnych' [Logical Content of Two Legal Principles] in G. Skąpska *et al.* (eds.), *Prawo w zmieniającym się społeczeństwie. Księga Jubileuszowa Profesor Marii Boruckiej-Arctowej*, Kraków 1992, pp. 145–146.

[184] In this notation, slightly modified in relation to the notation used by Woleński, symbols O and P, respectively, express deontic operators of obligation and permission, whereas symbol T expresses any tautology of classical propositional calculus (an example of which is the principle of the excluded middle), which is something necessary in a standard "world of logic".

[185] J. Woleński, *ibidem*, p. 146.

[186] It can be seen clearly that this is not the rule equivalent to the previously discussed principle of *necessitum nulla est obligatio*. If we write the latter as $\Box p \rightarrow {\sim}Op$ and the principle discussed here is in the form of $\Box p \rightarrow Pp$, these formulas are not equivalent, because the consequent ${\sim}Op$ is by no means equivalent to Pp, and that is simply because p, which is not obligatory, does not necessarily have to be permitted, since p may also be prohibited (of course, we disregard here the situation where p is necessary). Thus, in a standard system of deontic logic, the following theorem can be proved: ${\sim}Op \equiv P{\sim}p$, which is far from being absurd, even in the analysed context of an absolute necessity: just as death cannot be obligatory (since *necessitum nulla est obligatio*), but it must be permitted (since "That what is necessary, must be allowed") and from a legal and logical (deontic) point of view, ${\sim}p$ (human immortality) must also be permitted. On the admissibility of such norms, *see* a futuristic note 258 in Chap. 7 at p. 303.

Alexy's transcendental-pragmatic argument deals with the relation that occurs between the rules of making assertions r_a, which are not—according to the non-cognitivist standpoint adopted in this work—propositions (sentences in a logical sense) and, therefore, they cannot be directly substituted in place of propositional variables. However, there is the following possibility for application: if we accept the principle of parallelism of the logic of norms and deontic logic, justifying, inter alia, the isomorphism of reasoning (inferences) performed on the norms and deontic sentences (of descriptive character),[187] then it is relatively easy to show that the discussed implication $\Box r_a \rightarrow Or_a$ is false. Due to legibility, let us present the justification of this assessment in relation to the already used example of the discursive rule of non-contradiction: "No speaker may contradict him or herself". Transforming this principle into a deontic statement, we end up with the following: "It is obligatory that no speaker expresses contradictory statements". This sentence, being a deontic sentence of a descriptive character, is already a proposition (a sentence in the logical sense), and thus, it can constitute the argument p in the formula $\Box p \rightarrow Pp$, which expresses the principle: "What is inevitable, is permitted". Similarly, Alexy's implicit argument $\Box r_a \rightarrow Or_a$ can be generalised to the form: $\Box p \rightarrow Op$. Due to the fact that one of the theorems of the standard system of deontic logic is the implication $Op \rightarrow Pp$ (corresponding to an undoubtedly true statement: "What is obligatory, is permitted"), yet it is no longer the case with the equivalence $Op \equiv Pp$ (corresponding to a manifestly false sentence: "Something is obligatory if, and only if it is permitted"), the principle: "What is inevitable, is permitted" shows a logical falsehood of the thesis $\Box p \rightarrow Op$ and consequently of the thesis $\Box r_t \rightarrow Or_t$. Thus, the necessity implies permission and not obligation. Accordingly, the necessary rules of discourse do not have to be, but only can be valid.

At this point we could actually finish our search for the justification of Alexy's thesis. Nonetheless, it should come as no surprise that some logical systems allow the formulation of still another logical argument, based on the assertion (thesis), both contrary to the principle *necessitum nulla est obligatio* and to the principle: "What is inevitable, is permitted". In many systems of deontic logic based on, and combined with, modal logic (for example, in systems elaborated by Allan Ross Anderson—a precursor of them—or in the systems developed by Zdzisław Ziemba), one can prove the theorem $\Box p \rightarrow Op$,[188] which seems to directly justify

---

[187] The principle of parallelism between logic of norms and deontic logic was adopted, inter alia, by G.H. von Wright, *Norm and Action. A Logical Enquiry*, London 1963, pp. 100ff., 132ff., *cf. idem*, 'Deontic Logic: A Personal View', *RJ* 12 (1999), p. 32. The evidence of isomorphism of these two logical calculus terms can be found *e.g.* in C.E. Alchourrón, 'Logic of Norms and Logic of Normative Propositions', *LA* XII (1969), pp. 264–266. *See* also J. Woleński, 'Logika i normy' [Logic and Norms], *SF* 5 (1976), pp. 51ff. and *Z zagadnień analitycznej filozofii prawa*, *op. cit.*, pp. 66ff.

[188] *See e.g.*, Z. Ziemba, *Analityczna teoria obowiązku*, *op. cit.*, pp. 37, 91ff. It should be noted that this theorem is often rebutted – for example, J. Woleński, 'Treść logiczna dwóch zasad prawnych', *op. cit.*, p. 146, elegantly shows that it cannot be regarded as an axiom of deontic logic. According

the correctness of the implication $\Box r_a \rightarrow Or_a$ (when using the transformation of discourse rules into deontic sentences of a descriptive character—analogically, as in the discussion of the previous argument). Yet, deontic logicians interpret the claim $\Box p \rightarrow Op$ very restrictively, stating that it deals with an absolute rather than with a relative necessity. As pointed out by Ziemba: "Only this is impossible which invalidates laws of logic, semantic postulates of a given language, or laws of nature".[189] Thus, what should be *a contrario* considered as absolutely necessary are only the laws and postulates listed in the quoted passage of Ziemba's *Analytic Theory of Duty*. If we accept such an interpretation of the scope of application of the theorem $\Box p \rightarrow Op$, then it turns out that the accuracy of the analysed implication $\Box r_t \rightarrow Or_t$ can be demonstrated by means of the latter only when the necessity of rules of making assertions is of absolute character in one of the above-indicated meanings. Without a doubt, it is difficult to understand the necessity of discourse rules as a necessity having the nature of natural law (let us recall here that Alexy refers to human nature only in relation to the relative necessity of making assertions) or necessity being the consequence of the laws of logic; therefore, we should examine only the third possibility, according to which the necessity of discourse rules would be a meaning postulate of a certain language. Therefore, it seems that we are facing a very complicated problem, the solution of which should be preceded with a further explanation of what language we are dealing with. However, when we recall the full text of the second premise of the transcendental-pragmatic argument, assuming the form: $\Diamond a \rightarrow (\Box r_a \equiv Or_a)$, it becomes clear that there can be no absolute necessity of discourse rules (in the sense of a meaning postulate) because such a necessity is implicated by the possibility of making

to Woleński, the negation of this theorem, which can be expressed by the formula $\sim O(p \vee \sim p)$, does not lead to a contradiction but to the situation of a total normative indifference ("normative anarchism"), because this formula can be transformed into $Pp \wedge P\sim p$ (namely, everything is permitted, and no prohibition is possible). In the context of further analysis, let us add that from a practical point of view, the theorem $\Box p \rightarrow Op$ is of course unacceptable (and even absurd) for lawyers. After all, no lawyer-practitioner or law dogmatist shall hold that, for example, in any actual legal system the independent source of the law are the laws of nature, laws of logic or meaning postulates, because then they would have to consistently hold that in any system of law there are such valid norms as, for example: "Every man shall die" (based on the law of nature), "Everyone shall take a bribe or not take bribes" (based on the law of logic – the principle of the excluded middle) and "Every single man shall be an unmarried man" (based on the meaning postulate). Therefore, we reject this theorem, which however, as I believe, does not fully exempt us from the scientific obligation to discuss the possibilities of justifying the implication $\Box r_a \rightarrow Or_a$ on this basis. It cannot be thus denied that some deontic logicians do approve this theorem (yet, admittedly, in a rather restrictive interpretation, which shall be discussed later). It should also be added that recognising as valid such norms, whose validity should be justified by the necessity of behaviour (states of affairs) prescribed by them, falsifies a positivist Practical Difference Thesis, because the extra-legal necessity of certain behaviour (states of affairs) excludes that in this respect the law can play any role (motivational or informational) in the structure or content of practical reasoning, influencing the change in human behaviour (I leave aside here the situations, which are difficult to imagine, in which, due to the knowledge of valid legal norms, a man finds that, for example, she/he must die one day).

[189] Z. Ziemba, *Analityczna teoria obowiązku*, *op. cit.*, p. 92.

assertions. What is more, when we recall the overall structure of the transcendental argument,[190] it is evident that this argument is to serve the purpose of, inter alia, justifying the necessity of practical discourse rules. Meanwhile, in my opinion, it cannot be reasonably argued that the meaning postulates of a certain language, usually having the form of stipulative (synthetical) definitions,[191] should be justified by means of transcendental arguments. Even Alexy defends himself not only against the objection of arbitrariness of the necessary discourse rules (defined by him), but also against the objection that his characteristics of speech acts of assertion and his formulating discourse rules that concern the latter have the character of a "definitional trick".[192] Thus, he excludes the possibility of perceiving these rules as meaning postulates expressed by means of arbitrary, stipulative definitions. It should, therefore, be assumed that the assertion $\Box p \rightarrow Op$ does not allow us to justify the correctness of the implication $\Box r_a \rightarrow Or_a$.

To sum up the analysis, we must conclude that the first of the above-discussed arguments of "juristic logic" does not refute the implication $\Box r_a \rightarrow Or_a$. The second argument strongly undermines it (unless we believe that it directly refutes it). Whereas, the third argument certainly does not justify this implication, even if we assume the correctness of the theorem $\Box p \rightarrow Op$, which is hard to accept from the practical (particularly legal) point of view. Thus, despite the efforts that have been undertaken, we have failed to find a justification for Alexy's claim of the "indisputable" validity of the necessary discourse rules that enable making (the speech acts of) assertion.[193]

---

[190] *See supra*, pp. 94–99.

[191] On the arbitrariness of definitions that constitute the meaning postulates of a certain language *see* K. Ajdukiewicz, 'Trzy pojęcia definicji' [Three Concepts of Definition] in *idem*, *Język i poznanie*, Vol. II, Warszawa 1960, pp. 297, 304ff. and 'Zagadnienie uzasadnienia zdań analitycznych' [The Problem of Justifying Analytical Propositions], trans. H. Mortimer, in K. Ajdukiewicz, *ibidem*, pp. 309ff.

[192] *See* R. Alexy, 'A Discourse-Theoretical Conception of Practical Reason', *op. cit.*, p. 241 [German version, p. 21] and 'Diskurstheorie und Menschenrechte', *op. cit.*, pp. 138ff. [English version, pp. 216ff.].

[193] It should be added that from among the critics of the transcendental-pragmatic argument, it is only S. Wesche ('Robert Alexys diskurstheoretische Menschenrechtsbegründung', *op. cit.*, pp. 84–85) who indirectly challenges the validity of the necessary discourse rules, pointing out – in reference to Hart's analyses – the ambiguity of the concept of the rule that can refer both to the norms as well as to habits (non-normative practices), and providing the reasons for which the normativity of the discourse rules developed by Alexy can be objected to. From the standpoint of J. R. Searle's theory of speech acts, Wesche's argumentation can be supplemented by the following observation: among the rules for making successful speech acts, undoubtedly the most important is the essential rule, having the form of a constitutive rule ("X counts as Y"). However, according to Searle (*Speech Acts*, *op. cit.*, p. 41), at least some constitutive rules (and, in my opinion, among them certainly the rules defining the essential conditions for non-institutional speech acts) do not have a normative character, but – to put it very simply – they have primarily creative and definitional functions. Consequently, if they are not norms, we cannot in any way talk of their "validity". For more on the issue of constitutive rules and the problem of their semiotic status, *see* S. Czepita, *Reguły konstytutywne a zagadnienia prawoznawstwa* [Constitutive Rules and the

4.5.3 Conclusion of the Analysis of the Transcendental-Pragmatic Argument

The transcendental-pragmatic argument has been proved to be logically correct. However, its material external justification is very questionable and limited. The first premise of the argument $\Box_{rs}a$ may indeed be regarded as true, but due to the highly relative nature of the necessity of making assertions, its content is rather trivial. The first of the theses contained in the second premise $\Diamond a \rightarrow (\Box r_a \equiv Or_a)$, providing the catalogue of the necessary rules of making assertions, is—quite paradoxically—irrefutable just because it is highly arbitrary; moreover, the possibility of challenging this thesis is excluded due to relativisation included in the formulation of the first premise. The lack of alternatives to the discourse rules provided by Alexy is also relative to the content of the first premise. Yet, the thesis $\Box r_a \equiv Or_a$, implicitly contained in the second premise, even after it is weakened to the form of implication $\Box r_a \rightarrow Or_a$, may be regarded as valid only when we assume that it deals with instrumental (technical) validity of discourse rules, since Alexy's whole argument lacks any particular reasons in favour of adopting their non-instrumental validity. In addition, both these premises are so relatively formulated that it is difficult to speak of a "universal validity" of discourse rules. It therefore comes as no surprise that Alexy presents two additional arguments that serve to justify the universal validity of discourse rules formulated by him.

4.5.4 Additional Elements of the Justification of the Universal Validity of the Rules of Practical Discourse

As previously noted, the complementary components of Alexy's argumentation are: the argument from the maximisation of individual utility (referring to Hobbes' philosophy) and an anthropological thesis concerning human interest in correctness (having its roots in the Aristotelian tradition).[194] Alexy provides these arguments because the transcendental-pragmatic argument justifies only the hypothetical validity of discourse rules in an actual sense, which is dependent on whether, and to what extent human motivations and aspirations that comply with the rules of discourse actually exist. The transcendental-pragmatic argument cannot itself bring about that people will have such motives and aspirations. Hence, the necessity arises of supplementing the transcendental-pragmatic argument with two additional empirical arguments.

Problems of Jurisprudence], Szczecin 1996, in particular, pp. 26ff., 97ff., together with the extensive literature cited therein.

[194] *See* R. Alexy, 'A Discourse-Theoretical Conception of Practical Reason', *op. cit.*, pp. 242–244 [German version, pp. 23–24ff.] and 'Diskurstheorie und Menschenrechte', *op. cit.*, pp. 142–144 [English version, pp. 219–220].

According to the first of the above-mentioned supporting arguments, even the people who are only interested in maximising their own profit (for example, the ruling élite that exploits the members of the subject group), because of their interest to remain in power, should, due to purely strategic reasons, act in such a way as to, by dint of the argumentation (discourse), obtain the legitimacy for their actions. According to Alexy, it is a better way to keep oneself in power, than to use pure violence, which is expensive, and the order thus obtained is unstable and risky for the rulers.[195] The fact that this ruling élite, when arguing, usually uses poor arguments or pure propaganda is—according to Alexy—irrelevant; what is decisive is that it is in some way involved in the discourse. The second complementary argument justifies why joining the discourse is optimal for the ruling élite. It is an empirical anthropological thesis concerning the human pursuit of correctness. Accordingly, one must reckon with the fact that many people (though certainly not all) are really interested in correctness. Thus, their efforts must be taken into account by those who rule. The role of this empirical argument in justifying the universal validity of discourse rules consists primarily in that it allows us to combine the transcendental-pragmatic argument with the argument from the maximisation of individual utility. As a result, according to Alexy, the objective (or institutional—as he also defined it[196]) validity of discourse rules can be proved: they are objectively binding even for those who do not have any subjective motivation or interest in achieving correctness.[197] However, they are binding subjectively only for those people who do have such motivations and interests.

---

[195] Alexy again makes use of the argument, already used in the nonpositivist analytical argumentation (in the evolutionary version of *Unrechtsargument*) – *see* Chap. 3 at p. 39. This argument is, of course, nothing new – Tacitus Publius Cornelius wrote in his *Historiarum* II, paragraph 92, that *nec umquam satis fida potentia, ubi nimia est.*

[196] R. Alexy, 'A Discourse-Theoretical Conception of Practical Reason', *op. cit.*, p. 243 [German version, p. 23] and 'Diskurstheorie und Menschenrechte', *op. cit.*, p. 143 [English version, p. 220]. Equating the objective validity with the institutional one can hardly be surprising at first glance: in Alexy's theory, a rational system of law, understood as a system of a democratic constitutional state, constitutes a necessary institutionalisation of discursive practical reason, whereas according to the procedural four-step model of the legal system (*Vier-Stufen-Modell des Rechtssystems*), the procedure of a general practical discourse is its first component – *see* R. Alexy, 'Die Idee einer prozeduralen Theorie der juristischen Argumentation', *op. cit.*, pp. 184ff., 'Rechtssystem und praktische Vernunft', *op. cit.*, pp. 417ff., 'Idee und Struktur eines vernünftigen Rechtssystems', *op. cit.*, pp. 36ff., 'Ota Weinbergers Kritik der diskurstheoretischen Deutung juristischer Rationalität', *op. cit.*, pp. 152ff., and 'Die juristische Argumentation als rationaler Diskurs', *op. cit.*, pp. 119ff.; *cf.* M. Atienza, 'Entrevista a Robert Alexy', *op. cit.*, p. 685. However, as noted by Alexy in the penultimate of the indicated works (p. 153), the procedure of general practical discourse has a non-institutional character and, thus, the suspicion of an antinomy resulting from an ambiguous concept of institutionalism arises: the discourse rules are institutionally valid because they constitute a component of a legal system, and at the same time, they do not have an institutional nature because they are not positivised in this system.

[197] In connection with such an understanding of the objectivity of discourse rules, it should be noted that it does not entail the objectivity consisting of "coming from the object", "universal validity (acceptability)" or "impartiality" (on this distinction of the basic meanings of objectivity, *see* T. Gizbert-Studnicki, 'Podstawy argumentacji prawniczej', *op. cit.*, pp. 36ff.), but the

Before going on to evaluate the discussed supporting arguments, let us first note that their aim is to transform a hypothetical actually limited validity of discourse rules (which is one of the conclusions of the transcendental-pragmatic argument), into objective, institutional validity (i.e., independent of the actual, subjective and individual aspirations of people), which—though unfortunately Alexy fails to explain this directly—constitutes the universal validity of practical discourse that is sought by him. Yet, these two additional arguments do not seem fully convincing.[198] First, the argument from maximisation of individual utility implies that the ruling élite are interested in long-term maintenance of its privileged status. Nonetheless, it does not seem necessary: unfortunately, as history teaches us, rulers can be just as interested only in quickly plundering and killing their subjects. We often encounter such situations, not only in antiquity and the Middle Ages, but also in times that are more recent. Secondly, in relation to the anthropological thesis on human interest in correctness, Alexy's analysis lacks the consideration as to whether the ruled (subjects) always have such an interest and whether their subjective motivation is sometimes different. Let us take the example of the totalitarian state in which the authority governs by means of terror and its political opponents are deprived of their life and property. In this state, human basic desire, dictated by fear, will be providing the possibility of survival. In this context, we can recall the phenomenon of the "inner emigration" of many people living in totalitarian states, which undeniably recognised correctness as a positive value. Moreover, it is highly disputable whether having achieved such a state of complete subordination of the citizens, the ruling élite will continue to need—in order to maximise its profits—to conduct any dialogue, let alone rational practical discourse with the enslaved subjects. Thirdly, if the objective (universal) validity of discourse rules is to be proved, inter alia, by the fact that the rulers use pure propaganda or bad arguments for the legitimacy of their power, the suggestion arises that it might be better if discourse rules were not objectively (institutionally) valid, because after all, they can be used in a manipulative way to obtain the legitimisation for the rule of tyrants

objectivity which derives from the fact that the categorical discourse rules impose the same obligations on all its participants (objectivity O_1 according to the distinction proposed by R. Caracciolo, 'Moral Realism vs. Legal Positivism', *AS* 4 (2000), pp. 219ff.). If this observation is correct, then the objective validity of discourse rules is justified by the universal nature of discourse rules in their substantive aspect, which has already been mentioned. The latter, nonetheless, raises considerable doubts: the rules that have both a general and common character (taking into account the method of determining their addressee) are "objectively" valid, because due to their generality and common character, each person (the participant of the most general *Lebensform*) is their current addressee. It seems that such an automatic justification for the objective validity of discourse rules, based on their generality and common character, is out of the question; therefore, the objectivity of the validity of discourse rules must be understood differently than has undertaken by Alexy; namely, in relation to the heteronomous (and in this sense non-subjective) character of these rules.

[198] *See e.g.*, P. Gril, 'Alexys Version einer transzendental-pragmatischen Begründung der Diskursregeln im Unterschied zu Habermas', *op. cit.*, pp. 214–215 and *Die Möglichkeit praktischer Erkenntnis aus Sicht der Diskurstheorie*, *op. cit.*, pp. 147–149. In the text, I refer to some critical arguments raised by him.

and despots. Let us mention, in this context, that in the communist Polish People's Republic we also had a Parliament (*Sejm*) which seemingly had the role of the highest legislative authority. It should therefore be considered—taking into account all the pros and cons—that the objective validity of practical discourse rules was not satisfactorily proved by Alexy. We can only agree with the fact that these rules are subjectively (and thus hypothetically) valid only for those participants in the discourse who—for any reason—accept it and decide to participate in the practical discourse regulated by them.[199] The validity of these rules may thus be conceived merely instrumentally: if someone wants to achieve the correct (in Alexy's procedural sense) solution of a practical issue, then she/he should abide by those rules.

4.5.5 *Is the Discursive Rehabilitation of Practical Reason Successful?*

Even such a strong critic of the theory of legal discourse as Eric Hilgendorf, stresses that Alexy's theory actually allows us to critically analyse the problems of discursive ethics, rather than to limit oneself to asking a constantly repeated question: "What exactly does the author have in mind?".[200] This assessment, also shared by other commentators (e.g., Helmut Rüßmann and Ulfrid Neumann[201]), concerns the theory of practical and legal discourse presented by Alexy in his *Theory of Legal Argumentation*.

This positive evaluation, however, must be modified in relation to the argumentation developed by Alexy in favour of the existence of discursive practical reason. The succinctness of extensive excerpts of the analysis presented by him, the serious arbitrariness of many arguments relying on empirical grounds, yet not being justified empirically, but on intellectual grounds, disregarding the historical and cultural aspects that are inextricably connected with empirical arguments (i.e., with the supporting arguments justifying the universal validity of practical discourse rules), methodological eclecticism of the justification itself (transcendentalism plus empiricism), and finally, using at least five different concepts of the validity of practical discourse rules (universal, ideal, real, objective, namely institutional and subjective validity) without a full explanation of the conceptual relations between them mean that the interpreter often has to guess what the author of the conception at issue has in mind. It is therefore not surprising that Alexy's attempt at the discursive rehabilitation of practical reason encountered a decidedly critical attitude

[199] The first critic who drew attention to it was H. Rüßmann – *see* his review of R. Alexy's book: *Theorie der juristischen Argumentation*, *RT* 10 (1979), pp. 112–113. The list of the critics of Alexy's discourse theory who adopted the same position is too long to present it here.

[200] E. Hilgendorf, *Argumentation in der Jurisprudenz*, *op. cit.*, p. 128.

[201] H. Rüßmann, *ibidem*, p. 120 *in fine*; U. Neumann, *Juristische Argumentationslehre*, *op. cit.*, p. 95.

in jurisprudential literature, both in German-speaking (except the already mentioned Ota Weinberger, Armin Engländer, Peter Gril, Eric Hilgendorf and Steffen Wesche, also Arthur Kaufmann can be listed among fierce critics of the discursive-theoretical conception of practical reason based on the theory of practical discourse[202]) and international texts (due to their representativeness, it is primarily worth mentioning here the critical works of Manuel Atienza, Jerónimo Betegón, Alfonso García Figueroa, Enrique Haba and James Herget, as well as somewhat less critical papers by Tomasz Gizbert-Studnicki, Kaarlo Tuori, Georg Henrik von Wright and Aulis Aarnio[203]). These critics unanimously emphasise that Alexy's conception (or more specifically, German discursive ethics) can be, at best, treated as a way of understanding the correctness (or acceptability) of practical propositions and evaluations in Western European civilization in the late twentieth century.[204] It is difficult to argue with such an assessment, since the analyses carried out above also lead to the conclusion that Alexy failed to justify the universal (in the proper sense of the word) validity of the rules of practical discourse. As I have tried to demonstrate, these rules apply (though only in an instrumental sense) only to those who decide to join the practical rational discourse, so that their validity depends on a subjective volitional element. These rules can neither be regarded as universal in temporal terms, because, even when taking into account historically changing canons for justifying theoretical and practical statements (in particular, norms and normative propositions, which are contained in judicial decisions and their justifications), we cannot assume that the claim to justifiability—characteristic for the speech act of assertion—meant (and, looking ahead, will mean) the same: always and everywhere.[205] Moreover, as Alexy admits in the *Preface* to a collection of essays *Recht*, *Vernunft*, *Diskurs* of 1995,[206] his theoretical conceptions can be understood as an expression of analytical liberalism, which further supports their non-universal character in a methodological–ideological aspect. It is not necessary,

---

[202] *See* A. Kaufmann, *Rechtsphilosophie in der Nach-Neuzeit*, *op. cit.*, pp. 46ff.

[203] *See* M. Atienza, *Las Razones del Derecho*, *op. cit.*, pp. 216ff.; J. Betegón, 'Sobre la pretendida corrección de la pretensión de corrección', *op. cit.*, in particular, pp. 179ff.; A. García Figueroa, *Principios y positivismo jurídico*, *op. cit.*, in particular, pp. 343ff.; E.P. Haba, 'Teorización constructivista como "forma de vida" (Sobre "reglas y formas" del discurso jurídico en los tribunales inexistentes)', *DOXA* 21/I (1998), pp. 147–170; J.E. Herget, *Contemporary German Legal Philosophy*, *op. cit.*, pp. 53ff.; T. Gizbert-Studnicki, 'Podstawy argumentacji prawniczej', *op. cit.*, in particular, pp. 42–43; K. Tuori, 'Discourse Ethics and the Legitimacy of Law', *RJ* 2 (1989), pp. 125–143; G.H. von Wright, A. Aarnio, 'On Law and Morality. A Dialogue', *RJ* 3 (1990), in particular, pp. 324 and 330. A synthetic description of the debate concerning Alexy's conception can be found in R. Vigo, 'Balance de la teoría jurídica discursiva de Robert Alexy', *DOXA* 26 (2003), pp. 203–224.

[204] C. Braun was the first critic who pointed out the culturally relative character of Alexy's discourse theory – *see idem*, 'Diskurstheoretische Normenbegründung in der Rechtswissenschaft', *op. cit.*, p. 254.

[205] This argument was introduced by A. Engländer, 'Zur begrifflichen Möglichkeit des Rechtspositivismus', *op. cit.*, p. 452.

[206] R. Alexy, 'Vorwort' to *Recht, Vernunft, Diskurs*, *op. cit.*, p. 10.

but only possible (and, for followers of this method of practising philosophy and this ideology—also desirable) to apply the analytical method in combination with the liberal ideas of autonomy and universality.

Alexy's conception of practical reason (practical rationality) does not refute Weinberger's non-cognitivist allegations, which have already been mentioned.[207] As I believe, the fundamental problem, insoluble from a non-empirical perspective, is that Alexy's discourse theory (which he himself explicitly admits) implies that the discourse participants are generally able to distinguish between good and bad reasons; that is, they have the ability to judge in the practical sphere.[208] Even if, contrary to Weinberger, we suppose that this assumption is true (although life experience speaks rather for its limited scope, because it is difficult to regard it as referring to all human beings[209]), and that practical discourse rules were properly defined by Alexy, procedural correctness of the opinions or decisions arrived at through practical discourse cannot satisfy Weinberger. The reason is obvious—people must want to use their competence to distinguish good from evil, because it is only then that the result of discourse can raise claims to correctness exceeding the formal and procedural dimension, and it is this very correctness that Weinberger has in mind. The analysis of the empirical elements of justifying the universal validity of practical discourse rules showed that this willingness ultimately depends on the (not always) free will of the discourse participants, whereas the mere fact of taking part in it may also be dictated (as in the case of the ruling élite) by purely strategic reasons; for example, the desire to manipulate the subjects in order to convince them of the legitimacy of the power exercised by the élite. Accordingly, we come to the conclusion that the partial reinforcement of the conception of practical reason based on empirical premises leads to the rebuttal of Alexy's moderately cognitivist metaethical standpoint due to the counterarguments also having an empirical character.

On the other hand, we must appreciate Alexy's effort to construct a comprehensive practical discourse theory. If his conception proved to be fully justified, the supporters of non-cognitivism, let alone the lawmakers or judges, would be grateful to him for that. Achieving certain practical knowledge is the eternal goal of moral philosophy, which cannot be denied even by the most extreme non-cognitivists, despite the fact that according to them it is impossible for humans to reach for this. Many people, not only judges and scientists, strive to have certain knowledge about

---

207 *Cf. supra*, pp. 84–86.

208 In Alexy's view, this assumption is the "missing link" between discourse rules and the correctness of its results, but it should not be interpreted as a requirement of procedural discourse theory – *see idem*, 'Probleme der Diskurstheorie', *op. cit.*, p. 89 and 'A Discourse-Theoretical Conception of Practical Reason', *op. cit.*, pp. 236–237 [German version, pp. 16–17]. For more on the consequences of this assumption, connected with the possibility of monologic 'discourses', *see* P. Gril, *Die Möglichkeit praktischer Erkenntnis aus Sicht der Diskurstheorie*, *op. cit.*, pp. 151–153. We shall come back to this problem – which is only pointed out here – in Chap. 9 at pp. 465ff.

209 For more on this *see* M. Atienza, *Las Razones del Derecho*, *op. cit.*, pp. 208–209, who indicates the empirical falsity of this assumption.

what is good (right) and what is wrong (unjust). Unfortunately, Alexy's theory does not allow us to achieve certainty in terms of practical judgments. Perhaps these conclusions are somewhat exaggerated in relation to his conception of practical reason, since, as already shown above, he relatively perceives the correctness of normative propositions and norms, repeatedly stressing the non-finality of the outcomes of practical rational discourse. I wish I was wrong, but it seems that even a relative correctness of norms and practical judgments cannot be granted by Alexy's discursive-theoretical conception of practical reason (practical rationality).

4.6 Is the Nonpositivist Conception of Law Truly Nonpositivist?

We have already tried to demonstrate the fallacy of classifying Dreier's and Alexy's nonpositivist conception as another natural law doctrine.[210] Now we shall analyse the opposite allegation, which can be indeed considered as an additional argument for the rejection of natural law characteristics of the conception at hand. This allegation, formulated primarily in relation to Alexy's nonpositivist conception, reflects its insufficiently antipositivist or even crypto-positivist character.

4.6.1 Arguments Justifying Suspicions of Crypto-Positivism

In order to show the possibility of justifying the objection of crypto-positivism, let us start our discussion by reporting some of the objections raised in the jurisprudential literature in relation to the discursive theory of legal argumentation developed by Alexy. Ernst Tugendhat, when analysing the theory of general practical discourse and juristic discourse, presented by Alexy in *Theorie der juristischen Argumentation*, points out that while the first one is purely normative, his theory of juristic discourse is based on a descriptive analysis of the forms of argumentation used in this discourse, on legal canons of interpretation and on a reinforced understanding of legal dogmatics.[211] In Alexy's theory, those elements, characteristic for juristic discourse, constitute the institutional limit of the requirements of practical rationality, expressed by means of rules and forms of general practical discourse. Tugendhat holds that one could expect more from Alexy's discursive theory; namely, that on the basis of the concept of rational practical discourse, he

[210] *Cf.* Chap. 2, pp. 15ff.

[211] *See* E. Tugendhat, 'Zur Entwicklung von moralischen Begründungsstrukturen in modernem Recht', *ARSP* Bh. 14 (1980), p. 4. Approvingly – U. Neumann notes that Alexy, in his theory of legal discourse, surprisingly uncritically (*kritiklos*) and willingly (*bereitwillig*) accepts commonly used canons of legal interpretation, borrowed from the traditional *juristische Methodenlehre* – *see* his review of R. Alexy's book: *Theorie der juristischen Argumentation, op. cit.*, pp. 213–214 and *Juristische Argumentationslehre, op. cit.*, p. 89.

will try to determine normatively the most rational form of institutionalisation of this discourse in its special case, which is the legal discourse. Meanwhile, Alexy did not do that, which probably leads to an unintended conclusion that our world is the "best of all conceivable legal worlds" (*die beste aller denkbaren juristischen Welten*).[212] The theory of argumentation developed by the scholar from Kiel is similarly assessed by David Richards.[213] He notes that Alexy adopted a positivist canon of sources of law and his understanding of his own theory is not sufficiently antipositivist. In particular, Alexy's discursive theory contains a too strict division between the general practical discourse and legal materials used in juristic discourse, which—according to Richards—constitute a kind of "unreasonable residue of the spirit of German legal positivism".[214] Following in his criticism along the same line as Tugendhat, the American philosopher also shows the schematic and insufficiently nuanced way in which Alexy applied the conception of general practical discourse (discourse ethics) in the sphere of legal reasoning. When summing up both the criticisms, it can be concluded that in Alexy's theory, legal discourse is a too specific and too independent (autonomous) case of general practical discourse.

While the above objections did not yet directly concern Alexy's nonpositivist conception of law, but only certain elements of its justification, the objections raised by Alfonso García Figueroa already refer to it directly.[215] The Spanish author argues that what can be observed in Alexy's conception are some elements of "latent positivism" (*positivismo latente*). This assumption is justified by several arguments. First, García Figueroa notes that Alexy's conception—deprived of its basic element, namely the claim to correctness,[216] which is the indispensable basis of justifying both the argument from un-law (injustice) as well as the argument from principles—loses its nonpositivist character, and thus "becomes" a positivist conception. Secondly, he draws attention to the fact that Alexy recognises the correctness of the positivist conception of law from the perspective of the observer[217]; that is, from the typical research perspective of legal positivism. Thirdly, according to the philosopher of Toledo, the characteristic feature of Alexy's conception is that he refers to many of the fundamental theses of nonpositivist argumentation as "weak" ones. In this context, he indicates Alexy's moderately cognitivist metaethical standpoint based on a weak version of the

---

[212] E. Tugendhat, *ibidem*.

[213] *See* D.A. Richards' review of R. Alexy's book: *A Theory of Legal Argumentation*, *RJ* 2 (1989), pp. 304–317, in particular, pp. 306, 313 and 316.

[214] *Ibidem*, p. 313.

[215] *See* A. García Figueroa, *Principios y positivismo jurídico*, *op. cit.*, pp. 327ff., in particular, pp. 329–330, 363, 368–370, 397–398 and 'La tesis del caso especial y el positivismo jurídico', *op. cit.*, pp. 207ff.

[216] Anticipating the results of the analyses presented in the next section, it should be added that it is indeed the case, because the claim to correctness (and, consequently the argument from correctness based on the latter) was not satisfactorily justified by Alexy.

[217] *Cf.* Chap. 3, pp. 38 and 53.

transcendental-pragmatic argument, on a weak thesis about the connection of law and morality (*schwache Verbindungsthese*) and on a weak version of the one right answer thesis.[218] The occurrence of positivist elements in Alexy's conception is due the fact that he tries eclectically to combine two traditions, which are very difficult to reconcile; namely, German legal positivism with German antipositivism. It can, therefore, be concluded that Alexy tries to justify the correctness of his nonpositivist conception of law by means of a series of theses and specific arguments, whose "weak" nature is to facilitate their acceptance by the law philosophers who represent positivist positions as well as by practising lawyers who, as a rule, also lean towards a positivist understanding of law.

These attempts to justify the objection of insufficiently antipositivist, and even—at least in some passages—quite a positivist character of a nonpositivist conception of law can still be supplemented with the argument related to the resolution of the problem of legal certainty, as proposed in Dreier's and Alexy's conception. The authors take a unanimous position, which undermines the positivist thesis of judicial discretion, arguing that, also in this sphere, the judges—in line with the argument from principles, and in particular *Optimierungsthese*—are legally obliged to apply the procedure of balancing the principles and the formulation of a legal decision that corresponds to the results of applying this procedure.[219] In particular, in many of his several older as well as latest works, Alexy has tried to develop a catalogue of strict rules of weighing principles, which helps to achieve unambiguous results in applying this procedure, similar to the certainty of the results of subsumption of the legal rules.[220] Undoubtedly, one of the consequences of the nonpositivist argument from principles is to achieve at least some degree of legal certainty in the sphere in which legal positivists explicitly exclude certainty of law.[221] Nonpositivism, with its moderate moral cognitivism, tries to accomplish the

---

218 These "weak" elements of Alexy's conception have already been presented or they will soon be presented – *see supra*, pp. 86ff. (moderate cognitivism), *supra*, pp. 100ff. ("weak" version of the transcendental-pragmatic argument), Chap. 3 at pp. 47ff. and *infra*, pp. 162ff. (*schwache Verbindungsthese*). The "weakened" version of Dworkin's conception of one right answer – as adopted by Alexy – shall be referred to in the next paragraph of this section, at p. 120.

219 *See* Chap. 3, pp. 33–34, 43. For more on *Optimierungsthese see* R. Alexy, 'Zur Struktur der Rechtsprinzipien', *op. cit.*, pp. 32ff. [English version, pp. 295ff.].

220 Besides Alexy's paper, indicated in the previous note, *see* also R. Alexy, 'Zum Begriff des Rechtsprinzips', *op. cit.*, in particular, pp. 75ff., 'Rechtsregeln und Rechtsprinzipien', *op. cit.*, in particular, pp. 21ff., *Theorie der Grundrechte*, *op. cit.*, pp. 79ff. [English version, pp. 44ff.], 'Grundrechte, Abwägung und Rationalität', *AI* 7 (2002), pp. 113–125 [English version: 'Constitutional Rights, Balancing, and Rationality', *RJ* 16 (2003), pp. 131–140], and 'On Balancing and Subsumption. A Structural Comparison', *RJ* 16 (2003), pp. 433–449. It is worth noting that in the last of these papers, Alexy presents a formal scheme of balancing in the form of a *Weight Formula*, based on arithmetic rules which – apart from the nonorthodoxy of connecting a moderate cognitivism with arithmetics – triggers some associations with purely positivistic ideas of mechanical jurisprudence.

221 *See e.g.*, H.L.A. Hart, 'El nuevo desafío al positivismo jurídico', *op. cit.*, p. 11 and the last paragraph of his 'Postscript', P.A. Bulloch, J. Raz (eds.), in *idem*, *The Concept of Law*, 2nd ed, Oxford 1994, p. 276. According to Hart, Dworkin's objection against a positivist understanding of

task that non-cognitivist and axiologically relativistic legal positivism is unable to perform. Yet, it should be stressed that the nonpositivist legal certainty is not final, because Alexy, in contrast to Dworkin, does not accept the thesis about the existence of the one right answer, but only the thesis of the existence of at least one right practical solution,[222] which is a direct result of him assuming a relative understanding of practical correctness and the non-definitive character of the normative solutions arrived at through general practical discourse.[223]

To sum up, the positivistic element, which can be identified within German nonpositivism, can be described as follows. The solution to the problem of legal certainty proposed by nonpositivists is indeed contrary at least to some components of the positivist position on judicial discretion, but it is in full compliance with the positivist axiology. Legal certainty is unquestionably one of the core values approved by legal positivism. It should be further noted that the representatives of legal positivism by no means give up the completion of the postulate of legal certainty because they exclude the aspiration of law to pursue the idea of justice,[224] but only because of their views (based on the non-cognitivist position adopted by them on axiological relativism that follows from the latter) on the impossibility of an objective and fully conclusive resolution of moral problems.[225] Let us also add that the nonpositivist proposal, founded on the acceptance of the non-relativist position of moderate cognitivism, allows the realisation of one more value, usually associated with legal positivism; namely, the increase of the citizens' feeling of legal security. Under the nonpositivist conception, the citizen (or broadly speaking:

---

judicial discretion, concerning the injustice of retrospective lawmaking by a judge in a situation of judicial discretion (i.e., in hard cases), is entirely irrelevant, because in such situations legal regulation is incomplete, and therefore there can be no legitimate expectations of any individuals to determine legal consequences of their actions under the law, whose content is determined at the time of undertaking these actions.

[222] *See* R. Alexy, 'Die Idee einer prozeduralen Theorie der juristischen Argumentation', *op. cit.*, p. 183 and 'Probleme der Diskurstheorie', *op. cit.*, pp. 90–91. Let us note that even this thesis – though moderate and fully consistent with the positivist position – has been subject to criticism by M. Atienza, who accuses Alexy of disregarding the so-called tragic cases (*casos trágicos*), in which – roughly speaking – there is no morally correct solution of a case, that does not at the same time violate the law in force – *see idem*, *Las Razones del Derecho*, *op. cit.*, p. 232. Atienza presents his conception of "tragic cases" in the most complete way in 'Los límites de la interpretación constitucional. De nuevo sobre los casos trágicos', *IS* 6 (1997), pp. 7–30.

[223] *Cf. supra*, p. 88.

[224] This idea has been most distinctly expressed by H. Kelsen, 'Was ist juristischer Positivismus?', *op. cit.*, p. 468: "Die Trennung des Rechts von der Moral bedeutet natürlich nicht – wie vielfach mißverstanden wird – die Ablehnung der Forderung, daß das Recht der Moral und insbesondere der Moralnorm der *Gerechtigkeit* entsprechen, daß das Recht gerecht sein soll". An almost identical standpoint has been expressed by N. Hoerster, 'Zur Verteidigung der rechtspositivistischen Trennungsthese', *op. cit.*, p. 28.

[225] It is a metaethical standpoint characteristic of legal positivism – *see e.g.*, H. Kelsen, *ibidem* and 'Law and Morality', trans. P. Heath, in H. Kelsen, *Essays in Legal and Moral Philosophy*, O. Weinberger (ed.), Dordrecht/Boston 1973, pp. 87ff.; *cf.* H.L.A. Hart, 'Positivism and the Separation of Law and Morals', *op. cit.*, pp. 624ff.

the addressees of legal norms) who knows that in cases of an indeterminacy of the law (which can be caused, for example, by the open texture of legal rules, defeasibility of legal reasoning or the existence of real gaps in the system of positive law) her/his behaviour will be judged according to the standards of correct morality and so can be more confident of her/his legal situation. The addressee of legal norms can act in compliance with the maxim: "Obey the law, and when it is silent, or if you have doubts as to its proper interpretation, act in a way which is morally right". Naturally, such can also be the reasoning of a person who comprehends law under a positivist conception, yet there is indeed a significant difference here: German nonpositivism explicitly assumes the possibility of legal control of substantively moral judicial reasoning, lying in the sphere of judicial discretion, and it tries to develop methods of such reasoning in the form of a catalogue (formulas) of rules of weighing principles.[226] It is indeed, inter alia, for that reason—which was strongly emphasised by Dreier[227]—that the nonpositivist conception of law, with its theory of principles, is much better suited to describing and criticising the legal reality (the phenomena in the sphere of law) than is legal positivism.

4.6.2 Identification of the Opponent: *Trennungsthese*

Let us now consider the objection of crypto-positivism supported by critical arguments that have been put forward. The question, which we seek to answer, is as follows: Is not the nonpositivist conception of law, in its essence, another "softened" version of legal positivism? In order to answer this question that is seemingly paradoxically and inherently contradictory, let us first deal with the manner in which Dreier and Alexy identify the conception of legal positivism—which is competitive vis-à-vis nonpositivism. This is a crucial issue, since the objections raised in the critical literature concerned, inter alia, the insufficient clarification (identification) of the version of legal positivism that the nonpositivist conception of law tries to rebut. What is more, there were even a few attempts to demonstrate that some, although very few, versions of the positivist doctrine are by

[226] It should be added that Alexy, besides his efforts to limit judicial discretion by means of the *Weight Formula*, also examines the broader question of "discretionary errors" – *see idem*, 'Ermessensfehler' in R. Alexy, H.-J. Koch, L. Kuhlen, H. Rüßmann, *Elemente einer juristischen Begründungslehre*, *op. cit.*, pp. 251–286.

[227] R. Dreier, 'Neues Naturrecht oder Rechtspositivismus?', *op. cit.*, pp. 382ff. For more on the completeness of the nonpositivist conception of law, presenting a vision of law taking into account not only its idea of justice, but also the value of certainty of law, *see* S. Bertea, 'How Nonpositivism Can Accommodate Legal Certainty' in G. Pavlakos (ed.), *Law, Rights and Discourse*, *op. cit.*, pp. 69–82.

no means violated by the nonpositivist conception of law (in particular, in terms of the consequences of basing it on "Radbruch's formula") in relation to the problem of statutory unlawfulness; namely, extremely unjust law.[228]

Let us begin by recalling that both Dreier and Alexy identify their positivist opponent mainly by attributing to it the thesis of the lack of any necessary connection between law and morality; that is, the Separation Thesis (*Trennungsthese*).[229] Primarily because of the possible ways of its justification, the creators of the nonpositivist conception of law allow three interpretations of the positivist thesis of separation of law and morality and its negation—the nonpositivist thesis of necessary connection between law and morality (*Verbindungsthese*)—namely, an analytical, normative and empirical interpretation.[230] Therefore, in formulating different versions of the nonpositivist *Verbindungsthese*, they distinguish the analytically (conceptually), normatively or empirically necessary connection between law and morality.[231] Both Alexy (directly) and Dreier (indirectly) assume that the positivist *Trennungsthese* and nonpositivist *Verbindungsthese* determine how the concept of law should be defined.[232] The first of the theses excludes the possibility that this definition includes any moral elements, whereas the second thesis postulates the necessary presence of such elements.

However, the creators of the nonpositivist conception of law are of a different opinion regarding several important points relating to the understanding of both theses. Firstly, Dreier, influenced by Hoerster's criticism on determining the epistemological status of Kelsen's and Hart's positivist definitions of law,[233] attributes, both to the positivist Separation Thesis and to the nonpositivist Connection Thesis, the epistemological status of "definitional proposal" (*Definitionvorschlag*) or of

---

[228] *See e.g.*, W. Krawietz, bibliographic note on R. Alexy's book: *Begriff und Geltung des Rechts*, *RT* 24 (1993), pp. 249–250 and W. Ott, *Der Rechtspositivismus*, *op. cit.*, pp. 190ff.

[229] *See* R. Dreier, 'Der Begriff des Rechts', *op. cit.*, pp. 890ff. and 'Some Remarks on the Concept of Law', *op. cit.*, p. 113; R. Alexy, 'On Necessary Relations between Law and Morality', *op. cit.*, pp. 167ff., 'Zur Kritik des Rechtspositivismus', *op. cit.*, pp. 9ff., *Begriff und Geltung des Rechts*, *op. cit.*, pp. 15ff., 39ff. [English version, pp. 3ff., 20ff.], and 'The Nature of Arguments about the Nature of Law', *op. cit.*, pp. 9–10.

[230] *See* R. Dreier, 'Zur gegenwärtigen Diskussion des Verhältnisses von Recht und Moral in der Bundesrepublik Deutschland', *op. cit.*, p. 57. *Cf.* R. Dreier, 'Recht und Moral', *op. cit.*, pp. 180ff. and R. Alexy, *Begriff und Geltung des Rechts*, *op. cit.*, pp. 40ff. [English version, pp. 20ff.].

[231] R. Alexy, *ibidem*, p. 44 [English version, p. 23]; *see* also R. Dreier, 'Zur gegenwärtigen Diskussion des Verhältnisses von Recht und Moral in der Bundesrepublik Deutschland', *op. cit.*, pp. 57ff. Let us once more recall that Alexy, as opposed to Dreier, does not present an independent empirical argumentation.

[232] *See e.g.*, R. Dreier, *ibidem*, p. 57; R. Alexy, 'On Necessary Relations between Law and Morality', *op. cit.*, p. 168 and 'Zur Kritik des Rechtspositivismus', *op. cit.*, pp. 9–10.

[233] *See* N. Hoerster, 'Zur Verteidigung des Rechtspositivismus', *op. cit.*, pp. 2480ff., 'Die rechtsphilosophische Lehre vom Rechtsbegriff', *op. cit.*, pp. 187–188 and 'Zur Verteidigung der rechtspositivistischen Trennungsthese', *op. cit.*, p. 27. Hoerster's criticism concerns Dreier's analyses from 'Der Begriff des Rechts', *op. cit.*, p. 894.

"normative stipulation" (*normative Festsetzung*) dictated by purposeful considerations.[234] Alexy, on the other hand, opposes Hoerster's criticism because the position of the philosopher of Mainz on the status of both theses assumes that the connection between law and morality is neither impossible, nor conceptually necessary. Alexy approves the first assumption, but obviously rejects the second one (admittedly, to a methodologically limited extent), since in his view, from the perspective of a participant, conceptually, as well as normatively there is a necessary connection between law and morality.[235] Secondly, Alexy acknowledges that by means of the terms *Trennungsthese* or Separation Thesis one may determine not only the thesis concerning the proposed way of defining law, but also the main analytical argument in favour of such a thesis, proclaiming a lack of conceptually necessary connection between law and morality, or between the law as it is and the law as it should be.[236] Undoubtedly, Alexy rightly distinguishes these two ways of understanding; however, there are no legitimate reasons why the one adopted by him should be considered as a more appropriate understanding of the Separation Thesis, and, furthermore, despite the undeniable conceptual indeterminacy of the concept of *Trennungsthese* in the literature, it is difficult to accept Alexy's fully conscious consent to such an ambiguity.

However, let us leave these minor objections aside and move on to the next issue that requires consideration. The point here is whether identifying (defininig) legal positivism by means of attributing to it the thesis of the lack of the necessary connection between law and morality is correct and whether Alexy is right when he holds that the only common element of many versions of legal positivism is *Trennungsthese*.[237]

It is a truism, and perhaps even a cliché, to argue that legal positivism, due to the enormous number and diversity of the conceptions of law created in its frames, is

[234] *See* R. Dreier, 'Zur gegenwärtigen Diskussion des Verhältnisses von Recht und Moral in der Bundesrepublik Deutschland', *op. cit.*, p. 57 and note 5.

[235] R. Alexy, *Begriff und Geltung des Rechts*, *op. cit.*, pp. 42–44 [English version, pp. 22–23]. *Cf. idem*, 'On Necessary Relations between Law and Morality', *op. cit.*, p. 169 and 'Zur Kritik des Rechtspositivismus', *op. cit.*, p. 11.

[236] R. Alexy, 'On Necessary Relations between Law and Morality', *op. cit.*, p. 169 and 'Zur Kritik des Rechtspositivismus', *op. cit.*, p. 11. Alexy herein criticises Hoerster, who – in his opinion – does not distinguish between these two meanings. On the issue of this minor polemic, *see* M.P. Förster, 'Auseinandersetzung zwischen Norbert Hoerster und Joachim Hruschka', *op. cit.*, p. 532. Incidentally, Hoerster, in turn, in his later work 'Richtigstellung über den Rechtspositivismus', *op. cit.*, p. 416, determines the thesis of basically identical content as the one which Alexy referred to as *Trennungsthese*, calling it *Neutralitätsthese*. It is as follows: "Der Begriff des Rechts ist inhantlich neutral zu definieren".

[237] R. Alexy, *Begriff und Geltung des Rechts*, *op. cit.*, p. 39 [English version, p. 20]. Nonetheless, it is worth adding that in his later work, 'The Nature of Arguments about the Nature of Law', *op. cit.*, p. 10, Alexy slightly weakened the uncompromising character of this assertion, holding that the Separability Thesis, being a necessary premise of legal positivism, constitutes an element of its nature, but it is by no means exhaustive. On the criticism of Alexy's position, *see* J. Raz, 'The Argument from Justice, or How Not to Reply to Legal Positivism' in G. Pavlakos (ed.), *Law, Rights and Discourse*, *op. cit.*, pp. 18ff. and Alexy's response, 'An Answer to Joseph Raz', *op. cit.*, pp. 38ff.

very difficult to define.[238] Consequently, many philosophers and theorists of law treat legal positivism as a family notion,[239] whereas among the researchers who take up this complex issue it is far more popular to identify legal positivism (referring to the method used for the first time by H.L.A. Hart in his famous lecture at Harvard University in 1957[240]), consisting of reconstructing the fundamental theses (views, statements) that convey its essence. Even after a very rough review of the vast literature on the subject, we can easily see that the basic theses of legal positivism, adopted by individual researchers, differ as to the quantity, content and order of presentation.[241] However, it is impossible to deny that in most cases, the thesis of the separation of law and morality (formulated in various ways, more or less referring to the famous dictum of John Austin: "The existence of law is one

[238] A very fair presentation of several versions of legal positivism, which, unfortunately, do not include the last decades of the development of this doctrine, can be found in the monograph of W. Ott, *Der Rechtspositivismus*, *op. cit. See* also *idem*, 'Was heißt "Rechtspositivismus"?' in D. Mayer-Maly, P.M. Simons (eds.), *Das Naturrechtsdenken heute und morgen*, *op. cit.*, pp. 413–425. As regards the possible definitions of legal positivism from an analytical perspective, *see* A. Aarnio, 'The Form and Content of Law. Aspects of Legal Positivism', *AIC* XIII (1980), pp. 21ff.

[239] *See e.g.*, A. Aarnio, *ibidem*, pp. 17ff.; O. Weinberger, 'Beyond Positivism and Natural Law', *op. cit.*, pp. 115ff.; G.H. von Wright, 'Is and Ought' in E. Bulygin *et al.* (eds.), *Man, Law and Modern Forms of Life*, Dordrecht 1985, p. 277 (with the reference to Aarnio's work).

[240] H.L.A. Hart, 'Positivism and the Separation of Law and Morals', *op. cit.*, note 25 at pp. 601–602. This characterises the "meanings" of legal positivism, in the form of five positivist theses, and is also presented by him (with minimal changes) in the notes to *The Concept of Law*, *op. cit.*, pp. 253–254. It should be noted that Hart characterises his own positivist theory by means of three theses: the thesis of the conceptual separation of law and morality, the thesis of the social sources of law and the thesis of judicial discretion – *see idem*, 'El nuevo desafío al positivismo jurídico', *op. cit.*, pp. 4ff.

[241] These differences cannot be naturally discussed here in detail, yet as an example, let us indicate some works, noting at least the number of the basic theses of legal positivism directly attributed to it. Two theses are adopted by: A. Ross, 'Validity and the Conflict between Legal Positivism and Natural Law', *RJBA* IV (1961), pp. 50ff.; N. MacCormick, 'Law, Morality and Positivism', *op. cit.*, pp. 128ff.; T. Pietrzykowski, '"Miękki" pozytywizm i spór o regułę uznania' ["Soft" Positivism and Controversy over the Rule of Recognition], *SFP* 1 (2001), pp. 99ff.; P.E. Navarro, 'Tensiones conceptuales en el positivismo jurídico', *DOXA* 24 (2001), pp. 136ff.; M. Atienza, 'Is Legal Positivism a Sustainable Legal Theory?' in T. Gizbert-Studnicki, J. Stelmach (eds.), *Law and Legal Cultures in the 21st Century. Diversity and Unity*, Warszawa 2007, p. 240. Three theses, apart from Hart's – mentioned in the previous note – are adopted by: R. Dworkin, *Taking Rights Seriously*, *op. cit.*, pp. 17ff.; J. Raz, 'Legal Positivism and the Sources of Law' in *idem*, *The Authority of Law*, *op. cit.*, pp. 37ff.; G.H. von Wright, 'Is and Ought', *op. cit.*, pp. 277ff.; A. Engländer, 'Grundzüge des modernen Rechtspositivismus', *Jura* 22/3 (2000), pp. 113ff.; L. L. Hierro, '¿Por qué ser positivista?', *DOXA* 25 (2002), pp. 278ff.; K.E. Himma, 'Inclusive Legal Positivism', *op. cit.*, pp. 125ff. Four theses are adopted by L. Morawski, 'Hard Positivism, Soft Positivism and Dead Positivism', *op. cit.*, pp. 160ff. Five theses are adopted by: L.L. Fuller, *The Morality of Law*, 2nd ed., New Haven/London 1969, pp. 191ff. and N. Hoerster, 'Einleitung' in *idem* (ed.), *Recht und Moral*, Stuttgart 2002, p. 12. In turn, six theses of positivism are provided by L.M. Sánchez Fernández, 'Ironías, falacias, perversiones, enigmas: sobre el positivismo y la tesis de la separación', *DOXA* 25 (2002), pp. 342ff. and seven by: J.M. Broekmann, 'The Minimum Content of Positivism. Positivism in the Law and in Legal Theory', *RT* 16 (1985), pp. 350ff. and J. Stelmach, B. Brożek, *Methods of Legal Reasoning*, Dordrecht 2006, p. 8.

thing, its merit or demerit is another"[242]) takes a prominent place.[243] Therefore, the way of identifying a positivist opponent—as adopted by Dreier and Alexy—is probably acceptable, although the fact that Alexy recognises the Separation Thesis as the only element common to the positivist understanding of law is questionable, not least because of the number of core theses attributed to legal positivism in jurisprudential literature.[244]

In my opinion, the previous considerations lead to the conclusion that in order to conduct a more detailed comparative analysis of nonpositivism and positivism, allowing us to resolve the issue of the correctness of the crypto-positivism objection, it will be most appropriate to choose a particular version of legal positivism. Indeed, it seems pointless to analyse this objection based on some multipartite *quasi*-definition of legal positivism, the indisputability of which will probably never be achieved—even if we assume that the above-mentioned authors, who treat legal positivism as a family notion, are wrong because an adequate purely descriptive (analytical) definition of positivism is possible.

We can indicate many good reasons in favour of choosing Hart's positivist theory as a benchmark that allows us to confirm or refute the objection concerning the crypto-positivist character of the nonpositivist conception of law. Firstly, Hart's sophisticated legal positivism can certainly be regarded as the prototype of soft (inclusive) legal positivism, which will allow us to take into consideration the version of legal positivism that has undoubtedly experienced the greatest development in recent years. Secondly, due to the subject matter of this book—the juristic concept of legal validity—it would be essential to refer to the concept of the rule of recognition, also introduced by Hart. Thirdly, the authors of the nonpositivist conception of law, when analysing legal positivism, which is competitive to the nonpositivist conception of law, directly alluded to the opinions of the author of *The Concept of Law*,[245] so the comparison of certain elements of these two theories seems most natural and justifiable. Fourthly, Hart's concept of law is, at least in

[242] J. Austin, *The Province of Jurisprudence Determined* and *The Uses of the Study of Jurisprudence*, London 1954, p. 184.

[243] Among the works mentioned in the penultimate note, only Fuller and von Wright do not mention the Separation Thesis. Yet it is well known that Fuller has repeatedly criticised this thesis of legal positivism – *see e.g.*, *idem*, 'Positivism and Fidelity to Law – A Reply to Professor Hart', *op. cit.*, pp. 630ff. On the other hand, von Wright does not mention the positivist Separation Thesis probably because he, in fact, acknowledges its rightness in so far as it opposes natural law conceptions that blur the distinction between law and morality, yet he also emphasises the fallacy of legal positivism to the extent to which the latter insists on excluding moral considerations from the spheres of legislation, law application and hermeneutical aspects of legal dogmatics – *see idem*, 'Is and Ought', *op. cit.*, p. 279.

[244] I leave aside here the opinions according to which this thesis cannot be generally treated as an element of the definition of legal positivism – *see e.g.*, V. Villa, 'A Definition of Legal Positivism', *ARSP* Bh. 70 (1997), pp. 27ff.

[245] *See* R. Dreier, 'Der Begriff des Rechts', *op. cit.*, pp. 890ff. and 'Some Remarks on the Concept of Law', *op. cit.*, pp. 113ff.; R. Alexy, *Begriff und Geltung des Rechts*, *op. cit.*, pp. 38, 194ff. [English version, pp. 18–19, 121ff.].

outline, known even to unprofessionals, which may positively affect the readability of the following arguments.

4.6.3 Hard Positivism, Soft Positivism and Nonpositivism

Before we compare the nonpositivist conception with Hart's soft positivism in terms of legal validity (which we are primarily interested in), let us adopt *ad usum* in our analyses the following, quite evident distinction.[246]

Firstly, "softening" the positivist rule of recognition can rely on the fact that one of the criteria of validity of legal norms may be a requirement (condition) of non-contradiction between their content and the content of moral norms. In other words, the legal norms established by a competent legislator (and fully compliant with the positivist test of pedigree) may not be valid (may be considered invalid) if, according to the rule of recognition appropriate to the particular legal system, their validity will also depend on them fulfilling certain substantive moral criteria. In the jurisprudential literature, this type of "soft" rule of recognition and the respective version of legal positivism are named in different ways.[247] Without going into terminological issues, hereafter the role played by morality (moral norms) in the so-constructed rule of recognition shall be called a "negative (derogatory) validating function of morality" because this term seems to be clear and easy to understand intuitively. It is beyond any discussion, that in cases of such a rule of recognition, morality affects law in a negative (derogatory) way, establishing a necessary condition of the validity of law, which—when not complied with—eliminates immoral norms from the set of valid legal norms.

---

[246] This distinction is naturally not only adopted *ad usum*, but it also has an *ad hoc* character. Nevertheless, I think that it is clear enough and does not require any detailed explanation or justification. Similar distinctions adopted in the recent literature on the subject are mentioned in the next note. Let me note that within Polish legal theory, an analogous distinction, though in a slightly broader context of systemic connections of law and morality, was proposed by W. Lang, *Prawo i moralność* [Law and Morality], Warszawa 1989, pp. 127ff.

[247] For example, S.J. Shapiro proposes a distinction of the *necessity version* and *sufficient version* of inclusive legal positivism, based on a similar idea – *see idem*, 'On Hart's Way Out' in J.L. Coleman (ed.), *Hart's Postscript*, *op. cit.*, pp. 182ff. M.H. Kramer calls these two versions: "inclusive legal positivism" and "incorporationism" (respectively) – *see idem*, 'How Moral Principles Can Enter into the Law', *LT* 6 (2000), p. 83, 'Throwing Light on the Role of Moral Principles in the Law: Further Reflections', *op. cit.*, pp. 115–116 and *Where Law and Morality Meet*, *op. cit.*, pp. 2ff. Finally, K.E. Himma distinguishes the *necessity component* and *sufficiency component* of the thesis of incorporationism (which holds that the systems of law in which the criteria of validity include substantive moral norms are conceptually possible) – *see idem*, 'Inclusive Legal Positivism', *op. cit.*, p. 136.

Secondly, "softening" the rule of recognition can also conceptually mean something quite different[248]; namely, adopting within the rule of recognition such criterion according to which the norms that are not established by a competent legislator (and not meeting the positivist test of pedigree) become a part of valid law, providing that their content is equivalent to the content of moral norms. In other words, in accordance with such a constructed rule of recognition, compliance of a given norm with morality (for example, the one used by the judge in the resolution of some hard case) provides a sufficient condition for it to be a valid legal norm. For similar reasons as above, the role played in this case by morality shall be regarded by us as a "positive (law-creating) validating function of morality". In the case indicated above, morality affects law in a positive way, not decreasing (as in the case of a negative–derogatory function), but increasing the number of valid legal norms in a given legal system.

En passant let us discuss a question of utmost importance for our analysis. When we speak of "incorporating" moral rules into valid law, of "inclusive" legal positivism or of "incorporationism", we must always be aware of the notorious indeterminacy of the expressions and terms in which we use the concepts of incorporation and inclusion. I think that this indeterminacy, although very simple to identify, is not always taken into account by the authors who develop or comment on the various theoretical versions of soft positivism. It can often lead to confusion or unnecessary disputes, having purely a verbal character. Indeterminacy of these concepts in the context of the connections between law and morality—being of interest to us here—consists of the fact that the incorporation or inclusion of moral norms (standards, requirements) to the legal system can stand for three different phenomena. Firstly (and this is the understanding which is currently most debated among positivists), it may involve the inclusion of moral elements into the rule of recognition (using Hart's conceptual instrumentarium—to one of the secondary rules of legal system). Secondly, we can in this way refer to the introduction of moral norms (standards, requirements) to the system of valid norms (especially the primary rules and those secondary rules of change or adjudication, which—contrary to the rule of recognition—may be regarded

[248] This difference is also obvious, so let us just be content with indicating that both functions of morality are independent: the positive function is neither entailed by the negative function, nor vice versa. This is because the elimination of immoral (e.g. extremely unjust) legal norms from a legal system does not automatically imply supplementing this system with new legal norms which have a purely moral source. On the other hand, the incorporation of moral norms into a system of law and granting them the status of legal norms, does not necessarily have to (but only can) result in losing this status through the legal norms that up to that point belonged to a particular system. Let us note, for instance, that in the famous case used in Dworkin's antipositivist argumentation (*Riggs v. Palmer*), the recognition of the principle *neminem doluus suus prodesse debet* as a component of law, did not result in the loss of validity of such legal rules (norms) that regulate the validity of testamentary succession, but the reinterpretation of their scope of application (incidentally, this was exceptional in the judicature of the US courts), as a result of which, the killer of his grandfather was deprived of his inheritance – *see* R. Dworkin, *Taking Rights Seriously*, *op. cit.*, pp. 23, 28ff., in particular, p. 37 and *Law's Empire*, *op. cit.*, pp. 15–20. A detailed discussion of the reasoning underlying this ruling is provided by R. Beehler, 'Legal Positivism, Social Rules, and *Riggs v. Palmer*', *L&Ph* 9 (1990), pp. 285–293.

as valid or not). Thirdly, we could have in mind a combination of these two extensionally different types of incorporation of morality into law. Usually, the context of a particular expression can indeed allow us to comprehend which understanding of incorporation or inclusion the author has in mind.[249] Nonetheless, on account of the clarity of further arguments, let us emphasise that in our deliberations we shall adopt the first meaning. In the analysis to follow, we are only interested in the incorporation (inclusion) of moral elements (criteria, requirements) into the secondary rule of recognition of a legal system.

When moving forward to compare Hart's soft positivism with Dreier's and Alexy's nonpositivism, we shall first reconstruct the position of the philosopher from Oxford. As far as the negative (derogatory) validating function of morality is concerned, it is undisputed that Hart explicitly accepts the possibility of a rule of recognition under which morality fulfils such a function. When arguing—like other legal positivists—that there is no necessary conceptual connection between law and morality, Hart, practically throughout the entire period of his scientific activity, allowed for the possibility that among the validity criteria, which comprise the rule of recognition, content conditions of a purely moral character can occur.[250] Any doubts about his standpoint have been definitively dispelled during the famous polemics with Fuller,[251] whereas in the posthumously published *Postscript* to *The Concept of Law*, he explicitly referred to the version of legal positivism that was defended by him as "soft positivism".[252] What constitutes the subject of

---

[249] The fact that the problem of interpretation, related to the above-mentioned ambiguity, can actually occur, is relatively easy to demonstrate. For example, Hart in 'El nuevo desafío al positivismo jurídico', *op. cit.*, p. 7, uses the concept of incorporation in both senses, writing first about the incorporation of moral principles into the legal system, consisting of the courts recognising these principles as a fundamental criterion of validity (i.e., concerning incorporation of morality within the rule of recognition), and then about the incorporation of moral principles into the legal system through general clauses (i.e., incorporation concerning the sphere of the primary rules).

[250] *Cf.* Hart's analysis of J. Bentham's and J. Austin's position in 'Positivism and the Separation of Law and Morals', *op. cit.*, pp. 594ff. and his comments on the explicit incorporation of "principles of justice or substantive moral values" to the rule of recognition in the legal system of the United States of America in *The Concept of Law*, *op. cit.*, p. 199. *See* also Hart's papers pointed out in the next two notes.

[251] It is worth quoting here *in extenso* the view expressed by Hart in his review of L.L. Fuller's book: *The Morality of Law*, *HLR* 78 (1965), p. 1294: "There is, for me, no logical restriction on the content of the rule of recognition: so far as 'logic' goes it could provide explicitly or implicitly that the criteria determining validity of subordinate laws should cease to be regarded as such if the laws identified in accordance with them proved to be morally objectionable. So a constitution could include in its restrictions of the legislative power even of its supreme legislature not only conformity with due process but a completely general provision that its legal power should lapse if its enactments ever conflicted with principles of morality and justice". For more on Hart–Fuller polemics *see e.g.*, H.J.M. Boukema, 'The Hart–Fuller Debate', *RT* 14 (1983), pp. 29–59; N. Lacey, 'Philosophy, Political Morality, and History: Explaining the Enduring Resonance of the Hart–Fuller Debate', *NYULR* 83/4 (2008), pp. 1059–1087; J. Zajadło, *Dziedzictwo przeszłości*, *op. cit.*, pp. 222ff.

[252] H.L.A. Hart, 'Postscript', *op. cit.*, p. 250.

controversy is the issue as to whether Hart's version of positivism also accepts a positive (law-creating) validating function of morality. One can observe a dispute in the jurisprudential literature about whether Hart's positivism is a weaker version of inclusive legal positivism and agrees with the possibility that morality plays only a negative derogatory role in reference to immoral legal norms, or whether it is a stronger version (namely incorporationism in the full sense of the word) and recognises also the possibility that morality has a positive validating function. The participants in this dispute emphasise unanimously that in Hart's writings there is no evidence that he accepted a strong version of inclusive legal positivism and, therefore, they seek to determine his position by means of various arguments, usually based on the analysis of the internal consistency of his theory.[253]

Undoubtedly, the issue of the internal consistency of Hart's conception cannot be addressed here, because it would direct our discussion along tracks that are too remote from the subject at hand.[254] Let us, therefore, content ourselves with the finding, which seems crucial for understanding the essence of his sophisticated legal positivism, that this dispute is at least partially redundant, because—contrary to widespread belief—textual evidence exists that Hart also accepted, albeit reluctantly, a strong version of soft positivism. At this point, we have in mind the lecture *New Challenge for Legal Positivism*, delivered by Hart at the Autonomous University of Madrid in October 1979, the translation of which—nota bene undertaken by the distinguished Spanish legal philosophers (Liborio Hierro, Francisco Laporta and Juan Ramón de Páramo)—was directly authorised by Hart.[255] In his lecture, Hart, after a brief characteristic take on his own version of legal positivism, takes the polemics with Dworkin's views set out in *Taking Rights Seriously*, which

[253] For example, M.H. Kramer, 'How Moral Principles Can Enter into the Law', *op. cit.*, p. 84 and *Where Law and Morality Meet*, *op. cit.*, pp. 4–5, is explicitly in favour of attributing to Hart only a weaker version of inclusive legal positivism, whereas K.E. Himma, 'Inclusive Legal Positivism', *op. cit.*, pp. 138ff., attributes to him its strong version; namely, a full incorporationism.

[254] The main problem naturally concerns the consistency of inclusive positivism (not only in Hart's version) with the Practical Difference Thesis formulated by Shapiro (the name of this thesis was introduced by Coleman) – *see* S.J. Shapiro, 'On Hart's Way Out', *op. cit.*, pp. 177ff. For more on this issue *see e.g.*, J.L. Coleman, 'Incorporationism, Conventionality, and the Practical Difference Thesis', *op. cit.*, pp. 101, 121ff., and 'Practical Difference' in *idem*, *The Practice of Principle*, *op. cit.*, pp. 134–148; W.J. Waluchow, 'Authority and the Practical Difference Thesis: A Defense of Inclusive Legal Positivism', *LT* 6 (2000), pp. 72ff.; K.E. Himma, *ibidem*, pp. 157ff.; J.J. Moreso, 'In Defense of Inclusive Legal Positivism', *op. cit.*, pp. 115ff.; M.H. Kramer, *Where Law and Morality Meet*, *op. cit.*, pp. 17ff.

[255] H.L.A. Hart, 'El nuevo desafío al positivismo jurídico', *op. cit.* This authorisation is confirmed in the translators' note at p. 3. According to the oral relation of one of the translators of this lecture – Francisco Laporta – Hart, known for his perfectionism, discussed with them the details of the translation and he delivered the lecture in Spanish. The effort in preparing this speech certainly paid off, because the text of the lecture is – in my opinion – one of the most accurate and brilliant of Hart's achievements. For the record, we should add that several of its fragments were later used in a 'Postscript' to the second edition of *The Concept of Law*.

constitute the "new challenge" for legal positivism. What is strongly advisable for all those interested in Hart's theory of law, and, unfortunately, not yet clearly known to the participants of the above-mentioned dispute, are the passages of the lecture in which Hart explicitly allows for the possibility that morality has a positive (law-creating) validating function vis-à-vis law. When analysing Dworkin's objections that are related, inter alia, to the theory of adjudication developed by the American philosopher and based on a theoretical construct of an ideal judge—Hercules[256]—Hart states that this theory in no way falsifies the fundamental theses of his own version of legal positivism (i.e., not only the thesis of judicial discretion, but also the thesis of the conceptual separation of law and morality as well as the thesis of the social sources of law).[257] According to Hart, Dworkin—in his critique on legal positivism—does not take into account the possibility of such a constructed rule of recognition, in which there is a requirement for using the "Hercules procedure" (*procedimiento hercúleo*) as a basis for judicial decisions in situations where other sources of law are vague (and thus they do not indicate the contents of the judicial decision). Hart writes:

> Basically, there is no reason why such a rule would not provide for Hercules procedure among the criteria that [the rule of recognition – *A.G.*] determines for the identification of law. It is of course true that this will make moral arguments and moral judgments relevant for legal decision, but this relevance in such jurisdictions will simply be an example of a contingent incorporation of moral principles to legal system.[258]

The quoted statement leaves no doubt—the incorporation of the "Hercules procedure" into the rule of recognition (causing the introduction of moral principles into the legal system) is clearly an example of morality having a positive (law-creating) validating function. Thus, Hart's soft positivism constitutes incorporationism in the fullest sense of this term; namely, a strong version (accepting both validating functions of morality) of inclusive legal positivism.

Having resolved this issue, let us now compare Hart's positivism with Dreier's and Alexy's nonpositivist conception of law. Due to the differences between the positions of the German philosophers, we shall attempt this comparison in two stages. Firstly, we shall briefly examine the similarities and differences between

[256] On judge Hercules and his methods of adjudication *see* R. Dworkin, *Taking Rights Seriously*, *op. cit.*, pp. 105ff. Due to chronological reasons, Hart's critique does not apply to the development of the conception by Dworkin, who uses the construct of judge Hercules in his later works – *see e.g.*, *Law's Empire*, *op. cit.*, pp. 239ff., 313ff.

[257] H.L.A. Hart, 'El nuevo desafío al positivismo jurídico', *op. cit.*, p. 14.

[258] *Ibidem*. Let us add that a similar thesis was formulated by Hart in 'Postscript', *op. cit.*, p. 265, where he claims that "no general argument that the inclusion of principles as part of the law entails the abandonment of the doctrine of a rule of recognition could succeed". It should also be added that Dworkin anticipates the possibility of extending the rule of recognition in such a way so as non-positivised principles and standards were, in accordance with this rule, recognised as a valid law (yet, he does not mean here introducing to it the "Hercules procedure"), but he explicitly rejects such a possibility – *see e.g.*, R. Dworkin, *Taking Rights Seriously*, *op. cit.*, pp. 39ff. and, in particular, pp. 43–44, 64ff. *See* also his response to Soper, *ibidem*, pp. 345ff.

Hart's conception and Dreier's original version of the nonpositivist conception[259] and then we shall conduct a comparative analysis with respect to the nonpositivist conception of law as developed by Alexy. In order to highlight more clearly the similarities and differences between the conceptions at hand, in both cases this comparison will be made on two levels: theoretical and practical.

When challenging the positivist thesis of the separation of law and morality, Dreier metaphorically states that it "cuts off the umbilical cord between reason and positive law".[260] By rejecting the positivist thesis of the lack of any necessary (conceptual) connection between law and morality, he refrains from its categorical nonpositivist negation; namely, from adopting the necessity of such a connection.[261] He rather tries, as do inclusive legal positivists, to demonstrate the possible relation of law and morality, with a very limited power and scope. For example, when examining the relations between law and morality in their normative aspect, Dreier rejects both the thesis of the primacy (*Vorrang*) of law in respect to morality, as well as the opposite thesis—of the primacy of morality in respect to law—seemingly accepting that law, as a rule, has a dominant position, and only in exceptional circumstances should priority be given to morality.[262] This view, referring to "Radbruch's formula" and generally anticipating Alexy's subsequent formulation of *schwache Verbindungsthese*, allows us to conclude that on a theoretical level, Dreier's original nonpositivist conception comes down to a very limited (to exceptional situations) rejection of the positivist Separation Thesis, with no practical consequences—as we will see in a moment—which a moderate, inclusive legal positivist would not be able to accept.

Turning to practical issues, let us recall that in Dreier's nonpositivist conception, the basic role is played by two arguments that are fundamental for nonpositivism. The first one, namely the argument from un-law (*Unrechtsargument*), refers to law as it is understood apragmatically (as a product of the lawmaking process), implying a negative validating function of morality within the rule of recognition: legal norms, not ethically justified to at least a minimal extent, lose their legal character and they are eliminated from the legal system. The second one, the argument from

[259] When writing about "Dreier's original version of the nonpositivist conception", I have in mind the independent form of his conception, which did not yet take into consideration the amendments and additions introduced by Alexy, and subsequently accepted by Dreier. His version of nonpositivism was synthetically presented in Chap. 3 at pp. 29–35.

[260] R. Dreier, 'Some Remarks on the Concept of Law', *op. cit.*, p. 113. By the way, this metaphor is not very accurate – after all, children in their infancy are still strongly connected with their parents, and only in time, do they become independent (and – let us add, though that does not directly undermine this metaphor – they become rational, indeed).

[261] In Dreier's basic works (from the period before he accepted the amendments and additions of the nonpositivist conception of law as introduced by Alexy), not only will we not find such a claim, but we can even see that Dreier refrains from deeper considerations so as to characterise the modality of the Separation Thesis and Connection Thesis. It is not changed by the fact that Dreier, although very rarely, mentions "a (conceptually) necessary connection of law and morality" – *see e.g., idem*, 'Recht und Moral', *op. cit.*, p. 181.

[262] *Ibidem*, pp. 184ff.

principles (*Prinzipienargument*), refers already to law that is conceived pragmatically (and thus primarily to the process of law application and, more generally, to the legal discourse), implying a positive validating function of morality within the rule of recognition—because of the "openness" of law towards morality that arises out of this argument, norms, standards and moral arguments gain in legal status (of valid legal norms) and they are incorporated into the legal system. However, a closer analysis of Dreier's definition of law in respect to the nonpositivist version of the rule of recognition that corresponds to the latter, shows that in this definition, Dreier takes into account only the first—negative (derogatory)—function of morality, by introducing the requirement of at least minimum ethical justification or the possibility of such a justification in relation to the state or international legal system and all legal norms (constitutional ones and those of a lower rank) that are its components.[263] Yet, he does not include in his definition the consequences of *Prinzipienargument*, and hence, a positive (law-creating) validating function of morality. In his view, the argument from principles, in its validity version (which is of interest to us here), does not go beyond the positivist understanding of law[264] as it relates to the interpretation and application of law (understood pragmatically). Accordingly, its influence may be omitted in the very concept of law (that is understood apragmatically by Dreier).[265] Thus, the rule of recognition that is possible to infer from Dreier's original nonpositivist conception, can be characterised as a rule that corresponds in its content to the type of rules of recognition which are approved by the weaker version of inclusive legal positivism (recognising only the negative validating function of morality). We must, therefore, agree with Dreier when he characterises his concept of law as a mere modification of the positivist concept of law, consisting of its enrichment.[266]

In sum, the analysis of the original version of Dreier's conception leads to the conclusion that, taking into account both theoretical as well as practical aspects, only Dreier's approval of the nonpositivist conception of law developed by Alexy allows us to classify the philosopher of Göttingen as a nonpositivist rather than as a soft positivist. His original nonpositivist conception is indeed—in a theoretical plane—a very balanced, circumspect and indeed delicate attempt to overcome the positivist paradigm. It leads—at the practical level—to the corresponding rule of recognition, fully acceptable for soft (inclusive) legal positivism, even in its weaker version, than that admitted by Hart.

Within his conception of law—that is very critical of positivism—Alexy is far more radical than Dreier. He rejects not only the positivist Separation Thesis, but he

---

[263] This definition was presented and tentatively discussed in Chap. 2 at pp. 15–19. *See* also Chap. 5, pp. 193ff. and Chap. 7, pp. 349ff.

[264] *See* Chap. 3 at p. 34.

[265] *See* R. Dreier, 'Der Begriff des Rechts', *op. cit.*, p. 895.

[266] *Ibidem.*

also adopts the strongest form of its denial; namely, the thesis of a necessary (and not just possible) conceptual connection of law and morality. According to the fundamental thesis of Alexy's nonpositivist conception, such a connection exists and, therefore, legal positivism fails as a comprehensive theory.[267] Alexy also rejects the so-called negative legal positivism; namely, the thesis (since it is impossible to call it a "theory") espousing a logical possibility of a legal system where the rule of recognition does not contain any moral elements[268] and the thesis of the conventional character of this rule.[269] He also negates all the versions of soft (inclusive) legal positivism, namely those theories which negative legal positivism can be derived from,[270] accepting only the possibility (and not—as in his nonpositivist conception—necessity) of the conceptual connection of law and morality.[271] Therefore, we can conclude without any doubt that in the theoretical plane, Alexy's conception is a nonpositivist conception *par excellence*, although—what should be once more emphasised—only to a methodologically limited extent (i.e., to the participant's perspective).

Yet, when we go on to the practical analyses, aimed at the issue of the content of the nonpositivist rule of recognition—being directly related to the problem of legal validity that we are interested in—then the nonpositivist character of Alexy's theory almost completely disappears. Although Alexy indeed completes Dreier's nonpositivist argumentation with the third argument, fundamental in its sense, namely the argument from correctness (*Richtigkeitsargument*), his definition of law allows us to formulate the rule of recognition that is compatible with the stronger version of soft positivism; that is—for example—with the rule of recognition with the content approved by Hart.

The elements of material (substantive) correctness incorporated by Alexy into the nonpositivist definition of law[272] can be reduced to three nonpositivist (moral) conditions for its validity. Firstly, according to the argument from correctness, a legal system must lay claim to correctness. Alexy himself admits that this is a condition generally devoid of practical consequences, since all modern legal systems meet it.[273] Moreover, this requirement has no direct influence on the content of the

[267] R. Alexy, 'On Necessary Relations between Law and Morality', *op. cit.*, p. 167 and 'Zur Kritik des Rechtspositivismus', *op. cit.*, p. 9.

[268] The concept of negative legal positivism was coined by J.L. Coleman, 'Negative and Positive Positivism', *JLS* 11/1 (1982), pp. 140ff. *See* also *idem*, 'Incorporationism, Conventionality, and the Practical Difference Thesis', *op. cit.*, p. 128, note 44, where Coleman defines negative positivism as follows: "Negative positivism is the view that there must be one logically possible legal system in which morality is not a condition of legality".

[269] R. Alexy, 'The Nature of Arguments about the Nature of Law', *op. cit.*, pp. 10, 14–15.

[270] *See* J.L. Coleman, 'Incorporationism, Conventionality, and the Practical Difference Thesis', *op. cit.*, p. 128, note 44 *in fine*.

[271] *See* R. Alexy, *O pojęciu i naturze prawa / On the Concept and the Nature of Law*, *op. cit.*, pp. 37–38.

[272] *See* Chap. 2, pp. 16–17, Chap. 5, pp. 193ff, and Chap. 7, pp. 351ff.

[273] R. Alexy, *Begriff und Geltung des Rechts*, *op. cit.*, p. 202 [English version, p. 127] and 'Bulygins Kritik des Richtigkeitsarguments', *op. cit.*, p. 236.

rule of recognition, because the latter is of infra-systemic character—it provides the criteria for the validity of legal norms in a given legal system,[274] but of course it no longer concerns the validity of a legal system as such, but rather the foundation of its existence.[275] Secondly, this argument also affects—but already jointly with the argument from un-law—the validity of individual legal norms, which may not be extremely unjust. This nonpositivist condition entails that morality has a negative (derogatory) validating function within the rule of recognition. Thirdly, the consequence of *Richtigkeitsargument* and of the argument from principles is the fact that the system of law also comprises non-positivised (not complying with the positivist test of pedigree) normative (moral) principles and arguments. Therefore, we deal here with a positive (law-creating) validating function of morality. This condition, however, also does not refute—from a practical point of view—the positivist rule of recognition. As pointed out by Hart in his reply to Dworkin's antipositivist challenge,[276] and accepted by his successors,[277] it is only the *proprio vigore* incorporation of moral norms that refutes a still positivist, although already maximally "softened" rule of recognition, as well as the positivist thesis of the conceptual separation of law and morality. The third section of Alexy's nonpositivist definition of law does not deal with an incorporation *proprio vigore* of moral norms into the legal system, since moral requirements are explicitly listed; therefore, we can state that they are also included in the nonpositivist rule of recognition. Arguably, an incorporation based on the application of the rule of recognition is not an incorporation *proprio vigore*. Moreover, the incorporation postulated by Alexy is purposeful. According to the nonpositivist rule of recognition, the system of law includes only those extra-legal (non-positivised) principles and normative arguments that are necessary to satisfy the claim to correctness within the application of law, rather than any moral norms that are correct or right.[278] Thus, the rule of recognition, which can be reconstructed on

---

[274] *Cf.* H.L.A. Hart, *The Concept of Law*, *op. cit.*, pp. 92ff. Although these issues are relatively well known, for the record, however, let us quote Hart's original statement that confirms this assertion: "To say that a given rule is valid is to recognise it as passing all the tests provided by the rule of recognition and so as a rule of a system" (*ibidem*, p. 100). *See* also Chap. 7 at pp. 286ff.

[275] *See ibidem*, pp. 97ff. On the first of the cited pages, Hart notes that the explanation of the most important features of modern systems of law is possible only in terms of a complex social situation in which the rule of recognition is accepted and used to identify the primary rules, which may be referred to as "the foundations of legal system".

[276] H.L.A. Hart, 'El nuevo desafío al positivismo jurídico', *op. cit.*, p. 14 and *see* also *ibidem*, p. 7.

[277] *See e.g.*, J.L. Coleman, 'Negative and Positive Positivism', *op. cit.*, p. 152, who states that the rule: "the law is whatever is morally right" could never constitute the rule of recognition in a positivist sense. *Cf. idem*, 'Authority and Reason' in R.P. George (ed.), *The Autonomy of Law. Essays on Legal Positivism*, Oxford 1996, note 5 at pp. 315–316.

[278] I believe that this assessment is not changed by the fact that Alexy argues that the legal duty of respecting principles and moral arguments results only from their "substantial correctness" (*inhaltliche Richtigkeit*), which constitutes a definitional element of law in a nonpositivist sense – *see idem*, 'Law and Correctness', *op. cit.*, p. 218 [German version, p. 16]. These claims have, in fact, a theoretical (conceptual) sense rather than a practical one. For more on this issue *see* comments on the dilemma of nonpositivism presented in the Epilogue at pp. 538–539

the basis of the nonpositivist definition of law developed by Alexy, has the content acceptable by a stronger version of soft positivism (i.e., full incorporationism), in its version which was—though very reluctantly—admitted to even by Hart and currently is developed mainly by Coleman.[279] In this rule, morality fulfils two above-mentioned validating functions vis-à-vis law.

In conclusion, as far as in the theoretical dimension, Dreier's and Alexy's nonpositivist conception of law indeed deserves the name of "nonpositivism" (and, hence, we cannot speak of "crypto-positivism"). Yet, in terms of its practical consequences—that is, in relation to a nonpositivist rule of recognition that we can infer from it—this conception does not go beyond the limits of a weaker version of the soft (inclusive) legal positivism (Dreier) or its stronger, fully incorporative version (Alexy).

Before any final conclusions as to the merits of the objection of crypto-positivism, it is worth supplementing the analysis with the identification of the methodological consequences of the positivist Separation Thesis and nonpositivist Connection Thesis. These theses directly influence not only the conceptual sphere, or the question of the legal validity of norms, but they also have an impact on the way of understanding and practising legal sciences; in particular, the theory and philosophy of law. The most outstanding twentieth-century legal positivists, namely Hans Kelsen, with his conception of purely normative legal science (*reine Normwissenschaft*)[280] and H.L.A. Hart, with the idea of the descriptive theory of law, devoid of any justifying purposes,[281] have with one accord accepted the idea of the science (theory) of law which, due to the conceptual separation of law and morality, is completely morally neutral. This methodological aspect of the

[279] Let us note that in the English jurisprudential literature, Philip Soper is regarded as the author who first noticed the possibility of the stronger version of soft (inclusive) legal positivism – *see* E.Ph. Soper, 'Legal Theory and the Obligation of a Judge: The Hart/Dworkin Dispute', *MLR* 75 (1977), pp. 473–519, in particular, pp. 487–488, 509ff. Yet, in reality, the author who was the first – already in 1970 – to formulate the basic idea of soft (inclusive) legal positivism was Hart's student, Argentinian philosopher of law – Genaro R. Carrió – *see* J.J. Moreso, *In Defense of Inclusive Legal Positivism*, *op. cit.*, note 11 at p. 101 and M. Atienza, 'Is Legal Positivism a Sustainable Legal Theory?', *op. cit.*, p. 239.

[280] *See e.g.*, H. Kelsen, 'Was ist juristischer Positivismus?', *op. cit.*, p. 468, *Reine Rechtslehre*, 2nd ed., *op. cit.*, pp. 1, 65ff. [English version, pp. 1, 63ff.], and 'Law and Morality', *op. cit.*, pp. 92–93. From the vast literature commenting on Kelsen's fundamental methodological idea of legal sciences free from evaluations, whose primary task is *wertfreie Beschreibung* of the valid law, it is worth recalling a classic work of N. Bobbio, '"Sein" and "Sollen" in Legal Science', *ARSP* 56 (1970), pp. 7–30 and – in the recent literature – U. Neumann, 'Wissenschaftstheorie der Rechtswissenschaft bei Hans Kelsen und Gustav Radbruch. Zwei "neukantianische" Perspektiven' in St.L. Paulson, M. Stolleis (eds.), *Hans Kelsen. Staatsrechtslehrer und Rechtstheoretiker des 20. Jahrhunderts*, Tübingen 2005, pp. 35–55, in particular, pp. 45ff.

[281] *See* J.R. de Páramo, 'Entrevista a H.L.A. Hart', *op. cit.*, pp. 348ff. and H.L.A. Hart, 'Postscript', *op. cit.*, pp. 239ff. For more on Hart's methodological ideas *see e.g.*, St.R. Perry, 'Hart's Methodological Positivism' in J.L. Coleman (ed.), *Hart's Postscript*, *op. cit.*, pp. 311, 319ff. and J. Dickson, 'Methodology in Jurisprudence: A Critical Survey', *LT* 10 (2004), pp. 117–156, and the references cited therein.

Separation Thesis has been most succinctly expressed by Neil MacCormick, who rightly argued that the positivist legal theories maintain that the law can be analysed and explained "in terms independent of any thesis about moral principles or values".[282] According to legal positivists, the issues of moral justification or evaluation of the positive law are beyond the research scope of legal sciences. Such a position, sometimes referred to as "methodological legal positivism",[283] seems to be a necessary metatheoretical consequence of the positivist thesis of the conceptual separation of law and morality.[284]

We can easily observe that in the methodological aspect, the nonpositivist character of Dreier's and Alexy's conception is revealed in all its fullness. Assuming the nonpositivist *Verbindungsthese*, German authors consistently and unanimously opt for the introduction of ethical issues into the science of law—both in the already discussed joint methodological paper,[285] as well as in a number of independent works. It was already in the publications of the second half of the seventies of the last century[286] that Dreier first considered the possibility of the theory of *richtigen Recht* as a scientific theory, and then, analysing the epistemological aspect of legal sciences, he adopts its division into three parts; namely, the philosophy, theory and sociology of law. What is important is that he claims that the first of these disciplines examines law in terms of its substantive correctness (*materiale Richtigkeit*). Alexy, on the other hand, when presenting, quite recently, his vision of the philosophy of law, strongly rejects its restrictive form, directed primarily on jurisdiction (juridical theory of law), treating it as non-philosophy.[287] Being a supporter of adopting a broad range of research concerning the philosophy of law, comprising also the issue of correctness or legitimisation of law, he is in favour of two theses. Firstly, the General Nature Thesis, which states that within the

---

282 N. MacCormick, 'Natural Law and the Separation of Law and Morals' in R.P. George (ed.), *Natural Law Theory. Contemporary Essays*, Oxford 1992, p. 107.

283 St.R. Perry, 'Hart's Methodological Positivism', *op. cit.*, pp. 311ff. For more on methodological interpretation of the positivist Separation Thesis *see* V. Villa, 'A Definition of Legal Positivism', *op. cit.*, pp. 28–29 and L.M. Sánchez Fernández, 'Ironías, falacias, perversiones, enigmas: sobre el positivismo y la tesis de la separación', *op. cit.*, pp. 342ff. Generally on methodological interpretation of legal positivism as the way of practising jurisprudence *see* a classic text by N. Bobbio, 'Sur le positivisme juridique' in (collaborative ed.), *Mélanges en l'honneur de P. Roubier*: *Théorie générale du droit et droit transitoire*, Paris 1961, pp. 54ff.

284 Let us refer again to John Austin who, "in a single breath", refers to this relation in a presumably most quoted passage of *The Province of Jurisprudence Determined*, *op. cit.*, p. 184: "The existence of law is one thing; its merit or demerit is another. Whether it be or be not is one enquiry; whether it be or be not conformable to an assumed standard, is a different enquiry".

285 R. Alexy, R. Dreier, 'The Concept of Jurisprudence', *op. cit.*, discussed in Chap. 3 at pp. 23–28. Let us recall that according to their common methodological position – as expressed therein – on the normative level, jurisprudence (theory of law) intends to develop theories of right law and good legal science.

286 *See* R. Dreier, *Was ist und wozu Allgemeine Rechtstheorie?*, *op. cit.*, pp. 27ff. and 'Bemerkungen zur Rechtserkenntnistheorie', *op. cit.*, pp. 100ff.

287 *See* R. Alexy, 'The Nature of Legal Philosophy', *op. cit.*, pp. 67–68.

philosophy of law all possible problems of general philosophy may appear. Secondly, the Special Relation Thesis, according to which there exists a specific relation of the philosophy of law with other areas of practical philosophy; in particular, with moral and political philosophy.

Taking into account the methodological dimension of the nonpositivist thesis of the necessary conceptual connection of law and morality leads to the conclusion that the objection of crypto-positivism is not accurate. Rejecting the accusation of crypto-positivism in respect to the nonpositivist conception of law, it should nonetheless be kept in mind that the analyses showed that on the practical level, related to the issue of legal validity, German nonpositivism is consistent with soft (inclusive) positivism in the sense that the rules of recognition, postulated or at least approved by these two doctrines essentially coincide, only differing in some minor details. Practical proximity by means of the opposition, or—as can be more accurately expressed today—by means of the convergence of these two trends of the modern theory of law, is not surprising or startling. Both doctrines, to the extent that they relate to the content of the rule of recognition, after all, refer to the same substantive scope, which generally can be described as law that is conceived pragmatically (as a kind of social practice), rather than just apragmatically, as the *law in books*. I believe, though, that their proximity is not due to the fact that the nonpositivist conception is insufficiently antipositivist, but more due to the fact that the contemporary soft (inclusive) legal positivism—which is in its genesis a search for the "third way" between hard positivism and Dworkin's antipositivism—is legal positivism only in name.[288] It is noteworthy that some researchers do not hesitate to use, in their analyses of inclusive positivism, the term "crypto-iusnaturalism",[289] whereas according to others, a positivist, very "soft" rule of recognition in the version of a full incorporationism does not differ in any respect from entelecheia—as deftly defined by Luis Manuel Sánchez Fernández.[290] Therefore, it cannot be surprising that more and more critics of legal positivism argue its self-destruction or

---

[288] *See e.g.*, J.R.-Toubes Muñiz, 'Is Soft Positivism a Positivism?', *ARSP* Bh. 70 (1997), pp. 44–48; L. Morawski, 'Hard Positivism, Soft Positivism and Dead Positivism', *op. cit.*, pp. 177ff.; M. La Torre, 'On Two Distinct and Opposed Versions of Natural Law: "Exclusive" versus "Inclusive"', *op. cit.*, pp. 213ff.

[289] L.L. Hierro, '¿Por qué ser positivista?', *op. cit.*, p. 292. Similar objections are raised by R.N. McLaughlin, 'On a Similarity between Natural Law Theories and English Legal Positivism', *PhQ* 39 (1989), pp. 445–462. A lapidary, modal response of inclusive positivists to such objections can be found in J.L. Coleman, 'Practical Difference', *op. cit.*, pp. 147–148. In his opinion, inclusive legal positivism is not a natural law conception because it allows only a possibility, and not the necessity, of incorporating moral principles to the rule of recognition and to the legal system. This response, however, involves a certain vision of natural law doctrine, which we do not have to agree with.

[290] L.M. Sánchez Fernández, 'Ironías, falacias, perversiones, enigmas: sobre el positivismo y la tesis de la separación', *op. cit.*, p. 354. For more on – in my opinion – exaggerated "openness" and thus the almost tautological character of the positivist rule of recognition in the form accepted by the strong version of inclusive positivism, *see* Chap. 9 at pp. 456–457.

degeneration,[291] announcing—but perhaps prematurely—the transition of the contemporary theory and philosophy of law to the stage of postpositivist jurisprudence.[292]

4.7 The Problem of Justification of the Argument from Correctness

Among the arguments used by Alexy in analytical argumentation, the argument from correctness (*Richtigkeitsargument*) definitely comes to the fore. It constitutes Alexy's original contribution to the nonpositivist conception, while being—in his opinion[293]—the equivalent of a "somewhat opaque" Radbruch's definition of law from *Rechtsphilosophie*: "Law is the reality whose meaning is to serve legal values; the idea of law".[294] As can be seen from the previously undertaken reconstruction,[295] in Alexy's original analytical argumentation, this argument fulfils its essential function in justifying the nonpositivist *Verbindungsthese*. On the other hand, in the subsequent and—so far—final version of his nonpositivist argumentation, presented in *Begriff und Geltung des Rechts*, this argument also constitutes the foundation of the other nonpositivist arguments (the argument from un-law and argument from principles). Moreover, what I have tried to demonstrate elsewhere,[296] is that this argument, directly and independently of other analytical and normative arguments, leads to the necessity of adopting the nonpositivist concept of law. The only supplement needed to reach such a conclusion is to accept the validity

[291] *See e.g.*, J.D. Goldsworthy, 'The Self-Destruction of Legal Positivism', *OJLS* 10/4 (1990), pp. 449–486 and L. Morawski, 'Hard Positivism, Soft Positivism and Dead Positivism', *op. cit.*, pp. 159, 178. A thorough analysis of most of the important arguments that justify the thesis of self-destruction of modern legal positivism is provided by P.E. Navarro, 'Tensiones conceptuales en el positivismo jurídico', *op. cit.*, pp. 135ff.

[292] A. Calsamiglia, 'Postpositivismo', *DOXA* 21/I (1998), pp. 209–220 and L. Morawski, 'Hard Positivism, Soft Positivism and Dead Positivism', *op. cit.*, p. 178. Due to the highly polemical – in respect to positivism – way of creating his own theory of law, Ronald Dworkin is sometimes treated as the first postpositivist – *see* M. Atienza, *El sentido del Derecho*, Barcelona 2001, pp. 306ff. As for other authors, it merits noting N. MacCormick, who characterises his conception as "a post-positivist institutional theory of law" – *see idem*, 'Foreword' in *idem*, *Legal Reasoning and Legal Theory*, 2nd ed. 2, Oxford 1994, p. xv. The issue of the transition of modern jurisprudence (theory of law) to the postpositivist stage, which I aimed only to mention at this point – will be further addressed in the Epilogue at pp. 539–541.

[293] R. Alexy, *Begriff und Geltung des Rechts*, *op. cit.*, p. 62, in particular, note 43 [English version, p. 34, in particular, note 64].

[294] G. Radbruch, *Rechtsphilosophie*, *op. cit.*, p. 34. In the original: "Recht ist die Wirklichkeit, die denn Sinn hat, dem Rechtswerte, der Rechtsidee zu dienen".

[295] *See* Chap. 3, pp. 40ff., 46ff., 54.

[296] *See* A. Grabowski, 'Sonderfallthese – Its Critique and Interpretation', *op. cit.*, pp. 381–382 and T. Gizbert-Studnicki, A. Grabowski, 'Kilka uwag o niepozytywistycznej koncepcji prawa', *op. cit.*, pp. 65–67.

of the principle *impossibilium nulla est obligatio* in the sphere of practical and legal discourse. The consequence of adopting the claim to correctness (which is the essence of this argument) in the legal discourse is, in fact, inter alia, imposing on a judge the duty of the correct solution of a case. This obligation is impossible to fulfil if the judge is legally obliged to apply an unjust or unreasonable law.[297] The fact that also weighs in favour of this thesis is that Alexy himself admitted—when interviewed by Manuel Atienza in 2001—that his theory of legal argumentation has, from the very outset (i.e., long before formulating the argument from correctness and other nonpositivist arguments) presupposed a nonpositivist concept of law.[298] In addition, the claim to correctness (*Anspruch auf Richtigkeit*) also plays a key role in justifying the Special Case Thesis.[299] It is therefore reasonable to assume that convincing us of the justification of *Richtigkeitsargument*, in general, and of the claim to correctness, in particular, are essential for evaluating the cogency of Alexy's nonpositivist conception of law. If their justification can be rebutted, then—as emphasised by the commentators—Alexy's nonpositivist conception of law will "become" a positivist theory.[300] Indeed, if the nonpositivist definition of law—as formulated by him—is devoid of the elements that refer to the substantive correctness of the law as well as individual norms and legal decisions, then it will be fully acceptable, not only in practical terms (i.e., in the context of the content of a nonpositivist rule of recognition—considered in the preceding section), but also in a theoretical sense, at least for the advocates of soft positivism.

4.7.1 Justification by Means of *Performativer Widerspruch*: Preliminary Remarks

The core of the argument from correctness is the claim to correctness (*Anspruch auf Richtigkeit*), which—according to Alexy—constitutes an essential component of law. It should be recalled that Alexy justifies the necessity of the claim to correctness in law, using examples of two utterances, burdened with the error of

[297] The inability of the judge to meet this obligation is illustrated by the following examples of two opposing rulings, issued on the basis of an unjust law, which can be hardly regarded as being in full compliance with the law: "Mr N. is hereby sentenced to ten years' imprisonment on the grounds of an unjust law" – R. Alexy, 'Problems of Discursive Rationality in Law', *ARSP* Bh. 42 (1990), p. 178 and: "Given that the law applicable in the case is unjust, Mr N. is not condemned to a penalty determined by it" – M. Atienza, *Las Razones del Derecho*, *op. cit.*, p. 225.

[298] *Cf.* M. Atienza, 'Entrevista a Robert Alexy', *op. cit.*, p. 672. Alexy also admits therein that the failure to develop a nonpositivist concept of law was one of the weak points of his dissertation.

[299] *See* A. Grabowski, 'Sonderfallthese – Its Critique and Interpretation', *op. cit.*, pp. 374ff., and the references cited therein.

[300] It is held, inter alia, by A. García Figueroa, *Principios y positivismo jurídico*, *op. cit.*, p. 330.

"performative contradiction" (*performativer Widerspruch*).[301] Firstly, the article of the Constitution: "*X* is a sovereign, federal, and unjust republic"; and secondly, a court ruling: "The defendant is hereby sentenced to life imprisonment, albeit wrongly, because valid law was interpreted incorrectly". Then Alexy applies the eliminating argument (referred to by him as *Was-der-sonst-Schluß* or *Was-der-sonst-Argument*[302]), by which he attempts to demonstrate that the absurdity of these sentences can be fully explained only in such a way that their authors make conceptual faults, and not just technical, moral, conventional or legal ones (excluding in the course of analysis the possibility of such explanations). In the case of the first sentence, "performative contradiction" exists between the claim to justice (which Alexy treats as a special case of a general claim to correctness), implicitly contained in the act of creating the constitution, and the assertion stating injustice of the state X—explicitly expressed in this article. In the second case, the contradiction exists between the claim to correctness—implicitly contained in every act of ruling and the assertion stating its falsity—explicitly expressed in the analysed ruling.

Before we examine the merits of Alexy's argumentation based on the recognition of "performative contradiction" in relation to the above-mentioned examples of statements, we should make some comments on its previous criticism, as well as amendments and additions introduced by Alexy in his later works. Firstly, let us recall that the second of the examples of utterances (in a somewhat simpler form, then revised in response to Ulfrid Neumann's criticism[303]) appears already in *Theorie der juristischen Argumentation*, where Alexy uses it in order to argue in favour of the thesis under which juristic discourse adopts the claim to

[301] *Cf.* Chap. 3, pp. 41–42. Apart from the further analysed two basic examples, Alexy still occasionally uses the two other examples of utterances burdened with this error. One of them has already been mentioned (*supra*, p. 103) and it will become the subject of our discussion in the next section. The second sentence, referring to Ulpian's classic formula, has been presented by Alexy in 'Bulygins Kritik des Richtigkeitsarguments', *op. cit.*, note 34 at p. 247: "Iuris praecepta sunt haec: inhoneste vivere, alterum laedere, suum cuique non tribuere", and he repeats it in 'Law and Correctness', *op. cit.*, p. 212 [German version, p. 9] and 'On the Thesis of a Necessary Connection between Law and Morality: Bulygin's Critique', *op. cit.*, p. 142. In none of these works, however, does Alexy discuss it, so in our analysis it will also be left aside.

[302] *See* R. Alexy, 'Bulygins Kritik des Richtigkeitsarguments', *op. cit.*, *pp.* 244, 249 and 'Recht und Richtigkeit', *op. cit.*, pp. 8, 10.

[303] *See* Chap. 3, note 70 at p. 41. Let us add, however, that the change to the original wording of this example has also been criticised by Neumann – *see* his review of R. Alexy's book: *Begriff und Geltung des Rechts*, *op. cit.*, pp. 244–245. The point is that in a detailed, new version of this example of ruling, Alexy explains the absence of good reasons and the fallacy of this ruling in the spirit of positivism, writing about basing it on "an incorrect interpretation of law", rather than in a nonpositivist moral sense, writing, for example, about the "injustice of valid law". Therefore – as rightly observed by Neumann – the example of ruling provided by Alexy has a less argumentative power than it could have. For the record, let us recall that in one of his letter works ('Problems of Discursive Rationality in Law', *op. cit.*, p. 178), Alexy uses such a form of this example, which corresponds to Neumann's proposal: "Mr N. is hereby sentenced to ten years' imprisonment on the grounds of an unjust law". Yet, he does it only to illustrate the general aspect (rather than it being restricted to the framework of a specific valid legal system) of the claim to correctness, relating to singular legal decisions.

correctness.[304] It was already in the very same book that the idea appeared that the fallacy of such a ruling is not only of moral character, and that there was the indication of its resemblance to the famous speech act analysed repeatedly by John L. Austin: "The cat is on the mat, but I do not believe it is".[305] Later, in the works presenting Alexy's analytical nonpositivist argumentation, both these examples were provided and analysed; it was also in these works that the concept of "performative contradiction" appeared for the first time.[306] In the meantime, many critics of German discursive ethics raise the objection of the circularity in respect of the method of justification used by the authors (in particular, Karl-Otto Apel, Jürgen Habermas and Wolfgang Kuhlmann), which was based on demonstrating a "performative contradiction" to identify and ultimately justify the basic rules of ethical discourse.[307] The critics of Alexy's conception also raise the *circulus vitiosus* objection in relation to his method of justifying the claim to correctness based on the recognition of "performative contradiction".[308] This circularity lies in the fact that we can speak of "performative contradiction" only when discourse rules are valid earlier, and when this condition is not met, such a contradiction cannot be identified. It follows, therefore—explicitly acknowledged by Alexy in a series of works published in the nineties—that by means of this method of justification, we can only "show" (*zeigen*) that practical discourse rules are valid. Yet, we cannot—without falling into a vicious circle—substantiate their validity.[309] Alexy, nonetheless, still advocates the idea that although we cannot speak here of justification understood as "justifying one sentence by another independent sentence", the argument based on "performative contradiction" does provide us with a certain justification (in the broader sense of the word), because "a better justification cannot be achieved when dealing with basic questions".[310] Finally, in the polemics with Bulygin,[311] Alexy clarifies his understanding of

---

[304] For more *see* Chap. 3 at pp. 36–37.

[305] *See* R. Alexy, *Theorie der juristischen Argumentation*, *op. cit.*, p. 266 [English version, p. 215].

[306] *See* R. Alexy, 'On Necessary Relations between Law and Morality', *op. cit.*, pp. 178ff., 'Zur Kritik des Rechtspositivismus', *op. cit.*, pp. 19ff., 'Nachwort (1991): Antwort auf einige Kritiker', *op. cit.*, pp. 428ff., and *Begriff und Geltung des Rechts*, *op. cit.*, pp. 64ff. [English version, pp. 35ff.].

[307] *See e.g.*, W.D. Fusfield, 'Can Jürgen Habermas's "Begründungsprogramm" Escape Hans Albert's *Münchhausen Trilemma*?', *JRh* 8 (1989), pp. 74ff., in particular, p. 77; E. Hilgendorf, 'Zur transzendentalpragmatischen Begründung von Diskursregeln', *op. cit.*, pp. 194–196; R. Gebauer, *Letzte Begründung. Eine Kritik der Diskursethik von Jürgen Habermas*, München 1993, pp. 128ff., in particular, p. 133.

[308] *See e.g.*, P. Gril, 'Alexys Version einer transzendental-pragmatischen Begründung der Diskursregeln im Unterschied zu Habermas', *op. cit.*, pp. 212–213 and A. Engländer, 'Zur begrifflichen Möglichkeit des Rechtspositivismus', *op. cit.*, p. 448, and the references cited therein.

[309] *See supra*, notes 169–170 at p. 103, with the corresponding text.

[310] R. Alexy, 'Bulygins Kritik des Richtigkeitsarguments', *op. cit.*, pp. 249–250 and 'Law and Correctness', *op. cit.*, p. 213 [German version, pp. 10–11].

[311] *Cf.* Bulygin's and Alexy's works listed *supra*, note 13 at p. 63.

"performative contradiction", characterising it as based on the classical approach of contradiction between sentences.[312] According to him, the only difference between the "performative contradiction" and a logical contradiction is that the former is specific (it can be said that it is narrower in scope), since it occurs only between the propositional content of a given speech act and its necessary assumptions, and the latter also takes place between sentences independent from each other. Thus, when interpreting the example—provided by Alexy—of the article of the constitution burdened with the error of *performativer Widerspruch*, it can be stated that there is a logical contradiction between the statement: "The constitution of the state *X* is unjust" and the claim to justice implicitly contained in the act of making the constitution, which is expressed in the statement: "The constitution of state *X* is just".[313] The issue is similar in respect to the example of an incorrect judicial decision.

4.7.2 From *Cogito, Ergo Sum* to Claim to Correctness

When Descartes formulated the fundamental principle of his philosophy in the form of a famous statement: "Cogito, ergo sum", he could not naturally assume that it would someday be treated as the starting point for Alexy's analytical argumentation in favour of the nonpositivist concept of law. This thesis may of course be puzzling, because what does *Cogito* have to do with the necessity of adopting the claim to correctness in law? However, this relation is remarkably close and surprisingly easy to demonstrate—both at the conceptual level, and in the plane of general philosophy.

When setting about the analysis of this relation in the conceptual sphere, it should be noted that it was more than three centuries after the work of Descartes, in which the statement: "Cogito, ergo sum" was formulated,[314] namely in 1962, when it became a subject of reflection for an eminent philosopher and logician, Jaakko Hintikka.[315] The Finnish philosopher, when examining the possible understanding

[312] *See* R. Alexy, 'On the Thesis of a Necessary Connection between Law and Morality: Bulygin's Critique', *op. cit.*, pp. 139–141. Let us recall that the formulation of the examples of utterances burdened with the "performative contradiction" mistake, and analysed in this section, come from this very work.

[313] *See ibidem*, p. 140.

[314] *See* R. Descartes, *Rozprawa o metodzie* [Discourse on the Method], trans. T. Boy-Żeleński, Kraków 2004, pp. 25ff. and *Medytacje o filozofii pierwszej* [Meditations on First Philosophy], trans. J. Hartman, Kraków 2004, pp. 34ff.

[315] J. Hintikka, '*Cogito, Ergo Sum:* Inference or Performance?', *PhilRev* LXXI (1962), pp. 3–32 and *cf. idem*, '*Cogito, Ergo Sum* as an Inference and Performance?', *PhilRev* LXXII (1963), pp. 487–496. The second of the indicated works was Hintikka's response to two critical papers referring to his first work – *see* J.R. Weinberg, '*Cogito, Ergo Sum*: Some Reflections on Mr. Hintikka's Article', *PhilRev* LXXI (1962), pp. 483–491 and J.D. Carney, '*Cogito, Ergo Sum* and *Sum Res Cogitans*', *PhilRev* LXXI (1962), pp. 492–496. Obviously, we have no room

of Cartesian intuition, suggested an interpretation based on the notion of "existential inconsistency", which has a performative or performatory character.[316] Hintikka tried to demonstrate that by means of this concept, we can explain and understand the gist of Descartes' statement far better than when using the traditional interpretation by inference (though rejected by Descartes himself and by his many critics and commentators), according to which we deal here with the syllogism, whose major enthymematic premise is as follows: "Everyone who thinks, exists".[317] By introducing the category of "existential inconsistency", he stressed that it primarily applies to statements, namely utterances (speech acts) performed by the speakers by means of sentences, formulated in the first person singular.[318] According to Hintikka, expressing by anyone the sentences: "I do not exist", "I think, but I do not exist" (and also—in a conversation with someone—the sentence: "You do not exist") is existentially inconsistent; it is an "existentially self-defeating" utterance.[319] Using the examples given by Hintikka, the sentences: "De Gaulle does not exist" and "Descartes does not exist", or even "Homer does not exist", obviously are not self-contradictory (i.e., contradictory due to pure logical reasons). The absurdity arises only if, for example, General de Gaulle uses the first of these sentences to make assertions concerning his existence: "I – Charles de Gaulle – do not exist".[320] Thus, the "existential inconsistency" of these utterances has a performative character, because only performing (expressing) them triggers the contradiction. It should be strongly emphasised that the concept of performativity is used by Hintikka regardless of the views held by the creator of the theory of performatives; namely John L. Austin—as proven not only by the lack of any mention of this theory in the cited source texts,[321] but also by the fact that the

for a discussion about the correctness of the performative interpretation of Descartes' principle proposed by Hintikka – on this issue, *see* two articles strongly questioning its accuracy: R. Grimm, 'Cogito, ergo sum', *Theoria* XXXI (1965), pp. 162ff. and F. Feldman, 'On the Performatory Interpretation of the *Cogito*', *PhilRev* LXXXII (1973), pp. 345–363.

[316] *See* J. Hintikka, '*Cogito, Ergo Sum:* Inference or Performance?', *op. cit.*, pp. 10ff. and '*Cogito, Ergo Sum* as an Inference and Performance?', *op. cit.*, pp. 489ff.

[317] J. Hintikka, '*Cogito, Ergo Sum:* Inference or Performance?', *op. cit.*, p. 20. Incidentally, in his work, Hintikka has shown that the logical interpretation of Descartes' reasoning, undertaken in the language of modern predicate logic, is inadequate due to at least three reasons: firstly, it is based on existential assumptions; secondly, with such inferential interpretation, it is impossible to distinguish the existence of living individuals from the existence of fictitious persons, such as Hamlet; and thirdly, with this interpretation, Descartes could also assume the following statement to be the basis for his philosophy: "Ambulo [I go], ergo sum" (this objection was already raised by Pierre Gassendi – the most famous critic of Descartes, contemporary to the latter) – for more *see ibidem*, pp. 6ff.

[318] Specifically: sentences in which the speaker refers to himself using the pronoun "I" – *ibidem*, p. 14.

[319] *Ibidem*, p. 13 and note 28 at p. 15. *Cf.* J. Hintikka, '*Cogito, Ergo Sum* as an Inference and Performance?', *op. cit.*, p. 489.

[320] J. Hintikka, '*Cogito, Ergo Sum:* Inference or Performance?', *op. cit.*, pp. 10–14, 19.

[321] Naturally, this is not a complaint against Hintikka, but only a statement of fact that is likely to be explained by the fact that Austin's posthumous *opus magnum*, namely *How to Do Things with*

Finnish philosopher does not mean "doing Things with Words" but—simply—performing utterances. We should not be deceived by the similarity of grammatical form of most of the examples given by Hintikka with the basic grammatical form of performatives in Austin's sense (i.e., the first person singular present tense of the active voice[322]). After all, when uttering the sentences: "I exist", "You do not exist" and the like, we are not able in any way to change the reality (of course with a common sense belief that it exists). Undoubtedly, these are the examples of statements—defined by Austin as "constatives"—whose purpose is to describe, rather than to change extra-linguistic reality. On the other hand, when uttering the statement: "I promise that tomorrow I will visit you", according to Austin, we change the reality by means of a performative (or, more broadly speaking, a speech act): making the promise becomes reality.

The next philosopher in the intellectual "chain" that links the thought of Descartes with Alexy's argumentation in favour of the claim to correctness is Karl-Otto Apel. This precursor of German discourse ethics attempts to demonstrate—in response to the famous *Münchhausen Trilemma* expressed in the late 1960s by Hans Albert[323]—that we have a method of an ultimate foundation (*Letztbegründung*) of our knowledge (and in particular, the rules of discourse ethics), which is not refuted by this trilemma, since it relates solely to the justifications having the nature of logic (deduction, induction or abduction) and it does not take into account the possibility of justification which is not based on deductive proof.[324] Of course, at this point we can present Apel's reasoning only in

Words, had been issued for the first time in 1962, so it was in the same year when Hintikka published the first of the articles referred to there. On the other hand, it cannot be excluded, however, that Hintikka loosely alluded to the concept of performatives, introduced into the philosophy of ordinary language by J.L. Austin.

[322] For more on J.L. Austin's theory of performatives and their differentiation on the basis of grammatical criterion – *see e.g.*, A. Grabowski, *Judicial Argumentation and Pragmatics*, Kraków 1999, pp. 63ff., and the references cited therein.

[323] *See* H. Albert, *Traktat über kritische Vernunft*, 5th ed., Tübingen 1991, pp. 15ff. According to the content of the trilemma, the search for certain foundaments or the ultimate grounds of our knowledge always leads to one of three alternatives: regress into infinity, a logical *circulus vitiosus* or to breaking the chain of justifications and relying on some arbitrarily adopted dogmatic assertion – namely on "Rekurs auf ein *Dogma*".

[324] *See e.g.*, K.-O. Apel, 'Das Apriori der Kommunikationsgemeinschaft und die Grundlagen der Ethik. Zum Problem einer rationalen Begründung der Ethik im Zeitalter der Wissenschaft' in *idem*, *Transformation der Philosophie*, Band II: *Das Apriori der Kommunikationsgemeinschaft*, Frankfurt am Main 1973, pp. 405ff. [English version: 'The *A Priori* of the Communication Community and the Foundations of Ethics', trans. G. Adey, D. Frishy, in *idem*, *Towards a Transformation of Philosophy*, London 1980, pp. 262ff.], 'Das Problem der philosophischen Letztbegründung im Lichte einer transzendentalen Sprachpragmatik. Versuch einer Metakritik des "kritischen Rationalismus"' in *idem*, *Auseinandersetzungen in Erprobung des transzendentalpragmatischen Ansatzes*, Frankfurt am Main 1998, pp. 35ff., in particular, pp. 41ff. [English version: 'The Problem of Philosophical Fundamental Grounding in Light of a Transcendental-Pragmatic of Language', trans. K.R. Pavlovic, *M&W* 8 (1975), pp. 240ff., in particular, pp. 244ff.], and 'Fallibilismus, Konsenstheorie der Wahrheit und Letztbegründung', in *idem*, *Auseinandersetzungen in Erprobung des transzendentalpragmatischen Ansatzes*, *op. cit.*, pp. 156ff. Nota bene,

a nutshell. In his view, justification always boils down to argumentation. Thus, when we argue, we must adopt some transcendental-pragmatic assumptions, which, however, cannot be proven deductively without making the *petitio principii* error (understood by Apel as a fallacy of circularity), but which are indisputable, because each speaker who tries to refute them makes the mistake of "performative self-contradiction" (*performativer Selbstwiderspruch*).[325] According to Apel, when someone claims that:

> on the basis of arguments, I contest the notion that I argue and that I therefore must recognize as irrefutable the presuppositions about the very existence of, and rules for, valid argumentation,[326]

he contradicts himself. The postmetaphysical "principle (criterion) of avoiding performative self-contradiction" (*Prinzip (Kriterium) des zu vermeidenden performativen Selbstwiderspruch*), namely, the necessity of avoiding the contradiction of one's own statements with their necessary argumentative presuppositions—in his opinion—is a test that allows the distinction between the transcendental-pragmatic method of the ultimate foundation of knowledge from the methods of empirical or metaphysical character.[327]

Fortunately, the correctness of Apel's transcendental-pragmatic reasoning is not the subject of our analyses,[328] since we are interested only in the origin and

---

Apel in this way tries to circumvent the trilemma formulated by Albert, although the latter did not limit its scope of validity to logical (deductive) justifications, but explicitly stated that it also concerned other – non-deductive – ways of justification – *see* H. Albert, *Traktat über kritische Vernunft*, *op. cit.*, p. 17.

[325] Let us recall here two, undoubtedly most cited statements that constitute the credo of Karl-Otto Apel's transcendental-pragmatic philosophy: "If I cannot challenge something without actual self-contradiction and I also cannot deductively ground it without a formal-logical *petitio principii*, then that thing belongs to those transcendental-pragmatic presuppositions of argumentation, which one must always have recognised, if a language game of argumentation has to preserve its *meaning*. Therefore, one can call this transcendental-pragmatic pattern of argumentation the *sinnkritische Form der Letzbegründung*" – "Das Problem der philosophischen Letztbegründung im Lichte einer transzendentalen Sprachpragmatik", *op. cit.*, p. 69 [English version, p. 264]. *See* also *idem*, 'Transcendental semiotics and the paradigms of First Philosophy', in *idem*, *From a Trancendental-Semiotic Point of View*, M. Papastephanou (ed.), Manchester/New York 1998, p. 60, where Apel synthetically presents the sense of the transcendental-pragmatic method by means of the following formula: "All those principles can be considered to be grounded ultimately (*letztbegründet*) that cannot be denied without committing a performative self-contradiction of arguing and, precisely for that reason, cannot be grounded by deduction without committing a '*petitio principii*'".

[326] K.-O. Apel, 'Can an Ultimate Foundation of Knowledge Be Non-metaphysical?', trans. B. Gregg, in *idem*, *From a Trancendental-Semiotic Point of View*, *op. cit.*, p. 91.

[327] *See e.g.*, *ibidem*, pp. 90–92 and 'Fallibilismus, Konsenstheorie der Wahrheit und Letztbegründung', *op. cit.*, pp. 159ff.

[328] "Fortunately" – because by leaving this issue aside, we are likely to avoid a blunt conclusion such as the one presented by W.D. Fulsfield, who claims that Apel, Habermas and other discourse ethics – attempting to find ultimately justified knowledge by using the method based on finding the "performative contradiction" of utterances – should take remedia logic courses – *see idem*, 'Can Jürgen Habermas's "Begründungsprogramm" Escape Hans Albert's *Münchhausen Trilemma*?',

history of the *performativer Widerspruch* concept. By introducing the concept of "performative self-contradiction", Apel expressly referred to the previously discussed analysis of Hintikka, thus highlighting, yet not too clearly, the performative aspect of "existential inconsistency" and using the examples of sentences provided by the Finnish philosopher.[329] It can easily be noted that Hintikka's thought (and, indirectly, also that of Descartes) has been greatly twisted (if not distorted) by Apel.

The most important and immediately striking difference is that Apel identifies thinking (*denken*) with argumentation (*argumentieren*).[330] Hintikka's analyses clearly showed[331] that Descartes, aware of the possibility of a performative interpretation of the basic principles of his philosophy (that is the thesis: "Cogito, ergo sum"), allowed for the possibility of replacing *cogito* only by relevant grammatical forms of a few verbs, called by Hintikka "verbs of intellectus", such as *dubio* or *profero*. Thus, when Apel writes:

> [j]etzt kann ich, wie schon Descartes selbst angedeutet hat, die *Evidenz* der notwendigen Koinzidenz meines Denkens bzw. Argumentierens und meines Existerens *entdecken*,[332]

it seems that this statement can only be accepted provided that we understand argumentation as a self-reflexive "discussion" with oneself and not as an externalised, real discussion (argumentation) with others.[333] In the latter case, the

op. cit., p. 79, note 11. Let us note that one can easily challenge the correctness of Apel's reasoning, even relying solely on his theory. For example, one can raise the objection that he himself made an error of *performativer Selbstwiderspruch*, because one can attribute to him a curious assertion (at least from a logical point of view), which has a justifying function: "*Petitio principii* error cannot apply to my ultimate foundation of knowledge" (*cf. supra*, quotations presented in note 325 at p. 145). Certainly, if one adopts such an assumption – even openly – then she/he can freely construct such an "ultimate foundation of knowledge".

[329] *See e.g.*, K.-O. Apel, 'Das Problem der philosophischen Letztbegründung im Lichte einer transzendentalen Sprachpragmatik', *op. cit.*, pp. 70ff. [English version, pp. 265ff.], 'Fallibilismus, Konsenstheorie der Wahrheit und Letztbegründung', *op. cit.*, pp. 159ff., 179ff., and 'Grenzen der Diskursethik? Versuch einer Zwischenbilanz', *ZphF* 40 (1986), pp. 11ff.

[330] K.-O. Apel, 'Fallibilismus, Konsenstheorie der Wahrheit und Letztbegründung', *op. cit.*, p. 180. Similarly in 'Grenzen der Diskursethik?', *op. cit.*, p. 11.

[331] *See* J. Hintikka, '*Cogito, Ergo Sum:* Inference or Performance?', *op. cit.*, pp. 17, 19, 23ff. and '*Cogito, Ergo Sum* as an Inference and Performance?', *op. cit.*, pp. 489–490.

[332] K.-O. Apel, 'Fallibilismus, Konsenstheorie der Wahrheit und Letztbegründung', *op. cit.*, p. 180.

[333] It is worth quoting here a very short fragment of Descartes' *Second Meditation*, which most emphatically weighs in favour of such an – introspective – understanding of performative interpretation of the thesis "Cogito, ergo sum", which in the Latin original reads as follows: "denique statuendum sit hoc pronunciatum, *ego sum*, *ego existo*, QUOTIES A ME PROFETUR, VEL MENTE CONCIPITUR, necessario esse verum" [emphasis in capital letters – *A.G.*].

statement: "Argumentiere, ergo sum" would have the same evidential (cognitive) value as the sentence "Ambulo, ergo sum" (I walk, therefore I am), rejected by Descartes himself.

Moreover, when Hintikka was introducing the concepts of "existential inconsitency" and "existentially self-defeating sentences", he insisted that the existentially self-defeating character of such an expression as: "I do not exist", is considerably different from the non-existentially self-defeating character of such a statement as: "I doubt everything".[334] Meanwhile, when Apel is introducing the concept of "performative self-contradiction" and the principle of avoiding it, he treats this principle as *Kriterium der selbstreflexiven Diskursrationalität*, which allows him—in a non-deductive way—to ultimately justify not only existential assertions (such as: "I exist", "You exist" etc.), but also numerous and quite complex rules of discourse ethics. Apel refers here to, inter alia, Habermas's four validity claims (*Geltungsansprüche*),[335] and to the principle of equality (*Gleichberechtigung*) of all members of real communities of communication or even all imaginable members of an ideal community of communication.[336]

Finally, it should be added that when interpreting Hintikka's analysis, Apel assumes[337] that the Finnish philosopher based his argumentation on John L. Austin's theory of performatives. Apel's assumption leads to the ambiguity of the concept of performativity [(1) performing an utterance—Hintikka; (2) an utterance of a certain grammatical form, characteristic for performatives—Austin's grammatical criterion of performatives; (3) the change of reality by means of words—Austin's functional

---

[334] *See* J. Hintikka, '*Cogito, Ergo Sum* as an Inference and Performance?', *op. cit.*, note 5 at p. 489, and the references cited therein.

[335] On the category of "validity claims" (*Geltungsansprüche*) *see e.g.*, J. Habermas, 'Vorbereitende Bemerkungen zu einer Theorie der kommunikativen Kompetenz (Vorlage für Zwecke einer Seminardiskussion)' in J. Habermas, N. Luhmann, *Theorie der Gesellschaft oder Sozialtechnologie – Was leistet die Systemforschung?*, Frankfurt am Main 1971, pp. 114ff., 123ff., 'Vorlesungen zu einer sprachtheoretischen Grundlegung der Soziologie' in *idem*, *Vorstudien und Ergänzungen zur Theorie des kommunikativen Handelns*, Frankfurt am Main 1984, pp. 80ff., 104ff., and 'Was heißt Universalpragmatik?' in: *ibidem*, pp. 354ff., 417ff.

[336] K.-O. Apel, 'Fallibilismus, Konsenstheorie der Wahrheit und Letztbegründung', *op. cit.*, p. 181. It is hard here not to make a rather unfriendly comment that this criterion is reminiscent of the Golden Fish from the Brothers Grimm famous tale, living – not just in my opinion – in an imaginary world of post-metaphysical pseudoscience, in which the *Münchhausen Trilemma* is not applicable and which fulfils all the wishes of the creators of discourse ethics, in particular, as it provides the "ultimate foundation" of many discourse rules which are of a purely ideological character. For more on this issue, *see e.g.*, H. Albert, 'Die angebliche Paradoxie des konsequenten Fallibilismus und die Ansprüche der Transzendentalpragmatik', *ZphF* 41 (1987), pp. 421–428, and the references cited therein. In his paper, Albert uses an even more pictorial comparison, characterising transcendental pragmatics as a project that "consists of pulling rabbits from the empty cylinder" (p. 427). Nothing more, nothing less.

[337] *See* K.-O. Apel, 'Das Problem der philosophischen Letztbegründung im Lichte einer transzendentalen Sprachpragmatik', *op. cit.*, p. 70 [English version, p. 265]. Let us recall that, as I have tried to demonstrate above, there is no immediate reason to adopt such a pedigree for Hintikka's thought – *cf. supra*, note 321 at p. 143, with the corresponding text. One may only speculate on this.

criterion of performatives] and, consequently, to the indeterminacy of the concept of "performative self-contradiction".[338] On the one hand, Apel—as I believe—very rightly insists on the fact that the "performative self-contradiction" is not of logical character.[339] In his view, the essence of it is a "clash" of propositional content of a given assertion (for example: "I do not exist") with the act of performing it (the utterance: "I claim that I do not exist").[340] However, on the other hand, Apel often translates the analysed statements into a grammatical form characteristic for performatives (in Austin's sense), as a result of which, in the case of non-existentially self-defeating statements, logical contradiction of the speaker's beliefs is fully manifested. Let us consider the following statements quoted by him: "Ich behaupte mit Verständlichkeitsanspruch, daß ich keinen Verständlichkeitsanspruch habe" or: "Ich behaupte als wahr, daß ich keinen Wahrheitanspruch habe".[341] Hence, many commentators and critics of his transcendental-pragmatic method of the ultimate fundamental grounding of knowledge recognise that the essence of the "performative self-contradiction" lies in the logical contradiction; therefore, they formulate a view under which utterances (speech acts), showing a "performative self-contradiction" constitute a subset of logically contradictory statements (speech acts).[342] This, in turn, implies that each *performativer Selbstwiderspruch* is a logical contradiction in the Aristotelian sense, even if it cannot be fully reduced to it.

Finally, the last philosopher who links Cartesian *Cogito* with the justification of Alexy's argument from correctness based on the recognition of "performative contradiction" is Jürgen Habermas. The creator of universal pragmatics, stressing Apel's merits in renewing a transcendental, non-deductive way of justifying ethical norms, borrows from him the concept of "performative contradiction" (*performativer Widerspruch*), defining it in a pragmatic-logical manner. In his view, "performative contradiction" within the meaning of Apel, occurs

---

[338] *See e.g.*, M. Kettner, 'Ansatz zu einer Taxonomie performativer Selbstwidersprüche' in A. Dorschel *et al.* (eds.), *Transzendentalpragmatik. Ein Symposion für Karl-Otto Apel*, Frankfurt am Main 1993, pp. 187ff., who identifies several types of *performativer Selbstwiderspruch* and presents an ordered list of sentences analysed by Apel, having the character of "performative self-contradiction" (*cf.* note 10 at p. 196).

[339] *See e.g.*, K.-O. Apel, 'Fallibilismus, Konsenstheorie der Wahrheit und Letztbegründung', *op. cit.*, p. 165ff., in particular, pp. 179–183. For more on this issue, *cf.* Apel's works indicated *supra*, note 324 at p. 144.

[340] *See e.g.*, K.-O. Apel, *ibidem*, pp. 180, 182.

[341] The examples are taken from K.-O. Apel, 'Fallibilismus, Konsenstheorie der Wahrheit und Letztbegründung', *op. cit.*, p. 160.

[342] *See e.g.*, R. Gebauer, *Letzte Begründung*, *op. cit.*, pp. 128ff., and the references cited therein. The view expressed here is based mainly on the analyses of M. Kettner, which show that most, but not all of Apel's examples of performatively self-contradictory statements can be interpreted as a logical contradiction – in particular, these are all acts referred to by Kettner as "performative logical contradictions"; whereas this concept is considered by Kettner as the only adequate explanation of the concept of *performativer Selbstwiderspruch* – *see idem*, 'Ansatz zu einer Taxonomie performativer Selbstwidersprüche', *op. cit.*, pp. 206ff., in particular, p. 208.

> when a certain constative speech act (*Sprechhandlung*) "Kp" is based on non-contingent assumptions whose propositional content contradicts the affirmative expression "p".[343]

Thus, the Habermasian interpretation of the concept of "performative contradiction" boils its essence down to a logical contradiction. Using an example taken over from Hintikka, the philosopher from Frankfurt maintains that this contradiction takes place between the utterance: "Ich existiere (hier und jetzt) nicht" and the inevitable existential premise, which is adopted by the speaker in making this utterance (*indem er sie äußert*), the propositional content of which reads: "Ich existiere (hier und jetzt)".[344] Based on the analysis of the "performative contradiction", Habermas also presents a list of some of the necessary assumptions of the argumentation.[345]

In this way, we now find the last chain in this short history of the concept of "performative contradiction". In Alexy's works, in which he uses this concept, we do not find any explanation of its origin; nonetheless, the only evidence of the text—one of the footnotes in the paper *Problems of Discursive Rationality in Law* of 1990,[346] repeated in the "Afterword" to the second edition of *Theorie der juristischen Argumentation* of 1991[347]—shows just the above-indicated work of Habermas. By using, in his analyses, the method based on identifying "performative contradiction", Alexy indeed refers to one of the works of Neil MacCormick,[348] but

---

343 J. Habermas, 'Diskursethik – Notizen zu einem Begründungsprogramm' in *idem*, *Moralbewußtsein und kommunikatives Handeln*, 6th ed., Frankfurt am Main 1996, p. 90.

344 *Ibidem*, pp. 90–91.

345 *Ibidem*, pp. 100ff.

346 R. Alexy, 'Problems of Discursive Rationality in Law', *op. cit.*, note 7 at p. 175.

347 R. Alexy, 'Nachwort (1991): Antwort auf einige Kritiker', *op. cit.*, note 64 at p. 428.

348 R. Alexy, 'On Necessary Relations between Law and Morality', *op. cit.*, p. 178, note 14 and 'Zur Kritik des Rechtspositivismus', *op. cit.*, p. 19, note 39. Alexy refers to the argument presented by MacCormick in 'Law, Morality and Positivism', *op. cit.*, p. 141, which concerns the requirements of the sincerity of legislative acts. MacCormick asks whether it will not be pragmatically self-contradictory, even if it is not contradictory in the logical sense, when the British Parliament passes a bill under the absurd title of "Unjust Restraints Act on Picketing Act 1970" or "The Unjust Taxation of the Wealthy Act". However, let us note that the similarity with the first Alexy example (i.e., the article of a constitution) is very loose here. Firstly, MacCormick uses the imaginary titles of statutes, and not the examples of articles (provisions) contained in them and, secondly, he explicitly excludes the logical explanation of the absurdity of the titles cited. Moreover, according to MacCormick, this argument only shows that the legislator should make laws on the basis of sincerely accepted values. Incidentally, it should be added that MacCormick himself firmly rejects accepting or expressing any claims (including the claim to correctness) by law as such – *see idem*, 'Why Law Makes No Claims' in G. Pavlakos (ed.), *Law, Rights and Discourse*, *op. cit.*, pp. 59–67. For more on this issue *see* E.Ph. Soper, 'Law's Normative Claims' in R.P. George (ed.), *The Autonomy of Law*, *op. cit.*, pp. 220 and p. 242, note 11. Soper is trying to justify the existence of claims in law (for example, the claim to justice), but recognises that the essence of MacCormick's examples comes down to the following truism on human behaviour, "that conscientious people (unless they are engaging in some odd joke of the Monty Python sort) do not offer advice, much less issue demands or take actions that affect others, unless they implicitly believe that what they are doing – advising, acting, ordering – is based on morally defensible (sincerely held) beliefs about what it is permissible or right to do". Soper also points out that many authors (in his opinion, including Alexy) overestimate the importance of this fact – since

given the similarity in terminology (let us recall that Alexy does not use in any of his works the concept of "existential inconsistency" introduced by Hintikka, or the concept of "performative self-contradiction" proposed by Apel), as well as his own logical interpretation of "performative contradiction", as was described earlier, we can assume that what constitutes the reference point for him is a Habermasian understanding of "performative contradiction". Incidentally, Habermas, in turn, analyses the necessary assumptions of argumentation by using the catalogue of the rules and forms of practical discourse, created by Alexy.[349]

Before going on to the critical analysis of the justification of the argument from correctness, we still have to prove the accuracy of the second thesis that was formulated at the beginning of this section. It should be explained why we claim that the close relationship of the Cartesian first principle of philosophy with Alexy's justification of the necessity to adopt the claim to correctness in law is easy to demonstrate also at a general philosophical level. In this aspect, we naturally mean a methodological relation, or more broadly speaking, epistemological one. The basic merit of Descartes was a breakthrough in the process of justification of human knowledge—an Archimedean point of philosophy has been found by him in self-knowledge, in the discovery of *Cogito*. As Władysław Tatarkiewicz wrote:

> Descartes has shown that the foundation of knowledge is to be sought not in the external world, but in man, not in the object, but in the subject, not in matter but in the conscious spirit.[350]

This Cartesian study of the self initiated modern philosophy, in which knowledge is based primarily on the study of reason; on the analyses of the cognitive powers of the mind. As noted by Jan Hartman, whose analyses we use here, the Cartesian system initiates the philosophy, which in its mature form (since Kant) is called a "critical" or "transcendental" philosophy.[351] Following this path of reasoning, it can be undoubtedly concluded that the transcendental method used in Kant's critical philosophy constitutes a certain development of the rationalist epistemological ideas of the author of *Discours de la Métode*. From this point, it is only one step to Alexy's nonpositivist argumentation, referring in many points to Kantianism, in particular, under a transcendental-pragmatic justification of the validity of the rules of general practical discourse, which has a key role in his conception of practical reason. Yet, only the existence of this kind of reason,

---

the fact that conscientious people believe that they act rightly, does not prove that this is actually so; therefore, the latter cannot constitute the basis to undermine the positivist thesis of the lack of the necessary connection between law and morality.

[349] *See* J. Habermas, 'Diskursethik – Notizen zu einem Begründungsprogramm', *op. cit.*, pp. 97ff.

[350] W. Tatarkiewicz, *Historia filozofii* [History of Philosophy], vol. II: *Filozofia nowożytna do roku 1830* [Modern Philosophy to 1830], 10th ed., Warszawa 1983, p. 48.

[351] J. Hartman, 'Posłowie: Tylko dla dorosłych' [Afterword: For Adults Only] in R. Descartes, *Rozprawa o metodzie*, *op. cit.*, pp. 54–55.

without which the whole nonpositivist conception becomes meaningless, allows him, among other things, to formulate the thesis of the necessity of adopting the claim to correctness in law.

4.7.3 Justification of *Richtigkeitsargument* by Means of Recognition of "Performative Contradiction"

Before we criticise Alexy's application of the method based on the recognition of *performativer Widerspruch*, it is worth noting that if we do not take into account the philosophical origin of this concept—reconstructed in the previous section—then the "performative contradiction" can be associated with such speech acts as: "I promise to visit you tomorrow, but I do not intend to do it". This association is even strengthened by Alexy's repeatedly expressed view that the incorrectness or defectiveness (*Fehlerhaftigkeit*) of the examples of sentences analysed by him is similar,[352] or that they show a "certain analogy"[353] to a speech act repeatedly analysed by Austin: "The cat is on the mat but I do not believe it is". This initial intuition, however, proved to be illusory.[354] This kind of speech act, for which the classic archetype is the so-called Moore's paradox: "I went to the pictures last Tuesday but I do not believe that I did" (or: "It is raining, but I do not believe it"),[355] indeed belong—according to Austin—to the group of performatives (speech acts) that

[352] R. Alexy, *Theorie der juristischen Argumentation, op. cit.*, p. 266 [English version, p. 215].

[353] R. Alexy, 'On Necessary Relations Between Law and Morality', *op. cit.*, note 15 at p. 179, 'Zur Kritik des Rechtspositivismus', *op. cit.*, note 40 at p. 20, and *Begriff und Geltung des Rechts, op. cit.*, note 45 at p. 68, [English version, note 66 at p. 38].

[354] In the discussion to follow, I mainly focus on the issue of contradiction, thus skipping one more argument for the rejection of the mentioned initial intuition. The point is that the statement like: "I promise to visit you tomorrow, but I do not intend to do so" cannot be treated as a promise at all, since its author explicitly denies one of the necessary and sufficient conditions of its successful performance ("happiness") – *see e.g.*, U. Neumann review of R. Alexy's book: *Begriff und Geltung des Rechts, op. cit.*, p. 244; identically T. Gizbert-Studnicki, A. Grabowski, 'Kilka uwag o niepozytywistycznej koncepcji prawa', *op. cit.*, s. 64. Meanwhile, the two examples of utterances given by Alexy are only defective, which means that the imaginary article of the constitution is the article of the constitution, and the convicting sentence is a convicting sentence. Such standpoint assumed by Alexy is easy to explain: let us recall that he accepts only a qualifying (not classifying) nature of the connection between law and morality in relation to particular legal norms and decisions, so the defectiveness of the cited article of the constitution and court ruling does not result in the loss of their legal character – *cf.* Chap. 3, pp. 41ff.

[355] More on "Moore's paradox" (the name of the paradox comes from L. Wittgenstein) *see* T. Czarnecki, *Moore i Wittgenstein. Niekartezjańskie rozwiązania problemu pewności* [Moore and Wittgenstein. Non-Cartesian Solutions of the Problem of Certainty], Kraków 2001, pp. 103ff., and the references cited therein. *See* also L.W. Forguson, 'On "It's Raining, But I Don't Believe It"', *Theoria* XXXIV (1968), pp. 89–101, who discusses and considers, inter alia, the analyses of statements like: "*p* but I do not believe that *p*", provided by G.E. Moore, J. Hintikka, M. Black, and J.L. Austin (p. 91–93).

"abuse procedures" and thus are not implemented or consummated,[356] or to a group of "self-defeating" speech acts (according to a later terminology of Daniel Vandervaken and John Searle,[357] referring, as one might assume, to Hintikka's terminology), but in these acts we do not deal with contradiction in a logical sense. Austin and other representatives of the speech act theory emphasise unanimously[358] that the fact that "the cat is on the mat" is not in any sense contradictory to the fact that "I do not believe it". The latter can be perfectly seen when one changes the grammatical subject of the second sentence: "The cat is on the mat, but he does not believe it", or the tense of the two sentences: "The cat was on the mat, but he did not believe it". It is after all obvious that "the cat being on the mat" is independent of anybody's belief that this is so or not, and the relation between sentences, which constitute locutionary acts within the analysed speech acts, does not have a logical character.[359] The essence of the error lies in the fact that, for example, when uttering the sentence: "It is raining, but I do not believe it", we explicitly deny one of the conditions (in this case it is the sincerity condition, also called a responsibility condition), whose fulfilment, in turn, conditions the fact as to whether uttering this sentence will be a successful ("happy" in the language of Austin's theory) act of assertion. Meanwhile, Alexy's two examples pointed out, from the very outset, a logical contradiction (the fact that the German scholar stated it only in 2000, is of course irrelevant). Let us add that this difference comes to light even more emphatically in the case of the already mentioned complex speech act, which Alexy used in order to define assertions: "Ich behaupte, daß es regnet, und ich betone dabei, daß dies falsch ist".[360] This act "contains in itself" a logical contradiction, taking place between the propositional content of an act of assertion (*Behauptung*): "it is raining",

---

[356] J.L. Austin, *How to Do Things with Words. The William James Lectures delivered at Harvard University in 1955*, 2nd ed., J.O. Urmson, M. Sbisà (eds.), Oxford 1976, p. 16.

[357] *See* D. Vanderveken, 'Illocutionary Logic and Self-defeating Speech Acts' in J.R. Searle *et al.* (eds.), *Speech Act Theory and Pragmatics*, Dordrecht/Boston/London 1980, pp. 249ff., 264ff. and J.R. Searle, D. Vanderveken, *Foundations of Illocutionary Logic*, *op. cit.*, pp. 148ff.

[358] *See* J.L. Austin, *How to Do Things with Words*, *op. cit.*, pp. 48ff. *Cf.* J.L. Austin, 'The Meaning of a Word' in *idem*, *Philosophical papers*, *op. cit.*, pp. 63ff., 'Performative utterances', in *ibidem*, p. 248, and 'Performative-Constative', trans. G.J. Warnock, in J.R. Searle (ed.), *The Philosophy of Language*, Oxford 1971, p. 17; L.W. Forguson, 'On "It's Raining, But I Don't Believe It"', *op. cit.*, pp. 89–90.

[359] The fact that Austin speaks in this context of "implying", should not mislead us, because he stresses that he uses the concept of implication in the sense referring to the one identified by Moore, whereas the implication of a logical character is expressed by him with the word "entails" (*see e.g.*, J.L. Austin, *How to Do Things with Words*, *op. cit.*, pp. 47–49). On the other hand, the fact that there is no logical connection here is very easy to prove (as demonstrated, among others, by Austin and Forguson in the above-mentioned works). Namely, if the sentence: "The cat is on the mat" implied – in a logical sense – the sentence: "I believe that the cat is on the mat" then, according to the law of transposition $(p \rightarrow q) \equiv (\sim q \rightarrow \sim p)$, the sentence: "It is not true that I believe that the cat is on the mat" should imply the sentence: "It is not true that the cat is on the mat". However, it is not the case.

[360] Alexy uses this example in 'Diskurstheorie und Menschenrechte', *op. cit.*, p. 136 [English version, p. 214]. *Cf. supra*, note 170 at p. 103, with the corresponding text.

and the propositional content of a subsequent act of emphasis (*Betonung*): "but it is false"; namely "it is not true that it is raining". Therefore, this example has nothing to do with "Moore's paradox" or Austin's example. The only thing that distinguishes it from other examples studied by Alexy is the fact that in the quoted assertion, a classic logical contradiction occurs between propositional contents of the components of this complex utterance, expressed directly by the speaker.

So what might Alexy have in mind when he mentions the similarity of his examples of utterances to those of Austin? One may reasonably infer that he means the following similarity. When someone says, "The cat is on the mat, but I do not believe it", then he clearly contradicts the sincerity condition of the assertions, according to which we should believe in (or at least take responsibility for) what we state. When comparing this speech act with the examples studied by Alexy, it should be recalled that—in his opinion—the author of the constitution, enacting the article which sets forth the injustice of state X, explicitly denies that state X ought to be just (i.e., he denies the claim to justice, which is regarded here as a special case of the claim to correctness[361]); while the judge, speaking of the erroneous conviction, explicitly denies that this judgment ought to be correct (i.e., she/he denies the claim to correctness). Yet, does such an analogy actually take place? It can obviously be long argued over, but—in my opinion—it is undisputed that the violation of the sincerity condition of the assertions consists in a failure of fulfilling it by the speaker. This failure of fulfilling the condition is of a functional character; it takes place in the "world of human actions", even if they only have a linguistic character of speech acts. Therefore, when we aim at interpreting them in the form of a classic logical contradiction, we make a categorial mistake, since the logical contradiction concerns only propositions, or extra-linguistic reality or, ultimately, our beliefs (in accordance with, respectively, logical, ontological and psychological interpretation of the Aristotelian principle of contradiction: $\sim (p \land \sim p)$[362]), but it cannot refer to things (entities) that belong to different ontological categories. Formulating the thesis that performing a certain act of assertion is logically contradictory with the condition of its satisfaction (happiness) results in treating a logical contradiction as a relation that exists between the sincerity condition (and thus a certain linguistic directive) and the speaker's behaviour. It is—as I believe—an obvious nonsense; then we would have to argue, by analogy, that there is a logical contradiction between the sanctioned legal norm encoded, for example, in Article 233 § 1 of the Polish Penal Code[363] and the behaviour (action) of the person that testifies untruthfully.[364]

[361] *Cf.* Chap. 3, note 73 at p. 41, with the corresponding text.

[362] *See* J. Łukasiewicz, *O zasadzie sprzeczności u Arystotelesa* [On the Principle of Contradiction in Aristotle], J. Woleński (ed.), Warszawa 1987, pp. 9ff.

[363] This provision reads: "Whoever, by submitting evidence to serve as evidence in court proceedings or other proceedings conducted under the statute, testifies untruthfully or conceals the truth, shall be liable to imprisonment for up to 3 years".

[364] Let us add that a possible defence of the thesis that we are dealing here with a logical contradiction, which consists in assuming that such a contradiction does not occur between the legal norm and the behaviour, but between the norm and the description of the perpetrator of the

Moreover, in such cases, one may only metaphorically speak of a "contradiction"—stating a contradiction of an Ought (expressed respectively in the sincerity condition or in a legal norm) with an Is (human behaviour) resembles a naturalist fallacy, which is well-known to theorists. It is therefore hardly surprising that philosophers of language, analysing the problem of defective speech acts, do not usually mention the logical contradictions (and only sometimes "illocutionarily inconsistent performative sentences"[365]), but they study these acts in extra-logical terms of their successful performance (in the jargon of Austin's theory of performatives: their "felicity" or "happiness"[366]).

Leaving this critical topic aside, this is where we come to the essential issue, which—so as not to make a categorial mistake—should be expressed in the form of the following questions. Can a logical contradiction occurring between propositional contents of the quoted article of the constitution and a court ruling and (respectively) their necessary (according to Alexy) argumentative assumptions at least illustrate the existence of a claim to correctness in practical and legal discourse? Do these examples in some way justify the thesis about the necessity of adopting a claim to correctness in law?

This may sound slightly sophistic, but let us answer these two questions clearly and unmistakably: of course it is not the case, because in a logical sense, everything results from the contradiction (from a pair of contradictory sentences); namely, both the fact that the claim to correctness occurs in that discourse and that it does not occur there. Another conclusion that can be drawn is that Alexy is not a co-creator of the nonpositivist conception of law, but rather a hard legal positivist and so forth.

In order not to leave any doubt, let us consider the consequences of a logical principle of the excluded middle: $p \vee \sim p$. If we assume that the basic laws of logic are still valid in a practical (normative) discourse and that instead of truth in this discourse we use the concept of practical correctness, it would seem that according to *tertium non datur*, out of a pair of contradictory statements, one must be correct and the other incorrect. Thus, this principle seems to entail that the article of the constitution stating that "State *X* is just", should be regarded as correct, whereas the article of the constitution "State *X* is not just" should be regarded as incorrect (and similarly in the case of a conviction). This conclusion, however, is a crude misunderstanding, at least due to two reasons. The first and more important reason is of an external nature to Alexy's theory: a mere logical principle of the excluded middle does not yet allow us to decide which sentence out of a pair of contradictory statements is correct (or true) and which is incorrect (or false). The second, somewhat less important reason is of an internal character because it is based on Alexy's findings under the theory of practical discourse. He emphasises repeatedly

crime, is also unacceptable. If we approve a non-cognitivist position, then we consider legal norms to be devoid of logical values. Thus, even with such an interpretation, we would have to ridiculously argue that there is a logical contradiction between the norm, which does not have a logical value, and a proposition that *ex definitione* has a logical value.

[365] *See* D. Vanderveken, 'Illocutionary Logic and Self-defeating Speech Acts', *op. cit.*, p. 249.

[366] *See* J.L. Austin, *How to Do Things with Words*, *op. cit.*, pp. 14ff.

that a procedural understanding of correctness allows for the possibility of recognising as legitimate normative sentences (or norms) which are mutually contradictory; a possible result of rational practical discourse can be thus both normative sentences, (or norms) *N*, as well as ~*N*.[367] Thus, according to his theory, the principle of contradiction, and therefore also the principle of the excluded middle, which is a logical consequence of the former, are not fully valid within the practical and legal discourse[368] (which is also indirectly shown by Alexy's rejecting Dworkin's one right answer thesis, as already mentioned earlier).

When we summarise previous arguments, it appears that the application of the method of identifying "performative contradiction" does not allow us to achieve the goals set for it by Alexy. To put this more generally, the belief of discursive philosophers that by showing contradictions between sentences (expressing the propositional contents and the necessary conditions of speech acts), we can reach the knowledge about the basic elements of a linguistic or extra-linguistic reality (for example, about the necessary claims in the practical discourse), is logically unjustifiable and—from the epistemological point of view—puzzling. In our view, we must therefore agree with the assessment of William Fusfield, who—when analysing the application of the method based on recognising "performative contradiction" by Habermas and other creators of discursive ethics—uses the term "Abracadabra Epistemology".[369] Indeed, if our cognition of the world was to be based on uttering pairs of contradictory statements and then claiming that due to this logical contradiction, one of them must be true, then the choice of the true (or practically correct) sentence would have to be dictated by extra-logical reasons; accordingly, logic does not in any autonomous way imply which sentence is true. Let us illustrate it with a simple example. The sentence: "John likes strawberries" is contradictory to the sentence: "It is not true that John likes strawberries". Can we only, on the basis of a mere contradiction of the contents of these sentences or by

[367] *See e.g.*, R. Alexy, 'Die Idee einer prozeduralen Theorie der juristischen Argumentation', *op. cit.*, p. 183, note 19, 'Probleme der Diskurstheorie', *op. cit.*, pp. 89ff., 'Nachwort (1991): Antwort auf einige Kritiker', *op. cit.*, pp. 413ff., and 'Ota Weinbergers Kritik der diskurstheoretischen Deutung juristischer Rationalität', *op. cit.*, p. 151, note 24.

[368] "Not fully" – because these principles apply only to individual participants in the practical discourse within the systems of normative statements or norms adopted by them, in accordance with the first basic rule (*Grundregel*) of practical discourse (1.1): "Kein Sprecher darf sich widersprechen". For more on this topic, *see* Alexy's works indicated in the previous note. Let us add that a rather peculiar assumption arises in this context; namely, that by means of the identification of the "performative contradiction" of utterances, we can only reach the knowledge available to particular individuals (because the quoted contradiction rule concerns each of these people individually), but not the knowledge which is common (non-individual and non-subjective). This assumption is by no means meaningless. It should be recalled that the transition from "Cogito, ergo sum" to a certain, common knowledge of the existence of the material world is provided to us only, according to Descartes, by the existence of a perfect God – on this issue, *see e.g.*, W. Tatarkiewicz, *Historia filozofii*, *op. cit.*, p. 49 and J. Hartman, 'Posłowie: Tylko dla dorosłych', *op. cit.*, pp. 62ff.

[369] W.D. Fusfield, 'Can Jürgen Habermas's "Begründungsprogramm" Escape Hans Albert's *Münchhausen Trilemma*?', *op. cit.*, p. 81.

uttering them, logically infer anything about whether John likes strawberries or does not like them? It is undisputed that, in this way, we cannot determine—unless purely arbitrarily—which of these sentences is true. Gaining moral knowledge in such a way seems *a priori* impossible without adopting additional, substantive (extra-logical) premises of choice.

This brings us to the last issue, associated with the method based on identifying the "performative contradiction" of statements, which should be discussed. At first glance, the objection of an arbitrary choice of correct (true) sentences seems to be inaccurate in relation to Alexy's nonpositivist argumentation for the necessity of adopting a claim to correctness in law. In his more recent works, Alexy uses the feature of "absurdity" as an indicator of practical incorrectness of the examples of "performatively contradictory" statements analysed by him.[370] If we therefore admit, after Alexy, that the quoted article of the constitution and the conviction are indeed absurd, then the arbitrariness objection will be, if not rebutted, at least severely weakened. Thus, it can be maintained that on account of the absurdity of one of the contradictory sentences, the other must be at least non-absurd, if not practically correct (true).[371] Let us discuss from this point of view both the examples provided by Alexy.

To begin, let us recall that the examples of statements analysed by Alexy deal with the absurdity that may be—according to the eliminating argument used by him—explained in full only when we treat the faults made by the authors of these statements as conceptual (and not only as technical, moral, conventional or legal faults). Many critics of Alexy's analytical nonpositivist argumentation (most of all, Eugenio Bulygin[372] and Ulfrid Neumann[373]) try to demonstrate that—contrary to Alexy's opinion—these statements are wrong in another sense (e.g., legal, political or social), but that these are not conceptual faults. In the analysis to follow, we will try to refute Alexy's thesis in a slightly different way; namely, by identifying situational contexts in which the absurdity of these statements is out of the question.[374]

---

[370] *See e.g.*, R. Alexy, 'Law and Correctness', *op. cit.*, p. 209ff. [German version, pp. 7ff.], 'The Nature of Arguments about the Nature of Law', *op. cit.*, pp. 11ff., and 'The Nature of Legal Philosophy', *op. cit.*, p. 72.

[371] As to the merits of such a "transition" from non-absurdity to correctness (truth) of normative sentences and norms, *see* comments in the last paragraph of this section at p. 159.

[372] *See* E. Bulygin, 'Alexy und das Richtigkeitsargument', *op. cit.*, pp. 21ff. and 'Is There a Conceptual Connection between Law and Morality?', *op. cit.*, pp. 54ff. It should be added that, in both papers, Bulygin, when analysing Alexy's examples, shows that if we treat them as prescriptions (norms), then these statements simply become meaningless (*sinnlos*), by which – perhaps unintentionally – he supports the thesis of their absurdity.

[373] *Cf.* U. Neumann's review of R. Alexy's book: *Theorie der juristischen Argumentation*, *op. cit.*, p. 213, *Juristische Argumentationslehre*, *op. cit.*, pp. 89ff., and his review of R. Alexy's book: *Begriff und Geltung des Rechts*, *op. cit.*, pp. 243ff.

[374] This form of criticism is indirectly pointed out by Alexy himself, by distinguishing in the course of the polemics with Bulygin two ways of understanding a court ruling (*das Urteil im engeren / weiteren Sinne*): in the narrower sense – corresponding to the very tenor of the ruling, and in a wider sense, in order to demonstrate that the judge can use – within a broadly understood

Let us start with the second example, because it is relatively easier to demonstrate non-absurdity of the judge's statement. When analysing this example ("The defendant is hereby sentenced to life imprisonment, albeit wrongly, because valid law was interpreted incorrectly"), we can observe that its absurdity disappears in those legal systems which use the majority rule in determining the content of the court ruling, and which, at the same time, have the institution of dissenting opinion (*votum separatum*), or, alternatively, which adopt individual judicial justification of legal decisions, drawn up by the judges who are members of the bench—as is the case in many countries whose legal systems belong to the system of common law.[375] In such legal systems, it is undoubtedly most legitimate and possible that the same judge (outvoted during the deliberation) first signs the guilty verdict (thus convicting the accused), and then, when giving reasons for his dissent, she/he can claim that this ruling is incorrect because the interpretation of the law applied in the case was erroneous. In the case of the analysed verdict, the judge's fault consists only of the fact that she/he expressed her/his belief in an erroneous interpretation of law already in the sentence of the guilty verdict, and not in its justification. Yet, apart from this purely legal issue, do her/his statements contain something absurd in conceptual terms? The judge, who considers the ruling incorrect and informs about it, undoubtedly acts in compliance with the general competence conferred on him by law, which is by no means absurd, since the majority principle in rendering judgments is, if not more effective, then at least as equally acceptable as the principle of unanimous decisions. Allowing the judge who has a dissenting opinion as to the correctness of the decision to express this view, also deserves approval, from both the legal as well as moral standpoint.[376]

In conclusion, it can be argued that the judge makes a mistake of a legal nature, or that—from a legal point of view—such a verdict is certainly bizarre, yet there is no "conceptual absurdity". The existence of the institution of dissent (*votum separatum*) proves that judges may be institutional co-authors of verdicts that they consider to be wrong. In addition, the mere fact that the judge expresses his dissent and justifies it already in the verdict can be hardly considered as a sufficient premise to assume "conceptual absurdity".[377] Alexy's example therefore retains its

ruling – descriptive statements, for example, specifying the court, the parties, the date and the legal basis for the decision. *See* R. Alexy, 'Bulygins Kritik des Richtigkeitsarguments', *op. cit.*, pp. 248ff. It should also be added that, with respect to the first example (concerning a "performative contradiction" of an imaginary first article of the constitution), an argument similar to that used below in the main text is formulated by B. Bix, 'Robert Alexy, Radbruch's Formula, and the Nature of Legal Theory', *op. cit.*, pp. 147–148.

[375] For more on this issue *see* J. Wróblewski, '*Votum separatum* w teorii i ideologii sądowego stosowania prawa' [*Votum Separatum* in the Theory and Ideology of the Judicial Application of Law], *SPE* XV (1975), pp. 7–30.

[376] *See ibidem*, pp. 14ff., in particular, p. 22. According to Wróblewski, the institution of dissent does not deserve to be approved only when adopting the ideology of bound judicial decision-making, which – frankly speaking – nowadays is aptly regarded as an anachronism.

[377] Without going deeper into dogmatic considerations, it can be noted that under the Polish penal procedure (*cf.* Article 114 § 1 of the Code of Penal Procedure: "At the moment of affixing [the

full argumentative force only in the case of judgments rendered by a single-judge panel. Nonetheless, doubt arises as to whether even in such case (i.e., when the judge, by means of the analysed ruling, expresses his dissent against the ruling given by himself) we would be willing to consider such a ruling to be a sufficient reason for justifying the adoption of the claim to correctness in law (legal discourse), or rather as a reason to grant the judge sick leave and send him for psychiatric treatment on account of suspecting "legal schizophrenia".[378]

The first example analysed by Alexy ("*X* is a sovereign, federal, and unjust republic") also seems very doubtful. Imagine a constitution in which the latter article is followed by another, stating that: "Our state, however, seeks to achieve such a degree of justice, which alone is possible". When we subject them to interpretation, these two articles undoubtedly sound strange, but they allow for quite a reasonable interpretation, in the light of which they are neither absurd, nor contradictory. We can say this: the creator of the constitution containing these two articles appears to be a realist, and therefore, as a sceptic in terms of the possibility of achieving an absolute justice, which he openly and frankly admits in the first of the articles cited. However, as evidenced by the second article, this author declares to do his utmost to reduce injustice and promote justice. With such an interpretation, we cannot quite see what the "conceptual absurdity" of the first of the quoted articles was to rely on. Let us also note that by applying Alexy's reasoning, one could just as easily justify the fact that in the legal discourse (or more broadly speaking, in the law as understood pragmatically) there occurs a "claim to state sovereignty". Suppose that the first article of the constitution reads as follows: "State *X* is a non-sovereign, federal and just republic". The application of the method of recognising a "performative contradiction" in the case of this article shows that its content is contrary to the sentence: "State *X* is sovereign". Further, following Alexy's line of reasoning, one could argue that because of the absurdity of this article, we must necessarily adopt a "claim to state sovereignty" in the

verdict] with the signature, a member of the adjudicating panel has the right to indicate his dissenting opinion in the verdict, stating in which part and in which direction he questions it") and civil one (*cf.* Article 324 § 2 of the Code of Civil Procedure, which reads, inter alia, that: "The judge who, when voting, disagreed with the vote of a majority, may, when signing the operative part of the ruling, express a dissenting opinion and is required to justify it in writing before signing the justification") the act of expressing *votum separatum* may already be made and recorded when signing the verdict. The judge who dissents, may write: "Dissenting opinion: I disagree with this decision, I believe that the claim should have been allowed" (the example is taken from B. Bladowski, *Czynności sądowe w sprawach cywilnych* [Court Actions in Civil Cases], Kraków 1999, p. 234). Thus, the judge implicitly states the fallacy of the verdict that was earlier signed by him. In the context of the example considered by Alexy, the only mistake that could be found here – from a dogmatic point of view – is that it is therefore a premature indication of the cause of this error; namely, incorrect interpretation of the law (which should only appear in the justification of the dissenting opinion).

378 It should be yet added that this suspicion may turn out to be completely unjustified. The analysed ruling might be the manifestation of the most meaningful judicial opposition as to the interpretation of valid law that has been imposed on him, for example, in the form of a legally valid interpretation determined by the constitutional court. Therefore, in such a situation there can be no "conceptual absurdity" in the text of the quoted ruling.

juristic discourse (or in the legal system). What is worse, we could, in a similar way, demonstrate the validity of many other—by no means necessary—claims.[379]

Overall, the way to reach the ultimate practical knowledge by applying the method of identifying *performativer Widerspruch*, used by Alexy, indeed, fully deserves to be called "abracadabra". Consequently, the justification of the necessity of adopting the claim to correctness in law, which is based on this method, must be rejected. The latter fact means that the argument from correctness, which is based on this claim, also cannot be justified in this way. Even if we deem the above-mentioned, undoubtedly slightly sophistic counterexamples provided by me as insufficient to refute Alexy's thesis on the "conceptual absurdity" of the examples analysed by him, it will not give us much. In order to justify *Richtigkeitsargument* by following this pattern, we would also have to adopt a very controversial premise that the absurdity of a given (normative) sentence justifies the correctness (practical truth) of the sentence that is logically contradictory to it. Additionally, such a premise—for example, on account of the conceptual indeterminacy and vagueness of the very concept of absurdity itself—is, in my opinion, impossible to prove. Would anyone indeed find the following principle (thesis) reasonable: "Out of a pair of contradictory statements, one (that is non-absurd) must be true and both cannot be false"? The mere thought of such an "interpretation" of the principle of the excluded middle[380] would probably make Aristotle turn in his grave.

4.7.4 *Justification by Means of the Argument from Alternative*

Alexy also largely anticipates the objection that by means of identifying the "performative contradiction" and an eliminating argument, one cannot justify the necessity of adopting *Anspruch auf Richtigkeit* in law. Therefore, he provides another way of justifying that necessity, based on demonstrating the unacceptability

[379] Let us add that Alexy anticipates this objection, considering its validity in relation to the article of the constitution that introduces the republican system in the state, which so far has been a monarchy. However, by challenging this objection, he states only that *Ungerechtigkeitsklausel* included in the imaginary article of the constitution, has "something absurd" (*etwas absurdes*) in it, which cannot be said of *Republikklausel* contained in the imaginary article of the constitution – *see idem*, 'Bulygins Kritik des Richtigkeitsarguments', *op. cit.*, pp. 243–244. It is doubtful whether such a counterargument is sufficient to rebut the objection about the possibility of using, by analogy, Alexy's method to justify the "necessity" of other claims in law, because undoubtedly the "non-sovereignty clause" has "something absurd" in it as well. And, accordingly, does not an obvious absurdity of the provision of property law: "The owner can always be expropriated by the State, without giving any reason and without any compensation" justify – using the method of recognising *performativer Widerspruch* – the "necessity" to adopt "a claim to inviolability of property rights" in civil law?

[380] To express this Aristotelian principle, I used the formulation provided by T. Kotarbiński, *Wykłady z dziejów logiki* [Lectures on the History of Logic], Warszawa, 1985, p. 25, which reads: "Out of a pair of contradictory statements, one must be true and both cannot be false".

of adopting a "power claim" (*Machtanspruch*),[381] which constitutes an alternative to the claim to correctness. In his view, if we abandon the claim to correctness in law, we will, at the same time abandon the social practice defined by distinguishing the correctness from the incorrectness, truth from falsehood, objectivity from subjectivity and justice from injustice. Thus, we will replace the categories constitutive of this practice—namely those of truth, correctness, objectivity, and even obligation—with the categories of the power, emotion, subjectivity and will. Such practice will no longer constitute a system of law, but a system of pure power, manipulation and emotional, subjective responses. In addition, our mode of acting and talking about law will become completely different. Therefore, the claim to correctness is indeed necessary in law: firstly, in conceptual terms, because without it there is no law, secondly, in a relative sense, since the possibility of replacing this claim by *Machtanspruch* demonstrates that this necessity is relativised to a certain social practice, and, thirdly, in a non-instrumental (independent) sense, as opposed to the necessity of coercion in law, which is instrumental in nature, dictated by considerations of legal certainty and the effectiveness of law.[382]

Alexy's argumentation—as presented above—having undoubtedly a highly persuasive nature, seems right and worthy of acceptance, at least from the axiological point of view. Undoubtedly, both participants in legal discourse, as well as addressees of legal norms (although certainly not all of them) tend to favour correctness, truthfulness, objectivity and justice (rather than incorrectness, falsehood, subjectivity and injustice). Yet, does this argumentation justify the relative necessity of the claim to correctness? I think that it is not the case, because the silent assumption of the argument from the alternative (resembling a Manichean perception of reality) seems to be extremely questionable. The point is that Alexy accepts the dichotomy of many conceptual categories, passing over the possibility of the existence of a legal system that accepts intermediate standpoints.[383] I am not convinced that the only alternative to correctness in law is "pure force of authority" because between correctness and incorrectness, objectivity and subjectivity, justice and injustice, and even (in the context of practical discourse) between truth and falseness, we can identify some intermediate standpoints. By means of example, let us consider a pair of concepts: justice–injustice. Alexy's own analyses show that between these extremes there are many intermediate positions: when referring to the legal system, we can talk about just law, partially just law and partially unjust, extremely unjust law and so on. The other pairs of concepts in the practical sphere, which includes law, also seem to be the extremes of a certain continuum. Therefore, axiological approval of the aims of Alexy's argumentation cannot hide the fact that it is not convincing.

---

[381] *See* R. Alexy, 'Law and Correctness', *op. cit.*, pp. 213ff. [German version, pp. 11ff.] and 'The Nature of Arguments about the Nature of Law', *op. cit.*, pp. 12ff.

[382] R. Alexy, 'The Nature of Arguments about the Nature of Law', *op. cit.*, p. 13. *Cf.* R. Alexy, 'The Nature of Legal Philosophy', *op. cit.*, pp. 71ff.

[383] In this context, it is worth noting that Hart has already drawn attention to the nonexhaustive nature of the (apparent) dichotomy between "law based merely on power" and "law which is accepted as morally binding" – *see idem*, *The Concept of Law*, *op. cit.*, pp. 198ff.

In sum, the basis of Alexy's nonpositivist argumentation—namely, the argument from correctness—should be regarded as unjustified. Even if we assume the thesis of legal essentialism—controversial as it is—according to which there are fixed and necessary features of law[384] (universal in relation to time and place), then correctness does not constitute *universalium iuris*, or at least it cannot be inferred from Alexy's nonpositivist analytical argumentation. It is neither by using the method of identifying the "performative contradiction" of utterances, nor from falsely—as I believe—adopted exclusive disjunction of the claim to correctness and claim to authority (power), that one might infer and justify the correctness of the thesis of the analytically necessary conceptual connection of law and morality, which has its basis (and its manifestation) in the necessity to adopt the claim to correctness in pragmatically perceived law.

4.8 Critique of Normative Argumentation

The rebuttal of the analytical foundation for justifying a nonpositivist conception of law (namely *Richtigkeitsargument*) does not yet resolve the dispute over the concept of law between legal positivists and supporters of nonpositivism. As Alexy repeatedly stresses,[385] a nonpositivist may even agree with a positivist that there is no analytically necessary conceptual connection between law and morality, justifying *Verbindungsthese* only by means of the non-analytical, normative arguments.[386] Therefore, a legal positivist, in order to demonstrate the inaccuracy of nonpositivism, should also prove that the better practical (normative) reasons weigh in favour of adopting such a definition of law that does not contain moral elements, in accordance with the positivist Separation Thesis.

Let us now consider some of the objections raised against, or in the context of nonpositivist normative argumentation. Before starting our investigation, it should be recalled that some of these arguments have already been analysed by us. Accordingly, a positivist argument from language (*Sprachargument*), setting forth

[384] Alexy argues most strongly in favour of his view about the existence of necessary, universal formal and substantive features of law (which he refers to as "universalism" and not as "essentialism") in 'Law, Discourse, and Time', *op. cit.*, pp. 101ff. *See* also *idem*, 'The Nature of Legal Philosophy', *op. cit.*, pp. 70ff. and 'An Answer to Joseph Raz', *op. cit.*, pp. 52ff. In such a metaphysical context it merits acquainting oneself with the attempt to justify the necessity of the claim to correctness and the connection between law and morality, which refers to the metaphysical requirements of normative knowledge, undertaken by Alexy's student – G. Pavlakos, 'On the Necessity of the Interconnection between Law and Morality', *RJ* 18 (2005), pp. 64–83.

[385] *See* R. Alexy, 'On Necessary Relations between Law and Morality', *op. cit.*, pp. 168–170, 'Zur Kritik des Rechtspositivismus', *op. cit.*, pp. 10–11, and *Begriff und Geltung des Rechts*, *op. cit.*, p. 41 [English version, p. 21]. *Cf. idem*, 'Zur Verteidigung eines nichtpositivistischen Rechtsbegriffs', *op. cit.*, pp. 86–87.

[386] *See* the reconstruction of Alexy's normative nonpositivist argumentation in Chap. 3 at pp. 44–51.

that it is linguistically pointless to use moral elements in the definition of law because it prevents a nonpositivist from providing conceptual characteristics of norms which, according to the standpoint adopted by her/him, are devoid of a legal nature due to their extreme injustice has already been discussed (and rejected) when analysing the first general objection against nonpositivist argumentation (*lex iniustissima non est lex*).[387] Additionally, the positivist argument from relativism (*Relativismusargument*), challenging not only the possibility of separating the cases of extreme and non-extreme injustice, but also objective knowledge and rational justification of practical claims (e.g., concerning moral rightness or justice) has already been considered (and accepted) in the course of analysis of Alexy's attempt to undertake the discursive-theoretical rehabilitation of practical reason.[388] In addition, in the previous section we have tried to demonstrate the lack of analytical justification of the argument from correctness which—due to the enormous role played by this argument also in nonpositivist normative argumentation—negatively affects the evaluation of the latter.

4.8.1 Argument from Efficiency

Let us begin with a positivist objection referred to by Alexy as the "argument from efficiency" (*Effektivitätsargument*)[389] and by Dreier as the "ethical–pedagogical argument" (*ethisch–pädagogisches Argument*).[390] In the context of Radbruch's *Wehrlosigkeitsthese*, this argument casts doubt on the nonpositivist view that the inclusion of moral elements in the definition of law can provide effective protection against "statutory un-law"; namely, extremely unjust law. It should be recalled that when analysing this argument, Alexy distinguishes—absolutely rightly—two specific positivist objections against the effectiveness of the nonpositivist conception (concept) of law. The first one holds that this conception does not prevent the development and application of unjust law, because one cannot change reality by means of a mere definition of law containing a reference to morality. The second suggests that this conception can uncritically legitimise unjust laws; if we, in fact, include moral elements in the concept of law, then there is a risk—according to the positivists—of identifying the requirements of law and morality (which implies the impossibility of moral criticism of the unjust laws).

Before presenting my own position, let us summarise Alexy's nonpositivist response to these objections.[391] Alexy first attempts to refute the second of them, stressing that the nonpositivist conception is based on a weak thesis of the

[387] *Cf. supra*, pp. 77ff.

[388] *Cf. supra*, pp. 86ff.

[389] *Cf.* Chap. 3 at pp. 47–48, together with the source texts cited therein.

[390] *See* R. Dreier, 'Recht und Moral', *op. cit.*, pp. 191–192.

[391] For more *see* Chap. 3 at pp. 47ff.

connection between law and morality (*schwache Verbindungsthese*). According to this thesis, a nonpositivist's only priority is that extremely unjust norms should not have a legal status. However, a nonpositivist does not enforce the requirement that the legal system should consist exclusively of just norms (compatible with just morality, i.e., the morality that is justifiable by means of practical discourse). According to the nonpositivist conception of law, there is no equivalence of these two normative systems, but only a limited, negative (derogatory) impact of morality on law. Thus, the positivist thesis of the possibility of an uncritical legitimation of not extremely unjust laws is defeated because the effect of applying "Radbruch's formula" is only the denial of the legitimacy of the norms that exceed a threshold of extreme injustice, rather than a positive legitimisation of norms below this threshold, which may still be subject to moral evaluation (e.g., as not extremely unjust, morally indifferent, just fair etc.). As for the first objection, in a situation in which the nonpositivist conception of law is accepted in legal practice of a Law-Governed State (*Rechtsstaat*), or when it was adopted there before the beginning of the totalitarian un-law state, the risk of making judges accountable for applying "statutory un-law" (*Risikoeffekt* resulting from adopting a nonpositivist concept of law) leads to the nonpositivist position turning out to be at least not less effective than the positivist one, if we take into account the eradication or prevention of the moral injustice of the state and law.

While retaining the order of reasoning adopted by Alexy, let us first deal with the issue of the uncritical legitimation of law, which consists of preventing moral criticism of law as a result of adopting a nonpositivist concept of law.[392] At first glance, Alexy's clear and unambiguous position falsifies this objection. It is, however, I believe, based on a false premise, which is an unauthorised extension of Radbruch's views.[393] Let us recall that in the nonpositivist definition of law formulated by Alexy, its nonpositivist component, corresponding to the argument from un-law, is formulated negatively—as a lack of extreme injust norms within the legal system (as opposed to Dreier's earlier nonpositivist definition, in which the requirement of at least minimum ethical justification of norms in the system of law is a positive constraint).[394] Yet, does this negative formulation change anything if

[392] Such objections are, of course, nothing new and they have already been raised in relation to the conceptions combining law with morality – apart from the already mentioned objections of Hart and Hoerster, *see e.g.*, H. Kelsen, 'Law and Morality', *op. cit.*, pp. 92–93, whereas, in reference to German discourse ethics, *see e.g.*, K. Tuori, 'Discourse Ethics and the Legitimacy of Law', *op. cit.*, p. 142.

[393] Let us recall that, according to *Unerträglichkeitsthese*, positive law is valid even if it is purposeless or unjust in content, and only in exceptional situations, where a conflict with justice reaches "such a level that cannot be borne", will the norms of positive law lose their legal status – for more on this issue, *see* Chap. 2 at p. 12 and *supra* pp. 70ff. From an analytical point of view it is impossible to find any error in this thesis, just as in the distinction of the concept of law in its narrower and broader sense – as introduced by Hart in relation to Radbruch's conception (*see idem*, *The Concept of Law*, *op. cit.*, pp. 204ff.). Yet, the problem arises when we interpret it in the context of the issue of legitimisation of law in the manner suggested by Alexy.

[394] The content of these definitions has been presented in Chap. 2 at pp. 15–19.

we take into account the necessity of determining whether a given norm (in terms of its ethical justification or lack of extreme injustice) is a norm of a legal nature (that is, a norm belonging to the legal system)? Certainly it does not change anything, because in order to solve this problem—regardless of whether we will use a positively formulated condition of Dreier's definition or a negatively worded condition of Alexy's definition—after all, in each of the analysed cases we would have to determine whether a given norm exceeds the threshold of extreme injustice or not. Therefore, when resolving this question, we will always—at least indirectly—morally legitimise those legal norms that are not considered to be extremely unjust.[395] Furthermore, the conviction that the nonpositivists have about the possibility of determining the "external borders" (*äußerste Grenze*) of positive law[396] by eliminating from its domain extremely unjust norms, associated with a "witty"[397] application of "Radbruch's formula" in the form of *schwache Verbindungsthese*, is also a pipe dream. As Ingeborg Maus[398] convincingly demonstrates, the incorporation of moral principles into the concept of law leads to the elimination of its borders in social reality and, worse still, the borders of state legal regulations. The "remoralization of law" (*Remoralisierung des Rechts*)—as defined by her—that is associated with such an incorporation, in fact leads to: (1) extending the autonomy of state organs which, by considering moral norms in their own conduct, can easily go beyond the extension of their legal (in the positivist sense) obligations and authority; (2) loss of a legally indifferent sphere (i.e., a sphere free from state intervention), because—due to the indeterminateness of moral principles—their introduction into the legal system means that virtually every conceivable state of affairs can be considered as legally relevant; and

[395] A similar argument, yet of a purely logical character (based on the law of transposition) is raised by N. Hoerster, 'Zur Verteidigung der rechtspositivistischen Trennungsthese', *op. cit.*, p. 32. Hoerster demonstrates that the nonpositivist *Verbindungsthese* entails the thesis: "If a given norm is legal, then it is moral". Let us add, for the record, that Alexy, emphasising the "weakness" of the thesis of the connection between law and morality, and the unique nature of exceeding the threshold of extreme injustice, explicitly rejects this argument (yet, considers its merits when adopting *starke Verbindungsthese*) – R. Alexy, 'Zur Verteidigung eines nichtpositivistischen Rechtsbegriffs', *op. cit.*, pp. 97–98 and *Begriff und Geltung des Rechts*, *op. cit.*, pp. 82ff. [English version, pp. 46ff.]. *Cf.* the criticism of O. Weinberger ('Logische Analyse als Basis der juristischen Argumentation', *op. cit.*, pp. 174ff.) concerning the natural-law formulation of *Grundnorm*, proposed by A. Aarnio, R. Alexy and A. Peczenik, 'The Foundation of Legal Reasoning', *op. cit.*, p. 144.

[396] *See* R. Alexy, *Mauerschützen*, *op. cit.*, p. 4, *Der Beschluß des Bundesverfassungsgericht zu den Tötungen an der innerdeutschen Grenze vom 24. Oktober 1996*, *op. cit.*, p. 11, 'Law and Correctness', *op. cit.*, p. 218 [German version, p. 16] and 'The Nature of Legal Philosophy', *op. cit.*, p. 74.

[397] *See* Chap. 3, note 98 at p. 50, with the corresponding text.

[398] *See* I. Maus, 'The Differentiation between Law and Morality as a Limitation of Law' in A. Aarnio, K. Tuori (eds.), *Law, Morality and Discursive Rationality*, Helsinki 1989, pp. 141ff. There is no need to add that considerably similar arguments are raised by a number of positivist critics of *Verbindungsthese* – for example *see* interesting deliberations of H. Dreier, 'Die Radbruchsche Formel – Erkenntnis oder Bekenntnis?', *op. cit.*, pp. 132ff.

(3) the changes in the very structure of the legitimisation of law, since an institutionalised democratic participation of citizens in the creation and criticism of the law can be easily replaced by non-institutionalised decision-making processes of political bodies, in which the participation of citizens is excluded (that is, by the usurpation of power, replacing the democratic control functions with moral argumentations). For a nonpositivist, the vision of a "moral" state and law, which arises here, triggers quite unpleasant associations with an essentially totalitarian system in which state power, by monopolising moral discourse, can easily assume that, on account of its moral omniscience, it knows best what is good and bad for people.[399]

The above considerations lead to an even further-reaching, fundamental objection of the superfluousness of law.[400] This objection refers to the "paradox of superfluousness of law in practical reasoning" (*la paradoja de la superfluidad del Derecho en el razonamiento prático*), formulated by the Argentinian philosopher of law and politics, Carlos Santiago Nino.[401] This paradox lies in highlighting the difficulties associated with finding a satisfactory answer to the fundamental question that is addressed to the authors who accept the existence of the necessary connection between law and morality. It reads as follows:

> Why do we need, in the ultimate sense, governments and laws made by the latter, if they cannot justify our actions in a different way than by a reference, in the last instance, to moral principles? If the laws are consistent with those principles, then they are superfluous, and if they are not consistent, then we should not pay any attention to them.[402]

---

[399] Perhaps at this point it is worth quoting a term referring to such a system of government, used in a slightly different context by Maus: "expertocracy of justice" – *see idem*, 'The Differentiation between Law and Morality as a Limitation of Law', *op. cit.*, pp. 156, 161. The problem consists in that even the best experts on morality cannot replace *vox populi* in a democratic state. Furthermore – as evidenced by history – psychopathic monocrats have often had claims to moral omniscience. Thus, the "risk effect" – resulting from the adoption of a nonpositivist conception of law – is an ambiguous term, because the acceptance of such a concept of law also poses the risk of creating an anti-democratic and anti-liberal state of "moral (or religious) totalitarianism" or of "moral (or religious) autocracy". In this context *see* the remarks of J. Woleński, 'O pozytywizmie prawniczym', *op. cit.*, p. 16, who – referring to historical examples – strongly emphasises that the adoption of the ideology of natural law certainly does not protect against arbitrariness of law, which remains valid, *mutatis mutandis*, also in relation to the nonpositivist conception of law.

[400] This objection should not be confused with the positivist argument from superfluousness (*Unnötigkeitsargument*) – analysed by Alexy – which relates to the non-necessity of using "Radbruch's formula" in order to eliminate the consequences of "statutory un-law" in reference to the cases outside the domain of penal law – for more on this topic *see* Chap. 3 at pp. 49–50.

[401] *See* C.S. Nino, *Derecho, Moral y Política. Una revisión de la teoría general del Derecho*, Barcelona 1994, pp. 130ff. It should be noted that Nino deems this paradox apparent and provides its solution, based on the analysis of the relations of law and politics – *see ibidem*, pp. 134ff. and *idem*, *El constructivismo ético*, Madrid 1989, pp. 116ff.

[402] C.S. Nino, *Derecho, Moral y Política*, *op. cit.*, p. 131. Let us note that, in principle, the same paradox, resulting from adopting the existence of a privileged, genuine morality, is perceived by Bulygin, who formulates it even more succinctly: "¿Para qué dictar normas jurídicas si ya sabemos qué debemos hacer?" [Why enact legal norms, if we already know what we ought to do?] – R. Caracciolo, 'Entrevista a Eugenio Bulygin', *DOXA* 14 (1993), p. 511.

If we assume that in the context of the problem of legitimisation of law that the nonpositivist conception of law is based essentially on a masked (hidden) *starke Verbindungsthese*, then—according to the cited paradox—it leads to at least partial self-destruction of "the law of nonpositivists". Let us make this observation more plausible by adducing one more reason: if the general practical discourse is the ultimate source and, at the same time, the criterion of the correctness of practical and legal judgments, then law—from a practical (moral) point of view—becomes at least partially superfluous, because it does not play any independent role in decision-making processes concerning the ways in which we act.[403]

As far as I know, Alexy does not directly contemplate such a decisive objection in any of his works. Yet, it is relatively easy to reconstruct his highly probable answer to the question posed by Nino: law is necessary because a practical (and especially moral) discourse is often (though not always) non-conclusive. A rational system of law (*vernünftiges Rechtssystem*), including rules, principles and procedures, and laying the claim to correctness, is, for the philosopher of Kiel, the consequence and, at the same time, the emanation and an attempt to institutionalise the practical reason, i.e., the principles of practical rationality.[404] Let us recall that Alexy in *Theorie der juristischen Argumentation*, after formulating (at analytical and normative level) the catalogue of rules and forms of general practical discourse, undertakes a reconstruction—in principle, fully approving—of rules and forms of legal discourse, at least implicitly recognising that they comply with the rules of general practical discourse (practical rationality). Yet, can such an explanation of the necessity of law (and legal discourse) be considered as refuting the mentioned paradox? In my opinion, not necessarily, because in order to achieve the decidability of practical disputes (e.g., legal ones), it is sufficient to appoint proper arbiters (judges) and equip them with the authority of conclusive dispute resolution. Accordingly, it is possible to have exclusively procedural law that does not contain any material norms. Consequently, that would be equivalent to at least the partial self-destruction of "the law of nonpositivists". In order to demonstrate that this argumentation does not resemble science fiction, we can just point to the legal systems of some Islamic countries (e.g., Saudi Arabia), in which judges (*kadi*) rule based on the Koran and Sunnah of the Prophet, rather than on substantive positive law (perceived in the sense proper for the West European legal culture).

---

[403] An analogical reason constitutes the basis of the criticism of the inclusive (soft) positivist's rule of recognition in the context of the Practical Difference Thesis – for more on this *see* works cited *supra*, note 254 at p. 129. This thesis should naturally be somewhat mitigated, because it cannot relate to the regulation of behaviour, which morality is silent about. For example, according to Bulygin, by assuming the existence of moral truths, we reduce the role of positive law to the regulation – complementary to morality – of morally indifferent matters; for example, the direction of traffic or the printing colour of legal texts – *see* R. Caracciolo, *ibidem*.

[404] R. Alexy, 'Rechtssystem und praktische Vernunft', *op. cit.*, pp. 416ff., 'Idee und Struktur eines vernünftigen Rechtssystems', *op. cit.*, pp. 36ff., 'The Special Case Thesis', *op. cit.*, p. 383, 'Die juristische Argumentation als rationaler Diskurs', *op. cit.*, pp. 119ff.

Let us now consider the problem of the preventive and educational function of nonpositivism. Can the adoption of the nonpositivist concept of law in legal practice prevent—if only minimally—the creation or application of extremely unjust law? There are no reasons why the positivists' argument that it is not the case could be regarded as justified. The nonpositivist conception of law undeniably introduces the concept of "risk effect" in both unlawful states and in democratic ones.[405] Ralf Dreier argues that the assessment of such a nonpositivist counterargument can only be based on empirical research.[406] Yet I think that there are also teleological reasons that weigh in favour of rejecting the positivist objection. If we want (and we probably do) the study of law (in particular the theory and philosophy of law) to be at least to a minimal degree useful in combating "statutory un-law" (*gesetzliches Unrecht*), which we still encounter in many modern states, then the nonpositivist conception of law has an obvious advantage over the positivist one. The latter, after all, not only accepts the principle of *dura lex, sed lex*, but even—in the last instance—the thesis *lex iniustissima, sed lex*, which makes it impossible for a positivist to find any legal remedy for positivised "statutory injustice".[407] We also know that prevention is better than cure, even if the effectiveness of preventing the emergence of new totalitarianism (more broadly: the unlawful states) by means of scientific theories is close to zero and the views expressed here may be treated as an expression of extreme naivety. However, is not optimistic naivety more appropriate here than positivist, sometimes cynical scepticism?

In the context of efficiency in preventing the "statutory lawlessness" due to the adoption of the nonpositivist concept of law, a significant detailed problem arises, related to the issue of the possible influence on reality by means of defining concepts. As Hoerster[408] points out, indirectly referring to Hart's earlier criticism, based on differentiating the narrower and the wider concept of law,[409] we cannot change reality by using mere definitions:

> [w]e change (often immoral) *reality* of state coercion by refusing to grant it the attribute of "law" to such a small degree (*so wenig*), as if we changed the reality of prostitution by denying to grant the prostitute (*Dirne*) the attribute of "woman".[410]

Alexy recognises the merits of such an argument, assuming that the philosophical definitions of law cannot by themselves change the reality.[411] This opinion is

---

[405] I mean here only the "risk effect", considered by Alexy, that involves the threat of accountability for judges applying extremely unjust laws in an unlawful state, and not the risk – identified above – of creating a "morally totalitarian (autocratic)" state without law.

[406] R. Dreier, 'Recht und Moral', *op. cit.*, p. 192.

[407] *Cf. supra*, note 81 at p. 82, and the references cited therein.

[408] *See* N. Hoerster, 'Die rechtsphilosophische Lehre vom Rechtsbegriff', *op. cit.*, pp. 186ff.

[409] *See* H.L.A. Hart, *The Concept of Law*, *op. cit.*, pp. 204ff.

[410] N. Hoerster, 'Die rechtsphilosophische Lehre vom Rechtsbegriff', *op. cit.*, p. 187.

[411] R. Alexy, 'Zur Verteidigung eines nichtpositivistischen Rechtsbegriffs', *op. cit.*, p. 98 and *Begriff und Geltung des Rechts*, *op. cit.*, p. 86 [English version, p. 49].

difficult to challenge, but it seems that this argument results, at least partially, from a misunderstanding, because we deal here with the performative function of legal language utterances, as well as with the fact that law, as such, is not a brute fact, but an institutional fact.[412] Firstly, it should be noted that when the constitutional court considers a given legal norm to be invalid (even if not necessarily in a nonpositivist spirit, namely due to its extreme injustice, but equally from any other reasons, for example, procedural ones) then, by means of a performative—the court's decision on the unconstitutionality of such a norm, after all—it changes not only the legal, but also social reality. The analysed norm ceases to be a valid legal norm, and the potential addressees of that norm (with the exceptions that can be left aside here) are exempt from an obligation to obey it. Thus, the concept (definition) of law—adopted by the constitutional court in the course of adjudication—indirectly affects the reality *tout court*. Secondly, let us note that the comparison of the phenomena of the world consisting of the brute facts with the world of institutional facts, demonstrates, in particular, the differences between these worlds, and not their similarities. Without a doubt, it is true that by calling an apple a "tomato", we are not able to change reality (an apple remains an apple), but it is also undeniable that, when an authorised state organ (for example, a civil court) deems the current holder to be the owner of the property, then he becomes its owner, at least in legal terms (an analogous change in legal reality may also be undertaken by a legislator; for example, by amending the legal definitions). Hence, the comparison applied by Hoerster, as well as the objection justified by the latter should be regarded as inadequate, at least to such an extent to which the brute facts (such as being an apple) are different from the institutional facts (e.g., being the owner), and the images of the world expressed in everyday language and in legal language differ in many respects.[413]

The summary of the analysis of the positivist argument from efficiency is not easy, since the results of its respective topics are varied. Undoubtedly, the advantage was gained by the arguments in favour of recognising its relevance. Accordingly, the above-identified risk of creating the states of "moral (or religious) totalitarianism (or autocracy)" and the threat of self-destruction of "the law of nonpositivists" is not compensated for by a preventive and educational role of the nonpositivist concept of law. Therefore, in the substantive scope of the controversy, determined by the content of *Effektivitätsargument*, I am inclined to agree with the positivists. By fully consciously exaggerating the consequences of incorporating moral elements into the concept of law, let us emphasise that the possibility of the manipulative use of the nonpositivist concept of law by psychopaths (such as Hitler)—convinced of their "moral" superiority over other people—by religious

[412] On the distinction of brute and institutional facts *see* G.E.M. Anscombe, 'On Brute Facts', *Analysis* 18/3 (1958), pp. 69–72; *cf.* J.R. Searle, *Speech Acts*, *op. cit.*, pp. 50ff.

[413] For more on these differences *see* T. Gizbert-Studnicki, 'Język prawny a obraz świata' [Legal Language and the Picture of the World] in G. Skąpska *et al.* (eds.), *Prawo w zmieniającym się społeczeństwie*, *op. cit.*, pp. 153ff.

fanatics or extreme cynics, arouses fear, like the administration of justice based on "edified" law with fuzzy borders. Incidentally, in a similar context, the positivist argument from legal certainty (*Rechtssicherheitsargument*) seems, contrary to Alexy's standpoint,[414] at least partially (*in abstracto*) justified. After all, the uniqueness of exceeding the threshold of extreme injustice by the legislator does not guarantee us the certainty that even the application of "Radbruch's formula" to such a limited extent (to *legi iniustissimae*) cannot be abused by the state authority for shameful purposes.[415]

4.8.2 Argument from Candour

The argument from candour (*Redlichkeitsargument*) challenges the nonpositivist conception of law as it leads to the circumvention of the principle of *nulla poena sine lege* in penal cases. According to Hart,[416] if we do not want to exempt from liability the people who benefited from the state of un-law, then what is more honest than the courts applying "Radbruch's formula", is a blatant enactment of retroactive penal laws by the legislature, in no way hiding (and in this sense, it is honest) that we sacrifice—as "the lesser evil"—the principle of *nulla poena sine lege*.

Let us begin the discussion of this positivist argument by noting that it is, in a sense, paradoxical that it is the positivist who accuses axiologically involved nonpositivism of a lack of candour (sincerity).[417] Therefore, it should be first clarified in relation to whom or what the nonpositivist conception of law, approving the application of "Radbruch's formula" also within the penal law, may be regarded as unfair. The answer seems to be *prima facie* quite simple. It can be argued that Dreier's and Alexy's nonpositivism is unfair only to the beneficiaries of the state of un-law (*Unrechtsstaat*), who were its officers or who abused extremely unjust "law". On the other hand, this conception is undeniably honest in relation to all those people who were injured by the totalitarian state of un-law, while being its

[414] *Cf.* Chap. 3, p. 48.

[415] Such risk is recognised by Alexy himself – *see idem*, 'Zur Verteidigung eines nichtpositivistischen Rechtsbegriffs', *op. cit.*, p. 103, where he notes the possibility of abusing the nonpositivist concept of law in a society dominated by Nazi morality (*Nazimoral*) and *Mauerschützen*, *op. cit.*, p. 24, where he writes about "moral blindness" (*moralische Blindheit*), which can be based on ideological blindness, ossified tradition and fanaticism, which limits the fundamental rule of recognising extreme injustice: "Unlawfulness is the more evident, the more extreme it is". In terms of this rule, combining the substantive aspect of the problem with its epistemological perspective, *see* R. Alexy, 'Zur Verteidigung eines nichtpositivistischen Rechtsbegriffs', *op. cit.*, p. 101 and *Begriff und Geltung des Rechts*, *op. cit.*, p. 91 [English version, p. 52].

[416] *Cf.* Chap. 3, p. 50.

[417] It is worth adding that the admissibility of such a positivist objection can be questioned – *cf.* comments on issues of "enlightened" morality in the next subsection, which, *mutatis mutandis*, also apply to the positivist argument from candour. *See* also *infra*, note 453 at p. 179.

victims. In analysing the objection related to the nonpositivist thesis of *lex iniustissima non est lex*, it was one of the reasons why we have already opted for nonpositivism,[418] not wanting to indirectly participate in the totalitarian "perfect crime". The construction of this crime is most succinctly expressed by the following observation:

> First to kill with impunity in the time of a dictatorship, and then seek protection in the prohibition of the retroaction that is a principle of the Law-Governed State – that would be the perfect murder.[419]

Nonetheless, Hart certainly has in mind something other than a lack of candour or sincerity in reference to the creators and officials of totalitarian states. The essence of his argument may be somewhat metaphorically (and in a some reference to Lon Fuller's famous paper concerning, inter alia, the problem of the fidelity to law[420]) interpreted as follows: within the argument from candour (sincerity), the positivist has in mind candour vis-à-vis the positive law, rather than candour related to law's addressees. The principles of *nullum crimen sine lege* and *nulla poena sine lege poenali anteriori* belong to the foundaments of penal law; therefore, any deviation from them should be based on a sound legal argument, referring to the regulation of positive law and should not be hidden under the pretence of moral reasoning used by the courts. If we accept such an—undoubtedly—extensive interpretation of the argument under consideration, then the assessment of its validity should be based on an examination of the extent to which the application of "Radbruch's formula" is acceptable (justifiable) from a purely legal standpoint.

Unfortunately, this kind of analysis proves to be impossible, and that is due to at least three reasons. Firstly, one can at least theoretically try to prove the legitimacy or acceptability of applying "Radbruch's formula" by means of the analysis of such post-war judicial decisions that were based on it. Yet, in doing so, we would confuse reason with the consequence, because the formula would have to be considered as legally acceptable (worthy of recognition) by courts, before they even started to apply it (and Hart just meant that they should not do so). Therefore, on the basis of the analysis of jurisdiction, we can only determine its practical usefulness or necessity in resolving court cases consistent with the sense of justice.[421] Secondly, one can try to prove legal acceptability of "Radbruch's formula" by means of analysing a supporting extra-legal (nonpositive, moral) normative

---

[418] *Cf. supra*, pp. 79–84.

[419] The quotation comes from a press article published in *Hannoversche Allgemeine Zeitung* of 13 November 1996. I quote after R. Ogorek, '"Mauerschützen" (BverfGE 95, 96ff.)', *KVfGR* 83/3–4 (2000), p. 341.

[420] *See* L.L. Fuller, 'Positivism and Fidelity to Law – A Reply to Professor Hart', *op. cit.*, pp. 630ff. What I mean here, obviously, is "fidelity to law" understood in positivist terms, and not – as in Fuller – in natural law ones.

[421] It is undertaken by W. Ott, 'Die Radbruch'sche Formel', *op. cit.*, pp. 337ff. For more on the application of "Radbruch's formula" in German and European jurisdiction, *see infra*, pp. 184ff., together with the rulings and references cited therein.

argumentation. As a result, however, we are likely to fall into *circulus vitiosus*, because the argument from candour (sincerity)—as discussed here—is precisely one of the normative arguments. Thirdly, our analysis could theoretically be based on the interpretation of positive law, but it is also unfeasible, since "Radbruch's formula" has not been positivised (introduced into the legal system) and cannot be deduced from the legislative acts (statutes) which are valid, for example, in Germany. Thus, we have to admit—although very reluctantly—that the legal legitimacy and admissibility of courts applying "Radbruch's formula" cannot be assessed by the methods that the legal positivist would find satisfactory.

In this state of affairs, the only thing left is a thought experiment based on a counterfactual hypothesis. Let us suppose that the German legislator has explicitly incorporated "Radbruch's formula" into the legal system by, for example, formulating Article 20 Section 3 of *Grundgesetz*[422] in an even more nonpositivist (or even natural law) spirit. Will then the positivist argument from candour (sincerity) continue to have its *raison d'être*? It seems that it will be the case, but its meaning would be significantly altered. Hart certainly could no longer be able to accuse any state authority (particularly the legislator or the courts) of dishonesty (insincerity), but he might have reservations about the fact that the introduction of "Radbruch's formula" into a legal system (more precisely: into the rule of recognition of this system) leads to normative conflicts in its framework, whereas its application by courts violates penal law principles of *nullum crimen* and *nulla poena sine lege*. Yet, he would not be able in any way to challenge the legal validity of the formula positivised in such a way. Let us note that not only did Hart not negate the moral and legal acceptability, but he even recommended solving the problem of the accountability of the beneficiaries of the state of un-law by means of retroactive penal laws.[423] Moreover, taking into account the standpoint of soft

[422] It reads as follows: "Die Gesetzgebung ist an die verfassungsmäßige Ordnung, die vollziehende Gewalt und die Rechtsprechung sind an Gesetz und Recht gebunden" [The legislative power is bound by the constitutional order, while the executive and the judiciary are bound by the statute and law]. In the genesis of this provision, which introduced into the German legal system the constitutional principle of "being bound by the statute and law", an essential role was played by Radbruch's post-war antipositivist works (incidentally, one of them, published in January 1947, was entitled 'Gesetz und Recht'). From the vast German literature on the subject, *see e.g.*, A. Kaufmann, 'Gesetz und Recht' in T. Würtenberger *et al.* (eds.), *Existenz und Ordnung. Festschrift für Erik Wolf zum 60. Geburtstag*, Frankfurt am Main 1962, pp. 357–397; R. Dreier, 'Der Rechtsstaat im Spannungsverhältnis zwischen Gesetz und Recht', *JZ* 40 (1985), pp. 353–359; J. Neuner, *Die Rechtsfindung contra legem*, München 1992, pp. 5ff.; B. Hoffmann, *Das Verhältnis von Gesetz und Recht*, *op. cit.* For those interested in a broader historical context, it is worth recommending the work by Ch. Perelman, 'Gesetz und Recht' in D. Mayer-Maly, P.M. Simons (eds.), *Das Naturrechtsdenken heute und morgen*, *op. cit.*, pp. 427–435 and J. Zajadło, 'The Notion of "Gesetz und Recht" in Contemporary German Legal Theory and Practice', trans. T.Z. Wolański, *Ius et Lex* I/1 (2005), s. 35–50, whereas for those interested in a linguistic aspect of the issue at hand, it is worth noting the analysis of G.P. Fletcher, 'In Honour of "Ius et Lex". Some Thoughts on Speaking about Law', *Ius et Lex* I/1 (2005), pp. 13–33.

[423] It could be treated as a curiosity that Fuller, in 'Positivism and Fidelity to Law – A Reply to Professor Hart', *op. cit.*, p. 661, also prefers to resolve the problem of the liability of those who

positivism—adopted by him in his later works[424]—it seems clear that the soft (inclusive) rule of recognition may include "Radbruch's formula". In fact, many faults can be found in the latter (for example, inefficiency caused by its conceptual indeterminacy and vagueness), but it cannot be accused of being unfair in any moral sense. In conclusion, our thought experiment shows that Hart had to pose an objection of lack of candour just because he was a positivist, and thus he did not acknowledge the identification (recognition) of valid legal rules on any other basis than the rule of recognition. In view of the proposed experimental interpretation, a positivist objection of dishonesty, expressed by the argument from candour, and related to the application of "Radbruch's formula" by the German courts boils down to the fact that the valid (according to the rule of recognition) fundamental principles of penal law are being circumvented by means of "Radbruch's formula", which—according to Hart's rule of recognition understood in the sense expressed in the first edition of *The Concept of Law*—is not legally valid.[425]

I think that the proposed thought experiment explains, on the one hand, that Hart's opposition had a deeper sense than just a moral one—in fact, it concerned the fundamental question of the proper comprehension of law. On the other hand, it proves that any compromise between the positivist and nonpositivist is out of the question. Accordingly, a positivist cannot be convinced of the candour of "Radbruch's formula" and its application by courts not only by a nonpositivist, but even by the legislator, as the latter—by incorporating it into the legal system or, more precisely, to the rule of recognition—causes the whole problem simply to cease to exist, not only for a soft positivist but even for a hard one.

4.8.3 The Problem of an "Enlightened" Morality

Doubt may arise as to why I claim that the fact of incorporating "Radbruch's formula" to the rule of recognition by the lawmaker causes the problem of the candour of this formula ceasing to exist for positivists. Does it mean that its positivisation (by its introduction into valid law) automatically entails the impossibility of accusing courts that apply this formula of a lack of sincerity or honesty? We shall explain this issue when analysing yet another problem related to

abuse "the law" in *Unrechtsstaat* by means of retroactive laws; after all, not because of the candour or sincerity of such a solution, but only due to the fact that it allows us to "a sharp break with the past" and effectively restore proper meaning to the idea of the fidelity to law.

[424] *Cf. supra*, pp. 128–130.

[425] Time relativisation of this claim is necessary because Hart's "softened" rule of recognition from his 'Postscript' does not allow even the formulation of an objection of a lack of candour towards the application of "Radbruch's formula" in such a way in which Hart did at the end of the 1950s. If, in the meantime, he allowed the incorporation of the the "Hercules procedure" into the rule of recognition (*cf. supra*, p. 130), he should even more so allow an analogous incorporation of even a nonpositivised "Radbruch's formula", which, after all, fulfils only a negative (derogatory) validating function vis-à-vis law.

nonpositivist normative argumentation (in particular, to a positivist argument from relativism); namely, the issue of an "enlightened" morality.

When a connection between law and morality—be it necessary or not—is being postulated or assumed, there immediately arises the problem of a precise definition of morality—both in quantitative as well as qualitative terms. When analysing such a possible connection of law and morality, Kelsen stresses[426] that if we treat this relation in terms of content, we must assume the existence of only one, uniquely valid (binding) and absolute morality—morality *par excellence*. The snag is that such morality—according to positivist non-cognitivist ethical relativism—does not exist. An equivalent thesis, which is only a conversion of Kelsen's claim, is expressed by Bulygin. The Argentine philosopher assumes that departing from ethical scepticism (relativism), "obliges us to abandon the thesis of the separation of law and morality".[427] The nature of the dispute between the natural law conceptions (to which Bulygin also includes Alexy's nonpositivist conception) and legal positivism, is neatly explicated by him by means of logical analysis, which allows us easily to understand the quantitative aspect of morality that the nonpositivist *Verbindungsthese* refers to.[428] Using the method of logical analysis proposed by Peter Geach, Bulygin holds that the thesis: "Every legal order must conform (*tiene que adecuarse*) to morality" might logically be interpreted in two ways:

(1) $\forall x\,(Lx \rightarrow \exists y\,(My \land Cxy))$
(2) $\exists x\,(Mx \land \forall y\,(Ly \rightarrow Cyx))$

The first sentence means that for every legal order (L) there is some (but not necessarily the same) moral system (M) that this order corresponds to (C). In turn, the second sentence expresses the view that there is such a moral system (M) that all legal systems (L) correspond to (C).

Bulygin undoubtedly rightly assumes that the first formalisation expresses "a wholly trivial truth" that even the most extreme (we could say: hard) positivist does not negate—because every legal system is an expression of some positive morality of a given society, or at least of those who are in power, and the officials of a given state. Nonetheless, the dispute between the supporters of natural law (and nonpositivists) with legal positivists concerns the second formalisation—the truth of this sentence implies the existence of a unique, privileged, perfect moral system, which is: (1) objectively true, (2) accessible to human knowladge, and—as Bulygin

426 *See* H. Kelsen, 'Law and Morality', *op. cit.*, pp. 87, 90.

427 R. Caracciolo, 'Entrevista a Eugenio Bulygin', *op. cit.*, p. 511.

428 *Cf.* E. Bulygin, '¿Hay vinculación necesaria entre derecho y moral?' in R. Vázquez (ed.), *Derecho y moral. Ensayos sobre un debate contemporáneo*, Barcelona 1998, pp. 220–221 and 'Is There a Conceptual Connection between Law and Morality?', *op. cit.*, p. 50.

complements in the context of Alexy's nonpositivist theory, especially in the context of his claim to correctness—(3) shared by all lawmakers.[429]

In response to Bulygin's objections, Alexy—which is essential and certainly slightly surprising—explicitly rejects the former's allegation that his nonpositivist conception presupposes the existence of the one ond only objective morality, shared by all lawmakers.[430] This declaration, having paramount importance for understanding and evaluating Alexy's nonpositivist conception of law, is only pointed out here, since it will become the subject of consideration in the next section. For now, let us focus on another specific issue, also directly resulting from *Verbindungsthese* being adopted by nonpositivists; namely, the problem of an "enlightened" morality. In short, we need to consider the question of whether there is any guarantee that this morality (no matter whether it is the one and only morality or not) is indeed a legitimate morality, protecting us against extremely unjust "law", and not just a collection of superstitions and prejudice. In other words, does the nonpositivist conception of law protect us from the fact that its appeal to morality will not constitute a reference to, for example, the "morality" of the Nazis or the supporters of apartheid?

Objections of this type are raised by many representatives of legal positivism and we shall indicate some of them only by way of example. In Hart's writings, this objection is very general (it concerns any theory of law adopting the Connection Thesis) and, obviously, it has not been formulated in the context of the nonpositivist conception of law, which was established about a quarter of a century after the publication of *The Concept of Law*. The philosopher from Oxford, when examining the question of a possible moral critique of law in a situation where we assume a necessary connection between law and morality, poses a question[431] as to whether the morality that law shall conform to in order "to be good" should stand for "the accepted morality of the group whose law it is" even if it "may rest on superstition". Or does morality, to which we refer, stand for "enlightened" morality, in the sense that it consists of standards (moral principles) based "on rational beliefs", concerning reality and accepting the fact that all human beings have the right to equal treatment and respect? In other words, Hart raises the question of whether the necessary connection of law and morality is to be understood as a relation with any, not necessarily "enlightened" morality of a given society (which might be self-contradictory, dogmatic or irrational), or with a critical morality that recognises at least the above-mentioned human rights and which, therefore, may be treated as a "true morality".[432]

[429] *See* E. Bulygin, 'Is There a Conceptual Connection between Law and Morality?', *op. cit.*, pp. 50–51 and 'Alexy's Thesis of the Necessary Connection between Law and Morality', *op. cit.*, p. 134.

[430] R. Alexy, 'On the Thesis of a Necessary Connection between Law and Morality: Bulygin's Critique', *op. cit.*, pp. 143–144.

[431] H.L.A. Hart, *The Concept of Law*, *op. cit.*, p. 201. *Cf.* also *ibidem*, p. 196. For more on Hart's differentiation between critical and positive morality – directly related to the problem of "enlightened" morality – *see* N. MacCormick, 'The Concept of Law and *The Concept of Law*' in R.P. George (ed.), *The Autonomy of Law*, *op. cit.*, p. 168, with Hart's works cited therein.

[432] In order to avoid a possible misunderstanding, it has to be explained that this last question is obviously of a purely hypothetical character, because Hart – as a non-cognitivist and moral relativist – denies the existence of a "true morality".

Similar objections, already explicitly referring to Dreier's and Alexy's nonpositivist concept of law, are formulated by Bulygin, Hoerster and Krawietz. Bulygin's charge is of an indirect nature, because—as already indicated—he primarily challenges the quantitative thesis, which he inappropriately attributed to Alexy, concerning the existence of a single, privileged morality, which is shared by all lawmakers.[433] In this context, however, Bulygin raises an additional objection, which already relates directly to a qualitative problem of "enlightened" morality. Accordingly, by challenging the thesis of the existence of a unique morality, privileged vis-à-vis other moralities, he poses a question as to whether, in fact, moral systems, and in particular the concepts of moral correctness and justice, which the legislators alluded to, were identical in the case of law enacted by Genghis Khan, Philip II of Spain, Henry VIII, Khomeini or Pinochet. Given a choice of the characters, we can undoubtedly assume that Bulygin, at the same time, undermines the "enlightened" nature of morality, which Alexy's nonpositivism postulates a necessary conceptual connection with. The problem of "enlightened" morality appears in its purest form just in Hoerster's critique of Dreier's nonpositivist conception.[434] The philosopher from Mainz formulates his objection in a manner that—due to its clarity—may be regarded as a model one, stating that:

> There is no guarantee or at least likelihood that this morality, which the judge or a citizen interested in determining the law incorporate into their concept of law, is indeed "enlightened" (*aufgeklärte*) morality!

What is more, Hoerster in the context of the example of the legal regulation of capital punishment rightly adds that:

> However, nothing at all suggests that the *moral imagination* of any specific people or any specific societies are in any sense more enlightened (for example, more "humane" or "fair") than *positive legal norms* in the respective states.

The presented positivist objection of "unenlightened" morality is undoubtedly very difficult to rebut, both for the representatives of the doctrines of natural law[435] as well as for nonpositivists.[436] Both Dreier and Alexy try at least to diminish its

---

[433] *See* E. Bulygin, 'Alexy's Thesis of the Necessary Connection between Law and Morality', *op. cit.*, p. 134.

[434] *See* N. Hoerster, 'Zur Verteidigung des Rechtspositivismus', *op. cit.*, p. 2482, where the examples in the text below were taken from. This argument has been repeated by W. Krawietz, 'Neues Naturrecht oder Rechtspositivismus?', *op. cit.*, pp. 214–215.

[435] By way of example, *see* Fuller's attempt to rebut it, presented in his 'Positivism and Fidelity to Law – A Reply to Professor Hart', *op. cit.*, pp. 635ff. Fuller's standpoint was reconstructed by R. S. Summers, *Lon L. Fuller*, London 1984, pp. 33ff., in particular, p. 61. According to Summers' reconstruction, among all Fuller's arguments against the mentioned positivist objection, two are the most essential. Firstly, that in the legal systems which are "open to morality", it is more likely to introduce to law "good" and not "bad" ("unenlightened") moral values. Secondly, that the possible immorality of the legal system that is "open to morality" does not by any means have to be greater than in the case of a legal system "closed to morality", in which there operate only purely formal tests of validity of legal norms, consistent with the positivist Separation Thesis.

[436] *Cf.* an interesting attempt of a partial and indirect rebuttal of this objection, undertaken by A. Aarnio and A. Peczenik, 'On Values. Universal or Relative?', *RJ* 9 (1996), pp. 321–330.

importance, using a primarily antirelativistic legal-ethical argumentation already used by Radbruch. The philosopher of Heidelberg, in *Five Minutes of Legal Philosophy*, formulated the view under which the principles of natural law or the law of reason were developed over the centuries with "such a far-reaching agreement" and codified in the various Declarations of Human Rights that this allows us to believe that many of these principles can be questioned only by a "wilful scepticism" (*gewollte Skepsis*).[437] Alexy, referring in his argumentation to Radbruch's view, accurately points out that the reference to historical facts or to the unanimity of the international community does not refute the metaethical relativistic position (and thus the argument from "unenlightened" morality) and that it merely brings us closer to its rebuttal.[438] Therefore, he tries to refute the positivist *Relativismusargument* by means of the discursive rehabilitation of practical reason and by demonstrating discursive possibilities for justifying basic human rights.[439] Dreier, on the other hand, explicitly recognising the importance of the objection from "unenlightened" morality,[440] seeks to demonstrate that, despite its general correctness, the application of an ethically enriched nonpositivist concept of law is more appropriate than the application of the positivist concept, not containing moral elements. In order to prove the latter, Dreier presents a three-stage model of juristic concepts of law (*Dreistufenmodell des juristischen Rechtsbegriffs*), briefly analysing (from the perspective of a participant) the relevance of competing concepts of law in relation to: (1) a particular system of law (here Dreier uses the example of German law), (2) systems of law appropriate for the type of states that are constitutional democracies, and (3) law in general. In his opinion, in each case under consideration, the nonpositivist concept of law manifests an advantage over a positivist concept, particularly in the context of the interpretation of legal principles (stage 1), restrictions of ethical relativism due to defining the states of a constitutional democracy by means of a catalogue of the principles common for them (stage 2) and the possibility of an adequate analysis of the "struggle for law" (*Kampf ums Recht*), taking place at an international level (stage 3).[441]

---

[437] G. Radbruch, 'Fünf Minuten Rechtsphilosophie', *op. cit.*, p. 210 [English version, p. 15].

[438] R. Alexy, 'Zur Verteidigung eines nichtpositivistischen Rechtsbegriffs', *op. cit.*, p. 103. Naturally, Alexy is not able to claim that even the universal consensus within the international community could refute moral relativism, since he would then be in conflict with his procedural conception of the practical correctness of normative sentences and norms – *cf. supra*, pp. 86ff.

[439] *Cf. supra*, pp. 91ff., in particular, the references cited in note 136 at pp. 93–94.

[440] *See* R. Dreier, 'Neues Naturrecht oder Rechtspositivismus?', *op. cit.*, p. 380 and 'Zur gegenwärtigen Diskussion des Verhältnisses von Recht und Moral in der Bundesrepublik Deutschland', *op. cit.*, note 5 *in fine* at p. 57.

[441] R. Dreier, 'Neues Naturrecht oder Rechtspositivismus?', *op. cit.*, pp. 381–382.

The dispute over the legitimacy of the positivist argument from "unenlightened" morality seems far from the final substantive resolution, if such is at all possible. However, due to demonstrating the defectiveness of Alexy's discursive-theoretical method of rehabilitating the practical reason[442] and the possibility of using "Radbruch's formula" for shameful purposes,[443] the only coherent position can be admitting that positivists were right in this matter because they recognised the relativism of moral judgments. Anyway, to paraphrase to a certain degree Alf Ross's thesis on natural law doctrines, it can be generally assumed that there is no ideology (which is reflected in the content of positive law) which could not be defended by means of resorting to morality.[444] This, however, does not provide a final resolution to the dispute, because there still exists a certain not substantive, but formal way by means of which a nonpositivist or even a supporter of the law of nature may prove the inadequacy of the positivist objection. It is amazing that this method—as can be expected, due to its obviousness, which, sometimes paradoxically, hinders cognition—has not yet appeared in its pure form during the debate on the issues of "enlightened" morality.

The crucial point is that the positivist objection of "unenlightened" morality, which could serve as a reference point for the nonpositivist concept of law (in accordance with the nonpositivist *Verbindungsthese*) is inadmissible in the light of the following reasoning. Let us note at first that the legal positivist accepts (according to the Separation Thesis) that positive law can be immoral, or even extremely unjust.[445] It should also be noted that, according to the positivist methodology, the thesis of the separation between law and morality prohibits the positivist undertaking the moral evaluation of law within (pure—Kelsen, descriptive and devoid of any justifying function—Hart) jurisprudence (in particular, the theory and philosophy of law).[446] Thus, ethical relativism—adopted by the positivists and usually associated with non-cognitivism—excludes the possibility

[442] *See supra*, pp. 111ff.

[443] *See supra*, pp.163ff., in particular, note 415 at p. 169.

[444] A. Ross, *On Law and Justice*, trans. M. Dutton, London 1958, p. 261. In the original, this thesis reads as follows: "The ideology does not exist that cannot be defended by an appeal to the law of nature". Of course, Alexy directly rejects this thesis, pointing out that morality must be justified, i.e., it must withstand the test of rational practical discourse – *see e.g.*, R. Alexy, 'Zur Verteidigung eines nichtpositivistischen Rechtsbegriffs', *op. cit.*, p. 103 and 'On the Thesis of a Necessary Connection between Law and Morality: Bulygin's Critique', *op. cit.*, p. 144.

[445] *See e.g.*, Hart's formulation of this thesis, taken from 'Postscript', *op. cit.*, p. 268: "[T]hough there are many different contingent connections between law and morality there are no necessary conceptual connections between the content of law and morality; and hence morally iniquitous provisions may be valid as legal rules or principles. One aspect of this form of the separation of law from morality is that there can be legal rights and duties which have no moral justification or force whatever". *See* also *supra*, pp. 82 and 167.

[446] *Cf. supra*, pp. 135ff.

of rational judgments about whether a given morality is "enlightened" or "unenlightened". In this regard, a positivist must keep agnostic silence, as long as she/he is and wants to remain a legal positivist *par excellence*.

We have therefore come to the conclusion that the legal positivist cannot accuse a nonpositivist that the incorporation of the principles and moral standards into the concept of law (or to the rule of recognition of a given legal system) may result in law becoming immoral. Accordingly, she/he cannot pose the objection of "unenlightened" morality until she/he revises her/his own relativistic and non-cognitivist position. In formulating such an objection, a positivist ceases to be a theorist (philosopher) of law,[447] and he "becomes" an ethicist; yet even then, his criticism might be viewed as inappropriate because it leads to contradictions or, at least, to inconsistencies in her/his views. Indeed, a positivist (as a theorist of law) first recognises that *Gesetz ist Gesetz*, thus allowing and accepting the possible immorality of positive law, and then (already as a moralist) criticises the authors of nonpositivist or natural law conceptions that may—in the positivists' opinion—lead to such an immorality of law or at least facilitate it. It seems that one can even risk a thesis that such a positivist *doublethink* (to once again refer to Orwell's terminology, this time from *Nineteen Eighty-Four*[448]) is a *contradicto in adiecto*—or, more gently speaking—a manifestation of the positivist's intellectual schizophrenia. How else to assess the position of the person who first explicitly accepts that the positive law can, for example, allow racial discrimination or active euthanasia of mentally ill people, and then criticises the conceptions that can—after all, in the exceptional cases of abuse—lead to such obviously immoral legislation. In this sense, the positivists' emphasis on the conceptual separation of law and morality, which aimed, inter alia, to allow for a methodologically pure moral criticism of law, has huge side effects.

Jerzy Kalinowski, in one of the critical works on positivist conceptions, argues (with reference to the concept of the ontological unity of man)[449] that, while distinguishing the legal obligations from the moral ones is somewhat reasonable, the separation of these obligations is irrational.[450] At first glance, it could be argued, by analogy, that while we can distinguish, on a conceptual level, a purely legal and purely moral criticism of the law, yet at the time of undertaking any criticism of the law, these two dimensions must be addressed simultaneously, and one of them must be recognised by the person undertaking the criticism as decisive. Otherwise, she/he will suffer from a legal and moral split personality. However, as I believe, this analogy is not fully justified. If law and morality are in conflict and they impose

[447] In formulating this thesis, I use the positivist, "pure" way of grasping the methodological character of the theory and philosophy of law.

[448] *Cf.* G. Orwell, *Animal Farm* and *1984*, *op. cit.*, pp. 289ff.

[449] *See* J. Kalinowski, 'Théorie, métathéorie ou philosophie du droit. Réflexions sur *The Concept of Law* de H.L.A. Hart et *On Law and Justice* d'Alf Ross', *APhD* XV (1970), pp. 188–189.

[450] Interestingly, an essentially identical position is taken by E. Bulygin, who is undoubtedly a hard legal positivist – *see* R. Caracciolo, 'Entrevista a Eugenio Bulygin', *op. cit.*, p. 511.

different (in particular, contradictory) obligations on man, then—as a rule—the decision on how to act, and the subsequent behaviour that results from the latter cannot be both consistent with law and with morality. Conversely, if we make an exclusively intellectual assessment of the positive law, which does not have a direct impact on our subsequent behaviour, it seems possible to make two independent evaluations (from the legal and moral perspective), and only then—in a situation that forces us to take practical decisions—can we make the preferential choice of the point view which we deem reliable.

It appeared, therefore, that although Dreier's and Alexy's nonpositivist conception does not substantively rebut the objection of "unenlightened" morality, yet taking into account the mentioned formal methodological reasons, nonpositivists may completely ignore this objection, if it is formulated by the authors who regard themselves as legal positivists. If a positivist wants to remain a positivist, he must (*nota bene*, in the manner probably most unattainable for a man[451]) completely abstain from any moral criticism of law and its conceptions. If a positivist does not say *ignoramus et ignorabimus*, then she/he will "become" a nonpositivist or the follower of iusnaturalism, or she/he will even cease to be a theoretician (philosopher) of law and will "become" an ethicist. Conceptual separation of law and its moral value, incidentally, sometimes treated as an example of the so-called analyticity error,[452] leads to the fact that the legal positivist cannot pose an objection of "unenlightened" morality, because it would be inconsistent with the positivist methodology.[453] Only if this objection were formulated by the followers of other nonpositivist conceptions of law or by the representatives of the theory of natural law, would their defence against such an objection probably be qualitatively different from that outlined above. Accordingly, the basic problem would consist of considering and determining which particular philosophical or legal conception is better (i.e., more effective) in the context of ensuring the moral correctness of positive law. Such a dispute would, therefore, only be carried out in "the family of antipositivists".

---

[451] The abundant evidence of scientific and political activity of the leading representatives of legal positivism (*e.g.*, Kelsen and Hart), who defend democracy and human rights, shows that the positivists also cannot hide the fact that they are supporters of law which complies with moral requirements (in the sense of critical morality). With regard to Kelsen's views, *cf. supra*, p. 120, whereas in terms of Hart's views, *see e.g.*, J.R. de Páramo, 'Entrevista a H.L.A. Hart', *op. cit.*, pp. 356ff. *See* also interesting observations on the progressive nature of the views and reformatory activities of the leading legal positivists (Bentham, Austin, Kelsen, Hart and MacCormick) made by F. Schauer, 'Positivism as Pariah' in R.P. George (ed.), *The Autonomy of Law*, *op. cit.*, p. 37, and the references cited therein.

[452] *See* L.M. Sánchez Fernández, 'Ironías, falacias, perversiones, enigmas: sobre el positivismo y la tesis de la separación', *op. cit.*, p. 359.

[453] It is also applicable in relation to the positivist objection against the possible incorporation of "Radbruch's formula" into the system of positive law. Let us repeat once again that in such a case, the problem of the candour of already incorporated formula cannot arise for legal positivists.

4.9 Some Remarks About Nonpositivist Empirical Argumentation

Let us start the analysis of nonpositivist empirical argumentation with a few comments on Ralf Dreier's conception, since this author directly utilises empirical arguments to justify both the argument from un-law (referring here to the examples of the judicial decisions of the German courts that apply "Radbruch's formula") and the argument from principles; in particular, in relation to *Inkorporationsthese* and *Optimierungsthese* (where, in addition to relying on the jurisdiction of the Federal Constitutional Court, he also examines the norms contained in the German *Grundgesetz* and in international law).[454] Such frequent use of empirical arguments can raise doubts, because the concept of law that was proposed by him is of a normative character, which Dreier repeatedly emphasises.[455] Does it amount to making a naturalistic fallacy not only by the supporter, but also by an expert in Kant's philosophy? Of course not, as it can be demonstrated by the following reasons.

First of all, Dreier, in response to Krawietz's criticism, explicitly states that his conception is not about changing the concept of law (from a positivist to a nonpositivist one), but that he reconstructs the concept, actually adopted in the German jurisdiction, which—in his view—is already nonpositivist in its essence.[456] Therefore, the application of empirical arguments is, in this case, not only appropriate but even indispensable. Accordingly, the fact that the concept of law, proposed by him, is normative, that it is a concept—to use Dreier's words—"that the judge ought to accept *ex officio*" (*Richter von Amts wegen haben sollte*)[457]—does not cause any methodological contradiction. On the other hand, such reliance on empirical arguments once again brings to mind Tugendhat's previously cited opinion concerning Alexy's theory, according to which we now live in the "best of all conceivable legal worlds".[458] Avoiding naturalistic fallacy in Dreier's argumentation results from his implicitly adopted standpoint that it is the case that the judges in Germany use such a concept of law, which—in light of Dreier's nonpositivist conception—they should accept and apply. Leaving aside the question as to whether Dreier's reconstruction of the judicial concept of law is adequate (and there is no reason why it should be otherwise[459]), we cannot escape the impression that his argumentation is, at least to some extent, circular and somewhat redundant:

---

[454] *Cf.* the reconstruction of Dreier's nonpositivist argumentation presented in Chap. 3 at pp. 29–35.

[455] *See* Chap. 3, notes 30–31 at p. 29, with the corresponding text.

[456] R. Dreier, 'Neues Naturrecht oder Rechtspositivismus?', *op. cit.*, p. 368.

[457] R. Dreier, 'Der Begriff des Rechts', *op. cit.*, p. 894. *Cf. idem*, 'Zur gegenwärtigen Diskussion des Verhältnisses von Recht und Moral in der Bundesrepublik Deutschland', *op. cit.*, p. 67.

[458] *See supra*, pp. 117–118.

[459] The demonstration of the accuracy of Dreier's nonpositivist empirical theses has been provided by U. Neumann, 'Positivistische Rechtsquellenlehre und naturrechtliche Methode. Zum

why should one convince the judges to adopt such a concept of law that they have already accepted?

Secondly, the reason for rejecting a possible objection of the naturalistic fallacy is the fact that Dreier's nonpositivist argumentation is of an analytically "soft" character (to use an expression popularised recently in the Polish jurisprudential literature[460]). He does not use any formal arguments based on deduction, in which the premises would belong to the "world of Is", whilst conclusions to the "world of Ought". He only lends credence to his arguments and conclusions by reference to the facts.

Alexy, on the other hand, although he allows for the possibility of nonpositivist empirical argumentation—due to the subsidiary character of such arguments—rejects the possibility of basing the nonpositivist concept of law on purely empirical justification.[461] In arguing for the nonpositivist conception of law, Alexy uses the concepts of analytical and normative necessity—basically ignoring empirical necessity. It should be noted that, although even the hard positivists do not deny the existence of numerous empirical (actual) interconnections between law and morality,[462] from an empirical point of view it is obviously unreasonable to speak about the necessity of a conceptual connection between law and morality (substantive correctness). Numerous examples of legal systems (and legal cultures) of the states of the continental system-type of enacted (statutory) law, in which we still deal with a positivist comprehension of law, illustrate the fact that any empirical necessity of the nonpositivist concept of law is out of the question. The approval of the nonpositivist *Verbindungsthese* is by no means necessary in order for a certain, positivistically defined system of norms to function as the law of a given society in an undoubtedly effective way.

However, as can easily be observed due to the previously presented reconstruction of Alexy's nonpositivist argumentation and thorough analysis of the justification of the universal validity of the rules of general practical discourse—as provided by him—he applies the empirical arguments more often than Dreier does. What is even worse is that many points are not justified empirically, but on purely intellectual grounds (by way of example, let us recall here the justification of an analytical evolutionary argument, the essential elements of which were also later used in the support of the argument from maximisation of individual utility and the anthropological argument concerning human interest in correctness[463]). Without repeating

---

Alltagsnaturrecht in der juristischen Argumentation', *ARSP* Bh. 37 (1990), pp. 145ff. For more on the results of empirical research described by Neumann, *see* Chap. 5 at p. 211.

[460] *See e.g.*, R. Sarkowicz, J. Stelmach, *Teoria prawa* [Theory of Law], Kraków 1996, pp. 31ff. and J. Stelmach, B. Brożek, *Methods of Legal Reasoning*, *op. cit.*, pp. 2ff.

[461] *Cf.* Chap. 3, note 17 at p. 26, with the corresponding text.

[462] It is worth emphasising that even Hart explicitly recognises the existence of the "necessary connexion of law and morals", understood empirically as an undeniable influence of morality on law – *see idem*, *The Concept of Law*, *op. cit.*, pp. 199–200. *Cf. e.g.*, L. Green, *Positivism and the Inseparability of Law and Morals*, NYULR 83/4 (2008), pp. 1044ff.

[463] *See supra*, pp. 112–114 and Chap. 3, pp. 38–40.

the previously presented criticism of these arguments, it should only be noted that the nonpositivist arguments used by Alexy can be, in many cases, faced with an objection of a lack of convincing justification of empirical theses that the latter are based on.

What is crucial in evaluating the validity of nonpositivist empirical arguments is the assumed scope of the concept of law postulated by the creators of the nonpositivist conception of law. Undoubtedly, one can adopt the following proportion here: the more they mean the universal concept of law (as opposed to the concept of law relativised to a particular legal culture or the state legal system), the more universally valid should be the empirical theses used in nonpositivist argumentation. From this perspective, Dreier's nonpositivist conception is much more modest than Alexy's conception, because the philosopher of Göttingen, despite allowing for the possibility of developing nonpositivist theories that have a much wider extension,[464] characterises his conception as the one which concerns the concept of law applicable to the democratic (and social) Law-Governed State (*demokratischen (und sozialen) Rechtsstaats*), clearly leaving aside the question as to whether and to what extent the claim to the universal validity of this concept may be justified.[465] In connection with this specific scope of applying Dreier's nonpositivist concept of law, the empirical arguments used by him do not raise objections; in particular, one cannot accuse them of being inadequate.

In relation to Alexy's nonpositivist conception, the matter is somewhat more complicated and controversial, as his theory adopts the mentioned claim to universality. The nonpositivist concept of law—as developed by him—is to be characteristic for law as such, rather than only for a specific legal culture (system of law). According to Alexy, the dispute over the concept of law between positivists and nonpositivists constitutes the dispute over what law is.[466] As already noted,[467] the necessary conceptual connection between law and morality—underlying Alexy's nonpositivist concept of law—is by no means based on assuming the only objective morality, shared by all lawmakers, but on the premise of the idea of a correct morality, justified by means of universal practical discourse, which is an expression of practical rationality (practical reason).[468] Thus, empirical arguments and theses applied by Alexy should first and foremost justify the universal (i.e., independent of

[464] *See* R. Dreier, 'Zur gegenwärtigen Diskussion des Verhältnisses von Recht und Moral in der Bundesrepublik Deutschland', *op. cit.*, p. 66, wherein Dreier considers the development of a universal nonpositivist legal theory at four levels, related to: (1) a particular system of law, (2) a group of ethically similar legal systems, (3) all systems of law recognised by the international community, and (4) all actual or possible legal systems.

[465] R. Dreier, 'Der Begriff des Rechts', *op. cit.*, p. 895. *Cf. idem*, 'Zur gegenwärtigen Diskussion des Verhältnisses von Recht und Moral in der Bundesrepublik Deutschland', *op. cit.*, pp. 55, 66.

[466] *See* R. Alexy, *Begriff und Geltung des Rechts*, *op. cit.*, p. 18 [English version, p. 5].

[467] *Cf. supra*, the text corresponding to note 430 at p. 174.

[468] R. Alexy, 'On the Thesis of a Necessary Connection between Law and Morality: Bulygin's Critique', *op. cit.*, p. 144. *Cf.* A. García Figueroa, 'La tesis del caso especial y el positivismo jurídico', *op. cit.*, pp. 207ff.

time and place, or more broadly: the existing legal culture) nature of the rules of practical discourse. There is no denying that Alexy is trying to prove this on the basis of empirical theses that concern not only the contemporary legal culture of constitutional democracies, but also even with respect to the regulation of slavery in Roman law,[469] whereas when seeking the justification of *Richtigkeitsargument* by identifying a "performative contradiction", he also uses an example of a revised definition of law derived from Ulpianus (*Iuris praecepta sunt haec: inhoneste vivere, alterum laedere, suum cuique non tribuere*).[470] On the other hand, the above analyses of justifying the universal validity of practical discourse rules (based on the transcendental-pragmatic argument and two complementary empirical arguments) showed[471] that his theory of practical discourse can be considered adequate only in relation to European legal culture of the late twentieth century characteristic for democratic countries.

Following this line of criticism of Alexy's conception, we have reached a reservation of a more general nature. If anyone attempts to justify some concept of law (no matter whether it is a positivist, or nonpositivist or natural law one) by using the empirical arguments, he can easily encounter the objection of confusing two issues. As it is very clearly formulated by Bernd Rüthers, referring to Kant's views,[472] the local question addressed to legal science about what law prescribes in a specific place and time (*Quid sit iuris?*) is one thing, and a global question of what law is (*Quid est ius?*) is another.[473] Similar objections on confusing (or a failure to distinguish) these two issues are often raised in the debate on the concept of law—both by the legal positivists and their opponents. By way of example, we can mention here the charges against Dworkin's antipositivist theory, formulated in different contexts by a number of representatives of legal positivism, pointing—generally speaking—at the American author's failure to distinguish or at his improper differentiation of law as such and the law as a particular system of a state's law.[474] We can also recall Dworkin's very similar allegations against the theory of Hart and other legal positivists.[475] In this context, Alexy's nonpositivist

---

[469] *Cf. supra*, note 74 at p. 80.

[470] *Cf. supra*, note 301 at p. 40, and the references cited therein.

[471] *Cf. supra*, pp. 99–117.

[472] *See* I. Kant, *Metafizyczne podstawy nauki prawa* [Metaphysical Foundations of the Science of Law], trans. W. Galewicz, Kęty 2006, pp. 41–42.

[473] B. Rüthers, *Rechtstheorie. Begriff, Geltung und Anwendung des Rechts*, München 1999, pp. 36–37. For more *see* R. Sartorius, 'The Concept of Law', *ARSP* 52 (1966), pp. 162ff.

[474] On various ways of formulating such objections, *see e.g.*, J.D. Goldsworthy, 'The Self-Destruction of Legal Positivism', *op. cit.*, pp. 451ff., in particular, note 15, and the references cited therein; J.L. Coleman, 'Normativity and Naturalism' in *idem*, *The Practice of Principle*, *op. cit.*, pp. 180ff. *Cf.* H.L.A. Hart, 'Comment' in R. Gavison (ed.), *Issues in Contemporary Legal Philosophy. The Influence of H.L.A. Hart*, Oxford 1987, pp. 39–40.

[475] *See* R. Dworkin, *Law's Empire*, *op. cit.*, pp. 31ff. Hart's very decisive response can be found in his 'Postscript', *op. cit.*, pp. 246ff., whereas Dworkin's other response was presented in 'Hart's Postscript and the Character of Political Philosophy', *OJLS* 24/1 (2004), p. 36.

conception, undoubtedly seeking the answer to a global question ("What is law?"), is exposed to the same objection, at least in this respect, in which its author uses local arguments of empirical character, relativised to the contemporary legal culture of Western democracies, or—even more specifically—referring to the post-war jurisdiction of German courts.[476]

Nonetheless, it should be strongly emphasised that it is impossible to challenge the fact that German jurisdiction (and also in recent years, European jurisdiction) provides strong empirical support for the nonpositivist conception of law and the concept of law postulated by nonpositivists. In particular, having in mind the jurisdiction of the Federal Constitutional Court and the German dogmatics of constitutional law, we should agree with the opinion expressed by the eminent German constitutionalist, Christian Starck, who describes it as an "applied philosophy of law" (*angewandte Rechtsphilosophie*).[477] Numerous German court decisions—related to the Germans reviewing the period of Nazi rule and, since the reunification of Germany, also concerning the accountability for the unlawfulness in the former GDR (in particular the trials over the "Berlin Wall shootings")—constitute excellent material to deepen the theoretical analyses related primarily, but not only, to the application of "Radbruch's formula" in judicial practice.

Let us familiarise with the fragments of the two rulings of the Court of Karlsruhe, which—due to nonpositivist theses presented expressly therein—appear to be the most representative ones and are often cited by the authors of the nonpositivist theory of law.

The first flagship example, showing the reception of "Radbruch's formula" in the German constitutional jurisdiction, is the *Bundesverfassungsgericht* (German Federal Constitutional Court) ruling of 14 February 1968 (the so-called *Staatsangehörigkeitsbeschluß*) on the already mentioned[478] case of the Eleventh Ordinance (*Verordnung*) of 25 November 1941, issued pursuant to the Statute on Reich Citizenship (*Reichsbürgergesetz*) of 15 September 1935. The reviewed case concerned the question of appropriate law (Dutch or German) in inheritance proceedings after a German national of Jewish descent, who emigrated to the Netherlands shortly before the war, and therefore—in accordance with §2 of the quoted regulation—was deprived of German citizenship.[479] Article 116 Section 2 of the German *Grundgesetz*, which restores the citizenship to German citizens who

---

[476] I will return to this issue, only indicated here, in the course of the discussion on the objection of Alexy's failure to differentiate between the concept and the conception of law, in Chap. 5 at pp. 196–199.

[477] I quote Starck's opinion after R. Dreier, 'Hauptströmungen gegenwärtiger Rechtsphilosophie in Deutschland', *op. cit.*, p. 180.

[478] *Cf.* Chap. 3, p. 31.

[479] *See* R. Alexy, *Begriff und Geltung des Rechts*, *op. cit.*, pp. 18–22 [English version, pp. 5–7]; R. Dreier, 'Recht und Moral', *op. cit.*, pp. 189–190, 'Gesetzliches Unrecht im SED-Staat?', *op. cit.*, p. 58, and 'Some Remarks on the Concept of Law', *op. cit.*, p. 116; W. Ott, 'Die Radbruch'sche Formel', *op. cit.*, pp. 338–339.

were deprived of it by the Nazis due to political, racial or religious reasons, however, on condition of their residence in Germany after 8 May 1945, and provided they did not express different intent, was not applicable in this case as that man was deported in 1942 from Amsterdam and his later fate was unknown. Therefore, the German Federal Constitutional Court had to decide on the validity of this regulation. The theses of the ruling, stating the retroactive (*ex tunc*) invalidity of this regulation, are as follows[480]:

1. The national socialist provisions of "law" may be denied their validity as law (*die Geltung als Recht*) if they are in such an evident contradiction with the fundamental principles of justice, that the judge who wishes to apply them or to recognize their legal effect, would adjudicate un-law in the place of law (*Unrecht statt Recht sprechen würde*).
2. In the Eleventh Ordinance to *Reichsbürgergesetz* of 25 October 1941 (RGbl. I, p. 772) the contradiction with justice has reached such an intolerable level (*so unerträgliches Maß erreicht*) that it must be considered invalid (*nichtig*).
3. Once established statutory un-law (*gesetztes Unrecht*), which clearly violates the constitutive principles of law (*konstituierende Grundsätze des Rechts*), shall not become law on the basis that it will be applied and obeyed.

The second example, no longer justifying the nonpositivist argument from un-law, but the argument from principles (or, more generally, the fulfilling of the positive validating function by morality within the rule of recognition[481]), refers to the so-called judicial development of law (*richterliche Rechtsfortbildung*)—which takes place in the German jurisdiction—sometimes even assuming the form of a *contra legem* interpretation.[482] The case of Iranian princess Soraya Esfandiary-Bakhtiari, the former wife of the last Shah of Iran, concerned the damages for infringing her personal interests.[483] This infringement occurred as a result of the publication in one of the German tabloids of a wholly imaginary interview with the princess on the details of her private life. The case was settled by German civil courts in the years 1962–1964; the princess was awarded damages amounting to 15,000 DM. The problem is that these decisions were contrary to the German Civil Code (*BGB*), which grants the right to compensation for non-pecuniary damage only in cases strictly regulated by law, which did not include the case at hand. Therefore, the rulings of the civil courts have become the subject of a constitutional

---

[480] I quote them after R. Dreier, 'Recht und Moral', *op. cit.*, p. 190. The quotation mark in the original.

[481] *Cf. supra*, p. 127.

[482] For more *see* J. Neuner, *Die Rechtsfindung contra legem*, *op. cit.*, in particular, pp. 47ff., 132ff.

[483] *Beschluß des Ersten Senat vom 14. Februar 1973* (1 BvR 112/65), published in *Entscheidungen des Bundesverfassungsgerichts* 34 (1973), pp. 269–293. For more on nonpositivist elements in this ruling *see* R. Dreier, 'Some Remarks on the Concept of Law', *op. cit.*, pp. 119–120 and R. Alexy, *Begriff und Geltung des Rechts*, *op. cit.*, pp. 22–26 [English version, pp. 8–10].

complaint, which the Federal Constitutional Court rejected in the ruling of 14 February 1973 (the so-called *Rechtsfortbildungsbeschluß*), recognising that the jurisdiction of the civil courts awarding compensation for serious violation of personal rights, also in the case of such non-pecuniary damage that took place in the discussed case, is consistent with the Constitution. In the justification of its decision, the Court, recognising it as its indisputable right and at the same time as the judge's duty to undertake—in the framework provided by the German constitution—"creative finding of law" (*schöpferische Rechtsfindung*), expressed an opinion which—due to its representativeness—is worth quoting *in extenso*:

> IV. 1. Traditional bounding of the judges by the statute, the basic element of the principle of the separation of powers, and thus the rule of law (*Rechtsstaatlichkeit*), has been modified in the *Grundgesetz* in that way that the jurisdiction is bound by "the statute (*Gesetz*) and the law (*Recht*)" (Article 20 Section 3). According to a common opinion, the narrow statutory positivism (*enger Gesetzpositivismus*) was thus rejected. This formula makes it aware that, although in general the statute and the law actually overlap, yet it is not always necessary and it does not always take place. The law is not identical to the totality of written statutes. In addition to positive lawmaking by the state authority, there may in certain circumstances occur a surplus of law (*ein Mehr an Recht*), having its source in the constitutional legal order perceived as a sensible whole (*Sinngänze*), and capable of correction functions vis-à-vis the written law; the task of the jurisdiction is to find it and make real (*zu verwirklichen*) in the undertaken decisions. According to the Constitution, a judge is not limited to the application of the legislator's directives in particular cases only within the limits of their possible linguistic meaning. Such understanding would imply that the positive state's legal order is in principle free of gaps, what is acceptable as the basic postulate of legal certainty, but unattainable in practice (*praktisch unerreichbar*). Judicial activity does not consist only in recognising and announcing the decision of the legislator. In particular, the role of the jurisdiction may be to meet the requirement of bringing to light and realising within the court judgment, by means of the act of evaluative cognition (*Akt des bewertenden Erkennens*), not deprived of the volitional elements, the ideas of values (*Wertvorstellungen*), which are immanent to the constitutional legal order, but which are not or are imperfectly expressed in the texts of statutes. The judge must at the same time refrain from arbitrariness; her/his decision must be based on rational argumentation. It must be possible to demonstrate by means of reasoning that the written statutory law (*geschriebenes Gesetz*) does not fulfil its function of a just resolution of a legal question (*ein Rechtsproblem gerecht zu lösen*). In this way the judge's decision fills this gap in accordance with the touchstone of practical reason (*nach den Maßstäben der praktischen Vernunft*) and the "entrenched general ideas of justice of community" (*fundierten allgemeinen Gerechtigkeitsvorstellungen der Gemeinschaft*) (BverGE 9, 338 [349]).[484]

The quoted passages of court judgments, given the unambiguous meaning, do not require any comments. The nonpositivist elements contained in them have been expressed by the Federal Constitutional Court clearly and unmistakably, which of course does not mean that they cast no doubt for the adherents of legal positivism. Yet, the latter is not the subject of discussion here. Undoubtedly, in addition to the

---

[484] *Entscheidungen des Bundesverfassungsgerichts* 34 (1973), pp. 286–287. Let us add that the statement in this passage, stating judicial duty to rely on "the rational argumentation" (in the case of finding and realising "the surplus of law"), was used by Alexy as a motto in his *Theorie der juristischen Argumentation*, *op. cit*., pp. 15, 44ff. [English version, pp. vii, 25ff.].

above paradigmatic examples, we could also cite several post-war decisions of the German courts, in which nonpositivist, or even natural law elements can be easily identified.[485] Nonetheless, taking into account the present times, we deal with a nonpositivist understanding of law primarily in connection with the undisputed renaissance of the interest in Radbruch's post-war views and the formula created by him,[486] which must be regarded as a result of a series of court judgments in the cases known collectively as the trials over the "Berlin Wall shootings" (*Mauerschützenprozesse*). In the context of these judgments, one can easily observe the need to develop such a conceptual apparatus, on the basis of which the analysis of their philosophical and jurisprudential status will become possible. The approval of the German courts in applying "Radbruch's formula" in decisions of the European Court of Human Rights of 22 March 2001, is also a fact that must be taken into account in the jurisprudential reflection, if the latter does not want to lose its contact with the practice. There is no doubt that the mentioned court rulings weigh strongly in favour of a modification of the positivist concept of law or a positivist conception of its validity, at least due to this seemingly prosaic reason that the latter are utterly useless in the analyses of the judgments discussed here.[487] In our further considerations, for reasons that will soon be presented, we shall follow the second

[485] As an example, from the vast German literature on the subject, *see* H. Weinkauff, 'Der Naturrechtsgedanke in der Rechtsprechung des Bundesgerichtshofes' in W. Maihofer (ed.), *Naturrecht oder Rechtspositivismus?*, Darmstadt 1962, pp. 554–576; A. Kaufmann, 'Die Naturrechtsrenaissance der ersten Nachkriegsjahre – und was daraus geworden ist', *op. cit.*, pp. 109ff.; W. Ott, 'Die Radbruch'sche Formel', *op. cit.*, pp. 337ff.; F. Saliger, *Radbruchsche Formel und Rechtsstaat*, *op. cit.*, pp. 32ff.

[486] This renaissance has been mentioned, inter alia, by H. Dreier, 'Gustav Radbruch und die Mauerschützen', *op. cit.*, pp. 424ff. and J. Zajadło, 'Formuła Radbrucha – geneza, treść, zastosowanie', *op. cit.*, pp. 26ff. It is hard to deny that *Mauerschützenprozesse* aroused great interest not only among legal dogmatists, but also theorists and philosophers of law – by way of example, let us indicate here the work of Germany's leading representatives of the latter discipline: R. Alexy, *Mauerschützen*, *op. cit.* and *Der Beschluß des Bundesverfassungsgericht zu den Tötungen an der innerdeutschen Grenze vom 24. Oktober 1996*, *op. cit.*; R. Dreier, 'Gesetzliches Unrecht im SED-Staat?', *op. cit.*; A. Kaufmann, 'Die Radbruchsche Formel vom gesetzlichen Unrecht und vom übergesetzlichen Recht in der Diskussion um das im Namen der DDR begangene Unrecht', *op. cit.*; U. Neumann, 'Positivismo jurídico, realismo jurídico y moralismo jurídico en el debate sobre "delincuencia estatal" en la anterior RDA', trans. F. Puigpelat Martí, *DOXA* 17–18 (1995), pp. 435–444; J.-R. Sieckmann, 'Die "Radbruch'sche Formel" und die Mauerschützen', *op. cit.* This issue has also been discussed in a theoretical monograph, published in 1999 by K. Seidel, *Rechtsphilosophische Aspekte der "Mauerschützen"-Prozesse*, *op. cit.* Having in mind the remaining literature, what is particularly worth recommending are the works of judges being at the same time researchers – *see e.g.*, R. Wassermann, 'Zur Anwendung der sogenannten Radbruchschen Formel auf Unrechtsurteile der DDR-Justiz', *NJW* 45 (1992), pp. 878–879 and W. Hassemer, 'Odpowiedzialność prawnokarna w odniesieniu do przestępczości państwowej w kontekście politycznej zmiany systemu w świetle okoliczności wyłączających bezprawność' [Criminal Liability in Relation to the State Crime in the Context of Political System Change in the Light of Circumstances Excluding Unlawfulness] in A. Eser, A. Zoll (eds.), *Prawo karne a problem zmiany ustroju politycznego*, Kraków 1998, pp. 73–91.

[487] For more on the inadequacy of the positivist conceptual apparatus for describing and analysing the judicial application of law *see* Chap. 5 at pp. 209–212.

of the identified ways, modifying the positivist concept of legal validity in the postpositivist direction.

Summarising the comments on the nonpositivist empirical argumentation, let us quote an accurate paraphrase by Jerzy Zajadło[488]: *Strasbourg locuta, causa finita.* The contemporary theory and philosophy of law should not ignore the examples of multiple application of the—essentially nonpositivist—"Radbruch's formula" in the most modern German and European jurisdictions, if it still wants to keep contact with the European practice of law application and another fundamental jurisprudential debate that accompanies the latter. Thus, as far as the creators of the nonpositivist conception of law refer to judicial decisions, their nonpositivist empirical argumentation should definitely be deemed appropriate and legitimate. Indeed, one does not discuss with the facts, as even the most declared legal positivists would surely agree with.

4.10 An Attempt at Evaluating the Nonpositivist Conception of Law

The evaluation of the nonpositivist conception of law created by Ralf Dreier and Robert Alexy is very difficult and complicated. Indeed, the discussion of the nonpositivist concept of law and its justification is still pending, and there is no sufficient historical perspective that would enable a fully objective and balanced judgment. Furthermore, it should be noted that this conception was developed as a reaction to the positivist theory, which is why many of the nonpositivist arguments have a highly polemical character, which makes the assessment a much more difficult task. To make a full, objective assessment, one should indeed compare the nonpositivist conception with the positivist doctrine in a more systematic way than was done above.

Nonetheless, taking into account the presented critical analysis of the nonpositivist conception, one could provide its overall evaluation, without any claims to finality or completeness. The first observation that arises concerns Dreier's conception and argumentation, which is much more modest, and certainly less controversial than Alexy's. The arguments raised in it prove more difficult to challenge (especially the empirical arguments, which are willingly used by Dreier). The reluctance of the philosopher of Göttingen to useless speculations and to expressing each thesis, even a trivial one, in an over-sophisticated way, also speaks in favour of Dreier's conception. It is indeed relatively easy to understand, not only for theorists of law (provided, of course, they actually want to understand it), but also for judges and other participants in the legal system, to whom Dreier indirectly addresses his argumentation. Alexy's conception and argumentation, on the other hand, constitutes a part of a much more elaborate theory, which—given its scale

[488] J. Zajadło, *Odpowiedzialność za mur. Procesy strzelców przy Murze Berlińskim* [Responsibility for the Wall. *Mauerschützenprozesse*], Gdańsk 2003, p. 171.

and substantive scope that arouse respect—can be, without a doubt, referred to as "Robert Alexy's philosophy of law". It consists of intertwined theories of a practical and legal discourse, the fundamental rights, legal principles and their balancing, discursively justified human rights and, finally, the nonpositivist conception of law, which is the direct subject of the present analysis. The effort taken by Alexy for the past 30 years in order to develop the various elements of his philosophy of law unquestionably deserves a positive assessment. Yet, the results of his deliberations are at many points considerably controversial. We will not repeat here the detailed conclusions drawn in respect to the analyses of particular objections against Alexy's nonpositivist argumentation (especially since some of the objections will be discussed further in later parts of the book[489]). Let us, therefore, finish the overall evaluation of Alexy's conception by the following ascertainment. Leszek Kołakowski begins his excellent book *Metaphysical Horror* with a painfully honest reflection:

> A modern philosopher who has never experienced the feeling of being a charlatan is such a shallow mind that his work is probably not worth reading.[490]

Not wanting to be misunderstood (especially on account of the criticism of the nonpositivist conception of law, as presented above) it should definitely and without a trace of irony or malice be emphasised that Robert Alexy's works are "worth reading". In most cases, Alexy's "charlatanism" is very subtle, and his books and papers in which he undoubtedly struggles with the most fundamental philosophical and jurisprudential problems, are very inspiring, not only for philosophers and theorists of law.

The conclusions from the mentioned criticism that I adopt as a starting point for further analyses are as follows. Firstly, I think that the nonpositivist conception of law and the nonpositivist concept of law proposed in its framework have not been satisfactorily justified at the analytical level. Nonpositivists have failed to rebut noncognitivist objection (i.e., to undertake discursive rehabilitation of practical reason) and, what appears to be even more important, to justify the analytical necessity for adopting the claim to correctness in law. According to the analyses provided above, Alexy's repeated reference to correctness of law and of particular norms and legal decisions turned out to be a merely highly persuasive nonpositivist mantra. Secondly, from the perspective of normative argumentation, the nonpositivist conception seems to be possible (but no longer necessary) to adopt. Some normative arguments and nonpositivist theses prove acceptable, but one has to agree with the positivists in relation to the others. Finally, in the empirical dimension, this conception seems possible to accept and worth recommending mainly due to the requirement of the practical utility of scientific theories. The nonpositivist conceptual apparatus manifests an advantage (in relation to legal practice) over traditional positivism, because it allows us to adequately describe and subject to criticism

---

[489] For more *see* Chap. 5 at pp. 194ff., Chap. 7 at pp. 349ff., and Chap. 9 at pp. 463ff.

[490] L. Kołakowski, *Metaphysical Horror*, Oxford 1988, p. 1.

nonpositivist elements (what I have in mind here is mainly, though not exclusively, "Radbruch's formula") which occur in modern jurisprudence, not only German, but also European jurisprudence. The advantage of the nonpositivist conceptual instrumentarium, in many ways benefiting from the achievement of contemporary theories of legal argumentation, over the conceptual apparatus of the positivist *juristische Methodenlehre* is—in my opinion—indisputable.[491] In the simplest terms, let us put it in the following way: if we do not want philosophical and legal analysis of such judgments as quoted or referred to above—that is, the decisions of the German courts and the rulings of the European Court of Human Rights—to be limited to deeming their "dishonesty" (in Hart's sense) and to adopting that the nonpositivist elements, contained in the justification of these judgments, cannot be dealt with by legal science, since they have a moral character, then we need another set of jurisprudential concepts; namely, nonpositivist, or even better, neutral (and unbiased) ones with respect to the positivism–nonpositivism controversy. *Tempus fugit* and since the times of Hart's complaints over an "obsessive concentration" of the legal theory to the problems of jurisdiction, associated with the so-called rule-scepticism, and his critique of Dworkin's theory of law (principally subsidiary in respect to the jurisdiction),[492] our discipline has undergone a huge transformation. In my opinion, its principal objective is to restore the practical dimension of analytical jurisprudence and to develop new methods—more theoretically adequate and applicable in practice than positivist ones—of jurisprudential analysis of legal phenomena in order to reduce the uncertainty arising from the imperfections of positive law regulations.[493] Therefore, it is hardly surprising that many scholars stress the inadequacy or incompleteness of legal positivism in terms of the description and analysis of modern legal systems in general and the practice of lawmaking as well as of law interpretation and application.[494] Anticipating the results of the analysis presented in

[491] For more on the advantage of – to a large extent nonpositivist – theories of legal argumentation over the traditional positivistic *Methodenlehre*, *see e.g.*, U. Neumann, 'Juristische Methodenlehre und Theorie der juristischen Argumentation', *RT* 32 (2001), pp. 239ff. *Cf.* W. Hasemmer, 'Juristische Methodenlehre und richterliche Pragmatik', *RT* 39 (2008), pp. 1–22.

[492] *See* H.L.A. Hart, 'American Jurisprudence through English Eyes: The Nightmare and the Noble Dream' in *idem*, *Essays in Jurisprudence and Philosophy*, *op. cit.*, pp. 123ff., *The Concept of Law*, *op. cit.*, pp. 132ff., and 'Comment', *op. cit.*, pp. 36ff.

[493] By way of example, what can be indicated here, apart from the nonpositivist conception of law, is R. Dworkin's antipositivist theory of law and the numerous theories of legal argumentation, in particular, N. MacCormick's rhetorical theory of argumentation (legal reasoning) – *see idem*, *Rhetoric and the Rule of Law. A Theory of Legal Reasoning*, Oxford 2005, pp. 12–31.

[494] *See e.g.*, A. Calsamiglia, 'Postpositivismo', *op. cit.*, pp. 212, 215; L.M. Sánchez Fernández, 'Ironías, falacias, perversiones, enigmas: sobre el positivismo y la tesis de la separación', *op. cit.*, p. 364; L. Morawski, 'Hard Positivism, Soft Positivism and Dead Positivism', *op. cit.*, pp. 172ff.; T. Gizbert-Studnicki, T. Pietrzykowski, 'Positivismo blando y la distinción entre Derecho y moral', trans. R. Gama Leyva, *DOXA* 27 (2004), pp. 67–70, 79; K. Dybowski, 'Fikcyjność pozytywistycznego paradygmatu' [The Fictitiousness of Positivistic Paradigm] in L. Morawski (ed.), *Wykładnia prawa i inne problemy filozofii prawa*, Toruń 2005, pp. 161–170; Z. Pulka, 'Czy nastąpił zmierzch pozytywistycznej koncepcji prawa i prawoznawstwa?' [The Fall of the Positivist

subsequent parts of the book,[495] the antidote to the shortcomings of the methodology and the conceptual framework of legal positivism need not be the nonpositivism that has been—so far—insufficiently justified (at least in Dreier's and Alexy's version). Such a remedy may turn out to be the postpositivist theory of law, which—in my opinion—should remain impartial in relation with traditional jurisprudential disputes concerning the existence and the character of the conceptual relations between law and morality.

Conception of Law and Legal Science?], *AUW* 2878 (2006), pp. 147–177. On the reasons of such a state of things *see* Chap. 5 at pp. 209ff.

[495] *See* Chap. 5 at pp. 207–213 and Chap. 9 at pp. 455–458.

Chapter 5
The Nonpositivist Conception of Law and the Juristic Concept of the Validity of Law

5.1 General Objections Against the Nonpositivist Definitions of Law

The analysis of nonpostivist definitions of law (which, according to Dreier's and Alexy's nonpositivism, also play a role in the definitions of valid law) in terms of their theoretical correctness and practical utility will be initiated by considering some general methodological objections. In order to facilitate the understanding of the nature and the assessment of the merits of the criticisms below, let us first recall the original wording of these definitions. According to Dreier's proposal:

> Law consists of those norms which belong to the constitution of a system of norms organized in a state or on the international level, if this system is on the whole socially effective and, in a minimal sense, ethically justifiable, and of those norms which are laid down according to this constitution, if these, taken by themselves, are socially effective or have at least the chance to become socially effective and which are, in a minimal sense, ethically justifiable.[1]

According to the nonpositivist definition formulated by Alexy, law is a system of norms that:

1. Lays the claim to correctness (*Anspruch auf Richtigkeit*);
2a. Consists of the totality of norms that belong to a constitution by and large (*im großen und ganzen*) socially efficacious and that are not extremely unjust;
2b. As well as the totality of norms that are enacted in accordance with this constitution, norms that manifest a minimum social efficacy or the chance of becoming socially efficacious and that are not extremely unjust;

[1] R. Dreier, 'Der Begriff des Rechts', *op. cit.*, p. 896 and 'Some Remarks on the Concept of Law', *op. cit.*, note 32 at pp. 123–124.

A. Grabowski, *Juristic Concept of the Validity of Statutory Law*,
DOI 10.1007/978-3-642-27688-0_5, © Springer-Verlag Berlin Heidelberg 2013

3. And, finally, comprises the principles and other normative arguments on which the procedure of law application is and/or must be grounded in order to satisfy the claim to correctness.[2]

The first objection that immediately comes to mind after reading these definitions is that they are not axiologically neutral, but have the character of persuasive definitions.[3] This objection can be justified by pointing to the characteristic features of this kind of definition. Firstly, both nonpositivist definitions of law include the constraints of a decidedly positive emotional tinge ("ethical justification", "claim to correctness", "satisfying the claim to correctness") as well as a negative one ("extreme injustice"). Secondly, these definitions modify the extension of the concept of (valid) law in relation to the positivist definition of law. In this aspect, in accordance with the typology developed by Tadeusz Pawłowski, they belong to these types of persuasive definition that aim at changing the extension of *definiendum*.[4] Let us add here an obvious remark that both of these definitions mainly refer to a still very lively tradition of the German philosophy of law, whose ultimate aim is to develop not just an axiologically neutral concept of law, but rather the concept of the right law (*richtiges Recht*). Thirdly, in the already cited source texts of Dreier (*Der Begriff des Rechts*) and Alexy (*Begriff und Geltung des Rechts*), in which the formulations of nonpositivist definitions of law appear for the first time, they constitute a conclusion of nonpositivist argumentation. Thus, they also fit quite well at this point within the characteristics of persuasive definitions provided by Pawłowski:

> A persuasive definition often occurs in conjunction with persuasive arguments, thus forming its constituent argument. Sometimes it is a kind of summary that in a concise and emphatic form presents the essence of a given argumentation.[5]

Fourthly, what is also recognised in the methodological literature as an important feature of persuasive definitions is the fact that the authors of such definitions combine the concepts of a real and nominal definition (as will soon be explained in detail). Summing up, although persuasiveness (as such) does not deprive these definitions of their possible cognitive value, it can result in an additional objection

---

[2] *See* R. Alexy, *Begriff und Geltung des Rechts*, *op. cit.*, p. 201 [English version, p. 127] and 'A Definition of Law', *op. cit.*, p. 102.

[3] The concept of the persuasive definition was introduced by Ch.L. Stevenson, 'Persuasive Definitions', *Mind* 47 (1938), pp. 331–350. In the deliberations that follow, I rely on the analyses of persuasive definitions provided by T. Pawłowski, *Tworzenie pojęć w naukach humanistycznych* [Creation of Concepts in Humanistic Sciences], Warszawa 1986, pp. 149ff., as well as on more specialised jurisprudential analyses of these kinds of definitions, provided by Z. Ziembiński, *Wstęp do aksjologii dla prawników*, *op. cit.*, pp. 35ff. and 'Definicje perswazyjne w prawoznawstwie' [Persuasive Definitions in Jurisprudence] in J. Pogonowski (ed.), *Eufonia i Logos*, Poznań 1995, pp. 673–680. It is worth mentioning that Ziembiński explicitly considers denying – as he puts it – "strikingly unjust norms of the written law" their attribute of law as a classic persuasive argument – *see idem*, '"Lex" a "ius" w okresie przemian', *op. cit.*, p. 5.

[4] *See* T. Pawłowski, *ibidem*, pp. 152ff.

[5] *Ibidem*, p. 149.

of a lack of scientific objectivity (understood primarily as an axiological and ideological impartiality). Regardless of whether we accept the liberal doctrine or not, the objection of methodologically illegitimate ideologisation of the concept of law can be primarily raised against Alexy who—as already mentioned—explicitly defines his nonpositivist theory as "an analytical liberalism".[6]

The second objection concerns the character of the discussed definitions. The problem consists in resolving whether these are real or nominal definitions.[7] At first glance, due to the arguments that support them and due to the unreserved intentions of their authors, these definitions have to be recognised as real ones. Both the German philosophers try to explain the actual, and in the case of Alexy's nonpositivist conception—also the necessary—essence of law, answering the question of what law is.[8] On the other hand, in nonpositivist argumentation, one can also find passages in which both Dreier and Alexy treat their nonpositivist definitions of law as nominal definitions, fulfilling a regulative function. Regarding Dreier's nonpositivist argumentation, it should be recalled that the concept of law developed by him is of such a normative character that "the judge should adopt [this concept] *ex officio*".[9] Whereas, in relation to Alexy's argumentation, it is worth recalling his analyses of the normative linguistic argument, of the argument from clarity as well as of the problem of "enlightened" morality,[10] under which much of the reasoning of the scholar from Kiel is understandable only if we perceive his nonpositivist definition of law as a nominal one, relating primarily to the meaning of words, rather than to the essence of things. Anyway, Alexy himself, in the famous polemics with Joseph Raz, admits that the concept of law is of a dual nature: it is both particular (conventional) and universal. On the one hand (indeed, as each concept), it constitutes the result of cultural conventions governing the meaning of words, while on the other hand, to the extent to which it adequately responds to the nature of its subject—it has a perfect ideal dimension, combined with universal validity.[11] It may therefore be assumed that Alexy's definition has a hybrid nature. A particular-conventional nature of the concept of law—as adopted by him—justifies its

[6] R. Alexy, 'Vorwort' to *Recht, Vernunft, Diskurs*, *op. cit*, p. 10.

[7] For more on these types of definitions and the possible criteria of differentiating them *see e.g.*, J. Kotarbińska, 'Definicja' [Definition] in *eadem*, *Z zagadnień teorii nauki i teorii języka*, Warszawa 1990, pp. 131ff. and K. Ajdukiewicz, 'Trzy pojęcia definicji', *op. cit.*, pp. 296ff.

[8] It can be most clearly seen in Alexy's position, who directly states that "Der Streit um den Rechtsbegriff ist ein Streit darüber, was Recht ist"– *Begriff und Geltung des Rechts*, *op. cit.*, p. 18 [English version, p. 5]. *Cf. idem*, *O pojęciu i naturze prawa / On the Concept and the Nature of Law*, *op. cit.*, pp. 31, 35, 41ff. Let us still recall that this question is of a "global" character for Alexy – *cf.* Chap. 4 at pp. 183–184.

[9] R. Dreier, 'Der Begriff des Rechts', *op. cit.*, p. 894. *Cf. idem*, 'Zur gegenwärtigen Diskussion des Verhältnisses von Recht und Moral in der Bundesrepublik Deutschland', *op. cit.*, p. 67.

[10] *Cf.* (respectively) Chap. 3 at pp. 46–47 and Chap. 4 at pp. 172–179.

[11] R. Alexy, *O pojęciu i naturze prawa / On the Concept and the Nature of Law*, *op. cit.*, pp. 42–44. *Cf. idem*, 'On Two Juxtapositions: Concept and Nature, Law and Philosophy', *op. cit.*, pp. 163ff. and 'Hauptelemente einer Theorie der Doppelnatur des Rechts', *ARSP* 95 (2009), pp. 151–166.

classification as a nominal one, while its ideal-universal dimension implies the real nature of his definition of (valid) law.

Nonetheless, from a methodological point of view, this objection does not completely discredit nonpositivist definitions of law. Kazimierz Ajdukiewicz shows in his analyses that the concepts of the real and nominal definition remain in an extensional relation of an overlapping. Ajdukiewicz even claims that all the real definitions formulated in the language in which the "ordinary laws and rules of logic are adopted" can be regarded as nominal definitions of the terms of this language.[12] Based on this—as I believe—accurate view, it may be assumed that the mixed (nominal–real) nature of the discussed definitions is not an error that would preclude their scientific accuracy or practical usefulness. However, at this point a fundamental question arises as to whether they can effectively fulfil both roles simultaneously. If we consider the role of nonpositivist definitions of law, understood as nominal definitions, then due to their complexity, a simultaneous dual nature is highly disputable, particularly with regard to the possibility of applying this in legal practice. On the other hand, when it comes to their real nature, there arises the problem of the extent to which these definitions provide an unambiguous characterisation of law, adequately giving its essential features. The analysis of these issues will be undertaken in the next section in the context of the theoretical correctness and practical usefulness of the nonpositivist definitions of law for lawyers.

The third objection is, to a large extent, surprising. Undoubtedly, Dreier and Alexy, to put it colloquially, "play in the same league" and they "fight on the same side" as Dworkin when they try to rebut legal positivism, inter alia, through the argument from principles, referring directly to the quasi-logical distinction of legal rules and principles, introduced into the contemporary conceptual instrumentarium of the analytical philosophy of law by the author of *Taking Rights Seriously*.[13] It seems, nonetheless, that one of the main antipositivist objections formulated by Dworkin in relation to the so-called semantic theories of law,[14] and consisting of a lack of differentiation between the concept of law and the conception of law,[15] is

[12] *See* K. Ajdukiewicz, 'Trzy pojęcia definicji', *op. cit.*, pp. 305–307. However, it should be noted that in addition to the position that combines real definitions with the nominal ones, what seems more prevalent is the view on their extensional exclusion – for more on this subject (in the context of the definitions applied in legal sciences) *see* W. Patryas, *Definiowanie pojęć prawnych* [Defining Legal Concepts], Poznań 1997, pp. 103ff., and the references cited therein. *Cf.* Chap. 7, pp. 261ff.

[13] Of course, we can easily identify many other points of nonpositivist argumentation in which the considerations of German authors are similar to Dworkin's antipositivist analyses. For example, the distinction – adopted by Alexy during the analysis of the argument from language (*see* Chap. 3 at pp. 46–47) – between "*prima facie* law" and "definite law" is broadly in line with Dworkin's analyses concerning the existence of the Nazi law, in relation to which the claim of the existence of a "*prima facie* law" is of a pre-interpretative character, whereas nonpositivist thesis denying the Nazi law its nature of law belongs to the later stages of constructive interpretation (*see* R. Dworkin, *Law's Empire*, *op. cit.*, pp. 101ff.).

[14] *See* R. Dworkin, *ibidem*, pp. 31ff.

[15] *Ibidem*, pp. 70–72, 90ff. *Cf. idem*, *Taking Rights Seriously*, *op. cit.*, pp. 134ff.

also applied—at least in relation to Alexy's nonpositivist conception. This peculiar categorial error (as aptly characterised by Zbigniew Pulka[16]) lies in the fact that some philosophers of law try to find answers to fundamental questions of jurisprudence (such as the question of the interrelation between law and morality, and the like) on the level of the concept of law, while—according to Dworkin—these problems can be resolved only at the level of the particular conceptions (theories) of law, which constitute certain interpretations of this concept. Referring to this objection, let us note that both authors of the nonpositivist conception[17] of law undertake their deliberations at the level of the concept (*Begriff*) of law, which is already evident even in the titles of their fundamental works. However, while in relation to Alexy's concept we can further assume that it has—to a large extent—a semantic nature in Dworkin's understanding of this word (since Alexy indeed examines, in a very broad manner, analytically and normatively necessary conceptual relations between law and morality, often using the methods of linguistic analysis), in Dreier's analyses, the semantic element is present to a much lesser extent. When analysing this objection, it should also be taken into account that the authors of the nonpositivist conception of law anticipate it to a certain extent (albeit not in such a direct form as H.L.A. Hart[18] and his follower, John Rawls[19]), repeatedly stressing that, in addition to the jurisprudential concepts of law developed by them, there are also the concepts of law that are characteristic of other legal sciences (e.g., sociology or the philosophy of law[20]), and noting that their nonpositivist definitions are valid only from the perspective of a participant.[21] These reservations militate in favour of the fact that Dreier and Alexy use the term "concept of law" in a way that corresponds to Dworkin's "conception of law", in the light of which, the thesis on the accuracy of the discussed objection vis-à-vis

---

[16] *See* Z. Pulka, 'Hart–Dworkin – dwa warianty "wewnętrznego" postrzegania prawa' [Hart–Dworkin: Two Versions of the "Internal" Comprehension of Law], *AUW* 2142 (1999), pp. 21–42. For more on the distinction between concepts and conceptions introduced by Ch. Perelman, *see e.g.*, D. Buchwald, *Der Begriff der rationalen juristischen Begründung. Zur Theorie der juridischen Vernunft*, Baden-Baden 1990, pp. 52–54.

[17] It should be noted that I use here, as in other parts of the work, the term "conception" not in Dworkin's understanding but in the everyday sense, referring in this way to a set of propositions differentiated on the basis of the subjective criterion (i.e., separated by identifying their authors) as well as the objective one. Obviously, conceptions understood in such way do not always meet the requirements for being considered as theories from the methodological point of view.

[18] *See* H.L.A. Hart, *The Concept of Law*, *op. cit.*, pp. 156ff. and 'Postscript', *op. cit.*, pp. 246–247.

[19] *See* J. Rawls, *A Theory of Justice*, Cambridge (Mass.) 1971, pp. 5–6, 10, in particular note 1 at p. 5, which indicates Rawls' reference to Hart's ideas.

[20] This sentence directly corresponds to Dreier's metatheoretical position – for more on this issue *see* Chap. 3 at p. 25 and his 'Bemerkungen zur Rechtserkenntnistheorie', *op. cit.*, pp. 100ff. Alexy, on the other hand, repeatedly admits (albeit usually indirectly) to the existence of different concepts of law, analysing the various (juristic, sociological and ethical) concepts of the validity of law – *see idem*, *Theorie der Grundrechte*, *op. cit.*, pp. 49ff. [English version, pp. 27ff.] and *Begriff und Geltung des Rechts*, *op. cit.*, pp. 139ff. [English version, pp. 85ff.].

[21] On Dreier's standpoint *see* Chap. 3, pp. 29ff., and on Alexy's position *see* Chap. 3, pp. 40ff.

the conceptual apparatus adopted by German authors should be weakened, since a possible dispute seems to be, at least partly, not substantial, but only verbal in nature. However, these additional objections—by which Alexy and Dreier restrict the scope of reference and, thus, the validity of their own conceptions—raise a number of serious doubts.

Firstly, to recognise that the various legal sciences operate with different concepts of law is to point out a fact which cannot be questioned, but which can be—at the most—regrettable. Nevertheless, it can be clearly seen that the creators of the nonpositivist conception of law, to a certain extent probably unintentionally, fulfil the integrative function of the theory and philosophy of law in such a way that, in their definitions of law, they try to combine the essential elements presented in sociological, ethical and even dogmatic definitions of the concept of law.[22] It would be hard to raise any objections against such a line of reasoning because the theory of law differs from other legal sciences in that, inter alia, the concept of law constitutes the primary object of its considerations, while other legal sciences usually focus on more specific issues. In this context, the integrative function of the theory of law implies the need to take into account the achievements in other legal sciences (the so-called internal integration of jurisprudence) and extra-legal sciences (the so-called external integration).[23] The most accurate recognition of this function by theorists of law weighs in favour of perceiving the theory of law as a discipline which plays an important supportive role in relation to other legal disciplines and legal practice, relying, in particular, on the development of such a conceptual apparatus that will be useful for the representatives of specific sciences (e.g. legal dogmatics), and lawyer-practitioners.[24] It is impossible, however, to question the fact that the nonpositivist concept of law—as proposed by Dreier and Alexy—is only one of the possible jurisprudential concepts of law, since the question of its universality remains open. The analyses of nonpositivist argumentation, carried out in the previous chapter,[25] proved that the nonpositivist conception of law—not only because its authors take advantage of the arguments of an empirical character—is deeply rooted in the tradition of the German philosophy of law and is related to German and European jurisdictional practice. Hence, it constitutes—to once more use Dworkin's language—a certain, yet not necessarily the most appropriate interpretation of the

[22] *Cf.* Chap. 2, pp. 16ff. and Chap. 4, pp. 180ff.

[23] On integrative tasks of jurisprudence, and legal theory in particular, *see* K. Opałek, 'Swoistość prawoznawstwa a problem integracji' [Specific Character of Jurisprudence and the Problem of Integration], *PiP* 4–5 (1966), pp. 628–641 and 'Law and Integration of Social Sciences', *AIC* IV (1971), pp. 7–24.

[24] In this context, it is worth noting Dworkin's passionate and emphatic appeal addressed to young legal philosophers to try to cultivate this discipline in an interesting way, not only for more abstract sciences than the philosophy of law, but primarily for lawyers and judges – *see idem*, 'Hart's Postscript and the Character of Political Philosophy', *op. cit.*, pp. 36–37.

[25] On the universality of Alexy's nonpositivist conception *see* Chap. 4, pp. 91ff., 182ff. Whereas on Dreier's conception, who – as we recall – abandons the claim to its universality, *see* Chap. 4, p. 182.

European continental (i.e., related to the legal system-type of statutory positive law) legal culture of democratic states of the late twentieth century.

What raises even more doubts is the second methodological restriction adopted by Dreier and Alexy; that is, the reference to the validity of their theory only from the participant's point of view. Hart had previously stressed the weakness of any theory of law that, in the description of the complexity of legal reality, leaves aside internal or external points of view. As he wrote: "One of the difficulties facing any legal theory [. . .] is to remember the presence of both these points of view and not to define one of them out of existence".[26] Accordingly, the philosopher from Oxford adopted a hermeneutic, moderately external point of view in his research—combining these two perspectives.[27] Naturally, neither Dreier nor Alexy deny the existence of the external point of view. Yet, it does not change the fact that the whole nonpositivist conception is constructed and justified from the internal point of view of the participant in the legal system (more precisely: from the perspective of the judge). What is more, Alexy, in his nonpositivist argumentation, explicitly acknowledges that the competitive positivist conception of law is the only correct one from the external point of view of an external observer, at least with respect to individual norms and legal decisions. It is worth noting that it is precisely in the context of such a duality of research perspectives that Bulygin formulates a principled objection of the relativisation of truth. Based on the correspondence theory of truth, he emphasises—undoubtedly accurately—that the dependence of the truth of jurisprudential theses on the adopted point of view is something incomprehensible. Adopting the criterion of the correspondence of judgments with reality that provides the objective dimension of the truth, in fact excludes the possibility of simultaneous truth and falsity of identical statements (e.g., concerning the relation between law and morality). Thus, the relativisation of the logical value as to who and from which perspective a given statement is uttered is out of the question.[28] Further consideration of these allegations would by far exceed the adopted scope of research; moreover, it does not seem necessary. It is important, nonetheless, to understand the lesson that comes from the criticism of Hart and Bulygin: when conducting theoretical jurisprudential analyses, it is essential to take into account both approaches to the legal reality.[29]

---

[26] H.L.A. Hart, *The Concept of Law*, *op. cit.*, p. 88.

[27] Concerning the points of view adopted in legal theory and jurisprudential analyses, *see* Chap. 6 at pp. 226ff.

[28] E. Bulygin, '¿Hay vinculación necesaria entre derecho y moral?', *op. cit.*, pp. 217–218 and 'Is There a Conceptual Connection between Law and Morality?', *op. cit.*, pp. 47–48. Another hard positivist – J. Raz – argues in a similar vein in 'The Argument from Justice, or How Not to Reply to Legal Positivism', *op. cit.*, pp. 24–25.

[29] This necessity is also perceived by Alexy – *see idem*, 'The Nature of Legal Philosophy', *op. cit.*, pp. 65–66. However, he constantly stresses the supremacy of a nonpositivist vision of law, developed from the viewpoint of the participant, over the positivist conceptions of law, in his opinion created from the viewpoint of the observer – *see e.g.*, *idem*, *O pojęciu i naturze prawa / On the Concept and the Nature of Law*, *op. cit.*, pp. 50–51.

The last of the general objections seems to be the most crucial, at least from the perspective of our further research concerning the concept of the validity of law. The objection that can be—as I believe—legitimately raised against the authors of the nonpositivist conception of law is that, in their definitions, they mix the meaning of defined concepts with the criteria of their application. This objection is naturally closely related to the one that has been just discussed. It can just be noted that in response to Dworkin's argument of the "semantic sting",[30] Hart equates the distinction of concept and conception with the distinction of the meaning of the concept and the criteria for its application.[31]

As far as the previously analysed objection pertained mainly to Alexy's theory, the currently discussed objection relates primarily to Dreier's nonpositivist conception. Yet, is it accurate? At first glance, it seems that both German authors construct a purely criterial definition of law. They, after all, provide a number of conditions that must be met by a system of norms (such as "social effectiveness", "minimum ethical justificability" or "raising the claim to correctness"), and by the norms, principles and normative arguments belonging to a legal system (e.g., "the enactment in accordance with the constitution", "not being extremely unjust" or "satisfying the claim to correctness") in order to refer to them as law. However, the conclusion about the inappropriateness of the objection at hand would be premature, as it can be relatively easy to refute. With respect to Dreier's position, the following quotation—containing a statement of purpose of the strategy to construct a nonpositivist concept of law, adopted by the philosopher of Göttingen—is instructive:

> Sein Zweck ist, den Kontakt der Rechtstheorie zur Rechtspraxis zu wahren und mit der Explikation des Rechtsbegriffs zugleich die rechtlichen Kriterien zu entwicklen, nach denen die Richter schwerige Fälle im allgemeinen tatsächlich entscheiden und vernünftigerweise entscheiden sollten.[32]

Without a doubt, we deal here with two elements: "an explication of the concept of law" and "the development of the legal criteria", allowing the judge to identify law, especially in hard cases. In relation to Alexy's conception, it should be noted that by recognising this epistemological problem in the context of his discursive-procedural theory of the correctness of normative statements and norms, the author of Kiel strongly advocates in favour of the criterial definitions of concepts.[33] Nonetheless, when arguing in favour of the nonpositivist concept of law, in several

---

[30] *See* R. Dworkin, *Law's Empire*, *op. cit.*, pp. 43ff. Among the numerous, largely critical comments on this argument of Dworkin, it is worth examining J. Raz's essay 'Two Views of the Nature of the Theory of Law: A Partial Comparison' in J.L. Coleman (ed.), *Hart's Postscript*, *op. cit.*, pp. 11ff.

[31] *See* H.L.A. Hart, 'Postscript', *op. cit.*, p. 246 and D. Sugarman, 'Hart Interviewed: H.L.A. Hart in Conversation with David Sugarman', *JL&S* 32/2 (2005), p. 287.

[32] R. Dreier, 'Zur gegenwärtigen Diskussion des Verhältnisses von Recht und Moral in der Bundesrepublik Deutschland', *op. cit.*, p. 67. *Cf. idem*, 'Der Begriff des Rechts', *op. cit.*, pp. 894ff.

[33] *See* R. Alexy, 'Probleme der Diskurstheorie', *op. cit.*, pp. 87–88 or 'Nachwort (1991): Antwort auf einige Kritiker', *op. cit.*, pp. 410–411.

of his works he also refers to "the substance of law", its "perfect dimension" or the "necessary elements of law", by which he undoubtedly refers to the problem of meaning, and not to the criteria of applying the concept of law. We can therefore conclude that the creators of the nonpositivist conception of law definitely put a stronger emphasis on determining a variety of criteria, whose fulfilment allows us to speak about law, although the elements of a noncriterial semantic analysis are also visible in their deliberations at some points.

However, in the context of the purposes of our research, the following observation is of fundamental importance. When analysing the definitions proposed by Dreier and Alexy, it is very easy to perceive that the criterial definition of law somehow inherently entails that the nonpositivist definitions are primarily aimed at determining the extension of the concept of law. This means that its intension (i.e., its meaning in the most intuitive sense of this term) remains on the sidelines of the mainstream investigation.[34]

5.2 Specific Objections from the Point of View of Legal Theory and Legal Practice

In the second chapter, we have already pointed out some doubts relating to the fact that Dreier and Alexy proposed such a construction of nonpositivist definitions of law in which the concept of law embraces the concept of the validity of law.[35] In particular, according to the semantic argument formulated therein, it turned out that one consequence of adopting nonpositivist definitions of law is that the term "valid law" becomes a pleonasm, because under the nonpositivist conception, the criteria of the validity of law become the criteria of law. Accordingly, applying the concept of the validity of law is, at least *prima facie*, completely unnecessary—the application of the mere concept of law is enough. Moreover, in an earlier analysis doubt also arose regarding the nature of the term "invalid law" and an objection concerning the depletion of the conceptual apparatus of jurisprudence of the concept of valid law, which causes both theoretical (in particular, conceptual) and practical difficulties in the analysis of the functioning of modern systems of positive law.

Before we discuss the doubts stemming from the construction of nonpositivist definitions of law and present arguments in favour of the legitimacy of the already mentioned objection, let us examine briefly the question of the nature of the term "invalid law" by means of the conceptual apparatus of "logic of adjectives",

---

[34] For more on the concepts of extension and intension used here, and on the indications – resulting from the above comments – concerning the structure of the analyses of the juristic concept of the validity of statutory law *see* Chap. 6 at pp. 218ff.

[35] *Cf.* Chap. 2, pp. 20ff.

provided by Kazimierz Twardowski,[36] which was already applied by us in the analysis of the concept of statutory un-law in the previous chapter. Our doubts can be expressed in the form of the following question: is "invalid law" an empty name, due to the fact that the qualifier "invalid" is of purely abolitive character, or is it a non-empty name, since this qualifier serves a modifying (abolitive-determining) function? The answer seems relatively simple. Let us apply the following test: due to the fact that Roman law is undoubtedly "invalid law", the assumption that the latter name is empty, implies that "Roman law" is also an empty name (a name without designates). From the logical point of view, what should be taken into account is the fact that the concepts of designatum and denotation can be used not only in relation to things that actually exist, but also to those things existing in the past or the future,[37] which is why this matter cannot be unambiguously resolved. Yet, without having to ask a historian of Roman law for his opinion, we can assume that, at least from the viewpoint of legal language terminology, it is unacceptable to accept an abolitive, rather than a modifying character for the term "invalid". It is the case because if the abolitive interpretation of this attribute was adopted, researchers would analyse, and students would learn about something that could only be (at most) referred to as "Roman non-law". The linguistic absurdity of such a determination speaks, therefore, in favour of adopting a modifying function of this attributive in legal language. Thus, "invalid law" should be treated as a non-empty name.

It should, however, be noted that the very concept of invalid law is ambiguous. In the previous paragraph, it was implicitly assumed that it refers to law that was (or will be) valid somewhere and sometime. The second interpretation is also possible. According to the latter, "invalid law" means law(?) that has never been valid anywhere and never will be valid (for example, a bill that has never been, and will never be passed). The question mark introduced in the preceding sentence already suggests what we now want to say: in this case, the attribute "invalid" is of a purely abolitive character. "Invalid law", understood in such a way—as noted by Kazimierz Opałek—"in effect is 'non-law'",[38] and so we are dealing here with an empty name. Consequently, but only with such a narrow interpretation of the concept of invalid law, the name "valid law" can actually be classified as a pleonasm.[39]

After these necessary explanations, let us set about analysing the concerns that arise from the method of constructing nonpositivist definitions of law adopted by Dreier and Alexy. The first, relatively general objection that arises, is the objection

---

[36] *See* K. Twardowski, 'Z logiki przymiotników', *op. cit.*

[37] *See* W. Marciszewski, 'Denotacja' [Denotation] in *idem* (ed.), *Mała encyklopedia logiki*, 2nd ed., Wrocław/Warszawa/Kraków/Gdańsk/Łódź 1988, p. 46.

[38] K. Opałek, 'Der Begriff des positiven Rechts', *ARSP* 68 (1982), p. 457.

[39] It should be added that this stands for the approval – yet to such a limited extent – of Kelsen's standpoint, who argues that "[e]ine geltende Norm ist ein Pleonasmus. Eine nicht geltende, ungültige Norm ist eine contradictio in adjecto" – *Allgemeine Theorie der Normen*, *op. cit.*, p. 137. As for legal positivists adopting the same point of view, *see* W. Lang, *Obowiązywanie prawa*, *op. cit.*, pp. 212ff.

of an unjustified introduction of synonymy between the concepts of law and valid law. Without the need for some extensive proof, it can be assumed that the concept of valid law is ambiguous, which is a direct result of the fact that, in jurisprudential and philosophical literature, the different (and often conflicting, or even contradictory) juristic concepts (definitions) of the validity of law are adopted.[40] In this context, the methodological procedure undertaken by Dreier and Alexy, which consists of the inclusion of the concept of validity in the concept of law, in my opinion needlessly complicates the matter: the assumed synonymy of these two concepts does not, in fact, eliminate the homonymy of the concept of legal validity, but rather—due to similar ambiguity of the very concept of law—leads to the synonymy of two ambiguous concepts, and therefore to a puzzle that is really extremely difficult to solve. Naturally, it cannot be disputed that if we look at the history of legal philosophy and analytical jurisprudence, then we can easily identify both these philosophies and theories of law that recognise "legal validity" as an immanent (definitional) feature of law (for example, the substantive theories of natural law[41] or the phenomenological philosophy of law[42]) or that equate law with valid law, indirectly defining the validity of law by means of a definition of the very concept of law (as undertaken by numerous representatives of legal positivism).[43] Nevertheless, it appears that treating these two concepts as synonyms does not correspond with the way the concept of law and the concept of its validity function in the modern legal discourse. If one perceives law from an internal perspective of a judge, then it is probably correct to say that a judge identifies law with valid law.[44] Yet, it should be noted that in determining the legal basis for her/his decision, a judge applies different tests for recognising whether a certain norm is a legal norm and whether that norm is valid. Therefore, it can be reasonably argued that the judge applies validity tests (or even more generally, she/he considers the issue of legal validity) only in respect to such norms that she/he has previously considered as legal norms (and not, for example, as moral, social or religious norms). It implies

---

[40] *See* Chap. 6, note 3 at p. 217 and Chap. 7, pp. 248ff., and the references cited therein.

[41] *See* J. Stelmach, 'Obowiązywanie prawa w sensie absolutnym i relatywnym' [Validity of Law in the Absolute and Relative Sense] in (teamwork ed.), *Teoria prawa. Filozofia prawa*, *op. cit.*, p. 318.

[42] *Cf. ibidem*, pp. 322ff.; R. Sarkowicz, J. Stelmach, *Teoria prawa*, *op. cit.*, pp. 135ff.; U. Neumann, 'Problem obowiązywania prawa', *op. cit.*, p. 36.

[43] Naturally, the standpoint which identifies law with valid law is adopted by a number of contemporary positivists – *see e.g.*, J. Raz, 'Legal Validity', *op. cit.*, p. 339, who expresses it clearly: "A valid law is a law, an invalid law is not", and O. Weinberger, 'Ontologie, Hermeneutik und der Begriff des geltenden Rechts', *ARSP* Bh. 27 (1985), p. 109, who claims: "Geltendes Recht ist Recht; ungültiges Recht ist kein Recht". *See* also Kelsen's statement quoted *supra*, note 39.

[44] For more about the correctness of this claim *see* Chap. 9 at pp. 506ff. At this point, I will confine myself to expressing the view that this claim is not falsified by the fact that in juristic language the sentence: "The court applied an invalid norm" is meaningful – yet only if we treat it as a peculiar and presumably inaccurate thought short-cut, referring to a relativised concept of legal validity and describing, for instance, the way an intertemporal legal problem is resolved by the judge.

that the two concepts should remain available to those directly involved in a legal discourse or to those researching it.[45]

The second, also quite obvious, objection sets forth that the nonpositivist definitions of law, perceived as criterial definitions of valid law, strike home with their vagueness and the use of multiple blurred, evaluative terms (e.g. "minimal ethical justification" or "minimal social effectiveness"). What is even worse is that German authors also write about the "chances" of such justification or effectiveness, which, in principle, excludes the possibility of operationalising these features in the form of requirements whose fulfilment by a given legal system or by its norms can be recognised and stated without doubt. Although, in relation to the analyses of Jerzy Wróblewski and Aleksander Peczenik, it should be recognised that modern systems of law are "fuzzy",[46] the extensional vagueness of a legal system should not be further strengthened by means of jurisprudential definitions, whose practical usefulness in solving the problems concerning legal validity seems negligible. Moreover, in both nonpositivist definitions, the so-called legal concept (i.e., not identical with the juristic concept) of validity (Dreier and Alexy use the terms *rechtlich geltendes Recht* or *rechtliche Geltung*[47]) is assumed by means of expressing a condition of "establishing norms in accordance with the constitution", but it remains unexplained. It can be naturally maintained that at the level of a quite abstract and general jurisprudential analysis, such explication is not necessary (or it can be claimed that it is trivial for the philosopher of law), yet on the other hand, it is difficult to deny its great importance in jurisprudential considerations and in the practice of law application, where disputes often relate to the constitutionality of enacted statutory norms.

The above-mentioned deficiencies of the discussed definitions cause the dogmatist of law seeking to use the nonpositivist definitions of law, or the judge, seeking to make the decision concerning the legal validity of norms on the basis of them, to be forced into independently developing a more detailed juristic definition—and thus a more suitable definition for a direct application—of the valid law.[48]

[45] As noted in a slightly different context by J. Stelmach, 'Obowiązywanie prawa w sensie absolutnym i relatywnym', *op. cit.*, p. 324: "The concept of validity of law cannot simply be eliminated from both legal and juristic language, and the search for 'synonyms' only pretends to be the solution of this problem".

[46] *See* J. Wróblewski, 'Nieostrość systemu prawa' [Vagueness of the Legal System], *SPE* XXXI (1983), pp. 7–24 and A. Peczenik, J. Wróblewski, 'Fuzziness and Transformations: Towards Explaining Legal Reasoning', *Theoria* LI (1985), pp. 26ff. A similar standpoint has been adopted by Z. Ziembiński, *Szkice z metodologii szczegółowych nauk prawnych* [Sketches on the Methodology of Particular Legal Sciences], Warszawa/Poznań 1983, p. 15, when writing about "the wobbled legal system". This problem is analysed in Chap. 7 at pp. 277ff.

[47] *See* R. Dreier, 'Recht und Moral', *op. cit.*, pp. 194ff., 'Der Begriff des Rechts', *op. cit.*, p. 894, and 'Neues Naturrecht oder Rechtspositivismus?', *op. cit.*, p. 376; R. Alexy, *Begriff und Geltung des Rechts*, *op. cit.*, pp. 142ff. [English version, pp. 87ff.].

[48] More on the uselessness of Alexy's nonpositivist definition of law, reinterpreted as a definition of the juristic concept of the validity of statutory law norms, for legal dogmatics and legal practice *see* Chap. 7 at pp. 351ff.

Furthermore, with regard to the third point of Alexy's nonpositivist definition of law, it should be noted that its formulation inevitably leads to the "fuzziness" of the extension of legal system, because this system also "comprises the principles and other normative arguments on which the procedure of law application is and/or must be grounded in order to satisfy the claim to correctness". Contrary to the holistic standpoint represented, for example, by Dworkin who—when sharing the American *Noble Dream*[49]—assumes that principles constitute an element of a legal system even before they are applied by courts, which merely reconstruct law by means of interpretation, Alexy argues forcefully in favour of a procedural conception of the integration of principles and other practical arguments (mainly moral ones).[50] Hence, the conclusion that it is the procedural correctness of "principles and other normative arguments" that weighs in favour of including them into the legal system. Due to the fact that the resolution of the issue of their procedural correctness often occurs only when resolving a particular case, a judge is not bound by those elements of law until the very resolution of the case, when she/he discursively justifies that the principles and normative arguments applied in the case at hand are correct. The fundamental importance of this objection is weakened by adding a modal clause by Alexy, as expressed by the phrase "must be grounded", but even when taking the latter into account, the objection in reference to Alexy's conception of making the legal system more "fuzzy" remains in force. The determination of the principles and normative arguments that the judge should rely on in order to correctly decide a case is impossible *ex ante*.[51] The latter cannot be predicted because we are not able to predetermine, *nota bene* only a relatively correct outcome of a particular legal discourse.[52] In this sense, such a modal clause ("must") is irrelevant because it does not allow in any way for the abstract determination of what specific practical arguments need to be included into the legal system. The procedural conception of integrating principles and other normative (practical) arguments, therefore, seems to lead to something that is certainly unacceptable, not only for lawyers; namely, to undermining the principle of a judge being bound by law, which is, after all, the essence of the rule of law principle. As aptly noted by Alfonso García Figueroa, whose analyses we refer to here,[53] if we are to recognise as law any principles and normative arguments applied in judicial reasoning, then we are faced with the necessity of solving a puzzle similar to the

---

[49] Of course, such label of Dworkin's standpoint is borrowed from Hart – *cf. idem*, 'American Jurisprudence through English Eyes: The Nightmare and the Noble Dream', *op. cit.*, pp. 125, 137ff. The question of whether such characteristics of Dworkin's theory are accurate cannot be dealt with here.

[50] *See* R. Alexy, 'The Special Case Thesis', *op. cit.*, pp. 383–384 and 'Law and Correctness', *op. cit.*, pp. 217ff. [German version, pp. 14ff.].

[51] *See* W. van der Burg, 'Two Models of Law and Morality', *AS* 3 (1999), p. 77.

[52] For more on the relative character of the concept of correctness assumed in Alexy's theory *see* Chap. 4 at pp. 87–88.

[53] *See* A. García Figueroa, *Principios y positivismo jurídico*, *op. cit.*, p. 391 and 'La tesis del caso especial y el positivismo jurídico', *op. cit.*, p. 217.

one formulated by Plato in *Euthyphro* (the famous "Euthyphro dilemma")[54]: Does something become law due to the fact that judges apply it, or do judges apply that which is law? In this context, Alexy's nonpositivist conception can be interpreted as either opting for the first of the identified alternatives (but then, the state of a judge being bound by law is very limited), or—due to the nonpositivist desire to reduce or even eliminate judicial discretion (mostly thanks to the application of the argument from principles)—as opting simultaneously for both alternatives, despite the fact that they are contradictory, as argued by Plato.[55]

Another quite obvious objection is that the two definitions—if treated as definitions of valid law—try to simultaneously define two extensionally different concepts: the first referring to the system of law (understood as a whole), and the second pertaining to individual norms inside this system. Using the terminology introduced independently by Aleksander Peczenik and Aulis Aarnio, it should be noted that these definitions apply to both the external and internal validity of law.[56] Without going deeper into a more detailed discussion here,[57] it can be noticed that an attempt at an overall solution of these two issues by using one definition can lead to a blurring of important differences that exist between internal and external legal validity. External validity of law may flow from the validity of individual norms of the legal system; namely, from their internal validity, or it can be a separate quality of the system as a whole, irreducible in such a manner.[58] However, it must indeed be recognised that the objection that has been raised may be slightly weakened if we pay attention to the fact that Dreier's and Alexy's nonpositivist definitions are, on the one hand, theoretical jurisprudential definitions and, on the other hand, oriented at the practice of law.[59] Hence, it seems necessary that these definitions combine the two understandings of the concept of legal validity, which in the Polish theory of law tends to be commonly referred to as the absolute and relative validity of law, respectively.[60]

---

[54] In this dialogue, Socrates, when considering the problem of distinguishing between what is pious and what is impious, raises the following question (incidentally, anticipating a medieval dispute between "intellectuals" who consider that God may want only that which – regardless of his will – is good, and "voluntarists", who recognise that something is good only because God wants it to be so): "Is the piety loved by the gods because it is piety, or is it piety because the gods love it?" – Plato, *Euthyphro*, section 10 a.

[55] *Ibidem*, section 11 a.

[56] A. Peczenik, 'The Structure of a Legal System', *RT* 6 (1975), p. 4 and A. Aarnio, *The Rational as Reasonable. A Treatise on Legal Justification*, Dordrecht/Boston/Lancaster/Tokyo 1987, p. 34.

[57] I address this issue in Chap. 6 at pp. 349ff.

[58] *See* A. Rojek, 'Kilka uwag o obowiązywaniu prawa' [Some Remarks on the Validity of Law] in M. Borucka-Arctowa *et al.* (eds.), *Prawo – władza – społeczeństwo – polityka. Księga jubileuszowa profesora Krzysztofa Pałeckiego*, Toruń 2006, pp. 148–149. She proposes defining the indicated possibilities of understanding the external validity of law as "individualism of validity" and "holism of validity". For more on this issue *see* Chap. 7 at pp. 285ff.

[59] *Cf.* Chap. 3, p. 23.

[60] *See* K. Opałek, 'The Problem of the Validity of Law', *AIC* III (1970), pp. 8–19; K. Opałek, J. Wróblewski, *Zagadnienia teorii prawa* [The Problems of Legal Theory], Warszawa 1969,

To conclude, in my opinion, a nonpositivist attempt to resolve the basic conceptual problem of jurisprudence—namely, defining the concept of law—will fail when we assess it from the standpoint of the theory and practice of law and treat the definitions provided by Dreier and Alexy as indirect contextual definitions of the concept of valid law. Moreover, as already mentioned, the nonpositivist definitions of law also seem unsuitable for the description and analysis of many phenomena typical of the developed systems of positive law. Let us point out what phenomena (legal institutions) this objection may deal with. For example, let us mention only three of them: the institution of *vacatio legis*, the intertemporal law regulations and the derogation. These phenomena are related to the temporal dimension of validity, which cannot be analysed based on the given definitions. For example, do they clarify anything about a disputable issue of the validity of legal norms during *vacatio legis*, or regarding the validity of formally repealed provisions that are, nonetheless, still applied under the intertemporal law, as they bind the authorities that apply the law? Such detailed questions must remain unanswered, because the level of abstraction of these definitions precludes any reasonable discussion. Therefore, we cannot agree on depleting the conceptual jurisprudential apparatus of the concept of valid law that a nonpositivist concept of law indirectly leads to. Even if we accepted the standpoint that "valid law" is a pleonasm, and "invalid law" does not exist, it does not imply that we cannot examine the very concept of the validity of law. This is because the concepts of valid law and the validity of law are certainly neither synonymous nor equal from an extensional perspective, if only due to the fact that they relate to different ontological categories: valid law is a kind of law and the validity of law (legal validity) in not law, but something ontologically diverse, probably a kind of relation.

5.3 The Need for an Axiologically Detached and Impartial Concept of the Validity of Law

When we try to summarise the critical analysis of nonpositivist definitions of law (understood as indirect contextual definitions of legal validity) presented in this chapter, as well as the criticism of nonpositivist argumentation provided in earlier

pp. 114ff.; J. Stelmach, 'Obowiązywanie prawa w sensie absolutnym i relatywnym', *op. cit.* In the context of the undertaken criticism, it should be noted, however, that due to the increasing orientation of philosophers and theorists of law to legal practice and the dogmatics of law, that distinction seems to lose its original significance. The philosopher or the theorist of law, when formulating their definition of validity, must, on the one hand, deal with its absolute sense – undoubtedly primary in the context of the considerations that aim at developing the concept of the validity of law – but, on the other hand, they must also take into account the interests and needs of practising lawyers (in particular, judges) and the dogmatists of law who focus on the questions of relative (intra-systemic) legal validity. Therefore, in our further considerations we will leave the distinction of an absolute and relative legal validity aside, considering a less interpretatively controversial distinction between the external and the internal legal validity, as proposed by Peczenik and Aarnio, to be the basic one.

chapters, it becomes apparent that Ralf Dreier's and Robert Alexy's conception has several shortcomings. Regarding the main subject of our deliberations, it also appears that this conception does not provide any conception of the validity of law that could be accepted from a theoretical (jurisprudential) and practical point of view. The consequence of the undertaken criticism is also that the conclusion is that the concept of the validity of law should be defined in an axiologically detached and impartial way.[61] Naturally, this conclusion could easily be considered to be insufficiently justified, because antipositivist theories might exist other than the German nonpositivist conception of law discussed above, that are better justified and which do not allow us to rebut the thesis of a necessary conceptual connection between law and morality. Nonetheless, it is equally evident that it is impossible to examine within one study all theories postulating such a connection, and it can reasonably be assumed that most of them will be exposed to objections identical to those already analysed in the previous chapter in the context of Dreier's and Alexy's nonpositivism. It should be emphasised that this conclusion is far from a compromise between the positions of legal positivism and antipositivist theories of law, but it allows us only to go beyond their dispute over the concept of law. The adoption of an axiologically detached and impartial concept of validity is a consequence of fully consciously abstracting from the problem of the modal nature of the conceptual interconnections between law and morality. I believe that many reasons, related to the weaknesses of competing theories, weigh in favour of accepting the standpoint proposed herein, which I tentatively refer to as a "postpositivist" one. Let us explain some of these reasons.[62]

Firstly, let us recall that there is no sufficient analytical justification for the necessity of taking into consideration moral requirements (e.g., substantive correctness) in the definition of the concept of law and the concept of its validity. This claim is a consequence of rebutting some of the basic elements of Alexy's

---

[61] "Axiological impartiality" does not prejudice the independence of the validity of law from moral issues, but it has to point at refraining from a definitional and, in this sense, *a priori* solution of the controversy between positivism and nonpositivism. Theoretically, this term could be replaced by "axiological neutrality", which is nonetheless not undertaken by us because the term "an axiologically neutral concept of the validity of law" is already used in jurisprudential literature, in which it is very often applied to characterise the traditional position of legal positivism – *see e.g.*, W. Lang, *Prawo i moralność*, *op. cit.*, pp. 120ff. Using the analogy of a dispute over the existence of God, in short, we believe that "axiological impartiality" stands for an agnostic position ("We do not know whether there exist necessary conceptual relations between law and morality in the sphere of legal validity") rather than hard positivist "atheism" ("There are no connections between law and morality in the sphere of validity"), which is indeed described (somewhat confusingly – *cf.* Chap. 4, note 81 at p. 82) as an "axiologically neutral position". For more on the "atheism" of legal positivists, as expressed by the Neutrality Thesis, *see e.g.*, V. Villa, 'Legal Theory and Value Judgments', *L&Ph* 16 (1997), pp. 449ff. and J. Morauta, 'Three Separation Theses', *L&Ph* 23 (2004), pp. 112, 128ff.

[62] Arguments in favour of axiological impartiality of the juristic concept of the validity of statutory law will be supplemented in later parts of the book – in particular, in Chap. 6 at pp. 234ff.

nonpositivist argumentation.[63] On the other hand, numerous nonpositivist normative arguments and—above all—empirical reasons, militate strongly in favour of constructing such a definition of the validity of law, which would not preclude, at least *a priori*, the application of nonpositivist arguments in a discourse on legal validity. What also weighs in favour of allowing such arguments are the consequences of such a discourse. Namely, when taking into account the imperfections of the not always correct legislative activity of lawmakers, increasing the field of legal reasoning on validity issues may prove useful and helpful both for law-applying authorities (primarily judges) and legal domaticians in the realisation of the task—after all, not an easy one—of correcting the legislator's mistakes. It should be noted that providing these subjects only with the rules of collision (such as *lex superior derogat legi inferiori*) and directives of the legal interpretation—largely positivist in nature—may be insufficient in many cases. Yet, it should be strongly emphasised that allowing nonpositivist or natural law arguments in a discourse concerning the validity of legal norms, as a consequence of adopting an axiologically detached and impartial definition of the validity of law, does not in any way prejudge their effectiveness, particularly their superiority over the typical positivist arguments.

What strongly weighs in favour of adopting a concept of the validity of law, detached and impartial vis-à-vis the classical dispute over the concept of law, is a criticism of a positivist comprehension of law and legal-dispute resolution—still dominant in several European countries; for example, in Poland.[64] It has already been mentioned that a number of philosophers and theoreticians of law emphasise the inadequacy of the positivist conceptual apparatus in describing and analysing the functioning of modern systems of law.[65] Leaving aside the already discussed nonpositivist criticism of legal positivism, and the arguments formulated by other authors with a nonpositivist (or even postpositivist) orientation (e.g., Manuel Atienza, Lech Morawski and Aleksander Peczenik) or antipositivist one (e.g., Lon Fuller and Ronald Dworkin), let us examine a few reasons—recognised even by the positivists themselves—that support the thesis concerning the inadequacy of positivism.

Some of these reasons are of an intra-systemic character—the modern application of law cannot be done without taking into account the requirements (norms) of morality. As noted by Tomasz Gizbert-Studnicki and Tomasz Pietrzykowski, it is trivial to observe that moral norms meet the applicative function (related to the settlement of legal cases) and validity function (related to the constitutional control

[63] *Cf.* Chap. 4, pp. 188ff.

[64] On the dominating role of so-called primordial legal positivism in the Polish legal culture, *see* M. Zirk-Sadowski, 'Pozytywizm prawniczy a filozoficzna opozycja podmiotu i przedmiotu poznania' [Legal Positivism and Philosophical Opposition of the Subject and the Object of Cognition], *SFP* 1 (2001), pp. 83 ff. and 'Legal Culture and Epistemological Stressing' in T. Biernat *et al.* (eds.), *Stressing Legal Decisions*, Kraków 2004, pp. 86ff.

[65] *Cf.* Chap. 4, in particular the studies referred to in note 494 at p. 190.

of the legislation) in a broadly understood process of the application of law.[66] The thesis on the connection between the application of law and moral argumentation not only concerns the systems of statutory (enacted) law,[67] but it also retains its adequacy in the common law system.[68] H.L.A. Hart pointed to the role of the standards of morality and justice in resolving hard cases.[69] His student—Neil MacCormick—who is, in fact, only a soft (inclusive) legal positivist (like Hart himself), does not hesitate in claiming that no researcher of legal reasoning can have doubts that any system of positive law "necessarily contains some non-positive norms"; namely, the norms "of sound reasoning".[70] The hard (exclusive) legal positivists also assume that moral principles are binding in resolving hard cases,[71] and that the theory of jurisdiction itself constitutes—as noted by Joseph Raz—a moral theory.[72] As previously indicated,[73] another leading representative of legal positivism—Georg Henrik von Wright—stresses the fallacy of positivist theory to the extent that it interprets the thesis of the separation of law and morality too broadly and thus it adheres to the exclusion of moral considerations from the spheres of legislation, law application and hermeneutical aspects of legal dogmatics. Finally, as also discussed above,[74] a number of inclusive legal positivists

---

[66] T. Gizbert-Studnicki, T. Pietrzykowski, 'Positivismo blando y la distinción entre Derecho y moral', *op. cit.*, pp. 64ff.

[67] In Polish jurisprudential literature, the role of moral argumentation in legal reasoning has been analysed by many authors – *see e.g.*, Z. Ziembiński, 'Argumentacje moralne stosowane przez prawników' [Moral Arguments Applied by Lawyers], *Etyka* 2 (1967), pp. 95–108 and 'Moralność jako czynnik kształtujący stosowanie prawa' [Morality as a Factor That Shapes Law Application], *Etyka* 5 (1969), pp. 89–111; L. Leszczyński, 'O aksjologii stosowania prawa' [On the Axiology of Law Application] in B. Czech (ed.), *Filozofia prawa a tworzenie i stosowanie prawa*, Katowice 1992, p. 143–152; J. Wróblewski, 'Oceny i normy moralne w wykładni prawa' [Moral Evaluations and Norms in Law Interpretation], *ZNUŁ NHS* I/22 (1961), pp. 3–18.

[68] As noted by J. D. Goldsworthy, 'The Self-Destruction of Legal Positivism', *op. cit.*, p. 467, the decision to apply *ratio decidendi* – previously identified by the court – to the settlement of the case or to apply the procedure of *distinguishing*, always requires applying a moral judgment concerning the issue as to whether the facts of the settled case require the application of this procedure. It must be a moral judgment, because the norms of positive law (i.e., the earlier precedents) do not regulate this issue – after all, the settlement concerns the issue of whether they should be applied or not, distinguishing the case under consideration from the earlier cases. Thus, according to Goldsworthy: "A moral judgment must be therefore made in every case at common law, even if it is made *sub silentio*".

[69] *See e.g.*, H.L.A. Hart, 'Problems of the Philosophy of Law', *op. cit.*, p. 107.

[70] N. MacCormick, 'Natural Law and the Separation of Law and Morals', *op. cit.*, pp. 120–121.

[71] *See e.g.*, M.H. Kramer, 'How Moral Principles Can Enter into the Law', *op. cit.*, p. 100.

[72] J. Raz, 'The Problem about the Nature of Law', in *idem*, *Ethics in the Public Domain. Essays in the Morality of Law and Politics*, Oxford 1994, p. 193. The interconnections of legal reasoning with moral reasoning have been broadly discussed by J. Raz in his paper 'On the Autonomy of Legal Reasoning', in: *ibidem*, pp. 310–324. In this paper, Raz justifies, inter alia, a more complex thesis under which "Legal reasoning is an instance of moral reasoning" (p. 324).

[73] *Cf.* Chap. 4, note 243 at p. 125.

[74] *See* Chap. 4, pp. 128ff.

openly formulate statements based on the role that morality (norms and moral standards) is performing within a "softened", but still positivist, rule of recognition.

The above opinions of the leading representatives of legal positivism come as no surprise, given that they are supported by empirical research. By way of example, let us mention here the results of German case studies presented by Ulfrid Neumann.[75] The analysis of about a hundred decisions of German higher federal courts revealed, inter alia, that taking into account the requirements of practical correctness in the judicial decision-making process is treated by judges as an element of the legal sphere (and not the moral or political sphere not determined by law), while the argumentation that refers to justice without exception outweighs other arguments; in particular, the argument that refers to the literal wording of the statute (*Argument des Wortlauts des Gesetz*) was a typical defeating argument.[76] Empirical studies naturally cannot independently resolve philosophical or jurisprudential disputes,[77] yet—taking into account primarily the usefulness of jurisprudential concepts for the practice of law application—their results cannot be underestimated.

Reflecting more deeply on why even legal positivists cannot deny the existence of moral reasoning in the process of law application, we can discover more fundamental causes. It seems that somehow, by the very nature of law, it cannot fully determine its interpretation[78] or method of application—it must always be determined by man.[79] The ideal of "a perfect norm", which itself determines both its interpretation and scope of application, is highly problematic.[80] Examples of the implications of these truths—obvious for contemporary researchers of law—include phenomena discovered by the twentieth-century philosophy and theory of law such as judicial discretion, the open texture of law, the application of general clauses by the legislator and defeasibility of legal concepts and legal reasoning. Accordingly, the conclusion that can be drawn is that not only does every legal

---

[75] *See* U. Neumann, 'Positivistische Rechtsquellenlehre und naturrechtliche Methode', *op. cit.*, pp. 145ff.

[76] *Ibidem*, pp. 146–147.

[77] Even more so due to the fact that the research conducted on other empirical bases can lead to less clear-cut conclusions. For example, the analysis of the conflict between the values of legality and justice in the jurisdiction of the Polish Constitutional Tribunal shows that the Tribunal only sometimes rules that the legal provisions do not comply with the Constitution when they are legally enacted, but that they are unjust, thereby favouring justice over legality – *see* S. Tkacz, *Rozumienie sprawiedliwości w orzecznictwie Trybunału Konstytucyjnego* [Understanding Justice in the Jurisdiction of the Constitutional Tribunal], PNUŚ (2003), pp. 69ff., in particular pp. 79–82.

[78] N. MacCormick, 'Argumentation and Interpretation in Law', *RJ* 6 (1993), p. 29.

[79] As Hart wrote: "Rules cannot claim their own instances, and fact situations do not await the judge neatly labelled with the rule applicable to them. Rules cannot provide for their own application, and even in the clearest case a human being must apply them" – *idem*, 'Problems of the Philosophy of Law', *op. cit.*, p. 106. Similar argumentation was put forward by K. Günther, 'Critical Remarks on Robert Alexy's "Special-Case Thesis"', *op. cit.*, p. 148.

[80] *See* K. Günther, *Ein normativer Begriff der Kohärenz für eine Theorie der juristischen Argumentation*, *op. cit.*, pp. 167ff. [English version, pp. 156ff.].

system correspond to a certain positive morality of a given society—which is not even questioned by the positivists[81]—but also that its members (mainly lawyers undertaking the interpretation and application of law) use their own moral judgments wherever law explicitly requires it, or where it remains indeterminate or vague. The need for lawyers to apply moral argumentation results not only from deficiencies of positive law regulations that can never be fully eliminated, but also, indirectly, from the fact that so-called law in action constitutes the result of human activity of the subjects that have certain moral convictions. Thus, as long as the reasons for the necessity of applying moral argumentation in a legal discourse are on the side of law—if not the necessity (as assumed by some philosophers of law[82])—then at least the possibility of this type of argumentation follows directly from the human capacity for moral thinking. This thesis seems so obvious that in my view it does not require any further arguments *in favorem*. If the latter is the case, then the positivist conceptual apparatus, constructed on the basis of the crucial thesis of the separation of law and morality, must also be regarded as not fully adequate which, inter alia, implicitly justifies the attempt—undertaken in the second part of this work—to develop a postpositivist, axiologically detached and impartial conception of the validity of law. I mean here the conception that constitutes an alternative to both an axiologically involved conception of law, adopted in antipositivist, nonpositivist or natural law theories, as well as to a supposedly axiologically neutral conception of the validity of law, which is one of the main components of traditional legal positivism.

* * *

Let us conclude the first part of the work with the following remark. Although due to its descriptive–critical nature, the issue of the validity of law was raised only incidentally within its frames (because the creators of the German nonpositivist conception of law have rarely directly tackled the problem of legal validity), I believe that we have already resolved the most fundamental problem. Critical analysis of contemporary German nonpositivism has led us to conclude that the validity of law shall not be made dependent upon its moral correctness or other requirements of moral character. The second part of the work will hopefully be less complicated and easier to understand than the reconstruction and criticism of Ralf Dreier's and Robert Alexy's nonpositivist conception of law that has been

---

[81] *See* Chap. 4, pp. 173ff. *Cf.* H.L.A. Hart, 'Positivism and the Separation of Law and Morals', *op. cit.*, p. 623, wherein Hart writes about the natural necessity of the fact that all legal systems coincide with morality at "such vital points" as the rules forbidding murder, violence and theft. *Cf. idem*, *The Concept of Law*, *op. cit.*, pp. 199–200, wherein Hart concedes the existence of the necessary connection between law and morals, understood empirically as a correspondence of a number of legal institutions and the application of law with morals.

[82] As claimed by the hard legal positivist, J. Raz, there are values and reasons that unconditionally govern our thinking and some of them are moral, because morality includes the "background considerations" to which humans, as "rational animals", that is "reasoning animals", must resort – *see idem*, 'On the Autonomy of Legal Reasoning', *op. cit.*, pp. 313–314. Ultimately, as Raz writes: "Even judges are humans" – *idem*, 'Incorporation by Law', *LT* 10 (2004), pp. 2ff.

undertaken so far. However, it should be noted that the proposals and conclusions indicated herein will often be highly controversial, especially for numerous adherents to the positivist comprehension of the phenomenon of legal validity. While the conclusions of the first part of this work may appeal to them, the analyses contained in the second part of this study are likely, at least at some points, to disturb their positivist good mood. I have to admit that I believe that such a mood is manifestly unjustified in light of the current state of research relating to the analytical theory of law which, incidentally, still remains in a very close interrelation with legal positivism.

Part II
Clarification of the Juristic Concept of the Validity of Statutory Law

Chapter 6
Preliminaries to the Clarification of the Juristic Concept of the Validity of Statutory Law

6.1 The Idea of Clarification

As stressed by Jan Woleński, the identification of valid law does not cause any considerable difficulties for practising lawyers.[1] Yet, the issue of the meaning of the predicate "valid" starts to be somehow complicated in the area of legal dogmatics and it becomes "dramatically difficult" within the theory of law. Woleński aptly notes the following pattern:

> The difficulties with validity increase with the transition from an "operative" comprehension of validity to a more conceptual one.[2]

The accuracy of such a standpoint can be indirectly proved by the existence of at least a dozen, *prima facie* equally convincingly justified and coherent, yet competitive, jurisprudential concepts of legal validity.[3] It seems that this state of affairs confirms the opinion of Hart, who began his inaugural lecture at Oxford University with the following, only apparently banal remark: "In law, as elsewhere, we can know and yet not understand".[4] Lawyers who apply law, usually know whether a particular legal norm is valid, and what normative consequences it entails, yet they do not necessarily have to understand what it means, that a norm is valid. In legal practice, lawyers need such an understanding only in exceptional situations—usually

[1] J. Woleński, 'Uwagi o pojęciu obowiązywania' [Remarks on the Concept of Validity] in *idem*, *Z zagadnień analitycznej filozofii prawa*, *op. cit.*, p. 98.

[2] *Ibidem.*

[3] In the analytical theory and philosophy of law, the conceptions of legal validity that can been regarded as the most widely discussed ones are those developed by E. Bulygin, R. Guastini, H.L.A. Hart, H. Kelsen, J. Raz, A. Ross, G. Sartor and G.H. von Wright. In Polish legal theory, we can mention the concepts of the validity of law elaborated by W. Lang, L. Nowak, A. Peczenik, J. Woleński, J. Wróblewski and Z. Ziembiński together with M. Zieliński. We will refer to a number of them in the subsequent parts of the study, in particular in Chapts. 7 and 8.

[4] H.L.A. Hart, *Definition and Theory in Jurisprudence. An Inaugural Lecture delivered before the University of Oxford on 30 May 1953*, Oxford 1953, p. 3.

A. Grabowski, *Juristic Concept of the Validity of Statutory Law*,
DOI 10.1007/978-3-642-27688-0_6, © Springer-Verlag Berlin Heidelberg 2013

labelled as hard cases. In most (clear) cases, in order to correctly apply the law, it is sufficient to have the knowledge of, and ability to use the validity criteria that allow for the decision as to whether a given legal norm is valid or not. Yet, such a problem is of utmost importance for a theorist and a philosopher of law, because their task is not to accurately apply law, but indeed to understand and explain the basic phenomena of legal reality, among which, the validity of law is one of the most fundamental.

Taking into account the previous findings made during our discussion of general epistemological objections against Dreier's and Alexy's nonpositivist definitions of law,[5] it should be noted that a precise division between the analysis of the meaning of the concept[6] of legal validity and the analysis of the extension of this concept, is of paramount importance for understanding the essence of the validity of law and for developing its adequate juristic conception. However, we have to concretise the above thesis in the context of the needs of legal discourse through a clear separation of two problems. On the one hand, the explanation of the meaning of the expression "A norm is valid"[7] and, on the other hand, the determination of the extension of the concept of valid law based on the investigation of the methods help to decide whether or not a given legal norm is valid (in the juristic sense of this concept).[8] Using the traditional logical terminology, which refers to the distinction introduced by the co-founder of analytic philosophy, Gottlob Frege,[9] in the subsequent investigations we will therefore carefully distinguish between the issues of

---

[5] *Cf.* Chap. 5, pp. 200ff.

[6] Speaking about the analysis of the "meaning of the concept" (and probably also of the "extension of the concept") may give rise to concerns from the perspective of traditional logic, where the concept is often defined as "the meaning of the name" or "the meaning of the term". Nonetheless, the pattern adopted in this study corresponds with a typical application of the term "concept" in the legal sciences, in which we usually talk about a number of legal and juristic concepts (and not about legal names or terms) when trying to explain and/or to define them. This linguistic custom of lawyers does not seem serious enough to warrant correction. A broader discussion of this issue is provided by W. Patryas, *Definiowanie pojęć prawnych*, *op. cit.*, pp. 10ff.

[7] The issue of why we refer validity to legal norms, rather than to legal systems, legislative (normative) acts or legal provisions will be explained *infra* at pp. 237ff.

[8] This way of concretising our tasks can naturally give rise to concern, as the discussion of the concept of legal validity is, at the same time, reduced to the analysis of the meaning of the expression stating the validity of a given legal norm and to the analysis of the extension of the concept of valid law. Such doubt in the context of W. Lang's conception of the validity of law has been raised by Z. Ziemba, 'Zwrot "norma *N* obowiązuje" w języku prawnym i prawniczym' [The Expression "norm *N* is valid" in "Legal and Juristic Language"], *SF* 3–4 (1963), p. 105. Nonetheless, I assume that such concretisation is justified, for it does not seem possible to question the idea that an adequate and practically useful conception of legal validity must first and foremost enable the answer to two questions: "What does it mean that the legal norm is valid?" and "What legal norms can be considered valid?". Hence, when we talk about the meaning (intension) and the extension of the juristic concept of the validity of statutory law, then it should be treated as a "thought shorthand", with its meaning so defined. Other arguments in favour of the adopted concretisation are presented *infra* at pp. 238ff. and in Chap. 7 at pp. 247ff.

[9] G. Frege, 'Über Sinn und Bedeutung', *ZPh&phK* 100 (1892), pp. 25–50. [English version: 'On Sense and Reference', trans. M. Black, in A.W. Moore (ed.), *Meaning and Reference*, Oxford 1993, pp. 23–42].

intension and extension of the concept of legal validity.[10] We can arguably predict that a failure to distinguish between these two problems can lead to many misunderstandings, controversies and disputes, which are easy to avoid, for the distinction of the meaning (intension) and the extension of concepts constitutes the canon of modern analytical methodology and it often provides the basis for jurisprudential studies of legal and juristic concepts.[11]

We therefore encounter two tasks that, due to the requirements of clarity, will have to be accomplished, as much as possible, independently,[12] assuming the following sequence of considerations. After discussing several methodological issues that are crucial in the context of further analyses, we will first explain the problem of intension of the juristic concept of legal validity (in Chaps. 7 and 8), and then we will go on to propose an argumentative way of solving the problem of the extension of this concept (in Chap. 9). The analytical method that will be applied when carrying out the indicated tasks is tentatively defined as "clarification". This term can certainly be associated primarily with the concept of a clarificative theory of legal interpretation developed by Jerzy Wróblewski,[13] yet it is also sometimes used to denote the process of "making meaning more clear". Maciej Zieliński refers to this process—which is something more than just the elimination of semantic indeterminacy or ambiguity—as "clarification in a broader sense".[14] However, given the scope of our research, our intention is to add an even broader sense to

[10] It should be noted that there is a considerable terminological confusion when it comes to the translation of terms "Sinn" and "Bedeutung", used by Frege. In English literature, "Sinn" tends to be translated as: "sense", "meaning", "concept", "intension", "connotation" and "designation"; whereas "Bedeutung" is translated as: "meaning", "referent", "nominatum", "object", "extension" and "denotation" (these terms were catalogued by A. Stroll, *Twentieth-Century Analytic Philosophy*, New York 2000, p. 27). In spite of this terminological confusion, it seems that what is least likely to cause confusion is the use of a pair of terms "intension"–"extension", popularised by Frege's student, Rudolf Carnap, who re-developed this distinction in *Meaning and Necessity. A Study in Semantic and Modal Logic*, Chicago 1947.

[11] Let us add that it is most likely the failure to distinguish between the issues of intension and extension that underlies a frequent disagreement, which consists in wrongly equating the concept of the valid norm and the concept of the validity of a norm, which has been pointed out by M. Zieliński and Z. Ziembiński, *Uzasadnianie twierdzeń, ocen i norm w prawoznawstwie*, *op. cit.*, p. 72. For more on this issue *see* Chap. 7 at p. 264.

[12] I would like to emphasise that in doing so, we do not prejudge that these are fully independent issues. The interconnections between intension and extension of the concept of the validity of law seem *prima facie* unquestionable, and it can be, in particular, assumed that the ignorance of the meaning of this concept entails difficulties in determining its extension (in the sense indicated *supra*, note 8 at p. 218) and vice versa.

[13] *See e.g.*, J. Wróblewski, *Sądowe stosowanie prawa*, 2nd ed., Warszawa 1988, pp. 112ff. [English version: *The Judicial Application of Law*, trans. Z. Bańkowski, N. MacCormick, Dordrecht/Boston/London 1992, pp. 87ff.].

[14] M. Zieliński, *Wykładnia prawa*, *op. cit.*, p. 242. Let us add that in the Polish theory of law we can identify such studies in which clarificative function of jurisprudential analyses is assumed directly – *see e.g.*, B. Kanarek, *Teoretyczne ujęcia derogacji* [Theoretical Grasp of Derogation], Szczecin 2004, p. 16.

the concept of clarification, referring indirectly to the elements of Wróblewski's conception. The author of *The Judicial Application of Law*, when presenting the basic assumptions of his clarificative conception of legal interpretation, assumed that some of the concerns that lead to a legal interpretation *sensu stricto* having to be undertaken, are also connected with the extensional vagueness ("fuzzy" character) of linguistic expressions that are contained in legal texts.[15] According to the clarificative conception of legal interpretation, the interpretation of law has to eliminate not only the uncertainty associated with semantic indeterminacy, or ambiguity, but also with the vagueness (extensional indeterminacy) of the interpreted concepts and expressions of legal language. Thus, the clarification will be, by analogy, understood by us as a procedure of eliminating—to the extent to which it is possible—both semantic indeterminacy and the vagueness of the analysed concept. Our purpose will therefore be clarification of intension, and then of extension of the juristic concept of the validity of statutory law.

The mere identification of the essence of the subsequent analysis does not relieve us from at least a brief explanation of the methods used in the process of clarification. It seems that clarification understood in the way indicated above, without doubt referring to the methods of analysis used by the representatives of the analytical philosophy of law,[16] bears a strong resemblance to one of the basic analytical procedures, namely explication. The purpose of explication "is not merely to paraphrase the definiendum into an outright synonym, but actually to improve upon the definiendum by refining or supplementing its meaning".[17] Therefore, in so far as our further analysis will serve the purpose of clarifying the meaning of the concept of legal validity (solving the problem of intension), we can use some guidance on the conditions to be fulfilled by a good *explicatum*. Based on the original conception of explication developed by Rudolf Carnap[18] and on the analysis of Tadeusz Pawłowski[19] and Jan Woleński,[20] which help to adapt this method to the specifics of the humanities, such conditions should be understood by

[15] K. Opałek, J. Wróblewski, *Prawo. Metodologia, filozofia, teoria prawa*, *op. cit.*, p. 253.

[16] At this point I in particular have in mind the analytical philosophy of law developed by H.L.A. Hart whose primary purpose was the elucidation of concepts (*see idem*, *The Concept of Law*, *op. cit.*, p. 208) as well as the elaboration of "an explanatory and clarifying account of law" (*idem*, 'Postscript', *op. cit.*, p. 239). On Hart's justification of the necessity of general, descriptive and clarificative theory of law *see idem*, 'Comment', *op. cit.*, pp. 36ff. *Cf.* N. Stavropoulos, 'Hart's Semantics' in J.L. Coleman (ed.), *Hart's Postscript*, *op. cit.*, pp. 72ff. and J. Dickson, 'Methodology in Jurisprudence: A Critical Survey', *LT* 10 (2004), pp. 118ff.

[17] W.V.O. Quine, 'Two Dogmas of Empiricism' in *idem*, *From a Logical Point of View. Nine Logico-Philosophical Essays*, 2nd ed., Cambridge (Mass.)/London 1961, p. 25.

[18] *See* R. Carnap, *Meaning and Necessity*, *op. cit.*, pp. 7–8 and *Logical Foundations of Probability*, London 1971, pp. 3ff.

[19] T. Pawłowski, *Tworzenie pojęć w naukach humanistycznych*, *op. cit.*, pp. 97ff.

[20] J. Woleński, *Z zagadnień analitycznej filozofii prawa*, *op. cit.*, pp. 44–46.

means of four particular goals: the similarity of the *explicatum* to the *explicandum*, its exactness (precision), scientific fruitfulness and simplicity. What also seems crucial in the context of further analysis are Pawłowski's findings on the phases of the explication procedure. He distinguishes three phases:

1. The selection of *explicandum*,
2. A preliminary explanation of *explicandum*,
3. The formulation of strict determination of *explicatum* and its inclusion into a wider system of concepts which, for example, constitutes a scientific theory.[21]

We shall follow this pattern accordingly in our pursuits, but it should be noted that the preliminary explanation of *explicandum*, as well as formulating its precise determination, namely *explicatum* (in the form of a regulative definition[22]) will be undertaken in the course of clarifying the intension of the juristic concept of legal validity in Chaps. 7 and 8, while the second component of the third phase (i.e., including *explicatum* to a wider system of concepts) will take place in the last part of our research that aims at clarifying the extension of this concept, particularly by means of two new concepts; namely, the concept of the validity discourse and the concept of the juristic presumption of the validity of statutory law norms, both introduced in Chap. 9.

[21] T. Pawłowski, *Tworzenie pojęć w naukach humanistycznych*, *op. cit.*, pp. 99ff.

[22] What can raise doubt is the fact that we intend to present the result of explication in the form of a regulative definition, contrary to the intentions of Carnap himself, who knowingly uses the term *explicatum* (rather than *explicans*) in order to, inter alia, avoid associations with the term *definiens* – usually used in the analysis of the definition's structure – *see idem*, *Logical Foundations of Probability*, *op. cit.*, p. 3. Nonetheless, it seems that the application of a regulative definition is justified due to at least two reasons. Firstly, let us recall that clarification, understood in the abovementioned way, and aiming to formulate an appropriate regulative definition, is not identical to explication, but merely similar to it, which gives us a certain methodological leeway. Secondly, based on Polish literature, it can be easily perceived that a number of commentators indicate a high similarity between explication and a regulative definition (*cf.* T. Pawłowski, *Tworzenie pojęć w naukach humanistycznych*, *op. cit.*, p. 112 and W. Marciszewski, 'Explication' in *idem* (ed.), *Mała encyklopedia logiki*, *op. cit.*, p. 53) or they acknowledge that a regulative definition may be regarded as a special case of explication (*cf.* J. Woleński, *Z zagadnień analitycznej filozofii prawa*, *op. cit.*, p. 45). Some Polish authors go even further, equating – at least terminologically – these two concepts by referring to the regulative definition as an "explication" (*cf.* Z. Ziembiński, *Logiczne podstawy prawoznawstwa. Wybrane zagadnienia* [Logical Basis for Jurisprudence. Selected Issues], Warszawa 1966, p. 153 and W. Marciszewski, 'Definicja' [Definition] in *idem* (ed.), *Mała encyklopedia logiki*, *op. cit.*, pp. 265–266), or by regarding explication as a certain version of a stipulative (synthetic) definition (*cf.* W. Patryas, *Definiowanie pojęć prawnych*, *op. cit.*, note 51 at p. 118).

6.2 Setting the Objectives of the Clarification of the Juristic Concept of the Validity of Statutory Law

Before we begin our clarificative efforts related to the juristic concept of the validity of statutory law, it seems useful to briefly present and justify the assumed objectives of clarification. This will allow for a better understanding of the choice and appropriateness of arguments applied in the course of the clarification.

Firstly, since we intend to clarify the juristic concept of the validity of law; that is, the concept that belongs to the conceptual apparatus of juristic language, and which is used every day by lawyers, the objective of clarification will be to provide such a meaning of the analysed concept that would not only be theoretically correct (or at least not raising substantial doubts from the point of view of contemporary analytical theory and the philosophy of law), but also linguistically (semantically) acceptable—especially for the dogmatists of law and practising lawyers. To put the matter more broadly, it can be stated that as far as possible, our aim during the analysis is to avoid the violation of lawyers' intuitions—*nota bene*, not only linguistic ones,[23] which play an important role in legal cognition, legal interpretation and the application of law. Naturally, providing that they are not intuitions that shall prove deceptive in the light of an on-going analysis and of applied arguments.[24] Referring to the methodological hint of Joseph Raz,[25] we recognise the fact that the linguistic evidence, and, in particular, a reference to the linguistic intuition of lawyers and/or the methods of applying concepts in a dogmatic and judicial legal discourse, have only an auxiliary function in relation to jurisprudential concepts—they can justify, yet they cannot replace them. It seems obvious that developing an adequate juristic conception of the validity of law cannot be purely descriptive, not least due to the considerable indeterminacy and instability of the linguistic habits of lawyers and a contradiction of a number of—*prima facie*—self-evident juristic intuitions.[26] Thus, in advance, we assume that the conception of legal validity elaborated below can ignore or reject some of the lawyers' common intuitions.

---

[23] For more *see* J. Stelmach, 'Intuicja prawnicza' [Legal Intuition] in J. Halberda (ed.), *Dziedzictwo prawne XX wieku*, Kraków 2001, pp. 31–40 and Z. Pulka, *Struktura poznania filozoficznego w prawoznawstwie* [The Structure of Philosophical Cognition in Jurisprudence], AUW 2697 (2004), pp. 197ff.

[24] As aptly pointed out by A. Kozak, *Granice prawniczej władzy dyskrecjonalnej* [The Limits of Juridical Discretion], Wrocław 2002, p. 67, a legal theorist who examines legal intuitions of lawyers assuming an internal point of view has to question their obviousness – without it, she/he would not be able to explain them. Therefore, a theorist must adopt a critical evaluative attitude towards current internal vision of legal system – which will be discussed in more details in the next section.

[25] *See* J. Raz, 'Legal Positivism and the Sources of Law', *op. cit.*, p. 41 and 'The Problem about the Nature of Law', *op. cit.*, note 12 at p. 187.

[26] On other reasons that weigh in favour of rejecting a purely descriptive method of analysis *see infra*, pp. 235ff.

Secondly, we will also endeavour to create such a conception of legal validity that will be useful not only in jurisprudential theoretical discourse, but also in dogmatic discourse as well as in the practice of lawmaking and law application (in particular within the judicial argumentation). During the clarification, we will therefore take into consideration not only the purely scientific, but also the practical utility of the proposed way of understanding the concept of validity of the norms of statutory law. We are well aware that such a universal formulation of the goal of clarification will undoubtedly make it more difficult (and it will thus facilitate the criticism of its results), but we see no reason to resign in advance from developing an integrative conception; that is, the conception combining operative (judicial), dogmatic and jurisprudential approaches to the validity of law (which necessarily results in taking into account in our deliberations the relative as well as the absolute dimension of the validity of law). The main reason in favour of adopting such an objective in the undertaken clarification is the standpoint of many theorists and philosophers of law—also shared by us—according to which theoretical analysis should be of practical value and it should, in particular, provide (both for the dogmatists of law as well as practising lawyers involved in the process of lawmaking and law application) a conceptual apparatus that will facilitate—rather than hinder—the solution of practical problems (in the context of the subject of our study, this postulate refers primarily to broadly understood problems of legal validity). By way of example, the scholars who directly adopt such a practical approach are, apart from Ralf Dreier and Robert Alexy,[27] Neil MacCormick[28] and Ronald Dworkin.[29] On the other hand, as far as the Polish legal theory is concerned, due to the nature of the studies published in recent years and an explicitly declared "target group" of readers, the list of scholars oriented at practice includes Leszek Leszczyński,[30] Lech Morawski,[31] Maciej Zieliński,[32] Marek Zirk-Sadowski[33] and

---

[27] *Cf.* Chap. 3, pp. 23–24.

[28] *See* N. MacCormick, *Legal Reasoning and Legal Theory*, *op. cit.*, p. v and *Rhetoric and the Rule of Law*, *op. cit.*, pp. v, 12ff.

[29] *See* Chap. 3, note 4 at p. 23 and Chap. 5, note 24 at p. 198, as well as the comments on the concept of law as integrity, which combines jurisprudence (legal theory) with jurisdiction, presented by R. Dworkin in *Law's Empire*, *op. cit.*, pp. 410ff. For more on the lack of distinction between the theory of law and the adjudication practice in Dworkin's legal theory *see* Z. Pulka, *Struktura poznania filozoficznego w prawoznawstwie*, *op. cit.*, pp. 182ff. *See* also J. Raz's critical comments on Dworkin's views, in 'Two Views of the Nature of the Theory of Law: A Partial Comparison', *op. cit.*, pp. 27ff.

[30] *See* L. Leszczyński, *Zagadnienia teorii stosowania prawa. Doktryna i tezy orzecznictwa* [The Problems of the Theory of the Application of Law. Doctrine and Theses of Jurisdiction], Kraków 2001, in particular p. 11.

[31] *See* L. Morawski, *Wykładnia w orzecznictwie sądów* [Interpretation in Courts' Decisions], Toruń 2002, in particular p. 12.

[32] *See* M. Zieliński, *Wykładnia prawa. Zasady. Reguły. Wskazówki* [Legal Interpretation: Principles, Rules, Hints], Warszawa 2002, in particular pp. 13–15.

[33] *See* M. Zirk-Sadowski, *Wprowadzenie do filozofii prawa*, *op. cit.*, in particular p. 7.

Jerzy Stelmach[34]—most strongly emphasising the moment of application of jurisprudential considerations and the intention of influencing the practice of law.

Thirdly, in relation to the results of the studies conducted in the first part of this work, our aim will be to develop such a conception of the validity of statutory law that will in no way prejudge the admissibility of the arguments that do not have a positivist character in the discourse of validity. It should be recalled that the previous analysis—conducted in the context of criticism of the German nonpositivist conception of law—revealed[35] that both the empirical reasons and, partly, normative arguments weigh in favour of constructing the concept of the validity of law in such a way that it could also be applied in these systems of law in which the legal culture and the adopted conception of the sources of law allow the use of, in the course of validity discourse, inter alia, "Radbruch's formula" or other reasons which go well beyond the positivist concept of law. When attempting the clarification, we will bear in mind that the concept of the validity of statutory law should remain impartial vis-à-vis the debate between hard legal positivism and nonpositivism, without resolving (in advance) this controversy *ex vi terminorum*.

Fourthly, we intend to undertake such a clarification that will be consistent with the facts. This means that when the considered theoretical conceptions and related terminological conventions will distort or definitely lack conformity to the legal reality (namely, to the phenomena taking place in pragmatically perceived law), then we will consider them as not being worthy of acceptance. Taking into account the achievements of the legal sciences, one should be aware that jurisprudential reflection co-creates (primarily together with the dogmatics of law) the juristic image of law (in particular, it reconstructs the law as a legal system possessing certain characteristic features[36]), and hence it is difficult to talk about the applicability of the classical (correspondence) theory of truth to eliminate false theoretical conceptions. Yet, it seems that even common sense suggests not accepting any primacy of theory over reality—it just suffices to recall years of the dominance of Marxist pseudo-science in Poland (and other allegedly independent East-European States, in reality, that were fully controlled by the Soviet Union after the Second World War) largely subordinated to an ideology based on a utopian theory of socio-economic background, whose ultimate aim was the conversion of society into a classless one. We are far from questioning the fact that the theory of law may seek

---

[34] *See* J. Stelmach, *Kodeks argumentacyjny dla prawników*, *op. cit.*, in particular pp. 9–14. For more on the problems connected with the relations between legal sciences and legal practice *see* K. Pałecki, 'Towards Better Formulation of the Problem: Can Legal Research Affect Law-Making and Judicial Practice?' in K. Pałecki, A. Peczenik (eds.), *Legal Research in Dynamic Society. A Polish–Swedish Research Project*, Kraków 2000, pp. 183–188.

[35] *Cf.* Chap. 4, pp. 188–191 and Chap. 5, pp. 207–212.

[36] In Polish literature *see* K. Płeszka, T. Gizbert-Studnicki, 'Obraz systemu prawa w dogmatyce prawniczej' [The Image of the System of Law in Legal Dogmatics] in S. Wronkowska, M. Zieliński (eds.), *Szkice z teorii prawa i szczegółowych nauk prawnych*, Poznań 1990, pp. 151–171. For more on the concept and the methodological aspects of the reconstruction of legal systems *see* Chap. 7, pp. 280–284 and Chap. 8, pp. 434–435.

to change the legal reality in the future; nevertheless, it should not distort its current state in order to achieve short-term ideological ends. Therefore, the undertaken studies adopt a moderately realistic point of view,[37] in particular stressing the primacy of the common-sense approach to reality over the speculative or ideological ones.

Finally, it is important for us that the result of the clarification—the juristic conception of the validity of statutory law, does not prove unfair. This is evidently a certain "thought shorthand", which can be explained as follows. Ralf Dreier in his study *Some Remarks on the Concept of Law*[38] draws attention to the special duty imposed on philosophers and theorists of law who study the concept of law. In his view, they must take care that the concepts (or conceptions) of law developed by them do not, in consequence, lead to decisions that are adverse to the citizens.[39] At this point, we touch upon the general problem of the responsibility of a theorist or a philosopher of law for the consequences of their theory being applied in practice. Dreier's reflection seems not only correct, but also extremely important, especially since this issue is rarely raised.[40] Due to the fact that the subject matter of our clarificative analysis will not be the concept of law, but the concept of legal validity, Dreier's postulate, will be referred to the second concept, whose essential function is to enable a correct identification of valid legal norms. Therefore, taking into account Dreier's postulate means that our aim during clarification will be to avoid any potential objection that the juristic concept of the validity of statutory law, as developed below, must lead to an unfair settlement of specific validity problems in legal practice or in the dogmatics of law. In the context of the possible harm of the addressees of legal norms, undoubtedly the strongest relation exists between the identification (recognition) of valid law and the principles of *ignorantia iuris nocet* and *ignorantia legis neminem excusat*. This issue will be revisited in the final parts

[37] At this point it should be clarified that we refer to it as "realistic" because we assume that a reality composed of legal phenomena exists, independent of the perception of legal scholars, and as "moderate", because we recognise that scholars of law, in particular, dogmatists and legal theorists, are the co-creators of legal reality because due to their analyses and reconstructions we obtain the access to some important parts of this reality – such as the systematisation of law, legal interpretation and so forth.

[38] R. Dreier, 'Some Remarks on the Concept of Law', *op. cit.*, p. 116.

[39] Dreier's comment reads as follows: "The legal theorist [...] should take care to see that discussion on the concept of law does not lead to results which are at the expense of the citizens". In considering the dispute on the concept of law in the context of resolving the problem of Nazi law, a similar conclusion is reached by F. Haldemann, 'Gustav Radbruch vs. Hans Kelsen: A Debate on Nazi Law', *op. cit.*, p. 176: "Theoretical disputes over the concept of law should not be carried out on the backs of the oppressed and the defenceless". Such moral arguments are naturally directed against a seemingly axiologically neutral positivist concept of law – *cf. infra*, note 95 at p. 236 and Chap. 9, pp. 526ff.

[40] For more on the various ways of understanding the responsibility of analytical philosophers *see* L. Koj, 'Uwagi o analizie w filozofii' [Remarks on the Analysis in Philosophy] in J. Hartman (ed.), *Filozofia i logika. W stronę Jana Woleńskiego*, Krakow 2000, p. 168ff. However, Koj considers, only marginally, the responsibility for the consequences of applying the analytical theory in practice.

of the study,[41] yet at this point, we will confine ourselves to the observation that the abovementioned third objective of clarification in the form of developing an axiologically impartial conception of the validity of law, which does not exclude the application of nonpositivist arguments in the juristic discourse of validity, to some extent already provides protection against unfair legal decisions on the validity of statutory norms.

6.3 The Point of View and the Moral Aspect of the Legal Theory Statements

The analysis of nonpositivist argumentation, undertaken in the first part of the study, has revealed the utmost importance of a correct identification of the point of view from which a given argumentation is carried out, in order to assess its accuracy. Since the introduction by Hart, the distinction between an internal and external point of view (and the corresponding aspects of legal rules), as well as internal and external statements, this matter constitutes a constant subject of inquiries and methodological controversies within the analytical philosophy and theory of law. Taking into account the mainly argumentative character of clarificative analysis, we consider it necessary to pay attention to the issue of determining the proper perspective for jurisprudential considerations and to the characteristics of statements, propositions and arguments formulated in legal theory. Considering that the purpose of the clarification is to develop the axiologically impartial concept of the validity of law, the following considerations will concentrate on explaining the moral aspect of statements and jurisprudential analyses, leaving aside, at least at this point, the question of their linguistic and logical characteristics.[42]

Even a superficial inspection of the literature shows large scale possibilities for adopting diverse points of view in jurisprudential theoretical reflection. This spectrum is co-created by the conceptions developed both in relation to Hart's basic distinction, as well as formulated independently from the idea of the author of *The Concepts of Law*. According to Alexy's remark (which is, by the way, rather disputable[43])—the possible points for the pre-understanding of law ranges from

[41] *Cf.* Chap. 9, pp. 529–533.

[42] We will provide such characteristics in Chap. 8 at pp. 367–400.

[43] What raises doubts here is Alexy's treating the perspective of a "bad man" as an instance of an "external point of view". For, as demonstrated by R. Sarkowicz, *Poziomowa interpretacja tekstu prawnego* [Levels of the Interpretation of Legal Text], Kraków 1995, pp. 102–104, the category of a "bad man" introduced by O.W. Holmes constitutes the equivalent of a "cognitive-internal point of view" (i.e., one of the categories distinguished by N. MacCormick – *see infra*, note 52 at p. 227, with the corresponding text), because – in relation to the analysis of L.L. Fuller – the point of view of a "bad man" requires a reference to a fully internal point of view of a "good man". In addition, what is equally disputable is that Alexy uses a cluster of concepts of external and detached points of view. As clearly shown by the further analysis presented in this section, these are clearly distinct concepts.

the perspective of a "bad man"—"a rather detached external point of view"—to the perspective of the judge Hercules—"a rather idealistic internal one".[44] In my opinion, the identifiable extreme points of this scale should be more broadly marked, however. On account of the studies of the authors who participate in the discussion on the points of view (research perspectives) in legal cognition, what appears to be the first extreme is undeniably a maximally external perspective of "men from Mars",[45] while the second appears as a fully internal position of the ideal law-abiding citizen[46] or of the *homo juridicus*.[47] Between these two extremes, there exist a number of possible points of view (research perspectives), which typically constitute a modification of the categories derived from the original distinction developed by Hart, such as: "extreme external point of view" and "non-extreme external point of view"; that is, the "hermeneutic point of view"[48] (also known as the "moderate external point of view"[49] or "detached point of view"[50]), the "hermeneutic point of view of an observer" and "hermeneutic point of view of the participant"[51] and, finally, the "cognitively internal point of view" and "volitionally internal point of view".[52] As if these possibilities were not enough, many philosophers and legal theorists use, in their analyses, a number of theoretical constructs of ideal judges (of such judges as Hercules, Herbert and Hermes,[53]

---

[44] R. Alexy, 'The Nature of Legal Philosophy', *op. cit.*, p. 66.

[45] *See* N. MacCormick, 'Law, Morality and Positivism', *op. cit.*, pp. 130–131.

[46] *See* J. Raz, *Practical Reason and Norms*, Oxford 1999, p. 171: "The ideal law-abiding citizen is the man who acts from the legal point of view. He does not merely conform to law. He follows legal norms and legally recognized norms as norms and accepts them also as exclusionary reasons for disregarding those conflicting reasons which they exclude".

[47] *See* N. MacCormick, 'Further Thoughts on Institutional Facts', *IJSL* V/13 (1992), pp. 11ff. and 'Powers and Power-Conferring Norms' in St.L. Paulson, B. Litschewski Paulson (eds.), *Normativity and Norms. Critical Perspectives on Kelsenian Themes*, Oxford 1998, pp. 504ff. In the latter study, the *homo juridicus* is defined as "an ideal-typical person whom we suppose always to act with regard to legal requirements, permissions, and empowerments" (p. 505).

[48] *See* N. MacCormick, *H.L.A. Hart*, London 1981, pp. 36ff. As noted by MacCormick (*ibidem*, p. 32), the commentator who first referred to Hart's method of legal research as "hermeneutic" was Peter Hacker – *see idem*, 'Hart's Philosophy of Law' in P.M.S. Hacker, J. Raz (eds.), *Law, Morality and Society. Essays in Honour of H.L.A. Hart*, Oxford 1977, pp. 9ff.

[49] *See* M. Van Hoecke, F. Ost, 'Epistemological Perspectives in Legal Theory', *RJ* 6 (1993), pp. 42ff. and L. J. Wintgens, 'The Relation of Law and Economics: Perspectives from Legal Theory', *SPhL* 3 (2007), pp. 41–42.

[50] *See* J.D. Goldsworthy, 'The Self-Destruction of Legal Positivism', *op. cit.*, p. 450, F. Laporta, 'Derecho y moral: vindicación del observador crítico y aporía del iusnaturalista' in R. Vázquez (ed.), *Derecho y moral, op. cit.*, pp. 254–255 and N. Lacey, *A Life of H.L.A. Hart. The Nightmare and the Noble Dream*, Oxford 2004, p. 336.

[51] *See* L. J. Wintgens, 'Legisprudence: Elements for a New Theory of Legislation', *op. cit.*, pp. 193ff.

[52] *See* N. MacCormick, *Legal Reasoning and Legal Theory*, *op. cit.*, pp. 288ff. and *H.L.A. Hart*, *op. cit.*, pp. 33ff.

[53] R. Dworkin, *Taking Rights Seriously*, *op. cit.*, pp. 105ff. (judge Hercules), pp. 125ff. (judge Herbert), and *Law's Empire*, *op. cit.*, pp. 239ff. (judge Hercules), p. 317ff. (judge Hermes).

Jupiter, Hercules and Hermes[54] or Rhadamanthus[55]), undoubtedly also introduced in order to show varied research perspectives of law and to recognise its nature and scope. Even a brief description, not to mention a thorough analysis of the said kinds of viewpoints and imaginary judges, goes well beyond the scope of this study. Yet, their analysis does not seem indispensable, since the goal of the discussions undertaken at this point is merely a justification of adopting a morally detached and impartial point of view in the subsequent clarificative analysis, combined with the general characteristics of the moral aspect of detached legal statements (propositions, arguments), formulated by legal theorists. Let us take a closer look at the reasoning that leads to the recognition of a morally detached and impartial point of view as methodologically appropriate for jurisprudential analysis and investigation.

The basic premises of such reasoning are the conclusions resulting from the analysis of the evolution of Hart's views on the research perspective assumed by a theorist of law, adequate for developing such a theory of law, which—according to his metatheoretical standpoint—is simultaneously general and descriptive.[56] In order to reconstruct this evolution, we have to go back to the beginning of the issue at hand, namely to 1959, when Hart published an essay devoted to Scandinavian realism[57]; more precisely, to a certain form of this realism, as presented by Alf Ross in *On Law and Justice* published a year before. In his critique, Hart focused mainly on the predictive conception of legal validity developed by Ross.[58] In this context, Hart, for the first time—according to my knowledge—proposed a distinction between external and internal legal statements. The external statements are formulated by an external observer, who neither accepts nor endorses the rules of a given social group and thus she/he may describe these rules in the form of statements of facts. The internal statements are made by the members of the given social group, who use a distinctive normative vocabulary (containing such words as "ought", "must", "should", "may", "right", "wrong", "duty", "obligation") in order to express their approval for these rules and to evaluate and criticise both their own behaviour, as well as the behaviour of other members of the group.[59]

[54] F. Ost, 'Jupiter, Hercule, Hermès: trois modèles du juge', in P. Bouretz (ed.), *La force du droit. Panorama des débats contemporains*, Paris 1991, pp. 241–272.

[55] J. Mackie, 'The Third Theory of Law', *op. cit.*, pp. 168ff.

[56] *Cf.* Chap. 4, pp. 135ff., in particular note 281 at p. 135.

[57] H.L.A. Hart, 'Scandinavian Realism' in *idem*, *Essays in Jurisprudence and Philosophy*, *op. cit.*, pp. 161–169.

[58] *See ibidem*, pp. 164–169. On the subject matter of Hart's criticism *see* A. Ross, *On Law and Justice*, *op. cit.*, pp. 11ff., 29ff. Interestingly enough, Ross, as was later followed by Hart and Raz, based his views concerning the nature of legal statements on a critical analysis of Kelsen's theory – *see ibidem*, in particular note 4 on pp. 9–10.

[59] H.L.A. Hart, 'Scandinavian Realism', *op. cit.*, pp. 166–167. It is worth noting that Hart partially anticipated the distinction between these two types of legal statements already in his lecture of 1953, *Definition and Theory in Jurisprudence*, *op. cit.*, pp. 9ff. When analysing the statements of lawyers on one's rights or obligations, he referred to them as "conclusions of law", precisely

As can be clearly noted, in this original form of Hart's distinction we can find its characteristic ambiguity.[60] The interpretation of the meaning and scope of reference of the features of "internality" and "externality" leads to the conclusion that they are understood and referred to by Hart in two different ways. Firstly, Hart uses these concepts to distinguish between two semantically and pragmatically different categories of statements. Secondly, he also uses them in order to identify the position of people who make these statements by means of determining the degree of acceptance and support of social standards (rules), in particular legal ones. It therefore comes as no surprise that in *The Concept of Law*, published 2 years later, Hart tried to eliminate this ambiguity by using two correlated distinctions.[61] Firstly,

distinguishing them from statements which establish the legal rules or which refer to such rules. For more on another interesting issue of the sources of Hart's inspiration (which we shall leave aside in our presentation) *see idem*, *The Concept of Law*, *op. cit.*, p. 242, note to p. 54, and p. 244, note to p. 86; N. MacCormick, *Legal Reasoning and Legal Theory*, *op. cit.*, pp. 278–279; N. Lacey, *A Life of H.L.A. Hart*, *op. cit.*, pp. 230–231. Let us add for the record only that Hart drew the terminology from Anders Wedberg – *cf.* L. Lindahl, 'Norms, Meaning, Postulates, and Legal Predicates' in E. Garzón Valdés *et al.* (eds.), *Normative Systems in Legal and Moral Theory*, *op cit.*, p. 294.

[60] The opinion on the ambiguity, as formulated here, that occurs within the categories differentiated by Hart, should not be confused with MacCormick's objection, which concerned the ambiguity of the criterion that constituted the basis of this distinction – *see idem*, *Legal Reasoning and Legal Theory*, *op. cit.*, pp. 291ff. The Scottish legal philosopher articulates his complaint in the form of a question as to whether Hart's distinction refers to different levels of understanding law, or to different degrees of volitional commitment in relation to law. As R. Sarkowicz aptly points out in *Poziomowa interpretacja tekstu prawnego*, *op. cit.*, p. 101: "The adoption of the first option is more cognitively valuable and methodologically safer" and the second option is generally excluded because, as can be clearly seen from the subsequent reconstruction of Hart's position, the degree of acceptance of law (i.e., as it can be maintained – volitional commitment in MacCormick's sense) is irrelevant for its understanding in the sense that such acceptance is not a necessary precondition for a correct recognition (identification) and understanding of law. It was already Kelsen who pointed out that even people who "emotionally reject the law as a coercive order" (such as anarchists), put in the position of a professor of law, "could describe positive law as a system of valid norms, without having to approve of this law" – *idem*, *Reine Rechtslehre*, 2nd ed., *op. cit.*, note ** at pp. 224–225, [English version, note 82 at p. 218]. As noted by Z. Bańkowski, N. MacCormick, R.S. Summers, J. Wróblewski, 'On Method and Methodology' in N. MacCormick, R.S. Summers (eds.), *Interpreting Statutes. A Comparative Study*, Aldershot/Brookfield/Hong Kong/Singapore/Sydney/Vermont 1991, p. 23: "if one rejects the system's values or some important subset of them, this does not disable one from a clear and objective reconstruction of it". Similar opinions, formulated already in the context of Hart's distinction, have been presented by a number of commentators – *cf. e.g.*, L.L. Hierro, '¿Por qué ser positivista?', *op. cit.*, pp. 266ff. and A. Kozak, *Granice prawniczej władzy dyskrecjonalnej*, *op. cit.*, p. 66.

[61] There can naturally be some doubts as to why I write about two rather than three distinctions. Apart from substantive reasons, left aside in further deliberations (since they are irrelevant in the context of their purpose), on account of which I consider as acceptable identifying an "internal aspect of rules" with an "internal point of view" (and, respectively, an "external aspect of rules" with an "external point of view"), I based my reconstruction on the opinion of Hart himself, who, in the 'Postscript', *op. cit.*, p. 254, refers only to two distinctions concerning statements about law and aspects of law. I think it is obvious that the concepts of the internal and external aspects of law,

he made a distinction between the concepts of the internal statement and external statement. Secondly, he also distinguished the concept of the internal aspect of rules—essentially inseparable from the internal point of view, and the concept of the external aspect of rules—corresponding to a research perspective referred to as the external point of view.[62] Yet, while Hart retained the second distinction as unchanged,[63] the distinction of internal and external statements was substantially modified by him in subsequent studies in a way that we intend to reconstruct below.

The third time Hart took up the issue concerning the nature of the statements on law was in a report—incidentally, not devoid of self-criticism—of the public debate that he held with Kelsen in November 1961 at the University of Berkeley.[64] In preparation for the debate, Hart, being in a sense the guest of Kelsen, who since 1945 was the professor of this university, chose as the first subject of the discussion the concept of rules of law in a descriptive sense, introduced by Kelsen, which Hart considered as particularly difficult to understand.[65] During the discussion with

as used by him in the above study, altogether cover the relevant aspects of rules and points of view; therefore, a recognition of three distinctions would no longer be a reconstruction, but rather a modification of Hart's views.

[62] *See* H.L.A. Hart, *The Concept of Law*, *op. cit.*, p. v, 55–56, 86–88, 96, 99–107, 197–99. We do not present Hart's position from his *opus magnum*, limiting merely to a few observations which are necessary to preserve the coherence of arguments, because it has been already repeatedly discussed. Instead, we will reconstruct next steps in the evolution of Hart's methodological views which were unfortunately typically ignored or only fragmentarily presented in the literature.

[63] *See* H.L.A. Hart, 'Postscript', *op. cit.*, pp. 254–255. This assessment is not changed by the fact that he also used the concept of the hermeneutic point of view, as expanded upon in a moment.

[64] H.L.A. Hart, 'Kelsen Visited' in *idem*, *Essays in Jurisprudence and Philosophy*, *op. cit.*, pp. 286–308. For more on the details of the debate *see* N. Lacey, *A Life of H.L.A. Hart*, *op. cit.*, pp. 249ff.

[65] This difficulty at least partly resulted from the unfortunate translation of German terminology used by Kelsen. Hart, who used a reprint (of 1949) of Kelsen's book, *General Theory of Law and State*, trans. A. Wedberg, Cambridge (Mass.) 1945, probably did not realise that the German counterpart of the terms of "rule of law" and "legal rule", as used by Kelsen, was probably the term "Rechtssatz", which should rather be translated as a "statement about law", or ultimately, as a "legal statement" and certainly not as "legal rule". For more on Kelsen's German original terminology and doubts relating to its translation into English *see* U.U. Bindreiter, '"Descriptive Normativity": Kelsen's *Sollsatz* in the Light of Some Later Theories', *AS* 5 (2001), pp. 71ff., in particular note 2 at p. 73. It should be pointed out that Kelsen, in a number of his German-language papers published after 1953, knowingly used the terminology that deviated from a commonly accepted, synonymous usage of the terms "Rechtsnorm" and "Rechtssatz" in the German juristic language – *cf. e.g.*, *idem*, *Allgemeine Theorie der Normen*, *op. cit.*, p. 124. While Kelsen's ideas and terminology remain outside our research, in order to facilitate the understanding of the nature of his dispute with Hart, let us explain, as briefly as possible and in a considerable simplification, that Kelsen (*see ibidem*, pp. 119–124, and *idem*, 'Eine "Realistische" und die Reine Rechtslehre. Bemerkungen zu Alf Ross: On Law and Justice', *ÖZÖR (NF)* X (1959), p. 5ff. or *Reine Rechtslehre*, 2nd ed., *op. cit.*, pp. 73ff. [English version, pp. 71ff]) made a distinction between these two subtypes of ought-statements ("Sollsätze"), in such a way that the term "Rechts*norm*" referred to the norms established by the legislator who uses the concept of ought (*Sollen*) in a prescriptive sense, while the term "Rechts*satz*" – to the statements about legal norms – was formulated by the science of law, in which ought had a merely descriptive sense. According to

Kelsen, he suggested that the statements of the normative science of law, that belong to this category, which—according to Kelsen—use the concept of the ought in a descriptive sense, be characterised based on the analytical distinction between the use and the mention of words.[66] On account of this distinction, it could be argued that the legislator uses certain words when enacting law, whereas a lawyer, when interpreting law, just talks about those words. Kelsen strongly rejected Hart's proposal, stressing that the discussed statements of the normative science of law are neither metalinguistic statements, nor paraphrases. Hart was then convinced that Kelsen was wrong, yet, in a paper published 2 years later, he admitted that Kelsen was right and recognised the jurists' statements representing the law as "a specific kind of use of language and not a mention of it".[67]

One of the main issues that became a permanent subject of Hart's interest was the concept of legal obligation. Hart struggled with this problem for many years, trying to find a remedy for shortcomings and mistakes of the conception presented in *The Concept of Law*.[68] In the context of the undertaken reconstruction of the evolution of Hart's standpoint, among the ideas that he attempted to widely use in developing a new conception of obligation, the one that deserves special attention is Hart distinguishing the third category of statements about law, called detached statements.[69] Hart used the distinction introduced by his pupil, Joseph Raz, who

Kelsen, the latter are propositions (in logical sense), because they constitute a description – free from any evaluations – of the object of cognition of the "pure theory of law". For more *see* R.J. Vernengo, 'Kelsen's *Rechtssätze* as Detached Statements' in R. Tur, W. Twining (eds.), *Essays on Kelsen*, Oxford 1986, pp. 99ff., N. Bobbio, '"Sein" and "Sollen" in Legal Science', *op. cit.*, pp. 21ff. and U.U. Bindreiter, *ibidem*, pp. 71ff., as well as the works of J. Raz referred to *infra*, note 70 at p. 232.

[66] *See* H.L.A. Hart, 'Kelsen Visited', *op. cit.*, pp. 292ff.

[67] *Ibidem*, p. 295. It is puzzling that the author of an excellent bibliography of Hart, N. Lacey, *A Life of H.L.A. Hart*, *op. cit.*, p. 252, presents a discussion between Hart and Kelsen in a different manner, in particular she assigns Hart as expressing, during this debate, the idea of "detached normative statements", which one can hardly agree with. Hart, when commenting on his debate with Kelsen more than twenty years later, explicitly acknowledged that although he had already then "some glimmer" of an idea as to how to distinguish between committed and detached statements, he did not perceive that Kelsen had the latter in mind when he wrote about "rules in a descriptive sense", formulated by legal scientists – *see* H.L.A. Hart, 'Introduction' in *idem*, *Essays in Jurisprudence and Philosophy*, *op. cit.*, p. 15; *see* also his praise of Kelsen's anti-reductionist position in J.R. de Páramo, 'Entrevista a H.L.A. Hart', *op. cit.*, p. 351. Incidentally, admitting that Kelsen was right and giving him the priority, constitutes one of numerous pieces of evidence concerning the scientific honesty of Hart. For more on Hart's interpretation of the category of "rules of law in a descriptive sense" *see* U.U. Bindreiter, 'Presupposing the Basic Norm', *RJ* 14 (2001), pp. 166ff.

[68] H.L.A. Hart, *The Concept of Law*, *op. cit.*, pp. 79ff., 163ff. On Hart's self-critical assessment and his attempts to create an error-free conception of legal obligation *see* J.R. de Páramo, *ibidem*, pp. 343ff. and N. Lacey, *ibidem*, pp. 222–229, 335–336.

[69] H.L.A. Hart, 'Introduction', *op. cit.*, pp. 10 and 14. Hart admitted therein that in his critical essay on A. Ross' theory (*cf. supra*, notes 57–59 at p. 228, along with the corresponding text), he wrongly concluded that "normative vocabulary" can be used only in internal statements. *See* also

suggested—*nota bene* also as a result of a critical analysis of Kelsen's views[70]—a distinction of committed and detached statements.[71] According to Raz, committed statements (equated by him with internal statements in Hart's sense[72]) are formulated by those who accept law (rules of law) as binding; thus, only they deserve the name of "full-blooded normative statements".[73] The detached statements that are "parasitic" on internal ones,[74] define the rights and obligations of the subjects of law in such a way that does not oblige the author to normative views expressed by means of them.[75] As Raz writes, these are statements that express:

> what a speaker believes the law requires, without commitment on his part as to whether there is any reason to act as the law requires.[76]

Using the category of detached statements in order to develop a new theory of obligation, devoid of previous mistakes, was to enable Hart, inter alia, to retain the standpoint which he had always presented, which involved separating legal and moral obligations. It therefore comes as no surprise that Hart understood committed and detached statements in a specific way; in particular, he rejected such a possibility of interpreting Raz's distinction, which would be based on distinguishing the moral attitude of people that undertake it (according to such an interpretation, *nota bene* also proposed by Hart,[77] committed statements express a belief in a moral binding force of law which they relate to, whereas detached statements involve

---

the explication of Hart's understanding of this category of normative statements in J.R. de Páramo, *ibidem*, pp. 351–352.

[70] *See* J. Raz, *The Concept of a Legal System. An Introduction to the Theory of Legal System*, 2nd ed., Oxford 1980, pp. 234ff. and 'Kelsen's Theory of the Basic Norm' in *idem*, *The Authority of Law*, *op. cit.*, pp. 140ff. On the question of the correctness of Raz's analyses *see* R.J. Vernengo, 'Kelsen's *Rechtssätze* as Detached Statements', *op. cit.*, pp. 100ff.

[71] *See* J. Raz, *ibidem*, and *Practical Reason and Norms*, *op. cit.*, pp. 170ff., 'Legal Validity', *op. cit.*, pp. 346ff., 'On The Nature of Law', *ARSP* 82 (1996), pp. 8, 17. As regards the evolution of Raz's conception – from the one that complies with Hart's axiologically neutral views, to the one that adopts a moral involvement of committed statements – *see* J.D. Goldsworthy, 'The Self-Destruction of Legal Positivism', *op. cit.*, pp. 461ff., in particular the notes 91–92, along with the corresponding text.

[72] J. Raz, 'Legal Validity', *op. cit.*, p. 351. Let us note that the discussion on Raz's distinction is based mainly on this work of his for two reasons. Firstly, it seems highly likely – even on account of chronological reasons – that it was this very work that Hart relied on when adapting Raz's distinction in 1983 in his 'Introduction' to the *Essays in Jurisprudence and Philosophy*, *op. cit.* Secondly, in this work, Raz presents and discusses the distinction at issue in the most profound way.

[73] *Ibidem*, p. 347. Raz's quoted statement indeed relates to internal statements, yet given the fact, as indicated above, that Raz identified them with committed statements, it seems legitimate to attribute such a characteristic to them.

[74] *Ibidem*, pp. 351–352.

[75] *Ibidem*, p. 346.

[76] J. Raz, 'On The Nature of Law', *op. cit.*, p. 8.

[77] *See* J.R. de Páramo, 'Entrevista a H.L.A. Hart', *op. cit.*, note 5 at p. 351. *Cf.* H.L.A. Hart, 'Introduction', *op. cit.*, p. 10.

taking into account this belief without the actual necessity of sharing it). When adapting Raz's distinction, he maintained that committed statements by no means entail the need for belief in the moral binding force of law, whereas detached statements are made by means of adopting the point of view of the people who accept legal rules, yet these statements do not stand for sharing this acceptance. Thus, Hart conceived detached statements—in the spirit of his own, in this aspect, classical legal positivism—as an expression of a morally entirely neutral point of view.[78]

Let us try to draw the conclusions resulting from the above reconstruction. Hart's recognition of the third category of statements about law, allows us to distinguish two ways of using a "normative vocabulary" (the committing way in internal statements and the non-committing way in detached statements) and, thus, it opens up the possibility for a meaningful explanation of the nature of normative dogmatic and jurisprudential statements. It is certainly a truism to say contemporarily that when undertaking the study of law, it is necessary to adopt a critical approach to the analysed phenomena of the legal reality and to the content of positive law, regardless of whether we approve of the abovementioned standpoints of Kelsen, Hart and Raz, clearly regarding the legal statements made by the lawyers as the *Rechtssätze* (i.e., the statements that describe the legal ought), or as detached statements, and thus inherently critical. Despite recognising normative detached statements as an appropriate way of formulating legal assertions and the arguments that support them (naturally along with many other categories of normative[79] and non-normative legal statements), we must proceed with considerable caution. Adopting Hart's entirely morally neutral interpretation of this category of statements would remain in an obvious conflict with the previously formulated postulate of developing an axiologically impartial, rather than neutral, juristic concept of the validity of statutory law. Therefore, we shall understand detached statements in the spirit of Raz's original conception, regarding them to be such normative statements of lawyers, which, although they do not imply moral or any other acceptance and support for the norms of positive law, do not preclude such acceptance and support from their authors. Incidentally, only such an interpretation seems to be appropriate and to correspond with the facts. It is difficult to require that the statements of legal theorists—including those who share a belief in the moral

[78] It is therefore not surprising that J.R. de Páramo, *ibidem*, pp. 351ff., in order to present Hart's interpretation of "detached legal statements", aptly uses the Spanish term "enunciados jurídicos neutrales", instead of "distanciados".

[79] Taking into account the undertaken analyses, among the vast literature concerning linguistic aspects of jurisprudence, it is worth paying attention to the only study – to the best of my knowledge – in which normative detached statements have been subjected to a logico-linguistic analysis; namely, the paper of J. Wróblewski, 'Semantics and Pragmatics of Normative Qualification Statements', *IJSL* III/7 (1990), pp. 35–53. For more details on the different types of statements formulated in legal science *see* the monograph of M. Zieliński and Z. Ziembiński, *Uzasadnianie twierdzeń, ocen i norm w prawoznawstwie*, *op. cit.*, in particular pp. 83ff.

binding force of law—have to take the form of axiologically entirely neutral detached statements in Hart's sense.

Thus, we reach the final question; namely, the determination of the research perspective proper for legal theory, or at least for such a postpositivist form of it that we try to develop in this study. As already noted, Hart in *The Concept of Law* stressed the need to consider both external as well as internal points of view in jurisprudential research[80]; nonetheless, he did not explain very accurately his own position on this issue. This is one of the reasons why this methodological aspect of Hart's conception has become the subject of numerous analyses,[81] which have led, inter alia, to the formulation of a number of intermediate concepts, of the mixed (external–internal) points of view that have served the purpose of explaining or modifying his metatheoretical position.[82] Among these clarifications, Hart chose the standpoint (approach) referred to as the "hermeneutic point of view", developed by his disciples—Peter Hacker and Neil MacCormick.[83] Hart first used it mainly in order to characterise the point of view of the individuals who make detached statements, whereas he merely mentioned a "hermeneutic point of view",[84] and only later did he expand its scope by applying it directly to his own methodology of jurisprudential research (at the same time, resigning from this inopportune term[85]). As he claimed, a theorist of law, in order to describe how law essentially functions, must "put himself in the place" of those who assume an internal point of view.[86] He stressed, nevertheless, that even if his critics are right when they argue that an internal point of view out of necessity entails a kind of moral commitment

[80] *Cf.* Chap. 5, note 26 at p. 199, with the corresponding quotation in the main text.

[81] On the doubts resulting from a not entirely precise description of Hart's position, particularly concerning the ambiguity of the concepts of internal and external points of view, *see* G.J. Postema, 'Jurisprudence as Practical Philosophy', *LT* 4 (1998), pp. 335ff.

[82] *Cf. supra*, notes 48–52 at p. 227, with the corresponding text.

[83] *Cf. supra*, studies indicated in note 48 at p. 227.

[84] H.L.A. Hart, 'Introduction', *op. cit.*, pp. 13–14.

[85] The fact that Hart in his later works refrained from using the term "hermeneutic point of view" results probably from the fact that he realised its inadequacy. It is hard not to notice that the only element that connects his research approach with hermeneutics was his emphasis of the need to understand the essence of assuming an internal point of view. In his studies, there are indeed no other conceptual categories, typical for philosophical or legal hermeneutics, such as the concepts of pre-understanding, application or of the hermeneutic circle or spiral. Neither can it be excluded that Hart wished to emphasise in this way the diversity of his approach from that of R. Dworkin, who openly admitted his connection with hermeneutics – for more *see* M. Zirk-Sadowski, 'Wprowadzenie' [Introduction] in R. Dworkin, *Imperium prawa*, Warszawa 2006, pp. XXII ff. Yet this is only a hypothesis. Moreover, it is worth noting a substantive comment made by J. Wróblewski, 'Semantics and Pragmatics of Normative Qualification Statements', *op. cit.*, note 15 at p. 47, who questions the validity of distinguishing the "hermeneutic approach", arguing that all normative statements are based on understanding treated as a form of cognition.

[86] H.L.A. Hart, 'Comment', *op. cit.*, p. 39 and 'Postscript', *op. cit.*, p. 242.

(involvement),[87] then from that research perspective, it is still possible to describe—in an axiologically neutral way—the behaviour and moral conviction of people involved in the social practice called law. Hart's position is certainly appropriate for the positivist, particularly for the sophisticated legal positivist (the primordial legal positivism of Jeremy Bentham and John Austin left entirely aside the internal point of view), yet it cannot be adopted in our research due to the reasons which have already been partly presented in a discussion on the concept of detached legal statements. Let us add here an argument under which an axiologically entirely neutral description of legal reality does not seem possible due to quite prosaic reasons: every researcher of law has, after all, certain moral convictions, which they cannot completely disregard,[88] otherwise they could be faced with an objection of insincerity. Incidentally, even if it was possible to achieve a completely positivist axiological neutrality for describing law, it seems that those philosophers of law who maintain that hardly anything interesting can be said about law from a methodologically "pure" point of view; that is, a research perspective that entirely disregards the axiology and moral issues, are in the right.[89] Contemporary philosophy and theory of law, as it was accurately foreseen over 30 years ago by Norberto Bobbio,[90] has become a science that is not free from

[87] H.L.A. Hart, 'Postscript', *op. cit.*, p. 243. It should be added that apart from MacCormick (to whom Hart refers his remark), a number of other commentators consider that an internal perspective stands for adopting a moral point of view, and internal statements are of a morally committing character – *cf. e.g.*, J.D. Goldsworthy, 'The Self-Destruction of Legal Positivism', *op. cit.*, p. 486; N.E. Simmonds, 'The Nature of Propositions of Law', *RT* 15 (1984), pp. 99ff.; S. Urbina, 'Which Positivism?', *ARSP* 80 (1994), p. 316; R. Holton, 'Positivism and the Internal Point of View', *L&Ph* 17 (1998), pp. 597ff.

[88] *See* Chap. 5, note 82, with the corresponding text at p. 212. *Cf. infra*, note 95 at p. 236.

[89] *See e.g.*, the opinion expressed by N. MacCormick, 'Four Quadrants of Jurisprudence' in W. Krawietz *et al.* (eds.), *Prescriptive Formality and Normative Rationality in Modern Legal Systems*, *op. cit.*, p. 67, who claims that: "The school or schools of pure legal exegesis are things of the past, perhaps because they did their work pretty well. Very little of the more interesting contemporary work is absolutely pure in the Kelsenian sense". Similarly, M. Zieliński, Z. Ziembiński, *Uzasadnianie twierdzeń, ocen i norm w prawoznawstwie*, *op. cit.*, p. 84. J. Stelmach goes even further in 'Epistemologiczna perspektywa ponowoczesnej filozofii prawa' [Epistemological Perspective of the Postmodern Philosophy of Law] in M. Borucka-Arctowa *et al.* (eds.), *Prawo – władza – społeczeństwo – polityka*, *op. cit.*, p. 44, when he states that: "All versions of *Reine Rechtslehre* are simply a theoretical fiction". Incidentally, the programmatic methodological "purity" of Kelsen's normativism is very often questioned – *see e.g.*, A. Ross, 'Validity and the Conflict between Legal Positivism and Natural Law', *op. cit.*, pp. 78ff.; R. Lippold, 'Geltung, Wirksamkeit und Verbindlichkeit von Rechtsnormen', *RT* 19 (1988), pp. 463ff.; D. Beyleveld, R. Brownsword, 'Normative Positivism: The Mirage of the Middle-Way', *op. cit.*, pp. 473ff. For more *see* Chap. 8 at pp. 402ff.

[90] N. Bobbio, '"Sein" and "Sollen" in Legal Science', *op. cit.*, pp. 14ff. In his view, a strongly ideological prescriptive meta-jurisprudence, characteristic of legal positivism, which postulated methodologically "pure" descriptive jurisprudence, is being replaced by descriptive meta-jurisprudence, which reveals anew "the eternal prescriptive function of the jurist in society" (*ibidem*, p. 15). It should nevertheless be stressed that the metatheoretical (methodological) dispute between descriptive and normative (prescriptive) ways of practising the theory of law (jurisprudence) is far

evaluation—also moral evaluation—having at least partly a prescriptive character.[91] In particular, it is difficult to specify reasonable grounds on account of which a theorist of law should always be confined to an axiologically neutral description and analysis of moral reasoning, which often takes place—as contemporarily it remains beyond dispute[92]—in the practice of law and in dogmatic sciences. In this sense, the methodological approach, as proposed here, merely justifies the conduct of numerous philosophers and theorists of law who often use moral argumentation and usually do not shun participation in law-related discussions of an ethical character (e.g., concerning the issue of euthanasia, the death penalty, the rights of sexual minorities or the admissibility of abortion). What is worth emphasising is that such argumentations and moral discussions cannot be classified as irrationally pointless, because even such hard legal positivists as, for instance, Joseph Raz, openly admit that the statement that "all factual matters are non-controversial" is equally as false as the statement claiming that "all moral propositions are controversial".[93]

To conclude, we claim that the appropriate perspective that should be adopted for jurisprudential deliberations is the one that we should hereafter refer to—also in view of terminological coherence—as a morally detached and impartial point of view.[94] Instead of suspending one's own moral judgment in the name of the apparent axiological neutrality of allegedly purely descriptive jurisprudence[95]—as recommended by the legal positivists—in our analysis we assume an attitude of

from being settled – *see e.g.*, a critique of Hart's descriptive methodology provided by R. Dworkin, 'Hart's Postscript and the Character of Political Philosophy', *op. cit.*, pp. 2ff. and J.L. Coleman's defence of the descriptive methodology of legal theory in 'Beyond the Separability Thesis: Moral Semantics and the Methodology of Jurisprudence', *OJLS* 27/4 (2007), pp. 581–608.

[91] For more *see* Z. Ziembiński, 'Prescriptive and/or Descriptive Language in Legal Sciences' in W. Krawietz, J. Wróblewski (eds.), *Sprache, Performanz und Ontologie de Rechts. Festgabe für Kazimierz Opałek zum 75. Geburtstag*, Berlin 1993, pp. 85–92.

[92] *Cf.* Chap. 5, pp. 209–212.

[93] J. Raz, 'Authority, Law, and Morality' in *idem*, *Ethics in the Public Domain*, *op. cit.*, p. 218.

[94] On the concept of impartiality *cf.* Z. Tobor, T. Pietrzykowski, 'Roszczenie do bezstronności' [The Claim to Impartiality] in J. Stelmach (ed.), *Filozofia prawa wobec globalizmu*, *op. cit.*, pp. 57–73. When taking into consideration philosophical texts, it is worth recommending the text of T. Czyżowski, 'O rzetelności, obiektywności i bezstronności w badaniach naukowych' [On the Reliability, Objectivity and Impartiality in Scientific Research] in *idem*, *Odczyty filozoficzne*, Toruń 1958, pp. 306ff.

[95] Let us recall that in reference to the axiological (moral) neutrality of legal positivism, it can be reasonably argued that it is an illusion, because adopting a positivistic pattern of understanding the law often leads to opting for one of the litigants, which could *de facto* mean adopting a moral position – *cf.* Chap. 4, p. 82, in particular note 81, and the references cited therein. Also *see* R. Dworkin, 'Hart's Postscript and the Character of Political Philosophy', *op. cit.*, p. 20. Let us add that even legal positivists acknowledge that the theory of law is not a value-free science, especially at the metatheoretical level; however, the jurisprudential evaluations do not necessarily have to be based on moral arguments – *see e.g.*, H.L.A. Hart, 'Comment', *op. cit.*, p. 39; J. Raz, 'The Problem about the Nature of Law', *op. cit.*, pp. 192–193 and 'On The Nature of Law', *op. cit.*, p. 15. For more on the problem of the moral neutrality of a sophisticated legal positivism *see* G.J. Postema, 'Jurisprudence as Practical Philosophy', *op. cit.*, pp. 330ff.

impartiality which, on the one hand, involves refraining from firm moral decisions but, on the other hand, entails taking into account, in a detached way, both other's as well as our own moral views, in situations where moral reflection proves necessary on account of the purpose of the undertaken research or the content of the arguments provided.[96] At the level of metatheoretical reflection, this impartiality will stand for *par excellence* agnostic moral (axiological) indifference in the process of constructing legal concepts (in particular, the concept of the validity of statutory law, which—let us note—will be constructed in a way that distances it from the dispute over the relations between law and morals). Whereas at the theoretical level, impartiality will consist in the fact that in any consideration or application of moral arguments, we present only a certain moral position; with a reservation as to its validity, i.e., a full awareness of the fact that other people's moral views may be more appropriate (i.e., better justified). Thus, any normative statements of the theorists of law concerning the positive law, shall be interpreted as detached statements within the meaning indicated above—namely, as not excluding the moral acceptance of law, rather than as internal statements or detached ones (as both defined by Hart), committed statements (in Raz's sense) or external statements, which (and here we fully agree with Hart[97]) cannot be regarded as normative statements at all.

6.4 The Referent of the Concept of Legal Validity

Two questions directly related to the preliminary explanation of the chosen *explicandum* have still to be discussed. Let us recall, that in order to clarify the intension of the juristic concept of the validity of statutory law, we are going to apply the method based on analysing the meaning of the expression "A norm is valid".[98] Therefore, firstly it should be explained why we decided to refer the feature of validity to legal norms. Secondly, the concept of legal norm that we will use in clarificative analysis should be elucidated.

Even a superficial analysis of the literature and of the linguistic habits of lawyers shows that the concept of the validity of law is indeterminate in substantive terms—undoubtedly, in juristic discourse the predicate "is valid" is referred to different objects. Without the claim to completeness, we can mention the following six

---

[96] It does not mean that we are going to abuse moral argumentation. In fact, in this study we use it mostly during the discussion on moral critical arguments relating to "Radbruch's formula" – *cf.* Chap. 4, pp. 169ff. and Chap. 9, pp. 526ff. Besides, we refer to the moral arguments only exceptionally, for example, when determining the requirement of the fair clarification of the concept of legal validity with respect to the subjects of law – *cf. supra*, pp. 225–226, and the relations between the juristic presumption of the validity of statutory law norms and the principles of *ignorantia iuris nocet* and *ignorantia legis neminem excusat* – *cf.* Chap. 9, pp. 529–533.

[97] *Cf.* H.L.A. Hart, *The Concept of Law*, *op. cit.*, pp. 87–88.

[98] *Cf. supra*, note 8 at p. 218, and Chap. 7, pp. 247ff.

categories of objects that—in relation to the continental system-type of statutory law (a system-type of *ius civile*)—can be deemed to be valid, without violating the intuitions that are characteristic for juristic language[99]:

1. The statutory (enacted) law as such
2. The concrete system of law (domestic or international)
3. The law-creating acts (constitutions, international agreements, statutes, administrative acts etc.), usually somewhat confusingly called "normative acts"[100]
4. Legal provisions (precepts)
5. Legal norms directly or indirectly expressed by the lawmaker[101] (or—in another terminology—legal norms explicitly enacted by the legislator[102])
6. Legal norms capable of being inferred, on the basis of the accepted juristic rules of inference,[103] from the norms indicated in the previous point (or—in another terminology—legal norms which are formal or interpretive consequences of them[104])

Taking into account the previously identified objectives of clarification, and in particular the intention to develop a juristic conception of the validity of law that is also practically useful, let us consider why it is most accurate to treat legal norms that belong to categories 5 and 6 as the most appropriate referent, to which the predicate "is valid" will be related in our postpositivist conception of the validity of statutory law.

---

[99] In compiling this list, as well as in further considerations, I primarily refer to Polish legal terminology. However, given the similarity of the legal system in continental Europe – as belonging to the system-type of statutory law – I assume that despite of some terminological discrepancies, the categories included in our list are easy to understand. The reason why I refer to Polish juristic terminology is quite obvious, and – as we hope – methodologically justified: this is a terminology which I am familiar with, and the comparative analysis of the terminologies used in other countries will go well beyond the assumed scope of research.

[100] *Cf.* Z. Ziembiński, '"Akt normatywny" czy "akt prawotwórczy"' ["Normative Act" or "Law-Creating Act"], *PiP* 11–12 (1993), p. 96.

[101] I use here the terminology of M. Zieliński, *Interpretacja jako proces dekodowania tekstu prawnego* [Interpretation as the Process of Decoding Legal Text], Poznań 1972, pp. 17ff., 46ff.

[102] In the terminology of J. Wróblewski – *see idem*, *Sądowe stosowanie prawa*, *op. cit.*, p. 96 [English version, p. 77] and K. Opałek, J. Wróblewski, *Prawo. Metodologia, Filozofia, Teoria Prawa*, *op. cit.*, p. 241.

[103] *See* M. Zieliński, *Interpretacja jako proces dekodowania tekstu prawnego*, *op. cit.*, pp. 17ff., 28. For more on the rules on inference in the legal system (such as *argumentum a fortiori*, *argumentum a contario*, *argumentum a simile* etc.) *see* L. Nowak, *Interpretacja prawnicza. Studium z metodologii prawoznawstwa* [Legal Interpretation. A Study on the Methodology of Jurisprudence], Warszawa 1973, pp. 65ff.; Z. Ziembiński, *Metodologiczne zagadnienia prawoznawstwa* [Methodological Issues of Jurisprudence], Warszawa 1974, pp. 146ff. and *Problemy podstawowe prawoznawstwa* [Basic Problems of Jurisprudence], Warszawa 1980, pp. 299ff.

[104] In the terminology of J. Wróblewski – *see idem*, *Sądowe stosowanie prawa*, *op. cit.*, pp. 96–97 [English version, pp. 77–78] and K. Opałek, J. Wróblewski, *Prawo. Metodologia, Filozofia, Teoria Prawa*, *op. cit.*, pp. 242–243.

The first two categories seem to be inadequate, primarily due to the fact that in the discourse of validity, associated with the practice of law application,[105] the questions of the validity of statutory law as such, or the validity of a particular system of law (the so-called external legal validity in terminology introduced by Peczenik and Aarnio[106]), are devoid of practical significance. It is indeed difficult to imagine a situation in which arguments such as: "This legal norm is not valid because law is not valid at all" or "This legal norm is not valid because the legal system to which it belongs is not valid", would be frequently used, even in the states of un-law. As history has shown, only a few participants in the court trials in these states (usually the accused in the political cases), have the courage to raise heroic and usually ineffective arguments such as: "The law, under which you intend to convict me, is not valid, and you – 'judges' – are not judges at all, but criminals in robes". The infrequency of such arguments results from the fact that in the juristic practical discourse one usually conceives the validity of law in internal terms (in the sense of Peczenik–Aarnio's distinction) or in relative ones (as defined by Opałek–Stelmach),[107] by assuming the validity of not only the legal system in the context of which we resolve the problem of the validity of norms, but also the validity of law as such.

The above practical argument can be easily supplemented with an observation that in the work of philosophers and theorists of law who take up the issue of legal validity, both the question of the validity of law as such, as well as the validity of the legal system, are often fully consciously disregarded. Let us point out here the approach of Wiesław Lang, who in his monograph devoted to the validity of law totally ignores the issue of legal validity in relation to the legal system, by treating that problem as an "extra-normative issue".[108] In his later work, Lang clarifies his earlier position,[109] stressing that the issue of validity of the system of law can meaningfully be considered only from the external perspective and in the context of the simultaneous existence of many different legal systems. In such a case, nonetheless, we deal with a meta-systemic validity of a particular legal system, founded on its actual efficacy. This reasoning leads Lang to the conclusion that the feature of validity could be reasonably referred only to the norms or other elements of the legal system, rather than to the system which is viewed as a whole. Hence, as he claims: "the notion of the validity of a legal system has very little cognitive or practical value".[110]

---

[105] This basic type of discourse of validity is later defined as the validity discourse in the strict sense – *cf.* Chap. 9, pp. 471ff.

[106] *Cf.* Chap. 5, p. 206.

[107] Let us recall that the concepts of internal and relative validity should not be treated as synonyms – for more on this issue *see* Chap. 5, notes 56 and 60 at pp. 206–207, together with the corresponding text, and Chap. 7, note 290 at pp. 311–312.

[108] W. Lang, *Obowiązywanie prawa*, *op. cit.*, pp. 104, 291.

[109] *See* W. Lang, 'A Concept of the Validity of Law', *op. cit.*, pp. 100–101.

[110] *Ibidem*, p. 101.

A similar research approach is encountered in a number of studies on specific problems of validity. For example, Sławomira Wronkowska, when taking the issue of validity in the context of the conception of sources of law in Poland, leaves aside in her deliberations the problem of validity in an absolute sense (i.e., validity relating to the law in general), focusing on the validity relativised to a particular legal system. In this context, she formulates the view under which "the basic intuitions suggest that the feature of validity can be related to normative acts (as the products of legislation), provisions and norms"[111] (i.e., categories 3–6 in our list). A similar pattern is followed by the Spanish philosopher, Josep Aguiló Regla, who, when examining the issue of derogation—in a reference to the theory of Riccardo Guastini—assumes that the judgments on validity (*juicios de validez*) may be related to the normative acts, norms and formulas of norms.[112] The examples of this kind of intra-systemic approach to the problem of validity can be multiplied, yet we shall refrain from providing more of them, because one can also indicate some examples of the authors who take a broader perspective—for instance, concerning the issues of the validity of the legal system or an absolute validity of law. However, such counterexamples are not able to undermine the conclusion that within the basic jurisprudential research related to issues of the validity of law, the priority should be granted to the issue of internal validity, which—due to positivist habits (and perhaps the nature of things?)—prevails in jurisprudential deliberations and in the practice of the application of law.[113] This thesis—in the context of the undertaken research—is even strengthened if we take into account the postulate of developing a "non-painstaking" conception of the validity of statutory law, which will not only be theoretically correct, but also useful for legal dogmatics and the practice of lawmaking and law application.[114]

On account of the above arguments, it seems possible to choose either the third, or the fourth, or—jointly—the fifth and the sixth category of objects, to which legal validity will be attributed. Thus, we need to consider the fundamental problem:

---

[111] S. Wronkowska, 'O źródłach prawa i aktach normatywnych raz jeszcze', *op. cit.*, p. 119.

[112] J. Aguiló Regla, *Sobre la Derogación. Ensayo de Dinámica Jurídica*, 2nd ed., México 1999, pp. 75ff., 98–99. On the meaning of the term "formula of a norm" *see* Chap. 8, note 69 at p. 372.

[113] *Cf. e.g.*, J. Wróblewski, 'Obowiązywanie systemowe i granice dogmatycznego podejścia do systemu prawa' [Systemic Validity and the Limits of a Dogmatic Approach to the System of Law], *SPE* XXXVI (1986), pp. 23–36. As even more decidedly admitted by M. Zieliński and Z. Ziembiński, *Uzasadnianie twierdzeń, ocen i norm w prawoznawstwie*, *op. cit.*, p. 173: "The assertions on the validity of some norms as legal norms in any case must constitute assertions relativised to a particular legal system". A similar standpoint is expressed by H.L.A. Hart, who believes that the term "validity" is required only to resolve the questions "which arise *within* a system of rules" – *idem*, *The Concept of Law*, *op. cit.*, p. 105. For more on this issue *see* Chap. 7 at pp. 284ff., where we explain why referring the feature of "validity" to the legal system does not make any independent (intrinsic) sense.

[114] *Cf. supra*, pp. 223–224 (the fragment concerning the second objective of clarification) and Introduction, the text corresponding to the notes 15–16 at p. 8.

what should be considered as the basic "unit", "piece"[115] or "particle of law"[116] (in relation to the continental system of statutory law), to which we will assign the attribute of validity? We maintain that the stronger arguments speak for the third of the mentioned options, namely for referring the validity to the legal norms established either directly by the legislator or interpreted or inferred from them. In order to justify this choice, we can refer to a number of useful arguments formulated in the studies of the authors who belong to the Poznań school of legal theory.

The basic argument that can be labelled as the argument from derivation is based on several co-related premises. Firstly, it seems obvious that legal interpretation constitutes an essential element of the scientific as well as the practical professional activity of lawyers.[117] Secondly, the main objective of legal interpretation, and the unique goal in the case of the operative interpretation of law, is the validity purpose, which consists in "reconstructing the norm which is valid at some time".[118] Therefore—thirdly—we accept as legitimate the view of Leszek Nowak, who claims that the problems of legal interpretation are derivative to the issues of legal validity because "as the questions of validity concern norms, so they presuppose a certain solution of the question of the interpretation of legal provisions".[119] The approval of the indicated premises leads to the conclusion that the legal

[115] This term is used by J. Wróblewski, who also provides a number of arguments in favour of admitting that "units of law" are norms rather than legal provisions – *see idem*, *Zagadnienia teorii wykładni prawa ludowego* [Issues on the Theory of Interpretation of People's Law], Warszawa 1959, pp. 79ff.

[116] This term (in the original: *pieza del Derecho*) is used by M. Atienza and J. Ruiz Manero, who relate it to the interpreted (having a fixed meaning) "linguistic units of law", namely legal norms within the meaning characteristic for the analytical theory of law – *see iidem*, *Las piezas del Derecho. Teoría de los enunciados jurídicos*, Barcelona 1996, p. XIII, in particular note 2 [English version: *A Theory of Legal Sentences*, trans. R. Zimmerling, Dordrecht 1998, p. xi, in particular note 2].

[117] *See e.g.*, M. Zieliński, 'Aspekty zasady *clara non sunt interpretanda*' [Aspects of the Principle *clara non sunt interpretanda*] in S. Wronkowska, M. Zieliński (eds.), *Szkice z teorii prawa i szczegółowych nauk prawnych*, *op. cit.*, pp. 176ff. and 'Podstawowe zasady współczesnej wykładni prawa' [The Fundamental Principles of Modern Interpretation of Law] in P. Winczorek (ed.), *Teoria i praktyka wykładni prawa*, Warszawa 2005, pp. 118ff.; M. Zieliński, Z. Radwański, 'Wykładnia prawa cywilnego' [Interpretation of Civil Law], *SPP* 1 (2006), pp. 17ff.; P.E. Navarro, 'Acerca de la inevitabilidad de la interpretación', *IS* 22 (2005), pp. 99–122.

[118] The concept of validity purpose and the quotation are taken from B. Kanarek, M. Zieliński, 'Porządkująca faza wykładni prawa' [The Arranging Phase of Legal Interpretation], *RPEiS* LXIII/3 (2001), pp. 4–5.

[119] L. Nowak, *Interpretacja prawnicza*, *op. cit.*, pp. 32–33. Let us note that Nowak's thesis can be supported by the additional argument that refers to lawyers' linguistic intuitions. It seems that this intuition is not affected by the following sentence: "This norm is not valid, because it is the result of an erroneous interpretation of legal provisions", but it is no longer acceptable to utter the sentence which reads: "This norm is not valid, therefore it is the result of an erroneous interpretation of legal provisions" because it is relatively easy to identify situations that falsify it (for example, the invalidity of a norm resulting from the inconsistency of its enactment with the constitutional rules of the legislative procedure).

norms—treated as results of legal interpretation—constitute the "units of law" that we should attribute with the feature of validity. Without a doubt, it cannot be claimed that the results of legal interpretation are the law-creating acts or legal provisions (categories 3 and 4).

The second argument is related to the terminological postulate recently put forward in Polish jurisprudential literature by Beata Kanarek and Maciej Zieliński.[120] They propose the use of the terms "enactment" and "repeal" in reference to legal provisions (precepts of law), reserving the term "validity" for legal norms. On account of the way in which this postulate is justified by them, we can name it as the argument from precedence (or priority). They aptly point out that the juridical concepts of enactment and repeal of a legal provision, are—from the logical point of view—prior to the corresponding concepts of issuing and derogating a norm, usually combined in juristic discourse with the concept of legal validity. Let us add that, in the further considerations, we will strive to meet this demand, which protects us, inter alia, against encountering the apparent legal antinomies such as: "The court applied a valid legal norm which was decoded (inferred, interpreted) from invalid legal provisions".

The next argument, closely connected with the previous one, is already of a negative character. It is the argument from uselessness, based on a rather trivial observation that the theoretical and, above all, practical usefulness of the determination that a given act of law-creation (e.g., a statute) or legal provision is valid, is in many cases severely limited. It is indeed difficult to question the fact that lawyers often interpret legal acts or provisions which were formally repealed by the lawmaker and which—according to the intertemporal rules of law—form the normative basis for reconstructing currently valid norms.[121] The conceptual antinomies that arise in such situations, usually dealt with by means of highly arbitrary conceptual distinctions, also argue in favour of assuming that these are the legal norms that constitute the primary point of reference of the juristic concept of validity. This argument is reinforced if we take into account the distinction between legal norms and provisions, which is assumed in the previous deliberations and widely accepted in the Polish theory of law. This distinction, introduced at a conceptual level, and most clearly highlighted by the creators of the derivative conception of legal interpretation,[122] is combined with the purely syntactical definition of legal provision. For example, Maciej Zieliński defines it as a "one-

---

[120] *See* B. Kanarek, M. Zieliński, 'Porządkująca faza wykładni prawa', *op. cit.*, p. 6. Similarly, M. Zieliński, *Wykładnia prawa, op. cit.*, pp. 207–208 and P. Grabowski, M. Hermann, 'O normatywnym charakterze przepisów o wejściu w życie' [On the Normative Character of Provisions on Entrance into Force], *PiP* 9 (2006), note 13 at p. 71.

[121] For more *see* Chap. 9, pp. 506ff., and the references cited therein.

[122] *See* Z. Ziembiński, 'Przepis prawny a norma prawna' [Legal Provision and Legal Norm], *RPiE* XXII/1 (1960), pp. 105–122 and *Logiczne podstawy prawoznawstwa, op. cit.*, pp. 119ff. *Cf.* Z. Ziembiński, M. Zieliński, *Dyrektywy i sposób ich wypowiadania* [Directives and the Method of Expressing Them], BMS 17 (1992), pp. 104ff. and M. Zieliński, *Wykładnia prawa, op. cit.*, pp. 15ff.

sentence or several-sentence long editorial unit of the legal text of a legislative act",[123] and Lech Morawski refers to is as "an elementary systematizing unit of a given legal text".[124] In the context of such definitions of legal provision, it seems that the only non-absurd understanding of the phrase "the editorial unit of the legal text [i.e., legal provision] is valid" must refer to the concept of the membership of legal provisions in the legal system.[125] Meanwhile, anticipating the outcomes of further analyses,[126] it should be noted that the acceptance of the category of the "membership in the legal system" as a clarification of the intension of the juristic concept of the validity of statutory law turns out to be incorrect. Therefore, the uselessness of referring validity to legal provisions, identified in relation to the intertemporal legal cases, turns out to be more strongly justified than it might seem at first glance, since its jurisprudential explanation can be provided.

The last two arguments, strongly co-related and mutually supportive, are the argument from terminological consistency and the argument from adequacy. These arguments refer to the intra-systemic understanding of law, dominant both in legal dogmatics and in the legal practice of law application. The first one is based on the following, quite simple reasoning. If we use the concept of the legal system in order to clarify and resolve the problems of legal validity, then we should take into account that the elements of this system are generally considered legal norms of conduct, rather than provisions or legislative acts.[127] As noted (in a slightly overly

[123] M. Zieliński, 'Algorytm interpretacji przepisów prawnych' [Algorithm of the Interpretation of Legal Provisions] in J. Pogonowski (ed.), *Eufonia i Logos*, *op. cit.*, p. 657.

[124] L. Morawski, *Wstęp do prawoznawstwa*, 7th ed., Toruń 2004, p. 56. Numerous examples of similar definitions are provided by J. Nowacki, *Przepis prawny a norma prawna* [Legal Provision and Legal Norm], PNUŚ 973 (1988), pp. 9–11.

[125] The other understanding of the validity of legal provisions, for example, connected with their application, compliance or binding nature, are quite absurd on account of the very common legislative technique of fragmentation of the norms in the legal provisions. Nowak justifies the thesis that "the rationalised conception of validity", developed by him, can only refer to legal norms (rather than to provisions) by means of the argument which we now refer to: "It is hard to assume that a rational legislator first issues some legal norms, and then does not require from their addressees that they comply with these norms, but that they meet their 'fragments', 'scattered' in the various provisions" – L. Nowak, 'Cztery koncepcje obowiązywania prawa' [Four Conceptions of the Validity of Law], *RPEiS* XXXVIII/2 (1966), p. 102.

[126] *Cf.* Chap. 7, pp. 271–312.

[127] In the theory and philosophy of law, this position is taken in the first place (despite some differences in terminology, analysed by J. Wróblewski, 'Reguły prawne w analitycznej teorii prawa' [Legal Rules in the Analytic Theory of Law], *SPE* XXXIV (1985), pp. 7–26), by the leading representatives of legal positivism, such as Kelsen (hence the origin of the term "normativism"), Hart, Bulygin and many others. Let us add that in the international jurisprudential literature, there are even special terms such as "Normative Positivism" or "normativer Positivismus", denoting (in one of their meanings) such a trend in legal positivism, which identifies law with the norms that create legal obligations – *cf. e.g.*, D. Beyleveld, R. Brownsword, 'Normative Positivism: The Mirage of the Middle-Way', *op. cit.*, pp. 462ff.; J. Waldron, "Normative (or Ethical) Positivism", *op. cit.*, note 3 at p. 411, together with the corresponding text; J.-R. Sieckmann, *Regelmodelle und Prinzipienmodelle des Rechtssystems*, *op. cit.*, pp. 129ff.

categorical mode) by another representative of the Poznań school of legal theory, Jarosław Mikołajewicz, in the contemporary Polish theory of law, except for the studies on legislative technique, "it would be difficult to identify major works dealing with the legal system perceived differently than the set of the norms of conduct".[128] Therefore, the requirements for terminological consistency strongly militate in favour of referring validity to legal norms, otherwise we would be faced with significant inconsistencies between the systemic reconstruction of law and considerations related to the question of legal validity. Moreover, the juristic concept of intra-systemic validity would have to be redefined in a way that violates the basic juristic intuitions, because legal provisions, rather than norms would be intra-systemically (relatively) valid within the legal system consisting of legal norms. The second argument, whose name refers to the principle of adequacy, as formulated by Leon Petrażycki,[129] is also associated with a contemporarily dominant understanding of the legal system. The point is that considerations of both a theoretical and practical nature, militate in favour of assuming that the legal system also consists of the norms indirectly established by the lawmaker (category 6), which are inferred from the legal texts on the basis of systemic inference rules that, *nota bene*, are qualified as a type of validity rule.[130] In other words, using Jerzy Wróblewski's terminology, a correct construction of the legal system also includes, in addition to the enacted norms, their formal and interpretive consequences—in such a case we deal with the so-called LSIC system.[131] In the light of these observations, the conception of the validity of legislative (law-giving) acts or

[128] J. Mikołajewicz, *Prawo intertemporalne. Zagadnienia teoretycznoprawne* [Intertemporal Law. The Jurisprudential Problems], Poznań 2000, note 20 at p. 19. I believe that K. Płeszka's standpoint, provided in *Hierarchia w systemie prawa* [Hierarchy in the Legal System], ZNUJ PNP 33 (1988), pp. 16–17, is far more balanced. Płeszka recognises the perception of a legal system as a system of norms that are "the most common", and regarding legal provisions, as the elements of the system that are "relatively rare". *Cf.* K. Płeszka, T. Gizbert-Studnicki, 'Obraz systemu prawa w dogmatyce prawniczej', *op. cit.*, pp. 157ff. and R. Guastini, 'Proyecto para la voz "Ordenamiento jurídico" de un diccionario', trans. M. Atienza, J. Ruiz Manero, *DOXA* 27 (2004), pp. 248ff.

[129] L. Petrażycki, *Wstęp do nauki o prawie i moralności. Podstawy psychologii emocjonalnej* [Introduction to the Science of Law and Morality. Fundamentals of Emotional Psychology], trans. J. Lande, 2nd ed., Warszawa 1959, pp. 124ff. For more *see* A. Grabowski, *Judicial Argumentation and Pragmatics*, *op. cit.*, pp. 6–7, and the references cited therein.

[130] Such a nature of the inference rules has been most emphatically stressed by M. Zieliński, Z. Radwański, 'Wykładnia prawa cywilnego', *op. cit.*, p. 8. The same was assumed by Z. Ziembiński, *Metodologiczne zagadnienia prawoznawstwa*, *op. cit.*, pp. 146ff., who treated legal reasoning based on the inference rules as reasoning "concerning the validity of legal norms".

[131] *Cf.* J. Wróblewski, 'Nieostrość systemu prawa', *op. cit.*, pp. 13ff., 'Obowiązywanie systemowe i granice dogmatycznego podejścia do systemu prawa', *op. cit.*, pp. 28ff., and *Sądowe stosowanie prawa*, *op. cit.*, pp. 96ff. [English version, pp. 78ff.]; K. Opałek, J. Wróblewski, *Prawo. Metodologia, filozofia, teoria prawa*, *op. cit.*, pp. 241ff. In the context of the practice of the application of law, which is of interest to us, it should be noted that Wróblewski formulates the view, probably obvious to most continental lawyers, that the system of interpreted law (LSIC) is presupposed in the judicial application of law.

legal provisions would be inadequate and, more specifically, it would constitute the "lame theory" (in Pertażycki's terminology) related to a class of objects that is too narrow. It is indeed impossible to accept that a certain legislative act is inferred, or that it constitutes a formal or interpretive consequence of another law-giving act (and, similarly in the case of legal provisions). Thus, understanding the legal system as a system of norms entails the necessity of referring the feature of validity to legal norms as well.

The above five arguments strongly support the thesis that within the continental legal systems of statutory law the lawyers work on legal provisions, but they think—or should think—in the "language of norms"[132] and treat legal norms as primary "units" or "particles" of positive law. It also seems that these arguments justify the acceptance of the thesis that in the frame of juristic discourse the concept of validity should be related to legal norms (hereinafter understood as belonging to categories 5 and 6). Such acceptance does not mean that the problems related to the validity of other categories of objects indicated in the above list are completely unimportant for lawyers—yet, it is sufficient to recognise that they are significantly less important in the context of our research.

The last preliminary issue is to clarify what concept of legal norm will be used in our investigations. Undoubtedly, this concept, frequently aptly regarded as the theoretical construct of legal doctrine,[133] constitutes the fundamental component of lawyers' linguistic competence. Its explanation seems to be indispensable for the lucidity of our clarificative analysis, in particular due to the fact that there have been many sound and properly justified concepts of legal norms developed and used within the analytical theory of law. We feel exempt from the duty of presenting them and undertaking their comparative analysis, which would considerably exceed the scope of this study.[134] Instead of that, we will simply identify the concept of legal norm that we are going to use hereafter, and we shortly justify the choice of that concept. Thus, in what follows, we will use the so-called semantic concept of legal norm that constitutes the conceptual fundament of the derivative conception of legal interpretation, developed by Zygmunt Ziembiński and Maciej Zieliński.[135] Accordingly, we define a legal norm as:

> an utterance which sufficiently unambiguously orders (or prohibits) someone (the addressee) certain behaviour in certain circumstances.[136]

---

[132] *See* M. Zieliński, 'Języki prawne i prawnicze' [Legal and Juristic Languages] in W. Pisarek (ed.), *Polszczyzna 2000. Orędzie o stanie języka na przełomie tysiącleci*, Kraków 1999, pp. 63–64.

[133] A. Bator, *Użycie normy prawnej w regulacji stosunków gospodarczych* [The Use of the Legal Norm in the Regulation of Economic Relations], Wrocław 2000, pp. 141ff., in particular p. 160 and Z. Ziembiński, *Problemy podstawowe prawoznawstwa*, *op. cit.*, pp. 149ff.

[134] We can also add that this study is not devoted to the theory of legal norms.

[135] *See* the source texts indicated *supra*, note 122 at p. 242. To avoid misunderstanding, let us emphasise that in our analyses we neither assume nor reject the derivative conception of legal interpretation.

[136] M. Zieliński, 'Współczesne problemy wykładni prawa' [Contemporary Problems of Legal Interpretation], *PiP* 8–9 (1996), pp. 5–6.

We believe that this definition, given its simplicity, can constitute a neutral base—vis-à-vis jurisprudential disputes—for a clarificative analysis of the juristic concept of the validity of statutory law. Moreover, the semantic concept of legal norm contemporarily dominates in the Polish legal culture, and it has already found its direct reflection in Polish positive law, since Article 25 Section 1 of the currently valid *Principles of Legislative Technique*,[137] stipulates that:

> The provision of substantive law should possibly directly and clearly indicate who, in what circumstances, how ought to behave (the basic provision).

It should be added, however, that on account of the certain hesitancy of the abovementioned authors with respect to the *genus proximum* of the concept of legal norm,[138] we decide, in a slightly arbitrary fashion,[139] to classify the legal norm as an utterance (rather than as an expression or an indication), which will definitely help to harmonise the application of this concept with further pragmatic analyses.[140] Finally, given the earlier findings, according to which clarification will concern the juristic concept of the validity of statutory law that refers both to the norms directly enacted by a lawmaker (category 5 above), as well as to those inferred from them (category 6 above), it has also to be added that such a genetic aspect of legal norms is left aside in the adopted definition.

---

[137] *Zasady techniki prawodawczej. Załącznik do Rozporządzenia Prezesa Rady Ministrów z dnia 20 czerwca 2002 r. w sprawie "Zasad techniki prawodawczej"* [Principles of Legislative Technique. Annex to the Regulation of the Prime Minister of 20 June 2002 on "Principles of Legislative Technique"], published in *Dziennik Ustaw* [Journal of Statutes] 2002, No. 100, Item 908.

[138] Z. Ziembiński usually defined the norms of conduct (and thus also the legal norms) as "utterances" or "indications" – *cf. idem*, 'Przepis prawny a norma prawna', *op. cit.*, pp. 105ff. and 'Uwagi o negowaniu norm i wypowiedzi z normami związanych' [Comments on Negating Norms and Utterances Related to Norms], *SF* 2–3 (1985), p. 106. M. Zieliński mostly treats legal norms as "expressions", sometimes "even just the ones that someone thought of" – *see idem*, *Wykładnia prawa*, *op. cit.*, p. 16, while S. Wronkowska understands them as "utterances" – *see idem*, *Podstawowe pojęcia prawa i prawoznawstwa* [Basic Concepts of Law and Jurisprudence], 3rd ed., Poznań 2005, p. 13.

[139] The content of the previous note shows that such an approach has gained the advantage. Moreover, the arbitrariness is undermined by the arguments justifying the preference for "utterance" (ahead of "expression") provided by Ziembiński himself – *see idem*, 'O aparaturze pojęciowej dotyczącej sytuacji prawnych' [On the Conceptual Apparatus Concerning Legal Situations], *PiP* 3 (1985), p. 35 and, indirectly, in the paper 'W związku z artykułem K. Opałka "Dwoistość ujęcia normy w nauce prawa"' [A Propos K. Opałek's Paper "The Duality of the Understanding of Norm in Jurisprudence"], *PiP* 12 (1988), p. 105, reinforced with approving remarks by T. Gizbert-Studnicki's review of the book by Z. Ziembiński and M. Zieliński: *Dyrektywy i sposób ich wypowiadania*, *PiP* 3 (1993), p. 88.

[140] *See* Chap. 8, pp. 380ff., 422ff.

Chapter 7
Critique of the Jurisprudential Conceptions of Legal Validity

7.1 On the Method of Clarificative Analysis

In this chapter we shall examine some of the most well-known and influential jurisprudential conceptions of legal validity, assessing them in terms of their suitability for clarifying the intension of the juristic concept of the validity of statutory law. Using the recently popular jargon of postmodernists, it can be said that we will "deconstruct" this concept. Nevertheless—as it will soon be proved—in the course of the analysis we will not make use of any particular postmodern methods. The undertaken analyses will, in fact, be based solely on typical measures of analytical philosophy and the analytical theory of law, since the principal aim of the conception of the validity of statutory law—developed and presented in the next chapter—is to complete the project of the modern philosophy of law (so-called legal modernism) in the form of the postpositivist theory (of the validity) of law, which only partially dismantles the current positivist paradigm.

The modernist, rather than the postmodernist nature of the clarificative analysis is most clearly manifested in the method applied below, which was long ago named by Jeremy Bentham as "paraphrase". In short, this method calls for the analysis of the meaning (elucidation) of the legal and juristic concepts by means of the linguistic analysis of typical expressions (or utterances) in which these concepts are used. In contemporary analytical legal philosophy, Bentham's method of paraphrasing has been recalled and successfully applied by H.LA. Hart.[1] Independently of its origin, it has also often been applied in the jurisprudential analyses of legal validity. For example, Alf Ross, when developing a predictive conception of legal validity, has devoted a considerable part of his treatise *On Law and Justice* to the analysis of the assertion "D is valid law",[2] while many leading Polish theorists

[1] *See* H.L.A. Hart, *Definition and Theory in Jurisprudence*, *op. cit.*, pp. 8ff., 15ff.

[2] A. Ross, *On Law and Justice*, *op. cit.*, pp. 39ff., 75ff. Symbol D stands for directives that include legal norms.

A. Grabowski, *Juristic Concept of the Validity of Statutory Law*,
DOI 10.1007/978-3-642-27688-0_7, © Springer-Verlag Berlin Heidelberg 2013

and philosophers of law (including Wiesław Lang,[3] Leszek Nowak,[4] Kazimierz Opałek and Jerzy Wróblewski,[5] as well as Maciej Zieliński and Zygmunt Ziembiński[6]) tried to explain the meaning of the concept of legal validity or determine its nature by analysing the expression "Norm *N* is valid" or via its slightly extended versions (e.g., by semantic, systemic, territorial or temporal relativisation). The examination of the meaning of the expression concerning the validity of a legal norm should then be regarded as a methodologically legitimate means of clarificative analysis, especially since (as rightly pointed out by Opałek and Wróblewski[7]) the term "validity"—when used without any direct or indirect referent—has the character of an apparent name (pseudo-name), which is derived from the predicates used in phrases that contain the predicate "is valid". In light of the cited opinion, it can even be argued that it is necessary to adopt the method of the paraphrase. Therefore, without much resistance (and enjoying the venerable tradition), we shall apply this method to clarify the intension of the juristic concept of the validity of statutory law.

Given the enormous number and diversity of the conceptions of legal validity, created by many leading representatives of our discipline,[8] it can undoubtedly be maintained that the achievements of the analytical theory and philosophy of law in this area are extremely abundant. This basically forces us to undertake a clarification of the character of the modelling; that is, in a generalised and simplified way. The fact that also weighs in favour of adopting such a generalised and simplified pattern of clarification is that the analyses of the concepts (theories) of legal validity are usually of such a model-based nature,[9] and we only rarely

[3] *Cf.* W. Lang, 'Obowiązywanie normy prawnej w czasie w świetle logiki norm', *op. cit.*, pp. 48ff. and *Obowiązywanie prawa*, *op. cit.*, pp. 111ff.

[4] *Cf.* L. Nowak, 'Cztery koncepcje obowiązywania prawa', *op. cit.*, pp. 96ff.

[5] *See* K. Opałek, J. Wróblewski, *Zagadnienia teorii prawa*, *op. cit.*, pp. 125ff.; K. Opałek, 'Der Dualismus der Auffassung der Normen in der Rechtswissenschaft. Der Versuch seiner Überwindung', *RT* 20, pp. 435ff.; J. Wróblewski, *Sądowe stosowanie prawa*, *op. cit.*, pp. 94ff. [English version, pp. 76ff.].

[6] *Cf.* Z. Ziembiński, *Logiczne podstawy prawoznawstwa*, *op. cit.*, pp. 83ff.; Z. Ziembiński, M. Zieliński, *Dyrektywy i sposób ich wypowiadania*, *op. cit.*, pp. 32ff.; M. Zieliński, *Wykładnia prawa*, *op. cit.*, pp. 20–21.

[7] K. Opałek, J. Wróblewski, *Zagadnienia teorii prawa*, *op. cit.*, p. 126.

[8] *Cf.* Chap. 6, note 3 at p. 217.

[9] *See e.g.*, U. Neumann, 'Theorien der Rechtsgeltung' in V. Gessner, W. Hassemer (eds.), *Gegenkultur und Recht*, Baden-Baden 1985, pp. 21–41; O. Weinberger, *Norm und Institution. Eine Einführung in die Theorie des Rechts*, Wien 1988, pp. 122ff.; L. Nowak, 'Cztery koncepcje obowiązywania prawa', *op. cit.*, pp. 97ff.; Z. Ziembiński, *Logiczne podstawy prawoznawstwa*, *op. cit.*, pp. 80ff.; Z. Ziembiński, M. Zieliński, *Dyrektywy i sposób ich wypowiadania*, *op. cit.*, pp. 32ff.; K. Opałek, 'The Problem of the Validity of Law', *op. cit.*, pp. 9ff. Within Polish literature, it was Z. Ziembiński who directly wrote about "the modelling approach to the validity of legal norms" in *Problemy podstawowe prawoznawstwa*, *op. cit.*, pp. 176ff., whereas in the foreign literature, the modelling analysis, still limited to the normative conceptions of legal validity, has been presented by E. Garzón Valdés, 'Modelle normativer Geltung', *RT* 8 (1977), pp. 41–71.

encounter studies that present the results of these analyses in a monographic way.[10] Therefore, it is necessary to explain and, at the same time, to stress that even if we sometimes undertake our considerations in the context of the conceptions of legal validity that originate from the singular authors,[11] their application shall serve as an illustration and, thus, the following critique of successive model solutions for the problem of legal validity will not directly concern these conceptions. It is, in fact, clear that a scientifically reliable critique of someone's jurisprudential conceptions must be preceded by their precise reconstruction, which, however, cannot be attempted by us, since it would undoubtedly exceed the scope of our research and, at the same time, send it along a different track. Moreover, such a critique could be rightly exposed to the objection of inappropriateness (or, even worse—of scientific dishonesty), as the authors of the discussed conceptions prioritise different aspects of the concept of legal validity, as a result of which a number of existing theories of validity do not only concern the issue of the intension of the juristic concept of the validity of statutory law—which remains the main interest in this part of our study—but also encompass the issues of the extension of this concept or of the justification of the validity of law (or often all these problems simultaneously). We, on the other hand, intend to consider—with unrelenting consistency—an analytical distinction between three fundamental questions: about the intension (meaning) and the extension of the juristic concept of legal validity, and about the justification of validity,[12] where the latter will be regarded as primarily related to the issue of extension.[13] Thus, in the course of clarification of the intension of the juristic conception of the validity of statutory law, we will not even endeavour to establish any catalogue of the criteria (conditions) that allow for the determination of the practical problem as to whether a given legal norm is valid, but will focus on finding the proper way in which to determine the intension of this concept, expressed in the form of a noncriterial regulative definition.[14]

[10] I can point out only one contemporary monograph, which, incidentally, covers only some of the theories of legal validity: U. Wendland, *Geschichte der Geltungstheorien des Rechts seit Kant unter besonderer Berücksichtigung der Anerkennungstheorien*, Berlin 1999.

[11] This will include the conceptions of E. Bulygin and R. Alexy – *see infra*, pp. 321ff. and 349ff.

[12] *See* Chap. 6, pp. 218–219. *Cf.* the arguments in favour of differentiating the "definition of validity" and the "theory of the grounds for validity" presented by G. Sartor, 'Legal Validity as Doxastic Obligation: From Definition to Normativity', *L&Ph* 19 (2000), pp. 607ff., 623ff.

[13] As aptly pointed out by A. Peczenik: "The distinction between justification and identification of (valid) law is thus merely gradual: justification is more evaluative than identification" – *idem*, 'On the Nature and Function of the *Grundnorm*', *RT* Bh. 2 (1981), p. 291. A more detailed justification of the adopted standpoint is provided in Chap. 9 at p. 490.

[14] The emphasis is placed on the noncriterial character of the sought definition, mainly due to the fact that a criterial definition usually has an extensional character; therefore, it is aimed at resolving the problem of extension rather than of intension – *cf.* the comments on nonpositivist definitions of law presented in Chap. 5 at pp. 200ff., as well as P.E. Navarro, 'Enunciados jurídicos y proposiciones normativas', *IS* 12 (2000), pp. 125–126. Furthermore, it is also obvious that a criterial definition would have to be relativised to a particular system of positive law (for without such relativisation it would not be useful in practice), while we adopt a broader perspective of the

The following analyses will also have a modelling nature in the sense that we will undertake them in the context of a certain type of legal system. We adopt the research perspective, which does not refer to any particular legal system (usually positivistically understood as a set of legal norms that are valid in a given state within a specified time), but to the so-called continental system-type of statutory law[15] (also known, mainly in the Anglo-Saxon literature, as a system-type of *civil law*), which, moreover, includes, in addition to the legal systems of continental European countries, the legal systems of Latin America.[16] The reason for adopting such a perspective is clear: if we wanted to explain the concept of a legal validity characteristic, for example, for the Polish, French or German legal culture, our research would be largely descriptive, and one of the methods applied would be a formal-dogmatic analysis of the provisions of the Polish, French or German statutory law and judicial decisions (with a particular reference to the jurisdiction of the courts that are supreme in a given system of law). Leaving aside even the fact that due to the scientific competence that would be required, we do not feel equipped to perform such an analysis,[17] its outcome would, out of necessity, be merely "local" and, in addition, it would be easily defeasible from the theoretical point of view. In order to achieve the desired result of clarification—the elimination of the semantic indeterminacy and ambiguity of the juristic concept of legal validity—we would have to assume that in contemporary legal culture we operate only with one precise and well-determinate concept of legal validity, or we would have to at least assume that a concept exists that is dominant and commonly accepted. Yet, such assumptions are clearly counterfactual. For example, considering Polish legal theory, a number of theoretical disputes, as well as the ongoing disputes between the adjudicating bodies (e.g., the controversies over the problems of legal validity occurring between the Constitutional Tribunal and the Supreme Court, related to the so-called interpretive rulings[18]) are the best proof here. In addition, we indeed

system-type of statutory law, which we write about in the next paragraph. Finally, given the complicated nature of the various criteria, which need to be met in order to classify the norm as valid, it can be assumed in advance that a criterial definition could hardly be considered as a simple *explicatum*. As for the other reasons *see infra*, pp. 348ff. and Chap. 9 at pp. 455ff.

[15] At this point we shall confine ourselves only to the identification of the systems of statutory law, while the pattern of understanding the concept of statutory law itself – as adopted in this study – will be, mainly for editorial reasons, explained in Chap. 8 at pp. 434–435.

[16] For more *see e.g.*, H. Rot, W. Gromski, 'Prawo stanowione' [Enacted Law] in (teamwork ed.), *Główne kultury prawne współczesnego świata*, Warszawa 1995, pp. 32–86.

[17] Such studies should be conducted jointly with the dogmatists of law, in particular, with specialists of constitutional law.

[18] *Cf. e.g.*, A. Józefowicz, 'Orzeczenia interpretacyjne Trybunału Konstytucyjnego' [Interpretive Rulings of the Constitutional Tribunal], *PiP* 11 (1999), pp. 28–34; J. Trzciński, 'Orzeczenia interpretacyjne Trybunału Konstytucyjnego' [Interpretive Rulings of the Constitutional Tribunal], *PiP* 1 (2002), pp. 3–14; P. Czarny, 'Trybunał Konstytucyjny a wykładnia ustaw w zgodzie z Konstytucją' [The Constitutional Tribunal and Interpretation of Statutes in Accordance with the Constitution] in S. Wronkowska (ed.), *Polska kultura prawna a proces integracji europejskiej*, Kraków 2005, pp. 67ff.; L. Gardocki, 'Problem tak zwanych wyroków interpretacyjnych Trybunału Konstytucyjnego' [The Problem of the So-called Interpretive Rulings of the Constitutional Tribunal]

deal here with principal controversies. By virtue of an example, let us consider one of the jurisprudential disputes in Poland. According to the Poznań school of legal theory (Zygmunt Ziembiński, Maciej Zieliński, Sławomira Wronkowska), legal norms are valid during the *vacatio legis* (in the descriptive sense that they belong to a legal system).[19] This approach contrasts with the views of Wiesław Lang[20] and Jerzy Wróblewski,[21] who argue that the legal norms are valid (in the normative sense, in that we ought to follow them or apply them) only from the moment of their entry into force; that is, after the *vacatio legis* period. The existence of such controversies, still subject to intense polemics,[22] proves that adopting the Polish legal culture as the sole perspective for the clarificative analysis would also result in the necessity of considering some dogmatic issues—which turns out to be inappropriate because we are going to clarify the intension of the juristic (and not the legal) concept of the validity of statutory law. The concept should be universal in reference to the continental system-type of statutory law, and not particular and related only to the Polish, German, French or Spanish legal culture.

Before we begin the clarificative analysis, it is necessary to undertake some minor arbitrary selection of the concepts that will be examined in terms of their suitability for clarification of the intension of the juristic concept of the validity of statutory law. Taking into account the modelling nature of clarification, these will be: the concept of the membership of norms in the legal system (Sect. 7.2), the concept of the application of norms (Sect. 7.3), the concept of the applicability of norms (Sect. 7.4), and—considered jointly—the concepts of the observance and efficacy of norms (Sect. 7.5). We shall also briefly examine some of the combinations of concepts used in jurisprudential conceptions of legal validity (Sect. 7.6), with particular emphasis on the concepts applied in Robert Alexy's nonpositivist definition of law (Sect. 7.6.1). This choice is mainly justified by the role of these concepts in the development of philosophical and jurisprudential

---

in P. Winczorek (ed.), *Teoria i praktyka wykładni prawa*, *op. cit.*, pp. 153–157; A. Mączyński, 'O tak zwanych wyrokach interpretacyjnych Trybunału Konstytucyjnego' [On the So-called Interpretive Rulings of the Constitutional Tribunal] in P. Winczorek (ed.), *ibidem*, pp. 159–173.

[19] *Cf. e.g.*, Z. Ziembiński, *Logiczne podstawy prawoznawstwa*, *op. cit.*, p. 146; S. Wronkowska, M. Zieliński, *Problemy i zasady techniki redagowania tekstów prawnych* [The Problems and Principles of the Technique of Editing Legal Texts], Warszawa 1993, pp. 73–74; W. Patryas, 'Kilka uwag na marginesie koncepcji obowiązywania norm' [Some Comments on the Conception of the Validity of Norms] in J. Brzeziński *et al.* (eds.), *Odwaga filozofowania. Leszkowi Nowakowi w darze*, Poznań 2002, p. 268; S. Wronkowska, *Podstawowe pojęcia prawa i prawoznawstwa*, *op. cit.*, pp. 51–52.

[20] *See* W. Lang, 'Obowiązywanie normy prawnej w czasie w świetle logiki norm', *op. cit.*, p. 52 and *Obowiązywanie prawa*, *op. cit.*, p. 231.

[21] *See* J. Wróblewski, *Sądowe stosowanie prawa*, *op. cit.*, pp. 96ff. [English version, pp. 77ff.] and 'Obowiązywanie systemowe i granice dogmatycznego podejścia do systemu prawa', *op. cit.*, p. 27.

[22] *Cf.* P. Grabowski, M. Hermann, 'O normatywnym charakterze przepisów o wejściu w życie', *op. cit.*, pp. 71ff. and G. Wierczyński, '"Obowiązywanie" a "wejście w życie" – uwagi polemiczne' ["Validity" and "Entry into Force" – Polemical Remarks], *PiP* 2 (2007), pp. 108–112. The solution to the problem that constitutes the subject of this controversy will be proposed *infra* at pp. 304ff.

reflection concerning legal validity. Our choice is also substantiated from a methodological perspective, for all model conceptions of the validity of law analysed in this chapter have, at least *prima facie*,[23] a descriptive character in such a basic sense that they ascribe a descriptive, rather than a normative meaning to the expressions concerning the legal validity of statutory norms. It should be added that the normative conceptions of legal validity will by no means be left aside, yet due to the consistency of reasoning, they will be examined in the next chapter, in which we will present, inter alia, linguistic and logical characteristics of pragmatically varied statements concerning the validity of legal norms.[24]

7.1.1 On the Relativisation of the Expression: "A norm is valid"

We are well aware that the methodological considerations—characteristic of the theory of law—are often not very interesting or important, especially for legal dogmatists and practicing lawyers. Nevertheless, we feel obliged to discuss some specific methodological issues, in order to avoid unnecessary problems and errors that can easily be made when attempting a proper clarificative analysis. The first issue concerns the possible relativisation of the expression "A norm is valid", which is to constitute the *definiendum* of the definition of the juristic concept of the validity of statutory law that we are looking for. We shall point out that in the Polish jurisprudential studies, devoted to the meaning of this expression, its simple (related to a single aspect of validity)[25] or complex relativisation[26] is quite often assumed, while occasionally the scholars analyse its basic (non-relativised) form.[27] Let us therefore briefly examine the four most commonly encountered ways of relativising the expression on the validity of the norm; namely, semantic

[23] *Cf.* Chap. 8, pp. 370–400.

[24] *See* Chap. 8, pp. 413ff.

[25] A systemic relativisation is adopted by K. Opałek, 'The Problem of the Validity of Law', *op. cit.*, p. 18, as well as by J. Wróblewski, 'Obowiązywanie systemowe i granice dogmatycznego podejścia do systemu prawa', *op. cit.*, pp. 27ff. A temporal relativisation is adopted by L. Nowak, 'Cztery koncepcje obowiązywania prawa', *op. cit.*, pp. 99ff. Finally, a semantic relativisation can be found in Z. Ziembiński, *Logiczne podstawy prawoznawstwa*, *op. cit.*, p. 83 and M. Zieliński, *Wykładnia prawa*, *op. cit.*, pp. 20–21.

[26] A complex temporal–systemic–legislative relativisation is adopted by L. Nowak, *Interpretacja prawnicza*, *op. cit.*, p. 63, whereas a complex conceptual–systemic–spatiotemporal relativisation is used by J. Wróblewski, *Sądowe stosowanie prawa*, *op. cit.*, p. 101 [English version, pp. 81–83].

[27] *See e.g.*, W. Lang, *Obowiązywanie prawa*, *op. cit.*, pp. 111ff.; J. Jakubowski, 'Pojęcie obowiązywania, realizacji i skuteczności normy prawnej oraz podstawy ich rozróżniania' [The Concept of Validity, Realization and Effectiveness of Legal Norms and the Basis of their Distinction] in S. Ehrlich (ed.), *Studia z teorii prawa*, Warszawa 1965, p. 324; J. Woleński, 'Truth and Legal Validity', *ARSP* Bh. 25 (1985), p. 206; Z. Ziembiński, M. Zieliński, *Dyrektywy i sposób ich wypowiadania*, *op. cit.*, pp. 36–37; J. Mikołajewicz, *Prawo intertemporalne*, *op. cit.*, p. 24.

(conceptual), systemic, territorial and temporal relativisation. The discussion to follow will also indirectly take into account the requirements of good explication,[28] since it is obvious that the choice of a proper *explicandum* is of utmost importance in the context of meeting these requirements. Accordingly, the decisive criterion for acceptance of the specific relativisation (or rejection of it) will be for the sake of exactness (precision), simplicity, and the scientific as well as practical fruitfulness of the proposed clarification.

When we relativise the expression on the validity of the norm by means of indicating its specific meaning (e.g., thetic, behavioural and axiological—as the scholars from the Poznań school do[29]) or—indirectly—by means of differentiating various concepts of the validity of norms (e.g., systemic, factual and axiological validity—as adopted by Jerzy Wróblewski,[30] or the sociological, ethical and juridical concept of validity—as assumed by Ralf Dreier and Robert Alexy[31]), then from a jurisprudential point of view it is impossible to find any fault in the process. Nonetheless, in the context of our clarificative intentions, relativisation of this kind cannot be accepted, since it would be counter-productive. Firstly, such differentiations have a reporting or, alternatively, reconstructive character and our primary intent is neither a description nor a reconstruction of the conceptions of legal validity that exist in the literature and/or in legal practice, but the formulation of an accurate regulative definition of the concept of legal validity. Secondly, an important purpose of clarification is to eliminate the ambiguity (semantic indeterminacy) of the analysed concept. We intend to make a clarification of the juristic concept of the validity of statutory law, and not of an ethical, axiological or sociological concept of validity. In this regard, adopting any semantic or conceptual relativisation of the expression "A norm is valid" would only conserve the existing indeterminacy, in no way contributing to its elimination and—in principle—even making such elimination impossible.

It can be seen from the earlier observations and findings[32] that the practical validity discourse and dogmatic deliberations are dominated by an internal[33] and, therefore, intrasystemic grasp of legal validity, relativised to a particular legal system. Does it implicate that the expression about the validity of a norm should include such a relativisation? Several reasons weigh against such a consequence. First of all, let us note that such relativisation would determine *a priori* that the juristic concept of the validity of statutory law is inherently connected with the

---

[28] *Cf.* Chap. 6, pp. 220–221.

[29] *See e.g.*, Z. Ziembiński, *Logiczne podstawy prawoznawstwa*, *op. cit.*, p. 83; M. Zieliński, *Wykładnia prawa*, *op. cit.*, pp. 20–21; S. Wronkowska, *Podstawowe pojęcia prawa i prawoznawstwa*, *op. cit.*, pp. 16ff.

[30] *See e.g.*, J. Wróblewski, *Sądowe stosowanie prawa*, *op. cit.*, pp. 96ff. [English version, pp. 77ff.].

[31] *See e.g.*, R. Dreier, 'Recht und Moral', *op. cit.*, p. 194ff. and R. Alexy, *Begriff und Geltung des Rechts*, *op. cit.*, pp. 139ff. [English version, pp. 85ff.].

[32] *Cf.* Chap. 6, pp. 239–240.

[33] In the terminology of A. Peczenik and A. Aarnio – *cf.* Chap. 5, note 56 at p. 206.

concept of the legal system. Leaving aside even the question that the concept of the legal system itself is highly ambiguous,[34] and thus the adoption of systemic relativisation could negatively affect the practical usefulness and simplicity of the result of clarification, the acceptance of a systemic relativisation seems premature. We shall indeed attempt to discuss the question of the connection between the validity of norms and the legal system in the next section, in which we will examine the fruitfulness of the concept of the membership in the legal system for the clarification of the juristic concept of the validity of statutory law.[35] Moreover, what also weighs against systemic relativisation is the next argument of a purely logical character. If we adopted such relativisation of the expression which, after all, constitutes the *definiendum* of the regulative definition sought by us, and afterwards it would appear that even in the *definiens* we would have to use the concept of the legal system, then, for example, such a definition as: "A norm of statutory law is valid in a given legal system if, and only if it belongs to this system (or if it is applied, applicable, observed and/or effective in this system)", could be considered by critics to be partly burdened with the error of *idem per idem*, or—alternatively—of *ignotum per ignotum*. Without commenting on the question of whether such objections are indeed legitimate, we do not accept a systemic relativisation. We assume that the potential interconnection between the validity of statutory norms and the legal system shall be grasped by us in the *definiens*. In doing so, we will provide complete protection against the objections listed above, which is quite crucial to our position.

It would not pose a great difficulty for us to avoid considering other relativisations of the expression of the validity of a norm (i.e., territorial and temporal relativisations). Adopting the concept of a legal norm developed in the Poznań school of legal theory would allow us to ignore these issues since, according to this conception, the elements that concern the territorial and temporal—to use the terminology of Hans Kelsen[36]—sphere of validity, constitute substantive components of a legal norm. As Zygmunt Ziembiński wrote:

> If speaking about the validity of a certain norm in one or another meaning of this phrase, we will omit the term "in a given place and at given time", then it is due to the fact that the determination of the place and time in which the behaviour indicated in the norm should be undertaken by its addressees, is in principle included in the content of the norm.[37]

---

[34] For more *see infra*, the argument A–II at pp. 280ff.

[35] *See infra*, pp. 271ff.

[36] *Cf.* H. Kelsen, *General Theory of Law and State*, *op. cit.*, pp. 42ff., 207ff., 218ff., 233ff., *Reine Rechtslehre*, 2nd ed., *op. cit.*, pp. 12ff. [English version, pp. 12ff.], and *Allgemeine Theorie der Normen*, *op. cit.*, pp. 116ff.

[37] Z. Ziembiński, *Wstęp do aksjologii dla prawników*, *op. cit.*, p. 120., pp. 57ff. It is worth noting that the standpoint of the Poznań school of legal theory is identical in its essence with the views of Kelsen, who repeatedly pointed out that "[t]he sphere of validity (*Geltungsbereich*) of a norm is an element of its content" – *see idem*, *Reine Rechtslehre*, 2nd ed., *op. cit.*, p. 12 [English version, p. 13] and *Allgemeine Theorie der Normen*, *op. cit.*, p. 117. For more details *see* R. Thienel, 'Der

Yet, we will not use this option, for the importance of problems related to these two spheres of the validity of norms, particularly in the practical discourse of validity, weighs in favour of at least a brief discussion of the possibility of the territorial or temporal relativisation of the expression about a norm's validity. Thus, in this discussion we will briefly suspend the semantic conception of legal norm, at the same time recognising the theoretical admissibility of the territorial or temporal indexation of the validity of legal norms.

As for territorial relativisation, the issue seems quite simple. Without a doubt, we should consider it absurd to subject the meaning of the expression of the validity of a legal norm to the territory that this validity concerns (at least in reference to the systems of statutory law adopted for the purposes of our clarificative analysis). What seems utterly irrelevant for the analysis and clarification of the intension of the juristic concept of legal validity are otherwise evident facts that the norms of the Polish law are valid in Poland, the norms of the German law—in Germany, the norms of the French law—in France, whilst Argentinean legal norms are valid in Argentina. Nonetheless, the only fact worth noticing, yet only indirectly related to the territorial sphere of validity, is a purely linguistic aspect of the concept of legal validity—the legal and juristic terminology concerning validity issues—used in different natural languages that constitute the linguistic basis for specific legal cultures.[38] Yet, it suggests including relativisation in a specific, linguistically determined legal culture, not necessarily coinciding with the territory of the State (e.g., the French language is also basic for the French-speaking part of the legal culture of Belgium, Switzerland, Canada and some African countries). What is more, the application of territorial relativisation would trigger the need to examine a number of specific jurisprudential problems that, in the context of the significant differences between the various national systems of statutory law, does not seem possible due to the model-based and highly simplified nature of our clarificative analysis. Thus, bearing in mind the indicated reasons, we resign from the territorial relativisation of the expression on the validity of a norm.

The issue that still remains to be discussed is the possibility of the temporal relativisation of the expression of the validity of a norm. This relativisation is naturally irrelevant in terms of whether we talk about the meaning of the expression of the validity of norms in 1970, 1990 or 2005, for our analyses relate to the present time and are not of a diachronic character. Undoubtedly, we do not question the fact that over the years, the legal cultures of individual countries are subject to evolution, also regarding the understanding of legal validity, but it is not this aspect that lawyers have in mind when they invoke temporal relativisation. This kind of relativisation may be justified primarily for the sake of the practice of lawmaking and law application, in which we are confronted with a number of important specific validity problems related to the temporal sphere of legal validity. The

zeitliche Geltungsbereich von Normen im Lichte der Legistik' in H. Mayer (ed.), *Staatsrecht in Theorie und Praxis*, *op. cit.*, pp. 712ff.

[38] Due to its importance, this issue will be discussed separately *infra* at pp. 267–271.

issues of intertemporal law or retroactivity constitute the outstanding examples in this context. The theory of law also often undertakes temporal issues, reflected both in general[39] and in more specific monographs.[40] Yet, does it imply that in the *definiendum* of the sought definition we should temporally relativise the expression of the validity of legal norms? Taking into account the objectives and requirements of good clarification, we assume that it is not advisable and we provide three arguments to support this thesis.

The first argument concerns the ambiguity of a temporally relativised expression of the validity of a norm. This ambiguity stems from the fact that legal theorists try, in various ways, to solve the problems related to the temporal and, in particular, intertemporal aspect of the validity and application of law by proposing a number of conceptual constructs or forms of temporal indexation of norms. Let us examine three instructive examples. For the purpose of analysing the relationship between time and the validity of law, Eugenio Bulygin introduced the distinction between the "external time" (*tiempo externo*) and "internal time" (*tiempo interno*) of a legal norm.[41] Roughly speaking, the external time of a norm stands for the period during which a norm exists in the legal system—that is, belongs to it—while the internal time of a norm stands for the period in which a given norm is applicable.[42] Additionally, for the purposes of the analysis of intertemporal regulations, Åke Frändberg proposed a far-reaching distinction of three understandings of the phenomenon of being in force, related to legal rules.[43] Using the basic formula: "Rule *r* has x-force (is in x-force) during t_1–t_n", he distinguishes between an unspecified force, a case-related force and a decision-related force for legal rules. Finally, Ota Weinberger, when examining the issues of subsumption in relation to previously derogated norms, points to two possible temporal indexations of legal norms.[44] When using a symbolic form of a legal norm "p > !q" (which reads: "If *p*, then *q* ought to be"), Weinberger identifies two forms of depicting the validity of a norm in

[39] *See e.g.*, G. Winkler, *Zeit und Recht. Kritische Anmerkungen zur Zeitgebundenheit des Rechts und des Rechtsdenkens*, Wien/New York 1995.

[40] *See e.g.*, J. Aguiló Regla, *Sobre la Derogación*, *op. cit.*; J. Mikołajewicz, *Prawo intertemporalne*, *op. cit.*; W. Wróbel, *Zmiana normatywna i zasady intertemporalne w prawie karnym* [Normative Change and the Intertemporal Principles of Penal Law], Kraków 2003; T. Pietrzykowski, *Wsteczne działanie prawa i jego zakaz* [Retroactive Action of Law and Its Prohibition], Kraków 2004.

[41] *See* E. Bulygin, 'Time and Validity' in A.A. Martino (ed.), *Deontic Logic, Computational Linguistic and Legal Information Systems*, Vol. II, Amsterdam/New York/Oxford 1982, pp. 67ff. [a modified Spanish version: 'Tiempo y validez', trans. E. Bulygin, in C.E. Alchourrón, E. Bulygin, *Análisis lógico y Derecho*, Madrid 1991, pp. 198ff.], 'Algunas consideraciones sobre los sistemas jurídicos', *DOXA* 9 (1991), p. 266, and 'Normensystem und Rechtsordnung' in H. Mayer (ed.), *Staatsrecht in Theorie und Praxis*, *op. cit.*, pp. 100ff.

[42] On Bulygin's concept of legal validity understood as the applicability (*aplicabilidad*) of norms *see infra*, pp. 321–334.

[43] Å. Frändberg, 'Retroactivity, Simulactivity, Infraactivity', *ARSP* Bh. 64 (1995), pp. 59ff.

[44] O. Weinberger, 'Ontologie, Hermeneutik und der Begriff des geltenden Rechts', *op. cit.*, pp. 119–120.

a period t_0–t_i: "$(p > !q)_{t0-ti}$" or "$p_{t0-ti} > !q$". In his view, both indexations are basically equivalent, with the only difference being that the latter allows for a further application of a previously derogated norm.

These examples illustrate the ambiguity of the temporal relativisation of the expression "A norm is valid". Yet, this ambiguity undergoes a further multiplication when one considers that in traditional jurisprudence, as rightly pointed out by Zygmunt Ziembiński, the term "legal norm" does not stand for "one simple norm of conduct", but for "a set of two functionally interrelated norms of conduct"[45]; that is, the sanctioned norms (*normy sankcjonowane*) and the sanctioning norms (*normy sankcjonujące*). These two types of norms are directed to different addressees because the former type of norms stipulates the legal obligations of the ordinary addressees of norms—legal subjects—whereas the latter specifies the sanctions that ought to be imposed by law-applying authorities if the addressee of a sanctioned norm does not comply with it.[46] By their very nature, these norms are not necessarily valid in an identical period of time.[47] When we take into account this distinction, it turns out that adopting the temporal relativisation of the expression of the validity of a legal norm must lead—in my opinion—to the subsequent indeterminacy of the concept of the validity of statutory law, which, in fact, prevents an effective implementation of clarification. Different "times" (Bulygin), "forces" (Frändberg) or "indices of the time of validity" (Weinberger) of the two basic kinds of norms (Lande, Ziembiński) mean that the adoption of the temporal relativisation of the expression of the validity entails the necessity of a difficult and probably very hard choice: of either carrying out a separate clarificative analysis in respect to each of the various ways of understanding the temporal relativisation of the expressions on the validity of the sanctioned and sanctioning norms or of making a *de facto* arbitrary decision (at least at the current stage of research[48]) to grant

[45] Z. Ziembiński, *Teoria prawa* [Theory of Law], Warszawa/Poznań 1973, p. 29. *Cf. idem*, *Problemy podstawowe prawoznawstwa*, *op. cit.*, pp. 159–160.

[46] The distinction between the sanctioned norms and the sanctioning norms was introduced to the conceptual apparatus of the Polish theory of law by J. Lande, 'Nauka o normie prawnej' [The Science on the Legal Norm], *AUMCS-G: Ius* III (1956), pp. 7ff. For more details *see* M. Zieliński, *Wykładnia prawa*, *op. cit.*, pp. 32ff. According to an opinion expressed by H. Kelsen, *General Theory of Law and State*, *op. cit.*, pp. 63ff., the author who can be considered as a forerunner in distinguishing these two types of norms is J. Austin, who introduced the distinction of primary and secondary rights and duties.

[47] Let us consider the frequently encountered intertemporal regulation, known under its jurisprudential term of the "infraactivity" (Å. Frändberg) or "ultraactivity" (E. Bulygin) of law; namely, a construction – well known to legal dogmatists and practicing lawyers – of the prolonged activity of a former law, according to which, since the entry into force of new legal regulations, the sanctioned norms of the former law are no longer valid, but (to simplify a little) the sanctioning norms that are correlated with them are still applicable. Similar effects are sometimes triggered by applying the principle of *lex mitior agit* in criminal law – *see e.g.*, W. Wróbel, *Zmiana normatywna i zasady intertemporalne w prawie karnym, op. cit.* pp. 473ff.

[48] Such a decision will naturally have to be made in the course of our clarificative analysis, since without it, it is impossible to eliminate the ambiguity of the concept of the validity of statutory law.

priority to a particular way of understanding this expression (e.g., as an internal time of a sanctioned norm or as a case-related force of a sanctioning norm). The choice of the first option is not recommended, primarily due to the requirement of the simplicity and practical usefulness of clarification, since the introduction of complex semantic distinctions would clearly undermine its intuitive understanding, especially by practicing lawyers. The second option, in turn, is likely to lead to the inadequacy of further clarificative analyses, whose outcome could rightly be questioned due to the omission of one or another way of understanding the temporal indexation of the validity of either category of norms (sanctioned or sanctioning ones). This reasoning shows that it is more appropriate to dispense with the temporal relativisation of the expression of the validity of norms in the *definiendum* of the definition of the juristic concept of their validity and to undertake the clarification in such a way that the fixed meaning of this expression can be applied in relation to all the reasonable[49] ways of understanding the temporal relativisation of the validity of legal norms, both sanctioned and sanctioning ones.

The second argument has a conditional character. Although we have already resigned from the systemic relativisation of the expression of the validity of legal norms, we have also made a reservation that a potential conceptual connection between the validity of norms and the legal system shall be taken into consideration in the *definiens* of the developed definition of the juristic concept of the validity of statutory law.[50] If this is to be the case, it can be said in advance that, when relating the validity of norms to the legal system, lawyers usually have in mind a concrete system of law, which is valid *hic et nunc*.[51] Yet, sometimes, especially in dogmatic or historical considerations, the concept of the legal system is relativised to a certain, short or even very long period of time (e.g., let us take into account an intuitive temporal meaning of the expression "the American legal system"). The modern theory of law has elaborated a conceptual apparatus that allows grasping and dealing with such ambiguity, which is unfortunately typical in practical legal discourse. As proposed by Joseph Raz, we can distinguish between the momentary

---

Nonetheless, it will not be arbitrary, but justified by a proposed regulative definition of this concept – *cf.* Chap. 8, pp. 433ff.

[49] This reservation is necessary because some of them shall prove to be inadequate in the course of the analysis.

[50] *Cf. supra*, pp. 253–254.

[51] We refer here to the concept of a concrete legal system, in the sense proposed by J. Wróblewski, who defined it as "a set of norms that are valid in a given state at a given time" – *see* W. Lang, J. Wróblewski, S. Zawadzki, *Teoria państwa i prawa* [The Theory of State and Law], 3rd ed., Warszawa 1986, p. 390. *See* also U. Neumann, *Wahrheit im Recht. Zu Problematik und Legitimität einer fragwürdigen Denkform*, Baden-Baden 2004, p. 30, who emphasises that "Aussagen über die Rechtslage beziehen sich jeweils auf das *hic et nunc* geltende Rechtssystem", and a similar standpoint as expressed by P.O. Ekelöf, 'The Expression "Valid Rule": A Study in Legal Terminology', *SSL* 15 (1971), p. 61. What is more, according to Bulygin's view, a specific temporal relativisation of the legal system is even necessary: "If a legal system is to be conceived of as a set (e.g., a set of norms), then it must be a momentary system" – *idem*, 'Time and Validity', *op. cit.*, p. 66 [Spanish version, p. 197].

and non-momentary; that is, continuous legal systems.[52] A momentary system of law "contains all the laws of a system valid at a certain moment",[53] whereas a non-momentary system, also called an intertemporal legal system,[54] consists of norms that are valid at a certain period of time. An even more precise terminology—which nevertheless is considerably distinct from the everyday linguistic intuition of practicing lawyers—has been suggested by Carlos Alchourrón and Eugenio Bulygin. Argentine philosophers distinguish between the concept of legal system and the concept of legal order.[55] The former refers to a set of norms that are valid—which belong to the system of law relativised to a certain point in time—while the legal order is understood as an ongoing sequence of respective, consecutive momentary legal systems. An obvious conclusion can be drawn from the presented distinctions: with the possible adoption of a conceptual interconnection between the validity of norms with the legal system, the introduction of a temporal relativisation of the expression of the validity of a norm is unnecessary because the very legal system, in the context of which we talk about the validity of a legal norm or we resolve the various validity problems, is (or at least should be) always relativised to a particular moment or period of time.

The third argument, closely connected with the adopted methodology of research,[56] is more general. Let us recall that the analysis of the expression "A norm is valid" serves the purpose of clarifying the intension of the juristic concept of the validity of statutory law. Therefore, the question that we are now trying to answer is: What does it mean that a legal norm is valid? This question is evidently different from the question: When is a legal norm valid? The latter is directly related to the issue of the extension of the juristic concept of validity, since the decision as to whether the legal norm is valid is principally relativised in time. Let us note that an attempt to find the answer to the latter question, made without temporal relativisation, is doomed to failure.[57] Only by adopting the extreme natural law standpoint[58] that recognises the timeless, eternal validity of certain

---

[52] J. Raz, *The Concept of a Legal System*, *op. cit.*, pp. 34–35, 170–171, 189ff. and 'The Identity of Legal Systems' in *idem*, *The Authority of Law*, *op. cit.*, p. 81.

[53] J. Raz, *The Concept of a Legal System*, *op. cit.*, p. 34.

[54] Such terminology is used by Å. Frändberg, 'Retroactivity, Simulactivity, Infraactivity', *op. cit.*, p. 56.

[55] *See* C.E. Alchourrón, E. Bulygin, 'Sobre el concepto de orden jurídico', in *iidem*, *Análisis lógico y Derecho*, *op. cit.*, p. 397; E. Bulygin, 'Time and Validity', *op. cit.*, pp. 66–67 [Spanish version, p. 197], 'Algunas consideraciones sobre los sistemas jurídicos', *op. cit.*, pp. 259–260, and 'Normensystem und Rechtsordnung', *op. cit.*, pp. 97ff.

[56] *Cf.* Chap. 5, pp. 218–221.

[57] A question that is not relativised in time is too general, and its indeterminacy prevents a correct answer. For example, if we ask whether the norm prohibiting abortion due to social reasons is valid in Poland, then in order to provide the correct answer, it must be referred to a specific moment or period of time; for example, before and after 1993. The simple answer: "yes" or "no", is not possible.

[58] Adopting a more moderate conception of natural law with a variable content means that such a temporal question also becomes meaningless.

norms, might one be tempted to resolve such an issue, thus leaving aside the temporal aspect. What seems crucial from the standpoint of modern legal practice as well as of legal dogmatics are temporally relativised decisions on legal validity, because it is the law which is valid at a particular time or at a specified time period that constitutes the normative basis of judicial decisions and the primary object of jurisprudential, in particular dogmatic, analyses. Thus, it seems clear that the question about when the legal norm is valid is a question specific to the problem of the extension of the concept of legal validity. Therefore, the adoption of the temporal relativisation of the expression of the validity of a norm can lead to a confusion of the issues of the intension and extension of the clarified concept. The analyses of the nonpositivist conception of law have already demonstrated[59] that simultaneous attempts at definitional solutions to these two problems significantly hinder, if not prevent the clarification of the meaning of the concept of the validity of statutory law.

We believe that the presented arguments justify the need to abandon temporal relativisation of the expression of the validity of a legal norm, which naturally does not mean that we intend to completely ignore the problems associated with the temporal sphere of the validity of norms. While clarifying the intension of the juristic concept of the validity of statutory law, we shall often make use of the arguments related to the temporal aspect of the validity of law, while the argumentative juristic presumption of the validity of norms, developed in order to solve the problem of extension, as well as the discussion on the manner of argumentation in terms of legal validity—will be largely based on considering the impact of the temporal aspect of the changes in positive law on the validity of the statutory law norms.

7.1.2 The Nature, Linguistic Stylisation and Structure of the Definition of the Juristic Concept of the Validity of Statutory Law

It has already been set that the definition of the juristic concept of the validity of statutory law will be a regulative definition, aimed at eliminating the semantic indeterminacy of the defined concept.[60] The adoption of the method of the paraphrase in the clarificative analysis determines that it will also constitute a contextual definition—the intension of the juristic concept of legal validity shall be investigated by analysing the expression, a part of which is the predicate "is valid"—therefore, it will only constitute part of the *definiendum* of the constructed definition.

Nonetheless, what still remains to be considered are a number of specific methodological issues related to the nature, linguistic stylisation and construction

[59] *Cf.* Chap. 5, pp. 200–201.

[60] *Cf.* Chap. 6, p. 221.

of the definition, which will be the result of clarificative analysis. Due to the large margin of freedom provided by the contemporary theory of definition,[61] the following observations will primarily serve to explain our intentions and manner of proceeding, rather than to completely justify the choice of a particular type and form of definition. We deem this explanation to be necessary due to the requirements of legibility and the explicitness of clarification. It is also intended to facilitate the criticism of the conception of the validity of norms—as developed in this study—for those who recognise the proposed conception as incorrect.

It seems that the most important aspect here concerns the explanation of the nature of definition, which we will propose. The intention to regulate the meaning of the juristic concept of the validity of statutory law implies that it has to be a nominal definition. However, the method applied in formulating this definition—largely consisting of verifying the correctness of the existing conceptions of legal validity—is not only based on linguistic and logical arguments, but also on taking into account a number of the phenomena occurring in the course of lawmaking and law application, weighing in favour of attributing to it the character of a real definition, by means of which we shall attempt, at least partly, to explain the essence of legal validity. An additional, albeit not very strong argument for the real character of the discussed definition, results from taking into account the fact that it will be the definition of one of the basic juristic concepts, expressed in juristic language.[62] In this sense, it will be an intralinguistic definition, which is often considered as an important feature of real definitions. The above reasons favour the approval of the standpoint of Kazimierz Ajdukiewicz—already pointed out[63]—according to which the extensions of real and nominal definitions overlap. It is worth noting that this is not an isolated methodological position—another prominent representative of the Lvov–Warsaw school of analytical philosophy, Tadeusz Czeżowski, regarded the controversy concerning the functions of the definitions ("the characteristics of things, or attributing meaning to terms?") to be illusory. He wrote:

> It is indeed impossible to separate the two tasks: whoever wants to characterize the thing, has to name it, and when characterizing the thing he attributes meaning to its name; whereas whoever wants to attribute meaning to the name, at the same time describes things, to which it refers.[64]

[61] This freedom is primarily due to terminological disorder, which characterises the modern theory of definition – *see e.g.*, J. Kotarbińska, 'Definicja', *op. cit.*, pp. 128ff. and W. Patryas, *Definiowanie pojęć prawnych, op. cit.*, pp. 128–129.

[62] For more *see* Chap. 8 at pp. 360ff.

[63] The standpoint of Ajdukiewicz, which is referred to herein, is most succinctly expressed in the following quote, taken from *Logika pragmatyczna*, *op. cit.*, p. 62: "Many utterances which are nominal definitions of certain words on the basis of a specific vocabulary, at the same time present real definitions of certain objects, and vice versa. Nevertheless, the concepts of nominal and real definition are two concepts with different content". *Cf.* Chap. 5, p. 196.

[64] T. Czeżowski, 'O tradycyjnych rozróżnieniach wśród definicji' [On the Traditional Distinctions among Definitions] in *idem*, *Filozofia na rozdrożu (Analizy metodologiczne)*, Warszawa 1965, p. 19.

Bearing in mind the non-orthodox character of the position adopted hereinafter, we recognise, therefore, that the question of whether it is a nominal or real definition is an improper question—it is primarily essential to ask what functions the legal definitions created by us should fulfil. It is our intention that the definition we propose in the next chapter is a definition that first and foremost meets the function of the nominal definition, but also—to a lesser extent—the function of a real definition, which is a quite often used procedure in the legal sciences.[65] Let us add that the functionally "mixed" nature of the definition that we intend to present as a result of clarificative analysis entails the necessity of formulating it in a substantive (intralinguistic) stylisation, since the use of semantic or lexical stylisation, typical only for the nominal metalinguistic definitions, would exclude its real character.

We should, for a moment, focus on the issue of the structure of the discussed definition. The basic problem is to decide whether it should be constructed as a so-called normal definition (in which *definiendum* and *definiens* are in a relation of equivalence) or not. The fact that weighs in favour of another structure for the definition is that explication does not necessarily have to lead to a normal definition, but—what is even more often the case—a clarification of *explicatum* has the form of a partial definition or a definition by postulates.[66] This is because the relationship between *explicatum* and *explicandum* "is not subject to synonymy",[67] as explication is primarily a modification of the sense of an explicated concept. It should nevertheless be borne in mind that we intend to undertake clarification rather than explication, and we only use the subsidiary requirements of good explication, which—somewhat paradoxically—justify the formulation of the normal definition of the juristic concept of the validity of statutory law. Indeed, taking into consideration the requirements of exactness (precision) and scientific as well as practical fruitfulness, we consider it obvious that the concept of the validity of statutory law, which—according to the adopted assumption[68]—is constructed as a classifying concept (rather than as a typological concept or metric concept that are gradable) and which should be defined on the basis of a normal definition. The reasons are as follows. In the institutional validity discourse[69]—for instance, taking place during the proceedings before a public or constitutional court—it must be decidedly resolved whether a given legal norm is valid or not. A similar resolution is necessary for dogmatic analyses to be accurate. Accordingly, the use of the partial definition, which, by its nature, only partially clarifies the meaning of the juristic

[65] *See* W. Patryas, *Definiowanie pojęć prawnych*, *op. cit.*, pp. 18ff., 103ff.

[66] For more details *see* T. Pawłowski, *Tworzenie pojęć w naukach humanistycznych*, *op. cit.*, p. 101.

[67] J. Woleński, *Z zagadnień analitycznej filozofii prawa*, *op. cit.*, p. 45. *Cf.* Chap. 6, the quotation of the similar opinion of W.V.O. Quine, corresponding to note 17 at p. 220.

[68] *Cf.* Introduction, note 11 at pp. 4–5, with the corresponding text.

[69] This concept seems to be intuitively understandable, therefore at this point I leave it unexplained. For more *see* Chap. 9 at pp. 476–478.

concept of legal validity, would significantly hinder and limit the application of the developed conception. Therefore, providing a normal definition in order to resolve the problem of intension is considered a necessary—though naturally not sufficient—precondition to a subsequent attempt to resolve the problem of the extension of the analysed concept. A possibly[70] unambiguous and explicit definition of the meaning of the juristic concept of the validity of statutory law is a remedy for the errors of equivocation and verbal disputes, which often take place in juristic discourse on validity, in which the problem of extension is solved.

The second problem that relates to the construction of the definition of the concept of validity concerns the formulation of its *definiendum*. This concerns whether or not we should use the variable *N* in formulating the expression concerning the validity of a norm, giving it the following form: "A norm *N* of statutory law is valid". We believe that this is inappropriate. Firstly because the introduction of such a variable could give rise to associations that blur the methodological distinction—adopted for the sake of the clarificative analysis—between the issues of intension and extension of the analysed concept. The inclusion of a variable *N* to the *definiendum* would, in fact, suggest that the definition of the juristic concept of the validity of statutory law does not intend to elucidate the meaning of this concept, but to characterise and determine the set of valid norms, and thus to determine the extension of this name. Due to the fact that at this point our reasoning differs—as we believe—from the common intuition of jurists, we are forced to precisely explain the adopted position. We think that there are three main reasons for the rejection of the probably still commonly adopted thesis according to which the definitional determination of the meaning of the concept of the validity of statutory law is identical, or at least it entails the determination of the set of valid norms.[71] The first reason has a logico-linguistic character and it is based on a quite

---

[70] It should be emphasised that these possibilities are limited, inter alia, as a result of the open texture of legal and juristic concepts.

[71] This thesis naturally constitutes a certain juristic concretisation of a general argument provided by G. Frege, developed later in the semantics of A. Church, according to which *Sinn* (intension) determines *Bedeutung* (extension), and so the latter constitutes the function of the former. The frames of our study are too modest to enter deeper into the philosophical and logical problems of the relations between intension and extension, yet it should be noted that they constitute the subject of an on-going controversy, at least since the seventies of the last century, when Saul Kripke and Hilary Putnam presented a serious argument against Frege's thesis – *see* S. Kripke, *Naming and Necessity*, Oxford 1980, pp. 59ff.; H. Putnam, 'Is Semantics Possible?' in S.P. Schwartz (ed.), *Naming, Necessity, and Natural Kinds*, Ithaca/London 1977, pp. 102–118, 'Meaning and Reference' in *ibidem*, pp. 119–132, and 'The Meaning of "Meaning"' in *idem*, *Mind, Language and Reality. Philosophical Papers*, Vol. 2, Cambridge/London/New York/New Rochelle/Melbourne/Sydney 1975, pp. 215–271. The best known in this respect is Putnam's "Twin Earth Argument", which will be presented in a condensed form, to show what this criticism can concern (for more details *see* 'Meaning and Reference', *op. cit.*, pp. 120ff. and 'The Meaning of "Meaning"', *op. cit.*, pp. 223ff.). Let us imagine a twin planet, which is different from the Earth in that water does not have the chemical composition of H_2O, but a very complex chemical composition manifested in the formula *XYZ*. On *Twin Earth*, the oceans, seas and lakes are composed of *XYZ*, *XYZ* rain is raining there etc. The inhabitants of both planets operate with the same concept of water, but they

trivial observation that the expression concerning the validity of a norm (regardless of whether it contains a variable *N* or not) is an expression, while the term "valid norm" is a term. A second reason, related to the preceding one, has an ontological character. As already noted,[72] the concepts of legal validity and of valid law cannot be treated as synonymous, because—as aptly pointed out by Zygmunt Ziembiński and Maciej Zieliński—identifying a "valid norm" with a "validity of norm" leaves aside "the difference of ontological category, which these two terms refer to".[73] In fact, it is difficult to question the thesis that in legal discourse, the first of these terms serves primarily to identify a set (in a distributive sense) of valid legal norms—that is, a certain abstract object (for each set in a distributive sense, as opposed to the sets in the collective sense, is an abstract entity)—while the second refers to a certain phenomenon occurring in legal reality (or speaking more generally—existing in social reality). The third reason is of a pragmatic (functional) character: undoubtedly, different activities are undertaken by the researchers and/or by lawyers seeking to determine the intension of the juristic concept of legal validity, and different activities are undertaken by those who seek to establish its extension, even if they are not aware of it. The former indeed undertake the activities of an intellectual character, whereas the latter—even on account of the evaluative nature of a number of criteria of validity and the incompleteness of the rules of recognition, which are typical for the modern systems of statutory law[74]—are forced to take decisions based on the principles of practical rather than theoretical rationality in solving specific problems of validity.

Notwithstanding the foregoing reasons, leaving aside the variable *N* in *definiendum* probably helps to avoid the objection of incompleteness (inadequacy in an ordinary sense[75]) of the proposed definition. Such an objection was raised by Wojciech Patryas in relation to the modified definition of the validity of norms proposed by Leszek Nowak.[76] Generalising this complaint, it should be noted that any definition of validity, in the *definiendum* of which there is variable *N*, limits the set of norms in relation to which it can be applied. Patryas argues that the application of a variable means that in its place one can only substitute the norms formulated in the language of a lower degree than the language which the definition

refer it to different objects, and thus the meaning (intension), contrary to Frege's thesis, does not determine the reference (extension). Putnam's argument has been accessibly discussed and analysed by A. Stroll, *Twentieth-Century Analytic Philosophy*, *op. cit.*, pp. 230ff. Let us add that the way we proceed in the course of clarificative analysis seems to confirm the correctness of the criticism of Frege's thesis – some of the arguments used below assume the determinateness of the extension of the juristic concept of the validity of statutory law, treating it as an auxiliary indicator of the correctness of further model definitions of its intension.

[72] *Cf.* Chap. 5, p. 207.

[73] Z. Ziembiński, M. Zieliński, *Uzasadnianie twierdzeń, ocen i norm w prawoznawstwie*, *op. cit.*, p. 72.

[74] For more *see infra*, pp. 277–279.

[75] There cannot be a case of inadequacy in the logical sense, because this feature concerns only reporting (analytical) definitions, while the definition proposed by us will be regulative.

[76] *See* W. Patryas, 'Kilka uwag na marginesie koncepcji obowiązywania norm', *op. cit.*, p. 266.

of validity belongs to, and therefore any so-called metanorms cannot aspire to be valid because they are, in fact, formulated in the language of the same degree as the definition. Leaving aside doubts about the cognitive value of distinguishing degrees of language in the analyses of legal and juristic language,[77] let us note that Patryas' argument even implies the need to abandon the variable *N* in the analysed expression of the validity of a norm of statutory law. Otherwise, some of the legal norms would be left outside the scope of this definition. Thus, considering the arguments presented above, the expression that is subject to a clarificative analysis and, consequently, constitutes the *definiendum* of the proposed definition, would read as follows: "A norm of statutory law is valid".

The third and last problem connected with the construction of the definition of the juristic concept of the validity of statutory law is associated with the choice of an appropriate definitional connective (copula). The fact that we consider the construction of a normal definition, in which the *definiendum* consists of a certain expression, rather than a name, as well as the fact that we are going to use an intralinguistic stylisation, exclude a number of possibilities of expressing definitional equivalence (typically symbolised by $=_{\mathrm{df}}$ or $\stackrel{\mathrm{df}}{=}$) by means of such definitional connectives as: "is", "is the same as", "should be understood as", "means that" and many others. It seems that the best way to express the connective of a normal definition, suitable to the wording of *definiendum* and meeting other requirements, should be the conjunction "if, and only if", which is, *nota bene*, quite often used in the definitions of legal validity.[78] Applying this definitional connective in order to express the relation between the *definiendum* and *definiens*, it has to be emphasised—to avoid possible misunderstandings and over-interpretation—that it will stand for synonymy (semantic sameness), but not for the logical equivalence of the parts of the definition. We do not question that the connective "if, and only if" is used in the standard language of logic to express the relation of logical equivalence between propositions ($p \equiv q$), yet in the case of the definition of the juristic concept of the validity of law, such an interpretation is unacceptable for two reasons. Firstly, the concept of logical equivalence refers to propositions (sentences that do possess a truth-value): only they can be replaced *salva veritate*. Meanwhile, the expression that constitutes the *definiendum*, apart from its semantic incompleteness, is in many cases of its use in juristic language, deprived of logical value.[79] Secondly, even if

[77] These doubts result mainly from the fact that nowadays no one seems to deny that both in legal language as well as in juristic language there are expressions that belong to different levels of language – *see e.g.*, T. Gizbert-Studnicki, 'Język prawny a język prawniczy' [Legal Language and Juristic Language], *ZNUJ PP* 55 (1972), pp. 226ff.

[78] *See e.g.*, R. Guastini, 'Invalidity', *RJ* 7 (1994), p. 224; J. Raz, *Practical Reason and Norms*, *op. cit.*, p. 127; A. Marmor, 'Exclusive Legal Positivism', *op. cit.*, p. 106; L. Nowak, 'Cztery koncepcje obowiązywania prawa', *op. cit.*, p. 99; J. Woleński, *Z zagadnień analitycznej filozofii prawa*, *op. cit.*, pp. 103ff.; J. Wróblewski, 'Obowiązywanie systemowe i granice dogmatycznego podejścia do systemu prawa', *op. cit.*, p. 27.

[79] *Cf.* the arguments provided in Chap. 8 at pp. 380ff. At this point, we cannot address the issue of the truth-value of *definiens*, because we are still seeking it.

we do not accept the first argument, conservatively assuming that the sentences on the validity of legal norms do have truth-value, then the definition proposed below cannot be treated as establishing the logical equivalence between *definiendum* and *definiens*. In order to substantiate this thesis, we shall use the conception of equivalence derived from Rudolf Carnap.[80] This author provides the definition of material equivalence, consisting of the compliance of the extension; namely, the logical value of equivalent sentences, which reads:

> Two sentences are equivalent if and only if both have the same truth-value, that is to say, both are true or both are false.[81]

Yet, Carnap's definition of logical equivalence that results from mere semantic rules (*L-equivalence*) and relates to the identity of intension (and therefore, synonymy that is of interest to us) of equivalent sentences, takes the following form:

> Sentence Z_1 remains in relation of L-equivalence with the sentence Z_2 if and only if the sentence stating the relation of ordinary equivalence between these sentences is L-true.[82]

It can be inferred from the above definitions that in order to determine the equivalence of two sentences (expressions)—regardless of whether we have in mind the equivalence of the extension, or the equivalence of the intension resulting from the semantic rules of a certain language—it is necessary that the sentence stating such equivalence is in some way (extensionally or semantically) true. Having regard to the prosaic fact that the regulative definitions are deprived of logical value (and the definition that we propose shall indeed constitute an example of a regulative definition[83]), we cannot interpret them as expressing the equivalence between *definiendum* and *definiens* in any of the meanings indicated by Carnap.

---

[80] R. Carnap, *Meaning and Necessity*, *op. cit*., pp. 6ff. The choice of this conception is naturally justified by the fact that Carnap defines equivalence by means of the conceptual distinction between extension and intension.

[81] *Ibidem*, p. 6.

[82] *Ibidem*, p. 11. I quote the reading of Carnap's symbolic definition, provided by E. Grodziński, *Językoznawcy i logicy o synonimach i synonimii. Studium z pogranicza dwóch nauk* [Linguists and Logicians on Synonyms and Synonymy. Study on the Border of Two Sciences], Wrocław/Warszawa/Kraków/Gdańsk/Łódź 1985, p. 57.

[83] One can object that this argument does not take into consideration the mixed nature of the forthcoming definition – since its role, although to a lesser extent, is to fulfil the function of a real definition of legal validity, and thus it can be assessed from the perspective of its logical value. We believe that such an objection can nonetheless be left aside because when speaking of the truth of the real definition, we, as a rule, refer to its correspondence with reality. Meanwhile, in the case of the definition of a juristic concept of the validity of statutory law, we should, in advance, exclude the use of the classical corresponding theory of truth. This definition, in fact, applies to the reality composed of institutional facts, rather than of *facta bruta*; that is, co-created by the researchers (interpreters) of law. Moreover, as rightly indicated by S. Grzybowski, 'Przepisy prawa oraz normy prawne a zagadnienie wykładni i konstrukcji' [Legal Provisions and Legal Norms vis-à-vis the Problem of Interpretation and Construction], *KSP* XXI (1988), p. 11: "Legal constructions (and all legal concepts) [...] may prove useful or useless, and it is the only factor that determines their value; whereas the consideration of whether they are 'true' or 'false', would not make any sense".

Fortunately, it does not cause significant difficulties in undertaking clarificative analysis, because the synonymy constitutes a symmetric relation—as noted by Jerzy Kmita, the synonymy of two sentences takes place if, and only if the theses of a certain language consist of two conditionals: "If Z_1, then Z_2" and "If Z_2 then Z_1".[84] We shall repeatedly take into account this feature of synonymy when considering the pros and cons of the following conceptions of legal validity and the model definitions that express them.

Summing up this brief and probably controversial methodological discussion, we assume that the definition of the juristic concept of the validity of statutory law will be regulative, contextual, mixed (i.e., meeting at the same time the functions of both a nominal and real definition), normal and formulated in substantive (intralinguistic) stylisation. Additionally, it will begin with the words: "A norm of statutory law is valid if, and only if".

7.1.3 Linguistic and Terminological Remarks

A renowned *Encyclopaedic Dictionary of the Theory and Sociology of Law* (*Dictionnaire d'Éguilles*) reports[85] that the French term "validité" corresponds to the German "Geltung", English "validity", Spanish "validez" and Italian "validità". It would seem that in these languages, undoubtedly very crucial for the development of the European and American theory and philosophy of law, there is an established terminology, which easily allows for finding synonyms for the English term "validity". Nothing could be more wrong! It should be realised that this terminology is not plain and unambiguous and what is more, there is reasonable doubt as to whether these terms are actually adequate counterparts of the concept of validity in other languages. Therefore, we consider it necessary to pay attention to the issue of the meaning and translatability of juristic terminology concerning validity. The analysis of these issues is all the more important since it will reduce the possibility of misunderstandings and disputes arising from a merely approximate translatability (semantic equivalence) of the terms by which the different languages refer to the validity of law.[86]

---

[84] J. Kmita, *Wykłady z logiki i metodologii nauk* [Lectures on Logic and Methodology of Science], Warszawa 1977, p. 61. The symbol "Z" stands for the sentence (*zdanie* in Polish).

[85] A.-J. Arnaud (ed.), *Dictionnaire Encyclopédique de Théorie et de Sociologie du Droit*, Paris/Bruxelles 1988, p. 452.

[86] Such disagreements and disputes arising from them are not uncommon – the most famous one was a dispute over the concept of the validity of law between H.L.A. Hart and A. Ross, largely caused by the very inaccurate translation of the terminology used by Ross in *Om Ret og Retfærdidighed* from Danish to English in *On Law and Justice*, *op. cit.* This misunderstanding is explained by Ross in 'Validity and the Conflict between Legal Positivism and Natural Law', *op. cit.*, pp. 76–78, 84ff. and *Directives and Norms*, London/New York 1968, pp. 104–105. *Cf.* a funny comment made in this context by E. Bulygin, 'An Antinomy in Kelsen's Pure Theory

By limiting our necessarily rudimentary considerations to the most important issues in the context of further clarificative analyses, we must first point out a certain crucial difference that could have an impact on the linguistic intuitions of the authors who take up the issue of legal validity. It occurs between the languages in which the terms of our interest derive from Latin, originating from the verb *valeo* (meaning, among other things, "to have the power, value, significance"[87]) and from the adjective *validus* ("valid", "in force", "strong"[88]), and the languages in which this is not the case. In the former (namely in French, English, Spanish, Italian and many other languages), nouns and adjectives derived from Latin sources simultaneously fulfil two semantic functions in the legal discourse.[89] For example, the English noun "validity" and the adjective "valid" are used not only in the phrases "validity of law", "legal validity" and "valid law", but above all, to express the validity or legitimacy of legal actions (acts) and/or their consequences (such as in the expressions: "validity of a legal act/transaction", "validity of proofs", "validity of a will", "valid passport" or "valid contract"[90]). On the other hand, in the languages in which the terminology of interest to us is not derived from Latin, we deal with the two terms. For example, in Polish juristic language we use "obowiązywanie" and "ważność", in German a pair of terms "Geltung" and "Gültigkeit",[91] in Danish the pair of adjectives "gœldende" and "gyldig",[92] and in Swedish, the adjectives "gällande" and "giltig".[93] Nonetheless, in contrast to the

of Law', *RJ* 3 (1990), note 2 at p. 37, on the superiority of the Spanish translation over the English one.

[87] K. Kumaniecki, *Słownik łacińsko-polski* [Latin–Polish Dictionary], 16th ed., Warszawa 1986, p. 524.

[88] M. Kuryłowicz, *Słownik terminów, zwrotów i sentencji prawniczych łacińskich oraz pochodzenia łacińskiego* [Dictionary of Latin Terms, Phrases and Dictums, and of Latin Origin], 3rd ed., Kraków 2002, p. 94.

[89] *See e.g.*, J. Pieńkos, M. Szepietowski, K. Poklewski-Koziełł, *Słownik prawniczy polsko-francuski* [Polish–French Dictionary of Law], Wrocław/Warszawa/Kraków/Gdańsk/Łódź 1987, pp. 52, 63, 154, 238 and E. Muszalski, A. Makowski, W. Szyszkowski, M. Szerer, S. Sołtysiński, *Słownik prawniczy polsko-angielski* [Polish–English Dictionary of Law], Wrocław/Warszawa/Kraków/Gdańsk/Łódź 1986, pp. 52, 82, 133, 210.

[90] The examples have been taken from J. Pieńkos, *Polsko-angielski słownik prawniczy* [Polish–English Dictionary of Law], Kraków 2002, p. 416.

[91] *See e.g.*, K.M. Pospieszalski, B. Ostaszewski, J. Rezler, O. Wandmayer, *Słownik prawniczy polsko-niemiecki* [Polish–German Dictionary of Law], Wrocław/Warszawa/Kraków/Gdańsk/Łódź 1987, pp. 69, 107, 174, 241, 259. When referring to German terminology, it merits quoting N. Hoerster's standpoint under which, "den deutschen Begriffen 'geltend' und 'gültig' im Englischen nur *ein* wörtliches Äquivalent, nämlich 'valid' gegenübersteht" – *idem*, '"Wirksamkeit", "Geltung" und "Gültigkeit" von Normen. Ein empiristischer Definitionsvorschlag' in D. Mayer-Maly, P.M. Simons (eds.), *Das Naturrechtsdenken heute und morgen*, *op. cit.*, p. 595.

[92] *Cf.* the fragments of A. Ross' works indicated *supra*, note 86 at p. 267.

[93] *See* P.O. Ekelöf, 'The Expression "Valid Rule": A Study in Legal Terminology', *op. cit.*, pp. 61–62 and G.H. von Wright, *Norm and Action*, *op. cit.*, p. 195.

Polish juristic language, in these languages the said terms are often treated as synonyms.[94]

The indicated features of juristic terminology in different languages elucidate not only semantic differences—often subtle and difficult to understand for speakers who are not native speakers or fluent in the languages in question—but they also explain the problems associated with the translation of juristic terms into another language. When using the example of the English terminology, it is worth noting in this context that the Polish professional translators of the works by Hart, Raz or Dworkin[95] sometimes translate the English terms "validity", "legal validity" or "valid law" by means of the term "obowiązywanie" (and its derivatives), but more often they use the term "ważność" (and its derivatives), which should not come as a surprise. Yet, this is not the end of the terminological problems, because the most serious difference between the discussed foreign-language terminologies and the Polish terminology results from etymology and the semantic specificity of the Polish terms "obowiązywanie", "obowiązujący" and the like. Although the clarificative analysis of the intension of the juristic concept of the validity of statutory law will not be based on the etymological method, but on the conceptual one,[96] the assumption-free character of the undertaken analysis—as adopted in the Introduction—indeed does not imply ignoring the ordinary (non-professional) meaning of the concepts under consideration, especially since—as already indicated[97]—in the course of clarificative analysis we try not to interfere in lawyers' linguistic intuitions, which, after all, are necessarily based on the semantics of a given natural language. We shall therefore take a closer look at the etymology and ordinary, everyday meaning of the word "obowiązywanie" in the Polish language, also because this was the original language of this study.

Let us start with the obvious remark, which nonetheless surprisingly rarely appears in the Polish studies devoted to the validity of law,[98] that the term "obowiązywanie" (and the like), even if it is not semantically derived from the term "obowiązek" (English: "duty" or "obligation"), at least is directly associated with it. This observation is confirmed by a review of renowned Polish language dictionaries, which define (in the first place) the meaning of the verb

[94] *See* P.O. Ekelöf, *ibidem*, p. 62 and N. Hoerster, '"Wirksamkeit", "Geltung" und "Gültigkeit" von Normen', *op. cit.*, pp. 585–586.

[95] *Cf.* the Polish translations of works of H.L.A. Hart: *Pojęcie prawa* [The Concept of Law], trans. J. Woleński, Warszawa 1998 and *Eseje z filozofii prawa* [Essays in Jurisprudence and Philosophy], trans. J. Woleński, Warszawa 2001; of J. Raz: *Autorytet prawa* [The Authority of Law], trans. P. Maciejko, Warszawa 2000; and of R. Dworkin: *Biorąc prawa poważnie* [Taking Rights Seriously], trans. T. Kozłowski, Warszawa 1998 and *Imperium prawa* [Law's Empire], trans. J. Winczorek, Warszawa 2006.

[96] For more on this method *see* Chap. 8 at pp. 365–367.

[97] *Cf.* Chap. 6, p. 222.

[98] Among a dozen jurisprudential studies by Polish authors, referred to in the process of writing this book, this relation has been mentioned only by W. Lang – *cf.* W. Lang, J. Wróblewski, S. Zawadzki, *Teoria państwa i prawa*, *op. cit.*, p. 385.

"obowiązywać" by means of the expression "to be someone's duty".[99] The relation between "obowiązywanie" and "obowiązek" is also supported by etymological analysis. As presented by Wieslaw Boryś in the latest *Etymological Dictionary of the Polish Language*, the Polish verb "obowiązywać" (up to the sixteenth century "obowięzywać") derives from the Old-Church Slavonic word "obęzati" (Polish: "obwiązać"; English: "to tie"), whereas the archaic form "obowiązać"—used in the Polish language since the fifteenth century (preserved in the contemporary Polish language in the past participle form of "obowiązany") means the same as "to extend the duty, to impose obligation, to oblige".[100] Thus, we see that in the Polish language there is a semantic relationship between "obowiązywanie" and "obowiązek", which is not found in the foreign terminologies under discussion.[101] This fact implies that one cannot exclude the significant role that the semantic relationship, which occurs in the Polish language between "obowiązywanie" (English: "validity") and its derivatives and "obowiązek" (English: "duty" or "obligation"), played in formulating the conception of validity presented in this book.[102]

The fact that the choice of language in which a given concept of the validity of law is presented determines how it is linguistically expressed, can be most easily demonstrated by referring to one fragment of the theory of legal validity developed by Wiesław Lang. As already noted,[103] the author of *Obowiązywanie prawa* [The Validity of Law] argues that the legal norms are valid (in terms of the duty of their application) only from the date of their entry into force. In his later study, devoted to the validity of law, which was written in English, Lang already used two concepts of legal validity—the first, referred to by the terms "legal validity" and "valid law", and the second—manifested by the terms "law in force" and "binding law".[104] As can be easily seen, the second term directly corresponds to the Polish "obowiązywanie" (in terms of Lang), which is demonstrated in the following passage of his reflections:

---

[99] *Cf.* W. Doroszewski, *Słownik języka polskiego* [Polish Language Dictionary], Vol. V, Warszawa 1963, p. 512; M. Szymczak (ed.), *Słownik języka polskiego* [Polish Language Dictionary], 7th ed., Vol. II, Warszawa 1992, p. 419; H. Zgółkowa (ed.), *Praktyczny słownik współczesnej polszczyzny* [Practical Dictionary of Modern Polish], Vol. 25, Poznań 2000, p. 60.

[100] W. Boryś, *Słownik etymologiczny języka polskiego* [Etymological Dictionary of the Polish Language], Kraków 2005, pp. 374–375.

[101] *Cf.* A.-J. Arnaud (ed.), *Dictionnaire Encyclopédique de Théorie et de Sociologie du Droit*, *op. cit.*, p. 450, where we find the following counterparts of the Polish word "obowiązek": "obligation" (French), "Verpflichtung" and "Schuld" (German), "duty" and "obligation" (English), "obligación" (Spanish), and "obbligazione" (Italian).

[102] The need to consider this relation results explicitly from the fact that we aim at formulating a regulative definition, which is different from an entirely arbitrary synthetic definition of the juristic concept of the validity of statutory law. We should not, therefore, completely disregard the current usage of the term "validity" (and its derivative terms) in juristic and legal discourse.

[103] *Cf. supra*, p. 251.

[104] *Cf.* W. Lang, 'A Concept of the Validity of Law', *op. cit.*, pp. 87ff. On the nonsynonymy of the terms "valid" and "binding" *see* N. MacCormick, *Institutions of Law*, *op. cit.*, pp. 160ff.

> The law in force binding its addressees is by definition a valid law. But a valid [law] doesn't have to be necessarily the law in force. Usually there is an interval between the time of the official publication of a statute and the time of its coming into force (*vacatio legis*). During this period such a law is valid but not binding.[105]

It is hoped that the above linguistic and terminological observations, in spite of their general nature, will not only reduce possible confusion in understanding the following conception of legal validity, but they will also allow for a better comprehension of the arguments—applied in the clarificative analysis—that refer to the linguistic intuitions of the Polish natural language and, in particular, of the Polish juristic language. What should be stressed is that these intuitions, out of necessity, cannot be left aside in our deliberations.

7.2 Legal Validity Understood as the Membership of Norms in a Legal System

After the necessary methodological explanations, we can now proceed to the clarificative analysis. In the present section, we will examine the theoretical correctness and practical usefulness of the first model definition of the validity, having the following form: "A norm of statutory law is valid if, and only if it belongs to the legal system" (hereinafter labelled "D_1"). Since this definition expresses the conception of the validity of law that is probably most commonly adopted by lawyers (and especially by the supporters of legal positivism), its analysis requires particular diligence. The question is whether this definition can be regarded as such a clarification of the intension of the juristic concept of the validity of statutory law that is both accurate and meets the established goals and requirements of it.[106]

7.2.1 Introductory Remarks

The introduction to the analysis of the definition D_1 will consist of discussing two observations that are worth emphasising already at this stage of consideration. Firstly, given the intuitions of lawyers (and especially those of practitioners) and their typical manner of using the concept of legal validity in juristic language, it is obvious that jurists often perceive the validity of legal norms in two different ways—either "looking into the past" or "looking into the future".[107] On the one

[105] W. Lang, *ibidem*, p. 88.

[106] *Cf.* Chap. 6, pp. 222–226.

[107] It can be expressed in a non-metaphoric way that lawyers often treat the sentence on the validity of a norm either as a conclusion of the reasoning concerning validity or as a condition for the reasoning concerning the application of law. Let us add that in the following argument we shall use (with a slight

hand, the basic intuition of lawyers is to understand validity in the following form, so to speak, as a criterial validity implication: If the criteria $c_1, c_2, \ldots, c_n$ are met (sometimes only the criteria of competence and procedure, and sometimes also the substantive and systemic ones[108]), then the norm of statutory law is valid. In this case, lawyers "look into the past" by examining whether the norm has become a valid norm. As a rule, they typically understand the validity of the norm in terms of its membership in the legal system that is being analysed in this section. On the other hand, one of the basic intuitions of jurists consists of understanding validity in the manner associated with the applicative dimension of law. When applying a legal norm, lawyers assume (or better: we assume) the following relation (this time having the form of a consequential validity implication): If the norm of a statutory law is valid, then it entails legal consequences $lc_1, lc_2, \ldots, lc_n$ (provided in this norm). In this case, lawyers undoubtedly "look into the future", determining the legal consequences of certain facts of the case. Both these intuitions are indeed correct and the problem that we would like to point out is that when these two intuitions (expressed by means of "validity implications") are combined and taken together, then the concept of the validity of law can be deprived of any meaning. Using the terminology introduced by Alf Ross,[109] the term "validity of law" will become *tû-tû* and, therefore, talking about the validity will be a "pure nonsense".[110] When we apply, by analogy, the method of analysing legal concepts—as provided by Ross—we will obtain the following reasoning:

1. If the criteria $c_1, c_2, \ldots, c_n$ are met, then the norm of statutory law is valid;
2. If the norm of statutory law is valid, then it entails legal consequences $lc_1, lc_2, \ldots, lc_n$.

One does not need logical expertise to see that the so-formulated "validity implications", when eliminating the so-called medium term used in them, can serve as the basis for inferring the following conditional:

3. If the criteria $c_1, c_2, \ldots, c_n$ are met, then it entails legal consequences $lc_1, lc_2, \ldots, lc_n$.

Accordingly, "validity of law" becomes *tû-tû*, since replacing the phrase "the norm of statutory law is valid" with "*tû-tû*" (or any other word), does not change anything in the assessment of the formal logical correctness of the above

modification, which is indicated *infra*, note 111 at p. 273) the two formulations of "validity implications" (my term) provided by J.-R. Sieckmann, *Regelmodelle und Prinzipienmodelle des Rechtssystems*, *op. cit.*, p. 98, who recognises them as the subject matter of the theory of legal validity.

[108] *Cf.* the second introductory remark, concerning two meanings of the concepts of legal validity and the membership of norms at p. 274.

[109] *See* A. Ross, 'Tû-Tû', *HLR* 70 (1957), pp. 812–825. The word (term?) *tû-tû*, the meaning of which is – somewhat paradoxically – the lack of any meaning (in the sense of intension as well as extension), was applied by Ross in this famous paper to analyse the concept of ownership. For more about the concepts that have the function of "legal middle terms" in legal reasoning *see* L. Lindahl, 'Deduction and Justification in the Law. The Role of Legal Terms and Concepts', *RJ* 17 (2004), pp. 182–202.

[110] A. Ross, *ibidem*, p. 812.

reasoning.[111] It should be added that if someone wants to rebut this reasoning by means of referring to the concept of metalanguage (e.g., claiming that we can "transfer" the concept of the validity of law to a metalinguistic level), it would be in vain, because it would not change anything—the concept of validity would still be subject to elimination by means of applying the above procedure. Indeed, it cannot be denied that—as rightly observed by Manuel Atienza and Juan Ruiz Manero—the term "validity" is used in legal discourse as a "bridge predicate".[112] In spite of the fact that particularly the "criterial validity implication" refers primarily to the problem of extension, two conclusions—crucial also in the context of clarifying the intension of the analysed concept—can be inferred from the argument from *tû-tû* just presented. Firstly, we need to distinguish between understanding "validity" as a predicate that determines the outcome of a successful lawmaking act from understanding "validity" as an expression of the conclusion (of a reductive character) inferred from the fact that a given norm brings about legal consequences.[113] Secondly, we have to make every effort in the course of clarificative analysis so that the proposed definition of the juristic concept of the validity of statutory law did not make this concept superfluous, and thus that it does not require any definition,[114] because it would be a peculiarly circular *reductio ad absurdum* of our inquiries.

---

[111] One might try to refute such an objection by claiming that in the antecedent of the criterial validity implication we should not speak of undefined, non-specified "criteria" but of "the criteria of validity" and that by doing so the concept of legal validity is, at least indirectly, preserved. Such a defence, nonetheless, would be absurd, because determining the criteria for the concept that is *tû-tû*, resembles searching for criteria that allow identifying, for example, "an educated dwarf". More seriously, it seems indisputable from a practical standpoint, as well as from jurisprudential one, that the criteria referred to in the first implication constitute the criteria for a membership of a norm in a legal system. However, it is disputable whether these are also the criteria of validity – a positive answer to this question indeed presupposes the correctness of the definition D_1, which is being analysed now. Therefore, let us note that probably the easiest way to rebut the *tû-tû* objection is to refute the thesis of the equivalence of validity and the membership expressed in D_1, which – by the way – will soon be done. Without adopting this equivalence, Ross-like reasoning becomes erroneous, because then we deal with four terms (the *quaternio terminorum* fallacy): in the first validity implication, its consequent is expressed by the phrase: "the norm of statutory law belongs to the legal system", which differs from the antecedent of the second implication: "the norm of statutory law is valid".

[112] M. Atienza, J. Ruiz Manero, 'Preliminaries for a Theory of Legal Validity', a paper presented at the seminar of the Executive Committee of *IVR* "Validity and Applicability", in Paris, 30 June–1 July 2002, typescript, p. 1. *Cf. idem*, 'Seis acotaciones preliminares para una teoría de la validez jurídica', DOXA 26 (2003), p. 720. It should be added that Atienza and Ruiz Manero, unlike in the argument presented above, determine – in relation to Kelsen's conception of validity – the antecedent of the first and the consequent of the second validity implication, which is of no great importance at this point. The important factor is that they stress the differences in the intensions, which we shall often refer to in further analysis. On the function of the link, fulfilled in the legal discourse by the predicate "is valid" *see* L. Lindahl, 'Norms, Meaning Postulates, and Legal Predicates', *op. cit.*, pp. 304ff.

[113] For more details *see* Chap. 8 at pp. 441ff.

[114] Let us note that we do not need any definition of validity in order to carry out the above reasoning, expressed in sentences 1–3.

This concept must have some meaning, which cannot be eliminated in the way described by Ross. As we shall see, this last hint will soon lead us to very unorthodox conclusions, which justify the fact that jurisprudential correctness is questioned in both the above-mentioned implications.

The second introductory remark relates to the distinction between the two senses of the validity of legal rules, proposed by Riccardo Guastini.[115] The Italian legal theorist notes that in the dogmatic literature (and probably also at least in some jurisprudential literature), we can identify the use of two different concepts of validity. The first is the validity in the strong sense, defined as follows:

> [A] rule is valid within a certain legal system if, and only if, it meets *all* the criteria of identification which are peculiar to that legal system.

Secondly, we talk about validity in a weak sense, which consists of the fact that:

> [A] rule is valid if, and only if, it exists, i.e., it was actually created, laid down, namely formulated and enacted by a rule-creating authority.

This distinction may seem trivial, yet it has undeniable research value. Nonetheless, it cannot be directly applied in our analyses because that would stand for admitting that the validity of law comes down to the fact that norms fulfil certain criteria (all or some); namely, admitting their "strong" or "weak" membership in the legal system. This acceptance would be premature because, after all, we are in the process of considering this possibility, as expressed in the form of D_1. For the sake of clarificative analysis, we shall, though, assume, by analogy to Guastini's distinction, a working distinction between two ways of understanding the concept of the membership of the norm in the legal system, which will soon prove to be very helpful. The membership in the strong sense would mean that a norm meets all the membership criteria proper for a given legal system. On the other hand, membership in a weak sense means that a norm meets competence-procedural criteria; namely (very generally speaking), it was set up in a procedurally correct way by the competent legislative authority, which includes its proper announcement (promulgation). This distinction seems to be intuitively understood, yet in order to avoid any possible misunderstanding, let us add that its adoption implies that the set of the norms, which belong in the strong sense to the legal system, is contained in the set of norms that belong in a weak sense to the legal system, and only in this second set there exist conflicts between norms which are legal rules.[116]

---

[115] *See* R. Guastini, 'Invalidity', *op. cit.*, pp. 224–225, which is also the source of the quotations in the text.

[116] Conflicts between norms, which are legal principles (in the sense stipulated by Dworkin or Alexy), occur naturally in both these sets because "the possibility of collision" constitutes an immanent feature of principles that cannot be eliminated by determining *in abstracto* their hierarchy – *cf.* (in Polish literature) T. Gizbert-Studnicki, 'Zasady i reguły prawne', *op. cit.*, pp. 19ff.; M. Zirk-Sadowski, 'Pozytywizm prawniczy a filozoficzna opozycja podmiotu i przedmiotu poznania', *op. cit.*, p. 90; M. Dybowski, 'Ronalda Dworkina koncepcja zasad prawa', *op. cit.*, p. 102ff.; M. Kordela, 'Możliwość konstruowania ogólnej teorii zasad prawa', *op. cit.*, pp. 13ff.

7.2.2 Four Arguments

The analysis of the accuracy of definition D_1 will begin with the argument (hereinafter labelled as A–I),[117] which refers to the concept of the membership of norms in the legal system and is directly related to the above distinction between its two meanings. The basis of this argument is the concept of *prima facie* duties (obligations) developed by David Ross.[118] According to his conception, a *prima facie* duty is by no means identical to the duty or obligation determined "at first sight",[119] but it stands for a *pro tanto* duty[120]; that is, a duty valid to a certain extent that is limited by other *prima facie* duties. Due to the fact that we only aim at articulating some intuitions connected with the concept of a *prima facie* duty (obligation), we can use here a typical, though circular definition. We shall, therefore, assume that a *prima facie* duty of conduct *C* consists of the situation in which there is a duty to do *C* unless there is another, more important and, therefore, overriding *prima facie* duty to refrain from conduct *C*.[121] As can be easily seen,

---

[117] The arguments formulated in the course of the clarificative analysis are marked with Roman numerals in order to facilitate cross references in the text. Moreover, only some of them can be synthetically and meaningfully named, which also weighs in favour of introducing a single symbolic way of marking them.

[118] *See* W.D. Ross, *The Right and the Good*, Oxford 1930, pp. 18ff. and *Foundations of Ethics*, Oxford 1939, pp. 83ff. It should be added that Ross explicitly accepted that this term stands for a certain situation in a specific way related to the duty, rather than for duty "strictly speaking" – *cf. The Right and the Good*, note 1 at p. 18 and pp. 20ff. This objection is not taken into account in the subsequent analysis and we treat *prima facie* duties as a kind of duty, because it seems necessary. Otherwise, it would be difficult to say that some *prima facie* duties or obligations prevail over others (like Ross himself wrote about – *see infra*, note 121, followed by a number of ethicists and philosophers of law), thus Ross' conception would become self-contradictory. For more on the arguments in favour for such an interpretation of this slightly ambiguous conception developed by Ross *see* J.R. Searle, '*Prima Facie* Obligations' in J. Raz (ed.), *Practical Reasoning*, Oxford 1978, pp. 82ff., 86. Searle calls for abandoning the use of the concept under discussion; however, it cannot be accepted because his argumentation is not convincing – *cf. e.g.*, J.-R. Sieckmann, *Regelmodelle und Prinzipienmodelle des Rechtssystems*, *op. cit.*, pp. 80ff. and B. Loewer, M. Belzer, '*Prima Facie* Obligation: Its Deconstruction and Reconstruction' in E. Lepore, R. Van Gulick (eds.), *John Searle and His Critics*, Cambridge (Mass.)/Oxford 1991, pp. 362ff.

[119] W.D. Ross, *The Right and the Good*, *op. cit.*, p. 20. *Cf. idem*, *Foundations of Ethics*, *op. cit.*, p. 85.

[120] S. Rachels, "A Defense of Two Optimistic Claims in Ethical Theory", *PhS* 112 (2003), note 37 at p. 25 and F. von Kutschera, *Grundlagen der Ethik*, *op. cit.*, p. 203. *See* also the categories of *pro tanto* rules and *pro tanto* law in A. Peczenik, *Scientia Juris*, *op. cit.*, pp. 13ff., 155ff., respectively.

[121] It is a slightly modified version of the definition provided by F. Snare, who treats it as a point of departure for his restorative analyses in his study 'The Definition of *Prima Facie* Duties', *PhQ* 24 (1974), p. 235. This definition refers to what was pointed out by Ross himself in his analysis of an example of a promise: "[I]t seems clear that there are cases in which some other *prima facie* duty overrides the *prima facie* duty of fulfilling a promise" – W.D. Ross, *The Right and the Good*, *op. cit.*, p. 46. There is also the possibility of not only purely formal, but also axiologically oriented definitions of *prima facie* duties. For example, M.B.E. Smith proposes the definition: "[A] person

such an interpretation of Ross' conception allows for regarding the latter as the anticipation of one of the fundamental elements of Dworkin's theory of principles because the legal principles that "lose" in a given procedure of weighing and balancing are not at the same time derogated—they remain fully valid in a legal system.[122]

The concept of *prima facie* duty (obligation) enables us to explain the first complication that results from accepting definition D_1 as the clarification of the intension of the juristic concept of the validity of statutory law. Let us note that if we assume that the validity of a norm stands for its membership—in a weak sense—in the legal system, then all the duties or obligations imposed by legal norms that are in such a way "valid" will constitute—in a legal sense—merely *prima facie* duties or obligations. Therefore, the conception of validity—grounded on membership being understood in such a weak way—should be, by analogy, at best named as "the conception of the juristic *prima facie* validity of norms of statutory law".[123] In effect, every legal duty or obligation, drawn from the norms of statutory law, which belong, in a weak sense, to the legal system, may be indeed limited or even overridden[124] by the duties or obligations arising from other norms that might turn out to be "winners" in a situation of the conflict of norms. It would seem that a natural and effective remedy for the indicated weakness of the conception of

S has a prima facie obligation to do an act *X* if, and only if, there is a moral reason for *S* to do *X* which is such that, unless he has a moral reason not to do *X* at least as strong as his reason to do *X*, *S*'s failure to do *X* is wrong"– *idem*, 'Is There a Prima Facie Obligation to Obey the Law?', *op. cit.*, p. 951.

[122] *Cf. supra*, the studies indicated in note 116 at p. 274. In *The Right and the Good*, *op. cit.*, p. 28, we can find the fragment of analyses, which explicitly justifies the thesis on the anticipatory nature of Ross' conception with respect to the modern theory of principles: "When we think ourselves justified in breaking, and indeed morally obliged to break, a promise in order to relieve someone's distress, we do not for a moment cease to recognise a *prima facie* duty to keep our promise".

[123] To be more precise, we mean here "the conception of the juristic *prima facie* validity of the norms of statutory law, which are the rules of conduct applied by means of subsumption". Indeed, in relation to other types of norms, in particular legal principles, the problem of *prima facie* validity does not appear at all. Of course, it is sometimes controversial whether a given legal principle is valid; nevertheless, any possible non-validity of principles does not stem from their *prima facie* nature, because all the principles – according to R. Dworkin's or R. Alexy's theories – are of such character. For more details *see* O. Weinberger, '*Prima Facie* Ought. A Logical and Methodological Enquiry', *RJ* 12 (1999), pp. 239ff. At this point we leave aside the fact that some authors, as *e.g.*, R. Alexy, *Theorie der Grundrechte*, *op. cit.*, pp. 87ff. [English version, pp. 57ff.], maintain that legal rules also have a *prima facie* character, albeit in a different sense than legal principles, which is associated with the inability to predict the introduction of new exceptions to the rule (*Ausnahmeklausel*) by decision-making organs in these branches of law in which it is not prohibited. A similar standpoint is expressed by A. Peczenik, 'The Non-Positivist Conception of Law', *op. cit.*, p. 323, who indicates, inter alia, the possibility of applying legal rules *contra legem*. However, such an interpretation of the *prima facie* character of legal rules expressly refers to the phenomenon of the defeasibility of legal rules, and only indirectly – and by a slightly illegitimate extension of the meaning of *prima facie* property – to W.D. Ross' conception.

[124] Naturally, in this case the norm of statutory law cannot typically be regarded (except in the case of applying the *lex specialis* rule for normative conflicts) even as *prima facie* valid, because it will simply become an invalid legal norm.

validity, based on the concept of membership in the legal system in a weak sense, is to apply the concept of the membership in a strong sense. In such a case, duties or obligations imposed by legal rules that belong, in a strong sense, to the legal system, will constitute definitive duties or obligations and, therefore, according to the expression most commonly used in the literature, these will be the so-called all things considered duties or obligations.[125] Nevertheless, several reasons suggest that it is not always possible to determine with utmost certainty whether a given norm belongs in a strong sense to the legal system and, thus, whether it meets all the criteria for membership.

As already noted, modern systems of law are "fuzzy".[126] According to the analyses of Jerzy Wróblewski and Aleksander Peczenik, the "fuzziness" of legal validity lies in the fact that the "fuzzy" rules of recognition formulate the criteria of the validity of norms (understood, by definition, as the membership in the legal system[127]) in such a way that in respect of some legal norms it can be undoubtedly determined whether they are valid in a given legal system. Yet, in relation to other norms, this question is insoluble even if we have full knowledge about the norm (the status of which we assess), about the rules of recognition and other relevant properties of a given legal system.[128] The reasons for the "fuzziness" of the system of interpreted law (LSIC)[129] that are of interest here are primarily the decisional lee-ways of legal interpretation,[130] and indirectly—because it is the system that constitutes an extension of the legal system consisting merely of the norms directly enacted by the legislator (LSLE)[131]—also the concerns about the consequences of the explicit derogation and the application of the rule of normative conflict *lex*

[125] This term has probably been coined by J. Raz, 'Reasons for Action, Decisions and Norms', *Mind* 84 (1975), p. 484, in particular note 3, *cf.* also *idem*, 'Introduction' in J. Raz (ed.), *Practical Reasoning*, *op. cit.*, pp. 11ff. and accepted and popularised by J.R. Searle, '*Prima Facie* Obligations', *op. cit.*, pp. 85ff. The list of authors who apply this term is too long to be presented here.

[126] *Cf.* Chap. 5, p. 204.

[127] A. Peczenik, J. Wróblewski, 'Fuzziness and Transformations: Towards Explaining Legal Reasoning', *op. cit.*, p. 27.

[128] *Ibidem*, p. 30. *See* also J. Wróblewski, 'Nieostrość systemu prawa', *op. cit.*, p. 20 and "Obowiązywanie systemowe i granice dogmatycznego podejścia do systemu prawa", *op. cit.*, p. 34, where Wróblewski writes about the "instability" of the rules of recognition.

[129] *Cf. supra*, Chap. 6, note 131 at p. 244, with the corresponding text.

[130] We see that Wróblewski and Peczenik implicitly accept the thesis about the derivative character of the decisions on validity with respect to the interpretive ones – *cf.* the argument from derivation presented in Chap. 6 at pp. 241–242. It is worth noting that adopting the thesis on the reversed order of these decisions does not change anything, for in such a case, the "fuzziness" of interpretive statements is transferred to the statements of validity that are included in the former, what has been demonstrated by T. Mazzarese, 'Semantic and Pragmatic Fuzziness of Legal Language', *AIC* XXIX–XXX (1996–1997), p. 52.

[131] *See* J. Wróblewski, 'Dilemmas of the Normativistic Concept of the Legal System', *RT* Bh. 5 (1984), p. 323 and *Sądowe stosowanie prawa*, *op. cit.*, pp. 96–97 [English version, pp. 77–78].

specialis derogat legi generali.[132] Zygmunt Ziembiński reaches similar conclusions when writing about the "fickleness" of the legal system as a result of a lack of sufficiently precise grounds to allow for the identification of norms belonging to it.[133] In his opinion, this phenomenon is caused mainly by the vagueness and ambiguity of the rules of validity that make up the normative conception of the sources of law of a specific legal system and by the impossibility of presenting the set of these rules "in [an] entirely formalized manner".[134] Therefore, the act of solving a problem of validity is not purely intellectual in nature, but out of necessity, it has a decisional character.[135] Kazimierz Opałek, in turn, draws attention to the blurred limits of valid law within the system, stressing the existence of a considerable margin of "uncertain law".[136]

Thus, we see that the concept—frequently used by lawyers in juristic discourse—of a membership in a strong sense is definitely of an idealising character, which should not come as a surprise, since it was already Hart who repeatedly stressed the open texture and possible incompleteness of the rule of recognition.[137] When using his theory of legal validity, we can easily identify two additional reasons why the application of the rule(s) of recognition of a given legal system must lead to its "fuzziness" and why we can rarely be certain of the resolution of a problem concerning the legal validity of norms.[138] Firstly, if we take into account Hart's soft positivism,[139] then it is obvious that the rule of recognition may include moral standards, which are inherently highly imprecise and vague criteria of the membership of norms in the legal system. Secondly, the rule of recognition, like

[132] *See* A. Peczenik, J. Wróblewski, 'Fuzziness and Transformations: Towards Explaining Legal Reasoning', *op. cit.*, pp. 30–31 and J. Wróblewski, 'Nieostrość systemu prawa', *op. cit.*, pp. 20–21, and the references cited therein. Let us add that T. Mazzarese, 'Semantic and Pragmatic Fuzziness of Legal Language', *op. cit.*, p. 53, completes this list of reasons with the phenomenon of legal gaps and the related application of reasoning by analogy, whereas Z. Pulka stresses the "evaluative character of the criteria of systemic validity" – *idem*, 'Czy nastąpił zmierzch pozytywistycznej koncepcji prawa i prawoznawstwa?', *op. cit.*, p. 173.

[133] *See* Z. Ziembiński, *Szkice z metodologii szczegółowych nauk prawnych*, *op. cit.*, pp. 13ff. and 'Desuetudo', *PiP* 11 (1994), p. 4.

[134] Z. Ziembiński, *Szkice z metodologii szczegółowych nauk prawnych*, *op. cit.*, p. 16.

[135] *Ibidem*, pp. 14–15. Similarly, A. Peczenik, 'On the Nature and Function of the *Grundnorm*', *op. cit.*, p. 291, who emphasises the creative character of the acts of identifying valid law.

[136] K. Opałek, J. Wróblewski, *Prawo. Metodologia, filozofia, teoria prawa*, *op. cit.*, p. 228.

[137] *See* H.L.A. Hart, *The Concept of Law*, *op. cit.*, pp. 106, 119–120, 144ff., his review of L.L. Fuller's book: *The Morality of Law*, *op. cit.*, p. 1293, and 'Postscript', *op. cit.*, pp. 250ff. For more details *see e.g.*, J. Raz, 'The Identity of Legal Systems', *op. cit.*, pp. 93ff.; P.M.S. Hacker, 'Hart's Philosophy of Law', *op. cit.*, pp. 22ff.; Z. Pulka, *Legitymizacja państwa w prawoznawstwie* [Legitimization of the State in Jurisprudence], AUW 1885 (1996), pp. 129ff.

[138] I consciously restrain the firmness of the thesis that has been put forward here. In fact, the presented argumentation even justifies the standpoint that we are never able to achieve absolute certainty on decisions on validity, based on the criteria of the membership in the legal system, which, however, seems to be a too far-fetched and sceptical consequence of the indicated jurisprudential theses and, in particular, of the thesis on the open texture of the rule of recognition.

[139] For more *see* Chap. 4 at pp. 128ff.

any other customary rule (*regla consuetudinaria*),[140] in a natural way undergoes continuous, uncontrolled and unpredictable evolutionary changes—some of the membership criteria become obsolete, others change their content, and still others, which have not been dealt with so far by law-applying organs, become the new elements of the rule of recognition of a given legal system.

The conclusions of the presented argumentation arise quite naturally. An attempt to regard the membership in the legal system as a correct clarification of the intension of the juristic concept of the validity of statutory law means that if we do not want to create a conception relating only to a non-definitive *prima facie* validity of legal norms, then we need to use the concept of the membership in a strong sense. Nevertheless, although the latter concept appears in juristic discourse, and in particular in dogmatic discourse, lawyers are really, at most, capable of determining that a given legal norm belongs to the legal system in a so to speak medium sense, which is similar to a strong one, but not tantamount to it.[141] We are thus in a hopeless situation, because the low practical and theoretical usefulness of the definition of validity, making use of the concept of the membership in the medium sense, is quite obvious. Without denying the "fuzziness" of modern legal systems—the open texture and the variability of the criteria of the membership of norms in the legal system—we consider it inappropriate that the theory of law should reinforce this status quo through the use of an essentially descriptive (reporting) definition of legal validity. Jurists certainly need a definition regulating the intension of the juristic concept of the validity of statutory law, which would be indeed helpful in resolving specific problems of validity, without consolidating the state of uncertainty due to its imprecise nature.

In conclusion, if we take into consideration the consequences mentioned above, then applying the concept of the membership to the definition of the juristic concept of the validity of statutory law must be regarded as inappropriate. The definition constructed in such a way does not meet the assumed objectives and conditions of a good clarification, in particular, the requirements for exactness (precision) and the practical utility of its outcome.

Before we proceed to present the arguments that are directly related to the issue of the intension of the juristic concept of legal validity, we should supplement the foregoing deliberations with a complementing argument (A–I bis). To formulate it, let us assume for a moment that Wróblewski, Peczenik, Ziembiński, Opałek and Hart are wrong, and so legal systems are not fuzzy and it is possible to clearly define

---

[140] The Spanish term, used by Hart in 'El nuevo desafío al positivismo jurídico', *op. cit.*, p. 8. The English equivalent is used by J. Raz, 'The Identity of Legal Systems', *op. cit.*, p. 94 and *The Concept of a Legal System*, *op. cit.*, p. 198, as well as by P.M.S. Hacker, 'Hart's Philosophy of Law', *op. cit.*, p. 23.

[141] Contrary to appearances, it should not bother us too much, because such a determination usually suffices, or speaking more precisely, must suffice to resolve specific validity problems, especially in the process of the judicial application of law. For more on the consequences of the argument A–I in relation to the ways of solving the problem of the extension of the juristic concept of validity *see* Chap. 9 at pp. 457–458.

the criteria for membership in the strong sense, as well as to determine their unequivocal application in order to decide on the validity of individual legal norms. It should be noted that when making such an assumption, definition D_1 would *de facto* become a criterial definition (and thus an extensional one)—only indirectly clarifying the intension of the defined concept.[142] A full explanation of its intension that makes the comprehension of this concept possible would require the identification and analysis of a large number of criteria and arguments used by lawyers in the course of resolving specific problems of validity.[143] Thus, this definition would clearly violate the requirement of the simplicity of *explicatum*, which would also weigh in favour of rejecting it.

We are not going to hide the fact that the above arguments fall deeply into the issue of the extension of the juristic concept of the validity of statutory law. Although we have already explained that such a procedure is methodologically justified,[144] nevertheless, this fact undoubtedly undermines their argumentative force and value. Let us therefore go on to the arguments that are already directly associated with the issue of intension that will relate to the second of the concepts used in the *definiens* of D_1; namely, the concept of the legal system.

As in the case of the A–I argument, let us start the discussion by noting the ambiguity—this time of the concept of the legal system—which, in fact, is much more polysemic than the concept of the membership of legal norms in the legal system that was analysed within the previous argument. It is even evidenced by the differentiation of numerous theories of legal systems constructed by the whole array of legal theoreticians. The concepts of the legal system created by Adolf Merkl,[145] Hans Kelsen,[146] H.L.A. Hart,[147] Joseph Raz,[148] Carlos Alchourrón and

[142] *Cf.* the arguments against the criterial definition of legal validity, presented *supra*, note 14 at pp. 249–250.

[143] Such attempts are sometimes undertaken – *cf. e.g.*, definitions of the concept of validity DI–DXI, provided by L. Nowak, *Interpretacja prawnicza*, *op. cit.*, pp. 62–147. Without a doubt, a scientifically accurate definition of this type would necessarily have to assume a narrower research perspective than the one adopted in this study; namely, of a particular legal culture of a given state, rather than the continental system-type of the statutory law.

[144] *Cf. supra*, note 71 at pp. 263–264.

[145] *See* J. Behrend, *Untersuchungen zur Stufenbaulehre Adolf Merkls und Hans Kelsens*, Berlin 1977, pp. 13 ff., R. Walter, 'Die Lehre vom Stufenbau der Rechtsordnung', *AIC* XIII (1980), pp. 5–16, 'Adolf Merkl jako teoretyk prawa' [Adolf Merkl as Law Theoretician], trans. K. Opałek, *PiP* 2 (1991), pp. 33–34 and K. Płeszka, *Hierarchia w systemie prawa*, *op. cit.*, pp. 73ff., and the references cited therein.

[146] *See* H. Kelsen, *General Theory of Law and State*, *op. cit.*, pp. 110ff., *Reine Rechtslehre*, 2nd ed., *op. cit.*, pp. 196ff. [English version, pp. 193ff.], and *Allgemeine Theorie der Normen*, *op. cit.*, pp. 203ff., J. Raz, *The Concept of a Legal System*, *op. cit.*, pp. 93ff., J. Behrend, *ibidem*, pp. 49ff. and K. Płeszka, *ibidem*, pp. 67ff.

[147] *See* H.L.A. Hart, *The Concept of Law*, *op. cit.*, pp. 77ff., L. Leszczyński, 'Zagadnienia systemu prawa w koncepcji H.L.A. Harta' [The Issues of the Legal System in H.L.A. Hart's Conception], *AUMCS Sectio G: Ius* XXVI (1979), pp. 133–144 and N. MacCormick, *H.L.A. Hart*, *op. cit.*, pp. 92ff.

[148] *See* J. Raz, *The Concept of a Legal System*, *op. cit.*, pp. 121ff. and *Practical Reason and Norms*, *op. cit.*, pp. 149ff.

Eugenio Bulygin,[149] Robert Alexy[150] or Jan-Reinard Sieckmann[151] (to name but a few, the best known and widely discussed in jurisprudential literature) constitute irrefutable evidence that the unambiguity of the concept of the legal system is out of the question. Such ambiguity is equally obvious in the Polish legal theory: Jerzy Wróblewski alone elaborated a classification and characteristics of several concepts (models) of legal systems,[152] which should be supplemented with the theories of the legal system developed by Aleksander Peczenik,[153] Kazimierz Świrydowicz[154] and Krzysztof Płeszka.[155] As if this was not enough, the ambiguity of this concept is not by any means a kind of *differentia specifica* of the contemporary legal theory, because it also occurs in other legal such as the sociology of law or legal dogmatics. With regard to the latter, its theoretical analysis shows that the dogmatists of law assume and apply many concepts of the legal system, which differ, inter alia, in the manner of understanding the concept of the set that constitutes the legal system, identifying its elements as well as understanding their internal arrangement.[156]

The semantic indeterminacy of the concept of the legal system means that the prerequisite for recognising definition D_1 as the correct clarification of the intension of the juristic concept of the validity of statutory law is a clear identification and explanation of the concept of the legal system used in its *definiens*. Otherwise, this definition could not be considered as precise. Yet, before we attempt such an identification, we should first discuss a fundamental issue related to the concept of the legal system, which has great importance in the context of the undertaken

---

[149] *See* C.E. Alchourrón, E. Bulygin, *Normative Systems*, Wien/New York 1971 and 'Sobre el concepto de orden jurídico', *op. cit.* and E. Bulygin, 'Algunas consideraciones sobre los sistemas jurídicos', *op. cit.* and 'Normensystem und Rechtsordnung', *op. cit.*

[150] *See* R. Alexy's works indicated in Chap. 2, note 29 at p. 19.

[151] *See* J.-R. Sieckmann, *Regelmodelle und Prinzipienmodelle des Rechtssystems*, *op. cit.*, pp. 89ff. and 'Legal System and Practical Reason. On the Structure of a Normative Theory of Law', *RJ* 5 (1992), pp. 288–307.

[152] *See* J. Wróblewski, 'Modele systemów norm a system prawa' [Models of Normative Systems and the Legal System], *SPE* II (1969), pp. 23–48, 'Nieostrość systemu prawa', *op. cit.*, and 'Dilemmas of the Normativistic Concept of the Legal System', *op. cit.*; K. Opałek, J. Wróblewski, *Prawo. Metodologia, filozofia, teoria prawa*, *op. cit.*, pp. 230ff. Anticipating further discussion, let us add that Wróblewski treats the assumption of a systemic character of law as "one of the presuppositions of legal reasoning".

[153] *See* A. Peczenik, 'The Structure of a Legal System', *op. cit.*, 'On the Nature and Function of the *Grundnorm*', *op. cit.*, 'Sources of Law' in A. Aarnio *et al.* (eds.), *Rechtsnorm und Rechtswirklichkeit*, *op. cit.*, pp. 75–84, and 'Unity of the Legal System' in W. Krawietz *et al.* (eds.), *Prescriptive Formality and Normative Rationality in Modern Legal Systems*, *op. cit.*, pp. 71–81.

[154] *See* K. Świrydowicz, *Analiza logiczna pojęcia kompetencji normodawczej* [Logical Analysis of the Concept of Norm-giving Competence], Warszawa/Poznań 1981, pp. 13ff.

[155] *See* K. Płeszka, *Hierarchia w systemie prawa*, *op. cit.*, pp. 21ff.

[156] K. Płeszka, T. Gizbert-Studnicki, 'Obraz systemu prawa w dogmatyce prawniczej', *op. cit.*, p. 170.

clarificative analysis. Using a formulation derived from Krzysztof Płeszka and Tomasz Gizbert-Studnicki, let us consider whether the systemic character of law is its immanent or transcendent feature; namely,

> whether the law is given to us in the form of the system (i.e. whether the systemic character is "contained" in law as such) or whether its systemic character constitutes a result of lawyers' arranging attempts.[157]

Without a doubt, this problem is of fundamental importance and leaving it unresolved can lead to a series of misunderstandings that make it difficult, or even impossible to attempt a successful clarification of the concept of legal validity, undertaken by means of applying the concept of the membership in the legal system.

The clarification of the concept of the legal system is not the immediate object of our considerations; therefore, the problem of the systemic character of law can only be briefly discussed. We believe that the stronger arguments weigh in favour of the thesis that the legal system "cannot be treated as given as a consequence of legislator's actions"[158] but it is the result of a rational reconstruction of the raw legal material. The concept of rational reconstruction, which we refer to here, is rooted in Hans Kelsen's views on the creative function of legal science,[159] and it was introduced to the methodology of contemporary analytical theory of law by

---

[157] *Ibidem*, p. 153.

[158] As noted by Z. Pulka, 'Czy nastąpił zmierzch pozytywistycznej koncepcji prawa i prawoznawstwa?', *op. cit.*, p. 173. Similarly, A. Kozak, 'Kulturowy fundament decyzji interpretacyjnej' [Cultural Foundation of the Interpretive Decision] in A. Sulikowski (ed.), *Z zagadnień teorii i filozofii prawa*, *op. cit.*, p. 47, who recognises that: "The law by its very nature is not a system of norms or utterances of another type. [...] The sum of the political decisions of the legislator does not yet constitute the system".

[159] *Cf.* N. MacCormick, 'Powers and Power-Conferring Norms', *op. cit.*, pp. 497–498, in particular note 6. As Kelsen wrote, legal sciences create (in the epistemological sense) their objects, perceiving law as *sinnvolles Ganzes*. In his opinion: "Just as natural science, by means of its ordering cognition, turns the chaos of sensory impressions into a cosmos, that is, into nature as a unified system, so likewise legal science, by means of cognition, turns the multitude of general and individual legal norms issued by legal organs – the material given to legal science – into a unified system free of contradiction, that is, into a legal system" – H. Kelsen, *Reine Rechtslehre*, 2nd ed., *op. cit.*, p. 74 [the translation is provided by St.L. Paulson, 'Arriving at a Defensible Periodization of Hans Kelsen's Legal Theory', *OJLS* 19/2 (1999), p. 363]. On Kelsen's epistemological constructivism and his view on the constitutive role of juristic cognition *see* St.L. Paulson, 'Four Phases in Hans Kelsen's Legal Theory? Reflections on a Periodization', *OJLS* 18/1 (1998), pp. 159–160; P. Comanducci, 'Kelsen vs. Searle. A Tale of Two Constructivists', *AS* 4 (2000), pp. 33–48. It should be added that a similar standpoint is expressed by the authors who, unlike Kelsen, do not base their findings on the Kantian theory of cognition. For example, Z. Ziembiński, *Szkice z metodologii szczegółowych nauk prawnych*, *op. cit.*, p. 14, acknowledges that the specific legal sciences do not just "select the objects that constitute the subject of theirs research" but they also "to some extent create these objects" and determine "what is to be regarded as valid legal norms and what is not". As Ziembiński points out in 'Prescriptive and/or Descriptive Language in Legal Sciences', *op. cit.*, p. 91, "a dogmatic legal science becomes in practice an element co-creating the object of its research". *Cf.* J. Bengoetxea, 'Legal System as a Regulative Ideal', *ARSP* Bh. 53 (1994), pp. 65–80.

Zenon Bańkowski, Neil MacCormick, Robert Summers and Jerzy Wróblewski,[160] with reference to the idea of rational reconstruction, formulated back in the sixties of the last century by Martin Golding[161]—the commentator on Kelsen's pure theory of law. Rational reconstruction does not rely merely on the description of the facts, but it attempts to explain legal phenomena by means of referring to them as "theoretical objects", and thus fragmented, unstructured and often inconsistent data on "raw law" are recognised as the elements of a coherent and well-ordered whole, making them relatively easy to understand.[162] It is important that the method of rational reconstruction is, in fact, not entirely axiologically neutral, nevertheless, it allows for the reconstruction of even morally objectionable or evil normative orders in a relatively detached and disinterested way[163]; that is, from a morally detached and impartial point of view, which we consider most appropriate in jurisprudential analyses.[164] In terms of MacCormick, who most often uses the concept of rational reconstruction, the systemic nature of the law is the result of applying this method by the legal sciences. As noted by the Scottish philosopher of law:

> [t]he systematized character of law (where it exists) is a product of legal science and legal theory, not a datum for it.[165]

In the Polish theory of law, in addition to the already mentioned authors—Zbigniew Pulka and Artur Kozak—a similar approach to the systemic character of law has been presented by Andrzej Bator, who treats it as "a certain type of a

---

[160] Z. Bańkowski, N. MacCormick, R. S. Summers, J. Wróblewski, 'On Method and Methodology', *op. cit.*, pp. 10, 18ff. It should be added that the concept of rational reconstruction has been first used in MacCormick's study, 'Reconstruction after Deconstruction: a Response to CLS', *OJLS* 10/4 (1990), pp. 556ff. Nonetheless, the Scottish philosopher repeatedly emphasises that the methodological approach, defined by means of this concept, was jointly developed by the authors indicated in the text, with a particular role of Wróblewski – *cf.* N. MacCormick, *ibidem*, note 39 at p. 556, 'Four Quadrants of Jurisprudence', *op. cit.*, p. 57, and *Rhetoric and the Rule of Law*, *op. cit.*, p. 29. For more on the application of the method of reconstruction in the theory of law *see* V. Villa, 'Constructivismo y teoría del Derecho', trans. J. Aguiló Regla, *DOXA* 22 (1999), pp. 295ff., and the references cited therein. The problems connected with the systemic reconstruction of law have been presented in interesting way by P.E. Navarro, 'Legal Reasoning and Systematization of Law' in A. Soeteman (ed.), *Pluralism and Law*, Dordrecht/Boston/London 2001, pp. 251–277 and 'Legal Systems and Legal Statements', *AS* 6 (2002), pp. 75–88.

[161] *See* M.P. Golding, 'Kelsen and the Concept of "Legal System"', *ARSP* 47 (1961), pp. 357ff. Golding aptly notes that the concept of rational reconstruction originates from the tradition of logical positivism (in particular the Vienna Circle). For more on Golding's idea *see* U.U. Bindreiter, 'Presupposing the Basic Norm', *op. cit.*, pp. 164ff.

[162] *See* Z. Bańkowski, N. MacCormick, R.S. Summers, J. Wróblewski, 'On Method and Methodology', *op. cit.*, p. 19; N. MacCormick, 'Foreword' in *idem, Legal Reasoning and Legal Theory*, 2nd ed., *op. cit.*, pp. xiii–xiv and *Rhetoric and the Rule of Law*, *op. cit.*, p. 29.

[163] *See* Z. Bańkowski, N. MacCormick, R.S. Summers, J. Wróblewski, *ibidem*, pp. 20ff.

[164] For more *see* Chap. 6 at pp. 234–237.

[165] N. MacCormick, 'Powers and Power-Conferring Norms', *op. cit.*, p. 497, similarly in 'Four Quadrants of Jurisprudence', *op. cit.*, p. 57.

research approach to law", which consists of recognising its individual components such as its legal norms, institutions or the various branches of law in the framework of the legal system understood as a whole.[166]

The view on the transcendent nature of the systematised character of law can hardly be questioned because the lawyers—dogmatists and practitioners (in particular, judges)—are the creators (and not only "re-creators") of the legal system. Typically, lawyers rationally reconstruct only the fragment that constitutes the subject of detailed dogmatic analyses or a normative basis for a particular judicial decision. This view seems all the more obvious in the context of the assumption—most frequently encountered in jurisprudential literature—that the legal norms, being the result of legal interpretation, are the elements of the legal system.[167] Let us recall that the legal system, understood as a set (in the distributive sense) of norms, is merely an abstract object—as is any set of this kind—rather than something given (e.g., by the legislator) or existing in the social reality. Yet, it should be emphasised that the view on the transcendent source of the systematised character of law does not contradict the thesis that the so-called construction rules of legal system (understood as specific rules of the meaning of the conventional actions of lawmaking) are not determined solely by the science of law, but they constitute, at least in part, a consequence of the activities of the lawmaker.[168] Nevertheless, it does not change the fact that, according to MacCormick:

> [t]here is no single uniquely correct reconstruction of the raw material of law in the single canonical form of "legal system".[169]

After explaining our standpoint on the problem of the systematised character of law, let us now go on to present the A–II argument, associated with the identification and explanation of the concept of the legal system used in *definiens* of D_1. We will try to demonstrate that this concept in the context of applying it in the definition D_1 cannot stand for the legal system that we could attribute with the property of

---

[166] A. Bator, 'System prawa' [Legal System] in A. Bator, W. Gromski, A. Kozak, S. Kaźmierczyk, Z. Pulka, *Wprowadzenie do nauk prawnych. Leksykon tematyczny*, Warszawa 2006, p. 166. Unfortunately, due to the modest frames of the study, we cannot analyse and trace a very instructive history of the systemic approach to law – for more on this issue *see e.g.*, C.E. Alchourrón, E. Bulygin, *Normative Systems*, *op. cit.*, pp. 50–53, 65ff.; W. Krawietz, 'Rechtssystem und Rationalität in der juristischen Dogmatik', *RT* Bh. 2 (1981), pp. 318ff.; M. Błachut, J. Kaczor, P. Kaczmarek, A. Sulikowski, 'Systemowość w myśleniu prawniczym' [Systematization in Legal Reasoning] in O. Bogucki, S. Czepita (eds.), *System prawny a porządek prawny*, Szczecin 2008, pp. 89–107.

[167] *Cf.* the argument from terminological consistency, presented in Chap. 6 at pp. 243–244.

[168] For more *see* S. Czepita, 'Reguły konstrukcji systemu prawnego a prawotwórstwo" [The Rules of the Construction of Legal System and Law-creation], *RPEiS* LVI/4 (1994), pp. 31–38, and the references cited therein. It should be noted that the construction rules apply primarily to the legal system understood as a system of law-creating (normative) acts, rather than as a system of legal norms (i.e., the approach adopted in this study).

[169] N. MacCormick, 'On Institutional Normative Order: An Idea about Law' in E. Garzón Valdés *et al.* (eds.), *Normative Systems in Legal and Moral Theory*, *op. cit.*, p. 423.

"validity", which certainly reduces the value and usefulness of the definition D_1 in legal and juristic discourse.

The above-mentioned ambiguity of the origin of the legal system is even more noticeable if we take into account that the concept of the legal system can be constructed depending on, or—certainly more seldom—independently of attributing to such a system the feature of "validity". Let us recall that the external validity of the law (in the terminology of Peczenik–Aarnio)—namely, the validity of the legal system as such—may result from the validity of individual norms belonging to it (the so-called individualism of validity),[170] or it can rely on the fact that the legal system has a certain feature or a set of features (the so-called holism of validity).[171] Let us note that in juristic language we can express these two ways of understanding the validity of the legal system by using the phrases "the system of valid law" (which corresponds to the first possibility) and "the valid legal system" (the second possibility). By adopting such a linguistic convention, it can be easily perceived that if "membership in the legal system" (the concept that we refer to in *definiens* of D_1) is understood as "membership in the system of valid law",[172] then the definition under discussion will be obviously burdened with the *idem per idem* fallacy, depriving it of any cognitive value and practical utility. In effect, if we assume, firstly, that the intension of the concept of the validity of the norms of statutory law should be clarified by means of their membership in the system of valid law and, secondly, that the concept of the system of valid law would not stand for anything else than the system (an ordered set) of valid statutory norms, then we would find ourselves in a definitional *circulus vitiosus* from which there is no reasonable way out.[173] So we see that the only alternative, which merits a more detailed analysis, is the understanding of the legal system in definition D_1 as a "valid legal system"—and thus in the spirit of the holism of validity.

[170] The paradigmatic formulation of the thesis of the individualism of validity can be found in the studies of J. Raz who – while remaining under the undoubted influence of Kelsen's theory – believes that: "A normative system is valid if its norms are valid" – *Practical Reason and Norms*, *op. cit.*, p. 127 or that: "If we can say of the system itself that it is valid this is only in the sense that its rules are valid" – 'Legal Validity', *op. cit.*, p. 341. Kelsen himself indirectly expressed such an individualistic view in relation to the problem of the validity of statutes, when writing: "[D]ie Geltung eines aus mehreren Rechtsnormen bestehenden Gesetzes nicht anders ist als die Geltung dieser Rechtsnormen und nicht eine von der Geltung dieser Rechtsnormen verschiedene Geltung des Gesetzes" – *Allgemeine Theorie der Normen*, *op. cit.*, p. 91.

[171] *Cf.* Chap. 5, notes 56 and 58 at p. 206, with the corresponding text.

[172] It should be stressed here that the conception of treating the legal system as the system of valid law (i.e., a set of valid norms) is very common – *see e.g.*, J. Wróblewski's definition of a concrete legal system and J. Raz's definition of a momentary legal system, cited *supra* at pp. 258–259.

[173] Nevertheless, the attempts to find such a solution are indeed undertaken (for instance, by J. Raz or E. Bulygin) and they involve differentiating between several concepts of the validity of legal norms (rules) – for more *cf.* the next argument A–III, in particular notes 204–206 at pp. 292–293, with the corresponding text. Yet, they are useless for our clarificative analysis because of reasons discussed in the context of the possibility of conceptual relativisation of the expression on the validity of statutory norms – *see supra*, p. 253.

The issue of the validity of the legal system as such (i.e., the external legal validity) is an astonishingly rare object of inquiry for analytical theory and philosophy of law. In particular, it should be emphasised that the concepts of the highest norms of the legal systems, elaborated by the most prominent legal philosophers such as Kelsen's concept of *Grundnorm*, Hart's rule of recognition or von Wright's sovereign norm,[174] do not directly relate to the problem of external legal validity. These ultimate norms, in fact, belong to the legal system,[175] and can therefore constitute (at least according to the authors of these conceptions) a definitive basis for the validity or identification of the norms of this system, but not the validity of the legal system understood as a whole (consequently, they are in the spirit of the holism of validity).[176] Therefore, the authors who directly undertake the issue of the validity of the legal system generally understand it in sociological or moral terms,[177] or they treat the validity of the legal system as a hypothesis—the interpretation scheme—which allows us to understand and predict social behaviour related to the law; in particular, the behaviour of judges.[178] Nevertheless, in principle many legal theoreticians leave aside the issue of the validity of the legal system. There arises the question of why even philosophers and legal theorists particularly meritorious in solving complex jurisprudential problems related to the validity of law act this way; why does Hart maintain that "[w]e only need the word 'validity', and commonly only use it, to answer questions which arise *within* a system of rules",[179] and Lang considers the issue of the validity of the legal system

[174] For more on the various conceptions and ways of grasping the highest norms of the legal system *see* R. Alexy, *Begriff und Geltung des Rechts*, *op. cit.*, pp. 154ff. [English version, pp. 95ff.]; R. Guastini, 'Normas supremas', trans. J. Ferrer, *DOXA* 17–18 (1995), pp. 257–270; J. Stelmach, 'Norma podstawowa' [Basic Norm], *SFP* 1 (2001), pp. 64ff.

[175] This statement is naturally controversial in relation to the status of the basic norm – *cf. infra*, the argument A–III at pp. 295–299. Yet, even if we assume that the basic norm does not belong to the legal system, then – as demonstrated by K. Opałek – the attempt to clarify the concept of the validity of the legal system by referring to the basic norm is unsuccessful – *see idem*, 'The Problem of the Validity of Law', *op. cit.*, pp. 13–14 and K. Opałek, J. Wróblewski, *Zagadnienia teorii prawa*, *op. cit.*, p. 122.

[176] Such a vision of the legal system, which, like a logical system, *per se* justifies not only the validity of its components (which can be accepted under some conditions), but which also justifies its own validity as a whole, thus resembling Baron Münchhausen who, when drowning in a swamp, saves himself by pulling up his own hair, is – in my view – so unrealistic that it does not even have to be focused on. It should, nonetheless, be noted that such ideas also appear from time to time – *cf. e.g.*, S. Jørgensen, 'Grundnorm und Paradox', *RT* Bh. 5 (1984), pp. 179–191, in particular p. 188. *See* also *infra*, note 180 on the next page.

[177] For example, it is made by R. Alexy, *Begriff und Geltung des Rechts*, *op. cit.*, p. 144ff. [English version, pp. 89ff.], who analyses the collisions between the legal, social and moral validity, yet he also examines the possibility of a non-circular justification of the legal validity of norms by means of the basic norm – *see ibidem*, pp. 154ff. [English version, pp. 95ff.].

[178] *See e.g.*, A. Ross, *On Law and Justice*, *op. cit.*, pp. 34ff. His position resembles, in some respects, the above-discussed method of rational reconstruction and implicitly expresses the thesis of the transcendent origin of the systematised character of law.

[179] H.L.A. Hart, *The Concept of Law*, *op. cit.*, p. 105.

as an "extra-normative problem", highlighting the negligible cognitive and practical value of this concept.[180]

The first possible answer is of a logico-methodological character. Let us note that legal theorists are (no doubt rightly) interested in the first place in unravelling the problem of the internal validity of law; namely, the validity of individual legal norms. Some legal theorists—as for example the above-mentioned Hans Kelsen, H.L.A. Hart and Georg Henrik von Wright—to that end develop different conceptions of the highest norms, serving as an ultimate justification of the validity of other "ordinary" legal norms or as a criterion for identifying them. Other authors—such as Gustav Radbruch, Alf Ross and Joseph Raz—either argue that the juristic doctrine of validity must treat the constitution as *causa sui*,[181] or maintain that there is no "Archimedean point", allowing for a verification of the validity of the elements of the legal system in a manner that is independent of the legal system[182] or, finally, they observe that "law regulates its own validity".[183] Thus, they more or less openly admit that the criteria for the membership of norms in the legal system, and thus their validity (perceived as a membership) are of a circular character.[184] In this context, as rightly observed by Kazimierz Opałek, the justification of the internal validity of law by justifying the validity of the legal system as a whole (i.e., law's external validity) is meaningless, because it is based on a failure to differentiate between these two meanings of validity.[185] We therefore reach the conclusion that the fact that legal theoreticians leave aside the issue of the

---

[180] *See* Chap. 6, pp. 239–240. Let us add that the marginal cognitive and practical value of the concept of validity referring to the legal system can also easily be proven when adopting the perspective of the individualism of validity. Let us quote the argument formulated by R. Lippold, 'Geltung, Wirksamkeit und Verbindlichkeit von Rechtsnormen', *op. cit.*, pp. 472–473. According to the Austrian author, if we assume that the validity of a norm lies in its membership in the legal system, and that each legal system includes at least one norm ("Ohne Norm keine Normenordnung"), then the concept of a non-valid legal system is nonsensical, since it would have to be the system that no legal norm belongs to. Accordingly, it can be easily inferred that the position of the individualism of validity combined with the perception of law as defined in D_1, leads to the cognitive and practical uselessness of the concept of the validity of the legal system, because every legal system must be a system of valid law and there cannot be any non-valid legal systems (they are "unthinkable", as Lippold claims).

[181] In the original: "Die Verfassung selbst aber kann und muß eine solche rein juristischen Geltungslehre als eine causa sui auffassen" – G. Radbruch, *Rechtsphilosophie*, *op. cit.*, p. 79.

[182] A. Ross, *On Law and Justice*, *op. cit.*, p. 36.

[183] J. Raz, 'Legal Validity', *op. cit.*, p. 343, with a reference to Kelsen's views.

[184] The circularity of the ultimate criteria of validity/membership of norms is most clearly manifested when analysing the content of Hart's rule of recognition – for more details *see* Chap. 9 at pp. 456–457.

[185] *Cf.* K. Opałek, 'The Problem of the Validity of Law', *op. cit.*, p. 18 and K. Opałek, J. Wróblewski, *Zagadnienia teorii prawa*, *op. cit.*, p. 128. Opałek uses the distinction of validity in the absolute and relative sense (rather than the external and internal validity), but it does not change anything with regard to the merits of his criticism. Similarly, A. Peczenik, 'The Structure of a Legal System', *op. cit.*, p. 4, emphasises the differences in the means of establishing the external validity of the "total legal system" and the internal validity of "single legal rules".

validity of the legal system results from the belief that this is not a proper way to explain the problem of the validity of individual legal norms—in order to resolve it, it is enough to adopt the condition, presupposition, assumption or fiction (as followed by Kelsen, Hart and Peczenik in their theories) that the legal system is—as Kelsen wrote—*im großen und ganzen* effective.[186]

The second answer is of a semantic and normative character and it is directly related to the issue of the intension of the juristic concept of legal validity. If we take into account the relationship between "validity" and "being someone's duty", characteristic not only of the semantics of the Polish language, but also present in a number of theories of the validity of law (especially those having a normative character), then we can easily understand why the problem of the validity of the legal system is "extra-normative" (Lang) and why the term "validity" is used only when the solution of problems concerns the legal validity of norms, which arise within the legal system (Hart). The point is that the legal system does not impose any duties or obligations on the subjects of the law than those arising from individual legal norms of that system. When lawyers argue that "the legal system imposes obligations on citizens", it is only a certain shorthand, perhaps even justified on the grounds of economy of language because we cannot indeed identify any legal duty or obligation that would not have theirs source or basis in the legal norms, which constitute the elements of the system. Moreover, when recognising the thesis of the transcendent origin of the systemic character of law, under which the systematisation of law results from the ordering activities of lawyers, it is difficult in general to seriously talk about the "legal system imposing the duties or obligations", since it would mean an utter denial of the essence of the concept of the norm-giving competence. If the reconstruction of the legal system is undertaken, for example, by the dogmatist of constitutional law, then she/he has no legal authority to impose any duties or obligations on legal subjects, as this is reserved for the legislator, whereas the researcher can—to use Kelsen's language—apply the concept of ought only in a descriptive sense. We believe that such a categorical response helps to explain the position of Hart, Lang and many other philosophers and theorists of law who do not recognise the issue of the validity of the legal system as normative or who apply the concept of validity exclusively or mainly in respect of individual legal norms.

The argument A–II shows that the concept of the legal system that is used in *definiens* of D_1 can be understood neither as the system of valid law (individualism of validity), nor as the valid legal system (holism of validity). When analysing this definition, we must therefore use the concept of the legal system, which is not in any way attributed with the property of "validity". Referring to the content of this argument, let us add that the questions of the status and content of the *Grundnorm*, the rule of recognition or the sovereign norm undeniably constitute the issues of utmost importance for the theory and philosophy of law, yet it is difficult to assume that their explanation can be accepted as a clarification of the intension of the

---

186 For more details *see infra*, pp. 342ff., and the references cited therein.

juristic concept of legal validity. Undoubtedly, the highest norms of the legal system constitute the concepts (theoretical constructs) used in the jurisprudential analyses for identifying (recognising) valid norms and, above all, the legal justification for their validity; namely, they concern the issue of the extension of juristic concept of the validity of norms.[187]

The argument A–II is incomplete in the sense that it is of a negative character. Due to this argument, we have merely determined how the concept of the legal system, used in the *definiens* of D_1, cannot be comprehended. Before proceeding to the next argument, it is worth considering how the concept of the legal system should be understood in the context of the validity of law. Let us note that if we accepted that the definition under analysis should be interpreted in such a way that the membership of the norm in any non-valid but, for example, "existing" legal system stands for its validity then it would be an inaccurate interpretation. Adopting it would therefore entail the assertion that the norms of Roman law are valid, as they undoubtedly belong to the Roman law system. This legal system "exists", after all, in the same sense in which any other legal system does; namely, as a result of rational reconstruction, yet undertaken—and this is the only important difference (perhaps apart from difficult access to the *fontes iuris cognoscendi*)—not by the dogmatists and legal theoreticians, but by historians (dogmatists) of Roman law. In order to avoid such imprecision,[188] we should, in line with the earlier estimates,[189] at least indirectly relativise the concept of the legal system on a temporal basis. It seems obvious that when using the definition D_1, we can talk about the validity of the legal norm (in the present tense) only when we undertake the reconstruction of the legal system on the basis of the current state of positive law (at the moment of undertaking the said reconstruction).[190] We realise that this finding seems to be quite artificial—after all, it would be much easier to assume that what is meant here is the legal system which is valid *hic et nunc*. Nevertheless, argument A–II precluded the possibility of using the concept of the legal system—in such a sense—in the context of the analysed definition of validity.

Definition D_1 expresses the intensional identity of the validity of a norm and its membership in the legal system. The next argument, A–III, refers to the symmetry of this relation.[191] We shall attempt to determine in this argument whether it is possible to recognise as correct both the thesis: "If a norm of statutory law is valid, then it

---

[187] It will therefore be discussed only after having resolved the question of intension; namely, in Chap. 9 at pp. 456ff.

[188] The imprecision consists merely in that we – quite rightly – speak of the norms of Roman law in that they *were* valid and not that they *are* valid.

[189] *See supra*, pp. 258ff., in particular the second argument against temporal relativisation.

[190] This means that the basis for this reconstruction (among other sources of law) will consist of the legal provisions that were enacted and not repealed; however, sometimes during the reconstruction, the jurists shall also take into consideration repealed provisions if it becomes necessary to determine the content of legal norms which are part of that system – for more details *see* Chap. 9 at pp. 506ff.

[191] *Cf. supra*, pp. 266–267, in particular note 84, with the corresponding text.

belongs to the legal system" as well as its opposite: "If a norm of statutory law belongs to the legal system, then it is valid". Yet, before we examine the legitimacy of these implications, let us note that Joseph Raz, in his famous essay on the validity of law, poses a very similar, *prima facie* Euthyphro-like question about what the reason is here and what the consequence is: "Is a rule a part of a system because it is valid or is it valid because it is part of legal system?".[192] At this point, however, it should be stressed that argument A–III does not apply to the determination of the correct order of elements in the relation between validity and membership in the legal system in the conceptual terms of reasons and consequences, because in the case of the normal definition whose accuracy is considered here, it is irrelevant. Indeed, if we consider the definition $A =_{df} B$, then the question of what the reason is and what the consequence is, is meaningless: both A must be the reason of B and B must be the reason of A, as expressed by the implications drawn above.[193]

Let us begin our considerations with the first implication. We aim to determine whether it is justified to say that the validity of a statutory law norm implies its membership in the legal system (understood as being defined within the argument A–II). In most cases, it is undoubtedly correct, and this interrelation even constitutes the basis for constructing the concepts of a concrete (Wróblewski) or momentary (Raz) legal system. Nevertheless, we can also identify situations in which the implication at hand is unjustified.

The first counterexample is the *casus* of the applicability of a legal norm—discussed by Eugenio Bulygin and significantly modified for the purposes of our discussion—which has never belonged and does not belong to any legal system.[194] Let us consider what can be said about the validity and membership of a statutory law norm in the legal system in the situation when such a norm is unconstitutional (e.g., is was enacted in violation of procedural requirements or it remains in substantial contradiction to the constitutional norms), but the constitutional court will erroneously deem that it does not violate the constitution and, thus, will not derogate it. Although the ruling of the constitutional court in this case is purely declarative,[195] we do not usually deny that such a norm is valid. It is most likely how the effects of this ruling will be assessed by the dogmatists of law and lawyer-practitioners, especially since some of them (e.g., judges) are—as in the Polish law[196]—bound by the decisions of this highest authority on matters relating to legal

[192] J. Raz, 'Legal Validity', *op. cit.*, p. 341.

[193] It is worth noting that J. Raz, *ibidem*, pp. 341–342, argues that the proponents of the equivalence of the terms "validity" and "membership" are likely to answer negatively on both questions. However, they are wrong, as he states, since "validity" is not identical to "membership of a system".

[194] *Cf.* E. Bulygin, 'Algunas consideraciones sobre los sistemas jurídicos', *op. cit.*, pp. 267–268. *Cf.* also the comments on such "irregular norms" in J.J. Moreso, *Legal Indeterminacy and Constitutional Interpretation*, trans. R. Zimmerling, Dordrecht 1998, pp. 110–111. On the concept of the applicability of norms, *see infra* at pp. 321ff.

[195] For more details, *see* Chap. 8 at pp. 388–390.

[196] *Cf.* the Article 190 Section 1 of the Constitution of Poland: "The rulings of the Constitutional Tribunal have the force of universal validity and are definite".

validity. Yet, as Bulygin rightly notes, such a norm does not belong to the legal system, because the membership (even in the sense defined above as a weak one) does not, in fact, depend on whether someone (e.g., the court that is competent to decide on the constitutionality of laws) determines it, but rather on the fact as to whether the norm meets the criteria for the membership in the system or not. According to the Argentine philosopher, this claim should not come as a shock to lawyers, because it merely constitutes a logical consequence of the definition of membership, in which there is, after all, no criterion implying the need for judicial confirmation of the membership of the norm in the legal system.[197] This example illustrates the first of some possible situations in which the implication: "If a norm of statutory law is valid, then it belongs to the legal system" is inaccurate. It seems that the presented reasoning can be challenged only by endorsing the thesis (based inter alia on the failure to differentiate between the institutional validity of rulings and their correctness) that judges never make mistakes, which is, however, unacceptable from a jurisprudential point of view.[198]

The second counterexample refers to the phenomenon of the openness of modern legal systems, analysed by a number of legal theoreticians.[199] Joseph Raz can be regarded as the precursor of this type of consideration in contemporary jurisprudential discussion, undertaken within the context of Hart's rule of recognition. When examining the functions of this master secondary rule, he pointed out that the courts are often obliged to apply foreign law—that is, norms that belong to the legal systems of other states—and the legal systems often recognise religious, ethnic or tribal regulations that do not come from the state authority as well as the norms (rules) adopted in voluntary associations.[200] Andrei Marmor, Raz's student, added to this list the norms of public international law, which "can be valid in a

---

[197] Let us note that among the criteria of the membership of the norm in the legal system – which are generally adopted in the system-type of statutory law – one can only identify a negative condition of absence of determining the unconstitutionality of a given norm by the competent authority – usually the constitutional court. Yet, this is not the same as a positive condition of determining its membership, as indicated in the text, because without a doubt, the vast majority of legal norms are considered valid, although the constitutional court has never referred to them and especially, it did not confirm their legal validity.

[198] *See e.g.*, N. MacCormick's argumentation, 'Can Judges Make Mistakes?' in H. Jung, U. Neumann (eds.), *Rechtsbegründung – Rechtsbegründungen. Günther Ellscheid zum 65. Geburtstag*, Baden-Baden 1999, pp. 76–89. *Cf.* K.E. Himma, 'Final Authority to Bind with Moral Mistakes: On the Explanatory Potential of Inclusive Legal Positivism', *L&Ph* 24 (2005), pp. 15ff. and A. Aarnio, *The Rational as Reasonable*, *op. cit.*, pp. 42–43.

[199] *See e.g.*, J.J. Moreso, P.E. Navarro, 'The Reception of Norms, and Open Legal Systems' in St. L. Paulson, B. Litschewski Paulson (eds.), *Normativity and Norms*, *op. cit.*, pp. 273–291, in particular pp. 285ff., as well as J. Raz's and A. Marmor's studies indicated in two subsequent notes. It should be noted that the openness of legal systems analysed at this point should not be confused with their "fuzziness" (as defined by Wróblewski and Peczenik) or open texture (as defined by Hart).

[200] *See* J. Raz, 'The Identity of Legal Systems', *op. cit.*, p. 97, 'Legal Principles and the Limits of Law' in M. Cohen (ed.), *Ronald Dworkin and Contemporary Jurisprudence*, Totowa 1983, p. 74, *Practical Reason and Norms*, *op. cit.*, pp. 152ff., and 'Legal Validity', *op. cit.*, p. 342.

certain legal system, even if they do not belong to it".[201] Given the scope of our analysis, limited to the norms of statutory law, in discussing this example we will focus on issues of validity and the membership of foreign law norms, applied by domestic courts of a state under the rules of private international law, because they are undoubtedly statutory norms. The first question is: Are these norms valid?

In considering the answer to this question, we shall primarily note that it is not at all certain that the norms applied under private international law are currently valid (in the sense of their membership in the legal system) in the state where they were enacted.[202] For example, if a Polish civil court is obligated to apply German law, it may happen that, according to the intertemporal rules of private international law, the Polish court will have to consider as a law applicable in a given case such legal norms that have been, for a long time, no longer valid in Germany.[203] Nonetheless, the question that seems much more important is whether these norms of German law may be considered as valid within the Polish law. Legal theorists explicitly dealing with this issue, generally agree that these foreign norms are valid, but they use different concepts of validity of law to the concept that identifies the validity of norms with their membership in the legal system. For instance, in Raz's theory of legal validity, which constitutes the adaptation of Kelsen's theory, we can find the distinction between the validity of norms—conceived normatively by Raz and consisting of the obligation to comply with the legal norms due to some non-specific reasons—and the legal validity (i.e., the systemic validity of law), also normatively understood and consisting of the obligation of their compliance due to their membership in the legal system or their enforceability in that system.[204] In Raz's approach, the discussed norms of foreign law are legally (systemically) valid, because they are recognised and enforced in a given legal system (and therefore they entail legal consequences), yet despite this property, they do not become parts of this system (i.e., they do not belong to it).[205] In Eugenio Bulygin's theory of the validity of law, the norms of foreign law are valid in terms of their applicability and in normative terms (i.e., their observance and application is prescribed), yet they are

---

[201] A. Marmor, 'Exclusive Legal Positivism', *op. cit.*, p. 105.

[202] This fact has been pointed out by J.J. Moreso, P.E. Navarro, 'The Reception of Norms, and Open Legal Systems', *op. cit.*, p. 287.

[203] According to the Polish positive law, such a situation can take place, e.g., in connection with the disposition of Article 34 of the *Prawo prywatne międzynarodowe. Ustawa z dnia 12 listopada 1965 r.* [Private International Law. Statute of 12 November 1965], published in *Dziennik Ustaw* [Journal of Statutes] 1965, No. 46, Item 290, with amendments, which states that: "In matters of succession the national law of the deceased, valid at the time of his death, is applicable".

[204] *See* J. Raz, *Practical Reason and Norms*, *op. cit.*, pp. 127ff. and 'Legal Validity', *op. cit.*, pp. 342ff. Unfortunately, Raz juggles the terms "validity", "legal validity" and "systemic validity", therefore the interpretation of his view as provided in the text is not certain. I base it primarily on the definitions proposed by Raz in 'Legal Validity', *op. cit.*, p. 346.

[205] J. Raz, *Practical Reason and Norms*, *op. cit.*, pp. 152–154 and 'Legal Validity', *op. cit.*, pp. 342ff. The same is claimed by A. Marmor, 'Exclusive Legal Positivism', *op. cit.*, p. 105.

not valid in the sense of their membership in the domestic legal system.[206] Conversely, according to José Juan Moreso and Pablo Navarro, the norms of foreign law belong to the category of binding norms, and thus applicable ones, but not to the category of valid norms, since the norms of this category, according to the conceptual convention adopted by them, must belong to a given (domestic) legal system.[207]

The issue of the validity of foreign laws seems to imply the need to discuss the problem of our conceptual preferences, expressed in an unpretentious question: Which concept of legal validity is better than others? Such a discussion would be, nevertheless, pointless, because what conditions its meaningfulness is the existence of a number of conceptions of the validity of statutory law that are acceptable from the viewpoint of analytical legal theory. Otherwise, it would be considerations that were based on choosing the "lesser evil", which—as we believe—do not merit being called scientific. At the present stage of clarificative analysis, it is yet a too premature assumption, and in the course of further discussions it will prove to be erroneous. Therefore, we have to settle for the observation that in the jurisprudential discourse, the norms of foreign law, applied by domestic courts under the rules of private international law, are often referred to as "valid". This fact can be explained in several ways, yet we shall content ourselves with two reasons in favour of such a linguistic (terminological) usage. Firstly, these foreign norms—when interpreted as sanctioning norms—undoubtedly obligate domestic courts that apply them to take a decision based on the content specified by them; accordingly, they trigger legal consequences in relation to legal subjects that are not their direct addressees. In this respect, they do not differ from the valid norms of domestic law. Secondly, by attributing them with the property of validity, lawyers avoid the antinomy resulting from identifying the validity of statutory law norms with their membership in the legal system: if a valid (in terms of membership) norm of domestic law N_D requires the application of foreign legal norm N_F (which is not valid in the sense of membership, as expanded upon in a moment), then the domestic courts are legally bound to apply invalid law. The antinomy therefore consists in the fact that the valid law requires the application of invalid laws, and it is evident that a theoretically correct conception of legal validity should not lead to such a reconstruction of the application of foreign legal norms.[208]

---

[206] *Cf.* E. Bulygin, 'Algunas consideraciones sobre los sistemas jurídicos', *op. cit.*, pp. 266ff.

[207] J.J. Moreso, P.E. Navarro, 'The Reception of Norms, and Open Legal Systems', *op. cit.*, pp. 285ff.

[208] The appeals of this type are increasing in jurisprudential literature. For example, J. Mikołajewicz, *Prawo intertemporalne*, *op. cit.*, p. 119, postulates that: "We should revisit the concept of legal validity so as to avoid the absurd situation that we considered as invalid such legal norms whose application is subject to the obligation of certain legal organs". Similarly W. Wróbel, 'O niektórych problemach interpretacji pojęcia "obowiązujący akt normatywny" w orzeczeniach Trybunału Konstytucyjnego' [On Some Problems with Interpreting the Concept "Valid Normative Act" in the Rulings of the Constitutional Tribunal] in A Jankiewicz (ed.), *Działalność orzecznicza Trybunału Konstytucyjnego*, Warszawa 1994, p. 55, who rightly observes that: "There arises a

Let us now answer the second question: Do foreign law norms belong to the legal system of the state whose norms require their application? Contrary to appearances, the answer to this question also needs to be considered carefully. Although the above-mentioned authors assume unanimously that the norms of foreign law do not belong to the legal system of the state where they can be applied under private international law, it is difficult not to mention the opposite position of Hans Kelsen, who believed that:

> [t]he rule obliging the courts of a State to apply norms of a foreign law to certain cases has the effect of incorporating the norms of the foreign law into the law of this State.[209]

This position is clearly consistent with Kelsen's doctrine of the unity of law, based on his monistic theory of the relation between international public law and domestic (national) law.[210] The criticism of this doctrine, carried out by such authors as Hart[211] and Raz,[212] indirectly shows that adopting the thesis of incorporating foreign legal norms into the domestic legal system has certain unacceptable consequences. Without going into the details of this well-known critique, it is worth noting that this thesis is untenable, not least due to the fact that the statement on the membership of norms in the legal system of a given state depends, after all, on whether these norms meet the membership criteria proper for this domestic legal system. Meanwhile, when applying foreign law, national courts do not use the membership criteria appropriate to the domestic law, but the criteria for the membership, or for the applicability relevant for the foreign legal system[213] (Hart refers to this type of recognition of law—different from the ordinary one—as "derivative" recognition[214]), possibly supplemented—as in the Polish private international law[215]—with meta-rules limiting the possibility of applying foreign norms rather than of their membership in the domestic system of law.

---

fundamental doubt of whether any public authority may apply 'invalid law'. If, however, it is stated that such law may be applied by the authority, then it must be valid to some extent". Let us add that the method that enables us to avoid these types of antinomies in cases involving the application of intertemporal rules is presented in Chap. 9 at pp. 509–511. However, this method is based on a postpositivist conception of legal validity, which does not involve its identification with the membership in the legal system.

[209] H. Kelsen, *General Theory of Law and State*, *op. cit.*, p. 244.

[210] *Cf.* H. Kelsen, *General Theory of Law and State*, *op. cit.*, pp. 363ff. and *Reine Rechtslehre*, 2nd ed., *op. cit.*, pp. 328ff. [English version, pp. 328ff.].

[211] *Cf.* H.L.A. Hart, 'Kelsen's Doctrine of the Unity of Law' in *idem*, *Essays in Jurisprudence and Philosophy*, *op. cit.*, pp. 309–342.

[212] *Cf.* J. Raz, *The Concept of a Legal System*, *op. cit.*, pp. 100ff. and 'Kelsen's Theory of the Basic Norm', *op. cit.*, pp. 127ff.

[213] *Cf. e.g.*, the Article 5 of the *Prawo prywatne międzynarodowe*, *op. cit.*, which indirectly refers to these criteria, prescribing that: "If in a State whose law is applicable, the various legal systems are valid, the law of that State determines which of these systems ought to be applied".

[214] H.L.A. Hart, 'Kelsen's Doctrine of the Unity of Law', *op. cit.*, p. 342.

[215] *Cf. e.g.*, the Article 6 of the *Prawo prywatne międzynarodowe*, *op. cit.*: "The laws of a foreign State cannot be applied if their application would have effects contrary to the fundamental principles of Polish legal system".

We are well aware that the discussed counterexample may be questionable. In particular, it is not certain whether the norms of foreign law, applicable under the rules of private international law, can be regarded as a legitimate antecedent of the analysed implication: "If a norm of statutory law is valid, then it belongs to the legal system". Nevertheless, the discussed example has such an advantage that it reminds us that the concept of legal validity constructed under the concept of the membership in the legal system, is not very useful to describe the phenomena of the modern law, which assumes the form of a multicentric legal system,[216] and which—due to the progressive importance of supranational legal orders—can (and perhaps should be) reconstructed as a part of a global so-called network system of law.[217] Neither does the conception of legal validity, identifying it with the membership in the legal system, correspond to the different methods of using this concept in juristic and legal discourse. Let us note that during the litigation, wherein the norms of foreign law will constitute the basis of the final ruling, the counsels of the parties and the parties themselves probably will not hesitate to assert that those norms (interpreted as sanctioned norms) regulate the substantive rights and duties of the litigants and that they are valid (as sanctioning norms) in terms of determining the legal consequences which the court should authoritatively determine in the sentence. Yet, it is hard to believe that these norms will be considered by the court or by the parties as belonging to the domestic legal system under which the dispute is resolved.

The third counterexample, being the last to challenge the legitimacy of the first implication, concerns the characteristics of the *Grundnorm*—the transcendental response to the jurisprudential question about *arche* in Hans Kelsen's normativism. It is not an easy task to examine this example, because the characteristic feature of Kelsen's *Grundnorm* is the changeability of its formulations and its methodological (epistemological) status. As far as the first issue is concerned, as aptly noted by a

---

[216] In Polish jurisprudential literature *cf.* E. Łętowska, 'Multicentryczność współczesnego systemu prawa i jej konsekwencje' [Multicentric Character of Contemporary Legal System and Its Consequences], *PiP* 4 (2005), pp. 3–17; W. Lang, 'Wokół "Multicentryczności systemu prawa"' [About "Multicentric Character of Legal System"], *PiP* 7 (2005), pp. 95–99; A. Kustra, 'Wokół problemu multicentryczności systemu prawa' [About the Problem of the Multicentricy of Legal System], *PiP* 6 (2006), pp. 85–99; M. J. Golecki, B. Wojciechowski, 'Ekonomiczna analiza stosowania prawa wspólnotowego' [Economic Analysis of Applying Community Law] in J. Stelmach, M. Soniewicka (eds.), *Analiza ekonomiczna w zastosowaniach prawniczych*, Warszawa 2007, pp. 117ff.; A. Kalisz, 'Multicentryczność systemu prawa polskiego a działalność orzecznicza Europejskiego Trybunału Sprawiedliwości i Europejskiego Trybunału Praw Człowieka' [The Multicentric Character of the Polish Legal System and the Jurisdiction of the European Court of Justice and the European Court of Human Rights], *RPEiS* LXIX/4 (2007), pp. 35–49.

[217] On the theory of a multicentric network-system of law (the latter term introduced by W. Cyrul), elaborated by Belgian legal philosophers (François Ost, Michael van de Kerchove and Luc J. Wintgents) *see* W. Cyrul, *Dyskursywna teoria tworzenia prawa* [The Discursive Theory of Lawmaking], Kraków 2001 [unpublished PhD thesis], pp. 85ff. and W. Cyrul, B. Brożek, 'Globalny system prawa' [The Global Legal System], *SFP* 2 (2003), pp. 102ff., and the references cited therein.

prominent scholar and commentator on the pure theory of law—Stanley Paulson—due to Kelsen's constant struggle with the problem of the basic norm, "[a]ny attempt to precisely reconstruct the knowledge about *Grundnorm* leads to a maze of different terms, representations, concepts".[218] It suffices to add that the American scholar provides a list of ten different formulations of *Grundnorm* that come from Kelsen's studies, at the same time stressing that the list is still not exhaustive.[219] The same applies to the methodological status of the basic norm, which is subject to significant changes in subsequent phases of Kelsen's scientific work.[220] To mention only the most crucial approaches, it was conceived by him as: a hypothesis (understood as a non-verifiable assumption) of legal thinking, as the constitution in a legal and logical sense (*Verfassung in rechtslogischen Sinne*), as a transcendentally and logically necessary presupposition of law cognition, and finally, in the last, sceptical phase of scientific work (after 1962[221]), as a proper fiction (*eigentliche Fiktion*) in terms of the *Als-Ob* philosophy of the neo-Kantian philosopher, Hans Vaihinger.[222]

In the context of the analysed thesis: "If a norm of statutory law is valid, then it belongs to the legal system", it is essential to determine the status of the basic norm in terms of validity and membership, to which we shall limit our investigations. As for the first question, there is no doubt that *Grundnorm* is valid; more precisely, its validity is presupposed and cannot be questioned.[223] In the pure theory of law, its main function is to justify the validity of other legal norms, which, according to the author of *Reine Rechtslehre*, can only consist in the reference to *Sollen*; namely, to the validity of another higher norm. Additionally, it is indeed the basic norm that is the highest one, representing the beginning of all "chains of validity" in a given

[218] St.L. Paulson, 'Die unterschiedlichen Formulierungen der "Grundnorm"' in A. Aarnio *et al.* (eds.), *Rechtsnorm und Rechtswirklichkeit*, *op. cit.*, p. 55.

[219] *Ibidem*, p. 58ff. In particular, Paulson omitted such formulations in which Kelsen pointed to the possibility of interpreting *Grundnorm* as a norm of natural law – for more details *see* Chap. 8, note 191 at p. 403.

[220] On the contentious problem of periodisation of Kelsen's thought *cf.* J. Wróblewski, 'Dilemmas of the Normativistic Concept of the Legal System', *op. cit.*, p. 319; E. Bulygin, 'An Antinomy in Kelsen's Pure Theory of Law', *op. cit.*, pp. 30–31; St.L. Paulson, 'Four Phases in Hans Kelsen's Legal Theory?', *op. cit.* and "Arriving at a Defensible Periodization of Hans Kelsen's Legal Theory", *op. cit.*

[221] *Cf.* St.L. Paulson, 'Arriving at a Defensible Periodization of Hans Kelsen's Legal Theory', *op. cit.*, pp. 354–355.

[222] *See* two excellent studies, reconstructing the genesis and evolution of Kelsen's views on this matter: R. Walter, 'Die Grundnorm im System der Reinen Rechtslehre' in A. Aarnio *et al.* (eds.), *Rechtsnorm und Rechtswirklichkeit*, *op. cit.*, pp. 85–99 and U.U. Bindreiter, 'Presupposing the Basic Norm', *op. cit.*, pp. 144ff., and the source texts cited therein. The analysis of the status of *Grundnorm* from the perspective of the analytical theory of law has been presented by R. Alexy, *Begriff und Geltung des Rechts*, *op. cit.*, pp. 170ff. [English version, pp. 107ff.].

[223] For more on the basic norm *see* H. Kelsen, *Reine Rechtslehre*, 1st ed., *op. cit.*, pp. 62ff., *General Theory of Law and State*, *op. cit.*, pp. 115ff., *Reine Rechtslehre*, 2nd ed., *op. cit.*, pp. 196ff. [English version, pp. 193ff], and *Allgemeine Theorie der Normen*, *op. cit.*, pp. 203ff.

legal order (system).[224] Yet, what raises considerable controversies is the question of the membership of the basic norm in the legal system. In the jurisprudential literature one can encounter the standpoint that, according to Kelsen, this norm belongs to the legal system,[225] but there are also contrary opinions,[226] or relativised ("mixed") ones,[227] as well as the normative claims that the basic norm should[228] or should not[229] belong to the legal system. These controversies, as it seems, stem from imprecise statements formulated by Kelsen himself as well as from the fact that the commentators often mix two research perspectives: a descriptive-reconstructive and a critical-postulative one. It is one thing to attempt to find answers to the question as to whether *Grundnorm* belongs to the legal system according to the author of *Reine Rechtslehre* and quite another as to whether it should belong to this system due to some reasons. Naturally, there is no room in our study to deliberate over the second (normative) issue, that is why we shall focus on the descriptive approach, thus confining our analysis to the legal system understood (as Kelsen did) as a dynamic normative system.

It must be admitted that the statements made by the founder of normativism, relating to the membership of the basic norm in the legal system, are often unclear, yet we may indicate two source texts, whose interpretation provides a simple and unambiguous way to identify his position. The first one is the article *Was ist ein*

---

[224] On the chains of validity in Kelsen's theory, *see* J. Raz, *The Concept of a Legal System*, *op. cit.*, pp. 97ff., 105ff.

[225] *Cf. e.g.*, H.L.A. Hart, 'Kelsen's Doctrine of the Unity of Law', *op. cit.*, p. 338 and J. Raz, 'Kelsen's Theory of the Basic Norm', *op. cit.*, pp. 122, 144. Let us note that if we understand the legal system as a set of norms interconnected by "the chains of validity", then such a criterion of membership entails that the thesis of the membership of the basic norm in the legal system becomes not only justified, but even analytically necessary.

[226] *Cf. e.g.*, W. Lang, *Obowiązywanie prawa*, *op. cit.*, p. 199ff.; R. Alexy, *Begriff und Geltung des Rechts*, *op. cit.*, p. 173; W. Kersting, 'Neukantianische Rechtsbegründung. Rechtsbegriff und richtiges Recht bei Cohen, Stammler und Kelsen' in R. Alexy *et al.* (eds.), *Neukantianismus und Rechtsphilosophie*, *op. cit.*, p. 59; S. Kaźmierczyk, 'Norma podstawowa' [Basic Norm] in A. Bator, W. Gromski, A. Kozak, S. Kaźmierczyk, Z. Pulka, *Wprowadzenie do nauk prawnych*, *op. cit.*, p. 109. Let us add that Alexy, Kersting and Kaźmierczyk aptly refer their statements directly to the system of positive law.

[227] The clearest example is perhaps seen in U.U. Bindreiter's position from 'Presupposing the Basic Norm', *op. cit.*, who at first (correctly) notes that in Kelsen's theory the basic norm "is not really a part of positive law" (p. 145) and then (also correctly) concludes that the basic norm must be understood "as belonging to [...] legal system" (p. 150). Why both Bindreiter's statements are right will be justified shortly.

[228] *See e.g.*, K. Świrydowicz, *Analiza logiczna pojęcia kompetencji normodawczej*, *op. cit.*, p. 35, who believes that "for the clarity of the system's construction", we should assume that the basic norm belongs to the legal system, but he also rightly points out that in Kelsen's conception, this norm "does not belong to the system on the basis of its enactment".

[229] *See e.g.*, an interpretation of the basic norm as the highest norm of the static normative system, conceived in analogy to Kant's categorical imperative, presented by J. Stelmach, 'Norma podstawowa', *op. cit.*, pp. 65ff. In relation to dynamic legal systems, Stelmach considers as an open question "whether the basic norm constitutes a component of the system [...], or this norm does not belong to the system" (*ibidem*, p. 66).

Rechtsakt?, published in 1952 (in the classical period of the development of Kelsen's theory), which is a polemic with Alfred Verdross' views.[230] In this work, Kelsen stresses that if we want to define legal acts (*Rechtsakte*) by reference to the concept of legal order (*Rechtsordnung*), this concept cannot be limited to a positively established norm (contained in the constitution and normative acts of lower rank), but it must also include a presupposed (pre-posited)[231] basic norm. As he writes:

> If the norms of the Constitution are components of the legal order, then also the *Grundnorm* must be perceived as belonging to legal order,[232]

and therefore:

> The Constitution and the norms enacted on the grounds of Constitution only together with the basic norm, which is the fundament of the Constitution, constitute the legal order.[233]

Kelsen's position is thus based on the assumption that if we do not limit the concept of legal order (legal system)[234] only to positively enacted legal norms—namely to the system of norms issued by man (*durch menschliche Akte*)—then *Grundnorm* belongs to such a legal system.

Kelsen's second statement, which should be pointed out, comes from the second edition of *Reine Rechtslehre* of 1960. In this study, the author of normativism enters into polemics with the interpretation of his basic norm theory presented by Anders Wedberg, who argued that according to Kelsen, any legal system contains the basic norm. Let us again quote Kelsen's statement in which he firmly opposes Wedberg's interpretation:

> The *Grundnorm* is not "included" in a positive legal order, for it is not a positive, it means: enacted (*gesetzte*) [norm], but a norm presupposed (*vorausgesetzte*) in juristic thought.[235]

---

[230] H. Kelsen, 'Was ist ein Rechtsakt?' in R. Marcic *et al.* (eds.), *Internationale Festschrift für Alfred Verdross zum 80. Geburtstag*, München/Salzburg 1971, pp. 153–165 [English version: 'What is a Legal Act?', trans. B. Paulson, St.L. Paulson, *AJJ* 29 (1984), pp. 199–212].

[231] *Ibidem*, pp. 154–155 [English version, pp. 200–202]. Why the "presupposed" (*vorausgesetzt*) norm should be considered "pre-posited" has been convincingly explained by U.U. Bindtreiter, 'Presupposing the Basic Norm', *op. cit.*, pp. 148, 170.

[232] H. Kelsen, 'Was ist ein Rechtsakt?', *op. cit.*, p. 155 [English version, pp. 201–202].

[233] *Ibidem*, p. 163 [English version, p. 209].

[234] Kelsen virtually equates the concepts of the legal order and legal system – *see e.g.*, *Reine Rechtslehre*, 1st ed., *op. cit.*, p. 62, *General Theory of Law and State*, *op. cit.*, pp. 110, 113, *Reine Rechtslehre*, 2nd ed., *op. cit.*, p. 78 [English version, p. 75], and 'Vom Geltungsgrund des Rechts' in F.A. Frhr. v. d. Heydte *et al.* (eds.), *Völkerrecht und rechtliches Weltbild. Festschrift für Alfred Verdross*, Wien 1960, p. 157.

[235] H. Kelsen, *Reine Rechtslehre*, 2nd ed., *op. cit.*, note marked * at p. 201 [omitted in English translation]. Kelsen expresses a similar, albeit indirect view in 'Vom Geltungsgrund des Rechts', *op. cit.*, p. 165, where he discusses the allegation that positivism and positivist *Reine Rechtslehre* can justify the validity of positive law only by means of the norm which "keine Norm dieses positiven Rechts (im engeren Sinne des Wortes) ist".

The Austrian philosopher also points out that the elements of the positive order (*positive Ordnung*) are only the enacted norms (*gesetzt*); that is, positive ones.[236] This position, only *prima facie* contradictory to the previously presented one, should not raise any interpretive doubts. Kelsen undoubtedly correctly claims that *Grundnorm* does not belong to the order (system) of positive law due to a quite prosaic reason—namely, it is not a positive norm; that is, a norm established by man. It thus appears that the answer to the question of what Kelsen thought about the membership of the basic norm in the legal system is relativised to the way in which one understands its extension: if the legal system includes both positive and pre-positive (non-positive) norms, then *Grundnorm* belongs to it, and if the legal system includes only positive norms, then *Grundnorm* does not belong to it, because due to its origins (the way it is "created") it is not possible.

We cannot deal at this point with a problem of which concept of the legal system is more appropriate from a jurisprudential point of view—we limit ourselves in noting that Kelsen advocated a broader extension of it.[237] Coming back to the basic course of the argument, we shall conclude that the presented analyses show that *Grundnorm* is valid but it does not belong to the system of positive law, understood as a system containing only the norms established by man. Despite a tautological, and thus trivial justification, this counterexample—although it goes beyond the scope of the discussion adopted in our clarificative analysis, which is limited to the issue of the validity of statutory law norms—demonstrates that apart from statutory norms, mistakenly deemed constitutional, and foreign legal norms that are valid but do not belong to a domestic legal system, we can similarly characterise the basic norm. The *Grundnorm* is, in fact, not an established norm, but it is valid, though not belonging to the system of positive law (as defined by Kelsen). This counterexample is naturally only seemingly adequate,[238] yet it does illustrate the fact that in the jurisprudential discourse, the relation between validity and membership is not absolute; hence, it was worth bringing up and considering. In passing, let us add that the category of the basic norm—as evidenced in Bulygin's studies—is utterly redundant for lawyers in determining the membership of norms in the legal system: what is sufficient, is a properly formulated recursive definition of membership.[239]

---

[236] H. Kelsen, *Reine Rechtslehre*, 2nd ed., *op. cit.*, p. 201 [English version, p. 198].

[237] *Cf.* H. Kelsen, 'Was ist ein Rechtsakt?', *op. cit.*, p. 155 [English version, p. 202], where Kelsen makes the possibility of the positivist understanding of law (i.e., perceiving it as norms established by man) dependent on adopting the concept of the legal order (legal system), which includes *Grundnorm.*

[238] Since it directly refers to the thesis: "If a norm is valid, then it belongs to the system of positive law", as opposed – both in terms of antecedent as well as consequent – to the thesis: "If a norm of statutory law is valid, then it belongs to the legal system", which we discuss in the context of the correctness of definition D_1.

[239] *See* E. Bulygin, 'An Antinomy in Kelsen's Pure Theory of Law', *op. cit.*, pp. 40ff. *Cf. idem*, 'Algunas consideraciones sobre los sistemas jurídicos', *op. cit.*, pp. 263ff. In the Polish literature, a similar view on the redundancy of the construction of the basic norm has been expressed by Z. Ziembiński, *Problemy podstawowe prawoznawstwa*, *op. cit.*, pp. 210–211.

Let us now examine the correctness of the second implication: "If a norm of statutory law belongs to the legal system, then it is valid". There are also a number of examples that can be presented in order to undermine its legitimacy. Due to the symmetry of our arguments, we shall confine ourselves to the present three, as it seems, most important counterexamples.[240]

The first counterexample, the most obvious to philosophers and theorists of law, concerns Hart's rule of recognition. The topic of this rule has already been indicated in our study and we shall revisit this problem,[241] which should not come as a surprise given the enormous contribution of the philosopher from Oxford in clarifying the issue of the validity of law, which constitutes the main object of our inquiry. This time we will focus on a relatively non-complicated issue; namely, characterising this rule in terms of membership and validity. The rule of recognition as one of the secondary rules, undoubtedly belongs to the legal system (i.e., to the legal system constructed in accordance with Hart's positivist theory), but that is not all—its acceptance is one of two minimum conditions necessary and sufficient for its existence.[242] Nevertheless, as Hart insists, "it can neither be valid nor invalid" because the question of the validity of the rule of recognition does not come up at all.[243] The validity of the rule of recognition is not a condition of recognising the validity of individual legal norms (especially the primary rules) on the basis of the criteria that comprise this rule. The role of such a condition is fulfilled by its existence, *nota bene* identically, as in the case of the sovereign norm in von Wright's conception of validity.[244] As Hart stated:

> the rule of recognition exists only as a complex, but normally concordant, practice of the courts, officials, and private persons in identifying the law by reference to certain criteria. Its existence is a matter of fact.[245]

After all, according to Hart, the expression of this fact by means of the statement—in fact obscuring the merits of the issue—under which the validity of the rule of recognition is "assumed but cannot be demonstrated", recalls the assertion that we can assume, although we will never demonstrate that the standard metre bar in Paris, which is the ultimate test of the accuracy of all metric measurements, "is itself correct".[246]

---

[240] In fact, in the subsequent part of this subsection, we will discuss four counterexamples, but the last of them, due to its importance, will be presented as a separate argument, A–IV.

[241] *See supra*, pp. 278ff., Chap. 4, pp. 128–130, and Chap. 9, pp. 456–457.

[242] H.L.A. Hart, *The Concept of Law*, *op. cit.*, p. 113.

[243] H.L.A. Hart, *ibidem*, p. 105. *Cf.* J. Woleński, 'Obowiązywanie prawne w ujęciu H.L.A. Harta' [Validity of Law in H.L.A. Hart's Conception], *ZNUJ PP* 51 (1971), pp. 284ff.

[244] *See* G.H. von Wright, *Norm and Action*, *op. cit.*, pp. 196ff.

[245] H.L.A. Hart, *The Concept of Law*, *op. cit.*, p. 107.

[246] *Ibidem*, p. 106. Naturally, Hart opposes Kelsen here, who before 1962, treated the basic norm as presupposed, and the rule of recognition is not presupposed since – according to Hart – it, simply, exists. In effect, in such a context, the question as to whether the standard metre is one metre long, is absurd. For more on the differences between Hart's concept of the rule of recognition and

It is not surprising that this counterexample, like the above example of Kelsen's *Grundnorm*, is also not fully adequate.[247] The rule of recognition is not a norm of statutory law, but—as already mentioned[248]—a customary rule. Nevertheless, the analysis of the status of the rule of recognition in terms of membership and validity once more demonstrates that within jurisprudential discourse the relation between membership and validity is not absolute, and the fact that we do not deal with statutory norms does not appear to significantly undermine the argumentative force of this example.

The second counterexample, demonstrating the inaccuracy of the implication: "If a norm of statutory law belongs to the legal system, then it is valid", refers to the *desuetudo* phenomenon. The mass media frequently report on the fact that some norms that were "long forgotten" (particularly by the authorities obliged to apply the law) and are contemporarily nonsensical, are formally valid and even scientists do not usually shun recording examples that trigger widespread amusement.[249] For instance, we can quote a recently rediscovered, and still not formally repealed *Ban issued on 15 November 1894 by the Directorate of the Police in consultation with the Spiritual Authority and with Krakow Municipality*, according to which it was banned (and, formally speaking, still is)[250]:

1. To walk the streets, public places and venues dressed as St. Nicholas, an Angel or Devil on St. Nicholas day and on the eve of it.
2. To walk the streets, public places and venues singing carols and presenting nativity plays during Christmas.
3. To walk the streets, public places and venues disguised or masked during "Haman" holidays, according to Judaism.

Kelsen's *Grundnorm* theory *see* H.L.A. Hart, *ibidem*, note to p. 97 at pp. 245–246, *cf. e.g.*, J. Woleński, 'Obowiązywanie prawne w ujęciu H.L.A. Harta', *op. cit.*, pp. 285ff. and N. Lacey, *A Life of H.L.A. Hart*, *op. cit.*, pp. 249ff.

[247] For it directly refers to the thesis: "If a norm belongs to the legal system, then it is valid", which differs – yet this time only in its antecedent – from the second implication: "If a norm of statutory law belongs to the legal system, then it is valid", analysed in the context of the correctness of D_1.

[248] *Cf. supra*, note 140 at p. 279, with the corresponding text.

[249] *Cf. e.g.*, Z. Ziembiński, *O stanowieniu i obowiązywaniu prawa*, *op. cit.*, p. 109, who in the context of *desuetudo* recalls administrative normative acts "associated with the rationing process of gutting herring or with setting the length of the stems of carnations classified as I, II and III category". T. Stawecki, P. Winczorek, *Wstęp do prawoznawstwa*, 2nd ed., Warszawa 1999, p. 79, give the example of the *Regulation of the Council of Ministers* of 1962, according to which the entrance to the railway platforms and other parts of the railway stations and bus stops is permitted only to holders of a rail ticket or platform ticket. And D. Heckmann, *Geltungskraft und Geltungsverlust von Rechtsnormen*, *op. cit.*, pp. 450ff., analyses (in the context of *desuetudo*) the "claim for compensation for maidenhood" (*Kranzgeldanspruch*), granted to "the bride of good repute" on the basis of the still formally valid § 1300 of *BGB*. In passing, let us add that legal theorists sometimes provide counterexamples, like Hart, who recalls a woman convicted by the English court in 1944 of divination, under the Witchcraft Act of 1735 – *see idem*, *The Concept of Law*, *op. cit.*, p. 60.

[250] M. Kozioł, 'Zakazane zostało' [It Was Banned], *Goniec* 8 (2005), p. 11.

Similar examples can be found, yet it does not change the fact that *desuetudo* rarely constitutes the subject matter of jurisprudential analysis, and the nature of this phenomenon is sometimes differently understood, which shall be illustrated by indicating three representative positions. For Hans Kelsen, *desuetudo* sometimes means the "negative legal effect of custom",[251] while sometimes it means the "rule of customary law".[252] For Jerzy Wróblewski, it is the phenomenon of a sufficiently long inapplication of systematically valid legal norms by the competent state authorities.[253] For Zygmunt Ziembiński, *desuetudo* designates:

> the cases in which some formally not repealed norms of the legal system, previously considered to be legally valid, are deemed no longer legally valid – due to their differently understood "outdatedness".[254]

It seems that the nature of *desuetudo* is best captured by the latter approach, more so in that both Kelsen and Wróblewski recognise that as a consequence of *desuetudo*, formally not repealed legal norms lose their validity.[255] If we consider that the formal failure to repeal a legal norm undoubtedly constitutes one of the basic criteria of its membership in the legal system (regardless of whether we talk about the membership in a weak sense, a medium or a strong one), the example of norms which lose their validity as a result of *desuetudo* makes us realise that membership in the legal system does not always entail their validity.

The third counterexample, concerning the thesis on entailing the validity of the norm by its membership in the legal system, refers to principles *necessitum nulla est obligatio* and *impossibilium nulla est obligatio*. One of the main components of the paradigm of legal positivism, associated with the argument on the separation of law and morality, is an acceptation that the norms of any content can constitute law—as it was expressed by Hans Kelsen in his classic formula: "Jeder beliebige Inhalt kann Recht sein".[256] It should be, at the same time, noted that when criticising legal positivism, it is often forgotten that even Kelsen (who was undoubtedly the archetypal hard positivist) assumed a certain limitation on the scope of this fundamental positivist principle. In his view, the content of legal norms cannot be human behaviour that is necessary or impossible.

In *Allgemeine Theorie der Normen*[257] Kelsen examines the examples of two mutually conflicting norms that violate the above limitation: "Die Menschen sollen sterben" (which cannot be infringed, because it prescribes something necessary),

[251] H. Kelsen, *General Theory of Law and State*, *op. cit.*, p. 119.

[252] *Ibidem*, p. 156.

[253] J. Wróblewski, *Sądowe stosowanie prawa*, *op. cit.*, p. 98 [English version, p. 79].

[254] Z. Ziembiński, 'Desuetudo', *op. cit.*, p. 3.

[255] *Cf.* H. Kelsen, *General Theory of Law and State*, *op. cit.*, pp. 119, 173, *Reine Rechtslehre*, 2nd ed., *op. cit.*, p. 220 [English version, p. 213], and *Allgemeine Theorie der Normen*, *op. cit.*, p. 113; J. Wróblewski, *Sądowe stosowanie prawa*, *op. cit.*, pp. 98–99 [English version, pp. 78–79].

[256] *Cf.* Chap. 2, note 35 at p. 20, where we provide the original wording of an extended version of Kelsen's formula and we indicate the source texts.

[257] H. Kelsen, *Allgemeine Theorie der Normen*, *op. cit.*, p. 45.

and: "Die Menschen sollen nicht sterben" (which, in turn, cannot be observed because it prescribes impossible behaviour).[258] One should agree with Kelsen that the norms of such content are senseless[259] and cannot be valid ("kann keine Geltung haben").[260] Thus, what Kelsen certainly does not hide, only when leaving aside the discussed limitations, "kann das Sollen einer Norm jeden beliebigen Inhalt haben".[261] Interestingly, as it seems one can observe here a common sense (and, therefore, somewhat necessary aspect, because common sense should not be an understated feature of only some of the jurisprudential conceptions) compliance of legal positivism with natural law doctrines—for example, Lon Fuller, in his procedural conception of natural law assumes the principle of *impossibilium nulla est obligatio* as one of the conditions of the internal morality of law. As he states:

> [The] law commanding the impossible seems such an absurdity that one is tempted to suppose no sane lawmaker, not even the most evil dictator, would have any reason to enact such a law.[262]

The consequences of the discussed counterexample in relation to the accuracy of the analysed implication are unambiguous and irrefutable from the analytical point of view. We shall illustrate them by referring to another example of the norm provided by Kelsen; namely, a legal norm prohibiting hunting for certain species of animals.[263] If, despite the prohibition of killing, a certain species—protected by positive law—is extinct, then such a legal norm still continues to belong to the legal system, but it loses its validity irrespective of the possible intervention of the legislator, because it can no longer be followed or applied. In this case, the principle of *necessitum nulla est obligatio* intersects with the principle of *cessante ratione*

[258] We have already analysed these examples in Chap. 4 at pp. 106–107. Given the rapid development of genetics and transplantology, it may slightly futuristically be noted that both examples will probably become inadequate in the near future and, sooner or later, a law may be established that orders the death of a man, for example, upon reaching the age of 150, due to religious, moral or economic reasons. Yet, any possible justification of such norms already constitutes the area of inquiry for bioethics and biojurisprudence, and so far, Kelsen's examples remain valid. However, one cannot fail to note that such norms are already beginning to appear, although for different reasons. For example, as recently reported by the mass media, under the decree of 13 February 2008, the mayor of Sarpourenx imposed a ban on dying in respect of the 260 inhabitants of this Pyrenean village, unless they have purchased space in the local cemetery, and they want to be buried there, at the same time threatening them with severe penalties – fortunately, unspecified – if this prohibition is violated. In the atmosphere of pure nonsense introduced by the said decree (Sarpourenx residents would probably happily die of laughter when reading the mayor's decree, if they were allowed to), it is worth noting that this is not an entirely suitable example of the norm that violates the principle of *impossibilium nulla est obligatio* because these people who have not secured a place for their burial, may yet leave Sarpourenx and legally die elsewhere.

[259] H. Kelsen, *Reine Rechtslehre*, 2nd ed., *op. cit.*, p. 11 [English version, p. 11].

[260] H. Kelsen, *Allgemeine Theorie der Normen*, *op. cit.*, p. 113.

[261] *Ibidem*, p. 45.

[262] L.L. Fuller, *The Morality of Law*, *op. cit.*, p. 70.

[263] *See* H. Kelsen, *Allgemeine Theorie der Normen*, *op. cit.*, p. 113.

legis cessat ipsa lex, which—incidentally—rightly justifies (in the context of Kelsen's last examples) the incorrectness of the considered implication: "If a norm of statutory law belongs to the legal system, then it is valid".

When concluding on all the six presented counterexamples, it should be stated that they do show that in many cases there is no intensional (meaning) equivalence between the validity of norms and their membership in the legal system. Even if some of the considered examples relate to a situation that is not very frequently encountered in everyday legal practice, it does not change the fact that the A–III argument weighs strongly in favour of rejecting the definition D_1. This definition is not only inconsistent with the reconstruction of a system of positive law, carried out under the guidance of Kelsen's pure theory of law or Hart's sophisticated legal positivism, but it also fails in the case of applying foreign law norms, the phenomenon of *desuetudo*, erroneous rulings of constitutional courts or the activities of an "insane" legislator who establishes norms that are objectively unnecessary or impossible to meet. It is also worth noting that all of these counterexamples are not due to (and do not constitute the elements of) nonpositivist, antipositivist or natural law argumentation, but they refer to the analysis or the conceptions developed by the leading, mostly hard legal positivists,[264] probably rightly labelled as the "apostles of made law".[265] This fact highlights how the legal positivists themselves are responsible for the destruction of one of the essential elements of their own doctrine; namely, the identification of the validity of statutory norms with their membership in the legal system.

As already noted, the last argument A–IV constitutes a kind of continuation of the reasoning set out in the final part of the A–III argument. When discussing the objectives of the undertaken clarification of the intension of the juristic concept of the validity of statutory law, we have stressed our desire to create such a conception of validity, which, in addition to jurisprudential correctness, will not jeopardise legitimate juristic intuition and which will be useful in practice.[266] The analysis of the symmetry of the alleged synonymy that, in accordance with the definition D_1, takes place between the validity of a statutory law norm and its membership in the legal system, leads directly to the next argument under which we will try to prove that adopting such a definition entails an analytically necessary imprecision of applying the concept of the validity of law in a way—we believe—that is contrary to the legitimate insights of jurists; in particular, the dogmatists of law and practicing lawyers. The problem that this argument will directly affect is a questionable issue (at least in the Polish jurisprudential discussions)[267] of the validity of statutory legal norms in the period of *vacatio legis*.

---

[264] The analysed counterexamples used, inter alia, the ideas and examples from the work of E. Bulygin, H.L.A. Hart (the only soft positivist in this circle), H. Kelsen, J. Raz, J. Wróblewski and Z. Ziembiński.

[265] The term derived from L.L. Fuller, *Anatomy of the Law*, New York 1968, p. 112.

[266] *Cf.* Chap. 6, pp. 222–223.

[267] *Cf. supra*, the references cited in notes 19–22 at p. 251, and the corresponding text.

In order to present the argument A–IV in a maximally clear and readable way, we shall use a specific example from the Polish positive law. The currently valid Polish Penal Code, issued on the 6th of June 1997, was promulgated in the *Journal of Statutes* of the 2nd of August 1997.[268] In accordance with Article 1 of the *Introductory Provisions to the Penal Code*,[269] the new Penal Code came into force on the 1st of September 1998 (i.e., more than a year after its promulgation). Let us now consider[270] how we can characterise the validity of statutory norms contained (encoded) in the former Penal Code of April 19, 1969,[271] and in the new Penal Code in respect of the period in which the latter remained in the state of *vacatio legis*. From a purely theoretical point of view, we have a choice of four options. We can argue that in the period of more than 1 year (from the 6th of June 1997 to the 1st of September 1998), i.e., in the *vacatio legis* of the new Penal Code:

1. neither the norms of the former Penal Code, nor of the new Penal Code were valid;
2. the norms of the former Penal Code were valid and the norms of the new Penal Code were not valid;
3. the norms of the former Penal Code were not valid and the norms of the new Penal Code were valid; or
4. both the norms of the former as well as of the new Penal Code were valid.

Let us now examine these possibilities in the context of definition D_1; namely, in relation to the conception of validity based on the concept of membership of norms in the legal system. Regarding the first option, let us just record its absurdity. Leaving aside the question of the membership of the norms of the old and the new Penal Code in the Polish legal system, we take for granted that the institution of *vacatio legis* does not consist of the fact that the legislator, when making legal amendments, temporarily introduces more than a one-year-long state of normative anarchy within the criminal law, meaning that neither the old repealed law, nor the new introduced one is valid.

The second option corresponds—which we allow ourselves to assume without proof (in particular, without examining the studies that support or challenge this position)[272]—to a common sense approach of the dogmatists of law, practicing

[268] *Kodeks karny. Ustawa z dnia 6 czerwca 1997 r.* [Penal Code. Statute of 6 June 1997], published in *Dziennik Ustaw* [Journal of Statutes] 1997, No. 88, Item 553.

[269] *Przepisy wprowadzające kodeks karny. Ustawa z dnia 6 czerwca 1997 r.* [Introductory Provisions to the Penal Code. Statute of 6 June 1997], published in *Dziennik Ustaw* [Journal of Statutes] 1997, No. 88, Item 554. Amendments concerning the end of *vacatio legis* of the new Penal Code were published in *Dziennik Ustaw* 1997, No. 160, Item 1083, and in *Dziennik Ustaw* 1998, No. 113, Item 715.

[270] Naturally, in the following discussion we omit the detailed issues of applying the penal law principle of *lex mitior agit* as well as intertemporal rules that can justify the validity of the norms interpreted from formally repealed legal provisions.

[271] *Kodeks karny. Ustawa z dnia 19 czerwca 1969 r.* [Penal Code. Statute of 19 June 1969], published in *Dziennik Ustaw* [Journal of Statutes] 1969, No. 13, Item 94.

[272] We do not need to provide such proof since the essence of the argument A–IV is to highlight complications arising from adopting definition D_1, in particular the criticism of the defects of the fourth option of the description of the *vacatio legis* phenomenon. For the record, it should be

lawyers, as well as non-professional addressees of legal norms to the issues of legal validity.[273] We should add only that by supporting this option, linguistic intuitions of lawyers and non-lawyers are based—at least in regard to the Polish juristic language—on the already discussed semantic relation that takes place in Polish language between "validity" and "being someone's duty".[274] No one disputes (including the supporters of definition D_1) that the obligations set by the legal norms are actualised only at the time when the new law enters into force, which is also lexically confirmed.[275] Yet, the second option cannot be accepted by the supporters of definition D_1, because the assumption that a properly promulgated norm (or a legislative act) belongs to the legal system also during the *vacatio legis* period cannot be rebutted—as rightly stated by Sławomira Wronkowska—at the moment when the legislative act has been promulgated;

> [it] becomes the element of the legal system and it may be modified or eliminated from it only in accordance with procedural rules of legislation.[276]

pointed out that jurisprudential argumentation in favour of the second option is presented by T. Pietrzykowski, 'Temporalny zakres obowiązywania prawa' [Temporal Scope of the Validity of Law], *PiP* 4 (2003), pp. 46ff. and *Wsteczne działanie prawa i jego zakaz*, *op. cit.*, pp. 38ff. Polemically P.J. Grabowski, 'W sprawie zakresu temporalnego obowiązywania prawa' [On the Scope of the Temporal Validity of Law], *PiP* 4 (2004), pp. 96ff.

[273] The consequence of adopting this option, which we strongly advocate, is the above-mentioned similarity of the situation envisaged in argument A–IV to the cases analysed in the second part of the previous argument A–III: legal norms that remain in the period of *vacatio legis* belong to the legal system, yet they are not valid.

[274] *Cf. supra*, pp. 269–270. A similar linguistic argument is used by G. Wierczyński, '"Obowiązywanie" a "wejście w życie" – uwagi polemiczne', *op. cit.*, pp. 109–110. It should be added that this position is confirmed by normative theories of legal validity, since it is indeed hard to deny that the institutional duty of applying valid legal norms concerns the period after *vacatio legis* has elapsed.

[275] *See e.g.*, H. Zgółkowa (ed.), *Praktyczny słownik współczesnej polszczyzny*, *op. cit.*, p. 60, where the meaning of the adjective "valid" is as follows: "that which is legally binding, is up to date, has been put into effect", or D. Ludwiczak *et al.* (eds.), *Słownik wyrazów bliskoznacznych* [Thesaurus], Warszawa 1998, p. 133, where the expression "to come into force" is the second out of three synonyms of the expression "to be valid". In Polish jurisprudential literature, the same position was taken by W. Lang, *Obowiązywanie prawa*, *op. cit.*, p. 231, who argues that the statutory phrase "the law comes into force on ...", is synonymous with the phrase "the law is valid". S. Wronkowska, although she is a supporter of the opposite terminological convention, also admits that in legal and in juristic language, "the expression 'norm N has come into force' relatively often renders the meaning of 'norm N is valid'. Accordingly, these expressions are construed as synonyms" – *Podstawowe pojęcia prawa i prawoznawstwa*, *op. cit.*, p. 54. *See* also a similar opinion of A. Aarnio, 'On the Validity, Efficacy and Acceptability of Legal Norms' in *idem*, *Philosophical Perspectives in Jurisprudence*, APhF XXXVI (1983), pp. 152, 154ff.

[276] S. Wronkowska, 'Glosa do wyroku Trybunału Konstytucyjnego z dnia 26 października 1999 r. (sygn. akt K 12/99) [A Gloss on the Constitutional Tribunal Ruling of 26 October 1999 (sign. K 12/99)], *PS* 3/38 (2000), p. 101. The list of the authors presenting an identical standpoint is provided by T. Pietrzykowski, *Wsteczne działanie prawa i jego zakaz*, *op. cit.*, note 35 at p. 21; *see* also similar opinions of E. Bulygin, 'Time and Validity', *op. cit.*, p. 68 [Spanish version, p. 199] and of P.E. Navarro, 'Legal Reasoning and Systematization of Law', *op. cit.*, p. 262.

Thus, according to D_1, the new Penal Code was valid during *vacatio legis*, and therefore the advocates of this definition have to choose between the third and fourth option.

At first glance, the third option seems as absurd as the first option—because the thesis that since the 2nd of August 1997, the former Penal Code was not valid, whereas the new Penal Code was valid, is utterly inconsistent with the second option, which we have already advocated for. Nevertheless, the third option at least releases us from the obligation of having to recognise the temporal "co-validity" of both these codes and, moreover, if we assumed a kind of isomorphism of systemic consequences of enacting and repealing legal acts (or norms), it would be theoretically possible to defend the position that, like the act of establishing a norm (whose last stage is its proper promulgation), entails its immediate membership in the legal system, its derogation entails an immediate (i.e., taking place when promulgating a derogating norm) loss of membership in the legal system. Defending such a position is, nevertheless, a task doomed to failure if we, for example, take into account the example—albeit not very frequently encountered—of temporary (episodic) acts of law, whose provisions also define the final moment of their validity. When analysing this institution in the context of the *Principles of Legislative Technique*, Sławomira Wronkowska and Maciej Zieliński rightly point out that on the date of the entry into force of the episodic law;

> there takes place the act of determining the time when the validity of the statute expires (rather than the act of the expiry of its validity).[277]

Adopting a contrary position, in fact, leads to the absurd: the episodic statutes (normative acts) would cease to be valid at the moment of their entry into force and they would be valid (in the meaning of their membership in the legal system) only during the period of *vacatio legis*.

What therefore remains is the fourth option—the only one consistent with the definition that identifies the validity of statutory norms with their membership in the legal system. Yet, its proponents are forced to conclude that during the *vacatio legis* of the new Penal Code both codes and legal norms contained therein would be simultaneously valid ("co-valid"). Contrary to appearances, this position is neither self-contradictory nor does it lead to contradictions,[278] since the conception of the legal norm—derived from the Poznań school of legal theory and adapted for the purpose of this study—allows us to reconstruct (decode) legal norms contained in both Penal Codes in such a way that there can be no contradiction caused by the

---

[277] S. Wronkowska, M. Zieliński, *Komentarz do zasad techniki prawodawczej z dnia 20 czerwca 2002 r.* [Commentary on the Principles of Legislative Technique of 20 June 2002], Warszawa 2004, p. 56.

[278] We could speak of a possible contradiction only if we assume that lawmaking acts (as opposed to legal norms) constitute the valid elements of the legal system, which we have previously disagreed with – *cf.* Chap. 6 at pp. 240ff. Moreover, it is not quite certain what this contradiction would involve, if it were not the contradictions between individual legal norms contained in both codes, which – as we explain in the text – do not take place.

adoption of definition D_1. It is the case because the provisions on the entry into force co-determine (along with other provisions) the content of the legal norms contained in those codes.[279] As already noted by Zygmunt Ziembiński in 1966, when using the example of the Polish Civil Code of 1964,[280]

> the norms under which from the 1st of January 1965 one should act in a certain way in civil transactions and adjudicate in a certain way in civil cases, are valid from the date of promulgating the code.[281]

Thus, the norms of both codes cannot be in contradiction due to the simple reason that—roughly speaking and ignoring, in particular, the intertemporal issues, mainly related to the sanctioning norms—the norms of the old code regulate human behaviour until the entry into force of the new code, whereas the norms of the latter do so from that very moment.

Nonetheless, lack of contradictions does not protect the supporters of D_1 against the allegation of an analytically necessary linguistic (semantic) imprecision, stemming from the acceptance of the fourth option. The imprecision arising from the application of this "simplistic concept of validity"[282] lies in the fact that definition D_1 does not allow for a linguistically (terminologically) easy differentiation between legal norms remaining in the state of *vacatio legis* and the norms which have already entered into force—both the former as well as the latter belong to the legal system and, therefore, they are valid *ex definitione*. Although one can provide particular reasons in favour of adopting the conception of the validity of law that is considered in this section,[283] when also taking into account the above arguments

---

[279] As noted by S. Wronkowska and M. Zieliński, *Komentarz do zasad techniki prawodawczej z dnia 20 czerwca 2002 r.*, *op. cit.*, p. 100: "The provision on the entry into force can be therefore considered as supplementing every norm expressed in any legislative act, in which it is included, namely supplementing it with the initial moment of its validity". The detailed arguments in favour of treating the provisions on the entry into force as supplementing the content of legal norms, contained in a given legislative act (and not as independent metanorms) are presented by J. Mikołajewicz *Prawo intertemporalne*, *op. cit.*, pp. 71ff. and P. Grabowski, M. Hermann, 'O normatywnym charakterze przepisów o wejściu w życie', *op. cit.*, pp. 72ff. It should be added that we agree with this line of argumentation – for more *see infra*, pp. 323ff.

[280] *Kodeks cywilny. Ustawa z dnia 23 kwietnia 1964 r.* [Civil Code. Statute of 23 April 1964], published in *Dziennik Ustaw* [Journal of Statutes] 964, No. 16, Item 93, with amendments. Let us add that this *Dziennik Ustaw* was issued on 18 May 1964.

[281] Z. Ziembiński, *Logiczne podstawy prawoznawstwa*, *op. cit.*, p. 146. To avoid possible confusion, which may, for example, originate from the content of our earlier observations (in particular, *cf. supra*, note 37 at p. 254), let us add that Kelsen did not identify the moment of promulgation with the beginning of validity, explicitly allowing for the possibility of commencing the validity of the norm before (in the case of retroactive norms) and after the time of its enactment, as well as identifying the period of its validity (until its derogation) with the time specified in the temporal sphere of the norm; namely, undoubtedly with the time, whose initial moment corresponds to the end of *vacatio legis* – *see idem*, *Allgemeine Theorie der Normen*, *op. cit.*, p. 138.

[282] The term used by S. Wronkowska, 'O źródłach prawa i aktach normatywnych raz jeszcze', *op. cit.*, p. 120.

[283] Due to the nature of things (or maybe better: human nature) it cannot come as a surprise (or be the subject of severe criticism) that the conception of validity, understood as the membership of

A–I, A–II and A–III, we find no rational reason for applying the concept of validity expressed by D_1, which—as the argument A–IV illustrates—leads to an inaccurate description of the situation of a normative change, which is frequently encountered in modern systems of statutory law. Additionally, what can an "ordinary" native speaker of any natural language (that is not a jurist familiar with legal and juristic concepts) understand from information where, during some period, both Penal Codes were valid simultaneously? Probably nothing.

Argument A–IV can be further enhanced by providing a series of detailed theoretical reasons in favour of rejecting definition D_1 on account of its consequences related to the institution of *vacatio legis*. Generally speaking, this definition entails the need to reformulate a number of commonly assumed concepts and methods of jurisprudential analysis. This thesis shall be illustrated by means of one of the possible examples,[284] indirectly indicated by Włodzimierz Wróbel who—when advocating for recognising the moment of the entry into force as the initial moment of validity of legal norms—no doubt rightly notes that:

> the consequence of the validity of the individual norm, even if it is not yet applicable, is its derogatory impact based on the juristic rules of normative conflicts.[285]

Therefore, if we want to consistently apply the definition that identifies the validity of the norms of statutory law with their membership in the legal system, then the legal theory on the normative conflict resolution (based on the juristic rules *lex superior*, *lex specialis*, *lex posterior* and so forth) would also have to be adequately harmonised with such a conceptual convention, for it is commonly accepted that the statutory norms have no derogatory force in the *vacatio legis* period.

---

norms in the legal system from the moment of their promulgation, is eagerly accepted by the judges of the Polish Constitutional Tribunal who thus want, as it seems, to justify the fact of extending the scope of its jurisdiction – *see e.g.*, Z. Czeszejko-Sochacki, L. Garlicki, J. Trzciński, *Komentarz do Ustawy o Trybunale Konstytucyjnym z dnia 1 sierpnia 1997 roku* [Commentary on the Statute on the Constitutional Tribunal from 1st of August 1997], Warszawa 1999, p. 24. In passing, let us add that the definition, presented in the next chapter, being the result of clarifying the intension of the juristic concept of the validity of statutory law, also indirectly expands this scope, yet it does not usually lead to recognising legal norms that remain in the period of *vacatio legis* as valid ones.

[284] Another example of jurisprudential conceptions requiring a reformulation may be the analysis of reconstructing the normative basis of legal decisions, since – as L. Leszczyński aptly observes in *Zagadnienia teorii stosowania prawa*, *op. cit.*, p. 158 – statutory provisions (and, therefore, also statutory norms) that are 'waiting' for entry into force, may not constitute the source of such a reconstruction, despite the fact that (let us recall), according to definition D_1, they are already valid.

[285] W. Wróbel, *Zmiana normatywna i zasady intertemporalne w prawie karnym*, *op. cit.*, p. 39.

7.2.3 Conclusions

Let us now recapitulate the arguments that weigh against the model conception of legal validity as expressed in the form of the definition: "A norm of statutory law is valid if, and only if it belongs to the legal system" (D_1).

The argument A–I demonstrated that primarily due to the "fuzzy" nature of modern legal systems, this conception assumes the form of the conception of the juristic *prima facie* validity of statutory norms, whose accuracy and practical usefulness is severely limited. Familiarity with the intension of the juristic concept of the validity of statutory law, as defined by means of D_1, and therefore necessarily based on the concept of the membership in the legal system in at most the medium sense, can be of little help to lawyers in solving specific problems of validity concerning the extension of the concept at issue. It is the case because it does not provide for any "intrinsic added value" that might help lawyers to apply the criteria of membership in the legal system, which are undoubtedly crucial in determining the validity of individual legal norms.

The argument A–II has shown that the concept of the legal system, used in the *definiens* of D_1, cannot stand for such a legal system, which we could attribute with the feature of validity. It can be neither "the system of valid law" (individualism of validity), nor "the valid legal system" (holism of validity). Although terminological uniformity is not a value in itself, however, it should be stressed that adopting the conception of validity as expressed by definition D_1 means that jurisprudential discourse on the validity of law cannot apply the concepts of a concrete (Wróblewski) or momentary (Raz, Bulygin) legal system, which significantly reduces the utility of this conception. Or even—on account of the fact that according to some authors (such as Bulygin), the reconstruction of the legal system as a system of norms implies that it must be a momentary system, consisting of norms that are valid at a particular moment[286]—the discussed model conception of validity has to be completely rejected. In any case, the definition D_1 results in the incoherence of the conceptual apparatus of the analytical theory of law.

The argument A–III has already been summarised,[287] let us therefore only recall that it demonstrates the non-synonymy of the concepts of the validity of statutory norms and their membership in the legal system. Six examples, discussed in its framework, have also proved that legal positivists themselves, whose ideas and conceptions we have referred to in this argument, deconstruct—thus acting like proper postmodernists—one of the main components of the positivist paradigm; namely, the conception of validity expressed in the form of D_1. Worse still, this conception of the validity of law precludes not only the application of the concepts of the concrete or momentary legal system (as already mentioned), but also the application of the two still very influential positivist theories of the structure of legal systems, which have already found their permanent and prominent place in legal thinking. Firstly, with respect to Kelsen's pure theory of law, the analysis showed

[286] *Cf. supra*, note 51 *in fine* at p. 258.

[287] *Cf. supra*, p. 304.

that the legal system—membership in which was indicated by definition D_1—can only be the system of positive law, containing a non-positive basic norm; namely, a basic norm not established by anyone but being a necessary juristic hypothesis, presupposition or fiction (as Kelsen finally claimed).[288] Secondly, in principle, the analysed definition of validity precludes the application of the concept of the legal system as proposed by Hart, as the rule of recognition that constitutes the part of the legal system falsifies the thesis on the intensional equivalence of the concepts of validity and membership in jurisprudential discourse.

The last argument A–IV allowed for the justification of the thesis on the necessary—due to analytical reasons—linguistic (semantic) imprecision, which constitutes an inevitable consequence of grasping the validity of statutory norms by means of a reference to the concept of their membership in the legal system. In fact, definition D_1 "lumps together" the legal norms that remain in the period of *vacatio legis* and the norms that are already in force.[289] This leads to recognising as valid both categories of norms, greatly distinct in terms of validity, whose cognitive (informative) value is negligible. What is more, the application of the concept of validity based on definition D_1 may easily mislead non-professional addressees of legal norms (or at least trigger their cognitive dissonance). Let us indeed consider how they could, for example, understand a press release, issued more or less 10 years ago, that since the 2nd of August 1997 to the 1st of September 1998 both Polish Penal Codes were valid? We shall leave this question unanswered, or more precisely, we shall leave the answer to the theorists of law (usually legal positivists) who opt for such a conception of validity that expresses the intension of the juristic concept of validity by means of definition D_1.

The above-mentioned arguments lead to the conclusion that the juristic concept of the validity of statutory law and the definition that expresses the essence of this concept should not be based on the concept of membership of the norm in the legal system.[290] The natural remedy for the deficiencies disclosed in definition D_1, its

---

[288] Let us add that the requirement under which a system of positive law has to contain non-positive norms, leads to *contradictio in terminis* (or – as some maintain – to pseudo-positivism) in Kelsen's pure theory of law. *Cf.* Chap. 8, pp. 402ff.

[289] Thus, by means of definition D_1, we in effect create an "inadequate theoretical class" because – as we pointed out at the end of the A–IV argument – many of the existing juristic methods and jurisprudential theories are obviously inadequate (more precisely: they turn into "jumping theories" in terms of L. Petrażycki's methodology) in relation to the so-defined class of valid norms. For more on the principle of adequacy and the basic methodological concepts of Petrażycki *see e.g.*, J. Woleński, 'Metodologiczne dążenia Petrażyckiego a współczesna teoria nauki' [Petrażycki's Methodological Aspirations and Contemporary Theory of Science] in K. Opałek (ed.), *Z zagadnień teorii prawa i teorii nauki Leona Petrażyckiego*, Warszawa 1969, pp. 161–172 and A. Grabowski, *Judicial Argumentation and Pragmatics*, *op. cit.*, pp. 6–7, and the references cited therein.

[290] Thus, the question as to whether the intension of the juristic concept of the validity of statutory law, understood in terms of the internal validity (in Peczenik–Aarnio's terminology), should be determined as the validity in a relative sense (in Opałek's terminology), consisting of the membership of the norm in the legal system, is answered in the negative. Nonetheless, it does not mean that we have to use the concept of legal validity in an absolute sense, but rather (as already indicated in Chap. 5, note 60 at pp. 206–207 and Chap. 6 at p. 223) that the distinction

unacceptable consequences leading to a number of inconsistencies and antinomies[291] in jurisprudential, dogmatic or purely practical analyses of the problem of the validity of statutory norms, is to develop a different conception that would aptly clarify the intension of the juristic concept of validity. It should nevertheless be stressed that this conclusion by no means implies that the concept of the membership of the norm in the legal system is completely useless in solving specific problems of validity. On the contrary, it plays a decisive role in determining whether a given norm of statutory law is valid (namely, in relation to the problem of the extension of the clarified concept). As we shall see, the conception of the juristic presumption of the validity of statutory norms—presented in the penultimate chapter of the book[292]—designed to clarify the issue of the extension of the juristic concept of validity, will be based on some of the most basic positivist criteria of the membership of the norm in the legal system; in particular, related to the concept of so-called thetic justification (of the validity) of legal norms.

7.3 Legal Validity Understood as the Application of Norms

In this section we examine the theoretical correctness and practical usefulness of the second model definition, under which "A norm of statutory law is valid if, and only if it is applied" (hereafter D_2). The question again is whether this definition could be regarded as a successful clarification of the intension of the juristic concept of the validity of statutory law. As long as the concept of legal validity—most entrenched in traditional legal thinking—understood in terms of the membership of statutory norms in the legal system, required special care and attention in the selection and analysis of counterarguments, this time only three general arguments seem to be sufficient to reject the conception of validity based on the concept of law application. Moreover, such a conception is very rarely encountered in its pure form, as the authors who investigate the conceptual problem of legal validity, if they already use the concept of norm application, typically place it in a more complex conceptual context.[293] Therefore, our arguments will also serve as the introduction to the analysis of some of the conceptions of validity (which constitute

between absolute and relative validity becomes less important and in clarificative analysis we will need to take into account both senses of legal validity.

[291] It should be noted that, following the thesis *argumenta non numeranda, sed ponderanda sunt*, we have left aside some possible arguments showing conceptual antinomies and contradictions, related to the application of the rules of intertemporal law, which could be caused by the adoption of definition D_1. Some of them are analysed in Chap. 9 at pp. 505ff.

[292] *Cf.* Chap. 9, pp. 484–491.

[293] For example, we deal with such a situation in the case of predictive conceptions of legal validity (O.W. Holmes, A. Ross, and other legal realists), which interpret it in terms of predictions or prognoses of how courts will apply legal norms, and in normative conceptions of legal validity, which interprets utterances on the validity of a legal norm as the prescription (command or order) for applying it.

the subject of the discussion in the subsequent parts of the book[294]), which, in a more or less direct way refer to the concept of the application of norms.

What shall serve as the starting point for the first argument (labelled A–V) will be the definition of the application of law recently proposed by Leszek Leszczyński:

> Generally speaking, the application of law shall be understood as the decision-making process undertaken by the competent state authority (or other authorized organ), resulting in issuing a binding decision of an individual (and specific) character. The content of this decision is the qualification of the state of facts from the standpoint of the criteria set out in its normative basis and the determination of the legal consequences of this qualification.[295]

Without a doubt, this definition accurately recognises the meaning of the concept of the application of law, as traditionally adopted in Polish legal theory, which may be evidenced by its similarity to the definitions provided by other scholars.[296] Yet, the problem is that although Leszczyński rightly considers this definition as "the most general", it is still too narrow in the context of possibly recognising the definition D_2 as a correct clarification of the intension of the juristic concept of the validity of statutory law. This is because the application of law in the sense indicated by Leszczyński directly refers only to the application of sanctioning norms,[297] which are mainly addressed to competent state authorities. Depending on the adopted terminology, these recipients are referred to as "primary addressees", for example, by Hans Kelsen, Alf Ross and Wiesław Lang, or as "secondary addressees", as for example by Franciszek Studnicki and H.L.A. Hart.[298] Accordingly, if we do not want definition D_2 only to be indirectly applicable in relation to sanctioned norms, mainly addressed to the recipients who are not state authorities, we need to extend the concept of law application both in terms of its meaning as well as in terms of its scope of reference.

---

[294] In particular, we mean here the conceptions of validity based on the concept of the applicability of legal norms (*see infra*, pp. 321–334), or determined by means of a combination of the concepts of membership and applicability (*see infra*, pp. 347–349), or understood normatively – as someone's ought to follow or apply valid legal norms (*see* Chap. 8 at pp. 413–422).

[295] L. Leszczyński, *Zagadnienia teorii stosowania prawa*, *op. cit.*, p. 15.

[296] *Cf. e.g.*, K. Opałek, J. Wróblewski, *Zagadnienia teorii prawa*, *op. cit.*, pp. 283ff.; Z. Ziembiński, *Problemy podstawowe prawoznawstwa*, *op. cit.*, pp. 415ff., J. Wróblewski, *Sądowe stosowanie prawa*, *op. cit.*, pp. 7ff. [English version, pp. 1ff.]; R. Sarkowicz, J. Stelmach, *Teoria prawa*, *op. cit.*, pp. 93ff.; K. Pałecki, *Prawoznawstwo – zarys wykładu. Prawo w porządku społecznym* [Lecture on Jurisprudence. Law in Social Order], Warszawa 2003, p. 144; T. Pietrzykowski, *Wsteczne działanie prawa i jego zakaz*, *op. cit.*, pp. 28ff.

[297] Let us recall that sanctioned norms prescribe legal obligations and duties of the ordinary addressees of norms – legal subjects; whereas sanctioning norms determine the sanctions that ought to be imposed by law-applying authorities if the addressee of a sanctioned norm does not comply with it. *Cf. supra*, p. 257, and the references cited in notes 45–46.

[298] *See* J. Jakubowski, 'Pojęcie obowiązywania, realizacji i skuteczności normy prawnej oraz podstawy ich rozróżniania', *op. cit.*, pp. 315–316, and the references cited therein.

In the Polish jurisprudential literature, such a proposal of extending this concept was introduced nearly half a century ago by Lang, thus distinguishing between the "application of legal norms" and "adherence to legal norms".[299] In his view, this distinction "has long been known in the science of law" (especially the German one),[300] whereas the application of norms and adherence to norms are "practically inseparable".[301] Both the phrase "norms N should be applied" as well as the phrase "norm N should be adhered to" mean the same as: "norm N should be regarded as the criterion of evaluation and the basis of the decision"[302]; the only difference lies in who is evaluated (the person themself or others), and in relation to whom the decision is taken.[303] In accordance with Lang's definition, the adherence to law means either:

> recognizing the norm as the criterion for assessing one's own conduct,

or:

> behaving in accordance with the content of the norm-making decisions provided for in the norm and implementing the situations set forth in the disposition of the norm.[304]

Nonetheless, Lang's terminological proposals did not catch on, mainly because the term "adherence to law" is essentially a synonym for more commonly used terms: "observance of law" and "compliance with law".[305] It is worth noting, however, that the analysis of Lang, who in his deliberations took into account not only the sanctioned norms that impose duties and obligations, but also the norms that entitle one to certain actions, indirectly show that we can talk about law application even if the addressee of the norm exercises the power or competence ascribed to her/him. There are indeed no purely linguistic or terminological contraindications so as not to speak, for example, for applying the constitutional norms by the parliament that enacts statutes[306] or for applying law to the parties

---

[299] *See* W. Lang, *Obowiązywanie prawa*, *op. cit.*, pp. 167ff.

[300] *Ibidem*, p. 169. Lang maintains that the categories introduced by him correspond to the German terms *Normenanwendung* and *Normenbefolgung*, which is questionable in relation to the latter, meaning "observance of norms" or "following the norms" rather than "adherence to norms".

[301] *Ibidem*, p. 171.

[302] *Ibidem*, p. 169.

[303] *Ibidem*, pp. 170–171.

[304] *Ibidem*, pp. 169–170.

[305] *Cf.* Z. Ziembiński, *Problemy podstawowe prawoznawstwa*, *op. cit.*, p. 415.

[306] *See e.g.*, *ibidem*, p. 419, where Ziembiński rightly notes that the normative acts of establishing legal norms of subconstitutional rank are always based on applying the competence norms of law-creating, and J. Woleński, 'Uwagi o racjonalności decyzji prawnych' [Notes on the Rationality of Legal Decisions] in H. Rot (ed.), *Problemy metodologii i filozofii prawa*, Wrocław 1988, p. 179, who similarly argues that in the continental legal systems, lawmaking activity is the subject of legal regulation, and thus lawmaking acts are "almost always the application of some norms, at least procedural ones". In the context of the concept of the legal system, which also includes individual norms, H. Kelsen stresses that law application (*Rechtsanwendung*) – contrary to traditional beliefs – is usually the act of its creation (*Rechtserzeugung*) – *cf. idem*, *Reine Rechtslehre*, 2nd ed., *op. cit.*, p. 240 [English version, pp. 234–235].

concluding a contract of employment.[307] If we use the terminology introduced by Alf Ross, the application of law may involve not only the substantive (duty-imposing) legal norms, but also the norms of competence—both those that create "public authority" as well as those that form "private autonomy".[308]

Yet, does such an expanded concept of, so to say, the law application *sensu largo*, referring not only to sanctioning norms but also the norms of competence, protect us from the allegation of extensional incompleteness of the concept of legal validity as expressed by definition D_2? The answer is unfortunately in the negative, because the sanctioned norms continue to remain outside the direct scope of this definition,[309] whereas sanction-free norms (*leges imperfectae*) do not belong to it at all—they are, by definition, not interconnected with any corresponding sanctioning norms. Worse still, such an extended concept of law application *sensu largo* demonstrates with full force a fundamental complication that might arise from recognising D_2 as a proper clarification of the intension of the juristic concept of the validity of statutory law. Our objective was to construct the concept of legal validity as a classifying concept and thus not subject to gradation.[310] Meanwhile, particularly in terms of the application of the norms belonging to the category of competence norms of "personal autonomy" naturally leads to the transformation of the concept of legal validity into a gradable concept. Let us consider the above-mentioned example of concluding an employment contract. The phenomenon of illegally employing workers shows that the norms of competence that govern the possibility of concluding employment contracts, are applied by their addressees only to some extent, which can perhaps be estimated or determined as a percentage. However, even if it could be so determined, what would it stand for that, for example, 80 % of workers in Poland are employed under contracts resulting from the application of the relevant legal regulations, and the remaining 20 % work without any contracts or permits. If we take such a statement into consideration, then according to D_2 we would have to consequently state that the norms of Polish labour law governing the ways of employing workers are valid in 80 % of cases.

---

[307] *Cf. e.g.*, S. Wronkowska, Z. Ziembiński, *Zarys teorii prawa* [An Outline of Legal Theory], Poznań 1997, p. 213 ff. where they provide the basic meaning of the term "application of law", pointing to the relationship between applying law and "exercising the powers which are granted to a certain entity by a given legal norm".

[308] *Cf.* A. Ross, *Directives and Norms*, *op. cit.*, pp. 132–133.

[309] Will the jurists say that someone does not kill a man because she/he applies the norm of penal law that prohibits killing? Undoubtedly, this sentence sounds a lot better if we replace "applies" with "complies with" or "follows". The supporters of definition D_2 are, therefore, left with using the construction of the interconnection of the sanctioned and sanctioning norms, by claiming that the former are applied indirectly. Nevertheless, as we have already opposed 'lumping together' the norms in the state of *vacatio legis* and the norms that are already in force, in this case we also have to oppose the same classification of sanctioning norms, which are applied by the competent legal authorities, and sanctioned norms, whose validity would only result from the application of sanctioning norms, corresponding with them.

[310] *See supra*, Introduction, note 11 at p. 4, with the corresponding text.

The theoretical and practical uselessness of the concept of legal validity conceived in this way requires no further comments.

Let us now recapitulate the presented argumentation. Firstly, even if we expand the concept of law application as it seems to the maximum extent allowed by the semantic rules of juristic language, relating it also to the norms of competence, then some categories of legal norms, namely sanctioned norms, will be placed within the scope of the application of the considered definition only indirectly—by means of their interconnection with sanctioning ones; whereas other, namely sanction-free norms, will entirely remain outside its scope. Secondly, definition D_2, applied to the norms of competence of "personal autonomy" leads to the gradability of the feature of validity[311]—which can be remedied only by an arbitrary convention that such norms are valid which are applied, for example, in more than 50 %, 60 % or 75 % of cases.

The second argument (hereafter labelled A–VI) refers to the symmetry of the relation indicated in model definition D_2.[312] Within this argument, we shall attempt to determine whether we can recognise as correct the thesis, which states that: "If a norm of statutory law is valid, then it is applied", and its reverse counterpart: "If a norm of statutory law is applied, then it is valid".

In reference to the first implication, we can easily identify several situations in which there is no equivalence between validity and the application of norms, since valid norms are not applied by the authorities that are obligated to do so. The first example refers to the phenomenon of *desuetudo*, already discussed in the previous section.[313] It should be pointed out that before the norms subject to *desuetudo* actually lose their validity, they are not applied for a relatively long period of time (usually corresponding to the period of the formation of custom) by the relevant state authorities. Without a doubt, in this period such norms are valid, yet they are not applied—otherwise there is no effect of *desuetudo*, consisting in loss of legal validity by formally valid, yet non-applied legal norms. The second example concerns the phenomenon of the so-called symbolic law (statute),[314] namely such lawmaking acts which only pretend to create valid law, with no real intention of the

[311] The gradability of the concept of legal validity is expressly assumed by the authors who use the concept of law application in the definition of validity. For instance, as A. Ross writes in *On Law and Justice*, *op. cit.*, p. 45: "It can also be said that a rule can be valid law to a greater or lesser degree varying with the degree of probability with which it can be predicted that the rule will be applied".

[312] This argument is based on reasoning analogous to the one presented in argument A–III at pp. 289–304.

[313] *Cf. supra*, pp. 301–302.

[314] This particular type of law is also referred to as "apparent legislation" – *see e.g.*, U. Moś, 'Ustawodawstwo symboliczne, czyli o możliwości działań pozornych w prawie' [Symbolic Legislation, That Is the Possibility of Apparent Actions in Law], *CC* 6/41–1/42 (1988–1989), note 2 at p. 47, or as "ideological law" – *see* K. Pałecki, *Prawoznawstwo – zarys wykładu*, *op. cit.*, p. 162.

legislator ensuring that the legal norms contained in them are implemented.[315] A good Polish example of such a symbolic law, taken from the relatively recent past, is a statute known as "*lex* 203 zlotys",[316] in which—among other legislative errors[317]—the Polish legislator did not indicate the sources of funding for the increase of 203 zlotys in the salaries of the employees of public health-care facilities. Thus, this statute, despite its validity, was not implemented, which resulted in numerous social protests (particularly of hunger strikes among Polish nurses). The third example relates to the phenomenon of constructive (structural) legal gaps,[318] which can be, unfortunately, often encountered, at least in the system of Polish positive law. When a given administrative authority, despite its so-called statutory delegation, did not issue a lawmaking executive act, while being obligated to do so, then the norms of such a statute are undoubtedly valid, yet some of them may not be applied because it is not known what their application would consist of.[319] Finally, the last, fourth example refers to the concept, introduced by Kelsen, of the ideal case of the validity (*Idealfall der Geltung*).[320] According to the author of *Reine Rechtslehre*, we deal with the ideal case of the validity of a legal norm if a sanctioned norm is 100 % efficient—all legal subjects follow it, and therefore the courts do not have to apply the corresponding sanctioning norm at all. Although the concept introduced by Kelsen is quite utopian, this example also illustrates the incorrectness of the analysed implication: "If a norm of statutory law is valid, then it is applied" because, at least theoretically, we cannot exclude the possibility that the situation envisaged by Kelsen takes place.

Let us now consider the correctness of the reverse implication: "If a norm of statutory law is applied, then it is valid". When we reflect on the possible counterexamples that prove the incorrectness of this implication, the first thought

---

[315] As U. Moś observes, *ibidem*, p. 47: "Generally speaking, symbolic legislation constitutes a variation of the so-called bad law which (in this case) is created not in order to be applicable but in order to exist". As can be seen, the definitional feature of symbolic law is its non-application.

[316] *Ustawa z dnia 22 grudnia 2000 r. o zmianie ustawy o negocjacyjnym systemie kształtowania przyrostu przeciętnych wynagrodzeń u przedsiębiorców oraz o zmianie niektórych ustaw i ustawy o zakładach opieki zdrowotnej* [Statute of 22 December 2000 amending the statute on the negotiating system of regulating the increase of average wages in enterprises and on amending certain statutes and the statute on health care facilities], published in *Dziennik Ustaw* [Journal of Statutes] 2001, No. 5, Item 45.

[317] These errors were presented in an interesting way by H. Jadacka, 'Wymierne i niewymierne koszty niejasności tekstów prawnych' [Tangible and Intangible Costs of Non-clarity of Legal Texts] in E. Malinowska (ed.), *Język – Prawo – Społeczeństwo*, *op. cit.*, pp. 153ff.

[318] On the concept of constructive (structural) legal gaps *see e.g.*, Z. Ziembiński, *Problemy podstawowe prawoznawstwa*, *op. cit.*, pp. 223ff.; S. Wronkowska, Z. Ziembiński, *Zarys teorii prawa*, *op. cit.*, p. 185; R. Sarkowicz, J. Stelmach, *Teoria prawa*, *op. cit.*, p. 169.

[319] We disregard here the relatively rare situations in which the constructive (structural) gaps may be removed based on the methods adopted in a given legal culture such as with *per analogiam* reasoning or comparative interpretation.

[320] *Cf.* H. Kelsen, 'Eine "Realistische" und die Reine Rechtslehre', *op. cit.*, p. 20 and *Reine Rechtslehre*, 2nd ed., *op. cit.*, p. 11 [English version, pp. 11–12].

naturally concerns the views of those legal theoreticians who recognise that in intertemporal situations we can deal with the application of invalid norms (decoded from formally repealed legal provisions). Nevertheless, as already indicated,[321] this mode of describing past law in an intertemporal situation ("applying invalid law in accordance with valid rules of intertemporal law"), as we believe, leads to antinomy and, thus, we regard it as incorrect.[322] Therefore, we shall not use this counterexample, though it would explicitly call into question the correctness of the debated implication. We will, in turn, try to demonstrate that this implication leads either to the circularity of the definition D_2 or to the ambiguity of the concept of legal validity defined by means of it.

For the ease of understanding in fact a very simple argument, we will refer our considerations to the type of law application that is most widely discussed in the literature; namely, the judicial application of law. Let us consider the substantive decisional model of the judicial application of law developed by Jerzy Wróblewski.[323] According to this model, often treated as a starting point for jurisprudential analyses of law application,[324] the first element of the judicial application of law is a decision on validity, involving inter alia the determination of the validity of legal norms applied by the court in a given case.[325] Thus, it must be assumed that the resolution of the problem of validity constitutes one of the stages of judicial law application. In other words, a discourse of validity can be regarded as a part of the discourse of application.[326] In the context of the implication under analysis: "If a norm of statutory law is applied, then it is valid", it becomes clear that its antecedent needs to be properly extended, taking into account the decision on validity that takes place during the judicial application of law. It means that this implication should be reformulated as follows: "If a norm of statutory law is valid, then it is applied, and therefore it is valid". Such an extended form of this implication can be interpreted in two ways. Firstly, we can conclude that the predicate "is valid"—used twice—has the same meaning in both cases. However, in the context of such an interpretation, what turns out to be obvious is the circularity (tautological nature) of the definition D_2, since the implication under analysis assumes the following form: "If a norm of statutory law is valid, then [. . .] it is valid". The second possible interpretation consists of assuming that we deal with two concepts of validity: the first one—proper when taking the decision on validity and the second—expressed by the definition D_2—identifying the validity

---

[321] *Cf. supra*, note 208 at p. 293 and Chap. 5, note 44 at p. 203.

[322] The means of describing this situation in a jurisprudentially correct way, not leading to antinomies, will be presented in Chap. 9 at pp. 508–511.

[323] *See* J. Wróblewski, *Sądowe stosowanie prawa*, *op. cit.*, pp. 42–49, 93ff. [English version, pp. 30–35, 75ff.].

[324] *Cf. e.g.*, L. Leszczyński, *Zagadnienia teorii stosowania prawa*, *op. cit.*, pp. 17–19, 62ff. and B. Brożek, *Rationality and Discourse*, *op. cit.*, pp. 82–90, 257–261, 268ff.

[325] *See* J. Wróblewski, *Sądowe stosowanie prawa*, *op. cit.*, pp. 43–44, 93ff. [English version, pp. 30–32, 75ff.].

[326] For more details *see* Chap. 9 at pp. 473–476.

with the application of a norm. Consequently, the discussed implication reads: "If a norm of statutory law is valid$_D$, then it is applied, and therefore it is valid$_A$". This interpretation no longer leads to *circulus in definiendo*, yet it still leaves open the question of determining what concept of legal validity we use when we are about to make the decision on validity. Naturally, it may not be the concept of validity understood as the application of the law because in such case we would come back to *circulus vitiosus*. Accordingly, the implication: "If a statutory law norm is applicable, then it is valid", turns out to be completely useless for clarifying the intension of the juristic concept of the validity of statutory law.

The argumentation against the analysed implication can be further supported by paying attention to another counterexample. There is no doubt that sometimes the state authorities apply (or try to apply) the norms, which later turn out to be invalid, in accordance with constitutional court rulings. It may happen that those rulings are of *ex tunc* force—as an example we can recall the German Federal Constitutional Court ruling of 14 February 1968 (*Staatsangehörigkeitsbeschluß*) concerning the Eleventh Ordinance of 25 November 1941.[327] In point three of this ruling, the constitutional court formed the view that directly falsifies the analysed implication:

> Once established statutory un-law, which clearly violates the constitutive principles of law, shall not become law on the basis that it will be applied and obeyed.

This counterexample certainly does not settle a controversial theoretical issue, concerning the possibility of, in fact, a retroactive annulling of the law (legal validity), yet it reveals the fact that the application of certain laws does not always entail their validity. Hence, it is not only from the nonpositivist perspective[328] that one can defend the view under which courts sometimes apply the law which turns out not to be a valid law.

The argument A–VI shows that the equivalence between validity and the application of statutory norms does not take place. In fact, at this point, we could terminate our analysis; nevertheless, we will still draw attention to the axiological aspect of the discussed issue. Leaving aside the above-mentioned analytical arguments, we cannot help but notice that the concept of legal validity, determined by means of definition D_2, would be unjust, and possibly even extremely unjust. We shall explain and justify this objection on the basis of the last argument—hereafter labelled A–VII—which is against the analysed method of clarifying the intension of the juristic concept of the validity of statutory law.

[327] *Cf.* Chap. 4, pp. 184–185.

[328] A similar situation can be encountered in the legal systems of those states where positive law permits a ruling on the unconstitutionality of lawmaking acts with *ex tunc* effect – for example, in Germany, Spain and Portugal, where the rulings of constitutional courts may retroactively deprive the unconstitutional legal norms of their validity – *cf.* L. Garlicki, *Sądownictwo konstytucyjne w Europie Zachodniej* [Constitutional Jurisdiction in Western Europe], Warszawa 1987, pp. 271ff. In these countries, it turns out, yet *ex post*, that the unconstitutional legal norms were applied, but they were not legally valid.

For the purposes of argument A–VII, let us tentatively suppose that the definition D_2 is correct, and therefore the norms of statutory law are valid if, and only if they are applied. Accepting such a concept would certainly affect the resolution of specific problems of validity; namely, the issues concerning the extension of the concept under discussion. It should be noted in this context that if we treated this definition seriously (e.g., when accepting, after behavioural realism, that "law is valid because it is applied"[329]), the addressees of legal norms would not be able to recognise (identify) valid norms in the period between their entry into force and their first application, and the judges or other state organs with competence to apply the law would not be in any way bound by new legal norms.[330] Consistent application of the definition D_2 in solving practical problems would therefore lead to extremely unfair situations, because the principles of *ignorantia iuris nocet* and *ignorantia legis neminem excusat* would have an entirely new dimension that could be manifested by means of a classic totalitarian adage attributed to Stalinist prosecutor Andriej Wyszynskij: "Give me a man, and a I will find a paragraph [for her/him]". In fact, any change in the law would entail a state of uncertainty close to normative anarchy, while the determination of the initial moment when law starts to be valid would remain at the theoretically and practically unlimited discretion of law-applying authorities. Worse, the first application of the new law would not lead to an automatic improvement of the functioning of positive law in society: the addressees of legal norms (precisely, sanctioned norms) would have to constantly follow the case law in terms of the application of sanctioning norms in order to find out which norms of statutory law are valid.[331] This argument may seem purely demagogic, yet it is hard to deny that under the case law systems, the analysed situation sometimes does indeed take place, at least in those branches of the legal system in which the precedent decisions are of a lawmaking nature. Nonetheless, as regards the scope of our analysis, namely the system-type of statutory law, the absurdity of the above situation is obvious.[332]

In sum, the concept of the application of law does not help to clarify the intension of the juristic concept of the validity of statutory law. After all, as in relation to the concept of the membership of norms in the legal system—analysed in the previous section—one cannot deny that various arguments connected with the application of legal norms may be applied in the discourse of validity, such as the argument from *desuetudo* or the argument from symbolic law (legislation).

---

[329] *Cf.* the analysis of such a variant of legal realism in A. Ross, *On Law and Justice*, *op. cit.*, pp. 70ff., in particular p. 73, where the cited quote was taken from.

[330] At this point, we can again use – *mutatis mutandis* – the argument based on Plato's "Euthyphro dilemma".

[331] Incidentally, the knowledge of the current judicial jurisdiction would also be indispensable in order to learn which norms of statutory law are no longer valid.

[332] The objection of absurdity may be justified, in particular, by noting that the consistent use of the definition D_2 in legal discourse must lead to the conclusion that, for example, the norms of the Polish Constitution of 1997 concerning the States of Emergency (Chapter XI, Articles 228–234), that have not been applied so far, are not yet valid.

7.4 Legal Validity Understood as the Applicability of Norms

In this section, we shall examine the theoretical correctness and practical usefulness of the next model definition: "A norm of statutory law is valid if, and only if it is applicable" (hereafter D_3). Contrary to previous considerations, the point of reference for clarificative analysis will be a particular jurisprudential conception, developed by the doyen of modern hard legal positivism, the Argentinean legal philosopher Eugenio Bulygin. Our analysis will nevertheless retain the existing synthetic form, since Bulygin's conception shall be treated as the basis for a model analysis.[333] The objective of the analysis remains unchanged—we will try to determine whether this definition is useful in order to clarify the intension of the juristic concept of the validity of statutory law.

Before we proceed to the analysis of the conception of validity defined by means of the concept of the applicability of norms, it must be at least briefly presented; in particular, because the knowledge about it among English-speaking scholars is probably scant.[334] Bulygin introduced his conception in the study *Time and Validity* of 1982,[335] and then he developed and modified it in several subsequent works.[336] Our analysis will rely primarily on the paper *Tiempo y validez* of 1991, in which the conception of legal validity, conceived in terms of the applicability of norms, is presented in the fullest possible way and—given the language in which the paper was written—it certainly most accurately reflects the views of its author.[337]

The Argentine philosopher distinguishes three basic concepts of legal validity occurring in the juristic language (discourse). The first one is a descriptive-relational concept of validity (i.e., related to a system of norms), understood as the

---

[333] It is even more justified to undertake model analyses in that Bulygin's conception is still undergoing some changes, which will be discussed mainly in the footnotes so as not to interfere with the basic argument presented in the main text.

[334] In the Spanish jurisprudential literature, this conception is often commented upon and applied, and it was also extended by P.E. Navarro and J.J. Moreso, 'Applicability and Effectiveness of Legal Norms', *L&Ph* 16 (1997), pp. 201–219. *See* also J.J. Moreso, *Legal Indeterminacy and Constitutional Interpretation*, *op. cit.*, pp. 105ff.; P.E. Navarro, 'Enunciados jurídicos y proposiciones normativas', *op. cit.*, pp. 137ff. and 'Legal Reasoning and Systematization of Law', *op. cit.*, pp. 259ff.

[335] E. Bulygin, 'Time and Validity', *op. cit.*, pp. 66ff.

[336] *Cf.* E. Bulygin, 'Tiempo y validez', *op. cit.*, pp. 196ff., 'Algunas consideraciones sobre los sistemas jurídicos', *op. cit.*, pp. 266ff., 'Normensystem und Rechtsordnung', *op. cit.*, pp. 100ff., and '¿Está (parte de) la filosofía del Derecho basada en un error?', *DOXA* 27 (2004), pp. 19ff.

[337] Although it is undoubtedly Bulygin who created this conception – despite the fact that the concept of applicability (*Anwendbarkeit*) also appears in the studies of some German authors (*cf.* T. Pietrzykowski, *Wsteczne działanie prawa i jego zakaz*, *op. cit.*, note 54 at p. 27, in which he recalls the studies of G. Winkler and A. Vonklich) – it must be emphasised that from a methodological point of view it has a descriptive nature, like the other two conceptions of validity identified and analysed by Bulygin. For Bulygin merely reconstructs the concepts that are already present in juristic discourse, rather than creating a new normative approach that establishes a proper way of understanding and applying the concept of legal validity.

membership of norms in the legal system. The second one is a normative-absolute concept of validity, understood as a prescription that obligates legal subjects to obey the law and judges or administrative organs to apply legal norms. The third way of comprehending legal validity, identified by Bulygin, is the conception that makes use of the concept of the applicability of norms (*aplicabilidad*, *Anwendbarkeit*), which is characterised as follows:

> If there is a norm N_i, that prescribes the obligation to apply another norm N_j in a given case, it should be stated that N_j is valid in the sense that, according to N_i, it ought to be applied. Such a concept of validity is also *relative*, but it deals with a triad relation between the norms N_i and N_j and the case (*caso*) C_k: the norm N_i prescribes that the norm N_j should be applied in the case C_k. We also deal here with a *descriptive* conception because to say that a given norm is valid in such a sense does not stand for issuing a prescription, but confirming the existence of a prescription, according to which the indicated norm should be applied in a given case. Accordingly, the utterance "p is valid" is a descriptive proposition, even though this proposition is referred to the norm. I will use the term "applicability" when referring to this third concept of validity.[338]

According to the terminology proposed by Bulygin, the norms of category N_i, which prescribe the application of other norms (of N_j type), are called "applicability norms" (*normas de aplicabilidad*, *Anwendungsnormen*) or "criteria of applicability" (*criterios de aplicabilidad*). Their sources are varied: they can be established in positive law (in the constitution or in statutes), they can derive from the practice of judicial decisions or they may even be settled by legal science (dogmatics of law).[339] The examples of applicability norms (criteria of applicability), referred to and analysed by Bulygin, are inter alia, the constitutional principle of *nullum crimen, nulla poena sine praevia lege*, the statutory principle of penal law—*lex mitior agit*— as well as the metanorms that regulate the moment of the entry into force of individual lawmaking acts. In contrast, the norms of the category N_j are referred to by Bulygin as "applicable norms" (*normas aplicables*). It should be noted that in Bulygin's theory, the distinction between applicability norms and applicable norms is closely related to the differentiation between the external time and the internal time of a legal norm, which has already been described in this study.[340] In order to allow for a better understanding of the following analysis, it should be recalled that the external time of a legal norm stands for the period (or periods) in which the norm exists in a given legal system—that is, it belongs to it—whereas the internal time of a norm is a period (or periods) in which a given norm is applicable: the latter is therefore, as Bulygin claims, "the function of its applicability".[341]

---

[338] E. Bulygin, 'Tiempo y validez', *op. cit.*, p. 196. *Cf.* earlier formulation in 'Time and Validity', *op. cit.*, p. 66, and later ones in 'Normensystem und Rechtsordnung', *op. cit.*, pp. 100–101, and '¿Está (parte de) la filosofía del Derecho basada en un error?', *op. cit.*, pp. 19–20.

[339] E. Bulygin, 'Tiempo y validez', *op. cit.*, pp. 202–203 and 'Time and Validity', *op. cit.*, pp. 70–71.

[340] *See supra*, p. 256.

[341] E. Bulygin, 'Tiempo y validez', *op. cit.*, p. 199, 'Algunas consideraciones sobre los sistemas jurídicos', *op. cit.*, p. 266, and 'Normensystem und Rechtsordnung', *op. cit.*, p. 101.

Going on to the analysis of a model conception of validity, understood in terms of the applicability of norms, it should first be noted that it appears to be devoid of certain errors of the previously analysed conceptions. For example, arguments A–IV and A–VII lose their *raison d'être*. Let us recall that the first argument is directed against the understanding of validity as the membership of norms in the legal system and it concerns the validity of statutory law norms in the period of *vacatio legis*. In relation to Bulygin's conception, this argument is no longer justified, because the norms before the moment of their entry into force are obviously not applicable, thus, they are not valid. The second argument, referring to the conception of validity understood as the application of norms and exposing the injustice of the practical consequences of such an understanding, loses its grounds because Bulygin distinguishes applicability norms N_i, and by means of them it is possible to determine in advance the applicability of the applicable norms N_j, so their validity does not remain suspended until their first application by the competent authority. Moreover, it seems (at least at first glance) that this conception is based on an adequate description of the process of applying legal norms, which brings it closer to practice. In light of our objectives that consist of clarifying the juristic concept of the validity of statutory law,[342] Bulygin's conception provides an important advantage. Nevertheless, one can also easily formulate three major arguments that weigh in favour of rejecting the discussed conception of the validity due to its unsuitability in clarifying the intension of the juristic concept of the validity of statutory law.

The first argument (hereafter A–VIII) is the most principal, for it disputes the accuracy of the distinction between applicability norms and applicable norms, which constitutes the conceptual grounds of the conception of the validity of norms, understood as their applicability. Referring to Hart's distinction between primary and secondary rules, Bulygin states that the applicability norms belong to the category of secondary rules and, as such, they have the nature of metanorms in relation to applicable primary rules,[343] except for the ultimate (*últimos*) applicability norms, which belong to an even higher category of third-level metanorms. These norms govern the applicability of norms that are secondary rules[344] (including "normal" applicability norms, such as the principle of *lex mitior agit*).

Let us discuss the example of a metanorm—repeatedly analysed by Bulygin—that is identified as an "ultimate applicability norm"; namely, the norm set out in Article 303 of the Argentine Penal Code of 1921, which established the 6-month period of *vacatio legis* of that statute.[345] Bulygin believes that in the case of this

---

[342] *Cf.* Chap. 6, pp. 223–224 (a fragment concerning the second objective of clarification).

[343] E. Bulygin, 'Normensystem und Rechtsordnung', *op. cit.*, p. 102.

[344] E. Bulygin, 'Tiempo y validez', *op. cit.*, pp. 202–204. It is worth noting that in 'Time and Validity', *op. cit.*, pp. 70–71, Bulygin does not yet use the concept of the "third-level norms" (*normas de tercer nivel*), while in 'Normensystem und Rechtsordnung', *op. cit.*, pp. 102–103, he no longer uses this concept. These changes are not discussed here, since they are of no importance in the context of argument A–VIII; however, it can be stated that this element of Bulygin's conception is not satisfactorily elaborated.

[345] *Cf.* E. Bulygin, 'Time and Validity', *op. cit.*, pp. 68ff., 'Tiempo y validez', *op. cit.*, pp. 199ff., and 'Normensystem und Rechtsordnung', *op. cit.*, pp. 101ff.

metanorm there is no difference between its external and internal time. He emphasises that Article 303 has been applicable since its promulgation, and thus its membership in the legal system and its applicability concern an identical time period.[346] From the point of view of the Poznań conception of legal norm, adopted in this study, a doubt arises as to whether the provisions of the entry into force may give rise to a decoding of the self-reliant, independent intertemporal metanorms, or whether they only co-determine the content of the applicable legal norms.[347] Accordingly, what emerges is a crucial question as to whether at least some of the examples of applicability norms N_i, identified by Bulygin, are indeed legal norms and not merely provisions containing elements of applicable norms N_j that determine the temporal scope of their application.

In seeking an answer to this question, let us consider the arguments formulated by the representatives of the Poznań school of jurisprudence (Jaroslaw Mikołajewicz, Paweł Grabowski and Mikołaj Hermann),[348] which justify the opposite position to that adopted by Bulygin with respect to a normative interpretation of the provisions of the entry into force. Firstly, these authors note that the interpretation of the interim legal provisions (which undoubtedly include the provisions on the entry into force) as metanorms (i.e., ultimate applicability norms in Bulygin's terminology) that compel the implementation (compliance, application) of other legal norms (i.e., applicable norms) from the moment indicated in them, constitutes only an apparent solution to the issue of the validity of norms in time (in particular, the validity of the norms of former law), because it merely shifts the intertemporal problem on the level of metanorms. The evaluation of this argument is not an easy

---

[346] E. Bulygin, 'Time and Validity', *op. cit.*, p. 70 and 'Tiempo y validez', *op. cit.*, p. 202. Regrettably, at this point, we also have to note the inconsistent changes in Bulygin's position, since in his later work 'Normensystem und Rechtsordnung', *op. cit.*, p. 103, he extends – in my opinion wrongly – the scope of the claim about the identity of the "external time" with the "internal time" on all applicability norms, which is a mistake in relation to those of them that still remain in the *vacatio legis* period. On the other hand, even in his later work '¿Está (parte de) la filosofía del Derecho basada en un error?', *op. cit.*, p. 22, under the influence of von Wright's analyses, Bulygin assumes that the chain of applicability norms terminates with the ultimate applicability norm, which is neither applicable nor non-applicable (and the question of the applicability of applicability norms is meaningless) – for more details *see infra*, note 378 at p. 332. Accordingly, it must, consequently, be concluded that the "internal time" of such an ultimate applicability norm cannot be determined and, thus, the thesis of identity fails.

[347] *Cf. supra*, note 37 at p. 254 and pp. 307–308. Let us add that in this section we use the concepts of applicability norms, applicable norms and metanorms within Bulygin's concept of legal norm, although argument A–VIII demonstrates that these concepts are incorrect (since the expressions of juristic language that are referred to by him by means of these concepts are not at all norms in the meaning adopted by us). Yet, we have no choice, because the attempt to replace these three Bulygin's concepts by different ones would probably result in utterly incomprehensible arguments; however, one should keep this reservation in mind.

[348] *Cf.* J. Mikołajewicz, *Prawo intertemporalne*, *op. cit.*, pp. 71ff. and P. Grabowski, M. Hermann, 'O normatywnym charakterze przepisów o wejściu w życie', *op. cit.*, pp. 72ff. In the discussion, we slightly change the sequence and the content of the arguments presented in these studies, and we adjust them to Bulygin's terminology.

task. From a jurisprudential standpoint, it is not convincing, because Bulygin's conception by no means belongs to a type of spurious solution—at best, it is an incorrect solution. It is equally difficult to regard as spurious, multiple jurisprudential conceptions developed by other authors (Kelsen, von Wright or Raz), who, when studying the question of legal validity, use differently understood constructions of "chains of validity". In these conceptions, the validity of a lower norm is justified by a reference to the validity (e.g., Kelsen) or existence (e.g., von Wright) of the norm that constitutes a higher link in the chain, and thus the issue of validity is being shifted in these conceptions also at the level of metanorms. It should be noted, nevertheless, that the authors of the discussed argument are undoubtedly right when they argue that the adoption of a metanormative character of applicability norms complicates the picture of the legal system and its functioning in practice: determining the obligations of the addressees of applicable norms or applying them in order to resolve a certain case always requires determining the content (reconstruction) of corresponding applicability norms, which is impractical and, which—let us add our view—does not exactly correspond with the practice of law application. We believe that it is an exaggeration to say that each application of law includes the settlement of intertemporal issues.

Secondly, the interpretation of the provisions of the entry into force in the form of applicability metanorms leads to a typical problem of identifying the metanorms of respective (higher) levels, compelling (or at least justifying) the applicability of applicability norms. When referring this argument to Bulygin's conception, we can observe that there arises the problem of the applicability of the ultimate applicability norms. As already noted,[349] the Argentine philosopher avoids *ad infinitum* regress by settling this particular validity version of *Münchhausen Trilemma*[350] in a manner similar to that of both Hart and von Wright. As we recall, these authors argue that the problem of validity does not concern the highest norms of the legal system (respectively, the rule of recognition and the sovereign norm).[351] Bulygin, in a similar vein, considers the question of the applicability of the ultimate applicability norms to be pointless. Indeed, it is hard to find (i.e., reconstruct) the norms that prescribe the application of metanorms determining the entry into force of lawmaking acts. Nonetheless—in my opinion—it remains an open question as to whether the solution proposed by Bulygin (just like Hart's and von Wright's solutions) does not merely constitute only a circumvention (and not a real solution) of the trilemma formulated by Albert.[352]

[349] *Cf. supra*, note 346 at p. 324.

[350] As for the content of this trilemma *see* Chap. 4, note 323 at p. 144.

[351] *See supra*, p. 300. In our present consideration, we refer the content of this trilemma to the question of the ultimate justification of the validity of legal norms.

[352] At this point, we will leave this question unresolved and revisit it in Chap. 9 at pp. 456–458, as we consider it as related to the issue of the justification of the validity of legal norms, which – as already mentioned (*cf. supra*, p. 249) – belongs to the problems related to the extension of the juristic concept of the validity of statutory law.

While the two above arguments seem inconclusive, the third argument seems to be decisive. If we consider "an utterance which sufficiently unambiguously orders (or prohibits) someone (the addressee) certain behaviour in certain circumstances" as being legal norm,[353] it can easily be seen that the distinction between applicability norms and applicable norms is inconsistent with such a definition of a legal norm. If we treat applicability norms N_i (including the metanorms that define the moment of the entry into force of the applicable norms) as independent legal norms, then the corresponding applicable norms N_j cannot include in their scope of application the element which determines their initial point of application (because it would make the ultimate applicability norms utterly useless[354]). At the same time, applicable norms (as defined by Bulygin) are obviously incomplete and difficult to regard as sufficiently clear utterances indicating the circumstances in which a given behaviour is ordered or prohibited for a certain addressee.[355] It follows that legal norms (as defined in this study) can be reconstructed (decoded) only when we, at the same time, take into account—to put it in a conceptual grid of Bulygin's

[353] This definition, formulated by M. Zieliński, has been adopted as the basis for our clarificative analysis in Chap. 6 at p. 245.

[354] These norms may also be considered as redundant for another reason. Let us consider an undoubtedly correct thesis on the normative superfluity of legal provisions "which would prescribe the application (or implementation) of the norms contained in valid normative acts", formulated by S. Wronkowska and M. Zieliński in *Komentarz do zasad techniki prawodawczej z dnia 20 czerwca 2002 r.*, *op. cit.*, pp. 34–35. The authors from Poznań justify this thesis by arguing that the valid normative acts determine the ought of a certain conduct for the addressees of the norms included in these acts, and therefore it is unnecessary to prescribe such an ought for the second time. In the context of the analysed distinction between applicability norms and applicable norms, this objection can be understood in such a way that if we treat Bulygin's interpretation of the provisions on the entry into force as the ultimate applicability norms that order the application of other norms, then in terms of the normative aspect, they are completely unnecessary – they cannot function as the order to apply valid norms, but only as a clarification of the scope of application of applicable norms in the temporal aspect.

[355] In passing, let us add that a similar argument from incompleteness can be formulated in reference to the applicability norms, which, in turn, incompletely determine the ought of a certain behaviour of their addressees since they are only blank rules. In effect, without identifying the content of the sanctioning norm that the judge is bound by, the judge is not able to behave in the manner prescribed by the applicability norm (if it is at all possible, in the sense that there exists an abstract behaviour, capable of being identified or described as "the application of applicable norms"). Only when the judge does so, will she/he be able to apply the decoded applicable sanctioning norm and thus – but only indirectly – fulfil the obligation created by the applicability norm. This note reveals that Bulygin's conception forces us to a conceptually unnecessarily complicated description of law application, which is also highly debatable. For such a description presupposes the possibility of iterating the obligations – for more on that last point, *see* Chap. 8 at pp. 402–418; *cf.* also the standpoint of S. Wronkowska and M. Zieliński presented in previous note, which also supports this argument. It should be noted, however, that Bulygin strongly opposes the arguments expounded in this and the previous note, arguing that the duty imposed on judges by the applicability norms is not superfluous, since "it does not coincide with the obligations established by other legal norms", but unfortunately he does not provide any argument to support his position – *see idem*, '¿Está (parte de) la filosofía del Derecho basada en un error?', *op. cit.*, p. 20.

conception—the contents of applicable norms and the corresponding applicability norms, since without this, it is not possible to reach a level of "sufficient clarity". It therefore comes as no surprise that the theorists of the Poznań school of legal theory, whose arguments were applied in the above critical analysis, emphatically reject the metanormative interpretation of the provisions of the entry into force and they advocate treating the latter as supplementing (or more specifically, modifying) the content of legal norms.[356] In the context of the undertaken clarificative analysis, this argument can be further strengthened by noting that the consequence of adopting the concept of validity proposed by the Argentine philosopher concerns the need to identify each time (by way of interpreting the applicability norms) the internal time of applicable norms. Without meeting such a requirement, the statement that a given norm is valid (in terms of its applicability) would often be completely useless in the practice of law application.[357] Thus, if we accepted this conception, the statements on the validity of applicable norms would have to be relativised in time and we have already advocated against this solution because such relativisation is not advisable when clarifying the intension of the juristic concept of the validity of statutory law.[358]

In sum, the fundamental nature of the A–VIII argument challenges the distinction between applicability norms and applicable norms as an ineligible "dismemberment" of legal norms, resulting in neither applicability norms nor applicable norms being considered as legal norms within the meaning adopted for the purposes of our clarificative analysis. In addition, and also in connection with the above reasoning, this argument undermines the accuracy of recognising applicability norms as metanorms, as Bulygin does.[359] Yet, we cannot deny that the authors who opt for a different understanding of the concept a legal norm will find this argument inappropriate and the applicability norms may be considered as metanorms requiring the application of applicable norms. Therefore, at this point we shall not yet complete the critical analysis, but rather go on to present the next argument, directed against the conception of validity expressed in the form of model definition D_3.

The second argument (referred to as A–IX) is very similar to the A–V argument, formulated in the preceding section in relation to the conception of the legal validity of statutory norms, understood as the application of norms. The point is that the now analysed concept of validity, understood as the applicability of norms, does not

---

[356] *Cf.* J. Mikołajewicz, *Prawo intertemporalne*, *op. cit.*, pp. 72ff.; P. Grabowski, M. Hermann, 'O normatywnym charakterze przepisów o wejściu w życie', *op. cit.*, pp. 73ff.; S. Wronkowska, M. Zieliński, *Komentarz do zasad techniki prawodawczej z dnia 20 czerwca 2002 r.*, *op. cit.*, p. 100.

[357] In particular, it would be insufficient in such court cases in which an intertemporal legal problem takes place.

[358] *Cf.* three arguments against the temporal relativisation of the expression on the validity of statutory norms presented *supra* at pp. 256–260.

[359] Yet, it should be noted that Bulygin prefers to use the concept of applicability criteria than of applicability norms, perhaps realising the arguable use of the latter concept, which – as I believe – was demonstrated in argument A–VIII.

refer to a number of types of legal norms, thus the scope of reference of the definition D_3 is even narrower than in the case of the definition D_2. Definition D_3 cannot therefore be seen as an accurate clarification of the juristic concept of the validity of statutory law norms, because such a clarification should undoubtedly include all (or at least the vast majority) of the types of statutory law norms and not just some of them.

Let us recall that Bulygin defines applicable norms as norms that, under the applicability norms, should be applied when resolving legal cases. Applicability norms—as he writes in *Tiempo y validez*—have a "form of directives—addressed to judges—which determine what norms they ought to apply in a given case".[360] It can undoubtedly be concluded that in the light of the distinction between sanctioned and sanctioning norms—as adopted in this study[361]—the concept of applicable norms is essentially identical in its extension to the concept of sanctioning norms (with the exception of non-ultimate applicability norms, as explained below). What therefore remains outside the extension of this definition are sanctioned norms and the norms of competence (which Bulygin—after Hart—considers to be secondary rules, thus distinguishing them from the applicability norms[362]), not to mention the norms without sanctions, which by definition are not affiliated with any applicability norms and, therefore, as *leges imperfectae* they do not belong to the category of applicable norms. Moreover, as already noted,[363] the problem of the applicability of applicability norms—ambiguously resolved in Bulygin's conception—is solved in his latest studies in such way that the ultimate applicability norms can be considered neither as applicable nor as non-applicable.

Thus, the definition that provides for the equivalence of the validity of statutory norms with their applicability can be used only in relation to sanctioning norms and some of the applicability norms. Additionally, it is only in relation to these types of norms that we could rule on their validity on the basis of definition D_3, which for obvious reasons, is not satisfactory. Such a clarification would drastically reduce the scope of reference and, therefore, the practical usefulness of the concept of the validity of the norms of statutory law.

Before proceeding to the next argument, we should very briefly discuss the modification of Bulygin's conception proposed by Pablo Navarro and José Juan Moreso, because—at least at first glance—it definitely weakens the power of the A–IX argument, as it extends the concept of the applicability of norms and, therefore, the concept of validity based on it. They distinguish between the external applicability and internal applicability of legal norms. The first concept refers directly to the concept of applicability introduced by Bulygin, yet it is more

[360] E. Bulygin, 'Tiempo y validez', *op. cit.*, p. 203. Identically in 'Time and Validity', *op. cit.*, p. 71, '¿Está (parte de) la filosofía del Derecho basada en un error?', *op. cit.*, p. 20, and similarly in 'Normensystem und Rechtsordnung', *op. cit.*, p. 102.

[361] *Cf.* the studies indicated *supra*, notes 45–46 at p. 257.

[362] E. Bulygin, 'Normensystem und Rechtsordnung', *op. cit.*, p. 102.

[363] *Cf. supra*, note 346 at p. 324 and p. 325.

accurate and defined in a multi-relativised manner (temporarily, substantively and systemically):

> A norm N_i is *externally applicable* at the moment t to a certain individual case c, which is an instance of the generic case C, if and only if a norm N_j, belonging to a legal system LS at t, prescribes (obliges or empowers) the application of N_i to the individual cases which are instances of C.[364]

Such a definition of externally applicable norms indirectly broadens the scope of reference of definition D_3, because the characteristic of applicability norms is thus extended. As far as Bulygin's original conception goes, these are only the norms that constitute obligations and in the conception of Navarro and Moreso, these are also the norms of competence that empower law-applying authorities with the competence to apply applicable norms. As already noted, non-ultimate applicability norms are, at the same time, norms that belong to the category of applicable norms, so the scope of reference of the latter concept is thus extended. This extension is even further strengthened by the concept of the internal applicability of norms—entirely new in respect to Bulygin's original conception—which is defined by Navarro and Moreso in the following way:

> A norm N_i is *internally applicable* at moment t to an individual case c if and only if c is an instance of the generic case C, and C is defined by the spatial, material, personal and temporal spheres of validity of N_i.[365]

If, within the analysis of argument A–IX, we have to consider internally applicable norms, namely the category that undoubtedly includes the set of sanctioned norms, then this argument would not be very convincing. If we took into account the modifications introduced by Navarro and Moreso, the concept of applicable norms would comprise not only externally applicable sanctioning norms and some norms of competence, but also internally applicable sanctioned norms. Indeed, definition D_3 would therefore still not include all statutory norms, but almost all of the most crucial statutory norms from the perspective of legal practice. Nonetheless, such conclusions would be premature because the concept of the internal applicability of norms is highly dubious.

Navarro and Moreso introduce the concept of the internal applicability of norms for the purposes of the logical analysis of the structure and truth-conditions of the statements concerning the applicability and effectiveness of legal norms, thus recognising that the effectiveness of legal norms depends on their observance by the addressees.[366] It may not cause surprise that the concept of the internal applicability of norms is indispensable for them, since it relates directly to sanctioned norms, and it is in relation to them that we usually argue whether they are

---

[364] P.E. Navarro, J.J. Moreso, 'Applicability and Effectiveness of Legal Norms', *op. cit.*, p. 203. Let us add that concepts of the individual case and generic case used in this definition are also derived from Bulygin – *cf.* C.E. Alchourrón, E. Bulygin, *Normative Systems*, *op. cit.*, pp. 27ff.

[365] P.E. Navarro, J.J. Moreso, *ibidem*, p. 206. This definition naturally uses the concept of the spheres of validity that was introduced by H. Kelsen – *cf.* his studies cited *supra*, note 36 at p. 254.

[366] *Ibidem*, p. 201.

observed or not. Thus, without introducing this concept, Navarro's and Moreso's analyses would be significantly incomplete—they could, in fact, refer only to relations between the applicability of sanctioning norms and their observance. Yet, when referring to sanctioned norms, is it possible at all to state that they are applicable? It does not seem reasonable, even if only for the reasons for which we have already challenged the accuracy of the statements about the application of sanctioned norms.[367] It can certainly be much more easily expressed and in a manner not prejudicial to the juristic linguistic intuitions when we say that the sanctioned norms regulate someone's behaviour or that they are observed rather than that they are applicable. "Applicability" is thus an important feature of sanctioning norms—in fact, they are applied by the courts and other law-applying authorities because they are, by definition, their only addressees. We are dealing here with the semantic intuitions of juristic language, which are by their very nature not entirely clear and are difficult to grasp, yet this image definitely brightens and becomes clearer when we briefly revisit Bulygin's original conception. According to the quoted original definition,[368] the essence of the applicability consists of the relation between the norms that belong to two conceptually distinct categories; namely, applicability norms and applicable norms. Meanwhile, the concept of the internal applicability of norms, introduced by Navarro and Moreso, breaks this relation: legal norms are internally applicable as they themselves determine their scope of application, and not because there are some applicability norms that correspond to them. Consequently, as I believe, internal applicability is something generically totally different from the applicability in Bulygin's sense of that notion. The conceptual category of internally applicable norms introduced by them cannot be regarded as an extension of the definition of applicability provided by Bulygin, and consequently of the scope of reference for the definition D_3. Thus, we return to the position according to which the sanctioned norms do not fall under applicable norms, which discredits the definition of legal validity understood as the applicability of statutory law norms on account of its too narrow scope of reference.

Following the beaten track of clarificative analysis, we should now proceed to reconsider the symmetry of the intensions of the concepts of the validity and applicability of norms, as constructed in definition D_3.[369] We would have no

[367] *See supra*, pp. 313–316, in particular note 309 at p. 315. In order to adjust the argument presented in note 309 to the present discussion, we should ask whether we say that someone does not kill a man because the sanctioned norm of penal law that prohibits killing is applicable (in relation to her/him). Is it not an artificial and unnecessarily complicated way of describing someone's behaviour in the context of penal law, which can be expressed in the form of a simple and easily understood assertion that someone does not kill a man because the sanctioned norm of penal law prohibits killing a man?

[368] *Cf. supra*, the quotation from Bulygin's 'Tiempo y validez' at p. 322.

[369] This manner of reasoning has already been applied in argument A–III (*cf. supra*, pp. 289ff.) directed against the definition that identifies the validity of statutory norms with their membership in the legal system, as well as in argument A–VI (*cf. supra*, pp. 316ff.), which undermines the definition of validity based on the concept of the application of norms.

difficulties in formulating and justifying the argument that proves the asymmetry of the semantic relation between these two concepts, since both Bulygin[370] and his followers[371] cite and analyse many examples of legal norms that are valid, yet they are not applicable, and vice versa. Nevertheless, we shall not make use of these analyses and neither will we present the argument against symmetry that corresponds to them, for it would be manifestly incorrect for two reasons. Firstly, when we operate the concept of the validity of norms, understood as their applicability, and then we confront it with the concept of validity—understood as the membership of norms in the legal system (Bulygin, Navarro and Moreso often act in such a way, as expanded in the next argument A–X)—then naturally we can easily identify numerous examples of the norms that belong to the legal system, and that are not applicable (e.g., new legal norms in the period of *vacatio legis*), and—on the other hand—the norms which do not belong to a given legal system, yet which are applicable within it (e.g., the norms of foreign law). Such argumentation would be nonetheless based on the ambiguity of the concept of validity, which is unacceptable for us because our clarification aims at eliminating the ambiguity of this concept. Secondly, demonstrating the asymmetry of the alleged equivalence between the validity (understood as a membership) and the applicability of legal norms would be contrary to the results of previous analyses. The concept of the validity of statutory norms, based on the concept of their membership in the legal system, has already been rejected by us, which excludes the possibility of applying it in order to rebut the considered concept of validity presented by means of definition D_3. Any argument would therefore be similarly worthless, like an argument that undermines some particular thesis on human nature by means of the thesis which wrongly proclaims that, for example, all men are xenophobes. For these reasons, the argument challenging the symmetry of the equivalence of intensions between the validity and applicability of norms must be omitted, but in the next and, at the same time last argument against the definition D_3, we will directly refer to the objection of the ambiguity of the concept of the validity of legal norms, which Bulygin's conception necessarily leads to.

The last argument (hereafter A–X), refers primarily to the question of the validity of norms that belong to the category of applicability norms. Bulygin repeatedly emphasises that applicability norms must belong to the legal system (and in this sense they must be valid),[372] having in mind the momentary legal system valid at the moment when the judge makes a decision. Such a legal system is

[370] *Cf.* E. Bulygin, 'Time and Validity', *op. cit.*, pp. 68ff., 'Tiempo y validez', *op. cit.*, pp. 199ff., 'Algunas consideraciones sobre los sistemas jurídicos', *op. cit.*, pp. 266ff., and 'Normensystem und Rechtsordnung', *op. cit.*, pp. 101ff.

[371] *Cf.* P.E. Navarro, J.J. Moreso, 'Applicability and Effectiveness of Legal Norms', *op. cit.*, pp. 209ff.; J.J. Moreso, *Legal Indeterminacy and Constitutional Interpretation*, *op. cit.*, pp. 108ff.; P.E. Navarro, 'Legal Reasoning and Systematization of Law', *op. cit.*, pp. 262ff.

[372] *Cf.* E. Bulygin, 'Time and Validity', *op. cit.*, p. 70, 'Tiempo y validez', *op. cit.*, p. 202, 'Algunas consideraciones sobre los sistemas jurídicos', *op. cit.*, p. 267, and 'Normensystem und Rechtsordnung', *op. cit.*, p. 103.

referred to by Bulygin as a "privileged system" (*sistema privilegiado*) or "present system" (*gegenwärtigen System*). The same pattern is followed by Navarro and Moreso, who already in the definition of external applicability (which expands the concept of applicability introduced by Bulygin) directly express the requirement of the membership of applicability norms in the legal system that is temporarily relativised by the moment of taking the decision about the application of applicable norms.[373] Thus, it can be easily noticed that the authors of the analysed conception not only apply two descriptive[374] concepts of validity (applicability and membership)—*nota bene* terminologically strongly preferring the latter one[375]—but they also construct the concept of validity, understood as the applicability of legal norms, on the basis of the assumption of the membership of applicability norms in a momentary legal system. As Navarro claims: "[A] norm is applicable in virtue of the fact that another norm belongs to the legal system".[376] Naturally, such a construction is necessary in order to avoid *regresus ad infinitum*.[377] Such a regress could occur as a consequence of the assumption that applicable norms can be identified on the basis of applicability norms (applicability criteria), which, in turn, are subject to identification on the basis of applicability metanorms (metacriteria), and so on *ad infinitum*.[378] The system of norms that includes

---

[373] *Cf. supra*, the text of the quotation corresponding to note 364 at p. 329.

[374] We should not be confused by the fact that Bulygin in his latest work '¿Está (parte de) la filosofía del Derecho basada en un error?', *op. cit.*, pp. 19–20, characterises the concept of applicability as normative, because what he means is an otherwise obvious fact that applicability norms constitute prescriptions that stipulate the legal obligations of judges. It does not change anything with regard to the descriptive nature of the sentences stating the applicability of legal norms.

[375] *Cf. e.g.*, E. Bulygin, 'Algunas consideraciones sobre los sistemas jurídicos', *op. cit.*, p. 264, where Bulygin adopts the convention based on the synonymy of the terms "membership" (*pertenencia*) and "validity" (*validez*), as well as 'Normensystem und Rechtsordnung', *op. cit.*, pp. 101 and 103, where he treats as synonyms the German-language equivalent terms: *Zugehörigkeit* and *Geltung*. A similar conceptual convention is adopted by Navarro and Moreso, who recognise as valid only those norms that belong to the legal system – *see supra*, the text corresponding to note 207 at p. 293.

[376] P.E. Navarro, 'Legal Reasoning and Systematization of Law', *op. cit.*, p. 262.

[377] Bulygin differently justifies the necessity of using the concept of validity, understood as the membership of norms in the legal system, in respect to applicability norms. He believes that this is the only way that we can avoid another logical error; namely, the possible circularity likely to occur between the concept of applicability norms and the concept of the legal system (it would be the case if applicability norms or criteria served the purpose of identifying the extension of the legal system, whereas the legal system would provide us with the applicability criteria) – *see idem*, 'Time and Validity', *op. cit.*, p. 77 and 'Tiempo y validez', *op. cit.*, p. 212.

[378] As already noted, Bulygin – in our opinion, only apparently – avoids *regressus ad infinitum*, by assuming only the need of the existence and not the applicability of the applicability norms – *cf. supra*, note 346 at p. 324 and p. 325. In this context, it has to be explained that Bulygin uses, by analogy, the conception of the relative validity of norms, developed by G.H. von Wright, *Norm and Action*, *op. cit.*, pp. 194ff., in particular, pp. 196ff. and 199–200. For more on von Wright's conception *see* J. Woleński, *Z zagadnień analitycznej filozofii prawa*, *op. cit.*, pp. 99ff. and D. González Lagier, *Acción y norma en G.H. von Wright*, Madrid 1995, pp. 370ff. We shall briefly

applicability norms must therefore be identifiable by means of the criterion independent from the concept of the applicability of norms such as—for example—the criterion of the membership of norms in a (momentary) legal system. It thus appears that the conception of legal validity understood as the applicability of the norms (expressed in the definition D_3) not only applies two concepts of validity, which in itself is not acceptable in our clarificative analysis, but—even worse—it must use the concept of validity understood as the membership of norms in the legal system, which has already been rejected by us. Consequently, we must conclude that in the light of the A–X argument, the analysed conception is not suited to clarifying the intension of the juristic concept of the validity of statutory law.

Important conclusions can be drawn from the foregoing reflections on the conception of legal validity understood as the applicability of legal norms. The argument A–X has highlighted the ambiguity of the concept of legal validity constituting a necessary feature of this conception. In the context of further clarification of the juristic concept of legal validity, it should be noted that this ambiguity is twofold. Firstly, to simplify slightly (thus leaving aside the issue of the applicability of applicability norms), we can say that, according to Bulygin and his followers, the legal norms "are valid" in two senses[379]: either they are applicable (applicable norms N_j) or they belong to the legal system (applicability norms N_i). Secondly, what seems essential in the context of our discussion is that they are also valid in two different ways (that is, in two domains). While applicability norms belong to a given legal system, applicable norms are applied (and enforced)—to put it somewhat metaphorically—in the institutional frames of a given legal system; namely, by law-applying organs, constituted in this system. As I believe, this is a very important point for our analysis. We should, therefore, once more emphasise the conclusion that can be drawn from the undertaken criticism of Bulygin's conception: legal validity may be related either to a given legal system or to the institutional framework of a given legal system. This observation will be crucial in the developed conception of legal validity, especially on account of the fact that the first possibility—that is, understanding validity with regard to the legal system—was, in fact, already excluded by us.[380]

explain that according to von Wright, we are dealing with the relative validity of a norm when it is dependent on the existence of a hierarchically higher norm that empowers the norm-giver to its enactment, whereas we are dealing with absolute validity (also called "validity in the system") if its enactment is ultimately reinforced by a sovereign norm, which is situated at the top of the hierarchical chain of norms belonging to the system. What is important, in von Wright's approach, is that the concept of validity in the absolute sense has a secondary character because it presupposes the relative concept of the validity of norms. As can be seen, von Wright's distinction is not identical with the differentiation between the validity in an absolute and in a relative sense, as adopted in the Polish legal theory (Opałek, Stelmach), which has been repeatedly referred to in our previous deliberations.

[379] We disregard here the third normative-absolute concept of validity identified by Bulygin, which is of no importance for the conception of validity based on the concept of the applicability of legal norms.

[380] *See supra*, pp. 253–254 and 284–289.

In summary, the conception of legal validity, understood in terms of the applicability of norms, must be rejected, as the three presented arguments do not allow recognising it as the clarification of the intension of the juristic concept of the validity of statutory law. Naturally, it does not mean that such a conception is utterly devoid of value, since both the distinction between applicability norms and applicable norms, as well as a number of detailed conceptual analyses of the phenomena of applicability and the application of legal norms, undertaken by Bulygin and his followers, have undeniable explanatory value. For example, it seems that this conception can constitute a starting point of analysis of a law-application process in a multicentric legal system, yet on the condition of adopting a different conception of a legal norm than the one assumed in this study.[381]

7.5 Legal Validity Understood in Terms of Observance or Efficacy

In the present section, we will examine the theoretical correctness and practical usefulness of the definitions of legal validity, in which we will use the concepts of the observance and efficacy (effectiveness) of legal norms. Let us emphasise that we do not yet go on to analyse the possible combinations of concepts that might constitute the *explicatum* of the juristic concept of the validity of statutory law, but we want to discuss two separate definitions of its intension in tandem: "A norm of statutory law is valid if, and only if it is observed" (referred to as D_4) and "A norm of statutory law is valid if, and only if it is efficacious" (referred to as D_5). We join together the analysis of these two model definitions, because the arguments formulated below generally apply to both of them, so there is no need to present them twice. Adopting such a method of clarificative analysis is also justified by the conceptual relationships between the observance and the efficacy of legal norms; in particular, the efficacy of law is often defined by means of the concept of its observance. The question is whether any of these definitions can be regarded as an accurate and useful clarification of the intension of the juristic concept of the validity of statutory law.

The arguments against the definitions D_4 and D_5 will be presented in a condensed way due to the fact that in most cases they are very similar to the arguments that have already been formulated in relation to the previously considered model concepts of legal validity. The first argument (hereafter A–XI) is primarily focused on the gradability of the concept of legal validity, understood in terms of its observance or efficacy. It is based on the reasoning that has been

[381] It should be noted, however, that the conventional adopting of another concept of a legal norm will not, by itself, release us from the problems connected with the discussed model conception of validity understood as the applicability of legal norms.

already applied in the A–V argument, directed against the definition of validity based on the concept of the application of norms.[382] To begin, let us note that in light of the previous analyses concerning the validity consequences of the principles *necessitum nulla est obligatio* and *impossibilium nulla est obligatio*, only those norms that prescribe the ought of the behaviour, which are both possible and not necessary to accomplish, can be regarded as valid. The futility of norms that violate this requirement is most clearly emphasised by Kelsen.[383] Therefore, it can be legitimately argued that the possibility of non-observance or inefficacy is an inherent feature of valid legal norms. When we move on to an empirical (factual) perspective, it is not surprising that legal theorists who take up the issue of the observance or efficacy of legal norms—regardless of whether the latter is understood as behavioural, motivational (psychological) or of finistic efficacy (effectiveness)[384]—unanimously emphasise the gradability of both these characteristics: legal norms can be observed or efficacious to a lesser or greater extent.[385]

Nonetheless, the following counterargument can be raised. We are able, at least sometimes,[386] to determine empirically, and thus objectively, whether a given legal norm is observed and/or efficacious. It follows that formulating a definition of legal validity by means of one of these concepts would have the advantage over the other definitions in the context of solving the problem of extension, because the juristic concept of the validity of statutory law, constructed in this way, would permit the use of certain criteria of empirical verifiability in determining the validity of the legal norm.

Let us consider the examples related to some of the particular concepts of efficacy (effectiveness) of legal norms that can be found in the jurisprudential literature. Article 65 Section 5 of the Polish Constitution[387] states that:

---

[382] *Cf. supra*, pp. 315–316.

[383] *Cf. supra*, pp. 302–304.

[384] On the differentiation of the indicated ways of understanding the efficacy of legal norms *see* W. Lang, J. Wróblewski, S. Zawadzki, *Teoria państwa i prawa*, *op. cit.*, pp. 494ff.; K. Pałecki, *Prawoznawstwo – zarys wykładu*, *op. cit.*, pp. 169ff.; Z. Ziembiński, *O stanowieniu i obowiązywaniu prawa. Zagadnienia podstawowe* [On Enacting and the Validity of Law. Basic Problems], Warszawa 1995, pp. 102ff.

[385] *Cf. e.g.*, W. Lang, J. Wróblewski, S. Zawadzki, *ibidem*, pp. 495, 531; K. Pałecki, *ibidem*, p. 171; J. Jakubowski, 'Pojęcie obowiązywania, realizacji i skuteczności normy prawnej oraz podstawy ich rozróżniania', *op. cit.*, p. 319; Z. Ziembiński, M. Zieliński, *Dyrektywy i sposób ich wypowiadania*, *op. cit.*, p. 36; H. Kelsen, 'Eine "Realistische" und die Reine Rechtslehre', *op. cit.*, p. 21; N. Hoerster, '"Wirksamkeit", "Geltung" und "Gültigkeit" von Normen', *op. cit.*, p. 592; P. Ingram, 'Effectiveness', *ARSP* 69 (1983), p. 485.

[386] Apart from other limitations of the procedures appropriate for empirical research, we need to exclude in advance the possibility of determining the degree of observance or efficacy of legal norms in a situation where these two concepts are understood in psychological terms – for example, as motives or reasons that guide the people who obey the law.

[387] *Konstytucja Rzeczypospolitej Polskiej z dnia 2 kwietnia 1997 r.* [Constitution of the Republic of Poland of 2 April 1997], published in *Dziennik Ustaw* [Journal of Statutes] 1997, No. 78, Item 483.

> Public authorities shall pursue policies aiming at full, productive employment by implementing programs to combat unemployment, including organizing and supporting guidance and vocational training as well as public and intervention works.

The finistic efficacy (effectiveness) of the programme norm, which can be interpreted from the quoted legal provision, could—theoretically speaking—be empirically estimated based on unemployment rates in Poland provided by the Central Statistical Office (*GUS*). Let us suppose that in this way we could assess that the effectiveness of this norm is 90 % (counterfactually assuming that only the right policy of the Polish government and other public authorities, rather than the entrepreneurship or mobility of the Poles employed abroad determines the 10 % unemployment rate among professionally active people). Theoretically, we might by analogy determine the behavioural effectiveness (efficacy) of the sanctioned norm encoded, for example, in the Article 148 § 1 of the Polish Penal Code[388] or in other norms of penal, civil or administrative law, empirically determining the degree of their observance by the addressees. Yet, can such an objectivised factual concept of legal validity, expressed by definitions D_4 or D_5, be regarded as an accurate clarification of the intension of the juristic concept of the validity of statutory law? We can easily point to some major theoretical and practical reasons in favour of a negative answer to that question.

Firstly, determining the degree of the observance or efficacy (effectiveness) of legal norms can only be made *ex post*. No legislator, even the most rational one, can yet foresee to what extent the law enacted by him will be observed or effective (with any understanding of efficacy). As rightly pointed by Zygmunt Ziembiński—whose analyses we refer to here—this fact makes the criterion of effectiveness "defective from the standpoint of legal practice", since the resolution of the issue of the validity of a legal norm "must be provided before choosing the conduct which should be affected by a given norm".[389] In effect, the definitions of legal validity in which we use the concepts of observance or efficacy (effectiveness), seem obviously to confuse the reason with the consequence, which is best seen in relation to the legal norms that have just come into force. As far as their validity can be regarded as the reason for their observance or efficacy (effectiveness), the reasoning in the opposite direction gives rise to serious suspicions of circularity, which we shall consider in the next argument A–XII.

Secondly, the gradability of legal validity arising from the gradability of the observance or efficacy (effectiveness) of legal norms is not acceptable, not simply because we have assumed a classifying character of the juristic concept of the validity of statutory law.[390] Even if such an assumption were not made, then the gradability of legal validity that results from adopting the definitions D_4 or D_5

---

[388] This is a basic provision of Polish penal law that prohibits the intentional killing of a man.

[389] Z. Ziembiński, *Problemy podstawowe prawoznawstwa*, *op. cit.*, p. 178. The dilemma of effectiveness has been similarly presented by A. Aarnio, 'On the Validity, Efficacy and Acceptability of Legal Norms', *op. cit.*, pp. 155ff. *Cf. idem*, *The Rational as Reasonable*, *op. cit.*, p. 42, where Aarnio quotes identical opinions to S. Jørgensen, T.M. Benditt and K. Makkonen.

[390] *Cf.* Introduction, note 11 at pp. 4–5, with the corresponding text.

would still have consequences that were unacceptable for lawyers (particularly practitioners). To treat any of these definitions seriously would be tantamount to "playing pseudo-mathematization",[391] consisting of the fact that the authorities applying the law would have to abstain from resolving whether a given legal norm is valid until they empirically determine the degree of its observance or efficacy, and only then would they rule on the basis of the norms valid in 98 %, 72 % or 56 % of cases. Such "pseudo-mathematization" of the concept of validity understood in terms of observance or efficacy (effectiveness) could be avoided by establishing a minimum degree of observance or efficacy of the norm, which could justify recognising it as valid—yet the problem is that, so far, no one has succeeded in determining such a degree in a rational way and even the mere possibility of the non-arbitrary determination of such a minimum threshold is highly questioned.[392]

It is therefore necessary to agree with Ulfrid Neumann, who recognises the socio-realistic model of legal validity (namely, the conceptions of validity based on the concepts of the application, observance or effectiveness of the law) as the grotesque failing to tally the understanding of the legal system, especially from the perspective of the judge.[393] As he states:

> A judge is considering whether the statute should be respected or applied by the judiciary. The same question is raised by legal dogmatics, which serves the function of preparing judicial decisions. Both the judge and the lawyer-dogmatist must be oriented at the normativity of the legal system, rather than at the actual proceeding in accordance with the norms of this system.[394]

Similar conclusions are justified, albeit quite rarely, by empirical research on legal validity. Per Olof Ekelöf describes his *par excellence* reality-based legal research—carried out among the judges of the first-instance courts and the prosecutors—concerning the application of certain provisions of the Swedish *Procedural Code*.[395] According to him, the respondents provided two conflicting responses, in the proportion of 50 % to 50 %, to one of the important questions. The Swedish researcher poses an open question (resembling in its assumption the above opinions of Ziembiński and Neumann) of how judges should act in such a case. He aptly notes that the effectiveness of the regulation at issue is significantly reduced; nevertheless, he doubts whether it can be said that the analysed legal rule is "valid in 50%". Ekelöf is undoubtedly right when he says that it is rational to adopt that the view of half of the respondents is wrong.[396] However, he does not add a remark, probably due to its self-evident nature, that when we sociologically research this

[391] The term is borrowed from Z. Ziembiński, *Problemy podstawowe prawoznawstwa*, *op. cit.*, pp. 177–178. Ziembiński defines, in this way, the procedures related to predicting the degree (probability) of obedience; namely, the behavioural observance or effectiveness of legal norms.

[392] *Cf. e.g.*, Z. Ziembiński, *ibidem* and P. Ingram, 'Effectiveness', *op. cit.*, pp. 485ff.

[393] U. Neumann, 'Problem obowiązywania prawa', *op. cit.*, p. 34.

[394] *Ibidem*, p. 37.

[395] P.O. Ekelöf, 'The Expression "Valid Rule": A Study in Legal Terminology', *op. cit.*, p. 65.

[396] We should strongly emphasise that this view is wrong, regardless of whether we consider the concept of the validity as a classifying or gradable concept.

issue, it is impossible to determine which half of the judges and prosecutors is right and which is wrong. Thus, we see that from the perspective of legal practice, the identification of the validity of law with its gradable observance or efficacy (effectiveness) is not only ludicrous, but it also prevents adopting any reasonably justified decision on validity, especially in the case of a stalemate. As, in the case described by Ekelöf, the only resolution, at least that is formally just, would be a coin toss or similar "decisions" on legal validity.

Let us now move on to the next argument A–XII, which will deal with the conceptual relations between the validity, observance and efficacy (effectiveness) of legal norms analysed in the context of a highly probable circularity of the definitions D_4 and D_5. Their circularity follows from the fact that the theorists and sociologists of law who use the concept of law observance (or compliance), unanimously recognise the need for the knowledge about the validity of a legal norm as a condition for the possibility of observing it by the subject obligated to do so.[397] As Sławomira Wronkowska remarks:

> The norm is observed by the one who implements it consciously, so at least knows that such a norm with such a content is valid, or even – under its influence – modifies his behaviour.[398]

It is clear that, as in the argument A–VI, directed against the definition of legal validity based on the concept of its application, one can easily demonstrate that the definition D_4 (directly) and definition D_5 (indirectly) both result in *circulus in definiendo*. Indeed, if according to the former, we will accept the intensional equivalence of the validity and observance of statutory norms, and in light of the quoted opinions, the observance of a norm requires—as Zygmunt Ziembiński wrote[399]—"by its very definition" that the law-observing person knew about the validity of the norm, then we obtain indisputably circular reasoning: "The norm is valid – its addressee knows that the norm is valid – the norm is observed – the norm is valid (under D_4)". On the other hand, if we accept, according to definition D_5, the meaning equivalence of the validity and efficacy (effectiveness) of statutory norms, then, given that both behavioural as well as motivational efficacy (effectiveness) also *ex definitione* require the knowledge of the addressees of the norms about their validity,[400] it emerges that the definition D_5 is thus fraught with the same fallacy.[401]

[397] To confine this only to the Polish literature *see e.g.*, L. Nowak, 'Cztery koncepcje obowiązywania prawa', *op. cit.*, p. 98, Z. Ziembiński, *Problemy podstawowe prawoznawstwa*, *op. cit.*, pp. 414, 423, L. Leszczyński, *Zagadnienia teorii stosowania prawa*, *op. cit.*, p. 16, K. Pałecki, *Prawoznawstwo – zarys wykładu*, *op. cit.*, p. 137 and S. Wronkowska, *Podstawowe pojęcia prawa i prawoznawstwa*, *op. cit.*, p. 121.

[398] S. Wronkowska, *ibidem*, p. 120.

[399] Z. Ziembiński, *Problemy podstawowe prawoznawstwa*, *op. cit.*, p. 423.

[400] Let us note, without an unnecessary indication of studies of the authors who present the same standpoint, that talking about the efficacy (effectiveness) of invalid norms or their empirical research is meaningless, at least from the practical perspective of the application of statutory law.

[401] Resorting to the finistic comprehension of the efficacy of legal norms cannot rescue us here, because – as Ziembiński aptly notes – this concept "is not generally taken into account when determining the validity of legal norms" – *idem*, *O stanowieniu i obowiązywaniu prawa*, *op. cit.*, p. 103.

To conclude, the recognition of the definitions D_4 or D_5 as proper clarification of the intension of the juristic concept of the validity of statutory law leads to an even more absurd solution—at least from a juristic point of view—of the validity version of the "Euthyphro dilemma"[402] than in case of the definition that identifies the validity of law with its application. To avoid the said circularity of the analysed definitions, it would have to be assumed that statutory norms become valid due to their observance or efficacy (effectiveness), namely as a result of the collective decision of their addressees, who, by means of choosing such conduct, which complies with (implements) a given norm or not, would, in fact, resolve the problem of the extension of the juristic concept of validity. From the standpoint of the essence of law, and in particular its normativity, manifested in the form of the binding force of law, it is clearly unacceptable, and it seems that the only remedy appears to be adopting a different conception of legal validity than the ones that present the definitions analysed in this section. In light of the indicated argument, it is necessary to conceptually distinguish between the validity, observance and efficacy (effectiveness) of legal norms, since otherwise we fall into a vicious circle in defining, which we can escape only when we grant the right to decide on legal validity to the group of the addressees of legal norms, as a result of which, law will be deprived of its coercive nature and will become something akin to a voluntary game; for example, chess.

The last argument (referred to as A–XIII) is based on the reasoning—already recalled several times in the course of the clarificative analysis—which concerns the scope of reference of the examined model conception of legal validity.[403] The problem lies in the fact that both definition D_4 as well as definition D_5 do not seem to comprise all types of statutory norms that are or can be valid, according to the common jurist linguistic usage of this term. As far as the definitions D_2 and D_3 examined in the two preceding sections turned out to be too narrow because they directly pertained only to sanctioning norms, the definitions that identify the validity of law with its observance or efficacy (effectiveness) seem—at least at first sight—to be directly related only to sanctioned norms.

Let us begin by considering the scope of reference of the definition that clarifies the intension of the juristic concept of legal validity by means of the concept of its observance (D_4). When focusing our attention on the terminology and the manner of using the concept of observance in juristic discourse, we will clearly note that the observance of law is usually only related to sanctioned norms, while the sanctioning norms are said to be applied. As pointed out by Jerzy Jakubowski more than 40 years ago, such terminology "in principle corresponds with a linguistic convention

[402] *Cf. supra*, pp. 319–320 and Chap. 5, pp. 205–206.

[403] *Cf. supra*, pp. 313–316 (argument A–V directed against the definition of validity understood as the application of legal norms) and pp. 327–331 (argument A–IX, concerning the definition of validity by means of the concept of the applicability of legal norms).

that is already well-known in jurisprudence".[404] A similar convention can be found in the studies of the authors who contemporarily take up the issue of the observance of law; for example, Leszek Leszczyński emphasises that:

> the concept of the observance of law is mainly associated with the activities of the so-called ordinary addressees of legal norms,[405]

having also in mind the addressees of the sanctioned rather than the sanctioning norms. Naturally, it does not mean that the semantic rules of juristic language preclude the use of the concept of observance in relation to sanctioning norms and the norms of competence; namely, the observance of law called "institutional" or "public".[406] Nevertheless, in this case the analyses of the practices of public authorities are usually conducted in the context of the legitimacy or legality of their actions[407] involving the application of sanctioning norms or norms of competence, yet not in terms of the observance of law.

With regard to the scope of reference of the definition D_5, which clarifies the intension of the juristic concept of legal validity by means of the concept of its efficacy (effectiveness), at first glance, the objection of its too limited scope seems to be unfounded. Let us consider two similar definitions of the efficacy (effectiveness) of the law. In the classic approach of Hans Kelsen, who, incidentally, strongly resisted identifying the concepts of the validity and efficacy of legal norms (as expanded upon in a moment), the efficacy (*Wirksamkeit*) of a norm lies in the fact that "the norm is actually observed (*tatsächlich befolgt*) and if it is not observed, then it is applied".[408] In the conception of Zygmunt Ziembiński, the so-called behavioural justification of validity refers directly to a factual (real) effectiveness of the sanctioned norm and only indirectly—in the case of the non-observance of a sanctioned norm—to the formal effectiveness of a sanctioning norm. The norms are recognised as valid if one can assume with a "sufficiently high" level of probability that they will be observed by their addressees, and in the case of their non-observance, that there is a "sufficiently high" probability of executing a sanction by a competent authority.[409] Thus, it would seem that the substantive scope of the definition D_5 covers both sanctioned as well as sanctioning norms. Yet, it cannot be

---

[404] J. Jakubowski, 'Pojęcie obowiązywania, realizacji i skuteczności normy prawnej oraz podstawy ich rozróżniania', *op. cit.*, p. 317.

[405] L. Leszczyński, *Zagadnienia teorii stosowania prawa*, *op. cit.*, p. 16. Similar conclusions can be drawn from the examination of the factors that affect the observance of law – *cf.* Z. Ziembiński, *Problemy podstawowe prawoznawstwa*, *op. cit.*, pp. 423ff.

[406] *Cf. e.g.*, K. Pałecki, *Prawoznawstwo – zarys wykładu*, *op. cit.*, pp. 142ff., who considers the legislation, application and enforcement of law as the forms of the institutional observance of law.

[407] For more details *see e.g.*, Z. Tobor, *Teoretyczne problemy legalności* [Theoretical Problems of Legality], PNUŚ 1721 (1998), in particular pp. 88ff.

[408] H. Kelsen, *Allgemeine Theorie der Normen*, *op. cit.*, p. 3 and *see* also an identical definition of the efficacy of the normative order provided by Kelsen on p. 111.

[409] *Cf.* Z. Ziembiński, *Problemy podstawowe prawoznawstwa*, *op. cit.*, pp. 176–178 and Z. Ziembiński, M. Zieliński, *Dyrektywy i sposób ich wypowiadania*, *op. cit.*, pp. 35–36.

ignored that a number of authors who take up the issue of the efficacy of a legal norm, refer primarily or exclusively to the degree of observance of law by their ordinary addressees (citizens),[410] indirectly confirming Ziembiński's observation that "the effectiveness of a sanctioned norm is substantially more important than the effectiveness of a sanctioning norm".[411] In fact, the basic conceptual intuitions of lawyers regarding the concept of the efficacy (effectiveness) of legal norms and law, as such undoubtedly relate to the degree of observance of law by ordinary addressees of legal norms—the members of a given community—rather than the degree of their institutional observance understood as the application of sanctioning norms, which is usually (but not always) a consequence of the non-observance of sanctioned norms. Let us consider whether the following statement can be recognised as correct: "This legal norm is efficacious, although the vast majority of people do not observe it, because those who do not observe it always bear the legal consequences of their unlawful conduct". We believe that the jurist would rather be inclined to say about such a sanctioned norm that it is not efficacious, and the question of even 100 % efficiency of the corresponding sanctioning norm would be utterly irrelevant; for example, for a legislator seeking to actually modify the conduct of the ordinary addressees of legal norms. Generally speaking, extending the concept of efficacy (effectiveness) on sanctioning norms entails the risk—as we believe—of a highly artificial terminological convention: the efficacy of sanctioning legal norms is to a quite large extent independent of the conduct of the addressees of sanctioned norms.[412] Although it is possible to encounter such conceptions that relate the efficacy of law with the degree of law application,[413] nevertheless, the above observations suggest the reference of the concept of the efficacy of law primarily to the category of sanctioned norms. Hence, we do believe

---

[410] *Cf. e.g.*, J. Jakubowski's review of W. Lang 's book: *Obowiązywanie prawa*, *PiP* 10 (1962), p. 640; N. Hoerster, '"Wirksamkeit", "Geltung" und "Gültigkeit" von Normen', *op. cit.*, p. 589; P.E. Navarro, J.J. Moreso, 'Applicability and Effectiveness of Legal Norms', *op. cit.*, p. 201. For more *see* P. Ingram, 'Effectiveness', *op. cit.*, pp. 492ff.

[411] Z. Ziembiński, *Problemy podstawowe prawoznawstwa*, *op. cit.*, p. 177.

[412] Given the inevitability of judicial errors and, on the other hand, the degree of detecting illegal behaviour, we can conclude that the non-observance of sanctioned norms is neither a prerequisite nor a sufficient condition for the application (and thus the potential effectiveness) of sanctioning norms.

[413] *See* P. Ingram, 'Effectiveness', *op. cit.* Naturally, the authors who recognised the legal system as consisting of sanctioning norms – such as H. Kelsen and A. Ross – primarily or exclusively referred to them the concept of efficacy (effectiveness). *Cf. e.g.* H. Kelsen, *General Theory of Law and State*, *op. cit.*, p. 62: "[T]hough the efficacy of law is primarily its being applied by the proper organ, secondarily its efficacy means its being obeyed by the subjects" and A. Ross, *On Law and Justice*, *op. cit.*, p. 35: "The effectiveness which conditions the validity of the norms can therefore be sought solely in the judicial application of the law, and not in the law in action among private individuals". Nonetheless, our analyses leave such conceptions aside because nowadays it is generally accepted that the legal system is composed of various categories of norms – in particular, also of sanctioned norms and not just sanctioning ones.

that the view, expressed nearly half a century ago by Hart, who conceived the efficacy of law as "the fact that a rule of law which requires certain behaviour is obeyed more often than not",[414] preserves its accuracy.

In light of the above arguments, it is not surprising that a number of leading representatives of the twentieth-century positivist theory of law (among whom we can mention the two most prominent—Hans Kelsen and H.L.A. Hart) strongly reject the possibility of understanding the validity of law in terms of its observance or efficacy, but this does not mean that these concepts are utterly irrelevant in the context of legal validity. For Kelsen, whose position seems the most representative here, a relative (*im großen und ganzen*) efficacy of law (legal order) constitutes the condition of both its validity as a whole and the validity of individual legal norms.[415] Nevertheless, it is a *conditio sine qua non*, rather than a *conditio per quam*.[416] Kelsen often stressed that the effectiveness of law is only a necessary condition and not the reason (*Grund*) for its validity,[417] rightly noting that "[a] condition cannot be identical with that which it conditions".[418] Contrary to appearances, a similar approach to the relationship between the validity and efficacy (effectiveness) of law can be found in Hart's sophisticated legal positivism. Although the author of *The Concept of Law* openly claims that his understanding of the relationship between validity and efficacy differs from Kelsen's conception (in particular, there may be special circumstances in which the reasonableness of the claims about validity is preserved, despite the fact that a given legal system is no longer efficacious),[419] nevertheless, he assumes that the normal context in which the claims about validity are made relates to the efficacy of the legal system. The reconstruction of Hart's views, undertaken by Jan Woleński,[420] shows that the British philosopher defines the interrelation between efficacy and the validity of law by means of a presupposition method, typical of analytical linguistic philosophy. As Hart writes, the "normal use" of internal statements about the validity of norms presupposes "the truth of the external statement of fact that the system is generally efficacious".[421] It is easy to perceive a peculiar analogy here: both Kelsen

---

[414] H.L.A. Hart, *The Concept of Law*, *op. cit.*, p. 100.

[415] *Cf. e.g.* H. Kelsen, *General Theory of Law and State*, *op. cit.*, pp. 41ff., 173, *Reine Rechtslehre*, 2nd ed., *op. cit.*, pp. 10, 218ff. [English version, pp. 11, 211ff.], and *Allgemeine Theorie der Normen*, *op. cit.*, pp. 112ff. A synthetic description of the manner of understanding the efficacy in Kelsen's pure theory of law can be found in P. Ingram, 'Effectiveness', *op. cit.*, pp. 488–490 and R. Lippold, 'Geltung, Wirksamkeit und Verbindlichkeit von Rechtsnormen', *op. cit.*, pp. 468–469, 473ff.

[416] H. Kelsen, *General Theory of Law and State*, *op. cit.*, p. 119.

[417] *Ibidem*. *Cf.* H. Kelsen, 'Eine "Realistische" und die Reine Rechtslehre', *op. cit.*, p. 10 and 'Was ist juristischer Positivismus?', *op. cit.*, p. 467.

[418] H. Kelsen, *Reine Rechtslehre*, 2nd ed., *op. cit.*, p. 219 [English version, p. 212].

[419] H.L.A. Hart, *The Concept of Law*, *op. cit.*, note to p. 100 at p. 247.

[420] J. Woleński, 'Obowiązywanie prawne w ujęciu H.L.A. Harta', *op. cit.*, pp. 282–284.

[421] H.L.A. Hart, *The Concept of Law*, *op. cit.*, p. 101. *Cf. idem*, 'Scandinavian Realism', *op. cit.*, p. 168, where Hart identically defines the "normal context" of internal normative statements.

and Hart reject the equivalence of the validity and efficacy (effectiveness) of law, inter alia, due to the differences between the statements about the validity and the statements about the efficacy of law. In Kelsen's theory, the statement about the validity refers to the sphere (world) of *Sollen*, whereas the statements about the efficacy of law relate to facts (*Seins–Tatsache*), from the sphere of *Sein*. As Kelsen writes:

> That the law is "valid" ("*gilt*") means that it *ought* to be observed or applied, [whereas] that it is efficacious means that it *is* observed or applied.[422]

In contrast, in Hart's theory, the former statements are regarded as internal statements (by means of which—let us recall[423]—the normativity of law is being expressed) whereas the latter are external statements of fact.

The similarity of comprehending the relation between the validity and efficacy (effectiveness) of law by Kelsen and Hart is additionally strengthened if we take into account the views of the two philosophers concerning the basis of the existence of the legal system. For Kelsen, the basic norm—which undoubtedly constitutes the basis of the existence of the legal system—prescribes the conduct conforms with the established and *im großen und ganzen* effective constitution and also with *im großen und ganzen* efficacious statutory norms, issued on its basis.[424] For Hart, in turn, the statement that the legal system exists, has a "Janus face"—when uttering it, we look on the one hand at the observance of law by the ordinary people (and thus at the efficacy of primary rules, which undoubtedly are sanctioned norms), and on the other hand, at the fact that the officials approve a given system of secondary rules as the official critical patterns of their behaviour.[425]

Summing up the presented considerations, we are forced to assume that neither the concept of law observance nor the concept of its efficacy (effectiveness) can be used to clarify the intension of the juristic concept of the validity of statutory law. This view is justified by the gradability of the concept of legal validity conceived in terms of the observance or efficacy (effectiveness) of legal norms (discussed in the argument A–XI), the circularity of definitions D_4 and D_5 (shown in the argument A–XII) and their far too limited scope of reference (identified in the argument A–XIII). It should be yet added (as it was in the case of the previously analysed concepts) that the discourse of validity discourse by means of which we try to solve the problem of the extension of the concept of legal validity, applies a number of arguments related to the observance or efficacy (effectiveness) of legal norms.

---

[422] H. Kelsen, 'Was ist juristischer Positivismus?', *op. cit.*, p. 467.

[423] *Cf.* Chap. 6, pp. 228ff.

[424] H. Kelsen, *Reine Rechtslehre*, 2nd ed., *op. cit.*, p. 219 [English version, p. 212]. Let us note that the concept of efficacy ceases to be merely the condition of legal validity, since it becomes the element of the content of the basic norm – for more on interpretive problems connected with this issue *see* G. Hughes, 'Validity and the Basic Norm', *CLR* 59 (1971), pp. 701ff.

[425] H.L.A. Hart, *The Concept of Law*, *op. cit.*, p. 113.

7.6 Legal Validity Defined by Means of the Combination of Concepts

At this point, we shall briefly examine the theoretical correctness and practical usefulness of some definitions of the juristic concept of the validity of statutory law formulated by means of a combination of concepts. In contemporary jurisprudence, one can encounter many such proposals, therefore it would not be possible to analyse all of them. Accordingly, we should consider only a few such combined conceptions that were elaborated in Polish legal theory, and then—also in order to complement the critical analysis of nonpositivism presented in the first part of the study—in a separate section we will examine Robert Alexy's nonpositivist definition of law, treating it as a combined definition of the validity of legal norms. It should be stressed that the clarificative analysis, which is to follow, will not concern the theories of the authors who—following Hans Kelsen[426]—openly accept the ambiguity of the concept of legal validity, but will concern such conceptions in which the concept of legal validity is presented by means of two or more primitive concepts; for example, the concepts of the membership in the legal system, observance, application or applicability of legal norms.

The existence of the conceptions of legal validity based on a combination of concepts cannot come as a surprise. Lawyers are accustomed to the fact that while resolving the practical question of the validity of legal norms, they typically apply a variety of different (e.g., formal, logical, sociological, axiological) criteria that have to be met in order to justify the claim on the validity of a given norm. Accordingly, there naturally appear the attempts to capture such practices by defining the meaning of the concept of legal validity by means of using a combination of concepts, which generally correspond to the applied criteria and express them in a synthetic way. Moreover, the use of combinations of concepts, at least at first glance, could prevent definitions formulated in this way from many objections raised in the previous sections in respect of such model conceptions of legal validity that try to grasp the intension of the juristic concept of the validity of statutory law by means of only one concept. For example, it seems that the use of the combination of the concepts of the observance and application of legal norms protects us against the argument of a too narrow scope of reference of the definitions based purely on

[426] The ambiguity of the concept of legal validity in the pure theory of law follows from the fact that Kelsen conceived the validity of legal norms in three ways: firstly, ontologically ("Geltung *qua* Existenz") – as their specifically legal existence; secondly, normatively ("Geltung *qua* Verbindlichkeit") – as an obligation (ought) of their observance or application; and thirdly, dynamically ("Geltung qua Zugehörigkeit") – as their membership in the legal system, based on the competence relations between norms. For more *see e.g.*, D.W.P. Ruiter, 'Legal Validity Qua Specific Mode of Existence', *L&Ph* 16 (1997), pp. 479ff. and St.L. Paulson, 'Die unterschiedlichen Formulierungen der "Grundnorm"', *op. cit.*, pp. 58ff. *Cf.* a synthetic discussion of the basic theses of Kelsen's theory of validity in E. Garzón Valdés, 'Modelle normativer Geltung', *op. cit.*, pp. 41ff.

one of these concepts[427]: it can be, in fact, argued that we observe sanctioned norms, whereas we apply sanctioning norms and the norms of competence, thus the above-mentioned objection becomes unfounded.

Moving on to the analysis, let us begin by recalling the study of Leszek Nowak, *Four Concepts of Legal Validity*, of 1966,[428] in which he catalogued as many as 16 different combinations of three basic concepts of legal validity, arguing that at least nine of them can be encountered in jurisprudential studies.[429] Nowak's catalogue, illustrating the various possibilities of combining the formal (thetic) concept of validity ("*F*-validity") with two sociological concepts of validity, based on the concept of the fulfilment of sanctioning and sanctioned norms (respectively: "*S*-validity" and "*P*-validity"), served him to develop his own "rationalised conception" of the validity of legal norms. According to this, the expression "Norm N is valid" means that the legislator demands or wishes "that the norm is fulfilled by the addressees, and if violated – sanctioned by the state authorities" (i.e., it should be *P*-valid or *S*-valid).[430] In this way, Nowak interprets the statement that a given norm has been enacted and has not been repealed.

Nowak's conception shows a significant, probably unintended resemblance to the conception of legal validity outlined 1 year earlier by Jerzy Jakubowski, who also assumed that the concept of the validity of a legal norm is determined by the interconnection between the state authority that establishes law and the norm enacted thereby. In his view, the claim that a given norm is valid means that "this authority expresses its will that it shall be implemented", namely observed by its primary addressees (legal subjects), or—in the case of its non-observance—applied by the secondary addressees (state authorities).[431] It can be perceived that the only difference, albeit very slight, consists in formulations proposed by both authors. When clarifying the concept of legal validity, Nowak writes about "demanding" or "wishing", whereas Jakubowski writes about the "expression of will" of the law-creating authority. It is worth noting that Jakubowski, like Nowak, does not hesitate to add that the claim about the validity of a norm "means only that this norm has been established and has not been repealed".[432] Both conceptions are therefore very strongly associated with the so-called thetic understanding of the validity of legal norms and they explain rather the sense of the conventional act of law-creating than the concept of legal validity. This statement can be supported by the comparison of Nowak's and Jakubowski's definitions with the definition of lawmaking provided recently by Sławomira Wronkowska. She defines it as:

---

[427] *Cf. supra*, the argument A–V at pp. 313–316 and the argument A–XIII at pp. 339–342.

[428] L. Nowak, 'Cztery koncepcje obowiązywania prawa', *op. cit.*

[429] *Ibidem*, pp. 99–100.

[430] *Ibidem*, p. 101.

[431] J. Jakubowski, 'Pojęcie obowiązywania, realizacji i skuteczności normy prawnej oraz podstawy ich rozróżniania', *op. cit.*, pp. 312–313, 320, 328.

[432] *Ibidem*, p. 313.

> a conventional act of the competent state authority by means of which this authority "demands" that the legal norms of the content determined by it were realised.[433]

In light of this comparison, which does not require any comment, we can conclude that the above-mentioned conceptions in fact result in adopting the meaning equivalence of the concepts of the validity of norms and their enactment. Such equivalence can be expressed by means of the following definition of legal validity, based on the conceptions developed by Jakubowski and Nowak: "A norm of statutory law norm is valid if, and only if the lawmaker 'demands' ('wishes', 'expresses his will') that the norm was observed or applied; that is, the legislator issues the norm and does not repeal it" (hereafter referred to as D_6). Let us analyse its acceptability.

If we take a look at the *definiendum* and the final part of the *definiens* of this definition, we can easily see that it is burdened with the error that resembles the *idem per idem* fallacy (which assumes here the form of an indirect vicious circle in defining), for the norm of statutory law is valid if, and only if it has been enacted and has not been repealed; that is, when it constitutes the norm of statutory (i.e., enacted) law. This observation leads to the conclusion that the conceptions under discussion equate the concept of the valid legal norm of statutory law with the concept of the norm that has been enacted and has not been repealed. Therefore, they constitute the exemplifications (greatly simplified) of the conception of a formal (systemic, thetic) validity of legal norms. When we take into account the fact that the concept of the norms which have been enacted but have not been repealed undoubtedly corresponds, at least roughly, to the concept of the norms that belong in the legal system, it turns out that these conceptions inappropriately clarify the intension of the juristic concept of the validity of statutory law due to the arguments against the definition, which equates the validity of statutory law norms with their membership in the legal system (D_1), provided for and discussed above.[434]

The analysed conceptions of Nowak and Jakubowski cannot be regarded as an appropriate clarification of the intension of the juristic concept of the validity of statutory law also due to the fact that they do not offer any "intrinsic added value" that might be useful for lawyers in solving the problem of the extension of the concept of legal validity, and thus in deciding whether a given norm of statutory law is valid or not. Indeed, if—in accordance with the views of Jakubowski and Nowak—the expression that the legislator "demands", "wishes" or "expresses his will" that the norm be observed or applied, comes down to determining that such a norm has been enacted and has not been repealed, then the practical usefulness of such a clarification of intension is hardly discernible. As we will soon see, the structure of the discourse on validity and the methods of validity argumentation are much more complicated nowadays, thus resulting in the fact that resolving the issues of the validity of particular norms of positive law does not merely consist of determining that they were issued and have not been repealed.[435] Anticipating the

[433] S. Wronkowska, *Podstawowe pojęcia prawa i prawoznawstwa*, *op. cit.*, p. 23.

[434] *See supra*, pp. 271–312.

[435] *See* Chap. 9, pp. 478ff.

results of the analyses of the validity discourse *sensu stricto*, it should be noted that the conceptions of Jakubowski and Nowak or—broadly speaking—the conception based on a thetic justification of the validity of statutory norms will form the basis of the juristic presumption of the validity of statutory law norms.[436] In this sense, the analysed conceptions will help us in specifying the starting point for argumentation concerning the extension of the juristic concept of the validity of the norms of statutory law.

Let us now examine the second model conception of the validity of statutory law, this time capturing the validity by means of the combination of the concepts of the membership of norms in the legal system and their applicability. According to Tomasz Pietrzykowski's conception of the temporal scope of the validity of legal provisions, the concept of the time of validity of legal provisions comprises "the conjunction of the periods of their membership in the legal system and their applicability".[437] Leaving aside the question of the correctness of Pietrzykowski's conception, established in the context of the analysis of understanding the temporal scope of validity in the jurisdiction of the Polish Constitutional Tribunal,[438] let us discuss the theoretical correctness and practical usefulness of the clarification of the intension of the juristic concept of the validity of statutory law undertaken by means of a model definition under which: "A norm of statutory law is valid if, and only if it belongs to the legal system and is applicable" (hereafter referred to as D_7).

At first glance, it seems that due to the fact that this definition uses the conjunction (rather than the alternative) of the concepts of the membership in the legal system and the applicability of legal norms, we do not accumulate the errors encountered in the conceptions based on one of these two concepts, but we reduce them. From the perspective of the extension of legal validity, it seems obvious that the Cartesian product of the sets of legal norms that belong to the legal system and that are applicable is certainly smaller than the sum of these sets. Nonetheless, when we once more consider the arguments raised against the definition D_1 (which presents validity by means of the concept of membership) and the definition D_3 (based on the concept of the applicability of norms), it turns out that what loses its

[436] *Cf. supra*, p. 312.

[437] T. Pietrzykowski, 'Temporalny zakres obowiązywania prawa', *op. cit.*, p. 54. *Cf. idem*, *Wsteczne działanie prawa i jego zakaz*, *op. cit.*, p. 39, where Pietrzykowski equates the period of the validity of a legal provision with the conjunction of the periods of the membership of legal provision in the legal system and the obligation of its application.

[438] Let us add that in order to identify the temporal scope of the validity of legal provisions, the Polish Constitutional Tribunal makes use of an alternative, not a conjunction, of the periods of their membership in the legal system and their applicability – for more *see* A. Grabowski, B. Naleziński, 'Kłopoty z obowiązywaniem', *op. cit.*, pp. 224–229, 248ff. In the present clarificative analysis, we leave aside the model conception of the validity of statutory law that corresponds to conceiving the temporal scope of the validity of legal norms as an alternative to these two concepts, since it is obvious that as such it would only sum up the errors of model conceptions that present the juristic concept of the validity of statutory law in terms of the membership of norms in the legal system and their applicability. Yet, we do not prejudge here that this conception is erroneous in relation to the issue of the extension of the clarified concept.

raison d'être is only the argument A–IV, referring to the analytically necessary linguistic (semantic) imprecision of using the concept of legal validity in relation to legal norms that remain in the state of *vacatio legis* and those norms that are still in force.[439] In fact, the concept of the applicability of norms, used in the definition D_7, protects us from the simultaneous validity of these two categories of norms, since the norms that remain in the period of *vacatio legis* are not applicable, *ergo* they are not valid. Yet, the other three arguments (A–I, A–II and A–III)[440] against the definition D_1, as well as three arguments (A–VIII, A–IX and A–X)[441] against the definition D_3 preserve their accuracy, which already suffices to reject the analysed model definition D_7. This is the case because, contrary to appearances, if we look from the perspective of the extension of the concept of legal validity, this definition does not lead to overlapping the scopes of the extensions of norms belonging to the legal system and applicable norms, but rather to identifying a set of applicable norms, which constitute a subset of the norms that belong to the legal system. Let us note that the lawyer who wishes to apply the definition D_7 when resolving whether a given norm of statutory law is valid, will probably first have to determine whether it belongs to the legal system and only then, whether it is applicable.[442] Moreover, we shall recall that it is not possible to independently identify the elements of the sets of norms belonging to the legal system and applicable norms, which has already been shown in the A–X argument.[443] By virtue of this argument, the identification of applicable norms requires a prior determination as to whether applicability norms that prescribe the application of the former belong to the legal system.

A model conception of legal validity, expressed by means of the definition that combines the concepts of the membership in the legal system and the applicability of legal norms, cannot be regarded as a theoretically correct and practically useful clarification of the intension of the juristic concept of the validity of statutory law also due to the fact that it leads to a criterial definition. Perhaps because of the genesis of this conception, the basic problem, which we shall try to solve by means of definition D_7, is the problem of the temporal scope of the validity of legal norms

[439] *Cf. supra*, pp. 304–309.

[440] Let us recall that these are: the argument concerning the conception of the juristic *prima facie* validity of norms of statutory law based on the concept of the membership of norms in the legal system, the argument that excludes the use of the concept of the legal system that is valid *hic et nunc* in the *definiens* of the definition D_1 and the argument showing intensional inequivalence of the concepts of validity and membership of norms in the legal system – *cf. supra*, pp. 275–304.

[441] These are the arguments that question the legitimacy of distinguishing the applicable norms and applicability norms, that indicate a too limited scope of reference of the definition D_3 and that demonstrate the necessity of using the two concepts of legal validity, which leads to ambiguity – *cf. supra*, pp. 323–333.

[442] It would be inconsistent with the rules of the economy of thought to adopt the reverse order, due to the fact that the applicable norms may also fail to belong to a particular legal system (as in the case of foreign law norms – *cf. supra*, pp. 291–295): why determine the applicability of norms that do not belong to the legal system if, under the definition D_7, the membership in the legal system is one of *sine qua non* conditions for recognising the norm as valid?

[443] *Cf. supra*, pp. 331–333.

that can be manifested in the form of the following question: When is the norm of statutory law valid? When seeking answers to this question, lawyers who initially try to determine the membership in the system and then the applicability of a given norm, will probably consider whether a given norm meets the criteria of the membership that are characteristic for the relevant legal system, and then applicability criteria that determine the application of applicable norms. Thus, the *definiens* of the analysed definition remains only as a guideline for deciding the specific problems of validity until it has been developed by providing these two groups of criteria (for membership and applicability). Incidentally, we can also predict with a high degree of probability that the application of the analysed definition will lead to such antinomies—common in juristic discourse—which we have strongly opted against.[444] These antinomies mean that we will have to admit the statements about the application of non-valid norms arising from the content of valid norms, which prescribe the application of the norms that do not belong to a given legal system. Thus, such a combined definition of the juristic concept of the validity of statutory law is also not suitable for clarifying the intension of the concept at issue.

7.6.1 Is the Nonpositivist Definition of Law a Clarification?

A critical analysis of the nonpositivist definitions of law has already been undertaken in Chap. 5. These definitions were rendered inadequate due to the numerous objections raised therein concerning, inter alia, the persuasiveness of the nonpositivist definitions of law, their criterial nature and the fact that by means of them Ralf Dreier and Robert Alexy try to simultaneously (and indirectly) define the two concepts of valid law: the first—referring to the legal system as such, and the second—referring to particular norms of that system.[445] Currently, our purpose is to consider whether the definition based on the concepts used in the nonpositivist definitions of law is suited to clarifying the intension of the juristic concept of the validity of statutory law. Dreier's definition will be left aside in the subsequent considerations and it will be Alexy's nonpositivist definition of law—more complex in relation to the former and, thus, more interesting in the context of a combined understanding of legal validity—that will serve as the subject of the model analysis.

Before we proceed to the clarificative analysis, it merits making a brief comment of a more general nature. When examining the strategies of constructing the concepts (or a concept) of legal validity, we can identify three typical patterns which can be illustrated—taking into account the extensions of these concepts—on the basis of the following schemes (see Fig. 7.1 on the next page)[446]:

[444] *Cf. supra*, pp. 293–294 and 317–318.

[445] *Cf.* Chap. 5, p. 206.

[446] This schematic presentation assumes the existence of three basic concepts of legal validity, unquestionably the most prevalent in the literature; for example, in the theories of legal validity developed by H. Kelsen, E. Bulygin, R. Dreier and R. Alexy, the Poznań school of jurisprudence and J. Wróblewski.

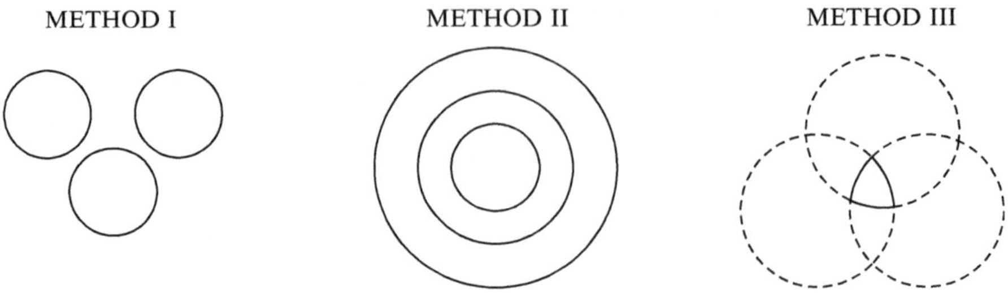

Fig. 7.1 The methods of constructing the concepts of legal validity

The first method consists of recognising the ambiguity of the concept of legal validity and subjecting its individual meanings to a relatively independent analysis.[447] The second method—in a sense, an indirect one—also originates from accepting the ambiguity of the concept of legal validity, yet it leads to such a determination of its meanings that other concepts of validity constitute a "superstructure" of the earlier ones, and thus their extensions are more and more narrow (because the extension is inversely proportional to the intension).[448] Finally, the third method, involving the approval of the thesis of the ambiguity only in a reporting aspect or in not recognising such ambiguity at all,[449] leads to only one concept of legal validity, often referred to as the "juristic" one. In light of the presented typology, it should be kept in mind that Alexy's nonpositivist conception of law is constructed in this very way.[450]

---

[447] Classic examples of such a pattern are the analyses of various concepts of legal validity carried out by E. Bulygin and by the Poznań school of jurisprudence. The latter example may be questionable, because the representatives of this school sometimes summarise the results of their studies in graphic form corresponding to the third of the identified methods of analysis – *see e.g.*, Z. Ziembiński, M. Zieliński, *Dyrektywy i sposób ich wypowiadania*, *op. cit.*, p. 36 and S. Wronkowska, *Podstawowe pojęcia prawa i prawoznawstwa*, *op. cit.*, p. 17. Yet it is of no great importance in relation to the concepts of a thetic, axiological and behavioural validity of legal norms – developed by this school – because it shows only that the extensions of the norms whose validity is justified under the various conceptions can overlap.

[448] Such a strategy was adopted by J. Wróblewski when developing the concepts of the systemic, factual and axiological validity – *see idem*, *Sądowe stosowanie prawa*, *op. cit.*, pp. 96ff. [English version, pp. 77ff.], albeit that he exceptionally defined the three concepts independently of one another (and thus following the method indicated as the first one) – *see idem*, 'Semantics and Pragmatics of Normative Qualification Statements', *op. cit.*, p. 41.

[449] An example of such a construction can be found in L. Nowak, who – when developing his "formal–axiological–sociological concept of legal validity" – strongly withdraws his previous position (expressed in the study 'Cztery koncepcje obowiązywania prawa', *op. cit.*) and stresses that in juristic language the term "validity" is not ambiguous – *see idem*, *Interpretacja prawnicza*, *op. cit.*, pp. 92–93, 111, 160–161.

[450] *Cf. e.g.*, R. Alexy, *Begriff und Geltung des Rechts*, *op. cit.*, pp. 139ff. [English version, pp. 85ff.]. It can be added that our aim in this study is to develop a single integrated juristic concept of the validity of statutory law – *cf.* Chap. 6 at p. 223 (a fragment concerning the second goal of clarification).

Our clarificative analysis must begin with a model definition of validity, based on parts 1, 2a and 2b of Alexy's nonpositivist definition of law.[451] It is clear already at this point that due to the fact that Alexy differently determines the conditions of the membership of constitutional norms and ordinary norms in the legal system, we are, in fact, compelled to formulate two definitions.[452] With regard to constitutional norms, the definition reads as follows: "A constitutional norm of statutory law is valid if, and only if it belongs to a by and large (*im großen und ganzen*) socially efficacious constitution (which raises the claim to correctness) and is not extremely unjust" (hereafter D_{8A}). Additionally, in relation to other legal norms of a lower rank, we obtain the following definition: "An ordinary norm of statutory law is valid if, and only if it is enacted in accordance with a by and large socially efficacious constitution (which raises the claim to correctness), manifests a minimum social efficacy or the chance of becoming socially efficacious, and is not extremely unjust" (hereafter D_{8B}). As usual, we pose the question as to whether these definitions may be regarded as fulfilling the requirements of good clarification.

First of all let us note that formulating two model definitions of the validity of statutory norms relieves the nonpositivist conception of validity from the objection of simultaneously defining the concepts of the validity of the legal system (i.e., external validity) and the validity of the individual norms of this system (i.e., internal validity). Both definitions are related only to the concept of internal validity. At the same time, nevertheless, another objection can be raised; namely, that the above definitions provide different meanings of the validity of the constitutional norm and of the validity of the other, ordinary legal norms. Such a solution seems difficult to accept because the concept of internal validity, which is of interest here, becomes ambiguous. Let us consider whether this is not by any chance an indelible ambiguity and what its possible consequences are when constructing the juristic concept of the validity of statutory law.

When analysing the definitions given, one can provisionally assume[453] that they include a combination of two (in the case definition D_{8A}) or three (in the definition D_{8B}) fundamental concepts of the substantial correctness (let us call it a "moral component"), the social efficacy (let us call it a "sociological component") and the due enactment (let us call it a "formal or thetic component"), which, however, is used only in the second definition.[454] On the one hand, leaving aside the formal

---

[451] This definition has been presented twice already, so we will not quote it again – *see* Chap. 2 at p. 16 or Chap. 5 at pp. 193–194. Let us add a somehow obvious comment that at this point we omit the third part of Alexy's definition, because it does not concern the norms of statutory law, but nonpositivised "principles and other normative arguments".

[452] Theoretically, it is possible to present Alexy's nonpositivist conception in the form of a single definition, yet it would then not be very clear.

[453] It will turn out in the course of the analysis that, apart from the indicated concepts, there is yet another one; namely, the concept of the membership in the legal system that has been assumed in these definitions.

[454] These concepts are derived from Alexy – *cf.* his "definitional triangle of law", presented in Chap. 2 at p. 17.

(thetic) component in the definition of the validity of constitutional norms (D_{8A}) seems realistic, because in the case of the new constitutions that were created by the revolutionary authorities or military junta, the process of their enactment often proceeds without observing the constitutional rules that determine the acceptable procedure for amending or changing the existing constitution. On the other hand, even in such cases, the revolutionary authorities or junta sometimes attempt to keep up the appearance of amending the constitution in accordance with the existing rules of lawmaking. Indeed, it is a rule in modern democratic states that the adoption of the new constitution follows the procedure provided for in the previous constitution, or—as happened in Poland in the nineties of the last century—it takes place on the basis of a special episodic constitutional act[455] that regulates the procedure for the creation of a new constitution. Nevertheless, these counterexamples (of non-democratic issuance of a constitution) do not invalidate the conclusion that due to them, the ambiguity of the nonpositivist concept of the validity of statutory law is justified—at least from the empirical perspective. Yet, in the context of constructing the concept of the legal validity of statutory law, we can hardly come to terms with such an ambiguity, more so because it can be relatively easily eliminated. It suffices to note that the lack of a formal (thetic) component in the definition D_{8A} justifies the statement that the concept of the due enactment of norms is not an essential element that must be reflected in the definition of the juristic concept of the validity of statutory law. Accordingly, if the constitutional norms do not need to satisfy this requirement in order to be considered valid, then it should not be treated as indispensable.

Following the same vein of thinking, we can observe that there is a possibility of formulating a unified nonpositivist definition of the validity of statutory law, which will include the elements common for the definitions D_{8A} and D_{8B}. Let us carry out the reasoning—undoubtedly having the status of a thought experiment[456]—that will result in determining the content of such a definition (which we shall denote as D_8).

The first common component of the definitions D_{8A} and D_{8B} is the concept of substantial correctness. This ethical element, characteristic of the nonpositivist conception of law, is expressed in the content of both definitions by means of two conditions: firstly, the system of norms, referred to as law, has to lay the claim to correctness and, secondly, the norms that belong to this system should not be extremely unjust. The first condition can be left aside when formulating definition D_8, since, as already indicated in the reconstruction of the nonpositivist rule of

[455] For example, the present Polish Constitution of 1997 was created according to *Ustawa konstytucyjna z dnia 23 kwietnia 1992 r. o trybie przygotowania i uchwalenia Konstytucji Rzeczypospolitej Polskiej* [Constitutional Statute of 23 April 1992 on the mode of preparation and adoption of the Constitution of the Republic of Poland], published in *Dziennik Ustaw* [Journal of Statutes] 1992, No. 67, Item 336.

[456] The reservation that it is a thought experiment seems essential in order to avoid the objection of distorting or over-simplifying the nonpositivist conception of law.

recognition, even Alexy admits that all modern legal systems fulfil it.[457] Therefore, the only necessary ethical element in the content of D_8, resulting from "Radbruch's formula", will be the substantive requirement of the absence of extreme injustice, referring to the content of valid norms.

The second common component of the definitions D_{8A} and D_{8B} is the concept of social efficacy. In the definition of the validity of the constitutional norms, this sociological element is expressed in the form of a requirement under which the constitution should basically be (*im großen und ganzen*) socially efficacious. On the other hand, according to the definition of the validity of sub-constitutional legal norms, their characteristic feature should be "at least minimum social efficacy or the chance of becoming socially efficacious". We believe that this is not considered to be too simplistic if these requirements are put together in the form of one condition under which the system of norms called "law" is basically socially efficacious. The concept of the efficacy of the system of norms undoubtedly covers the efficacy of its elements; namely, individual legal norms.

This brings us to the following, extensionally complete (i.e., encompassing both constitutional norms, as well as ordinary ones) nonpositivist definition of legal validity: "A norm of statutory law is valid if, and only if it is not extremely unjust and it belongs to the system of norms that is basically socially efficacious" (hereafter D_8).

Before we provide four general arguments for rejecting this definition, let us note that when we subject it to a more thorough analysis, it can be seen that what can be found in its *definiens*, in addition to the ethical concept of extreme injustice and the sociological concept of social efficacy, is the concept of the membership in the system of norms, to which this definition refers indirectly. Therefore, the following critical arguments will focus on three concepts. Finally, let us add that these objections will largely be based on the earlier analyses, so they will be presented in a very concise way.[458]

Let us begin with the arguments that have already been justified in our study. Firstly, it is worth noting in relation to the concept of extreme injustice—used in the definition D_8—which gives it a clear moral tone, that the criticism of the nonpositivist conception of law carried out in the first part of the study has led us to believe that the juristic concept of legal validity must remain axiologically unbiased.[459] The standardised nonpositivist definition of legal validity, as reconstructed above in the form of D_8, does not meet this requirement, therefore we cannot accept it. Secondly, the concept of social efficacy used in D_8 has already been rejected by us in the preceding section. Thirdly, the same can be said about the concept of the membership of norms in the legal system, because the above-mentioned arguments (as presented in Sect. 7.2) against the comprehension of

[457] *Cf.* Chap. 4, p. 133.

[458] In the following argumentation, we will leave aside the objections raised in Chap. 5 at pp. 194ff.

[459] *Cf.* Chap. 5, pp. 207ff.

legal validity as the membership of norms in the legal system (probably with the sole exception of the argument A–II) also remain valid. Therefore, we cannot endorse the definition formulated in the form of the conjunction of these three concepts (i.e., the concepts of extreme injustice, social efficacy and membership in the legal system).

These arguments shall be supplemented with the fourth and final objection, which require a brief discussion. An additional flaw of the definition based on Alexy's nonpositivist conception of law is that it does not contain any element that would manifest the normative nature of law and its validity. It is indeed difficult to recognise that it is sufficient to assume that the law consists of norms. Let us note that the three concepts used in definition D_8 are of a descriptive-evaluative nature, and none of them, even to a minimal extent, attempts to explain the binding force of law (the requirement of the lack of extreme injustice of a given norm can hardly be considered as its explanation; moreover, it would indeed lead to iusnaturalism). In particular, this definition does not take into account the semantic relation between "validity" and "obligation".[460] Perhaps it is the case due to the fact—as we have already pointed out[461]—that the nonpositivist definition of law and, consequently, the model nonpositivist definition of legal validity are mainly oriented at solving the problem of the extension rather than intension of these concepts.

To sum up the clarificative analysis of the nonpositivist conception of legal validity, let us consider the problem that seems most crucial from the perspective of the method of constructing the juristic concept of the validity of statutory law. The undertaken comparison of the contents of definitions D_{8A} and D_{8B}, resulting in a unified definition D_8, revealed that the formal (thetic) element of "the enactment in accordance with the constitution" does not need, and should not be included in the content of the definition that we sought to find, if we do not want the juristic concept of legal validity to be ambiguous. This is an important conclusion, which weighs strongly in favour of rejecting the attempt to clarify this concept using the definition based on the formal component. In addition, with regard to the model conception, analysed in this subsection, which has been derived from Alexy's nonpositivist definition of law, we conclude that the arguments presented do not allow us to recognise it as a proper clarification of the intension of the juristic concept of the validity of statutory law.

7.7 *En passant* Comment

We have analysed eight model definitions of the juristic concept of the validity of statutory law. The critical arguments, only seemingly complicated, that were used in the clarificative analysis, have led us to conclude that neither the definitions

[460] For more *see supra*, at pp. 269–270.

[461] *Cf.* Chap. 5, p. 201.

based on one concept (membership, application, applicability, observance or efficacy), nor on selected combinations of concepts, can be considered as a proper clarification of the intension of the concept at issue. This conclusion comes as a surprise, because it was a difficult task to expect that the conceptions of legal validity—typical for the analytical theory of law—can be so easily "deconstructed", incidentally almost exclusively by means of the arguments of a purely analytical or even positivist character.[462] It can indeed be assumed that the outcome of our inquiries is at least partly caused by the fact that we have assumed that we were seeking the conception accurately clarifying the intension of the juristic concept of the validity of statutory law, and the analysed conceptions do not only concern intension, but they are targeted, to an equal or greater extent, at solving the problem of the extension of that concept. Yet, it does not change the fact that the analysed conceptions and the model definitions that correspond to them proved unsuitable for the adopted method and for the purposes of clarification.

Let us now reconsider the consequences of our previous inquiries with respect to the further analysis and the content of a regulative definition that is supposed to serve as a clarification of the intension of the juristic concept of the validity of statutory law.

First of all, we must note that the conceptions analysed in this chapter endeavour to clarify the intension of the concept of legal validity by demonstrating the feature or features (in the case of combined definitions) of legal norms that are identical to their validity. Accordingly, a general form of the analysed definitions can be expressed in the following schematic formulation: "A norm of statutory law is valid if, and only if it has feature C (or features C_1, C_2, ..., C_n)".[463] The fact that these conceptions have been, without exception, rejected, makes us realise that—to put it colloquially—"we are on the wrong track". Such a clarification of the intension of the juristic concept of the validity of statutory law that would be correct and actually useful for lawyers must be sought elsewhere. Therefore, in the next chapter we shall modify the current method of clarificative analysis. We will try to understand and clarify the concept of the validity of statutory law norms in a manner independent of its past jurisprudential theories that adopted the above definitional pattern.[464]

---

[462] The only argument that went beyond the traditional domain of the analytical theory of law was argument A–VII, directed against the understanding of the validity of norms by means of the concept of their application, and having a partly moral nature – *cf. supra*, pp. 319–320.

[463] Certain interpretive doubts can only be raised in respect to the definition D_6, based on the conceptions of validity developed by L. Nowak and J. Jakubowski, which is, nevertheless, ultimately based also on a combination of two features: "the enactment" and "lack of derogation" of a legal norm by the legislator – *see supra*, p. 346.

[464] In order to deem the analysis complete, we shall still discuss the normative conception of legal validity – *see* Chap. 8 at pp. 413ff. However, it has to be added that this conception is no longer based on the reconstructed definitional pattern.

The presented analyses and, in particular, the criticism of the definitions of legal validity based on the concepts of the membership of norms in the legal system and their applicability has shown that the concept of legal validity should not be construed as the concept of the validity of norms in the legal system, but within its institutional frames.[465] Let us recall that if we aim at including the issue of the validity of applicable norms in the definition of the juristic concept of the validity of statutory law, which undoubtedly constitutes a problem of great importance for the practice of law application, we must abstract from the purportedly direct interconnection between the concept of legal validity and the membership of legal norms in the State legal system and replace it with the relativisation of this concept to the practice of the institutions (legal authorities) that apply the law within a given system; namely, to "law in action". What is particularly important, due to the critique against a unified nonpositivist model definition of the validity of legal norms, is that we do realise that when formulating the postpositivist regulative definition, we should not use the formal element related to the thetic justification of norms.[466] Otherwise, the constructed concept of the validity of statutory law will be ambiguous, which we cannot accept.

Furthermore, thanks to formulating several critical arguments against the model conceptions of validity analysed in this chapter, we are aware of what errors to avoid in clarifying the intension of the juristic concept of the validity of statutory law. The errors that seem of utmost importance are the ones identified and considered in the arguments that repeat similar or even adopt identical layouts of argument. These include: the error of the intensional inequivalence between *definiendum* and *definiens*,[467] the fallacy of the circularity of the definition[468] and the error of a too narrow scope of reference for the proposed definition.[469] Naturally, the subsequent clarificative analysis should also take into account the content of other specific arguments.

Finally, it should be noted that when undertaking the clarificative analysis we have incidentally particularised one of the requirements of good clarification. We have accepted that its scientific (theoretical) relevance and practical usefulness must in the first place mean that the developed conception of validity will offer a certain "intrinsic added value", which consists of the fact that the clarification of the intension of the juristic concept of the validity of statutory law will turn out to be helpful in solving the problems of its extension related to the vagueness of this

[465] *Cf. supra*, pp. 253–254, 284–289, 333.

[466] *Cf. supra*, pp. 351–353.

[467] *Cf. supra*, pp. 289–309 (arguments A–III and A–IV) and 316–319 (argument A–VI).

[468] *Cf. supra*, pp. 316–319 (argument A–VI) and 338–339 (argument A–XII).

[469] *Cf. supra*, pp. 313–316 (argument A–V), 327–331 (argument A–IX), and 339–343 (argument A–XIII).

concept. In this context, let us recall that we have in fact rejected some conceptions of legal validity because they do not provide any "intrinsic added value",[470] whereas we have resigned from other conceptions—resulting in the gradability of the concept of legal validity—due to the fact that they hinder or even prevent the resolution of the issues concerning the extension of that concept.[471]

[470] In particular, they are: the conception of legal validity understood as the membership of norms in the legal system – *see supra* at pp. 271–312 and the conceptions of legal validity developed by L. Nowak and J. Jakubowski – *see supra* at pp. 345–347.

[471] We mean here a group of factual conceptions of legal validity, recognised by means of the concepts of its application, observance or efficacy – for more *see supra*, pp. 315–316 (argument A–V *in fine*) and pp. 334–338 (argument A–XI).

Chapter 8
The Postpositivist Concept of the Validity of Statutory Law

8.1 Juristic Language, Types of Juristic Concepts and Modes of Their Creation

The distinction between legal language and juristic language (or various juristic languages) and the analyses of the linguistic status and mutual relations of these languages, attempted in the broader context of the concepts and characteristics of the ethnic, natural, official and ordinary language, undeniably constitute the *spécialité de la maison* of Polish legal theory. Many authors have taken up these issues since the conceptual differentiation between legal and juristic language was first elucidated in the pioneering work of Bronisław Wróblewski, published posthumously in 1948.[1] Chronologically, one should mention especially the works of Jerzy Wróblewski,[2] Jan Woleński,[3] Zygmunt Ziembiński,[4] Tomasz Gizbert-Studnicki,[5] Marek Zirk-Sadowski,[6]

---

[1] B. Wróblewski, *Język prawny i prawniczy* [Legal and Juristic Language], Kraków 1948.

[2] J. Wróblewski, *Zagadnienia teorii wykładni prawa ludowego*, *op. cit.*, pp. 230ff. and 'Legal Language and Legal Interpretation', *L&Ph* 4 (1985), pp. 239–255; K. Opałek, J. Wróblewski, *Zagadnienia teorii prawa*, *op. cit.*, pp. 39ff.

[3] J. Woleński, 'Język prawny w świetle współczesnych metod analizy semantycznej' [Legal Language in the Light of Modern Methods of Semantic Analysis], *ZNUJ PP* 31 (1967), pp. 141–156.

[4] Z. Ziembiński, 'Le langage du droit et le langage juridique. Les critères de leur discernement', *APhD* XIX (1974), pp. 25–31 and *Problemy podstawowe prawoznawstwa*, *op. cit.*, pp. 81ff.

[5] T. Gizbert-Studnicki, 'Język prawny a język prawniczy', *op. cit.*, 'Czy istnieje język prawny?' [Does Legal Language Exist?], *PiP* 3 (1979), pp. 49–60, *Język prawny z perspektywy socjolingwistycznej* [Legal Language from Sociolinguistic Perspective], ZNUJ PNP 26 (1986), and 'Język prawny a obraz świata', *op. cit.*

[6] M. Zirk-Sadowski, 'Rola pragmatyki w badaniach języka prawnego' [The Role of Pragmatics in the Research on the Legal Language], *AUL FI* 6 (1981), pp. 41–57, *Rozumienie ocen w języku prawnym* [Understanding Evaluations in Legal Language], Łódź 1984, and 'Language and Law' in B. Lewaszkiewicz-Petrykowska (ed.), *Rapports polonais*, Łódź 1998, pp. 7–20.

A. Grabowski, *Juristic Concept of the Validity of Statutory Law*,

DOI 10.1007/978-3-642-27688-0_8, © Springer-Verlag Berlin Heidelberg 2013

Andrzej Bator[7] and Jerzy Pieńkos,[8] as well as the recently published studies of Maciej Zieliński[9] and his followers.[10] It can be assumed that virtually every Polish legal theorist is accustomed to analysing and solving the many conceptual problems of jurisprudence, perceiving them through the prism of the mentioned distinctions. Yet this still does not constitute a sufficient reason to continue our clarificative investigations in such a traditional way. What is crucial are the substantive reasons—after all, we intend to clarify the juristic concept of the validity of statutory law; namely, a certain concept that belongs to the conceptual apparatus of juristic language. Let us consider to what extent the achievements of the Polish theory and philosophy of law can be helpful in our clarificative analysis.

First of all, we have to remember that one of the main objectives of our analysis is to develop an integrative conception of the validity of statutory law, which will not only be correct from the jurisprudential point of view, but also useful, both in the scientific discourse—in particular, in discourse within legal dogmatics—as well as in the practice of lawmaking and law application.[11] Therefore, we intend to propose a definition of a juristic concept of the validity of statutory law that will determine the intension of this concept, which is—in our view—proper in relation to at least two specific juristic languages; namely, the juristic language of legal science and the juristic language of jurisdiction (or, more broadly, the judicial practice). Accordingly, it should be emphasised that the manner in which the concept of legal validity is used in the Polish (or any other) legal language (i.e. the language used by lawmakers in legal texts) remains outside the scope of our considerations.

The second issue, which shall be merely indicated at this point,[12] concerns the necessity of undertaking not only semantic, but also pragmatic analyses when researching the content, meaning and extension of juristic concepts. We believe that pragmatic analyses can turn out to be very helpful when clarifying the intension

---

[7] A. Bator, 'O konserwatyźmie językowym nauki prawa', *op. cit.* and 'Język prawniczy wobec zmian w prawie' [Juristic Language in the Face of Changes in Law], *SP* 1 (1991), pp. 3–16.

[8] J. Pieńkos, *Podstawy jurysIingwistyki. Język w prawie – Prawo w języku* [The Fundamentals of Jurislinguistics. Language in Law – Law in Language], Warszawa 1999. Let us add that this study also presents a synthetic analysis of modern international literature that has been left aside in this work (pp. 36ff.).

[9] M. Zieliński, 'Języki prawne i prawnicze', *op. cit.* and 'Język prawny, język administracyjny, język urzędowy' [Legal Language, Language of Administration, Official Language] in E. Malinowska (ed.), *Język – Prawo – Społeczeństwo*, *op. cit.*, pp. 9–18.

[10] The most interesting are the works of A. Choduń, 'Język prawny a język potoczny' [Legal Language and Ordinary Language] in E. Malinowska (ed.), *Język – Prawo – Społeczeństwo*, *op. cit.*, pp. 77–86, 'Leksyka tekstów aktów prawnych' [The Lexis of the Texts of Legal Acts], *RPEiS* LXVIII/1 (2006), pp. 19–30, and *Słownictwo tekstów aktów prawnych w zasobie leksykalnym współczesnej polszczyzny* [The Vocabulary of the Texts of Legal Acts in the Contemporary Polish Lexical Resource], Warszawa 2007.

[11] *Cf.* Chap. 6, pp. 223–224 (the fragment on the second goal of clarification).

[12] For more *see infra*, at pp. 380ff. and 427ff.

of the concept of legal validity, especially because the model conceptions of legal validity, discussed in the previous chapter, mostly leave aside the pragmatic dimension of juristic language, thus focusing on its semantics. Therefore, in clarificative analysis, we will investigate the pragmatic aspect of expressions on the validity of statutory norms, which are formulated in the two above-mentioned juristic languages.[13] We will also use a certain pragmatic concept of legal norm in order to determine the content of the postpositivist definition of the juristic concept of the validity of statutory law.

The third point, which should at least be briefly discussed, concerns the characteristics of the concept of the validity of statutory law as the concept of juristic language. For this purpose, we will use the typology of juristic concepts developed by Kazimierz Opałek and Jerzy Wróblewski.[14] These authors distinguish between four groups of juristic concepts: juristic concepts that are the "repetition" of the meanings of legal terms contained in the legal texts of statutes, regulations etc. (A), juristic textual concepts (B), juristic ordering concepts (C) and other juristic concepts, often borrowed from other disciplines than the jurisprudence such as sociology, psychology, logic or ethics (D). In light of this typology, it seems clear that the juristic concept of the validity of statutory law can only belong to group B or C. Our analysis will thus recapitulate the characteristics of these two types of juristic concepts provided by Opałek and Wróblewski, and then we will explore which classification is more apt when considering the concept of legal validity.[15]

Let us begin with a synthetic discussion of the juristic textual concepts (B). According to Opałek and Wróblewski, these are the concepts that constitute the meanings of the terms which occur both in the legal, as well as in the juristic language (e.g., "right", "contract", "ownership", "legal person" and so forth). Unfortunately, the characteristics of the juristic textual concepts provided by these terms are considerably laconic. Let us therefore use the comments provided by Marek Zirk-Sadowski, who notes that concepts of this type:

> may be present in both these languages, but the legal language determines their extension, while the juristic language – by means of the theories constructed within the particular legal dogmatics – attributes meaning to them.[16]

---

[13] It means that for the purposes of the analysis, we will consider them as languages in the sense of *la parole*, rather than *la langue*. For more on the uselessness of linguistic analyses (in relation to norms) at the level of *la langue see* M. Zirk-Sadowski, 'Legal Norm as a Pragmatic Category', *ARSP* 65 (1979), pp. 206ff., in particular p. 213.

[14] *See* K. Opałek, J. Wróblewski, *Zagadnienia teorii prawa*, *op. cit.*, pp. 69–71. Given the character of the style, the author of the fragment – discussed and quoted below – was most probably Wróblewski; nonetheless, we shall use the term "the conception of Opałek and Wróblewski". The analysis to follow also takes into account the modifications of this conception, proposed by M. Zirk-Sadowski, *Wprowadzenie do filozofii prawa*, *op. cit.*, pp. 217ff.

[15] It is worth noting at this point that our investigations will be limited to the classification and characterisation of the concept of the validity of statutory law, which we are now developing, thus leaving aside the typical jurisprudential concepts of legal validity, which we have analysed (and rejected) in the previous chapter.

[16] M. Zirk-Sadowski, *Wprowadzenie do filozofii prawa*, *op. cit.*, p. 218.

What is essential from the point of view of our discussion is the fact that Opałek and Wróblewski emphasise that the juristic textual concepts are *ex definitione* determined by the legal language, and thus they cannot be "richer" in a logical sense than legal concepts.[17] The authors most possibly have in mind the extension of these concepts.[18] To conclude this brief characterisation, let us add that the concepts of type B can be associated with a particular system of positive law, with a group of systems that are, in some respects, similar (e.g., a system-type of statutory law), or with law in general.

Let us now discuss juristic ordering concepts (C). These concepts do not occur in the legal language, but they are created for the purposes of jurisprudence in order to analyse, systematise, apply and interpret the valid law (e.g., "legal system", "legal reasoning", "legal gap"[19]). What is particularly important in terms of our consideration on the matter—according to Opałek and Wróblewski—is that one of the tasks of jurisprudence that is to be met by juristic ordering concepts relates to solving problems (which we can refer to as the problems of validity) by means of utterances such as: "Norm N is valid in the system S at the time T".[20] Analogous to juristic textual concepts, the concepts that belong to group C may be associated with the law on three levels (with a particular legal system, system-type of law or law in general).

In the light of the characteristics of juristic textual and ordering concepts, it should not come as a surprise that by means of clarificative analyses, we attempt to construct the concept of the validity of statutory law that belongs to the category of juristic ordering concepts (C). Such a classification is justified by a number of factors. First, the adopted scope of reference for our research—namely, a continental system-type of statutory law[21]—in principle precludes the possibility of treating the concept of legal validity as a juristic textual concept. In fact, it is impossible to analyse the various meanings and applications of this concept that are characteristic for specific state legal systems that belong to this system-type. It is doubtful whether, by way of such analyses—which have a comparative rather than a theoretical character—we would be able to obtain a sufficiently universal and sound clarification of the juristic concept of the validity of statutory law. Moreover, anticipating the results of the analysis on validity discourse, it can be argued that the concept of the validity of statutory law and, in particular, its extension, is only partly determined by the will of the lawmaker, as expressed through legal provisions.[22] Thus, it is difficult to accept a potential claim that it is a concept

---

[17] K. Opałek, J. Wróblewski, *Zagadnienia teorii prawa*, *op. cit.*, p. 70.

[18] In this way, M. Zirk-Sadowski interprets this feature of "juristic textual concepts" in *Wprowadzenie do filozofii prawa*, *op. cit.*, p. 218.

[19] The examples are provided by M. Zirk-Sadowski, *ibidem*, p. 219.

[20] K. Opałek, J. Wróblewski, *Zagadnienia teorii prawa*, *op. cit.*, p. 70. Let us add a somewhat obvious comment that the role attributed to the juristic ordering concepts weighs strongly in favour of recognising the juristic concept of the validity of statutory law as an ordering concept, because we certainly try to elaborate a conception that would be useful in practice, rather than just meeting the cognitive objectives.

[21] *Cf.* Chap. 7, pp. 250–251.

[22] For more *see* Chap. 9 at pp. 470ff.

"determined by the legal language", which—according to Opałek and Wróblewski—constitutes a defining feature of juristic textual concepts (B).

One can also express doubt as to whether the lawmakers actually use the concept of the validity of norms in the texts of legislative acts. By narrowing our analysis to the semantic specifics of the Polish legal texts, we can indicate, without difficulty—even currently in the Polish Constitution—examples of such provisions in which the legislator applies the concept of validity with respect to legal provisions[23] or legislative acts.[24] Yet, it is difficult to identify cases where the lawmaker would use the concept of validity in respect to legal norms,[25] thus referring it—as we have assumed—to the "unit of law" that is adequate in the context of the juristic concept of the validity of statutory law.[26] What is more, we shall shortly prove that in many cases purely normative utterances about the validity (regardless of whether they are related to legal provisions, legislative acts or legal norms) are utterly redundant—in fact, the only meaningful use of this concept is to apply it when conducting derogation ("authentic" or "tribunal").[27] Therefore, categorising the concept of legal validity—understood in the manner adopted in this study (i.e., as it refers to legal norms)—as juristic textual concept (B), does not seem accurate.[28] We will therefore treat it as a juristic ordering concept (C).

---

[23] *Cf.* Article 236 Section 2 and Article 238 Sections 1 and 3 of the Polish Constitution, which refer to "the validity of legal provisions" and "valid legal provisions".

[24] *Cf.* Article 241 Section 7 of the Polish Constitution, which speaks of "valid bylaws".

[25] This is the case probably because, as already demonstrated twenty years ago by J. Nowacki, in the texts of Polish legislative acts (and therefore in the legal language), the Polish lawmaker uses the concept of a legal provision or the names of systemising units of the legal texts ("article", "paragraph", "section" etc.), in principle, without using the concept of a legal norm – *cf. idem*, *Przepis prawny a norma prawna*, *op. cit.*, pp. 31ff. Let us note that when using one of the most popular legal databases in Poland, containing the texts of current legislation, we will find only one act – at the statutory level – in which the legislator uses (four times) the concept of valid norms (more specifically, he uses the descriptive term "norms valid in the Member States of the European Union") – *see* Article 11 Section 8, Article 15 Section 6, and Article 41 Section 2, Points 1 and 2 of the *Ustawa z dnia 7 czerwca 2001 r. o leśnym materiale rozmnożeniowym* [Statute of 7 June 2001 on forest reproductive material], published in *Dziennik Ustaw* [Journal of Statutes] 2001, No. 73, Item 761, with amendments. However, only in relation to the first of the cited provisions under which: "The minister responsible for the environmental affairs shall determine, by means of a regulation, the organisational structure of the Bureau of Forestry Seed, taking into consideration the nature of the tasks defined in Article 10 and norms which are valid in this area in the Member States of the European Union", can it be stated that the legislator does not use here a secondary meaning of the term "norm" – most commonly encountered in lawmaking acts (namely, a norm defined as a "pattern", "measure", "standard" etc.). For more on the secondary meaning of "norm" *see* M. Zieliński, Z. Ziembiński, *Uzasadnianie twierdzeń, ocen i norm w prawoznawstwie*, *op. cit.*, p. 82 and J. Nowacki, *ibidem*, pp. 35ff., together with numerous examples of such secondary uses of this term in the law.

[26] For more *see* Chap. 6 at pp. 237–246.

[27] *Cf. infra*, pp. 390ff. and Chap. 9 at pp. 478ff.

[28] The legitimacy of categorising the juristic concept of the validity of statutory law as a juristic ordering concept is also supported by the comments made by J. Wróblewski, who stresses that the terminology of the theory of law "does not in principle use textual terms" – *cf. idem*, 'Zagadnienia terminologii nauk prawnych' [The Problems of the Terminology of Legal Sciences], *NP* XXXII/3 (1984), p. 82.

Opałek and Wróblewski do not limit the analysis of juristic concepts simply to the proposal of their appropriate typology, but they also investigate the modes of creating juristic textual and ordering concepts, which are applied in jurisprudence.[29] Since the juristic concept of the validity of statutory law belongs to the latter group, we will now consider what method of constructing concepts should be adopted for the purposes of clarifying its intension. Let us recall that in the previous chapter we sought to find such a definition of the juristic concept of the validity of statutory law that would be correct from a jurisprudential point of view and that would meet the assumed goals of clarification. We endeavoured to do so by means of the critical analysis of the model theoretical conceptions of legal validity; thus, in a way that could be described as inductive. Although this method is recommended and often applied in jurisprudential conceptual analysis,[30] our efforts were in vain, because we managed to obtain only some guidelines, mostly negative in content, which determined how the clarification should further proceed.[31] Thus, we will—with one minor exception[32]—abandon the inductive method and we will take efforts to develop a certain conceptual convention that will be justified due to the fact that it meets the assumed goals of clarification. Accordingly, we will adopt such a method of constructing juristic concepts that is regarded by Opałek and Wróblewski as being the "most radical"[33]; however, we will try to give it the least arbitrary form possible.[34] It should be added that the research that has been conducted so far has been, in fact, methodologically varied: in addition to the basic inductive method, we used the elements of etymological analysis,[35] and our deliberations also took into account many juristic intuitions. We have thus already

[29] K. Opałek, J. Wróblewski, *Zagadnienia teorii prawa*, *op. cit.*, pp. 71ff. *See* also a modified version of this conception, elaborated by M. Zirk-Sadowski, *Wprowadzenie do filozofii prawa*, *op. cit.*, pp. 220ff.

[30] It is worth noting that this is exactly the way in which the authors of the discussed conception carry out their conceptual analyses – *cf.* K. Opałek, J. Wróblewski, 'Sporne zagadnienia pojęć teoretycznoprawnych' [Controversial Issues of Jurisprudential Concepts], *RPEiS* XXXIV/1 (1972), pp. 91–92.

[31] *Cf.* Chap. 7, pp. 355–357.

[32] Indeed, we are still left to discuss the definition corresponding to the normative concept of legal validity – *see infra* at pp. 413–422.

[33] K. Opałek, J. Wróblewski, *Zagadnienia teorii prawa*, *op. cit.*, p. 75.

[34] We are very interested in the non-arbitrariness of clarificative analysis and its results because we treat the proposals of purely arbitrary definitions of the fundamental concepts of jurisprudence, one of which is undoubtedly the concept of legal validity, as useless in terms of implementing the primary cognitive function of legal theory; namely, the progress in our understanding of the law and legal practice. Arbitrariness, in fact, considerably limits the possibility of a rational discussion and substantive rather than just purely verbal polemics. In addition, it may be questionable whether there is a possibility of creating absolutely discretionary conventional concepts – *cf.* J. Kaczor, 'Konwencjonalny charakter pojęć prawniczych' [The Conventional Nature of Juristic Concepts], a report presented at the 16th National Congress of the Departments of Theory and Philosophy of Law "The Polish legal culture and the process of European integration" in Gniezno, 26–28 September 2004, typescript, pp. 2ff.

[35] *Cf.* Chap. 7, pp. 267–271.

applied the methods that are typically recommended when creating concepts in the humanities.[36] Nonetheless, they have not yielded the desired result.

The observation that the juristic concept of the validity of statutory law is expected to have an ordering character and the decision for adopting the conventional manner regarding its creation, do not by themselves provide us with any detailed and precise guidance as to the manner of conducting a further clarificative analysis. Given that the method of conceptual analysis used in this study can be generally described as analytical, let us consider for a moment whether we can obtain any such guidelines by discussing the characteristics of this method. Even a cursory review of the literature shows that contemporary analytical philosophy uses a number of different methods of analysis,[37] and analytic philosophers disagree even as to the most fundamental question; namely, what that very analysis is.[38] It is not our intention to examine these disputable and extraordinarily complex methodological problems.[39] Instead, we shall base our deliberations on a specific conception by analysing and constructing an analytical theory developed by Peter Strawson, as it seems to be useful in determining the methods of the research that follow.

In considering the question of the proper form for the systematic analytical theory, Strawson makes a distinction between two models of conceptual analysis.[40] He distinguishes between a reductive (atomistic) model and a connective model. The first one attempts to clarify the meaning of concepts by finding completely simple ideas that are "free from internal conceptual complexity"; namely, a clarification of complex meanings by means of reducing them to "simple meanings".[41] The English philosopher considers the program of such reductive conceptual analysis to be unacceptable and instead he proposes a model of analysis based on searching for connections within a certain system or systems of concepts. As he postulates:

> Let us abandon the notion of perfect simplicity in concepts; let us abandon even the notion that analysis must always be in the direction of greater simplicity. Let us imagine, instead, the model of an elaborate network, a system of connected items, concepts, such that the function of each item, each concept, could, from the philosophical point of view, be properly understood only by grasping its connections with the others, its place in the system – perhaps better still, the picture of a set of interlocking systems of such a kind.[42]

[36] *Cf.* T. Pawłowski, *Tworzenie pojęć w naukach humanistycznych*, *op. cit.*, pp. 29ff. Pawłowski discusses the etymological, inductive and intuitive method in reference to the construction of analytical definitions, emphasising that there are no methods of constructing regulative definitions. It is not yet excluded that these methods can be applied in a subsidiary way for the latter purpose.

[37] *Cf. e.g.*, J. Woleński, *Z zagadnień analitycznej filozofii prawa*, *op. cit.*, pp. 44ff.

[38] *See e.g.*, A. Stroll, *Twentieth-Century Analytic Philosophy*, *op. cit.*, pp. 6ff., and the references cited therein.

[39] In our study, we have adopted the strategy of analysing only these methodological issues that serve to explain the grounds and procedures for the clarificative analysis.

[40] P.F. Strawson, *Analysis and Metaphysics. An Introduction to Philosophy*, Oxford 1992, pp. 17ff.

[41] *Ibidem*, pp. 17–18.

[42] *Ibidem*, p. 19.

The differences between the two models of analysis are most clearly illustrated by Strawson's observations concerning the general charge of circularity in the analysis. While in the case of a reductive model this error "is damaging, indeed fatally damaging" to the undertaken analysis, in the case of the second model—according to Strawson—it should not worry us if, when looking for the interconnections between the concepts, we return to the starting point of our analyses, or pass by it, because in this case "we might have moved in a wide, revealing, and illuminating circle".[43]

Due to the above distinction, the following reflection arises on how to conduct the clarificative analysis and construct the juristic concept of the validity of statutory law. Certainly, the model concepts of legal validity that have been analysed so far were based on a reductive model of conceptual analysis, which can be best seen in the case of the combined definitions of the juristic concept of legal validity.[44] They attempt—to put it somewhat metaphorically—to break down the concept of the validity of statutory norms into constituent parts, indicating the attributes of norms that correspond to their validity. The definitions, based on a simpler pattern: "A norm of statutory law is valid if, and only if it has a feature C", which grasp validity by means of using the concepts (attributes) of the membership in the legal system, application, applicability, observance and efficacy (effectiveness) of the norms of statutory law also undoubtedly rely on the same reductive model. It is thus difficult to find in their formulations the network or system (systems) of concepts characteristic of the model based on the analysis of the connections between the concepts. Furthermore, when discussing the model conceptions of validity we have twice encountered the objection—in our opinion "fatally damaging" these conceptions—of the circularity of the definitions that express them,[45] which also constitutes a distinctive feature of a reductive model of the analysis, according to Strawson's methodological insights.

A reductive model of analysis, used perhaps not fully consciously by the authors of the conceptions of legal validity discussed so far, did not prove useful when clarifying the intension of the juristic concept of the validity of statutory law.[46] This

---

[43] *Ibidem*, pp. 18–20.

[44] *Cf.* Chap. 7, pp. 344–354.

[45] *See* Chap. 7, the argument A–VI at pp. 316–319 and the argument A–XII at pp. 338–339.

[46] It can hardly come as a surprise from a wider perspective on contemporary jurisprudential reflection, since – as evidenced by Peczenik – many reductionist theories of law, such as the economic analysis of law, the psychological theory of law developed by Petrażycki or the theories that reduce the rational legal reasoning to the rules of formal logic, despite achieving some valuable results, contemporarily no longer withstand the criticism, primarily because of their "imperialist" attempts to obtain an intellectual monopoly. Interestingly, Peczenik suggests – similarly to Strawson – a circular justification for our beliefs (knowledge), based on the idea of coherence. He writes: "Metaphorically speaking, a coherent belief system is like a network of argumentative circles, mostly quite large ones" – *see idem*, 'Against Reductionism', *AS* 2 (1998), pp. 101–103, 114ff. For more on the concept of coherence promoted by A. Peczenik *see idem*, 'Coherence, Truth and Rightness in the Law', *op. cit.*, 'Law, Morality, Coherence and Truth', *op. cit.*, 'The Passion for Reason. Some Remarks on Coherence in the Law' in E. Garzón Valdés

leads to the conclusion that in the further clarificative analysis and when constructing the concept of validity we should adopt the model of the analysis based on a search for connections between (at least some) primitive concepts. When following Strawson's methodological guidance, one must firstly identify and define the concepts that will create a certain system of concepts, which are connected—in a more or less close way—with the concept of the validity of statutory law, and then, by means of analysing the relations that take place between them, formulate the *definiens* of the sought regulative definition. The problem, nevertheless, lies in the question of what concepts to choose and how to justify their choice, so as to minimise the arbitrariness of the developed conception, thus allowing for a rational discussion and criticism, which is a precondition for its eventual approval.

8.2 Linguistic and Logical Characterisation of Utterances Concerning the Validity of Norms in Juristic Language

Before we propose the concepts that will constitute a conceptual basis for the clarification of the intension of the juristic concept of the validity of statutory law, we shall devote some attention to the analysis of the utterances concerning legal validity performed in the juristic language of legal sciences and in the juristic language of jurisdiction. There are several reasons to support the research aimed at the linguistic and logical characterisation of these utterances.

First and foremost, it has to be recalled that the concept of legal validity, which we are trying to clarify, should be useful in the legal discourse—in particular, in jurisprudential and practical discourse (associated with law application), rather than only correct from the point of view of the current state of the analytical theory and philosophy of law. Therefore, in order to determine the meaning of the concept of legal validity it would prove useful to consider how lawyers apply this concept in everyday life and what semantic intuitions accompany it. In particular, the identification and explanation of the nature of the utterances on validity will serve to clarify the status of the sentence that constitutes the *definiendum* of the regulative definition of the juristic concept of the validity of statutory law, which will soon be proposed. Naturally, the primary issue is to determine whether the expression: "A norm of statutory law is valid" should be regarded as a descriptive sentence or a non-descriptive one (a norm or evaluation), or whether it has a mixed character, which is not clearly identifiable by means of the traditional categories of semantic and logical analyses.

---

et al. (eds.), *Normative Systems in Legal and Moral Theory*, *op. cit.*, pp. 309–321, 'Certainty or Coherence?' in W. Krawietz *et al.* (eds.), *The Reasonable as Rational?*, *op. cit.*, pp. 157–171, and *Scientia Juris*, *op. cit.*, pp. 115ff., 137ff.

What also weighs in favour of the linguistic characterisation of the utterances on validity is the method of paraphrasing adopted in our clarificative analysis.[47] When applying it, we try to clarify the juristic concept of the validity of statutory law by means of a multi-dimensional analysis of the expression: "A norm of statutory law is valid". In our view, it is difficult to challenge the claim that the clarificative analysis cannot lack the considerations related to the conditions of using[48] this expression in juristic discourse. In order to avoid a possible misunderstanding, at this point it should be explained that the intention to examine the conditions of using the expression on the validity of the statutory norm does not mean that the clarification of the intension of the juristic concept of the validity of statutory law will be based on the theory of meaning stemming from the famous Ludwig Wittgenstein's theorem: "meaning is use".[49] The regulative definition that we shall formulate, will, in fact, not say anything explicit about the conditions or ways of using the concept of the validity of statutory law, but it will only indirectly (contextually) determine its meaning by pointing to two—in our view—linguistically equivalent expressions.[50] Nevertheless, the analysis of the ways of using the expression on the validity of the statutory norm will allow us to extend the clarificative analysis so that we may examine the pragmatic dimension of the juristic expressions on the validity of statutory law, which will, in turn, complement the semantic and logical analyses.

---

[47] *Cf.* Chap. 7, pp. 247–248.

[48] It seems clear that, when carrying out the analyses, we must adopt a position similar to so-called semantic antirealism (which identifies the meaning of sentences with the conditions for their application or possibility of their being stated), since the use of the conception of so-called semantic realism (which identifies the meaning of sentences with the conditions of their truthfulness) would be tantamount to making the fallacy of begging the question. This fallacy would consist of the fact that we have not yet settled on whether the truth-values do apply to juristic utterances on the validity of norms (and more precisely, their propositional content, as expanded upon in a moment). Therefore, we cannot assume that it is the case. Generally, on realism and antirealism in the semantic sense *see* J. Woleński, *Epistemologia* [Epistemology], Vol. 3: *Prawda i realizm* [Truth and Realism], Kraków 2003, pp. 193–194, 196ff., and the references cited therein; whereas in relation to the analysis of juristic utterances *see* D. Patterson, *Law and Truth*, Oxford/New York 1996, pp. 5ff.

[49] This thesis was expressed by Wittgenstein in § 43 of *Philosophical Investigations*, *op. cit.*, p. 20e, which is worth quoting *in extenso* (trans. G.E.M. Anscombe): "For a *large* class of cases – though not for *all* – in which we employ the word 'meaning' it can be defined thus: the meaning (*Bedeutung*) of a word is its use (*Gebrauch*) in the language (*Sprache*)". Italics and quotation marks in the original.

[50] The fact that synonyms (semantically equivalent expressions) typically have identical conditions for their use in the language is irrelevant here, because it is one thing to talk about how to use the expression, and quite another to say that one expression has the same use as another. We will illustrate the latter through example because the presented thesis may seem unbelievable. If we tell someone that the English terms "French fry" and "chip" have the same linguistic usage, then what will she/he know about the situations in which these terms can be used in a way consistent with the semantic rules of English. This argument is borrowed from W.P. Alston, 'Meaning and Use' in G.H.R. Parkinson (ed.), *The Theory of Meaning*, Oxford 1968, pp. 159ff.

When we start to analyse the utterances on the validity of norms, we are struck by a great conceptual confusion characteristic of the jurisprudential literature devoted to semiotic analysis of the utterances related to legal norms.[51] One can risk the opinion that the scholars who take up this issue in fact abound *praeter necessitatem* the terminology concerning the utterances on norms.[52] However, there is no universally accepted network of appropriate concepts or terms, thus they probably feel compelled to do so. Yet, it does not bother them to hold a number of substantive disputes concerning, inter alia, the issue that is of our immediate interest; namely, the linguistic and logical characterisation of the utterances on the validity of legal norms.

Having the latter in mind, before we proceed to discuss the views on issues of interest to us, it appears necessary to at least provisionally determine the scope of our analysis. To this end, we shall assume probably the simplest possible distinction between two types of utterances about the validity of the norms of statutory law (validity utterances)[53]: positive validity utterances (which assume the form: "Norm

[51] This opinion was already formulated in 1985 by Z. Ziembiński, 'Uwagi o negowaniu norm i wypowiedzi z normami związanych', *op. cit.*, p. 106. Naturally, during the last 20 years this state has undergone some changes, yet, unfortunately, for the worse, as evidenced by the next note.

[52] Let us look at some instructive examples drawn from the English literature. G.H. von Wright uses the terms "normative statement", "norm-proposition" and "deontic sentence" (while we should add that "deontic sentence" may be of a descriptive or prescriptive character) – *see e.g., idem, Norm and Action, op. cit.*, pp. 105ff. and 'On Norms and Norm-Propositions. A Sketch' in W. Krawietz *et al.* (eds.), *The Reasonable as Rational?*, *op. cit.*, p. 173. J.J. Moreso examines several categories of "legal propositions" such as "deontic legal statement", "conceptual legal statement", "pure legal statement", "applicative legal statement" and "norm proposition" – *see idem, Legal Indeterminacy and Constitutional Interpretation, op. cit.*, pp. 47 ff. and 'On the Truth-conditions of Norm Propositions', *AS* 6 (2002), pp. 63ff. A record in this field has probably been beaten by A. Aarnio, since in his studies we can read about: "norm statement", "interpretive statement", "norm proposition", "norm contention", "norm recommendation", "interpretation proposition", "meaning proposition" and "interpretive proposition" – *see* A. Aarnio, R. Alexy, A. Peczenik, 'The Foundation of Legal Reasoning', *op. cit.*, pp. 425ff.; A. Aarnio, 'On Truth and the Acceptability of Interpretative Propositions in Legal Dogmatics', *RT* Bh. 2 (1981), pp. 44ff. and *The Rational as Reasonable*, *op. cit.*, pp. 49ff. As for the history of the diverse terminology of the normative utterances and sentences about norms, derived from the distinction between "genuinely normative sentences" and "spuriously normative sentences", made in 1941 by the Swedish philosopher Ingemar Hedenius – *see* L. Lindahl, 'Norms, Meaning Postulates, and Legal Predicates', *op. cit.*, pp. 293ff. (in particular, the scheme on p. 294, comparing the terminologies of I. Hedenius, A. Wedberg, H.L.A. Hart, G.H. von Wright, C.E. Alchourrón and E. Bulygin, as well as H. Kelsen); *cf.* T. Mazzarese, '"Norm Proposition": Epistemic and Semantic Queries', *RT* 22 (1991), pp. 39ff. Let us recall that the terminologies of Kelsen, Hart and Raz have been roughly discussed in Chap. 6 at pp. 230–234, although we did not consider there the problem of the logical value of the utterances about legal validity, which we are trying to explain now.

[53] We want to emphasise that by means of this distinction we do not try to multiply, but rather to reduce and simplify the current terminology. However, soon we will have to extend it, by adapting it to the needs of the analyses of the possible – lawmaking or non-lawmaking – solutions of validity discourse – *cf. infra*, pp. 380ff. and Chap. 9 at pp. 478–481.

N is valid" or the like[54]) and negative validity utterances ("Norm N is not valid" etc.).

According to the traditional positivist model of axiologically neutral jurisprudence,[55] the act of resolving the problems of validity is of a cognitive character. An important component of the paradigm of positivist-oriented legal dogmatics is the concept of the systemic validity of law, on the basis of which the validity of a legal norm can be descriptively stated. This is accompanied by the cognitive theory of legal interpretation, according to which the interpretation consists in discovering either the objective and proper meaning of the legal text, or the subjective intention of the legislator—depending on the adopted normative theory of interpretation.[56] Therefore, the statements on the validity of norms, relativised to the legal system created by the lawmaker,[57] are regarded as having logical value.

This traditional approach, often supported by superficial reasons and stereotypes of legal thinking[58] can be contrasted with a number of arguments that challenge its

---

[54] The attempt to establish some canonical form of positive and negative validity utterances seems inappropriate, given the diversity of the forms of utterances on validity that are made by lawyers. From the extensional perspective, the proposed distinction is to be understood in such a way that in positive validity utterances the predicate "is valid" is used in relation to the norms of statutory law, while in negative validity utterances we use the phrase "is not valid".

[55] Within Polish legal theory, the essential features of the positivist model were identified and widely discussed in the studies of J. Wróblewski, 'Paradygmat dogmatyki prawa a prawoznawstwo' [A Paradigm of Legal Dogmatics and Jurisprudence] in S. Wronkowska, M. Zieliński (eds.), *Szkice z teorii prawa i szczegółowych nauk prawnych*, *op. cit.*, pp. 34ff.; Z. Pulka, *Struktura poznania filozoficznego w prawoznawstwie*, *op. cit.*, pp. 45ff. and 'Czy nastąpił zmierzch pozytywistycznej koncepcji prawa i prawoznawstwa?', *op. cit.*, pp. 148ff.; K. Płeszka, 'O paradygmacie dogmatyki prawa' ['On the Paradigm of Legal Dogmatics] in J. Czapska *et al.* (eds.), *Zasady procesu karnego wobec wyzwań współczesności*, *op. cit.*, pp. 763–773.

[56] *See* R. Guastini, 'Interpretive Statements' in E. Garzón Valdés *et al.* (eds.), *Normative Systems in Legal and Moral Theory*, *op. cit.*, pp. 279–280.

[57] *See* J. Wróblewski, 'Paradygmat dogmatyki prawa a prawoznawstwo', *op. cit.*, pp. 34–35 and Z. Pulka, 'Czy nastąpił zmierzch pozytywistycznej koncepcji prawa i prawoznawstwa?', *op. cit.*, p. 151. Let us recall that the conception of an ontologically immanent source of the systemic character of law, according to which the legal system is allegedly only a product of the lawmaker's actions, has already been criticized in Chap. 7 at pp. 282–284, where we opted for the transcendent origin of such a character.

[58] Let us indicate some of them. When analysing the legal dogmatists' anxiety about whether the dimension of truth/falsehood applies to the statements of legal dogmatics, T. Gizbert-Studnicki suggests two reasons for such concerns. Firstly, an unjustified inferiority complex of legal scholars and the representatives of other humanistic sciences towards natural sciences, is based on the naive belief that the latter provide an objective and certain knowledge. Secondly, there is the conviction of the auxiliary function of legal dogmatics in relation to the practice of law. In order for this role to be fulfilled, it is necessary that dogmatic statements about the legal system are true. Otherwise, it is doubtful whether the practice of the judicial application of law, partly based on those statements, can reach certain values and objectivities, essential for this practice. *See* T. Gizbert-Studnicki, 'How Many Theories of Truth Are Needed in Jurisprudence?', *ARSP* Bh. 25 (1985), p. 153. R. Guastini underlines the fallacy of the assumptions of the positivist, cognitive theory of legal interpretation, that consists in accepting that the words have the "proper" intrinsic meaning, depending on the objective relationship between words and things (objects), that lawmakers (being usually a collegial organ) have an univocal and recognisable "will" or "intention" and

accuracy. It therefore comes as no surprise that in the contemporary analytical theory of law it is increasingly more common to adopt the standpoint that questions the descriptive character and the ascription of truth-value to jurisprudential and, in particular, dogmatic utterances on the validity of norms. Let us now indicate some jurisprudential conceptions that offer a different, non-descriptive characterisation of them.

No later than in the eighties of the last century, some suggestions appeared in the literature that directly or indirectly supported the view that the juristic utterances on the validity of legal norms lacked truth-value. Aulis Aarnio, for example, generally challenged the application of the concept of truth in the context of legal dogmatics, and he proposed replacing it with the concept of acceptability.[59] Zygmunt Ziembiński stressed that the language of legal sciences also formulates, apart from descriptive and prescriptive utterances, such utterances, which,

> in the practice of lawyers' discussions (and sometimes even in theoreticians' discussions about the methodological models of different legal sciences) have a hybrid character: they are interpreted unconsciously in one way or another.[60]

On the other hand, Jerzy Wróblewski, who in a series of studies directly referred to a simplified systemic concept of the validity of legal norms—characteristic for legal dogmatics—defended the view that the criteria of systemic validity are not applied (except in extremely simple situations) in a descriptive way, and that "they do not determine the only true answer related to the validity of a particular norm",[61] because they require evaluation and they are relativised to the assumed, often "soft" rules (criteria) for recognising the norms as valid. Therefore, in many cases, the "fuzziness" of legal validity brings about the statements concerning legal validity,

---

that the legal system must be complete and consistent – *see idem*, 'Interpretive Statements', *op. cit.*, p. 280. Finally, let us add that the view according to which statements about the validity of norms have logical value is indirectly supported by deontic logicians, who have, for a long time, assumed, without any evidence (because the logic – as an axiomatic and non-empirical science – certainly cannot provide such evidence), that the so-called norm propositions (which are descriptive deontic propositions) are the propositions in a logical sense even if they refer to the legal norms, and not just to very simple examples of imaginary norms, usually analysed by logicians – *see e.g.*, G.H. von Wright, *Norm and Action*, *op. cit.*, pp. 105–106 and 'On Norms and Norm-Propositions', *op. cit.*, p. 173; E. Bulygin, 'On Norm Propositions' in W. Krawietz *et al.* (eds.), *The Reasonable as Rational?*, *op. cit.*, pp. 129–130. The view that the juristic validity utterances do have truth-values is also supported by the belief – entrenched in the legal reasoning, yet not based on any evidence – that juristic statements *de lege lata* are purely descriptive, therefore they possess a logical value due to the sufficient reason that they differ from utterances *de lege ferenda*, which have a normative character, and thus are deprived of such value – for more *see e.g.*, A. Peczenik, *Scientia Juris*, *op. cit.*, pp. 4–5.

[59] A. Aarnio, 'On Truth and the Acceptability of Interpretative Propositions in Legal Dogmatics', *op. cit*, pp. 46–47, 51. For more on Aarnio's concept of acceptability *see infra*, note 125 at p. 384.

[60] Z. Ziembiński, 'Prescriptive and/or Descriptive Language in Legal Sciences', *op. cit*, p. 92.

[61] J. Wróblewski, 'Obowiązywanie systemowe i granice dogmatycznego podejścia do systemu prawa', *op. cit.*, p. 35. *Cf. idem*, 'Problems Related to the One Right Answer Thesis', *RJ* 2 (1989), pp. 243ff.

based on evaluation, to be insoluble.[62] As he wrote: "Not every norm can be descriptively ruled that it belongs or does not belong to the system".[63] The analyses led Wróblewski to the conclusion that the utterances on the validity of norms are semantically indeterminate—they can be descriptive or evaluative, except if we assume the factual concept of legal validity—since in such a case they are, by definition, of descriptive character.[64]

The above remarks aimed at introducing the jurisprudential atmosphere of those times. Now we shall go on to discuss two conceptions that clearly undermine the theses of a purely descriptive character and of the logical value of juristic utterances concerning the validity of legal norms. We need to present them in a possibly exhaustive manner, since, so far, they have seldom been discussed in the jurisprudential literature. The first concerns the conception of the so-called norm propositions, presented by the Italian legal philosopher Tecla Mazzarese in 1991,[65] according to which, they are of a non-descriptive character and cannot be qualified as true or false. The second relates to the theory of the "fused modality" of lawyers' propositions *de lege lata*, developed since 1996 by Norwegian theorist Svein Eng.[66]

Mazzarese tentatively assumes that the term "norm proposition" stands for the statements on the validity of norms that take the following form: "The norm *n* is valid".[67] In her view, those statements can be considered as a disguised conjunction of at least two statements; namely, an interpretive and validity statement.[68] The first describes what a given norm requires ("The norm formulation *NF*[69] expresses the

[62] *See* J. Wróblewski, 'Nieostrość systemu prawa', *op. cit.*, pp. 19ff. and A. Peczenik, J. Wróblewski, 'Fuzziness and Transformations: Towards Explaining Legal Reasoning', *op. cit.*, pp. 26ff. *Cf.* Chap. 7, pp. 277–278.

[63] J. Wróblewski, 'Paradygmat dogmatyki prawa a prawoznawstwo', *op. cit.*, p. 39.

[64] J. Wróblewski, 'Semantics and Pragmatics of Normative Qualification Statements', *op. cit.*, p. 41. Yet, it should be kept in mind that the statements on legal validity, based on the factual concept of legal validity, are never absolutely certain, as they are always highly relative, as stressed by one of the creators of this conception – A. Ross, *On Law and Justice*, *op. cit.*, pp. 44–45.

[65] *See* T. Mazzarese, '"Norm Proposition": Epistemic and Semantic Queries', *op. cit.*, pp. 42ff.

[66] *See* S. Eng, *Analysis of Dis/agreement – with particular reference to Law and Legal Theory*, Dordrecht 2003 [the first Norwegian edition in 1998, based on his doctoral thesis of 1996] and 'Fusion of Descriptive and Normative Propositions. The Concepts of "Descriptive Proposition" and "Normative Proposition" as Concepts of Degree', *RJ* 13 (2000), pp. 236–260.

[67] Thus, her deliberations refer directly to those validity utterances that we have identified above as positive ones.

[68] *See* T. Mazzarese, '"Norm Proposition": Epistemic and Semantic Queries', *op. cit.*, pp. 40, 42ff.

[69] Mazzarese does not define "norm formulation" and this term is not often used in jurisprudential studies. Therefore, it has to be explained that "norm formulation" usually stands for the wording of a normative utterance, which is then subjected to legal interpretation. Mazzarese writes, for example, that it is hard to defend the standpoint that a norm formulation expresses only one norm. Moreover, she rightly states that one single norm can have different norm formulations. Yet, it is not always the case because, according to the author, the concept of norm formulation also applies to unwritten norms (such as the norms of customary law) and, more importantly, a norm formulation may be the outcome of legal interpretation (as in the case of the norms of judge-made

norm *n*"); while the second describes the (alleged) fact that a given norm is valid ("*NF* belongs to the sources of law"). After having discussed the terminology and the conceptual network usually used to analyse the utterances that describe valid norms or state their validity, the Italian author ascertains that the concept of the norm proposition was introduced by deontic logicians[70] in order to solve the problem of creating the logic of norms (which, in accordance with the non-cognitivist position, do not have a truth-value) by means of an intuitively credible concept of the norm proposition that stands for such a descriptive statement about the norm that has logical value. Mazzarese argues that this concept is "tricky", because it is based on problematic presuppositions, doubtful both from the epistemic as well as the semantic point of view and, moreover, it is used to support a number of disputable theses.[71]

As for interpretive statements ("The norm formulation *NF* expresses the norm *n*"), Mazzarese proves that, in fact, they are not descriptive, because the interpretation of law is based on ascribing the meaning, and not—as it is usually recognised in the jurisprudential works—on its discovery and/or clarification.[72] Interpretive statements cannot be considered as the bearers of truth-values, because the multiplicity of the criteria for the interpretation of law (Mazzarese examines the criteria related to the wording of a norm formulation, *ratio legis*, the systemic aspect of the law and *analogia iuris*) prevents the determination of "one to one correspondence between norm formulations and interpretive statements".[73] Apart from the ambiguity of expressions, typical for every non-artificial language, the one who interprets the law has yet to deal, inter alia, with the semantic indeterminacy of legal terms and the problems of interpretation that arise from the application of technical legal terms, standards or general clauses in legal texts. As a result, the formula (wording) of the norm does not express only one norm but a set of different possible norms, while the interpretive statement suggests or ascribes the content to a given formula. Therefore, it seems reasonable to doubt whether the interpretive statements are descriptive and can be conceived as true or false.

In turn, the validity statements ("*NF* belongs to the sources of law") are not descriptive truth bearers because they give rise to three types of epistemic

---

law, interpreted from the content of judicial precedents). Let us add that Mazzarese most likely uses the term "norm formulation" in a way quite similar to G.H. von Wright, who defined this term in *Norm and Action*, *op. cit.*, p. 93, as "the sign or symbol (the words) used in enunciating (formulating) the norm".

[70] Mazzarese has here in mind Erik Stenius and Georg Henrik von Wright, who (independently of each other and in reference to Ingemar Hedenius's distinction, which was mentioned *supra*, note 52 at p. 369) have introduced this term to the conceptual apparatus of deontic logic in 1963 – *see* T. Mazzarese, '"Norm Proposition": Epistemic and Semantic Queries', *op. cit.*, pp. 42–44, in particular, notes 11 and 17, and the works of Stenius and von Wright indicated therein.

[71] T. Mazzarese, *ibidem*, pp. 41, 47ff. In the context of our analysis, the assumption which proves to be most important among these "problematic presuppositions" and "debatable theses" is the one under which norm propositions have truth-values. This problem will be further discussed in more detail.

[72] *Ibidem*, pp. 48ff.

[73] *Ibidem*, pp. 48–49.

problems.[74] Firstly, the doubts relate to the catalogue and internal hierarchy of the sources of law—the main question is whether a given norm formulation may be regarded as belonging to a particular source of law. Secondly, problems arise in respect of those norm formulations—often highly controversial—that constitute the result of legal interpretation; namely, the norms of customary law and the norms of judge-made law (interpreted from the content of precedents). Thirdly, a number of specific problems are associated with determining whether a given formula of a norm indeed expresses a valid norm. Generally speaking, according to Mazzarese, irrespective of which concept of validity shall be applied, these problems may arise when: (1) the legislative act, in which a given norm was formulated, is not valid; (2) the *desuetudo* has taken place; (3) the norm has been implicitly derogated; (4) the norm remains in conflict with a higher norm or a previously enacted norm; and (5) the norm is not accepted by the legal community. Mazzarese draws the conclusion that the validity statement is, in itself, a disguised conjunction of a number of specific statements, which deny the occurrence of the above-mentioned five situations. Yet these statements are not descriptions or declarations, since they are usually the expression of the interpreter's decisions based on evaluation.

The presented analyses justify Mazzarese's conclusion that norm propositions expressed in the form of the statement "The norm *n* is valid" are, in fact, a function of two sets of variables.[75] The first set includes different interpretive statements, which a norm formulation can lead to, whereas the second one consists of different validity statements concerning the same norm formulation. It is very doubtful that both types of statements are descriptive and that they are bearers of logical values. Thus, similar doubts can also arise in relation to the descriptive character of, and the ascription of truth-values to norm propositions that are a disguised conjunction of interpretive and validity statements.

Mazzarese's conception is not without disputable theses and questionable opinions. It has been already criticised by authors who defend the traditional outlook; that is, a descriptive and truth-oriented comprehension of the utterances about norms.[76] On the other hand, it has been confirmed (at least partially) in the Polish legal theory in the form of a recently presented analysis of the nature of juristic dogmatic statements developed by Zbigniew Pulka.[77] Mazzarese's

---

[74] *Ibidem*, pp. 56ff.

[75] *Ibidem*, pp. 58–59.

[76] *See e.g.*, I. Niiniluoto, 'Norm Propositions Defended', *RJ* 4 (1991), pp. 367–373 and E. Bulygin, 'On Norm Propositions', *op. cit.*, pp. 130ff.

[77] Pulka, like Mazzarese, comes to the conclusion that dogmatic deontic propositions (understood descriptively – as describing the language of legal acts, or a set of postulated worlds, designated by the legal texts) strongly presuppose (in the semantic sense) the propositions formed by combining two types of dogmatic statements; namely, validity and interpretive ones. Pulka believes that these statements are neither empirically determinable (as regards their truth-value) nor axiologically neutral, because their premises of validity are axiological and normative reasons, related to the adopted criteria of validity and to the directives of legal interpretation, which are often evaluative in nature. Pulka, nonetheless, does not go as far as Mazzarese, because he assumes that the

understanding of the utterances about the validity of legal norms (leaving aside the fact as to whether we call them "norm propositions" or not[78]) is clear: they are recognised as non-descriptive and are deprived of logical value. Yet, is this vision appropriate? Before attempting to answer this question, we shall present the second innovative conception, directed against the traditional way of understanding the utterances about the validity of norms, developed by Svein Eng.

Eng's theory, in fact, does not directly apply—as does Mazzarese's conception—to the utterances about the validity of legal norms, yet its scope undoubtedly covers them, since the subject of this theory concerns lawyers' propositions (statements) *de lege lata*.[79] Eng introduces the concept of fused modality, since he believes that the concepts of the descriptive proposition and normative proposition[80] constitute the extreme points of a certain graduated continuum, passing "from the purely descriptive to the purely normative".[81] The author does not deny that purely descriptive and purely normative legal statements exist, yet in accordance with his empirical theory, lawyer's utterances, which concern *de lege lata* questions, are characterised by an inherent descriptive–normative modality—they

---

dimension of truth/falsity can be applied to dogmatic deontic propositions. However, their truth is of an analytical nature and cannot be understood in a classic way, but at most, in the spirit of the consensual theory of truth – *see* Z. Pulka, *Struktura poznania filozoficznego w prawoznawstwie*, *op. cit.*, pp. 46–51 and 'Czy nastąpił zmierzch pozytywistycznej koncepcji prawa i prawoznawstwa?', *op. cit.*, pp. 160ff., 174–176.

[78] Bulygin claims that there is no reason to believe (as adopted by Mazzarese) that norm propositions must concern valid norms because they may well refer, for example, to the norms contained in the draft of a statute, which are invalid – *see* E. Bulygin, 'On Norm Propositions', *op. cit.*, p. 132. It is a question of terminology, worthy of noting, but irrelevant to the undertaken analysis of juristic validity utterances.

[79] In presenting Eng's theory, I rely on his own summary provided in 'Fusion of Descriptive and Normative Propositions', *op. cit.* For more *see idem*, *Analysis of Dis/agreement – with particular reference to Law and Legal Theory*, *op. cit.*, pp. 312ff. A synthetic description of Eng's theory can be found in A. Peczenik, 'Legal Research – Normative and Descriptive', *AIC* XXIX-XXX (1996–1997), pp. 20–21 and *Scientia Juris*, *op. cit.*, pp. 100–101; *see* also U.U. Bindreiter, '"Descriptive Normativity": Kelsen's *Sollsatz* in the Light of Some Later Theories', *op. cit.*, pp. 84–90.

[80] In order to avoid any misunderstanding, we have to clarify one terminological issue. The term "normative proposition" is often used by the authors who analyse the utterances about norms (e.g., C.E. Alchourrón and E. Bulygin, R. Guastini, P.E. Navarro, G.H. von Wright) as a synonym for "norm proposition". Yet, it is very misleading, because when understood in such a way, the term "normative proposition" stands – at least according to the indicated authors – for descriptive propositions about norms (i.e., propositions about their existence, content, validity etc.), as pointed out by L. Lindahl, 'Norms, Meaning Postulates, and Legal Predicates', *op. cit.*, note 1 on p. 293. Eng uses this term in a different way and – in my opinion – an accurate manner. Namely, a term "normative proposition" stands for non-descriptive propositions (directives, evaluations etc.) concerning human conduct and is devoid of truth-values. It is how we also use this concept in our analyses, incidentally, in accordance with the understanding of the term "normative proposition" that is usually adopted in the Polish jurisprudential and semiotic works.

[81] S. Eng, 'Fusion of Descriptive and Normative Propositions', *op. cit.*, pp. 236, 251.

are "fused descriptive and normative propositions".[82] Importantly, Eng points out that the concept of the fused descriptive and normative proposition does not include the propositions in which descriptive and normative elements could be in any way separated. As he writes, the relation of fused propositions to descriptive and normative propositions corresponds to "the relationship of the colour grey to white and black",[83] because the fused propositions, as such, are not a combination but a fusion of descriptive and normative propositions.

Eng's theory of juristic propositions *de lege lata* is unorthodox and intriguing. The representatives of legal sciences are accustomed to the vision of mixed juristic discourse, in which the theoretical discourse (carried out by means of analytical and descriptive propositions attributed with logical value) and the practical discourse (with normative propositions deprived of such value) are intermingling and coinherent.[84] In order to evaluate Eng's theory, which definitely destroys this image by introducing the category of modally fused juristic propositions, we shall first take a closer look at its justification.

Eng defines lawyers' propositions *de lege lata* as propositions concerning the issue of what the law is, no doubt having in mind the valid law.[85] The question of whether these propositions are descriptive, normative or fused is treated by him as an open empirical question, stressing that the widely adopted presupposition that those propositions are either descriptive or normative (and there is no third option) is a superstition.[86] According to him, lawyers' propositions *de lege lata* constitute the paradigm case of fused propositions, since their subjective meaning—namely, the meaning adopted by the author or interpreter[87]—cannot be reduced to a purely descriptive or purely normative meaning.

The basic empirical evidence of Eng's theory is based on analysing the reaction of the users of juristic language (in particular, the author of propositions *de lege lata*) that can be encountered in a situation of a discrepancy between the statement and reality; namely, when the juristic proposition *de lege lata* does not coincide with the subsequent judicial decision or the opinion of other legal dogmaticians. Eng undoubtedly rightly assumes that if the author of any proposition that has a

---

[82] *Ibidem*, pp. 236, 239ff.

[83] *Ibidem*, p. 252.

[84] *Cf. e.g.*, J. Stelmach, B. Brożek, *Methods of Legal Reasoning*, *op. cit.*, pp. 125ff.

[85] S. Eng, 'Fusion of Descriptive and Normative Propositions', *op. cit.*, pp. 239ff.

[86] *Ibidem*, pp. 237 and 240.

[87] Eng stresses that his theory is not about the objective linguistic meaning, which nevertheless does not seem to diminish the value of his theory, if we consider the controversies over the objective meaning of sentences. In the context of analysing jurisprudential statements it is worth noting that, as shown by T. Gizbert-Studnicki, even the assumption that the meaning of legal texts is (in some sense) objective, does not provide any objective foundation for dogmatic interpretive propositions – *see idem*, 'How Many Theories of Truth Are Needed in Jurisprudence?', *op. cit.*, pp. 158ff. Although the analysis of Gizbert-Studnicki is referred to dogmatic interpretive propositions, his conclusions can be extended to validity utterances that are at the core of our interests, as justified by the views of J. Wróblewski, T. Mazzarese and Z. Pulka, which have been analysed above.

discrepancy with the reality, when noting the discrepancy, tries to correct it, then such conduct indicates that her/his intention was to formulate a descriptive proposition. On the other hand, if she/he tries to change (correct) reality so that it matches her/his words, then such a reaction indicates that she/he intended to advance a normative proposition.[88] Eng argues that when lawyers' dogmatic propositions are not supported by the court decisions or by dogmatic literature, the lawyers "will seldom say quite simply that they made a mistake and unilaterally correct their own propositions *de lege lata*"[89] and, therefore, they rarely consider them as purely descriptive. On the other hand, lawyers equally rarely understand their statements in a purely normative way, by only criticising the court decision or the opinions of other dogmatists. According to Eng, after having examined jurisprudential literature, one can speak of lawyers' characteristic openness to the determination of what ought to be corrected: the proposition *de lege lata* or the reality. The Norwegian philosopher perceives that in the situation of a discrepancy, lawyers pursue reconsidering the arguments in favour of their previous propositions before taking the decision as to what should be adjusted: the proposition *de lege lata* to the decisions/opinions of other lawyers, or vice versa.[90]

The criterion of the reaction to the discrepancy between propositions *de lege lata* and reality is not the only component of justifying the theory of fused modality. Eng maintains that this criterion does not allow for distinguishing the fused propositions from purely descriptive and purely normative ones because, in the case of such modally pure statements, a specific response to their divergence from reality also takes place. A juristic proposition *de lege lata* can be of modally fused character even if the author merely corrects its content or only tries to adjust the reality relating to it. Therefore, Eng adopts two auxiliary tests for identifying fused propositions.[91] First, the criterion of how open the reaction of the author of a proposition *de lege lata* is to the discrepancy between the content of the proposition and the reality—allows for the identification of fused propositions in the situation when their author does not anticipate the decision of what she/he will correct after such a discrepancy occurs. Second, is the criterion of recognising the discrepancy as an important argument in the debate concerning the choice of what is to be corrected.

[88] S. Eng, 'Fusion of Descriptive and Normative Propositions', *op. cit.*, p. 238. Those who are familiar with the conceptual apparatus of the theory of speech acts can easily see that at this point Eng's considerations show a far-reaching similarity with the standard pragmatic analyses of the so-called directions of fit of assertions, which have word-to-world direction of fit [↓] and directives, which have an opposite, i.e. world-to-word direction of fit [↑] – for more *see* J.R. Searle, 'A Taxonomy of Illocutionary Acts' in K. Gunderson, *Language, Mind, and Knowledge*, MSPhS VII (1975), pp. 346–347 and J.R. Searle, D. Vanderveken, *Foundations of Illocutionary Logic*, *op. cit.*, pp. 52ff., 92ff.

[89] S. Eng, 'Fusion of Descriptive and Normative Propositions', *op. cit.*, p. 246.

[90] *Ibidem*, pp. 246ff.

[91] *Ibidem*, p. 238.

Eng's descriptive theory highlights a certain specific use of juristic language in lawyers' propositions *de lege lata*, which is a fact, because it is empirically observable. Eng does not limit his analyses to formulating the theory of fused modality; he also tries to explain the conditions of the possibility for and the reasons for the existence of fused propositions.[92] In short, the tangible source of the descriptive component of fused propositions *de lege lata* is the fact that lawyers (legal dogmatists) can always enter into discussion regarding what norms motivate law-enforcing organs. Moreover, a general feature of lawyers' argumentation *de lege lata* is to take into consideration the opinion of other lawyers. Therefore, the lawyers who formulate propositions *de lege lata* adopt a perspective of "the generalised lawyer", which, incidentally, is also the condition of making modally fused juristic propositions.[93] On the other hand, the primary source of the normative component is that lawyers are involved in a process of solving conflicts, thus seeking reasonable and just decisions.[94] In order for a proposition *de lege lata* to lead to such results, it cannot be based solely even on true statements regarding previous rulings, opinions of other dogmatists or statements of compliance with morality or religious precepts. In a word, in order to find a "reasonable and just solution" that is expected from lawyers not only by the parties of a given conflict, they must undertake evaluations and make axiological choices.

Like Mazzarese's conception, the theory of the fused modality of juristic propositions *de lege lata* is controversial, especially because—as Eng openly admits—modally fused propositions do not have to find their linguistic expression, but they are identifiable primarily on account of the patterns of legal argumentation (particularly the dogmatic one).[95] In relation to the previously discussed ideas and theories of other authors, this one has such an advantage, as Eng directly analyses the pragmatic aspect of juristic utterances, so that his theory becomes descriptive and empirical. Eng's theory was particularly welcomed by Aleksander Peczenik, who, apart from recognising its merits, pointed out that by introducing the third modality—that is, the fused modality of juristic statements—this theory finally breaks with the traditional distinction (introduced by Ingmar Hedenius[96]) between "genuinely normative sentences" and "spuriously normative sentences", which for many years, like a "sacred cow", has dominated the Scandinavian analytical jurisprudence.[97] In turn, Peczenik's student, Uta Bindreiter, presented the possibility of explaining Kelsen's theory of the basic norm, subconsciously presupposed in

[92] *Ibidem*, pp. 241ff.

[93] *Ibidem*, pp. 250ff. According to Eng, it is "a fundamental consciousness perspective" of the lawyers who loyally take into account the opinion of other lawyers and law practitioners. What constitutes an important element of this perspective is a specific legal method, expressed in the argumentation made in juristic language, based on specialised knowledge on law application and on the views expressed by other lawyers.

[94] *Ibidem*, pp. 244ff.

[95] *Ibidem*, pp. 256ff.

[96] *Cf. supra*, note 52 at p. 369.

[97] A. Peczenik, *Scientia Juris*, *op. cit.*, p. 101.

legal thinking, and his conception of ought-sentences (*Sollsätze*)[98] by means of the concept of fused descriptive and normative modality.[99]

Eng's theory of fused modality also encountered strong criticism. Taking into account the purpose of our investigation, it is worth noting Eng's recent controversy with Christian Dahlman,[100] which clearly demonstrates the methodological choice of conceptual apparatus that we are facing if we want to determine the logical status of lawyers' propositions relating to valid law. Dahlman calls for rejecting Eng's theory, assessing it as having no value for legal theory. In his view, the category of "fused modality" is nothing other than a "confused modality", because the lawyers who—according to Eng—formulate modally fused propositions are merely lawyers who do not realise the logical nature of their utterances.[101] Moreover, Dahlman argues that Eng's theory and, in particular, the lawyers' reactions that it predicts in the event of discrepancies between their propositions *de lege lata* and legal reality, do not exclude the possibility that these statements are based on a combination of two easily separable classic modalities (descriptive and normative ones). He admits that people are not always willing to explain whether they state that something is or that something ought to be; however, such clarity and precision can be demanded from solicitors, judges or law professors, because there is no excuse for obscuring the logical nature of their statements pertaining to the law.[102]

Dahlman's criticism has forced Eng to clarify his own standpoint and has prompted him to present interesting arguments against the traditional methodology and conceptual network that constituted the basis of Dahlman's objections. When addressing these objections, Eng argues that the phenomenon of fused modality of lawyers' propositions *de lege lata* cannot be understood within the traditional naturalistic methodology, based on "an empiricist and logical paradigm of atemporal cognition and control".[103] The conceptual apparatus used by Dahlman does not enable us to conceptualise two particular aspects of legal thinking about the law.[104] Firstly, the temporal aspect, in the sense of the determination of what the law is, is constantly subject to lawyers' analyses, and Dahlman, in his criticism, ignores it, assuming a specifically atemporal understanding of the law as a fixed fact that constitutes the subject of legal cognition. Secondly, the institutional aspect, which is manifested in the fact that legal reasoning takes place within the institutional order where there are bodies (courts) vested with the powers of a binding interpretation and application of the law. While the propositions classified by Dahlman as

[98] For more on Kelsen's concepts of "Sollsatz" and "Rechtssatz" *see* Chap. 6, note 65 at p. 230.

[99] U.U. Bindreiter, '"Descriptive Normativity": Kelsen's *Sollsatz* in the Light of Some Later Theories', *op. cit.*, pp. 90ff.

[100] *See* Ch. Dahlman, 'Fused Modality or Confused Modality?', *RJ* 17 (2004), pp. 80–86 and S. Eng, 'Fused Modality. An Integral Part of Lawyers' Form of Life', *RJ* 18 (2005), pp. 429–433.

[101] Ch. Dahlman, *ibidem*, pp. 82ff.

[102] *Ibidem*, pp. 85–86.

[103] S. Eng, 'Fused Modality. An Integral Part of Lawyers' Form of Life', *op. cit.*, pp. 429ff.

[104] *Ibidem*, pp. 431ff.

"modally confused" do not provide us with any information other than about the confused state of mind of their authors, the propositions with fused modality—being the result of the lawyer's clear and conscious choice—provide the information about actual and normative aspects of reality; namely, about something that directly affects and interests us.[105] Finally, according to Eng, his theory demonstrates the interrelation between the legal dogmatic concept of law and the normativity and morals, manifested in *de lege lata* legal thinking in the form of lawyers' fused propositions.[106]

The presented polemics highlight a fundamental methodological controversy that accompanies, and perhaps even provides the basis for the discrepancies concerning the nature of the juristic utterances about the law and, in particular, the nature of the statements about the validity of legal norms. Let us note in this context that Eng's and Mazzarese's conceptions do not undermine the traditional distinction between purely descriptive and purely normative propositions. Mazzarese does not present any standpoint on this issue at all,[107] focusing her attention on demonstrating the lack of truth-value and the non-descriptive character of the statements about the validity of legal norms, whilst Eng proposes introducing the new category of fused legal propositions—by no means denying the existence of purely descriptive and purely normative legal statements.[108] I believe that there are some reasons that weigh in favour of accepting the conceptual network developed by Eng. Firstly, its explanatory value, certainly higher than that of the traditional theory based on a simple dichotomy(?) of descriptivity and normativity. Secondly, its *a posteriori* nature, resulting from the empirical justifiability of the majority of Eng's theses. And thirdly, the fact that the analyses of the Norwegian author also include pragmatic aspects of legal dogmatic utterances, basically ignored in the traditional theory, which is rather focused on the semantics of the juristic language.

8.2.1 Pragmatic Analysis of Juristic Utterances Concerning Validity

Adopting a tripartite division of juristic (in particular, dogmatic) legal statements (i.e., descriptive, normative and fused ones) as a tool for our clarificative analysis does not yet resolve the question concerning the logical and linguistic status of the

[105] *Ibidem*, pp. 430, 432.

[106] *Ibidem*, p. 432.

[107] It can be interpreted in such a way that Mazzarese's conception does not undermine the very distinction, but its application in relation to juristic utterances concerning valid law.

[108] *Cf.* S. Eng, 'Fusion of Descriptive and Normative Propositions', *op. cit.*, pp. 241, 251–252.

juristic utterances pertaining to the validity of statutory norms.[109] As already noted,[110] we believe that only the fact of taking into account the pragmatic aspect allows us to formulate their accurate linguistic characterisation and to resolve the controversy over the question as to whether they possess logical value. What also weighs in favour of identifying and examining the pragmatically varied types of juristic utterances on the validity of legal norms are the faults of the previous jurisprudential analyses. Probably most crucial is to avoid the fallacy of illegitimate generalisation of the theses formulated within such analysis. Let us brood awhile upon this error, since its consequences are devastating and its analysis will only reinforce the justification of the suitability of pragmatic analysis.

We shall discuss an example directly related to the problem we are currently dealing with. When commenting on Mazzarese's analysis of norm propositions, Bulygin accuses her of committing the fallacy of illegitimate generalisation,[111] no doubt rightly arguing that, for instance, the following statement should be regarded as logically incorrect: "If in some cases it is doubtful whether a given norm is valid, then it is always doubtful regarding all norms that they are valid".[112] This fallacy lies in the fact that we draw an inference from a particular sentence (beginning with an existential quantifier) to the general sentence (with a universal quantifier) without any additional premises or arguments that justify it. Such a fallacy is difficult to avoid in the heat of jurisprudential polemics, which is proven by the somewhat amusing fact that Bulygin himself probably makes the very same error when he concludes his critique of Mazzarese's conception with the thesis concerning norm propositions: "[T]he fact that they are true (or false) in clear cases is enough to maintain that they have truth-values".[113] It seems that the fallacy of illegitimate generalisation is a consequence of *par excellence* ontological conviction of numerous legal theorists and philosophers in that if an object has a certain feature, then such a feature also constitutes a property of all the objects that are related thereto; a belief that Lech Morawski calls "a universalist error".[114] We

[109] We therefore do not make a fallacy of *petitio principii* which can be, as I believe, legitimately imputed to the traditional theory. Adopting the traditional distinction of juristic utterances into two categories, namely purely descriptive and purely normative ones, in principle determines the result of the characteristics of juristic validity utterances because – as we shall prove in the next section – the purely normative statements about the validity of norms are utterly redundant both from the legal point of view as well as from the pragmatic perspective of linguistic communication.

[110] *Cf. supra*, pp. 360–361.

[111] In logical literature, this error is named *fallacia fictae universalitatis*.

[112] E. Bulygin, 'On Norm Propositions', *op. cit.*, p. 132. The correctness of this statement does not naturally determine that Mazzarese actually made such an error. For more on the controversy between Mazzarese and Bulygin *see* R. Guastini, 'Eugenio Bulygin e Tecla Mazzarese su interpretazione e proposizioni normative', *D&QP* 6 (2006), pp. 97–100.

[113] E. Bulygin, 'On Norm Propositions', *op. cit.*, p. 134. Let us note that if we even leave the logical objection aside, then Bulygin's thesis also raises substantive doubts – *see* P.E. Navarro, 'Enunciados jurídicos y proposiciones normativas', *op. cit.*, pp. 152ff.

[114] *See* L. Morawski, 'Zasady prawne – komentarz krytyczny', *op. cit.*, p. 81, and the references cited therein.

should agree with Morawski that our world (and thus the world of legal phenomena), fortunately, is not a coherent, regular, orderly and logocentric whole, which strongly suggests that its examination shall begin in a maximally concrete and detailed way, and only then go on to higher levels of abstraction. Given that pragmatics is the least abstract part of semiotics, it seems that a pragmatic analysis of the utterances about the validity of norms may prove to be a remedy for inaccuracies, or even errors of more abstract semantic analyses as well as the most abstract studies in formal logic.

Before we begin a pragmatic analysis, we should first explain the concepts that it applies, because many of them have nothing to do with everyday juristic terminology. This necessity also results from the above-mentioned lack of a uniform conceptual network that would allow for linguistic and logical analyses of juristic utterances. The fundamental controversies undoubtedly concern, inter alia, the concept of truth applied in linguistic jurisprudential analyses and an accurate definition of "truth bearers".[115] A thorough analysis of these issues would far exceed the scope of this study; we shall, therefore, confine ourselves to explaining the basic concepts that will be applied in the pending analysis, and we will justify their choice only to the extent necessary.

Firstly, in accordance with the standard theory of speech acts,[116] we will assume (to somewhat simplify the problem) that the structure of the utterance about the validity of the norm will be reduced to a general form F(P), where F stands for the so-called illocutionary force, allowing us to identify the speech act performed, whereas P stands for its propositional content. For example, the utterance: "I promise to visit you tomorrow" can be interpreted as a promise (F) that tomorrow I will visit you (P). In order to analyse the problem of truth-values that are attributed to the utterances about the validity of norms, it is crucial to assume that the logical value is attributed to the propositional content of only some speech acts. In fact, we accept the view expressed by the founder of speech acts theory—John L. Austin—who emphasised that, "The truth or falsity of a statement depends not merely on the meanings of words but on what act you are performing in what circumstances".[117] Thus, according to our analysis, the only possible "truth bearers" will be in the propositional content of those speech acts, which were collectively defined by us as the utterances relating to the validity of norms (validity utterances). Let us note that for lawyers, especially legal theoreticians, there is nothing surprising in such a selective treatment of the propositional content of juristic speech acts in terms of its logical value. By way of example, let us consider the two ways of understanding

[115] Philosophical literature on the concept of truth is too vast to present it here, yet it merits indicating two very interesting jurisprudential monographs devoted to the issue of truth in law and in legal discourse – D. Patterson, *Law and Truth*, *op. cit.* and U. Neumann, *Wahrheit im Recht*, *op. cit.*

[116] Let us add that by "standard theory of speech acts" we refer to the J.R. Searle's theory of speech acts, being the extension of J.L. Austin's original conceptions of performatives and illocutionary acts.

[117] J.L. Austin, *How to Do Things with Words*, *op. cit.*, p. 145.

deontic propositions[118] that can be encountered in jurisprudential literature.[119] This involves a distinction between deontic propositions of a prescriptive and descriptive character. The basis for this distinction is a pragmatic criterion of the purpose of using a deontic proposition. If we use it in order to create a norm, then it is a prescriptive use and if our aim is to present the content or characteristics of the norm—we are dealing with a description of it. Thus, the proponents of this distinction assume that deontic propositions of prescriptive character express norms, whereas deontic propositions of descriptive character express the so-called norm propositions, already discussed in the previous section.

Secondly, as regards the concept of truth, the basis of our analyses will be the realist conception of truth, developed by one of the leading analytic philosophers, William Alston.[120] It is both relatively simple, and yet—as we believe—largely corresponds to the intuitions of lawyers. According to his conception, which belongs to the family of the minimalist theories of truth, "[a] statement (proposition, belief...) is true if and only if what the statement says to be the case actually is the case".[121] This definition means that when we, for example, analyse the sentence: "The grass is green", then the only necessary and sufficient condition for its truth is the "grass's *being* green"[122] and nothing more, as expressly pointed out by Alston. We believe that this conception can be accepted as a basis for our analyses also due to the fact that lawyers continually strive for objectivity, trying to make dogmatic statements, which—at least in their view—are objective (in the sense of "originating from the object"[123]). The realist conception of truth is ideally suited to this pursuit, since the "truth maker" is something objective in relation to the "truth bearer"; it is the actual occurrence of what we state.[124] We believe that it would be difficult to challenge the thesis that the dogmatics of law and other lawyers indeed have in mind such a state of "overlapping" when they utter the propositions about the validity of legal norms. Yet it does not determine that their utterances indeed have a truth-value, because their goal may also depend on something other than the formulation of a genuine validity statement. It can also be the case that the "truth maker" of validity statements is not a legal reality but, for example, the opinions of other lawyers, as argued by the proponents of the application of the consensual

[118] The term "deontic proposition" is derived from Greek – τὸ δέον means "what is to be" or "what ought to be". Both usages are, therefore, semantically acceptable. For more *see e.g.*, J. Kalinowski, 'Logika prawnicza a logika deontyczna' [Legal Logic and Deontic Logic] in S. Wronkowska, M. Zieliński (eds.), *Szkice z teorii prawa i szczegółowych nauk prawnych*, *op. cit.*, pp. 347ff. and 'Ontic and Deontic', *IJSL* III/8 (1990), p. 136.

[119] *See e.g.*, E. Bulygin, 'On Norm Propositions', *op. cit.*, pp. 129–130; G.H. von Wright, 'Deontic Logic: A Personal View', *op. cit.*, p. 31 and 'On Norms and Norm-Propositions', *op. cit.*, p. 173.

[120] W.P. Alston, *A Realist Conception of Truth*, Ithaca 1996, pp. 5ff., 22ff.

[121] *Ibidem*, p. 5.

[122] *Ibidem*, p. 7. Italics in the original.

[123] For more on the ways of understanding the objectivity in legal and juristic discourse *see* T. Gizbert-Studnicki, 'Podstawy argumentacji prawniczej', *op. cit.*, p. 36 ff.

[124] W.P. Alston, *A Realist Conception of Truth*, *op. cit.*, p. 7.

theory of truth in relation to juristic statements. Nevertheless, this theory does not seem to us to be more adequate than the adapted Alston's realist theory.[125] For one thing is certain: the conceptions of Mazzarese and Eng—presented in the preceding section—both critical to the traditional jurisprudential view on the truth-value of juristic utterances, at least show that nothing can be assumed here without discussion.

If we intend to use Alston's theory of truth, we need to take into account the specificity of legal discourse, in many respects different from philosophical or logical reasoning. In the context of the truth-values of juristic speech acts, attention needs to be primarily drawn to a peculiar way of understanding the feature of "possessing a truth-value" in terms of juristic utterances. It is peculiar for legal thinking, as can be clearly visible in Wróblewski's opinions on "fuzziness" of the systemic concept of legal validity and in Mazzarese's theory of a non-descriptive character of the utterances about legal validity. This peculiarity stems from the fact that lawyers, and legal scholars in particular, quite correctly leave it up to the philosophers to tackle the basic controversies surrounding the concept of truth, thus recognising that the major problem is in distinguishing between those juristic utterances that have logical value and those that do not. Moreover, what constitutes

[125] A. Aarnio has been the most consistent advocate of the consensual theory of truth, based on the concept of acceptability – *see idem*, 'On Truth and the Acceptability of Interpretative Propositions in Legal Dogmatics', *op. cit.*, pp. 46 ff., 'On the Validity, Efficacy and Acceptability of Legal Norms', *op. cit.*, pp. 160ff., and *The Rational as Reasonable*, *op. cit.*, p. 188 ff. In Polish literature, following Aarnio, the consensual theory of truth in relation to juristic interpretive propositions has been adopted by T. Gizbert-Studnicki, who nevertheless also recognises the need to use the correspondence theory of truth in jurisprudence – *see idem*, 'How Many Theories of Truth Are Needed in Jurisprudence?', *op. cit.*, in particular pp. 160–161. It should be noted that in the context of our analyses, the idea of applying the consensual theory of truth in the form proposed by the Finnish philosopher to the characteristics of validity utterances is out of question because it constitutes a version of the conception of the axiological legal validity of J. Wróblewski, which Aarnio explicitly acknowledges – *cf. idem*, 'On the Validity, Efficacy and Acceptability of Legal Norms', *op. cit.*, p. 154 and *The Rational as Reasonable*, *op. cit.*, p. 33. The application of this theory would thus be inconsistent with a detached and axiologically impartial methodological approach to the jurisprudential clarification of the juristic concept of the validity of statutory law as adopted in this study – *cf.* Chap. 6, pp. 234–237. Let us add that even the fact of applying the consensual theory of truth within the area of jurisprudence is controversial in itself. For example, J. Wróblewski challenges the manner of understanding dogmatic utterances as utterances about the views of the juristic audience rather than as utterances about law – *see idem*, 'Paradygmat dogmatyki prawa a prawoznawstwo', *op. cit.*, pp. 41–42. In turn, U. Neumann, in the context of the consensual theory of truth in the German theory of practical discourse, formulates the objection concerning the relationship between the concepts of truth and consensus. He raises the question as to which of these concepts is the "active part" and which the "passive" one. Neumann believes that it is not clear whether the statement is true because of its "ability" to achieve consensus, or – conversely – if it is "capable" of reaching consensus because it is true – *see idem*, *Wahrheit im Recht*, *op. cit.*, p. 25. Similar argumentation has been presented by J.J. Moreso, who questions the usefulness of the consensual theory of truth in relation to the problem of norm existence, emphasising that the consent of a certain legal community as to the existence of the norm can only be a symptom but not the criterion of its existence – *see idem*, 'On the Truth-conditions of Norm Propositions', *op. cit.*, pp. 65ff.

the basis of such a distinction for lawyers is the availability of methods, criteria or tests, whereby they are able to determine the truth-value of the propositional content of the utterances formulated in the juristic language. Such an operational approach is certainly very practical, in our opinion, and deserves to be approved, although from a logical point of view it may raise some doubts,[126] not to mention possible philosophical objections. Nevertheless, the determination and application of the methods (criteria, tests) that allow us to ascribe logical value to a given type of juristic utterance is a real problem for lawyers and, moreover, it generates significant practical consequences. In fact, what can be achieved by stating that certain types of utterances about the law have a truth-value, when we do not know if, or how such a value can be determined at all? Thus, one can assume that the set of utterances whose propositional content lawyers are eager to attribute with the status of the truth-value, is far less populated than would appear from a purely philosophical (especially epistemological) or logical analysis conducted by the representatives of other humanistic disciplines.

A pragmatic analysis shall begin by considering the question of whether any positive or negative juristic validity utterances exist that can be regarded as purely descriptive and attributed with a truth-value. Aulis Aarnio, in one of his studies, recalls "the trivial case of legal dogmatical statements" that possess a truth-value in the classic sense of the correspondence theory of truth, when referring to the statements under which the legal text contains certain words or sentences ("The law text contains the sentence *P*").[127] By analogy, let us try to formulate a "trivial utterance" about the validity of statutory law norms, and then to characterise it, using the adopted conceptual network.

Let us, for example, consider a legal dogmatic utterance: "In the Polish civil law a norm: 'Who at his fault caused damage to another person, is obliged to repair it' is valid". At first glance, this is a descriptive deontic sentence that has a truth-value. It can be said that if we faithfully quoted the wording of Article 415 of Polish Civil Code,[128] it is true, and if we made a mistake, it is false, because its propositional content would then not comply with the legal text, fulfilling here the function of the "truth maker". Yet, the following doubt arises: can the above sentence in single quotation marks actually be considered as the expression of a legal norm in the

---

[126] One can, in fact, support the idea, widely adopted among logicians, that the truth-value is the property which is also attributed to such propositions in relation to which we do not have any effective method allowing for us to determine their logical value; it is sufficient that they describe reality. Let us note that in our analyses we adopted the standpoint expressed by lawyers rather than by logicians, because this study is addressed to the former (which, contrary to appearances, seems to us a quite reasonable argument). It is also worth noting that the standpoint on the extension of the utterances (propositions) having logical value, which we attribute to lawyers, largely resembles anti-metaphysical views formulated, for example, by the representatives of *Wiener Kreis*, concerning the necessity of "susceptibility to the verification" of the scientific judgments and theories.

[127] A. Aarnio, R. Alexy, A. Peczenik, 'The Foundation of Legal Reasoning', *op. cit.*, p. 427.

[128] *Kodeks cywilny. Ustawa z dnia 23 kwietnia 1964 r.* [Civil Code. Statute of 23 April 1964], published in *Dziennik Ustaw* [Journal of Statutes] 964, No. 16, Item 93, with amendments.

meaning adopted in this study[129]; namely, as the wording of a "sufficiently unambiguous" utterance? Naturally, it is not the case, as evidenced even by the necessity of its proper interpretation.[130] Therefore, the analysed positive utterance about legal validity is devoid of truth-value as its presupposition is false[131]: a sentence in French quotation marks is not a wording of a legal norm but a repetition of the wording of a legal provision. Thus, the analysed utterance has to be "trivialised" to an even greater extent. To this end, we will replace the quoted content of the mentioned provision of the Polish Civil Code with the name of the norm and we will state the following: "In the Polish civil law there is a valid norm that prescribes the compensation for wrongful damage". In respect of such an utterance, it is difficult to deny that it is descriptive and it has the truth-value (because the name of the norm need not be "sufficiently unambiguous"). Thus, it appears that in the set of juristic validity utterances there are utterances whose linguistic and logical character is in line with the traditional (positivist) approach to the utterances about legal norms. We do not believe that in relation to the utterances, formulated in the juristic language, such as, for example: "In Poland the legal norm that prohibits active euthanasia is valid" or "In France the norm that prescribes to employ only Polish plumbers is valid", one could reasonably question their descriptive nature. Moreover, such a need does not arise even from the jurisprudential perspective, though, incidentally, it can be seen that the above examples refer to the utterances that are not specific for legal dogmatics or for judicial practice, since they can be just as well made by a layperson—a citizen who has only a superficial knowledge of valid law.

Although we have already managed to identify "trivial" utterances about the validity, having a descriptive and truth-oriented character, it would be advisable to find at least one more type of validity utterance of an identical nature. Let us, therefore, discuss the second type of juristic validity utterances, this time a specific—long since institutionalised—namely; the utterances that are a part of judicial decisions, in particular, performed by the judges of constitutional courts who settle validity problems. Utterances about the validity made by those judges need to be analysed, because from a pragmatic point of view, they are—in a specific way—analytically true, as a result of their explicit performative nature (in fact, they belong

[129] For more *see* Chap. 6, pp. 245–246. Let us recall that a legal norm is defined as "an utterance which sufficiently unambiguously orders (or prohibits) someone (the addressee) certain behaviour in certain circumstances".

[130] *See e.g.*, G. Bieniek, H. Ciepła, S. Dmowski, J. Gudowski, K. Kołakowski, M. Zychowicz, T. Wiśniewski, C. Żuławska, *Komentarz do kodeksu cywilnego. Księga trzecia: Zobowiązania* [Commentary to the Civil Code. Book Three: Obligations], 3rd ed., Warszawa 2001, where the explanatory notes on the interpretation of Article 415 of Polish Civil Code take up 16 pages (pp. 216–233).

[131] We apply here the concept of presupposition in the sense referring to the views of Frege and Strawson, rather than Russell. Moreover, we have in mind the so-called strong presupposition ("resistant to negation"); namely, that it is identical for a positive and negative utterance about the validity of norms – for more *see* R. Sarkowicz, *Poziomowa interpretacja tekstu prawnego*, *op. cit.*, pp. 133 ff., and the references cited therein.

to the category of linguistic declarations in accordance with Searle's terminology[132]). Let us now look at some examples to consider whether this very simple, purely linguistic (non-institutional) analytic accuracy has any implications in relation to the linguistic and logical character of the juristic utterances about the validity of norms.

We shall begin our analysis with the positive validity utterances ("Norm N is valid" and the like). How can one characterise the utterance about the validity of a given norm[133] if it constitutes a part of the ruling issued by a constitutional court vested with legal power to settle validity disputes? If such a court holds that a certain statutory norm is consistent with the constitution and that it is valid, then its utterance is of an explicitly performative character, whereby the sentence claiming that "the constitutional court rendered this norm valid" becomes analytically true. It is a cliché, but an interesting and far from banal question actually arises for lawyers, as to whether the constitutional court's decision implies that every subsequent juristic (in particular, dogmatic) utterance, secondary to the former one, and stating the validity of this norm, will be *eo ipso* purely descriptive and true. In other words, the question as to whether the positive decision of the constitutional court entails the truth of the positive utterances about validity that refer to the norm considered in this decision.[134] This issue is very controversial and difficult to explain from a jurisprudential perspective because the answer depends on several factors, such as: the legal regulation of the binding force of rulings rendered by the constitutional courts, the normative conception of the sources of law adopted in a given legal culture, the standpoint of the doctrine and, more importantly, the judiciary in the lawmaking role of the constitutional courts.

---

[132] For more on declarations *see* J.R. Searle, 'A Taxonomy of Illocutionary Acts', *op. cit.*, pp. 358ff. and 'How Performatives Work', *Lin&Ph* 12 (1989), pp. 540ff.; J.R. Searle, D. Vanderveken, *Foundations of Illocutionary Logic*, *op. cit.*, pp. 56ff., 95ff. *Cf.* A. Grabowski, *Judicial Argumentation and Pragmatics*, *op. cit.*, pp. 83ff., and the references cited therein. It should be added that in the following analysis, we deliberately avoid the use of not very well-known conceptual network of speech acts theory and we try to express the pragmatic analysis in a terminologically simplified form.

[133] For the purposes of the undertaken pragmatic analysis, we shall assume that in the system-type of statutory law the constitutional courts rule and present the standpoint on the validity of norms and not of legal provisions. Such assumption seems acceptable, because even if the constitutional court directly refers in its ruling to the validity of legal provisions, its utterances – at least indirectly – undoubtedly concern the validity of legal norms.

[134] If we deal with the conceptual network of Searle's speech acts theory, one needs to consider whether the positive validity utterances of the constitutional courts belong to the category of extra-linguistic declarations, which – by definition – result in the truth of their propositional content, which would, in turn, entail the necessity of the truth of jurisprudential utterances that have the identical content. For more about this category of speech acts *see* the works indicated in note 132 above. It should be added that in our analysis we use the findings made in these works, thus knowingly leaving aside the question of the logical value of performatives and the methods of their conceptual recognition (e.g., in terms of analytic, self-confirming, non-falsifying or self-descriptive propositions) – for more on this *see e.g.*, L. Åqvist, 'Some Remarks on Performatives in the Law', *AI&L* 11 (2003), pp. 110ff. and W. Patryas, *Performatywy w prawie* [Performatives in Law], Poznań 2005, pp. 61ff., and the references cited therein.

A comprehensive analysis of this multifaceted problem undoubtedly goes beyond the scope of this study and it even does not seem necessary. Let us note that we should answer in the negative, and thus refuse to acknowledge the automatic truth of the secondary positive utterances about the validity of the norm that are subsequent to the constitutional tribunal's decision, regardless of whether we approve of the theory based on Hans Kelsen's distinction between the "positive" legislators (parliament), and "negative" ones (the constitutional courts)[135] or whether we reject it. Accordingly, if we accept the view—which seems to still dominate in the Polish legal culture—that the constitutional court is only a "negative" legislator and not (at least in some cases) a "positive" one, then a confirming ruling of this court cannot entail the truth of the secondary juristic utterances about the validity of the norm that constituted the subject of the court's ruling. According to the proponents of the theory of a "negative" legislator, due to the declaratory character of confirmatory rulings,[136] which do not contribute anything (in a lawmaking sense) to the system of positive law, it is unlikely that lawyers would find it as a sufficient reason for the truth of their subsequent positive utterances about the validity of the legal norm analysed by the constitutional court.[137] Moreover—as already noted[138]—the constitutional court can make a mistake when it rules that the contested norm is consistent with the constitution. Yet, if we reject the theory of the "negative" legislator and we believe that the constitutional courts make law (for example, by means of the so-called interpretive or applicative rulings), there is also no reason to believe that the secondary juristic validity utterances will become true. Indeed, if the constitutional court holds that a certain norm (with the content given by the court) is valid, then its utterance about the validity of this norm will be the element of a conventional institutionalised activity of judicial lawmaking.[139] Thus,

[135] Kelsen probably first used this distinction in his famous lecture in Vienna in April 1928, entitled 'Wesen und Entwicklung der Staatsgerichtsbarkeit', *VVDS* 5 (1929), pp. 30–88, where, on p. 56, we find the terms "der positive Gesetzgeber" and "der negative Gesetzgeber". From the jurisprudential perspective, for more on Kelsen's theory on the "negative" legislator and its shortcomings *see* S. Wronkowska, 'Kilka uwag o "prawodawcy negatywnym"' [Some Comments on the "Negative Legislator"], *PiP* 10 (2008), pp. 5ff.

[136] The view about the declarative nature of such a ruling results from approving the theory of a "negative" legislator. We use here the concepts of declaratory and constitutive rulings according to the manner adopted in the Polish dogmatics of the constitutional law – the former rulings do not change the valid law, while the latter do so. At this point it is worth noting the critical remarks on the distinction between these concepts, formulated from the jurisprudential perspective by S. Kaźmierczyk, 'Orzeczenia konstytutywne i deklaratywne' [Constitutive and Declaratory Rulings] *AUW* 211 (1973), pp. 25–38 and 'Charakter prawny orzeczeń Trybunału Konstytucyjnego' [The Legal Nature of the Constitutional Court Rulings], *AUW* 1037 (1987), pp. 271–294.

[137] Let us recall that a confirming ruling of the constitutional court can hardly be considered as a condition of the systemic validity of norms – *cf.* Chap. 7, note 197 at p. 291.

[138] *Cf.* Chap. 7, pp. 290–291.

[139] It should be added that in this case, due to purely conceptual reasons, it is difficult to speak of a "mistake" by the constitutional court, because we are dealing here with lawmaking and not with the examination of its compliance with the constitution. In turn, when lawyers talk about "judicial mistakes", they do not refer to a "legislative mistake" as that means something else – for example,

the constitutional court ruling cannot by itself result in the fact that the subsequent juristic utterances about the validity of this norm—secondary vis-à-vis that ruling—will be true, because we are dealing here with a situation analogous to the act of lawmaking performed by the legislator. Without a doubt, no one will contemporarily assume that the mere fact of enacting the legal norm entails the correctness of the subsequent juristic utterances about its validity. It suffices to note that, just as with the norms of law enacted by the legislator, the legal norms established by the constitutional courts (or, as in the case of Switzerland[140] and probably in many other countries, even by the courts of general jurisdiction) can also be regarded as invalid, for example, due to the application of *lex superior*, or *lex posterior* rules, the occurrence of *desuetudo* or a number of other well-known reasons that deprive these norms of their validity.

The positive validity utterances of constitutional courts, regardless of whether we interpret them as confirming or lawmaking utterances, do not therefore mean that the secondary juristic (dogmatic) positive utterances about the validity of legal norms gain a descriptive and truth-oriented character.[141] They only show the correctness of the utterances, which state that the constitutional court deemed a given norm valid; namely, the utterances that do not directly refer to the issue of the

an instrumentally incorrect choice of the method of legal regulation by the legislator or a serious violation of the rules in terms of legislative technique.

[140] We mean here a famous provision, yet rarely used in practice; namely, Article 1 Section 2 of the Swiss Civil Code, under which – in the absence of applicable legal regulation – the court should rule on the basis of customary law, and in the absence of such law, it should rule "selon les règles qu'il établirait s'il avait à faire acte de législateur" – the quotation after H. Kelsen, *General Theory of Law and State*, *op. cit.*, p. 147. It should be added that in our analyses we deliberately ignore the fundamental controversy regarding the lawmaking activity of courts in the continental system-type of statutory law. On this question, it is worth indicating an important standpoint of the leading representative of hard legal positivism – E. Bulygin – who presented his affirmative answer in 'Los jueces, ¿crean derecho?', *IS* 18 (2003), pp. 7–25. I think that today's lawmaking activity of the courts is the fact; therefore, the principle of the separation of powers can be regarded as an ideological mystification, unfortunately, often supported by legal doctrine. Yet, this is already a topic for another study. In this context, from the recent Polish literature *see e.g.*, A. Gomułowicz, *Aspekt prawotwórczy sądownictwa administracyjnego* [Legislative Aspect of the Administrative Jurisdiction], Warszawa 2008, in particular pp. 91ff.

[141] Let us note that the results of the undertaken analysis can be *mutatis mutandis* referred to the positive validity utterances that are made by the courts of general jurisdiction or by administrative courts, in relation to which one can also argue whether they are of a purely confirming character or – at least sometimes – lawmaking one. It should be also pointed out that although judges and other law enforcing entities tend to be bound by the content of the constitutional court rulings, this fact does not bear any consequences as to the linguistic character or the logical value of the utterances about validity – this binding force is of a normative and institutional character rather than of a cognitive one. It would be absurd to assume that the judges, due to the fact of being bound by the content of the constitutional court rulings, undertake merely true, purely descriptive statements about the validity of legal norms.

validity of norms but to the content of the court rulings, which are nevertheless irrelevant from the perspective of the scope and purposes of our analysis.[142]

Let us now go on to another type of utterances about the validity—this time negative judicial utterances—and let us try to determine (as in the above-analysed case of positive utterances) their linguistic and logical nature as well as possible consequences in relation to the secondary juristic negative utterances about the validity of the norms in question. At the outset, let us note an easily perceptible ambiguity of the negative validity utterances. The utterance "Norm N is not valid" (and the like) can mean that a given norm has never been valid (for example, due to the fact that it is merely a postulated norm or that it is decoded in the draft of a statute that has never become valid). When applying such an interpretation, the analysed utterance undoubtedly gains a descriptive and truth-oriented status, since it seems as equally simple from the linguistic and logical point of view as the "trivial" dogmatic validity statements analysed above. Yet, what seems much more essential—in theory and in practice—is the second understanding of this utterance, according to which the negative validity utterance means that a certain norm is not currently valid, although previously it was valid. As in the case of a positive validity utterance, from a pragmatic point of view, the negative utterances about the validity of norms can be of two different kinds: either they will not be the lawmaking utterances (that do not trigger any changes in the legal system), which claim that a certain legal norm is not valid, or derogatory utterances, which eliminate a given norm from the set of valid norms.

Let us first deal with derogatory utterances, which in the continental system-type of statutory law are typically formulated by the constitutional courts, because they are more important for lawyers, rather than negative validity utterances, which have no lawmaking effect. It is usually assumed that the ruling about the unconstitutionality results in depriving the norm at issue of its validity; namely, eliminating the unconstitutional norm from the set of valid norms by means of the so-called tribunal derogation made by the constitutional court.[143] A pragmatic analysis of derogatory utterances leads to the conclusion that they are of performative character in the very sense of that notion,[144] and therefore they constitute the example—to use the famous dictum of John L. Austin—of "doing things with words". It should be noted that the judgment of the constitutional court about the invalidity of a given

[142] Naturally, we do not question that the jurisprudential utterances concerning the content of the constitutional court rulings have descriptive and truth-oriented character. We only claim that this fact does not determine the linguistic and logical nature of the juristic (in particular: dogmatic) positive validity utterances which refer to the confirming or "positive" lawmaking decisions of the constitutional courts.

[143] On the concept of tribunal derogation (performed by a constitutional court) and its differences to the so-called authentic derogation (carried out by the legislator) *see* Chap. 9, pp. 479–480, and the references cited therein.

[144] According to the institutional (formal) classification of speech acts, derived from the Searlean taxonomy of speech acts, the utterances of the constitutional courts that derogate legal norms belong to the category of "extra-linguistic declarations".

legal norm entails not only the correctness of the descriptive sentence, proclaiming that the court deprived it of its validity, but also that the legal norm, deemed unconstitutional, in fact ceases to be valid. Accordingly, this utterance is true by definition, just as when the ruling of the criminal court that passes a guilty verdict implies that the accused is convicted. The fact that the constitutional court formulates a negative (derogatory) validity utterance means that its propositional content is true from the moment when the constitutional court's ruling becomes legally effective and when it triggers the change of the legal order.

By means of a pragmatic analysis, we have managed to identify this very specific type of utterance relating to the validity of norms, since these utterances are non-descriptive, yet they are true by definition. This is due to their institutional nature; in particular, the consequences that positive law attributed to them. Moreover, it should be noted that if the secondary negative utterances about validity refer to the norms that had been previously derogated by the constitutional courts, in that case they acquire a descriptive and truth-oriented status, since they describe—correctly or incorrectly—the fact that a given norm has been definitively deprived of its validity. Although such a ruling on unconstitutionality can be a mistake, a potential protest expressed by the legal dogmatists or judges can only relate to the content of the constitutional court's ruling and not its effect—namely, the institutional fact—in the sense that a given norm is no longer valid—in the same way that a jurisprudential criticism can refer to the content and to the justification of the criminal court's ruling, but not to the institutional fact that the accused has been convicted under a valid sentence. If that happened, it is simply a fact, which lawyers cannot question.[145]

Let us summarise the results of the foregoing pragmatic analysis, which enabled us to identify several types of validity utterances, having a clearly determined logical character. Firstly, in the juristic language, "trivial" validity utterances are formulated, which are descriptive and attributed with truth-values. Secondly, negative validity utterances exist, which concern merely postulated (planned) norms and also have a descriptive and truth-oriented nature. Thirdly, the institutional validity discourse consists of negative utterances about validity, by means of which the constitutional courts deprive legal norms of their validity. These derogatory utterances have a specific linguistic and logical character—they are non-descriptive, because they are performative, yet not only do they have truth-value, but they

[145] One can only metaphorically say that the fact of the loss of validity can be "questioned" by the legislator, but in order to do that, a new legal norm, identical in its content to the one derogated by the constitutional court, needs to be enacted by him. Nevertheless, it cannot come as a surprise that in the case in which the legislator undertakes such extraordinary steps to evade the consequences of the "tribunal derogation" carried out by the constitutional court, the negative jurisprudential utterances concerning the previously derogated norm cease to be true – because there will indeed be a change of the "truth maker"; namely, the positive law, which always outdates the part of juristic utterances that refer to the previous law regulations.

are also true by definition.[146] And finally, the fourth type of utterances consists of the secondary negative juristic utterances about the validity of norms (referring to derogation carried out by the constitutional court), which have a descriptive and truth-oriented nature. In addition, we also managed to establish that, except as indicated above, the remaining utterances about the validity of norms (both positive and negative) are not of a descriptive and truth-oriented character. Thus, a question arises as to how they can be characterised.

To answer that question, we do not need to go deeper into pragmatic analysis, because the image of the remaining juristic validity utterances, which emerges from the previously presented standpoints of Aulis Aarnio, Zygmunt Ziembiński and Jerzy Wróblewski, as well as from the theories of Tecla Mazzarese (confirmed by the analyses of Zbigniew Pulka) and Svein Eng,[147] and also—already in a negative way—from the pragmatic analysis carried out in the current section, is sufficiently clear. Therefore, we shall confine ourselves to indicating the basic arguments supporting the thesis of the mixed, namely "modally fused" character of positive and negative validity utterances, which do not belong to one of the above-mentioned four types of juristic utterances about the validity of norms.

Firstly, it is currently difficult to challenge the fact that legal reasoning is based on valuations. Even the hard legal positivists—such as, for example, Ota Weinberger—openly admit that valuation plays a decisive role in juristic discourse and argumentation.[148] As Krzysztof Płeszka states, in legal dogmatics "it is not disputable that dogmatic reflexion expresses valuations".[149] A similar situation can be encountered in the contemporary theory and philosophy of law, where many authors (even legal positivists) allow value judgments and evaluations. To give an example, related to Anglo-Saxon analytical jurisprudence, let us mention such authors who greatly contributed to the development of modern jurisprudential thought such as Joseph Raz, Wilfrid Waluchow, Neil MacCormick and Frederick Schauer.[150] Value judgments and evaluations are crucial in the juristic discourse

---

[146] The fact that they are "true by definition" due to their fully performative character is not in contradiction with the statement that their propositional content, as well as the semantically identical propositional content of the secondary negative jurisprudential validity utterances is also true in the sense of Alston's realistic conception of truth that we apply in this study.

[147] *Cf. supra*, pp. 371–380.

[148] *Cf.* O. Weinberger, 'Wartość, wartościowanie i doświadczanie wartości w argumentacji prawniczej', *op. cit.*, pp. 264, 277ff. and 'Wertediskurs in Moral, Recht und Politik', *op. cit.*

[149] K. Płeszka, 'O paradygmacie dogmatyki prawa', *op. cit.*, p. 771. A similar opinion was formulated by J. Wróblewski when he wrote about going beyond the traditional paradigm of jurisprudential deliberations – *see* K. Opałek, J. Wróblewski, *Prawo. Metodologia, filozofia, teoria prawa*, *op. cit.*, pp. 38ff. *Cf.* the criticism of the traditional paradigm of legal dogmatics presented by Z. Pulka, 'Czy nastąpił zmierzch pozytywistycznej koncepcji prawa i prawoznawstwa?', *op. cit.*, pp. 160ff.

[150] My comments are based on the reconstruction of the standpoint expressed by these authors, provided by V. Villa, 'Legal Theory and Value Judgments', *op. cit.*, pp. 460ff. In this context, it is worth to familiarise with Villa's interesting argumentation in favour of the necessity of value judgments in jurisprudence – *see ibidem*, pp. 472ff.

mostly due to the essential role played in this discourse by moral standards and requirements, which has been repeatedly drawn attention to.[151] Moreover, when we consider the analyses of the moral aspect of juristic statements, associated with the points of view adopted by lawyers (in particular, theorists and dogmatists of law), we will be able to recall here that only external statements, which by their very definition do not express an approval for the analysed law, are fully non-valuating.[152] Nonetheless, it does not seem an exaggeration to consider that in the juristic discourse, the external statements can only incidentally assume the form of *de lege lata* utterances about the validity of legal norms—for example, it can be the case when we formulate the validity utterance in relation to the norms of foreign law.

Secondly, due to the already identified shortcomings of the still-dominant positivist vision of the systemic validity of law, value judgments are also necessary in juristic validity discourse.[153] Using some metaphorical phrases, typically applied in this context,[154] we must admit that the "fuzziness" of modern legal systems (Wróblewski, Peczenik, Mazzarese), related to the "fickleness" of the criteria of validity and the "unstable" normative conception of the sources of law (Ziembiński), in particular resulting from the "open texture" of the customary rule of recognition (Hart) that can also include—unfortunately for the positivists—moral standards (Hart and inclusive legal positivists), not only leads to the existence of "uncertain law" (Opałek), but also entails the inability to recognise most of the utterances about the validity of norms as being descriptive and truth-oriented.[155] If these utterances could be purely descriptive and true (respectively, false), then any uncertainty would likely be eliminated. The lawyers who have non-valuating, unambiguous descriptive validity criteria could easily decide whether a given norm of statutory law is valid or not. There is no doubt that the latter is not the case, as confirmed by the existence of the constitutional courts and its role in resolving controversies concerning legal validity.

Thirdly, there are a number of reasons in favour of the "modally fused" character of most juristic utterances concerning the validity of legal norms. These reasons are

[151] *Cf.* Chap. 4, pp. 126–130 and Chap. 5, pp. 209–212.

[152] *Cf.* Chap. 6, pp. 228–237. Let us recall that the other categories of juristic utterances either express the acceptance for the law (the committed statements) or they can express such approval (the detached statements in Raz's sense, adopted in our analyses, and the internal statements in Hart's sense).

[153] *Cf. supra*, pp. 371–372 and Chap. 7, pp. 277–279.

[154] It is symptomatic that legal positivists tend to excessively use metaphors when they struggle with the non-conclusiveness of the solutions to validity problems that they themselves suggest, yet we must admit that they usually try to explain these metaphors in analytic terms.

[155] The presented argument is valid providing that we approve the specific juristic understanding of the truth of juristic validity utterances – *cf. supra*, note 126 at p. 385, with the corresponding text, referring to the analyses of J. Wróblewski and T. Mazzarese. For if we indeed assume a broader (i.e., logical) understanding of truth, then the fact that we cannot determine the logical value of some juristic utterance (more precisely, of its propositional content) about legal validity does not entail that it does not have the truth-value.

related to the thesis about the derivative nature of validity decisions vis-à-vis interpretive ones, as assumed in the course of our clarificative analysis.[156] This thesis implies that the specific features of juristic interpretive statements "transfer" onto validity statements. In the literature, one can encounter observations—to our mind, correct ones—that law "can never completely regulate its own interpretation" (MacCormick),[157] and none of the conceptions of legal interpretation developed in the jurisprudence that were to remedy it, can, in a "satisfactory way", control the judicial interpretation of law (Morawski).[158] It is also stressed that demonstrating the existence of the objective meaning of the text constitutes "a breakneck task" from the perspective of the philosophy of language (Sarkowicz).[159] Therefore, the interpretation of law can often be "creative" and the real controversy relates mainly to the problem of adequately determining the scope of this "creative" and "reproductive" interpretation.[160] In the context of the Polish jurisprudential debate, it can be added that according to two theories of legal interpretation, fundamental to modern Polish legal culture—namely, clarificative and derivative conception—cognitive and non-cognitive processes intertwine in legal interpretation; however, the modern theory of legal interpretation seems to be dominated by the approaches that "emphasise its non-cognitive character" (Kozak).[161] Today, there are also greater expectations that the legal interpretation should fulfil a "supplementary and creative" role in the legal practice (Zieliński).[162] These observations lead to the conclusion that recognising validity utterances, other than those identified and analysed in the earlier pragmatic analysis, as descriptive and truth-oriented utterances, must be rejected. It can therefore come as no surprise that even those legal theorists who apply the concept of the norm propositions, sometimes openly

---

[156] *Cf.* Chap. 6, pp. 241–242 and Chap. 7, note 130 at p. 277.

[157] N. MacCormick, 'Argumentation and Interpretation in Law', *op. cit.*, p. 29.

[158] L. Morawski, 'Kilka uwag na temat wykładni' [Some Comments on Interpretation'] in S. Wronkowska (ed.), *Polska kultura prawna a proces integracji europejskiej*, *op. cit.*, p. 41.

[159] R. Sarkowicz, 'Uwagi o współczesnej interpretacji prawniczej' [Comments on the Modern Legal Interpretation] in S. Wronkowska (ed.), *Polska kultura prawna a proces integracji europejskiej*, *op. cit.*, p. 28. A similar standpoint – already in relation to legal interpretation – has been expressed by E. Bulygin, 'On Norm Propositions', *op. cit.*, pp. 130–131 and R. Guastini, 'Interpretive Statements', *op. cit.*, pp. 280ff.

[160] We refer here to the recent controversy between L. Morawski and T. Gizbert-Studnicki, concerning the theory of interpretation assumed by the Polish Constitutional Tribunal – *cf.* R. Sarkowicz, *ibidem*, pp. 25ff.

[161] A. Kozak, *Pojmowanie prawa w teorii wykładni* [The Comprehension of Law in the Theory of Interpretation], AUW 1987 (1997), pp. 40ff. *Cf.* R. Guastini, 'Interpretive Statements', *op. cit.*, pp. 281ff., who presents jurisprudential characterisation of a "mixed" theory of legal interpretation; namely, neither "cognitive" (which can also be called "traditional") nor "sceptical" (which is sometimes referred to as "nihilistic").

[162] M. Zieliński, 'Współczesne problemy wykładni prawa', *op. cit.*, p. 9. Zieliński's thesis is supported by the demands formulated in legal practice – *see e.g.*, A. Gomułowicz, *Aspekt prawotwórczy sądownictwa administracyjnego*, *op. cit.*, pp. 57ff., and the references cited therein.

admit, in a manner that raises suspicion of *contradictio in terminis*, that some norm propositions remain indeterminate with respect to their truth-value (Moreso).[163]

These arguments and prior pragmatic analyses lead to the conclusion that the remaining juristic validity utterances (certainly more common in juristic discourse than the four identified above specific categories) should be characterised as "modally fused", or more precisely, as utterances devoid of the logical value and having a mixed, descriptive–evaluative–normative nature. Let us note that by adding an evaluative component we propose a certain modification of Eng's theory, which constituted the basis of our analyses.[164] In our view, it is essential explicitly to express the often-dominant evaluative element that is directly related to value judgments and decisions taken by lawyers who formulate the statements about the validity of legal norms. It is an indispensable element, since the previous analyses precluded the possibility of treating validity utterances as purely descriptive ones, and from a legal point of view, it is also impossible to assume that they have a purely normative character, as we shall justify in the next section.

The results of the pragmatic analysis are illustrated in the following table (see Table 8.1).

Table 8.1 The linguistic and logical characterisation of validity utterances

Type of utterance	Specific features	Linguistic status	Logical status
"Trivial" validity utterances	They contain the names of norms	Descriptive	They have truth-value
Negative validity utterances	They concern the postulated or planned norms	Descriptive	They have truth-value
Negative—derogatory validity utterances	They are contained in the constitutional court rulings	Performative	True by definition
Secondary negative validity utterances	They concern norms derogated by the constitutional courts	Descriptive	They have truth-value
The remaining juristic validity utterances	They are of *de lege lata* character	"modally fused"	They do not have truth-value

At this point, we could just finish the linguistic and logical analysis of the utterances about the validity of norms that are performed in juristic language. We have indeed established that the concept of the validity of the statutory law can be

[163] J.J. Moreso, 'On the Truth-conditions of Norm Propositions', *op. cit.*, p. 68.

[164] In passing, it should be pointed out that the views on the possibility of a descriptive, evaluative or normative interpretation of the juristic utterances about the validity of legal norms are nothing new. As an example, we could quote a fragment of J. Jakubowski's review (from 1962) of the W. Lang's book: *Obowiązywanie prawa*, *op. cit.*, p. 639: "It should be assumed that the expression 'legal norm N is valid' can be either a proposition about the norm or a norm about the norm or, ultimately, an evaluation of the norm. The question of what it is in a particular case, can be answered only by means of analysis of the particular utterance and, necessarily, of its context, yet even after such analysis has been completed, there still can remain some doubts". The standpoint expressed by Jakubowski cannot be regarded as anticipating Eng's theory, since "doubts" are not the same as the "modally fused" character of validity utterances; nevertheless, one can still perceive a strong resemblance here – at least in the approach to the logical nature of juristic utterances about valid law.

used in validity statements that have varied logico-linguistic status: from descriptive and truth-oriented utterances, through performative, and by definition true utterances, to the most common "modally fused" utterances (of descriptive–evaluative–normative character), which are devoid of truth-values. This implies that the phrase "A norm of statutory law is valid"—which constitutes the *definiendum* of the sought definition—must be treated by us as the sentence including the concept of validity that lawyers most commonly apply when they formulate non-descriptive statements that are devoid of truth-value. Therefore, for the sake of the simplicity of our clarificative analysis—let us assume that the *definiendum* of the definition of the juristic concept of the validity of statutory law is such an expression that can be attributed with the dominant evaluative character.

Yet, the above comment is not complete. The pragmatic analysis allows us to provide a certain alternative and, at the same time, a complementary (in relation to the theory of Mazzarese, Eng and the opinions of other authors) explanation of the reasons resulting in the fact that validity utterances (except for the above-identified four specific types) are "modally fused" and are devoid of logical value. In order to present it, we need to briefly suspend the methodological assumption of the "philosophical minimalism" of the analysis carried out in this study.[165] Our explanation undeniably enters the area of philosophical reflection because it is based on a speculative distinction of two worlds—typical for neo-Kantianism[166]—that may constitute the subject of the utterances formulated in the legal or juristic language; namely, the world of Is and the world of Ought.[167]

The contradistinction of *Sein* and *Sollen* is associated primarily with Kelsen's pure theory of law. However, it is aptly recognised that the author of *Reine Rechtslehre* failed to maintain a strict distinction, even within the concept of *Grundnorm*, fundamental for normativism.[168] We will leave aside the problem of

---

[165] *Cf.* Introduction, p. 4.

[166] *See e.g.*, St.L. Paulson, 'Faktum/Wert-Distinktion, Zwei-Welten-Lehre und immanenter Sinn. Hans Kelsen als Neukantianer' in R. Alexy *et al.* (eds.), *Neukantianismus und Rechtsphilosophie*, *op. cit.*, pp. 226ff. and U. Neumann, 'Wissenschaftstheorie der Rechtswissenschaft bei Hans Kelsen und Gustav Radbruch', *op. cit.*, pp. 37 ff.

[167] For more on the dualism of Is and Ought *see e.g.*, J. Wróblewski, 'Byt i powinność a błąd naturalistyczny w normatywizmie' [Is and Ought and the Naturalistic Mistake in Normativism], *SPE* XXIX (1982), pp. 24ff.; N. Bobbio '"Sein" and "Sollen" in Legal Science', *op. cit.*, pp. 19ff.; R. Dreier, 'Sein und Sollen', *op. cit.*, pp. 218ff.; G.H. von Wright, 'Is and Ought', *op. cit.*, pp. 263ff. In the following explanation, it is quite irrelevant whether the dualism of Is and Ought is interpreted in ontological or epistemological terms; yet its content will be presented in the language of an ontological approach, thus leaving aside the epistemological, methodological and logical aspect of this distinction. On this last aspect *see* K. Opałek, J. Woleński, 'Is, Ought, and Logic', *ARSP* 73 (1987), pp. 373–385.

[168] This cornerstone of Kelsen's theory refers in its content to the sphere of *Sein* in the form of the requirement of *im großen und ganzen* social efficacy of the (first) constitution and the norms of a given legal system established on its base – *see e.g.*, J. Wróblewski, *Krytyka normatywistycznej teorii prawa i państwa Hansa Kelsena* [Critique of Hans Kelsen's Normativist Theory of Law and State], Warszawa 1955, pp. 180ff. and a similar opinion of G. Hughes, cited in Chap. 7, note 424 at p. 343. For more on this issue *see* E. Bulygin, 'An Antinomy in Kelsen's Pure Theory of Law', *op. cit.*, pp. 33ff.

Table 8.2 The reference of juristic utterances

Reference → *The character of the utterance ↓*	The real world—the sphere of *Sein*	The postulated world—the sphere of *Sollen*
Descriptive utterances	A: description of reality	B: "description" of normative system
Normative utterances	C: "norm"—the change of social reality	D: norm—an ought of certain behaviour

the correctness of Kelsen's theory, especially as the dualism of Is and Ought can also be expressed in a less speculative language of "possible worlds", which refers to modal and deontic logic, by identifying the sphere of *Sein* as the "real world", while the sphere of *Sollen* is the "postulated world".[169] Let us examine a scheme (see Table 8.2 above), on the basis of which we will try to clarify—by means of the analysis of the pragmatic aspect of utterances—the origins (and perhaps even the necessity) of formulating "modally fused" juristic utterances, or at least to highlight their diversity from purely descriptive utterances (category A in the above scheme) and purely normative ones (category D).

The proposed explanation that has a character of a thought experiment, is as follows. The above scheme shows that we can first identify two ideal types of utterances formulated in the legal language and juristic language. Firstly, the utterances of a descriptive and truth-oriented nature (category A), by means of which lawyers describe the legal reality, for example, "trivially" claiming that in accordance with Polish civil law: "Who at his fault caused damage to another person, is obliged to repair it" and thus citing the wording of Article 415 of the Polish Civil Code, which acts here as the "truth maker". When applying the standard pragmatic concept of the direction of fit, it can be added that a characteristic feature of such assertions is the attempt to "make the words match the world"; that is, to obtain a "word-to-world" direction of fit, usually symbolised by [↓].[170] Secondly, utterances exist which are purely normative and devoid of truth-value—at least from a non-cognitivist perspective. Their purpose is to express (or to decode) legal norms in the texts of legislative acts or in judicial decisions of a lawmaking character (category D). These are, for example, legislator's or court's utterances, which indirectly establish legal norms—that is, by means of legal provisions, or directly—namely by formulating the content of the legal norms by the constitutional court in the so-called interpretive or applicative rulings, or by the court of the general jurisdiction by means of a precedent ruling. These utterances

[169] *See* J. Woleński, 'Semantyczne ujęcie dogmatyki prawa' [A Semantic Approach to Legal Dogmatics], *SF* 2–3 (1985), pp. 88ff., where Woleński admits that Kelsen's "sphere of Ought" can be identified with the "content of the class of postulated worlds". *Cf.* also *idem*, 'Możliwe światy teorii prawa' [Possible Worlds of the Theory of Law] in S. Wronkowska, M. Zieliński (eds.), *Szkice z teorii prawa i szczegółowych nauk prawnych*, *op. cit.*, pp. 15ff.

[170] Another group of juristic utterances that belong to category A, for example, are descriptive and truth-oriented statements concerning past court decisions, and many others.

belong to the group of directives that can be characterised by the opposite, "world-to-word" direction of fit [↑]. The aim of their authors is to fit "the real world", and, in particular, the manner of the conduct of the addressees of legal norms, to "the postulated world", expressed in the form of legal norms. Moreover, the presented scheme demonstrates the possibility of another two types of particular utterances about the law. Thirdly, we can deal with such normative utterances, formulated in the legal language, which in fact are not norms in accordance with the theory developed by the Poznań school of jurisprudence and adopted for the purposes of our analyses, yet which have a normative character in the common sense of this term, based on the general thesis about normativity (or at least the possibility of a normative interpretation) of legal texts (category C). To provide an example, we may present a legal provision of a recently enacted *Statute of 21 April 2005 on the formation of Kazimierz Wielki University in Bydgoszcz.*[171] It reads as follows:

> Article 1.1. On 1 September 2005 the University of Kazimierz Wielki is established, hereinafter referred to as "the University".
> 2. The seat of the University is the city of Bydgoszcz.
> 3. The University is a state university.

There is no doubt that the cited statutory provisions may be regarded as an example of a fully performative utterance (which belongs to the category of extra-linguistic declarations in accordance with Searle's taxonomy of illocutionary acts mentioned repeatedly in our study), by means of which the legislator introduces changes to the social reality (the sphere of *Sein*) and not only to a postulated world.[172] It is hard to deny (if we want to preserve common sense) that from 1 September 2005 in Bydgoszcz there exists the State University of *Kazimierz Wielki*, established by the legislator by means of the quoted legal provisions. Thus, what characterises these utterances is a "double" direction of fit [↕], as the legislator's utterance undoubtedly "does things with words", of course provided that the conditions of its legal (institutional) "felicity" are met.

Finally, we deal with the last category B, which includes *de lege lata* juristic utterances that are at the core of our interest, in particular, positive and negative validity utterances. We do believe that one can defend the view that normally these are not purely descriptive utterances, since they do not describe the "real world" (such as the utterances that belong to the category A), but they attempt to "describe", or more precisely, to interpret the sphere of *Sollen*; namely, a certain legal "postulated world". Yet, in most cases these are neither purely normative utterances (category D) because they do not prescribe (the ought) of the certain

[171] *Ustawa z dnia 21 kwietnia 2005 r. o utworzeniu Uniwersytetu Kazimierza Wielkiego w Bydgoszczy*, published in *Dziennik Ustaw* [Journal of Statutes] 2005, No. 90, Item 755.

[172] *See e.g.*, T. Gizbert-Studnicki, 'Język prawny a obraz świata', *op. cit.*, pp. 158ff., in particular p. 160, where he states that "by means of issuing a lawmaking act the changes in social reality take place". For more on the performative function of legal and juristic utterances and the real effects of performatives *see e.g.*, M. Zieliński, Z. Ziembiński, *Uzasadnianie twierdzeń, ocen i norm w prawoznawstwie*, *op. cit.*, pp. 17ff. and W. Patryas, *Performatywy w prawie*, *op. cit.*, pp. 90ff.

conduct of the addressees of legal norms (their authors are undoubtedly deprived of a norm-making competence since they are only the interpreters of the content of the world of *Sollen*). A specific linguistic and logical nature of *de lege lata* utterances is, therefore—as we believe—undeniable, and any attempts to recognise these utterances as "hybrid" (Ziembiński)[173] or "descriptive–normative" *Rechtssätze* (Kelsen)[174] appear in the context of the presented scheme as going in the right direction, although that direction is not precise enough. In light of our pragmatic analysis, these utterances are of a "modally fused" character (descriptive–evaluative–normative), which implies that as many as three directions of fit somehow coexist (or, better, compete) in them. Firstly, the "word-to-world" direction of fit [↓]—characteristic for assertions and corresponding to the lawyers' pursuit of the objective description of the normative state (the legal norms that belong to the sphere of *Sollen*). Secondly, the normative (directive) "world-to-word" direction of fit [↑]—related to the lawyers' desire to influence the opinions of other lawyers and the future, rational and just court's decisions. Thirdly, the most important, and specifically evaluative double (two-way) direction of fit, taking place between the "the postulated world" of *Sollen* co-created by lawyers, inter alia, by means of a creative reconstruction of the legal system,[175] and words [↕], or only between words alone [↔]—at least when the legal dogmatists, or—rarely—the theorists of law define the juristic textual or ordering concepts.[176]

The experimental status of the proposed clarification of the origin (or even necessity) of the "modally fused" and deprived-of-truth-value nature of the majority of the juristic utterances about the validity of legal norms (that belong to category B) allows us to ignore the more thorough justification of the pragmatic intuitions which were merely outlined here. It is not our intention to argue whether this highly simplified explanation deserves to be fully accepted.[177] Yet, in my opinion, it highlights an essential aspect of juristic utterances about law (in particular, dogmatic validity utterances that mainly belong to category B). The latter has been aptly manifested in Vittorio Villa's metaphor. The Italian philosopher acknowledges that contemporarily the minds of the representatives of legal science

---

[173] *Cf. supra*, p. 371. In passing, let us note that even G.H. von Wright attributes to deontic logic (from the period of *Norm and Action*, i.e., from the early 1960s) the status, which he defines as "hybrid" – *see idem*, 'Deontic Logic: A Personal View', *op. cit.*, p. 32. The Finnish philosopher has in mind that the deontic systems created by him were applicable not only in relation to (descriptively interpreted) norm propositions, but also to the norms that are prescriptive.

[174] *Cf.* Chap. 6, pp. 230–231. Yet, it should be recalled that according to Kelsen, *Rechtssätze* do possess a truth-value, which in light of the pragmatic analysis undertaken here, turns out to be partially incorrect – only some of the juristic validity utterances can be characterised in this way.

[175] *Cf. supra*, Chap. 7, pp. 282–284.

[176] On the textual and ordering juristic concepts, *cf. supra*, pp. 361–363.

[177] Perhaps it would be less speculative to provide an alternative explanation of the genesis of "modally fused" juristic utterances, which ignores the ontological aspect and is grounded in the description of relations between law and morality based on the distinction of internal, committed, detached and external juristic statements – for more on these categories *see* Chap. 6 at pp. 228–234.

no longer play the role of the mirror, but they act as a reflector, thus illuminating the world of legal phenomena.[178] We approve the idea that was the inspiration for the quoted metaphor due to the fact that it corresponds to the postpositivist vision of the law we strive to present here.

8.3 Logical Redundancy of Purely Normative Utterances Concerning the Validity of Norms

It is not disputed that from a pragmatic point of view many utterances about the validity of legal norms can be characterised as directive utterances (directives). Legal dogmatists can recommend or postulate that the law-enforcement authorities should recognise a certain norm of the statutory law as valid or invalid, the citizens seeking legal advice may ask questions about whether a certain norm is valid, whereas lawyers may advise their clients to treat a given legal norm as valid.[179] Yet, can positive or negative validity utterances ("Norm N is valid", "Norm N is not valid" etc.) also be regarded as purely normative utterances; that is, expressing the norms rather than just being recommendations, guidelines, instructions or advice? It seems advisable to discuss this problem not only because it will supplement the previous pragmatic analysis of the juristic validity utterances, but also on account of the fact that it will constitute a useful introduction to the criticism of the normative conceptions of legal validity that will be presented in the next subsection.

The first problem that has to be solved will assume the form of the following question: Can juristic validity utterances be recognised (in some context of verbal social communication) as legal norms? Let us begin with a fairly obvious observation, concerning the question as to whether the potential authors of validity utterances have a legal competence in norm-making.[180] In order not to unnecessarily complicate further discussions, let us assume—without proof—that the dogmatists of law, attorneys, prosecutors, legal counsellors or legal advisers do not have such competence. Thus, their validity utterances cannot be seen as creating or repealing valid legal norms. The only group of lawyers that can possibly be attributed with the norm-making competence in the system-type of statutory law are judges, in particular, the judges of the supreme courts and constitutional courts. As already indicated,[181] we do not intend to analyse the disputable problem of the lawmaking activity of courts in the continental system-type of statutory law. Yet,

[178] V. Villa, 'Legal Theory and Value Judgments', *op. cit.*, p. 469.

[179] The indicated speech acts (recommendations, proposals, questions and advice) belong to the pragmatic category of directives, since they have a suggestive (influential) function, which is their defining feature.

[180] For more on the concept of norm-making competence *see* the references cited *infra*, note 303 at p. 430.

[181] *Cf. supra*, note 140 at p. 389.

for the purposes of the current analysis, it seems reasonable to assume that the judges in such a legal system-type do sometimes create the so-called case law, otherwise further analysis of the issue at hand would become completely pointless for we would simply have to state that juristic utterances about the validity of norms can never be recognised as legal norms. It is obvious that it would be an apparent, rather than a real solution.

Let us consider the following example. The court, when confronted in the course of adjudication with a legal gap, formulates an abstract legal norm having the nature of a "normative novelty",[182] which is subsequently referred to as "valid" in the court's justification of the ruling. When analysing this example, it should first be noted that the positive validity utterance that we are dealing with, cannot be regarded as a legal norm due to the fact that the utterance "The norm is valid" prescribes neither the addressee and circumstances nor the ought behaviour. For the purposes of analysis, the validity utterance must therefore be treated as a part of a lawmaking judicial utterance that can, for example, assume the following form: "The norm: 'In the circumstances *C*, the behaviour *B* of an addressee *A* is ordered (prohibited)' is valid".[183] There arises the question as to whether the predicate "is valid", used in this utterance, can be interpreted purely normatively, and therefore as expressing the ought of someone's certain behaviour.[184]

Before presenting the argumentation that would demonstrate the redundancy of purely normative utterances about the validity of norms, we shall extend our analysis. Let us pose the second, more general question: Can juristic validity utterances be, in fact, interpreted as norms? When seeking the answer to such a question, it should be stressed that this time it concerns not only the utterances being a fragment of judicial lawmaking decisions, but any utterances about validity, and thus including those whose authors are legal dogmatists or lawyer-practitioners.[185] This question no longer deals with "legal norms", therefore we do not need to take into consideration the issue of norm-making competence in the legal sense. In order to formulate norms of conduct, it is undoubtedly sufficient to have linguistic competence, which is a natural attribute of those who use a given language. It is not possible to deny the fact that a lawyer can say: "Norm N should

[182] The concept of normative novelty was introduced by M. Zirk-Sadowski – *see idem*, 'Problem nowości normatywnej' [The Problem of Normative Novelty], *SPE* XXII, pp. 47–62, 'Tak zwana prawotwórcza decyzja sądowego stosowania prawa' [The so-called Lawmaking Decision of the Judicial Application of Law], *SP* 1–2 (1980), pp. 255ff. and 'Precedens a tzw. decyzja prawotwórcza' [The Precedent and the so-called Lawmaking Decision], *PiP* 6 (1980), pp. 74ff.

[183] This example is adjusted to the Poznań concept of legal norm, adapted in our clarificative analysis.

[184] Let us note that in the context of the purpose of our clarificative analysis, it is completely irrelevant whether we are dealing here with a behaviour prescribed by the norm which we recognise as valid or with any other behaviour. Nonetheless, in the further analysis, we will focus on the first possibility, because it is far more important from the jurisprudential point of view.

[185] Naturally, this also includes judicial validity utterances that do not have a lawmaking character, contained in the justifications of judicial decisions.

be observed" or "The application of norm N is obligatory". It nevertheless remains an open question as to whether these utterances have any sense from a legal point of view and, if so, then what.

In Chap. 4, when examining the possible justification of Alexy's transcendental-pragmatic argument, we have allowed the possibility of combining modal with deontic operators.[186] From the logical point of view, now it seems necessary to consider whether the iteration of normative operators is sensible. It is the case due to the fact that if we wanted to recognise a purely normative nature of validity utterances, then the utterance: "The norm: 'In the circumstances *C*, the behaviour *B* of an addressee *A* is obligatory' is valid" should be—at least at first glance—logically interpreted in the form of O(O*p*),[187] regardless of whether its author is a judge (the author of a legal precedent), a legal dogmatist or a practicing lawyer who expresses her/his opinion on the validity of this norm.

We shall now proceed to present the key argument, which will aim to demonstrate the redundancy (from a legal point of view) of purely normative utterances about the validity of legal norms. In other words, we will try to demonstrate that the validity utterances should not be interpreted normatively; namely, in the form of any orders or prohibitions that are legally relevant. This argument has been formulated by Alf Ross in the context of the criticism of Hans Kelsen's normative conception of legal validity and was used by Ross to show that, in effect, Kelsen is a *quasi*-positivist.[188] According to Ross, we cannot grasp the concept of legal validity in such a way that it stands for a legal duty to obey the law on account of the following reasoning[189]:

1. It is said that the "validity" or "binding force" of law means the duty to obey the law. What kind of duty do we have in mind here?
2. A duty is always a duty to behave in a certain way—for example, the duty to pay a debt.
3. So, what does the duty to obey the law consist of? It does not prescribe any behaviour that is not already prescribed by the law itself.
4. It follows that the duty to obey the law has to mean a duty that does not have a legal, but an extra-legal character; for example, a moral one. It can be demonstrated by the following argument:

   4.1. The norm: "The debtor is obligated to pay the debt" is valid,

[186] *See* Chap. 4, pp. 95ff.

[187] The formula O(O*p*) thus reads as follows: "It is obligatory that is it obligatory that *p*". It has to be stressed that in the course of the foregoing analysis the phrases "is obligatory" are both to be prescriptively interpreted.

[188] A. Ross, 'Validity and the Conflict between Legal Positivism and Natural Law', *op. cit.*, pp. 62ff. *Cf. idem, Directives and Norms, op. cit.*, pp. 156–157, where Ross formulates his argument in a condensed way.

[189] Ross's original reasoning is reconstructed and slightly modified.

4.2. Since this norm is valid, so—according to thesis (1)—the debtors (i.e., the addressees of this norm) have a duty to obey the norm "The debtor is obligated to pay the debt",

4.3. Therefore, the debtors are obligated to be obligated to pay the debt (alternatively: "they have the duty to have the duty to pay the debt"—which sounds even more absurd),

4.4. At this point Ross raises the crucial question: "What, then, is the meaning of saying that the individuals ought to do what they ought to do?".[190]

5. Thus, Kelsen, who defines "validity" by means of the ought of the individuals to behave as the norm stipulates, is a *quasi*-positivist.

We are not interested in the last point of the above reasoning,[191] but in the consequences of Ross's argument concerning the redundancy of iterated legal duties (obligations) in relation to the question of the legal normativity of positive validity utterances. It seems obvious that such utterances cannot be purely normative, because in such cases their authors would make the above-mentioned error, since they would *praeter necessitatem* multiply legal obligations. Therefore, if we accept the presented Ross argument, then the purely normative interpretation of juristic validity utterances is excluded because the iteration of a normative operator is utterly redundant from the legal point of view.

Let us return for a moment to the previously proposed formalisation of the utterance "The norm: 'In the circumstances *C*, the behaviour *B* of an addressee *A*

---

[190] A. Ross, 'Validity and the Conflict between Legal Positivism and Natural Law', *op. cit.*, p. 80.

[191] Although Ross does not pick up this topic in his criticism, it should be noted that Kelsen himself is not blameless here, because due to his statements, in which he recognised the similarity of *Grundnorm* to natural law, he undoubtedly contributed to the objection of *quasi*-positivism. For example, in the work *Natural Law Doctrine and Legal Positivism*, trans. W.H. Kraus, published as a supplement to the *General Theory of Law and State*, *op. cit.*, Kelsen firstly admits: "The basic norm is not valid because it has been created in a certain way, but its validity is assumed by virtue of its content. It is valid, then, like a norm of natural law, apart from its merely hypothetical validity" (p. 401), and then he adds: "If one wishes to regard it as an element of a natural-law doctrine despite its renunciation of any element of material justice, very little objection can be raised..." and "[T]he theory of basic norm may be considered a natural-law doctrine in keeping with Kant's transcendental logic" (p. 437). A similar standpoint is expressed by Kelsen in his study 'Vom Geltungsgrund des Rechts', *op. cit.*, p. 165, where he acknowledges a "certain similarity" (*gewisse Ähnlichkeit*) between natural-law doctrine and the pure theory of law; namely, that the theory of the validity of positive law in *Reine Rechtslehre* can only be justified by means of a norm that is no longer a positive norm. Leaving aside much more numerous fragments of Kelsen's studies, in which he explicitly rejects the natural-law interpretation of *Grundnorm*, thus highlighting the fallacy of natural law (for more on this issue *see e.g.*, J. Raz, 'Kelsen's Theory of the Basic Norm', *op cit.*, pp. 129ff.), it should be clarified that a decisive counterargument against attributing a natural law character to his theory of *Grundnorm* lies in the fact that this norm does not constitute a category of practical philosophy, but the transcendental-logical category and, thus – as aptly noted by Neumann – it "constitutes the normativity of law in the sense of deontic thinking, which is opposed to the form of thinking about what exists; yet it does not oblige the citizen or a judge – in the moral or specifically legal sense – to a certain behaviour" – *idem*, 'Problem obowiązywania prawa', *op. cit.*, pp. 39–40.

is ordered (prohibited)' is valid" in the form of $O(Op)$. Ross's argument shows that this utterance will become reasonable only when we differentiate the concept of duty (obligation)—occurring twice in its content—which can be expressed by means of the following logical formula: $O_X(O_L p)$, in which the normative operator O_X stands for the duty (obligation) of an extra-legal character (for example, moral, religious, praxeological or instrumental), whereas O_L stands for the duty (obligation) having a legal nature. Let us prove it via the example of a positive validity utterance made by a lawyer who is a proponent of the normative conception of legal validity and who assumes that the validity of legal norms must be understood as a duty (obligation) of their observance.[192] The reasoning is as follows:

1. A lawyer's positive validity utterance is made: "The norm N is valid".
2. Therefore, according to the normative conception of legal validity, adopted by the lawyer—the addressee of the norm N has the duty (obligation) to obey it.
3. Let us assume that the norm N prescribes that: "Everyone has the duty (obligation) to read the *Journal of Statutes* within two weeks from the date of its issuance".
4. Thus, the lawyer's utterance: "The norm N is valid" means the same as: "Everyone is obligated to be obligated to read the *Journal of Statutes* within two weeks from the date of its issuance".
5. In order for this sentence to make sense, its interpretation must rely on a distinction between two meanings of "obligation" or "duty", which can be, for example, expressed in the form of a norm: "Everyone has the moral (instrumental, religious etc.) duty (obligation) consisting in having the legal duty (obligation) to read the *Journal of Statutes* within two weeks from the date of its issuance".

The last sentence, expressing a norm, is entirely sound and reasonable. It can be seen that a lawyer's positive validity utterance: "The norm N is valid" can indeed be interpreted normatively, yet the essence of the problem lies in the fact that it cannot be legal normativity. When we interpret this utterance in the above-mentioned way, then it gets a moral, religious or any other character, but not a legal one. The lawyer's utterance: "Everyone has the moral (instrumental, religious etc.) duty (obligation) consisting in having the legal duty (obligation) to read the *Journal of Statutes* within two weeks from the date of its issuance" in fact does not stand in contradiction with adopting a morally detached and impartial point of view.[193] Yet, the fact of accepting

[192] For the sake of simplicity, hereafter we use the terms "duty" and "obligation" interchangeably.

[193] *Cf.* Chap. 6, pp. 234ff. This contradiction does not occur for at least two reasons. Firstly, let us recall that the perspective of legal research, referred to as "a morally detached point of view", does not preclude that the lawyers who formulate juristic statements about law, approve of them morally. Yet, it is hard not to notice that a purely normative (in the moral sense) method of interpreting juristic validity utterances, based on Ross's argument, strongly weighs in favour of recognising them as committed statements in Raz's sense, rather than as detached statements. Secondly, it does not seem necessary to assume – after Ross – that a legally redundant duty (obligation) of law obedience must be of a moral nature.

the possibility of an extra-legal normative interpretation of juristic validity utterances (resulting from Ross's argument) entails the consequences that can be accepted neither by the positivist nor—as I believe—by the postpositivist theory of law.[194] These consequences will be soon considered by us within the criticism of normative conceptions of validity, yet we should firstly discuss the question of the correctness of the argument presented by the author of *On Law and Justice*, that constituted the basis of the reasoning discussed above. If this argument proved incorrect, then the above analysis would also have to be deemed erroneous, and the conclusions which we intend to derive from it—unjustified.

The correctness of Alf Ross's argument about the redundancy of iterated legal duties (obligations) is confirmed—directly or indirectly—by the opinions of a number of renowned legal theorists and philosophers. What is particularly relevant and significant, is that they are expressed by the authors who are legal positivists. Let us begin this brief review by noting that in 1961—namely, the same year when Ross published the study containing the argument under discussion—*The Concept of Law* by H.L.A. Hart was published, in which the Oxford philosopher formulated a very similar objection in relation to Kelsen's theory of the basic norm.[195] When analysing the differences between the theory of *Grundnorm* and the conception of the rule of recognition, Hart expressed the view that if the constitution, which determines different sources of law, is accepted by the courts and officials of a given legal system, then its "needless reduplication" is the suggestion that there is an additional rule under which this constitution is "to be obeyed".[196] If, in a given system, there exist (i.e., is accepted) the rule of identifying valid norms, based even on an unwritten constitution, then according to Hart, speaking of "a rule that this rule be obeyed"[197] is mystifying. There is no doubt that the core of Hart's argument is identical with the essence of Ross's argumentation.

Eugenio Bulygin is the second and even hard legal positivist who already directly expresses the acceptance of Ross's argument. This doyen of modern legal positivism approves it with emphasis, thus highlighting the inconsistency of the conception of legal validity adopted by Kelsen, which is based on the concept of binding force (*obligatoriedad*), with Kelsen's positivist program of *Reine Rechtslehre*.[198] According to Bulygin, in order to ensure the consistency of a pure theory of law, one should either replace the idea of the basic norm with true principles and norms (which entails breaking with the positivism and accepting a

[194] *Cf. infra*, argument A–XIV presented at pp. 414–415. For the record, let us note that sometimes one can encounter the thesis about the possibility of reconciling the moral character of the propositions about law with legal positivism – *see e.g.*, N.E. Simmonds, 'The Nature of Propositions of Law', *op. cit.*, pp. 97ff.

[195] Let us add that both of the cited works demonstrate that Ross and Hart quite independently reached very similar conclusions about *Grundnorm* theory, which naturally strengthens the presumption of their correctness.

[196] H.L.A. Hart, *The Concept of Law*, *op. cit.*, p. 246, a note to p. 97.

[197] *Ibidem.*

[198] E. Bulygin, '¿Está (parte de) la filosofía del Derecho basada en un error?', *op. cit.*, pp. 18–19.

certain form of natural law theory) or give up the idea of normative validity (and thus remain a positivist).[199] For, as the Argentine philosopher believes, the validity understood as the binding force turns out to be a void (*vacuo*) concept, unless we interpret it in terms of moral validity.[200]

Pablo Navarro infers similar consequences from Ross's argument.[201] Navarro stresses that, in light of this argument, a legal obligation to obey a certain legal norm is "utterly redundant" (*completamente redundante*) and he concludes that the normative concept of validity cannot be accepted by a coherent positivism. As he concludes: "Attributing binding force (*fuerza vinculante*) to norms seems to be responsible for the crisis of the positivist program".[202] In turn, Jan-Reinard Sieckmann claims—quite independently from Ross's argument—that the concept of legal validity, having a genuinely normative sense, does not allow a reasonable question as to whether one ought to obey or apply a given norm, which is, in that sense, valid.[203]

As far as I know, Ross's argument about the redundancy of iterated legal obligations has not yet been analysed in the Polish jurisprudential literature. One can only note that a similar argumentative motif can be found in Zdzisław Ziemba's criticism of Wiesław Lang's normative conception of validity[204] and in Paweł Grabowski's study devoted to the phenomena of metalinguistics and metanormativity in legal language.[205] This does not mean, nonetheless, that the essence of this argument is unknown. On the contrary, it is even manifested in the Polish positive law. Accordingly, Paragraph 4 Section 4 of the *Principles of Legislative Technique*[206] reads as follows:

> The statute shall not contain the provisions that order the application of other normative acts ...";

whereas Paragraph 11 states that:

> The statute shall not contain the utterances which do not serve the purpose of expressing legal norms, in particular appeals, demands, recommendations, warnings and justifications of formulated norms.

---

[199] E. Bulygin, 'An Antinomy in Kelsen's Pure Theory of Law', *op. cit.*, pp. 43–44. Let us add that in his later study, '¿Está (parte de) la filosofía del Derecho basada en un error?', *op. cit.*, pp. 19ff., Bulygin proposed the interpretation of the normative validity of law in accordance with his own conception of legal validity – understood as the applicability of legal norms, which has already been analysed in Chap. 7 at pp. 321–334.

[200] E. Bulygin, '¿Está (parte de) la filosofía del Derecho basada en un error?', *op. cit.*, p. 19.

[201] P.E. Navarro, 'Tensiones conceptuales en el positivismo jurídico', *op. cit.*, pp. 146ff.

[202] *Ibidem*, p. 148.

[203] J.-R. Sieckmann, 'Basic Rights in the Model of Principles', *ARSP* Bh. 67 (1997), p. 30.

[204] Z. Ziemba, 'Zwrot "norma *N* obowiązuje" w języku prawnym i prawniczym', *op. cit.* We will use Ziemba's argumentation in the course of the critical analysis of normative conceptions of legal validity – *see infra*, pp. 418ff., in particular, the argument A–XVI.

[205] *Cf. infra*, note 225 at p. 410.

[206] *Zasady techniki prawodawczej. Załącznik do Rozporządzenia Prezesa Rady Ministrów z dnia 20 czerwca 2002 r. w sprawie "Zasad techniki prawodawczej"* [Principles of Legislative Technique. Annex to the Regulation of the Prime Minister of 20 June 2002 on "Principles of Legislative Technique"], published in *Dziennik Ustaw* [Journal of Statutes] 2002, No. 100, Item 908.

As previously noted,[207] when commenting on these provisions, Sławomira Wronkowska and Maciej Zieliński formulate the thesis about the normative redundancy of legal precepts, which prescribe the application or implementation of the norms contained in valid lawmaking acts.[208] This thesis undoubtedly coincides in its substance with the reasoning contained in Ross's argumentation. When discussing the quoted Paragraph 11 of the *Principles of Legislative Technique*, the authors point out that the legal text should contain only the utterances that would serve the purpose of expressing the norms of conduct or performing conventional acts, and therefore:

> it is erroneous to include in the legal text any utterances which serve a different purpose, such as a justification of issuing given norms, encouraging their implementation, reminding that these norms ought to be obeyed,[209]

and they refer to such "additional" utterances of the legislator as "non-normative" ones. We can see that when applying a peculiar scheme of *a maiori ad minus* reasoning, it could be argued that if even the legislator should not duplicate legal obligations,[210] then it should not be done by lawyers (in particular, theorists and dogmatists of law) through the adoption of a purely normative interpretation of validity utterances. Thus, Ross's argument is supported by the views put forward by Wronkowska and Zieliński, and it has found its specific institutional confirmation in the Polish positive law.

The reported views and opinions of legal positivists, who—as it would seem—should support Kelsen's normative theory of validity rather than Ross's criticism, present strong arguments in favour of the correctness of the argument that shows the redundancy of iterating legal duties (obligations). It does not mean, nevertheless, that this argument is not questioned sometimes. A nonpositivist, Robert Alexy, comes here to Kelsen's rescue, which is not surprising if we consider the common Kantian roots of their philosophy. The German legal theoretician, when seeking the *Grundnorm* structure corresponding to the nonpositivist conception of law, questions both Hart's thesis about the "needless reduplication" of the constitution by the basic norm as well as Ross's argument about the redundancy of iterating legal obligations.[211] We are interested only in the correctness of this argument;

---

[207] *Cf.* Chap. 7, note 354 at p. 326.

[208] S. Wronkowska, M. Zieliński, *Komentarz do zasad techniki prawodawczej z dnia 20 czerwca 2002 r.*, *op. cit.*, pp. 34–35.

[209] *Ibidem*, p. 48.

[210] In the context of this discussion, there appears to be an interesting question of the normativity of Article 83 of the Polish Constitution, which states that: "Everyone has an obligation to obey the laws of the Republic of Poland". I believe that even if we accept a legal redundancy of the "obligation to obey the law" expressed by this article, one can defend the view that this provision contains a normative element, because the term "everyone" – used in its formulation – can provide an important clue to facilitating the determination of the addressees of the individual legal norms in Polish legal order. Leaving aside the question of normativity, we believe that this provision is quite reasonable, not least because of its suggestive and educational function.

[211] R. Alexy, *Begriff und Geltung des Rechts*, *op. cit.*, p. 159 [English version, pp. 98–99].

therefore, we shall confine the analysis of the defence of the basic norm theory—provided by Alexy—to the example, which, according to him, demonstrates the incorrectness of Ross's reasoning. Alexy's example is as follows.[212] The sentence:

(i) Peter told me: "You are obligated (*verpflichtet*) to give me 100 marks",

does not entail the sentence:

(ii) I am obligated to give Peter 100 marks.

It is not possible to pass from the first sentence to the second, unless we adopt the norm with the following content:

(iii) I am obligated to do what Peter says I am obligated to do.[213]

According to Alexy, such a norm is necessary in order to reach the conclusion (ii) by means of syllogistic reasoning; hence, there can be no "needless reduplication" of legal obligations.

At first glance, Alexy's counterargument seems convincing. Yet, after a deeper analysis it turns out that it is mistaken, at least when it comes to the problem of the redundancy of iterating normative operators that express legal obligations. Firstly, let us note that the major premise (iii) provided by Alexy (i.e., the basic norm of the normative system in which Peter is the norm-giver) can also be expressed in the form of the following hypothetical norm (having a conditional structure):

(iv) When Peter says that I am obligated to do something, then I am obligated to do it.

The possibility of such a formulation of the sought premise, incidentally having a more linguistically natural structure than the one proposed by Alexy, justifies the statement that any iteration of legal obligations is out of the question here. Let us recall that the core of the problem of the redundancy of iterated legal obligations lies in the fact that, according to Ross and the above-mentioned theorists of law, the utterances of metanormative structure $O(Op)$ turn out to be legally redundant or lead to iusnaturalism. It is true that the obligation to do something is mentioned twice in the norm (iv); however, for the first time it is mentioned in its antecedent (i.e., norm's hypothesis) and for the second time—in the consequent (i.e., norm's disposition). When using, for example, the formalisation of normative logic proposed by Carlos Alchourrón,[214] the sentence (iv) can be most easily presented in the form: $NxOp \rightarrow \mathbf{O}sp$, which means that "if x has ruled (issued a norm to the effect)

[212] *Ibidem*, pp. 164–165 [English version, pp. 101–102].

[213] In the original: "Ich bin verpflichtet, das zu tun, wovon Peter sagt, daß ich verpflichtet bin, es zu tun" (*ibidem*, p. 165).

[214] C.E. Alchourrón, 'Logic of Norms and Logic of Normative Propositions', *op. cit.*, pp. 245ff. We use the notation proposed by Alchourrón because of its simplicity, but it has to be added that this is a notation of deontic logic, rather than in the logic of norms, which is nonetheless irrelevant here since the provided formula does not express any iteration of obligations, regardless of how – normatively or deontically – we will interpret it.

that *p* is obligatory, then *p* is strongly obligatory".[215] In such a formula we can find no iteration of obligations (of the type O(O*p*)), and therefore the example of the norm given by Alexy does not disprove Ross's argument.

It is also doubtful whether the sentence (iii) in fact expresses the norm and it is not simply a descriptive deontic proposition. Our concerns stem from the fact that it is an utterance performed in the first person singular, so it is an autonomous norm[216] in the sense that it is addressed to oneself ("I am obligated to ..."). These doubts would be weakened if Alexy expressed his example in the second person singular ("You are obligated to ..."), but it is obvious why he did not. Juristic intuitions related to Kelsen's theory of the basic norm justify that *Grundnorm* is presupposed by lawyers, and therefore—leaving aside the transcendental aspect of its necessity—it is also an autonomous norm. If we—lawyers—want to deal with the pure theory of law, and to present law in a form of a dynamic system of valid norms, then if we agree with Kelsen, we should regard the basic norm as the foundation of our knowledge about the law. Yet, leaving aside the relations of Alexy's example with the theory of *Grundnorm* and focusing on its linguistic formulation, can we unambiguously say that we are indeed dealing with the norm? I think that it is not the case, because the sentence: "I am obligated to do what the legislator says I am obligated to do" could more clearly be interpreted as generally defining—descriptively rather than normatively—the legal situation of a man who lives in a given legal order. Furthermore, let us note that even if we assume that the utterance (iii), beginning with the words: "I am obligated to", constitutes the norm, in order for Alexy's example to be effective in relation to Ross's argument, it should also be demonstrated that the second phrase "I am obligated" is purely normative and not deontic in a descriptive sense. At this point, we revisit the fundamental problem of the iteration of legal obligations, formalised by means of normative operators.

We have so far considered the correctness of Ross's argument in the context of the views presented by other leading theorists and philosophers of law. At this point, it seems desirable to supplement our discussions with a brief analysis of the views expressed by those logicians who are, simultaneously, legal theorists. We will narrow down our considerations to three highly renowned authors.

The question of whether norms can be the content of another norm has been directly examined by Georg Henrik von Wright.[217] In his opinion, it would be more

---

[215] In Alchourrón's deontic logic (which he called "normative", but it is just a matter of terminology that is opposite to the commonly accepted one, which should not mislead us) the proposition referred to in the text follows directly from the definition of the strong obligation; that is, an obligation clearly established by some norm-giving authority. This definition is as follows: $\mathbb{O}$s = NxO, whilst one of the fundamental theorems, being a consequence of this definition, has the following form: NxO*p* ≡ $\mathbb{O}$s*p* – *cf. ibidem*, pp. 249–250.

[216] According to the taxonomy of speech acts, elaborated by J.L. Austin and amended by J.R. Searle, this norm belongs to the category of commissives, i.e. those acts "whose point is to commit the speaker ... to some future course of action" – J.R. Searle, 'A Taxonomy of Illocutionary Acts', *op. cit.*, p. 356.

[217] *See* G.H. von Wright, *Norm and Action*, *op. cit.*, p. 189.

reliable to assume that these are rather norm propositions (i.e., deontic descriptive sentences) that may be the subject of normative regulation. Although von Wright considers the issue of the norms of higher order, he does not mean the norms about norms (metanorms), but the norms concerning normative acts (actions),[218] whose existence no modern lawyer can deny—their paradigmatic instances are the norms of the norm-making competence, which determine the legislative procedure and which can undoubtedly be found in all legal systems that belong to the continental system-type of statutory law. What is more, the Finnish philosopher explicitly acknowledges that in the context of the first systems of deontic logic, which he constructed in respect of actions—namely, on the basis of the ought of the *Tun-Sollen/Dürfen* type[219]—the iteration of normative operators is not only impossible, but—as he writes—"it makes no sense".[220] As can be seen, von Wright remains faithful to the view according to which

> [the] iteration of deontic operators to form complex symbols, such as *OO* or *PO* or *O~P*, etc., does not yield meaningful results,[221]

although some types of "iterations"[222] are certainly possible; namely, in the case of the above-mentioned norms of a higher order—prescriptions, prohibitions or permissions regarding the "acts of giving (other) prescriptions".[223]

A similar standpoint on a possible subject of legal norms has been presented by Carlos Alchourrón, who, in the above-indicated study, also considers the issue—analogous to the one that interests us—of the iterability of operators in deontic logic.[224] The Argentine philosopher argues that such an iteration is possible, for example, in the case of the formula: NyONxO*p*, which he reads as follows: "y has ruled that it is obligatory for x to rule that it is obligatory that *p*".[225] It can therefore

---

[218] *Ibidem*, pp. 190ff.

[219] For more on the two types of Ought (*Sein-Sollen/Dürfen* and *Tun-Sollen/Dürfen*), distinguished by von Wright, *see infra*, pp. 439–440.

[220] Let us quote the entire sentence which was the source of this opinion: "The forbidden thing can be an action (e.g. smoking), but its being forbidden is a norm and not an action; therefore it makes no sense (in this system) to speak of the permittedness of a prohibition" – G.H. von Wright, 'Ought to be – Ought to do' in *idem*, *Six Essays in Philosophical Logic*, APhF LX (1996), p. 63.

[221] G.H. von Wright, *Norm and Action*, *op. cit.*, p. ix. It should be noted that in the first system of deontic logic developed by von Wright, the possibility of the iterability of operators is not mentioned at all – *cf. idem*, 'Deontic Logic', *Mind* 60 (1951), pp. 1–15.

[222] G.H. von Wright, *Norm and Action*, *op. cit.*, p. ix. Quotation mark in the original.

[223] *Ibidem*.

[224] *See* C.E. Alchourrón, 'Logic of Norms and Logic of Normative Propositions', *op. cit.*, pp. 263ff.

[225] *Ibidem*, p. 264. This formula naturally arouses associations with the norms of a norm-making competence, which were thoroughly examined by P. Grabowski from the perspective of their potential metanormativity – *see idem*, *O metajęzykowości i metanormatywności języka prawnego* [On Matalinguisticity and Metanormativity of Legal Language], Poznań 2001, pp. 65–76 [an unpublished manuscript of a Master's thesis]. In the context of the correctness of Ross's argument, it is worth quoting in full the passage of his work, which contains arguments consistent with the

be seen that Alchourrón subjectively relativizes deontic operators by distinguishing between the authors of respective normative propositions, which he expresses by means of the parameters x and y used in this formula. Moreover, he supplements his analyses with a comment—crucial in the context of our discussion—that the iteration of deontic modalities in the context of the acts of self-referring normation (norm-giving) is also exceptionally possible, providing that norms are not identified with orders. In such a case, in the above formula x = y, which means that someone has issued a norm that obligates him to establish a norm of a specific content. This comment, however, does not prejudge whether it is possible to iterate normative operators (being a part of prescriptive deontic sentences).[226]

Last, but not least, it is worth mentioning the views presented by Jan Woleński, who, in one of his studies devoted to the analogy between the validity of norms and the truth of propositions, provides and analyses the following utterance: "It is valid that it is prescribed that the citizens with high income pay the equalization tax".[227] Woleński considered this statement to be admissible, reserving, however, that the part that follows the phrase "it is valid that" is a deontic proposition (by which he understands it as a deontic descriptive sentence, true or false). In his opinion, the structure of such an utterance is reflected in the formula V(*D*), which means "it is valid that *D*" where *D* represents any deontic sentence.[228] Therefore, any metanormativity of this utterance is out of the question.

A comparison of the opinions presented by the experts in deontic logic is not an easy task, yet there begs the observation that they all allow the possibility of combining normative with deontic operators, which means that the subject of the norm can be expressed by means of a descriptive deontic sentence. In the context of Alexy's example that was previously analysed, we can risk saying that they would

reasoning presented by the Danish philosopher. Grabowski, while considering the possibility of interpreting the norms of norm-making competence as metanorms, provides the following objection: "It can be moreover indicated that the norm of a norm-making competence does not meet the condition imposed on the legal norms, namely it is not itself suitable to independently identify what behaviour was ordered (prohibited) to a group of subjects in specific circumstances. Treating it as the norm which prescribes the behaviour consistent with further normative acts, sounds very vague and seems to be meaningless. Accordingly, the objection that can be raised in connection thereto is that this obligation is so indetermined that such expression should be denied the character of a norm. The legal norm should allow its addressee to recognise what actually her/his duties are, while the indication that it consists in behaving in accordance with some other norms that firstly, may not be implemented into the legal system, and secondly, may not be applicable, does not explain anything" (p. 71).

[226] Especially that – as Alchourrón emphasises – we must assume a "clear distinction" between the formulas OO*p* and ONxO*p* (= O**O**s*p*), and only in reference to the latter does he add that it has "a clear meaning" – C.E. Alchourrón, 'Logic of Norms and Logic of Normative Propositions', *op. cit.*, p. 263.

[227] J. Woleński, 'Obowiązywanie a prawdziwość', *op. cit.*, p. 15. It should be noted that Woleński provides another formulation of this utterance – for those who find the quoted one to be of a blatant style: "It is valid that the payment of the equalization tax by the citizens with high income is prescribed" – *ibidem*, note 5 at p. 16.

[228] *Ibidem*, p. 16.

agree to such an interpretation, according to which the utterance: "I am obligated to do what Peter says I am obligated to do", would be understood as a norm, whose subject (the argument of a normative operator) is a descriptive deontic sentence, for example, in the following form: "It is valid that I am obligated to give 100 marks to Peter". Yet, such an interpretation means that the example provided by Alexy does not rebut Ross's argument.

Finally, the inaccuracy of Alexy's counterargument to Ross's argument can be justified on account of the distinction between the three types (ways of understanding) of a binding force (*Verbindlichkeit*) of law: the subjective, the authoritative and the objective. Using the definitions set out by Rainer Lippold,[229] we can assume that the first one—*subjektive Verbindlichkeit*—lies in the fact that the norm is subjectively binding (*verbindlich*) for the addressee when she/he recognises her/his obligation to obey it. The second—*autoritative Verbindlichket*—takes place when it is the norm-maker who recognises the norm as binding; that is, obligating its addressees to obedience. Finally, the third—*objective Verbindlichkeit*—which can also be referred to as "institutional", boils down to the fact that, regardless of the assessments of the norm-giver or of the addressees, a given legal norm has binding force. This distinction, *nota bene* closely related to Kelsen's pure theory of law,[230] can be easily intuitively understood, and it allows us to articulate the next and final objection against Alexy's argument.

First, let us note that in the sentence (i): "Peter told me: 'You are obligated to give me 100 marks'", we are dealing with the binding force in the authoritative sense. For there is no doubt that Peter—the norm-giver—recognises the addressee of his utterance to be obligated to give him 100 marks, otherwise his utterance would be defective (it would violate the pragmatic condition of sincerity). On the other hand, the sentence (ii): "I am obligated to give Peter 100 marks" expresses a subjective sense of the binding force, because in this case it is the addressee of the norm established by Peter that explicitly recognises the obligation imposed on him. This brings us to an enthymematic premise; namely, the sentence (iii): "I am obligated to do what Peter says I am obligated to do" or the sentence (iv): "When Peter says that I am obligated to do something, then I am obligated to do it". In the context of Lippold's distinction, it is obvious that, regardless of whether we accept the sentence (iii) or (iv) as the missing premise of the syllogism, a normative sense of these utterances is the same: they allow for the conversion (transformation) of the subjective obligation, as expressed by sentence (ii), into the objective obligation. This implies that the aim of sentences (iii) and (iv) is that the obligation (duty) of the norm addressee was not only subjective or authoritative, but rather objective. Sentence (iii) should therefore be interpreted in the form (iii_A): "I am *objectively*

[229] *See* R. Lippold, 'Geltung, Wirksamkeit und Verbindlichkeit von Rechtsnormen', *op. cit.*, pp. 470–471.

[230] There is a relationship with a distinction – repeatedly used by Kelsen – between the objective and the subjective sense of Ought – *cf. e.g.*, *idem*, *Reine Rechtslehre*, 2nd ed., *op. cit.*, pp. 7ff., 45ff. [English version, pp. 7ff., 44ff.], 'Vom Geltungsgrund des Rechts', *op. cit.*, pp. 161ff., and *Allgemeine Theorie der Normen*, *op. cit.*, pp. 21–22, 43–44.

obligated to do what Peter says I am *authoritatively* obligated to do" (and by analogy with respect to sentence (iv)). Such a clarification of the essence of Alexy's example justifies the conclusion that it cannot be regarded as disproving Ross's argument about the redundancy of iterating legal obligations. This example, in fact, deals with the conversion of the authoritative obligation into an objective obligation. Ross undoubtedly wanted to demonstrate that it is meaningless to iterate legal obligations, which he certainly treated as objective rather than them being of a different type.

We believe that the presented objections against Alexy's example justify the above-posed thesis of the inappropriateness of his argument in relation to the problem of the iteration of normative operators. Ross's argument about the redundancy of iterating legal obligations (duties) is therefore not only confirmed in the views of a broad range of the representatives of the positivist legal theory and deontic logicians, but it is offered a peculiar institutional support in the provisions of the Polish *Principles of Legislative Technique*. Moreover, it is not rebutted by Alexy's counterargument. When critically analysing the normative conceptions of legal validity, we shall apply Ross's argument, thus being fully convicted of its rightness. In passing, it is also worth noting that the presented analysis, based on Ross's argument, showed that the juristic validity utterances cannot be interpreted in a purely normative way (in the legal as well as juristic sense of normativity).[231]

8.3.1 Normative Concept of Legal Validity

It is time to examine the theoretical correctness and practical usefulness of the definition of legal validity, whose *definiens* is purely normative; namely, as expressed by means of the norm (a deontic sentence of a prescriptive character). If we take into consideration the normative concepts of legal validity developed by Hans Kelsen[232] and Wiesław Lang[233]—undoubtedly the most well known and widely discussed in the Polish theory of law—the model definition of validity

---

[231] It should be emphasised that this conclusion applies to all juristic validity utterances – both positive and negative, including *prima facie* normative negative utterances about validity by means of which the constitutional courts deprive legal norms of their validity. As it has already been demonstrated, such derogatory utterances have a performative nature, so they are true by definition, which excludes their purely normative interpretation – *cf. supra*, pp. 390–391.

[232] Let us recall that in Kelsen's conception, the validity, understood normatively ("Geltung *qua* Verbindlichkeit"), consists in the ought to obey the law, and in case of non-obedience, in the ought to apply the law by the competent state authorities – *cf.* the definitions of the normative validity provided by Kelsen in the *General Theory of Law and State*, *op. cit.*, p. 39, *Reine Rechtslehre*, 2nd ed., *op. cit.*, p. 196 [English version, p. 193], 'Was ist juristischer Positivismus?', *op. cit.*, p. 465 and 467, and *Allgemeine Theorie der Normen*, *op. cit.*, p. 3 and 112.

[233] According to Lang's conception, the validity of a legal norm is defined by means of a categorical metanorm (a norm about the norm). In his view, both in legal and juristic language, the phrase: "Norm N is valid" means that: "One ought to apply norm N" – *see idem*,

that will be analysed by us, will read as follows: "A norm of statutory law is valid if, and only if one ought to obey or apply it" (hereafter labelled "D_9"). Although in the jurisprudential literature there were a number of normative conceptions of legal validity,[234] we nevertheless recognise that the critical analysis of the proposed model definition will be sufficient to answer the fundamental question of whether the clarification of the juristic concept of the validity of statutory law can be such a definition whose *definiens* is purely normative and expresses the obligation (duty) of observing or applying valid legal norms.

The normative conceptions of legal validity seek to explicitly capture and express the essential element of legal normativity of the validity of law; namely, its binding force. In this respect, they show an advantage over most of the conceptions of validity examined in the previous chapter, which—perhaps apart from constructing legal validity by means of the concept of a norm's applicability[235]—do not take into account the semantic relationship existing between "validity" and "being someone's duty".[236] Although the law in many respects resembles a game of chess,[237] there is no doubt that the validity of legal norms differs considerably from the validity of rules in voluntary games. As rightly noted by Ulfrid Neumann,

> the law is, so to speak, "a compulsory game", and no one has enough liberty to put oneself outside its rules.[238]

Therefore, we believe that the definition of the juristic concept of the validity of statutory law should, to some extent, take into consideration the normative aspect of legal validity. It does not appear, however, that equating the validity with the binding force of law in the form of a purely normative concept of its validity (expressed by the model definition D_9) was an acceptable method of meeting this demand. This standpoint will be proved by the forthcoming arguments.

Let us begin by formulating two critical arguments, which constitute a direct consequence of the analysis—presented in the preceding section—of a legal redundancy of iterating legal obligations. These arguments are alternative. The first one

'Obowiązywanie normy prawnej w czasie w świetle logiki norm', *op. cit.*, p. 49 and *Obowiązywanie prawa*, *op. cit.*, pp. 158–159.

[234] *See e.g.*, E. Garzón Valdés, 'Modelle normativer Geltung', *op. cit.*, where the Spanish philosopher reconstructs and discusses the conceptions of legal validity developed by H. Kelsen, J. Austin, H.L.A. Hart and G.H. von Wright. When considering the latest theories, it is worth noting the one presented by G. Sartor, who proposes a purely normative concept of legal validity as "doxastic obligation"; i.e., an obligation of accepting the valid legal norms (rules) in legal reasoning – *see idem*, 'Legal Validity as Doxastic Obligation: From Definition to Normativity', *op. cit.* and *Legal Reasoning. A Cognitive Approach to the Law*, Dordrecht 2005, pp. 331ff.

[235] *Cf.* Chap. 7, pp. 321–334.

[236] *Cf.* Chap. 7, pp. 269–270.

[237] The comparative analysis of legal rules and rules of chess has been made by many legal theorists – *e.g.*, by Cz. Znamierowski, H.L.A. Hart, Z. Ziembiński and G.H. von Wright. In the recent literature, *see* A. Marmor, 'How Law is Like Chess', *LT* 12 (2006), pp. 347–371.

[238] U. Neumann, 'Problem obowiązywania prawa', *op. cit.*, p. 42.

(hereafter referred to as A–XIV) holds that the normative concept of legal validity, expressed by means of the definition D_9, leads to some version of natural law. The line of reasoning provided by Ross, which leads us to such a conclusion, can be expressed as: $V(Op) \equiv O(Op) \equiv O_X(O_Lp)$.[239] The justification for the accuracy of this argument has already been presented; therefore, it only remains to consider the above-formulated thesis under which such a consequence of a normative understanding of legal validity can be approved neither by the positivist nor by the postpositivist theory of law. The second argument (referred to as A–XV) provides that if we do not want to become the supporters of iusnaturalism, we need to assume—as aptly noted by Bulygin[240]—that the concept of legal validity is semantically empty: $V(Op) \equiv O(Op) \equiv Op$. While the general arguments against regarding the term "valid law" as a pleonasm have already been presented,[241] it seems desirable to revisit this point, this time in the specific context of the consequences of adopting the normative concept of legal validity as a clarification of the intension of this concept.

As regards the justification of the thesis that neither legal positivism nor postpositivist legal theory can approve the natural law consequences of the normative concept of legal validity (shown in argument A–XIV), the case seems rather simple. Positivism cannot accept such a consequence, not only because of the thesis on the separation of law and morality (which constitutes an essential or perhaps even definitional element of this doctrine),[242] but first, and foremost because of the axiologically neutral approach adopted by the positivists in relation to the problems of legal validity. Let us recall that hard (exclusive) legal positivism acknowledges the full independence of legal validity and morality, while soft (inclusive) legal positivism only allows for a contingent and extensionally restricted dependence of the validity of these two normative systems. On the other hand, a postpositivist theory of law[243]—namely, the theory which forms the basis for our reflection on the juristic concept of the validity of statutory law—cannot accept the consequences of the normative concept of legal validity that arises out of the argument A–XIV. For legal postpositivism calls for developing an axiologically detached and impartial concept of legal validity, which will be indifferent to the traditional controversy about the concept of law that takes place between legal positivism and natural law theory.[244] Although the postpositivist standpoint does not preclude that there are validity relations between law and morality, adopting the normative conception of

[239] In this reasoning, the formula $V(Op)$ means that the norm Op is valid (V); the formula $O(Op)$ means that it is obligatory that p is obligatory; whereas the formula $O_X(O_Lp)$ means (in accordance with the previous analysis of Ross's argument) that it is obligatory in a certain, most probably moral sense (O_X) that p is obligatory in legal sense (O_Lp).

[240] *Cf. supra*, note 200 at p. 406, with the corresponding text.

[241] *Cf.* Chap. 5, pp. 201–202, 207.

[242] *Cf.* Chap. 4, pp. 123–125.

[243] For more on legal postpositivism *see* Epilogue, pp. 539–541.

[244] This problem has been discussed in Chap. 5 at pp. 207–212.

legal validity and its consequences (as shown by the argument under discussion) would be tantamount to a definitional solution of the controversy between positivism and natural law theories in favour of the latter. Accordingly, that would entail negating the primary postpositivist thesis of an axiological impartiality and a peculiarly detached approach to the law, which constitute the characteristic feature of the postpositivist concept of the validity of statutory law.

When it comes to the argument A–XV, it is worth pointing out Riccardo Guastini's logico-linguistic analysis of the concept of legal validity,[245] which has demonstrated that—from the positivist point of view—the sentences which can be symbolically formalised as: V(O*p*), O(O*p*) and O*p*, are logically equivalent. Naturally, their equivalence results from the fact that the Italian theorist implicitly assumes the redundancy of the iteration of deontic operators,[246] which express legal obligations (duties). In passing, let us add that similar conclusions can be drawn from the interpretations of some of the definitions of the normative concept of legal validity ("Geltung *qua* Verbindlichkeit"), formulated by Kelsen. Let us consider a typical definition, taken from his *General Theory of Law and State*: "Validity of law means that the legal norms are binding, that men ought to behave as the legal norms prescribe, that men ought to obey and apply the legal norms".[247] It seems that as far as the last sentence of this definition expresses a metanorm O (O*p*), in the case of the penultimate sentence, such an interpretation is not necessary, because it may as well be presented in the form of the formula O*p*.[248]

In his analysis, Guastini rightly points out that the logical equivalence of the sentences V(O*p*) and O*p* is incompatible with common juristic linguistic intuitions.[249] First of all, the sentence V(O*p*): "The norm 'It is obligatory that p' is valid" is the sentence about a norm, whereas the sentence O*p*: "It is obligatory

[245] *See* R. Guastini, '"Sollsätze". An Exercise in Hard Legal Positivism', *RT* 31 (2000), pp. 188ff.

[246] In Guastini's analysis, these are deontic and not normative operators, which is, however, irrelevant here, because they are still subject to reduction, indicated by him.

[247] H. Kelsen, *General Theory of Law and State*, *op. cit.*, p. 39.

[248] A similar interpretation seems to be acceptable in relation to the definition of the validity of a legal norm provided by Kelsen in *Reine Rechtslehre*, 2nd ed., *op. cit.*, p. 196 [English version, p. 193]: "Daß eine sich auf das Verhalten eines Menschen beziehende Norm 'gilt', bedeutet, daß sie verbindlich ist, daß sich der Mensch in der von der Norm bestimmten Weise verhalten soll". Here, on the other hand, the penultimate sentence seems to be of a metanormative character O(O*p*), while the last sentence – only of a normative one: O*p*. At this point, we need to clarify a certain doubt that may arise in relation to Kelsen's normative concept of legal validity, which is associated with the fact that he did not accept the "operational" standpoint on the extension of legal utterances, which can be attributed with a truth-oriented character (we touched upon this issue *supra*, at pp. 384ff.). The author of normativism emphasised that juristic utterances about validity (like other *Rechtssätze*) are true or false – *cf. e.g.*, *Allgemeine Theorie der Normen*, *op. cit.*, p. 177. This may arouse some doubts as to whether his conception of legal validity is indeed purely normative. Yet, such doubts are unfounded, since Kelsen repeatedly emphasised that the validity (*Geltung*) belongs to the realm of *Sollen*, and not of *Sein* – *see e.g.*, *Reine Rechtslehre*, 2nd ed., *op. cit.*, p. 10 [English version, p. 10] and 'Was ist juristischer Positivismus?', *op. cit.*, p. 467.

[249] *See* R. Guastini, '"Sollsätze". 'An Exercise in Hard Legal Positivism', *op. cit.*, p. 187.

that p", according to Guastini, "looks like the norm itself"[250]; therefore, it is certainly not a statement about a norm. Secondly, the sentence V(O*p*) attributes the feature of validity to a given norm (having a certain content O*p*, but this content is completely irrelevant, because this sentence can, in addition, only indicate the name of the norm: V(N)), whereas the sentence O*p* does not provide any information about the norm (as such) but it merely repeats (quotes) its content. Following this line of reasoning, it is easy to notice that the normative conception of legal validity, if not leading (in accordance with the A–XIV argument) to iusnaturalism, assumes the form of a deflationary conception of legal validity. The reasoning which forms the essence of the argument A–XV indeed shows that the concept of legal validity becomes semantically empty, which proves that this conception reduces itself *ad absurdum*. It is also crucial that in the context of the assumed purposes of the clarification of the juristic concept of the validity of statutory law, and in particular from the perspective of the requirement of its practical usefulness in solving validity problems, the analysed normative conception has no "intrinsic added value". If the utterance: "The norm: 'Everyone has the duty (obligation) to read the *Journal of Statutes* within two weeks from the date of its issuance' is valid" does not mean anything more than: "Everyone has the duty (obligation) to read the *Journal of Statutes* within two weeks from the date of its issuance", then such a deflationary comprehension of the intension of the juristic concept of validity is deprived of any practical value. This conclusion is confirmed indirectly by Jerzy Wróblewski, who, in his *opus magnum*, firstly states—in reference to Wiesław Lang's normative conception of legal validity—that the phrase about the validity of a norm in the juristic language used within legal practice "simply means that 'one ought to apply N'",[251] and then—when already seeking the solution to the problem of the extension ("the answer to the question of what is valid")—he constructs the criterial concepts of systemic, factual and axiological validity of law that have no substantive connection with the normative concept of legal validity.[252] Thus, we see that the semantic emptiness of the concept of validity threatens or even implies that it may become a *tû-tû* concept.[253] If lawyers who, for example, apply the criteria of systemic legal validity provided by Wróblewski, determine firstly that a certain norm is valid, and then—relying on the definition D_9—they state that this norm ought be obeyed or applied, then the concept of legal validity in fact proves useless and totally redundant, at least in the context of resolving specific problems of validity (the problem of extension).

Summing up the alternative arguments A–XIV and A–XV, and considering their implications for the clarification of the juristic concept of the validity of statutory law, it can be stated that the normative concept of legal validity cannot be accepted. The clarification of the intension of this concept in the manner proposed by this

[250] *Ibidem*.

[251] J. Wróblewski, *Sądowe stosowanie prawa*, *op. cit.*, pp. 94–95 [English version, p. 76].

[252] *See ibidem*, pp. 96ff. [English version, pp. 77ff.].

[253] *Cf.* the analysis of the "argument from *tû-tû*" in Chap. 7 at pp. 272–274.

conception in fact leads us either to natural law doctrine or to a minimalist deflationary conception of legal validity. Moreover, what weighs in favour of rejecting the normative concept of validity is the fact that we have already agreed that most of the juristic validity utterances are "modally fused"; namely, they are of a descriptive–evaluative–normative character.[254] Therefore, the attempt to provide a regulative definition of the juristic concept of the validity of statutory law, whose *definiens* would be purely normative (and more specifically, apparently metanormative) must also be criticised because of the requirement of the synonymity between the elements of such a normal definition. These conclusions also seem to justify the statement that if we wanted the sought definition to somehow include the normative element of legal validity—the binding force of law—then it should be formulated in such a way that there is no error of unnecessary multiplication (iteration) of the legal obligations. Otherwise, the arguments A–XIV and A–XV will thwart the result of the pursued clarification.

Although we believe that the uselessness of the normative concept of legal validity in clarifying the intension of the juristic concept of the validity of statutory law has already been proved, nevertheless, partly due to "theoretical caution", it seems apt to present yet another argument (referred to as A–XVI), which could additionally support such a negative opinion. It is hard to hide the fact that the previous criticism of the normative conception of legal validity is largely based on Ross's argument of the redundancy of iterating legal obligations and on highlighting the consequences of such an argument, which is deemed correct in light of the pursued analysis. The argument A–XVI, by means of which we will try to reinforce the belief in the inadequacy of the discussed conception for clarifying the juristic concept of validity, is therefore addressed primarily to those who have not yet been convinced by the current critical analysis.

This argument refers to one of the elements of the critique posed by Zdzisław Ziemba against Wiesław Lang's normative concept of legal validity.[255] According to the objection raised by Ziemba, the so-called directive of the verification of validity, introduced by Lang, is a nonsense. Lang formulates this directive as follows:

> The norm X is valid, if it is inferred from the norm Z and if the norm Z is valid.[256]

Leaving aside the aspect of terminology, related to at least a partly incorrect and extensionally chaotic application of the term "verification" by Lang,[257] we find that

[254] *Cf. supra*, pp. 380–396.

[255] *See* Z. Ziemba, 'Zwrot "norma *N* obowiązuje" w języku prawnym i prawniczym', *op. cit.*, pp. 108ff.

[256] W. Lang, *Obowiązywanie prawa*, *op. cit.*, p. 190.

[257] Lang indeed writes both about "the normative verification of validity" as well as about "the verification of the judgments that determine the validity of norms", which seems at least terminologically incorrect if we consider that he himself emphasises that these judgments are well founded or unfounded rather than true or false – *cf. ibidem*, pp. 187ff., in particular, p. 190. *Cf.* the critique of Z. Ziemba, 'Zwrot "norma *N* obowiązuje" w języku prawnym i prawniczym', *op. cit.*, pp. 108ff.

the essence of Ziemba's criticism comes down to the fact that if seemingly descriptive utterances about the validity of the norms X and Z—which are contained in this directive—are interpreted in accordance with Lang's normative conception of validity, then we obtain the following utterance:

> Apply the norm X, if the norm X is inferred from the norm Z and apply the norm Z.

Its absurdity results from the fact that although at first glance Lang's "directive of the verification of validity" appears to be a conditional proposition, whose elements are the propositions (sentences in the logical sense), the interpretation presented by Ziemba proves that it is not the case. If we express this directive having a general form: "*p*, if *q* and if *r*" in a simpler yet equivalent form: "if *q* and *r*, then *p*", we will obtain the following conditional:

> If the norm X is inferred from the norm Z and apply the norm Z (= norm Z is valid), then apply the norm X (= norm X is valid).

For Ziemba, the sentence in such a form is nonsensical primarily because in its antecedent we can find not only a description of the situation in which its addressee has to behave in a prescribed way, but also a call for the application of the norm Z, which means that that the said addressee is not able to know whether she/he has to behave in the way prescribed in its consequent ("apply the norm X").

According to my knowledge, Lang did not answer such a principled criticism posed by Ziemba. However, it can be assumed that Lang could provide the following defence against the objection of the nonsense of the proposed "directive of the verification of validity" (we leave aside the terminological aspect, which is irrelevant here). Let us note that the "inference" of the norm X from the norm Z is understood by Lang in terms of the relationship of a normatively dynamic nature that occurs between the legal basis of the norm X—namely, the norm of competence Z—and the norm X.[258] Accordingly, Lang recognises that in order to verify or justify the sentence about the validity of a given norm X, it is necessary to verify three sentences. The first one declaring that the norm X has been issued by the addressee of the norm of competence Z. The second one stating that the norm X has been issued in the way stipulated in Z. And the third sentence under which the norm of competence Z is valid.[259] There is no doubt that this line of reasoning about validity (leaving aside whether we will refer to it as "the verification of validity" or give up this unfortunate term) corresponds to the manner of justifying the validity of legal norms proposed or applied by those lawyers who recognise the dynamic relations between norms in a given legal system as essential ones. I believe that

---

It would be much easier if Lang held – just like Kelsen did – that the validity of a legal norm is unverifiable, but at most justifiable, whereas the utterances about the validity of norms can be verifiable – *cf. e.g.*, *idem*, *Allgemeine Theorie der Normen*, *op. cit.*, pp. 143–144. Although in light of the earlier pragmatic analysis of the juristic validity utterances, Kelsen's standpoint seems to be erroneous, it is at least consistent terminologically. Namely, according to him, these are the sentences in a logical sense (propositions) that are verifiable, and not metanorms, as Lang holds.

[258] *Cf.* W. Lang, *Obowiązywanie prawa*, *op. cit.*, pp. 190ff.

[259] *Ibidem*, p. 193.

many lawyers and theorists of law—even those who are not the supporters of the normative concept of validity—would tend to accept the following, unfortunately highly stereotyped reasoning in the style of traditional legal positivism: a given norm is valid, if it has been issued on the basis of the norms of norm-making competence by the thereto authorised organ (the norm-maker) and in the way prescribed by the norm of the norm-making competence. At first glance, this reasoning can be, in a simplified form, expressed by means of the following inference (wherein Op stands for the norm Z of norm-making competence, Oq—for the norm X established on the basis of the norm Z, while the symbol $\Rightarrow$ stands for the normative relation of "dynamic inference" of the lower norms (usually material ones) from the norms of a higher rank (norms of competence)):

$$\frac{\begin{array}{l}\mathrm{O}p \Rightarrow \mathrm{O}q \\ \mathrm{O}p\end{array}}{\mathrm{O}q}$$

This is how Lang could rebut Ziemba's objection, because—at least from a purely formal point of view—it is a logically correct inference of the *modus ponendo ponens* type. Consequently, it seems that the "directive of the verification of validity" can no longer be deemed nonsensical. It is worth noting that Lang—probably in anticipation of such an objection—presented a similar formula of inference, which constitutes the equivalent of "the directive of verifying the sentences that state the validity of legal norms",[260] which, due to the clarity of the provided comparisons, should be expressed in the following way (in this scheme V stands for the validity of a norm):

$$\frac{\begin{array}{l}\mathrm{V}(\mathrm{O}p) \rightarrow \mathrm{V}(\mathrm{O}q) \\ \mathrm{V}(\mathrm{O}p)\end{array}}{\mathrm{V}(\mathrm{O}q)}$$

It could seem that Lang's reasoning is entirely logically correct, whereas Ziemba's criticism is inaccurate. Yet, it is not the case. Let us note that when considering the original formulation of "the directive of the verification of validity": "The norm X is valid, if it is inferred from the norm Z and if the norm Z is valid" or in its expanded form: "If the norm X is inferred from the norm Z and apply the norm Z (= norm Z is valid), then apply the norm X (= norm X is valid)", we obtain the following scheme of inference that justifies ("verifies") the validity of legal norms:

O$p \Rightarrow$ Oq the norm X is "dynamically inferred" from the norm Z
V(Op) the norm Z is valid = apply the norm Z; i.e., O(Op)

[260] This formula reads as follows: $[(p > q) \cdot p] > q$, where the variables are replaced by "the sentences that state the validity of legal norms" – *ibidem*, p. 195. It is therefore logically equivalent to the scheme of inference presented in the text.

V(O*q*) the norm X is valid = apply the norm X; i.e., O(O*q*)

Leaving aside the question of the logical incompleteness of such an inference,[261] it can be observed that this inference scheme shows that adopting the normative conception of legal validity, combined with the dynamic (or even mixed) vision of the legal system[262] based on the relations of competence between legal norms, is incompatible with the modern juristic understanding of the legal validity phenomenon. One can risk the thesis that even the keenest followers of the pure theory of law would not accept as justified the thesis that the validity of a certain legal norm is ultimately and irrefutably determined (or justified) for the simple reason that it has been issued according to a higher norm of norm-making competence. Let us recall that even the creator of normativism—Hans Kelsen—acknowledged the effects of *desuetudo* and the influence of principles *impossibilium nulla est obligatio* and *necessitum nulla est obligatio* on the validity of legal norms.[263] He also stressed that the very act of issuing the norm (*Satzung einer Norm*) is only a condition (*Bedingung*), but not even the foundation (*Grund*) of its validity.[264] Thus, recognising such a condition of the validity of legal norms as being sufficient for establishing their validity is—to express it simply—absurd from the jurisprudential point of view.[265] It is worth recalling that the analysis of a combined, model nonpositivist definition of legal validity also showed that this is even not a *conditio sine qua non*, at least if our discussions concern the problem of the intension of the juristic concept of legal validity.[266]

---

[261] Let us note here the lack of a clear justification that the validity of the norm of competence Z implies the validity of the norm X; that is, the norm established on the basis and in accordance with Z. If we wanted to express such a missing premise, for example by means of the proposition: V(O*p*) → V(O*q*), then in order to obtain the logical correctness of the presented reasoning, we would have to prove that this premise is true, whereas undoubtedly this is not the case, as proved by the reasons presented in the text.

[262] For more *see e.g.*, K. Opałek, 'Statisches und dynamisches Normensystem' in H. Mayer (ed.), *Staatsrecht in Theorie und Praxis. Festschrift für Robert Walter zum 60. Geburtstag*, Wien 1991, pp. 507–518.

[263] *Cf.* Chap. 7, pp. 301–304.

[264] *Cf.* H. Kelsen, *Allgemeine Theorie der Normen*, *op. cit.*, pp. 136 and 144. Let us add that according to Kelsen, there never exists any "absolute guarantee" that the lower norm will correspond to a higher one which determines the creation and the contents of the former – *cf. idem*, *General Theory of Law and State*, *op. cit.*, pp. 154–155, and – in the context of law application – that the validity of a lower (individual) norm is not deduced from the validity of a higher (general) norm – *cf. idem*, *Allgemeine Theorie der Normen*, *op. cit.*, pp. 185ff. For more on this issue *see* L. Gianformaggio, 'Hans Kelsen on the Deduction of Validity', *RT* 21 (1990), pp. 198ff.

[265] Although it is obvious, let us note the fact that many legal norms are recognised by the constitutional courts as invalid, even though they have been established by the competent authority and under the proper, legally prescribed legislative procedure.

[266] *Cf.* Chap. 7, pp. 351–354.

When we summarise the argument A–XVI, it turns out that the fact of adopting the normative concept of legal validity leads to a definitely inaccurate clarification of the intension of the juristic concept of the validity of statutory law. This comes to light when we want to apply this conception to solve the problem of the extension of this concept and, in particular, to justify the validity of individual legal norms. Having also considered the previous pair of alternative arguments, A–XIV and A–XV, based on the thesis of the redundancy of iterating legal obligations (duties), we come to the conclusion that the conception analysed in this section must be rejected. We therefore should still pursue the clarificative analysis, since the normative conception of legal validity—being the last on our list to discuss—also proved to be unsatisfactory, which means that it is theoretically incorrect as well as useless in legal practice. Yet, it should be noted that during the analysis, we decided that the regulative definition of the juristic concept of the validity of statutory law, which we are attempting to find out, should in some way express the element of the normativity of legal validity, related to the binding force of law. It is yet another valuable hint which we will soon make use of.

8.4 The Legal Situation and the Pragmatic Approach to Law

After having analysed the juristic validity utterances and having demonstrated the inadequacies of the normative conception of legal validity, we shall come back to the main course of clarificative analysis. We will now present a list of primitive concepts, which will serve to clarify the intension of the juristic concept of the validity of statutory law, and will apply the model of analysis proposed by Peter Strawson, which consists in looking for the connections between these concepts.[267]

Previous considerations, and in particular the criticism of the most widespread jurisprudential conceptions of legal validity, weigh in favour of the fact that we should not apply the following concepts: the membership of norms in a legal system, the application or applicability of norms and the observance or efficacy of norms.[268] Although, theoretically speaking, it is possible that these concepts (or at least some of them) could constitute "a system of connected concepts" within Strawson's methodological conception, the analysis of some combined approaches of legal validity proves[269] that it would be very risky. Therefore, we will not make use of these concepts. Conversely, we will offer yet another concept, which, we believe, will be less controversial, and which will possibly allow us to minimise the arbitrariness of the developed conception of the validity of statutory law. When making a selection of these concepts, we will avail ourselves of the assumed goals of clarification; in particular, we will take into account not only the requirement of

[267] *Cf. supra*, pp. 365–367.
[268] *Cf.* Chap. 7, pp. 271–343.
[269] *Cf.* Chap. 7, pp. 344–349.

jurisprudential correctness but also that of the practical usefulness of the conception of validity in solving specific problems of validity (the "intrinsic added value" of clarification).

The first concept, the choice of which requires no justification, is the juristic concept of the validity of statutory law, which is subject to clarification. The second one will be the semantic concept of legal norm, developed in the Poznań school of jurisprudence and already adapted to the needs of our clarificative analysis. The choice of this concept has already been justified, so we do not have to repeat the reasons why we did so.[270] The third concept will be the concept of legal situation. Its choice, dictated—as we believe—by the necessary conceptual relations between this concept and the juristic concept of the validity of statutory law, will be justified in the first subsection below. The fourth component of our conceptual network will be the pragmatic concept of legal norm, which will prove to be very helpful in expressing the element of the normativity of legal validity (its binding force) in the regulative definition of the juristic concept of the validity of statutory law that we are going to propose. Its application will be justified in detail in the second subsection. Finally, the fifth element of the system of connected concepts will consist in the distinction between the norms of action and the norms of end, closely related to the pragmatic concept of norm, which will also be manifested in the *definiens* of the postpositivist definition of legal validity.[271]

When using the graphic scheme of the relations between the legal and juristic concepts, developed by Dietmar von der Pfordten,[272] the proposed system of connected concepts, which will constitute the basis for the clarification of the juristic concept of the validity of statutory law, can be presented in the form of the following scheme (see Fig. 8.1 on the next page).

In this scheme, the dashed lines, additionally marked with the character—(minus sign),[273] symbolise the differences between the concepts linked by them, while the solid lines indicate the existence of conceptual connections, which are additionally characterised by the modal categories of possibility ◇ or necessity □. It should be noted that in order to preserve the clarity of the above scheme, we have left aside a number of relations both between the rejected concepts as well as between those which we will use when formulating the regulative definition of the juristic concept of the validity of statutory law.

---

[270] *Cf.* Chap. 6, pp. 245–246.

[271] For editorial reasons, the content of this distinction and the reasons for including it in the system of connected concepts will be presented *infra* in the final part of the forthcoming Section 5, at pp. 438–440.

[272] *See* D. von der Pfordten, 'Zum Verhältnis von Begriffen, insbesondere im Recht' in B. Schünemann *et al.* (eds.), *Gerechtigkeitswissenschaft – Kolloquium aus Anlass des 70. Geburtstages von Lothar Philipps*, Berlin 2005, pp. 215ff.

[273] In the original graphic presentation, proposed by D. von der Pfordten, the differences between the concepts are expressed by means of a vertical character | (and not, as in the above diagram, a horizontal minus sign), for example "A | B" represents the difference between the general concepts A and B.

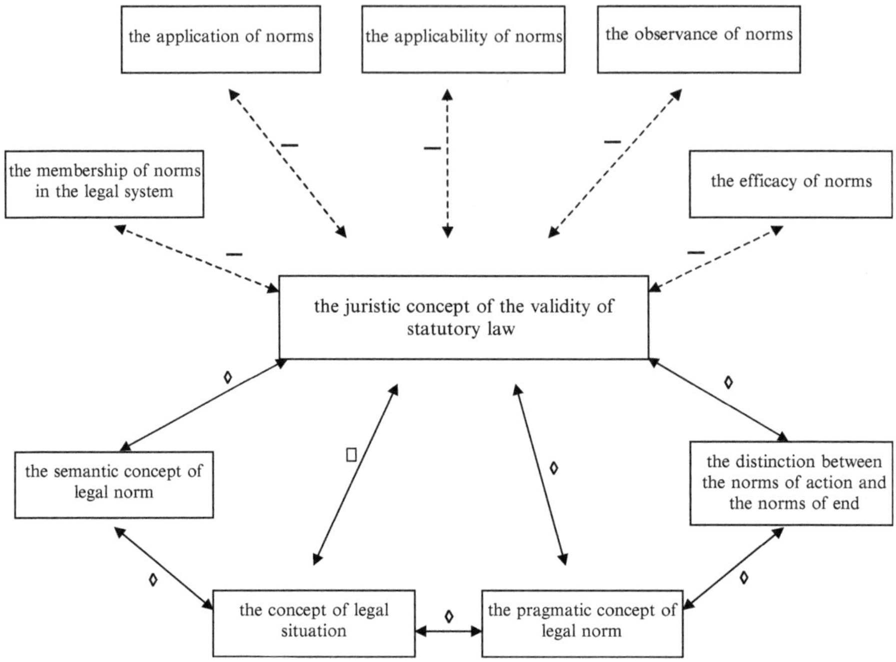

Fig. 8.1 The set of concepts related to the juristic concept of the validity of statutory law

8.4.1 The Concept of Legal Situation

The concept of legal situation is of paramount importance in clarifying the intension of the juristic concept of the validity of statutory law. It underpins the pursued postpositivist conception of legal validity primarily on account of the fact that it is the only concept which belongs to the proposed system of connected concepts, whose relationship with the concept of the validity of statutory norms is necessary. In short, the basic intuition that justifies such a perception of the role of the concept of legal situation lies in the very simple and—as it would seem—uncontroversial recognition of the inseparable conceptual interrelation between this concept and the concept of valid law. This interrelation boils down to the fact that these are the valid legal norms that constitute (create) the legal situation, and therefore—by converting this statement—we can almost tautologically assume that if any legal situation takes place, then we have to deal with valid legal norms.

The concept of legal situation, which we will use in order to formulate the regulative definition of the juristic concept of the validity of statutory law, has been coined in the modern theory of law by Sławomira Wronkowska.[274] She defined the

[274] *See* S. Wronkowska, *Analiza pojęcia prawa podmiotowego* [Analysis of the Concept of Subjective Right] Poznań 1973, pp. 17ff. *Cf. eadem*, *Podstawowe pojęcia prawa i prawoznawstwa*, *op. cit.*, pp. 163ff.

legal situation of a certain subject (person) as a situation characterised by the interrelation of four elements[275]:

1. The subject or subjects with specific properties,
2. The behaviour or type of behaviour of these subjects in certain circumstances,
3. The considered system of legal norms, and
4. The qualification of the behaviour of these subjects under certain circumstances, on account of the norms of the considered legal system S.[276]

The third element provided by Wronkowska is most crucial in the context of constructing the system of connected concepts that serve the purpose of clarifying the concept of validity. There is no doubt that "the considered system of legal norms" consists of currently valid norms,[277] which confirms the above intuition about the immanent interrelation of the concepts of the legal situation and legal validity.

Wronkowska distinguishes between the basic and derivative legal situations, as well as simple and complex ones.[278] What is at the core of our interest here is the so-called basic legal situation of the subject, which is always determined by the primary normative modalities; namely, the modalities of the actions performed by this subject, the most crucial of which are the orders or the prohibitions of a certain behaviour that constitutes the obligations of the subject in such a situation.[279] It is worth noting that the author of the analysed conception defines obligation in a manner consistent with the semantic concept of legal norm developed by the Poznań school of jurisprudence. As she writes:

> The obligation of a certain behaviour is set by the legislator in the situation when it either orders or prohibits a given subject to behave in a specific manner.[280]

Unfortunately, such an approach to the basic legal situation prevents us from directly applying this concept for the purpose of elucidating the meaning of the phrase relating to the validity of statutory norms. There are two main reasons for this. Firstly, the *definiendum* of the pursued definition of the juristic concept of the validity of statutory law already refers to the semantic concept of norm developed

[275] Let us note here a certain analogy to the method of conceptual analysis that was recommended by Strawson and is used by us in the undertaken clarification.

[276] S. Wronkowska, *Analiza pojęcia prawa podmiotowego*, *op. cit.*, p. 17.

[277] As Wronkowska states: "in case of lawyers' interests, we generally deal with situations that arise for particular subjects in relation with currently valid legal norms, rather than just merely postulated norms" – *ibidem*, p. 6.

[278] *Ibidem*, pp. 19ff.

[279] In addition to the obligatory actions, Wronkowska distinguishes permissible, optional and indifferent actions – *see ibidem*, pp. 19ff. *Cf. eadem*, *Podstawowe pojęcia prawa i prawoznawstwa*, *op. cit.*, pp. 163ff.; S. Wronkowska, Z. Ziembiński, *Zarys teorii prawa*, *op. cit.*, pp. 101ff.; Z. Ziembiński, 'O aparaturze pojęciowej dotyczącej sytuacji prawnych', *op. cit.*, pp. 38ff.

[280] S. Wronkowska, M. Zieliński, *Problemy i zasady techniki redagowania tekstów prawnych*, *op. cit.*, p. 34.

by the Poznań school of jurisprudence, and therefore if its *definiens* was directly based on the same concept, it could easily result in formulating a definition that is flawed with the *idem per idem* error. Secondly, the analysis of Ross's argument about the redundancy of iterating legal obligations weighs in favour of exercising particular caution in applying the concepts of legal obligation or duty, since the error of an unnecessary multiplication of obligations can be easily made, as evidenced by the criticism of the model normative definition of legal validity.

These comments do not mean, nevertheless, that the concept of legal situation is totally useless for our clarificative analysis. The application of this concept in various jurisprudential analyses has already proved its fruitfulness,[281] and there are many reasons that weigh in favour of using this concept. We will now try to identify and briefly discuss them.

The first reason is related to one of the assumed goals of clarification; namely, the usefulness of its outcome in everyday legal practice. When we consider the cases in which lawyers use the juristic concept of the validity of law (legal norms), it turns out that very often it takes place when one determines the legal situation of the subject who is interested in getting to know her/his/its situation. It is quite natural that people who seek legal advice are primarily interested in their legal situation. The determination of the legal situation (*Rechtslage*) is considered one of the basic tasks of dogmatics of law, particularly (though probably not only) in the German legal culture.[282] The second reason is of a negative nature. The analyses carried out in the previous chapter showed that the intension of the juristic concept of the validity of statutory law cannot be clarified (or at least it has not taken place so far) by means of a definition which specifies the feature or a set of features characteristic for valid norms.[283] It indirectly proves the correctness of Hans Kelsen's views, under which the validity of a legal norm is not its feature (*Eigenschaft*) but—as he wrote—"a dynamic process",[284] as well as Jan Woleński's opinion that "the validity of norms is not their semantic property".[285] Thus, if validity is not a feature, property or an attribute of legal norm, then there naturally arises the idea to present it by means of the concept of legal situation. Finally, the third reason—due to the concept under discussion it is possible to express in the pursued definition of legal validity the normative element—is the binding force of law, which is also essential for us, as was already repeatedly noted.

At this point, it is worth recalling yet another theory that applied the concept that was very similar to the concept of legal situation developed by Wronkowska; namely, the conception of legal norm elaborated by Krzysztof Grzegorczyk and

---

[281] *See e.g.*, Z. Ziembiński, 'O aparaturze pojęciowej dotyczącej sytuacji prawnych', *op. cit.* and J. Mikołajewicz, *Prawo intertemporalne*, *op. cit.*, pp. 57ff.

[282] I rely here on U. Neumann's opinion, expressed in his unpublished lecture 'Die Bedeutung der Rechtsdogmatik in der deutschen Rechtskultur', Frankfurt am Main 2001, p. 2.

[283] *Cf. supra*, pp. 366–367 and Chap. 7, p. 355.

[284] *See* H. Kelsen, *Allgemeine Theorie der Normen*, *op. cit.*, pp. 39ff, 167ff.

[285] J. Woleński, 'Obowiązywanie a prawdziwość', *op. cit.*, p. 24.

Tomasz Gizbert-Studnicki.[286] They define the concept of legal norm as a situation that takes place when having met eight features that characterise it.[287] This theory, probably developed independently from Wronkowska's conception, allows us directly to capture the essential aspect of connection of the concept of legal situation with the normativity of law. The authors claim that the normativity of law (legal regulation) is not founded (*ne réside pas*) in the very linguistic signs (by means of which legal norms—being situations—are created), but in their specific "productive" relation to the extra-linguistic reality, which involves the possibility of creating *situations normatives* by means of these signs.[288] Leaving aside a quite insignificant difference in terminology ("legal situation"—"normative situation"), what can be perceived in this theory of norms is a considerable similarity to the conception of legal situation as developed by Wronkowska.

Due to the above arguments, it seems fully justified to introduce the concept of legal situation to the system of connected concepts on the basis of which we shall define the juristic concept of the validity of statutory law. The act of taking into account the normative aspect of the latter concept in the pursued regulative definition has to be, nevertheless, founded on a different basis, since applying, at this end, the concept of obligation (or order) raises the concerns discussed above. In order to determine the essence of—so to speak—a primary legal (normative) situation, which is determined by valid legal norms, we will use the pragmatic conception of a legal norm,[289] which will supplement the semantic conception of a legal norm developed by the Poznań school of jurisprudence and applied so far in our analyses.

8.4.2 The Pragmatic Conception of Legal Norm

Hart, in the first chapter of *The Concept of Law*, devoted to jurisprudential "persistent questions", states that:

---

[286] K. Grzegorczyk, T. Gizbert-Studnicki, 'Les rapports entre la norme et la disposition légale', *APhD* XIX (1974), pp. 243–256.

[287] In short these features are: 1. a certain sign has been issued, 2. this sign is directed to an addressee and indicates certain conduct, 3. the sign has been created in accordance with the accepted procedure, 4. the conduct indicated by the sign is classified positively or negatively, 5. the legislator associates the indicated conduct with a certain conventional effect, 6. the addressee of the sign exists, 7.-8. the indicated behaviour is neither necessary nor impossible – *ibidem*, pp. 252–253.

[288] *Ibidem*, pp. 253ff. For more on the category of the "productive use of utterances" *see* T. Gizbert-Studnicki, 'Język prawny a język prawniczy', *op. cit.*, pp. 229ff.

[289] The identification of a conceptual relation between a legal norm understood as a certain situation or an element of such a situation, and the pragmatic conception of a legal norm is naturally nothing new. Let us quote here J. Wróblewski, who wrote: "The legal norm exists as a part of a given situation whose elements are persons, their behaviour and experience. Such approach may be related to pragmatic understanding of the norm as a 'speech act', which serves a suggestive function, thus influencing the conduct of certain people" – W. Lang, J. Wróblewski, S. Zawadzki, *Teoria państwa i prawa*, *op. cit.*, p. 343.

> The most prominent general feature of law at all times and places is that its existence means that certain kinds of human conduct are no longer optional, but in *some* sense obligatory.[290]

The problem of the normativity of law, which this quote expresses in classic form, is beyond the scope of our inquiry. We are interested only in the question of how the normative element of legal validity,[291] in particular its binding force, can be properly expressed in the definition of the juristic concept of the validity of statutory law. The achievements of modern analytical theory and philosophy of law and the wide range of diverse jurisprudential conceptions undoubtedly provide a number of opportunities for presenting this element in the *definiens* of the sought definition.[292] To that purpose, we shall apply a pragmatic concept of legal norm, because we believe that the pragmatic approach to law,[293] which is much less abstract than the semantic or logical one, since it also takes into account the senders and recipients of the utterances, as well as their linguistic behaviour and reactions accompanying it, may constitute a useful supplement to traditional, largely semantic and logical jurisprudential analyses of legal norms, often neglecting their pragmatic aspect. The application of the pragmatic concept of legal norm is, to some extent, also justified by the fact that it harmonises with the pragmatic analyses of the juristic utterances about the validity of norms, which have already been carried out in this chapter. Besides, as Marek Zirk-Sadowski writes, "the principle of the primacy of pragmatics holds for all intensional languages"[294]; that is, the kind of languages to which the juristic language undoubtedly belongs.

Pragmatic approaches to analyse legal norms and to clarify their nature can quite often be encountered in the Polish theory of law.[295] Pragmatic foundations (in the

---

[290] H.L.A. Hart, *The Concept of Law*, *op. cit.*, p. 6. Italics in the original.

[291] We should add a comment – somehow obvious in the light of the previous analyses and their goals – that the problem of the normativity of law is interpreted here as the problem of explaining the use of normative concepts in validity utterances which are formulated in juristic language.

[292] There are two possibilities that are most likely to be brought to mind in this context (apart from the already discussed concept of legal situation). Firstly, one can apply the thesis on the firmness (i.e., peremptory character) of legal norms – often encountered in the Polish jurisprudential literature, and in particular in the studies of K. Opałek. According to him, in contrast to the weaker directives without a rigid influence, the legal norms leave their addressees no choice in deciding how to behave – *cf. e.g.*, K. Opałek, *Z teorii dyrektyw i norm* [On the Theory of Directives and Norms], Warszawa 1974, pp. 152ff. [German version: *Theorie der Directiven und der Normen*, Wien/New York 1986, pp. 97ff.] and K. Opałek, J. Wróblewski, *Prawo. Metodologia, filozofia, teoria prawa*, *op. cit.*, pp. 192ff. Secondly, one can rely on the conception of norms as exclusionary reasons, developed by J. Raz – *cf. e.g.*, *idem*, 'Reasons for Action, Decisions and Norms', *op. cit.*, pp. 482ff. and *Practical Reason and Norms*, *op. cit.*, pp. 35ff., 73ff., 182 ff.

[293] For more *see* M. Zirk-Sadowski, 'Rola pragmatyki w badaniach języka prawnego', *op. cit.*, and 'Legal Norm as a Pragmatic Category', *op. cit.*; A. Bator, *Użycie normy prawnej w regulacji stosunków gospodarczych*, *op. cit.*, pp. 75ff.

[294] M. Zirk-Sadowski, 'Legal Norm as a Pragmatic Category', *op. cit.*, p. 204.

[295] *Cf.* A. Grabowski, *Judicial Argumentation and Pragmatics*, *op. cit.*, pp. 87ff. When considering the international theory of law, C.E. Alchourrón's and E. Bulygin's expressive conception of norms is most similar to the pragmatic conception of norms presented below – *see iidem*, 'The Expressive Conception of Norms' in R. Hilpinen (ed.), *New Essays in Deontic Logic*, Dordrecht/

form of John L. Austin's doctrine of performatives) can be undeniably attributed to the non-linguistic conception of norms created by Jan Woleński and Kazimierz Opałek,[296] whereas the analyses of legal norms carried out by Marek Zirk-Sadowski and Andrzej Bator are of an explicitly pragmatic character.[297] Additionally, those Polish legal theorists who opt for a semantic approach to the legal norm that relies on defining norms by providing the content of expressions (or utterances) deemed as legal norms, often take up purely pragmatic issues in their studies, in particular when they consider the question of pragmatic functions performed by legal norms.[298] It follows that the pragmatic analyses can be regarded as complementary rather than competitive with respect to the semantic or even purely logical analyses of legal norms.

In order to formulate a regulative definition of the juristic concept of the validity of statutory law, we will use our own pragmatic conception of legal norm.[299] This conception is based on the model of analysing speech acts developed by John Searle,[300] and consists in identifying such pragmatic conditions which are necessary and sufficient to make a successful (in Austin's terminology—"happy") institutional (formal)[301] act of norm-making, the outcomes of which are legal norms. In formulating these conditions, I relied mostly on the achievements of the Polish theory and philosophy of law. My aim in doing so was to ensure the consistency of the developed conception with the views—expressed in the Polish jurisprudential literature—on a pragmatic aspect and function of legal norms. In particular, when formulating the essential (definitional) condition that constitutes the core of the pragmatic conception of norms, I assumed—thus following the

---

Boston/London 1981, pp. 95–124. *Cf.* O. Weinberger's interesting criticism in 'The Expressive Conception of Norms – An Impasse for the Logic of Norms', *L&Ph* 4 (1985), pp. 165–198.

[296] On the non-linguistic concept of legal norms *see e.g.*, J. Woleński, *Z zagadnień analitycznej filozofii prawa*, *op. cit.*, pp. 105ff.; K. Opałek, 'Der Dualismus der Auffassung der Normen in der Rechtswissenschaft', *op. cit.*; T. Gizbert-Studnicki, 'The Non-Linguistic Concept of Norm and Ontology' in W. Krawietz, J. Wróblewski (eds.), *Sprache, Performanz und Ontologie de Rechts. Festgabe für Kazimierz Opałek zum 75. Geburtstag*, Berlin 1993, pp. 423–434; A. Bator, *Użycie normy prawnej w regulacji stosunków gospodarczych*, *op. cit.*, pp. 97ff.

[297] M. Zirk-Sadowski, 'Legal Norm as a Pragmatic Category', *op. cit.* and A. Bator, *ibidem*, pp. 75ff.

[298] *See e.g.*, Z. Ziembiński, M. Zieliński, *Dyrektywy i sposób ich wypowiadania*, *op. cit.*, pp. 14ff. and *Uzasadnianie twierdzeń, ocen i norm w prawoznawstwie*, *op. cit.*, pp. 11ff.

[299] *Cf.* A. Grabowski, B. Naleziński, 'Kłopoty z obowiązywaniem', *op. cit.*, pp. 242ff. and A. Grabowski, 'Dylemat Jørgensena z perspektywy pragmatycznej' [The Jørgensen's Dilemma from a Pragmatic Perspective] in Z. Tobor, I. Bogucka (eds.), *Prawoznawstwo a praktyka stosowania prawa*, PNUŚ 2052 (2002), pp. 205ff.

[300] *See e.g.*, J.R. Searle, 'What is a Speech Act?' in M. Black (ed.), *Philosophy in America*, London 1965, pp. 231ff. and *Speech Acts*, *op. cit.*, pp. 54ff.

[301] For more on the conception of secondary institutional (formal) speech acts, based on the ideas of D. Wunderlich, N. MacCormick and Z. Bańkowski, *see* A. Grabowski, *Judicial Argumentation and Pragmatics*, *op. cit.*, pp. 44ff. and 'Dylemat Jørgensena z perspektywy pragmatycznej', *op. cit.*, pp. 199ff., and the references cited therein.

analyses of Maciej Zieliński and Zygmunt Ziembiński—that the dominant pragmatic function of legal norms is their suggestive function that consists in "influencing the conduct of a given subject".[302] I also used the concept of norm-making competence frequently analysed in the Polish jurisprudential literature.[303] At this point, I use the definition of "the rule of competence for symbolic activities of lawmaking", proposed by Marek Zirk-Sadowski.[304] It should be noted that the content of the essential (definitional) condition has also been determined with reference to the pragmatic analyses of foreign authors, which shall be expanded upon in a moment.

The pragmatic conception of norm is expressed by the necessary and sufficient pragmatic conditions for the successful performance of the institutional acts of norm-making, the outcome of which are legal norms. In the formulation of these conditions, *L* stands for the legislator (norm-maker), *A* represents the addressee of the norm, *B* stands for the manner of behaviour of the addressee of the norm that has been determined by this norm, whereas *G* represents the goal, whose achievement is required by a norm. And the conditions run as follows:

Preparatory conditions:

1. *A* is capable of fulfilling (implementing) the norm and *L* believes so.
2. *L* has the appropriate norm-making competence; namely, it is someone whom the higher legal norms entitles to undertake the act of norm-making.[305]

Propositional content condition:

The future and not necessary manner of behaviour *B* of the addressee *A* or the achievement of the goal *G* by the addressee *A*.

The condition of sincerity (responsibility):

L wants that *A* behaves in the manner *B* or that *A* achieves the goal *G*.

---

[302] For more on the suggestive and the similar pragmatic functions of legal norms *cf.* M. Zieliński, Z. Ziembiński, *Uzasadnianie twierdzeń, ocen i norm w prawoznawstwie*, *op. cit.*, pp. 16–17; J. Wróblewski, 'Reguły prawne w analitycznej teorii prawa', *op. cit.*, p. 14; M. Zirk-Sadowski, 'Legal Norm as a Pragmatic Category', *op. cit.*, pp. 210, 213ff.

[303] Among the notably impressive Polish literature *see e.g.*, K. Świrydowicz, *Analiza logiczna pojęcia kompetencji normodawczej*, *op. cit.*; M. Zieliński, 'Dwa nurty pojmowania "kompetencji"' [Two Trends of Understanding "Competence"] in H. Olszewski, B. Popowska (eds.), *Gospodarka. Administracja. Samorząd*, Poznań 1997, pp. 581–607; A. Bator, *Kompetencja w prawie i prawoznawstwie* [Competence in Law and Jurisprudence], AUW 2602 (2004); M. Matczak, *Kompetencja organu administracji publicznej* [Competence of the Organ of Public Administration], Kraków 2004, in particular pp. 75ff.

[304] M. Zirk-Sadowski, 'Tak zwana prawotwórcza decyzja sądowego stosowania prawa', *op. cit.*, pp. 254ff. Let us add that this rule is directly manifested in the second preparatory condition.

[305] *Cf. ibidem*, p. 254.

The essential (definitional) condition:

The act of norm-making performed by *L* counts as an attempt to persuade *A* to behave in the manner *B* or to achieve the goal *G*, which is based on *L's* norm-making competence under which *A* cannot refuse to fulfil (implement) the norm.

What proves to be of utmost importance for the clarificative analysis of the juristic concept of the validity of statutory law is the essential condition, which assumes the form of a constitutive rule and—at the same time—it provides a definition of the pragmatic concept of legal norm. This begs the following comment. The basis of the essential condition, apart from the above-mentioned borrowings from the Polish legal theoreticians (related to the concept of the suggestive function and the concept of the norms of norm-making competence) are the results of pragmatic analyses carried out by John Searle and Daniel Vanderveken, which concerned the illocutionary verbs "command" and "order".[306] What was particularly inspiring was their observation that one of the characteristics of illocutionary acts, performed by means of these verbs, is the self-commitment of the authors not to give the addressees (recipients) of such acts the "option of refusal".[307] What also proved useful in formulating the essential (definitional) condition were the analyses of the Spanish legal theoretician—Daniel González Lagier—who presented the pragmatic characteristics of the directives, also based on Searle's theory of speech acts.[308] In the essential condition, we also use the concept of the fulfilment (implementation) of norms. At this point, it should be explained that this concept is understood in relation to sanctioned norms as their observance, whereas in relation to sanctioning norms and norms of competence as their application.[309] The primary objective of applying the concept of norm fulfilment (implementation) in the formulation of the essential condition is the possibly simplest expression of the subjective scope of the pragmatic conception of legal norm, including the mentioned, diverse types of legal norms. Finally, it should be added that within the essential condition (as with the propositional content condition and sincerity condition) we assume the distinction between the norms of action and the norms of end—the fifth and final element of the system of connected

[306] *See* J.R. Searle, *Speech Acts*, *op. cit.*, p. 66 and J.R. Searle, D. Vanderveken, *Foundations of Illocutionary Logic*, *op. cit.*, pp. 37ff., 100–101, 201.

[307] J.R. Searle, D. Vanderveken, *ibidem*, p. 201. Let us note that in the above-proposed essential condition, the absence of the option of refusal is understood more broadly, since in the institutional context of creating legal norms, the self-commitment of a legislator to deny the addresses of norms the "option of refusal" is meaningless – the law mostly consists of heteronomous norms which define someone else's rather than one's own commitments (obligations). Moreover, it is obvious that the legislator may change the valid laws at any time.

[308] *See* D. González Lagier, *Acción y norma en G.H. von Wright*, *op. cit.*, p. 278ff.

[309] *Cf. e.g.*, J. Jakubowski, 'Pojęcie obowiązywania, realizacji i skuteczności normy prawnej oraz podstawy ich rozróżniania', *op. cit.*, pp. 313ff.; Z. Ziembiński, *Problemy podstawowe prawoznawstwa*, *op. cit.*, pp. 412ff.; S. Wronkowska, *Podstawowe pojęcia prawa i prawoznawstwa*, *op. cit.*, p. 120; K. Pałecki, *Prawoznawstwo – zarys wykładu*, *op. cit.*, pp. 137ff.

concepts, which helps to clarify the intension of the juristic concept of the validity of statutory law. These distinctions will be discussed in the final part of the next section.

The pragmatic conception of legal norms, and in particular the essential (definitional) condition of the institutional (formal) act of norm-making, can be treated as a pragmatic interpretation of Kazimierz Opałek's thesis about the firmness of legal norms which differentiates them from other weaker directives that do not have a firm nature.[310] When taking into consideration the semantic concept of legal norm, developed by the Poznań school of jurisprudence, which we have made use of in the course of clarificative analysis, the primary concept was undoubtedly the normative concept of an order, closely linked with the concept of legal obligation (duty).[311] In the pragmatic conception of legal norm, the element of the legal normativity of legal validity has been expressed by the concept of the lack of an option on the part of the norm's addressee to refuse its fulfilment (implementation). By doing so, we identify something that—to our mind—can be defined as "a primary legal (normative) situation", determined by the valid legal norms. This concept has been inspired by the concept of legal situation, developed by Wronkowska, and by the concept of normative situation, elaborated by Grzegorczyk and Gizbert-Studnicki. The main difference between these three concepts lies in the fact that the primary legal (normative) situation is a situation involving the minimal and, simultaneously—as we believe—the crucial element of the normativity of legal validity, usually referred to as the "binding force of law". The invitation to play chess can encounter a negative response, but when being the addressee of legal norms we may not refuse (naturally in the legal sense and not, for example, in the logical, dynamic, axiological or psychological sense[312]) to fulfil (implement) the norm. The need to use the concept of refusal in the definition of the juristic concept of the validity of statutory law also results from the fact that the above-indicated reasons[313] make it impossible to base such a definition on the concept of legal order, duty or obligation. This fact justifies the inclusion of the pragmatic concept of legal norm to the system of connected concepts, which has been established for the purposes of clarification.

[310] *Cf. supra*, note 292 at p. 426.

[311] *Cf.* S. Wronkowska, *Analiza pojęcia prawa podmiotowego*, *op. cit.*, p. 16.

[312] We refer here to the distinction between the five modal interpretations of ought-utterances, containing the modal verb "may", provided by Z. Ziembiński, *Practical Logic*, *op. cit.*, pp. 146ff.

[313] *Cf.* the arguments against the normative comprehension of legal validity, discussed *supra* at pp. 425–426.

8.5 The Regulative Definition of the Juristic Concept of the Validity of Statutory Law

We have finally reached the point at which we are able to present the result of the clarificative analysis of the juristic concept of the validity of statutory law, carried out in the second part of this work. The clarification of the intension of this concept, consisting in elucidating the meaning of the expression concerning the validity of statutory norms in juristic language, has led us to the following regulative definition, which we hereafter label as "postpositivist":

> A norm of statutory law is valid if, and only if the potential addressee of this norm does not have any legal options of refusing to behave in the way prescribed by it or to take action aimed at achieving the end determined by it.

In our opinion, this definition explains what meaning should be attributed to the juristic utterance stating that the norm of statutory law is valid (within the continental system-type of statutory law). Since this is a regulative definition, there arises the question of its proper understanding or interpretation. Jerzy Wróblewski emphasises this problem with the following words: "The attempts of definitions which regulate more or rather less precise practical usage create the risk of the misunderstandings arising from the inertia of the already existing conceptual associations which are not effectively remedied by the efforts to provide definitions".[314] Therefore, what is presented below is an "authentic interpretation" of the proposed definition, which assumes the form of a commentary to terms and expressions used in it.

A. "NORM". Due to the fact that there may arise an erroneous impression that we use here a pragmatic concept of legal norm, it should be stressed that this is not the case. We took into account the pragmatic conception of legal norm, which was crucial for us only in order to present in a maximally uncontroversial way from a jurisprudential point of view, the normative component of the validity of law (namely, its binding force) in the *definiens* of the postpositivist definition. Although this is not a descriptive but a regulative definition, we do not intend to propose any alterations of the understanding or application of the semantic concept of legal norm—still dominant in contemporary jurisprudence, and in particular, we do not intend to replace it by a pragmatic one. Thus, having also in mind the importance of making the postpositivist definition clear for lawyers who do not specialise in the theory and philosophy of law, as well as its possible practical applications, we assume that the concept of norm used in the proposed definition of the validity of statutory law is still the same concept which we used in the course of the clarificative analysis; namely, it is the concept defined by the authors of the Poznań school of legal theory. Let us recall here Maciej Zieliński's definition of legal norm under which it is "an utterance which sufficiently unambiguously orders (or

[314] J. Wróblewski, 'Metody logiczno-językowe w prawoznawstwie' [Logico-Linguistic Methods in Jurisprudence] in A. Łopatka (ed.), *Metody badania prawa*, Wrocław 1973, p. 69.

prohibits) someone (the addressee) certain behaviour in certain circumstances".[315] Finally, let us add one rather obvious remark. In the postpositivist definition of validity, we refer to the norms of statutory law, which means the abstract and general norms, rather than individual and concrete ones.

B. "STATUTORY LAW". It should be recalled that already in the Introduction we decided to narrow down the scope of our research to the problem of the validity of statutory law. By doing this, we wanted to restrict the field of inquiry so that it was possible to omit the specific problems of the validity of customary norms as well as non-positivised legal principles in the sense provided by Dworkin or Alexy. Nevertheless, the very concept of statutory law has not yet been clarified; therefore, a few words of comment seem necessary. As it was pointed out by Kazimierz Opałek, the concept of lawmaking (*Rechtssetzung*) is by no means well determined and clear.[316] We do not aim precisely to determine the intension or the extension of this concept, even more so since the role of these remarks is only to explain the terms applied in the proposed definition. We will therefore limit our remarks to the explanation of which understanding of the concept of statutory law was tacitly adopted in this research.

The statutory law is used here as a synonym of the enacted written law. There is no doubt that the paradigm, or—as Lon Fuller writes—"the prototype" of law of this kind is a legal act that assumes the form of a statute.[317] Statutory law (i.e., enacted law in the strict sense)[318] is usually the result of a unilateral lawmaking act of the competent state authority, which, in the continental legal systems, assumes the form of a statute or of executive acts (regulations, decrees, ordinances etc.). It is sometimes the case that contract law is regarded as statutory law,[319] which is nevertheless irrelevant in the context of the discussed definition. What seems much more crucial is the fact that, taking into account the earlier findings regarding the scope of the reference of the juristic concept of validity,[320] the status of statutory law norms was also attributed to the norms which are treated in a given legal culture as acknowledged consequences (inferential or interpretive) of the norms that are

---

[315] M. Zieliński, 'Współczesne problemy wykładni prawa', *op. cit.*, pp. 5–6.

[316] K. Opałek, 'Der Begriff des positiven Rechts', *op. cit.*, p. 453. A similar opinion in the context of Polish legal culture has been expressed by H. Rot and W. Gromski, 'Prawo stanowione', *op. cit.*, pp. 38ff.

[317] L.L. Fuller, *Anatomy of the Law*, *op. cit.*, p. 43. Fuller uses the term "made law" instead of "statutory law", but it does not make any difference. Similarly H. Rot, W. Gromski, *ibidem*, pp. 35–36.

[318] The concept of the enacted law in the strict sense is applied by L. Morawski, *Wstęp do prawoznawstwa*, *op. cit.*, p. 96.

[319] In Polish literature *cf. e.g.*, H. Rot, W. Gromski, 'Prawo stanowione', *op. cit.*, p. 36 and S. Wronkowska, *Podstawowe pojęcia prawa i prawoznawstwa*, *op. cit.*, pp. 21, 24ff. For more on this form of lawmaking in the context of the Polish legal order *see* T. Chauvin, 'Próba wprowadzenia do teorii umów prawotwórczych' [The Attempt of Introduction to the Theory of Lawmaking Contracts] in J. Stelmach (ed.), *Filozofia prawa wobec globalizmu*, *op. cit.*, pp. 83–90.

[320] *Cf.* Chap. 6, pp. 237–245.

directly expressed in legal texts. On the other hand, the point which can no longer be disputed—at least in the Polish legal theory—is that the norms of customary law, of case law (judge-made law) or the so-called juristic law (made by legal scholars) cannot be regarded as the norms of statutory law.[321]

It has already been pointed out that the question of whether the law created by means of international or internal public agreements belongs to the extension of the concept of statutory law remains irrelevant in the context of the proposed definition of validity. This is the case because we are dealing here with a regulative definition. Thus, the problem of a logically understood adequacy of the proposed definition is merely an apparent problem—since only descriptive definitions are subject to such a qualification. However, we do not preclude that the postpositivist definition of the juristic concept of the validity of statutory law may also prove accurate in relation to other categories of legal norms—such as norms of customary law or case law (judge-made law). If it is the case, we do not have anything against such a broader extension of the *definiendum* of the postpositivist definition of validity. Yet, it should be kept in mind that in the course of the clarificative analysis we have entirely left aside the phenomenon of the validity of the norms of non-statutory law; therefore, the issue under discussion would presumably require additional analyses and, consequently, a modified argumentation. In conclusion, it can be stated that when undertaking the clarificative analysis we have applied—probably not fully consciously—the method that resembles one of the classic methods of philosophical analysis—the argument from the ideal type.[322] We have considered that the ideal type of legal validity is the validity of statutory law norms understood in the manner clarified above.

III. "IS VALID". The meaning of this predicate cannot be explained without falling into the *circulus in definiendo* fallacy. This is the purpose of the entire proposed definition. It should yet be remembered that this definition applies to the juristic concept of the validity of statutory law, and therefore it does not deal with the validity understood morally or in any other way apart from the juristic one. In particular, this definition does not apply to the way of understanding validity in the legal language (used by legislators), which remained outside the scope of our analysis.

IV. "IF, AND ONLY IF". At this point, we shall also confine ourselves to recalling that this definitional connective (copula) should be interpreted in the sense of synonymy (the sameness of meanings) rather than via logical equivalence of the parts of a postpositivist definition.[323] Being a regulative definition, it has no truth-value. Moreover, the pragmatic analyses of the juristic validity utterances

---

[321] *See e.g.*, H. Rot, W. Gromski, 'Prawo stanowione', *op. cit.*, p. 39; L. Morawski, *Wstęp do prawoznawstwa*, *op. cit.*, pp. 97ff.; S. Wronkowska, *Podstawowe pojęcia prawa i prawoznawstwa*, *op. cit.*, pp. 24ff.

[322] For more on this method, typical for analytical philosophy *see e.g.*, J. Woleński, *Z zagadnień analitycznej filozofii prawa*, *op. cit.*, pp. 52ff.

[323] *Cf.* Chap. 7, pp. 265–267.

have already demonstrated that the expression which constitutes its *definiendum* is mostly used by lawyers to formulate utterances of the "modally fused" variety; namely, of descriptive, evaluative and normative character.[324] Therefore, the claim of logical equivalence of the parts of this definition is out of the question.

V. "THE POTENTIAL ADDRESSEE OF THE NORM". This is a very broad term. For the sake of the simplicity of the outcome of clarification, we did not use a more descriptive term, which could, for example, assume the form: "the potential addressee of the norm in the circumstances (factual or legal) clearly specified by it". Thus, the definition has completely ignored the element of legally relevant circumstances in which a legal norm is applicable. At the same time, in order to understand or to determine who should be regarded as "the potential addressee of the norm", it will be necessary to interpret the scope of the application of a given legal norm, also including—besides the circumstances indicated by the norm—the interpretation of its personal, temporal and territorial aspect. This seems to be the task of legal interpretation, which—according to the standpoint adopted in this study—precedes the validity discourse; that is, is prior to the solutions of validity questions that concern legal norms, which are the product of legal interpretation.[325]

It should be emphasised that we have in mind the potential addressee, otherwise we would encounter the factual relativisation of the juristic concept of the validity of statutory law.[326] The intension of this concept cannot in any way be conceptually linked to the occurrence or solution of a specific validity question, for example, in the context of a case concerning a given actual addressee of a norm. It seems obvious that the application of the concept of the addressee of the norm, without characterising him as a "potential" one, could be construed as restricting the use of the proposed definition in the juristic (particularly dogmatic) discourse. The representatives of legal sciences indeed consider the problems of validity *in abstracto*, and not in relation to specific legal subjects, identified by individual names, whose legal (normative) situation is also created by the valid legal norms. Naturally, the use of the term "potential" does not exclude the application of this definition in the judicial discourse, since it is difficult to deny that each real addressee of the norm is at the same time its potential addressee (leaving aside a peculiar and unique case of "jurisdictional mistakes", consisting in a flawed interpretation that wrongly indicates the addresses of legal norms). The element of "potentiality" is also important due to the fact that it helps to avoid the objections which might arise in relation to the accuracy and usefulness of applying the proposed definition in such cases in which there is no actual addressee of a given legal norm.

---

[324] *Cf. supra*, pp. 370–400. Let us add that probably the *definiens* of the postpositivist definition also has a "modally fused" status, yet this is only a speculation, which will be verified in the next chapter, devoted to the extension of the juristic concept of the validity of statutory norms.

[325] *Cf.* Chap. 6, pp. 241–242 and Chap. 7, note 130 at p. 277.

[326] Let us recall that we are dealing with the factual relativisation of validity within the conception of legal validity founded on the concept of the applicability of norms – *cf.* Chap. 7, pp. 321ff.

VI. "DOES NOT HAVE ANY LEGAL OPTIONS OF REFUSING". This fragment of the proposed definition is probably the most controversial one, while being at the same time prone to over-interpretation or misunderstanding. Let us explain first that we fully consciously apply here the concept of an option rather than, for example, the concepts of authority, competence, entitlement, permission or, ultimately, the right of refusal that are prevalent in legal and juristic language. A "legal option" is treated as a generic name, not necessarily having any legal basis in statutory law. It is directly related to a very broad understanding of law underlying the postpositivist conception of legal validity that is being developed herein. According to Marek Zirk-Sadowski's comprehension of law from a hermeneutic perspective:

> the law is never a complete object, to be studied like other natural objects around. The law "comes into being" through discourse, i.e. through communicative actions.[327]

This statement most accurately explains the manner of understanding law as adopted in this study. It is also worth recalling at this point the discursive theory of law developed by Robert Alexy, who claims that the legal system consists of a "passive side"—the legal norms (rules and principles) and "active side"—the processes of making and applying law as well as the discursive analysis of law.[328] When using yet another, classic Anglo-Saxon jurisprudential terminology introduced by legal realism, we might as well say that the concept of law, which we shall refer to in the *definiens*, consists both of "law in books" as well as of "law in action".

These statements imply that the concept of the legal options of refusing should be interpreted very broadly. This option may be grounded on the positive law (in the sense of hard legal positivism) or may have its basis, for example, in extra-legal arguments justified in the legal discourse, or even in the general practical discourse. Let us indicate, by way of example, that the option of refusing may be based on the arguments from the impossibility or necessity of norm implementation (*impossibilium nulla est obligatio* and *necessitum nulla est obligatio*), on the argument from extreme injustice (the "Radbruch formula") or on the argument from the so-called symbolic law, which often go beyond the positivist concept of law.[329] This does not naturally prejudge that the indicated arguments will prove to be the reliable reasons for such refusal.

Three points of a technical nature still remain to be clarified. Firstly, when we speak of "the legal option of refusing", we mean such a refusal that is effective (conclusive). We are therefore not concerned with a legal option of refusing, which consists in raising some legally ineffective or nonsensical validity arguments (objections). According to the provided postpositivist definition, we should thus

---

[327] M. Zirk-Sadowski, 'Rationality of Legal Discourse in Relation to Legal Ethics' in W. Krawietz *et al.* (eds.), *The Reasonable as Rational?*, *op. cit.*, p. 615. Quotation marks in the original.

[328] *Cf.* Chap. 2, p. 19, and the references cited in note 29.

[329] For more on the arguments used in validity discourse *see* Chap. 9, pp. 500–503, 521ff.

use the concept of validity for expressing our opinion on a statutory norm, according to which, in relation to such a norm, the legally conclusive option of refusal does not exist. The question as to whether this is the case is naturally entirely irrelevant here, because the clarification of the intension of the juristic concept of the validity of statutory law seeks to find the answer to the question of what it means for the norm of statutory law to be valid and not to answer the question as to whether (or, possibly, when) a given norm is valid (i.e., solving the problem of extension). The second technical question concerns the relationship between the concept of the legal option of refusing and the concept of legal system. During clarificative analysis, we have found that the juristic concept of legal validity should not be related to the legal system (usually understood as a concrete or momentary system) but to the institutional framework of a given legal system, determined by the activities of the authorities (or, more broadly, institutions), which are constituted in a given system in order to apply and enforce the law.[330] This, in turn, means that when considering the extension of the juristic concept of validity, we will assume a somehow obvious thesis that the ultimate instance in validity issues is a broadly understood judicature (courts of general jurisdiction, administrative and constitutional courts). Finally, the last technical point concerns the very concept of refusal. Although this concept appears both in the legal and juristic language (for example, we may speak of "a refusal to recognise the debt", "a refusal to testify" or "the right of first refusal"), it is important that we understand it in a manner proper for the natural language. In the context of the postpositivist definition of legal validity, "refusal" therefore stands for "lack of approval to do something".[331] Let us note, however, that such a lexical concept of refusal has already been, to some extent, modified by the above remarks.

VII. "TO BEHAVE IN THE WAY PRESCRIBED BY IT OR TO TAKE ACTION AIMED AT ACHIEVING THE END DETERMINED BY IT". In this formulation, we refer to the distinction between the norms of action and the norms of end. This distinction constitutes the fifth and final element of the system of connected concepts, which is the basis of the postpositivist definition of the juristic concept of the validity of statutory law. The analysis of the origins and the nature of this distinction shall constitute the final part of the "authentic interpretation" of the proposed definition.

Let us begin the analysis by presenting the origins of this distinction. We are not able to determine who first introduced this distinction, which is, in principle, very simple and intuitively easy to grasp for lawyers, but we can undoubtedly state whose conceptions and analyses we refer to when adapting it for the purposes of a postpositivist definition that aims at "elucidating" the intension of the juristic concept of the validity of statutory law.

---

[330] *Cf.* Chap. 7, pp. 253ff., 284ff., 333.

[331] M. Bańko, *Inny słownik języka polskiego PWN* [The *PWN*'s Different Dictionary of Polish Language], Vol. I, Warszawa 2000, p. 1113.

Firstly, this distinction has been introduced (without indicating any earlier source) by Manuel Atienza and Juan Ruiz Manero in the treatise *Las piezas del Derecho*, published in 1996.[332] In their conception, the legal theorists from Alicante relied on the two-partial concept of norm, as developed by Carlos Alchourrón and Eugenio Bulygin.[333] Following this conception, Atienza and Ruiz Manero define legal norms as utterances which capture the interrelations (*correlaciones*) occurring between two elements: generic cases (*casos genéricos*), expressed by the sets of properties of a given state of affairs and decisions (*soluciones*); that is, normative qualifications of certain conduct.[334] Then they expand this conception by arguing that the consequent of a legal norm may involve not only the qualification of a conduct, but also the deontic qualification that concerns the attainment of a certain state of affairs (*obtención de un cierto estado de cosas*). The Spanish authors proposed that the first type of norms was called "rules of action" (*reglas de acción*), while the second, "rules of end" (*reglas de fin*), and they stipulate their canonical forms[335]:

> Rules of action: "If a state of affairs X is given, then Z ought to take an action Y".
> Rules of end: "If a state of affairs X is given, then Z ought to achieve an end (a state of affairs) F".

The second conception, which we shall refer to in the analysed formulation, is the distinction—substantially similar to the one presented above—between two ways of the linguistic expression of ought (obligatoriness) and permission (permittedness). It has been presented (independently from the conception of Atienza and Ruiz Manero) by Georg Henrik von Wright in the paper *Ought to be – Ought to do*, coincidentally, also published in 1996.[336] The Finnish philosopher argues that in this distinction he refers to the long-established German terminology, according to which conceptual clusters of *Sein-Sollen/Dürfen* and *Tun-Sollen/Dürfen* stand for two ways of using the concepts of ought or permission.[337] In his opinion, in all natural languages known to him, there are phrases that express the said concepts. For instance, in English these are the phrases "ought to

[332] *See* M. Atienza, J. Ruiz Manero, *Las piezas del Derecho, op. cit.*, pp. 7ff. [English version, pp. 7ff.].

[333] What is meant here is a hyletic conception of norms presented by C.E. Alchourrón and E. Bulygin in *Normative Systems, op. cit.*, pp. 15ff., 28ff., 34ff.

[334] M. Atienza, J. Ruiz Manero, *Las piezas del Derecho, op. cit.*, pp. 7–8 [English version, pp. 6–7].

[335] *Ibidem*, pp. 180–181 [English version, pp. 178–179].

[336] *See* G.H. von Wright, 'Ought to be – Ought to do', *op. cit*, pp. 63–64, 68ff. Yet, it should be noted that von Wright used this distinction already in his earlier works – *see e.g.*, *idem*, *Norm and Action, op. cit.*, pp. 13ff. For more *see* D. González Lagier, *Acción y norma en G.H. von Wright, op. cit.*, pp. 431ff.

[337] Von Wright does not refer to any specific German sources in the analysed study, yet in the earlier treatise, *Norm and Action, op. cit.*, notes 1–2 on p. 14, he points at Nicolai Hartmann and – indirectly – at Max Scheler, whereas among the Anglo-Saxon philosophers he mentions G.E. Moore.

be" (*Sein-Sollen* type of ought) and "ought to do" (*Tun-Sollen* type of ought). Similarly, in relation to permission, we can use the phrases "may be" (*Sein-Dürfen*) and "may do" (*Tun-Dürfen*). Following this first distinction, von Wright secondly distinguishes between two types of norms (and it is at this point that his conception coincides with that of the Spanish authors); namely, between the norms of the *Sein-Sollen/Dürfen* type and of the *Tun-Sollen/Dürfen* type. He also states that the norms that belong to the former type are the primary ones (they determine the obligatory or permitted state of affairs rather than the obligatory or permitted behaviour).[338]

We believe that the comparison and more detailed discussion of the presented conceptions in the context of differentiating between the norms of action and the norms of end is useless, since a simple linguistic intuition underlying it seems obvious.[339] We assumed that the *definiens* of the proposed definition should present these two ways of determining the legal ought because there is no doubt that the disposition (consequent) of legal norms may be both the behaviour of their addressees as well as the desired states of affairs. The best example of the norms that determine the end (desired states of affairs) are the so-called programme norms in relation to which the adopted distinction between the norms of action and the norms of end has already proved cognitively useful.[340] What weighs in favour of taking such a distinction into account is also the fact that the reducibility of the ought expressed through the norms of conduct to the ought expressed by the norms of end is often questioned,[341] whereas the converse reduction is out of the question: the norms of end *ex definitione* do not determine the required manner of conduct for their addressees, leaving them with a choice of behaviour in order to achieve the indicated goal.

Due to the accuracy of the *definiens* of the proposed regulative definition, it is essential that the analysed formulation also allows for the inclusion in this definition such norms of statutory law—being, for example, legal principles in Alexy's sense—which do not directly prescribe the required behaviour but only determine the end which the addressee of the norm ought to attain. Thus, the scope of

[338] G.H. von Wright, 'Ought to be – Ought to do', *op. cit.*, p. 68.

[339] In particular, we believe that there is no risk of confusing the norms of end with the teleological norms (directives), i.e. norms in which we deal with the instrumental relation between the means and the ends. For more on teleological norms *see e.g.*, Z. Ziembiński, *Problemy podstawowe prawoznawstwa*, *op. cit.*, pp. 126ff. and T. Gizbert-Studnicki, 'Normy celowościowe a reguły konstytutywne w prawie' [Teleological Norms and Constitutive Rules in Law] in A. Bodnar *et al.* (eds.), *Prawo i polityka*, Warszawa 1988, pp. 102–112, and the references cited therein.

[340] *Cf.* T. Gizbert-Studnicki, A. Grabowski, 'Normy programowe w Konstytucji' [Programme Norms in the Constitution] in J. Trzciński (ed.), *Charakter i struktura norm konstytucji*, Warszawa 1997, pp. 101ff.

[341] *Cf. e.g.*, G.H. von Wright, 'Ought to be – Ought to do', *op. cit.*, p. 69 and J. Stelmach, B. Brożek, *Methods of Legal Reasoning*, *op. cit.*, pp. 40ff.

reference of the proposed definition is subject to a justified linguistic extension, when compared to the semantic definition of legal norm adopted so far in this study.[342]

8.6 The Overview of the Clarification of the Intension of the Juristic Concept of the Validity of Statutory Law

In Chap. 6, we identified five objectives of the clarification of the juristic concept of the validity of statutory law.[343] Although the clarification of the extension of this concept has not yet been finished, we can already consider whether these objectives were achieved when clarifying the intension of the concept under discussion.

The first purpose was such an "elucidation" of a clarified concept to make it not only accurate from the jurisprudential point of view but also acceptable for lawyers, and in particular, in terms of not violating juristic intuitions. It is extremely difficult to assess whether such a goal was achieved. By presenting a certain jurisprudential conception—here in the form of the postpositivist conception of the validity of statutory law, its author is naturally committed (due to the pragmatic condition of responsibility–sincerity) to acknowledge its correctness, which does not yet prejudge anything as regards its real objective value. In order to, at least partly, examine this issue, we shall briefly reconsider the three basic arguments by means of which we have criticised the jurisprudential conceptions of legal validity discussed in the previous chapter. These are the argument justifying non-synonymity of *definiendum* and *definiens*, the argument indicating the fallacy of the circularity of the definition and the argument showing the error of a too narrow objective extension of the model definitions of legal validity. The question is whether we managed to avoid these errors within the postpositivist conception of legal validity.

The first of the indicated arguments was constructed on the basis of analysing the symmetry of the semantic relation expressed by the model definitions of validity.[344] Taking into account the postpositivist definition of validity, we should therefore examine the correctness of two implications based on it; that is, the conditional:

(1) if a norm of statutory law is valid, then the potential addressee of this norm does not have any legal options of refusing to behave in the way prescribed by it or to take action aimed at achieving the end determined by it,

---

[342] It should be noted, however, that we introduce here only the linguistic modification of the formulation used in the definition of legal norms developed by the Poznań school of jurisprudence, since the authors and supporters of this conception interpret it in such a way that this concept includes, besides the norms of action, also the norms of end. The difference lies only in the applied terminology – *cf. e.g.*, M. Zieliński, Z. Ziembiński, *Uzasadnianie twierdzeń, ocen i norm w prawoznawstwie*, *op. cit.*, pp. 59ff. and S. Wronkowska, *Podstawowe pojęcia prawa i prawoznawstwa*, *op. cit.*, p. 164.

[343] *Cf.* Chap. 6, pp. 222–226.

[344] *Cf.* Chap. 7, the arguments A–III and A–IV (directed against understanding the legal validity of norms as their membership in the legal system) at pp. 289–309 and the argument A-VI (against defining validity by means of the concept of law application) at pp. 316–319.

and its converse:

> (2) if the potential addressee of a statutory norm does not have any legal option of refusing to behave in the way prescribed by it or to take action aimed at achieving the end determined by it, then this norm of statutory law is valid.

Leaving it to critics to identify potential counterexamples, we shall confine our discussion to the attempt at rebutting the first of the indicated implications by referring to the phenomenon of civil disobedience.[345] It is obvious that civil disobedience does not, by itself, pose any threat to the formulated definition because—as demonstrated by Aleksandra Wilczyńska in her conceptual analyses—it lies in its very nature that valid law is violated by the acts of civil disobedience.[346] Thus, the acts of civil disobedience by their very definition do not fall within the concept of the legal option of refusal. It was obvious, but the issue gets complicated when civil disobedience becomes the subject of legal regulation and it takes the form of a positivised right to (usually passive) resistance. For instance, such a right has been set forth by the German *Grundgesetz*, which, in Article 20 Section 4, gives all German people the right to resistance (*Recht zum Widerstand*) against anyone who tries to overthrow the constitutional legal order, reserving, however, the condition under which "it is not possible to rectify it otherwise".[347] We believe that in certain situational contexts this right can be seen as the legal option of refusal within the meaning of the postpositivist definition of validity. At first glance, this leads to the conclusion that the first implication can be challenged. Yet, if one takes into account the purpose of this right and the scarce situations in which it is properly exercised by the citizens, it does not seem that this argument was crucial enough so as to lead to the rejection or the need to reformulate the presented definition by establishing an exception related to civil disobedience. It can also be noted that in the case of the German regulation, the purpose for which one can exercise the right to resistance is to defend the constitutional legal order. It can therefore be argued that if someone effectively exercises this right, she/he will at the same time demonstrate the unconstitutionality of a given action (at this point we are mainly focused on legal actions in the form of making new legal regulations or legal norms that violate the constitution). Thus, it would probably result in the fact that the new legal regulation, aiming to overthrow the constitutional legal order, will be considered as invalid,[348] which proves the correctness of the postpositivist definition (and, in particular, the synonymy of its parts). Accordingly,

---

[345] *See* A. Wilczyńska, 'Wokół definicji cywilnego nieposłuszeństwa' [Around the Definition of Civil Disobedience] in T. Pietrzykowski (ed.), *W kręgu teorii prawa i zagadnień prawa europejskiego*, Sosnowiec 2007, pp. 133–148, and the references cited therein.

[346] *Ibidem*, pp. 134, 137ff.

[347] In the original: "Gegen jeden, der es unternimmt, diese Ordnung zu beseitigen, haben alle Deutschen das Recht zum Widerstand, wenn andere Abhilfe nicht möglich ist".

[348] We will therefore deal with a situation similar to that which may arise, for example, when the citizen uses the institution of constitutional complaint, claiming that a given legal provision or statute is unconstitutional.

the implication at issue will be somewhat actually (empirically) negated only in the situation when no one wants to exercise their right to resistance.[349] On the other hand, the refusal—based on this right or on the civil disobedience doctrine—to fulfil (implement) such a legal norm, which does not aim to overthrow the constitutional legal order, will be, in most cases, deemed absurd in validity discourse. "I have the constitutional right to resistance, so I refuse to pay my debt owed to Schmidt"—indeed sounds bizarre and surely does not have any impact on the legal validity of norms regulating the duty to pay the debt.

Let us now move on to the argument from the circularity of the definition. When constructing the system of connected concepts, which constituted the basis for the postpositivist definition of validity, we have relied on the method of analysis that allows for a circularity understood as being reciprocal circular relations between some connected concepts.[350] Nevertheless, it is worth considering whether the proposed definition is not burdened with such an error. The problem once again concerns the concept of the legal option of refusal. As already noted, probably many of these options (though not all of them) will be anchored in the valid norms of positive statutory law.[351] Let us consider whether it leads to the circularity of the postpositivist definition of validity.

When we applied the argument from circularity in relation to several traditional jurisprudential conceptions of validity, it turned out that the model definitions that expressed them were burdened with the error of *circulus in definiendo*, usually assuming the form of a direct vicious circle.[352] We have indeed shown that if we want to present the validity of statutory law by means of the concepts of the application, observance or efficacy of norms, we will fall into a vicious circle. In order to use these definitions in the legal discourse, it is necessary to first determine that a given norm is applied, observed or effective (efficacious). To be able to determine this, one first needs to know whether this norm is valid, and therefore validity cannot be defined by means of the aforementioned conceptual categories.

Yet, in the case of the postpositivist definition of the validity of statutory norms, the situation is fundamentally different. To make use of this definition, we need not predetermine or know in advance whether a given norm is valid or invalid. Due to the negative wording of its *definiens*, the validity of other norms of statutory law may be the basis of the invalidity of the norm (and not its validity), because these norms can provide the potential addressee with legal options of refusing the

---

[349] In such a case, the legal norm is usually regarded by lawyers as valid, even though there exists a legal option of refusing its fulfilment (implementation). Such empirical negation of the analysed implication is naturally utterly irrelevant in the context of the correctness of the definition under discussion. This definition, in fact, talks about the existence of "legal options of refusing" rather than about making actual use of them by legal subjects.

[350] *Cf. supra*, p. 366.

[351] Cf. *supra*, pp. 437–438.

[352] *Cf.* Chap. 7, the argument A–VI (against the definition of validity understood as a norm application) at pp. 316–319 and the argument A–XII (against the definitions of validity understood as an observance or efficacy of norms) at pp. 338–339.

fulfilment (implementation) of a given norm. Thus, the validity of other norms can at best determine the invalidity but not the validity of a given norm—and those are two different issues, since the norm may not be valid also in the situation when no valid legal norm constitutes the basis for the legal options of refusal. Thus, any circularity of the proposed definition is out of the question. Naturally, we do not deny that modern systems of statutory law may be "looped" with respect to validity relations—namely, apart from the linear dynamic and static connections between the norms, constituting the relations of the hierarchy (both in the aspect of norm-making competence and derogation)[353]—yet in the system of legal norms, relations (interconnections) of a circular nature can take place. Such situations are nevertheless an example of mutual circular validity relations in the legal system, which are irrelevant for the problem of the circularity of the definition proposed above. Even if legal validity—when we look at it in terms of justifying the validity of norms—sometimes has such a circular "looped" nature, it does not mean that the same applies to the very concept of validity (in the sense described by the definition under discussion).

Finally, the last argument that we used in the clarificative analysis concerned an error of a too narrow scope of reference of the model definitions of legal validity.[354] The analysis of such an objection could be avoided by hiding behind a veil created by the conception of legal norms developed by the Poznań school of jurisprudence, which constituted the basis of a clarificative analysis. We could say that the presented regulative definition includes all those norms that are contained within the extension of Poznań's semantic concept of legal norm. Accordingly, if someone is not satisfied with the proposed objective extension of the presented definition, the allegations should focus on a different direction. Yet, we shall not do so, because we have chosen the conception of norms developed by the Poznań school of jurisprudence, therefore we do bear responsibility for this choice (*culpa in eligendo*). What is more, analysing the question of the objective extension of the postpositivist definition of validity seems advisable not only in terms of its jurisprudential correctness, but it is, in itself, important, especially as regards its practical applications.

The question of the objective extension of the definition of legal validity is strongly associated with the content of jurisprudential conceptions that recognise and characterise different types (categories) of legal norms. By way of example, let us recall that in the pure theory of law, which undoubtedly significantly influenced the contemporary legal thinking about legal norms, there is a distinction between four functionally basic (though not necessarily fully independent) categories of norms: the prescribing (*Gebieten*), the authorising (*Ermächtigen*), the permitting

[353] On the concept of normative hierarchy in the aspects of competence and of derogation, *see* K. Płeszka, *Hierarchia w systemie prawa*, *op. cit.*, pp. 53ff., 65ff.

[354] *Cf.* Chap. 7, the argument A–V (against the definition of validity understood as the application of norms) at pp. 313–316, the argument A–IX (against the definition of validity understood as the applicability of norms) at pp. 327–331, and the argument A–XIII (against the definitions of validity understood as the observance or efficacy of norms) at pp. 339–343.

(*Erlauben*) and the derogatory (*Derogieren*) norms.[355] The distinction might seem exaggerated for legal theorists who present a somewhat reductive attitude, for example, those who seek to bring all the legal norms down to prescribing (ordering) and prohibiting ones, whereas others—more descriptively or structurally oriented—may treat it as an oversimplification. Probably the most detailed classification of the legal norms in contemporary legal theory has been developed by Manuel Atienza and Juan Ruiz Manero, who distinguish and characterise between up to 19 "particles" of law; that is, the interpreted utterances of the legislator performed in legal language.[356] The assumed frames of our study naturally do not allow us to examine the correctness of these distinctions, typologies or classification of norms, nor to consider all the categories of legal norms identified in the literature, in the context of the completeness of the objective extension of the proposed definition of validity. Therefore, we shall focus our discussion on those categories of norms that are most important for lawyers (not only in theory but also in legal practice).

There is no doubt that the proposed wording of the *definiens* allows us to apply the postpositivist definition of validity in reference to the ordering and prohibiting norms, to the sanctioned and sanctioning norms, and (on account of the assumed distinction of the norms of action and norms of end[357]) to the so-called programme norms and even to the legal principles within the meaning of Dworkin or Alexy (with the only exception that in view of the adopted scope of *definiendum*, these principles must be positivised; i.e., expressed in the form of statutory norms). In relation to the norms of competence, it can also be assumed that they are covered by the proposed definition, provided that we recognise the possibility of their interpretation in the form of the norms of conduct—as acknowledged, inter alia, by Hans Kelsen[358] and Alf Ross,[359] and expressly assumed in the Polish theory of law by Zygmunt Ziembiński in his comprehensive conception of competence and norms of competence.[360] On the other hand, the postpositivist definition of validity certainly

[355] *See e.g.*, R. Walter, 'Normy prawne' [Legal Norms], trans. K. Opałek, *KSP* XXI (1988), pp. 98ff. *Cf.* H. Kelsen, *Allgemeine Theorie der Normen*, *op. cit.*, pp. 76ff.

[356] *See* M. Atienza, J. Ruiz Manero, *Las piezas del Derecho*, *op. cit.*, in particular, the schematic classification of these utterances at pp. 177ff. [English version, pp. 175ff.]. *Cf.* D.W.P. Ruiter, 'Eine rechtstheoretisch fundierte Typologie gesetzlicher Rechtsnormen', *RT* 17 (1986), pp. 478–500.

[357] *Cf. supra*, pp. 438–439.

[358] *Cf.* H. Kelsen, *Allgemeine Theorie der Normen*, *op. cit.*, pp. 83, 210ff. It should yet be added that Kelsen's standpoint on implicating prescribing norms (*Gebieten*) by authorising norms (*Ermächtigen*), or the reductibility of the latter to the former ones concerned only the authorisation (competence) to establish the norms (*Normsetzung*). *See* also *idem*, *Reine Rechtslehre*, 2nd ed., *op. cit.*, pp. 15–16, 55ff., 123ff. [English version, pp. 15–16, 54ff., 118ff.].

[359] Ross wrote: "The norms of competence are reductible to norms of conduct..." – *On Law and Justice*, *op. cit.*, p. 33 and *cf.* also *ibidem*, pp. 50, 162 and *Directives and Norms*, *op. cit.*, pp. 118ff. In the Polish literature, Ross's views on the reductibility of the norms of competence to the norms of conduct can be found in K. Świrydowicz, *Analiza logiczna pojęcia kompetencji normodawczej*, *op. cit.*, pp. 51–52 and M. Matczak, *Kompetencja organu administracji publicznej*, *op. cit.*, pp. 84ff.

[360] *Cf.* the reconstructions of Ziembiński's conception in M. Zieliński, 'Dwa nurty pojmowania "kompetencji"', *op. cit.*, p. 583 and M. Matczak, *ibidem*, pp. 91ff., and the references cited therein.

does not apply in relation to permitting norms, which not only do not fall within the concept of legal norm within the meaning adopted by the Poznań school of jurisprudence,[361] but they also cannot be considered as norms in light of the pragmatic conception of norms—applied alternatively in our analyses—because there is no doubt that they do not independently fulfil the suggestive function.

To dispel any possible doubts arising from the wording of the *definiens* of the proposed definition, it is worth noting that its extension also includes sanction-free norms[362] and the norms expressed by means of dispositive provisions (*iuris dispositivi* norms).[363] Yet, as far as the legal norms in the *vacatio legis* period are concerned, under the postpositivist definition of validity they cannot be qualified as valid.

The analysis of the objective scope of the proposed definition leads to the conclusion that we cannot use it for all categories of legal norms distinguished in the jurisprudential literature. The utterances—sometimes regarded as being norms—which directly or indirectly do not order or prohibit anything, remain outside its scope,[364] but this is relevant only providing that we consider these are indeed legal norms. Overall, it appears that most utterances—undoubtedly being legal norms—fall within the scope of reference of this definition, due to which the analysed objection is then—if not rebutted—at least significantly weakened.

The first of the adopted objectives of clarification also includes a postulate of the consistency of clarificative analysis with the juristic intuitions and the requirement that its results should be acceptable for lawyers. Again, it is very difficult to assess whether these constraints are satisfied. It should be noted that—to the best of my knowledge—the attempt to define the juristic concept of legal validity by means of the concept of legal options to refuse the fulfilment (implementation) of the norm has not yet been introduced in the jurisprudential literature. Among the dozens of studies devoted to the issue of legal validity, which I have analysed during the research at hand, only one includes a thesis that resembles the proposed definition. It comes from the work of Pablo Navarro of 2002, in which he analyses, inter alia, the relations between validity, binding force and the applicability of legal norms. The remark made by him is as follows: "A legal norm is institutionally binding only

[361] *See* K. Świrydowicz, S. Wronkowska, M. Zieliński, Z. Ziembiński, 'O nieporozumieniach dotyczących tzw. "norm zezwalających"' [On Misunderstandings Concerning the So-called Permitting Norms], *PiP* 7 (1975), pp. 57–64.

[362] *Cf. infra*, note 388 at p. 452, with the corresponding text.

[363] The power to independently shape the content of the legal relationship undoubtedly cannot be regarded as "the legal option of refusing" in the sense of the postpositivist definition of validity, since we are dealing here with the problem of the application of law, rather than validity of norms – for more *see* M. Piotrowski, *Normy prawne imperatywne i dyspozytywne* [Imperative and Dispositive Legal Norms], Warszawa/Poznań 1990, pp. 21ff., and the references cited therein.

[364] It would be naturally absurd to provide such an interpretation of the proposed definition under which all "norms" that are not orders or prohibitions are valid, because there is certainly no possibility of refusing the implementation of such norms which do not designate any ought behaviour for their addressees.

when judges must not ignore it at the moment of deciding a particular case".[365] Naturally, the phrase "must not ignore" only loosely resembles the phrase about "any legal option of refusing", yet there is indeed a certain similarity between them, which can best be demonstrated when we interpret Navarro's thesis by referring it to the concept of the invalidity of norms. In such a case, we will end up with the following sentence: "A legal norm is not valid (i.e., it is not institutionally binding) only when judges may ignore it when deciding a particular case". At this point, we can perceive a certain analogy, because "the possibility of ignoring" clearly resembles "the option of refusing". Unfortunately, the similarity ends here, because Navarro interprets his thesis in the normative categories of the judges' legal duty to apply norms,[366] whereas it has to be emphasised that no such legal duty or obligation can be inferred from the postpositivist definition of validity.

The jurisprudential literature devoted to legal validity indeed lacks the references to the concept of the absence of legal options of refusing the fulfilment (implementation) of legal norms, yet does it actually mean that the proposed definition violates juristic intuitions and is unacceptable for lawyers? This is certainly not the case, because the reason why the legal theoreticians refrain from applying this concept is probably that the basic idea expressed in the postpositivist definition of law is obvious for them. In other words, I believe that the reason why such a conception of validity has not yet been used in the literature is not that it violates juristic intuitions but—somewhat paradoxically—that many authors interested in, and working on the problems of legal validity find it too intuitive and obvious (presumably in a pejorative sense). In my opinion, the obviousness of the results of clarifying the intension does not come as a shortcoming—I consider it to be a positive value, which the conceptual analysis should aim at, thus trying to avoid presenting the simple relations in a needlessly complicated or over-intellectualised way.[367] We might raise a hopefully rhetorical question as to whether it is indeed better if we highly value those conceptions of legal validity which prove to be theoretically incorrect and/or inapplicable in legal practice, yet which are not obvious.

As for the postulate of the result of the clarification being consistent with the intuitions of lawyers, it seems that the application of the proposed definition of validity will lead to inconsistency with at least some of them. Let us return briefly to the already analysed case of foreign law norms[368]—applied by domestic courts under the rules of international private law—which, according to the postpositivist definition of validity, should be regarded as valid, since the national courts have no legal option of refusing to implement the norms of foreign law; namely, refusing to

[365] P.E. Navarro, 'Legal Systems and Legal Statements', *op. cit.*, p. 77.

[366] *Ibidem*, p. 78.

[367] *Cf.* A. Grabowski, *Judicial Argumentation and Pragmatics*, *op. cit.*, pp. 190ff., and the references cited therein. We have also assumed – as one might recall – that simplicity is one of the conditions of a good clarification – *cf.* Chap. 6, p. 221.

[368] *Cf.* Chap. 7, pp. 291–295.

decide the case in accordance with their content. Does recognising these foreign norms as legally valid violate legal intuitions? Probably yes, but only because the basis of such intuitions is the identification of the validity of norms with their membership in a domestic legal system. Meanwhile, the postpositivist conception of validity negates such an inter-conceptual relation.[369] It seems that when we take into account such a reservation, then the inconsistency with juristic intuitions can only take place when we advocate the idea of a conceptual relation between the validity of legal norms and their membership in the legal system, which we previously deemed erroneous.

On the other hand, we may also identify such juristic intuitions that prove to be fully consistent with the postpositivist definition, yet they are inconsistent with several previous conceptions of legal validity. Let us note that the postpositivist definition of the validity of statutory law leads us to recognise as valid also such legal norms, applied on the basis of the rules of intertemporal law, which constitute the result of interpreting, inter alia, formally derogated legal provisions.[370] This precludes the statement that under the valid norms, which regulate the intertemporal issues, the judges apply norms that are not currently valid. In general, apart from a few exceptions, which are nevertheless indispensable in the light of legal practice,[371] the postpositivist definition of validity does not allow for the possibility of talking about the application of invalid legal norms by judges, which appears to be its advantage not only in the context of the juristic intuitions concerning the validity of law.

As can be seen, therefore, we cannot unequivocally determine the extent of meeting the postulate of the conformity of the clarificative analysis with juristic intuitions and the requirement of the acceptability of its result by the lawyers. Let us now go on to our second objective of clarifying the juristic concept of the validity of statutory law. Our purpose was to develop an integrative conception of legal validity, which should be useful not only for theorists of law but, above all, applied in the dogmatic juristic discourse as well as in the practice of lawmaking and law-application. We have specified this purpose in the course of the clarificative analysis by assuming that the developed conception of validity should offer a certain "intrinsic added value"; namely, that the clarification of the intension of the juristic concept of the validity of statutory law should be helpful in solving validity problems, related to the vagueness of the juristic concept of validity.[372]

When we consider the degree of achieving this second objective of clarification, what should first, and foremost be noted is the fact that the postpositivist definition

---

[369] *Cf.* Chap. 7, pp. 253–254.

[370] For more on the validity of norms applied according to the rules of intertemporal law *see* Chap. 9 at pp. 506–511.

[371] Let us recall that judges sometimes apply the law, which, in the light of a subsequent constitutional court's ruling, turns out not to be invalid – *cf.* Chap. 7, p. 319.

[372] *Cf.* Chap. 7, pp. 356–357. The justification of the importance of "intrinsic added value" in the clarificative analysis also refers to one of the requirements of a good clarification; namely, its scientific fruitfulness – *cf.* Chap. 5, p. 221.

of the validity of statutory law is not a criterial definition. This definition merely explains what it means (in the juristic language) for a statutory norm to be valid, whereas it does not explain what conditions must be met to be able to state (or, better, to express an opinion having a "modally fused" character) that a given legal norm is valid. Its "intrinsic added value" lies in the fact that the postpositivist definition puts us on the right track—the argumentative–discursive method of solving the problem of the extension of legal validity, based on the juristic presumption of the validity of statutory law norms.[373] What turns out to be the most important task in the context of the problem of the extension of the juristic concept of validity is to realise that the *definiens* of the postpositivist definition of validity results directly in adopting the structure of validity discourse, which resembles the so-called negative theories of legal justification[374] that refer to the Popperian falsificationism.[375] Let us note that this definition refers to the absence of "legal options of refusing"; that is, to the lack of a broadly understood legal basis that could justify the invalidity and not the validity of a certain legal norm.

Moreover, it should be taken into account that the postpositivist concept of the validity of statutory law has an "intrinsic added value" in the sense that it is not a *tû-tû*; that is, a meaningless concept.[376] The proposed definition does not imply anything about the membership of the valid norms of statutory law in the legal system or about the obligation (duty) of their observance or application. Both "validity implications", identified in Chap. 7,[377] become completely irrelevant and meaningless in relation to the postpositivist concept of validity, since they provide no criteria of validity and neither do they specify the normative (legal) consequences of the validity of legal norms.

The third objective of clarification was to develop such a concept of legal validity that remains impartial (and detached) with respect to the traditional dispute between legal positivism and antipositivist conceptions, in particular non-positivism. This goal was fully met. The proposed definition of the validity of statutory law is axiologically impartial (and not neutral in the positivist sense), since a very broad and discursive understanding of law in the context of the concept of legal options of refusal that it contains,[378] allows for its direct application also in those countries where the legal culture (or, more narrowly, the validity discourse) approves the application of the nonpositivist validity arguments resembling the "Radbruch formula". Moreover, it is worth noting that the postpositivist conception

---

373 *See* Chap. 9, pp. 484ff.

374 *See e.g.*, N. Jääskinen, 'External Justification of Propositions in Legal Science' in E. Bulygin *et al.* (eds.), *Man, Law and Modern Forms of Life*, *op. cit.*, pp. 227ff. *Cf.* Chap. 9, pp. 500–502.

375 It should be emphasised that the similarity of validity discourse to the negative theories of legal justification and – indirectly – to falsificationism is purely structural, since the juristic validity utterances are in most cases deprived of truth-value.

376 *Cf.* Chap. 7, pp. 272–274.

377 *Cf.* Chap. 7, pp. 271–273.

378 *Cf. supra*, p. 437.

of validity can hardly be accused of *quasi*-positivism,[379] due to the "modally fused" and not purely normative logico-linguistic character of the vast majority of juristic utterances that contain the expressions constituting the parts of the proposed definition.

According to the fourth objective of the clarificative analysis, it should be carried out "in accordance with the facts", which resulted from a moderately realistic approach to legal reality that has been adopted in this study. Did we succeed in achieving this goal? There is no doubt that in the course of the clarification analysis we have repeatedly applied the arguments from common sense in order to rebut—as we believed—purely speculative jurisprudential conceptions or statements. Yet, it does not prejudge that the outcome of the clarification of the intension of the juristic concept of the validity of statutory law—namely, the postpositivist definition—is actually consistent with the facts. To be able to consider this question, we must examine the postpositivist definition, for a moment interpreting it as a real rather than nominal definition.

In passing, it can be noted that when we try to determine the nature of the proposed definition of validity, at first glance it seems not to be a regulative definition. If it is considered in isolation from the chain of the previous interconnected analyses and arguments, it may seem to be a descriptive (analytical) definition, mainly due to its—hopefully—intuitive obviousness. Nevertheless, it cannot be forgotten that the postpositivist definition of validity includes—though it is not directly expressed—a considerably negative stipulative element. Let us recall[380] that according to this definition, the concept of the validity of statutory law cannot be clarified by means of the concepts of the membership of the norm in the legal system, its application or applicability, its observance or efficacy, as well as by some combinations of them, as demonstrated in Chap. 7.[381] This definition indirectly also rejects the possibility of a purely normative understanding of legal validity, for example, in terms of an obligation (duty) to obey or apply legal norms.[382] Moreover, as it has been repeatedly pointed out, both its *definiendum* and *definiens* are usually used by lawyers to formulate "modally fused" (descriptive–evaluative–normative) utterances about the validity of norms, while only in borderline cases (for example, of "trivial" dogmatic utterances) may the validity utterances have truth-value. Accordingly, there is no doubt that this is a regulative definition, and thus also a nominal one, since only nominal definitions are regulative.

The fact of determining that the presented definition is a nominal regulative definition does not nevertheless preclude the attempt to find the answer to the question of the extent to which the fourth goal of clarification has been met. When presenting the methodological considerations relating to the methods of

---

[379] *Cf. supra*, notes 188–191 at pp. 402–403, with the corresponding text.

[380] *Cf. supra*, the scheme (Fig. 8.1) at p. 424.

[381] *Cf.* Chap. 7, pp. 271–357.

[382] *Cf. supra*, pp. 413–422.

clarificative analysis, we have accepted the standpoint expressed by Kazimierz Ajdukiewicz about the overlapping extensions of the nominal and real definitions.[383] This provides us with the possibility of presenting the interpretation of the postpositivist definition of the validity of statutory law as a real definition, which explains the essence (nature) of legal validity. This interpretation will bring us closer to answering the question as to whether the fourth objective of clarification—consistency with the facts—has been successfully met.

In the postpositivist definition, the element of legal normativity of the validity of law is captured by means of the concept of the absence of legal options of refusing the fulfilment (implementation) of the norm by its potential addressee. As already noted, when setting up the list of connected concepts, which constitute the conceptual foundation of the proposed definition, we have made the identification of the primary legal (normative) situation, determined by the valid legal norms.[384] The pragmatic conception of legal norm together with the concept of legal situation developed by Sławomira Wronkowska and the analyses of Krzysztof Grzegorczyk and Tomasz Gizbert-Studnicki[385] led us to conclude that the normativity of legal validity is manifested in the form of such a situation. It should be noted that the primary legal (normative) situation consists in circumstances which are expressed by the *definiens* of the postpositivist definition of validity: the potential addressee of the norm of statutory law has no legal options of refusing to fulfil the norm. Thus, it is not a "basic legal situation" within the meaning of Wronkowska, but something that analytically precedes this situation. It should also be emphasised that the absence of legal options to refuse serves as the explanation of the normativity of legal validity—the law's binding force, rather than the normativity of law as such. This last issue was not directly touched upon by our analyses or by the presented conception of validity.

When considering the fourth objective of the clarification, we need to ask whether such an explanation of the nature of legal validity is consistent with the facts; whether the normative element of legal validity is aptly presented through the postpositivist definition. We must admit that we are not certain of it. We should indeed point out that in the course of the critical analysis of the normative conception of legal validity,[386] we have applied the arguments that are significant in relation to the definition of validity which is of a nominal rather than real character. Therefore, we believe that no direct justification was provided to accept the postpositivist definition as the adequate explanation of the essence of legal validity, interpreted as the actual element of legal reality. Perhaps we managed to explain such a nature to some extent in the course of the clarificative conceptual analysis; perhaps we did not—and, unfortunately, we have to make do with such a

[383] *Cf.* Chap. 7, pp. 261–262.

[384] *Cf. supra*, p. 432.

[385] *Cf. supra*, pp. 422–432.

[386] *Cf. supra*, pp. 400–422.

conclusion.[387] Yet, what needs emphasising is the significance of the distinction between the normativity of law and the normativity of legal validity, which in our opinion at least brings us closer to the explication of the essence of legal validity in its real aspect. Let us note that the existence of the normativity of legal validity can best be illustrated when we examine the case of valid legal norms, which are sanction-free (*leges imperfectae*).[388] The potential addressee of the norm, which belongs to this category, may (similarly to the potential addressee of the norm containing the sanction) not observe a given sanction-free norm or may not apply it (the only difference is that there is no legal sanction for it). What is more, the postpositivist understanding of legal validity does not justify the thesis that the potential addressee of any legal norm has a legal obligation to obey or apply valid legal norms. Nevertheless, even in the case of *leges imperfectae*, we are dealing with the normativity of legal validity within the above meaning. For the potential addressee of a sanction-free norm cannot, after all, refuse to behave in the way prescribed by it, or to take action aimed at achieving the end determined by it on the basis that this norm does not provide any legal sanctions in case of its non-fulfilment. Clearly and demonstrably, the lack of sanction has nothing to do with the option to refuse.

The fifth of the assumed objectives of the clarification was the requirement that the developed conception of legal validity should not be unfair; namely, it should not entail the necessity of settling specific validity issues in the manner that would be unfair for the norm's addressees. At this point of the analysis, we are not able to comment on the extent to which this goal was achieved, yet we keep in mind that it was strongly related to the principles of *ignorantia iuris nocet* and *ignorantia legis neminem excusat*. We will comment on this in the penultimate section of the next chapter.[389]

When analysing dogmatic legal interpretation, Aulis Aarnio formulated an idea that is undoubtedly also crucial in relation to the postpositivist regulative definition of the juristic concept of the validity of statutory law. The Finnish legal theorist emphasises that the weakness of juristic regulative definitions lies in the fact that they are "open to agreement".[390] The above "authentic interpretation" of the postpositivist definition of legal validity, together with the comments on the extent to which the assumed objectives of clarification of the juristic concept of the validity of statutory law were achieved, were supposed not only to clarify the understanding and practical application of this definition, but also to bring such an agreement closer. This is also one of the main purposes of the following Chap. 9,

[387] It is not advisable at this point to take up a new purely philosophical investigation, especially since the clarificative analysis primarily aimed at formulating a nominal rather than a real definition.

[388] For more about this category of norms from the jurisprudential perspective *see* J. Jabłońska-Bonca, 'Przesłanki stanowienia norm bez sankcji' [The Conditions for Establishing Sanction-Free Norms], *RPEiS* XLVI/4 (1984), pp. 151–167, and the references cited therein.

[389] *See* Chap. 9, pp. 529–533.

[390] A. Aarnio, *The Rational as Reasonable*, *op. cit.*, p. 57.

in which we will present an argumentative–discursive model of analysing the methods of how lawyers deal with specific legal problems concerning the validity of statutory norms. We will try to show that the postpositivist conception of the validity of statutory law has indeed an "intrinsic added value", for it helps in solving the problem of the extension of the concept under analysis. It should be noted, nonetheless, that the subsequent and very synthetic chapter will have, in fact, a character of an appendix, since it will present only an outline of a certain conceptual network, enabling lawyers to grasp and to understand the structure of validity discourse. The decidedly innovative nature of the concepts introduced in the next chapter results from the fact that now we are indeed entering a "no-man's-land" of the contemporary theory and philosophy of law, because—to the best of my knowledge—the argumentative–discursive analyses of validity discourse have not yet been undertaken by the legal theorists.[391]

[391] As far as I know, the only study which applies the concept of validity discourse (understood intuitively) is the study of G. Sartor, 'Legal Validity as Doxastic Obligation: From Definition to Normativity', *op. cit.*, pp. 590ff. Yet, the Italian theorist of law uses it in a manner different from that proposed here – *cf.* Chap. 9, p. 470.

Chapter 9
Discourse of Validity and the Juristic Presumption of the Validity of Statutory Law Norms

9.1 The Argumentative Approach to the Clarification of Extension of the Juristic Concept of the Validity of Statutory Law

When getting down to the clarification of the juristic concept of the validity of statutory law, we have made a distinction between the problems of its intension and extension.[1] Let us recall that as far as the problem of extension is concerned, our goal is to indicate the juristic methods that help to determine whether a given norm of statutory law is valid (in the juristic sense of this concept, clarified from the postpositivist perspective in the previous chapter). In other words, the clarification of the extension of the juristic concept of the validity of statutory law deals with the extensional indeterminacy (vagueness) of the concept of valid law.[2]

Is the norm of statutory law valid? This is the fundamental practical question that is very important for legal practitioners as well as for legal dogmaticians. The theory of law typically undertakes efforts to explain how to find answers to this question in the form of a catalogue of criteria (requirements or conditions), the fulfilment of which would justify classifying a given legal norm valid. In the Polish jurisprudential literature, there have been some attempts to establish such a catalogue, developed by Leszek Nowak[3] and Jerzy Wróblewski.[4] The criteria of the validity of norms, as provided by these authors, can be considered as the

---

[1] *See* Chap. 6, pp. 218ff.

[2] It should be noted that when we consider the problem of the extension of the juristic concept of the validity of statutory law, we do not deal with the logical value of the utterances about the validity of norms, especially since in most cases they can be "modally fused", by which their logical value is entirely out of the question – *cf.* Chap. 8 at pp. 380–400.

[3] *See* L. Nowak, *Interpretacja prawnicza*, *op. cit.*, pp. 62ff.

[4] *See e.g.*, J. Wróblewski, 'Obowiązywanie systemowe i granice dogmatycznego podejścia do systemu prawa', *op. cit.*, pp. 26ff. and *Sądowe stosowanie prawa*, *op. cit.*, pp. 96ff. [English version, pp. 77ff.].

A. Grabowski, *Juristic Concept of the Validity of Statutory Law*,

DOI 10.1007/978-3-642-27688-0_9, © Springer-Verlag Berlin Heidelberg 2013

components of the rule of recognition, accepted in the Polish legal culture of the late twentieth century. However, the previous analyses strongly militate in favour of rejecting the clarification of the extension of the juristic concept of the validity of statutory law that is based on the rule of recognition composed of several, mainly systemic, criteria of validity. Let us recall that in the light of the earlier analyses, the rule of recognition proves to be an open textured and customary rule, probably incomplete and subject to constant evolutionary changes, and often containing (in accordance with the standpoint of soft positivism) moral criteria of evaluation, which directly leads to the "fuzziness" of modern legal systems.[5] Moreover, we can supplement the objections against Hart's conception of the rule of recognition that have been presented in the previous chapters with the objection of its circularity—quite frequently discussed in the jurisprudential literature.[6] If the content of the rule of recognition is determined by the conduct of judges and other officials who assume an internal point of view and take validity decisions (in terms of Jerzy Wróblewski's substantive decisional model of the judicial application of law[7]) within a given legal system, then the circularity of this rule is obvious. As the question of determining who is a judge or an official, after all, depends on the content of the valid legal norms, in particular on the secondary rules of adjudication (in Hart's terminology), which are, in turn, valid because they meet the criteria of validity contained in the rule of recognition.[8] The existence of the rule of recognition is therefore not just merely "a matter of fact"—as claimed by the Oxford philosopher.[9] Robert Alexy, when criticising Hart's position in relation to Kelsen's theory of *Grundnorm*, in the context of the validity of the constitution, rightly observes that:

> [i]t seems strange and artificial (*ungewöhnlich und konstruiret*) for a judge, asked why he follows the constitution, to answer: "I follow the constitution not because it is legally valid (*rechtlich gilt*), but exclusively because my colleagues and I accept and implement it. This is a fact, and there is nothing to add".[10]

---

[5] *Cf.* Chap. 4, pp. 128–130 and Chap. 7, the argument A–I at pp. 278–279.

[6] *See e.g.*, N. MacCormick, *H.L.A. Hart*, *op. cit.*, pp. 22, 28, 108ff. and F. Laporta, 'Derecho y moral: vindicación del observador crítico y aporía del iusnaturalista', *op. cit.*, p. 253. *Cf.* the polemics between E. Bulygin and J. Ruiz Manero concerning, inter alia, the circularity of the rule of recognition – E. Bulygin, 'Algunas consideraciones sobre los sistemas jurídicos', *op. cit.*, pp. 275ff.; J. Ruiz Manero, 'Normas independientes, criterios conceptuales y trucos verbales. Respuesta a Eugenio Bulygin', *DOXA* 9 (1991), pp. 290ff.; E. Bulygin, 'Regla de reconocimiento: ¿norma de obligación o criterio conceptual? Réplica a Juan Ruiz Manero', *DOXA* 9 (1991), pp. 316ff., and the references cited therein.

[7] *Cf.* J. Wróblewski, *Sądowe stosowanie prawa*, *op. cit.*, pp. 42ff., 93ff. [English version, pp. 30ff., 75ff.].

[8] We therefore deal here – as interpreted by N. MacCormick, *H.L.A. Hart*, *op. cit.*, p. 109 – with the "logical circle" that is composed of three elements: the two types of secondary rules (i.e., rules of recognition and adjudication) and the concept of the judge.

[9] *Cf.* Chap. 7, note 245 at p. 300.

[10] R. Alexy, *Begriff und Geltung des Rechts*, *op. cit.*, pp. 162–163 [English version, p. 100].

The attempt at reinforcing the validity of legal norms in Kelsen's theory of the basic norm also raises serious doubts among legal theorists. Aleksander Peczenik asks: "But how can a mere presupposition constitute a ground for legal validity? This is a puzzle".[11] It is indeed puzzling, especially since *Grundnorm* cannot be treated as a category of practical philosophy, but rather as a transcendental-logical category (which has already been drawn attention to).[12]

Thus, the jurisprudential proposals for solving the problem of the extension of the juristic concept of the validity of statutory law, based on purely positivist-oriented theories of legal validity, seem doomed to failure from an analytical point of view. Let us consider how we should evaluate the attempt to explain to the person sentenced to imprisonment that the ultimate justification—in the sense of validity—of her/his imprisonment, in addition to the reprehensibility of the committed crime and the efficiency of law enforcement and justice state organs, is the hypothesis made by lawyers, a transcendental presupposition or a fiction of the basic norms (Kelsen), or the circular, customary and open textured rule of recognition, usually morally involved, and grounded in the practice of judges and officials who accept the law from an internal point of view (Hart). Such an explanation would probably be treated as a cynical joke. Incidentally, another explanation based on a nonpositivist basic norm,[13] justified, inter alia, through the identification of *performativer Widerspuch* of certain legal or juristic utterances, would hardly be better rated.[14]

The clarification of the extension of the juristic concept of the validity of statutory law, which is based on careful examination of whether a given legal norm meets the criteria of validity, also seems inadvisable due to the demands of the economy of legal thinking and acting. The vision of the lawyer, who in order to determine the validity of a particular legal norm, shall scrupulously check whether it fulfils all the criteria of legal validity that are characteristic for a given legal culture, should be regarded as significantly differing from reality. This way to solve the problem of extension is much less worthy of approval on account of the fact that—as already shown—the result of such juristic examination can be, at most, the determination that a given norm of statutory law belongs to the legal system in the sense referred to by us as a "medium" one.[15] By doing so, we would solve the problem of extension in the spirit of the conception of the juristic *prima facie*

---

[11] A. Peczenik, 'On the Nature and Function of the *Grundnorm*', *op. cit.*, p. 282.

[12] *Cf.* Chap. 8, note 191 *in fine* at p. 403.

[13] *Cf.* the formulation of the nonpositivist *Grundnorm* proposed by R. Alexy, *Begriff und Geltung des Rechts*, *op. cit.*, pp. 169–170 [English version, p. 105].

[14] Although the works of legal theoreticians or philosophers are not addressed to the convicts (which considerably weakens the argument presented), it is undoubtedly recommendable for the legal scholars (or better: for us) to act with common sense and not to lose contact with social reality. In this context, the nonpositivist basic norm formulated by Alexy is at an advantage over positivist's one, since it contains elements of substantive correctness. Yet, the problem lies in its unsatisfactory analytical justification – *cf.* Chap. 4, pp. 91ff., 138ff.

[15] *Cf.* Chap. 7, p. 279.

validity of norms of statutory law.[16] Yet, it cannot be regarded as satisfactory, because lawyers, and in particular judges involved in the law application process, are not only legally obligated to definitively resolve the issue of the validity of a specific norm, but they actually do it every day, disregarding the jurisprudential dilemmas.

The postpositivist conception of the validity of statutory law—as outlined in the previous chapter—leads us to another way of solving the problem of the extension of the concept of legal validity, which, as we believe, is not only a proper one, but probably even necessary from a practical point of view. It is much easier and simpler to understand the nature of validity decisions and the activities undertaken for this purpose by the lawyers, if we abandon the traditional methods of solving specific validity problems—highly associated with the positivist comprehension of law and based on more or less extensive catalogues of the criteria of legal validity determined by the traditional *juristische Methodenlehre*—and instead present this process by adopting an argumentative perspective.[17] The theories of legal argumentation that we shall refer to in the next section, provide a useful base to develop a new conceptual apparatus that allows us to capture the nature of legal reasoning on validity problems, primarily on account of the fact that they constitute a natural alternative—already well-established in the literature—to the traditional legal science and methodology.[18] Anticipating the subsequent analyses of validity discourse, it is worth noting that the most important advantage of an argumentative approach to law and legal reasoning is that they place emphasis on the justification of legal decisions, which does not involve a simple, somehow mechanical compliance with predetermined criteria (methods) of correct legal reasoning, determined by *juristische Methodenlehre*, but a construction of such a reasoning that convinces us about the rationality or even rightness of the legal decision.[19] Therefore, our study will not seek to determine the catalogue of the criteria that could provide the basis for the method of finding the correct answer to the question as to whether a specific norm of statutory law is valid. In turn, we will carry out an argumentative analysis of the structure of validity discourse, in which the problem of the extension of the juristic concept of validity finds its actual, practically relevant solution.

---

[16] *Cf.* Chap. 7, pp. 274ff.

[17] The concept of an argumentative perspective has been touched upon by J. Stelmach, B. Brożek, *Methods of Legal Reasoning*, *op. cit.*, p. 144.

[18] For more *see* U. Neumann, 'Juristische Methodenlehre und Theorie der juristischen Argumentation', *op. cit.*, and the references cited therein.

[19] *See* U. Neumann, *ibidem*, pp. 245ff., 255. *Cf. idem*, *Juristische Argumentationslehre*, *op. cit.*, p. 4.

9.2 The Concept of Juristic Discourse

The concept of juristic discourse—as pointed out by Jerzy Stelmach and Bartosz Brożek—is particularly ambiguous and the formulation of its acceptable definition poses considerable difficulties.[20] This concept is derived from the theory of legal argumentation. Without a doubt, Robert Alexy played a decisive role in promoting it in the jurisprudential reflection (as presented in detail below). At this point, we will explain the concept of juristic discourse that will accompany the subsequent analyses of validity discourse and try to determine the appropriate methodology. To do this, we shall first concisely and briefly discuss the characteristics and some of the typologies of the theories of legal argumentation developed in the last half-century and then we will focus on the approach to juristic discourse proposed by the author of *Theorie der juristischen Argumentation*. The critique of this approach will enable us to determine our own position and to characterise the methods applied in further investigation.

The theories of legal argumentation, originating with the pioneering works of Theodor Viehweg,[21] Chaïm Perelman and Lucie Olbrechts-Tyteca,[22] published in the fifties of the last century, won a permanent place in the contemporary theory of law.[23] Their strong development took place in the eighties and nineties mainly due to two particularly important works, published in 1978 by Robert Alexy[24] and Neil MacCormick,[25] who independently contributed to the creation of the theory of legal argumentation that is currently labelled as "standard".[26] As far as the Polish theory

[20] J. Stelmach, B. Brożek, *Methods of Legal Reasoning*, *op. cit.*, p. 126.

[21] T. Viehweg, *Topik und Jurisprudenz. Ein Beitrag zur rechtswissenschaftlichen Grundlagenforschung*, 5th ed., München 1974 [1st ed. 1953; English version: *Topics and Law. A Contribution to Basic Research in Law*, trans. W. Cole Durham Jr., Frankfurt am Main/Berlin/Bern/New York/Paris/Wien 1993]. It is worth adding that some of Viehweg's statements resemble the theses presented a few years earlier by E.H. Levi, *An Introduction to Legal Reasoning*, Chicago/London 1949.

[22] Ch. Perelman, L. Olbrechts-Tyteca, *Traité de l'argumentation. La nouvelle rhétorique*, 5th ed., Bruxelles 1988 [1st ed. 1958; English version: *The New Rhetoric: A Treatise on Argumentation*, trans. J. Wilkinson, P. Weaver, Notre Dame/London 1969]; *see* also Ch. Perelman, *Logique juridique. Nouvelle rhétorique*, Paris 1976.

[23] For more *see* three monographs devoted to the theories of legal argumentation: U. Neumann, *Juristische Argumentationslehre*, *op. cit.*; M. Atienza, *Las Razones del Derecho*, *op. cit.*; E.T. Feteris, *Fundamentals of Legal Argumentation. A Survey of Theories on the Justification of Judicial Decisions*, Dordrecht/Boston/London 2011. On the ancient origins and the history of the theory of legal argumentation *cf.* F. Haft, E. Hilgendorf, 'Juristische Argumentation und Dialektik', *op. cit.*, pp. 94ff. and J. Stelmach, B. Brożek, *Methods of Legal Reasoning*, *op. cit.*, pp. 159ff.

[24] R. Alexy, *Theorie der juristischen Argumentation*, *op. cit.* A considerable contribution to the development of the contemporary theory of legal argumentation has also been made by the joint work by A. Aarnio, R. Alexy and A. Peczenik, 'The Foundation of Legal Reasoning', *op. cit.*

[25] N. MacCormick, *Legal Reasoning and Legal Theory*, *op. cit.*

[26] M. Atienza, *Las Razones del Derecho*, *op. cit.*, p. 235.

of law is concerned, in the 1980s, the argumentative trend also appeared,[27] initiated by the monograph by Lech Morawski.[28] However, the discursive approach to the analysis of legal phenomena,[29] preceded by the studies of Marek Zirk-Sadowski that were directly devoted to the very concept of discourse,[30] is now a dominant tendency among Polish scholars.

The characteristic feature of the theories of legal argumentation consists in a such high degree of methodological and philosophical differentiation, that Ulfrid Neumann (the author of one of the few monographs on legal argumentation) does not hesitate in saying that the term "theory of legal argumentation" stands not so much for a certain trend in legal reflection, but for a specific scope of jurisprudential problems.[31] However, the literature devoted to the problems at hand is full of typologies, or even classifications of these theories, undertaken from a methodological, substantive or descriptive-historical perspective.[32] It seems that it is most appropriate to distinguish three basic approaches to legal argumentation: logical, rhetorical (also called "rhetorical–topical") and dialogical (also known as "dialectical" or "procedural").[33]

---

[27] *Cf. e.g.*, J. Czaja, J. Stelmach, 'Teoria argumentacji prawniczej' [Theory of Legal Argumentation], *KSP* XXVI–XXVII (1993–1994), pp. 19–31; T. Gizbert-Studnicki, 'Podstawy argumentacji prawniczej', *op. cit.*; A. Grabowski, *Judicial Argumentation and Pragmatics*, *op. cit.*; J. Stelmach, *Kodeks argumentacyjny dla prawników*, *op. cit.*

[28] L. Morawski, *Argumentacje, racjonalność prawa i postępowanie dowodowe* [Argumentation, Rationality of Law and Hearing of Evidence], Toruń 1988.

[29] *Cf. e.g.*, W. Cyrul, *Dyskursywna teoria tworzenia prawa*, *op. cit.*; B. Wojciechowski, 'Uzasadnienie praw człowieka w koncepcji dyskursu prawniczego', *op. cit.* and 'Dyskursywny model sądowego stosowania prawa – wybrane aspekty', *op. cit.*; B. Brożek, *Rationality and Discourse*, *op. cit.*

[30] M. Zirk-Sadowski, 'Pojęcie dyskursu' [The Concept of Discourse], *KiS* XXXVI/2 (1992), pp. 61–74 and 'Dyskurs jako mowa regulowana wymogami moralnymi' [Discourse as Speech Regulated by Moral Constraints] in G. Skąpska *et al.* (eds.), *Prawo w zmieniającym się społeczeństwie*, *op. cit.*, pp. 185–195. *Cf.* also *idem*, 'Rationality of Legal Discourse in Relation to Legal Ethics', *op. cit.*

[31] U. Neumann, *Juristische Argumentationslehre*, *op. cit.*, pp. 1–2.

[32] Let us now look at some proposals for such classifications. R. Alexy distinguishes between empirical, analytical and/or normative theories of discourse – *cf. idem*, *Theorie der juristischen Argumentation*, *op. cit.*, pp. 224–225 [English version, p. 180]. U. Neumann distinguishes two approaches to legal argumentation: logico–analytical and topic–rhetorical, as well as the theory of legal argumentation based on practical discourse theory and the comprehensive model of legal argumentation – *see idem*, *ibidem*, pp. 16ff., 54ff., 70ff., 96ff. In Polish jurisprudential literature, L. Morawski distinguishes between three models of the rationality of legal argumentation: the epistemological–technological (scientistic), rhetorical–topical and communicative – *cf. idem*, *Argumentacje, racjonalność prawa i postępowanie dowodowe*, *op. cit.*, pp. 23ff.; M. Zirk-Sadowski distinguishes between rhetorical, communicative and hermeneutic theories of discourse – *cf. idem*, 'Pojęcie dyskursu', *op. cit.*, pp. 66ff. and 'Dyskurs jako mowa regulowana wymogami moralnymi', *op. cit.*, pp. 192ff.; J. Stelmach and B. Brożek distinguish between two conceptions of legal discourse: topical–rhetorical and procedural – *cf. iidem*, *Methods of Legal Reasoning*, pp. 130ff.

[33] *Cf.* E.T. Feteris, 'A Survey of 25 Years of Research on Legal Argumentation', *ARG* 11 (1997), pp. 358ff. and *Fundamentals of Legal Argumentation*, *op. cit.*, pp. 19ff., 163ff.

The logical approach to legal argumentation, initiated in the 1950s by Ulrich Klug[34] and the co-creators of deontic logic, Georg Henrik von Wright[35] and Jerzy Kalinowski,[36] and lately encountering its renaissance mainly due to the authors who deal with the systems of nonmonotonic defeasible logics (e.g., Henry Prakken, Giovanni Sartor, Jaap Hage and in Poland, Bartosz Brożek),[37] does not seem useful for an analysis of validity discourse and the arguments applied in it. The reason for this is, naturally, the "modally fused" nature of most juristic validity utterances, identified in the previous chapter. It should also be noted that the issues of the applicability and usefulness of logical analyses in relation to law and legal reasoning are the subject of perennial disputes,[38] which became particularly significant after Jørgen Jørgensen formulated the famous dilemma.[39] Nevertheless, some elements of logical analysis will be further applied to express the structure of the juristic presumption of the validity of statutory law norms, which is undoubtedly subjected to logical formalisation (in the broad sense of this term).

The rhetorical approach, initiated by Viehweg and Perelman,[40] and additionally reinforced by Stephen Toulmin's theory of practical argumentation,[41] based on the pattern of judicial argumentation, is also still applied in legal theory. Neil MacCormick was the most famous follower of Perelman's "New Rhetoric".[42] When analysing the possible routes for validity argumentation, we shall also refer

[34] *See* U. Klug, *Juristische Logik*, 4th ed., Berlin 1982 [1st ed. 1951].

[35] *See* G.H. von Wright, 'Deontic Logic', *op. cit.*

[36] *See* J. Kalinowski, 'Théorie des propositions normatives', *SL* I (1953), pp. 147–182. This study was largely based on the unpublished habilitation thesis of Kalinowski, *Logika zdań praktycznych. Z badań nad podstawami logicznymi poznania praktycznego* [Logic of Practical Propositions. Research on the Logical Basis of Practical Cognition] of June 1951.

[37] For more *see* B. Brożek, *Defeasibility of Legal Reasoning*, Kraków 2004, pp. 81ff. and J. Stelmach, B. Brożek, *Methods of Legal Reasoning*, *op. cit.*, pp. 49ff., and the references cited therein.

[38] *See e.g.* a recent polemics of S. Haack, 'On Logic in the Law: "Something, but not All"', *RJ* 20 (2007), pp. 1–31, with E. Bulygin, 'What Can One Expect from Logic in the Law? (Not Everything, but More than Something: A Reply to Susan Haack)', *RJ* 21 (2008), pp. 150–156. In the Polish literature *see* J. Wróblewski, 'Logika a teoria argumentacji: teoretyczne zagadnienia poprawności decyzji sądowej' [The Logic and the Theory of Argumentation: Theoretical Issues of the Correctness of Judicial Decision], *PiP* 7–8 (1986), pp. 5ff. and K. Opałek, 'Teoria rozumowania prawniczego – między logika i aksjologią' [The Theory of Legal Reasoning – Between Logic and Axiology] in *idem, Studia z teorii i filozofii prawa*, *op. cit.*, pp. 61–80. At this point, it is also worth recalling the sharp opinion of J. Stelmach, *Kodeks argumentacyjny dla prawników*, *op. cit.*, p. 12, who emphasises that "referring to non-classic logics, for example to deontic or modal logic, does not provide any practical significance for lawyers".

[39] J. Jørgensen, 'Imperatives and Logic', *ERK* 7 (1937–1938), pp. 288–296. This dilemma fully highlighted the problem of applying logic in the sphere of juristic normative reasoning, however – at least as evidenced by the contents of Haack's paper cited in the previous note – these controversies began at least half a century earlier.

[40] *Cf. supra*, the studies indicated in notes 21–22 at p. 459.

[41] *See* S.E. Toulmin, *The Uses of Argument*, Cambridge 1958.

[42] *See* N. MacCormick, *Rhetoric and the Rule of Law*, *op. cit.*, in particular pp. vii, 12ff., 162ff.

to this approach, particularly because the concept of the absence of a legal option for refusing the fulfilment (implementation) of a statutory norm—used in the postpositivist definition of the validity of statutory law—allows for the incorporation of a number of legal topics, which could form the basis of that refusal, into validity discourse.[43] Yet, it should be noted that it will be a highly general reference. First, because the model of analysis of validity discourse—as presented here—is a conception *in statu nascendi*, no doubt requiring further investigations, modifications and supplements.[44] Secondly, due to the fact that our considerations are very broadly relativised, since we refer them to the continental system-type of statutory law, and not directly to, for example, the Polish, German or French legal culture. Meanwhile, the legal reasons, arguments and topics that call for recognising a specific norm of statutory law as invalid, seem strongly to depend on the legal culture of a particular society.[45]

The dialogic (dialectical) approach to the research on legal argumentation is currently a dominant one.[46] As already noted, a paradigmatic example of such an approach is a procedural theory of juristic discourse and argumentation, developed by Robert Alexy. This theory should be paid more attention to, especially since it was indeed Alexy who proposed a procedural understanding of legal argumentation in terms of an ideal and rational discourse, where rules are strictly determined.[47] As Ulfrid Neumann notes, before the publication of *Theorie der juristischen Argumentation*, there was virtually no dispute about the fact that the specific conditions of judicial argumentation exclude the possibility of comprehending it as discourse,[48] although it is worth mentioning that, at times, the very notion of discourse has been used in relation to the utterances formulated by lawyers.[49] On account of the fact

[43] *Cf. infra*, pp. 500ff., 521ff.

[44] For more on this *see infra*, pp. 533ff.

[45] *Cf.* a similar view expressed by B. Naleziński and K. Wojtyczek, 'Konsekwencje wadliwości aktów normatywnych w polskim systemie prawnym' [The Consequences of the Defectiveness of Normative Acts in the Polish Legal System], *RPEiS* LV/4 (1993), p. 19.

[46] *Cf.* E.T. Feteris, 'A Survey of 25 Years of Research on Legal Argumentation', *op. cit.*, pp. 362–363 and 'Recent Developments in Legal Argumentation Theory: Dialectical Approaches to Legal Argumentation', *IJSL* VII/20 (1994), pp. 133–153.

[47] *Cf.* R. Alexy, *Theorie der juristischen Argumentation, op. cit.*, pp. 233ff., 361–367 [English version, pp. 187ff., 297–302]. The general rules of practical discourse in the context of their transcendental-pragmatic justification have already been referred to in Chap. 4, at pp. 91ff.

[48] U. Neumann, *Juristische Argumentationslehre, op. cit.*, p. 84. The same opinion has been expressed by A. Kaufmann, 'Läßt sich die Hauptverhandlung in Strafsachen als rationaler Diskurs auffassen?' in H. Jung, H. Müller-Dietz (eds.), *Dogmatik und Praxis des Strafverfahrens. Beiträge anläßlich des Colloquiums zum 65. Geburtstag von Gerhard Kielwein*, AUS 122 (1989), p. 21.

[49] In Polish jurisprudential literature, we can point to K. Opałek's work published in 1974, *Z teorii dyrektyw i norm, op. cit.*, pp. 131ff., in which we can find a chapter on "directival discourse". It is symptomatic that in the German version of his monograph, *Theorie der Directiven und der Normen, op. cit.*, pp. 86ff., published in 1986, Opałek refrained from using the concept of discourse. He writes there about "direktiven Sprachzusammenhanges", which probably indicates that he did not want to be associated with legal discourse theory based – as in the case of Alexy – on the German

that Alexy's theory of argumentation has been repeatedly presented in the literature, we shall leave aside its description and instead go straight to critical analysis. We will consider three specific topics: the problem of interpretation and relevance of *Sonderfallthese*; the problem of the monological nature of certain rules of juristic discourse (closely related to the somehow "reverse" problem of the so-called virtual discourses); and the problem of the scientific usefulness and practical applicability of determining the rules of general practical discourse and juristic discourse by means of mainly analytical analysis.

The development of Robert Alexy's theory of legal argumentation can be summarised through the identification of its three easily distinguishable stages.[50] The German philosopher first proposed the theory of a general practical discourse, which constitutes a procedural-discursive interpretation of Habermas' concept of the ideal speech situation (*ideale Sprechsituation*),[51] thus devoting most attention to establishing the catalogue of its universally valid rules and forms. Then he formulated the Special Case Thesis, according to which, juristic discourse has been recognised as a "special case" (*Sonderfall*) of general practical discourse. Finally, by using the distinction between the internal and external justification of legal decisions, as introduced by Jerzy Wróblewski,[52] Alexy elaborated and proposed the set of specific rules and forms of juristic discourse, incidentally, in a way that differs little from the traditional, positivist-oriented *juristische Methodenlehre*.[53]

The first of the specific issues that we would like to analyse in the context of the criticism of Alexy's theory of legal argumentation is the problem of the interpretation and adequacy of *Sonderfallthese*, which constitutes a link between the theories of general practical discourse and those of specific juristic discourse. Due to the fact that the standpoint on these topics has already been presented in a separate study,[54]

discourse ethics, which he did not refer to in his work at all, although he allowed the application of the very concept of discourse – *cf. ibidem*, note marked * at p. 86.

[50] *See* R. Alexy, *Theorie der juristischen Argumentation*, *op. cit.*, pp. 219ff. [English version, pp. 175ff.], and the references cited therein.

[51] For more in the Polish jurisprudential literature *see e.g.*, M. Zirk-Sadowski, 'Uniwersalna pragmatyka a teoria i filozofia prawa', *op. cit.*, pp. 29ff.; L. Morawski, *Argumentacje, racjonalność prawa i postępowanie dowodowe*, *op. cit.*, pp. 93ff. and 'Dyskurs w ujęciu Jürgena Habermasa a inne koncepcje argumentacji', *op. cit.*, pp. 130ff. *Cf.* E. Tugendhat, 'Die Diskursethik' in *idem*, *Vorlesungen über Ethik*, Frankfurt am Main 1993, pp. 163ff.

[52] *See* J. Wróblewski, 'Legal Decision and Its Justification', *LA* 53–54 (1971), pp. 412ff., 'Legal Syllogism and Rationality of Judicial Decision', *RT* 5 (1974), p. 39, 'Uzasadnienie i wyjaśnienie decyzji sądowej' [Justifying and Explaining Judicial Decisions], *SPE* XVI (1976), pp. 16ff., and 'Poziomy uzasadnienia decyzji prawnej' [The Levels of Justifying Legal Decisions], *SPE* XL (1988), pp. 25ff. For more on the application of this distinction in the modern jurisprudential reflection and on R. Alexy's, N. MacCormick's and A. Peczenik's related conceptions *cf.* A. Grabowski, *Judicial Argumentation and Pragmatics*, *op. cit.*, pp. 155ff., and the references cited therein.

[53] For more on the critique of this fragment of Alexy's theory of argumentation *cf.* Chap. 4, pp. 117ff.

[54] *Cf.* A. Grabowski, 'Sonderfallthese – Its Critique and Interpretation', *op. cit.*, and the references cited therein.

we shall narrow our forthcoming discussion to the most crucial conclusions of the analyses presented therein.

At first, it should be noted that the Special Case Thesis can be interpreted only as *Integrationsthese*; namely, as an essentially normative thesis, postulating the combination of general practical arguments with specific legal arguments in the course of juristic discourse (legal argumentation). This is the case because the other interpretations of *Sonderfallthese* analysed by Alexy (i.e., *Sekundaritätsthese*—the thesis about the façade character of legal discourse and *Additionsthese*—the thesis about the complementary character of general practical discourse)[55] did not allow for legal discourse to be grasped as a "special case" of general practical discourse. It should also be noted that *Sonderfallthese,* interpreted as a purely descriptive or empirical thesis, must be rejected, due to its inadequacy. This inadequacy relies on distorting the real picture of juristic discourse (legal argumentation), both with regard to the descriptive–theoretical part of legal dogmatic discourse and—to an even greater extent—in relation to judicial argumentation, which is indeed practical in nature, but it does not follow the numerous general rules of practical discourse set by Alexy. As an example, let us mention two of the basic rules of a general practical discourse (*Grundregeln*): the sincerity rule (1.2 in Alexy's notation) and the rule of preserving the identical meaning of the expressions used by various participants in the discourse (1.4).[56] There is no doubt that the compliance with those rules in the judicial discourse cannot be prescribed, even by means of legal provisions, because in relation to many legal subjects it would violate the principle of *impossibilium nulla est obligatio* (within its subjective understanding, mostly adopted by the litigant parties). Let us note that the provisions of procedural law often impose the duty of sincerity (understood as "telling the truth") with respect to the testimony of witnesses, but not in relation to the arguments of the litigants. The legislator probably realises that setting such rules that would impose on the litigants and their attorneys the duty of "speaking only of what they believe in" would be defunct ("dead") law. Moreover, numerous verbal disputes that seem inevitable in the course of court proceedings (concerning, for example, the correct interpretation of the law) also show that the rule under discussion cannot have its practical application here. Thus, from a methodological point of view, the *Sonderfallthese* should be understood only as an analytical-normative thesis, and only a few rules of general practical discourse, which can withstand the test of empirical adequacy in relation to the actual judicial application of law, may be used as secondary (but not specifically juristic) procedural criteria of the acceptability of the arguments provided by the participants in actual court proceedings.

---

[55] *See* R. Alexy, *Theorie der juristischen Argumentation, op. cit.*, p. 38 [English version, pp. 19–20]. Let us add that Alexy is also in favour of adopting the *Integrationsthese* as the proper interpretation of the Special Case Thesis.

[56] R. Alexy, *ibidem*, pp. 234ff. [English version, pp. 188ff.]. The first of these rules states that "Every speaker may assert only what she/he believes in", whereas the other states that "Different speakers may not use the same expression (*Ausdruck*) in different meanings".

With regard to Alexy's procedural theory of legal argumentation, we can raise two interrelated methodological objections concerning the nature of the rules of general practical discourse as determined by him. Firstly, the objection of a monological (and therefore purely semantic and not pragmatic) character of some of these rules. Secondly, a peculiarly opposite objection, relying on the thesis that legitimate and correct solutions for practical questions can also be reached through a "discourse" with oneself, therefore it is not necessary to observe these discourse rules which, in turn, are of a dialogic nature (and thus of pragmatic character *par excellence*).

As far as the first objection is concerned, let us explain first why—according to some critics of Alexy's conception—he did make this error. Ernst Tugendhat argues that is it the case because Alexy combines semantic and pragmatic rules.[57] This argument, however, seems irrelevant, because both Habermas, as well as Alexy—who developed Habermas' ideas—based their theories of discourse on the speech acts theory in which the pragmatic rules contain semantic rules. This approach, represented by many leading representatives of speech acts theory (for example, directly by John Searle and, indirectly, by John L. Austin) is by no means based on mixing these two domains of linguistic research, but it has its source in a broad understanding of pragmatics—as a discipline which also includes semantic analyses or even sometimes syntactic ones.[58] Thus, including both semantic and pragmatic rules in the catalogue of practical discourse rules does not seem to be something improper—except perhaps for the very definition of the former as "discourse rules". It should be added that Alexy, in his later works (related to the concept of practical reason), explicitly indicates which of the discourse rules established by him also concern the monologues, and which are only "specific rules of discourse".[59]

The second of the above-mentioned objections is much more serious. Many authors who take up the problem of characterising legal discourse and its rules, recognise the possibility of individual "discourses" conducted with oneself. They refer to them as "inner discourses" (Alexy),[60] "simulated argumentation" (Kaufmann),[61] "a dialogue with a virtual partner" or "virtual discourses"

---

[57] E. Tugendhat, 'Zur Entwicklung von moralischen Begründungsstrukturen in modernem Recht', *op. cit.*, pp. 6ff. *Cf.* U. Neumann, *Juristische Argumentationslehre*, *op. cit.*, pp. 94ff. and M. Atienza, *Las Razones del Derecho*, *op. cit.*, pp. 210ff. Alexy's response to Tugendhat's objections can be found in 'Nachwort (1991): Antwort auf einige Kritiker', *op. cit.*, pp. 404ff.

[58] For more *see* A. Grabowski, *Judicial Argumentation and Pragmatics*, *op. cit.*, pp. 10–13, 63ff., and the references cited therein.

[59] *Cf.* R. Alexy, 'A Discourse-Theoretical Conception of Practical Reason', *op. cit.*, p. 235 [German version, p. 15].

[60] R. Alexy, *Theorie der juristischen Argumentation*, *op. cit.*, note 11 at p. 224 [English version, note 11 at p. 179].

[61] A. Kaufmann, 'Über die Wissenschaftlichkeit der Rechtswissenschaft. Ansätze zu einer Konvergenztheorie der Wahrheit', *ARSP* 72 (1986), p. 433. Kaufmann's statement is quoted *infra*, note 64 *in fine* at the next page.

(Gizbert-Studnicki)[62] or "mono-discourses" (Stelmach).[63] In fact, many legal practitioners and, in particular—though not only[64]—judges, who individually adjudicate a court case and then justify their decisions by way of argumentation, are forced into what is sometimes called "adjudicating in mind".[65] The consequences that this fact has for the discourse theory seem to be devastating. Let us recall that in Alexy's theory of argumentation it is not the consensus, but rather the fact of complying with the discourse procedure (determined by the rules of discourse), that constitutes the basis of recognising a specific practical decision (norm or normative proposition) as being (relatively) correct.[66] If such a correct solution can be the result of "an internal discourse", it is clear that in the said "self-discourse" we cannot violate any rule of general practical discourse which has a dialogical (purely pragmatic) nature, because it has a monological nature in effect. What is more, a doubt arises as to whether the remaining rules of general practical discourse, which preserve their validity in respect to the monologues, are generally needed to achieve the desired effect. As already noted, Alexy's discourse theory is based, inter alia, on the assumption that the participants in the discourse are generally able to distinguish between good and bad reasons, and therefore they have the ability to judge in the practical area, which admittedly is not a requirement of procedural discourse theory, but it constitutes an essential "missing link" between the rules of discourse and the correctness of its results.[67] This assumption justifies the suspicion that can be expressed in the form of the hypothesis that those who undertake "an internal discourse" can ignore the rules of general practical discourse that are important for monologues, because their ability to judge in the practical sphere seems, in itself, to guarantee the practical correctness—naturally conceived differently than in Alexy's procedural theory—of the results of such "virtual discourses".

This brings us to the fundamental questions. Is it really worth setting the rules of general practical discourse (also valid, though indirectly due to *Sonderfallthese*, for the juristic discourse), which are not only deprived of an acceptable justification,[68]

---

[62] T. Gizbert-Studnicki, 'Podstawy argumentacji prawniczej', *op. cit.*, p. 43 and 'Rozkład ciężaru argumentacji w dyskursie interpretacyjnym' [The Distribution of the Burden of Argumentation in Interpretive Discourse], *SFP* 2 (2003), pp. 65–66.

[63] J. Stelmach, *Kodeks argumentacyjny dla prawników*, *op. cit.*, p. 35.

[64] Similar "internal discourses" are probably undertaken by legal practitioners (lawyers, legal counsellors or prosecutors) when they prepare arguments in favour of the theses, objections or applications submitted subsequently in court or administrative proceedings, as well as by the dogmatists and theorists of law. As A. Kaufmann states in 'Über die Wissenschaftlichkeit der Rechtswissenschaft', *op. cit.*, p. 433, a discourse "man freilich auch in seinem Arbeitszimmer simulieren kann, indem man die anderen Argumentationspartner in Form ihrer literarischen Äuserungen zu Wort kommen läßt".

[65] *See* Z. Openchowski, 'Wyrokowanie w myśli' [Adjudicating in Mind], *GSiP* 8 (1970), p. 6.

[66] *Cf.* Chap. 4, pp. 86–88.

[67] *Cf.* Chap. 4, p. 116.

[68] *Cf.* the criticism of justifying the universal validity of the rules of general practical discourse, based on the transcendental-pragmatic argument, presented in Chap. 4 at pp. 99–117.

but which need not be observed (in any sense of this phrase) by many participants of the legal discourse?[69] Is James Herget not right when he concludes the analysis of Robert Alexy's procedural theory of discourse with the following statement:

> We have known for a long time that a panel of judges who openly debate an issue are more likely to come up with a better decision than a single judge. Does legal discourse theory tell us anything more?[70]

It is very difficult to give a balanced and scientifically fair answer to the above questions. Admittedly, the analytical–descriptive part of Alexy's theory, devoted to specific rules and forms of juristic discourse, has been very well accepted and it is widely used in jurisprudential literature. Whereas its analytical–normative part, within which he developed the rules and forms of general practical discourse, encountered an equally significant criticism, which has been repeatedly mentioned. This criticism has often assumed a form that verges on the scientific rules of decorum.[71] It can also easily be perceived that the strategy of constructing argumentation theory, based on the pragmatic (dialogue, dialectic) conception of legal argumentation, is often equally contested.[72] On the one hand, it is possible and even probable that Robert Alexy's theory of general practical discourse would be better accepted if, instead of trying to prove the existence of the discursive practical reason (practical rationality), its author concluded—as Marek Zirk-Sadowski did—that (practical) discourse is "a speech governed by moral constraints"[73] and refrained from at least a partly arbitrary determination of the catalogue of its rules and forms. On the other hand, it seems that the discussed theory of general practical discourse is more than just a collection of scientifically unjustified postulates of "analytical liberalism".[74] This theory provides—probably not in a manner that is likely to please everyone—at least approximate acceptability criteria[75] of practical arguments in the European legal culture, which can be used, for example, during judges' deliberation, as mentioned by Herget. It is also difficult to refuse philosophers and legal theorists the opportunity to create normative

---

[69] It should be stressed that at this point we do not only mean those who undertake "internal discourses". What is important, it is not argued that a number of the rules of general practical discourse can never be fully implemented in practice by its participants.

[70] J.E. Herget, *Contemporary German Legal Philosophy*, *op. cit.*, p. 61. *Cf.* A. Kaufmann, 'Über die Wissenschaftlichkeit der Rechtswissenschaft', *op. cit.*, p. 433, who stresses that due to the necessary presence of normative and subjective moments in the process of discovering law (*Rechtsfindung*), "a lone thinker in his study" cannot be considered as "an ideal type" of lawyer.

[71] *Cf.* Chap. 4, note 24 *in fine* at p. 65.

[72] *Cf. e.g.*, T. Gizbert-Studnicki, 'Podstawy argumentacji prawniczej', *op. cit.*, pp. 38ff., 42ff., and the critique of E. Tugendhat and D.A. Richards discussed in Chap. 4 at pp. 117–118.

[73] *Cf.* M. Zirk-Sadowski, 'Dyskurs jako mowa regulowana wymogami moralnymi', *op. cit.*

[74] On the "analytical liberalism" as the ideology underlying Alexy's theory *cf.* Chap. 4, pp. 115–116.

[75] We prefer the term "acceptability criteria" rather than "criteria of correctness", because the observance of practical discourse rules neither decides its outcome (the field of "discursively possible" decisions is very large), nor does it guarantee – in a different sense than *ex definitione* – the objective correctness or rightness of those decisions.

theories of legal discourse, thus seeking answers to the question as to how lawyers should argue. Such attempts, no doubt intellectually interesting, are occasionally made.[76] They bring us closer to the understanding of the nature of juristic argumentative discourse.

The presented review of the typical approaches to the research of legal argumentation, and in particular the discussion of the shortcomings of its procedural-discursive comprehension in Alexy's theory, leads to several conclusions concerning the perception of validity discourse and conducting its analyses as well as the scope of the subsequent research.

Firstly, we shall understand validity discourse as a kind of juristic discourse of a real rather than an ideal nature.[77] Only such an approach corresponds with the moderately realistic perspective on legal reality that has been assumed in the course of our analyses. The main task will be to identify the structure of validity discourse and to express it in the form of an adequate theoretical model. Under this model, we shall propose a set of concepts that will also highlight the role that the postpositivist definition of the validity of statutory law—presented in the previous chapter—could have in validity discourse. In developing the model of analysis that is appropriate for the discourse of validity, we will also take into account the primary practical purpose of this research—making it easier for legal dogmatists and practising lawyers to reach the answer to the basic question as to whether a given norm of statutory law is valid.

Secondly, we assume that there are grounds to believe that, having regard to the practical usefulness of jurisprudential analyses, we should refrain from unnecessary speculations, and especially from determining the "binding" or "universally valid" rules of validity discourse. In our opinion, however, we should accept an important exception: as we shall shortly see, in validity discourse in the strict sense, an essential role is played by the rules of the burden of argumentation, which we will try to roughly identify. The lawyers, who deal with the rules of the burden of proof every day, intuitively understand the rules of the burden of argumentation, so there are no obstacles to devoting some attention to these rules in our subsequent deliberations. Their inclusion will be helpful in defining the interrelations between the legal presumption of the validity of statutory law norms and the principles *ignorantia iuris nocet* and *ignorantia legis neminem excusat,*[78] which, in turn, will bring us closer to the evaluation of the postpositivist conception of the validity of statutory law in terms of the fairness of the social effects caused by its application.[79]

---

[76] In the Polish theory of law *see e.g.*, B. Brożek, *Rationality and Discourse*, *op. cit.*, in particular pp. 226ff.

[77] A real (and not ideal – "angelic") character of legal discourse has been most emphatically stressed by O. Weinberger – *cf. idem*, 'Logische Analyse als Basis der juristischen Argumentation', *op. cit.*, p. 192, 'Conflicting Views on Practical Reason', *op. cit.*, pp. 259ff. [German version, pp. 38ff.], 'Grundlagenprobleme des Institutionalistischen Rechtspositivismus und der Gerechtigkeitstheorie', *op. cit.*, pp. 262ff., and 'Basic Puzzles of Discourse Philosophy', *op. cit.*, pp. 173ff.

[78] For more *see infra*, pp. 529ff.

[79] *Cf.* Chap. 6, pp. 225–226 (the fragment on the fifth objective of clarification).

Thirdly, there is no denying that the validity argumentation theory, presented in the following sections, will be of a hybrid methodological character. However, as noted by Tomasz Gizbert-Studnicki, *de facto* formulated theories of legal argumentation are typically of such a mixed character.[80] When speaking of methodologically mixed theories, we can, for example, indicate the theory of legal argumentation developed by Aulis Aarnio, Robert Alexy and Aleksander Peczenik, which is normative and analytical, as well as Neil MacCormick's theory of legal reasoning, which is normative and descriptive,[81] whereas in the Polish legal theory, a hybrid nature is a characteristic feature of Jerzy Stelmach's theory of legal argumentation, which combines the elements of the discursive procedural theory and topics.[82] It seems that in relation to validity discourse, such a character is justified at least by the fact that the validity arguments used in it are very different in nature, which brings about the necessity of using the adequate methods of analysis corresponding to them. Therefore, from a methodological point of view, the following clarification of the extension of the juristic concept of the validity of statutory law will be of a hybrid (mixed) character. For instance, in the following analysis, we will apply the elements of a logical approach to legal argumentation when determining the structure of the juristic presumption of the validity of statutory law norms. We shall also apply the analysis that is typical for a rhetorical and topical approach in order to characterise the possible juristic validity arguments, because argumentation concerning legal validity has an undeniably open nature[83] that can best be explained by means of this approach. Nonetheless, what will prove essential for us is the dialogic approach (the dialectical, discursive one), interpreted analytically (since we will focus on analysing the structure of validity discourse), rather than normatively or empirically.

---

[80] *Cf.* T. Gizbert-Studnicki, 'Podstawy argumentacji prawniczej', *op. cit.*, p. 35 and J. Stelmach, B. Brożek, *Methods of Legal Reasoning*, *op. cit.*, pp. 111ff., and the references cited therein.

[81] As openly admitted by the authors of the theories indicated in the text – *see* A. Aarnio, R. Alexy, A. Peczenik, 'The Foundation of Legal Reasoning', *op. cit.*, p. 260; R. Alexy, *Theorie der juristischen Argumentation*, *op. cit.*, pp. 32–33 [English version, pp. 15–16]; N. MacCormick, *Legal Reasoning and Legal Theory*, *op. cit.*, p. 13.

[82] *See* J. Stelmach, *Kodeks argumentacyjny dla prawników*, *op. cit.*, in particular pp. 32ff.

[83] "Open" in the sense that it is unfeasible to provide an exhaustive catalogue of validity arguments, perhaps even in relation to a particular legal culture, and even more so on such level of analysis that is related to the system-type of statutory law. Let us add that the openness of legal argumentation understood in such a way was most clearly emphasised by the creators of the topical approach – *cf.* the studies of E.H. Levi and T. Viehweg indicated *supra*, note 21 at p. 459. In Polish literature the thesis about the openness of legal discourse (taken as an essential feature of interpretive argumentation) can be found in K. Płeszka, 'Reguły preferencji w prawniczych rozumowaniach interpretacyjnych' [Rules of Preference in Juristic Interpretive Reasoning], *SFP* 2 (2003), p. 83.

9.3 Validity Discourse

In principle, the argumentative analyses of validity discourse have not yet been undertaken.[84] The only study that can be recalled here that uses the concept of validity discourse is the already mentioned paper by Giovanni Sartor, in which he presents the normative conception of the validity (bindingness) of law, understood as a "doxastic obligation".[85] Sartor uses this concept in an intuitive way, without paying attention to its definition, since his primary purpose is to analyse a few simple examples of argumentative discussions concerning the validity of norms. Thus, one can assume that at this point of our clarificative analysis, we enter a jurisprudential "no-man's-land",[86] which has advantages and disadvantages. The positive element is that it is unlikely that we will be threatened by the objection that the following fragment of this work is just a "five hundred and second" study on validity discourse perceived through the prism of legal argumentation theory.[87] We have, therefore, complete freedom in choosing the specific issues and the method of analysing validity discourse and its structure. The downside of this situation, on the other hand, is the impossibility of confronting our ideas with the ones expressed by other legal theorists, which undoubtedly increases the probability of making errors. In particular, since our discussion will concern a certain validity-type of juristic discourse, which undoubtedly plays an important role in legal practice, we can be faced with the objection of the inadequacy of the theory of validity discourse outlined below. This inadequacy could mainly stem from leaving aside a number of important specific issues and presenting conceptual proposals and statements in a very general way, also due to the fact that we have adopted a considerably broad perspective in our research; namely, a continental system-type of statutory law. We accept such an objection in advance, hoping that in the future, the proposed theoretical model of validity discourse will be extended and made more precise, in collaboration with other scholars.[88]

We shall at first present the types and forms of validity discourse. Next, we identify and briefly characterise the possible outcomes of validity discourse *sensu stricto*. At this point, we will recall again that the proposed conceptual net is largely based on stipulative (synthetic) definitions of a purely conventional character.

---

[84] *Cf.* Chap. 8, p. 453.

[85] G. Sartor, 'Legal Validity as Doxastic Obligation: From Definition to Normativity', *op. cit.*, pp. 590ff. *Cf. idem*, *Legal Reasoning*, *op. cit.*, pp. 331ff.

[86] Although there are no studies devoted directly to validity discourse and its structure, our analysis will take advantage of many specific conceptions, created by the representatives of various legal disciplines, which indirectly relate to the topics discussed below – for example, to the studies on the structure of legal and juristic discourse, legal presumptions, the burden of argumentation, the particular validity arguments etc.

[87] *Cf.* the comments and arguments related to the "five hundred and first" study on legal argumentation theory in J. Stelmach, *Kodeks argumentacyjny dla prawników*, *op. cit.*, pp. 9–10.

[88] For more *see infra*, pp. 533ff.

9.3.1 *Types of Validity Discourse*

Identifying the various types of validity discourse and their characteristics will begin with us presenting a chart that shows the essence of the proposed typology (see Fig. 9.1).

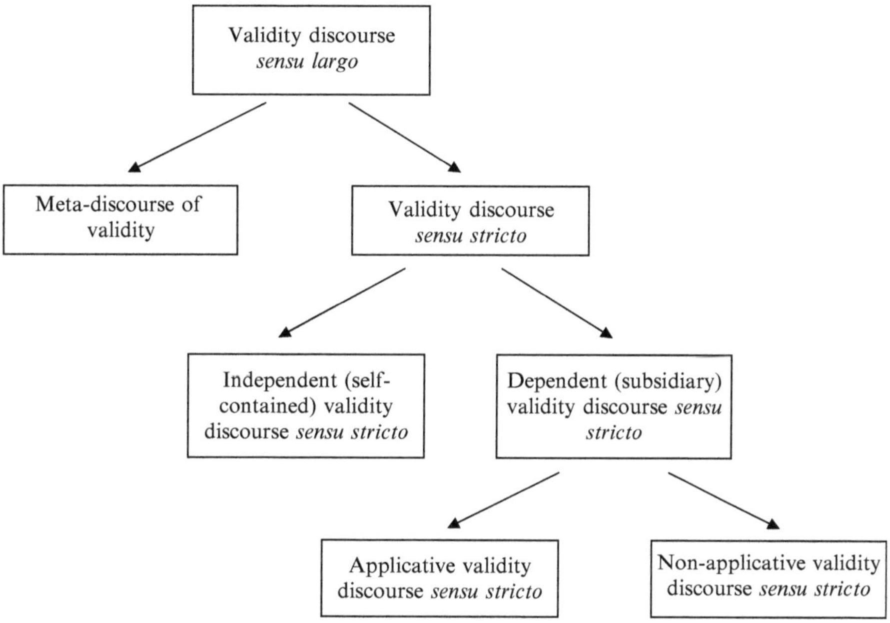

Fig. 9.1 The types of validity discourse

Validity discourse *sensu largo* (in the broad sense) is a superior and complex concept, whose definition will not be formulated here, since it would have to be so general that its cognitive value would remain minimal. Instead of that, we determine the extension of this concept. Validity discourse in the broad sense includes the meta-discourse of validity and the validity discourse *sensu stricto* (in the strict sense). These concepts are not extensionally disjunctive in the logical sense, but they are typological. These discourses can be characterised in a substantive and methodological way.

The subject matter of the meta-discourse of validity includes the basic concepts applied by jurists in order to define the essence of legal validity and to solve specific validity problems. In other words, from a practical perspective, this discourse aims to establish the network of abstract concepts that makes possible it to participate in juristic validity discourse in the strict sense. The most crucial of these concepts (which we label hereafter as "validity concepts"), both from a theoretical and practical point of view, are such juristic concepts as: legal validity, the binding force of law, the entry of provisions (norms) into force, derogation, the membership of norms in the legal system, the application of law, the social effectiveness of law, the substantial rightness of law, the sources of law etc. We can *quasi*-ostensively define this discourse by pointing to the work of the theorists, philosophers, logicians or sociologists of law, whose content can be treated as an example of participating in the meta-discourse of validity.[89] It can also be stated that all the considerations presented in the second part of this work constitute an example of participating in this type of validity discourse.

From the methodological perspective, the meta-discourse of validity is very diverse, because it can be undertaken not only on the basis of the methodology of the analytical theory and philosophy of law (applied in this study), but also by means of the other methods characteristic for jurisprudential analyses, or for axiological, logical, sociological, psychological, historical, cultural or anthropological research. What is important, in the context of differentiating between the meta-discourse of validity and validity discourse *sensu stricto*, is that the dogmatic method can also be used in the former case, especially when we try to define the concept of legal validity (or other validity concepts) in relation to the legal culture (or legal order) of a singular state or a group of states.

In turn, the subject matter of validity discourse *sensu stricto* is seeking (within a certain momentary legal system, be it national or international) an acceptable answer to the question as to whether a given legal norm is valid. Therefore, it is juristic discourse *par excellence* in which the most important role is played by dogmatic (legal) arguments, but the participants of it can also use theoretical (jurisprudential) arguments or purely practical (extra-legal, for instance moral) ones.[90] In the frame of validity discourse in the strict sense, we can distinguish between an independent (self-contained) and a dependent (subsidiary) validity discourse. The exclusive aim of an independent (self-contained) validity discourse *sensu stricto* is to solve the problem of the validity of a specific legal norm—the paradigmatic case of such a discourse is an argumentative discourse that accompanies the proceedings pending before the constitutional courts and concerns the constitutionality of statutory law norms. However, it may also take place in the course of dogmatic analyses, primarily focused on scientific purposes. A dependent validity discourse *sensu stricto* is of a subsidiary nature—the determination of the validity of a legal norm constitutes here only a part (a fragment) of settling some other legal problems. Within this type of validity discourse, we can distinguish between applicative validity discourse *sensu stricto* and non-applicative validity discourse. A more detailed definition of these two subtypes of the dependent (subsidiary) validity discourse *sensu stricto* will soon be proposed, after having

---

[89] In Polish legal theory, the following studies should be regarded as typical for the meta-discourse of validity: W. Lang, *Obowiązywanie prawa*, *op. cit.* and 'A Concept of the Validity of Law', *op. cit.*; L. Nowak, 'Cztery koncepcje obowiązywania prawa', *op. cit.* and 'Pojęcie obowiązywania prawa jako teoretyczne pojęcie prawoznawstwa' [The Concept of Legal Validity as A Theoretical Concept of Jurisprudence], *SM* III (1967), pp. 45–65; K. Opałek, 'The Problem of the Validity of Law', *op. cit.*; J. Wróblewski, 'Obowiązywanie systemowe i granice dogmatycznego podejścia do systemu prawa', *op. cit.*

[90] For more on the methods applied in this discourse *see infra*, pp. 494–525.

discussed, in the following section, the famous controversy of Klaus Günther and Robert Alexy concerning the distinction between the discourse of justification and application discourse.

The provided definitions of the respective subtypes of validity discourse *sensu largo* do not aspire to the role of strict and unambiguous definitions; however, due to their intuitiveness, we assume that they are sufficient to ensure the readability of the further analyses. We assume, therefore, that the provisional map of the "no-man's-land" is already outlined.

9.3.2 The Discourse of Justification and the Discourse of Application

Robert Alexy's Special Case Thesis has been accepted, with minor modifications or reservations, by many theorists of legal argumentation such as Neil MacCormick,[91] Aleksander Peczenik[92] and Jerzy Stelmach.[93] In relation to Alexy's thesis, it should be noted, however, that Klaus Günther developed an interesting dualistic theory of moral and legal (juristic) discourse, which competes with Alexy's theory of legal discourse and argumentation. In Günther's theory, the primary role is not granted to the discourse of justification (*Begründungsdiskurs*), but to the application discourse (*Anwendungsdiskurs*).[94] According to Günther, legal discourse is a "special case" of moral application discourse.[95] The reasoning that justifies this alternative to

[91] *Cf.* N. MacCormick, 'Moral Disestablishment and Rational Discourse' in H. Jung *et al.* (eds.), *Recht und Moral. Beiträge zu einer Standortbestimmung*, Baden-Baden 1991, p. 225 and 'Foreword' in *idem*, *Legal Reasoning and Legal Theory*, 2nd ed., *op. cit.*, pp. xii, xvi. It should be added that MacCormick anticipated Alexy's *Sonderfallthese*, claiming that legal reasoning constitutes "a special, highly institutionalised and formalized, type of moral reasoning" – *idem*, *Legal Reasoning and Legal Theory*, 1st ed., *op. cit.*, p. 272.

[92] *See* A. Peczenik, 'Legal Reasoning as a Special Case of Moral Reasoning', *RJ* 1 (1988), pp. 123–136.

[93] *Cf.* J. Stelmach, *Współczesna filozofia interpretacji prawniczej* [Contemporary Philosophy of Legal Interpretation], Kraków 1995, pp. 73ff.; J. Czaja, J. Stelmach, 'Teoria argumentacji prawniczej', *op. cit.*, pp. 19, 25ff.; J. Stelmach, *Kodeks argumentacyjny dla prawników*, *op. cit.*, pp. 27–28.

[94] *Cf.* K. Günther, *Der Sinn für Angemessenheit*, *op. cit.* [English version: *The Sense of Appropriateness*, *op. cit.*], and the studies of Günther indicated in the subsequent notes. When presenting his theory, I make use of the analysis already presented in my study 'Sonderfallthese – Its Critique and Interpretation', *op. cit.*, pp. 383ff. For more on the concepts of justification and on the discourse of justification *see* D. Buchwald, *Der Begriff der rationalen juristischen Begründung*, *op. cit.*, in particular pp. 277ff. and J. Stelmach, 'Zum Begriff Rechtsbegründung', *RT* 25 (1994), pp. 537–545, whereas, on the discourse of application, *see* U. Neumann, 'Die Geltung von Regeln, Prinzipien und Elementem' in B. Schilcher *et al.* (eds.), *Regeln, Prinzipien und Elemente im System des Rechts*, *op. cit.*, pp. 123ff.

[95] *See* K. Günther, 'Ein normativer Begriff der Kohärenz für eine Theorie der juristischen Argumentation', *op. cit.*, pp. 188ff. [a fragment left out in the abridged English version] and

Alexy's *Sonderfallthese* in based on following arguments. As already noted,[96] Günther rightly argues that no legal or moral norm alone can determine its own interpretation or application to singular cases. Therefore, *Begründungsdiskurs* (within the meaning of Alexy) can only justify a *prima facie* (discursive) validity of a norm (whereas it is not the validity in the formal legal sense, because the latter is presupposed in justification discourse),[97] but it cannot justify its application to a particular case. On the basis of this argument, Günther defines the correctness of normative propositions differently to that in Alexy's discourse theory. Such propositions can be deemed correct (*richtig*), not in cases when they are the result of applying a certain rational procedure of the discourse of justification, but only if they are "based on a valid norm and on its appropriate application".[98] Accordingly, the appropriate application of legal norms takes place only when two "Principles of Appropriateness" are met. Firstly, we need to provide a full description of the given case, taking into account all the relevant moral reasons, and secondly, we need to carry out a coherent interpretation of those, directly or indirectly relevant, moral reasons.[99]

Alexy, when responding to Günther's criticism, does not indeed question the need to distinguish between the discourse of justification and the discourse of application. However, he believes that treating the latter as an independent part of legal discourse that is equivalent to the discourse of justification is erroneous, because each discourse of application necessarily includes the discourse of justification, which, moreover, determines the outcome of an application of a legal norm.[100] According to Alexy, the idea of application discourse is both correct (because it evokes the hermeneutic condition of taking into account all points of view), empty (because it does not specify which points of view should be taken into account and how this should be done) and it can also lead to confusion (since the conceptual distinction between application discourses and justification discourses involves the risk of a non-universalist judicial practice).[101]

The commentators on Günther's conception of application discourse and on his criticism of Alexy's *Sonderfallthese* based on this conception formulate diverse

'Universalistische Normbegründung und Normanwendung in Recht und Moral', *ARSP* Bh. 45 (1992), pp. 70 ff.

[96] *Cf.* Chap. 5, p. 211.

[97] *See e.g.*, K. Günther, 'Ein normativer Begriff der Kohärenz für eine Theorie der juristischen Argumentation', *op. cit.*, p. 175 [English version, p. 160].

[98] In original: "Ein singulärer Normsatz kann beanspruchen, richtig zu sein, wenn er sich auf eine gültige Norm und ihre angemessene Anwendung stütz" – *ibidem*, p. 190 [a fragment left out in the abridged English version].

[99] K. Günther, 'Critical Remarks on Robert Alexy's "Special-Case Thesis"', *op. cit.*, p. 151. *Cf. idem*, *Der Sinn für Angemessenheit*, *op. cit.*, pp. 287ff. [English version, pp. 229ff.].

[100] *See* R. Alexy, 'Justification and Application of Norms', *op. cit.*, pp. 157ff., in particular p. 170 [German version, pp. 3ff., in particular pp. 16–17].

[101] R. Alexy, 'Jürgen Habermas' Theorie des juristischen Diskurses', *op. cit.*, pp. 171ff.

opinions,[102] among which the most important is Jürgen Habermas' standpoint, which strongly approves of the idea of application discourse.[103] In the Polish theory of law, the proposal to distinguish between application discourse and justification discourse, and to regard application discourse as the primary focus, went unnoticed, yet it should be noted that, regardless of the polemics between Günther and Alexy, the view, to some extent, is akin to the conception of application discourse, which has been presented by Stelmach, who states that "the general discourse, from the perspective of the possibility of its independent application, does not exist at all" because the argumentative discourse "by its very nature must be applied (realized)".[104]

Leaving aside the question of the correctness of Günther's theory of application discourse, let us consider whether the presented controversy may prove useful to distinguish between the subtypes of a dependent (subsidiary) validity discourse *sensu stricto*. We can undoubtedly point out the following criteria that allow us to distinguish the discourse of justification (within Alexy's meaning) from the discourse of application (within Günther's meaning); namely:

1. The nature of the legal norms that constitute the subject of a given discourse: within the discourse of justification these are universal; that is, general and abstract norms, whereas within the application discourse these are individual and concrete ones,
2. The fact that the discourse of justification is of a potentially abstract character—it need not necessarily be related to resolving a particular case, while the discourse of application is specific—and it is always connected to resolving a particular case,
3. The fact that in addition to the common, identical rules of discourse, probably each of these two discourses is attributed with specific rules and principles of undertaking it.

However, such a distinction between the discourse of justification and discourse of application—even if it is justified—does not seem to provide a useful basis from which to differentiate between the subtypes of dependent (subsidiary) validity discourse in the strict sense. When it comes to the concept of the discourse of justification, the fundamental problem lies in the fact that the independent (self-contained) validity discourse *sensu stricto* also has an undeniably justifying character (within Alexy's meaning of this term). Hence, the use of this concept is not

[102] *See* A. Grabowski, 'Sonderfallthese – Its Critique and Interpretation', *op. cit.*, p. 384, and the references cited therein.

[103] *See* J. Habermas, *Between Facts and Norms. Contributions to a Discourse Theory of Law and Democracy*, trans. W. Rehg, Cambridge (Mass.) 1996 [1st German ed. 1992], pp. 217ff., 230ff. Alexy responded to Habermas' objections against *Sonderfallthese* in 'Jürgen Habermas' Theorie des juristischen Diskurses', *op. cit.*, pp. 170ff. and 'The Special Case Thesis', *op. cit.*, pp. 376ff.

[104] J. Stelmach, *Kodeks argumentacyjny dla prawników*, *op. cit.*, p. 27. *Cf.* J. Stelmach, B. Brożek, *Methods of Legal Reasoning*, *op. cit.*, p. 183, where we read that the general practical discourse (and thus justification discourse in Alexy's meaning) "does not exist as such – it exists only in concrete applications, that is to say, as certain practical discourse".

recommended, because it can easily lead to misunderstandings. On the other hand, the use of the concept of application discourse (within Günther's meaning) seems to be out of the question, because the Frankfurt philosopher assumes that the formal legal validity of norms, whose potential application constitutes the subject of this discourse, is presupposed in it.[105] This, in turn, can lead to the self-contradiction of the concept of the applicative validity discourse *sensu stricto*, because—according to Günther—a particular problem of legal validity does not occur within it.

Günther's dispute with Alexy and the accompanying debate are certainly instructive, nevertheless, we believe that it is far more appropriate to distinguish and name the two subtypes of a dependent (subsidiary) validity discourse in the strict sense in a way that refers to the understanding of law application commonly adopted in the European legal culture. The proposed definitions, whose content is also determined by their assumed simplicity, are as follows. The applicative validity discourse *sensu stricto* will be hereafter understood as a dependent (subsidiary) type of validity discourse in the strict sense, accompanying the search for the answer to the question as to whether a given norm of statutory law is valid within the application discourse, whose primary objective is to apply the law in the strict sense of the word; namely, for making binding legal decisions of an individual character (i.e., having the form of individual and concrete norms) by the state authority duly empowered to act in such circumstances.[106] What can be considered as a paradigmatic example of application discourse is a juristic argumentative discourse that accompanies the judicial application of law within the meaning of the substantive decisional model of the judicial application of law as developed by Jerzy Wróblewski.[107] In addition, the non-applicative validity discourse *sensu stricto* will be understood as any dependent (subsidiary) validity discourse in the strict sense, which does not take place during the process of law application, but, for example, in the course of a dogmatic interpretation or systematisation of the law or negotiations that lead to the conclusion of a contract.

9.3.3 The Forms of Validity Discourse

Independently of the above distinction between the types and subtypes of validity discourse, we could also differentiate between its forms. Accordingly, the discourse of validity may be institutional or non-institutional in nature. The former is governed by positive law—the juristic validity discourse takes place, at least in

[105] Let us note that this assumption coincides with the substance of the argument that we applied when criticising the conception of validity understood as the application of norms – *cf.* Chap. 7, pp. 313ff., in particular the part of the argument A–VI concerning the correctness of the "reverse implication" at pp. 317–319.

[106] For more *see* Chap. 7, the argument A–V at pp. 313–316.

[107] *Cf.* J. Wróblewski, *Sądowe stosowanie prawa*, *op. cit.*, pp. 42ff. [English version, pp. 30ff.].

part, under a specific procedure determined by law. The participants of this discourse can be the actors set forth by the law, while its objective as well as its temporal scope are subject to legal restraints. On the other hand, the non-institutional form is legally indifferent. This distinction, widely accepted in relation to legal discourse,[108] naturally makes sense in so far as it affects the differentiation of the types of discourse, whereas this influence is, unfortunately, very slight, as should be—at least briefly—demonstrated.

As for the meta-discourse of validity, it has a non-institutional character because it is undertaken within legal science (mainly the theory and philosophy of law and the dogmatics of constitutional law) or other humanistic sciences. Positive law does not specifically regulate this discourse.[109] The argumentations that are characteristic for the meta-discourse of validity can also be encountered within validity discourse in the strict sense, and then they could be institutional in nature. For example, they are often present in an independent (self-contained) validity discourse *sensu stricto,* which is undertaken when settling a case pending before the constitutional court.

The independent (self-contained) validity discourse in the strict sense can take both forms. Such discourse cannot only be undertaken in the course of the proceedings pending before the constitutional courts, but also within dogmatic analyses. Therefore, it can be both an institutional as well as a non-institutional juristic discourse.

The dependent (subsidiary) applicative validity discourse in the strict sense is always of an institutional character, since it takes place within the judicial (or other type of) application of law. On the other hand, the dependent (subsidiary) non-applicative validity discourse in the strict sense is usually non-institutional in nature due to the fact that it is primarily undertaken within legal dogmatics. However, it may also take an institutional form in the situation when (for example) a specific legal system of a given state provides for an institutional interpretation of law carried out by a (constitutional or high) court empowered to do so. In such cases, in accordance with the terminology adopted in this study and in the Polish theory of law, we do not deal with the application of law in the strict sense of the word (i.e., the situation when a competent state authority makes a binding individual legal decision), but it is indeed the positive law that regulates the way in which such a type of juristic argumentation on validity is carried out.

At this point we have reached conclusions that are somehow uninteresting from the cognitive point of view: all the previously listed types and subtypes of validity discourse *sensu largo*—with one exception of the dependent (subsidiary)

---

[108] Apart from the studies of the theorists of legal argumentation, it is also worth noting an interesting analysis of the institutionalisation of legal discourse, undertaken from the perspective of linguistics by P. Goodrich, *Legal Discourse. Studies in Linguistics, Rhetoric and Legal Analysis*, Houndmills/London 1987, pp. 144–146, 170ff.

[109] We do not deny that the positive law – yet only non-specifically – also regulates the methods of conducting scientific argumentation, for example, by means of the legal provisions for copyright protection.

applicative validity discourse in the strict sense (which is always institutional in the meaning adopted here)—may take both institutional and non-institutional forms. Nevertheless, in our opinion, it does not mean that we should ignore the distinction between these two forms of discourse, because it is crucial in order to properly identify the characteristics of each type of validity discourse. In particular, the distinction between the two forms of validity discourse will have implications for identifying the juristic and/or legal rules of the burden of argumentation on legal validity.[110]

9.3.4 Possible Solutions for Validity Discourse

The solutions for the meta-discourse of validity—provided that they can indeed be at all referred to as "solutions"—cannot be subjected to any simple characterisation or classification. A number of competing conceptions of legal validity developed by the theorists and philosophers of law offer a variety of explanations, or even definitions of various validity concepts. Most of them can be assigned to the existing theories of law (positivist, nonpositivist, natural law etc.),[111] yet it is questionable as to whether the creation of a specific classification or typology of the solutions of the meta-discourse of validity would have any intrinsic cognitive value, or if this would not merely just be a cliché of the typology of contemporary theories of law.

In turn, it seems relatively easy to determine the possible solutions of validity discourse *sensu stricto*. We have indirectly addressed this problem in the previous chapter, where we analysed the juristic validity utterances from a pragmatic point of view.[112] Let us recall that we have distinguished between the positive and negative utterances about the validity of norms. The former are of a purely confirmatory nature, while the latter can express both non-derogatory decisions on validity (being, for example, the result of a dogmatic analysis), which do not cause that a specific norm of law ceases to be valid, as well as derogatory decisions on validity (typically taken by the constitutional courts), which cause that a given norm of law ceases to be valid. Therefore, there are three theoretically possible solutions of validity discourse *sensu stricto*:

1. A positive (confirmatory) solution,
2. A negative non-derogatory solution,
3. A negative derogatory solution.

In addition, it should be explained that, in our opinion, we cannot speak of "a positive solution of validity discourse *sensu stricto*" having lawmaking character,

110 *Cf. infra*, pp. 491ff.

111 For more *see* Epilogue at pp. 537ff.

112 *Cf.* Chap. 8, pp. 369–370, 380ff.

because if one formulated a positive validity utterance within the judicial decision of a lawmaking nature, it would be difficult to conclude that it is the result of validity discourse.[113]

Given the scope of the further analyses concerning the structure of validity discourse in the strict sense and the methods of validity argumentation, it is also worth presenting a synthetic characterisation of negative derogatory solutions. For this purpose, we shall apply the comparison of this category of solutions with a derogation that is not the result of an independent (self-contained) validity discourse in the strict sense, but which results from the decision of the legislator (a so-called authentic derogation carried out by the legislator). Moreover, due to the fact that in the continental system-type of statutory law the authors of the negative validity decisions of a derogatory character are primarily the constitutional courts, for the sake of simplicity, in the said comparison we will refer to them as "tribunal derogation".[114]

The most important differences between the derogation of legal norms carried out by the legislator (i.e., "authentic derogation") and the derogation resulting from the institutional independent (self-contained) validity discourse in the strict sense, taking place before the constitutional court (i.e., "tribunal derogation"), are as follows[115]:

1. The difference in the functions that these derogations fulfil: the "authentic derogation" allows the legislator to make changes in the positive law, while the "tribunal derogation" prevents new regulations or changes in the positive law introduced by the legislator from violating the valid law, and in particular the constitution of a given state,
2. The difference in the normative consequences caused by these two types of derogation, as "authentic derogation" (undertaken by means of the derogation of

---

[113] *Cf.* Chap. 8, pp. 388–389.

[114] For more *see* A. Grabowski, B. Naleziński, 'Kłopoty z obowiązywaniem', *op. cit.*, pp. 251–252. The term "tribunal derogation" is related to the name of the Polish Constitutional Court: *Trybunał Konstytucyjny*. I suppose that "tribunal derogation" is a better term than "judicial derogation" because the latter can create a false intuition that in this case we are dealing with a derogatory decision made by any court (not necessarily a constitutional one).

[115] We focus here on differences that are perceptible from the jurisprudential point of view. Thus, we leave aside those that have a specific dogmatic nature, associated with the content of the relevant regulations in a particular legal system. It should be added that the description of these differences (except for the last two) is based on the analysis provided by the Spanish legal theorist J. Aguiló Regla, who identified them in order to distinguish between the institution of derogation (undertaken by the norm-giver) and the voidability (*anulabilidad*) of legal norms (by judicial authorities) – *see idem*, *Sobre la Derogación*, *op. cit.*, p. 100. For more on these differences from a theoretical point of view *cf.* R. Guastini, 'A Theory of Derogation (with Special Reference to Italian Law)' in A.A. Martino, F. Socci Natali (eds.), *Automated Analysis of Legal Texts. Logic, Informatics, Law*, Amsterdam 1986, pp. 497ff. and P. Radziewicz, 'Przywrócenie mocy obowiązującej przepisu prawnego jako skutek orzeczenia Trybunału Konstytucyjnego' [Restoring the Validity of Legal Provision as a Result of the Constitutional Tribunal Ruling], *PS* 3 (2005), pp. 29ff.

certain legal provisions) usually does not involve the fact that the derogated provisions shall cease to be the basis for interpreting (on account of intertemporal regulations, in particular the principle *tempus regit actum*) legal norms that are valid, while the effect of "tribunal derogation" is a prohibition of such an interpretation of the repealed legal provisions,[116]
3. The difference in the author of the derogation; namely, either the legislator or the specific judicial organ that applies the law (in a broad sense)—usually the constitutional court or tribunal,
4. The difference in the appropriate procedure required to effectively carry out derogation (a procedure of legislation vs. judicial procedure),
5. The difference in the assessment, which consists in the fact that "authentic derogation" does not necessarily imply a negative assessment of the current legal regulation, while "tribunal derogation" is in principle associated with a critical, negative evaluation of the law as unconstitutional,
6. The difference in suability,[117] which consists in the fact that "authentic derogation" undertaken in the form of repealing legal provisions may be challenged and may become the subject of "tribunal derogation", yet not vice versa,
7. The difference in the possible subject of derogation, which is akin to the previous one, because it boils down to the fact that "authentic derogation" does not entirely exclude the possibility of a subsequent "tribunal derogation" of the norms previously repealed by the legislator.

The above differences seem to be so obvious that they do not require any additional comment. However, it was worth indicating them, since the distinction between "authentic derogation" and "tribunal derogation" will play a major role in identifying and examining the methods of validity argumentation, some of which are linked exclusively to one or the other type of derogation.[118]

Let us finally add that the analysis of the possible solutions (decisions) on legal validity justifies the assumption—adopted in the Introduction—about the classifying nature of the juristic concept of the validity of statutory law. We cannot, in fact, identify such solutions of validity discourse in the strict sense, which would rely on the determination that a certain statutory norm is in a peculiar "transitive"

[116] In reference to the Polish legal system, *cf.* K. Gonera, E. Łętowska, 'Artykuł 190 Konstytucji i jego konsekwencje w praktyce sądowej' [Article 190 of the Constitution and Its Consequences in Judicial Practice], *PiP* 9 (2003), pp. 7ff. and 'Wieloaspektowość następstw stwierdzania niekonstytucyjności' [Multifacetedness of the Consequences of Unconstitutionality], *PiP* 5 (2008), pp. 30ff.; R. Hauser, J. Trzciński, *Prawotwórcze znaczenie orzeczeń Trybunału Konstytucyjnego w orzecznictwie Naczelnego Sądu Administracyjnego* [The Legislative Significance of the Rulings of the Constitutional Tribunal in the Jurisdiction of the Supreme Administrative Court], Warszawa 2008, pp. 43ff. For more *see infra*, pp. 505ff.

[117] This difference can also be defined as the difference in the degree of certainty (understood here as stability) of the outcomes of the two derogations or the difference consisting in the superiority of the derogation made by the constitutional courts over the derogation undertaken by the legislator.

[118] *Cf. infra*, pp. 498ff., 513ff.

category between validity and invalidity. A dogmatist of law can say *ignoramus* and deal only with the interpretation of a given norm, yet in such a case it is difficult to state that she/he in fact settles any issue of validity.

9.4 The Structure of Validity Discourse *Sensu Stricto*

According to the postpositivist definition of the juristic concept of the validity of statutory law, the lack of an option on the part of the norm's addressee to refuse its fulfilment (implementation) means that a given statutory norm is valid. As already noted, this definition leads us to the idea of the argumentative clarification of the extension of the analysed concept by means of validity discourse *sensu stricto*, whose structure shall be based on reasoning reminiscent of falsification, rather than of verifying a particular hypothesis.[119] The structure of validity discourse in the strict sense is based—to put it simply and in a manner consistent with lawyers' intuitions—on the juristic presumption of the validity of norms set forth by the legislator, which subsequently constitutes the subject matter of validity argumentation. Let us review some arguments that justify the thesis that it is indeed the juristic presumption of legal validity that constitutes the axis of the analysed type of validity discourse *sensu stricto*.

Firstly, let us recall for the last time that a criterial method of defining legal validity, and, in particular, the attempt to solve the problem of the extension of the juristic concept of the validity of statutory law, does not deserve approval. If we followed this strategy, we would be able merely to determine the "*prima facie* validity of legal norms".[120] Little is changed by replacing the catalogue of validity criteria with the catalogue of invalidity criteria that specifies the legal possibilities of refusing the fulfilment (implementation) of a given norm. Such a negative catalogue, which can be referred to as "a postpositivist rule of non-recognition", will be burdened with the same defects as the substantively positive (or mixed) rule of recognition. Besides, it would be worthless if it did not contain at least one positive condition of validity. The remedy seems to be the proposed structure of validity discourse based on the presumption. Generally speaking,[121] the juristic presumption of the validity of statutory law norms will play a positive role here, while validity arguments—aimed at rebutting this presumption—will have a negative function.

Secondly, the adoption of the structure of validity discourse in the strict sense, based on the juristic presumption of legal validity, is strongly supported by a

[119] *Cf.* Chap. 8, p. 449. Let us recall that one can speak here only about the structural similarity, since most of the juristic validity utterances are devoid of logical value and thus they are not subject to falsification in the strict sense of the word.

[120] *Cf. supra*, pp. 457–458 and Chap. 7, pp. 276–277.

[121] In reality, the methods of validity argumentation are far more varied – *cf. infra*, pp. 494–520.

phenomenon—identified by Hart[122]—of the defeasibility of legal concepts and rules, and juristic reasoning.[123] This presumption expresses the assumption that the enacted legal norms are valid until their authentic or tribunal derogation occurs. This assumption is inherently "rebuttable" in a much broader sense than proposed in the modern systems of nonmonotonic defeasible logic. As we shall shortly see, the presumption can be rebutted not only by means of the validity arguments but, for example, it can also be blocked or circumvented. Accordingly, adopting the structure of the validity discourse *sensu stricto*, based on the presumption, allows us to dispense with the conceptions (systems) of defeasible logic, and thus protects against the possible objection that we apply logical analysis in relation to the mixed reasoning of validity, in which a significant role is most typically played by "modally fused" utterances about the validity of legal norms.

Thirdly, when we begin to analyse the structure of validity discourse in the strict sense, what immediately strikes home is the fact that this discourse is highly specific compared with other types of juristic discourse. Let us note that court proceedings (that are pending before the courts of common jurisdiction) very rarely involve argumentative disputes or discussions concerning the validity of norms (or legal provisions) that are relevant to the solution of a particular case. There is no doubt that within the continental system-type of statutory law, an essential role in the court proceedings is played by the *iura novit curia* principle,[124] under which the court knows the law *ex officio*. The knowledge of the law, which the cited principle refers to, undoubtedly applies to the questions of the legal validity of norms, and not just to the interpretation of the law. Yet, even in the case of an institutional, independent (self-contained) validity discourse in the strict sense—pending before the constitutional court—in which the outcome of a particular problem of validity of the specific statutory law norm constitutes the primary task, the argumentation in favour of a positive (confirmatory) decision does not necessarily have to be taken in order for the court to ultimately adopt such a decision. This is due to the presumption—adopted in the constitutional judicature (although with some exceptions concerning, for example, the sub-statutory norms)—of the constitutionality (compliance with the constitution) of statutory law norms, which shifts the burden of argumentation onto the party who questions the constitutionality and, thus, the validity of a specific legal norm.[125]

---

[122] H.L.A. Hart, 'The Ascription of Responsibility and Rights' in A.G.N. Flew (ed.), *Logic and Language, First Series*, Oxford 1951, pp. 147ff.

[123] In the Polish literature, *see* B. Brożek, *Defeasibility of Legal Reasoning*, *op. cit.*, in particular pp. 13ff. and *Rationality and Discourse*, *op. cit.*, pp. 28ff., 119ff.

[124] Let us note that this principle is, in fact, a fragment of a more complex principle: *Facta probantur, iura novit curia* [Facts are subject to proof, the court knows the law]. For more on the role of this principle in the validity discourse *see infra*, at pp. 492–494.

[125] For more in the context of the Polish legal system, *see* K. Wojtyczek, 'Ciężar dowodu i argumentacji w procedurze kontroli norm przez Trybunał Konstytucyjny' [The Burden of Proof and of Argumentation in the Procedure of Reviewing Norms by the Constitutional Tribunal], *PS* 1 (2004), pp. 19ff., with the extensive literature and rulings of the Constitutional Tribunal cited therein. It is worth noting that we can speak of juristic reasoning based on the presumption – this

What ultimately weighs in favour of adopting a presumption-based structure of validity discourse *sensu stricto* are the criterial conceptions of legal validity, which imply the method of clarifying the extension of this concept, based on analysing the extent to which the conditions of the validity of the norm at issue have been met. Let us look at the conception of the systemic validity of norms developed by Jerzy Wróblewski, which is one of the basic conceptions existing in the Polish legal culture.[126] According to this conception, a norm N is valid in a legal system (LS) if, and only if:

1. N was enacted (passed and promulgated) according to the rules valid in the LS,
2. N has come into force,
3. N has not been explicitly derogated by the norm valid in the LS,
4. N is not contradictory to the other norms that are valid in the LS,
5. And if N is contradictory to the other norms that are valid in the LS, then either N does not lose its validity on account of the rules about conflict between legal norms, or N is interpreted in such a way that having the meaning established through legal interpretation, it is not yet contradictory to any other norm that is valid in the LS.

When wc look at the conditions proposed by Wróblewski, then we find (leaving aside the fourth condition, which is logically redundant) that the first two conditions are of a positive character and they generally determine a set of norms in relation to which, it may be presumed,[127] they are legally valid. On the other hand, the latter two conditions are no doubt worded negatively: the norms "has not been explicitly derogated...", "does not lose its validity..." and "it is not yet contradictory to...". In our opinion, we do not need to comment on the fact that the order and the wording of the respective criteria of systemic validity, elaborated by Wróblewski, can easily be reinterpreted in the form of a presumption of legal validity: the positive conditions (1 and 2) will form its basis, whereas the negative conditions (3 and 5) express the negation of the so-called evidence to the contrary ("N has not been explicitly derogated" and so forth).[128]

---

time not of the constitutionality, but of legal force (which is undeniably the analogue of validity in relation to individual norms) also in case of administrative decisions – *cf. e.g.*, M. Kamiński, 'Konstytucyjne podstawy domniemania ważności decyzji administracyjnej' [The Constitutional Basis of the Presumption of the Legal Force of Administrative Decisions], *PiP* 9 (2007), pp. 56–67, and the references cited therein.

[126] *See* J. Wróblewski, 'Obowiązywanie systemowe i granice dogmatycznego podejścia do systemu prawa', *op. cit.*, p. 27 and *Sądowe stosowanie prawa*, *op. cit.*, p. 96 [English version, p. 77]. The following quotation in the text has been taken from the former study.

[127] According to my knowledge, Wróblewski did not use the concept of presumption in the context of legal validity, but it seems linguistically and logically justified – *cf.* the remark about Lang's terminology based on the conception developed by Wróblewski, *infra*, p. 486.

[128] For more on the structure of presumptions *see infra*, p. 487, and the references cited in note 144. Let us add that the logical structure of the presumption, whose possible reconstruction is described by us, is as follows: $(BP \wedge \sim EC) \rightarrow VN$, where 'BP' stands for the basis of the presumption, 'EC'

9.4.1 *The Juristic Presumption of the Validity of Statutory Law Norms*

The reasons and arguments, on account of which we recognise that the structure of juristic validity discourse *sensu stricto* is based on the presumption of the validity of statutory norms, have just been indicated and explained. Before describing the structure and the content of this presumption, let us remark that so far a considerably small number of legal theorists have made use of the concept of presumption (or related concepts) in their analyses of *Geltungsdiskurs*.[129]

In chronological terms, the first of these authors is Stanley Paulson, who, in his study *Neue Grundlagen für einen Begriff der Rechtsgeltung*, published in 1979, introduced the conception of the presumption of the validity of a legal norm (*Vermutung der Geltung der Rechtsnorm*, *Geltungsvermutung*), based on the then very fashionable theory of speech acts.[130] Referring to the pragmatic conception of the conditions of the "happiness" (successful performance) of speech acts (in the version proposed by John Searle), and taking into account the postulate of the certainty of law, the American scholar proposed a conventional solution to the problems of legal validity in the form of a presumption of validity, which combines the element indicating the basis of the presumption (i) and—in a negated form—the evidence to the contrary (ii).[131] This presumption, in the form of a constitutive rule, runs as follows:

> The lawmaker's utterance: "The law was passed" is regarded as establishing of a valid norm, if (i) the formal condition of promulgating the act has been satisfied and (ii) until it has not been proved in accordance with the law that [the remaining – *A. G.*] verifiable conditions are not fulfilled.[132]

---

for the evidence to the contrary, and 'VN' for the conclusion of the presumption; namely, a positive validity utterance about a norm N.

[129] It should be added that this reference is only of an informative character, because when constructing the juristic presumption of the validity of statutory law norms, we will not refer directly to any of these conceptions due to the reasons explained later on. We need to also make an obvious reservation that I probably leave aside the studies of many theorists and philosophers of law who have also used the concept of the presumption of legal validity, but their work is not known to me. However, I consciously leave aside a conception of "a rebuttable presumption of validity" (*widerlegbare Geltungsvermutung*), proposed by D. Heckmann, *Geltungskraft und Geltungsverlust von Rechtsnormen*, *op. cit.*, pp. 60ff.

[130] St.L. Paulson, 'Neue Grundlagen für einen Begriff der Rechtsgeltung', *ARSP* 65 (1979), pp. 1–19, in particular pp. 12ff.

[131] The logical structure of this presumption is: (BP $\wedge$ ~EC) $\rightarrow$ VN. It is therefore identical with the structure that may be determined by a presumptive reinterpretation of the concept of the systemic legal validity developed by J. Wróblewski – *cf. supra*, p. 483.

[132] St.L. Paulson, 'Neue Grundlagen für einen Begriff der Rechtsgeltung', *op. cit.*, p. 17. Paulson stresses that such wording is only "a preliminary approximation" to determine the concept of legal validity.

It should be noted that "the remaining verifiable conditions" are competence-based or substantive (material) in nature and they are determined by the constitution of a specific legal order. Paulson claims that, in accordance with the presumption, we should accept that the validity of a legal norm is only a presumptive validity. Lawyers should make do with such a surrogate (*Ersatz*) on account of the principle of legal certainty until the moment when one of the competence-based or material (substantive) conditions of validity proves to be unfulfilled.[133]

Another theorist of law worth mentioning here is Frederick Schauer—the author of the conception of presumptive legal positivism.[134] Although in his conception there is not any direct reference to the presumption of the validity of legal norms, some ideas are certainly worth noting. Schauer applies the concept of presumption to describe the force of legal rules, which consists in the fact that they are applied, unless there are "particularly exigent reasons" that justify their non-application.[135] What is more, he indirectly refers to the issue of validity by using the concept of a pedigreed set of legal rules that do not have absolute force—undeniably having in mind a presumptive binding force of these rules.[136] In his opinion, presumptive legal positivism is a descriptive theory (rather than a conceptual one, as in the case of soft legal positivism developed by Hart, Coleman and other inclusive positivists), determining both the status of "pedigree norms" (within the meaning of Dworkin), as well as those which contribute to this normative universe, although they do not meet the test of pedigree. At this point, we enter the sphere of the typical Anglo-Saxon disputes that focus around the consequences of Hart's rule of recognition for the positivist doctrine and the adequate visions (of the system) of law, which lie outside the scope of the current analyses. However, it cannot go unnoticed that Schauer's conception is based on similar, however more abstractly interpreted intuitions, whose clarification was attempted by Paulson.

As for the Polish jurisprudence, similar ideas can be found in the above-mentioned work by Wiesław Lang, dedicated to the concept of legal validity.[137] Yet, the use of the concept of the presumption of validity of legal norms has a very limited nature and it does not constitute a significant element of his normative conception of legal validity. Lang acknowledges that this presumption applies to legal norms "enacted by a competent authority in a proper way defined by the procedural rules of law making"[138] and it entails only a *prima facie* validity of norms that meet such a minimum condition of systemic validity. Obviously, this is a rebuttable ("defeasible" in Lang's words) presumption and its most important role is that it shifts the

---

[133] *Ibidem*, p. 17; *see* also p. 8, where Paulson provides the general characteristics of these two groups of legal conditions of "happy" lawmaking.

[134] F. Schauer, *Playing by the Rules. A Philosophical Examination of Rule-Based Decision-Making in Law and in Life*, Oxford 1991, pp. 196ff.

[135] *Ibidem*, p. 203.

[136] *Ibidem*, pp. 203–204.

[137] *See* W. Lang, 'A Concept of the Validity of Law', *op. cit.*, pp. 94ff.

[138] *Ibidem*, p. 95.

burden of proof of the incompatibility of such a *prima facie* valid norm with other valid norms to the party who challenges its validity.[139]

Before presenting a conception of the presumption of the validity of statutory law norms—in my opinion, the foundation and the core concept for the validity discourse in the strict sense—we shall first explain why we do not restrict our analyses to the acceptance of Paulson's or Lang's proposals.[140] We believe that both these conceptions are too simplistic, since they overlook some important elements of this presumption, and they prevent a full representation of the diversity and complexity of the validity discourse *sensu stricto*, which is much more argumentatively open than would appear from their proposals. In particular, both scholars, either implicitly (Paulson) or explicitly (Lang—directly referring to the theory of legal validity developed by Wróblewski),[141] refer to the criterial conceptions of systemic legal validity, adopting the following scheme of validity reasoning; the first criterion of the systemic validity of law (concerning a formally correct enactment of a norm) is transformed into the presumption of legal validity, whereas the remaining criteria (generally included either in its structure—as in Paulson's conception, or outside of it—as in Lang's proposal) nullify its result in cases where they are not met, which implies and justifies the statement that a given legal norm is not valid. Hence, the authors of the analysed conceptions are not able to identify the actual structure and the various ways of conducting validity discourse, and they must settle for taking a position that this presumption justifies the thesis that a valid norm is, in fact, "a norm which is presumptively valid" (Paulson), or "a *prima facie* valid" (Lang), up to the moment when it turns out that, in effect, it is not valid. In our opinion, such reasoning leads to an absurd conclusion that is clearly contrary to the legal reality evidenced by an everyday juristic discourse on legal validity. As, on the basis of Paulson's or Lang's conceptions, the norms of statutory law are either *prima facie* valid or they are not valid—*tertium non datur*.[142] However, in the practice of validity discourse, especially within the dependent (subsidiary) applicative discourse of validity in the strict sense, law-applying organs settle cases every day, undoubtedly relying on the norms that are definitively valid (at a given time). We do not hesitate to use the concept of

[139] *Ibidem*. In the latest work by W. Lang, 'System prawa i porządek prawny' [The Legal System and Legal Order] in A. Bogucki, S. Czepita (eds.), *System prawny a porządek prawny*, *op. cit.*, p. 17, we can find a complex formulation of this rebuttable presumption of the validity of a norm: "It suffices to say that the legal provision which the norm is decoded from, has been issued by the competent authority and published in the relevant official gazette, and that the time indicated in a given provision or in the provisions on the date of entry into force has elapsed".

[140] We cannot use Schauer's proposal since it is too abstract.

[141] *Cf.* W. Lang, 'System prawa i porządek prawny', *op. cit.*, notes 15–16 at pp. 17–18.

[142] The authors of the analysed conceptions would probably protest against the provided interpretation; however, in light of our previous analyses, concerning the incompleteness and the open texture of a customary and circular rule of recognition, which typically has a "soft" character, in fact, *tertium non datur*. For more about the rule of recognition *see supra*, notes 5–9 at p. 456, and the references cited therein.

absurdity, because how else can one determine the ruling issued by the court that contains the following wording: "According to the norm N, which is *prima facie* valid, the court rules as follows: . . .".[143] What sounds similarly absurd is a dogmatic interpretive utterance partially resulting from a dependent (subsidiary) non-applicative validity discourse *sensu stricto*: "The norm N, whose validity is presumed, states that . . .". In general, the idea that the subject of the jurisprudential analyses should be only *prima facie* valid norms (or presumptively valid norms), would seriously call into question the correctness of the judicial application of law and the scientific character of legal dogmatics.

The above general objections may be supported by more detailed ones. What negatively strikes in Paulson's presumption of the validity of a legal norm is—we believe—the fact of leaving aside a rather obvious point that the norms formally derogated by a legislator or by a constitutional court are not covered by the scope of this presumption. It is indeed difficult to conclude that this circumstance has been taken into consideration by him in the second part of the presumption (ii), because in most cases it is impossible to speak of "proving" that the derogation of the norm has taken place—the derogation is usually a notorious fact that need not to be proved during the court proceedings. Moreover, the fact that the American author adopted the structure of the presumption according to which its content includes both its basis as well as negated evidence to the contrary,[144] seems inappropriate due to two reasons. Firstly, it is impossible to present—even in very general terms—all the reasons resulting in a rebuttal of the presumption. Validity discourse in the strict sense is of an open character, even on account of the fact that it poses a considerable difficulty in identifying any regulation of a positive law or a commonly accepted jurisprudential conception that would exhaustively determine the reasons of invalidity (or a loss of validity) of statutory norms. Secondly, reducing validity discourse *sensu stricto* to such a form in which the only method of validity

[143] Calling the consequences of a certain conception "absurd" is undoubtedly very strong; however, in our opinion, it is justified. Let us note that this absurdity is fully demonstrated when we compare the effects of applying the juristic presumption of the validity of statutory law norms with the effects of applying a certain legal presumption. As an example, let us consider the court's ruling, based on the legal presumption of paternity, which would read as follows: "The court recognises *prima facie* paternity of Mr X". Incidentally, apart from the absurdity of such a decision, doubt arises as to what the said *prima facie* means here – certainly not *pro tanto*, yet probably also not "at first glance".

[144] We use here the concepts of the basis of presumption and of the evidence to the contrary *per analogiam* to the concepts commonly used in relation to the structure of legal presumptions. It should be noted, however, that the presumption of the validity of statutory law norms is a juristic presumption; it means that this is not a legal presumption. For more on the structure of legal presumptions, *see* J. Wróblewski, 'Domniemania w prawie – problematyka teoretyczna' [Presumptions in Law – Theoretical Issues], *SPE* X (1973), pp. 11ff.; T. Gizbert-Studnicki, 'Znaczenie terminu "domniemanie prawne" w języku prawnym i prawniczym' [The Meaning of the Term "Legal Presumption" in Legal and Juristic Language], *RPEiS* XXXVI/1 (1974), pp. 103ff. and 'Spór o domniemania prawne' [The Dispute over Legal Presumption], *PiP* 11 (1977), pp. 69–70; J. Nowacki, *Domniemania prawne* [Legal Presumptions], PNUŚ 142 (1976), pp. 9ff., 75ff.

argumentation would be that which seeks to rebut the presumption of validity, is highly unjustified. There are, after all, also different methods of validity argumentation applied in this discourse, as shall be indicated and discussed more thoroughly in the next section. On the other hand, in regard to Lang's proposal, the objection of leaving aside the act of formal derogation must be weakened. Although he does not mention it in the very formulation of the presumption, he indicates derogation as one of the reasons for the loss of validity of a legal norm. Moreover, he briefly examines the negative doctrinal rules of validity, referring to them as "derogation rules".[145] However, in relation to Lang's conception, what still remains justified is the above-mentioned objection of a too simplistic image of validity discourse in the strict sense, which—incidentally—comes as no surprise, nor can it form the basis of the direct criticism of this conception, because its author does not undertake to study the structure of validity discourse.

We shall begin the presentation of the juristic presumption of the validity of statutory law norms with the schematic expression of its structure. We assume that it has the general form:

$$F \rightarrow VN$$

(where F stands for the facts constituting the basis of the presumption, and VN for the validity of a norm N). On account of the wording of the presumption, which will be presented in a moment, and, in particular, due to the fact that, in our opinion, only the conjunction of two facts constitutes the basis of the presumption, the developed ("fully-grown") formula of the structure of the presumption is as follows:

$$(F_1 \wedge F_2) \rightarrow VN$$

As can be seen, in the structure of the juristic presumption of the validity of statutory law norms we leave aside the reservation of the evidence to the contrary,[146] for the reasons that have just been pointed out when criticising the structure of the presumption as proposed by Paulson. Accordingly, on the basis of two empirically verifiable complex facts, in this presumption we arrive to the

[145] *Cf.* W. Lang, 'A Concept of the Validity of Law', *op. cit.*, pp. 93–94.

[146] As far as the Polish discussion is concerned (*cf. supra*, note 144 at p. 487), J. Wróblewski and T. Gizbert-Studnicki voted for including the reservation of the evidence to the contrary in the structure of legal presumptions, whereas J. Nowacki strongly opposed this. This issue also remains disputable in international literature – *cf. e.g.*, D. Mendonca, 'Presumptions', *RJ* 11 (1998), p. 408 (a vote for including a negation of the evidence to the contrary in the structure of legal presumption) and E. Ullmann-Margalit, 'On Presumption', *JPh* LXXX/3 (1983), pp. 147ff. (a vote against inclusion). We do not discuss this controversy, since the specific reasons provided in the text justify the choice of a simpler structure of the juristic presumption of validity; moreover, this dispute concerns legal, rather than juristic presumptions, therefore in this aspect we use the freedom of "no man's land".

conclusion concerning the validity of a given norm of statutory law.[147] Any naturalistic fallacy (in the sense of "Hume's guillotine") is out of question here, since the intension of the juristic concept of validity of statutory norms, postpositivistically defined in the previous chapter, as well as the pragmatic analysis of juristic validity utterances, have shown that this conclusion is not of a purely normative character, but "modally fused". It can be therefore seen that to some extent (from a methodological point of view) we make *a maiori ad minus* inference here. The sentences stating the occurrence of facts F_1 and F_2 are rather descriptive in nature, whereas the conclusion VN in most cases has a fused, descriptive–evaluative–normative, character.

At this point, we will clarify the content of the presumption by characterising the facts which we refer to in it. We assume that we should begin with the following "working" form:

> If a norm N has been enacted, promulgated in accordance with the procedure of promulgating legal norms and entered into force (F_1), and its derogation by means of a derogatory norm D, established and promulgated in accordance with the procedure of promulgating legal norms, has not entered into force (F_2), then the norm N is valid (VN).

Now, bearing in mind the requirement of the simplicity of the proposed presumption, we shall express it in a simplified form, which we consider as final at this stage of research. We will use "the rule of correspondence for the term 'enacting a legal norm'", elaborated by Leszek Nowak, under which a procedurally correct promulgation of the norm stands for its enactment.[148] This brings us to the formulation of the final version of the juristic presumption of the validity of statutory law norms:

> If a norm N has been promulgated in accordance with the procedure of promulgating legal norms and entered into force (F_1), and its derogation by means of a derogatory norm D, promulgated in accordance with the procedure of promulgating legal norms, has not entered into force (F_2), then the norm N is valid (VN).

It can easily be seen that the proposed wording of the presumption refers not only to the conception of formal validity developed by Leszek Nowak,[149] but also

---

[147] Let us emphasise again that this is not a presumption of the "*prima facie* validity of norms" – *cf. supra*, note 143 at p. 487, which shows the absurdity of such an understanding of the results of applying this presumption in validity discourse. Moreover, in most cases the legal norms covered by this presumption are valid *tout court*.

[148] L. Nowak, 'Pojęcie obowiązywania prawa jako teoretyczne pojęcie prawoznawstwa', *op. cit.*, pp. 57ff. This rule reads as follows: "If a norm N is presented in the relevant journal of laws J in accordance with the procedural conditions C_P, then the norm N is enacted". What can be observed here is a strong resemblance to the analysed conceptions of St.L. Paulson and W. Lang, in which the concept of a formally correct promulgation of a legal norm appears in the content of the presumption. Let us note that in the juristic presumption of the validity of statutory law norms, as presented in the following part of our study, we apply an analogous rule of correspondence for the concept of a derogation of a legal norm, which is explicitly allowed by Nowak (although he does not, in fact, write about "derogation", but about "repealing" a given norm) – *see ibidem*, p. 58.

[149] *See* L. Nowak, 'Pojęcie obowiązywania prawa jako teoretyczne pojęcie prawoznawstwa', *op. cit.*, pp. 49ff. and 'Cztery koncepcje obowiązywania prawa', *op. cit.*, pp. 97ff. For more on Nowak's conception *see* Chap. 7, pp. 345–347.

to the conception of so-called thetic justification of (the validity of) legal norms, proposed by the Poznań school of jurisprudence and originating from the conception of thetic norms developed by Czesław Znamierowski.[150] The only difference (yet very important difference) is that we propose here a rebuttable juristic presumption of the validity of statutory law norms, which plays a key role in clarifying the extension of the juristic concept of the validity of statutory norms that consists in solving the practical question as to whether a given legal norm is valid, rather than in justifying its validity.[151] It should be stressed that although the complex fact F_2 is of a negative nature ("derogation ... has not entered into force"), there is no question of any similarity to the structure of the presumption of the validity of the legal norm elaborated by Paulson, because the fact that such derogation has not entered into force does not serve the purpose of rebutting the presumption, but constitutes the element of its foundation.

The content of legal presumptions originates from the valid law. The proposed presumption of the validity of statutory law norms is a kind of juristic presumption,[152] which raises the question of its acceptable justification. From the negative perspective, this justification stems from the presented criticism of the formulas proposed by Paulson and Lang. Yet it is worth considering whether our proposal can be justified in a positive way. Edna Ullmann-Margalit identifies three types of justifications used in relation to legal presumptions: the justification based on inductive-probabilistic considerations, value-related (normative) and procedural (which can also be called "praxeological") justifications.[153] The first of these justifications is related to the degree of likelihood of the occurrence of something indicated in the conclusion of the presumption in the situation when we are dealing with the occurrence of facts determined by its basis. It is accepted without proof that

---

[150] *Cf.* Z. Ziembiński, 'Normy tetyczne a normy aksjologiczne w koncepcji Cz. Znamierowskiego' [Thetic Norms and Axiological Norms in Cz. Znamierowski's Conception], *SF* 2 (1963), pp. 88ff. and S. Czepita, *Koncepcje teoretycznoprawne Czesława Znamierowskiego* [Jurisprudential Conceptions of Czesław Znamierowski], Poznań 1988, pp. 46ff.

[151] For more on the justification of the validity of statutory law norms in the course of validity discourse in the strict sense *see infra*, at pp. 502ff.

[152] By way of historical interest, let us note that in the early days of the constitutional courts, they were authorised only to examine whether the act of law was duly promulgated – *see* S. Wronkowska, 'O wadliwych aktach normatywnych w ujęciu wiedeńskiej szkoły teorii prawa' [On Defective Normative Acts in Terms of the Vienna School of Legal Theory], *SFP* 1 (2001), p. 212. In the context of the Polish legal system, it is also worth recalling the wording of Article 65 Section 5 of the so-called *April Constitution* from 1935, published in *Dziennik Ustaw* [Journal of Statutes] 1935, No. 30, Item 227: "The courts have no right to examine the validity of duly promulgated legislative acts". It seems, therefore, that the proposed presumption of the validity of statutory law norms, in which we use the concept of promulgation, could have been regarded in those times as legal presumption, at least in reference to the dependent (subsidiary) applicative discourse of validity *sensu stricto*.

[153] E. Ullmann-Margalit, 'On Presumption', *op. cit.*, pp. 157ff. Although her analyses concern legal presumptions, they also seem to be of value in analysing juristic ones.

in this aspect the above-proposed juristic presumption of validity is probable to a high degree. Although the conjunction of the facts F_1 and F_2 is (presumably) not a *condition sine qua non*, much less a sufficient condition for the positive solution of the problem of the validity of a given legal norm, undeniably, in the vast majority of cases, lawyers do recognise their consequence, VN, expressed by the conclusion of the presumption. The discussions concerning values also seem to justify the proposed content of the presumption of validity. As rightly pointed out by Ullmann-Margalit, as far as the inductive-probabilistic consideration "had to do with the *chance* of error", the normative (value-related) consideration, in turn, "has to do with the *acceptability* of error".[154] This problem will be separately discussed later, when analysing the practical consequences of applying the juristic presumption of the validity of statutory law norms in the context of the principles of *ignorantia iuris nocet* and *ignorantia legis neminem excusat*.[155] At this point, we shall content ourselves with recalling—in reference to Paulson's analyses—that it is the principle of legal certainty that presumably plays the most essential role in the axiological justification of this presumption. Finally, the third type of the considerations on justification, referred to as "procedural", involves primarily the question of "what presumption will be most useful to adopt" in legal (judicial) practice; namely, whether it is an appropriate starting point for legal deliberations.[156] Indirect evidence that the juristic presumption of the validity of statutory law norms is also positively justified in this aspect can be found in the next section, where we examine the methods of validity argumentation, which are closely connected with, and related to, the said presumption. Yet, already at this point we can make an observation that this presumption is most beneficial for judges who are bound (within the continental system-type of statutory law) by the principle *iura novit curia*.

9.4.2 The Rules of the Burden of Juristic Argumentation on Validity

According to the presented standpoint, when undertaking argumentative analyses of validity discourse *sensu stricto* (understood as a real, rather than an ideal discourse), we shall refrain from attempting to identify or establish its rules, while making an exception in relation to the rules of the burden of validity argumentation.[157] Identification and characterisation of these rules seem advisable not only in the context of the fairness of the results achieved in the undertaken clarification of the extension of the juristic concept of the validity of statutory law

---

[154] *Ibidem*, p. 159. Italics in original.

[155] *Cf. infra*, pp. 529–533.

[156] E. Ullmann-Margalit, 'On Presumption', *op. cit.*, p. 162.

[157] *Cf. supra*, p. 468.

norms, but also due to the fact that the rules of the burden of validity argumentation co-constitute the respective methods of this argumentation.[158] Identification of these rules, however, is not an easy task, mainly for two reasons. The first one involves the need for clarifying an undoubtedly ambiguous concept of the burden of argumentation and determining its possible meanings in a way that will allow us to apply this concept in analysing the various forms of validity argumentation. The second reason for the difficulties connected with applying the concept of the burden of argumentation in the analysis of validity discourse in the strict sense, is directly related to a high degree of abstraction of the undertaken clarificative analysis, which does not refer to any national (e.g., German, French or Polish) legal culture, but to a juristic discourse characteristic for the continental system-type of statutory law.

As for the first of the above-indicated problems, let us note that when analysing the rules of the burden of validity argumentation, we can apply, by analogy, the conceptions related to the concept of the burden of proof, in which we usually deal with a distinction of its various meanings. Such a method was implemented by Krzysztof Wojtyczek, who, in his analyses of the burden of argumentation in the proceedings before the Polish Constitutional Tribunal, uses the distinction—borrowed from the dogmatics of penal procedural law—between a general (praxeological), material and formal meaning of the burden of argumentation.[159] We can also adapt the conceptual convention—based on a dogmatic theory of the burden of proof—proposed by Tomasz Gizbert-Studnicki, who distinguishes between the burden of argumentation in the pragmatic sense as well as in the weak and strong procedural sense.[160] However, there arises a fundamental problem of applying this type of distinction in relation to validity discourse, associated with the role that the principle *iura novit curia* plays in it. In the context of the burden of argumentation in the interpretative discourse, Gizbert-Studnicki maintains that, on account of this principle:

> at least with respect to operative interpretation, a failure of raising a particular argument by the parties of the interpretative dispute, does not absolve the court from the obligation to consider all the arguments for and against each of the possible interpretive decisions,[161]

which can also be *mutatis mutandis* applied to validity discourse. In turn, when referring directly to validity argumentation, Wojtyczek draws attention to the widespread standpoint—also based on the principle *iura novit curia*—that:

---

[158] The basic element constituting validity discourse in the strict sense is – we believe – the juristic presumption of the validity of statutory law norms, as proposed in this study.

[159] *See* K. Wojtyczek, 'Ciężar dowodu i argumentacji w procedurze kontroli norm przez Trybunał Konstytucyjny', *op. cit.*, pp. 14ff., and the references cited therein.

[160] *See* T. Gizbert-Studnicki, 'The Burden of Argumentation in Legal Disputes', *RJ* 3 (1990), pp. 120ff. and 'Rozkład ciężaru argumentacji w dyskursie interpretacyjnym', *op. cit.*, pp. 67ff., and the references cited therein.

[161] T. Gizbert-Studnicki, 'Rozkład ciężaru argumentacji w dyskursie interpretacyjnym', *op. cit.*, p. 68.

> the court is required to determine the content of valid legal norms and apply them regardless of the activity of the litigants,[162]

especially having in mind this type of discourse, which we defined above as an institutional dependent (subsidiary) validity discourse in the strict sense.[163] The question of the burden of validity argumentation turns out to be very complicated because—on the one hand—the principle *iura novit curia* seems to at least minimise the importance of any validity argumentation for the institutional settlement of the question as to whether a given norm of statutory law is valid, but—on the other hand—the juristic presumption of the validity of statutory law norms is, after all, a rebuttable presumption, making it difficult to ignore the possibility of the validity argumentation of the litigants against this presumption or in the context of it.

When considering the second reason for the difficulties that can be encountered in analysing the rules of the burden of validity argumentation, it should be stressed that adopting a considerably general research perspective (though—as we think—this is justified by the projecting nature of the proposed conception of the clarification of the extension of the juristic concept of the validity of statutory law norms based on the argumentative approach), significantly prevents a precise identification and characterisation of these rules. Let us recall that the two subtypes of validity discourse in the strict sense—the most important and interesting from a practical point of view—namely, an independent (self-contained) validity discourse and an applicative discourse of validity, are mostly of institutional character.[164] Thus, these discourses are at least partially regulated by positive law, which is not taken into consideration in the undertaken analyses. This raises a problem that the actual operating rules of the burden of validity argumentation may remain unrecognised by us at the adopted level of the abstract, supra-systemic jurisprudential analysis. Some consolation was provided by Gizbert-Studnicki, who acknowledges that "the legal system (in itself) has no such rules".[165] In terms of the burden of argumentation in the proceedings before the Polish Constitutional Tribunal, this opinion is confirmed by Wojtyczek's analyses showing that the Polish legal system lacks an adequate statutory regulation. Therefore, the Constitutional Tribunal has been forced to define the rules of the burden of argumentation in its rulings.[166] We believe that carrying out the analyses within a given legal system

---

[162] K. Wojtyczek, 'Ciężar dowodu i argumentacji w procedurze kontroli norm przez Trybunał Konstytucyjny', *op. cit.*, p. 16.

[163] After all, this principle is essential only to some extent within the institutional independent (self-contained) validity discourse in the strict sense – *see ibidem*, p. 19.

[164] *Cf. supra*, pp. 476–478. Let us recall that the dependent (subsidiary) applicative discourse of validity in the strict sense is always institutional, whereas the independent (self-contained) validity discourse in the strict sense, although it may also take place in the course of dogmatic considerations, can be more often encountered during the proceedings before the constitutional courts.

[165] T. Gizbert-Studnicki, 'The Burden of Argumentation in Legal Disputes', *op. cit.*, p. 119.

[166] K. Wojtyczek, 'Ciężar dowodu i argumentacji w procedurze kontroli norm przez Trybunał Konstytucyjny', *op. cit.*, pp. 19 ff. It is worth quoting one of the conclusions made by Wojtyczek,

should be left to specialists in this field—that is, to dogmatists of law. Yet, the general jurisprudential intuitions connected with the problem of the burden of validity argumentation may prove to some extent useful for them in undertaking such intra-systemic analyses related to a given legal system.

When analysing the methods of validity argumentation, taking into account the above observations, we shall primarily focus on determining whether, in the context of the *iura novit curia* principle and the juristic presumption of the validity of statutory law norms (whose correctness is assumed here), any validity argumentation is necessary in effect. If the argumentation on validity proves to be unnecessary, then analysing the question of its burden will become virtually pointless. Otherwise, we will try to determine whom the burden of validity argumentation rests on and what the consequences are of a failure to meet them by its authors. Let us add that having regard to the readability of the undertaken analyses of the burden of validity argumentation, we will leave aside the non-institutional validity discourse in the strict sense, which by its very nature is not necessarily conclusive. We will, in turn, focus on two types of institutional validity discourse; namely, independent (self-contained) validity discourse *sensu stricto* (as a rule taking place before the constitutional court) and dependent (subsidiary) applicative discourse *sensu stricto* (taking place in the proceedings before the courts of general jurisdiction and administrative courts).[167] They are indeed most crucial for legal practice.

9.5 Methods of Validity Argumentation

The main objective of the clarification of the extension of the juristic concept of the validity of statutory law norms is to eliminate an extensional indeterminacy (vagueness) of this concept. The foundation of the proposed argumentative approach to the practical question of whether a given norm of statutory law is valid is the juristic presumption of the validity of statutory law norms. In the temporal aspect, this presumption calls for recognising as valid those norms in respect of which there takes place fact F_1 (promulgation and entrance into force of the norm N) and fact F_2 (the absence of promulgation and/or the absence of entry into force of derogatory norm D, which derogates norm N).[168] The duration of the validity of a statutory law norm covered by the presumption is illustrated by the

which demonstrates that there is no simple solution to the discussed problems: "Contrary to a common belief, the regulation of the burden of proof and argumentation in the material sense in the Polish constitutional law does not come down to a formula under which the burden of proof rests on those who question the constitutionality of a given normative act" (*ibidem*, p. 26).

[167] More on types and forms of validity discourse *see supra*, at pp. 471–473, 476–478.

[168] For more *see supra*, at pp. 484–491. It is necessary to present the consequences of adopting the juristic presumption of the validity of statutory law norms in temporal aspect because temporally non-relativised answer to the question of whether a given statutory norm is valid, is completely pointless – *cf.* Chap. 6, pp. 259–260.

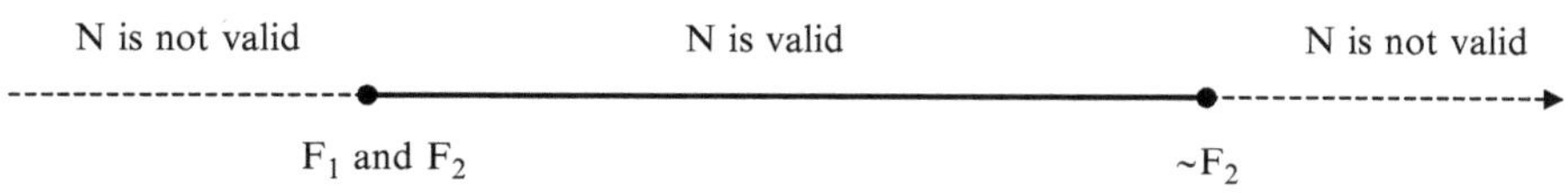

Fig. 9.2 The juristic presumption of the validity of statutory law norms

following scheme (see Fig. 9.2), in which the bold line indicates the duration of the validity of a statutory norm, while the thin dashed line—the time of its invalidity[169]:

The validity discourse *sensu stricto*, in which lawyers present validity argumentation that aims at resolving the problem of the extension of the clarified concept, can be very diverse. When analysing the possible types of juristic argumentation directed against legal presumptions, Daniel Mendonca distinguishes between the blockage strategy and the strategy of destruction of the presumption.[170] The former consists in the fact that we try to show that the basis of a presumption has not been proven or that its negation has been proven, whereas the latter comes down to proving the negation of the conclusion of a presumption. If we applied this distinction vis-à-vis the juristic presumption of the validity of statutory law norms, having the form $(F_1 \wedge F_2) \rightarrow VN$, then the blockage strategy would attempt to demonstrate that $\sim(F_1 \wedge F_2)$, whereas the destruction strategy—that $\sim VN$. However, we will not use the distinction proposed by the Spanish theorist, because validity argumentation can take more forms and be based on different strategies than just those two. Furthermore, we believe that the terminology applied by Mendonca, probably adequate in relation to the argumentation seeking to rebut legal presumption, does not seem to be most appropriate if we want to refer it to the methods of validity argumentation that can be encountered within validity discourse in the strict sense. Therefore, we are forced to create an extensive conceptual network,[171] by means of which we will try to identify and briefly explain the methods of argumentation that are used (or can be used) by lawyers in the validity discourse *sensu stricto*.

Before presenting the methods and strategies of validity argumentation, it is worth noting that in validity discourse in the strict sense we can question a "modally fused" opinion that the statutory law norm covered by the presumption is valid (and thus aim at a negative decision on validity) or question the opposite opinion under which a legal norm is not valid, even though it is not covered by the presumption (and seek—contrary to the presumption—a positive decision on validity). These two kinds of validity argumentation are hereafter referred to as "negative validity

[169] In the following schemes, illustrating the different methods and strategies of validity argumentation, we use the same graphical convention. Let us add that the bold dashed line, used in some of the following schemes, represents the doubt (uncertainty) concerning the validity of a norm of statutory law.

[170] *See* D. Mendonca, 'Presumptions', *op. cit.*, pp. 410ff.

[171] The proposed conceptual apparatus will also include the concepts of blockage and destruction of presumption, yet they will be attributed with the meaning different from the conceptual distinction of the Spanish theorist presented in the text.

argumentation" and "positive validity argumentation". As a consequence, it should be emphasised that juristic validity discourse in the strict sense can be a discourse addressed directly against the conclusion of the presumption, or a discourse undertaken in connection with it (directly or indirectly contesting the appropriateness of its adoption).

We propose to identify and distinguish between ten methods of validity argumentation, relativised to its outcome or its subject matter.[172] It should be noted that this enumeration is most likely incomplete, because the real juristic argumentation on validity may take other forms, probably more complex than those indicated and analysed below. A negative validity argumentation may be aimed at, or related to: the blockage of presumption, the expiry or the cancellation of presumption, or the rebuttal or the destruction of presumption and its suspension. Whereas a positive validity argumentation can take the form of the circumvention of presumption (the initial or the final one), or it may concern its revival or resumption.

It should be added that the following analysis most vividly reveals the provisional and conceptually synthetic character of our considerations. In fact we do not go into detailed analysis but we only offer a conceptual network being a starting point for further analysis and investigation of validity discourse in specific national legal cultures.[173] In this aspect our additional analyses on the burden of validity argumentation (which—let us recall—are related only to the institutional forms of two subtypes of the validity discourse in the strict sense: an independent and an applicative one) are also of a rudimentary character.

9.5.1 *The Blockage of Presumption*

We will say that the juristic presumption of the validity of statutory law norms is blocked when the complex fact F_1 did not occur. The purpose of referring to the blockage of presumption in the validity discourse is the justification of the correctness of the negative decision of validity; namely, the opinion that a norm N is not valid. The essence of the blockage of presumption is illustrated in the following scheme (see Fig. 9.3).

Due to the fact that F_1 is a complex positive fact (it consists of the promulgation and entry into force), the blockage of presumption may indicate that the statutory norm N has not been promulgated in accordance with the procedural rules of promulgation[174] or that it has not entered into force.

---

[172] We do realise that the primary shortcoming of the proposed typology is that in order to identify the methods and strategies of validity argumentation, we use the terms (names) of the outcomes or subject matter of validity discourse in the strict sense. Thus, we combine two different categories, which nevertheless seems necessary, at least at this stage of research, because we cannot find another, equally simple way to distinguish between the different methods of validity argumentation.

[173] For more on this *see infra*, at pp. 533ff.

[174] Due to the simplicity of the validity argumentation, we do not mention here the situation where a norm of statutory law has not been promulgated at all.

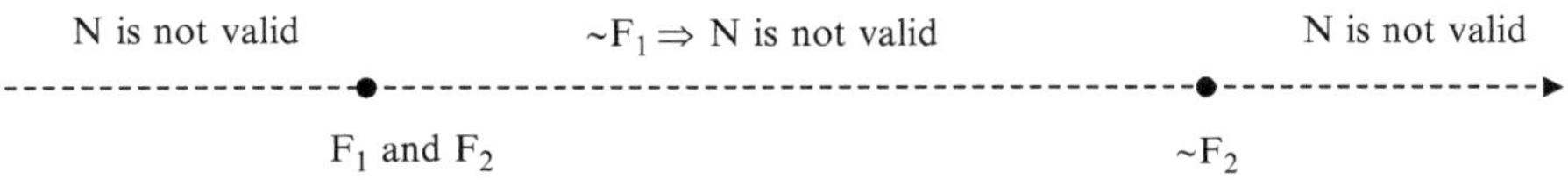

Fig. 9.3 The blockage of the juristic presumption of the validity of statutory law norms

The blockage of presumption is probably rare, yet it is not impossible, especially when viewed through the prism of the Polish experience. As regards the issue of promulgating norms (normative acts), let us recall the manner of promulgating *the decree of 12 December 1981 on martial law*[175] which has become—directly or indirectly—the subject of many court proceedings.[176] On the other hand, in relation to the situation when a properly promulgated norm failed to enter into force, let us consider the cases of legal norms whose *vacatio legis* was subject to extension by the legislator. In the system-type of statutory law, we cannot rule out a farther-reaching possibility of a situation when a legal norm had been derogated by a lawmaker even before its entry into force.

As for the burden of validity argumentation, due to the frequent self-evident nature of the above-mentioned facts, which result in the blockage of presumption, it seems that in most cases, speaking about the burden of argumentation is out of the question. At most, if a court did not take these circumstances into account *ex officio*, the court would have to be referred to them or reminded about them. Nevertheless, there is at least one exception; namely, if the procedural conditions for promulgating legal norms are complicated in a specific legal system, there may arise a dispute as to whether a given legal norm has been correctly promulgated. In this case, we can already speak of the burden of validity argumentation concerning the blockage of presumption, which rests—we believe—equally on both parties of such a validity dispute. This is the case because the legal norm that the dispute relates to is not covered by the juristic presumption of the validity of statutory law. Thus, both the supporter of the opinion that a given norm of statutory law is not valid due to the blockage of presumption, as well as its opponent, who considers that the norm has been properly promulgated—and thus it is valid (naturally, due to its entry into force) according to presumption—shall, to an equal extent, seek to

[175] In the text, we consciously provide the name of this infamous act of the communist un-law written with small letters. This decree, introducing Martial Law in Poland, was published in *Dziennik Ustaw* [Journal of Statutes] 1981, No. 29, Item 154, predated as of December 14, 1981, and formally speaking, it remained in force until October 2002 (sic!).

[176] Among the recent rulings, it is worth noting a grotesque (at least from the standpoint of legal philosophy) *Resolution of the Supreme Court – Penal Chamber*, from 20 December 2007, sign. I KZP 37/2007 (published in *OSNKW* 2007, No 12, Item 86). Under this resolution, the communist judges, adjudicating in criminal cases under this decree, were not discharged from the legal duty to apply retroactive statutory penal provisions. In that regard *see* an interesting theoretical gloss – in my opinion slightly too soft – by J. Zajadło, *Po co prawnikom filozofia prawa?* [What do Lawyers Need Legal Philosophy for?], Warszawa 2008, pp. 169ff.

justify their positions. However, their validity argumentation will be merely subsidiary, since what applies here is the principle *iura novit curia*—both in an applicative validity discourse *sensu stricto* and, although the issue is not entirely clear from a theoretical point of view, also in the institutional independent (self-contained) validity discourse *sensu stricto* before the constitutional court.

At this point, we should emphasise the need to distinguish between a blockage of presumption and the situation referred to as an "initial circumvention of presumption", which we deal with in a case of positive validity argumentation in favour of the validity of a specific norm, although the presumption of its validity has been blocked.[177]

9.5.2 *The Expiry and the Cancellation of Presumption*

We will say that the juristic presumption of the validity of statutory law norms expires (due to "authentic derogation") or it is cancelled (due to "tribunal derogation") when a complex fact F_2 does not occur ($\sim F_2$). Since this fact is expressed in a negative way ("the derogation of a norm N by means of a derogatory norm D, promulgated in accordance with the procedure of promulgating legal norms, has not entered into force"), we can use the logical principle of double negation and describe this situation in an easier, purely positive manner. Accordingly, we shall say that the juristic presumption of the validity of statutory law norms expires if a derogatory norm D, made by the legislator, was promulgated in accordance with the procedural rules of promulgation and has entered into force. On the other hand, the presumption is cancelled if a derogatory norm D, issued by the constitutional court, was promulgated in accordance with the procedural rules of promulgating legal norms and has entered into force. As with the blockage of presumption, the aim of referring, in validity discourse, to the expiry or the cancellation of presumption,[178] is to justify the correctness of a negative solution for the problem of validity; namely, the opinion or decision that a norm N, derogated by means of D, is not valid anymore. The nature of the expiry as well as the cancellation of presumption is illustrated by the following scheme (see Fig. 9.4).

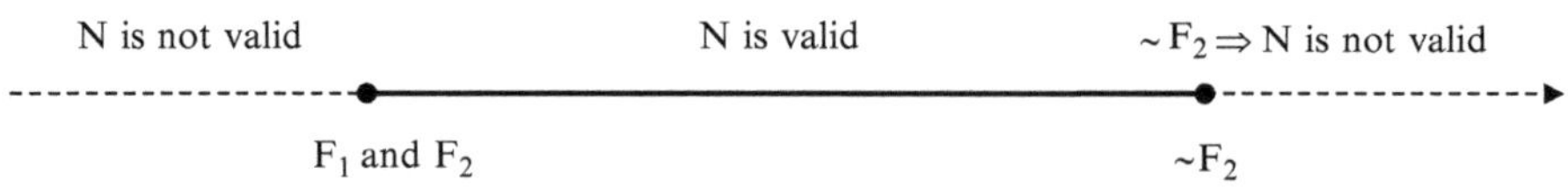

Fig. 9.4 The expiry and the cancellation of the juristic presumption of the validity of statutory law norms

[177] *Cf. infra*, pp. 503ff.

[178] It is worth noting that the cancellation of presumption can be both the subject matter of a negative validity argumentation, as well as the result of the institutional independent (self-contained) validity discourse in the strict sense.

A conceptual distinction between the expiry and the cancellation of presumption is necessary due to the substantial differences taking place between "authentic derogation" and "tribunal derogation".[179] Among these differences, in the context of undertaking validity argumentation, the most crucial is the difference of the normative consequences of these derogations, which is of utmost importance in the case of the final circumvention of presumption,[180] and the difference in the suability—which might lead to a revival of the presumption only in case of its prior expiration.[181] In turn, the difference that strongly militates in favour of the distinction between the expiry and the cancellation of the juristic presumption of the validity of statutory law norms is undeniably the difference in the possible subject matter of derogation, which consists in the fact that "authentic derogation" does not preclude the subsequent "tribunal derogation" in relation to the norms previously derogated by the legislator.[182] This means that the cancellation of the presumption precludes (or makes pointless) its subsequent expiry, but not vice versa.[183]

The expiry of presumption is very common, and due to the frequent changes in positive law, one can sometimes fail to notice that a given legal norm has been effectively derogated by the legislator. The cancellation of presumption occurs less frequently, but there may also arise some doubts as to the scope of the impact that the "tribunal derogation" of a given norm has on the validity of other norms that belong to a certain legal system, as was most vividly emphasised by

---

[179] These differences have been described *supra*, at pp. 479–480. As regards the effects of "tribunal derogation" with respect to the Polish legal system, *see* the monograph of M. Florczak-Wątor, *Orzeczenia Trybunału Konstytucyjnego i ich skutki prawne* [The Constitutional Tribunal Rulings and Their Legal Effects], Poznań 2006, pp. 132ff. Let us add that due to the synthetic nature of our conceptual proposals and on account of the simplicity of the presented conception of the validity discourse in the strict sense, when analysing the methods of validity argumentation, we leave aside the problem (highly contentious in the Polish legal culture) of whether "tribunal derogation" has *ex tunc* or *ex nunc* effectiveness. For more on this particular issue *see e.g.*, M. Florczak-Wątor, *ibidem*, pp. 67ff.; A. Zoll, 'Skuteczność orzeczeń polskiego Trybunału Konstytucyjnego' [The Effectiveness of the Polish Constitutional Tribunal Rulings] in A. Dębiński *et al.* (eds.), *Ius et Lex. Księga jubileuszowa ku czci Profesora Adama Strzembosza*, Lublin 2002, pp. 245ff.; K. Pietrzykowski, 'Problem skuteczności *ex tunc* albo *ex nunc* orzeczeń Trybunału Konstytucyjnego w orzecznictwie Sądu Najwyższego' [The Problem of *Ex Tunc* or *Ex Nunc* Effectiveness of the Constitutional Tribunal Rulings in the Jurisdiction of the Supreme Court] in *ibidem*, pp. 277–292; M. Safjan, 'Skutki prawne orzeczeń Trybunału Konstytucyjnego' [Legal Effects of the Rulings of the Constitutional Tribunal], *PiP* 3 (2003), pp. 11ff., and the references and court decisions cited in these studies.

[180] *Cf. infra*, pp. 504ff.

[181] *Cf. infra*, pp. 518ff.

[182] In Polish positive law, *cf.* the Article 39 Section 3 of *Ustawa z dnia 1 sierpnia 1997 r. o Trybunale Konstytucyjnym* [Statute of 1 August 1997 on the Constitutional Tribunal] (published in *Dziennik Ustaw* [Journal of Statutes] 1997, No. 102, Item 643), added under the amendment of 9 June 2000 (published in *Dziennik Ustaw* [Journal of Statutes] 2000, No. 53, Item 638), which excludes the application of the provisions on the dismissal of proceedings "if issuing the ruling on a normative act, which lost its validity before rendering the ruling, is necessary to protect constitutional liberties and rights".

[183] Theoretically, it is possible to circumvent the cancellation of presumption by the legislator who re-enacts a legal norm identical in its content to the norm derogated by the constitutional court, which nevertheless – as we do believe – is in fact more similar to the revival of presumption. For more on this *see infra*, pp. 518ff.

Carlos Alchourrón.[184] As regards the burden of validity argumentation, the observations on the blockage of presumption remain valid, which means that apart from exceptional cases, speaking about the burden of argumentation is pointless, whereas the validity argumentation will be at most of a subsidiary character.

Let us add that the controversial issue of the exact moment when legal norms lose their validity as a result of a deferred "tribunal derogation" will be analysed in a separate subsection devoted to the suspension of presumption.[185] Let us conclude with the remark that the expiry of presumption should not be confused with the case of the final circumvention of presumption, which involves a positive validity argumentation in favour of the validity of a given legal norm, even though the juristic presumption of its validity has already expired.[186]

9.5.3 The Rebuttal and the Destruction of Presumption by Means of Validity Arguments

We will say that the juristic presumption of the validity of statutory law norms has been rebutted when the conclusion of presumption has been effectively undermined by means of negative validity argumentation. This means that the validity discourse in the strict sense has led to the negative solution of the problem of legal validity; namely, to adopting the opinion or taking a decision that a norm N (covered by the scope of presumption) is not valid, even though the juristic presumption of validity has not been blocked, has not expired and has not been cancelled. The rebuttal of presumption is illustrated by the next scheme (see Fig. 9.5).

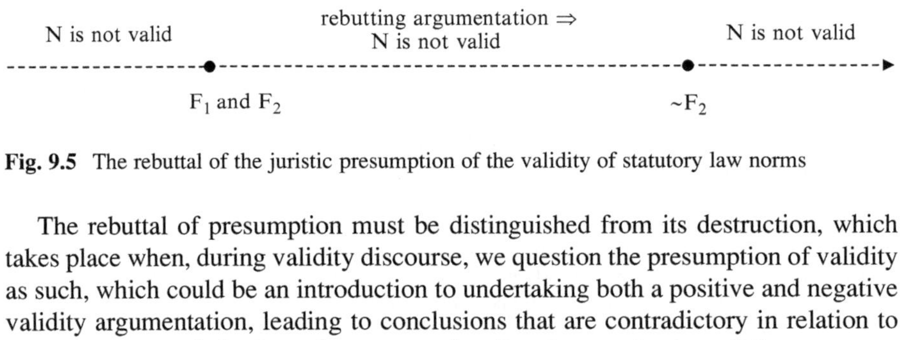

Fig. 9.5 The rebuttal of the juristic presumption of the validity of statutory law norms

The rebuttal of presumption must be distinguished from its destruction, which takes place when, during validity discourse, we question the presumption of validity as such, which could be an introduction to undertaking both a positive and negative validity argumentation, leading to conclusions that are contradictory in relation to those that we can infer from the presumption. In other words, the validity argumentation, aiming at the destruction of the juristic presumption of the validity of statutory law norms comes down to formulating the arguments against the proposed conception of the presumption of legal validity, which means that we enter the level

[184] For more on this intriguing problem, which is merely indicated here, *see e.g.*, B. Kanarek, *Teoretyczne ujęcia derogacji*, *op. cit.*, pp. 118ff., and the references cited therein.

[185] *Cf. infra*, pp. 513ff.

[186] *Cf. infra*, pp. 505ff.

of the meta-discourse of validity. This should not come as a surprise, since such a type of argumentation is very likely to be encountered in the course of institutional independent (self-contained) validity discourse in the strict sense, usually taking place before the constitutional court. The essence of the destruction of presumption and its possible consequences within validity discourse *sensu stricto* are presented in the next scheme (see Fig. 9.6), in which the bold dashed line represents the doubt (uncertainty) concerning the validity of a norm of statutory law:

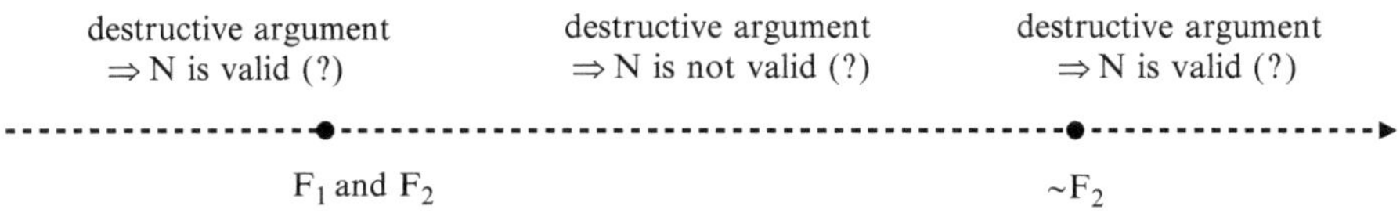

Fig. 9.6 The destruction of the juristic presumption of the validity of statutory law norms

The particular validity arguments, aiming at the rebuttal or destruction of presumption, can be very diverse, both in aspects of their content and in their epistemological character. In order not to complicate the presentation of the methods of validity argumentation, we devote a separate section to them.[187] At this point, we shall confine ourselves to stating that, in accordance with the postpositivist conception of the validity of statutory norms, the rebutting arguments—we believe—should be interpreted as an attempt to prove that the potential addressee of a statutory norm does have legal options for refusing the fulfilment (implementation) of it.[188] Let us add that the presumptive structure of the validity discourse in the strict sense, as proposed here, is an example of applying the so-called negative (coherent) theories of justification.[189] A juristic presumption of the validity of statutory norms plays a positive role in clarifying the extension of the concept of legal validity, while the validity arguments—as most evident in the argumentation which seeks to rebut the presumption—provide the reasons for rejecting the conclusion of this presumption. Thus, although the clarification of the extension primarily aims to find the correct answer to the question as to whether a given norm of statutory law is valid, it also implies the argumentatively-discursive model of justifying specific solutions of validity discourse *sensu stricto*,[190] which is synthetically manifested by a simple basic thesis that the juristic opinion or judicial decision on the validity of a statutory law norm,

---

[187] *See infra*, pp. 521.

[188] We leave aside an exceptional situation where the argumentation aiming at the destruction of presumption has the form of positive validity argumentation: the one who argues aims at destroying the presumption so as to subsequently justify the validity of the norm of statutory law that is not covered by the scope of presumption. This issue will be revisited at the end of this subsection.

[189] We have already mentioned this aspect of the postpositivist conception of validity in Chap. 8 at p. 449.

[190] For more *see infra*, pp. 533ff.

based on the presumption, is regarded as justified until the arguments in favour of adopting the contrary opinion are acknowledged.

In respect of the question relating to the burden of validity argumentation, it should be noted that this problem seems very complex, and, at the level of abstract jurisprudential analysis that is adopted in this study (which does not take into account the positive law regulations of the institutional types of validity discourse in the strict sense), difficult to explain. Therefore, let us content ourselves with expressing merely general intuitions.

As for the burden of rebutting argumentation, which takes place within a dependent (subsidiary) applicative discourse *sensu stricto*, it will, as a rule, rest on its author. We will presumably encounter some exceptions related to the situation in which a specific rebutting validity argument will be of a dogmatic (formal) character and it will be, to a considerable extent, accepted in a given legal culture (the example appropriate for the system-type of statutory law is the argument challenging the competence of the creator of the normative act to issue this act or the argument alleging a material violation of the legislative procedure). Then, in accordance with the *iura novit curia* principle, the rebutting argumentation becomes subsidiary. On the other hand, in relation to those rebutting arguments whose status in a given legal culture is disputed (for example, the nonpositivistic axiological arguments), the burden of validity argumentation will rest on the party that undertakes the negative validity argumentation, which is not subsidiary, but is necessary in such a case.

In relation to the rebutting argumentation that takes place in the course of the proceedings pending before the constitutional courts (i.e., within the institutional independent validity discourse in the strict sense), the analysed problem is—in our opinion—slightly different. We believe that determining any general rule of the distribution of the burden of validity argumentation that would result from the jurisprudential analysis—is out of the question.[191] The decisive role must be attributed to positive law regulations, depending on whether the proceedings before the constitutional court are based on the procedural principle of its instructive or adversarial nature. In both cases, the rules of the burden of validity argumentation will be framed in different ways. From the standpoint of legal theory, one can only express a certain intuition, according to which, in the proceedings concerning the constitutionality of legal norms, the juristic presumption of the validity of statutory norms, as proposed in this study, which in these proceedings usually assumes a peculiar form of the presumption of constitutionality, should be considered as a starting point for an independent (self-contained) validity discourse *sensu stricto*.[192]

[191] *Cf.* the opinion of K. Wojtyczek, quoted *supra*, note 166 at pp. 493–494.

[192] It is a rather secondary issue for the clarificatory analysis undertaken here; however, it can be stated from the axiological point of view that during the proceedings before the constitutional courts, it is the presumption of validity, rather than of constitutionality that should constitute the axis of the independent (self-contained) validity discourse in the strict sense, as the content of the presumption of the validity of statutory law norms does not imply anything as regards the question of the constitutionality of legal norms that are controlled by constitutional courts. *Cf. infra*, pp. 534–535.

With respect to validity argumentation aiming at the destruction of presumption, one can assume that the burden of this type of validity argumentation rests on the party who relies on this presumption, in particular, on the author of this work and on those who accept the idea of the juristic presumption of the validity of statutory law norms. Yet, we do hope that one can indeed defend the view under which the proposed conception is based on the intuitions and perceptions shared by many participants of the validity discourse in the strict sense. In fact, it does not seem to be erroneous when a lawyer or a citizen, being the addressees of a legal norm, adopts the assumption that the norms of statutory law, properly promulgated, not derogated and already in force, constitute the basis for further considerations, aiming to determine the legal situation of a certain legal subject. If this supposition is correct, then the burden of validity argumentation will rest on the party who intends to destroy the presumption. It should be further noted that when assessing whether the destruction of presumption in fact occurred, one should consider the ultimate objective of validity argumentation; namely, not only the argumentative justification for the negative validity decision, but also a positive settlement, usually in a way that will be referred to as "the circumvention of presumption".

9.5.4 The Initial Circumvention of Presumption

Another method of validity argumentation is the initial circumvention of presumption. It consists in the fact that the validity argumentation is of a positive nature and thus it supports the opinion or decision that a given statutory norm is valid, although the complex fact F_1 did not take place. In other words, we are dealing with this method of validity argumentation when we try to demonstrate that a norm of statutory law is valid, even though the juristic presumption of the validity of statutory law norms has been blocked; namely, a given statutory norm has not been promulgated in accordance with the procedural rules of promulgation or it has not entered into force. The essence of the initial circumvention of presumption is presented in the following scheme (see Fig. 9.7 on the next page).

Without a doubt, the only reasonable basis for the initial circumvention of presumption may be such an argument that challenges the basis of this presumption by questioning the thesis that the promulgation of a statutory norm in a manner that is consistent with the procedural legal rules of promulgation is necessary for its validity. In turn, we do not accept the argumentation under which the norm of statutory law is valid although it has not entered into force.[193] The initial circumvention of presumption is therefore connected with a partial destruction of the

[193] Such argumentation is excluded by the earlier critical analysis of the conception of legal validity, understood as the membership of norms in the legal system, in particular the argument A–IV formulated against this conception – *cf.* Chap. 7, pp. 304ff. This argumentation is also excluded by the postpositivist conception of legal validity presented in the previous chapter, because the fact that the statutory norm has not entered into force undoubtedly constitutes an example of an acceptable basis for the legal possibility of refusing its fulfilment (implementation).

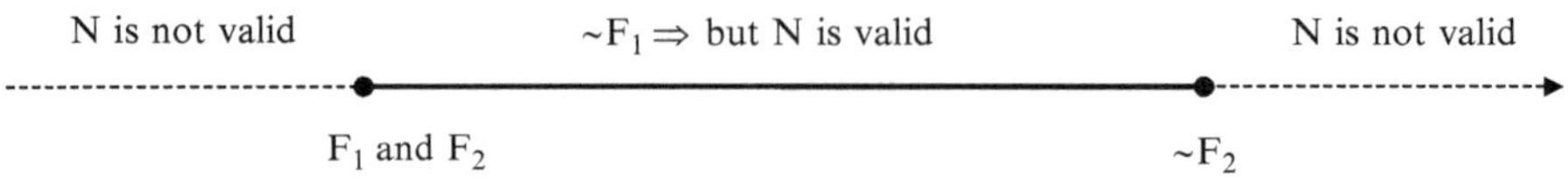

Fig. 9.7 The initial circumvention of the juristic presumption of the validity of statutory law norms

juristic presumption of the validity of statutory law norms, which we touched upon in the previous subsection.

Naturally, such a method of validity argumentation is unusual and unorthodox, in particular in those states where the requirement of promulgating valid laws is constitutional (as in Poland, in accordance with Article 88 of the Polish Constitution). However, even in such cases, this argumentation is indeed possible, as evidenced by recent proceedings pending before the Polish courts, and before the European Court of Human Rights on matters related to the property of Polish citizens left beyond the Bug River after the Second World War. What can be observed therein is the argumentation of the litigant parties seeking to make an initial circumvention of presumption by providing arguments for the legal validity of the unpublished "Republican Treaties".[194]

As for the burden of validity argumentation in case of the initial circumvention of the presumption of the validity of statutory law norms, it seems justified to maintain that it rests entirely on the party that argues in such a way. If the author of the argumentation fails to demonstrate the merits of her/his thesis in the validity discourse, it will be rejected without the need for providing any counterargument—it is sufficient to rely on the norms of positive law that establish the obligation to promulgate law or on the presumption of validity, as proposed in this study. Thus, the analysed argumentation related to the initial circumvention of presumption is necessary during the validity discourse *sensu stricto*.

9.5.5 The Final Circumvention of Presumption

The circumvention of presumption will also take place when someone argues that the norm N is valid, despite the fact that norm D, derogating the norm N, has come into force after having been promulgated in accordance with the legal rules of promulgation ($\sim F_2$). Thus, in such a case, we are dealing with the final circumvention of presumption that is the consequence of a positive argumentation in favour of the validity of a given statutory norm, undertaken in the situation when the

[194] *See* K. Michniewicz-Wanik, *Mienie zabużańskie. Prawne podstawy realizacji roszczeń* [Property Left Beyond the Bug River. Legal Basis of Implementing Claims], Wrocław 2008, pp. 24ff., 97ff., 178ff., and the references and rulings of the Polish courts and the European Court of Human Rights cited therein.

presumption of its validity has already expired.[195] The essence of this method of validity argumentation is shown in the next scheme (see Fig. 9.8) that is only of a provisional character, which will be demonstrated in the subsequent analysis:

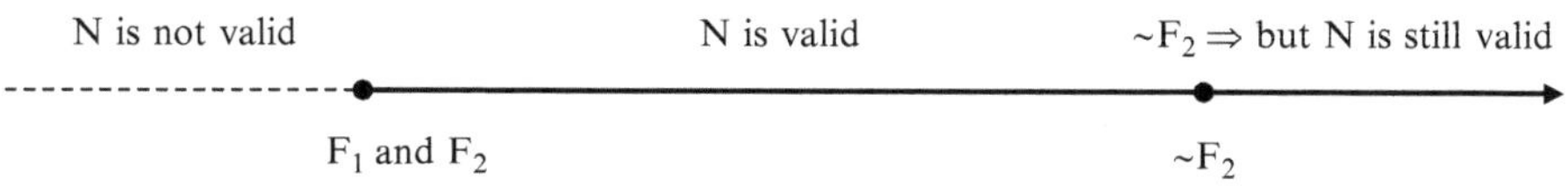

Fig. 9.8 The final circumvention of the juristic presumption of the validity of statutory law norms (working version)

At this point, we enter the conceptually most complex area of validity discourse *sensu stricto*. The characteristic feature of this kind of validity argumentation (in particular, taking place during the dependent applicative validity discourse in the strict sense), is a number of different ways of argumentation, mostly related to solving intertemporal problems resulting from normative changes in the positive law.[196] This is also an area of juristic discourse where one can easily encounter antinomies manifested in often self-contradictory utterances on validity questions. To provide an example, we can cite a fragment of the judicial justification of one of the recent resolutions rendered by the Polish Supreme Court in which we can find the following, *prima facie* self-contradictory opinions:

> The temporal scope of validity and application of a given provision does not necessarily overlap and, as evidenced by judicial practice with regard to legal provisions repealed in the distant past, as a rule it does not overlap, since it is difficult to assume that there will not be revealed the events occurred before the derogation of a provision. The loss of validity of the normative act as a consequence of its derogation or lapse of time for which this act was established, is therefore not synonymous with the loss of validity. Such a definite loss of validity takes place when a given provision cannot anymore be applied at all.[197]

It is easy to observe that in the beginning and in the end of the second quoted sentence we find an explicit contradiction ("The loss of validity [...] is therefore not synonymous with the loss of validity"). Yet, after taking into account the content of the remaining sentences, this contradictory statement no longer sounds absurd, since its meaning can be expressed in a non-contradictory way: "The *formal*

---

[195] Let us recall that in the case of the cancellation of presumption as a consequence of "tribunal derogation" any final circumvention of it is out of the question.

[196] On the change of law from the perspective of legal theory, *see* J. Mikołajewicz, *Prawo intertemporalne*, *op. cit.*, p. 39 ff., whereas from the perspective of legal dogmatics, *see* W. Wróbel, *Zmiana normatywna i zasady intertemporalne w prawie karnym*, *op. cit.*, p. 37 ff., 194 ff., and the references cited therein.

[197] *Resolution of the Supreme Court – Civil Chamber* from 30 May 2003, sign. III CZP 29/2003 (published in *OSNC* [Records of the Supreme Court Rulings, the Civil Chamber] 2004, No. 4, Item 50). I express my gratitude to Tomasz Pietrzykowski for drawing my attention to the content concerning the justification of this resolution.

loss of validity[198] [...] is therefore not synonymous with the *definite* loss of validity", which seems to be acceptable for the lawyers. However, even in this short passage of the cited resolution, we can see that the Supreme Court presents a "juggling of concepts", which is typically the consequence of attempts at the unambiguous description of multifaceted relations between the concepts of legal validity and judicial application of law in the context of intertemporal legal regulations.

A positive validity argumentation aiming at the final circumvention of presumption is undeniably strongly associated not only with intertemporal legal problems, but also with the question of the normative consequences of "authentic derogation" in reference to the legal validity of norms, which is highly contentious in the jurisprudential literature.[199] It is not our intention to discuss all of the topics related to derogation, since it would require analysing many interrelated conceptual issues which, at this current initial stage of considerations, does not seem advisable.[200] Therefore, we will focus on what seems crucial in the context of analysing the methods of validity argumentation; namely, clarifying the essence of the final circumvention of presumption. Due to the fact that we are exploring the area of theoretical jurisprudential reflection, in which we do not deal with a universally accepted conceptual apparatus, we will use an example of a case illustrating a simple intertemporal situation.[201] On the basis of the discussion of this case, we will try to explain the real nature of the final circumvention of presumption and, in addition, to propose the pattern of a jurisprudential interpretation of such an intertemporal situation that does not lead to antinomies or conceptual inconsistencies, nor to contradictions within the legal system.

So, let us imagine a case in which the employer terminates the contract with the employee. According to the legal norm of the former law N_F, which is valid at the date of terminating the contract and applicable in this case, the employer pays the employee a severance package in the amount of two months' salary. After some time (say, after half a year), there is a change in the law, and the new statutory norm N_N comes into force. According to the norm N_N, in the case of terminating an employment contract, the employee is entitled to receive a severance package equal to one month's salary. Having learnt of this, the employer files a lawsuit against a

[198] At this point, we follow Polish jurisprudential terminology, according to which the term "formal derogation" is equivalent to "authentic derogation"; that is, a derogation made by the legislator – *cf.* J. Wróblewski, *Sądowe stosowanie prawa*, *op. cit.*, p. 96 [English version, p. 77]; I. Bogucka, S. Bogucki, 'O derogacji i pojęciach pokrewnych' [On Derogation and Related Concepts], *PiP* 6 (1992), pp. 80ff.; B. Kanarek, *Teoretyczne ujęcia derogacji*, *op. cit.*, pp. 14–15.

[199] We confine ourselves to indicating only jurisprudential monographs – *cf.* D. Heckmann, *Geltungskraft und Geltungsverlust von Rechtsnormen*, *op. cit.*, pp. 193ff.; J. Aguiló Regla, *Sobre la Derogación*, *op. cit.*; B. Kanarek, *Teoretyczne ujęcia derogacji*, *op. cit.*

[200] Our task is merely to propose a conceptual network, useful for the analysis of validity discourse in the strict sense, which focuses on the juristic presumption of the validity of statutory law norms.

[201] We use the concept of the intertemporal situation introduced by J. Mikołajewicz, *Prawo intertemporalne*, *op. cit.*, pp. 59ff.

former employee, claiming reimbursement for half of the previously paid severance pay. The legal basis for this claim, as provided by the employer, is the new legal norm N_N. The case is obviously very simple from the perspective of legal practice: the court dismisses the lawsuit (or even—depending on the legal regulations of a given legal system—rejects it), because it applies the norm N_F (of the former law) and refers to the appropriate intertemporal legal rules or to the *tempus regit actum* principle. The problem is how to describe this situation in the language of legal theory, which is sometimes too far away from legal practice. Let us note that probably no practising lawyer (for example, a judge) or dogmatist of law has any doubt in this matter,[202] but the theorist of law has several, mutually conflicting interpretations and possibilities of conceptualising this simple case.

The first possible interpretation is a classic positivist one.[203] The norm of the new law N_N has brought about the so-called tacit derogation (understood as the complete loss of validity) of previously valid norm N_F. This derogation is based on the rule of normative conflicts *lex posterior derogat legi priori.*[204] Thus, the norm of the former law N_F is no longer valid in the present, momentary legal system (if it were valid, there would be a contradiction in this system between N_N and N_F, which is excluded by classic positivists). However, the court shall dismiss the lawsuit because it is obligated to apply invalid legal norms (i.e., the norm N_F in the case at issue) due to valid rules of intertemporal law or the principle *tempus regit actum.* This interpretation thus leads to the antinomy that we have already criticised.[205]

The second possible description is more complicated. The former norm N_F has brought about the derogation (also understood as a complete loss of validity and based on the *lex posterior* rule) of the former sanctioned norm—$N_{F\text{-}SD}$: "The employer has a legal duty to pay to the dismissed employee a severance package equal to two months' salary", but not of the sanctioning norm $N_{F\text{-}SG}$: "If the employer violates the norm $N_{F\text{-}SD}$, the court is obligated to award the dismissed employee the severance package equal to two months' salary, which has to be paid by the employer". Thus, a sanctioning norm of the former law $N_{F\text{-}SG}$ continues to be valid in a momentary legal system (if it were not valid, the court would probably have to support the employer's action, which seems to be clearly absurd). Due to the fact that the sanctioning norm $N_{F\text{-}SG}$ is not applicable (because the sanctioned norm $N_{F\text{-}SD}$ has not been violated), the court dismisses the lawsuit, on account of the lack of a legal basis for the employer's claim. The above interpretation, at least at first

[202] One can also ask whether this case does not differ too much from reality; nevertheless, let us assume that our hypothetical employer can file such a lawsuit – after all, he is vested with the right to court.

[203] This interpretation alludes to the views of E. Bulygin, 'Time and Validity', *op. cit.*, pp. 76–78 [Spanish version, pp. 211–213] and J. Wróblewski, *Sądowe stosowanie prawa*, *op. cit.*, pp. 107–108 [English version, pp. 83–84].

[204] To avoid unnecessary complications, the analysed example assumes that we are dealing with an indirect (tacit) derogation resulting from the juristic rules of normative conflicts (similar to the *lex posterior* rule) rather than from a direct derogation made by the legislator.

[205] *Cf.* Chap. 7, p. 293, in particular note 208. More on the antinomies in validity discourse *cf.* W. Lang, *Obowiązywanie prawa*, *op. cit.*, pp. 158ff.

glance, leads to contradictions in the legal system. If the sanctioning norm of the former law $N_{F\text{-}SG}$ is still valid in this system, and the sanctioning norm of the new law $N_{N\text{-}SG}$ is also valid within this system, then in the momentary legal system there are two different sanctioning norms, one of which requires the court to determine the severance package in the amount of two months' salary, while the second, new one—to one month's remuneration. This is naturally an apparent contradiction, as shown in the following, third jurisprudential description of the analysed case. The problem, however, lies in the fact that one cannot rebut another objection under which this description leads to such an understanding of derogation that is incompatible with common juristic intuitions and jurisprudential conceptual apparatus. It is difficult to identify the studies that would have defended the view that the sanctioning norms are not subject to derogation, but they are infinitely valid (or at least valid until the limitation of claims or rights which they relate to is reached).

Let us now present the third jurisprudential description of the analysed case, which—in our opinion—is adequate and conceptually consistent. The norm of the new law N_N caused a derogation (i.e., a complete loss of validity, based on the *lex posterior* rule), of both the former sanctioned norm $N_{F\text{-}SD}$ ("The employer has a legal duty to pay to the dismissed employee a severance package equal to two months' salary"), as well as the former sanctioning norm $N_{F\text{-}SG}$ ("If the employer violates the norm $N_{F\text{-}SD}$, the court is obligated to award the dismissed employee the severance package equal to two months' salary, which has to be paid by the employer"). Thus, none of the norms of the former law is valid after the change of positive law. The question arises, under what legal basis will the court dismiss the legal action of the employer, if the only valid sanctioning norm, which *prima facie* appears to be legally relevant, is the sanctioning norm of the new law $N_{N\text{-}SG}$, providing one month's severance pay (and therefore consistent with the employer's legal claim). It should be noted, however, that the event which the discussed case concerns (i.e., termination of employment and payment of two month's severance), took place at the moment that is not covered by the temporal scope of validity of a sanctioning norm $N_{N\text{-}SG}$.[206] This norm is, in fact, applicable to cases of termination and severance pay that took place after its entry into force, because only then did the sanctioned norm $N_{N\text{-}SD}$—linked to the latter—begin to be valid. Before the sanctioning norm of the new law $N_{N\text{-}SG}$ came into force, its potential addressee (i.e., the court competent to hear such cases) certainly had a legal option of refusing the fulfilment (implementation) of this norm; namely, awarding one month's severance pay.[207] Thus, we return to the question of which valid legal norm constitutes the basis for the court when resolving the analysed case. It is an important question, because in order to avoid the antinomy, we aim to demonstrate that courts decide cases on a normative basis consisting of currently valid legal norms, rather than formerly valid ones.

---

[206] We assume here that the new law is not retroactive.

[207] For instance, it could effectively block the juristic presumption of validity.

The explanation is very simple, yet unorthodox (although the conceptions that resemble it have already been encountered in the literature,[208] especially the Polish literature[209]). We will present it in several points, showing the reasoning that leads to a jurisprudential description of the analysed case, hopefully free of the defects of its previously presented interpretations.

1. In accordance with the position adopted by many theorists of law, even the smallest change of any of the parts (i.e., components of the content) of a legal norm is considered as its derogation.[210] In other words, the legislator may make changes in the law, yet may not change norms, but only replace one legal norm by another.[211] In the analysed case, issuing the norm N_N is therefore a derogation of the norm N_F, since the former sets forth a one month's severance package, while the latter provides for a two-month package. From the point of view of legal theory, these two norms should not therefore be understood as one and the same norm, with a merely changed content, but as two different norms.
2. "Authentic derogation" is undertaken by the legislator by means of repealing legal provisions (in the form of abrogation—when the repealed provisions were not replaced by new ones or by means of obrogation in the strict sense—when

[208] The theory that differs to the greatest extent from the traditional understanding of derogation was developed by R. Guastini, 'A Theory of Derogation (with Special Reference to Italian Law)', *op. cit.*, pp. 500ff. The Italian theorist of law does not recognise derogation as a phenomenon that concerns validity of norms, but which consists in reducing their temporal scope (of applicability). It is worth noting the criticism of Guastini's conception in B. Kanarek, *Teoretyczne ujęcia derogacji*, *op. cit.*, pp. 101ff, who nevertheless recognises that his conception has an unquestionable advantage; namely, it helps to explain why a derogated norm can still constitute the basis of judicial decisions (*ibidem*, p. 112). It should be stressed that, although our reasoning aims in a similar direction, we undoubtedly understand derogation in traditional terms in the sense that it concerns the validity of norms, rather than only their temporal scope (of applicability).

[209] The reasoning that follows leads to the conclusion that is convergent (or perhaps even identical) with the view expressed by M. Zieliński and Z. Ziembiński in the context of the criticism of W. Lang's conception of legal validity – *cf. iidem*, *Uzasadnianie twierdzeń, ocen i norm w prawoznawstwie*, *op. cit.*, note 32 at p. 174, and the so-called conception of partial derogation developed by W. Wróbel, *Zmiana normatywna i zasady intertemporalne w prawie karnym*, *op. cit.*, pp. 44–45, which seems to resemble some of the theses of R. Thienel's theory of derogation – *see idem*, 'Derogation. Eine Untersuchung auf Grundlage der Reinen Rechtslehre' in R. Walter (ed.), *Schriftenreihe des Hans Kelsen-Institut* 12 (1988), pp. 35ff. It should be noted, nevertheless, that E. Bulygin qualifies this solution as "a rather cumbersome and artificial construction" – *idem*, 'Time and Validity', *op. cit.*, p. 78 [Spanish version, p. 213]. I disagree with Bulygin, though the approach proposed below can be undoubtedly described as unorthodox – *cf. infra*, note 218 at p. 512.

[210] Such a standpoint, in the context of changes of law, connected with derogation of norms, has been explicitly presented by H. Kelsen, 'Derogation' in *idem*, *Essays in Legal and Moral Philosophy*, *op. cit.*, pp. 266ff. and E. Bulygin, 'Time and Validity', *op. cit.*, p. 78 [Spanish version, pp. 212–213].

[211] *See* M. Zieliński, Z. Ziembiński, *Uzasadnianie twierdzeń, ocen i norm w prawoznawstwie*, *op. cit.*, p. 167, where we can encounter a similar idea: "If we understand the norm of conduct as an utterance explicitly prescribing or prohibiting certain behaviour to specified addressees in certain circumstances, then such a norm cannot, by the very conceptual nature, be subject to changes".

the existing legal provisions have been repealed and replaced with new ones). Moreover, as presented in the above case, "authentic derogation" may take the form of the amendment—if the legislator does not repeal the legal provisions directly, but changes (modifies) their content.[212] Regardless of the used form of "authentic derogation", it is commonly known that very often the repealed or amended legal provisions, taken in its former version (a version before the change of law), does not cease to be the basis for decoding (interpreting) the legal norms that are still applied (due to intertemporal regulations or principles).

The above two points are probably hardly disputable. Yet, it is no longer the case with the following ones.

3. If we refer "authentic derogation" to legal provisions, it becomes an inadequate concept (or even an empty name, since something like this in fact does not exist), because the legislator does not derogate legal provisions (if derogation is understood as the complete loss of validity), but he repeals them or amends their content.[213] In our opinion, the fact that the legislator can use the following clause in the legal text: "The [following] legal provisions are losing their validity [or: binding force]: ..."[214] is irrelevant—after all, he does not use the juristic concept of the validity of legal norms that constitutes the core of our analyses.
4. The repeal or change of the content of the legal provisions causes the loss of validity of some norms, which could have been interpreted by lawyers on the basis of these provisions (and only in this respect can we speak of "authentic derogation" at all), yet—and this is the hardest to accept, although it seems obvious—repealing or modifying the content of legal provisions causes that new norms start to be valid, because they can be interpreted (reconstructed, decoded), *inter alia*, from the provisions of the former law. These norms are valid under the rules of intertemporal law or such principles as *tempus regit actum*, which act as applicability norms in the Bulygin sense of that notion.[215]

[212] For more about the terminology applied here, *see* A. Grabowski, B. Naleziński, 'Kłopoty z obowiązywaniem', *op. cit.*, pp. 246ff. It should be noted that it is largely based on conceptual analyses of I. Bogucka, S. Bogucki, 'O derogacji i pojęciach pokrewnych', *op. cit.* and B. Kanarek, 'Analiza teoretyczna pojęcia "derogacja"' [Theoretical Analysis of the Concept of "Derogation"] in L. Leszczyński (ed.), *Zmiany społeczne a zmiany w prawie. Aksjologia, konstytucja, integracja europejska*, Lublin 1999, pp. 235–244. Naturally, the change of the content of legal provisions is understood as an indirect derogation of the former provisions.

[213] As we believe, what is confirmed at this point are the semantic intuitions presented by B. Kanarek and M. Zieliński, which we presented within the argument from precedence (priority) in Chap. 6 at p. 242.

[214] For more about the expressions used by the Polish legislator in order to repeal legal provisions *see* B. Kanarek, 'Moc obowiązująca i moc prawna a zagadnienie derogacji' [Binding Force and Legal Force vis-à-vis the Issue of Derogation] in Z. Tobor, I. Bogucka (eds.), *Prawoznawstwo a praktyka stosowania prawa*, *op. cit.*, pp. 187ff.

[215] *Cf.* Chap. 7, pp. 322ff. B. Kanarek and M. Zieliński write in this context about "anti-derogatory provisions" – *cf. iidem*, 'Porządkująca faza wykładni prawa', *op. cit.*, p. 7.

5. Therefore, since the entry into force of the legal norm N_N, what starts to be valid within the legal system (understood in postpositivist terms, as adopted in this study) is a negative interim (temporary) sanctioning norm $N_{I\text{-}SG}$, which reads as follows: "In case of non-infringement of the sanctioned norm of the former law $N_{F\text{-}SD}$, within the time when it was valid and applicable, the court is obligated to dismiss the lawsuit which is based on the currently valid sanctioned norm of the new law $N_{N\text{-}SD}$".[216]

We assume that the jurisprudential description of the analysed case, as presented in point 5, is correct from the theoretical point of view. The fact that legal norm $N_{I\text{-}SG}$ is valid despite the "authentic derogation" of the norm N_F by the legislator, is clear to us in light of the postpositivist conception of legal validity. The court certainly has no legal option of refusing the fulfilment (implementation) of the sanctioning norm $N_{I\text{-}SG}$, which results in issuing the ruling that dismisses the employer's lawsuit in the case at hand. Let us add that there is no normative contradiction in the new legal system, because the interim (temporary) sanctioning norm $N_{I\text{-}SG}$ is not in conflict with the sanctioning norm of the new law $N_{N\text{-}SG}$ (which is also valid in this momentary system). Both of them differ in their scope of application (and more precisely, in the temporal element of these scopes), making it impossible to recognise them as inconsistent. The former determines how to settle court cases relating to the severance payment due under the termination of the employment contract on the basis of the former law, while the latter—under the new law.

When revisiting the concept of the final circumvention of the presumption of the validity of statutory law norms, we need to ask an important question; namely, when has the interim (temporary) sanctioning norm $N_{I\text{-}SG}$ been issued? As it would seem, we should not state that it happened already at the time of establishing the norm of the former law N_F, after which the norm $N_{I\text{-}SG}$ remained somewhat "dormant", waiting for the "authentic derogation" of the norm N_F. It is indisputable that in order to determine the content of the interim (temporary) sanctioning norm $N_{I\text{-}SG}$, we need to know the actual date at which the norm of the new law N_N has entered into force. This, in turn, cannot be determined before "authentic derogation" has taken place, and even the most rational legislator is unable to predict at which moment the derogation of the norms established by him shall be deemed appropriate.[217] Thus, the moment at which the interim (temporary) sanctioning norm $N_{I\text{-}SG}$ enters into force is identical to the moment in which the norm of the

[216] Naturally, in a more likely case in which the employer failed to pay the severance to the dismissed employee, we would apply a "positive" interim norm $N_{I\text{-}SG}$, which reads as follows: "In case of infringing the sanctioned norm of the former law $N_{F\text{-}SD}$ within the time when it was valid and applicable, the court is obligated to allow the employee's lawsuit filed on that basis; that is, to award the severance pay amounting to two months' remuneration".

[217] We disregard here the problem of the episodic statutes (lawmaking acts) which *ex ante* determine the loss of their validity at a particular moment. The validity argumentation concerning them is analysed in the next subsection.

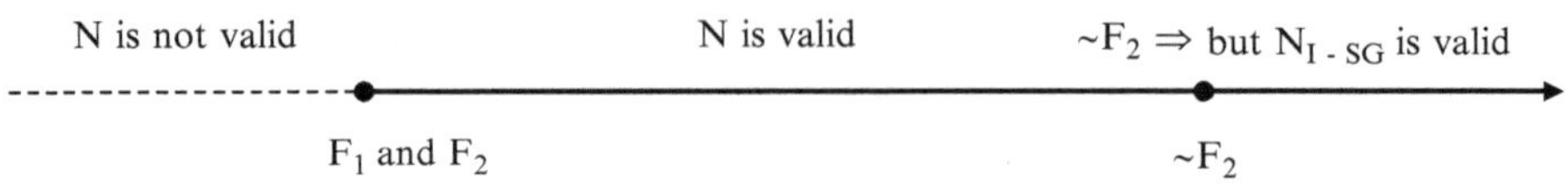

Fig. 9.9 The final circumvention of the juristic presumption of the validity of statutory law norms (final version)

former law N_F loses its validity, and the norm of the new law N_N acquires it by the fact of entering into force.[218]

Our analysis leads to the following modification of the previously proposed scheme of the final circumvention of presumption (see Fig. 9.9).

Therefore, the final circumvention of presumption can only be of a purely apparent character.[219] To avoid any misunderstanding, let us add that this method of positive validity argumentation cannot deal with proving that a particular derogatory norm D is not, in fact, the norm which derogates statutory norm N (namely, derogating such a legal norm whose validity was implied by presumption). Such validity argumentation, also taking place in the validity discourse in the strict sense, can be encountered in the situation of a dispute as to whether the juristic presumption of the validity of statutory law norms in fact expired or has been cancelled,[220] or in the situation connected with the revival of presumption.[221]

---

[218] The unorthodox consequence of this reasoning is that derogation seems to be, at the same time, the creation of the law; namely, the interim (temporary) sanctioning norms. Such a "complex consequence" of the so-called partial derogation is mentioned by W. Wróbel, who states: "On the one hand, there is a derogation of a currently valid norm, and on the other hand, there takes place the enactment of a new norm with the identical scope of application, except that with the time constraints" – *idem, Zmiana normatywna i zasady intertemporalne w prawie karnym, op. cit.*, p. 44. Similarly, M. Zieliński and M. Ziembiński, who mention in this context "the norm with the revised content which is valid on the base of another set of lawmaking acts" – *iidem, Uzasadnianie twierdzeń, ocen i norm w prawoznawstwie, op. cit.*, note 32 at p. 174. From the point of view of legal theory, these views are by no means particularly controversial – let us even note a kind of symmetry, which consists in the fact that the lawmaking acts are, in turn, at the same time usually the acts of derogating the norms of the former law. However, we do believe that we can propose a different conceptualisation of the analysed phenomenon of normative changes of the law, which indeed seems to be less controversial? In our opinion, derogation need not be treated as an act of establishing interim (temporary) sanctioning norms, such as $N_{I\text{-}SG}$, if we consider that, according to the dominant view, the statutory law also consists of such norms, which are interpreted or inferred from the legal norms directly issued by the legislator and, thus, they are understood as "acknowledged (accepted) consequences" of them – for more on this issue *cf.* Chap. 6, pp. 243–245 (the argument from adequacy). Thus, interim (temporary) sanctioning norms can be considered an example of "acknowledged (accepted) consequences" of the norms directly enacted by the legislator.

[219] We are thus tempted to rename this method of positive validity argumentation, which we nevertheless resist doing, since we cannot find a more appropriate term than "an apparent final circumvention of presumption".

[220] *Cf. supra*, pp. 498–500.

[221] *Cf. infra*, the text corresponding to note 244 at p. 520.

We are still left to consider the issue of the burden of validity argumentation in the case of—as it turned out, apparent—final circumvention of presumption. We believe that this burden does not rest entirely on the arguing party, since what applies here again is the principle *iura novit curia*. Thus, a positive validity argumentation, seeking to justify the opinion or decision on the validity of the interim (temporary) sanctioning norm $N_{I\text{-}SG}$ will be of a subsidiary character. Regardless of the arguments raised by the parties to the dispute, it is highly probable that this norm will be *ex officio* considered as valid, provided, of course, that we do not have to deal with a retroactive or retrospective action of the new law.[222]

9.5.6 The Suspension of Presumption

We will say that the juristic presumption of the validity of statutory law norms has been suspended when we cannot use this presumption in the course of validity discourse *sensu stricto* because of the lawmaking action of the legislator or due to the constitutional court ruling. We propose to use, by analogy to the distinction between the two types of derogation, the subjectively relativised concepts of "authentic suspension" and "tribunal suspension" of presumption (respectively). What decidedly differentiates these phenomena from each other is that in the case of the "authentic suspension" of the juristic presumption of the validity of statutory law norms, we can also talk about its "resumption". However, in the case of the "tribunal suspension", this possibility does not exist, because it is inseparable from "tribunal derogation".

The "authentic suspension" of presumption takes place in two situations, very similar to each other from the point of view of validity. The first one involves the enactment of an episodic statute by the legislator. This kind of particular normative act of lawmaking determines in advance the date when their validity expiries. In the continental system-type of statutory law, the episodic statutes can include such regulations that prohibit the application of legal norms contained in other statutes for as long as the episodic statute remains valid. As we believe, it is precisely in relation to these norms, whose application during the validity of an episodic statute is excluded, that we can speak of the "authentic suspension" of the presumption of their validity. The second situation in which we can encounter the suspension of presumption is the special legislation of emergency states or the state of war (martial law)—also essentially episodic in nature—that may not only exclude the application of other ordinary laws, but even restrict a number of civil liberties and rights provided for in the constitution.[223] In this case, the "authentic suspension" of the juristic presumption of the validity of statutory law norms can apply even to the

[222] For more on the concepts of retroactivity and retrospection of law *see* T. Pietrzykowski, *Wsteczne działanie prawa i jego zakaz*, *op. cit.*, pp. 77ff., and the references cited therein.

[223] *Cf. e.g.*, Article 233 of Polish Constitution or Articles 115 d and 115 k of the German *Grundgesetz*.

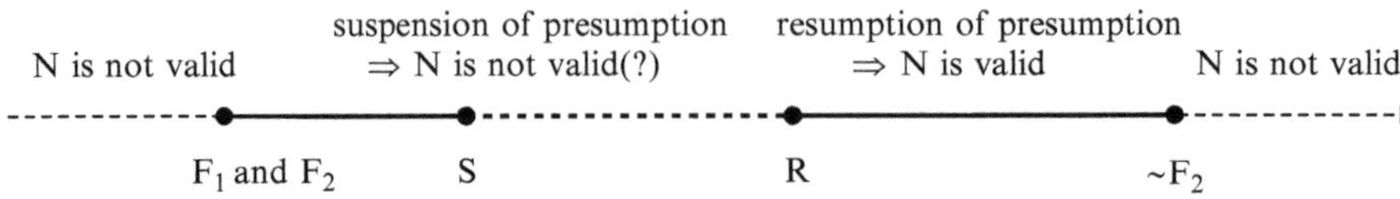

Fig. 9.10 The "authentic suspension" of the juristic presumption of the validity of statutory law norms

constitutional norms. Of course, in both indicated normative situations we can also talk about the resumption of presumption that occurs when the episodic statutes or statutes introducing the state of emergency or declaring the martial law lose their validity. Thus, the essence of the "authentic suspension" of presumption is presented in the following scheme (see Fig. 9.10 above).

Let us add that the reason for distinguishing an "authentic suspension" of juristic presumption of the validity of statutory law norms from its expiry, is that the episodic statutes or statutes introducing the state of emergency or martial law do not usually derogate the "ordinary" legal norms that they merely temporarily "replace" within a specific legal system.[224] Accordingly, it can be argued that the "authentic derogation" of them does not usually occur, and therefore any expiry of presumption is *ex definitione* out of the question.[225] It can be maintained that the juristic intuitions speak in favour of assuming that the legal norms whose application is temporarily restricted or excluded by the legislator, are still legally valid.[226] Yet, when we take into consideration the postpositivist concept of the validity of statutory law norms, the validity of such temporarily non-applied norms is hardly possible. For example, the obligation of the non-application of specific legal norms (contained in statutes introducing the state of emergency or martial law) undoubtedly constitutes the option of refusing the fulfilment (implementation) of these norms by their potential addressees.

All in all, we will leave open the question as to whether a given norm in relation to which there occurred an "authentic suspension" of presumption, is valid or not (as expressed by means of a question mark in the above scheme). At this point, it is not a particularly essential problem for us, because we aim to identify the methods of validity argumentation rather than to determine the correct outcomes of validity discourse in the strict sense.[227] Therefore, we assume that the "authentic suspension" of the juristic presumption of the validity of statutory law norms involves only such a consequence that this presumption can no longer be applied in the course of validity discourse.

[224] For example, Article 115 k Section 1 of the German *Grundgesetz,* which indicates the possibility of temporarily leaving such norms "beyond application" (*außer Anwendung*).

[225] *Cf.* a synthetic definition of the expiry of the presumption of validity, presented *supra* at p. 498.

[226] These intuitions are naturally associated with a (in our opinion, erroneous) conception of legal validity understood as the membership of norms in the legal system – *cf.* Chap. 7, pp. 271ff.

[227] Moreover, these are the judges and dogmatists of constitutional law (rather than legal theorists) who have the final word on this matter.

What seems much more controversial, at least at first glance, is a "tribunal suspension" of presumption. Here we have in mind a situation of issuing a ruling on rendering a specific legal norm unconstitutional, which brings about its "tribunal derogation". According to Katarzyna Gonera and Ewa Łętowska, "the official declaration of the unconstitutionality of the [legislative] act takes place already upon issuing the ruling", which stands for "rebutting the presumption of constitutionality".[228] In the context of validity discourse in the strict sense, there arises an essential question of what significance the constitutional court ruling has for the methods of validity argumentation. This is a particularly urgent question from the axiological point of view in the situation when—as in the case of the Polish legal system—there can even be a one and a half year long postponement of the loss of validity of the norms that are subject to "tribunal derogation".[229] This problem particularly concerns the proceedings pending before the courts of common jurisdiction (and thus it takes the institutional form of a dependent applicative validity discourse in the strict sense), because these are, in fact, judges—as aptly noted by Monika Florczak-Wątor[230]—who find themselves in the situation of a particular "conflict of conscience". On the one hand, they already know that a specific norm of positive law is unconstitutional and its "tribunal derogation" will soon enter into force, while on the other hand, this norm is still valid, at least formally speaking, in the sense of its membership in the legal system, since its derogation has not yet entered into force. The validity of a statutory law norm in this "peculiar *vacatio legis*, characteristic for derogation",[231] which can be labelled as *vacatio derogationis*, is undoubtedly highly controversial, especially from an axiological point of view. Therefore, without attempting to provide any substantive solution, which, as we believe, can be adopted only based on an in-depth analysis of a

---

[228] K. Gonera, E. Łętowska, 'Artykuł 190 Konstytucji i jego konsekwencje w praktyce sądowej', *op. cit.*, p. 14.

[229] For more on the constitutional tribunal rulings with the postponement clause, *see e.g.*, M. Florczak-Wątor, *Orzeczenia Trybunału Konstytucyjnego i ich skutki prawne*, *op. cit.*, pp. 117ff., 158ff.; R. Hauser, J. Trzciński, *Prawotwórcze znaczenie orzeczeń Trybunału Konstytucyjnego w orzecznictwie Naczelnego Sądu Administracyjnego*, *op. cit.*, pp. 65ff.; A. Wróbel, '"Odroczenie" przez Trybunał Konstytucyjny utraty mocy obowiązującej przepisu niezgodnego z Konstytucją. Zagadnienia wybrane' ['Postponing' of the Loss of Validity of Unconstitutional Provision by the Constitutional Tribunal. Selected Issues], in J. Góral *et al.* (eds.), *Ratio est anima legis. Księga jubileuszowa ku czci Profesora Janusza Trzcińskiego*, Warszawa 2007, pp. 105–126; K. Gonera, E. Łętowska, 'Odroczenie utraty mocy niekonstytucyjnej normy i wznowienie postępowania po wyroku Trybunału Konstytucyjnego' [Postponement of the Loss of Force of an Unconstitutional Norm and Resumption of Proceedings after the Constitutional Tribunal Ruling], *PiP* 6 (2008), pp. 3–21, and the constitutional tribunal rulings cited therein.

[230] M. Florczak-Wątor, *ibidem*, p. 125. *Cf.* K. Gonera, E. Łętowska, *ibidem*, pp. 5ff. and 'Wieloaspektowość następstw stwierdzania niekonstytucyjności', *op. cit.*, pp. 25ff.

[231] Such a term is used by W. Wróbel, *Zmiana normatywna i zasady intertemporalne w prawie karnym*, *op. cit.*, p. 43.

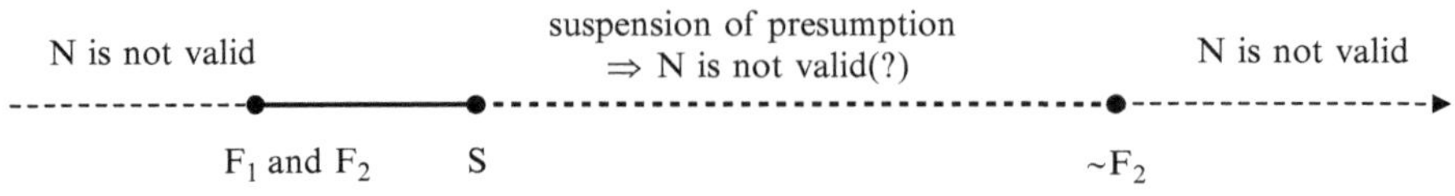

Fig. 9.11 The "tribunal suspension" of the juristic presumption of the validity of statutory law norms

specific legal regulation in a given legal system, we acknowledge that in the analysed case, we also deal with the suspension of the juristic presumption of the validity of statutory law norms, which this time has an irreversible character, as shown in the following scheme (see Fig. 9.11 above).

What remains to be discussed is the burden of validity argumentation related to the suspension of the juristic presumption of the validity of statutory law norms. In the case of "authentic suspension", connected with episodic legislation, this issue seems relatively simple. We claim that the burden of validity argumentation rests here on the party who seeks to demonstrate that the "ordinary" legal norms, which were "replaced" by the norms of episodic statutes, are valid. For we deal here with the suspension of the presumption of validity and, consequently, a validity discourse *sensu stricto* starts anew.[232] We do not think, however, that positive validity argumentation is of particular importance here, because especially in dependent (subsidiary) applicative validity discourse *sensu stricto,* the judicial argumentation of the parties will probably centre around the problem of applicability, rather than the validity of legal norms relevant to the outcome of the litigation. Besides, a significant role will be also played by the *iura novit curia* principle, which in the case of "authentic suspension" of presumption is fully applicable, thus making the arguments of the parties subsidiary.

On the other hand, in the case of the "tribunal suspension" of presumption, the problem of the burden of validity argumentation is much more complex. The conflict of conscience characteristic for the judge who is to issue a ruling based on legal norms which remain in *vacatio derogationis*, is quite real and resembles a "tragic case"—a conceptual category introduced by Manuel Atienza.[233] From the perspective of the proposed postpositivist conception of validity in this study, the core of the problem lies in determining whether the very act of issuing the ruling by the constitutional court, declaring the derogation of a given legal norm due to its unconstitutionality, constitutes a judge's option of refusing its fulfilment (implementation). We believe that it ought to be so, yet—given the moderately realistic approach adopted in this study—it does not, in fact, mean that it is the case. In

[232] It is hard to deny that the presented approach is strongly associated with the herein adopted postpositivist conception of legal validity, because the episodic legislation, and more specifically, the temporary valid legal norms of episodic statutes, undeniably constitute "legal options of refusing" the fulfilment (implementation) of non-episodic legal norms whose application is temporarily excluded.

[233] On Atienza's conception *cf.* Chap. 4, note 222 at p. 120, and the references cited therein.

judicial practice, one can probably encounter various decisions on validity, depending on positive law regulations and legal culture, characteristic of a particular legal system.[234] We believe that on a very general level of analyses, which have been adopted in this study, the legal theorist can only assume that in the analysed situation of the "tribunal suspension" of presumption, the burden of validity argumentation will rest on the party who seeks a positive (confirmatory) solution of validity discourse; namely, a decision that the unconstitutional statutory norm is valid until the "tribunal derogation" enters into force. This view is based on the conviction that it is difficult to defend a rather unreasonable view that a legal norm, deprived by the constitutional court of its validity, remains in compliance with the constitution in the period of *vacatio derogationis*, and ceases to be in such compliance at the time when the tribunal's ruling with the postponement clause has entered into force. In turn, it can be more confidently argued that due to the suspension of the presumption of validity both the positive as well as the negative validity argumentation can play a decisive role in the decision-making process undertaken by the judge who will find the mere *iura novit curia* principle of little use.

In this context, we would like to draw attention to a specific aspect of "tribunal suspension", so far generally overlooked in the Polish jurisprudential literature. We opt for adopting the view under which the burden of validity argumentation in relation to the unconstitutional legal norm in *vacatio derogationis* rests on the agent who supports the thesis on its validity, also due to the fact that we take into account one of the previously assumed objectives of the clarification of the juristic concept of the validity of statutory law. Let us recall that we have assumed, following Ralf Dreier's ideas, that the clarification of the juristic concept of validity should not necessary lead to such validity decisions that would be unfair to the citizens (legal subjects).[235] From the standpoint of a citizen, the question of the validity of unconstitutional norms whose "tribunal derogation" has been postponed by the constitutional court, is very simple and can be described as follows. From the perspective of a citizen (legal subject), what is undoubtedly valid in a given legal system is the constitution. Moreover, it is also clear that a certain state authority—the parliament—has enacted statutory norms inconsistent with this constitution, which have been ultimately and unquestionably determined by another state authority; namely, the constitutional court. Yet, during *vacatio derogationis*, these unconstitutional legal norms are formally valid—and this means that the citizen has no option of refusing their fulfilment (implementation). However, this normative situation is by no means the citizen's fault, because it was the lawmaker who

[234] The way in which Polish courts handle "tragic cases" has been most thoroughly analysed in R. Hauser, J. Trzciński, *Prawotwórcze znaczenie orzeczeń Trybunału Konstytucyjnego w orzecznictwie Naczelnego Sądu Administracyjnego*, *op. cit.*, pp. 71ff. and K. Gonera, E. Łętowska, 'Odroczenie utraty mocy niekonstytucyjnej normy i wznowienie postępowania po wyroku Trybunału Konstytucyjnego', *op. cit.*, pp. 5ff.

[235] *Cf.* Chap. 6, pp. 225–226 (the fifth objective of clarification).

established the unconstitutional norms, therefore the citizen deserves at least an explanation of what the grounds are on which the unconstitutional norms should still be valid, even for as long as a year and a half, as Polish positive law allows. Why can a citizen be held liable for violating unconstitutional law, and why will a judge, when deciding this case, have to apply unconstitutional legal norms? In light of such reasoning, stating that it is the citizen (legal subject) that needs to prove the invalidity of legal norms whose "tribunal derogation" has already been ruled, seems ethically unacceptable. When referring to the Polish legal regulation, there arises an unavoidable postulate *de lege ferenda* to immediately eliminate this systemically dysfunctional and ethically reprehensible institution of "prolonging"[236] the validity of unconstitutional norms by means of rulings with a postponement clause, or at least to definitely extend the catalogue of the legal subjects that obtain "the privilege of benefits"[237] in the period of *vacatio derogationis* of unconstitutional statutory norms.

9.5.7 The Revival of Presumption

The last method of validity argumentation in our provisional list is the argumentation connected with the revival of the presumption. We will say that the juristic presumption of the validity of statutory law norms revives, when, due to the derogation of repealing or amending norms,[238] we can again invoke this presumption in the validity discourse in the strict sense in relation to those norms that have been previously repealed or amended (and thus formally derogated). The following diagram (see Fig. 9.12) illustrates the essence of the revival of presumption, based on such a "double" derogation, which to some extent, resembles its resumption[239]:

In the Polish jurisprudential literature, the situation that we refer to here, has been, for many years, the subject of numerous discussions, usually as a problem of the "revival" (of the validity) of legal provisions, less often legal norms. At least

[236] For more about "prolonging" the validity of unconstitutional legislative acts *see* R. Hauser, J. Trzciński, *Prawotwórcze znaczenie orzeczeń Trybunału Konstytucyjnego w orzecznictwie Naczelnego Sądu Administracyjnego*, *op. cit.*, pp. 70ff.

[237] For more on this institution, *see* P. Radziewicz, '"Przywilej korzyści" jako skutek prawny orzeczenia Trybunału Konstytucyjnego' ['Privilege of Benefits' as the Legal Consequence of the Constitutional Tribunal Ruling], *PL* 4 (2006), pp. 9–34.

[238] Due to the highly general nature of our discussion, we ignore the differences between these two normative forms of derogation (repealing and amending).

[239] It should be clarified that with this scheme we presuppose the theory of voidability (*Vernichtsbarkeitslehre*) rather than the theory of invalidity (*Nichtigkeitslehre*), because in the latter case, the moments marked as $\sim F_1$ and $\sim\sim F_2$ should be identical, as shown in the next scheme.

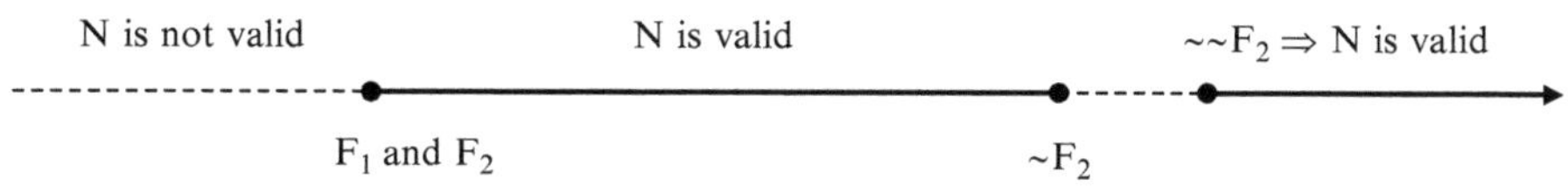

Fig. 9.12 The revival of the juristic presumption of the validity of statutory law norms

since a landmark ruling of the Polish Constitutional Tribunal from 20 December 1999,[240] many authors analysed this issue,[241] trying to clarify the essence of restoring the validity to the statutory norms after their prior unconstitutional "authentic derogation" by the legislator. A detailed discussion of this question requires a separate study, taking into account the specificity of the Polish legal culture and the regulation of positive law. At this point, the aim of our investigations of the validity discourse is different and, therefore, we only propose an alternative conceptual approach to the problem of the restoration of legal validity, based on the juristic presumption of the validity of statutory law norms. According to this approach, the consequences of constitutional court rulings concerning the unconstitutional derogation are interpreted in the form of the revival of the juristic presumption of validity, rather than the "revival" of the validity of unconstitutionally derogated norms of the former law.

However, the revival of the presumption of validity can be encountered not only in the case of the "tribunal derogation" of the norms that repealed or amended previously valid legal norms. As we believe, an "authentic derogation" of amending norms can also bring about the revival of the presumption of validity of previously valid statutory norms. We have here in mind such a case in which the legislator first introduces a new wording of specific legal norms or, more precisely,[242] it replaces the norms of the former law with the norms of a new law, thus, indirectly (or, as lawyers say, tacitly) repealing the former due to the juristic rules of normative conflicts that operate in a given legal order, in particular the *lex posterior* rule.

---

[240] *Ruling of the Constitutional Tribunal* from 20 December 1999, sign. K 4/99 (published in *Dziennik Ustaw* [Journal of Statutes] 1999, No. 106, Item 1215). *See* also the accompanying interpretive *Decision of the Constitutional Tribunal* from 21 March 2000, sign. K 4/99 (published in *OTK ZU* 2000, No. 2, Item 65). In addition to the studies cited in the next note, it is worth mentioning the work of A. Mączyński, who, being a judge of the Polish Constitutional Tribunal, has rendered a ruling in this case – *see idem*, 'Kontrola konstytucyjności przepisów uchylających i zmieniających' [The Control of the Constitutionality of Repealing and Amending Provisions] in F. Rymarz, A. Jankiewicz (eds.), *Trybunał Konstytucyjny. Księga XV-lecia*, Warszawa 2001, pp. 157–167.

[241] The current state of discussion has been exhaustively presented by P. Radziewicz, 'Przywrócenie mocy obowiązującej przepisu prawnego jako skutek orzeczenia Trybunału Konstytucyjnego', *op. cit.* Among the latest studies *see* S. Wronkowska, 'O źródłach prawa i aktach normatywnych raz jeszcze', *op. cit.*, pp. 127ff., in particular pp. 133–134; M. Florczak-Wątor, *Orzeczenia Trybunału Konstytucyjnego i ich skutki prawne*, *op. cit.*, pp. 143ff.; R. Hauser, J. Trzciński, *Prawotwórcze znaczenie orzeczeń Trybunału Konstytucyjnego w orzecznictwie Naczelnego Sądu Administracyjnego*, *op. cit.*, pp. 102ff., and the references cited therein.

[242] *Cf. supra*, notes 210–211 at p. 509, together with the corresponding text.

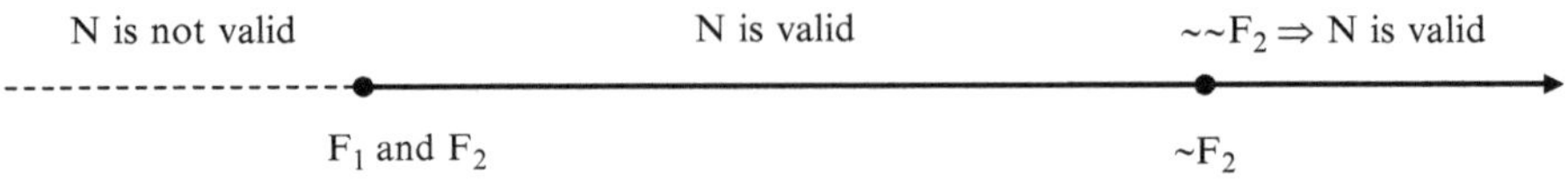

Fig. 9.13 The apparent revival of the juristic presumption of the validity of statutory law norms

Then the legislator "authentically derogates" this new regulation by means of abrogation; that is, by repealing legal provisions without replacing them with new ones. In this situation, undoubtedly quite sporadic in the systems of statutory law, yet indeed possible, the presumption of the validity of the norms of a former law also revives because the rule of *lex posterior derogat legi priori* is no longer applicable due to the absence of *legi posteriori*.[243]

Finally, we should also mention the apparent revival of presumption that can be illustrated in the form of the following scheme (see Fig. 9.13).

We can encounter this method of positive validity argumentation when debating whether the juristic presumption of validity of statutory law norms has expired or has been cancelled.[244] In other words, in the course of validity argumentation, one of the parties argues that the norm D is not actually the norm that derogates norm N, thereby undermining the thesis of the opponent under which there occurred a complex fact $\sim F_2$; namely, the norm D that derogates norm N (covered by the presumption) has entered into force after having been promulgated in accordance with the rules of promulgating legal norms.

The question of the burden of validity argumentation, related to the revival of the juristic presumption of the validity of statutory law norms, is undoubtedly very complex. On the one hand, the revival of the presumption of validity is an unusual situation, sometimes even excluded in advance by some legal theorists.[245] On the other hand, the revival of the presumption of the validity of statutory law norms seems fully justified, in particular from the axiological point of view, since it is the result of "restoring the constitutionality" of statutory law by the constitutional court. Due to the fact that at this point the axiological arguments clearly outweigh the theoretical ones, and having regard to the fairness of validity decisions, we are committed to attributing the burden of argumentation to that party who challenges the revival of the presumption. However, its argumentation will be subsidiary, since the validity of statutory law norms covered by the presumption of validity due to its revival is undoubtedly in the field of the application of the *iura novit curia* principle.

---

[243] For more *see* A. Grabowski, B. Naleziński, 'Kłopoty z obowiązywaniem', *op. cit.*, p. 254.

[244] *Cf. supra*, pp. 498–500.

[245] This position has been, inter alia, adopted by Kelsen, who assumed that derogation is irreversible and a derogatory norm can be derogated only on condition that it had not yet entered into force – *see idem*, 'Derogation', *op. cit.*, pp. 262–263. There is not much room here to prove that Kelsen's position was erroneous, let us therefore make do with stating that our standpoint fully coincides with the view expressed by Mączyński, who notes that "the thesis of an automatic and irreversible effect of a repealing provision constitutes an arbitrary assumption" – *idem*, 'Kontrola konstytucyjności przepisów uchylających i zmieniających', *op. cit.*, p. 159.

9.6 Remarks on Possible Classifications and Ways of Analysing Validity Arguments

According to the postpositivist conception of the validity of statutory law, the validity arguments that aim at rebutting the juristic presumption of the validity of statutory law norms are intended to demonstrate that the potential addressee of a legal norm has a legal option of refusing its fulfilment (implementation).[246] These arguments have already been analysed by us, in particular when highlighting the complex and institutionally diverse nature of the rules of the burden of negative validity argumentation that aims at rebutting the conclusions of the juristic presumption of validity.[247] We have also stressed that validity arguments (being at least in part topical in nature) strongly depend on the legal culture of a specific juridical society[248]; therefore, from the perspective of legal theory, their analysis at the level of the system-type of statutory law encounters considerable difficulties. It is undoubtedly a highly abstract level, which prevents a clear and unambiguous identification of validity arguments, determination of their force in validity discourse in the strict sense and specification of the burden of argumentation characteristic for them. This type of discussion and analysis should be conducted in the context of a particular state or supranational legal order in an integrative manner; namely, in the form of the cooperation between the representatives of different legal sciences, in particular the dogmatists of constitutional law, experts in legal procedure, specialists in European law as well as theorists and philosophers of law, and—last but not least—legal practitioners.[249]

However, it seems that even at such a level of abstraction, as adopted in this study, a theorist of law may conduct a preliminary analysis of the possible classifications or typologies of validity arguments, whose usefulness will be subject to verification in the course of the analyses relativised to the specific legal order and legal culture. When undertaking such a task, it should be first noted that—as far as I know—in the Polish theory of law there are no studies devoted to this issue, while, as for the foreign legal theory, they are very rare.[250] Therefore, probably some of the proposed classifications or typologies will have to be refined or rejected upon their application. It is also worth noting that the following proposals are largely

---

[246] For more on this *cf.* Chap. 8, pp. 437–438.

[247] *Cf. supra*, the text corresponding to notes 188–192 at pp. 501–503.

[248] *Cf. supra*, note 45, with the corresponding text at p. 462.

[249] For more on this *see infra*, pp. 533–535.

[250] The only study written from the perspective of legal theory, in which we can find a direct analysis of the reasons for the invalidity of legal norms in the continental system-type of statutory law, is the paper by R. Guastini, 'Invalidity', *op. cit.*, which we shall refer to during our deliberations. Some guidance can also be found in the work of D. Heckmann, *Geltungskraft und Geltungsverlust von Rechtsnormen*, *op. cit.*, pp. 193ff., in particular pp. 272ff., which is nevertheless closely related to the German juridical culture and legal system and at considerably numerous points it is of a dogmatic rather than theoretical character (which is by no means any objection against this valuable study).

correlated with the results of the current clarificative analyses, in particular with the results of the analysis of the methods of validity argumentation, focused around the juristic presumption of validity.

We propose seven jurisprudential classifications or typologies of validity arguments that can be applied to rebut the juristic presumption of the validity of statutory law norms.[251] It should be noted that when presenting the following list, we are primarily driven by practical utility, since the classifications or typologies of validity arguments may not be an art in itself, but they should serve the purpose of analysing particular arguments applied in validity discourse *sensu stricto*. In other words, the classifications or typologies as presented in this study,[252] are intended to constitute a point of departure (and at the same time a means) of analysing validity arguments.

The first classification, quite obvious from a theoretical point of view, is the distinction between thetic, factual and axiological arguments. It corresponds to the tri-partial division, often adopted in the jurisprudential literature, of the kinds, meanings or justifications of the validity of norms. As an example, let us recall here a distinction, already entrenched in the Polish legal culture, between thetic, behavioural and axiological justification (of the validity) of legal norms developed by the Poznań school of legal theory,[253] or the equally well-known conception of systemic, factual and axiological legal validity elaborated by Jerzy Wróblewski.[254] This distinction is also quite commonly adopted in the international jurisprudence—let us recall, for example, the distinction between the juristic, sociological and ethical concept of legal validity, adopted by the creators of the nonpositivist conception of law—Ralf Dreier and Robert Alexy.[255] It can therefore be seen that, despite differences in terminology, by analogy to the above distinctions, we can differentiate between three types of validity arguments using the criterion of their character. Generally speaking, thetic validity arguments concern the defects of the legal norm resulting from its improper issuance, sociological arguments are based on analysing the process of applying legal norms and their functioning in society,

[251] In the analysis, we leave aside the arguments aimed at the destruction of presumption, yet it can be assumed that some of the proposed classifications may also be applied in relation to them.

[252] In the subsequent considerations, we leave aside the question as to whether the divisions proposed by us have the logical character of classifications or typologies (and we use only the first term). At the present stage of research, it does not seem important, and what is more, without specifying the membership of respective validity arguments to a given category, it is difficult to assess whether we are dealing with a classification or typology. Our working hypotheses on this issue are provided *infra*, in note 267 at p. 525.

[253] *See e.g.*, Z. Ziembiński, *Logiczne podstawy prawoznawstwa*, *op. cit.*, p. 83; M. Zieliński, *Wykładnia prawa*, *op. cit.*, pp. 20–21; S. Wronkowska, *Podstawowe pojęcia prawa i prawoznawstwa*, *op. cit.*, pp. 16ff.

[254] *See e.g.*, J. Wróblewski, *Sądowe stosowanie prawa*, *op. cit.*, pp. 96ff. [English version, pp. 77ff.].

[255] *See e.g.*, R. Dreier, 'Recht und Moral', *op. cit.*, p. 194ff. and R. Alexy, *Begriff und Geltung des Rechts*, *op. cit.*, pp. 139ff. [English version, pp. 85ff.].

while axiological validity arguments are grounded in the values that the law is to implement or whose implementation we expect from the law.

The second classification seems equally obvious. We can distinguish between validity arguments based on the positive law and those that do not have such a foundation. When using Robert Alexy's terminology, which we refer to here,[256] the former will be called "institutional" arguments of validity, while the latter—"non-institutional". According to Alexy, the institutional arguments, applied in juristic discourse, may take the form of linguistic arguments (based on the linguistic meaning of the expressions in legal language), genetic arguments (based on the determination of the actual will of the historical legislator, yet which are—as Alexy believes—rarely used in modern juristic discourse) and systematic arguments (referring to the idea of the unity and coherence of the legal system). On the other hand, non-institutional arguments constitute the result of general practical discourse. We believe that this general classification of juristic arguments, despite a number of previously raised objections against Alexy's theory of discourse,[257] can be applied in relation to validity arguments, or at least we should not exclude it from the outset. This opinion is also justified by the fact that the criterion of basing the argument on the positive law is a natural counterpart of the starting point for constructing particular validity arguments and, moreover, it plays an important role in identifying the distribution of the burden of validity argumentation.

The third classification is of a less general nature than the already discussed ones. We find it useful to distinguish between the validity arguments that are applicable to all statutory law norms (we shall refer to them as "full-range arguments") from those that seek to rebut the presumption of the validity of legal norms that were previously inferred (interpreted) from the norms directly expressed by the legislator in legal texts (the so-called "non-full-range arguments"). This distinction is associated with a commonly adopted view that the legal system also consists of the norms which are considered as acknowledged (accepted) consequences of explicitly enacted legal norms.[258] This enables us to apply the criterion of the extension of validity arguments, the result of which is the proposed distinction.

The fourth classification directly relates to the analyses of the reasons for invalidity of legal norms provided by Riccardo Guastini. He distinguishes between the invalidity of legal norms arising from the fact that they have not been produced in accordance with the meta-rules governing the lawmaking process, from the invalidity resulting from the inconsistency of enacted norms with the superior (i.e. higher-ranked) norms that belong to the same legal system.[259] According to this distinction, we can differentiate between procedural-competence and substantive validity arguments, based on the criterion of their subject matter: the former

[256] *Cf.* R. Alexy, 'Die juristische Argumentation als rationaler Diskurs', *op. cit.*, pp. 120–122.

[257] *Cf. supra*, pp. 462–468 and Chap. 4, pp. 91ff.

[258] *Cf.* Chap. 6, the argument from adequacy presented at pp. 243–245.

[259] R. Guastini, 'Invalidity', *op. cit.*, pp. 212ff.

concern the lawmaking process, while the latter—its result; namely, the content of the established legal norms.[260]

The fifth classification is also related to the analyses of the Italian theorist. Guastini conceptually distinguishes the weak (plain) invalidity (i.e., invalidity *tout court*) and the strong invalidity; that is, the non-existence of norms.[261] He assumes that in addition to competence or substantive errors that lead to the weak invalidity of legal norms, one can also talk about the non-existence of norms in the situation when a legal norm "was produced by a subject lacking any power to create that kind of [legal] source".[262] Guastini provides the example of a "statute" passed by the executive authority—a legal act that does not exist at all and does not deserve to be called a "statute". He aptly adds that generally:

> infringement of a *single* procedural rule simply involves invalidity, while infringement of *all* the procedural rules involves non-existence.[263]

The degree of violating the legal rules of lawmaking, which Guastini indirectly refers to, is certainly considerably difficult to determine. Marek Safjan, a long-standing President of the Polish Constitutional Tribunal, observes in a similar context that:

> [t]he catalogue of "essential defects" is difficult to precisely define and exhaustively enumerate, what is more, there is a lack of precise criteria to distinguish crucial from non-crucial defects [...]. On the other hand, it can be reasonably held that the provision deprived of the minimum (necessary) features required from legal regulation should be regarded as not existing in the system from the very beginning, as not creating any legal states ....[264]

Thus, the degree of the intensity of the legislative defects may be various; however, it seems possible to propose a classification of juristic validity arguments that would be based on the criterion of the purpose of a validity argument. Accordingly, we can distinguish between validity arguments aiming to demonstrate the invalidity of a specific legal norm and those that intend to prove its non-existence. This distinction seems to be sound and significant because—and we are not alone in claiming that[265]—the non-existence of a legal norm can be stated by any court or any other authority that applies law, without resorting to a procedure of control before the constitutional court.

---

[260] It should be added that this distinction evokes theoretical suspicions, because one can have doubts as to the logical separation (disjunctive character) of these two groups of arguments since, for example, the infringement of the rules of lawmaking, which determine the possible content of the enacted law, can also cause a substantive inconsistency of the norms of a higher and lower rank.

[261] R. Guastini, 'Invalidity', *op. cit.*, pp. 222ff.

[262] *Ibidem*, p. 223.

[263] *Ibidem*. Italics in the original.

[264] M. Safjan, 'Skutki prawne orzeczeń Trybunału Konstytucyjnego', *op. cit.*, p. 9.

[265] *Cf. e.g.*, R. Guastini, 'Invalidity', *op. cit.*, p. 223.

The sixth and seventh classifications are directly related to the argumentative model of validity discourse in the strict sense, as presented above. The sixth distinction is based on the criterion of the force of the validity argument. In theory, we can distinguish between those validity arguments that independently rebut the presumption of the validity of statutory law norms and those that do not have such a consequence and, therefore, have to be supplemented by additional validity arguments, without which the argumentation intended to rebut the presumption will fail. We will call them "sufficient" and "insufficient" validity arguments, respectively. In turn, distinction number seven concerns the burden of validity argumentation. As already stated, it depends on the argument that we raise in the validity discourse because, from the theoretical point of view, we did not manage to identify any general rule for the distribution of the burden of validity argumentation.[266] The previous analyses have shown only that in relation to certain types of validity argumentation can we talk about their subsidiary nature (resulting from the influence which the principle *iura novit curia* has on validity discourse *sensu stricto*), while other validity arguments are indeed necessary. Thus, the criterion of the distribution of the burden of argumentation shall be applied by us individually to each of the analysed arguments that aim at rebutting the juristic presumption of the validity of statutory law norms.

The proposed classifications or typologies[267] of validity arguments that could be a starting point for their further detailed characterisation, are compiled in the following table (see Table 9.1).

Table 9.1 The types of validity arguments

The criterion of distinguishing validity arguments	Types of validity arguments that aim at rebutting the juristic presumption of the validity of statutory norms
The nature of the argument	Thetic, sociological or axiological arguments
The reference to positive law	Institutional or non-institutional arguments
The extension of the argument	Full-range or non-full-range arguments
The subject matter of the argument	Procedural-competence or substantive arguments
The purpose of the argument	Arguments showing the invalidity or non-existence of norms
The force of the argument	Sufficient or insufficient arguments
The distribution of the burden of validity argumentation	Subsidiary or necessary arguments

[266] *Cf. supra*, pp. 491–494.

[267] The undertaken jurisprudential analyses lead us to believe that the first, fourth and fifth distinction have the nature of the typology, the remaining ones are classifications in a logical sense.

9.6.1 An Example of the Analysis of Validity Arguments: The Argument from "Radbruch's Formula"

The vast majority of negative validity arguments that aim at rebutting the juristic presumption of the validity of statutory law norms are based on positive law. The assessment of their adequacy must therefore be made in the context of a specific legal order (or, more broadly, legal culture), while the primary method of such an assessment is formal dogmatic analysis. Let us, for example, consider the negative validity argument based on the thesis of a closed catalogue (*numerous clausus*) of the legitimated sources of law. In those states where such a thesis is correct, it can form the basis of a sufficient validity argument that guarantees to rebut the presumption of validity. It can be then said: "So what that norm N was correctly promulgated and has entered into force, if it has been established by means of the normative act that is not an acknowledged source of the law in our legal system!". Yet, in the legal systems of those states where this thesis is unjustified, this argument would be ineffective.

Nevertheless, there also exist such validity arguments in respect to which a supra-systemic jurisprudential analysis seems possible.[268] One of them is the jurisprudential argument based on "Radbruch's formula", analysed and discussed many times in our study.[269] It should therefore not come as a surprise that this argument—taken as a negative validity argument—shall be subject to a brief analysis, thus concluding the discussion on the nonpositivist conception of law presented in the first part of the study.

The argument from "Radbruch's formula" shall be formulated as follows: "The norm of statutory law is not valid, despite the fact that it is covered by the presumption of validity, because it is extremely unjust".[270] According to the proposed scheme of analysis, we will begin with describing this argument by means of conceptual distinctions presented in the previous section, and then we will consider its legitimacy in validity discourse in the strict sense, characteristic for the continental systems of statutory law.

Due to its nature, we shall deem this argument axiological. The concept of extreme injustice applied in it, undoubtedly constitutes an indirect reference to the value of justice, which shifts validity discourse onto an axiological level. If we look at this argument from the perspective of its relation to the positive law, we can

[268] In addition to the argument from "'Radbruch's formula", which is analysed below, such arguments include, for example, the negative validity arguments based on the principles *impossibilium nulla est obligatio* and *necessitum nulla est obligatio*, as well as non-full-range arguments that claim the violation of normative inference rules, accepted in a specific legal culture.

[269] *Cf.* Chap. 2, pp. 12ff., Chap. 3, pp. 46ff., and Chap. 4, pp. 70ff., 162ff.

[270] When formulating this argument, we therefore rely solely on the content of *Unerträglichkeitsthese*, thus leaving aside *Verleugnungsthese*, which is usually not used in judicature – *cf.* Chap. 4, notes 55–56, with the corresponding text at p. 73.

assume that it is non-institutional. Yet, this is not entirely clear, since the application of the argument from "Radbruch's formula" in many rulings of the German as well as the European courts,[271] leads to the conclusion that it will certainly withstand the "test of institutional support" within the meaning of Dworkin.[272] It is therefore also possible to deem it institutional, yet on the condition of a broad understanding of law—as, for example, adopted in this study—that goes beyond the positivistic paradigm. The extension of the analysed argument is not in any way limited, thus it is of a full-range character. Interestingly, similarly to the juristic presumption of the validity of statutory law norms, the argument from "Radbruch's formula" can also be applied to the hierarchically highest norms (having constitutional status). As for its subject matter, there is no doubt that it is a validity argument of a substantive nature, since it postulates considering as invalid those statutory norms whose content exceeds the threshold of extreme injustice. The purpose of the argument from "Radbruch's formula" in its classical form is to demonstrate the invalidity of legal norms, rather than their non-existence, although its stronger interpretation is indeed permissible.[273] When it comes to its force, it is undeniably a sufficient argument, since the fact of proving that a statutory norm is extremely unjust should be regarded as sufficient to rebut the presumption of validity, even in the legal cultures of those democratic European countries that remain strongly positivist. Finally, due to the distribution of the burden of validity argumentation, characteristic for the application of the argument from "Radbruch's formula" in practice, it can be stated that from the jurisprudential point of view, the burden rests entirely on the party who raises such an argument. This is true both in an independent (self-contained) validity discourse *sensu stricto*, as well as in a dependent (subsidiary) applicative validity discourse. We believe, therefore, that the argumentation that supports it is necessary, since the exceptional nature of the validity argument from "Radbruch's formula" is indisputable.[274]

Before we formulate a jurisprudential argumentation that supports the negative validity argument from "Radbruch's formula", it should be noted that it has already been partly presented by us.[275] It should also be explained that in the following reasoning we use several specific arguments of a moral nature, which is not only acceptable, but even necessary, given its axiological character. It should be noted, however, that the following considerations should be interpreted in accordance with a detached, axiologically impartial way of perceiving legal reality, as adopted in

---

[271] *Cf.* Chap. 4, pp. 184–188.

[272] *Cf.* R. Dworkin, *Taking Rights Seriously*, *op. cit.*, pp. 39ff., 64ff.

[273] *Cf.* Chap. 4, pp. 70–75. Let us recall that this stronger interpretation, based on the formulation of *Unerträglichkeitsthese*, taken from 'Fünf Minuten Rechtsphilosophie' is adopted by modern nonpositivism in the form of the theorem: *lex iniustissima non est lex.*

[274] This may change due to the positive law regulation of validity discourse in a specific legal system.

[275] *Cf.* Chap. 4, pp. 83–84, where we formulated the argument supporting "Radbruch's formula", based on the principle of equality, examined and applied in the context of the principles *ignorantia iuris nocet* and *ignorantia legis neminem excusat.*

this study.[276] This means that the moral arguments, presented below, are the expression of the standpoint in relation to which we cannot be certain as to whether it deserves an approval; however, their formulation seems to be advisable for us.

When analysing the merits of the validity argument from "Radbruch's formula", first of all we find that it reduces legal certainty only minimally. This argument, by its very nature, will be applied in the extreme, exceptional cases. In our opinion, it is also erroneous to claim that the courts will not be able to handle the application of this argument in case it is approved in a given legal culture. Given that the judges have to apply highly blurred general clauses on a daily basis, one cannot assume that judges will oppose the introduction of the argument from "Radbruch's formula" into validity discourse (especially since it would most likely be very experienced judges of the supreme or constitutional courts). This reasoning leads us to yet another question: Against whom can this argument be used? This question seems to be posed incorrectly, since validity discourse relates to the validity of statutory norms, therefore validity arguments are directed against something—that is, against the juristic presumption of their validity, rather than against someone. However, when we look at this problem from a broader perspective of a certain social practice, namely law, its creation, application and observance, we can come to clear conclusions. Having adopted such a perspective, we note that in validity discourse, the analysed argument is directed against the legislator who establishes extremely unjust law. Accordingly, there arise further questions: Should the legislator who makes such a law be in some way protected? Should we allow him to do so? These questions are obviously very persuasive, but the argument used in the further analysis is not. It alludes again to the principles *ignorantia iuris nocet* and *ignorantia legis neminem excusat*, already applied when analysing the correctness of "Radbruch's formula".[277] We believe that one can defend the view under which the application of these principles in relation to extremely unjust norms is a misunderstanding that neither any lawyer nor anyone else can accept. Should non-compliance with extremely unjust norms lead to negative consequences for those who refuse to recognise such norms as law? Should courts merely *ex post* rehabilitate people who "committed a crime" when fighting against a totalitarian state, or when helping those persecuted or exterminated by the Nazi's or communist's *Unrechtsstaat*?

However, it is not this ethical argument that we consider decisive when determining the question of the admissibility of the objection of extreme injustice of legal norms in the validity discourse. What is, in fact, decisive, is the argument that draws attention to the fact that within the validity discourse *sensu stricto* (and probably not only the Polish one) we often deal with efficacious application of negative validity arguments that do not refer to such a fundamental value as justice, but to the so-called instrumental legislative values, such as the clarity and

[276] *Cf.* Chap. 6, pp. 234ff.

[277] *Cf.* Chap. 4, pp. 83–84.

comprehensibility of statutory law.[278] On account of a *minori ad maius* argument, it can be easily seen that it does not seem justified at all to claim that the constitutional courts should "punish" the legislator by repealing the provisions that are unclear or incomprehensible to the average citizen, while they cannot "punish" the legislator for enacting norms that exceed the threshold of extreme injustice.

To conclude, we believe that the analysed negative validity argument from "Radbruch's formula" is acceptable and effective in validity discourse in the strict sense. In the context of the Polish legal culture, it should be noted that in addition to the precursors and followers of legal nonpositivism, namely Aleksander Peczenik[279] and Lech Morawski,[280] and the greatest expert and promoter of Radbruch's conception, that is, Jerzy Zajadło,[281] the approval for it has been indirectly expressed by Sławomira Wronkowska,[282] Maciej Zieliński and Zygmunt Ziembiński,[283] and also—as it seems—by a silent supporter of the nonpositivist (or at least non-positivist[284]) conception of legal validity; namely, Wiesław Lang.[285]

9.7 Juristic Presumption of the Validity of Statutory Law Norms vis-à-vis *ignorantia iuris nocet* and *ignorantia legis neminem excusat* Principles

When attempting the clarification of the juristic concept of the validity of statutory law, one of its objectives was to seek such an outcome of clarification—the conception of the validity of statutory law—that would not be unjust; namely, it would not lead to unfair validity decisions in respect of the addressees of legal norms.[286] As we have repeatedly stated, the issue of achieving this objective is

[278] *Cf. e.g.*, S. Wronkowska, 'Postulat jasności prawa i niektóre metody jego realizacji' [The Demand of the Clarity of Law and Some Methods of Its Implementation], *PiP* 10 (1976), pp. 19–33 and M. Andruszkiewicz, U. A. Kosielińska-Grabowska, 'Prawodawca w labiryncie definicji legalnej' [The Lawmaker in the Maze of Legal Definition], *SPE* LXXV (2007), pp. 22ff., and the Polish Constitutional Tribunal rulings cited therein.

[279] *Cf.* the studies of A. Peczenik cited in Chap. 4, note 22 at p. 65.

[280] *Cf.* the studies of L. Morawski cited in Chap. 4, note 21 at p. 65.

[281] *Cf.* the studies of J. Zajadło, cited in Chap. 4, note 23 at p. 65.

[282] *Cf.* S. Wronkowska, 'O źródłach prawa i aktach normatywnych raz jeszcze', *op. cit.*, p. 116.

[283] *Cf.* M. Zieliński, M. Ziembiński, *Uzasadnianie twierdzeń, ocen i norm w prawoznawstwie*, *op. cit.*, p. 188.

[284] On the logical distinction between nonpositivism and non-positivism *cf.* Introduction, note 17 at p. 8 and Chap. 4, notes 70–71 at pp. 78–79.

[285] This thesis may be surprising, yet in my opinion, any doubt is dispelled by the following condition of the systemic validity of norms, explicitly formulated by Lang: "The norm is consistent with the ethical rules or principles to which the legal system refers or which are encoded in the legal culture" – *idem*, 'A Concept of the Validity of Law', *op. cit.*, p. 94.

[286] *Cf.* Chap. 6, pp. 225–226 (the fifth objective of clarification).

related to the validity aspects of *ignorantia iuris nocet* and *ignorantia legis neminem excusat* principles. Let us try to answer the emerging question as to whether the presented model of an argumentative clarification of the extension of the juristic concept of the validity of statutory law, and in particular basing such a clarification on the juristic presumption of the validity of statutory law norms, does not cause that the outcome of validity will be unfair for those whom "ignorance of law harms".

The starting point for considerations will be a recently presented and very inspiring analysis provided by Wiesław Lang, which concerns, inter alia, the interrelations between the principles of *clara non sunt interpretanda* and *ignorantia iuris nocet.*[287] In his deliberations, Lang distinguishes between two groups of subjects (to simplify, the individuals without legal training and not participating in the institutional discourse of law application—category A, and state authorities, legal persons and natural persons who are legally trained and who participate in such a discourse—category B). Referring to the previous analyses of Franciszek Studnicki,[288] Lang also differentiates between two types of basic information about law: the information partly replaceable by the substitute information of convergent or identical moral norms and the irreplaceable information (due to a lack of equivalents in extra-legal rules of conduct).[289] What is important in the context of the validity issues that remain at the centre of our interest, is that Lang explicitly acknowledges that the substitute information does not include the knowledge about the validity of legal norms.[290] Then, using the introduced distinctions, Lang explores the interrelations between these two principles in subjective and objective terms. He argues that:

> a complete rejection of the *clara non sunt interpretanda* principle and a strict implementation of the *ignorantia iuris nocet* principle would be possible only in a society of lawyers,[291]

while in relation to people who belong to category A, what can be at best assumed is a presumption of a pragmatic clarity of law[292] related to the basic knowledge about

---

[287] *See* W. Lang, 'Zasada *clara non sunt interpretanda* w kontekście zasady *ignorantia iuris nocet* oraz zasady zaufania obywateli do prawa' [Principle *clara non sunt interpretanda* in the Context of Principle *ignorantia iuris nocet* and Principle of Citizens' Trust in Law] in S. Wronkowska (ed.), *Polska kultura prawna a proces integracji europejskiej*, *op. cit.*, pp. 175ff.

[288] *See* F. Studnicki, 'Znajomość i nieznajomość prawa' [Knowledge and Ignorance of Law], *PiP* 4 (1962), pp. 577–597. *Cf. idem*, 'Obecna rola zasady "nie można zasłaniać się nieznajomością prawa"' [Current Role of the Principle "One Cannot Plead the Ignorance of the Law"], *SC* X (1967), pp. 3–42.

[289] *Cf.* W. Lang, 'Zasada *clara non sunt interpretanda* w kontekście zasady *ignorantia iuris nocet* oraz zasady zaufania obywateli do prawa', *op. cit.*, pp. 173, 177ff. Let us add that Lang also distinguishes "non-basic information about law".

[290] *Ibidem*, pp. 177–178.

[291] *Ibidem*, p. 177.

[292] For more on this concept, introduced by J. Wróblewski, *see idem*, 'Pragmatyczna jasność prawa' [Pragmatic Clarity of Law], *PiP* 4 (1988), pp. 3–13.

the law since setting them higher requirements violates the principle of the citizens' trust in law.[293]

Lang's conception demonstrates the problems created by adopting a fiction of the universal knowledge of the law, otherwise necessary for its functioning in modern societies. His reflections concern the implications of the *ignorantia iuris nocet* principle, analysed in the context of the theory of legal interpretation.[294] We are, however, interested in its validity aspect, and in particular in the question of which extensional approach to valid law constitutes the appropriate point of reference for the principles indicated in the title of the current section.

The undertaken analyses of validity discourse in the strict sense and the methods of validity argumentation revealed a great complexity of reasoning and argumentation leading to often controversial decisions of validity in the practice of law application. We believe that it is difficult to accept a full, unlimited liability of a legal subject for the ignorance of the valid law, just as it is impossible—as shown by Lang—to always blame them for the ignorance or erroneous interpretation of positive law. The proposed model of the analysis of validity discourse enables us to look at the scope of application and the consequences of *ignorantia iuris nocet* and *ignorantia legis neminem excusat* principles from the perspective of legal validity phenomenon. It seems that when taking into account the moral dimension of validity decisions, one can suggest a certain way of interpreting these principles, which, on the one hand, takes into consideration the need for the proper functioning of the legal system and, on the other hand, allows for a margin of tolerance, justified by the uncertainty of juristic, and in particular, institutional decisions of validity.

We believe that the possibility of determining the extension of the concept of valid law depends largely on the juristic presumption of the validity of statutory law norms. However, the thesis under which, in order to apply the principles of *ignorantia iuris nocet* and *ignorantia legis neminem excusat*, we must define the scope of the valid law based solely on the presumption of validity, does not seem justified to us. Apart from other reasons, it is a rebuttable presumption, which may be refuted by means of validity arguments. Moreover, what is also possible is its blockage, circumvention, suspension, resumption and revival.[295] Therefore, we believe that determining the scope of liability that arises from the ignorance of valid law should be objectively and subjectively relativised. Using Lang's distinction between two categories of subjects (A and B), it is assumed that we need to differently determine the extension of "valid law" for the purposes of specifying the degree of the responsibility borne by the actors who belong to these categories, as results from the ignorance (non-recognition) of the valid law.

---

[293] W. Lang, 'Zasada *clara non sunt interpretanda* w kontekście zasady *ignorantia iuris nocet* oraz zasady zaufania obywateli do prawa', *op. cit.*, p. 180.

[294] For more *see* L. Morawski, *Wykładnia w orzecznictwie sądów*, *op. cit.*, pp. 375ff., and the rulings cited therein.

[295] *Cf. supra*, pp. 496–498, 503–520.

In relation to the subjects who belong to category A, we propose to determine the extension of "valid law$_A$" based on the juristic presumption of the validity of statutory law norms, including the possibility of its initial blockage, final circumvention (in fact, an apparent one), "authentic suspension" (and the corresponding resumption) and the rebuttal by means of validity arguments, but only those that are widely accepted in a given legal culture, in particular those that aim at demonstrating the non-existence and not only the invalidity of statutory law norms. In turn, in relation to the subjects who belong to category B, the extension of "valid law$_B$" should correspond to its actual extension, with the reservation that in case of effective application in the validity discourse of those methods of argumentation which are highly contentious (for example, juristic argumentation related to the initial circumvention of the presumption, its revival or rebuttal by means of contentious, usually non-institutional validity arguments), the liability of the entities in category B, resulting from the principles of *ignorantia iuris nocet* and *ignorantia legis neminem excusat* should be limited. What can also prove useful in determining the degree of responsibility borne by the legal subjects for the ignorance of valid law is taking into account the rules of the burden of validity argumentation. It seems that only in cases where the validity decision is taken as a result of applying those methods of argumentation or such validity arguments in which validity argumentation is of a subsidiary character, can we at all speak about the responsibility of the subjects that belong to group A. However, this reservation does not apply to professionals; namely, those members of category B who have (or: are supposed to have) legal knowledge.

We are well aware of the fact that the presented proposals constitute a mere sketch of the idea that—we believe—might prove helpful in determining the level of the responsibility of individual entities for the ignorance of the law. This idea is undoubtedly highly controversial, since having in mind the fairness of the consequences of validity decisions, we have proposed the distinction between three different extensions of the concept of valid law ("valid law$_A$", "valid law$_B$" and law which is valid *tout court*). It should be noted, however, that we propose such a distinction only in the context of the application of *ignorantia iuris nocet* and *ignorantia legis neminem excusat* principles.

We believe that these clarifications will save us from the objection of unfair consequences of the postpositivist conception of the validity of statutory law norms, developed and presented in this study. In the context of the proposed argumentatively-discursive way of clarifying the extension of the juristic concept of the validity of statutory law, it should be added that this manner of analysis does not guarantee the fairness of validity decisions, since this cannot be generally guaranteed by any theory of law. However, adopting an axiologically impartial, postpositivist definition of the concept of the validity of statutory law[296] and opening the validity discourse in the strict sense to non-institutional validity

[296] *Cf.* Chap. 8, pp. 433–453.

arguments, often of an axiological character,[297] constitutes—in our opinion—a maximum protection against unfair validity decisions, that can be offered to the practitioners of law and legal dogmatists by the author, who is by no means an advocate of natural law theory.

9.8 Some Remarks About the Applicability of the Proposed Model of Analysing Validity Discourse *Sensu Stricto*

The presented theoretical model of validity discourse, along with the proposed network of concepts that aim at eliminating the extensional indeterminacy (vagueness) of the juristic concept of the validity of statutory law, is very general and largely stipulative. As we have repeatedly emphasised, it needs elaboration and probably numerous revisions, the necessity of which will undoubtedly arise at the moment when the model is applied to the validity discourse proper for a specific, for example Polish, French or Italian legal culture. Only then will it become apparent as to what extent the intuitions and ideas that formed the basis of its construction were accurate. Let us recall that the theories of legal validity, dominant in contemporary jurisprudence, seek to establish the methods for solving specific problems of validity by means of laborious analyses of the criteria that should be met by a statutory norm in order to be recognised as legally valid.[298] The presented model of discourse analysis and validity argumentation, based on the argumentative conception of the juristic presumption of the validity of statutory law norms, seems to be a jurisprudential alternative that is possible to take into consideration.

When constructing the model of the analysis of validity discourse *sensu stricto*, we tried to take into account a very important objective of our research—to make it easier for dogmatists of law and legal practitioners to find the answer to the basic practical question: Is the norm of statutory law valid? In this context, it should be noted that nothing specific can be said about applying the elaborated model in practice or dogmatic analyses, at least not before it is transformed and adjusted to a given system of statutory law and legal culture. This remark does not refer to the very postpositivist concept of the validity of statutory law, which can be directly applied in practice and dogmatic considerations, yet due to a noncriterial character, its practical value is also limited. It is indeed the case, because the postpositivist definition of the concept of the validity of statutory law constitutes the result of clarifying the intension rather than the extension of this concept. However, we are convinced that this conception has some "intrinsic added value", which was of

[297] *Cf. supra*, p. 523.

[298] In reference to the Polish jurisprudence *cf. supra*, notes 3–4 at p. 455, with the corresponding text.

utmost importance for us during clarificative analysis,[299] for it leads us to the construction of the juristic presumption of the validity of statutory law norms.

As for the theoretical application of the presented conception of the validity of statutory law, we do hope that it will meet its function, at least in the sense that it will motivate a greater group of the representatives of legal science (we have in mind here primarily the theorists and philosophers of law) to address the problems of validity, and in particular, the basic concept of legal validity. It is indeed true that even in view of the character of many of the proposed theses—which are far from the positivist paradigm—we expect severe criticism from the representatives of other schools of theory and philosophy of law. As for the possible application of the proposed model of the analysis of validity discourse within the specific legal disciplines, it seems that one cannot preclude its usefulness in the dogmatics of the constitutional law. We believe that when using the method of integrative research,[300] one can modify the proposed theoretical model and arrive at a new approach to the institutional validity discourse in the strict sense, pending before constitutional courts, which constitutes one of the main areas of research for the dogmatists of constitutional law. For instance, in the context of Polish jurisprudence, we can observe that the argumentative approach, applied when clarifying the extension of the juristic concept of the validity of statutory law, brings us to such a vision of validity discourse in which the key role is played by the juristic presumption of the validity of statutory law norms, in many ways different[301] from the presumption of constitutionality, adopted in the judicial practice of the Polish Constitutional Tribunal and understood as the presumption of the consistency of statutes (lawmaking acts) with the constitution.[302] One can hazard a guess that taking a look at validity discourse, undertaken during the proceedings before the Constitutional Tribunal, through the prism of the proposed model of validity discourse, and in particular the juristic presumption of the validity of statutory law norms, allows us to capture those specific features of validity argumentation that remain hidden, when we view this discourse in the context of the presumption of consistency of statutes (lawmaking acts) with the constitution. In this new perspective, the presumption of constitutionality in the current meaning may prove unnecessary, since it may assume a brand new meaning, similar to the one

[299] *Cf.* Chap. 8, pp. 448ff.

[300] Naturally at this point we have in mind the so-called internal integration of legal science; that is, the cooperation between particular disciplines belonging to legal science.

[301] In addition to its function, the clear difference is that the juristic presumption of validity refers also to the norms of constitution, what in the case of the presumption of constitutionality is *ex definitione* excluded.

[302] For more on this presumption from the perspective of legal theory *see e.g.*, L. Morawski, *Wykładnia w orzecznictwie sądów*, *op. cit.*, pp. 230–231, and the Constitutional Court rulings cited therein. The dogmatic literature concerning the presumption of constitutionality is too numerous to list it here.

presented by Sławomira Wronkowska in one of her works.[303] She comprehends the presumption of constitutionality as a foundation under which only certain state organs, usually constitutional courts or supreme courts, are authorised to determine the inconsistencies between the norms of lawmaking competence and statutory norms that constitute the result of using such a competence.

We shall conclude our discussion with a fairly general remark. When analysing the research programme on the theory of legal argumentation, Eveline Feteris distinguishes five main components of it: the philosophical, the theoretical, the analytical, the empirical and the practical one.[304] In the context of this distinction, the analyses presented in this chapter, in particular, the theoretical model of validity discourse in the strict sense, can be understood as a mere introduction to a complete theory of juristic argumentation on validity. In our discussion, we have, in fact, left aside, in a sense purposefully, the philosophical realm and—this time out of necessity—the empirical and the practical sphere of validity discourse.[305] To conclude, there still remains much to be done to achieve a satisfactory result.

---

[303] S. Wronkowska, 'W sprawie bezpośredniego stosowania Konstytucji' [On the Direct Application of the Constitution], *PiP* 9 (2001), p. 21.

[304] *See* E.T. Feteris, 'A Survey of 25 Years of Research on Legal Argumentation', *op. cit.*, pp. 363ff.

[305] What can serve as a certain, yet highly subjective justification, is the fact that this chapter, at least according to our view, constitutes merely a synthetic annex – *cf.* Chap. 8, p. 453. It is another matter that, in order to develop a complete theory of validity discourse, it is necessary to provoke the cooperation of the representatives of particular legal disciplines.

Chapter 10
Epilogue

I remember hearing somebody say,
"You know he's a positivist,
but he's quite a nice man".
(H.L.A. Hart[1])

The contemporary theory and philosophy of law offers a number of opportunities and methods for analysing the problems whose topicality is confirmed in everyday legal practice. If we confine ourselves to the analytical theory of law, then on the one hand, we can choose from the different versions of legal positivism, in particular the soft (inclusive) positivism and the hard (exclusive) one,[2] and on the other hand, we can opt for the German nonpositivism, whose conception, developed by Ralf Dreier and Robert Alexy, constituted the object of criticism presented in the first part of this study. Interestingly, in the context of a broadly understood legal nonpositivism, we can also consider two of its versions, *per analogiam* referred to as inclusive and exclusive nonpositivism.[3] These trends by no means exhaust the

[1] A comment heard by Hart during his stay at Harvard Law School from 1956–1957, quoted by him in an interview with D. Sugarman, 'Hart Interviewed: H.L.A. Hart in Conversation with David Sugarman', *op. cit.*, p. 279.

[2] *Cf.* the references cited in Chap. 2, note 17 at p. 14 and Chap. 4, note 17 at p. 64.

[3] *Cf.* M. La Torre, 'On Two Distinct and Opposed Versions of Natural Law: "Exclusive" versus "Inclusive"', *op. cit.*, pp. 199ff. and *Constitutionalism and Legal Reasoning*, Dordrecht 2007, pp. 135ff. According to La Torre, by analogy to inclusive and exclusive legal positivism, one can distinguish between inclusive and exclusive theories of natural law. According to him, the former theories include Habermas' and Alexy's discursive theories of law, while the latter – Finnis' theory of natural law and legal idealism of the Sheffield School (D. Beyleveld and R. Brownsword). The criterion of this distinction is a monologue or dialogical (discursive) method of the moral justification of law. However, these two concepts can also be analysed in the context of the "definitional triangle of law" proposed by Alexy – *cf.* Chap. 2, pp. 16ff. In such an approach, which we advocate for, when we relate it to a broadly understood nonpositivism, we can say that nonpositivism can be referred to as "inclusive" if, in the definition of law, besides the element of substantial correctness, the concepts of due enactment and social efficacy are also used, while it is "exclusive" if it bases this definition only on the first of these concepts. It should be noted that Alexy is very likely to

A. Grabowski, *Juristic Concept of the Validity of Statutory Law*,
DOI 10.1007/978-3-642-27688-0_10, © Springer-Verlag Berlin Heidelberg 2013

broad spectrum of contemporary jurisprudential reflection, because just as legal positivism and iusnaturalism obviously do not constitute a pair of dichotomous concepts, the same—though not so obviously—holds true for the concepts of legal positivism and nonpositivism.[4] This opens the door to constructing new jurisprudential theories and conceptions, largely eclectic ones[5] that seek to move beyond the traditional, probably futile dispute concerning the necessary conceptual relations of law and morality,[6] which are, at least *prima facie*,[7] of great importance in the context of constructing an adequate theory of legal validity.

In the undertaken research, we have not only provided a criticism of the German nonpositivist conception of law, but also of the modern, supposedly sophisticated legal positivism.[8] This criticism has confirmed the opinions, expressed by many theorists and philosophers of law, that legal positivism is a degenerating research program,[9] containing many self-destructive elements.[10] Yet, it is also legal nonpositivism that seems to be a conception leading to deliberate self-destruction, as evidenced when we consider the dilemma of nonpositivism formulated by Ulfrid Neumann[11] and Robert Alexy's attempt to resolve it.[12] According to the opinion

---

interpret this distinction precisely in this way when he concedes that nonpositivism based on "Radbruch's formula" constitutes an example of inclusive nonpositivism – *cf. idem*, 'Effects of Defects – Action or Argument? Thoughts about Deryck Beyleved and Roger Brownsword's *Law as a Moral Judgment*', *RJ* 19 (2006), p. 173.

[4] *See* A. García Figueroa, 'Bemerkungen zu einer dispositionellen Erklärung des Rechts anhand der Diskussion der Verbindungs- und Trennungsthese', *ARSP* 92 (2006), pp. 363ff. On the conceptual logical difference between nonpositivism and non-positivism *cf.* Introduction, note 17 at p. 8, and the references cited therein.

[5] *Cf.* L. Morawski, 'Hard Positivism, Soft Positivism and Dead Positivism', *op. cit.*, p. 179, who notes that in the frames of the postpositivist jurisprudence, eclecticism "does not necessarily have to be a bad thing".

[6] *Cf.* a similar opinion expressed by B. Brożek, *Rationality and Discourse*, *op. cit.*, p. 233, who emphasises the futility of the ontological debate about whether there is a necessary connection between law and morality.

[7] We devoted much room (i.e., the first part of the study) to reaching the conclusion that, all things considered, this dispute is irrelevant in the sense that the concept of the validity of law should be constructed independently.

[8] In particular, *see* Chap. 4, pp. 137ff., Chap. 5, pp. 209ff., and Chap. 7, pp. 271ff.

[9] L. Morawski, 'Hard Positivism, Soft Positivism and Dead Positivism', *op. cit.*, pp. 159ff.

[10] *Cf.* the references cited in Chap. 4, notes 288–291 at pp. 137–138.

[11] *See* U. Neumann's review of R. Alexy's book: *Begriff und Geltung des Rechts*, *op. cit.*, p. 246. In the context of the nonpositivist argument from principles, the Frankfurt philosopher calls into question the conceptual connection between law and morality. In short, the "Neumann's dilemma" is as follows: if taking into consideration a specific principle when settling a court case is legally obligatory, then it is indeed a legal principle and, accordingly, there does not arise the question of the necessary connection between law and morality; whereas as far as only the moral principle is concerned, taking it into consideration by the judge *ex definitione* cannot be legally obligatory, so this question also does not arise.

[12] *See* R. Alexy, 'Law and Correctness', *op. cit.*, pp. 217–219 [German version, pp. 15–16]. Simply put, according to him, the dilemma of nonpositivism resolves itself when we realise which concept of law – whether positivist or nonpositivist – we make use of.

expressed by the co-author of the German nonpositivist conception of law, upon adopting a nonpositivist conception of law "substantial correctness, and therefore morality, are already part of law".[13] It may perhaps solve "Neumann's dilemma", yet it does not, at the same time, lead to a somehow conscious self-destruction of the nonpositivist conception of law, because at the moment of the realisation of its basic postulate, any necessary conceptual relation between law and morality is out of the question: morality indeed becomes a part of valid law.[14] As Alexy remarks, in such a case "nothing is left to be connected".[15]

In the Introduction, we have basically adopted the assumption-free method of analysing the juristic concept of the validity of statutory law. This resulted, inter alia, in the fact that the methodological considerations that allowed us to develop the conception of validity, referred to as a "postpositivist" one, were conducted in parallel with the substantive analyses. If we want to briefly identify the essential features of the postpositivist theory of law, whose idea is a by-product of our investigations on validity issues, we can capture them by means of three theses[16]:

1. The postpositivist theory of law[17] is based on a moderately realistic approach to the law, understood as a phenomenon from the realm of social reality, existing independently of its cognition by legal scholars, yet co-created by them in the course of a rational reconstruction of a discursively (pragmatically) grasped legal system,
2. The postpositivist theory of law considers a detached and axiologically impartial point of view, going beyond the traditional dispute over the necessary relations between law and morality, to become a relevant research approach to the law,

[13] *Ibidem*, p. 219 [German version, p. 16].

[14] We disregard here the problem related to a self-destruction of "the law of nonpositivists", which we referred to in Chap. 4, at pp. 165ff. However, it is worth quoting Raz's thesis, though it is tempting to be, as he puts it, "provocative rather than accurate". The Oxford philosopher states that "one may say that the very existence of the law, even of morally legitimate law, means the exclusion of morality", and that is because otherwise the law will not have any impact ("make no difference") on the content of judicial decisions, in effect based on morality – *cf. idem*, "Incorporation by Law", *op. cit.*, p. 8.

[15] R. Alexy, 'Law and Correctness', *op. cit.*, p. 219 [German version, p. 16].

[16] For more on my ideas concerning the programme of the postpositivist theory of law *see* A. Grabowski, 'W stronę postpozytywizmu prawniczego. Szkic z metodologii prawoznawstwa' [In the Direction of Legal Postpositivism. A Sketch on the Methodology of Jurisprudence], *AUW* 3337 (2011), pp. 159ff.

[17] The postpositivist jurisprudence, yet in the context of the philosophy of the science which departs from the spirit of twentieth-century philosophical positivism, has already been discussed about twenty years ago by J. Leszczyński, 'Postpozytywistyczny obraz prawoznawstwa' [Postpositivist Image of Jurisprudence], *CC* 6/41–1/42 (1988–1989), pp. 53–60. We naturally use the concept of the postpositivist theory of law in another sense – what we have in mind here is the theory that follows legal positivism. Accordingly, such a use somehow resembles the way in which L. Morawski uses the concept of the post-positivist jurisprudence – *cf. idem*, 'Hard Positivism, Soft Positivism and Dead Positivism', *op. cit.*, p. 178, and A. Calsamiglia – the concept of postpositivism – *cf. idem*, 'Postpositivismo', *op. cit.* For more on other scholars (such as N. MacCormick, A. Somek, N. Forgó, M. Atienza and J. Ruiz Manero) who use this concept or related concepts *cf.* A. Grabowski, *ibidem*, pp. 157ff.

3. The postpositivist theory of law is based on the achievements of the analytical theory of law (in the sense of trying to "complete the programme of modernism"[18]), constructing juristic concepts in a moderately conventional way by means of analytical methods, and at the same time it also postulates an argumentatively-discursive approach (aiming to solve practical questions) to the clarification of their extension.

Jerzy Stelmach noted that "The dispute over the validity of the law is [...] a multi-faceted and complex one. The belief of some theorists of law that one can find one commonly acceptable solution is [...] utterly groundless".[19] Undoubtedly, the juristic concept of legal validity, which is at the core of our deliberations, is an example of the so-called essentially contested concepts.[20] It is difficult, however, to deny the right to undertake the attempts aiming at its explanation. Incidentally, we do not expect "a common acceptance" of the postpositivist conception of legal validity presented in this study, because it is indeed a radical attempt to break from both "hard" and "soft" versions of legal positivism, as well as with newly created and already very influential German nonpositivism. A detached and axiologically impartial postpositivism undermines the majority of the so far adopted conceptions of legal validity, yet unfortunately it does not offer the most important thing in return; namely, the explanation of its very essence.[21] What it does offer is only a method of understanding (the clarification of the intension) of the juristic concept of the validity of statutory law as well as an argumentatively-discursive clarification of its extension, based on the juristic presumption of the validity of statutory law norms. If one recognises as legitimate the views of Marek Zirk-Sadowski, who argues that, in particular, the Polish legal culture is still dominated by "the model of thinking about law characteristic for the primordial legal positivism",[22] and that our legal culture is currently in a disintegration phase, then the process of its reintegration ("positive integration"), predicted by him,[23] cannot be successfully done without such a theory of legal validity, which should be both theoretically correct and useful in legal practice. It is yet to be seen whether the postpositivist conception of the validity of statutory law will have any influence in such a reintegration. Decisions in this regard—as is generally the case—will not be made by a group of

---

[18] *Cf.* Chap. 7, p. 247.

[19] J. Stelmach, 'Obowiązywanie prawa w sensie absolutnym i relatywnym', *op. cit.*, p. 323.

[20] *Cf.* W.B. Galie, 'Essentially Contested Concepts', *PAS* LVI (1955–1956), pp. 167–198.

[21] What can come as a certain consolation is the fact that it was not the aim at all, and in light of the critical analysis we can state that also other jurisprudential conceptions of legal validity do not provide any commonly acceptable explanation of this phenomenon. Perhaps this is a task for philosophers.

[22] M. Zirk-Sadowski, 'Pozytywizm prawniczy a filozoficzna opozycja podmiotu i przedmiotu poznania', *op. cit.*, p. 83.

[23] *See* M. Zirk-Sadowski, 'Transformation and Integration of Legal Cultures and Discourses – Poland' in W. Sadurski *et al.* (eds.), *Spreading Democracy and the Rule of Law? The Impact of EU Enlargement on the Rule of Law, Democracy and Constitutionalism in Post-Communist Legal Orders*, Dordrecht 2006, pp. 310–311.

theorists and philosophers of law, but rather in the practice of law. It is only when practising lawyers, especially judges, have accepted the line of thinking that is inconsistent with the existing positivistic canons, that there will be a change in their way of understanding legal validity. I do believe that the task of the legal theorist is to provide such a conceptual apparatus and theoretical models of the phenomena occurring in the practice of law application that will allow Polish, Spanish, German or French judges and other participants in legal discourse to undertake such changes, when—someday—they decide to do so.

References

Aarnio, Aulis. 1980. The Form and Content of Law. Aspects of Legal Positivism. *Archivum Iuridicum Cracoviense* XIII: 17–36.

Aarnio, Aulis. 1981. On Truth and the Acceptability of Interpretative Propositions in Legal Dogmatics. *Rechtstheorie*, Beiheft 2: 33–51.

Aarnio, Aulis. 1983. On the Validity, Efficacy and Acceptability of Legal Norms. In *idem*, *Philosophical Perspectives in Jurisprudence*, Acta Philosophica Fennica XXXVI: 152–162.

Aarnio, Aulis. 1987. *The Rational as Reasonable. A Treatise on Legal Justification*. Dordrecht/Boston/Lancaster/Tokyo: D. Reidel.

Aarnio, Aulis, Aleksander Peczenik. 1996. On Values. Universal or Relative? *Ratio Juris* 9: 321–330.

Aarnio, Aulis, Robert Alexy, and Aleksander Peczenik. 1981. The Foundation of Legal Reasoning. *Rechtstheorie* 12: 133–158, 257–279, 423–448. German version: Grundlagen der juristischen Argumentation. In *Metatheorie juristischer Argumentation*, ed. W. Krawietz, R. Alexy, 9–87. Berlin: Duncker & Humblot, 1983.

Aguiló Regla, Josep. 1999. *Sobre la Derogación. Ensayo de Dinámica Jurídica*, 2nd ed. México: Fontamara. [1st ed. 1995.]

Ajdukiewicz, Kazimierz. 1960. Trzy pojęcia definicji [Three Concepts of Definition]. In *idem*, *Język i poznanie*, Vol. II, 296–307. Warszawa: Państwowe Wydawnictwo Naukowe.

Ajdukiewicz, Kazimierz. 1960. Zagadnienie uzasadnienia zdań analitycznych [The Problem of Justifying Analytical Propositions]. Trans. H. Mortimer. In *idem*, *Język i poznanie*, Vol. II, 308–321. Warszawa: Państwowe Wydawnictwo Naukowe.

Ajdukiewicz, Kazimierz. 1975. *Logika pragmatyczna* [Pragmatic Logic]. Warszawa: Państwowe Wydawnictwo Naukowe.

Albert, Hans. 1987. Die angebliche Paradoxie des konsequenten Fallibilismus und die Ansprüche der Transzendentalpragmatik. *Zeitschrift für philosophische Forschung* 41: 421–428.

Albert, Hans. 1991. *Traktat über kritische Vernunft*, 5th ed. Tübingen: Mohr Siebeck. [1st ed. 1968.]. English version: *Treatise on Critical Reason*. Trans. M. Varney Rorty. Princeton: Princeton University Press, 1985.

Alchourrón, Carlos E. 1969. Logic of Norms and Logic of Normative Propositions. *Logique et Analyse* XII: 242–268.

Alchourrón, Carlos E., Eugenio Bulygin. 1971. *Normative Systems*. Wien/New York: Springer.

Alchourrón, Carlos E., Eugenio Bulygin. 1981. The Expressive Conception of Norms. In *New Essays in Deontic Logic*, ed. R. Hilpinen, 95–124. Dordrecht/Boston/London: D. Reidel.

Alchourrón, Carlos E., Eugenio Bulygin. 1991. Sobre el concepto de orden jurídico. In *iidem*, *Análisis lógico y Derecho*, 393–407. Madrid: Centro de Estudios Constitucionales.

Alexy, Robert. 1978. *Theorie der juristischen Argumentation. Die Theorie des Rationalen Diskurses als Theorie der juristischen Begründung*. Frankfurt am Main: Suhrkamp. English

DOI 10.1007/978-3-642-27688-0, © Springer-Verlag Berlin Heidelberg 2013

version: *A Theory of Legal Argumentation. The Theory of Rational Discourse as Theory of Legal Justification*. Trans. R. Adler, N. MacCormick. Oxford: Clarendon Press, 1989.

Alexy, Robert. 1979. Zum Begriff des Rechtsprinzips. *Rechtstheorie*, Beiheft 1: 59–87.

Alexy, Robert. 1981. Die Idee einer prozeduralen Theorie der juristischen Argumentation. *Rechtstheorie*, Beiheft 2: 177–188.

Alexy, Robert. 1985. Rechtsregeln und Rechtsprinzipien. *Archiv für Rechts- und Sozialphilosophie*, Beiheft 25: 13–29.

Alexy, Robert. 1985. *Theorie der Grundrechte*. Baden-Baden: Nomos. English version: *A Theory of Constitutional Rights*. Trans. J. Rivers. Oxford: Oxford University Press, 2002.

Alexy, Robert. 1987. Rechtssystem und praktische Vernunft. *Rechtstheorie* 18: 405–419.

Alexy, Robert. 1989. On Necessary Relations between Law and Morality. *Ratio Juris* 2: 167–183. German extended version: Zur Kritik des Rechtspositivismus. *Archiv für Rechts- und Sozialphilosophie*, Beiheft 37 (1990): 9–26.

Alexy, Robert. 1989. Probleme der Diskurstheorie. *Zeitschrift für philosophische Forschung* 43: 81–93. English version: Problems of Discourse Theory. *Crítica* 20 (1988): 43–65.

Alexy, Robert. 1990. A Theory of Practical Discourse. Trans. D. Frisby. In *The Communicative Ethics Controversy*, ed. S. Benhabib, F. Dallmayr, 151–190. Cambridge (Mass.)/London: The MIT Press.

Alexy, Robert. 1990. Problems of Discursive Rationality in Law. *Archiv für Rechts- und Sozialphilosophie*, Beiheft 42: 174–179.

Alexy, Robert. 1991. Idee und Struktur eines vernünftigen Rechtssystems. *Archiv für Rechts- und Sozialphilosophie*, Beiheft 44: 30–44.

Alexy, Robert. 1991. Nachwort (1991): Antwort auf einige Kritiker. In *idem*, *Theorie der juristischen Argumentation. Die Theorie des Rationalen Diskurses als Theorie der juristischen Begründung*, 2nd ed., 399–435. Frankfurt am Main: Suhrkamp. Original Spanish version was published as 'Postfacio: Respuesta a algunos críticos' in R. Alexy, *Teoría de la argumentación jurídica. La teoría del discurso racional como teoría de la fundamentación juridical*, trans. M. Atienza, I. Espejo, 290–318. Madrid: Centro de Estudios Constitucionales, 1989.

Alexy, Robert. 1992. A Discourse-Theoretical Conception of Practical Reason. Trans. R. Adler, N. MacCormick. *Ratio Juris* 5: 231–251. German version: Eine diskurstheoretische Konzeption der praktischen Vernunft. *Archiv für Rechts- und Sozialphilosophie*, Beiheft 51 (1993): 11–29.

Alexy, Robert. 1992. *Begriff und Geltung des Rechts*. Freiburg/München: Karl Alber. English version: *The Argument from Injustice. A Reply to Legal Positivism*. Trans. B. Litschewski Paulson, St.L. Paulson. Oxford: Clarendon Press, 2002.

Alexy, Robert. 1992. Zur Verteidigung eines nichtpositivistischen Rechtsbegriffs. In *Öffentliche oder private Moral? Vom Geltungsgrunde und der Legitimität des Rechts. Festschrift für Ernesto Garzón Valdés*, ed. W. Krawietz, G.H. von Wright, 85–108. Berlin: Duncker & Humblot.

Alexy, Robert. 1993. *Mauerschützen. Zum Verhältnis von Recht, Moral und Strafbarkeit*. Hamburg: Joachim Jungius-Gesellschaft der Wissenschaften/Göttingen: Vandenhoeck & Ruprecht.

Alexy, Robert. 1993. Normenbegründung und Normanwendung. In *Rechtsnorm und Rechtswirklichkeit. Festschrift für Werner Krawietz zum 60. Geburtstag*, ed. A. Aarnio, St.L. Paulson, O. Weinberger, G.H. von Wright, and D. Wyduckel, 3–17. Berlin: Duncker & Humblot. English version: Justification and Application of Norms, *Ratio Juris* 6 (1993): 157–170.

Alexy, Robert. 1994. A Definition of Law. In *Prescriptive Formality and Normative Rationality in Modern Legal Systems.* Festschrift *for Robert S. Summers*, ed. W. Krawietz, N. MacCormick, and G.H. von Wright, 101–107. Berlin: Duncker & Humblot.

Alexy, Robert. 1994. Ota Weinbergers Kritik der diskurstheoretischen Deutung juristischer Rationalität. *Rechtstheorie*, Beiheft 14:143–157.

Alexy, Robert. 1995. Discourse Theory and Human Rights. In *Challenges to Law at the End of the 20th Century (17th IVR World Congress Bologna, 17-21 June, 1995)*, Vol. II, 22–28. Bologna: Cooperativa Libraria Universitaria Editrice Bologna.

Alexy, Robert. 1995. Diskurstheorie und Menschenrechte. In *idem*, *Recht, Vernunft, Diskurs. Studien zur Rechtsphilosophie*, 127–164. Frankfurt am Main: Suhrkamp. English version: Discourse Theory and Human Rights. *Ratio Juris* 9 (1996): 209–235.
Alexy, Robert. 1995. Jürgen Habermas' Theorie des juristischen Diskurses. In *idem*, *Recht, Vernunft, Diskurs. Studien zur Rechtsphilosophie*, 165–174. Frankfurt am Main: Suhrkamp. English version: Jürgen Habermas's Theory of Legal Discourse. *Cardozo Law Review* 17 (1996): 1027–1034.
Alexy, Robert. 1995. Law, Discourse, and Time. *Archiv für Rechts- und Sozialphilosophie*, Beiheft 64: 101–110.
Alexy, Robert. 1995. Vorwort. In *idem*, *Recht, Vernunft, Diskurs. Studien zur Rechtsphilosophie*, 7–10. Frankfurt am Main: Suhrkamp.
Alexy, Robert. 1997. Bulygins Kritik des Richtigkeitsarguments. In *Normative Systems in Legal and Moral Theory*. Festschrift *for Carlos E. Alchourrón and Eugenio Bulygin*, ed. E. Garzón Valdés, W. Krawietz, G.H. von Wright, and R. Zimmerling, 235–250. Berlin: Duncker & Humblot.
Alexy, Robert. 1997. *Der Beschluß des Bundesverfassungsgericht zu den Tötungen an der innerdeutschen Grenze vom 24. Oktober 1996*. Hamburg: Joachim Jungius-Gesellschaft der Wissenschaften/Göttingen: Vandenhoeck & Ruprecht.
Alexy, Robert. 1998. Law and Correctness. Trans. K. Bock. In *Legal Theory at the End of the Millenium*, ed. M.D.A. Freeman, 205–221. Oxford: Oxford University Press. German version: Recht und Richtigkeit. In *The Reasonable as Rational? On Legal Argumentation and Justification*. Festschrift *for Aulis Aarnio*, ed. W. Krawietz, R.S. Summers, O. Weinberger, and G.H. von Wright, 3–19. Berlin: Duncker & Humblot, 2000.
Alexy, Robert. 1999. The Special Case Thesis. *Ratio Juris* 12: 374–384.
Alexy, Robert. 2000. On the Thesis of a Necessary Connection between Law and Morality: Bulygin's Critique. *Ratio Juris* 13: 138–147.
Alexy, Robert. 2000. Zur Struktur der Rechtsprinzipien. In *Regeln, Prinzipien und Elemente im System des Rechts*, ed. B. Schilcher, P. Koller, and B.-Ch. Frank, 31–52. Wien: Österreich. Shortened English version: On the Structure of Legal Principles. *Ratio Juris* 13 (2000): 294–304.
Alexy, Robert. 2002. Grundrechte, Abwägung und Rationalität. *Ars Interpretandi. Jahrbuch für juristische Hermeneutik* 7: 113–125. English version: Constitutional Rights, Balancing, and Rationality, *Ratio Juris* 16 (2003): 131–140.
Alexy, Robert. 2003. Die juristische Argumentation als rationaler Diskurs. In R. Alexy, H.-J. Koch, L. Kuhlen, H. Rüßmann, *Elemente einer juristischen Begründungslehre*, 361–378. Baden-Baden: Nomos. English version: Legal Argumentation as Rational Discourse. *Rivista internazionale di filosofia del diritto* LXX/1 (1993): 165–178.
Alexy, Robert. 2003. Ermessensfehler. In R. Alexy, H.-J. Koch, L. Kuhlen, H. Rüßmann, *Elemente einer juristischen Begründungslehre*, 251–286. Baden-Baden: Nomos.
Alexy, Robert. 2003. Justicia como corrección. Trans. A. I. Haquín. *DOXA* 26: 161–171.
Alexy, Robert. 2003. On Balancing and Subsumption. A Structural Comparison. *Ratio Juris* 16: 433–449.
Alexy, Robert. 2003. The Nature of Arguments about the Nature of Law. In *Rights, Culture, and the Law. Themes from the Legal and Political Philosophy of Joseph Raz*, ed. L.H. Meyer, St.L. Paulson, and T.W. Pogge, 3–16. Oxford: Oxford University Press.
Alexy, Robert. 2003. The Nature of Legal Philosophy. *Associations* 7: 63–75.
Alexy, Robert. 2004. Menschenrechte ohne Metaphysik? *Deutsche Zeitschrift für Philosophie* 52/1: 15–24.
Alexy, Robert. 2005. Ralf Dreiers Interpretation der Kantischen Rechtsdefinition. In *Integratives Verstehen. Zur Rechtsphilosophie Ralf Dreiers*, ed. R. Alexy, 95–109. Tübingen: Mohr Siebeck.
Alexy, Robert. 2006. Effects of Defects – Action or Argument? Thoughts about Deryck Beyleved and Roger Brownsword's *Law as a Moral Judgment*. *Ratio Juris* 19: 169–179.

Alexy, Robert. 2006. *O pojęciu i naturze prawa / On the Concept and the Nature of Law*. Warszawa: Fundacja "Ius et Lex".

Alexy, Robert. 2007. An Answer to Joseph Raz. In *Law, Rights and Discourse. The Legal Philosophy of Robert Alexy*, ed. G. Pavlakos, 37–55. Oxford/Portland: Hart.

Alexy, Robert. 2007. On Two Juxtapositions: Concept and Nature, Law and Philosophy. Some Comments on Joseph Raz's "Can There Be a Theory of Law?". *Ratio Juris* 20: 162–169.

Alexy, Robert. 2009. Hauptelemente einer Theorie der Doppelnatur des Rechts. *Archiv für Rechts- und Sozialphilosophie* 95: 151–166.

Alexy, Robert. 2010. Between Positivism and Non-Positivism? A Third Reply to Eugenio Bulygin. A lecture presented at the 1st Conference on Philosophy and Law "Neutrality and Theory of Law", Girona 20-22 of May 2010. http://www.te.gob.mx/ccje/Archivos/r_aalexy.pdf. Accessed 20 September 2010.

Alexy, Robert, Ralf Dreier. 1990. The Concept of Jurisprudence. *Ratio Juris* 3: 1–13.

Alston, William P. 1968. Meaning and Use. In *The Theory of Meaning*, ed. G.H.R. Parkinson, 141–165. Oxford: Oxford University Press. [1st published in *The Philosophical Quarterly* 13 (1963): 107–124].

Alston, William P. 1996. *A Realist Conception of Truth*. Ithaca: Cornell University Press.

Amato Mangiameli, Agata C. 1994. Variazioni positivistiche e giusnaturalistiche sulla dialettica fra diritto e morale. Osservazioni in margine a "Begriff und Geltung des Rechts" di Robert Alexy. *Rivista internazionale di filosofia del diritto* LXXI/1: 3–35.

Andruszkiewicz, Marta, Urszula Anna Kosielińska-Grabowska. 2007. Prawodawca w labiryncie definicji legalnej [The Lawmaker in the Maze of Legal Definition]. *Studia Prawno-Ekonomiczne* LXXV (2007), s. 9–36.

Anscombe, Gertrude Elisabeth M. 1958. On Brute Facts. *Analysis* 18/3: 69–72.

Apel, Karl-Otto. „Grenzen der Diskursethik? Versuch einer Zwischenbilanz", *Zeitschrift für philosophische Forschung* 40 (1986), s. 3–31.

Apel, Karl-Otto. 1973. Das Apriori der Kommunikationsgemeinschaft und die Grundlagen der Ethik. Zum Problem einer rationalen Begründung der Ethik im Zeitalter der Wissenschaft. In *idem*, *Transformation der Philosophie*, Band II: *Das Apriori der Kommunikationsgemeinschaft*, 358–435. Frankfurt am Main: Suhrkamp. English version: The *A Priori* of the Communication Community and the Foundations of Ethics. Trans. G. Adey, D. Frishy. In *idem*, *Towards a Transformation of Philosophy*. London: Routledge & Kegan Paul, 1980, 225–300.

Apel, Karl-Otto. 1998. Can an ultimate foundation of knowledge be non-metaphysical? Trans. B. Gregg. In *idem*, *From a Trancendental-Semiotic Point of View*, ed. M. Papastephanou, 81–102. Manchester/New York: Manchester University Press.

Apel, Karl-Otto. 1998. Das Problem der philosophischen Letztbegründung im Lichte einer transzendentalen Sprachpragmatik. Versuch einer Metakritik des "kritischen Rationalismus". In *idem*, *Auseinandersetzungen in Erprobung des transzendentalpragmatischen Ansatzes*, 33–79. Frankfurt am Main: Suhrkamp. English version: The Problem of Philosophical Fundamental-Grounding in Light of a Transcendental Pragmatic of Language. Trans. K.R. Pavlovic. *Man and World* 8 (1975): 239–275.

Apel, Karl-Otto. 1998. Fallibilismus, Konsenstheorie der Wahrheit und Letztbegründung. In *idem*, *Auseinandersetzungen in Erprobung des transzendentalpragmatischen Ansatzes*, 81–193. Frankfurt am Main: Suhrkamp.

Apel, Karl-Otto. 1998. Transcendental semiotics and the paradigms of First Philosophy. In *idem*, *From a Trancendental-Semiotic Point of View*, ed. M. Papastephanou, 43–63. Manchester/New York: Manchester University Press.

Arnaud, André-Jean (ed.). 1988. *Dictionnaire Encyclopédique de Théorie et de Sociologie du Droit*. Paris: Libraire Générale de Droit et de Jurisprudence/Bruxelles: E. Story-Scientia.

Atienza, Manuel. 1993. *Las Razones del Derecho. Teorías de la argumentatión jurídica*. 2nd ed. Madrid: Centro de Estudios Constitucionales. [1st ed. 1991.]

Atienza, Manuel. 1997. Los límites de la interpretación constitucional. De nuevo sobre los casos trágicos. *Isonomía* 6: 7–30.

Atienza, Manuel. 2001. *El sentido del Derecho*. Barcelona: Ariel.

Atienza, Manuel. 2001. Entrevista a Robert Alexy. *DOXA* 24: 671–687.

Atienza, Manuel. 2003. Seis acotaciones preliminares para una teoría de la validez juridical. *DOXA* 26: 719–735.

Atienza, Manuel. 2007. Is Legal Positivism a Sustainable Legal Theory? In *Law and Legal Cultures in the 21st Century. Diversity and Unity (23rd IVR World Congress, August 1-6, 2007, Cracow, Poland*, ed. T. Gizbert-Studnicki, J. Stelmach, 229–245. Warszawa: Wolters Kluwer Polska.

Atienza, Manuel, Juan Ruiz Manero. 1996. *Las piezas del Derecho. Teoría de los enunciados jurídicos*. Barcelona: Ariel. English version: *A Theory of Legal Sentences*. Trans. R. Zimmerling. Dordrecht: Kluwer, 1998.

Atienza, Manuel, Juan Ruiz Manero. 2002. Preliminaries for a Theory of Legal Validity. A paper presented at the seminar of the Executive Committee of *IVR* "Validity and Applicability", in Paris, 30 June–1 July 2002 [typescript].

Augustyn, św. [St. Augustine]. 1998. *Państwo Boże* [De civitate Dei]. Trans. W. Kubicki. Kęty: Antyk.

Austin, John. 1954. *Province of Jurisprudence Determined* and *The Uses of the Study of Jurisprudence*. London: Weidenfeld and Nicolson.

Austin, John Langshaw. 1979. A Plea for Excuses. In *idem*, *Philosophical papers*, 3rd ed. by J.O. Urmson, G.J. Warnock, 175–204. Oxford/New York/Toronto/Melbourne: Oxford University Press.

Austin, John Langshaw. 1971. Performative-Constative. Trans. G. J. Warnock. In *The Philosophy of Language*, ed. J.R. Searle, 13–22. Oxford: Oxford University Press.

Austin, John Langshaw. 1976. *How to Do Things with Words. The William James Lectures delivered at Harvard University in 1955*, 2nd ed. by J.O. Urmson, M. Sbisà. Oxford: Oxford University Press. [1st ed. 1962.]

Austin, John Langshaw. 1979. Performative utterances. In *idem*, *Philosophical papers*. 3rd ed. by J.O. Urmson, G.J. Warnock, 233–252. Oxford/New York/Toronto/Melbourne: Oxford University Press.

Austin, John Langshaw. 1979. The Meaning of a Word. In *idem*, *Philosophical papers*. 3rd ed. by J.O. Urmson, G.J. Warnock, 55–75. Oxford/New York/Toronto/Melbourne: Oxford University Press.

Åqvist, Lennart. 2003. Some Remarks on Performatives in the Law. *Artificial Intelligence and Law* 11: 105–124.

Bańko, Mirosław (ed.). 2000. *Inny słownik języka polskiego PWN* [The *PWN*'s Different Dictionary of Polish Language], Vol. I. Warszawa: Wydawnictwo Naukowe PWN.

Bańkowski, Zenon, Neil MacCormick, Robert S. Summers, and Jerzy Wróblewski. 1991. On Method and Methodology. In *Interpreting Statutes. A Comparative Study*, ed. N. MacCormick, R.S. Summers, 9–27. Aldershot/Brookfield/Hong Kong/Singapore/Sydney/Vermont: Dartmouth.

Bator, Andrzej. 1990. O konserwatyźmie językowym nauki prawa [On Linguistic Conservatism of the Science of Law]. In *Prawo i prawoznawstwo wobec zmian społecznych*, ed. H. Rot, 18–30. Wrocław: Wydawnictwo Uniwersytetu Wrocławskiego.

Bator, Andrzej. 1991. Język prawniczy wobec zmian w prawie [Juristic Language in the Face of Changes in Law]. *Studia Prawnicze* 1/107: 3–16.

Bator, Andrzej. 2000. *Użycie normy prawnej w regulacji stosunków gospodarczych* [The Use of the Legal Norm in the Regulation of Economic Relations]. Wrocław: Kolonia.

Bator, Andrzej. 2004. *Kompetencja w prawie i prawoznawstwie* [Competence in Law and Jurisprudence]. Acta Universitatis Wratislaviensis 2602.

Bator, Andrzej. 2006. System prawa [Legal System]. In A. Bator, W. Gromski, A. Kozak, S. Kaźmierczyk, Z. Pulka, *Wprowadzenie do nauk prawnych. Leksykon tematyczny*, 166. Warszawa: Wydawnictwo Prawnicze LexisNexis.

Beehler, Rodger. 1990. Legal Positivism, Social Rules, and *Riggs v. Palmer*. *Law and Philosophy* 9: 285–293.

Behrend, Jürgen. 1977. *Untersuchungen zur Stufenbaulehre Adolf Merkls und Hans Kelsens*. Berlin: Duncker & Humblot.

Bengoetxea, Joxerramon. 1994. Legal System as a Regulative Ideal. *Archiv für Rechts- und Sozialphilosophie*, Beiheft 53: 65–80.

Bertea, Stefano. 2007. How Non-positivism Can Accommodate Legal Certainty. In *Rights and Discourse. The Legal Philosophy of Robert Alexy*, ed. G. Pavlakos, 69–82. Oxford/Portland: Hart.

Beschluß des Ersten Senat vom 14. Februar 1973 (1 BvR 112/65). In *Entscheidungen des Bundesverfassungsgerichts* 34 (1973): 269–293. Tubingen: Mohr Siebeck.

Betegón, Jerónimo. 1998. Sobre la pretendida corrección de la pretensión de corrección. *DOXA* 21/I: 171–192.

Beyleveld, Deryck, Roger Brownsword. 1989. Normative Positivism: The Mirage of the Middle-Way. *Oxford Journal of Legal Studies* 9/4: 463–512.

Bieniek, Gerard, Helena Ciepła, Stanisław Dmowski, Jacek Gudowski, Krzysztof Kołakowski, Marek Zychowicz, Tadeusz Wiśniewski, and Czesława Żuławska. 2001. *Komentarz do kodeksu cywilnego. Księga trzecia: Zobowiązania* [Commentary to the Civil Code. Book Three: Obligations]. 3rd ed. Warszawa: Wydawnictwo Prawnicze. [1st ed. 1996.]

Bindreiter, Uta U. 2001. "Descriptive Normativity": Kelsen's *Sollsatz* in the Light of Some Later Theories. *Associations* 5: 71–94.

Bindreiter, Uta U. 2001. Presupposing the Basic Norm. *Ratio Juris* 14: 143–175.

Bix, Brian. 2006. Robert Alexy, Radbruch's Formula, and the Nature of Legal Theory. *Rechtstheorie* 37: 139–149.

Błachut, Michał, Jacek Kaczor, Przemysław Kaczmarek, Adam Sulikowski. 2008. Systemowość w myśleniu prawniczym [Systematization in Legal Reasoning]. In *System prawny a porządek prawny*, ed. O. Bogucki, S. Czepita, 89–107. Szczecin: Wydawnictwo Naukowe Uniwersytetu Szczecińskiego.

Bladowski, Bogdan. 1999. *Czynności sądowe w sprawach cywilnych* [Court Actions in Civil Cases]. Kraków: Zakamycze. [1st ed. 1991.]

Bobbio, Norberto. 1961. Sur le positivisme juridique. In *Mélanges en l'honneur de P. Roubier: Théorie générale du droit et droit transitoire*, 53–73. Paris: Dalloz & Sirey.

Bobbio, Norberto. 1970. "Sein" and "Sollen" in Legal Science. *Archiv für Rechts- und Sozialphilosophie* 56: 7–30.

Bogucka, Iwona, Stanisław Bogucki. 1992. O derogacji i pojęciach pokrewnych [On Derogation and Related Concepts]. *Państwo i Prawo* 6/556: 80–83.

Boryś, Wiesław. 2005. *Słownik etymologiczny języka polskiego* [Etymological Dictionary of the Polish Language]. Kraków: Wydawnictwo Literackie.

Boukema, H.J.M. 1983. The Hart-Fuller Debate. *Rechtstheorie* 14: 29–59.

Braun, Carl. 1988. Diskurstheoretische Normenbegründung in der Rechtswissenschaft. *Rechtstheorie* 19: 238–261.

Broekmann, Jan M. 1985. The Minimum Content of Positivism. Positivism in the Law and in Legal Theory. *Rechtstheorie* 16: 349–366.

Brożek, Bartosz. 2004. *Defeasibility of Legal Reasoning*. Kraków: Zakamycze.

Brożek, Bartosz. 2007. *Rationality and Discourse. Towards a Normative Theory of Applying Law*. Warszawa: Wolters Kluwer Polska.

Brożek, Bartosz, Wojciech Cyrul. 2003. Zwischen Logik und Diskurs – Bemerkungen zur Geltung im globalen Rechtssystem. *Krakauer-Augsburger Rechtsstudien* 1: 19–38.

Buchwald, Delf. 1990. *Der Begriff der rationalen juristischen Begründung. Zur Theorie der juridischen Vernunft*. Baden-Baden: Nomos.

Bulygin, Eugenio. 1982. Time and Validity. In *Deontic Logic, Computational Linguistic and Legal Information Systems*, Vol. II, ed. A.A. Martino, 65–81. Amsterdam/New York/Oxford: North-Holland. Slightly modified Spanish version: Tiempo y validez. Trans. E. Bulygin. In C.E. Alchourrón, E. Bulygin, *Análisis lógico y Derecho*, 195–214. Madrid: Centro de Estudios Constitucionales.

Bulygin, Eugenio. 1990. An Antinomy in Kelsen's Pure Theory of Law. *Ratio Juris* 3: 29–45.

Bulygin, Eugenio. 1991. Regla de reconocimiento: ¿norma de obligación o criterio conceptual? Réplica a Juan Ruiz Manero. *DOXA* 9: 311–318.

Bulygin, Eugenio. 1992. Entrevista con Ota Weinberger. *DOXA* 11: 313–323.

Bulygin, Eugenio. 1993. Alexy und das Richtigkeitsargument. In *Rechtsnorm und Rechtswirklichkeit. Festschrift für Werner Krawietz zum 60. Geburtstag*, ed. A. Aarnio, St.L. Paulson, O. Weinberger, G.H. von Wright, and D. Wyduckel, 19–24. Berlin: Duncker & Humblot.

Bulygin, Eugenio. 1998. ¿Hay vinculación necesaria entre derecho y moral? In *Derecho y moral. Ensayos sobre un debate contemporáneo*, ed. R. Vázquez, 214–223. Barcelona: Gedisa.

Bulygin, Eugenio. 1999. Is There a Conceptual Connection between Law and Morality? *Associations* 3: 45–59.

Bulygin, Eugenio. 2000. Alexy's Thesis of the Necessary Connection between Law and Morality. *Ratio Juris* 13: 133–137.

Bulygin, Eugenio. 2000. On Norm Propositions. In *The Reasonable as Rational? On Legal Argumentation and Justification.* Festschrift *for Aulis Aarnio*, ed. W. Krawietz, R.S. Summers, O. Weinberger, and G.H. von Wright, 129–134. Berlin: Duncker & Humblot.

Bulygin, Eugenio. 2003. Los jueces, ¿crean derecho? *Isonomía* 18: 7–25.

Bulygin, Eugenio. 2004. ¿Está (parte de) la filosofía del Derecho basada en un error? *DOXA* 27: 15–26.

Bulygin, Eugenio. 2008. What Can One Expect from Logic in the Law? (Not Everything, but More than Something: A Reply to Susan Haack). *Ratio Juris* 21: 150–156.

Bulygin, Eugenio. 2010. Alexy between Positivism and Non-Positivism. A lecture presented at the 1st Conference on Philosophy and Law "Neutrality and Theory of Law", Girona 20-22 of May 2010. http://www.te.gob.mx/ccje/Archivos/eugenio_bulygin.pdf. Accessed 20 September 2010.

Bulygin, Eugenio. Algunas consideraciones sobre los sistemas jurídicos. *DOXA* 9: 257–279.

Bulygin, Eugenio. Normensystem und Rechtsordnung. In *Staatsrecht in Theorie und Praxis. Festschrift für Robert Walter zum 60. Geburtstag*, ed. H. Mayer, 97–103. Wien: Manzsche Verlags- und Univesitätsbuchhandlung.

Burg, Wibren, van der. 1999. Two Models of Law and Morality. *Associations* 3: 61–82.

Calsamiglia, Albert. 1998. Postpositivismo. *DOXA* 21/I: 209–220.

Caracciolo, Ricardo. 1993. Entrevista a Eugenio Bulygin. *DOXA* 14: 499–513.

Caracciolo, Ricardo. 2000. Moral Realism vs. Legal Positivism. *Associations* 4, 213–222.

Carnap, Rudolf. 1947. *Meaning and Necessity. A Study in Semantic and Modal Logic.* Chicago: University of Chicago Press.

Carnap, Rudolf. 1971. *Logical Foundations of Probability.* London: Routledge & Kegan Paul. [1st ed. 1950.]

Carney, James D. 1962. *Cogito, Ergo Sum* and *Sum Res Cogitans. The Philosophical Review* LXXI: 492–496.

Chauvin, Tatiana. 2003. Próba wprowadzenia do teorii umów prawotwórczych [The Attempt of Introduction to the Theory of Law-making Contracts]. In *Filozofia prawa wobec globalizmu*, ed. J. Stelmach, 83–90. Kraków: Wydawnictwo Uniwersytetu Jagiellońskiego.

Chisholm, Roderick. 1978. What is a Transcendental Argument? *Neue Hefte für Philosophie* 14, 19–22.

Choduń, Agnieszka. 2004. Język prawny a język potoczny [Legal Language and Ordinary Language]. In *Język – Prawo – Społeczeństwo*, ed. E. Malinowska, 77–86. Opole: Wydawnictwo Uniwersytetu Opolskiego.

Choduń, Agnieszka. 2006. Leksyka tekstów aktów prawnych [The Lexis of the Texts of Legal Acts]. *Ruch Prawniczy, Ekonomiczny i Socjologiczny* LXVIII/1: 19–30.

Choduń, Agnieszka. 2007. *Słownictwo tekstów aktów prawnych w zasobie leksykalnym współczesnej polszczyzny* [The Vocabulary of the Texts of Legal Acts in the Contemporary Polish Lexical Resource]. Warszawa: Trio.

Coleman, Jules L. 1982. Negative and Positive Positivism. *The Journal of Legal Studies* 11/1: 139–164.

Coleman, Jules L. 1989. On the Relationship between Law and Morality. *Ratio Juris* 2: 66–78.

Coleman, Jules L. 1996. Authority and Reason. In *The Autonomy of Law. Essays on Legal Positivism*, ed. R.P. George, 287–319. Oxford: Clarendon Press.

Coleman, Jules L. 2001. Inclusive Legal Positivism. In *idem, The Practice of Principle. In Defence of a Pragmatist Approach to Legal Theory*, 103–119. Oxford/New York: Oxford University Press.

Coleman, Jules L. 2001. Incorporationism, Conventionality, and the Practical Difference Thesis. In *Hart's Postscript. Essays on the Postscript to* The Concept of Law, ed. J.L. Coleman, 99–147. Oxford/New York: Oxford University Press.

Coleman, Jules L. 2001. Normativity and Naturalism. In *idem, The Practice of Principle. In Defence of a Pragmatist Approach to Legal Theory*, 175–217. Oxford/New York: Oxford University Press.

Coleman, Jules L. 2001. Practical Difference. In *idem, The Practice of Principle. In Defence of a Pragmatist Approach to Legal Theory*, 134–148. Oxford/New York: Oxford University Press.

Coleman, Jules L. 2007. Beyond the Separability Thesis: Moral Semantics and the Methodology of Jurisprudence. *Oxford Journal of Legal Studies* 27/4: 581–608.

Comanducci, Paolo. 2000. Kelsen vs. Searle. A Tale of Two Constructivists. *Associations* 4: 33–48.

Cyrul, Wojciech. 2001. *Dyskursywna teoria tworzenia prawa* [The Discursive Theory of Law-making]. Kraków [unpublished PhD thesis].

Cyrul, Wojciech, Bartosz Brożek. 2003. Globalny system prawa [Global Legal System]. *Studia z filozofii prawa* 2: 93–109.

Czaja, Jacek, Jerzy Stelmach. 1993–1994. Teoria argumentacji prawniczej [Theory of Legal Argumentation]. *Krakowskie Studia Prawnicze* XXVI–XXVII: 19–31.

Czarnecki, Tadeusz. 2001. *Moore i Wittgenstein. Niekartezjańskie rozwiązania problemu pewnoś ci* [Moore and Wittgenstein. Non-Cartesian Solutions of the Problem of Certainty]. Kraków: Politechnika Krakowska.

Czarny, Piotr. 2005. Trybunał Konstytucyjny a wykładnia ustaw w zgodzie z Konstytucją [The Constitutional Tribunal and Interpretation of Statutes in Accordance with the Constitution]. In *Polska kultura prawna a proces integracji europejskiej*, ed. S. Wronkowska, 67–91. Kraków: Zakamycze.

Czepita, Stanisław. 1988. *Koncepcje teoretycznoprawne Czesława Znamierowskiego* [Jurisprudential Conceptions of Czesław Znamierowski]. Poznań: Wydawnictwo Naukowe Uniwersytetu im. Adama Mickiewicza w Poznaniu.

Czepita, Stanisław. 1994. Reguły konstrukcji systemu prawnego a prawotwórstwo [The Rules of the Construction of Legal System and Law-creation"]. *Ruch Prawniczy, Ekonomiczny i Socjologiczny* LVI/4: 31–38.

Czepita, Stanisław. 1996. *Reguły konstytutywne a zagadnienia prawoznawstwa* [Constitutive Rules and the Problems of Jurisprudence]. Szczecin: Wydawnictwo Naukowe Uniwersytetu Szczecińskiego.

Czeszejko-Sochacki, Zdzisław, Leszek Garlicki, Janusz Trzciński. 1999. *Komentarz do Ustawy o Trybunale Konstytucyjnym z dnia 1 sierpnia 1997 roku* [Commentary on the Statute on the Constitutional Tribunal from 1st of August 1997]. Warszawa: Wydawnictwo Sejmowe.

Czeżowski, Tadeusz. 1958. O rzetelności, obiektywności i bezstronności w badaniach naukowych [On the Reliability, Objectivity and Impartiality in Scientific Research]. In *idem, Odczyty filozoficzne*, 305–309. Toruń: Towarzystwo Naukowe w Toruniu.

Czeżowski, Tadeusz. 1965. O tradycyjnych rozróżnieniach wśród definicji [On the Traditional Distinctions among Definitions]. In *idem*, *Filozofia na rozdrożu (Analizy metodologiczne)*, 19–28. Warszawa: Państwowe Wydawnictwo Naukowe.
Dąbrowska-Kardas, Małgorzata. 1996. Kara jako konflikt dóbr i kolizja norm w świetle koncepcji Roberta Alexy'ego konfliktu reguł i kolizji zasad. Rozważania na tle konstytucyjnych norm stanowienia i stosowania prawa [Punishment as a Conflict of Goods and Collision of Norms in the Light of Robert Alexy's Concept of the Conflict of Rules and Collision of Principles. Studies from the Perspective of Constitutional Norms of Enacting and Applying Law]. *Przegląd Sejmowy* 4/16: 20–33.
Dahlman, Christian. 2004. Fused Modality or Confused Modality? *Ratio Juris* 17: 80–86.
Darwall, Stephen, Allan Gibbard, and Peter Railton. 1992. Toward *Fin de siècle* Ethics: Some Trends. *The Philosophical Review* CI: 115–189.
Dekret z dnia 12 grudnia 1981 r. o stanie wojennym [Decree of 12 December 1981 on martial law]. *Dziennik Ustaw* [Journal of Statutes] 1981, No. 29, Item 154.
Delacroix, Sylvie. 2004. Hart's and Kelsen's Concepts of Normativity Contrasted. *Ratio Juris* 17: 501–520.
Descartes, René. 2004. *Rozprawa o metodzie* [Discourse on the Method]. Trans. T. Boy-Żeleński. Kraków: Zielona Sowa. [1st French ed. *Discours de la méthode*, 1637.]
Descartes, René. *Medytacje o filozofii pierwszej* [Meditations on First Philosophy]. Trans. J. Hartman. Kraków: Zielona Sowa. [1st Latin ed. *Meditationes de prima philosophia*, 1641.]
Dickson, Julie. 2004. Methodology in Jurisprudence: A Critical Survey. *Legal Theory* 10: 117–156.
Doroszewski, Witold (ed.). 1963. *Słownik języka polskiego* [Polish Language Dictionary], Vol. V. Warszawa: Państwowe Wydawnictwo Naukowe.
Dreier, Horst. 1991. Die Radbruchsche Formel – Erkenntnis oder Bekenntnis? In *Staatsrecht in Theorie und Praxis. Festschrift für Robert Walter zum 60. Geburtstag*, ed. H. Mayer, 117–135. Wien: Manzsche Verlags- und Universitätsbuchhandlung.
Dreier, Horst. 1997. Gustav Radbruch und die Mauerschützen. *Juristenzeitung* 52: 421–434.
Dreier, Ralf. 1975. *Was ist und wozu Allgemeine Rechtstheorie?* Tübingen: Mohr Siebeck.
Dreier, Ralf. 1979. Bemerkungen zur Rechtserkenntnistheorie. *Rechtstheorie*, Beiheft 1: 89–105.
Dreier, Ralf. 1981. Recht und Moral. In *idem*, *Recht – Moral – Ideologie. Studien zur Rechtstheorie*, 180–216. Frankfurt am Main: Suhrkamp.
Dreier, Ralf. 1981. Sein und Sollen. *Bemerkungen zur Reinen Rechtslehre Kelsens*. In *idem*, *Recht – Moral – Ideologie. Studien zur Rechtstheorie*, 217–240. Frankfurt am Main: Suhrkamp.
Dreier, Ralf. 1985. Der Rechtsstaat im Spannungsverhältnis zwischen Gesetz und Recht. *Juristenzeitung* 40: 353–359.
Dreier, Ralf. 1986. Der Begriff des Rechts. *Neue Juristische Wochenschrift* 39: 890–896.
Dreier, Ralf. 1986. *Rechtsbegriff und Rechtsidee. Kants Rechtsbegriff und seine Bedeutung für die gegenwärtige Diskussion*. Frankfurt am Main: Alfred Metzner.
Dreier, Ralf. 1987. Göttliches und menschliches Recht. *Zeitschrift zum evangelisches Kirchenrecht* 32: 289–316.
Dreier, Ralf. 1987. Neues Naturrecht oder Rechtspositivismus? In Erwiderung auf Werner Krawietz. *Rechtstheorie* 18: 368–385.
Dreier, Ralf. 1991. Zur gegenwärtigen Diskussion des Verhältnisses von Recht und Moral in der Bundesrepublik Deutschland. *Archiv für Rechts- und Sozialphilosophie*, Beiheft 44: 55–67.
Dreier, Ralf. 1993. Gesetzliches Unrecht im SED-Staat? Am Beispiel des DDR-Grenzgesetzes. In *Strafgerechtigkeit. Festschrift für Arthur Kaufmann zum 70. Geburtstag*, ed. F. Haft, W. Hassemer, U. Neumann, W. Schild, and U. Schroth, 57–70. Heidelberg: Müller.
Dreier, Ralf. 1994. Some Remarks on the Concept of Law. In *Prescriptive Formality and Normative Rationality in Modern Legal Systems*. Festschrift *for Robert S. Summers*, ed. W. Krawietz, N. MacCormick, and G.H. von Wright, 109–124. Berlin: Duncker & Humblot.
Dreier, Ralf. 1995. Hauptströmungen gegenwärtiger Rechtsphilosophie in Deutschland. *Archiv für Rechts- und Sozialphilosophie* 81: 155–163.

Dreier, Ralf. 2005. Deutsche Rechtsphilosophie in der zweiten Hälfte des 20. Jahrhunderts. Ein Rückblick. In *Integratives Verstehen. Zur Rechtsphilosophie Ralf Dreiers*, ed. R. Alexy, 215–223. Tübingen: Mohr Siebeck.

Dreier, Ralf, Stanley L. Paulson. 1999. Einführung in die Rechtsphilosophie Radbruchs. In G. Radbruch, *Rechtsphilosophie. Studienausgabe*, ed. R. Dreier, St.L. Paulson, 235–250. Heidelberg: Müller.

Dworkin, Ronald. 1977. *Taking Rights Seriously*. Cambridge (Mass.): Harvard University Press.

Dworkin, Ronald. 1986. *Law's Empire*. London: Fontana.

Dworkin, Ronald. 1998. *Biorąc prawa poważnie* [Taking Rights Seriously]. Trans. T. Kozłowski. Warszawa: Wydawnictwo Naukowe PWN.

Dworkin, Ronald. 2004. Hart's Postscript and the Character of Political Philosophy. *Oxford Journal of Legal Studies* 24/1 (2004): 1–37.

Dworkin, Ronald. 2006. *Imperium prawa* [Law's Empire]. Trans. J. Winczorek. Warszawa: Wolters Kluwer Polska.

Dybowski, Krzysztof. 2005. Fikcyjność pozytywistycznego paradygmatu [The Fictitiousness of Positivistic Paradigm]. In *Wykładnia prawa i inne problemy filozofii prawa*, ed. L. Morawski, 161–170. Toruń: Wydawnictwo Uniwersytetu Mikołaja Kopernika.

Dybowski, Maciej. 2001. Ronalda Dworkina koncepcja zasad prawa [Ronald Dworkin's Conception of Legal Principles]. *Ruch Prawniczy, Ekonomiczny i Socjologiczny* LXIII/3: 99–115.

Działocha, Kazimierz, Włodzimierz Gromski. 1995. Niepozytywistyczna koncepcja państwa prawnego a Trybunał Konstytucyjny [Nonpositivist Conception of the Law-Governed State and the Constitutional Tribunal]. *Państwo i Prawo* 3/589: 4–16.

Ekelöf, Per Olof. 1971. The Expression "Valid Rule": A Study in Legal Terminology. *Scandinavian Studies in Law* 15: 57–74.

Eng, Svein. 2000. Fusion of Descriptive and Normative Propositions. The Concepts of "Descriptive Proposition" and "Normative Proposition" as Concepts of Degree. *Ratio Juris* 13: 236–260.

Eng, Svein. 2003. *Analysis of Dis/agreement – with particular reference to Law and Legal Theory*. Dordrecht: Kluwer. [1st Norwegian ed. *U/enighetsanalyse: med særlig sikte på jus og allmenn rettsteori*, Oslo: Universitetsforlaget, 1998.]

Eng, Svein. 2005. Fused Modality. An Integral Part of Lawyers' Form of Life. *Ratio Juris* 18: 429–433.

Engländer, Armin. 1997. Zur begrifflichen Möglichkeit des Rechtspositivismus. Eine Kritik des Richtigkeitsarguments von Robert Alexy. *Rechtstheorie* 28: 437–485.

Engländer, Armin. 2000. Grundzüge des modernen Rechtspositivismus. *Jura* 22/3: 113–118.

Engländer, Armin. 2000. The Failure of Discourse Theory. Critical Remarks on Habermas' Moral and Legal Cognitivism. *Associations* 4: 223–251.

Engländer, Armin. 2002. *Diskurs als Rechtsquelle? Zur Kritik der Diskurstheorie des Rechts*. Tübingen: Mohr Siebeck.

Engländer, Armin. 2004. Moralische Richtigkeit als Bedingung der Rechtsgeltung? Eine erkenntnistheoretische Kritik". *Archiv für Rechts- und Sozialphilosophie* 90: 86–97.

Feldman, Fred. 1973. On the Performatory Interpretation of the *Cogito*. *The Philosophical Review* LXXXII: 345–363.

Feteris, Eveline T. 1994. Recent Developments in Legal Argumentation Theory: Dialectical Approaches to Legal Argumentation. *International Journal for the Semiotics of Law* VII/20: 133–153.

Feteris, Eveline T. 1997. A Survey of 25 Years of Research on Legal Argumentation. *Argumentation* 11: 355–376.

Feteris, Eveline T. 2011. *Fundamentals of Legal Argumentation. A Survey of Theories on the Justification of Judicial Decisions*. Dordrecht/Boston/London: Kluwer.

Finnis, John. 1989. *Natural Law and Natural Laws*. Oxford: Clarendon Press. [1st ed. 1980.]

Fletcher, George P. 2005. In Honour of "Ius et Lex". Some Thoughts on Speaking about Law. *Ius et Lex* I/1: 13–33.

Florczak-Wątor, Monika. 2006. *Orzeczenia Trybunału Konstytucyjnego i ich skutki prawne* [The Constitutional Tribunal Rulings and Their Legal Effects]. Poznań: Ars boni et aequi.

Forguson, L. W. 1968. On "It's Raining, But I Don't Believe It". *Theoria* XXXIV: 89–101.

Förster, Markus Philipp. 1997. Auseinandersetzung zwischen Norbert Hoerster und Joachim Hruschka. Eine Stellungnahme zur antirechtspositivistischen Argumentation. *Rechtstheorie* 28: 531–538.

Frändberg, Åke. 1995. Retroactivity, Simulactivity, Infraactivity. *Archiv für Rechts- und Sozialphilosophie*, Beiheft 64: 55–72.

Frege, Gottlob. 1892. Über Sinn und Bedeutung. *Zeitschrift für Philosophie und philosophische Kritik* 100: 25–50. English version: On Sense and Reference. Trans. M. Black. In *Meaning and Reference*, ed. A.W. Moore, 23–42. Oxford: Oxford University Press, 1993.

Fuller, Lon L. 1958. Positivism and Fidelity to Law – A Reply to Professor Hart. *Harvard Law Review* 71: 630–672.

Fuller, Lon L. 1968. *Anatomy of the Law*. New York: Frederick A. Praeger Publishers.

Fuller, Lon L. 1969. *The Morality of Law*. 2nd ed. New Haven/London: Yale University Press. [1st ed. 1964.]

Funke, Andreas. 2003. Überlegungen zu Gustav Radbruchs "Verleugnungsformel". Ein Beitrag zur Lehre vom Rechtsbegriff. *Archiv für Rechts- und Sozialphilosophie* 89: 1–16.

Fusfield, William D. 1989. Can Jürgen Habermas's "Begründungsprogramm" Escape Hans Albert's *Münchhausen Trilemma*? *Jahrbuch Rhetorik* 8: 73–82.

Galie, Walter B. 1955–1956. Essentially Contested Concepts. *Proceedings of the Aristotelian Society* LVI: 167–198.

García Figueroa, Alfonso. 1998. *Principios y positivismo jurídico. El no positivismo principialista en las teorías de Ronald Dworkin y Robert Alexy*. Madrid: Centro de Estudios Políticos y Constitucionales.

García Figueroa, Alfonso. 1999. La tesis del caso especial y el positivismo jurídico. *DOXA* 22: 195–220.

García Figueroa, Alfonso. 2006. Bemerkungen zu einer dispositionellen Erklärung des Rechts anhand der Diskussion der Verbindungs- und Trennungsthese. *Archiv für Rechts- und Sozialphilosophie* 92: 363–381.

Gardocki, Lech. 2005. Problem tak zwanych wyroków interpretacyjnych Trybunału Konstytucyjnego [The Problem of the so-called Interpretive Rulings of the Constitutional Tribunal]. In *Teoria i praktyka wykładni prawa. Materiały konferencji naukowej Wydziału Prawa i Administracji Uniwersytetu Warszawskiego odbytej w dniu 27 lutego 2004 roku*, ed. P. Winczorek, 153–157. Warszawa: Liber.

Garlicki, Leszek. 1987. *Sądownictwo konstytucyjne w Europie Zachodniej* [Constitutional Jurisdiction in Western Europe]. Warszawa: Państwowe Wydawnictwo Naukowe.

Garzón Valdés, Ernesto. 1977. Modelle normativer Geltung. *Rechtstheorie* 8: 41–71.

Gebauer, Richard. 1993. *Letzte Begründung. Eine Kritik der Diskursethik von Jürgen Habermas*. München: Fink.

Gianformaggio, Letizia. 1990. Hans Kelsen on the Deduction of Validity. *Rechtstheorie* 21: 181–207.

Gizbert-Studnicki, Tomasz. 1972. Język prawny a język prawniczy [Legal Language and Juristic Language]. *Zeszyty Naukowe Uniwersytetu Jagiellońskiego. Prace Prawnicze* 55: 219–233.

Gizbert-Studnicki, Tomasz. 1973. Stwierdzenie jako akt mowy [A Statement as a Speech Act]. *Studia Filozoficzne* 3/88: 83–97.

Gizbert-Studnicki, Tomasz. 1974. Znaczenie terminu "domniemanie prawne" w języku prawnym i prawniczym [The Meaning of the Term "Legal Presumption" in Legal and Juristic Language]. *Ruch Prawniczy, Ekonomiczny i Socjologiczny* XXXVI/1: 101–114.

Gizbert-Studnicki, Tomasz. 1977. Spór o domniemania prawne [The Dispute over Legal Presumption]. *Państwo i Prawo* 11/381: 68–74.

Gizbert-Studnicki, Tomasz. 1979. Czy istnieje język prawny? [Does Legal Language Exist?]. *Państwo i Prawo* 3/397: 49–60.

Gizbert-Studnicki, Tomasz. 1985. How Many Theories of Truth Are Needed in Jurisprudence? *Archiv für Rechts- und Sozialphilosophie*, Beiheft 25: 153–161.

Gizbert-Studnicki, Tomasz. 1985. Teoria prawa, filozofia języka, lingwistyka [Theory of Law, Philosophy of Language, Linguistics]. *Studia Filozoficzne* 2–3/231–232: 67–81.

Gizbert-Studnicki, Tomasz. 1986. *Język prawny z perspektywy socjolingwistycznej* [Legal Language from Sociolinguistic Perspective]. Zeszyty Naukowe Uniwersytetu Jagiellońskiego. Prace z nauk politycznych 26 (1986).

Gizbert-Studnicki, Tomasz. 1988. Normy celowościowe a reguły konstytutywne w prawie [Teleological Norms and Constitutive Rules in Law]. In *Prawo i polityka*, ed. A. Bodnar, J.J. Wiatr, and J. Wróblewski, 102–112. Warszawa: Państwowe Wydawnictwo Naukowe.

Gizbert-Studnicki, Tomasz. 1988. Zasady i reguły prawne [Legal Principles and Rules]. *Państwo i Prawo* 3/505: 16–26.

Gizbert-Studnicki, Tomasz. 1990. The Burden of Argumentation in Legal Disputes. *Ratio Juris* 3: 118–129.

Gizbert-Studnicki, Tomasz. 1992. Język prawny a obraz świata [Legal Language and the Picture of the World]. In *Prawo w zmieniającym się społeczeństwie. Księga Jubileuszowa Profesor Marii Boruckiej-Arctowej*, ed. G. Skąpska, J. Czapska, K. Daniel, J. Górski, and K. Pałecki, 149–161. Kraków: Wydawnictwo Adam Marszałek.

Gizbert-Studnicki, Tomasz. 1993. Book review: *Dyrektywy i sposób ich wypowiadania* by Z. Ziembiński and M. Zieliński. *Państwo i Prawo* 3/565: 87–89.

Gizbert-Studnicki, Tomasz. 1993. The Non-Linguistic Concept of Norm and Ontology. In *Sprache, Performanz und Ontologie de Rechts. Festgabe für Kazimierz Opałek zum 75. Geburtstag*, ed. W. Krawietz, J. Wróblewski, 423–434. Berlin: Duncker & Humblot.

Gizbert-Studnicki, Tomasz. 1995. Podstawy argumentacji prawniczej [Foundations of Legal Argumentation]. *Acta Universitatis Wratislaviensis* 1772: 35–43.

Gizbert-Studnicki, Tomasz. 2003. Rozkład ciężaru argumentacji w dyskursie interpretacyjnym [The Distribution of the Burden of Argumentation in Interpretive Discourse]. *Studia z filozofii prawa* 2: 65–76.

Gizbert-Studnicki, Tomasz, Andrzej Grabowski. 1997. Normy programowe w Konstytucji [Programme Norms in the Constitution]. In *Charakter i struktura norm konstytucji*, ed. J. Trzciński, 95–113. Warszawa: Wydawnictwo Sejmowe.

Gizbert-Studnicki, Tomasz, Andrzej Grabowski. 2003. Kilka uwag o niepozytywistycznej koncepcji prawa [Some Remarks on the Nonpositivist Conception of Law]. In *Prawo a wartości. Księga jubileuszowa Profesora Józefa Nowackiego*, ed. I. Bogucka, Z. Tobor, 55–68. Kraków: Zakamycze.

Gizbert-Studnicki, Tomasz, Tomasz Pietrzykowski, 2004. Positivismo blando y la distinción entre Derecho y moral. Trans. R. Gama Leyva. *DOXA* 27: 63–79.

Golding, Martin P. 1961. Kelsen and the Concept of "Legal System". *Archiv für Rechts- und Sozialphilosophie* 47: 355–386.

Goldsworthy, Jeffrey D. 1990. The Self-Destruction of Legal Positivism. *Oxford Journal of Legal Studies* 10/4: 449–486.

Golecki, Mariusz Jerzy, Bartosz Wojciechowski. 2007. Ekonomiczna analiza stosowania prawa wspólnotowego [Economic Analysis of Applying Community Law]. In *Analiza ekonomiczna w zastosowaniach prawniczych*, ed. J. Stelmach, M. Soniewicka, 115–165. Warszawa: Wolters Kluwer Polska.

Gomułowicz, Andrzej. 2008. *Aspekt prawotwórczy sądownictwa administracyjnego* [Legislative Aspect of the Administrative Jurisdiction]. Warszawa: Wolters Kluwer Polska.

Gonera, Katarzyna, Ewa Łętowska. 2003. Artykuł 190 Konstytucji i jego konsekwencje w praktyce sądowej [Article 190 of the Constitution and Its Consequences in Judicial Practice]. *Państwo i Prawo* 9/691: 3–27.

Gonera, Katarzyna, Ewa Łętowska. 2008. Odroczenie utraty mocy niekonstytucyjnej normy i wznowienie postępowania po wyroku Trybunału Konstytucyjnego [Postponement of the Loss of Force of an Unconstitutional Norm and Resumption of Proceedings after the Constitutional Tribunal Ruling. *Państwo i Prawo* 6/748: 3–21.

Gonera, Katarzyna, Ewa Łętowska. 2008. Wieloaspektowość następstw stwierdzania niekonstytucyjności [Multifacetedness of the Consequences of Unconstitutionality]. *Państwo i Prawo* 5/747: 20–37.

González Lagier, Daniel. 1995. *Acción y norma en G.H. von Wright*. Madrid: Centro de Estudios Constitucionales.

Goodrich, Peter. 1987. *Legal Discourse. Studies in Linguistics, Rhetoric and Legal Analysis*. Houndmills/London: MacMillan Press.

Grabowski, Andrzej. 1999. *Judicial Argumentation and Pragmatics. A Study on the Extension of the Theory of Legal Argumentation*. Kraków: Księgarnia Akademicka.

Grabowski, Andrzej. 2002. Dylemat Jørgensena z perspektywy pragmatycznej [The Jørgensen's Dilemma from a Pragmatic Perspective]. In *Prawoznawstwo a praktyka stosowania prawa*, ed. Z. Tobor, I. Bogucka, 193–218. Prace Naukowe Uniwersytetu Śląskiego w Katowicach 2052.

Grabowski, Andrzej. 2003. Sonderfallthese – Its Critique and Interpretation. *Rechtstheorie* 34: 371–392.

Grabowski, Andrzej. 2011. W stronę postpozytywizmu prawniczego. Szkic z metodologii prawoznawstwa [In the Direction of Legal Postpositivism. A Sketch on the Methodology of Jurisprudence], *Acta Universitatis Wratislaviensis* 3337: 147–161.

Grabowski, Andrzej, Bogumił Naleziński. 2001. Kłopoty z obowiązywaniem. Uwagi na tle orzecznictwa Trybunału Konstytucyjnego [Problems with Validity. Comments on the Basis of the Constitutional Tribunal Jurisdiction]. *Studia z filozofii prawa* 1: 219–257.

Grabowski, Paweł. 2001. *O metajęzykowości i metanormatywności języka prawnego* [On Matalinguisticity and Metanormativity of Legal Language]. Poznań. [An unpublished manuscript of a Master's thesis].

Grabowski, Paweł. 2004. W sprawie zakresu temporalnego obowiązywania prawa [On the Scope of Temporal Validity of Law]. *Państwo i Prawo* 4/698: 95–101.

Grabowski, Paweł, Mikołaj Hermann. 2006. O normatywnym charakterze przepisów o wejściu w życie [On the Normative Character of Provisions on Entrance into Force]. *Państwo i Prawo* 9/727: 69–79.

Gram, Moltke S. 1978. Do Transcendental Arguments Have a Future? *Neue Hefte für Philosophie* 14: 23–56.

Green, Leslie. 2008. Positivism and the Inseparability of Law and Morals. *New York University Law Review* 83/4: 1035–1058.

Gril, Peter. 1997. Alexys Version einer transzendental-pragmatischen Begründung der Diskursregeln im Unterschied zu Habermas. *Archiv für Rechts- und Sozialphilosophie* 83: 206–216.

Gril, Peter. 1998. *Die Möglichkeit praktischer Erkenntnis aus Sicht der Diskurstheorie. Eine Untersuchung zu Jürgen Habermas und Robert Alexy*. Berlin: Duncker & Humblot.

Grimm, Robert. 1965. Cogito, ergo sum. *Theoria* XXXI: 159–173.

Grodziński, Eugeniusz. 1985. *Językoznawcy i logicy o synonimach i synonimii. Studium z pogranicza dwóch nauk* [Linguists and Logicians on Synonyms and Synonymy. Study on the Border of Two Sciences]. Wrocław/Warszawa/Kraków/Gdańsk/Łódź: Zakład Narodowy im. Ossolińskich – Wydawnictwo Polskiej Akademii Nauk.

Grundgesetz für die Bundesrepublik Deutschland. Bonn: Bundeszentrale für politische Bildung, 1999.

Grzegorczyk, Krzysztof (Christophe), Tomasz Gizbert-Studnicki. 1974. Les rapports entre la norme et la disposition légale. *Archives de Philosophie du Droit* XIX: 243–256.

Grzybowski, Stefan. 1988. Przepisy prawa oraz normy prawne a zagadnienie wykładni i konstrukcji [Legal Provisions and Legal Norms vis-à-vis the Problem of Interpretation and Construction]. *Krakowskie Studia Prawnicze* XXI: 3–12.

Guastini, Riccardo. 1986. A Theory of Derogation (with Special Reference to Italian Law). In *Automated Analysis of Legal Texts. Logic, Informatics, Law*, ed. A.A. Martino, F. Socci Natali, 495–514. Amsterdam: Elsevier.

Guastini, Riccardo. 1994. Invalidity. *Ratio Juris* 7: 212–226.

Guastini, Riccardo. 1995. Normas supremas. Trans. J. Ferrer. *DOXA* 17–18: 257–270.

Guastini, Riccardo. 1997. Interpretive Statements. In *Normative Systems in Legal and Moral Theory*. Festschrift *for Carlos E. Alchourrón and Eugenio Bulygin*, ed. E. Garzón Valdés, W. Krawietz, G.H. von Wright, and R. Zimmerling, 279–292. Berlin: Duncker & Humblot.

Guastini, Riccardo. 2000. "Sollsätze". An Exercise in Hard Legal Positivism. *Rechtstheorie* 31: 185–196.

Guastini, Riccardo. 2004. Proyecto para la voz "Ordenamiento jurídico" de un diccionario. Trans. M. Atienza, J. Ruiz Manero. *DOXA* 27: 247–282.

Guastini, Riccardo. 2006. Eugenio Bulygin e Tecla Mazzarese su interpretazione e proposizioni normative. *Diritto & questioni pubbliche* 6: 97–100. http://www.dirittoequestionipubbliche.org/page/2006_n6/studi_02_Guastini.pdf. Accessed 8 August 2007.

Günther, Klaus. 1988. *Der Sinn für Angemessenheit. Anwedungsdiskurse in Moral und Recht*. Frankfurt am Main: Suhrkamp. English version: *The Sense of Appropriateness. Application Discourses in Morality and Law*. Trans. J. Farrell. Albany: State University of New York Press, 1993.

Günther, Klaus. 1989. Ein normativer Begriff der Kohärenz für eine Theorie der juristischen Argumentation. *Rechtstheorie* 20: 163–190. Shortened English version: A Normative Conception of Coherence for a Discursive Theory of Legal Justification. *Ratio Juris* 2 (1989): 155–166.

Günther, Klaus. 1992. Universalistische Normbegründung und Normanwendung in Recht und Moral. *Archiv für Rechts- und Sozialphilosophie*, Beiheft 45: 36–76.

Günther, Klaus. 1993. Critical Remarks on Robert Alexy's "Special-Case Thesis". *Ratio Juris* 6: 143–156.

Haack, Susan. 2007. On Logic in the Law: "Something, but not All". *Ratio Juris* 20: 1–31.

Haba, Enrique P. 1998. Teorización constructivista como "forma de vida" (Sobre "reglas y formas" del discurso jurídico en los tribunales inexistentes). *DOXA* 21/I, 147–170.

Habermas, Jürgen. 1971. Vorbereitende Bemerkungen zu einer Theorie der kommunikativen Kompetenz (Vorlage für Zwecke einer Seminardiskussion). In J. Habermas, N. Luhmann, *Theorie der Gesellschaft oder Sozialtechnologie – Was leistet die Systemforschung?*, 101–141. Frankfurt am Main: Suhrkamp.

Habermas, Jürgen. 1983. Vorlesungen zu einer sprachtheoretischen Grundlegung der Soziologie. In *idem*, *Vorstudien und Ergänzungen zur Theorie des kommunikativen Handelns*, 11–126. Frankfurt am Main: Suhrkamp.

Habermas, Jürgen. 1983. Was heißt Universalpragmatik? In *idem*, *Vorstudien und Ergänzungen zur Theorie des kommunikativen Handelns*, 353–440. Frankfurt am Main: Suhrkamp.

Habermas, Jürgen. 1996. *Between Facts and Norms. Contributions to a Discourse Theory of Law and Democracy*. Trans. W. Rehg. Cambridge (Mass.): The MIT Press. [1st German ed. *Faktizität und Geltung. Beiträge zur diskursiven Theorie des Rechts und des demokratischen Rechtsstaats*, Frankfurt am Main: Suhrkamp, 1992.]

Habermas, Jürgen. 1996. Diskursethik – Notizen zu einem Begründungsprogramm. In *idem*, *Moralbewußtsein und kommunikatives Handeln*, 6th ed., 53–125. Frankfurt am Main: Suhrkamp. [1st ed. 1983.]

Hacker, Peter M.S. 1977. Hart's Philosophy of Law. In *Law, Morality and Society. Essays in Honour of H.L.A. Hart*, ed. P. M. S. Hacker, J. Raz, 1–25. Oxford: Clarendon Press.

Haft, Fritjof, Hilgendorf Eric. 1993. Juristische Argumentation und Dialektik. Ein Streifzug durch die Geschichte der juristischen Argumentationsmethoden. In *Strafgerechtigkeit. Festschrift für Arthur Kaufmann zum 70. Geburtstag*, ed. F. Haft, W. Hassemer, U. Neumann, W. Schild, and U. Schroth, 93–109. Heidelberg: Müller.

Haldemann, Frank. 2005. Gustav Radbruch vs. Hans Kelsen: A Debate on Nazi Law. *Ratio Juris* 18: 162–178.
Hart, H.L.A. 1951. The Ascription of Responsibility and Rights. In *Logic and Language, First Series*, ed. A.G.N. Flew, 145–166. Oxford: Oxford University Press. [1st publ. in *Proceedings of the Aristotelian Society* XLIX (1948–1949): 171–194.]
Hart, H.L.A. 1953. *Definition and Theory in Jurisprudence. An Inaugural Lecture delivered before the University of Oxford on 30 May 1953*. Oxford: Clarendon Press.
Hart, H.L.A. 1958. Positivism and the Separation of Law and Morals. *Harvard Law Review* 71: 593–629.
Hart, H.L.A. 1961. *The Concept of Law*. Oxford: Clarendon Press.
Hart, H.L.A. 1965. Book review: *The Morality of Law* by Lon L. Fuller. *Harvard Law Review* 78: 1281–1296.
Hart, H.L.A. 1980. El nuevo desafío al positivismo jurídico. Trans. L.L. Hierro, F. Laporta, and J.R. de Páramo. *Sistema* 36: 3–18.
Hart, H.L.A. 1983. American Jurisprudence through English Eyes: The Nightmare and the Noble Dream. In *idem*, *Essays in Jurisprudence and Philosophy*, 123–144. Oxford: Clarendon Press.
Hart, H.L.A. 1983. Introduction. In *idem*, *Essays in Jurisprudence and Philosophy*, 1–18. Oxford: Clarendon Press.
Hart, H.L.A. 1983. Kelsen Visited. In *idem*, *Essays in Jurisprudence and Philosophy*, 286–308. Oxford: Clarendon Press.
Hart, H.L.A. 1983. Kelsen's Doctrine of the Unity of Law. In *idem*, *Essays in Jurisprudence and Philosophy*, 309–342. Oxford: Clarendon Press.
Hart, H.L.A. 1983. Problems of the Philosophy of Law. In *idem*, *Essays in Jurisprudence and Philosophy*, 88–119. Oxford: Clarendon Press.
Hart, H.L.A. 1983. Scandinavian Realism. In *idem*, *Essays in Jurisprudence and Philosophy*, 161–169. Oxford: Clarendon Press.
Hart, H.L.A. 1987. Comment. In *Issues in Contemporary Legal Philosophy. The Influence of H.L.A. Hart*, ed. R. Gavison, 35–42. Oxford: Clarendon Press.
Hart, H.L.A. 1994. Postscript. Ed. P.A. Bulloch, J. Raz. In *idem*, *The Concept of Law*, 2nd ed., 238–276. Oxford: Clarendon Press.
Hart, H.L.A. 1998. *Pojęcie prawa* [The Concept of Law]. Trans. J. Woleński. Warszawa: Wydawnictwo Naukowe PWN.
Hart, H.L.A. 2001. *Eseje z filozofii prawa* [Essays in Jurisprudence and Philosophy]. Trans. J. Woleński. Warszawa: Dom Wydawniczy ABC.
Hartman, Jan. 2004. Posłowie: Tylko dla dorosłych [Afterword: For Adults Only]. In R. Descartes, *Rozprawa o metodzie*, 53–68. Kraków: Zielona Sowa.
Hassemer, Winfried. 1998. Odpowiedzialność prawnokarna w odniesieniu do przestępczości państwowej w kontekście politycznej zmiany systemu w świetle okoliczności wyłączających bezprawność [Criminal Liability in Relation to the State Crime in the Context of Political System Change in the Light of Circumstances Excluding Unlawfulness]. In *Prawo karne a problem zmiany ustroju politycznego*, ed. A. Eser, A. Zoll, 73–91. Kraków: Zakamycze.
Hassemer, Winfried. 2008. Juristische Methodenlehre und richterliche Pragmatik. *Rechtstheorie* 39: 1–22.
Hauser, Roman, Janusz Trzciński, 2008. *Prawotwórcze znaczenie orzeczeń Trybunału Konstytucyjnego w orzecznictwie Naczelnego Sądu Administracyjnego* [The Legislative Significance of the Rulings of the Constitutional Tribunal in the Jurisdiction of the Supreme Administrative Court]. Warszawa: Wydawnictwo Prawnicze LexisNexis.
Heckmann, Dirk. 1997. *Geltungskraft und Geltungsverlust von Rechtsnormen. Elemente einer Theorie der autoritativen Normgeltungsbeendigung*. Tübingen: Mohr Siebeck.
Herget, James E. 1996. *Contemporary German Legal Philosophy*. Philadelphia: University of Pennsylvania Press.
Hierro, Liborio L. 2002. ¿Por qué ser positivista? *DOXA* 25 (2002): 263–302.

Hilgendorf, Eric. 1990. *Argumentation in der Jurisprudenz. Zur Rezeption von analytischer Philosophie und kritischer Theorie in der Grundlagenforschung der Jurisprudenz*. Tübingen.
Hilgendorf, Eric. 1995. Zur transzendentalpragmatischen Begründung von Diskursregeln. *Rechtstheorie* 27: 183–200.
Hilgendorf, Eric. 1996. Moralphilosophie und juristisches Denken. *Archiv für Rechts- und Sozialphilosophie* 82: 397–415.
Himma, Kenneth Einar. 2002. Inclusive Legal Positivism. In *The Oxford Handbook of Jurisprudence and Philosophy of Law*, ed. J.L. Coleman, S.J. Shapiro, 125–165. Oxford: Oxford University Press.
Himma, Kenneth Einar. 2005. Final Authority to Bind with Moral Mistakes: On the Explanatory Potential of Inclusive Legal Positivism. *Law and Philosophy* 24: 1–45.
Hintikka, Jaakko. 1962. *Cogito, Ergo Sum:* Inference or Performance? *The Philosophical Review* LXXI: 3–32.
Hintikka, Jaakko. 1963. *Cogito, Ergo Sum* as an Inference and Performance? *The Philosophical Review* LXXII: 487–496.
Hoerster, Norbert. 1979. Zum begrifflichen Verhältnis von Recht und Moral. *Neue Hefte für Philosophie* 17: 77–88.
Hoerster, Norbert. 1982. Rechtsethik ohne Metaphysik. Theodor Viehweg zur Vollendung des 75. Lebensjahres am 30. 4. 1982. *Juristenzeitung* 37: 265–272.
Hoerster, Norbert. 1983. "Wirksamkeit", "Geltung" und "Gültigkeit" von Normen. Ein empiristischer Definitionsvorschlag. In *Das Naturrechtsdenken heute und morgen. Gedächtnisschrift für René Marcic*, ed. D. Mayer-Maly, P.M. Simons, 585–596. Berlin: Duncker & Humblot.
Hoerster, Norbert. 1986. Zur Verteidigung des Rechtspositivismus. *Neue Juristische Wochenschrift* 39: 2480–2482.
Hoerster, Norbert. 1987. Die rechtsphilosophische Lehre vom Rechtsbegriff. *Juristische Schulung* 27: 181–188.
Hoerster, Norbert. 1990. Zur Verteidigung der rechtspositivistischen Trennungsthese. *Archiv für Rechts- und Sozialphilosophie*, Beiheft 37: 27–32.
Hoerster, Norbert. 1993. Richtigstellung über den Rechtspositivismus. *Archiv für Rechts- und Sozialphilosophie* 79: 416–420.
Hoerster, Norbert. 2002. Einleitung. In *Recht und Moral. Texte zur Rechtsphilosophie*, ed. N. Hoerster, 11–14. Stuttgart: Reclam.
Hoffmann, Birgit. 2003. *Das Verhältnis von Gesetz und Recht. Eine verfassungsrechtliche und verfassungstheoretische Untersuchung zu Art. 20 Abs. 3 GG*. Berlin: Duncker & Humblot.
Holmes, Oliver Wendell. 1897. The Path of The Law. *Harvard Law Review* 10: 457–478.
Holton, Richard. 1998. Positivism and the Internal Point of View. *Law and Philosophy* 17: 597–625.
Hruschka, Joachim. 1992. Vorpositives Recht als Gegenstand und Aufgabe der Rechtswissenschaft. *Juristenzeitung* 47: 429–438.
Hruschka, Joachim. 1993. Recht und Unrecht bei Norbert Hoerster. *Archiv für Rechts- und Sozialphilosophie* 79: 421–424.
Hughes, Graham. 1971. Validity and the Basic Norm. *California Law Review* 59: 695–714.
Ingram, Peter. 1983. Effectiveness. *Archiv für Rechts- und Sozialphilosophie* 69: 484–503.
Jääskinen, Niilo. 1985. External Justification of Propositions in Legal Science. In *Man, Law and Modern Forms of Life*, ed. E. Bulygin, J.-L. Gardies, and I. Niiniluoto, 221–231.
Jabłońska-Bonca, Jolanta. 1984. Przesłanki stanowienia norm bez sankcji [The Conditions for Establishing Sanction-Free Norms], *Ruch Prawniczy, Ekonomiczny i Socjologiczny* XLVI/4: 151–167.
Jadacka, Hanna. 2004. Wymierne i niewymierne koszty niejasności tekstów prawnych [Tangible and Intangible Costs of Non-clarity of Legal Texts]. In *Język – Prawo – Społeczeństwo*, ed. E. Malinowska, 151–156. Opole: Wydawnictwo Uniwersytetu Opolskiego.

Jakubowski, Jerzy. 1962. Book review: *Obowiązywanie prawa* by Wiesław Lang. *Państwo i Prawo* 10/200: 637–640.

Jakubowski, Jerzy. 1965. Pojęcie obowiązywania, realizacji i skuteczności normy prawnej oraz podstawy ich rozróżniania [The Concept of Validity, Realization and Effectiveness of Legal Norms and the Basis of their Distinction]. In *Studia z teorii prawa*, ed. S. Ehrlich, 303–331. Warszawa: Państwowe Wydawnictwo Naukowe.

Jørgensen, Jørgen. 1937–1938. Imperatives and Logic. *Erkenntnis* 7: 288–296.

Jørgensen, Stig. 1984. Grundnorm und Paradox. *Rechtstheorie*, Beiheft 5: 179–191.

Józefowicz, Adam. 1999. Orzeczenia interpretacyjne Trybunału Konstytucyjnego [Interpretive Rulings of the Constitutional Tribunal]. *Państwo i Prawo* 11/645: 28–34.

Kaczor, Jacek. 2004. Konwencjonalny charakter pojęć prawniczych [The Conventional Nature of Juristic Concepts]. A report presented at the 16th National Congress of the Departments of Theory and Philosophy of Law "The Polish legal culture and the process of European integration" in Gniezno, 26–28 September 2004 [typescript].

Kalinowski, Jerzy (Georges). 1953. Théorie des propositions normatives. *Studia Logica* I: 147–182.

Kalinowski, Jerzy (Georges). 1970. Théorie, métathéorie ou philosophie du droit. Réflexions sur *The Concept of Law* de H.L.A. Hart et *On Law and Justice* d'Alf Ross. *Archives de Philosophie du Droit* XV: 179–195.

Kalinowski, Jerzy (Georges). 1990. Logika prawnicza a logika deontyczna [Legal Logic and Deontic Logic]. In *Szkice z teorii prawa i szczegółowych nauk prawnych*, ed. S. Wronkowska, M. Zieliński, 345–357. Wydawnictwo Naukowe Uniwersytetu im. Adama Mickiewicza w Poznaniu.

Kalinowski, Jerzy (Georges). 1990. Ontic and Deontic. *International Journal for the Semiotics of Law* III/8: 133–146.

Kalisz, Anna. 2007. Multicentryczność systemu prawa polskiego a działalność orzecznicza Europejskiego Trybunału Sprawiedliwości i Europejskiego Trybunału Praw Człowieka [The Multicentric Character of the Polish Legal System and the Jurisdiction of the European Court of Justice and the European Court of Human Rights]. *Ruch Prawniczy, Ekonomiczny i Socjologiczny* LXIX/4: 35–49.

Kamiński, Marcin. 2007. Konstytucyjne podstawy domniemania ważności decyzji administracyjnej [The Constitutional Basis of the Presumption of the Legal Force of Administrative Decisions]. *Państwo i Prawo* 9/739: 56–67.

Kanarek, Beata. 1999. Analiza teoretyczna pojęcia "derogacja" [Theoretical Analysis of the Concept of "Derogation"]. In *Zmiany społeczne a zmiany w prawie. Aksjologia, konstytucja, integracja europejska*, ed. L. Leszczyński, 235–244. Lublin: Wydawnictwo Uniwersytetu Marii Curie-Skłodowskiej.

Kanarek, Beata. 2002. Moc obowiązująca i moc prawna a zagadnienie derogacji [Binding Force and Legal Force vis-à-vis the Issue of Derogation. In *Prawoznawstwo a praktyka stosowania prawa*, ed. Z. Tobor, I. Bogucka, 186–192. Prace Naukowe Uniwersytetu Śląskiego w Katowicach 2052.

Kanarek, Beata. 2004. *Teoretyczne ujęcia derogacji* [Theoretical Grasp of Derogation]. Szczecin: Wydawnictwo Naukowe Uniwersytetu Szczecińskiego.

Kanarek, Beata, Maciej Zieliński. 2001. Porządkująca faza wykładni prawa [The Arranging Phase of Legal Interpretation]. *Ruch Prawniczy, Ekonomiczny i Socjologiczny* LXIII/3: 1–12.

Kant, Immanuel. 2006. *Metafizyczne podstawy nauki prawa* [Metaphysical Foundations of the Science of Law]. Trans. W. Galewicz. Kęty: Wydawnictwo Marek Derewecki. [1st German ed. *Metaphysische Anfangsgründe der Rechtslehre*, 1797.]

Kaufmann, Arthur. 1962. Gesetz und Recht. In *Existenz und Ordnung. Festschrift für Erik Wolf zum 60. Geburtstag*, ed. T. Würtenberger, W. Maihofer, and A. Hollerbach, 357–397. Frankfurt am Main: Klostermann.

Kaufmann, Arthur. 1986. Über die Wissenschaftlichkeit der Rechtswissenschaft. Ansätze zu einer Konvergenztheorie der Wahrheit. *Archiv für Rechts- und Sozialphilosophie* 72: 425–442.

Kaufmann, Arthur. 1989. Läßt sich die Hauptverhandlung in Strafsachen als rationaler Diskurs auffassen? In *Dogmatik und Praxis des Strafverfahrens. Beiträge anläßlich des Colloquiums zum 65. Geburtstag von Gerhard Kielwein*, ed. H. Jung, H. Müller-Dietz, 15–24. Annales Universitatis Saraviensis 122.

Kaufmann, Arthur. 1991. Die Naturrechtsrenaissance der ersten Nachkriegsjahre – und was daraus geworden ist. In *Die Bedeutung der Wörter. Studien zur europäischen Rechtsgeschichte. Festschrift für Sten Gagnér zum 70. Geburtstag*, ed. M. Stolleis, 105–132. München: Beck.

Kaufmann, Arthur. 1992. *Rechtsphilosophie in der Nach-Neuzeit*. 2nd ed. Heidelberg: Decker & Müller. [1st ed. 1989.]

Kaufmann, Arthur. 1995. Die Radbruchsche Formel vom gesetzlichen Unrecht und vom übergesetzlichen Recht in der Diskussion um das im Namen der DDR begangene Unrecht. *Neue Juristische Wochenschrift* 48: 81–86.

Kaufmann, Arthur. 2004. Problemgeschichte der Rechtsphilosophie. In *Einführung in Rechtsphilosophie und Rechtstheorie der Gegenwart*, 7th ed. by A. Kaufmann, W. Hassemer, and U. Neumann, 26–147. Heidelberg: Müller. [1st ed. 1977.]

Kaźmierczyk, Stanisław. 1973. Orzeczenia konstytutywne i deklaratywne [Constitutive and Declaratory Rulings]. *Acta Universitatis Wratislaviensis* 211: 25–38.

Kaźmierczyk, Stanisław. 1987. Charakter prawny orzeczeń Trybunału Konstytucyjnego [The Legal Nature of the Constitutional Court Rulings]. *Acta Universitatis Wratislaviensis* 1037: 271–294.

Kaźmierczyk, Stanisław. 2006. Norma podstawowa [Basic Norm]. In A. Bator, W. Gromski, A. Kozak, S. Kaźmierczyk, Z. Pulka, *Wprowadzenie do nauk prawnych. Leksykon tematyczny*, 109. Warszawa: Wydawnictwo Prawnicze LexisNexis.

Kelsen, Hans. 1929. Wesen und Entwicklung der Staatsgerichtsbarkeit. *Veröffentlichungen der Vereinigung der Deutschen Staatsrechtslehrer* 5: 30–88.

Kelsen, Hans. 1934. *Reine Rechtslehre. Einleitung in die rechtswissenschaftliche Problematik*. Leipzig/Wien: Franz Deuticke. English version: *Introduction to the Problems of Legal Theory*. Trans. B. Litschewski Paulson, St.L. Paulson. Oxford: Clarendon Press, 1997.

Kelsen, Hans. 1945. *General Theory of Law and State*. Trans. A. Wedberg. Cambridge (Mass.): Harvard University Press.

Kelsen, Hans. 1945. *Natural Law Doctrine and Legal Positivism*, trans. W.H. Kraus. In *idem*, *General Theory of Law and State*, 389–446. Cambridge (Mass.): Harvard University Press. [1st German ed. *Die philosophischen Grundlagen des Naturrechts und des Rechtspositivismus*, Charlottenburg: R. Heise, 1928.]

Kelsen, Hans. 1959. Eine "Realistische" und die Reine Rechtslehre. Bemerkungen zu Alf Ross: On Law and Justice. *Österreichische Zeitschrift für öffentliches Recht (Neue Folge)* X: 1–25.

Kelsen, Hans. 1960. *Reine Rechtslehre*. 2nd ed. Wien: Franz Deuticke. English version: *Pure Theory of Law*. Trans. M. Knight. Berkeley/Los Angeles/London: University of California Press, 1967.

Kelsen, Hans. 1960. Vom Geltungsgrund des Rechts. In *Völkerrecht und rechtliches Weltbild. Festschrift für Alfred Verdross*, ed. F.A. Frhr. v. d. Heydte, I. Seidl-Hohenveldern, St. Verosta, and K. Zemanek, 157–165. Wien: Springer.

Kelsen, Hans. 1965. Was ist juristischer Positivismus? *Juristenzeitung* 20: 465–469.

Kelsen, Hans. 1971. Was ist ein Rechtsakt? In *Internationale Festschrift für Alfred Verdross zum 80. Geburtstag*, ed. R. Marcic, H. Mosler, E. Suy, and K. Zemanek, 153–165. München/ Salzburg: Wilhelm Fink. [1st ed. 1952]. English version: What is a Legal Act? Trans. B. Paulson, St.L. Paulson. *The American Journal of Jurisprudence* 29 (1984): 199–212.

Kelsen, Hans. 1973. Derogation. Trans. P. Heath. In *idem*, *Essays in Legal and Moral Philosophy*, ed. O. Weinberger, 261–275. Dordrecht/Boston: D. Reidel.

Kelsen, Hans. 1973. Law and Morality. Trans. P. Heath. In *idem*, *Essays in Legal and Moral Philosophy*, ed. O. Weinberger, 83–94. Dordrecht/Boston: D. Reidel.

Kelsen, Hans. 1979. *Allgemeine Theorie der Normen*, ed. K. Ringhofer, R. Walter. Wien: Manzsche Verlags- und Universitätsbuchhandlung. English version: *General Theory of Norms*. Trans. M. Hartney. Oxford: Oxford University Press, 1991.

Kersting, Wolfgang. 2002. Neukantianische Rechtsbegründung. Rechtsbegriff und richtiges Recht bei Cohen, Stammler und Kelsen. In *Neukantianismus und Rechtsphilosophie*, ed. R. Alexy, L.H. Meyer, St.L. Paulson, and G. Sprenger, 23–68. Baden-Baden: Nomos.

Kettner, Matthias. 1993. Ansatz zu einer Taxonomie performativer Selbstwidersprüche. In *Transzendentalpragmatik. Ein Symposion für Karl-Otto Apel*, ed. A. Dorschel, M. Kettner, W. Kuhlmann, and M. Niquet, 187–211. Frankfurt am Main: Suhrkamp.

Keuth, Herbert. 1983. Fallibilismus versus transzendentalpragmatische Letztbegründung. *Zeitschrift für allgemeine Wissenschaftstheorie* XIV/2: 320–337.

Klug, Ulrich. 1982. *Juristische Logik*. 4th ed. Berlin: Springer. [1st ed. 1951.]

Kmita, Jerzy. 1977. *Wykłady z logiki i metodologii nauk* [Lectures on Logic and Methodology of Science]. Warszawa: Państwowe Wydawnictwo Naukowe. [1st ed. 1973.]

Koch, Hans-Joachim. Zur Methodenlehre des Rechtspositivismus. Das Prinzipienargument – eine methodische Widerlegung des Rechtspositivismus? *Archiv für Rechts- und Sozialphilosophie*, Beiheft 37: 152–161.

Kodeks cywilny. Ustawa z dnia 23 kwietnia 1964 r. [Civil Code. Statute of 23 April 1964]. *Dziennik Ustaw* [Journal of Statutes] of 1964, No. 16, Item 93.

Kodeks karny. Ustawa z dnia 19 czerwca 1969 r. [Penal Code. Statute of 19 June 1969]. *Dziennik Ustaw* [Journal of Statutes] of 1969, No. 13, Item 94.

Kodeks karny. Ustawa z dnia 6 czerwca 1997 r. [Penal Code. Statute of 6 June 1997]. *Dziennik Ustaw* [Journal of Statutes] of 1997, No. 88, Item 553.

Koj, Leon. 2000. Uwagi o analizie w filozofii [Remarks on the Analysis in Philosophy]. In *Filozofia i logika. W stronę Jana Woleńskiego*, ed. J. Hartman, 166–176. Kraków: Aureus.

Kołakowski, Leszek. 1988. *Metaphysical Horror*. Oxford: Basil Blackwell.

Konstytucja Rzeczypospolitej Polskiej z dnia 2 kwietnia 1997 r. [Constitution of the Republic of Poland of 2 April 1997]. *Dziennik Ustaw* [Journal of Statutes] 1997, No. 78, Item 483.

Konstytucja Rzeczypospolitej Polskiej z dnia 23 kwietnia 1935 r. [The "April Constitution" of Poland]. *Dziennik Ustaw* [Journal of Statutes] 1935, No. 30, Item 227, with amendments.

Kordela, Marzena. 2007. Możliwość konstruowania ogólnej teorii zasad prawa. Uwagi do koncepcji Roberta Alexy'ego' [The Possibility of Constructing a General Theory of Legal Principles. Comments on Robert Alexy's Conception]. *Ruch Prawniczy, Ekonomiczny i Socjologiczny* LXIX/2: 11–28.

Kotarbińska, Janina. 1965. The Controversy over the Limits of Applicability of Logical Methods. *Logique et Analyse (Nouvelle série)* 29: 178–207.

Kotarbińska, Janina. 1990. Definicja [Definition]. In *eadem, Z zagadnień teorii nauki i teorii języka*, 128–151. Warszawa: Państwowe Wydawnictwo Naukowe.

Kotarbiński, Tadeusz. 1985. *Wykłady z dziejów logiki* [Lectures on the History of Logic]. Warszawa: Państwowe Wydawnictwo Naukowe.

Kozak, Artur. 1997. *Pojmowanie prawa w teorii wykładni* [The Comprehension of Law in the Theory of Interpretation]. Acta Universitatis Wratislaviensis 1987.

Kozak, Artur. 2002. *Granice prawniczej władzy dyskrecjonalnej* [The Limits of Juridical Discretion]. Wrocław: Kolonia.

Kozak, Artur. 2006. Kulturowy fundament decyzji interpretacyjnej. [Cultural Foundation of the Interpretive Decision]. In *Z zagadnień teorii i filozofii prawa. W poszukiwaniu podstaw prawa*, ed. A. Sulikowski, 31–48. Acta Universitatis Wratislaviensis 2878.

Kozioł, Michał. 2005. Zakazane zostało [It Was Banned]. *Goniec (Biuletyn Informacyjny Magistratu)* 8: 11.

Kramer, Matthew H. 2000. How Moral Principles Can Enter into the Law. *Legal Theory* 6: 83–108.

Kramer, Matthew H. 2002. Throwing Light on the Role of Moral Principles in the Law: Further Reflections. *Legal Theory* 8: 115–143.

Kramer, Matthew H. 2004. *Where Law and Morality Meet*, Oxford: Oxford University Press.

Krawietz, Werner. 1981. Rechtssystem und Rationalität in der juristischen Dogmatik. *Rechtstheorie*, Beiheft 2: 299–335.

Krawietz, Werner. 1987. Neues Naturrecht oder Rechtspositivismus? Eine kritische Auseinandersetzung mit dem Begriff des Rechts bei Ralf Dreier und Norbert Hoerster. *Rechtstheorie* 18: 209–254.

Krawietz, Werner. 1993. Bibliographic note: *Begriff und Geltung des Rechts* by Robert Alexy. *Rechtstheorie* 24: 249–250.

Kretzmann, Norman. 1988. Lex iniusta non est lex. Laws on Trial in Aquinas' Court of Conscience. *American Journal of Jurisprudence* 33: 99–122.

Kriele, Martin. 1979. *Recht und praktische Vernunft*. Göttingen: Vandenhoeck und Ruprecht.

Kriele, Martin. 1990. Rechtspflicht und die positivistische Trennung von Recht und Moral. In *idem*, *Recht, Vernunft, Wirklichkeit*, 453–470. Berlin: Duncker & Humblot.

Kripke, Saul. 1980. *Naming and Necessity*. Oxford: Basil Blackwell. [1st ed. 1972.]

Kumaniecki, Kazimierz. 1986. *Słownik łacińsko-polski* [Latin–Polish Dictionary]. 16th ed. Warszawa: Państwowe Wydawnictwo Naukowe.

Kuryłowicz, Marek. 2002. *Słownik terminów, zwrotów i sentencji prawniczych łacińskich oraz pochodzenia łacińskiego* [Dictionary of Latin Terms, Phrases and Dictums, and of Latin Origin]. 3rd ed. Kraków: Zakamycze.

Kustra, Aleksandra. 2006. Wokół problemu multicentryczności systemu prawa [About the Problem of the Multicentricy of Legal System]. *Państwo i Prawo* 6/724: 85–99.

Kutschera, Franz, von. 1982. *Grundlagen der Ethik*. Berlin/New York: Walter de Gruyter.

La Torre, Massimo. 2006. On Two Distinct and Opposed Versions of Natural Law: "Exclusive" versus "Inclusive". *Ratio Juris* 19: 197–216.

La Torre, Massimo. 2007. *Constitutionalism and Legal Reasoning*. Dordrecht: Springer.

Lacey, Nicola. 2004. *A Life of H.L.A. Hart. The Nightmare and the Noble Dream*. Oxford: Oxford University Press.

Lacey, Nicola. 2008. Philosophy, Political Morality, and History: Explaining the Enduring Resonance of the Hart-Fuller Debate. *New York University Law Review* 83/4: 1059–1087.

Lande, Jerzy. 1956. Nauka o normie prawnej [The Science on the Legal Norm]. *Annales Universitatis Mariae Curie-Skłodowska. Sectio G: Ius* III: 1–62.

Lang, Wiesław. 1960. Obowiązywanie normy prawnej w czasie w świetle logiki norm [Validity of a Legal Norm in Time in the Light of Logic of Norms]. *Zeszyty Naukowe Uniwersytetu Jagiellońskiego. Prace Prawnicze* 7: 47–88.

Lang, Wiesław. 1962. *Obowiązywanie prawa* [Validity of Law]. Warszawa: Państwowe Wydawnictwo Naukowe.

Lang, Wiesław. 1989. *Prawo i moralność* [Law and Morality]. Warszawa: Państwowe Wydawnictwo Naukowe.

Lang, Wiesław. 1996-1997. A Concept of the Validity of Law. *Archivum Iuridicum Cracoviense* XXIX–XXX: 87–101.

Lang, Wiesław. 2005. Wokół "Multicentryczności systemu prawa" [About "Multicentric Character of Legal System"]. *Państwo i Prawo* 7/713: 95–99.

Lang, Wiesław. 2005. Zasada *clara non sunt interpretanda* w kontekście zasady *ignorantia iuris nocet* oraz zasady zaufania obywateli do prawa [Principle *clara non sunt interpretanda* in the Context of Principle *ignorantia iuris nocet* and Principle of Citizens' Trust in Law]. In *Polska kultura prawna a proces integracji europejskiej*, ed. S. Wronkowska, 169–185. Kraków: Zakamycze.

Lang, Wiesław. 2008. System prawa i porządek prawny [The Legal System and Legal Order]. In *System prawny a porządek prawny*, ed. O. Bogucki, S. Czepita, 9–27. Szczecin: Wydawnictwo Naukowe Uniwersytetu Szczecińskiego.

Lang, Wiesław, Jerzy Wróblewski, Sylwester Zawadzki. 1986. *Teoria państwa i prawa* [The Theory of State and Law]. 3rd ed. Warszawa: Państwowe Wydawnictwo Naukowe. [1st ed. 1979.]

Laporta, Francisco. 1998. Derecho y moral: vindicación del observador crítico y aporía del iusnaturalista. In *Derecho y moral. Ensayos sobre un debate contemporáneo*, ed. R. Vázquez, 247–264. Barcelona: Gedisa.

Lec, Stanisław Jerzy. 1972. *Myśli nieuczesane* [Unkempt Thoughts]. 4th ed. Kraków: Wydawnictwo Literackie.

Leiter, Brian. 2001. Legal Realism, Hard Positivism, and the Limits of Conceptual Analysis. In *Hart's Postscript. Essays on the Postscript to* The Concept of Law, ed. J.L. Coleman, 355–370. Oxford/New York: Oxford University Press.

Leszczyński, Jerzy. 1988–1989. Postpozytywistyczny obraz prawoznawstwa [Postpositivist Image of Jurisprudence]. *Colloquia Communia* 6/41–1/42: 53–60.

Leszczyński, Leszek. 1979. Zagadnienia systemu prawa w koncepcji H.L.A. Harta [The Issues of Legal System in H.L.A. Hart's Conception]. *Annales Universitatis Mariae Curie-Skłodowska. Sectio G: Ius* XXVI: 133–144.

Leszczyński, Leszek. 1992. O aksjologii stosowania prawa [On the Axiology of Law Application]. In *Filozofia prawa a tworzenie i stosowanie prawa*, ed. B. Czech, 143–152. Katowice: Instytut Wymiaru Sprawiedliwości – Ośrodek Terenowy przy Sądzie Wojewódzkim w Katowicach.

Leszczyński, Leszek. 2001. *Zagadnienia teorii stosowania prawa. Doktryna i tezy orzecznictwa* [The Problems of the Theory of the Application of Law. Doctrine and Theses of Jurisdiction]. Kraków: Zakamycze.

Łętowska, Ewa. 2005. Multicentryczność współczesnego systemu prawa i jej konsekwencje [Multicentric Character of Contemporary Legal System and Its Consequences]. *Państwo i Prawo* 4/710: 3–17.

Levi, Edward H. 1949. *An Introduction to Legal Reasoning*. Chicago/London: The University of Chicago Press.

Lindahl, Lars. 1997. Norms, Meaning Postulates, and Legal Predicates. In *Normative Systems in Legal and Moral Theory.* Festschrift *for Carlos E. Alchourrón and Eugenio Bulygin*, ed. E. Garzón Valdés, W. Krawietz, G.H. von Wright, and R. Zimmerling, 293–307. Berlin: Duncker & Humblot.

Lindahl, Lars. 2004. Deduction and Justification in the Law. The Role of Legal Terms and Concepts. *Ratio Juris* 17: 182–202.

Lippold, Rainer. 1988. Geltung, Wirksamkeit und Verbindlichkeit von Rechtsnormen. *Rechtstheorie* 19: 463–489.

Loewer, Barry, Marvin Belzer. 1991. *Prima Facie* Obligation: Its Deconstruction and Reconstruction. In *John Searle and His Critics*, ed. E. Lepore, R. Van Gulick, 359–370. Cambridge (Mass.)/Oxford: Basil Blackwell.

Ludwiczak, Danuta, Alicja Piskadłowa, Ewa Tarska-Huczek. 1998. *Słownik wyrazów bliskoznacznych* [Thesaurus]. Warszawa: Wydawnictwo „Wiedza Powszechna".

Łabieniec, Paweł. 2004. *Prawo rozumu. O teorii prawa naturalnego Johna Finnisa* [Law of Reason. On John Finnis' Theory of Natural Law]. Łódź: Wydawnictwo Uniwersytetu Łódzkiego.

Łukasiewicz, Jan. 1987. *O zasadzie sprzeczności u Arystotelesa* [On the Principle of Contradiction in Aristotle]. Ed. J. Woleński. Warszawa: Wydawnictwo Naukowe PWN. [1st ed. 1910.]

MacCormick, Neil. 1978. *Legal Reasoning and Legal Theory*. Oxford: Clarendon Press.

MacCormick, Neil. 1981. *H.L.A. Hart*. London: Edward Arnold.

MacCormick, Neil. 1986. Law, Morality and Positivism. In N. MacCormick, O. Weinberger, *An Institutional Theory of Law. New Approaches to Legal Positivism*, 127–144. Dordrecht/Boston/Lancaster/Tokyo: D. Reidel.

MacCormick, Neil. 1990. Reconstruction after Deconstruction: a Response to CLS. *Oxford Journal of Legal Studies* 10/4: 539–558.

MacCormick, Neil. 1991. Moral Disestablishment and Rational Discourse. In *Recht und Moral. Beiträge zu einer Standortbestimmung*, ed. H. Jung, H. Müller-Dietz, and U. Neumann, 219–231. Baden-Baden: Nomos.

MacCormick, Neil. 1992. Further Thoughts on Institutional Facts. *International Journal for the Semiotics of Law* V/13: 3–15.
MacCormick, Neil. 1992. Natural Law and the Separation of Law and Morals. In *Natural Law Theory. Contemporary Essays*, ed. R.P. George, 105–133. Oxford: Clarendon Press.
MacCormick, Neil. 1993. Argumentation and Interpretation in Law. *Ratio Juris* 6: 16–29.
MacCormick, Neil. 1994. Foreword. In *idem*, *Legal Reasoning and Legal Theory*, 2nd ed., ix-xvi. Oxford: Clarendon Press.
MacCormick, Neil. 1994. Four Quadrants of Jurisprudence. In *Prescriptive Formality and Normative Rationality in Modern Legal Systems.* Festschrift *for Robert S. Summers*, ed. W. Krawietz, N. MacCormick, G.H. von Wright, 53–70. Berlin: Duncker & Humblot.
MacCormick, Neil. 1996. The Concept of Law and *The Concept of Law*. In *The Autonomy of Law. Essays on Legal Positivism*, ed. R.P. George, 163–193. Oxford: Clarendon Press.
MacCormick, Neil. 1997. On Institutional Normative Order: An Idea about Law. In *Normative Systems in Legal and Moral Theory.* Festschrift *for Carlos E. Alchourrón and Eugenio Bulygin*, ed. E. Garzón Valdés, W. Krawietz, G.H. von Wright, and R. Zimmerling, 411–425. Berlin: Duncker & Humblot.
MacCormick, Neil. 1998. Powers and Power-Conferring Norms. In *Normativity and Norms. Critical Perspectives on Kelsenian Themes*, ed. St.L. Paulson, B. Litschewski Paulson, 493–506. Oxford: Clarendon Press.
MacCormick, Neil. 1999. Can Judges Make Mistakes? In *Rechtsbegründung – Rechtsbegründungen. Günther Ellscheid zum 65. Geburtstag*, ed. H. Jung, U. Neumann, 76–89. Baden-Baden: Nomos.
MacCormick, Neil. 2005. *Rhetoric and the Rule of Law. A Theory of Legal Reasoning.* Oxford: Oxford University Press.
MacCormick, Neil. 2007. *Institutions of Law. An Essay in Legal Theory.* Oxford: Oxford University Press.
MacCormick, Neil. 2007. Why Law Makes No Claims. In *Law, Rights and Discourse. The Legal Philosophy of Robert Alexy*, ed. G. Pavlakos, 59–67. Oxford/Portland: Hart.
Mackie, John. 1983. The Third Theory of Law. *Philosophy and Public Affairs* 7/1: 3–16.
Mączyński, Andrzej. 2001. Kontrola konstytucyjności przepisów uchylających i zmieniających [The Control of the Constitutionality of Repealing and Amending Provisions]. In *Trybunał Konstytucyjny. Księga XV-lecia*, ed. F. Rymarz, A. Jankiewicz, 157–167. Warszawa: Biuro Trybunału Konstytucyjnego.
Mączyński, Andrzej. 2005. O tak zwanych wyrokach interpretacyjnych Trybunału Konstytucyjnego [On the So-called Interpretive Rulings of the Constitutional Tribunal]. In *Teoria i praktyka wykładni prawa. Materiały konferencji naukowej Wydziału Prawa i Administracji Uniwersytetu Warszawskiego odbytej w dniu 27 lutego 2004 roku*, ed. P. Winczorek, 159–173. Warszawa: Liber.
Marciszewski, Witold. 1987. Definicja [Definition]. In *Logika formalna. Zarys encyklopedyczny z zastosowaniem do informatyki i lingwistyki*, ed. W. Marciszewski, 256–266. Warszawa: Państwowe Wydawnictwo Naukowe.
Marciszewski, Witold. 1988. Definicja [Definition]. In *Mała encyklopedia logiki*, 2nd ed. by W. Marciszewski, 265–266. Wrocław/Warszawa/Kraków/Gdańsk/Łódź: Zakład Narodowy im. Ossolińskich – Wydawnictwo. [1st ed. 1970.]
Marciszewski, Witold. 1988. Denotacja [Denotation]. In *Mała encyklopedia logiki*, 2nd ed. by W. Marciszewski, 46. Wrocław/Warszawa/Kraków/Gdańsk/Łódź: Zakład Narodowy im. Ossolińskich – Wydawnictwo. [1st ed. 1970.]
Marciszewski, Witold. 1988. Eksplikacja [Explication]. In *Mała encyklopedia logiki*, 2nd ed. by W. Marciszewski, 53. Wrocław/Warszawa/Kraków/Gdańsk/Łódź: Zakład Narodowy im. Ossolińskich – Wydawnictwo. [1st ed. 1970.]
Marmor, Andrei. 2002. Exclusive Legal Positivism. In *The Oxford Handbook of Jurisprudence and Philosophy of Law*, ed. J.L. Coleman, S.J. Shapiro, 104–124. Oxford: Oxford University Press.

Marmor, Andrei. 2006. How Law is Like Chess. *Legal Theory* 12: 347–371.

Matczak, Marcin. 2004. *Kompetencja organu administracji publicznej* [Competence of the Organ of Public Administration]. Kraków: Zakamycze.

Maus, Ingeborg. 1989. The Differentiation between Law and Morality as a Limitation of Law. In *Law, Morality and Discursive Rationality. Contributions derived from an international symposium on LAW AND LEGITIMACY held in Murikka Centre, Finland, August 1988*, ed. A. Aarnio, K. Tuori, 141–164. Helsinki: Hakapaino Oy. German version: Die Trennung von Recht und Moral als Begrenzung des Rechts, *Rechtstheorie* 20 (1989): 191–210.

Mazzarese, Tecla. 1991. "Norm Proposition": Epistemic and Semantic Queries. *Rechtstheorie* 22: 39–70.

Mazzarese, Tecla. 1996–1997. Semantic and Pragmatic Fuzziness of Legal Language. *Archivum Iuridicum Cracoviense* XXIX–XXX: 43–58.

McLaughlin, Robert N. 1989. On a Similarity between Natural Law Theories and English Legal Positivism. *The Philosophical Quarterly* 39: 445–462.

Mendonca, Daniel. 1998. Presumptions. *Ratio Juris* 11: 399–412.

Mertens, Thomas. 2002. Radbruch and Hart on the Grudge Informer: A Reconsideration. *Ratio Juris* 15: 186–205.

Meyer, Lukas H. 2002. "Gesetzen ihrer Ungerechtigkeit wegen die Geltung absprechen". Gustav Radbruch und der Relativismus. In *Neukantianismus und Rechtsphilosophie*, ed. R. Alexy, L.H. Meyer, St.L. Paulson, and G. Sprenger, 319–361. Baden-Baden: Nomos.

Michniewicz-Wanik, Krystyna. 2008. *Mienie zabużańskie. Prawne podstawy realizacji roszczeń* [Property Left Beyond the Bug River. Legal Basis of Implementing Claims]. Wrocław: Wydawnictwo „Nortom".

Mikołajewicz, Jarosław. 2000. *Prawo intertemporalne. Zagadnienia teoretycznoprawne* [Intertemporal Law. The Jurisprudential Problems]. Poznań: Wydawnictwo Printer.

Morauta, James. 2004. Three Separation Theses. *Law and Philosophy* 23: 111–135.

Morawski, Lech. 1988. *Argumentacje, racjonalność prawa i postępowanie dowodowe* [Argumentation, Rationality of Law and Hearing of Evidence]. Toruń: Uniwersytet Mikołaja Kopernika.

Morawski, Lech. 1994. Państwo prawne – odpowiedź na uwagi prof. H. Rota [Law-Governed State – a Reply to Prof. H. Rot's Comments]. *Państwo i Prawo* 12/586: 84–87.

Morawski, Lech. 1994. Spór o pojęcie państwa prawnego [A Dispute over the Concept of the Law-Governed State]. *Państwo i Prawo* 4/578: 3–12.

Morawski, Lech. 1996. Zasada państwa prawnego – próba reinterpretacji [The Principle of the Law-Governed State – an Attempt at Reinterpretation]. *Acta Universitatis Nicolai Copernici – Prawo* XXXV/304: 3–22.

Morawski, Lech. 1997. Państwo prawa [The Law-Governed State]. In *Filozoficzno-teoretyczne problemy sądowego stosowania prawa*, ed. M. Zirk-Sadowski, 11–24. Łódź: Wydawnictwo Uniwersytetu Łódzkiego.

Morawski, Lech. 1999. *Główne problemy współczesnej filozofii prawa* [Main Problems of the Contemporary Philosophy of Law]. Warszawa: Wydawnictwa Prawnicze PWN.

Morawski, Lech. 2001. *Co może dać nauce prawa postmodernizm?* [What Postmodernism Can Offer to Legal Science?]. Toruń: Wydawnictwo "Dom Organizatora".

Morawski, Lech. 2001. Zasady prawne – komentarz krytyczny [Legal Principles – A Critical Commentary]. *Studia z filozofii prawa* 1: 71–81.

Morawski, Lech. 2002. *Wykładnia w orzecznictwie sądów. Komentarz* [Interpretation in Courts' Decisions. A Commentary]. Toruń: Wydawnictwo „Dom Organizatora".

Morawski, Lech. 2004. *Wstęp do prawoznawstwa* [Introduction to Jurisprudence]. 7th ed. Toruń: Wydawnictwo „Dom Organizatora". [1st ed. 1996.]

Morawski, Lech. 2005. Hard Positivism, Soft Positivism and Dead Positivism. Trans. T.Z. Wolański. *Ius et Lex* I/1: 153–179.

Morawski, Lech. 2005. Kilka uwag na temat wykładni [Some Comments on Interpretation]. In *Polska kultura prawna a proces integracji europejskiej*, ed. S. Wronkowska, 31–42. Kraków: Zakamycze.

Moreso, José Juan. 1998. *Legal Indeterminacy and Constitutional Interpretation*. Trans. R. Zimmerling. Dordrecht: Kluwer. Original Spanish version: *La indeterminación del derecho y la interpretación de la Constitución*, Madrid: Centro de Estudios Políticos y Constitucionales, 1997.

Moreso, José Juan. 2001. In Defense of Inclusive Legal Positivism. *Diritto & questioni pubbliche* 1: 99–117. http://www.dirittoequestionipubbliche.org/page/2001_n1/D_Q-1Moreso.pdf. Accessed 23 September 2007.

Moreso, José Juan. 2002. On the Truth-conditions of Norm Propositions. *Associations* 6: 63–73.

Moreso, José Juan, Pablo E. Navarro. 1998. The Reception of Norms, and Open Legal Systems. In *Normativity and Norms. Critical Perspectives on Kelsenian Themes*, ed. St.L. Paulson, B. Litschewski Paulson, 273–291. Oxford: Clarendon Press.

Moś, Urszula. 1988–1989. Ustawodawstwo symboliczne, czyli o możliwości działań pozornych w prawie [Symbolic Legislation, That Is the Possibility of Apparent Actions in Law]. *Colloquia Communia* 6/41–1/42: 47–52.

Muszalski, Edward, Aleksander Makowski, Wacław Szyszkowski, Mieczysław Szerer, Stanisław Sołtysiński. 1986. *Słownik prawniczy polsko-angielski* [Polish–English Dictionary of Law]. Ed. L. Bar. Wrocław/Warszawa/Kraków/Gdańsk/Łódź: Zakład Narodowy im. Ossolińskich – Wydawnictwo Polskiej Akademii Nauk.

Naleziński, Bogumił, Krzysztof Wojtyczek. 1993. Konsekwencje wadliwości aktów normatywnych w polskim systemie prawnym [The Consequences of the Defectiveness of Normative Acts in the Polish Legal System"]. *Ruch Prawniczy, Ekonomiczny i Socjologiczny* LV/4: 19–32.

Navarro, Pablo E. 2000. Enunciados jurídicos y proposiciones normativas. *Isonomía* 12: 121–155.

Navarro, Pablo E. 2001. Legal Reasoning and Systematization of Law. In *Pluralism and Law*, ed. A. Soeteman, 251–277. Dordrecht/Boston/London: Kluwer.

Navarro, Pablo E. 2001. Tensiones conceptuales en el positivismo jurídico. *DOXA* 24: 133–163.

Navarro, Pablo E. 2002. Legal Systems and Legal Statements. *Associations* 6: 75–88.

Navarro, Pablo E. 2005. Acerca de la inevitabilidad de la interpretación. *Isonomía* 22: 99–122.

Navarro, Pablo E., José Juan Moreso. 1997. Applicability and Effectiveness of Legal Norms. *Law and Philosophy* 16: 201–219.

Neumann, Ulfrid. 1981. Book review: *Theorie der juristischen Argumentation* by Robert Alexy. *Philosophische Rundschau* 28: 209–214.

Neumann, Ulfrid. 1985. Theorien der Rechtsgeltung. In *Gegenkultur und Recht*, ed. V. Gessner, W. Hassemer, 21–41. Baden-Baden: Nomos.

Neumann, Ulfrid. 1986. *Juristische Argumentationslehre*. Darmstadt: Wissenschaftliche Buchgesellschaft.

Neumann, Ulfrid. 1990. Positivistische Rechtsquellenlehre und naturrechtliche Methode. Zum Alltagsnaturrecht in der juristischen Argumentation. *Archiv für Rechts- und Sozialphilosophie*, Beiheft 37: 141–151.

Neumann, Ulfrid. 1994. Book review: *Begriff und Geltung des Rechts* by Robert Alexy. *Protosoziologie* 6: 241–247.

Neumann, Ulfrid. 1994. Rechtsphilosophie in Deutschland seit 1945. In *Rechtswissenschaft in der Bonner Republik*, ed. D. Simon, 145–187. Frankfurt am Main: Suhrkamp.

Neumann, Ulfrid. 1995. Positivismo jurídico, realismo jurídico y moralismo jurídico en el debate sobre "delincuencia estatal" en la anterior RDA. Trans. F. Puigpelat Martí. *DOXA* 17–18: 435–444.

Neumann, Ulfrid. 2000. Die Geltung von Regeln, Prinzipien und Elementem. In *Regeln, Prinzipien und Elemente im System des Rechts*, ed. B. Schilcher, P. Koller, and B.-Ch. Frank, 115–127. Wien: Österreich.

Neumann, Ulfrid. 2001. Die Bedeutung der Rechtsdogmatik in der deutschen Rechtskultur. Frankfurt am Main. [Unpublished manuscript].

Neumann, Ulfrid. 2001. Juristische Methodenlehre und Theorie der juristischen Argumentation. *Rechtstheorie* 32: 239–255.

Neumann, Ulfrid. 2004. *Wahrheit im Recht. Zu Problematik und Legitimität einer fragwürdigen Denkform*. Baden-Baden: Nomos.

Neumann, Ulfrid. 2005. Ralf Dreiers Radbruch. In *Integratives Verstehen. Zur Rechtsphilosophie Ralf Dreiers*, ed. R. Alexy, 141–157. Tübingen: Mohr Siebeck.

Neumann, Ulfrid. 2005. Wissenschaftstheorie der Rechtswissenschaft bei Hans Kelsen und Gustav Radbruch. Zwei "neukantianische" Perspektiven. In *Hans Kelsen. Staatsrechtslehrer und Rechtstheoretiker des 20. Jahrhunderts*, ed. St.L. Paulson, M. Stolleis, 35–55. Tübingen: Mohr Siebeck.

Neumann, Ulfrid. 2007. Problem obowiązywania prawa [The Problem of Validity of Law]. Trans. A. Grabowski. *Państwo i Prawo* 7/737: 32–46.

Neuner, Jörg. 1992. *Die Rechtsfindung contra legem*. München: Beck.

Niiniluoto, Ilkka. 1991. Norm Propositions Defended. *Ratio Juris* 4: 367–373.

Nino, Carlos Santiago. 1989. *El constructivismo ético*. Madrid: Centro de Estudios Constitucionales.

Nino, Carlos Santiago. 1994. *Derecho, Moral y Política. Una revisión de la teoría general del Derecho*. Barcelona: Ariel.

Nowacki, Józef. 1976. *Domniemania prawne* [Legal Presumptions]. Prace Naukowe Uniwersytetu Śląskiego w Katowicach 142.

Nowacki, Józef. 1988. *Przepis prawny a norma prawna* [Legal Provision and Legal Norm], Prace Naukowe Uniwersytetu Śląskiego w Katowicach 973.

Nowak, Leszek. 1966. Cztery koncepcje obowiązywania prawa [Four Conceptions of the Validity of Law]. *Ruch Prawniczy, Ekonomiczny i Socjologiczny* XXXVIII/2: 95–103.

Nowak, Leszek. 1967. Pojęcie obowiązywania prawa jako teoretyczne pojęcie prawoznawstwa [The Concept of Legal Validity as A Theoretical Concept of Jurisprudence]. *Studia Metodologiczne* III: 45–65.

Nowak, Leszek. 1973. *Interpretacja prawnicza. Studium z metodologii prawoznawstwa* [Legal Interpretation. A Study on the Methodology of Jurisprudence]. Warszawa: Państwowe Wydawnictwo Naukowe.

Ogorek, Regina. 2000. "Mauerschützen" (BverfGE 95, 96 ff.). *Kritische Vierteljahresschrift für Gesetzgebung und Rechtswissenschaft* 83/3–4: 323–343.

Opałek, Kazimierz. 1966. Swoistość prawoznawstwa a problem integracji [Specific Character of Jurisprudence and the Problem of Integration]. *Państwo i Prawo* 4–5/242–243: 628–641.

Opałek, Kazimierz. 1970. The Problem of the Validity of Law. *Archivum Iuridicum Cracoviense* III: 8–19.

Opałek, Kazimierz. 1971. Law and Integration of Social Sciences. *Archivum Iuridicum Cracoviense* IV: 7–24.

Opałek, Kazimierz. 1974. *Z teorii dyrektyw i norm* [On the Theory of Directives and Norms]. Warszawa: Państwowe Wydawnictwo Naukowe. German version: *Theorie der Directiven und der Normen*. Wien/New York: Springer, 1986.

Opałek, Kazimierz. 1982. Der Begriff des positiven Rechts. *Archiv für Rechts- und Sozialphilosophie* 68: 448–462.

Opałek, Kazimierz. 1989. Der Dualismus der Auffassung der Normen in der Rechtswissenschaft. Der Versuch seiner Überwindung. *Rechtstheorie* 20: 433–447. [1st Polish ed. 1988.]

Opałek, Kazimierz. 1991. Statisches und dynamisches Normensystem. In *Staatsrecht in Theorie und Praxis. Festschrift für Robert Walter zum 60. Geburtstag*, ed. H. Mayer, 507–518. Wien: Manzsche Verlags- und Universitätsbuchhandlung.

Opałek, Kazimierz. 1993. Normen: Bedeutung und Performanz. In *Rechtsnorm und Rechtswirklichkeit. Festschrift für Werner Krawietz zum 60. Geburtstag*, ed. A. Aarnio, St.L. Paulson, O. Weinberger, G.H. von Wright, and D. Wyduckel, 41–51. Berlin: Duncker & Humblot.

Opałek, Kazimierz. 1997. Główne kierunki niemieckiej teorii i filozofii prawa po II wojnie światowej [Main Currents in the German Theory and Philosophy of Law After the Second World War]. In *idem*, *Studia z teorii i filozofii prawa*, ed. R. Sarkowicz, J. Stelmach, 11–44. Kraków: Wydawnictwo Uniwersytetu Jagiellońskiego.

Opałek, Kazimierz. 1997. Teoria rozumowania prawniczego – między logika i aksjologią [The Theory of Legal Reasoning – between Logic and Axiology]. In *idem*, *Studia z teorii i filozofii prawa*, ed. R. Sarkowicz, J. Stelmach, 61–80.

Opałek, Kazimierz, Jerzy Wróblewski. 1969. *Zagadnienia teorii prawa* [The Problems of Legal Theory]. Warszawa: Państwowe Wydawnictwo Naukowe.

Opałek, Kazimierz, Jerzy Wróblewski. 1972. Sporne zagadnienia pojęć teoretycznoprawnych [Controversial Issues of Jurisprudential Concepts]. *Ruch Prawniczy, Ekonomiczny i Socjologiczny* XXXIV/1: 91–102.

Opałek, Kazimierz, Jerzy Wróblewski. 1991. *Prawo. Metodologia, filozofia, teoria prawa* [Law. Methodology, Philosophy, Legal Theory]. Warszawa: Państwowe Wydawnictwo Naukowe.

Opałek, Kazimierz, Woleński Jan. 1987. Is, Ought, and Logic. *Archiv für Rechts- und Sozialphilosophie* 73: 373–385.

Openchowski, Zdzisław. 1970. Wyrokowanie w myśli [Adjudicating in Mind]. *Gazeta Sądowa i Penitencjarna* X/8: 6.

Orwell, George (Eric Arthur Blair). 2003. *Animal Farm* and *1984*. Orlando: Harcourt.

Ost, François. 1991. Jupiter, Hercule, Hermès: trois modèles du juge. In *La force du droit. Panorama des débats contemporains*, ed. P. Bouretz, 241–272. Paris: Éditions Esprit.

Ott, Walter. 1983. Was heißt "Rechtspositivismus"? In *Das Naturrechtsdenken heute und morgen. Gedächtnisschrift für René Marcic*, ed. D. Mayer-Maly, P. M. Simons, 413–425. Berlin: Duncker & Humblot.

Ott, Walter. 1988. Die Radbruch'sche Formel. Pro und Contra. *Zeitschrift für Schweizerisches Recht* 107: 335–357.

Ott, Walter. 1992. *Der Rechtspositivismus. Kritische Würdigung auf der Grundlage eines juristischen Pragmatismus*. 2nd ed. Berlin: Duncker & Humblot. [1st ed. 1976.]

Ott, Walter, Franziska Buob. 1993. Did Legal Positivism Render German Jurists Defenceless during the Third Reich? *Archiv für Rechts- und Sozialphilosophie*, Beiheft 52: 92–105.

Pałecki, Krzysztof. 2000. Towards Better Formulation of the Problem: Can Legal Research Affect Law-Making and Judicial Practice? In *Legal Research in Dynamic Society. A Polish–Swedish Research Project*, ed. K. Pałecki, A. Peczenik, 183–188. Kraków: Ratio.

Pałecki, Krzysztof. 2003. *Prawoznawstwo – zarys wykładu. Prawo w porządku społecznym* [Lecture on Jurisprudence. Law in Social Order]. Warszawa: Difin.

Páramo, Juan Ramón, de. 1988. Entrevista a H.L.A. Hart. *DOXA* 5: 339–361.

Paroussis, Michel. 1995. *Theorie des juristischen Diskurses. Eine institutionelle Epistemologie des Rechts*. Berlin: Duncker & Humblot.

Patryas, Wojciech. 1997. *Definiowanie pojęć prawnych* [Defining Legal Concepts]. Poznań: Wydawnictwo Naukowe UAM.

Patryas, Wojciech. 2002. Kilka uwag na marginesie koncepcji obowiązywania norm [Some Comments on the Conception of the Validity of Norms]. In *Odwaga filozofowania. Leszkowi Nowakowi w darze*, ed. J. Brzeziński, A. Klawiter, T.A.F. Kuipers, K. Łastowski, K. Paprzycka, and P. Przybysz, 263–272. Poznań: Wydawnictwo Fundacji Humaniora.

Patryas, Wojciech. 2005. *Performatywy w prawie* [Performatives in Law]. Poznań: Wydawnictwo Forum Naukowe.

Patterson, Dennis. 1996. *Law and Truth*. Oxford/New York: Oxford University Press. [German version: *Recht und Wahrheit*, Baden-Baden: Nomos, 1999.]

Paulson, Stanley L. 1979. Neue Grundlagen für einen Begriff der Rechtsgeltung. *Archiv für Rechts- und Sozialphilosophie* 65: 1–19.

Paulson, Stanley L. 1990. Lässt sich die Reine Rechtslehre transzendental begründen? *Rechtstheorie* 21: 155–179.

Paulson, Stanley L. 1993. Die unterschiedlichen Formulierungen der "Grundnorm". In *Rechtsnorm und Rechtswirklichkeit. Festschrift für Werner Krawietz zum 60. Geburtstag*, ed. A. Aarnio, St.L. Paulson, O. Weinberger, G.H. von Wright, and D. Wyduckel, 53–74. Berlin: Duncker & Humblot.

Paulson, Stanley L. 1998. Four Phases in Hans Kelsen's Legal Theory? Reflections on a Periodization. *Oxford Journal of Legal Studies* 18/1: 153–166.

Paulson, Stanley L. 1999. Arriving at a Defensible Periodization of Hans Kelsen's Legal Theory. *Oxford Journal of Legal Studies* 19/2: 351–364.

Paulson, Stanley L. 2000. On the Puzzle Surrounding Hans Kelsen's Basic Norm. *Ratio Juris* 13: 279–293.

Paulson, Stanley L. 2002. Faktum/Wert-Distinktion, Zwei-Welten-Lehre und immanenter Sinn. Hans Kelsen als Neukantianer. In *Neukantianismus und Rechtsphilosophie*, ed. R. Alexy, L.H. Meyer, St.L. Paulson, and G. Sprenger, 223–251. Baden-Baden: Nomos.

Paulson, Stanley L., 2006. On the Background and Significance of Gustav Radbruch's Post-War Papers. *Oxford Journal of Legal Studies* 26/1: 17–40.

Pavlakos, George. 2005. On the Necessity of the Interconnection between Law and Morality. *Ratio Juris* 18: 64–83.

Pawłowski, Tadeusz. 1986. *Tworzenie pojęć w naukach humanistycznych* [Creation of Concepts in Humanistic Sciences]. Warszawa: Państwowe Wydawnictwo Naukowe.

Peczenik, Aleksander. 1975. The Structure of a Legal System. *Rechtstheorie* 6: 1–16.

Peczenik, Aleksander. 1981. On the Nature and Function of the *Grundnorm*. *Rechtstheorie*, Beiheft 2: 279–296.

Peczenik, Aleksander. 1988. Legal Reasoning as a Special Case of Moral Reasoning. *Ratio Juris* 1: 123–136.

Peczenik, Aleksander. 1990. Coherence, Truth and Rightness in the Law. In *Law, Interpretation and Reality. Essays in Epistemology, Hermeneutics and Jurisprudence*, ed. P. Nerhot, 275–309. Dordrecht/Boston/London: Kluwer.

Peczenik, Aleksander. 1993. Sources of Law. In *Rechtsnorm und Rechtswirklichkeit. Festschrift für Werner Krawietz zum 60. Geburtstag*, ed. A. Aarnio, St.L. Paulson, O. Weinberger, G.H. von Wright, and D. Wyduckel, 75–84. Berlin: Duncker & Humblot.

Peczenik, Aleksander. 1994. Law, Morality, Coherence and Truth. *Ratio Juris* 7: 146–176.

Peczenik, Aleksander. 1994. Unity of the Legal System. In *Prescriptive Formality and Normative Rationality in Modern Legal Systems.* Festschrift *for Robert S. Summers*, ed. W. Krawietz, N. MacCormick, and G.H. von Wright, 71–81. Berlin: Duncker & Humblot.

Peczenik, Aleksander. 1996–1997. Legal Research – Normative and Descriptive. *Archivum Iuridicum Cracoviense* XXIX–XXX: 17–27.

Peczenik, Aleksander. 1997. The Passion for Reason. Some Remarks on Coherence in the Law. In *Normative Systems in Legal and Moral Theory.* Festschrift *for Carlos E. Alchourrón and Eugenio Bulygin*, ed. E. Garzón Valdés, W. Krawietz, G.H. von Wright, and R. Zimmerling, 309–321. Berlin: Duncker & Humblot.

Peczenik, Aleksander. 1998. Against Reductionism. *Associations* 2: 101–120.

Peczenik, Aleksander. 1998. Non-Positivist Conception of Law. In *Teoria prawa. Filozofia prawa. Współczesne prawo i prawoznawstwo*, (teamwork ed.), 223–248. Toruń: Uniwersytet Mikołaja Kopernika.

Peczenik, Aleksander. 2000. Certainty or Coherence? In *The Reasonable as Rational? On Legal Argumentation and Justification.* Festschrift *for Aulis Aarnio*, ed. W. Krawietz, R.S. Summers, O. Weinberger, and G.H. von Wright, 157–171. Berlin: Duncker & Humblot.'

Peczenik, Aleksander. 2003. Stan obecny teorii i filozofii prawa w krajach zachodnich [Current State of Theory and Philosophy of Law in Western Countries]. *Studia z filozofii prawa* 2: 9–14.

Peczenik, Aleksander. 2005. *Scientia Juris. Legal Doctrine as Knowledge of Law and as a Source of Law.* In *A Treatise of Legal Philosophy and General Jurisprudence*, ed. E. Pattaro, Vol. 4. Dordrecht: Springer.

Peczenik, Aleksander, Jerzy Wróblewski. 1985. Fuzziness and transformations: Towards explaining legal reasoning. *Theoria* LI: 24–44.

Peczenik, Aleksander, Sebastián Urbina. 1995. Why Officials? On Legal Positivism Old and New. *Rechtstheorie* 27: 139–162.

Perelman, Chaïm. 1976. *Logique juridique. Nouvelle rhétorique*. Paris: Jurisprudence générale Dalloz.

Perelman, Chaïm. 1983. Gesetz und Recht. In *Das Naturrechtsdenken heute und morgen. Gedächtnisschrift für René Marcic*, ed. D. Mayer-Maly, P.M. Simons, 427–435. Berlin: Duncker & Humblot.

Perelman, Chaïm, Lucie Olbrechts-Tyteca. 1988. *Traité de l'argumentation. La nouvelle rhétorique*. 5th ed. Bruxelles: Éditions de l'Universite de Bruxelles. English version: *The New Rhetoric: A Treatise on Argumentation*. Trans. J. Wilkinson, P. Weaver. Notre Dame/London: University of Notre Dame Press, 1969.

Perry, Stephen R. 2001. Hart's Methodological Positivism. In *Hart's Postscript. Essays on the Postscript to* The Concept of Law, ed. J.L. Coleman, 311–354. Oxford/New York: Oxford University Press.

Petrażycki, Leon. 1959. *Wstęp do nauki o prawie i moralności. Podstawy psychologii emocjonalnej* [Introduction to the Science of Law and Morality. Fundamentals of Emotional Psychology]. 2nd ed. Trans. J. Lande. Warszawa: Państwowe Wydawnictwo Naukowe. [1st ed. 1930.]

Pfordten, Dietmar, von der. 2005. Zum Verhältnis von Begriffen, insbesondere im Recht. In *Gerechtigkeitswissenschaft – Kolloquium aus Anlass des 70. Geburtstages von Lothar Philipps*, ed. B. Schünemann, M.-T. Tinnefeld, and R. Wittmann, 205–224. Berlin: Berliner Wissenschafts-Verlag.

Piechowiak, Marek. 1992. *W poszukiwaniu ontologicznych podstaw prawa. Arthura Kaufmanna teoria sprawiedliwości* [In Search for Ontological Foundations of Law. Arthur Kaufmann's Theory of Justice]. Warszawa/Poznań: Instytut Nauk Prawnych PAN.

Pieńkos, Jerzy. 1999. *Podstawy juryslingwistyki. Język w prawie – Prawo w języku* [The Fundamentals of Jurislinguistics. Language in Law – Law in Language]. Warszawa: Oficyna Prawnicza MUZA.

Pieńkos, Jerzy. 2002. *Polsko-angielski słownik prawniczy* [Polish–English Dictionary of Law]. Kraków: Zakamycze.

Pieńkos, Jerzy, Maciej Szepietowski, Krzysztof Poklewski-Koziełł. 1987. *Słownik prawniczy polsko-francuski* [Polish-French Dictionary of Law]. Ed. L. Bar. Wrocław/Warszawa/Kraków/Gdańsk/Łódź: Zakład Narodowy im. Ossolińskich – Wydawnictwo Polskiej Akademii Nauk.

Pietrzykowski, Krzysztof. 2002. Problem skuteczności *ex tunc* albo *ex nunc* orzeczeń Trybunału Konstytucyjnego w orzecznictwie Sądu Najwyższego [The Problem of *Ex Tunc* or *Ex Nunc* Effectiveness of the Constitutional Tribunal Rulings in the Jurisdiction of the Supreme Court]. In *Ius et Lex. Księga jubileuszowa ku czci Profesora Adama Strzembosza*, ed. A. Dębiński, A. Grześkowiak, and K. Wiak, 277–292. Lublin: Wydawnictwo Katolickiego Uniwersytetu Lubelskiego.

Pietrzykowski, Tomasz. 2001. "Miękki" pozytywizm i spór o regułę uznania ["Soft" Positivism and Controversy over the Rule of Recognition]. *Studia z filozofii prawa* 1: 97–121.

Pietrzykowski, Tomasz. 2003. Temporalny zakres obowiązywania prawa [Temporal Scope of the Validity of Law]. *Państwo i Prawo* 4/686: 45–56.

Pietrzykowski, Tomasz. 2004. *Wsteczne działanie prawa i jego zakaz* [Retroactive Action of Law and Its Prohibition]. Kraków: Zakamycze.

Piotrowski, Mariusz. 1990. *Normy prawne imperatywne i dyspozytywne* [Imperative and Dispositive Legal Norms]. Warszawa/Poznań: Państwowe wydawnictwo Naukowe.

Plato. 2002. *Five Dialogues: Euthyphro, Apology, Crito, Meno, Phaedo*. 2nd ed. Trans. G.M.A. Grube. Indianapolis: Hackett.

Płeszka, Krzysztof. 1988. *Hierarchia w systemie prawa* [Hierarchy in the Legal System]. Zeszyty Naukowe Uniwersytetu Jagiellońskiego. Prace z nauk politycznych 33.

Płeszka, Krzysztof. 2000. O paradygmacie dogmatyki prawa [On the Paradigm of Legal Dogmatics]. In *Zasady procesu karnego wobec wyzwań współczesności. Księga ku czci*

Profesora Stanisława Waltosia, ed. J. Czapska, A. Gaberle, A. Światłowski, and A. Zoll, 763–773. Warszawa: Wydawnictwo Prawnicze PWN.

Płeszka, Krzysztof, Tomasz Gizbert-Studnicki. 1990. Obraz systemu prawa w dogmatyce prawniczej [The Image of the System of Law in Legal Dogmatics]. In *Szkice z teorii prawa i szczegółowych nauk prawnych*, ed. S. Wronkowska, M. Zieliński, 151–171. Wydawnictwo Naukowe Uniwersytetu im. Adama Mickiewicza w Poznaniu.

Pospieszalski, Karol M., Bronisław Ostaszewski, Jan Rezler, Otmar Wandmayer. 1987. *Słownik prawniczy polsko-niemiecki* [Polish–German Dictionary of Law]. Ed. L. Bar. Wrocław/Warszawa/Kraków/Gdańsk/Łódź: Zakład Narodowy im. Ossolińskich – Wydawnictwo Polskiej Akademii Nauk.

Postanowienie Trybunału Konstytucyjnego z dnia 21 marca 2000 r. [Decision of the Constitutional Tribunal from 21 March 2000]. Sign. K 4/99. *Orzecznictwo Trybunału Konstytucyjnego. Zbiór Urzędowy* [The Official Collection of the Jurisdiction of Constitutional Tribunal] 2000, No. 2, Item 65.

Postema, Gerald J. 1998. Jurisprudence as Practical Philosophy. *Legal Theory* 4: 329–357.

Prawo prywatne międzynarodowe. Ustawa z dnia 12 listopada 1965 r. [Private International Law. Statute of 12 November 1965]. *Dziennik Ustaw* [Journal of Statutes] 1965, No. 46, Item 290.

Przepisy wprowadzające kodeks karny. Ustawa z dnia 6 czerwca 1997 r. [Introductory Provisions to the Penal Code. Statute of 6 June 1997]. *Dziennik Ustaw* [Journal of Statutes] 1997, No. 88, Item 554.

Pulka, Zbigniew. 1996. *Legitymizacja państwa w prawoznawstwie* [Legitimization of the State in Jurisprudence]. Acta Universitatis Wratislaviensis 1885.

Pulka, Zbigniew. 1999. Hart–Dworkin – dwa warianty "wewnętrznego" postrzegania prawa [Hart–Dworkin: Two Versions of the "Internal" Comprehension of Law]. *Acta Universitatis Wratislaviensis* 2142: 21–42.

Pulka, Zbigniew. 2004. *Struktura poznania filozoficznego w prawoznawstwie* [The Structure of Philosophical Cognition in Jurisprudence]. Acta Universitatis Wratislaviensis 2697.

Pulka, Zbigniew. 2006. Czy nastąpił zmierzch pozytywistycznej koncepcji prawa i prawoznawstwa? [The Fall of the Positivist Conception of Law and Legal Science?]. *Acta Universitatis Wratislaviensis* 2878: 147–177.

Putnam, Hilary. 1975. The Meaning of "Meaning". In *idem*, *Mind, Language and Reality. Philosophical Papers*, Vol 2, 215–271. Cambridge/London/New York/New Rochelle/Melbourne/Sydney: Cambridge University Press.

Putnam, Hilary. 1977. Is Semantics Possible? In *Naming, Necessity, and Natural Kinds*, ed. S.P. Schwartz, 102–118. Ithaca/London: Cornell University Press.

Putnam, Hilary. 1977. Meaning and Reference. In *Naming, Necessity, and Natural Kinds*, ed. S.P. Schwartz, 119–132. Ithaca/London: Cornell University Press.

Quine, Willard Van Orman. 1961. Two Dogmas of Empiricism. In *idem*, *From a Logical Point of View. Nine Logico-Philosophical Essays*, 2nd ed., 20–46. Cambridge (Mass.)/London: Harvard University Press.

Rodríguez-Toubes Muñiz, Joaquín. 1997. Is Soft Positivism a Positivism? *Archiv für Rechts- und Sozialphilosophie*, Beiheft 70: 44–48.

Rachels, Stuart. 2003. A Defense of Two Optimistic Claims in Ethical Theory. *Philosophical Studies* 112: 1–30.

Radbruch, Gustav. 1999. Fünf Minuten Rechtsphilosophie. In *idem*, *Rechtsphilosophie. Studienausgabe*, ed. R. Dreier, St.L. Paulson, 209–210. Heidelberg: Müller. English version: Five Minutes of Legal Philosophy (1945). Trans. B. Litschewski Paulson, St.L. Paulson. *Oxford Journal of Legal Studies* 26/1 (2006): 13–15.

Radbruch, Gustav. 1999. Gesetzliches Unrecht und übergesetzliches Recht. In *idem*, *Rechtsphilosophie. Studienausgabe*, ed. R. Dreier, St.L. Paulson, 211–219. Heidelberg: Müller. English version: Statutory Lawlessness and Supra-Statutory Law (1946). Trans. B. Litschewski Paulson, St.L. Paulson. *Oxford Journal of Legal Studies* 26/1 (2006): 1–11.

Radbruch, Gustav. 1999. *Rechtsphilosophie. Studienausgabe*, ed. R. Dreier, St.L. Paulson. Heidelberg: Müller.

Radziewicz, Piotr. 2005. Przywrócenie mocy obowiązującej przepisu prawnego jako skutek orzeczenia Trybunału Konstytucyjnego [Restoring the Validity of Legal Provision as a Result of the Constitutional Tribunal Ruling]. *Przegląd Sejmowy* 3/68: 21–46.

Radziewicz, Piotr. 2006. "Przywilej korzyści" jako skutek prawny orzeczenia Trybunału Konstytucyjnego ["Privilege of Benefits" as the Legal Consequence of the Constitutional Tribunal Ruling]. *Przegląd Legislacyjny* XIII/4: 9–34.

Rawls, John. 1971. *A Theory of Justice*. Cambridge (Mass.): Harvard University Press.

Raz, Joseph. 1975. Reasons for Action, Decisions and Norms. *Mind* 84: 481–499.

Raz, Joseph. 1977. Legal Validity. *Archiv für Rechts- und Sozialphilosophie* 63: 339–353.

Raz, Joseph. 1978. Introduction. In *Practical Reasoning*, ed. J. Raz, 1–17. Oxford: Oxford University Press.

Raz, Joseph. 1979. Kelsen's Theory of the Basic Norm. In *idem, The Authority of Law. Essays on Law and Morality*, 122–145. Oxford: Clarendon Press.

Raz, Joseph. 1979. Legal Positivism and the Sources of Law. In *idem, The Authority of Law. Essays on Law and Morality*, 37–52. Oxford: Clarendon Press.

Raz, Joseph. 1979. The Identity of Legal Systems. In *idem, The Authority of Law. Essays on Law and Morality*, 78–102. Oxford: Clarendon Press.

Raz, Joseph. 1979. The Obligation to Obey the Law. In *idem, The Authority of Law. Essays on Law and Morality*, 233–249. Oxford: Clarendon Press.

Raz, Joseph. 1980. *The Concept of a Legal System. An Introduction to the Theory of Legal System*. 2nd ed. Oxford: Clarendon Press. [1st ed. 1970.]

Raz, Joseph. 1983. Legal Principles and the Limits of Law. In *Ronald Dworkin and Contemporary Jurisprudence*, 73–87. Totowa: Totowa: Rowman & Allanheld.

Raz, Joseph. 1994. Authority, Law, and Morality. In *idem, Ethics in the Public Domain. Essays in the Morality of Law and Politics*, 194–221. Oxford: Clarendon Press.

Raz, Joseph. 1994. On the Autonomy of Legal Reasoning. In *idem, Ethics in the Public Domain. Essays in the Morality of Law and Politics*, 310–324. Oxford: Clarendon Press.

Raz, Joseph. 1994. The Problem about the Nature of Law. In *idem, Ethics in the Public Domain. Essays in the Morality of Law and Politics*, 179–193. Oxford: Clarendon Press.

Raz, Joseph. 1996. On The Nature of Law. *Archiv für Rechts- und Sozialphilosophie* 82: 1–25.

Raz, Joseph. 1999. *Practical Reason and Norms*. 2nd ed. Oxford: Oxford University Press. [1st ed. 1975.]

Raz, Joseph. 2000. *Autorytet prawa* [The Authority of Law]. Trans. P. Maciejko. Warszawa: Dom Wydawniczy ABC.

Raz, Joseph. 2001. Two Views of the Nature of the Theory of Law: A Partial Comparison. In *Hart's Postscript. Essays on the Postscript to* The Concept of Law, ed. J.L. Coleman, 1–37. Oxford/New York: Oxford University Press.

Raz, Joseph. 2004. Incorporation by Law. *Legal Theory* 10: 1–17.

Raz, Joseph. 2007. The Argument from Justice, or How Not to Reply to Legal Positivism. In *Rights and Discourse. The Legal Philosophy of Robert Alexy*, ed. G. Pavlakos, 17–35. Oxford/ Portland: Hart.

Renzikowski, Joachim. 1995. Naturrechtslehre versus Rechtspositivismus – ein Streit um Worte? *Archiv für Rechts- und Sozialphilosophie* 81: 335–346.

Richards, David A. 1989. Book review: *A Theory of Legal Argumentation. The Theory of Rational Discourse as Theory of Legal Justification* by Robert Alexy. *Ratio Juris* 2: 304–317.

Rojek, Anna. 2006. Kilka uwag o obowiązywaniu prawa [Some Remarks on the Validity of Law]. In *Prawo – władza – społeczeństwo – polityka. Księga jubileuszowa profesora Krzysztofa Pałeckiego*, ed. M. Borucka-Arctowa, T. Biernat, J. Czapska, H. Opałek, A. Rojek, and M. Stępień, 147–157. Toruń: Wydawnictwo Adam Marszałek.

Ross, Alf. 1957. Tû-Tû. *Harvard Law Review* 70: 812–825.

Ross, Alf. 1958. *On Law and Justice*. Trans. M. Dutton. London: Stevens & Sons. [1st Danish ed. *Om Ret og Retfærdidighed*, København: Busck, 1953.]
Ross, Alf. 1961. Validity and the Conflict between Legal Positivism and Natural Law. *Revista Jurídica de Buenos Aires* IV: 46–88.
Ross, Alf. 1968. *Directives and Norms*. London: Routledge & Kegan Paul/New York: Humanities Press.
Ross, W. David. 1930. *The Right and the Good*. Oxford: Oxford University Press.
Ross, W. David. 1939. *Foundations of Ethics*. Oxford: Clarendon Press.
Rot, Henryk. 1994. W sprawie koncepcji prawa i praworządności [On the Conception of Law and the Rule of Law]. *Państwo i Prawo* 7–8/581–582: 109–111.
Rot, Henryk, Włodzimierz Gromski. 1995. Prawo stanowione [Enacted Law]. In *Główne kultury prawne współczesnego świata*, (teamwork ed.), 32–86. Warszawa: Wydawnictwo Naukowe PWN.
Ruiter, D.W.P. 1997. Legal Validity Qua Specific Mode of Existence. *Law and Philosophy* 16: 479–505.
Ruiter, D.W.P. 1986. Eine rechtstheoretisch fundierte Typologie gesetzlicher Rechtsnormen. *Rechtstheorie* 17: 478–500.
Ruiz Manero, Juan. 1991. Normas independientes, criterios conceptuales y trucos verbales. Respuesta a Eugenio Bulygin. *DOXA* 9: 281–293.
Russell, J.S. 2000. Trial by Slogan: Natural Law and Lex Iniusta Non Est Lex. *Law and Philosophy* 19: 433–449.
Rüßmann, Helmut. 1979. Book review: *Theorie der juristischen Argumentation* by Robert Alexy. *Rechtstheorie* 10: 110–120.
Rüthers, Bernd. 1999. *Rechtstheorie. Begriff, Geltung und Anwendung des Rechts*. München: Beck.
Safjan, Marek. 2003. Skutki prawne orzeczeń Trybunału Konstytucyjnego [Legal Effects of the Rulings of Constitutional Tribunal]. *Państwo i Prawo* 3/685: 3–18.
Salas, Minor E. 2001. ¿Qué pasa actualmente en la Teoría del Derecho alemana? Un breve bosquejo general. *DOXA* 24: 203–234.
Saliger, Frank. 1995. *Radbruchsche Formel und Rechtsstaat*. Heidelberg: Müller.
Sánchez Fernández, Luis Manuel. 2002. Ironías, falacias, perversiones, enigmas: sobre el positivismo y la tesis de la separación. *DOXA* 25: 333–367.
Sarkowicz, Ryszard. 1995. *Poziomowa interpretacja tekstu prawnego* [Levels of the Interpretation of Legal Text]. Kraków: Nakładem Uniwersytetu Jagiellońskiego.
Sarkowicz, Ryszard. 2005. Uwagi o współczesnej interpretacji prawniczej [Comments on the Modern Legal Interpretation]. In *Polska kultura prawna a proces integracji europejskiej*, ed. S. Wronkowska, 11–30. Kraków: Zakamycze.
Sarkowicz, Ryszard, Jerzy Stelmach. 1996. *Teoria prawa* [Theory of Law]. Kraków: Wydawnictwo Uniwersytetu Jagiellońskiego.
Sartor, Giovanni. 2000. Legal Validity as Doxastic Obligation: From Definition to Normativity. *Law and Philosophy* 19: 585–625.
Sartor, Giovanni. 2005. *Legal Reasoning. A Cognitive Approach to the Law*. In *A Treatise of Legal Philosophy and General Jurisprudence*, ed. E. Pattaro, Vol. 5. Dordrecht: Springer.
Sartorius, Rolf. 1966. The Concept of Law. *Archiv für Rechts- und Sozialphilosophie* 52: 161–193.
Schauer, Frederick. 1991. *Playing by the Rules. A Philosophical Examination of Rule-Based Decision-Making in Law and in Life*. Oxford: Clarendon Press.
Schauer, Frederick. 1996. Positivism as Pariah. In *The Autonomy of Law. Essays on Legal Positivism*, ed. R.P. George, 31–55. Oxford: Clarendon Press.
Searle, John R. 1965. What is a Speech Act? In *Philosophy in America*, ed. M. Black, 221–239. London: George Allen & Unwin.
Searle, John R. 1969. *Speech Acts. An Essay in the Philosophy of Language*. London: Cambridge University Press.

Searle, John R. 1975. A Taxonomy of Illocutionary Acts. In *Language, Mind, and Knowledge*, ed. K. Gunderson. Minnesota Studies in the Philosophy of Science VII: 344–369.

Searle, John R. 1978. *Prima Facie* Obligations. In *Practical Reasoning*, ed. J. Raz, 81–90. Oxford: Oxford University Press.

Searle, John R. 1989. How Performatives Work. *Linguistics and Philosophy* 12: 535–558.

Searle, John R., Daniel Vanderveken. 1985. *Foundations of Illocutionary Logic*. Cambridge/London/New York/New Rochelle/Melbourne/Sydney: Cambridge University Press.

Seidel, Knut. 1999. *Rechtsphilosophische Aspekte der "Mauerschützen"-Prozesse*. Berlin: Duncker & Humblot.

Shapiro, Scott J. 2001. On Hart's Way Out. In *Hart's Postscript. Essays on the Postscript to* The Concept of Law, ed. J.L. Coleman, 149–191. Oxford/New York: Oxford University Press.

Sieckmann, Jan-Reinard. 1990. *Regelmodelle und Prinzipienmodelle des Rechtssystems*. Baden-Baden: Nomos.

Sieckmann, Jan-Reinard. 1992. Legal System and Practical Reason. On the Structure of a Normative Theory of Law. *Ratio Juris* 5: 288–307. German version: Rechtssystem und praktische Vernunft. Zur Struktur einer normativen Theorie des Rechts. *Archiv für Rechts- und Sozialphilosophie* 78 (1992): 145–165.

Sieckmann, Jan-Reinard. 1997. Basic Rights in the Model of Principles, *Archiv für Rechts- und Sozialphilosophie*, Beiheft 67: 30–36.

Sieckmann, Jan-Reinard. 2001. Die "Radbruch'sche Formel" und die Mauerschützen. *Archiv für Rechts- und Sozialphilosophie* 87: 496–515.

Sieckmann, Jan-Reinard. 2007. Human Rights and the Claim to Correctness in the Theory of Robert Alexy. In *Rights and Discourse. The Legal Philosophy of Robert Alexy*, ed. G. Pavlakos, 189–205. Oxford/Portland: Hart.

Simmonds, Nigel E. 1984. The Nature of Propositions of Law. *Rechtstheorie* 15: 96–108.

Skąpska, Grażyna, Jerzy Stelmach. 1988–1989. Stare i nowe interpretacje filozofii prawa Arthura Kaufmanna [Old and New Interpretations of Arthur Kaufmann's Philosophy of Law]. *Colloquia Communia* 6/41–1/42: 75–81.

Smith, M. B. E. 1973. Is There a Prima Facie Obligation to Obey the Law? *The Yale Law Journal* 82: 950–976.

Smolak, Marek. 2003. *Uzasadnianie sądowe jako argumentacja z moralności politycznej* [Judicial Justification as the Argumentation from Political Morality]. Kraków: Zakamycze.

Snare, Frank. 1974. The Definition of *Prima Facie* Duties. *The Philosophical Quarterly* 24: 235–244.

Soper, E. Philip. 1977. Legal Theory and the Obligation of a Judge: The Hart/Dworkin Dispute. *Michigan Law Review* 75: 473–519.

Soper, E. Philip. 1996. Law's Normative Claims. In *The Autonomy of Law. Essays on Legal Positivism*, ed. R.P. George, 215–247. Oxford: Clarendon Press.

Stavropoulos, Nicos. 2001. In *Hart's Postscript. Essays on the Postscript to* The Concept of Law, ed. J.L. Coleman, 59–98. Oxford/New York: Oxford University Press.

Stawecki, Tomasz, Piotr Winczorek. 1999. *Wstęp do prawoznawstwa* [Introduction to Jurisprudence]. 2nd ed. Warszawa: C. H. Beck. [1st ed. 1995.]

Stelmach, Jerzy. 1994. Zum Begriff Rechtsbegründung. *Rechtstheorie* 25: 537–545. [1st Polish ed. 1993.]

Stelmach, Jerzy. 1995. *Współczesna filozofia interpretacji prawniczej* [Contemporary Philosophy of Legal Interpretation]. Kraków: Wydawnictwo Uniwersytetu Jagiellońskiego.

Stelmach, Jerzy. 1998. Obowiązywanie prawa w sensie absolutnym i relatywnym [Validity of Law in Absolute and Relative Sense]. In *Teoria prawa. Filozofia prawa. Współczesne prawo i prawoznawstwo*, (teamwork ed.), 315–327. Toruń: Uniwersytet Mikołaja Kopernika.

Stelmach, Jerzy. 2001. Intuicja prawnicza [Legal Intuition]. In *Dziedzictwo prawne XX wieku. Księga pamiątkowa z okazji 150-lecia Towarzystwa Biblioteki Słuchaczów Prawa Uniwersytetu Jagiellońskiego*, ed. J. Halberda, 31–40. Kraków: Zakamycze.

Stelmach, Jerzy. 2001. Norma podstawowa [Basic Norm]. *Studia z filozofii prawa* 1: 63–70.

Stelmach, Jerzy. 2003. *Kodeks argumentacyjny dla prawników* [An Argumentative Code for Lawyers]. Kraków: Zakamycze.

Stelmach, Jerzy. 2006. Epistemologiczna perspektywa ponowoczesnej filozofii prawa [Epistemological Perspective of the Postmodern Philosophy of Law]. In *Prawo – władza – społeczeństwo – polityka. Księga jubileuszowa profesora Krzysztofa Pałeckiego*, ed. M. Borucka-Arctowa, T. Biernat, J. Czapska, H. Opałek, A. Rojek, and M. Stępień, 43–52. Toruń: Wydawnictwo Adam Marszałek.

Stelmach, Jerzy, Bartosz Brożek. 2006. *Methods of Legal Reasoning*. Dordrecht: Springer.

Stevenson, Charlie Leslie. 1938. Persuasive Definitions. *Mind* 47: 331–350.

Stolleis, Michael. 1994. *Recht im Unrecht. Studien zur Rechtsgeschichte des Nationalsozialismus*. Frankfurt am Main: Suhrkamp.

Strawson, Peter F. 1992. *Analysis and Metaphysics. An Introduction to Philosophy*. Oxford: Oxford University Press.

Stroll, Avrum. 2000. *Twentieth-Century Analytic Philosophy*. New York: Columbia University Press.

Studnicki, Franciszek. 1962. Znajomość i nieznajomość prawa [Knowledge and Ignorance of Law]. *Państwo i Prawo* 4/194: 577–597.

Studnicki, Franciszek. 1967. Obecna rola zasady "nie można zasłaniać się nieznajomością prawa [Current Role of the Principle "One Cannot Plead the Ignorance of the Law"]. *Studia Cywilistyczne* X: 3–42.

Sugarman, David. 2005. Hart Interviewed: H.L.A. Hart in Conversation with David Sugarman. *Journal of Law and Society* 32/2: 267–293.

Summers, Robert S. 1984. *Lon L. Fuller*. London: Edward Arnold.

Summers, Robert S. 1985. Toward a Better General Theory of Legal Validity. *Rechtstheorie* 16: 65–83.

Summers, Robert S. 1992. Positivism, Natural Law and the Theory of Legal Validity. In idem, *Essays on the Nature of Law and Legal Reasoning*, 49–54. Berlin: Duncker & Humblot.

Szymczak, Mieczysław (ed.). 1992. *Słownik języka polskiego* [Polish Language Dictionary], Vol. II. 7th ed. Warszawa: Wydawnictwo Naukowe PWN. [1st ed. 1978.]

Szymura, Jerzy. 1982. *Język, mowa i prawda w perspektywie fenomenologii lingwistycznej J.L. Austina* [Language, Speech and Truth in the View of J.L. Austin's Linguistic Phenomenology]. Wrocław/Warszawa/Kraków/Gdańsk/Łódź: Zakład Narodowy im. Ossolińskich – Wydawnictwo Polskiej Akademii Nauk.

Świrydowicz, Kazimierz. 1981. *Analiza logiczna pojęcia kompetencji normodawczej* [Logical Analysis of the Concept of Norm-giving Competence]. Warszawa/Poznań: Państwowe Wydawnictwo Naukowe.

Świrydowicz, Kazimierz, Sławomira Wronkowska, Maciej Zieliński, Zygmunt Ziembiński. 1975. O nieporozumieniach dotyczących tzw. "norm zezwalających" [On Misunderstandings Concerning the So-called Permitting Norms]. *Państwo i Prawo* 7/353: 57–64.

Tacitus, Publius Cornelius. *Historiarum* II. http://www.sacred-texts.com/cla/tac/h02090.htm. Accessed 15 December 2007.

Tatarkiewicz, Władysław. 1983. *Historia filozofii* [History of Philosophy], vol. II: *Filozofia nowożytna do roku 1830* [Modern Philosophy to 1830], 10th ed. Warszawa: Państwowe Wydawnictwo Naukowe. [1st ed. 1931.]

Thienel, Rudolf. 1988. Derogation. Eine Untersuchung auf Grundlage der Reinen Rechtslehre. In *Schriftenreihe des Hans Kelsen-Institut* 12, ed. R. Walter, 11–43.

Thienel, Rudolf. 1991. Der zeitliche Geltungsbereich von Normen im Lichte der Legistik. In *Staatsrecht in Theorie und Praxis. Festschrift für Robert Walter zum 60. Geburtstag*, ed. H. Mayer, 709–726. Wien: Manzsche Verlags- und Univesitätsbuchhandlung.

Tkacz, Sławomir. 2003. *Rozumienie sprawiedliwości w orzecznictwie Trybunału Konstytucyjnego* [Understanding Justice in the Jurisdiction of the Constitutional Tribunal]. Prace Naukowe Uniwersytetu Śląskiego w Katowicach 2177.

Tobor, Zygmunt. 1998. *Teoretyczne problemy legalności* [Theoretical Problems of Legality]. Prace Naukowe Uniwersytetu Śląskiego w Katowicach 1721 (1998).

Tobor, Zygmunt, Tomasz Pietrzykowski. 2003. Roszczenie do bezstronności [The Claim to Impartiality]. In *Filozofia prawa wobec globalizmu*, ed. J. Stelmach, 57–73.

Toulmin, Stephen E. 1958. *The Uses of Argument*. Cambridge: Cambridge University Press.

Trzciński, Janusz. 2002. Orzeczenia interpretacyjne Trybunału Konstytucyjnego [Interpretive Rulings of the Constitutional Tribunal]. *Państwo i Prawo* 1/671: 3–14.

Tschentscher, Axel. 2000. *Prozedurale Theorien der Gerechtigkeit. Rationales Entscheiden, Diskursethik und prozedurales Recht*. Baden-Baden: Nomos.

Tschentscher, Axel. 2002. Der Konsensbegriff in Vertrags- und Diskurstheorien. *Rechtstheorie* 33: 43–59.

Tugendhat, Ernst. 1980. Zur Entwicklung von moralischen Begründungsstrukturen in modernem Recht. *Archiv für Rechts- und Sozialphilosophie*, Beiheft 14: 1–20.

Tugendhat, Ernst. 1993. Die Diskursethik. In *idem*, *Vorlesungen über Ethik*, 161–176. Frankfurt am Main: Suhrkamp.

Tuleja, Piotr. 2003. *Stosowanie Konstytucji RP w świetle zasady jej nadrzędności (wybrane problemy)* [The Application of the Polish Constitution in the Light of the Principle of Its Superiority (Selected Problems)]. Kraków: Zakamycze.

Tuori, Kaarlo. 1989. Discourse Ethics and the Legitimacy of Law. *Ratio Juris* 2: 125–143.

Twardowski, Kazimierz. 1911. *O czynnościach i wytworach* [On Acts and Results]. Kraków: Skład Główny w Księgarni Gubrynowicza i Syna we Lwowie.

Twardowski, Kazimierz. 1965. Z logiki przymiotników [From the Logic of Adjectives]. In *idem*, *Wybrane pisma filozoficzne*, 373–375. Warszawa: Państwowe Wydawnictwo Naukowe.

Uchwała Sądu Najwyższego – Izba Cywilna z dnia 30 maja 2003 r. [Resolution of the Supreme Court – Civil Chamber, from 30 May 2003] Sign. III CZP 29/2003. *Orzecznictwo Sadu Najwyższego – Izba Cywilna* [Records of the Supreme Court Rulings, the Civil Chamber] 2004, No. 4, Item 50.

Uchwała Sądu Najwyższego – Izba Karna z dnia 20 grudnia 2007 r. [Resolution of the Supreme Court – Penal Chamber, from 20 December 2007]. Sign. I KZP 37/2007. *Orzecznictwo Sadu Najwyższego – Izba Karna i Wojskowa* [Records of the Supreme Court Rulings, the Penal and Military Chamber] 2007, No. 12, Item 86.

Ullmann-Margalit, Edna. 1983. On Presumption. *Journal of Philosophy* LXXX/3: 143–163.

Urbina, Sebastián. 1994. Which Positivism? *Archiv für Rechts- und Sozialphilosophie* 80: 301–317.

Ustawa konstytucyjna z dnia 23 kwietnia 1992 r. o trybie przygotowania i uchwalenia Konstytucji Rzeczypospolitej Polskiej [Constitutional Statute of 23 April 1992 on the mode of preparation and adoption of the Constitution of the Republic of Poland]. *Dziennik Ustaw* [Journal of Statutes] 1992, No. 67, Item 336.

Ustawa z dnia 1 sierpnia 1997 r. o Trybunale Konstytucyjnym [Statute of 1 August 1997 on the Constitutional Tribunal]. *Dziennik Ustaw* [Journal of Statutes] 1997, No. 102, Item 643, with amendments.

Ustawa z dnia 22 grudnia 2000 r. o zmianie ustawy o negocjacyjnym systemie kształtowania przyrostu przeciętnych wynagrodzeń u przedsiębiorców oraz o zmianie niektórych ustaw i ustawy o zakładach opieki zdrowotnej [Statute of 22 December 2000 amending the statute on the negotiating system of regulating the increase of average wages in enterprises and on amending certain statutes and the statute on health care facilities]. *Dziennik Ustaw* [Journal of Statutes] 2001, No. 5, Item 45.

Ustawa z dnia 7 czerwca 2001 r. o leśnym materiale rozmnożeniowym [Statute of 7 June 2001 on forest reproductive material]. *Dziennik Ustaw* [Journal of Statutes] 2001, No. 73, Item 761, with amendments.

Ustawa z dnia 21 kwietnia 2005 r. o utworzeniu Uniwersytetu Kazimierza Wielkiego w Bydgoszczy [Statute of 21 April 2005 on the formation of Kazimierz Wielki University in Bydgoszcz]. *Dziennik Ustaw* [Journal of Statutes] 2005, No. 90, Item 755.

Van Hoecke, Mark, François Ost. 1993. Epistemological Perspectives in Legal Theory. *Ratio Juris* 6: 33–47.
Vanderveken, Daniel. 1980. Illocutionary Logic and Self-defeating Speech Acts. In *Speech Act Theory and Pragmatics*, ed. J.R. Searle, 247–272. Dordrecht/Boston/London: D. Reidel.
Vernengo, Roberto J. 1986. Kelsen's *Rechtssätze* as Detached Statements. In *Essays on Kelsen*, ed. R. Tur, W. Twining, 99–108. Oxford: Clarendon Press.
Viehweg, Theodor. 1974. *Topik und Jurisprudenz. Ein Beitrag zur rechtswissenschaftlichen Grundlagenforschung*. 5th ed. München: Beck. [1st ed. 1953.]. English version: *Topics and Law. A Contribution to Basic Research in Law*. Trans. W. Cole Durham Jr. Frankfurt am Main/ Berlin/Bern/New York/Paris/Wien: Peter Lang, 1993.
Vigo, Rodolfo. 2003. Balance de la teoría jurídica discursiva de Robert Alexy. *DOXA* 26: 203–224.
Villa, Vittorio. 1997. A Definition of Legal Positivism. *Archiv für Rechts- und Sozialphilosophie*, Beiheft 70: 22–29.
Villa, Vittorio. 1997. Legal Theory and Value Judgments. *Law and Philosophy* 16: 447–477.
Villa, Vittorio. 1999. Constructivismo y teoría del Derecho. Trans. J. Aguiló Regla. *DOXA* 22: 285–302.
Waldron, Jeremy. 2001. Normative (or Ethical) Positivism. In *Hart's Postscript. Essays on the Postscript to* The Concept of Law, ed. J.L. Coleman, 411–433. Oxford/New York: Oxford University Press.
Walter, Robert. 1980. Die Lehre vom Stufenbau der Rechtsordnung. *Archivum Iuridicum Cracoviense* XIII: 5–16.
Walter, Robert. 1988. Normy prawne [Legal Norms]. Trans. K. Opałek. *Krakowskie Studia Prawnicze* XXI: 97–108.
Walter, Robert. 1991. Adolf Merkl jako teoretyk prawa [Adolf Merkl as Law Theoretician]. Trans. K. Opałek. *Państwo i Prawo* 2/540: 26–34.
Walter, Robert. 1993. Die Grundnorm im System der Reinen Rechtslehre. In *Rechtsnorm und Rechtswirklichkeit. Festschrift für Werner Krawietz zum 60. Geburtstag*, ed. A. Aarnio, St.L. Paulson, O. Weinberger, G.H. von Wright, and D. Wyduckel, 85–99. Berlin: Duncker & Humblot.
Walther, Manfred. 1989. Hat der juristische Positivismus die deutschen Juristen im "Dritten Reich" wehrlos gemacht? Zur Analyse und Kritik der Radbruch-These. In *Recht und Justiz im "Dritten Reich"*, ed. R. Dreier, W. Sellert, 323–354. Frankfurt am Main: Suhrkamp.
Waluchow, Wilfrid J. 2000. Authority and the Practical Difference Thesis: A Defense of Inclusive Legal Positivism. *Legal Theory* 6: 45–81.
Waśkiewicz, Hanna. 1962. "Drugie Odrodzenie" prawa naturalnego ["Second Revival" of Natural Law]. *Roczniki Filozoficzne KUL, Etyka* X/2: 115–151.
Wassermann, Rudolf. 1992. Zur Anwendung der sogenannten Radbruchschen Formel auf Unrechtsurteile der DDR-Justiz. *Neue Juristische Wochenschrift* 45: 878–879.
Weinberg, Julius R. 1962. *Cogito, Ergo Sum*: Some Reflections on Mr. Hintikka's Article. *The Philosophical Review* LXXI: 483–491.
Weinberger, Ota. 1983. Die Naturrechtskonzeption von Ronald Dworkin. In *Das Naturrechtsdenken heute und morgen. Gedächtnisschrift für René Marcic*, ed. D. Mayer-Maly, P.M. Simons, 497–515. Berlin: Duncker & Humblot.
Weinberger, Ota. 1983. Logische Analyse als Basis der juristischen Argumentation. In *Metatheorie juristischer Argumentation*, ed. W. Krawietz, R. Alexy, 159–232. Berlin: Duncker & Humblot.
Weinberger, Ota. 1985. Ontologie, Hermeneutik und der Begriff des geltenden Rechts. *Archiv für Rechts- und Sozialphilosophie*, Beiheft 27: 109–126.
Weinberger, Ota. 1985. The Expressive Conception of Norms – An Impasse for the Logic of Norms. *Law and Philosophy* 4: 165–198.

Weinberger, Ota. 1985. Wartość, wartościowanie i doświadczanie wartości w argumentacji prawniczej [Value, Evaluating and Experiencing Values in Legal Argumentation]. Trans. T. Gliwiński. *Studia Prawnicze* 3–4/85–86: 264–286.

Weinberger, Ota. 1986. Beyond Positivism and Natural Law. In N. MacCormick, O. Weinberger, *An Institutional Theory of Law. New Approaches to Legal Positivism*, 111–126. Dordrecht/Boston/Lancaster/Tokyo: D. Reidel.

Weinberger, Ota. 1988. *Norm und Institution. Eine Einführung in die Theorie des Rechts*. Wien: Manzsche Verlags- und Universitätsbuchhandlung.

Weinberger, Ota. 1992. Conflicting Views on Practical Reason. Against Pseudo-Arguments in Practical Philosophy. *Ratio Juris* 5: 252–268.

Weinberger, Ota. 1994. Grundlagenprobleme des Institutionalistischen Rechtspositivismus und der Gerechtigkeitstheorie. *Rechtstheorie*, Beiheft 14: 173–284.

Weinberger, Ota. 1996. Basic Puzzles of Discourse Philosophy. *Ratio Juris* 9: 172–181.

Weinberger, Ota. 1999. *Prima Facie* Ought. A Logical and Methodological Enquiry. *Ratio Juris* 12: 239–251.

Weinberger, Ota. 2000. Aus intellektuellem Gewissen. Ein Rückblick auf mein wissenschaftliches Leben. In *idem*, *Aus intellektuellem Gewissen. Aufsätze von Ota Weinberger über Grundlagenprobleme der Rechtswissenschaft und Demokratietheorie*, ed. M. Fischer, P. Koller, and W. Krawietz, 11–35. Berlin: Duncker & Humblot.

Weinberger, Ota. 2000. Wertediskurs in Moral, Recht und Politik. In *The Reasonable as Rational? On Legal Argumentation and Justification.* Festschrift *for Aulis Aarnio*, ed. W. Krawietz, R.S. Summers, O. Weinberger, and G.H. von Wright, 347–364. Berlin: Duncker & Humblot.

Weinkauff, Hermann. 1962. Der Naturrechtsgedanke in der Rechtsprechung des Bundesgerichtshofes. In *Naturrecht oder Rechtspositivismus?*, ed. W. Maihofer, 554–576. Darmstadt: Wissenschaftlische Buchgesellschaft.

Wendland, Uwe. 1999. *Geschichte der Geltungstheorien des Rechts seit Kant unter besonderer Berücksichtigung der Anerkennungstheorien*. Berlin: Pro Businnes.

Wesche, Steffen. 1999. Robert Alexys diskurstheoretische Menschenrechtsbegründung. *Rechtstheorie* 30: 79–93.

Wierczyński, Grzegorz. 2007. "Obowiązywanie" a "wejście w życie" – uwagi polemiczne ["Validity" and "Entry into Force" – Polemical Remarks]. *Państwo i Prawo* 2/732: 108–112.

Wilczyńska, Aleksandra. 2007. Wokół definicji cywilnego nieposłuszeństwa [Around the Definition of Civil Disobedience]. In *W kręgu teorii prawa i zagadnień prawa europejskiego*, ed. T. Pietrzykowski, 133–148. Sosnowiec: Oficyna Wydawnicza „Humanitas".

Winkler, Günther. 1995. *Zeit und Recht. Kritische Anmerkungen zur Zeitgebundenheit des Rechts und des Rechtsdenkens*. Wien/New York: Springer.

Wintgens, Luc J. 1999. Legisprudence: Elements for a New Theory of Legislation. *Associations* 3: 185–209.

Wintgens, Luc J. 2007. The Relation of Law and Economics: Perspectives from Legal Theory. *Studies in the Philosophy of Law* 3: 37–50.

Wittgenstein, Ludwig. 1953. *Philosophische Untersuchungen/Philosophical Investigations*. Trans. G.E.M. Anscombe. Oxford: Basil Blackwell.

Wittgenstein, Ludwig. 1979. *Über Gewissheit/On Certainty*, ed. G.E.M. Anscombe, G.H. von Wright. Trans. D. Paul, G.E.M. Anscombe. Oxford: Basil Blackwell. [1st ed. 1969.]

Wojciechowski, Bartosz. 2001. Uzasadnienie praw człowieka w koncepcji dyskursu prawniczego [Justification of Human Rights in the Conception of Legal Discourse]. *Studia Prawno-Ekonomiczne* LXIII: 9–25.

Wojciechowski, Bartosz. 2003. Dyskursywny model sądowego stosowania prawa – wybrane aspekty [Discursive Model of Judicial Application of Law – Selected Aspects]. In *Filozofia prawa wobec globalizmu*, ed. J. Stelmach, 151–166. Kraków: Wydawnictwo Uniwersytetu Jagiellońskiego.

Wojciechowski, Bartosz. 2004. *Dyskrecjonalność sędziowska. Studium teoretycznoprawne* [Judicial Discretion. A Jurisprudential Study]. Toruń: Wydawnictwo Adam Marszałek.

Wojtyczek, Krzysztof. 2004. Ciężar dowodu i argumentacji w procedurze kontroli norm przez Trybunał Konstytucyjny [The Burden of Proof and of Argumentation in the Procedure of Reviewing Norms by the Constitutional Tribunal]. *Przegląd Sejmowy* 1/60: 9–27.
Woleński, Jan. 1967. Język prawny w świetle współczesnych metod analizy semantycznej [Legal Language in the Light of Modern Methods of Semantic Analysis]. *Zeszyty Naukowe Uniwersytetu Jagiellońskiego. Prace prawnicze* 31: 141–156.
Woleński, Jan. 1969. Metodologiczne dążenia Petrażyckiego a współczesna teoria nauki [Petrażycki's Methodological Aspirations and Contemporary Theory of Science]. In *Z zagadnień teorii prawa i teorii nauki Leona Petrażyckiego*, ed. K. Opałek, 161–172. Warszawa: Państwowe Wydawnictwo Naukowe.
Woleński, Jan. 1971. Obowiązywanie prawne w ujęciu H.L.A. Harta. [Validity of Law in H.L.A. Hart's Conception]. *Zeszyty Naukowe Uniwersytetu Jagiellońskiego. Prace prawnicze* 51: 277–289.
Woleński, Jan. 1976. Logika i normy [Logic and Norms]. *Studia Filozoficzne* 5/126: 45–56.
Woleński, Jan. 1980. *Z zagadnień analitycznej filozofii prawa* [Some Problems in Analytical Legal Philosophy]. Kraków: Wydawnictwo Uniwersytetu Jagiellońskiego.
Woleński, Jan. 1985. Semantyczne ujęcie dogmatyki prawa [A Semantic Approach to Legal Dogmatics]. *Studia Filozoficzne* 2–3/231–232: 83–92.
Woleński, Jan. 1985. Truth and Legal Validity. *Archiv für Rechts- und Sozialphilosophie*, Beiheft 25: 205–210.
Woleński, Jan. 1988. Uwagi o racjonalności decyzji prawnych [Notes on the Rationality of Legal Decisions]. In *Problemy metodologii i filozofii prawa*, ed. H. Rot, 179–190. Wrocław: Wydawnictwo Uniwersytetu Wrocławskiego.
Woleński, Jan. 1990. Możliwe światy teorii prawa [Possible Worlds of the Theory of Law]. In *Szkice z teorii prawa i szczegółowych nauk prawnych*, ed. S. Wronkowska, M. Zieliński, 15–29.
Woleński, Jan. 1992. Treść logiczna dwóch zasad prawnych [Logical Content of Two Legal Principles]. In *Prawo w zmieniającym się społeczeństwie. Księga Jubileuszowa Profesor Marii Boruckiej-Arctowej*, ed. G. Skąpska, J. Czapska, K. Daniel, J. Górski, and K. Pałecki, 143–148. Kraków: Wydawnictwo Adam Marszałek.
Woleński, Jan. 1998. O pozytywizmie prawniczym [On Legal Positivism]. In *Etyka a Prawo i Praworządność*, ed. J. Pawlica, 9–16. Kraków: Wydawnictwo Uniwersytetu Jagiellońskiego.
Woleński, Jan. 2003. *Epistemologia* [Epistemology], Vol. 3: *Prawda i realizm* [Truth and Realism]. Kraków: Aureus.
Wright, Georg Henrik, von. 1951. Deontic Logic. *Mind* 60: 1–15.
Wright, Georg Henrik, von. 1963. *Norm and Action. A Logical Enquiry*. London: Routledge & Kegan Paul.
Wright, Georg Henrik, von. 1985. Is and Ought. In *Man, Law and Modern Forms of Life*, ed. E. Bulygin, J.-L. Gardies, and I. Niiniluoto, 263–281. Dordrecht: D. Reidel.
Wright, Georg Henrik, von. 1996. Ought to be – Ought to do. In *idem*, *Six Essays in Philosophical Logic*, Acta Philosophica Fennica LX: 63–70.
Wright, Georg Henrik, von. 1999. Deontic Logic: A Personal View. *Ratio Juris* 12: 26–38.
Wright, Georg Henrik, von. 2000. On Norms and Norm-Propositions. A Sketch. In *The Reasonable as Rational? On Legal Argumentation and Justification.* Festschrift *for Aulis Aarnio*, ed. W. Krawietz, R.S. Summers, O. Weinberger, and G.H. von Wright, 173–178. Berlin: Duncker & Humblot.
Wright, Georg Henrik, von, Aulis Aarnio. 1990. On Law and Morality. A Dialogue. *Ratio Juris* 3: 321–330.
Wronkowska, Sławomira. 1973. *Analiza pojęcia prawa podmiotowego* [Analysis of the Concept of Subjective Right]. Poznań: Wydawnictwo Naukowe Uniwersytetu im. Adama Mickiewicza w Poznaniu.

Wronkowska, Sławomira. 1976. Postulat jasności prawa i niektóre metody jego realizacji [The Demand of the Clarity of Law and Some Methods of Its Implementation], *Państwo i Prawo* 10/368: 19–33.

Wronkowska, Sławomira. 2000. Glosa do wyroku Trybunału Konstytucyjnego z dnia 26 października 1999 r. (sygn. akt K 12/99) [A Gloss on the Constitutional Tribunal Ruling of 26 October 1999 (sign. K 12/99)]. *Przegląd Sejmowy* 3/38: 100–104.

Wronkowska, Sławomira. 2001. O wadliwych aktach normatywnych w ujęciu wiedeńskiej szkoły teorii prawa [On Defective Normative Acts in Terms of the Vienna School of Legal Theory]. *Studia z filozofii prawa* 1: 207–218.

Wronkowska, Sławomira. 2001. W sprawie bezpośredniego stosowania Konstytucji [On the Direct Application of the Constitution]. *Państwo i Prawo* 9/667: 3–23.

Wronkowska, Sławomira. 2005. O źródłach prawa i aktach normatywnych raz jeszcze [Once More on Sources of Law and Normative Acts]. In *Prawo prywatne czasu przemian. Księga pamiątkowa dedykowana Profesorowi Stanisławowi Sołtysińskiemu*, ed. A. Nowicka, M. Kępiński, A. Koch, Z. Radwański, A.J. Szwarc, and S. Wronkowska, 113–140. Poznań: Wydawnictwo Naukowe UAM.

Wronkowska, Sławomira. 2005. *Podstawowe pojęcia prawa i prawoznawstwa* [Basic Concepts of Law and Jurisprudence]. 3rd ed. Poznań: Ars boni et aequi, 2005. [1st ed. 2002.]

Wronkowska, Sławomira. 2008. Kilka uwag o "prawodawcy negatywnym" [Some Comments on the "Negative Legislator"], *Państwo i Prawo* 10/752: 5–20.

Wronkowska, Sławomira, Maciej Zieliński. 1993. *Problemy i zasady techniki redagowania tekstów prawnych* [The Problems and Principles of the Technique of Editing Legal Texts]. Warszawa: Urząd Rady Ministrów.

Wronkowska, Sławomira, Maciej Zieliński. 2004. *Komentarz do zasad techniki prawodawczej z dnia 20 czerwca 2002 r.* [Commentary to the Principles of Legislative Technique of 20 June 2002]. Warszawa: Wydawnictwo Sejmowe.

Wronkowska, Sławomira, Zygmunt Ziembiński. 1997. *Zarys teorii prawa* [An Outline of Legal Theory]. Poznań: Ars boni et aequi.

Wróbel, Andrzej. 2007. "Odroczenie" przez Trybunał Konstytucyjny utraty mocy obowiązującej przepisu niezgodnego z Konstytucją. Zagadnienia wybrane ["Postponing" of the Loss of Validity of Unconstitutional Provision by the Constitutional Tribunal. Selected Issues]. In *Ratio est anima legis. Księga jubileuszowa ku czci Profesora Janusza Trzcińskiego*, ed. J. Góral, R. Hauser, J. Repel, and M. Zirk-Sadowski, 105–126. Warszawa: Naczelny Sąd Administracyjny.

Wróbel, Włodzimierz. 1994. O niektórych problemach interpretacji pojęcia "obowiązujący akt normatywny" w orzeczeniach Trybunału Konstytucyjnego [On Some Problems with Interpreting the Concept "Valid Normative Act" in the Rulings of the Constitutional Tribunal]. In *Działalność orzecznicza Trybunału Konstytucyjnego. Referaty z konferencji zorganizowanej przez Trybunał Konstytucyjny w Popowie w dniach 25-26 stycznia 1994 r.*, ed. A. Jankiewicz, 49–58. Warszawa: Trybunał Konstytucyjny.

Wróbel, Włodzimierz. 2003. *Zmiana normatywna i zasady intertemporalne w prawie karnym* [Normative Change and the Intertemporal Principles of Penal Law]. Kraków: Zakamycze.

Wróblewski, Bronisław. 1948. *Język prawny i prawniczy* [Legal and Juristic Language]. Kraków: Nakładem Polskiej Akademii Umiejętności.

Wróblewski, Jerzy. 1955. *Krytyka normatywistycznej teorii prawa i państwa Hansa Kelsena* [Critique of Hans Kelsen's Normativist Theory of Law and State]. Warszawa: Państwowe Wydawnictwo Naukowe.

Wróblewski, Jerzy. 1959. *Zagadnienia teorii wykładni prawa ludowego* [Issues on the Theory of Interpretation of People's Law]. Warszawa: Wydawnictwo Prawnicze.

Wróblewski, Jerzy. 1961. 'Oceny i normy moralne w wykładni prawa' [Moral Evaluations and Norms in Law Interpretation]. *Zeszyty Naukowe Uniwersytetu Łódzkiego. Nauki Humanistyczno-Społeczne* I/22: 3–18.

Wróblewski, Jerzy. 1969. Modele systemów norm a system prawa [Models of Normative Systems and Legal System]. *Studia Prawno-Ekonomiczne* II: 23–48.

Wróblewski, Jerzy. 1971. Legal Decision and Its Justification. *Logique et Analyse* 53–54: 409–419.

Wróblewski, Jerzy. 1973. Domniemania w prawie – problematyka teoretyczna [Presumptions in Law – Theoretical Issues]. *Studia Prawno-Ekonomiczne* X: 7–36.

Wróblewski, Jerzy. 1973. Metody logiczno-językowe w prawoznawstwie [Logico-Linguistic Methods in Jurisprudence]. In *Metody badania prawa*, ed. A. Łopatka, 47–75. Wrocław: Zakład Narodowy im. Ossolińskich – Wydawnictwo.

Wróblewski, Jerzy. 1974. Legal Syllogism and Rationality of Judicial Decision. *Rechtstheorie* 5: 33–46.

Wróblewski, Jerzy. 1975. *Votum separatum* w teorii i ideologii sądowego stosowania prawa [*Votum Separatum* in the Theory and Ideology of the Judicial Application of Law]. *Studia Prawno-Ekonomiczne* XV: 7–30.

Wróblewski, Jerzy. 1976. Uzasadnienie i wyjaśnienie decyzji sądowej [Justifying and Explaining Judicial Decisions]. *Studia Prawno-Ekonomiczne* XVI: 7–30.

Wróblewski, Jerzy. 1982. Byt i powinność a błąd naturalistyczny w normatywizmie [Is and Ought and the Naturalistic Fallacy in Normativism]. *Studia Prawno-Ekonomiczne* XXIX: 23–34.

Wróblewski, Jerzy. 1983. Nieostrość systemu prawa [Vagueness of the Legal System]. *Studia Prawno-Ekonomiczne* XXXI: 7–24. English version: Fuzziness of Legal System. In *Essays in Legal Theory in Honor of Kaarle Makkonen*, ed. U. Kangas, 311–330. Vammala: The Society of Finnish Lawyers, 1983.

Wróblewski, Jerzy. 1984. Dilemmas of the Normativistic Concept of Legal System. *Rechtstheorie*, Beiheft 5: 319–333.

Wróblewski, Jerzy. 1984. Zagadnienia terminologii nauk prawnych [The Problems of the Terminology of Legal Sciences]. *Nauka Polska* XXXII/3: 75–86.

Wróblewski, Jerzy. 1985. Legal Language and Legal Interpretation. *Law and Philosophy* 4: 239–255.

Wróblewski, Jerzy. 1985. Reguły prawne w analitycznej teorii prawa [Legal Rules in the Analytic Theory of Law]. *Studia Prawno-Ekonomiczne* XXXIV: 7–26.

Wróblewski, Jerzy. 1986. Logika a teoria argumentacji: teoretyczne zagadnienia poprawności decyzji sądowej [The Logic and the Theory of Argumentation: Theoretical Issues of the Correctness of Judicial Decision]. *Państwo i Prawo* 7–8/485–486: 3–20.

Wróblewski, Jerzy. 1986. Obowiązywanie systemowe i granice dogmatycznego podejścia do systemu prawa [Systemic Validity and the Limits of Dogmatic Approach to the System of Law]. *Studia Prawno-Ekonomiczne* XXXVI: 23–36.

Wróblewski, Jerzy. 1988. Poziomy uzasadnienia decyzji prawnej [The Levels of Justifying Legal Decisions]. *Studia Prawno-Ekonomiczne* XL: 17–33.

Wróblewski, Jerzy. 1988. Pragmatyczna jasność prawa [Pragmatic Clarity of Law]. *Państwo i Prawo* 4/506: 3–13.

Wróblewski, Jerzy. 1988. *Sądowe stosowanie prawa*. 2nd ed. Warszawa: Państwowe Wydawnictwo Naukowe. [1st ed. 1972.]. English version: *The Judicial Application of Law*. Trans. Z. Bańkowski, N. MacCormick. Dordrecht/Boston/London: Kluwer, 1992.

Wróblewski, Jerzy. 1989. Problems Related to the One Right Answer Thesis. *Ratio Juris* 2: 240–253.

Wróblewski, Jerzy. 1990. Paradygmat dogmatyki prawa a prawoznawstwo [A Paradigm of Legal Dogmatics and Jurisprudence]. In *Szkice z teorii prawa i szczegółowych nauk prawnych*, ed. S. Wronkowska, M. Zieliński, 31–45. Wydawnictwo Naukowe Uniwersytetu im. Adama Mickiewicza w Poznaniu.

Wróblewski, Jerzy. 1990. Semantics and Pragmatics of Normative Qualification Statements. *International Journal for the Semiotics of Law* III/7: 35–53.

Wyrok Trybunału Konstytucyjnego z dnia 20 grudnia 1999 r. [Ruling of the Constitutional Tribunal from 20 December 1999]. Sign. K 4/99. *Dziennik Ustaw* [Journal of Statutes] 1999, No. 106, Item 1215.

Zajadło, Jerzy. 1988–1989. "Trzecie odrodzenie" prawa natury? (Uwagi metodologiczne) ["Third Revival" of Natural Law? (Methodological Remarks)]. *Colloquia Communia* 6/41–1/42: 111–118.

Zajadło, Jerzy. 1988–1989. Gustaw Radbruch i antynomie współczesnej filozofii prawa [Gustav Radbruch and the Antinomies of Modern Philosophy of Law]. *Colloquia Communia* 6/41–1/42: 63–74.

Zajadło, Jerzy. 2000. Formuła Radbrucha – geneza, treść, zastosowanie [Radbruch's Formula – Genesis, Content and Application]. *Państwo i Prawo* 6/652: 25–42.

Zajadło, Jerzy. 2000. Formuła Radbrucha a paradygmat niepozytywistycznej teorii prawa [Radbruch's Formula and the Paradigm of Nonpositivist Legal Theory]. *Gdańskie Studia Prawnicze* VII: 683–697.

Zajadło, Jerzy. 2001. *Formuła Radbrucha* [Radbruch's Formula]. Gdańsk: Arche.

Zajadło, Jerzy. 2002. The Notion of 'Gesetz und Recht' in Contemporary German Legal Theory and Practice. Trans. T. Z. Wolański. *Ius et Lex* I/1: 35–50.

Zajadło, Jerzy. 2003. *Odpowiedzialność za mur. Procesy strzelców przy Murze Berlińskim* [Responsibility for the Wall. *Mauerschützenprozesse*]. Gdańsk: Arche.

Zajadło, Jerzy. 2007. *Dziedzictwo przeszłości* [Inheritance of the Past]. Gdańsk: Arche.

Zajadło, Jerzy. 2008. *Po co prawnikom filozofia prawa?* [What do Lawyers Need Legal Philosophy for?]. Warszawa: Wolters Kluwer Polska.

Zasady techniki prawodawczej. Załącznik do Rozporządzenia Prezesa Rady Ministrów z dnia 20 czerwca 2002 r. w sprawie „Zasad techniki prawodawczej" [Principles of Legislative Technique. Annex to the Regulation of the Prime Minister of 20 June 2002 on "Principles of Legislative Technique"]. *Dziennik Ustaw* [Journal of Statutes] 2002, No. 100, Item 908.

Zgółkowa, Halina (ed.). 2000. *Praktyczny słownik współczesnej polszczyzny* [Practical Dictionary of Modern Polish]. Vol. 25. Poznań: Wydawnictwo Kurpisz.

Zieliński, Maciej. 1972. *Interpretacja jako proces dekodowania tekstu prawnego* [Interpretation as the Process of Decoding Legal Text]. Poznań: Wydawnictwo Naukowe Uniwersytetu im. Adama Mickiewicza w Poznaniu.

Zieliński, Maciej. 1990. Aspekty zasady *clara non sunt interpretanda* [Aspects of the Principle *clara non sunt interpretanda*]. In *Szkice z teorii prawa i szczegółowych nauk prawnych*, ed. S. Wronkowska, M. Zieliński, 173–186. Wydawnictwo Naukowe Uniwersytetu im. Adama Mickiewicza w Poznaniu.

Zieliński, Maciej. 1995. Algorytm interpretacji przepisów prawnych [Algorithm of the Interpretation of Legal Provisions]. In *Eufonia i Logos. Księga pamiątkowa ofiarowana Profesor Marii Steffen-Batogowej oraz Profesorowi Tadeuszowi Batogowi*, ed. J. Pogonowski, 657–668. Poznań: Wydawnictwo Naukowe Uniwersytetu im. Adama Mickiewicza w Poznaniu.

Zieliński, Maciej. 1996. Współczesne problemy wykładni prawa [Contemporary Problems of Legal Interpretation]. *Państwo i Prawo* 8–9/606–607: 5–15.

Zieliński, Maciej. 1997. Dwa nurty pojmowania "kompetencji" [Two Trends of Understanding "Competence"]. In *Gospodarka. Administracja. Samorząd*, ed. H. Olszewski, B. Popowska, 581–607. Poznań: Printer.

Zieliński, Maciej. 1999. Języki prawne i prawnicze [Legal and Juristic Languages]. In *Polszczyzna 2000. Orędzie o stanie języka na przełomie tysiącleci*, ed. W. Pisarek, 50–74. Kraków: Ośrodek Badań Prasoznawczych Uniwersytetu Jagiellońskiego.

Zieliński, Maciej. 2002. *Wykładnia prawa. Zasady. Reguły. Wskazówki* [Legal Interpretation: Principles, Rules, Hints]. Warszawa: Wydawnictwo Prawnicze LexisNexis.

Zieliński, Maciej. 2004. Język prawny, język administracyjny, język urzędowy [Legal Language, Language of Administration, Official Language]. In *Język – Prawo – Społeczeństwo*, ed. E. Malinowska, 9–18. Opole: Wydawnictwo Uniwersytetu Opolskiego.

Zieliński, Maciej. 2005. Podstawowe zasady współczesnej wykładni prawa [The Fundamental Principles of Modern Interpretation of Law]. In *Teoria i praktyka wykładni prawa. Materiały konferencji naukowej Wydziału Prawa i Administracji Uniwersytetu Warszawskiego odbytej w dniu 27 lutego 2004 roku*, ed. P. Winczorek, 117–125. Warszawa: Liber.

Zieliński Maciej, Zygmunt Ziembiński. 1988. *Uzasadnianie twierdzeń, ocen i norm w prawoznawstwie* [Justifying Statements, Evaluations, and Norms in Jurisprudence]. Warszawa: Państwowe Wydawnictwo Naukowe.

Zieliński, Maciej, Zbigniew Radwański. 2006. Wykładnia prawa cywilnego [Interpretation of Civil Law]. *Studia Prawa Prywatnego* 1: 1–38.

Ziemba, Zdzisław. 1963. Zwrot "norma *N* obowiązuje" w języku prawnym i prawniczym [The Expression "norm *N* is valid" in Legal and Juristic Language]. *Studia Filozoficzne* 3–4/34–35: 93–115.

Ziemba, Zdzisław. 1983. *Analityczna teoria obowiązku. Studium z logiki deontycznej* [Analytic Theory of Duty. A Study of Deontic Logic]. Warszawa: Państwowe Wydawnictwo Naukowe.

Ziemba, Zdzisław. 1987. Logika deontyczna [Deontic Logic]. In *Logika formalna. Zarys encyklopedyczny z zastosowaniem do informatyki i lingwistyki*, ed. W. Marciszewski, 331–337. Warszawa: Państwowe Wydawnictwo Naukowe.

Ziembiński, Zygmunt. 1960. Przepis prawny a norma prawna [Legal Provision and Legal Norm]. *Ruch Prawniczy i Ekonomiczny* XXII/1: 105–122.

Ziembiński, Zygmunt. 1963. Normy tetyczne a normy aksjologiczne w koncepcji Cz. Znamierowskiego [Thetic Norms and Axiological Norms in Cz. Znamierowski's Conception]. *Studia Filozoficzne* 2/33: 87–112.

Ziembiński, Zygmunt. 1966. *Logiczne podstawy prawoznawstwa. Wybrane zagadnienia* [Logical Basis for Jurisprudence. Selected Issues]. Warszawa: Wydawnictwo Prawnicze.

Ziembiński, Zygmunt. 1967. Argumentacje moralne stosowane przez prawników [Moral Arguments Applied by Lawyers]. *Etyka* 2: 95–108.

Ziembiński, Zygmunt. 1969. Moralność jako czynnik kształtujący stosowanie prawa [Morality as a Factor That Shapes Law Application]. *Etyka* 5: 89–111.

Ziembiński, Zygmunt. 1973. *Teoria prawa* [Theory of Law]. Warszawa/Poznań: Państwowe Wydawnictwo Naukowe.

Ziembiński, Zygmunt. 1974. Le langage du droit et le langage juridique. Les critères de leur discernement. *Archives de Philosophie du Droit* XIX: 25–31.

Ziembiński, Zygmunt. 1974. *Metodologiczne zagadnienia prawoznawstwa* [Methodological Issues of Jurisprudence]. Warszawa: Państwowe Wydawnictwo Naukowe.

Ziembiński, Zygmunt. 1976. *Practical Logic*. Trans. L. Ter-Oganian. Warszawa: Państwowe Wydawnictwo Naukowe/Dordrecht: D. Reidel. [1st Polish ed. 1956.]

Ziembiński, Zygmunt. 1980. *Problemy podstawowe prawoznawstwa* [Basic Problems of Jurisprudence]. Warszawa: Państwowe Wydawnictwo Naukowe.

Ziembiński, Zygmunt. 1983. *Szkice z metodologii szczegółowych nauk prawnych* [Sketches on the Methodology of Particular Legal Sciences]. Warszawa/Poznań: Państwowe Wydawnictwo Naukowe.

Ziembiński, Zygmunt. 1985. Deskrypcjonistyczna i rekonstrukcjonistyczna analiza języka w prawoznawstwie [Descriptionistic and Reconstructionistic Analysis of Language in Jurisprudence]. *Studia Prawnicze* 3–4/85–86: 329–341.

Ziembiński, Zygmunt. 1985. O aparaturze pojęciowej dotyczącej sytuacji prawnych [On the Conceptual Apparatus Concerning Legal Situations]. *Państwo i Prawo* 3/469: 32–47.

Ziembiński, Zygmunt. 1985. Uwagi o negowaniu norm i wypowiedzi z normami związanych [Comments on Negating Norms and Utterances Related to Norms]. *Studia Filozoficzne* 2–3/231–232: 105–116.

Ziembiński, Zygmunt. 1988. W związku z artykułem K. Opałka "Dwoistość ujęcia normy w nauce prawa" [A Propos K. Opałek's Paper "The Duality of the Approach to Norm in Jurisprudence"]. *Państwo i Prawo* 12/514: 105–108.

Ziembiński, Zygmunt. 1990. *Wstęp do aksjologii dla prawników* [Introduction to Axiology for Lawyers]. Warszawa: Wydawnictwo Prawnicze.

Ziembiński, Zygmunt. 1991. "Lex" a "ius" w okresie przemian ["Lex" versus "Ius" in a Period of Transition]. *Państwo i Prawo* 6/544: 3–14.

Ziembiński, Zygmunt. 1993. "Akt normatywny" czy "akt prawotwórczy" ["Normative Act" or "Law-Creating Act"]. *Państwo i Prawo* 11–12/573–574: 96–98.

Ziembiński, Zygmunt. 1993. Prescriptive and/or Descriptive Language in Legal Sciences In *Sprache, Performanz und Ontologie de Rechts. Festgabe für Kazimierz Opałek zum 75. Geburtstag*, ed. W. Krawietz, J. Wróblewski, 85–92. Berlin: Duncker & Humblot.

Ziembiński, Zygmunt. 1994. Desuetudo. *Państwo i Prawo* 11/585: 3–8.

Ziembiński, Zygmunt. 1995. Definicje perswazyjne w prawoznawstwie [Persuasive Definitions in Jurisprudence]. In *Eufonia i Logos. Księga pamiątkowa ofiarowana Profesor Marii Steffen-Batogowej oraz Profesorowi Tadeuszowi Batogowi*, ed. J. Pogonowski, 673–680. Poznań: Wydawnictwo Naukowe Uniwersytetu im. Adama Mickiewicza w Poznaniu.

Ziembiński, Zygmunt. 1995. *O stanowieniu i obowiązywaniu prawa. Zagadnienia podstawowe* [On Enacting and the Validity of Law. Basic Problems]. Warszawa: Wydawnictwo Sejmowe, 1995.

Ziembiński, Zygmunt, Maciej Zieliński. 1992. *Dyrektywy i sposób ich wypowiadania* [Directives and the Method of Expressing Them]. Biblioteka Myśli Semiotycznej 17.

Zirk-Sadowski, Marek. 1979. Legal Norm as a Pragmatic Category. *Archiv für Rechts- und Sozialphilosophie* 65: 203–222.

Zirk-Sadowski, Marek. 1979. Problem nowości normatywnej [The Problem of Normative Novelty]. *Studia Prawno-Ekonomiczne* XXII: 47–62.

Zirk-Sadowski, Marek. 1980. Precedens a tzw. decyzja prawotwórcza [The Precedent and the so-called Law-Making Decision]. *Państwo i Prawo* 6/412: 69–78.

Zirk-Sadowski, Marek. 1980. Tak zwana prawotwórcza decyzja sądowego stosowania prawa [The so-called Lawmaking Decision of the Judicial Application of Law]. *Studia Prawnicze* 1–2/63–64: 243–267.

Zirk-Sadowski, Marek. 1981. Rola pragmatyki w badaniach języka prawnego [The Role of Pragmatics in the Researches on the Legal Language]. *Acta Universitatis Lodziensis – Folia Iuridica* 6: 41–57.

Zirk-Sadowski, Marek. 1984. *Rozumienie ocen w języku prawnym* [Understanding Evaluations in Legal Language]. Łódź: Zespół Wydawnictw „Folia Iuridica".

Zirk-Sadowski, Marek. 1992. Dyskurs jako mowa regulowana wymogami moralnymi [Discourse as Speech Regulated by Moral Constraints]. In *Prawo w zmieniającym się społeczeństwie. Księga Jubileuszowa Profesor Marii Boruckiej-Arctowej*, ed. G. Skąpska, J. Czapska, K. Daniel, J. Górski, and K. Pałecki, 185–195.

Zirk-Sadowski, Marek. 1992. Pojęcie dyskursu [The Concept of Discourse]. *Kultura i Społeczeństwo* XXXVI/2: 61–74.

Zirk-Sadowski, Marek. 1998. Language and Law. In *Rapports polonais. Présentés au Quinzième Congrès International de Droit Comparé, Bristol, 26 juillet – 1er août 1998*, ed. B. Lewaszkiewicz-Petrykowska, 7–20. Łódź: Wydawnictwo Uniwersytetu Łódzkiego.

Zirk-Sadowski, Marek. 2000. Rationality of Legal Discourse in Relation to Legal Ethics. In *The Reasonable as Rational? On Legal Argumentation and Justification.* Festschrift *for Aulis Aarnio*, ed. W. Krawietz, R.S. Summers, O. Weinberger, and G.H. von Wright, 607–617. Berlin: Duncker & Humblot.

Zirk-Sadowski, Marek. 2000. *Wprowadzenie do filozofii prawa* [Introduction to Legal Philosophy]. Kraków: Zakamycze.

Zirk-Sadowski, Marek. 2001. Pozytywizm prawniczy a filozoficzna opozycja podmiotu i przedmiotu poznania [Legal Positivism and Philosophical Opposition of the Subject and the Object of Cognition]. *Studia z filozofii prawa* 1: 83–95.

Zirk-Sadowski, Marek. 2004. Legal Culture and Epistemological Stressing. In *Stressing Legal Decisions*, ed. T. Biernat, K. Pałecki, A. Peczenik, Ch. Wong, and M. Zirk-Sadowski, 81–97. Kraków: Polpress.

Zirk-Sadowski, Marek. 2006. Transformation and Integration of Legal Cultures and Discourses – Poland. In *Spreading Democracy and the Rule of Law? The Impact of EU Enlargement on the Rule of Law, Democracy and Constitutionalism in Post-Communist Legal Orders*, ed. W. Sadurski, A. Czarnota, and M. Krygier, 299–311. Dordrecht: Springer.

Zirk-Sadowski, Marek. 2006. Wprowadzenie [Introduction]. In R. Dworkin, *Imperium prawa*, XI–XXVI. Warszawa: Wolters Kluwer Polska.

Zoll, Andrzej. 2002. Skuteczność orzeczeń polskiego Trybunału Konstytucyjnego [The Effectiveness of the Polish Constitutional Tribunal Rulings]. In *Ius et Lex. Księga jubileuszowa ku czci Profesora Adama Strzembosza*, ed. A. Dębiński, A. Grześkowiak, and K. Wiak, 239–256. Lublin: Wydawnictwo Katolickiego Uniwersytetu Lubelskiego.

Index

A. Grabowski, *Juristic Concept of the Validity of Statutory Law*,
DOI 10.1007/978-3-642-27688-0, © Springer-Verlag Berlin Heidelberg 2013

MIX
Papier aus verantwortungsvollen Quellen
Paper from responsible sources
FSC® C105338
FSC
www.fsc.org

If you have any concerns about our products,
you can contact us on
ProductSafety@springernature.com

In case Publisher is established outside the EU,
the EU authorized representative is:
Springer Nature Customer Service Center GmbH
Europaplatz 3, 69115 Heidelberg, Germany

Printed by Libri Plureos GmbH
in Hamburg, Germany